FAMOUS FIRST EDITION

THIS IS COPY NUMBER

2,297

OF MARVEL COMICS LIBRARY.
FANTASTIC FOUR. VOL. 1. 1961–1963

IN A FIRST PRINTING OF FIVE THOUSAND COPIES
PRINTED & BOUND IN ITALY — SUMMER 2022

TASCHEN

IT WORKS! I REALLY AM INVISIBLE! COMPLETELY, TOTALLY INVISIBLE! THERE CAN BE NO DOUBT! NOW, ALL THAT REMAINS IS... MY MISSION!

THOSE WORDS... "THE FANTASTIC FOUR"! WHAT CAN THEY MEAN?
SO! THE TIME HAS COME!

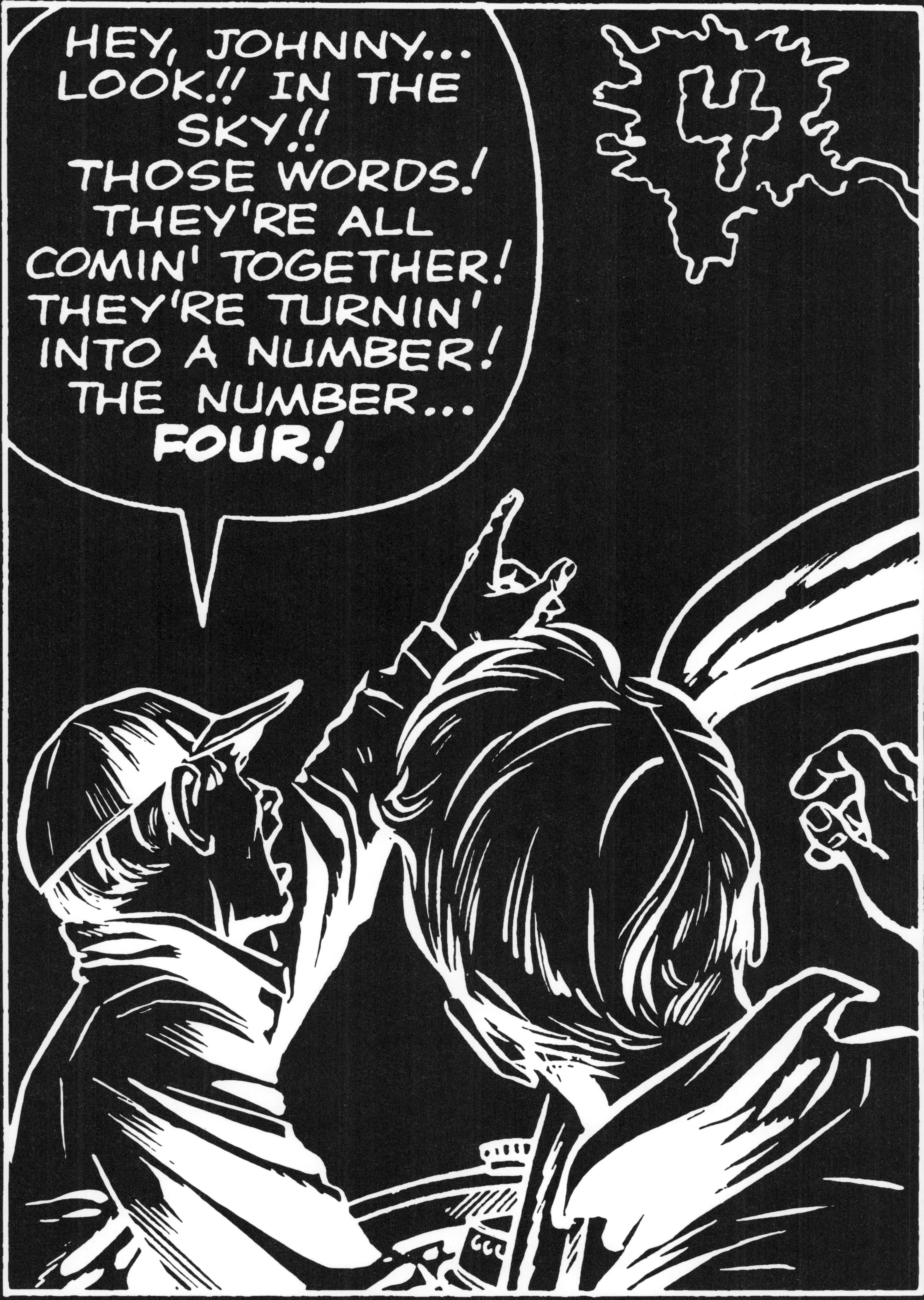
HEY, JOHNNY... LOOK!! IN THE SKY!! THOSE WORDS! THEY'RE ALL COMIN' TOGETHER! THEY'RE TURNIN' INTO A NUMBER! THE NUMBER... **FOUR!**
4

HALT!! HALT OR I'LL SHOOT!!
OKAY, I WARNED YOU!

NO TIME TO WAIT FOR OFFICIAL CLEARANCE! CONDITIONS ARE RIGHT TONIGHT! LET'S GO!

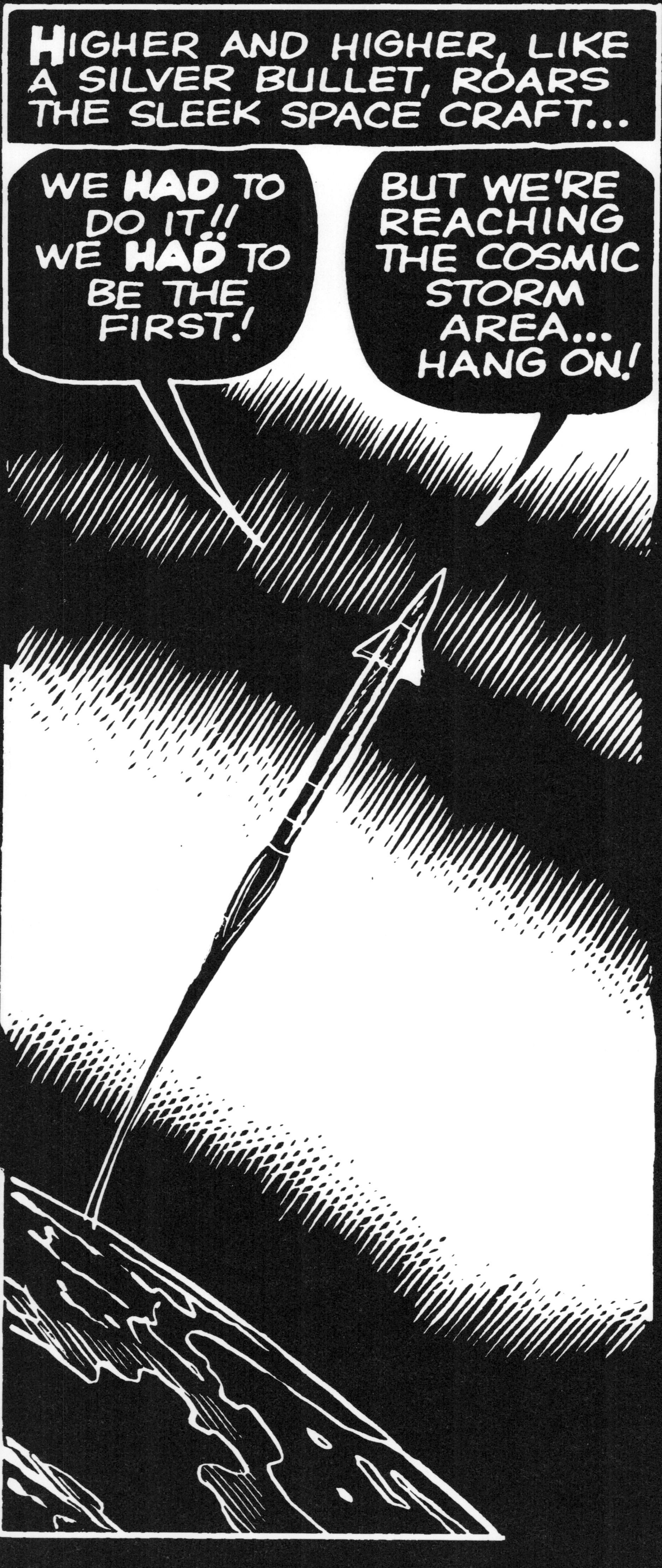
HIGHER AND HIGHER, LIKE A SILVER BULLET, ROARS THE SLEEK SPACE CRAFT...
WE HAD TO DO IT!! WE HAD TO BE THE FIRST!
BUT WE'RE REACHING THE COSMIC STORM AREA... HANG ON!

RAK TAC TA
HEAR THAT IT'S THE COSMIC RAY I--I WARNE YOU ABOUT 'EM!!

TAC TAC
THEY'RE PENETRATING THE SHIP!! OUR SHIELDING ISN'T STRONG ENOUGH!
BUT I DON'T FEEL ANYTHING!
NATURALLY! THEY'RE ONLY RAYS OF LIGHT! YOU CAN'T FEEL 'EM-- BUT THEY'LL AFFECT YOU JUST THE SAME!

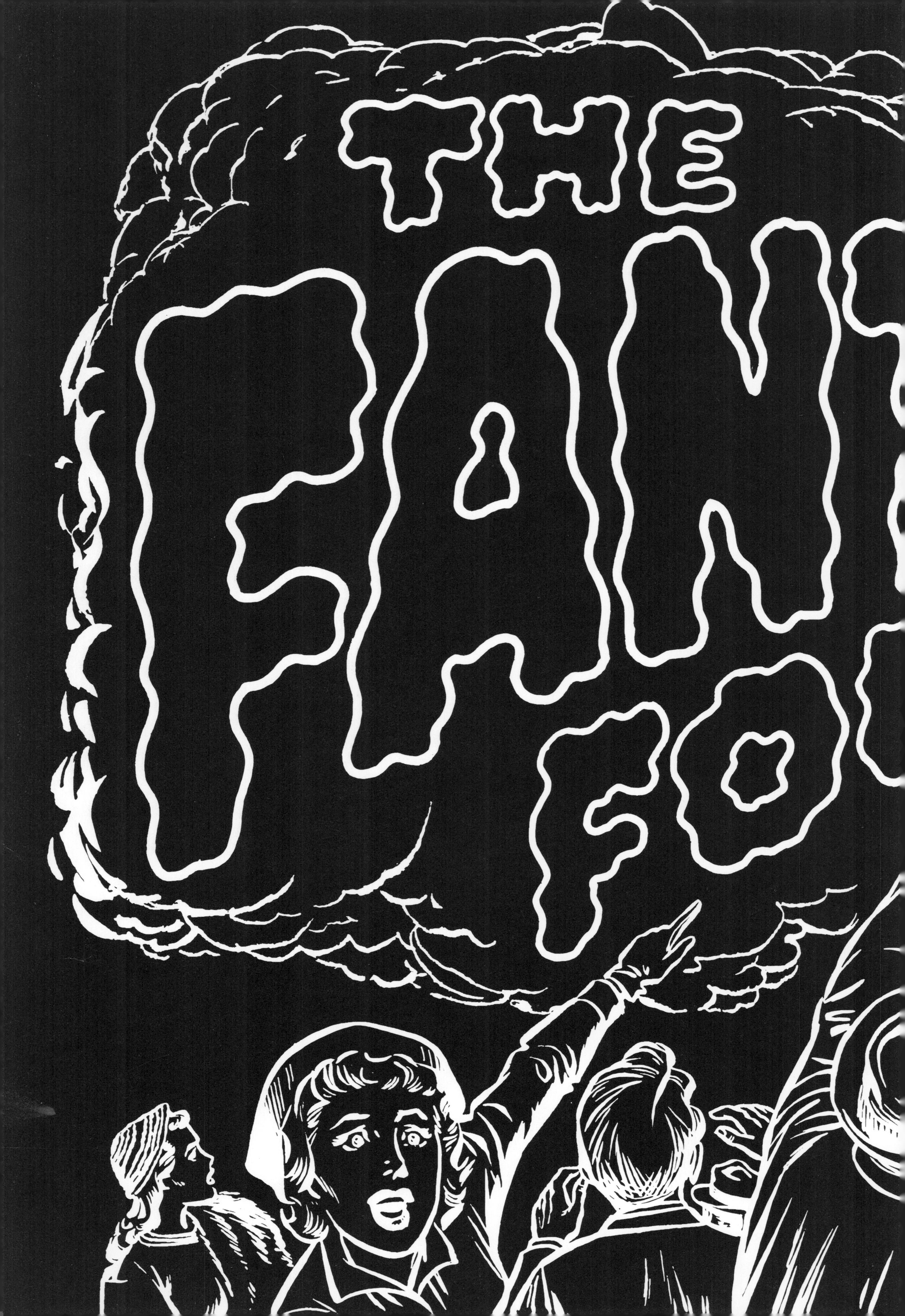
THE

ASTIC
R!
V-372

FOREWORD

Mike Massimino

MY DREAMS OF SPACE TRAVEL BEGAN when I was six years old watching Neil Armstrong take the first steps on the Moon. As I grew up, I enjoyed reading science fiction novels and comic books that were based on science. Jules Verne's novels and the *Fantastic Four* comics were favorites. They were educational and interesting, in addition to being pure fun to read. And they stoked my interest in becoming an explorer.

My father was an inspector for the Fire Department of the City of New York, and he instilled in me the importance of serving the public good, which the space program did in a very cool way. Brave astronauts were risking their lives for exploration, science, and—perhaps most of all in the early days—for the country. The Fantastic Four epitomized that feeling in the early 1960s, that it was of upmost importance for America to win the space race in a cold war battle of superpowers. It was crucial not to let "the commies beat us to it," as Fantastic Four team member Sue Storm put it. This was a goal set by a youthful President Kennedy that captured America's attention. The astronauts in the 1960s were known to the public, and fed the nation's desire for young heroes. The cool swagger, bravery, and intelligence that made me idolize the astronauts of that time was also captured in the Fantastic Four. On my most recent spaceflight, I was one of four spacewalkers who would occasionally jokingly refer to ourselves as the Fantastic Four.

By the time I was nine, I realized that I was never going to be a fearless test pilot astronaut like my hero Neil Armstrong. I didn't like heights or going fast, even on my bicycle. My dream of becoming an astronaut seemed impossible—I certainly didn't think I had the "right stuff." I was more of a math and science kid, not cut out for a fighter pilot career. I just figured that being an astronaut wasn't in the cards for someone like me. There were no science astronauts, and no gender or race diversity in the first few NASA astronaut groups.

The Fantastic Four accurately predicted what NASA would do years later. Reed Richards was a brilliant scientist, and Sue Storm made it to space two decades before Sally Ride became the first American woman in space as part of the NASA Astronaut Class of 1978—the first to include women and people of color. Even if many kids dreaming of going to space didn't see themselves in those original astronauts, they could read the *Fantastic Four* and imagine a different time to come that would lead to the diverse NASA astronaut program of today.

Comics like *Fantastic Four* have played an important role sparking interest in the space program among the recent generations of astronauts. With the help of the Fantastic Four, I am confident that future generations of astronauts will be inspired as well to look beyond their limitations and dream of what they can do to contribute to the next exciting phases of space exploration.

I CAN'T *HELP* MYSELF! THE PUPPET-MASTER IS MAKING ME ATTACK THE OTHERS!

DON'T, THING! WE MUSTN'T LET HIM CONTROL US!

THE WORLD'S GREATEST COMIC MAGAZINE!

Mark Waid

IN 1939, NEW YORKER MARTIN GOODMAN was well established as a successful publisher — not of high-class magazines or books, but of cheaply made but widely circulated fiction magazines called "pulps," referring to the low-cost, coarse wood-pulp paper upon which they were printed. As such, because Goodman kept a watchful eye on his newsstand competition, he couldn't help but notice those new-fangled "comic books." Ten-cent magazines aimed at kids and full of illustrated adventures, they'd become big business over the last few years. Alone, the first issue of some comic book called *Superman* clocked sales in excess of a million copies. Publishers were suddenly making money cranking out entire slates of comics starring other "super heroes," and Goodman wanted in.

At first, he scored big. Under the name Timely Comics Inc., Goodman gave readers Captain America, the Human Torch, the Sub-Mariner, and scores of other costumed crusaders. Timely was by far one of the most prominent and profitable comics publishers throughout World War II, collecting dimes not only from children nationwide, but from overseas servicemen looking for a quick, disposable read.

However, trends come and go; super heroes couldn't stay hot forever. Postwar, publishers rapidly pivoted toward other genres — horror, humor, funny animals — but they couldn't reverse a gradual sales decline industry-wide. Smaller companies were either folding or getting out of the game, leaving only a handful standing on relatively stable ground by the mid-1950s.

National Periodical Publications (later DC Comics) had heroes every child knew: Wonder Woman, Batman, and, most important, Superman, his sales bolstered heavily by the *Adventures of Superman* TV show. Archie Comics Group built most of its successful line on the shoulders of a red-headed teenager and his pals. Dell Comics remained a giant in the field, having licensed Donald Duck and Mickey Mouse and publishing *Walt Disney's Comics and Stories*, the best-selling comic in America with a circulation in the millions.

Timely Comics — by now rechristened Atlas after Goodman's distribution company — held its own in that crowd for four reasons. One was Goodman's notorious frugality — the rates he paid were, charitably put, unimpressive, and he printed his comics as cheaply as possible. The second, related, is that his shallow-bench in-house bullpen of creatives was headed by only one salaried editor, his wife's much younger cousin, whose job included writing most of Atlas's comics himself. The third was Goodman's continuing and unerring ability to seize upon market trends and flood the newsstands to exhaustion. In 1948, romance comics were big; Goodman rolled out 10 titles while the iron was hot. Westerns were the rage in 1955; overnight, Goodman launched far more cowboy comics than any of his competitors.

But the fourth reason Atlas thrived was that Goodman owned his magazine distribution company outright. Unlike rival publishers, Goodman didn't have to hand a share of his profits to an outside company in order to move his dozens and dozens of different magazines and comics to newsstands. Atlas Comics remained in a comfortable market position.

Until 1957, that is. Goodman, in an uncharacteristically disastrous business move, closed Atlas distribution after making a more profitable deal with the American News distribution company. Unfortunately, as comic book historian Gerard Jones explains, almost immediately "[American News] had been found guilty of restraint of trade and ordered to divest itself of the newsstands it owned. Its biggest client, George Delacorte, announced he would seek a new distributor for his Dell Comics and paperbacks. The owners of American News estimated the effect that would have on their income. Then they looked at the value of the New Jersey real estate where their headquarters sat. They liquidated the company and sold the land."[1]

With the abrupt loss of American News, Goodman quickly approached other distributors for help, but no one was giving it. They all remembered their former competitor grudgingly and unkindly. Goodman's only option was to contract with Independent News...a company owned by his chief rival, DC Comics. Independent took Atlas Comics in, but not before forcing Goodman to gut the line. In April of 1957, Goodman issued 41 different comics. In August, he published his new per-month limit of *eight*.

To add to his woes, Goodman discovered an office closet stuffed full of completed and paid-for stories, all unused, enough to fill dozens of books, and must have been aghast that he was simultaneously paying a bullpen of writers and artists to keep producing *new* work. Goodman subsequently fired nearly Atlas's entire staff. Industry legend has it that the layoffs happened because of the closet incident, but Atlas's remaining editor recalled them with a little more nuance:

> "[The layoffs] would never have happened just because he opened a closet door. But I think that I may have been in a little trouble when that happened. We had bought a lot of strips that I didn't think were really all that good, but I paid the artists and writers for them anyway, and I kinda hid them in the closet! And Martin found them, and I think he wasn't too happy. If I wasn't satisfied with the work, I wasn't supposed to have paid, but I was never sure it was really the artist's or the writer's fault. But when the job was finished, I didn't think that it was anything that I wanted to use. I felt that we could use it in inventory — put it out in other books. Martin, probably rightly so, was a little annoyed because it was his money I was spending."[2]

Fortunately for Goodman, but unfortunately for Atlas, he no longer counted a comics company among his prize assets. Throughout the 1940s and '50s, Goodman had created a line of conventional magazines and had entered the

(5) FONTOSTIC FOUR - MOR '62 (PART 2) V-735
FAN. 4 #5 - P.8

4.

I FOUND RRO ...THE THING FROM THE BOTTOMLESS PIT!

8.

(*Page 15*) With Sue Storm as his hostage, Dr. Doom holds all the cards in this original page from *Fantastic Four* No. 5, 1962. The villain made his first appearance in this issue.

(*Opposite*) Jack Kirby penciled this story from *Journey into Mystery* No. 58 in 1960. It was likely on his mind a year later when he drew the cover for *Fantastic Four* No.1, which featured a similar monster emerging from the depths.

(*Right*) Marvel's publisher, Martin Goodman, also had a line of true-crime detective magazines. In a case of waste not want not, he repurposed the Human Torch logo for a 1942 crime story.

(*Far right*) A 1942 house ad for the Human Torch's monthly series. Hyperbole aside, "America's most popular hero" (and Johnny Storm's predecessor) definitely led the charge for Marvel's first wave of Golden Age super heroes.

paperback book business. He was doing well enough that he could afford to let his comics line founder, even disappear, if the market dictated it. Atlas was reduced to a skeleton staff. "They were working out of a closet," said artist Gene Colan. "I'd call [the editor] for work, and he'd say, 'I'm sorry, I just don't have it.'"[3] Its lone editor did his best to keep things afloat, burning through the inventory, turning away freelance writers and artists—many of them personal friends—and began to wonder what he'd made of his life.

That editor was Stan Lee.

RETURN OF THE KING

In 1959, Jack Kirby needed work. A 20-year comics veteran, Kirby—together with his partner, Joe Simon—became an overnight success story by creating the best-selling *Captain America Comics* for Timely, only to leave when Goodman allegedly shorted the two on promised royalties. At DC, they created the Newsboy Legion—a "kid gang" of street urchins who assisted a cop-turned-super-hero named the Guardian—and a multinational group of young freedom fighters called the Boy Commandoes, who fought valiantly on the Allied front line. The Newsboys were popular, but the Commandoes for a short time became one of DC's best-selling features, second only to Superman. Jack was on his way to earning the nickname fans still use today: "King" Kirby.

Despite this success, after Kirby's career was interrupted by a stint in the Army, the World War II vet couldn't just pick up where he left off; in peacetime, the Simon / Kirby features were losing momentum. Worse, DC was demanding more editorial control than Kirby was used to. Jack and Joe meandered through the industry producing mostly crime comics before realizing that they could explore one key genre comics had never tackled: romance. Prize Comics was intrigued by the notion and backed the two on the condition that they'd be paid nothing up front and make their money off the back end.

They took the gamble and won big—for a while. *Young Love* and *Young Romance* were colossal hits and spawned dozens of imitators, but the good times couldn't last. Spearheaded by a headline-hungry psychiatrist armed with falsified data, Dr. Fredric Wertham, a sweeping campaign against comic books ran amok across America. Parents everywhere believed Wertham's unfounded claims that comics were a leading contributor to the scourge of juvenile delinquency and tossed their kids' "funnybooks" into giant bonfires. Congressional committees, responding to this backlash among their constituents, launched investigations. Industrywide, sales of comics plunged, and when Prize was no longer a lucrative option for Simon and Kirby, they took another gamble and established their own company, Mainline Publications.

"Fine comics. Wrong year for them. The crusaders were causing newsstands to stop carrying comics, and publishers were closing left and right. Every week, another one gone. In a panic, the majors banded together, formed a self-regulatory bureau, and proceeded to self-regulate crime, horror, and almost anything else that was entertaining out of everyone's product. Jack said it was like the business got together and said, 'You can't ruin our comics! We'll beat you to it!'"[4]

Simon and Kirby temporarily (and amicably) went their separate ways. For the first time in decades, Jack was on his own. He did a few jobs for Atlas until the implosion dictated by Independent News forced Stan Lee to use up his inventory in lieu of commissioning new work. Kirby returned to freelancing at DC, but he was miserable; his style was no longer in favor there, and what little work they did give him wasn't enough to keep him very busy and prompted soul-crushing lectures from editors about "making art the DC way." He fulfilled a boyhood dream by launching a newspaper strip called "Sky Masters," but it was short-lived, in part because Kirby was hit with a lawsuit from a DC editor who was suing for a commission for helping sell "Sky Masters" to the syndicate that placed it in newspapers. Worse, the suit caused Jack to find himself blackballed at DC.

As "Sky Masters" faltered, Kirby made do with a few odd jobs here and there—joining Simon at Archie Comics Group for a new super hero launch that was slight and only partially successful, and producing pages for the humor magazine *Cracked*. But when Lee was once more clear to buy new stories, Jack desperate to support his family, came back to Goodman.

Atlas didn't pay well, but there was work available.

There they were at Atlas, Stan Lee and Jack Kirby, neither of them happy, wrenching out formulaic romances, Westerns, and war stories. Halfheartedly filling the pages of comics like *Strange Tales* and *Tales to Astonish*, they began a seemingly endless stream of inconsequential monster stories about Godzilla-inspired creatures like Tim Boo Bah and Fin Fang Foom.

Both men had hit a creative nadir, and they were desperate to do something new.

Lee's wife, Joan, was a long-suffering witness to her husband's thwarted ambitions. She got weary of watching Stan moonlight with advertising copy and newspaper features in his spare time in hopes of "making it big," constantly chasing a brass ring but never grabbing it.

> "She wondered why I didn't put as much effort and creativity into the comics as I seemed to be putting into my other freelance endeavors. The fact is, I had always thought of my comic-book work as a temporary job—even after all those years—and her little dissertation made me suddenly realize that it was time to start concentrating on what I was doing—to carve a real career for myself in the nowhere world of

SYNOPSES: THE FANTASTIC FOUR JULY '61 SCHEDULE (#1)

STORY #1. INTRODUCTION. "MEET THE FANTASTIC FOUR"

This story is told in 2 chapters. Chapter one is 6 pages long. Chapter 2 is 5 pages.

There are four main characters:
1) REED RICHARDS. (Mr. Fantastic) He is young, handsome scientist. Leader of the four. Invents a space ship to go to Mars. Hopes to be first man to reach Mars.
2) SUSAN STORM. (Invisible Girl) She is Reed's girl friend. She's an actress. Beautiful, glamorous.
3) BEN GRIMM. (The Thing) Ben is very husky, brutish guy. He's a pilot. He falls for Susan also.
4) JOHNNY STORM. (Human Torch) He is Susan's kid brother. A teen-ager. 17 years old. High school star athlete.

Story might open up with a meeting of Fantastic Four. As meeting starts, caption tells reader that we will go back a few weeks to see how it all began....

Reed Richards tells Susan and her brother Johnny that his space ship is finally completed. He hopes to be first man to Mars. But he needs a pilot. They hire Ben Grimm. Ben is huge, surly unpleasant guy who doesn't want any part of project until he sees Susan. He falls for Susan, and she manages to coax him into piloting ship. Ben is crackerjack pilot, ex-war hero, best pilot available.

As the four are about to begin flight, they are warned against it by authorities. Told that no one yet knows what effect cosmic rays will have on human bodies so far out in space. But they decide to go anyway. They fear that if they don't go, Reds may beat us to it.

(NOTE: At the rate the Communists are progressing in space, maybe we better make this a flight to the STARS, instead of just to Mars, because by the time this mag goes on sale, the Russians may have already MADE a flight to Mars!)

So, without clearance from the authorities, in the dead of night, they take off for the nearest star-- very dramatically.

In space, on the way to the stars, POOOF! They are bombarded by cosmic rays which penetrate the ship and which affect all four of the occupants. They can't continue the trip-- have to turn back-- are lucky to land alive. But they are all different now- they sense it- although they don't yet quite know HOW they've changed.

Suddenly, they can't see Susan! But they know she's there! They can HEAR her. They realize she has become invisible. She can not become visible again. Later, she will buy a mask with a face like the one she had and she will have to wear that mask in order to be seen. Her clothes of course can be seen, so it is only her flesh that is invisible. When she takes her clothes off, she's completely invisible. (I hope this won't seem to sexy in art work. Better talk to me about it, Jack-- maybe we'll change this gimmick somewhat).

As for Johnny, Susan's brother, whenever he gets excited, he bursts into flame. Becomes a Human Torch, and can fly, as his body gets lighter than air. BUT doesn't last for more than 5 minutes. At end of five minutes, his flame goes out and he becomes normal again, until he gets excited again. But can't flame on for at least 5 minutes after he's gotten back to normal. Comics Association told me he may never burn anyone with flame, he may only burn ropes, doors, etc.--never people. And, he cannot toss fireballs as the old Human Torch could. His biggest asset is that he can fly.

more--

They think Reed Richards, the pilot, is unaffected by cosmic rays, as he seems normal-- UNTIL he tries to reach for something. Then they realize his arm has STRETCHED toward the thing he reached for. After awhile they realize Reed's body has become like RUBBER. He can get skinny, elongated, anything that you can do with rubber. He can squeeze thru keyholes, etc. Of course, the more stretched-out he gets, the weaker he gets-- but the point remains that he can twist and stretch his body into almost any shape. (He can even alter the appearance of his face to make himself look like someone else) BUT it is quite painful to do all this, so he can only maintain the strange shapes for a very short period of time until the pain gets to be unbearable.

Finally, Ben Grimm steps out of the shadows. They all gasp-- his body has changed in the most grotesque way of all. He's sort of shapeless-- he's become a THING. And, he's grown more fantastically powerful than any other living thing. He is stronger than an elephant. BUT, he is so heavy that he moves very slowly-- he's very ponderous, and those slow, ponderous movements should make him look very dramatic. He cannot alter his appearance as the others can, so he must wear a coat with turned-up collar, sunglasses, slouch hat, and gloves when he goes out in public. But when he takes 'em off, he is a THING!

So much for who they are and how they got that way. Now, here's a gimmick I think we might play up to advantage: Let's make The Thing the heavy- in other words, he's not really a good guy. He's part of the Fantastic Four because they all got that way together and they decide to remain a team, and also because he has a crush on Susan-- but actually, he is jealous of Mr. Fantastic and dislikes Human Torch because Torch always sides with Fantastic. Let's treat him so that reader is always afraid he will sabotage the Fantastic Four's efforts at whatever they are doing-- he isn't interested in helping mankind the way the other three are-- he is more interested in winning Susan away from Mr. Fantastic. (We might indicate that he feels he may return to his normal self at any time, because none of them know how long their strange powers will last- or whether or not the effect of the cosmic rays will one day wear off them).

Anyway, the four of them decide to form a unit-- they think it is an act of Fate which made them as they are and they think they owe it to fate to use their powers to help mankind. So they adopt their new names: HUMAN TORCH, MR. FANTASTIC, INVISIBLE GIRL, and THE THING, and vow to spend their lives fighting all sorts of evil menaces which the normal forces of the world cannot cope with. And, to keep it all from getting too goody-goody, there is always friction between Mr. Fantastic and The Thing, with Human Torch siding with Mr. F. Also, the other three are always afraid of The Thing getting out of their control some day and harming mankind with his amazing strength. Occasionally also, you might have the Thing wanting to do something for personal profit- and the other 3 try to stop him. In other words, the Thing doesn't have the ethics that the other three have, and consequently he will probably be the most interesting one to the reader, because he'll always be unpredictable.

So much for the introduction--- the preceding should have covered exactly 11 pages, consisting of 2 chapters. (Chapter one: 6 pages. Chapter 2: 5 pages)

The next two chapters, in which the Fantastic Four undertakes their first case, will ~~also~~ be ~~two~~ 3 chapters for a ~~total~~ total of ~~10~~ 13 pages-- ~~5 pages to each chapter~~ (3,5,5.)

comic books. I was really bored with what I was doing. This was about 1960. And my wife said, 'Before you leave, just once why don't you try to put out the kind of books you yourself would like to do?'"[5]

Meanwhile, Goodman had an idea of his own. DC Comics had begun a slow rollout of super hero revivals starting in 1956, remaking 1940s champions like Flash and Green Lantern for a modern audience, and they were selling like gangbusters. Industry legend has it that while playing golf with DC co-publisher Jack Liebowitz, Goodman learned that the first issue of their brand-new super hero team, *Justice League of America*, had sold in excess of 800,000 copies, absolutely dwarfing the sales figures of any of the Atlas books. Liebowitz later claimed that while he'd never actually played golf with Goodman, the gist of the story was true. The industry was small, and everyone knew one another's numbers.

Regardless of how exactly Goodman came upon his information, he spoke immediately to Stan. "'Stan,'" he said excitedly, "'can you come up with a team of super heroes like the Justice League?' Without waiting for an answer, he added, 'You could use our old Human Torch and Sub-Mariner and maybe Captain America. That'll save you from having to dream up any new characters.' Martin was nothing if not an incredibly clever thinker."[6]

"You know, Stan," reiterated Joan Lee, "if Martin wants you to create a new group of super heroes, this could be a chance for you to do it the way you've always wanted to. You could dream up plots that have more depth and substance to them, and create characters who have interesting personalities, who speak like real people."[7]

Kirby had his own version of the story: "I tried to work it out with Stan, to hint about super heroes. There were a few still going but they didn't have the big audience they had... I came in with presentations. I'm not gonna wait around for conferences. I said 'This is what you have to do.'"[8]

The two recollections aren't necessarily contradictory; everyone in comics noticed that super heroes were the latest trend, and timing is everything. What is indisputable is that both men sat down together to create Goodman's super-team. Or did they?

ONE PLUS ONE EQUALS FOUR

The way Stan always told the anecdote, he came up with the characters and their origin on his own, and there exists a two-page plot synopsis for Jack to illustrate that would seem to back up that claim. Jack, on the other hand, insisted he had far more to do with the team's invention than that. Specifically, he'd cite a feature that Simon and Kirby had sold to DC in 1957, *Challengers of the Unknown*. What mattered in the moment was what they produced together: the first issue of a comic magazine called *The Fantastic Four*.

It is not hyperbole to say that no one had ever read a super hero comic like this. Traditionally, costumed do-gooders were written and drawn for children. They wore bright colors, were eternally polite and good-tempered, lived in idyllic fictional cities, were handsome, had sidekicks and secret identities, and were adored by their public. And, for all their star power and inventiveness, they were about as deep as a soap dish.

Not these four, though. These four argued. They copped attitudes and downright brawled. One of them was physically grotesque and eternally sullen. Another was a kid, but not a sidekick — a full teammate. The "token" female wasn't a lovesick civilian; she was an active member of the team. Their adventures didn't wrap up neatly in 12-page installments. They didn't wear costumes. They lived in the very real New York City. They had money problems. And, most important, they had human emotions. They felt guilt; they wallowed in envy; they knew fear; they acted out in anger. They had genuine interpersonal relationships, and their world initially responded to them not with applause but with terror and trepidation. Stan and Jack struck gold by creating heroes whose problems we could actually identify with, gave them hopes and goals that were actually familiar to us. In one comic, they had redefined the super hero and changed comics history.

The Fantastic Four birthed the successor to Atlas Publishing, the company we know today as Marvel Comics, full of heroes whose personal lives matter to us as much as their thrilling exploits, who experience the same triumphs and tragedies as their audience. With the debut of the FF, Lee and Kirby established the blueprint for every subsequent comic book, TV show, video game, and blockbuster film under the Marvel banner, in turn forever influencing the entire super hero genre.

IND.
THE
Fantastic
10¢
APPROVED BY THE COMICS CODE AUTHORITY
MC
2 JAN.
THE THING
MR. FANTASTIC
FOUR
THEY HAD TAKEN A DEADLY OATH TO DESTROY THE FANTASTIC FOUR!!
THEY WERE MERCILESS! THEY WERE INHUMAN! THEY HAD POWERS FAR GREATER THAN EARTHMEN! THEY WERE THE DEADLY
"SKRULLS FROM OUTER SPACE!"
HUMAN TORCH
INVISIBLE GIRL
WE'RE TOO LATE!! TOO LATE!!
MY FLAME IS OUT!! I'M HELPLESS!

FAN. FOUR. #3 - P. 9
NEVER MIND THOSE MONSTERS, BOYS! LOOK WHAT I'VE GOT!
SUSAN! YOU DESIGNED A COSTUME FOR YOURSELF!
AND FOR YOU, TOO! IT'S TIME WE ALL HAD SOME COLORFUL COSTUMES!
BAH! COSTUMES... TIGHTS... THAT'S KID STUFF! WHO NEEDS 'EM?
WE DO, IF WE'RE IN THIS BUSINESS OF CRIME FIGHTING FOR REAL! IF WE'RE A TEAM, WE SHOULD LOOK LIKE A TEAM!
SAY! THIS ISN'T HALF BAD, SUE! EVER THINK OF WORKING FOR DIOR?
I'VE GOT ENOUGH TO DO ACTING AS NURSEMAID TO YOU THREE! HERE, THING, THIS EVEN MAKES YOU LOOK GLAMOROUS!
I AIN'T GONNA WEAR THIS FOOL OUTFIT!
REED! THING! LOOK! IT'S THE MIRACLE MAN! WHAT'S HE DOIN' AT THE PREMIERE?
HE--HE'S MAKIN' SOME KIND OF STRANGE GESTURE!
LOOK!!
THE MONSTER!! IT-- IT'S COME TO LIFE!!
7
9

(*Page 18*) Recollections may vary about how much Stan Lee and Jack Kirby contributed to the origins of this quartet of adventurers, but this two-page synopsis of the first issue by Lee definitively stands as an example of the collaborative "Marvel Method."

(*Page 19*) Reed, Sue, Johnny, and Ben saw their early adventures veer decidedly into sci-fi, as shown on this original cover art for *Fantastic Four* No. 2. The alien menace of the Skrulls, introduced in this issue, would evolve into a perennial thorn in the FF's side.

(*Opposite*) By *Fantastic Four* No. 3, Marvel's premier super heroes were finally looking the part, thanks to costumes designed by Sue Storm.

(*Above left and above*) These unpublished panels from *Fantastic Four* No. 3 show what could have been. Stan initially intended for Sue and Reed to go incognito with domino masks. After the final art arrived, Stan had them redrawn by production manager Sol Brodsky.

(*Left*) This is the original cover that Jack Kirby drew for *Fantastic Four* No. 3. It was replaced by a new cover that did not show the team in boxes.

FAN. FOUR. #3 - P. 14
CHAPTER III
"THE FLAME THAT DIED!"
Stan Lee J. KIRBY
THING!! LOOK!! IT'S THE TORCH!
HE'S FOUND THE MONSTER!
V-563
THAT MEANS ONE THING...
YEAH! THE MIRACLE MAN MUST BE THERE, TOO! LET'S GO!
YOU STAY HIDDEN, SUE, IN CASE WE NEED YOU!
AS FOR ME, I'M GETTIN' OUTTA THIS MONKEY SUIT SO I CAN MOVE!
11
14.

(*Opposite*) This early attempt at a costume for the Thing lasted only five pages. With some self-alterations, Ben adopted a more functional approach to his uniform.

(*Right and far right*) *The Comic Collector* was a popular fanzine that made its debut in 1961 and later reviewed the first issue of *Fantastic Four*. The young and effusive minds behind the fanzine were Jerry Bails (pictured here) and a young schoolteacher named Roy Thomas. Roy would go on to be a prolific comic book writer and at one point became Marvel's editor-in-chief.

(*Below*) Stan Lee responded to the *Fantastic Four* review in *Comic Collector*. Like a true salesman, he addressed their concerns, teased upcoming plots points for the series, and made sure to steer the fanzine toward the soon-to-launch title *Amazing Adult Fantasy*, the comic book series that would eventually introduce Spider-Man to the world.

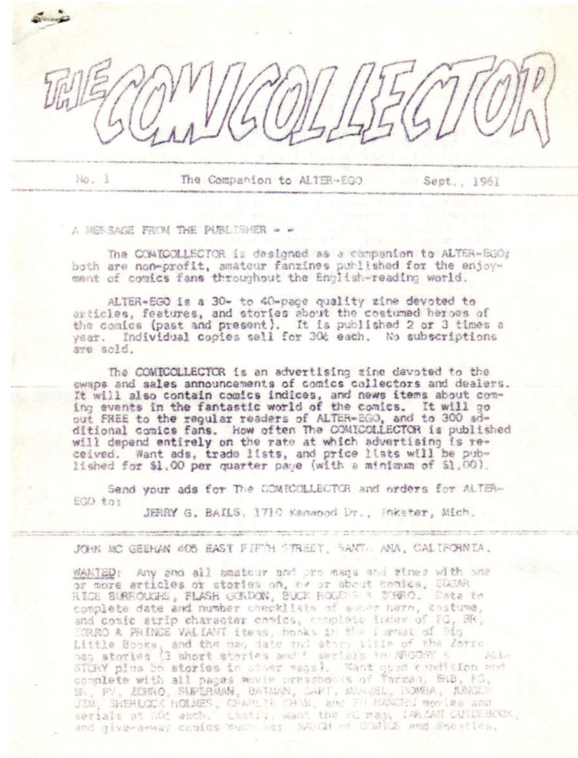

THE COMICOLLECTOR

No. 1 The Companion to ALTER-EGO Sept., 1961

A MESSAGE FROM THE PUBLISHER - -

The COMICOLLECTOR is designed as a companion to ALTER-EGO; both are non-profit, amateur fanzines published for the enjoyment of comics fans throughout the English-reading world.

ALTER-EGO is a 30- to 40-page quality zine devoted to articles, features, and stories about the costumed heroes of the comics (past and present). It is published 2 or 3 times a year. Individual copies sell for 30¢ each. No subscriptions are sold.

The COMICOLLECTOR is an advertising zine devoted to the swaps and sales announcements of comics collectors and dealers. It will also contain comics indices, and news items about coming events in the fantastic world of the comics. It will go out FREE to the regular readers of ALTER-EGO, and to 300 additional comics fans. How often The COMICOLLECTOR is published will depend entirely on the rate at which advertising is received. Want ads, trade lists, and price lists will be published for $1.00 per quarter page (with a minimum of $1.00).

Send your ads for The COMICOLLECTOR and orders for ALTER-EGO to:

JERRY G. BAILS, 1710 Kenwood Dr., Inkster, Mich.

JOHN MC GEEHAN 405 EAST FIFTH STREET, SANTA ANA, CALIFORNIA.

One of the major elements that made the Lee / Kirby team so strong was the creative chemistry between the men. At other comics companies, writers would turn in scripts complete with scene direction and dialogue. Artists, allowed little if any input into the stories, would simply illustrate their assigned scripts as written. Stan, because he was always writing for several artists at once, had developed out of necessity a different way of collaborating, still known today as the "Marvel Method."

"I'd be writing all the stories, and I'd be working on a *Fantastic Four* and the artist who's doing Dr. Strange would come in and say, 'Stan, I've finished my script. I need another.' But I've got the typewriter going for F.F., and I couldn't stop. And I couldn't let him sit around doing nothing.

MAGAZINE MANAGEMENT COMPANY

655 MADISON AVENUE, NEW YORK 21, N. Y. • TEmpleton 8-7900

SEP. 1 1961

8/29/61

Dear Jerry:

Enjoyed reading ALTER-EGO and the COMICOLLECTOR, and got a kick out of your little critique of THE FANTASTIC FOUR, written by Roy Thomas.

Just to correct a few small inaccuracies though, I'm not a "former" editor of Timely-- I've been editor and art director of that redoubtable institution for the past 21 years, and hope to continue ad infinitum. Also, it is doubtful that Mr. Thomas is the "only person who bought a copy" (although he said that humorously, of course) because judging by early sales reports, I think we have a winner on our hands!

As for the future of the F.F., we WILL have :
COSTUMES
A DIFFERENT TREATMENT (art-wise) OF THE TORCH
ADDITIONAL NEW CHARACTERS IN MONTHS TO COME
(Don't be too surprised to meet Sub-Mariner again, or Captain America! Who knows??)
AND A FEW MORE SURPRISES... so stay with us, pal!

Would be interested in your opinion of another new mag due to go on sale soon-- AMAZING ADULT FANTASY. We think it's a smash.

Regarding some of the various comments concerning the F.F., we have purposely refrained from letting invisible girl (oops, sorry!) Invisible Girl walk thru walls, and from giving TOO MUCH super powers to our characters, as we feel that effects like those are chiefly of appeal to the YOUNGER readers, and we are trying (perhaps vainly?) to reach a slightly older, more sophisticated group.

Enough for now- keep up the good work.

Regards,

Stan Lee

So I'd dream up a plot for him, tell him to draw it any way he wanted, and then I'd put in the dialogue later. It was a measure of expediency, so I wouldn't be the bottleneck. Then I found out it worked better."[9]

The Marvel Method played brilliantly to Kirby's strengths as a visual storyteller. From the start, Lee and Kirby sat together and talked out the Fantastic Four stories, after which Jack had free rein to plot and pace them as he saw fit. For the first handful of issues, remaining (and brief) plot synopses and rough diagrams by Stan on the back of existing pages of original art show that he kept a hand in every level of development. By the book's second year, though, the two men would simply have a conversation (sometimes as brief as, "Let's have them fight Doctor Doom this issue"), Jack would sit down in his home studio to draw it up, making margin notes for Stan as he went, and Stan would then put in dialogue based on the art. Both men were able to bring their best skills to the table, and it showed.

Watching Lee and Kirby, flying by the seats of their pants, develop and evolve the Four makes for fascinating reading. Every issue compiled in this collection contains a noteworthy milestone of some sort, to wit:

The unique world of the Fantastic Four established in their first issue was the world Jack and Stan were hungry to explore, and while the rough-hewn FF looked not at all like the gleaming Justice League of America, apparently Goodman was fine with that. In fact, some historians suspect Goodman deliberately guided them away from the more obvious super hero tropes. After all, here was Martin Goodman, trying to stealth-launch a new super hero comic while at the same time staying under the radar of Independent News. (DC Comics was known to be quite legally aggressive about protecting their monopoly on the genre.) Between the lack of capes and cowls, the bestial enemies, and the oddball, quirky, borderline fragile logo, *Fantastic Four* No. 1 could, at a glance, easily pass for just another of the company's monster comics, and that may well have been by design.

Bolstering this theory, there's a strong case to be made that the Fantastic Four wasn't originally intended to launch in its own comic at all. With the exception of Lee and Kirby's next creation, the Hulk, every other early Marvel hero debuted in a short story inside one of Goodman's anthology titles—Spider-Man in *Amazing Fantasy*, Ant-Man in *Tales to Astonish*, Thor in *Journey into Mystery*, Iron Man in *Tales of Suspense*. With that in mind, the entire back half of *Fantastic Four* No. 1 reads perfectly as a standalone tale, to be placed most likely in Lee and Kirby's *Amazing Adventures*.

On his blog, Marvel executive editor Tom Brevoort observes, "As with the monster stories that Lee and Kirby and others were doing during this time, this story is divided into chapters. Take away the first half of the book, and the chapter break approximates the structure of the typical monster story pretty well. The bottom tier [on page 20], where the Thing takes off his overcoat, is structured like a reveal. Which is strange, as we've already seen the Thing in

(*Left*) A 1962 house ad from *The Incredible Hulk* No. 1 features Marvel's first family in all their super heroic glory.

(*Opposite*) Johnny Storm and Ben Grimm love each other like brothers, with typical brotherly disputes. This page from *Fantastic Four* No. 5 illustrates the hilariously destructive behavior that often erupts in their relationship.

full light earlier in the issue. But if this was intended as a separate story, then it makes a bit more sense to do this unveiling in this manner."[10]

Reed Richards's sense of urgency to make his space flight may seem strange to a modern audience more accustomed to the idea of rocket launches, but it was perfect for its time. The Fantastic Four were born of the Space Race, the then-crucial competition between two Cold War rivals, the Soviet Union and the United States, to achieve firsts in spaceflight capability. NASA's space program was in its infancy, but it had already inspired children from coast to coast to look to the stars and imagine walking among them (while—bonus points—striking a parent-pleasing blow against the Commies).

Stan and Jack didn't produce each issue of the series single-handedly. Back then (and largely today), comics were made in an assembly line fashion. Jack would deliver story pages that were illustrated fully in pencil, then move onto the next story. An inker—freelancer George Klein for *Fantastic Four* Nos. 1 and 2, staffer Sol Brodsky on Nos. 3 and 4—would then go over Jack's lines with India ink so they would reproduce vividly, adding texture and dimension as he went. A letterer, typically Artie Simek, would put in all of Stan's accompanying dialogue and sound effects. Finally, colorist Stan Goldberg—the unsung production artist / cartoonist who made sure the early Marvels had a consistent look and feel—created and maintained color guides for the printer. Next issue, the cycle would start anew.

Roy Thomas, a 20-year-old schoolteacher who would later become Marvel Comics' editor-in-chief, was one of the fans who purchased this first issue. Shortly thereafter, Thomas wrote a review for a fan magazine (including an unwittingly prescient comment four issues ahead of its time):

> *The Fantastic Four* holds promise of becoming one of the better comics now on the stands, in this reviewer's opinion. Especially gratifying is the re-revival of the Torch, undoubtedly one of the most interesting super-hero ideas of all time. The Four's leader, Mr. Fantastic, is also a welcome character, as appearances by Elongated Man in *The Flash* have so far been too spotty to be satisfying.
>
> Unfortunately, this first issue also leaves a lot to be desired. Invisible Girl's power, apparently unsupplemented by the ability to walk through walls, etc. is such that her role is a minor one; the three humans wear drab clothing that would never really stand the rigors of a monster-filled adventure such as this first one; Mr. Fantastic's stretching power (like that of Elongated Man) is still too limited for him to be considered the true successor of Plastic Man or a great one in his own right; and, worst, of all, the drawing of this third version of the Human Torch is almost pathetic in many panels, *crying* for a return to something like the old Burgos version.
>
> It is too early yet to judge fully the Fantastic Four, but I, for one, cast my vote in favor of them. With a little added imagination in both stories and artwork—plus perhaps the addition of a fifth character, such as the Sub-Mariner or someone like the old Purple Claw—I think this comic would be worthy of a large circulation.[11]

Fantastic Four No. 2 presents more evidence that Goodman was still trying to avoid attention from DC. Though a preliminary version of the cover still exists, festooned with explosive blurbs calling out the names of the heroes, they were removed before going to print (along with bombastic word balloons from the characters, which is why the finished cover looks oddly empty). It certainly doesn't appear to be a super hero comic.

Stan and Jack stayed away from costumed super villains as well, instead hanging their story on an alien invasion by a chameleon race called the Skrulls, who've since gone on to become an integral part of Marvel's comics and movies. If—spoiler—you notice upon reading that one of the four villainous Skrulls is left unaccounted for, points for you. Stan threw in a hasty line of dialogue attempting to cover the mistake, but it became a plot point 10 years later when Roy Thomas and *Avengers* artist Neal Adams revealed the fourth to be a disguised senator who helped spark an intergalactic war with Earth caught in the middle. Just another example of how little seeds planted by Stan and Jack, even unwittingly, could eventually blossom into entire epics.

By issue No. 3, Goodman felt less nervous about DC's watchful eye and encouraged Stan to transform the Fantastic Four into more of a traditional super hero team—though, again, Stan and Jack put their own spin on the familiar fittings. Nowhere is that more obvious than in the costuming of the four. In the late 1980s, with the original art in hand, artist Greg Theakston noticed under Sol Brodsky's ink lines that Jack had originally penciled in domino masks for the team (as well as chest insignias that were an interlocking pair of F's). If you find yourself curious about that strange, nonsensical close-up on Sue's face on page seven, that was where she was originally showing off her mask. Once Jack's pages came in, Stan reconsidered and had inker Brodsky remove them.

Even the costumes themselves were offbeat, far more akin to astronaut suits than to tights and capes. Reed, Sue, and Johnny embraced theirs; Ben, not so much. To be honest, it's not like a creepy welder's mask was much of an improvement over his new natural look.

Another cliché Stan and Jack flipped was the typical secret hero headquarters. Over in Gotham City, no one knew where the Batcave was hidden, but the whole world knew that the Four made their home in the Baxter Building in midtown Manhattan. "The only reason I put the FF in a skyscraper headquarters," said Stan, "was that I wanted to definitely base them in New York. So I figured there were three things: they could be in a brownstone, in a subterranean subway or a skyscraper. I picked the skyscraper."[12] Just for fun, Jack provided a cutaway view of the FF's base on page five, a diagram he'd return to time and again on the probably accurate theory that kids loved hero headquarters.

MILES AWAY, IN THE HEART OF NEW YORK. A TOWERING SKY-SCRAPER BECOMES EMPTY AS ITS OCCUPANTS LEAVE FOR HOME AT THE END OF A TYPICAL WORK DAY...
ONE BY ONE THE BUILDING'S LIGHTS FLICKER OUT...
...ALL EXCEPT THOSE AT THE TOWER! THE TOWER WHICH SERVES AS HEADQUARTERS OF THE FANTASTIC FOUR!
AND, WITHIN THE TOWER WE FIND...
WHAT ARE YOU READING, JOHNNY?
A GREAT NEW COMIC MAG, REED! SAY! YOU KNOW SOMETHING--!
THE INCREDIBLE HULK
I'LL BE DOGGONED IF THIS MONSTER DOESN'T REMIND ME OF THE THING!
VER-RY FUNNY!
GIMME THAT MAG, SQUIRT! I'LL TEACH YA TO COMPARE ME TO A COMIC BOOK MONSTER!
HEY!
HULK
IF YOU WANT IT SO BAD, I'LL WARM IT UP FOR YOU, BIG MAN!
OWW!
COME BACK HERE!
COME 'N GET ME!
2
Jack Kirby
2

(*Far left*) The backup story in *The Amazing Spider-Man* No. 8 featured the Human Torch in what would be the first of many pairings with his fellow teenage hero/rival, Spider-Man.

(*Left*) These panels from *The Amazing Spider-Man* No. 1 in 1963 show Spidey's first meeting with the Fantastic Four. Soon, more characters would cross over from different series, as Stan and company built what would eventually become a shared Marvel Universe.

(*Opposite*) In 1963, the team also met the Incredible Hulk for the first time in the pages of *Fantastic Four* No. 12.

The issue's end was strikingly unusual for super hero comics of the day. Continuing storylines were quite rare — publishers didn't want to "penalize" a reader for missing an installment — and stories were almost always done in one issue. The infrequent two-part (or "continued") story would end part one with a traditional hero-in-danger cliffhanger, never on a character beat, but that's not what the readership came to Marvel for. They came to Marvel because, unlike other comics on the stands, actions had consequences. Characters grew and changed along clear, logical trajectories on an unpredictable playing field where anything could happen, and no one was safe. Each story built upon the last, with subplots lasting sometimes several issues before being resolved. Pulse-pounding perils and dynamic art captured the audience, but it was the soap opera that kept them coming back. Well, that and the showmanship.

Stan, a big personality who loved playing to the crowd, began leaning heavily into the role of carnival barker to promote the series. On the cover, he bannered issue No. 3 with the proclamation that *Fantastic Four* was "The Greatest Comic Magazine in the World!!" Inside, he took a page — literally — from the defunct EC Comics, a horror and fantasy publishing house (*Tales from the Crypt*, *Weird Science*) that launched the concept of a regular letters column that printed fan mail from the readers. Stan, whose skill at acknowledging and supporting Marvel fans and making them feel part of the creative process, clearly took joy in running "The Fantastic Four Fan Page," full of letters, snappy replies, and plugs for other upcoming Marvel projects. And while the kids reveled in it, the older readers — smaller in number but far more vocal — were likewise drawn in, devoting an increasing amount of coverage to the FF in their fan magazines and polls.

Having successfully resurrected a version of the original Human Torch, Stan and Jack turned their focus to another of Timely's best-selling super heroes, Namor the Sub-Mariner. Created by writer/artist Bill Everett, Namor was introduced in Goodman's very first comic, *Marvel Comics* No. 1, 1939. The son of a human sea captain and an Atlantean queen, Namor proclaimed himself king of the seven seas. Using his aquatic powers, he declared war on all land dwellers until he came to realize that the Nazis were his true enemy. Postwar, Namor remained largely on the side of good, though still haughty and short-tempered.

When Timely's super hero line ended in the late 1940s, the Sub-Mariner feature was retired. It was resuscitated in 1954–55, allegedly because Goodman was working to strike a deal for a television adaptation, but it was quickly forgotten. By the time *Fantastic Four* No. 4 was published, it's entirely likely that most readers had never heard of Namor; the common wisdom in those days, when comics were targeted exclusively at young children, was that the entire audience turned over about every five years.

Whether a known or unknown quantity, Namor became an integral character in the Fantastic Four cast. Amnesiac (to explain his absence since 1955), the Sub-Mariner was discovered purely by accident in a Bowery flophouse by Johnny Storm, who then restored Namor's memories — and, consequently, his loathing of land dwellers. Stan and Jack perfectly captured Namor's trademark arrogance and antihero qualities to create the series' most traditional super villain yet.

Momentum was building. Within its first year of publication, *Fantastic Four* nabbed Best Comic Book of the Year, Best Group of Heroes, Best Villain, and Best Supporting Character in the fan-driven Alley Awards. And when Stan plastered the phrase "The World's Greatest Comics Magazine!" on the cover of issue No. 4, it was more than a boast; it was a flag planted, a declaration that became the book's permanent tagline.

Next to the Fantastic Four themselves, the foe introduced in issue No. 5 is inarguably the most important character ever to debut in Marvel's flagship series. From the moment he first appeared, Doctor Victor von Doom immediately became the group's foremost nemesis and shows no sign of relinquishing the role. Here, his background and connection with Reed Richards is barely touched upon, but by 1964's *Fantastic Four Annual* No. 2, his complexity and the scope of his evil had been fully laid out.

As a boy, Victor Von Doom was a young Roma whose mother had been slain by villagers fearing her mystic powers. Doom thereafter dedicated his life to discovering some device, any device, that would allow him to retrieve her from the afterlife. Following years of development, his most promising invention failed and exploded, scarring his face — but only after he had ignored the warnings of college classmate Reed Richards, who tried and failed to bring Doom's attention to errors in the device's design. From that day forward, unable to accept that the error was his and choosing to believe that Richards had somehow sabotaged him, Doom dedicated his existence to humiliating and defeating Richards and his family. In a clever touch, Stan and Jack made Doom the leader of a small Balkan country called Latveria, giving him diplomatic immunity from any criminal prosecution.

Doom's face was never seen by readers. His ego was so gigantic that the scars he bore were to be forever hidden behind a mask. Though Stan wrote Doom as if he were hideously disfigured, Jack's theory was that Doom had suffered one scar so tiny as to be barely noticeable, but that his vanity caused him to view his face as monstrous.

This was the first *Fantastic Four* issue to be inked by Joe Sinnott, who would return to the book almost 40 issues later for a long tenure. By that time, Jack's pencils and characters were more polished and refined, and Sinnott's deft linework brought out fully the dimension and humanity in Jack's pencils. Their work together is widely considered the best of Kirby's 102-issue run.

Meanwhile, as the FF traveled through time to seek the treasure of Blackbeard the pirate, a timid teenager named Peter Parker was being bitten by a radioactive spider over in the pages of *Amazing Fantasy*. It wouldn't be long before he would cross paths with the FF — with arguably disastrous results.

FANTASTIC FOUR #12-16

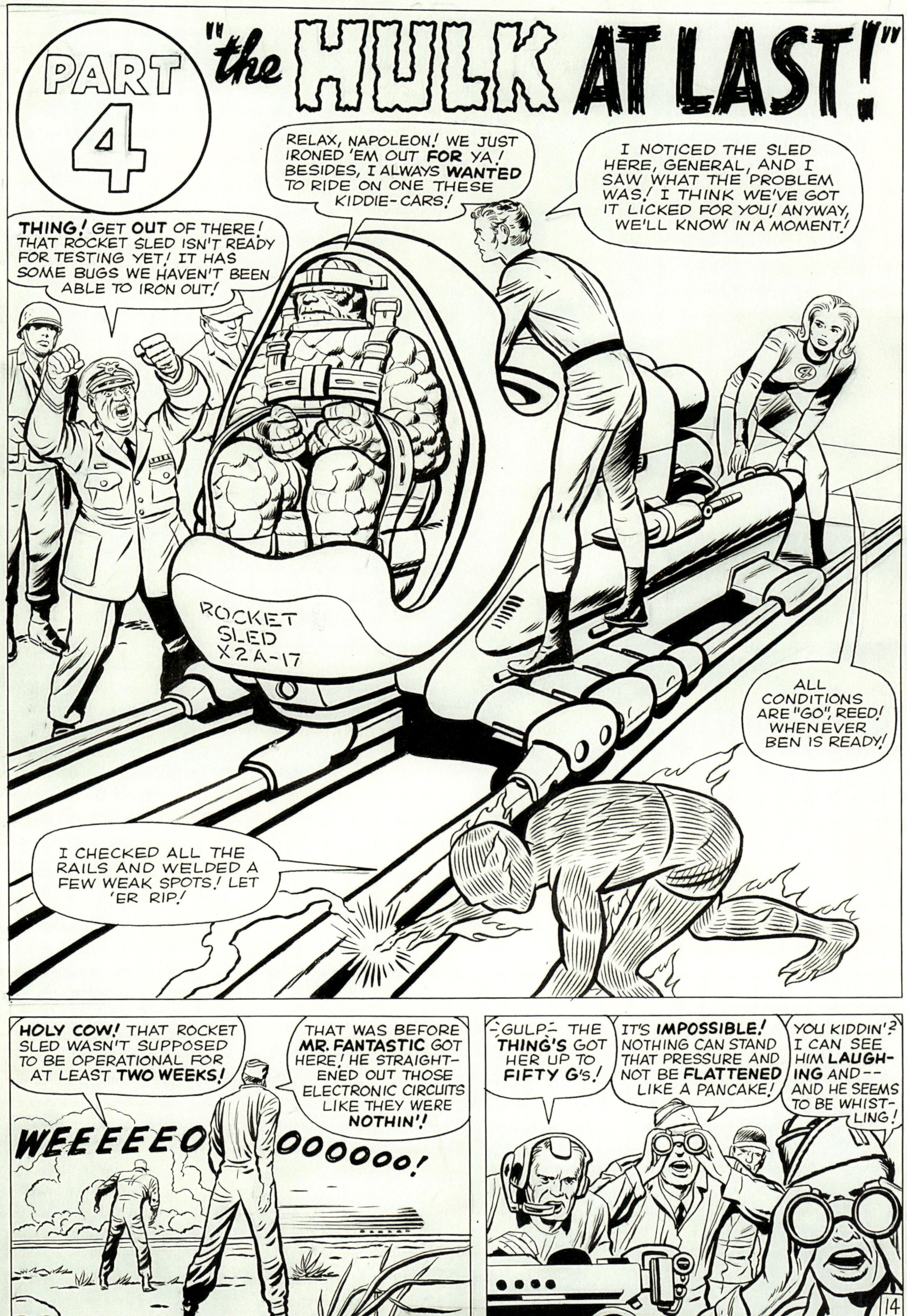

CONTINUED AFTER NEXT PAGE...

FANTASTIC FOUR - #13 - 15 EVOLVED

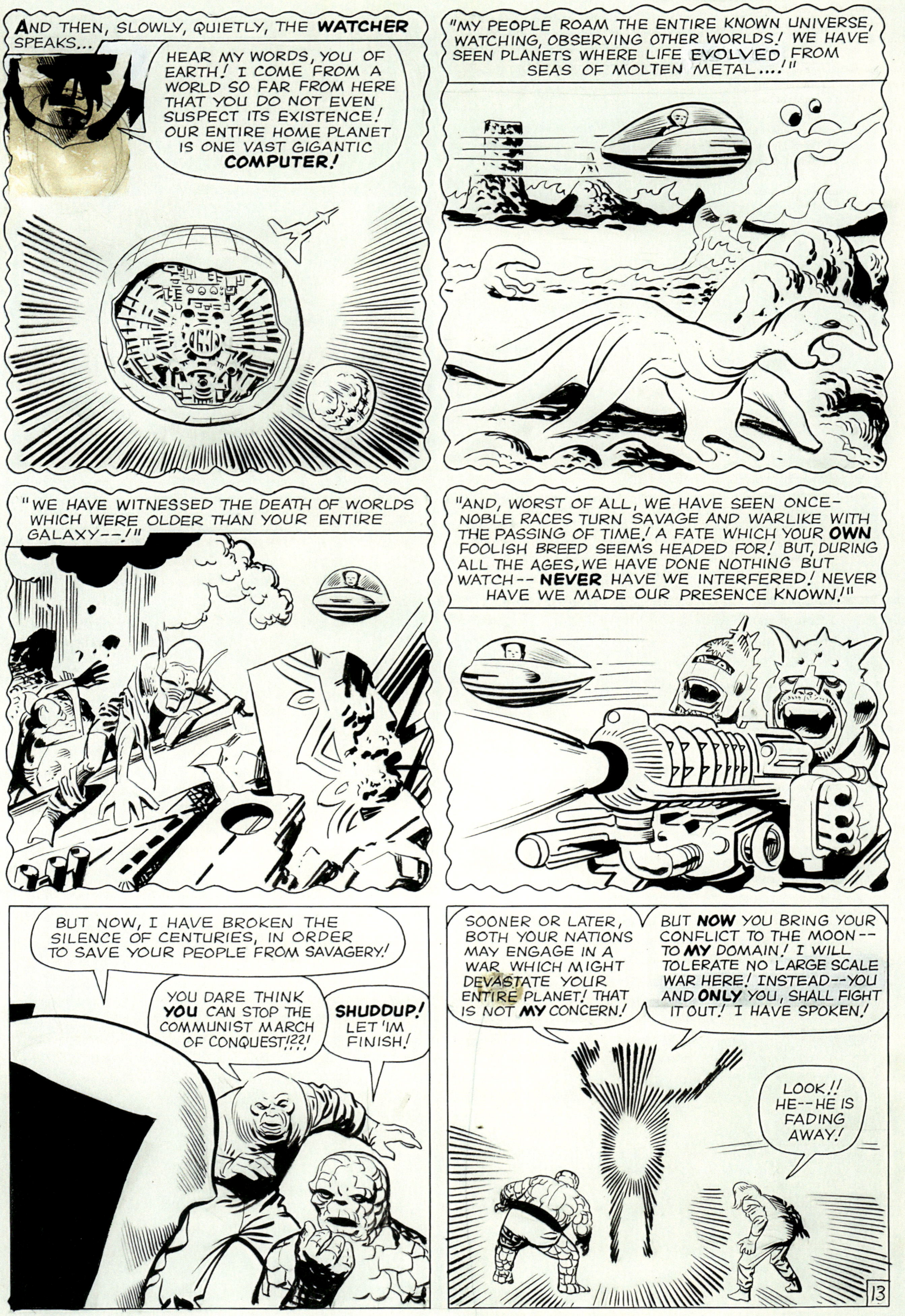

15.

(*Opposite*) *Fantastic Four* No. 13 chronicles another of Stan and Jack's creative leaps forward as they introduce the Red Ghost and his Super-Apes, the Blue Area of the Moon, and, most important, the Watcher, all make their debuts in this issue.

(*Below*) Stan Lee, who never passed on an opportunity to engage with Marvel's burgeoning fan base, provided this synopsis of *Fantastic Four* No. 8 to Jerry Bails, who would republish it in 1964's *CAPA-Alpha* No. 2. Bails contrasts Stan's as-yet-unnamed "Marvel Method" of plotting-by-synopsis to the formal script for an issue of DC's *Justice League of America*, and offers a pithy conclusion: "I say: Somewhere, there's a happy medium."

Doom, realizing his odds of defeating his nemeses were much stronger with Namor at his side, formed Marvel Comics' first super villain alliance in *Fantastic Four* No. 6. Like most of them, this one didn't last; Marvel's villains, despite their shared goals, inevitably turn on one another, and that pattern began here. In teaming up, however, both Doom and Namor show a new side to themselves. Namor, in the clinch, learns that he isn't as ruthless as he thought he was and acts heroically to save the Fantastic Four from certain death. Conversely, so intense is Doom's hatred for Reed Richards, the Doctor demonstrates that he'll backstab any ally without hesitation if it causes more pain to the Fantastic Four. (Befitting the regal stature he has adopted, Doom consistently describes himself as a man of honor and nobility, but he's fooling himself; actions speak louder than words.)

This issue also marks the first appearance of Ben's perpetual nemeses, the Yancy Street Gang. No Doom / Namor team, the YSG comprised a bunch of young pranksters who enjoyed nothing more than tormenting Ben with gag gifts like pepper bombs, pies in the face, and withering "fan" letters. (Years later, it would be established that Johnny himself was secretly behind a good number of the gags.) As you'd guess from their name, the Gang hailed from Manhattan's Lower East Side, specifically the fictional Yancy Street (named after the very real Delancey Street).

For the first time since their origin, the Fantastic Four travel off-world in issue No. 7. Abducted by Kurrgo, Master of Planet X, the team is held hostage, doomed to perish with the rest of Kurrgo's world unless Reed can conceive of some way to shield it from a swiftly approaching "runaway planet."

Alien worlds were a Kirby specialty. Whenever he got an opportunity to imagine a landscape free of Earthly restraints, every panel was bursting with wild gadgetry and bizarre architecture. In Kirbyspace, anything went, and the immutable laws of physics were, under Jack's pencil, mere guidelines. The Four may have failed in their initial space expedition, but this time they're able to save not only the human race but the entire population of Planet X. To spare him the embarrassment, please ignore the fact that Reed Richards, the greatest mind on Earth, confuses reducing and enlarging gases on the final page.

Sales on the series were increasing. With this issue, the publication frequency doubled from six times a year to monthly. Moreover, between issues seven and eight, Stan and Jack successfully launched the FF's first spin-off series, giving the Human Torch a side gig as the headliner of sister publication *Strange Tales* starting with issue No. 101. Spotlighting the Torch and, later, the Torch / Thing team, the feature was set in the fictional town of "Glenville" and lasted nearly three years. Much smaller in scale than its parent book, the Torch series introduced far fewer innovations to the Marvel Universe, in part because Lee and Kirby soon turned the writing and art over to others, briefly including Jerry Siegel, cocreator of DC's Superman.

Another new foe debuts in issue No. 8: The Puppet Master, a weird and gangly scientist who can control anyone by carving their likeness out of a special radioactive clay. The true significance of this issue is the introduction of the Puppet Master's blind stepdaughter, sculptress Alicia Masters. Forever sweet and forever tolerant, Alicia quickly became the first (non-villainous) member of the Four's supporting cast since, despite his grotesque exterior, Alicia had fallen for the man inside the Thing. As their romance blossomed, it lent a new twist to Ben's lamentations over his grotesque form: because Alicia loved him as he was, he never again endured another of Reed's failed attempts to cure him without fearing that Alicia might find his human form less attractive. (For those curious,

PLOT SYNOPSIS for FANTASTIC FOUR #8 "Prisoners of Puppet Master!"

(5 pages): Thing enters headquarters. Mr. F working on something in lab which he doesn't want Thing to see- tells Torch to keep Thing out. Torch tosses up wall of flame between them. Thing gets angry- feels they are keeping secrets from him. Says he's thru- storms out. I.G. runs after him- to cool him off. Becomes invisible so as not to attract attention to herself in her uniform- people stare at invisible gal talking to Thing. They suddenly see a guy about to jump off a bridge. I.G. shoots flare over guy's head. Mr. F sees it- tries to reach out of window to grab guy- too far to reach- Torch flies toward guy and saves him. Guy is in a daze- doesn't know why he did it- is a congressman. Across town the villain has observed what happened thru binoculars- angry- FF frustrated him. He has a small model of bridge and a small model of congressman on table- he made congressman walk off bridge by manipulating the small puppet of him. Now Puppet Master will make puppets of FF and destroy them! He has blind daughter - pretty. (He plans to demonstate his powers to the world, and then sell his services to nation which is the highest bidder).

(5 pages): Puppet Master figures easiest thing to do is let FF destroy themselves- he makes only <u>one</u> puppet- the Thing. He will let the Thing who is strongest destroy the others. He moves puppet to a model of his own apartment so that Thing will come to him. In street, Thing suddenly gets into a daze, and heads for Puppet Master's apt., followed by I.G. Thing, under PM's spell, reveals I.G.'s presence, some interesting scenes showing how PM tries to capture her, and he finally succeeds, helped by blind daughter who can sense things unseen. PM commands Thing to return and slay Mr. F and Torch-- he also tells his daughter to go WITH Thing, dressed in I.G.'s costume, to throw them off-guard. Then, PM makes puppet of warden of state prison- gonna get him to realize (sic) all the hundreds of dangerous prisoners, to prove his power. IG strains to escape bonds and stop him.

(3 pages): Thing enters FF headquarters with Blind gal. Starts to fight Mr. F- knocks out Torch before Torch can burst into flame. Mr. F runs into lab- Thing follows- gets exposed to artificial rays- becomes human- but only for as long as he is under rays- Mr. F tells him the rays are what he was working on earlier- to make Thing human- but didn't want Thing to know until they were perfected- because didn't want Thing to be disappointed. Not perfected yet- still has to find a way to make results more lasting. Blind gal can't understand- tells Thing she thinks he is handsome- his voice- his character- etc.- while in human form the Puppet Master's spell is broken- he is now ashamed of himself. Mr. F realizes blind gal is not I.G.- wonders where I.G. is- we switch to Puppet Master- he has opened prison gates (thru control of warden) and now is making a doll to finish off I.G......

....

EDITOR'S NOTE: The above portion of a FANTASTIC FOUR plot synopsis appears through the courtesy of Stan Lee, editor of the Marvel Group of Comics.

....

FANTASTIC FOUR #14 - 1
ONCE AGAIN, THE FANTASTIC FOUR FACE THE THREAT OF:
SUB-MARINER, and
"THE MERCILESS PUPPET MASTER"
PART 1
HAVING DEFEATED THE RED GHOST ON THE MOON LAST ISSUE, THE WORLD'S MOST POPULAR SUPER-HERO TEAM HEADS FOR HOME AND NEW ADVENTURE!
SCRIPT........STAN LEE
ART...........JACK KIRBY
INKING.......DICK AYERS
LETTERING..ART SIMEK
MOVE, BUTTERFINGERS! I'LL TAKE OVER THE CONTROLS NOW! IT'S ALMOST TIME TO LAND THIS CRATE!
I'M GRABBIN' FORTY WINKS! WAKE ME WHEN WE'VE LANDED!
OKAY, PARTNER! BUT THE WAY I DESIGNED THIS BIRD, SHE CAN PRACTICALLY LAND BY HERSELF!
WE'VE JUST RECEIVED RADIO LANDING CLEARANCE!
X-144
WONDER IF WE'LL RECEIVE MUCH OF AN OVATION WHEN WE LAND, REED?
AS THE FIRST EARTHMEN TO RETURN FROM A ROUND TRIP TO THE MOON? YOU CAN BET ON IT, LADY!
ALL AIR TRAFFIC HALTED WITHIN THOUSAND-MILE PERIMETER! FANTASTIC FOUR-- LAND AT WILL!
HERE THEY COME!
THEY MADE IT! THEY REALLY MADE IT!
1
Jack Kirby
1.

22 FANTASTIC FOUR APRIL '63 X-315
FANTASTIC FOUR #17-1
THE FABULOUS FANTASTIC FOUR...
STORY........STAN LEE
ART...........JACK KIRBY
INKING......DICK AYERS
LETTERING..ART SIMEK
"DEFEATED BY DOCTOR DOOM!"
HAPPY LANDINGS, ANT-MAN!
-SIGH- ISN'T HE THE CUTEST THING?!
I FEEL LIKE A MEATHEAD, WAVIN' TO SOMEONE THE SIZE OF A WORM!
LAST ISSUE, AIDED BY THE AMAZING ANT-MAN, THE FANTASTIC FOUR INVADED THE MICRO-WORLD OF DOCTOR DOOM, AND TRIUMPHED OVER THEIR ARCH-FOE! NOW, BACK HOME AGAIN, THEY BID ADIEU TO THEIR ANT-SIZED ALLY...
SO LONG, LITTLE PAL! YOU'RE A-OKAY IN OUR BOOK!
...AND SO BEGINS OUR NEW, EPIC TALE!
X-315
I'LL PUT AWAY THIS LITTLE LAUNCHING PLATFORM I BUILT FOR HIM! NEVER KNOW WHEN WE MIGHT NEED IT AGAIN!
WE COULD SURE USE A JOKER LIKE HIM IN OUR COMBO, EH, REED?
HE'D BE AN IMPROVEMENT OVER YOU, HOT-HEAD! WE WOULDN'T HAVETA KEEP A FIRE EXTINGUISHER HANDY WITH HIM AROUND!
WELL, WELL, YOU'RE TURNIN' INTO A REGULAR BOB HOPE!
ANT-MAN
1
4915
1.

(*Page 30*) The Fantastic Four returns to Earth after an adventure on the Moon, unaware that both the Puppet Master and a mind-controlled Sub-Mariner await them upon their return home to stir up trouble in this page from *Fantastic Four* No. 14.

(*Page 31*) *Fantastic Four* No. 17 sees the team bid adieu to Ant-Man after he aided them on a trip to the subatomic realm.

(*Opposite*) In issue No. 19, readers are introduced to the time-traveling pharaoh, Rama-Tut, who might be the descendant of Doctor Doom himself! This is a further example of Stan's commitment to building an inter-connected world with this new pantheon of super heroes.

(*Left*) A panel from the story "Return of the Ant-Man" sees Hank Pym, who debuted in a sci-fi story eight issues earlier, return to the Marvel Universe as a costumed adventurer for the first time in *Tales to Astonish* No. 37.

Ben and Alicia did eventually tie the knot — though not for another 57 (!) years.)

To his credit, Reed never stopped searching for a cure for Ben. Now and then, he was partially successful. Ben's monstrous transformation didn't fully "settle in" for a while, and he shifts randomly into human form several times in the issues collected here. Over time, Stan and Jack dropped this plot device, preferring to let Ben face his fate with courage and pathos.

Of all the Fantastic Four tales contained in this volume, the one from issue No. 9 is easily the most charmingly absurd. The Sub-Mariner launches a scheme against his enemies that's too clever by half and patently insane. Rather than simply come to New York once more, windmilling his arms in rage, he — in *one week* — learns that the Fantastic Four has gone broke, buys a successful Hollywood movie studio, baits his enemies into hitch-hiking to Los Angeles, and offers them a million dollars to star in a fake movie in order to trick them into walking into a series of poorly conceived deathtraps. Yet as goofy as it reads, the story serves two important purposes: first, to give Stan and Jack the opportunity to advance the budding romance of Sue Storm and Namor; second, to remind fans of the core philosophy of Marvel Comics — that its heroes have real-world, relatable problems just like us. The biggest weight on Superman's shoulders at this time was how to keep Lois Lane from discovering his secret identity; being cash-poor job-seekers seems a far more sympathetic plight.

Marvel's villains were very rarely captured and jailed. Instead, they met colorful ends (though at their own hands, never the FF's; the team had a strict no-killing rule) and reappeared with equal flourish. When last seen at the end of issue No. 6, Doctor Doom was hurtling through outer space on a speeding meteor, but he didn't simply return. Where's the surprise there? Instead, when he was found and rescued by alien spacefarers in *Fantastic Four* No. 10, he stole their technology and conned them into bringing him back home, becoming a greater threat than ever.

Lee and Kirby always pumped the dramatic stakes high, but they also took the time to have fun with the readers. Here, we find that in the world of the Fantastic Four, not only is there a comic book series dedicated to their exploits, but that it's based on "true" events: no plots can exist until Reed Richards reports to the Marvel offices to officially relate the details of the FF's latest exploit to Stan and Jack themselves!

The Fantastic Four weren't just adventurers or super heroes. They were your friends. Stan and Jack were masters at letting readers know their voices were heard, as seen in "A Visit With the Fantastic Four" in issue No. 11. This 11-pager doesn't have a villain or even a real conflict — it's just a series of clever exchanges and small, intriguing revelations about the team. It's here we first learn that Reed and Ben were college roommates and fellow combat veterans. We also get to see Reed Richards break the fourth wall to remind chauvinist readers that the Invisible Girl, despite her gender, is an integral part of the team who's saved them more than once. In an issue full of whimsy, we're also treated to the debut of the Impossible Man, an imp from the distant planet Poppup who torments the Four with his shape-changing powers until Reed realizes from his child-like behavior that he simply wants attention. Reed's plan is to just ignore him until he leaves, and it worked: readers didn't get to see the Four's most comical villain again for nearly 17 years.

Note also the first comic magazine appearance of the FF's mailman, Willie Lumpkin. Ever-hopeful to join the team, he even had his own "super-power." It wasn't exactly a qualifying ability, but it may have impressed Spider-Man's widowed Aunt May; the two were later an item for a brief time. The name "Willie Lumpkin" was a holdover from an eponymous newspaper strip by Stan and *Archie* artist and creator of *Josie and the Pussycats*, Dan DeCarlo. Starring a younger version of Willie, whose beat was (again) "Glenville," the strip ran from December 1959 to May 1961. Stan himself got the chance to ham it up as a live-action Willie in 2005's *Fantastic Four* feature film.

According to *The Incredible Hulk* No. 1, published between *Fantastic Four* Nos. 4 and 5, physicist Robert Bruce Banner was an advisor to the military who had invented a highly destructive "Gamma Bomb." During its trial run, however, Banner saw and rescued an innocent bystander who had blundered onto the test site. As a result, Banner was irradiated by the full force of the explosion, and from that moment on, the meek, mild scientist discovered he could, under the right circumstances, transform into a green-skinned, super-strong behemoth called the Hulk. As Stan and Jack's follow-up to the success of the FF, they must have been disappointed when the series couldn't find an audience and folded with its sixth issue. None-theless, Stan's faith in the character's potential didn't waver. Rather than relegate the jade giant to the junk heap of failure, he instead guest-starred the Hulk across the Marvel line for the next few years, keeping fans' awareness alive until the time was right to once more award him his own feature. Since then, the Hulk has prevailed to become one of Marvel's best known pop-culture icons, carrying numerous comics, TV shows, and feature films on his broad green shoulders.

This was no team-up, however. In *Fantastic Four* No. 12, It was a knock-down brawl, beginning the longest-lived ongoing rivalry in the Marvel Universe: Thing vs. Hulk, a battle that's been fought dozens of times since. Poor Ben, despite his fighting spirit, generally winds up on the losing side of their throwdowns, but they're still fun to watch. Everyone loves rooting for an underdog.

At the same time these strongmen were duking it out in their inaugural slobberknocker, the FF made their first guest appearance outside their own title (in *Amazing Spider-Man* No. 1). Peter Parker, aka Spider-Man, new on the scene, had come creeping into the Baxter Building to offer his services

FAN 4-#19-P.11
YES, I COME FROM THE YEAR 3,000.. THE GLORIOUS AGE OF ENLIGHTENMENT, THE CENTURY OF PEACE AND PROGRESS.. THE ULTIMATE IN CIVILIZATION AND CULTURE! AND I HATED IT!
"FOR I WAS THEN, AS I AM NOW, A MAN OF ACTION, AN ADVENTURER! BUT THERE WERE NO ADVENTURES IN THE YEAR 3,000...NO ENEMIES TO BATTLE, NO DRAGONS TO SLAY! ALL WAS PEACEFUL...HORRIBLY, UNBEARABLY PEACEFUL!!"
WHY WAS I BORN INTO AN AGE WHEN THE ONLY EXCITEMENT A MAN CAN FIND IS IN WATCHING 3-D STEREOVISIONS FROM A THOUSAND YEARS AGO?!!
"IT WAS WHILE WATCHING SUCH ANCIENT FILMS, PRESENTED BY OUR HISTORICAL SOCIETY, THAT I LEARNED OF THE EXISTENCE OF THE FANTASTIC FOUR! HOW I ENVIED YOUR DRAMATIC CAREERS!"
"THEN, ONE DAY, WHILE VISITING THE RUINS OF AN AMAZING ANCESTOR OF MINE, I CAME UPON WHAT WAS LEFT OF HIS GREATEST INVENTION...A TIME MACHINE!"
PART OF THE MACHINE STILL REMAINS...AND HERE ARE THE PLANS FOR ITS OPERATION!
IT WOULD BE SIMPLE FOR ME TO RECREATE IT, AND USE IT FOR MY OWN PURPOSES!
"I DEVOTED YEARS TO THE BUILDING OF THAT TIME MACHINE, FROM MY ANCESTOR'S PLANS! BUT, KNOWING THE SUPERSTITIOUS BELIEFS OF PEOPLE IN BYGONE DAYS, I SHAPED IT IN THE FORM OF A STRANGE CREATURE, IN THE FORM OF AN IDOL!"
"THEN AT LAST I WAS READY! READY TO TRAVEL TO LONG-DEAD AGES...READY TO BECOME A TIME LOOTER, WITH MY HEADQUARTERS IN ANCIENT EGYPT, WHERE, WITH MY VAST SCIENTIFIC KNOWLEDGE, I COULD BECOME AN ABSOLUTE RULER OF MANKIND!!"
10.

72 BIG PAGES
ANNUAL
APPROVED BY THE COMICS CODE AUTHORITY
Fantastic Four
IND.
MARVEL COMICS GROUP 25¢
ANNUAL
#1 1963
THE WORLD'S GREATEST COMIC MAGAZINE!
AT LAST! MIGHTY SUB-MARINER FINDS HIS LOST RACE! AND SO BEGINS THE MOST EAGERLY AWAITED BATTLE IN ALL COMICDOM -- THE FANTASTIC FOUR VS. THE LEGIONS OF PRINCE NAMOR! THE ONLY UNBROKEN 37-PAGE COMIC MAG TALE EVER PRINTED!!
IT HAD TO HAPPEN! SUB-MARINER IS ATTACKING THE HUMAN RACE!
ATTACK!! MANKIND MUST BOW TO THE SUB-MARINER!
NO MATTER WHO WINS, I LOSE SOMEONE I LOVE!
STAY BACK, ALL OF YOU! I WANT OL' FISH-FACE FOR MYSELF!
DON'T BE A MEAT-HEAD, TORCH! WE AINT PLAYIN' GAMES NOW! THIS IS FOR KEEPS!
ALSO IN THIS SPECTACULAR ISSUE:
THE MOST REQUESTED SAGA OF ALL TIME...
"THE ORIGIN OF THE FANTASTIC FOUR!"
PLUS ANOTHER F.F. FIRST:
"A GALLERY OF VILLAINS!"
THE MARVEL COMICS GROUP USHERS IN THE MARVEL AGE OF COMICS!!
SPIDER-MAN IS WAITING WITHIN THESE PAGES!
25¢
FANTASTIC FOUR ANNUAL
MARVEL COMICS GROUP

(*Opposite*) An unused cover for Marvel's game-changing *Fantastic Four Annual* No. 1. While DC Comics came up with the concept of oversized annual issues with reprinted material, Stan would one-up the competition with mostly original stories in the annual format.

(*Right*) *Fantastic Four Annual* No. 1 offered Lee a chance to revisit and expand upon the story of the FF's first meeting with Spidey that was originally presented in *Amazing Spider-Man* No. 1.

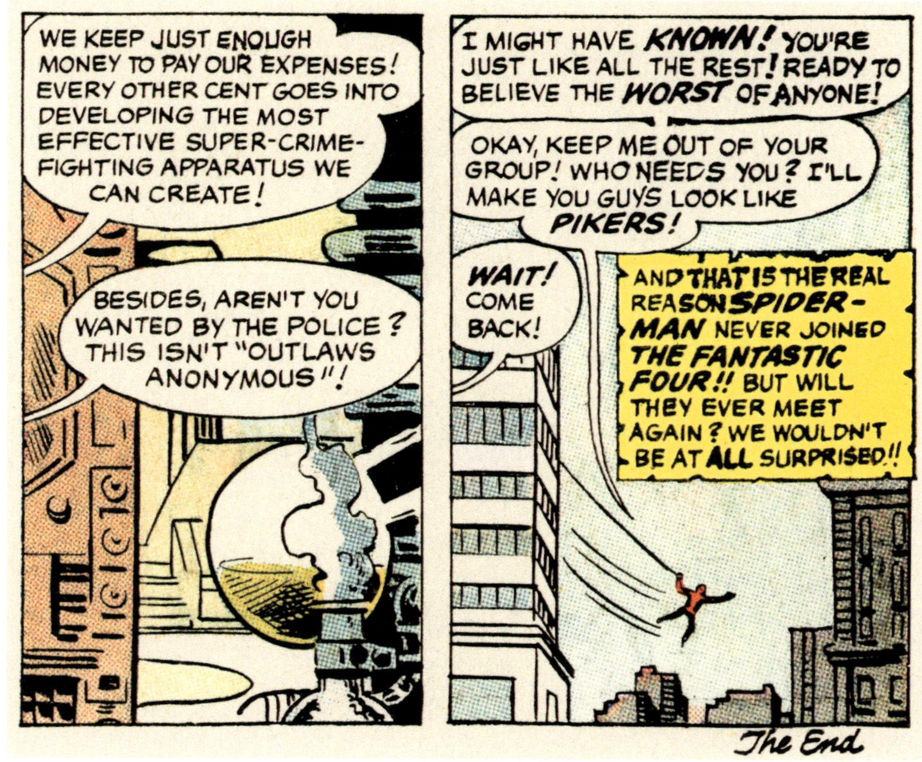

in hopes Reed would be willing to change the name of the team to the Fantastic Five. Following a bit of a dust-up (Ben especially had little patience with uninvited guests, and the wall-crawler was more than happy to "audition" his combat skills), Spidey explained himself, made his pitch . . . and bugged out once he was told how much the job paid. ("We pay *no* salaries or bonuses! Any profit we make goes into scientific research!" Reed didn't mince words.)

Fantastic Four No. 13 chronicles another leap forward in Stan and Jack's creativity, introducing not one but several concepts that have since become integral to the Marvel Universe as a whole. The Red Ghost and his Super-Apes is the least of them, though in an era marked not only by the Cold War with Russia but with the aforementioned Space Race, it was clever to mirror the FF's own origin with a Soviet astronaut and his three ape test subjects. Igor Kragoff and his hench-apes later went on to mix it up with (among others) Iron Man, Spider-Man, and Wolverine.

What makes this issue a true landmark in Marvel history, however, is the introduction of the Watcher and his home, the mysterious "Blue Area" of the Moon. The Watcher, we would learn in later Marvel comics, is a member of an ancient race who traveled the galaxy to gather knowledge and, in turn, used it to aid less-developed civilizations. However, after bestowing scientific advances to a planet of aliens who subsequently used them to war with one another and destroy their world, the Watchers vowed never again to interfere with the fate of others, only to watch and catalog data. Millennia later, Uatu, the Watcher of Earth, met the Four and gradually developed a fondness for the human race. Uatu succumbed often to the temptation of warning Earth's heroes and others about looming dangers, never fully dissuaded by the resultant punishments levied by his peers. (In the 1970s, readers learned that the Blue Area of the Moon was constructed not by the Watcher but by an alien race called the Kree. Like the Skrulls, the Kree — introduced in *Fantastic Four* No. 65 — quickly ascended to true archvillain status, becoming over dozens of appearances one of the most prominent and most dangerous alien races in the Marvel Universe.)

Yeoman inker Dick Ayers was spelled for this one issue by Steve Ditko, and the results are quite nice, offering a crispness to Jack's lines that Ayers's style did not. Sadly, the Kirby / Ditko pairing was only temporary. Normally, Ditko was busy inking his own pencils on the two strips he cocreated: *Spider-Man* and *Doctor Strange*.

Ongoing love triangles just didn't exist in super hero comics. The closest you'd come to finding one would be between Superman, Lois Lane, and Clark Kent, and since two of those are the same person, it doesn't really count. DC super heroes were nothing if not decisive (and ridiculously un-romantic). On the other hand, at Marvel, Cupid was firing his arrows right and left. Though committed to her love for good-if-dull guy Reed Richards, Sue Storm couldn't help but be attracted by bad boy Namor. Their running will-they / won't-they flirtation was an ongoing subplot in the book for decades, even after the wedding of Reed and Sue.

Since discovering, upon his reawakening, that his home of Atlantis had been destroyed by humanity's atomic bomb tests, Namor had been in search of his people, praying that they had not perished but had somehow survived and migrated. But the oceans are vast, and the failures of his quest did nothing to alleviate his rage toward land dwellers. So it comes as no surprise that he's once more attacking the surface world and the Fantastic Four in issue No. 14 — but, for a change, not deliberately. Instead, he's being mind-controlled by the Puppet Master. And even though she doesn't know that at the time, Sue saves him from a Fantastic Four beat-down because she's guessed what's really going on, and it's a very good guess — even by the story's conclusion, the FF never learn exactly who was pulling Namor's strings.

Beginning with issues dated May 1963, Marvel Comics got its official company name as seen on the covers of the books. Reportedly, Steve Ditko created the famous "corner box" design that allowed kids to spot Marvels instantly, whether fanned out on the newsstand shelves or pocketed in the ubiquitous wire "spinner racks" that could be found in drugstores, grocery stores, and convenience stores across the U.S.A.

At last, Reed Richards faced an enemy who was his mental match in *Fantastic Four* No. 15. The Mad Thinker was a criminal mastermind whose specialty was synthesizing observable data to predict future events with astonishing, down-to-the-second accuracy. (To be fair, he didn't refer to himself as mad: remember, villains tend to think of themselves as perfectly sane, even those who would happily label themselves with names like "Doctor Doom.") Though backed by human henchmen, the Thinker's real muscle was his Awesome Android, a featureless synthetic being who could adapt to most attacks. Spoiler: Willie Lumpkin to the rescue.

Another way early Marvel comics set themselves apart from other companies was the line-wide world-building at play. Since the 1930s, DC's heroes had been created independently of one another. Superman sprang from the minds of Jerry Siegel and Joe Shuster. Batman was the vision of Bill Finger and Bob Kane. Green Lantern, Flash, Wonder Woman — all from disparate imaginations. Aside from books like *Justice League of America* or *World's Finest Comics* featuring the Superman / Batman team, there was no sense of cohesion to what DC had built. Metropolis and Gotham City might as well have been on different planets as seldom as their champions interacted.

There, Stan had the advantage: with one writer / editor in charge of everything, working within a relatively small window of time, he and his artistic collaborators were able to create a consistency, a unity, between each Marvel series as they rolled out one after another. Marvel heroes were constantly dropping into one another's series to guest-star, which ended up

(*Left*) Artwork for a 1963 *Fantastic Four* No. 15 pin-up with best wishes from the Four: "Sincerely, Ben, Reed, Sue, + Johnny."

(*Opposite*) Kirby delivers an amazingly detailed cutaway of the Baxter Building in *Fantastic Four Annual* No. 1 from 1963. This drawing greatly expands on a simpler version of the team headquarters that he drew in *Fantastic Four* No. 3 two years earlier.

cross-promoting the entire line. If you were a young reader intrigued by Ant-Man's visit with the Fantastic Four, you'd likely drop another 12 cents on a copy of *Tales to Astonish,* where you'd discover that biochemist Hank Pym had developed shrinking and enlarging gases that allowed him and his partner, the Wasp, to command entire insect armies into helping them fight crime.

When last we saw Doctor Doom, he'd fallen afoul of his own shrinking ray and disappeared, dwindling helplessly to nothingness. But when the FF suddenly found themselves shrinking to tiny size while simultaneously receiving unexplained distress messages from thin air in *Fantastic Four* No. 16, they put two and two together — somehow, Doom had survived and was attacking them from a subatomic world. Summoning Ant-Man for help, the Four followed him into the microverse to find Doom indeed tyrannizing a microcosmic yet heavily populated planet. Overthrowing Doom's rule didn't put an end to his threat, however; using an enlarging ray, Doom returned to Earth and kidnapped Alicia Masters in order to bait the Four into a quartet of individual deathtraps. So menacing was Doom, threatening war on the entire nation, that President Kennedy himself was concerned. (He's there on page 11 of issue No. 17 — from the back and from the forehead up, at least. In the day, comics had a tradition of never directly showing or naming a sitting president "so as to preserve the dignity of the office.")

In their first appearance, the Skrulls took on the FF by duplicating their appearances — and lost. In issue No. 18, they came back fourfold, upping the ante by creating a Super Skrull who could actually duplicate (and even outdo) the powers of each of the team all at once. The ensuing battle was hard-fought, but the Four eventually triumphed through teamwork. The FF is often described as a "dysfunctional family" because of their squabbling and bickering, but they're not that at all. Reed and his crew are a distinctively *functional* family. In the real world, all families argue and fight, but none of them can combine their skills to defeat an undersea prince, an armored madman, or an alien mighty enough to be able to knock the Thing through the air like a Wiffle ball.

Again, part of the delight of reading early Marvel comes in watching the way its heroes, villains, and concepts progressively intertwine to create connections that even Stan and Jack never envisioned as they tossed out idea after idea with no apparent attempt at planning a future. *Fantastic Four* No. 19 is a prime example. While the man who would become Rama Tut is described here as a descendant of Doctor Doom, subsequent issues of *Fantastic Four* postulate that Rama Tut actually *is* Doom from a future era, later in Doom's personal timeline. Wait, it gets better — Marvel writers who followed not only confirmed that theory as canon, they established that Rama Tut would eventually become no fewer than *three* other noteworthy Marvel villains: Kang the Conqueror, the Scarlet Centurion, and Immortus, all masters of time travel.

Around this time, Marvel's chief competitor, DC, had begun issuing "Annuals" — not standard 32-page comics priced at 12 cents, but fat 80-page monsters costing a quarter. Not only did they sell very, very well, but they were ridiculously easy to produce; they consisted wholly of reprinted material, zeroing out DC's editorial cost in order to create a quite profitable package.

Stan decided to one-up his rivals. The first *Fantastic Four Annual* was only 72 pages compared to DC's 80, but it had only one 13-page reprint. The rest of the *Annual* was made up of brand-new material — pinups, fact files, diagrams, and two very special stories.

The lead tale, a blockbuster epic, took up half the book. (Even though Jack was one of the fastest artists in the business, how he found time to draw 37 pages atop all his other assignments is anyone's guess.) Good news: The Sub-Mariner had finally found the survivors of the Atlantean race and was crowned their king. Bad news: This only reminded Namor of his grudge against the surface world, and now he had an entire army ready to follow his orders. Namor declared full-blown war on the human race, and for once, the FF seemed utterly powerless to stop him. Atlantean soldiers swarmed New York City. Namor declared martial law. The Baxter Building was entombed in concrete. The United Nations was advised to stand by for action (despite the outrage of Russian premier Nikita Khrushchev himself!). And only the indomitable fighting spirit of Reed and his team allowed them to snatch victory from the jaws of defeat and achieve their greatest win to date.

But wait, there's more! "A Gallery of the Fantastic Four's Most Famous Foes!" clued latecomers into the first appearances and backgrounds of nearly every opponent the team had faced to date. A Q&A feature answered a long-standing question about how the FF's uniforms could withstand stretching and flames and could turn invisible along with Sue: The suits were made of "unstable molecules" that adapted to the powers of their wearers, "one of Reed's greatest discoveries." Jack even drew up an updated cutaway diagram of the team's headquarters that could be used as a pinup.

Best of all, however, was a six-page expanded retelling — from the FF's point of view this time — of Spider-Man's first encounter with the team (from *Amazing Spider-Man* No. 1). It was a fun romp that went into greater detail about their battle, probably so that the FF wouldn't look like such jobbers. (Spidey held them at bay with ease in the original telling.) It also allowed Stan to blurb Marvel's new breakout star on the cover ("Spider-Man waits within these pages!!").

There you have it: 20 comic books that changed the face of American pop culture. Without their success, there'd be no Avengers, no Hulk, no Marvel television shows or theme parks or blockbuster billion-dollar-grossing movies. In 1961, Stan and Jack and their peers began building a publishing empire featuring characters recognizable from Baltimore to Botswana.

If you enjoy the stories collected in this volume — and you will — tip your hat to Jack Kirby and Stan Lee. They deserve it.

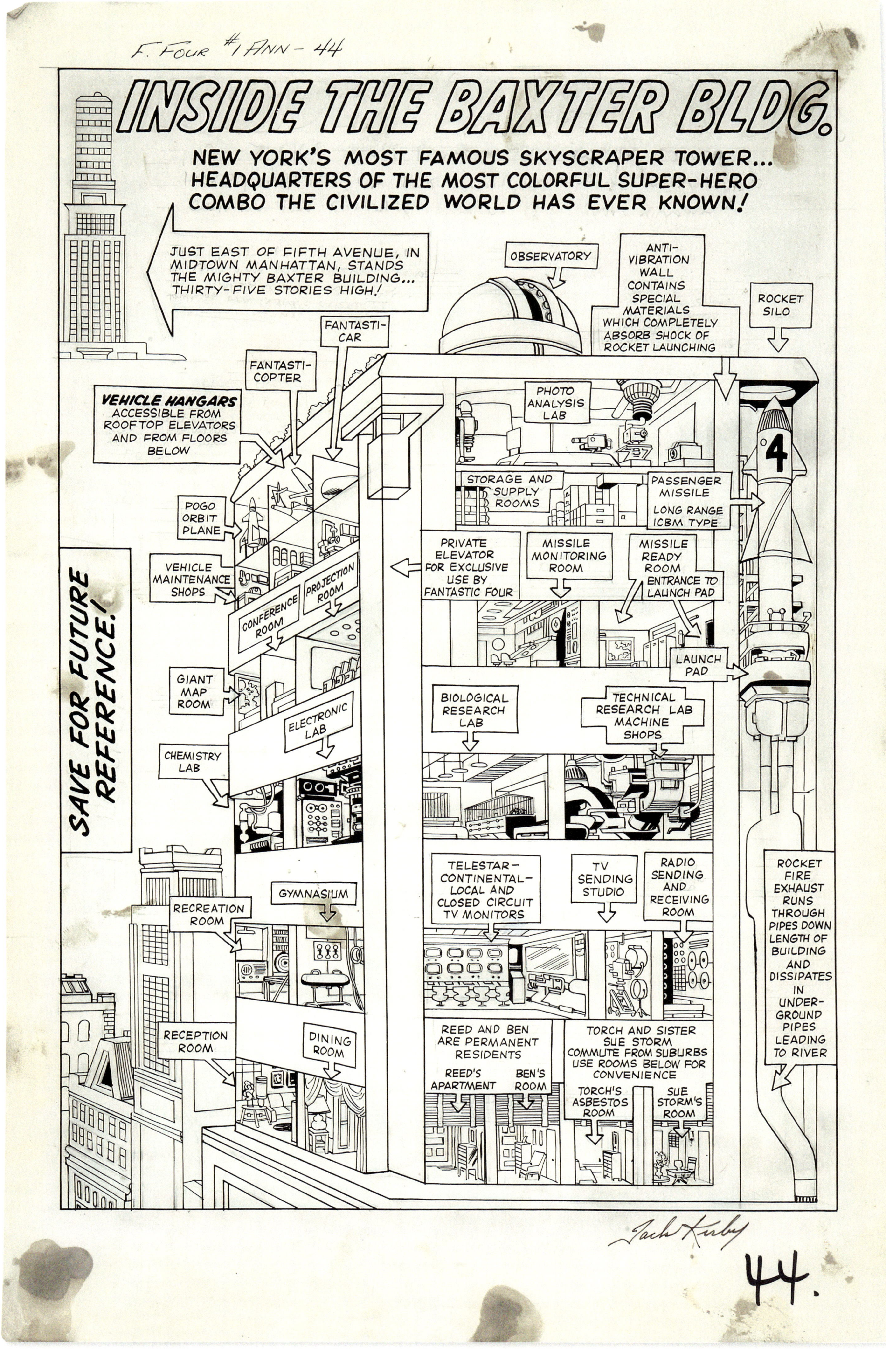
F. FOUR #1 ANN - 44
INSIDE THE BAXTER BLDG.
NEW YORK'S MOST FAMOUS SKYSCRAPER TOWER... HEADQUARTERS OF THE MOST COLORFUL SUPER-HERO COMBO THE CIVILIZED WORLD HAS EVER KNOWN!
JUST EAST OF FIFTH AVENUE, IN MIDTOWN MANHATTAN, STANDS THE MIGHTY BAXTER BUILDING... THIRTY-FIVE STORIES HIGH!
OBSERVATORY
ANTI-VIBRATION WALL CONTAINS SPECIAL MATERIALS WHICH COMPLETELY ABSORB SHOCK OF ROCKET LAUNCHING
ROCKET SILO
FANTASTI-CAR
FANTASTI-COPTER
VEHICLE HANGARS ACCESSIBLE FROM ROOFTOP ELEVATORS AND FROM FLOORS BELOW
PHOTO ANALYSIS LAB
4
STORAGE AND SUPPLY ROOMS
PASSENGER MISSILE LONG RANGE ICBM TYPE
POGO ORBIT PLANE
PRIVATE ELEVATOR FOR EXCLUSIVE USE BY FANTASTIC FOUR
MISSILE MONITORING ROOM
MISSILE READY ROOM ENTRANCE TO LAUNCH PAD
VEHICLE MAINTENANCE SHOPS
PROJECTION ROOM
CONFERENCE ROOM
SAVE FOR FUTURE REFERENCE!
LAUNCH PAD
GIANT MAP ROOM
BIOLOGICAL RESEARCH LAB
TECHNICAL RESEARCH LAB MACHINE SHOPS
ELECTRONIC LAB
CHEMISTRY LAB
TELESTAR-CONTINENTAL-LOCAL AND CLOSED CIRCUIT TV MONITORS
TV SENDING STUDIO
RADIO SENDING AND RECEIVING ROOM
ROCKET FIRE EXHAUST RUNS THROUGH PIPES DOWN LENGTH OF BUILDING AND DISSIPATES IN UNDER-GROUND PIPES LEADING TO RIVER
GYMNASIUM
RECREATION ROOM
RECEPTION ROOM
DINING ROOM
REED AND BEN ARE PERMANENT RESIDENTS
REED'S APARTMENT
BEN'S ROOM
TORCH AND SISTER SUE STORM COMMUTE FROM SUBURBS USE ROOMS BELOW FOR CONVENIENCE
TORCH'S ASBESTOS ROOM
SUE STORM'S ROOM
Jack Kirby
44.

NEDICKS

AT LEAST THEY ALL PARACHUTED TO SAFETY!
THAT SOUND-- IN THE DISTANCE! IT LOOKS LIKE--

I CAN'T ESCAPE IT... IT'S TOO FAST!! IT HAS A NUCLEAR WARHEAD... IF IT EXPLODES, I'M A GONER!
7

YOU'RE GASP FADING AWAY!!
OH, NO!! NO!!
IT'S IMPOSSIBLE!

LOOK!! I SEE HER!
I'M MYSELF AGAIN! IT HAPPENED SO SUDDENLY... ALL BY ITSELF!
11

THE COMICS

IND.
THE Fantastic Four
APPROVED BY THE COMICS CODE AUTHORITY
MC
1
NOV.
10¢
I--I CAN'T TURN INVISIBLE FAST ENOUGH!! HOW CAN WE STOP THIS CREATURE, TORCH?
JUST WAIT AND SEE, SISTER! THE FANTASTIC FOUR HAVE ONLY BEGUN TO FIGHT!
FEATURING: "THE THING!" "MR. FANTASTIC!" "HUMAN TORCH!" "INVISIBLE GIRL!" TOGETHER FOR THE FIRST TIME IN ONE MIGHTY MAGAZINE!
THE THREE OF YOU CAN'T DO IT ALONE! IT'S TIME FOR THE THING TO TAKE A HAND!
IT'LL TAKE MORE THAN ROPES TO KEEP MISTER FANTASTIC OUT OF ACTION!

THE FANTASTIC FOUR is published by CANAM PUBLISHERS SALES CORP. OFFICE OF PUBLICATION: 655 MADISON AVENUE, NEW YORK, N.Y. Published bi-monthly. Copyright 1961 by CANAM PUBLISHERS SALES CORP., 655 Madison Avenue, New York, N.Y. Vol. 1 No. 1, NOVEMBER 1961 issue. Price 10c per copy. Subscription rate $1.45 for 12 issues including postage. No similarity between any of the names, characters, persons, and/or institutions appearing in this magazine with those of any living or dead person or institution is intended, and any such similarity which may exist is purely coincidental. Printed in the U.S.A. by The Eastern Color Printing Co., Waterbury 20, Conn.

HERE THEY ARE...
DR. REED RICHARDS
BEN GRIMM
SUSAN STORM
JOHNNY STORM
Stan Lee + Jack Kirby
THE FANTASTIC FOUR!
V-372
WITH THE SUDDEN FURY OF A THUNDERBOLT, A FLARE IS SHOT INTO THE SKY OVER CENTRAL CITY! THREE AWESOME WORDS TAKE FORM AS IF BY MAGIC, AND A LEGEND IS BORN!!
LOOK! IN THE SKY-- WHAT IN BLAZES DOES IT MEAN?
I DUNNO, BUT THE CROWDS ARE GETTIN' PANICKY!
RUMORS ARE FLYIN' ABOUT AN ALIEN INVASION!
ABOVE ALL THE HUBBUB AND EXCITEMENT, ONE STRANGE FIGURE HOLDS A STILL-SMOKING FLARE GUN! ONE STRANGE MAN WHO IS SOMEHOW MORE THAN JUST A MAN--FOR HE IS THE LEADER OF... THE FANTASTIC FOUR!
IT IS THE FIRST TIME I HAVE FOUND IT NECESSARY TO GIVE THE SIGNAL! I PRAY IT WILL BE THE LAST!
1

IN ANOTHER PART OF TOWN, SUSAN STORM IS HAVING TEA WITH A SOCIETY FRIEND, WHEN SHE HEARS THE OMINOUS WORDS...
SUSAN... LOOK! THOSE WORDS IN THE SKY! WHAT DO THEY MEAN?
SO IT HAS HAPPENED AT LAST! I MUST BE TRUE TO MY VOW!
THERE CAN BE NO TURNING BACK!
SUSAN!! SHE--SHE'S GONE! BUT WHERE? HOW?
IT IS TIME FOR THE WORLD TO MEET... THE INVISIBLE GIRL!
HEY! WHAT'S GOIN' ON?
SOME--SOMETHING RUSHED PAST ME! SOMETHING UNSEEN!
STAND ASIDE! I HAVE NO TIME TO LOSE!
IT--IT'S A GHOST!
JUST WHAT I NEED... AN EMPTY CAB!
BOY, WHAT A DULL DAY!
I MIGHT AS WELL CRUISE AROUND UNTIL I PICK ME UP A FARE!
THANK YOU! I WILL GET OUT HERE!
OKAY...
HUH?!! WAIT-- WHO SAID THAT?? WHA--??
2

DON'T JUST SIT THERE GAPING, MAN! TAKE YOUR MONEY!
I--I'M HEARIN' THINGS! SEEIN' THINGS! OR--OR NOT SEEIN' THEM!!
GANGWAY! I'M GETTIN' OUT OF HERE!
IT WORKS! I REALLY AM INVISIBLE! COMPLETELY, TOTALLY INVISIBLE! THERE CAN BE NO DOUBT! NOW, ALL THAT REMAINS IS... MY MISSION!
BUT LET US LEAVE THE AMAZING INVISIBLE GIRL AND TURN OUR ATTENTION TO A MEN'S CLOTHING STORE, IN ANOTHER PART OF TOWN...
I'M SORRY, MISTER, I JUST DON'T CARRY ANYTHING BIG ENOUGH TO FIT A MAN YOUR SIZE!
BAH! EVERYWHERE IT IS THE SAME! I LIVE IN A WORLD TOO SMALL FOR ME!
LOOK! OUT THE WINDOW IN THE SKY!
THOSE WORDS... "THE FANTASTIC FOUR"! WHAT CAN THEY MEAN?
SO! THE TIME HAS COME!
WAIT, DON'T BOTHER TAKING OFF YOUR COAT... I TOLD YOU WE HAVEN'T ANYTHING IN YOUR SIZE...
YOUR--YOUR--SIZE...
OH NO...
WHAT A RELIEF TO GET RID OF THOSE TIGHT RAGS!
3

WHY MUST THEY BUILD DOORWAYS SO **NARROW?**
HOLY SMOKE!! A--A--**MONSTER!**
PETE, LOOK! WHAT'S **THAT?**
I DUNNO... BUT I AIN'T TAKIN' ANY **CHANCES** WITH IT!
HALT!! HALT OR I'LL SHOOT!!
OKAY, I **WARNED** YOU!
HIS FIRST SHOT MISSED BECAUSE HE WAS SO NERVOUS! BUT HE'LL NOT GET ANOTHER CHANCE!
DID YOU SEE **THAT?** HE RIPPED THE MANHOLE COVER OUT OF THE GROUND WITH HIS BARE HANDS!
IT'S **IMPOSSIBLE!**
I HAVE GONE FAR ENOUGH! I SHOULD BE UNDER MY DESTINATION BY NOW! BUT THERE IS NO MANHOLE ABOVE ME -- NO OPENING!
BAH! I CANNOT DELAY! I'LL **MAKE** AN OPENING!

WHAT IS THAT... RIGHT IN FRONT OF ME?? OH, NO... IT'S ALIVE!!
FOOL! DID YOU NOT SEE ME IN TIME?
IT'S A WALKING NIGHTMARE!! HELP!! HELP!!
LILY-LIVERED COWARDS!
IT AIN'T HUMAN! IT'S TOO BIG... TOO STRONG!! IT--IT'S A MARTIAN!
MINUTES LATER, THE POLICE RIOT SQUAD REACHES THE SCENE...
THERE'S NO ONE HERE!
STREET'S DESERTED!
THEN WHO PUT IN THAT DANGER CALL?
I DON'T KNOW HOW TO EXPLAIN IT, BUT THERE'S SOMETHING WEIRD HAPPENING IN CENTRAL CITY! THOSE WORDS IN THE SKY... THOSE SCATTERED REPORTS OF MONSTERS WALKING THE STREETS...
BUT WHAT DOES IT ADD UP TO, CHIEF? ...WHAT?
WHAT DOES IT ADD UP TO, INDEED? PERHAPS IF THE POLICE OFFICERS COULD WITNESS STILL ANOTHER SCENE IN A LOCAL SERVICE STATION, THEY WOULD FIND YET ANOTHER CLUE--AS WILL WE!
WE GOT HER PURRIN' GENTLE AS A LAMB, JOHNNY!
GOOD! THAT'S THE WAY I LIKE HER!
THERE'S ONLY ONE THING IN THE WORLD THAT INTERESTS ME MORE THAN CARS!
YEAH? WHAT'S THAT, JOHNNY?
5

HEY, JOHNNY... LOOK!! IN THE SKY!! THOSE WORDS! THEY'RE ALL COMIN' TOGETHER! THEY'RE TURNIN' INTO A NUMBER! THE NUMBER... FOUR!
4
JOHNNY! THAT HEAT! WHERE'S IT COMIN' FROM? WHA--? WHAT'S HAPPENING TO YOU?
DON'T WORRY, PAL!
YOU'RE TURNIN' INTO... GASP A-- A HUMAN TORCH!
REMEMBER ME SAYING THERE WAS ONLY ONE THING I CARE ABOUT MORE THAN CARS?
WELL, THIS IS IT!!
!
IMPOSSIBLE? INCREDIBLE? CALL IT WHAT YOU WILL, BUT THE FIGURE WHICH HAD BEEN JOHNNY STORM, SCANT SECONDS BEFORE, IS NOW A CAREENING HUMAN TORCH, FLASHING THRU THE SKIES ABOVE LIKE A FLAMING METEOR!
UNLESS WE'RE GOING MAD--IT'S SOME-THING HUMAN!
LOOK! A BLAZING, BURNING COMET!
NO!! IT'S NOT A COMET!! IT'S-- IT'S--
6

SECONDS LATER, THE MAYOR OF CENTRAL CITY ISSUES AN EMERGENCY ORDER...
CALL THE GOVERNOR! HAVE HIM ALERT THE NATIONAL GUARD!
MOVE, MAN!
Y-YES SIR!
AND BEFORE THE HOUR IS OUT, WASHINGTON HAS ALSO TAKEN IMMEDIATE ACTION!
RED DOG TO SQUADRON LEADER... ATTACK UNKNOWN FLAMING OBJECT OVER CENTRAL CITY...
FLAMING OBJECT? HUH! SOMEONE MUST HAVE FLIPPED HIS LID! OF ALL THE WILD GOOSE CHA-- HEY! WAIT!! WHAT'S THAT?
IT IS A FLAMING FLYING OBJECT! LET'S GET IT, GUYS!
NO! NO! STAY BACK! KEEP AWAY!
WHY WON'T THEY LISTEN?
I WARNED THEM!! I TRIED NOT TO BURN THEIR PLANES, BUT THEY CAME TOO CLOSE!!
AT LEAST THEY ALL PARACHUTED TO SAFETY!
THAT SOUND-- IN THE DISTANCE! IT LOOKS LIKE--
A HUNTER MISSILE! IT'S ZEROED IN ON ME! IT'S ATTRACTED TO MY FLAME!
I CAN'T ESCAPE IT... IT'S TOO FAST!! IT HAS A NUCLEAR WARHEAD... IF IT EXPLODES, I'M A GONER!

SUDDENLY, THE HUMAN TORCH'S FLAME BEGINS TO DIMINISH... AND, AS THE MISSILE IS ABOUT TO STRIKE HIM, TWO IMPOSSIBLY LONG ARMS REACH ABOVE THE ROOF-TOPS, AND...
GOT IT!!
MOVING WITH DAZZLING SPEED, ONE OF THE IN-CREDIBLE ARMS HURLS THE MIGHTY MISSILE FAR FROM SHORE, WHERE IT EXPLODES HARMLESSLY OVER THE SEA!
BUT, AS THE FLYING BOY'S FLAME FLICKERS OUT ALTOGETHER, HE BEGINS TO PLUMMET TOWARD EARTH... TOWARD A CERTAIN DOOM!
GRAB ME, JOHNNY BOY!! THAT'S IT!!
WHO IS THIS UNBELIEVABLE STRANGER WHO HAS SAVED THE HUMAN TORCH?
YOU'RE SAFE NOW, LAD! YOU'RE SAFE!
IN FACT, WHO ARE ALL FOUR OF THESE STRANGE AND ASTONISHING HUMANS? HOW DID THEY BECOME WHAT THEY ARE? WHAT MYSTIC QUIRK OF FATE BROUGHT THEM TOGETHER, TO FORM THE AWE-INSPIRING GROUP KNOWN AS THE FANTASTIC FOUR??
YOU ALL HEEDED MY SUMMONS!! GOOD!! THERE IS A TASK THAT AWAITS US... A FEARFUL TASK!
8

BUT, THERE IS TIME ENOUGH TO LEARN OF THE TASK WHICH FACES THE FANTASTIC FOUR! FIRST, LET US DISCOVER MORE ABOUT THEIR ORIGIN-- LET US GO BACK TO THAT MOMENTOUS DAY WHEN AN ANGRY BEN GRIMM CONFRONTED DR. REED RICHARDS...
IF YOU WANT TO FLY TO THE STARS, THEN YOU PILOT THE SHIP! COUNT ME OUT!
YOU KNOW WE HAVEN'T DONE ENOUGH RESEARCH INTO THE EFFECT OF COSMIC RAYS! THEY MIGHT KILL US ALL OUT IN SPACE!
BEN, WE'VE GOT TO TAKE THAT CHANCE... UNLESS WE WANT THE COMMIES TO BEAT US TO IT!
I-- I NEVER THOUGHT THAT YOU WOULD BE A COWARD!
A COWARD!! NOBODY CALLS ME A COWARD! GET THE SHIP! I'LL FLY HER NO MATTER WHAT HAPPENS!!
AND SO, LED BY A DETERMINED DR. REED RICHARDS, THE LITTLE GROUP SPED TOWARD THE SPACEPORT ON THE OUT-SKIRTS OF TOWN!
SUSAN, BEN AND I KNOW WHAT WE'RE DOING... BUT YOU--AND JOHNNY...
DON'T SAY IT, REED! I'M YOUR FIANCEE! WHERE YOU GO, I GO!
AND I'M TAGGIN' ALONG WITH SIS--SO IT'S SETTLED!
NO TIME TO WAIT FOR OFFICIAL CLEARANCE! CONDITIONS ARE RIGHT TONIGHT! LET'S GO!
BEFORE THE GUARD CAN STOP THEM, THE MIGHTY SHIP WHICH REED RICHARDS HAD SPENT YEARS CONSTRUCTING IS SOARING INTO THE HEAVENS...TOWARDS OUTER SPACE!
SHE'S BEHAVING LIKE A BABY! EVERYTHING IS PERFECT!
YEAH, EXCEPT THE COSMIC RAYS! NO ONE KNOWS WHAT THEY'LL DO...
9

HIGHER AND HIGHER, LIKE A SILVER BULLET, ROARS THE SLEEK SPACE CRAFT...
WE HAD TO DO IT!! WE HAD TO BE THE FIRST!
BUT WE'RE REACHING THE COSMIC STORM AREA... HANG ON!
RAK TAC TAC TAC TAC
HEAR THAT?? IT'S THE COSMIC RAYS!! I--I WARNED YOU ABOUT 'EM!!
THEY'RE PENETRATING THE SHIP!! OUR SHIELDING ISN'T STRONG ENOUGH!
BUT I DON'T FEEL ANYTHING!
NATURALLY! THEY'RE ONLY RAYS OF LIGHT! YOU CAN'T FEEL 'EM-- BUT THEY'LL AFFECT YOU JUST THE SAME!
MY HEAD!! IT--IT'S POUNDING AS THOUGH IT'S ABOUT TO BURST!!
BEN WAS RIGHT!! WE SHOULD HAVE WAITED... SHOULD HAVE GOTTEN HEAVIER SHIELDING!
JOHNNY! WHAT IS IT? WHAT'S HAPPENING TO YOU?
I DON'T KNOW, SIS! MY BODY FEELS HOT-- LIKE IT'S ON FIRE!! I-I FEEL LIKE I'M BURNING UP!!
UGH!! LISTEN TO ME...
...SOMEBODY ELSE TAKE THE CONTROLS... I CAN'T HANDLE THE SHIP ANY MORE! MY-- MY ARMS ARE HEAVY--TOO HEAVY-- CAN'T MOVE--TOO HEAVY-- GOT TO LIE DOWN-- CAN'T MOVE!!
BEN!
10

AT THAT MOMENT, THE POWERFUL SHIP'S AUTOMATIC PILOT TOOK OVER, AND MANAGED TO RETURN THE SLEEK ROCKET SAFELY TO EARTH, IN A ROUGH, BUT NON-FATAL LANDING!
I--I'M GRATEFUL WE'RE ALL ALIVE!! IT WAS MIGHTY CLOSE!
BUT, REED...WE FAILED!! AFTER ALL YOUR WORK... YOUR DEDICATION... WE FAILED!
BAH! WHAT'D YOU EXPECT?
BUT WE'RE STILL NOT COMPLETLY SAFE! WE STILL HAVE TO SEE WHETHER THE COSMIC RAYS AFFECTED US IN ANY WAY!
OH, REED... I FEEL SO STRANGE!
SUSAN! LOOK AT SUSAN!!
WHAT'S WRONG?
YOU'RE -GASP- FADING AWAY!!
OH, NO!! NO!!
IT'S IMPOSSIBLE!
SOMEHOW THE COSMIC RAYS HAVE ALTERED YOUR ATOMIC STRUCTURE...MAKING YOU GROW INVINSIBLE!
SIS! I CAN'T SEE YOU AT ALL ANY MORE!
HOW... HOW LONG WILL IT LAST?
THERE'S NO WAY OF KNOWING!!
WHA--WHAT IF SHE NEVER GETS VISIBLE AGAIN??
LOOK!! I SEE HER!
I'M MYSELF AGAIN! IT HAPPENED SO SUDDENLY...ALL BY ITSELF!
11

THANK HEAVENS!! YOU'RE ALL RIGHT, MY DARLING!
ALL RIGHT, EH? HOW DO YOU KNOW, WISE GUY? HOW DO YOU KNOW SHE WON'T TURN INVISIBLE AGAIN? HOW DO YOU KNOW WHAT'LL HAPPEN TO THE REST OF US?
BEN, I'M SICK AND TIRED OF YOUR INSULTS... OF YOUR COMPLAINING! I DIDN'T PURPOSELY CAUSE OUR FLIGHT TO FAIL!
AND I'M SICK OF YOU... PERIOD! IN FACT, I'M GONNA PASTE YOU RIGHT IN THAT SMUG FACE OF YOURS!
BEN, STOP! WAIT!! LOOK WHAT'S HAPPENING TO YOU! YOU'RE--CHANGING!
DON'T TRY TO TALK YOUR WAY OUT OF IT, MISTER! I'M GONNA MOP UP THE PLACE WITH YOU!
RUN, REED DARLING! HE'S TURNED INTO A-- A--SOME SORT OF A THING! HE'S STRONS AS AN OX!!
"REED DARLING"!! BAH! HOW CAN YOU CARE FOR THAT WEAKLING WHEN I'M HERE!?
I'LL PROVE TO YOU THAT YOU LOVE THE WRONG MAN, SUSAN! I'LL-- HEY! WHAT--??!
NO, YOU DON'T!!
YOU'VE HAD THIS COMING TO YOU FOR A LONG TIME, BEN!
OH, REED... REED... NOT YOU, TOO!! NOT YOU, TOO!!
WHAT AM I DOING? WHAT HAPPENED TO ME? TO ALL OF US?
12

YOU'VE TURNED INTO MONSTERS... BOTH OF YOU!! IT'S THOSE RAYS! THOSE TERRIBLE COSMIC RAYS!
NOW I KNOW WHY I'VE BEEN FEELING SO WARM! LOOK AT ME!! THEY'VE AFFECTED ME, TOO! WHEN I GET EXCITED I CAN FEEL MY BODY BEGIN TO BLAZE!
I'M LIGHTER THAN AIR!! I CAN FLY!! LOOK... I CAN FLY!!
MINUTES LATER, JOHNNY STORM'S FLAME SUBSIDED AND HE LANDED NEAR THE OTHER THREE! SILENTLY THEY WATCHED THE SMALL FIRE HE HAD STARTED IN THE UNDERBRUSH BURN ITSELF OUT!! SILENTLY THEY WERE EACH OCCUPIED WITH THEIR OWN STARTLING THOUGHTS!
WE'VE CHANGED! ALL OF US! WE'RE MORE THAN JUST HUMAN!
LISTEN TO ME, ALL OF YOU! THAT MEANS YOU TOO, BEN! TOGETHER WE HAVE MORE POWER THAN ANY HUMANS HAVE EVER POSSESSED!
YOU DON'T HAVE TO MAKE A SPEECH, BIG SHOT! WE UNDER-STAND! WE'VE GOTTA USE THAT POWER TO HELP MANKIND, RIGHT?
RIGHT, BEN, RIGHT!
I'M CALLING MYSELF THE HUMAN TORCH--AND I'M WITH YOU ALL THE WAY!
SAME GOES FOR ME... THE INVISIBLE GIRL!
THERE'S ONLY ONE STILL MISSING... BEN!!
I AIN'T BEN ANYMORE-- I'M WHAT SUSAN CALLED ME--THE THING!!
AND I'LL CALL MYSELF... MISTER FANTASTIC!!
AND SO WAS BORN "THE FANTASTIC FOUR!!" AND FROM THAT MOMENT ON, THE WORLD WOULD NEVER AGAIN BE THE SAME!!
13

WILL YOU
WORK SATURDAY MORNINGS
for $5.00 to $20.00 EXTRA?
THIS SPARE TIME SHOE BUSINESS CAN MAKE BIG MONEY FOR YOU...
DON'T Invest a Cent! We give you a
FREE SELLING OUTFIT!
It's just like having an EXTRA payday *every week* ... just for showing friends, relatives and neighbors how they'll *"walk on air"* in Mason comfort shoes! Many a man sells 2, 3, 4 or 6 pairs of Mason shoes on Saturday morning alone—and makes himself as much as $5 to $20 or more extra for 2 or 3 hours of his time. *You keep all of your profit!* We furnish you a FREE selling outfit containing everything you need to start making money right away. We carry the stock for you and ship the shoes for you—your profit is clear! You never invest a cent. And think what you'll save on your own shoes, too!
Here's Why You'll Make Money!
You'll take orders for over 230 different shoe styles for dress, sport or work, for men and women—a far greater selection than any neighborhood store can possibly stock. And you can fit almost anyone! You'll draw from our 300,000-pair stock with sizes ranging from 2½ to 15, widths AAAA to EEEE! You'll feature exclusive Velvet-eez shoes with foamy-soft air-cushion innersoles that let you "walk on air." You show many other exclusive features ... Ripple Sole Shoes, Oil-Resistant Work Shoes, Magic Shu-Lok Shoes, colorful styles for women—a line that's far beyond the reach of any store. That's why EVERYBODY is your prospect. And because Mason Shoes are never sold through stores, folks must buy from you!
Sales Equipment Absolutely FREE
Fill out and mail coupon below. We'll rush you your FREE selling outfit. Kit features 230 fast-selling shoe styles, plus foolproof measuring equipment—and "How To Make Extra Money" booklet. Send no money now or later. You get everything you need to start. Rush coupon for your FREE selling outfit ... have an EXTRA payday next Saturday! Act today!
MASON SHOE MFG. CO.
Dept. G-948
Chippewa Falls, Wisconsin
Opportunities for District Managers
If you have ambition, can sell, and can train and supervise others, we may have an opening for you as a District Sales Manager.
If you are qualified for this type of promotion, write us. Give age, education, sales and management experience. Personal interviews arranged with qualified men.
Write F. H. Froberg, Desk B, Mason Shoe Mfg. Company, Chippewa Falls, Wis.
RUSH STARTING OUTFIT
MR. NED MASON
Mason Shoe Mfg. Company, Dept. G-948 Chippewa Falls, Wis.
Dear Ned: Please rush FREE and postpaid my Starting Shoe Business Outfit with EVERYTHING I need to start making extra cash Saturday mornings.
Name
(PLEASE PRINT)
Address
Town
State

THE FANTASTIC FOUR MEET
THE MOLE MAN!
V-372
AND NOW, HAVING MET OUR FOUR AMAZING CHARACTERS, LET US RESUME OUR TALE...
I CALLED YOU TOGETHER BECAUSE I HAVE SOME PICTURES TO SHOW YOU!
PICTURES?
WHAT ARE THEY... PIN-UPS?
LOOK! ALL OF YOU! THIS USED TO BE AN ATOMIC PLANT BEHIND THE IRON CURTAIN!
WOW! WHAT HAPPENED TO IT?
14

THE SAME THING THAT HAPPENED TO THE OTHER ATOMIC PLANTS ON THOSE PHOTOS!
THIS ONE IS IN AUSTRALIA!
AND THIS IS IN SOUTH AMERICA!
THAT'S JUST IT! IT'S HAPPENING TO ATOMIC PLANTS ALL OVER THE WORLD! NO ONE KNOWS HOW--OR WHY!
WAIT!! ACCORDING TO THE STEADY IMPULSES ON MY RADAR MACHINE, ANOTHER CAVE-IN IS ABOUT DUE TO TAKE PLACE!!
AND, EVEN AS REED RICHARDS SPEAKS, HALF-WAY AROUND THE WORLD, IN FRENCH AFRICA, THE FOLLOWING SCENE IS TAKING PLACE...
WHAT IS WRONG, PIERRE?
I DO NOT KNOW! IT SOUNDS IN-SANE, BUT THE SAND BENEATH MY FEET SEEMS TO BE THROBBING!
...ALMOST AS IF SOMETHING IS MOVING BELOW US! ALMOST AS IF... LISTEN! DON'T YOU FEEL IT??
RUMBLE RUMBLE
HELP!!
RUMBLE ROAR
IT IS AN EARTHQUAKE! BUT HERE IN THE DESERT?? IMPOSSIBLE!!
IMPOSSIBLE OR NOT, PIERRE ALMOST FELL TO HIS DOOM!
WAIT!! THE GROUND IS TREMBLING AGAIN!! WHAT CAN IT BE??
SACRE BLEU!! THE EARTH IS GOING MAD!!
ROOOOOOMM

THE ENTIRE INSTALLATION!! IT--IT IS CAVING IN!
RRROOMM
BUT THE WORST IS YET TO COME!! FOR, LESS THAN THIRTY SECONDS LATER...
IN THE NAME OF HEAVEN!!
WHAT IS THAT?
WHAT INDEED?? IT IS A GIGANTIC PAIR OF CLAWS, THE LIKE OF WHICH HAVE NEVER BEEN SEEN ON EARTH, OR ON ANY PLANET IN THE UNIVERSE!! IT IS UNBELIEVABLE... MIND STAGGERING... BUT REAL!
ARTILLERY!! BRING THE ARTILLERY!! HURRY! HURRY!
ARTILLERY! OF WHAT USE IS ARTILLERY AGAINST A CREATURE WHOSE HIDE IS POWERFUL ENOUGH TO DIG ITS WAY UP THRU COUTLESS TONS OF ROCK-HARD EARTH??
ARTILLERY! OF WHAT USE IS ARTILLERY AGAINST A MONSTER WHO CAN CRUSH A HEAVY TANK WITH ONE HAND??
BUT, JUST AS IT SEEMS THAT NOTHING IN THE WORLD WILL HALT THE NIGHTMARE MENACE, THE SHRILL SOUND OF A COMMANDING VOICE IS HEARD... AND THE GOLIATH STOPS IN ITS TRACKS!
ENOUGH! RETURN TO EARTH'S CORE! OUR MISSION HERE IS FINISHED! GO!!
FOR EVEN SUCH A MONSTER HEEDS ITS MASTER! A MASTER KNOWN AS... THE MOLEMAN!!
16

BUT WE SHALL RETURN TO THE MOLEMAN BEFORE LONG! FIRST, LET US TURN OUR ATTENTION BACK TO THE FANTASTIC FOUR, AS THEY GAZE IN ASTONISHMENT AT DR. REED RICHARDS' SUPER-SENSITIVE RADARSCOPE...
THERE! IT HAS HAPPENED AGAIN! THIS TIME IN FRENCH EQUITORIAL AFRICA!
BUT HOW? WHY?
THAT'S WHAT WE'VE GOT TO FIND OUT!
BY STUDYING THE CAVE-INS CAREFULLY, I'VE PIN-POINTED AN ISLAND LOCATED EXACTLY BETWEEN THEM! THAT IS WHERE WE WILL FIND OUR ANSWER! IT IS KNOWN AS MONSTER ISLE!
MONSTER ISLE! THAT'S JUST A FAIRY TALE! THERE'S NO SUCH PLACE!
ONLY ONE WAY TO FIND OUT, BEN!
AND FIND OUT THEY DO! HOURS LATER, ABOARD THEIR SMALL, PRIVATE JET, THE FANTASTIC FOUR SEE A STRANGE MOUNTAIN RISING FROM THE SEA, LIKE AN UNEARTHLY GROTESQUE FACE!! THEY HAVE FOUND... MONSTER ISLE!
THERE IT IS!
4
LITTLE DREAMING WHAT AWAITS THEM, THEY CLIMB TO THE TOP OF THE FORBIDDING PEAK...
IF THIS IS JUST A WILD GOOSE CHASE, MISTER, I'LL MAKE SURE YOU LIVE TO REGRET IT!
SAVE YOUR BREATH FOR THE CLIMB, GRUE-SOME!
HOLD IT!! I HEAR SOMETHING!!
IT'S COMING FROM BELOW!
LOOK!! THOSE EYES...
SUDDENLY, A LIVING THREE-HEADED NIGHT-MARE HURLS ITSELF AT THEM FROM OVER THE EDGE OF THE PEAK OF MONSTER ISLE!
17

QUICK, SUE! TURN INVISIBLE!
SEEING ONE OF ITS INTENDED VICTIMS VANISH BEFORE ITS EYES, THE MONSTER HALTS... BEWILDERED!!
THERE'S JUST TIME FOR ME TO BECOME MR. FANTASTIC AGAIN! I'LL MAKE A HUGE LASSO OUT OF MY ARM!
GOT 'IM!!
I HAD HEARD THERE WAS A GIANT THREE-HEADED CREATURE GUARDING THIS ISLE... BUT HE SHALL GUARD IT NO LONGER!!
BUT BEFORE MR. FANTASTIC AND THE HUMAN TORCH CAN CATCH THEIR BREATH...
LOOK OUT!!
IT'S A CAVE-IN!
HOLD ON, JOHNNY! HOLD ON!
GULP! LUCKY SUE AND BEN WEREN'T WITH US AT THE EDGE!

CONTINUED AFTER NEXT PAGE..

BOYS — 12 or older —

Here's a swell way to MAKE $1 to $5 WEEKLY and Win Dandy FREE PRIZES Too!

over 30,000 boys **SELL GRIT** *"America's Greatest Family Newspaper"* IN SPARE TIME

Besides getting lots of spending money and winning prizes, selling GRIT gives boys valuable business training which helps them to become successful men.

GRIT will help you get started in a profitable business of your own. We send you complete, easy to understand selling instructions. You pay *only* for the papers you sell until you know how many to order.

GRIT sells for 15c
YOU MAKE 5¢ PROFIT *on every copy you sell*

—win these and many other prizes too.

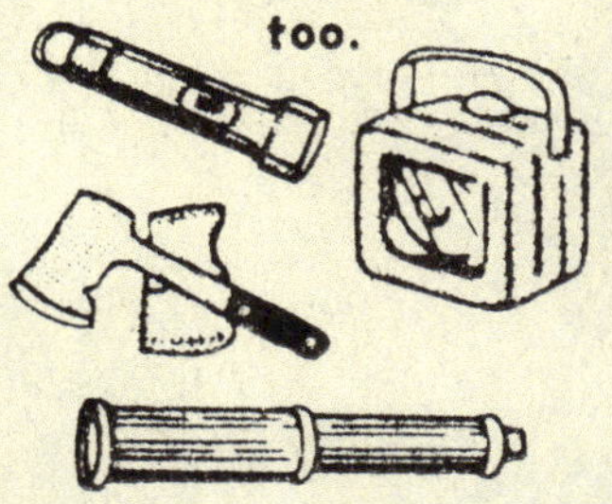

MAIL THIS COUPON ←

Today in an envelope or pasted on a post card

GRIT PUBLISHING CO., Williamsport, Pa.

Send my first bundle of papers, selling helps and prize offers. MC10-1

Name ....

Are You a Boy? ..... Age ..... Date Born .... Year ....

In Care of ....

Street and No. .... R. F. D. ....

Post Office .... State ....

Print Your Last Name Plainly Here

REWARD $2,000.00

FOR THIS COIN!

Illustrated: 1804 silver dollar — 19,000 minted, only 12 accounted for— where are the rest?

FOR CERTAIN COINS WE PAY UP TO:	
Pennies Before 1919	9,000.00
Silver Dollars Before 1936	8,000.00
Nickles Before 1945	6,000.00
Dimes Before 1946	5,000.00
Half Dollars Before 1947	4,500.00
Quarters Before 1941	3,500.00
Half Cents Before 1910	3,500.00
Lincoln Pennies Before 1940	200.00

Stop spending pocket change worth hundreds of dollars. New large illustrated catalogue lists the actual price we will pay for all United States Coins. Certain half cent coins are worth up to $3,500.00 for Canadian Coins. Our valuable Coin Book may reward you many thousands of dollars. Coins do not have to be old to be valuable. Thousands of dollars have been paid for coins dated as recently as 1940 to 1956. It's easy to learn the rare dates and to identify rare coins in your possession with our new 1961 catalogue. A fortune may be waiting for you. Millions of Dollars have been paid for rare coins. Don't sell your valuable coins for less than they are worth! Hold on to your coins until you obtain our catalogue. Send $1.00 for newest Coin Catalogue to: **BEST VALUES CO., COIN DEPT.115 403 MARKET ST. Newark, New Jersey.**

MAIL MONEY-SAVING NO-RISK FREE TRIAL COUPON NOW!

BEST VALUES CO., COIN DEPT. 115
403 Market St.
Newark, New Jersey

Rush your Latest Large Coin Catalogue listing the actual prices you will pay for United States Coins. I enclose $1. Send Postage Prepaid.

Name..

Address..

City.............................*State*..............

THE MOLEMAN'S SECRET!
BEFORE WE WITNESS THE BREATH-TAKING CONCLUSION OF OUR AMAZING TALE, LET US GATHER TOGETHER ALL THE LOOSE ENDS! LET US RETURN TO THE TWO MEMBERS OF THE FANTASTIC FOUR WHO DID NOT FALL BELOW DURING THE CAVE-IN...
REED... AND JOHNNY... GOT TO FIND THEM!!
WAIT! THAT NOISE-- BEHIND ME!! WHAT--??
BUT OTHER EARS ALSO HEAR THE MENACING SOUNDS... AND OTHER EYES BEHOLD THE FRIGHTENING SIGHT...
THE EYES OF... THE THING!!
DUCK, SUE! OUT OF THE WAY!
LET ME HANDLE 'IM!
20

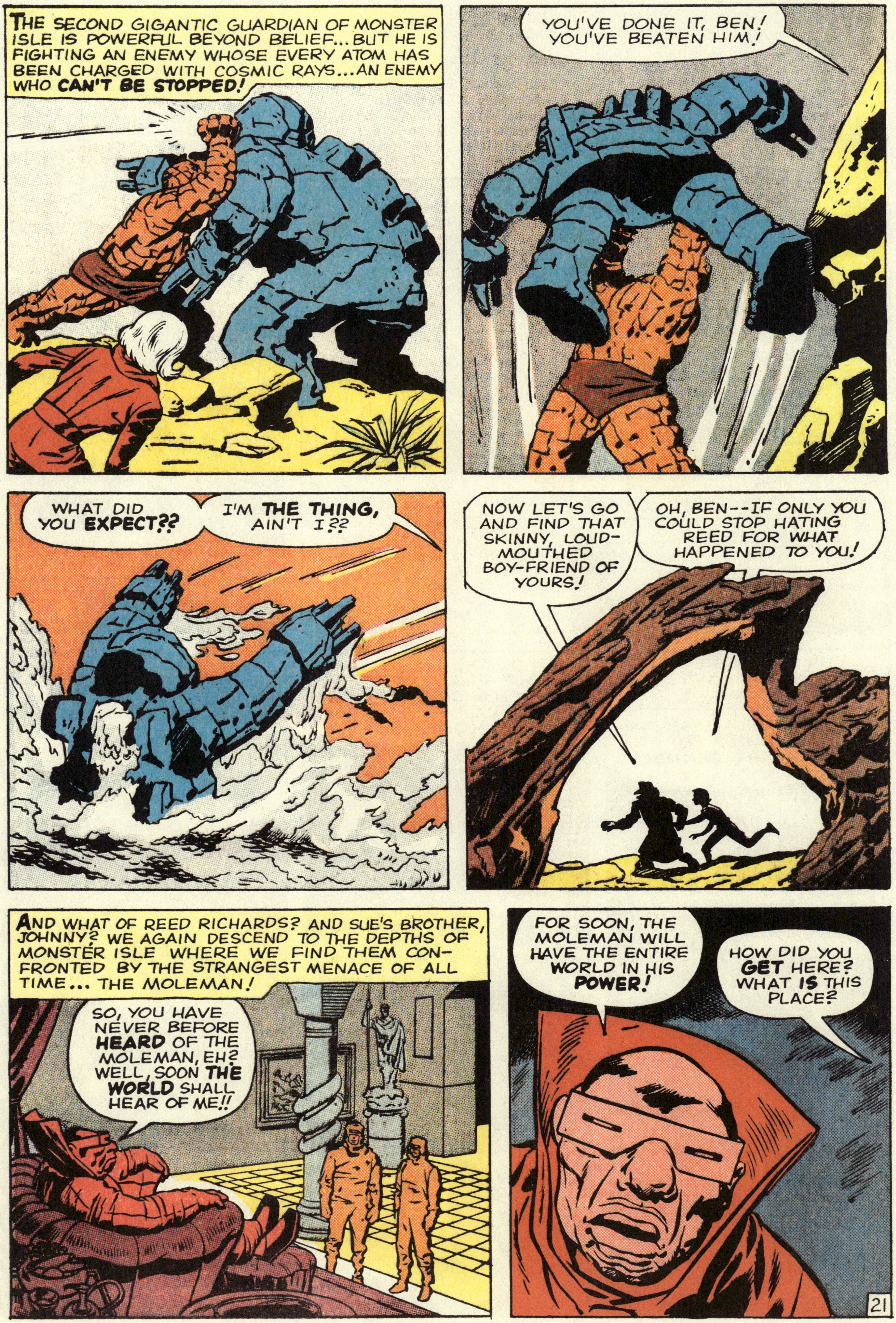
THE SECOND GIGANTIC GUARDIAN OF MONSTER ISLE IS POWERFUL BEYOND BELIEF... BUT HE IS FIGHTING AN ENEMY WHOSE EVERY ATOM HAS BEEN CHARGED WITH COSMIC RAYS... AN ENEMY WHO CAN'T BE STOPPED!
YOU'VE DONE IT, BEN! YOU'VE BEATEN HIM!
WHAT DID YOU EXPECT??
I'M THE THING, AIN'T I??
NOW LET'S GO AND FIND THAT SKINNY, LOUD-MOUTHED BOY-FRIEND OF YOURS!
OH, BEN--IF ONLY YOU COULD STOP HATING REED FOR WHAT HAPPENED TO YOU!
AND WHAT OF REED RICHARDS? AND SUE'S BROTHER, JOHNNY? WE AGAIN DESCEND TO THE DEPTHS OF MONSTER ISLE WHERE WE FIND THEM CON-FRONTED BY THE STRANGEST MENACE OF ALL TIME... THE MOLEMAN!
SO, YOU HAVE NEVER BEFORE HEARD OF THE MOLEMAN, EH? WELL, SOON THE WORLD SHALL HEAR OF ME!!
FOR SOON, THE MOLEMAN WILL HAVE THE ENTIRE WORLD IN HIS POWER!
HOW DID YOU GET HERE? WHAT IS THIS PLACE?

"IT ALL STARTED LONG AGO!! BECAUSE THE PEOPLE OF THE SURFACE WORLD MOCKED ME!"
WHAT? ME GO OUT WITH YOU? DON'T MAKE ME LAUGH!
I KNOW YOU'RE QUALIFIED, BUT YOU CAN'T WORK HERE! YOU'D SCARE OUR OTHER EMPLOYEES AWAY!
HEY, IS THAT YOUR FACE, OR ARE YOU WEARIN' A MASK? HAW HAW!
"FINALLY, I COULD STAND IT NO LONGER! I DECIDED TO STRIKE OUT ALONE...TO SEARCH FOR A NEW WORLD ...THE LEGENDARY LAND AT THE CENTER OF THE EARTH! A WORLD WHERE I COULD BE KING! MY TRAVELS TOOK ME ALL OVER THE GLOBE..."
EVEN THIS LONELINESS IS BETTER THAN THE CRUELTY OF MY FELLOW MEN!
"AND THEN, JUST WHEN I HAD ALMOST ABANDONED HOPE... WHEN MY LITTLE SKIFF HAD BEEN WASHED ASHORE HERE ON MONSTER ISLE, I FOUND IT!"
THAT STRANGE CAVERN! WHERE CAN IT LEAD TO?
"I SOON SAW WHERE IT LED... IT LED TO THE LAND OF MY DREAMS..."
DOWN THERE... BELOW-- I'VE FOUND IT!! IT'S EARTH'S CENTER!
"BUT IN THE DREAD SILENCE OF THAT HUGE CAVERN, THE SUDDEN SHOCK OF MY LOUD OUTCRY CAUSED A VIOLENT AVALANCHE, AND..."
"...WHEN IT WAS OVER, I HAD SOMEHOW MIRACULOUSLY SURVIVED THE FALL... BUT, DUE TO THE IMPACT OF THE CRASH, I HAD LOST MOST OF MY SIGHT! YES, I HAD FOUND THE CENTER OF EARTH--BUT I WAS STRANDED HERE...LIKE A HUMAN MOLE!!
22

THAT WAS TO BE THE LAST OF MY MISFORTUNES! MY LUCK BEGAN TO TURN IN MY FAVOR! I MASTERED THE CREATURES DOWN HERE-- MADE THEM DO MY BIDDING-- AND WITH THEIR HELP, I CARVED OUT AN UNDERGROUND EMPIRE!
A NOTE OF MADNESS CREEPS INTO THE MOLE'S VOICE AS HE SPEAKS OF HIS POWER! AND THEN, HE MAKES HIS FIRST FATAL MISTAKE...
I CONQUERED EVERYTHING ABOUT ME! I EVEN LEARNED TO SENSE THINGS IN THE DARK--LIKE A MOLE! HERE, I'LL SHOW YOU! TRY TO STRIKE ME WITH THAT POLE! TRY IT, I SAY!!
HAH! I SENSED THAT BLOW COMING! NOTHING CAN TAKE ME BY SURPRISE! AND, I HAVE DEVELOPED OTHER SENSES TOO, LIKE THOSE OF THE BAT--
I POSSESS A NATURAL RADAR SENSE... A WARNING SYSTEM WHICH ENABLES ME TO EVADE WHATEVER DANGER STRIKES AT ME!
COMPARED TO THE MOLE-MAN, YOU ARE SLOW... CLUMSY!! HAH HAH!!
SEE HOW EASILY I DEFEAT YOU... OR ANY OTHERS WHO TRY TO DEFY ME!
NOW, BEFORE I SLAY YOU ALL, BEHOLD MY MASTER PLAN! SEE THIS MAP OF MY UNDERGROUND EMPIRE! EACH TUNNEL LEADS TO A MAJOR CITY! AS SOON AS I HAVE WRECKED EVERY ATOMIC PLANT, EVERY SOURCE OF EARTHLY POWER, MY MIGHTY MOLE CREATURES WILL ATTACK AND DESTROY EVERYTHING THAT LIVES ABOVE THE SURFACE!
AND NOW, AT MY SIGNAL, THOSE CREATURES OF DARKNESS, MY DENIZENS OF EARTH'S CENTER, SHALL DISPOSE OF ALL OF YOU WITLESS INTRUDERS!
WE'LL SEE ABOUT THAT, MOLE!!
THE THING!!
23

TOO LATE, FOOL! THE DIE IS CAST! THERE IS NO TURNING BACK.!!
THING!! LOOK OUT... BEHIND YOU!
BONG! BONG!
HEARING THE MOLE'S SIGNAL, THE LARGEST AND MOST DEADLY OF HIS UNDERGROUND CREATURES PONDEROUSLY RAISES ITSELF INTO THE ROOM... ITS BRAINLESS RAGE DIRECTED AT THE FOUR ASTONISHED HUMANS!
AND THEN, THE FANTASTIC FOUR FLY INTO BLAZING ACTION...
LOOK OUT, REED! I'M GONNA BURN MY WAY OUTTA THIS MONKEY SUIT!
GOOD BOY, TORCH!
STAND ASIDE, GANG! IT'S GONNA GET MIGHTY WARM AROUND HERE!
BACK AND FORTH, BUZZING AROUND THE MONSTER'S HEAD LIKE A HORNET, FLIES THE HUMAN TORCH, AS THE GIGANTIC CREATURE VAINLY TRIES TO GRASP HIS FIERY FOE!
REED! THE MOLE MAN! HE'S ESCAPING!
NOT IF I CAN HELP IT, SUE!
AND HELP IT I CAN!
24

MOVING LIKE A WELL-OILED FIGHTING MACHINE, THE FANTASTIC FOUR, WITH THE DEADLY MOLEMAN IN THEIR GRASP, RACE FOR THE SURFACE... BUT THEN THEIR EVIL ANTAGONIST SEIZES THE SIGNAL CORD AGAIN, AND...
YOU HAVEN'T WON YET! EVEN YOU CAN'T DEFEAT ALL OF MY UNDER-EARTH HORDE!
HURRY, REED... HURRY!
CAN'T YOU EVEN HOLD ON TO ONE LITTLE GUY?
AND THEN THEY COME... LIKE FIGMENTS OF A MAD NIGHTMARE... ROARING, RUNNING, SNARLING... THE MOLEMAN'S ENTIRE ARMY OF UNDERGROUND GARGOYLES!!
BUT THEY HADN'T COUNTED ON THE UNBELIEVABLE POWER OF THE HUMAN TORCH! FLYING BETWEEN HIS FANTASTIC ALLIES, AND THE PURSUING HORDE, HE BLAZES A FIERY SWATH WHICH MELTS THE SOFT EARTH...
THIS WILL CAUSE A ROCKSLIDE, SEALING US OFF FROM THOSE CREATURES!
WE DID IT... WE'RE FREE!! AND THE ENTRANCE TO THE MOLEMAN'S EMPIRE IS SEALED FOREVER!
25
MOMENTS LATER...
BUT WHERE IS THE MOLEMAN?
I LEFT HIM BEHIND--HE'LL NEVER TROUBLE ANYONE AGAIN!
AND THE WORDS OF MR. FANTASTIC ARE INDEED PROPHETIC... AS, SECONDS LATER...
HE'S DESTROYED THE ENTIRE ISLE! HE'S SEALED HIMSELF BELOW--FOREVER!
IT'S BEST THAT WAY! THERE WAS NO PLACE FOR HIM IN OUR WORLD ...PERHAPS HE'LL FIND PEACE DOWN THERE... I HOPE SO!
I JUST HOPE WE HAVE SEEN THE LAST OF HIM!
BUT, WHETHER WE'VE SEEN THE LAST OF THE MOLEMAN OR NOT, WE WILL SEE MUCH MORE OF THE MOST AMAZING QUARTET IN HISTORY, IN THE NEXT GREAT ISSUE OF-- THE FANTASTIC FOUR!! DON'T MISS IT!!
THE END

IF YOU KNOW JUST 20 PEOPLE...

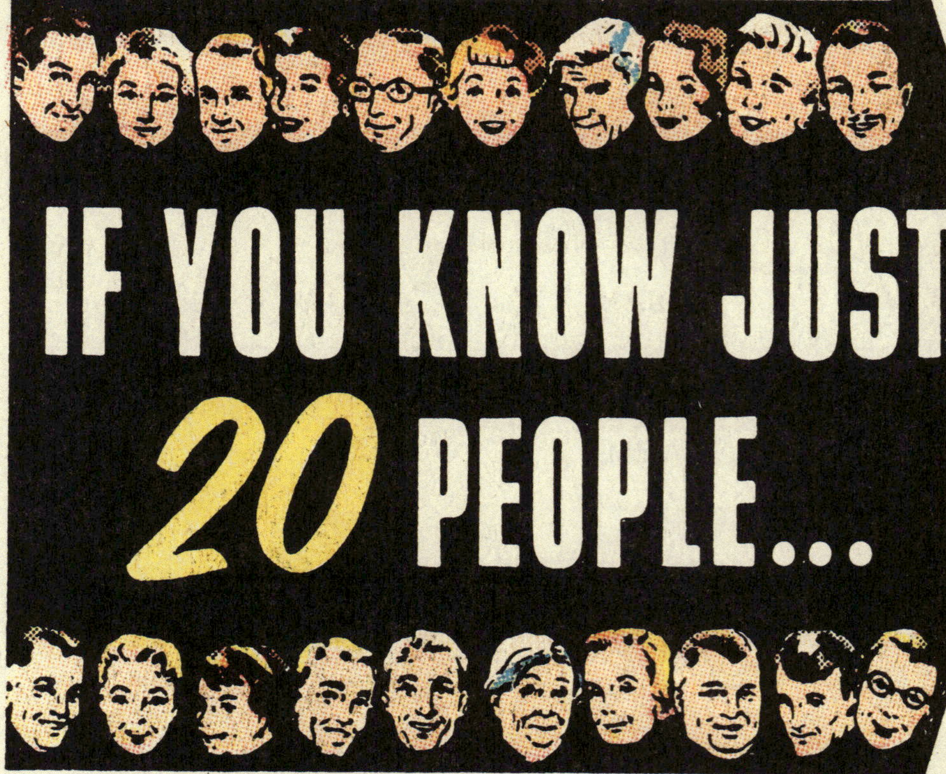

YOU CAN MAKE AT LEAST $50.00 -MORE LIKELY $100.00 to $200.00 IN YOUR SPARE TIME!

Get These 2 Assortments on Approval

REGAL LUSTRE ASS'T. 21 colorful DeLuxe cards on fabulous, lustrous Kromekote paper, in smart, tall shape, with brilliant decorations. A magnificent assortment!

FEATURE ASS'T. is a tremendous value! 21 gorgeous cards, beautiful designs rich with luxurious gold bronzing, sculptured embossing and sparkling glitter.

GET FREE CATALOG TOO – Send Coupon Below

Be first in your neighborhood to cash in on this easy way to extra money with the 1961 Wallace Brown Line of Christmas Cards and Gift Items. Mail coupon this minute! You'll get 2 boxes of Christmas Card Assortments on approval. And FREE Samples of Name-Imprinted Personal Christmas Cards. Plus FREE full-color catalog showing lots more money makers, including many Christmas Assortments, Everyday Greeting Card Assortments, Decorated Stationery, Gift Wrappings, Novelty Gifts, etc. Everything you need to start making money at once and we show you how. See how much fun making extra money can be. Just mail the coupon below today!

SEND NO MONEY
Paste Coupon on postcard or mail in envelope

WALLACE BROWN, INC.
11 East 26th St., Dept. R-134
New York 10, N.Y.

Send 2 Christmas Card Assortments on approval, plus FREE Samples of Personal Christmas Cards, FREE full-color Catalog, and details of simple money-making plan.

Name____________________

Address____________________

City & Zone________________ State______

If writing for an organization, give its name________________

Everyone You Know Needs Christmas Cards and Everyone Loves Wallace Brown Cards

Do you know 20 people? Of course, you do! Add up a half-dozen relatives, perhaps 5 neighbors, the butcher, the baker, the milkman, the grocer, your dentist, several friends and other tradespeople—and you've probably got a lot *more* than 20. So what are you waiting for? These folks alone can bring you in at least $50.00, probably $100.00 to $200.00, extra money in just a few hours spare time. And this is just a start! Most *everyone* you know needs Christmas Cards, and when you show them the spectacular, nationally famous 1961 Wallace Brown Line of Cards and Gift Items—it's love at first sight. They'll snap up 2, 3, 6 or more Christmas Card Boxes right on the spot. And you make up to 50¢ on each one! This is the *fun* way of making money because it's so easy. We send you samples that do the selling for you. You show such a beautiful selection of cards that you're bound to take orders from everybody. See for yourself without risking a penny by mailing coupon TODAY! You'll be glad you did!

FREE Samples of Popular-Priced, Name-Imprinted PERSONAL CHRISTMAS CARDS

Thrill your friends and neighbors and make even MORE MONEY for yourself with exquisite, custom-designed NAME-IMPRINTED Christmas Cards at amazingly low prices. A large variety of exclusive, original designs for folks who want the finest quality in Personalized Christmas Cards at prices everybody can afford. They sell just by being shown. It's so easy, too, because . . . *We ship direct to your customers and we pay postage* . . . You have no bother; no trouble and no wasted time making deliveries. Send coupon for your FREE Samples of the 4 Great New Lines of these fast-selling Personal Christmas Cards!

ORGANIZATIONS: Churches, clubs, veterans' auxiliaries, etc. can now add hundreds of dollars to their treasuries with these fast sellers. Give organization name on coupon for Fund-Raising Plan. Mail coupon NOW!

WALLACE BROWN, INC. 11 East 26th St., Dept. R-134 New York 10, New York

Learn Radio-Television Electronics

by Practicing at Home in Your Spare Time

WITHOUT EXTRA CHARGE NRI provides special kits that bring to life things you study. Makes learning easy, interesting, fast. All equipment yours to keep.

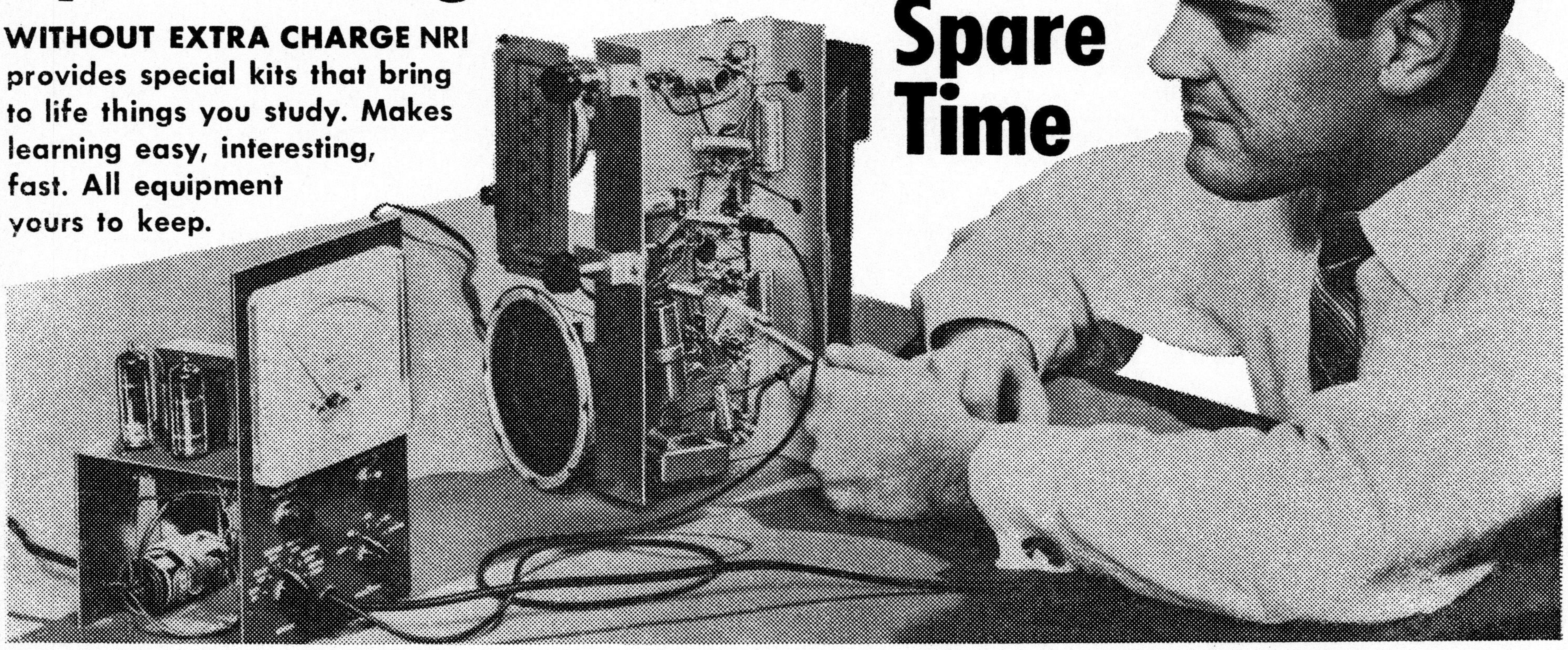

Fast Growth Offers You High Pay, Prestige, Bright Future

From Radio-TV Servicing and Broadcasting to missile launching sites like Cape Canaveral, NRI graduates share in the gigantic Electronics industry. Interesting jobs await you in studios, on ships and planes, in your own business. Mail coupon today for NRI catalog.

Many NRI graduates help build, install, operate and service automated electronic equipment for the new "Space Age" we live in—equipment used in offices, factories, the military. Others have important jobs as inspectors, laboratory technicans, etc., or hold essential civilian posts with the Government and Armed Forces.

J. M. SMITH
President

If you check the classified advertisements in your local newspaper, you will undoubtedly see more job opportunities available for men with Electronics training than for any other field. Hardly without exception, these are *better than average* jobs, with bright futures . . . jobs for which YOU could qualify through NRI training. Thousands of men like yourself—most of them without a high school diploma—have moved up to good pay and enjoy greater prestige in jobs with TV and Radio broadcasting stations, in industrial plants making Electronic equipment or in businesses of their own where they sell, install and service Radio and TV sets.

Train With The Leader

Join the many NRI graduates now taking advantage of career opportunities in this amazing Electronic Age. For 45 years, NRI has featured the best Radio-TV Electronics training for beginners—for men without previous experience. Throughout the U.S. and Canada, successful NRI graduates are proof that it's practical to train at home, in your spare time, at your own pace. Keep your present job while training. NRI supplies this training at low cost because it is the oldest and largest home-study Radio-TV Electronics school. In every respect, you will find the Electronics field a profitable one for the ambitious man. And the NRI "learn-by-doing" method is the most practical way for you to get into this exciting field quickly.

NRI Trained These Men

I was working in a textile factory trying to make ends meet. Now I own one of the most modern service shops in this section. ARGIE C. TAYLOR, Glasgow, Ky.

After graduating I was a shipboard radio operator. Now I am chief engineer at Station WARA. NRI was a wonderful foundation. RAYMOND D. ARNOLD, Attleboro, Mass.

Thanks to NRI I am in a top position with the Federal Aviation Agency in the Navaids Electronic Section. JOE DUCKWORTH, Fort Worth, Texas

Four months after starting your course I left my job in a hardware store to work at Raytheon Manufacturing. Now I am an engineering assistant in Microwave Power Tube Research and Development Laboratory. LEONARD BLOOM, Newton Centre, Mass.

Start Soon to Earn More

NRI training can bring prompt financial return. Soon after enrolling, NRI shows you how to earn $10, $15 and more a week extra fixing sets in your spare time. This can lead to a profitable Radio-TV business of your own. Others have found good paying jobs within a year after enrolling.

Mail the coupon below TODAY for our FREE CATALOG. It tells in words and pictures about the amazing field of Electronics. Read success stories. See the equipment you get. Find out about the NRI 60-day free trial enrollment offer and convenient monthly terms. National Radio Institute, Washington 16, D. C.

GET 64 PAGE CATALOG FREE

MAIL THIS COUPON NOW

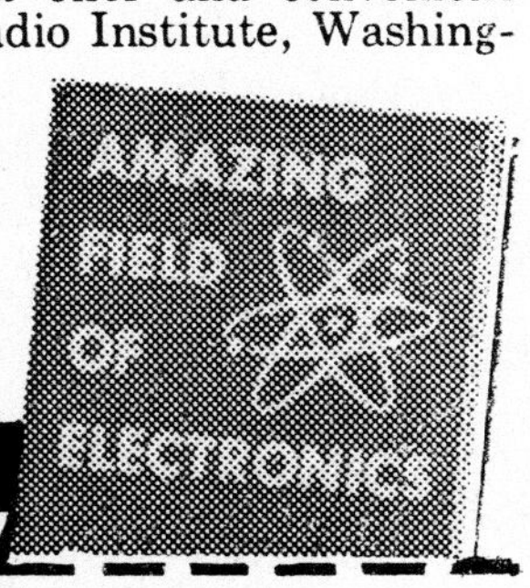

National Radio Institute
Washington 16, D.C. 1KM1

Send me full information without cost or obligation. No representative will call. (Please print.)

Name...Age.............

Address...

City.............................. ....Zone.....State..............

ACCREDITED MEMBER NATIONAL HOME STUDY COUNCIL

Albert Dorne – probably the greatest money-maker in the history of commercial art. At the height of his career, he began a full-time search for people who like to draw.

He's Looking for People Who Like to Draw

TODAY HUNDREDS of men and women who never thought they could be artists are working happily at easels and drawing boards, making pictures, and getting well paid for it. They all can thank Albert Dorne, a famous artist who devotes almost his full time to helping other people become artists.

Some of the people Dorne has helped

Don Smith of New Orleans is an example. A few years ago, he knew nothing about art, even doubted he had talent. Now he is an illustrator with a large advertising agency.

John Busketta is another. He was a pipefitter's helper in a big gas company. Today he still works for the same company, but as an artist in the advertising department, with a big increase in pay.

Harriet Kuzniewski was bored with an "ordinary" job before she heard of Albert Dorne. Today she does high-style fashion illustration in New York.

With the right training, Wanda Pickulski gave up her typing job to become fashion artist for a local department store.

John Whitaker of Memphis was an airline clerk two years ago. Recently he won a national cartooning contest and was signed to do a newspaper comic strip.

Long before Albert Dorne started looking for people who like to draw, they came to him for advice and help. Since he alone could only help a few of these people he called together America's most successful artists – men like Norman Rockwell, Jon Whitcomb, Stevan Dohanos and Al Parker.

A Plan To Help Others

He said: "All over America, there are people who like to draw, who could be turned into good artists. Why can't we give these people the training they need—including all the trade secrets and know-how we've learned over the years? I'm suggesting a new kind of school—a home-study art school that would give talented people the best professional art training, no matter where they live."

The famous artists agreed. Taking time from their busy careers, they spent several years creating a remarkable series of art lessons covering every aspect of drawing and painting. They illustrated their lessons with over 5,000 "here's-how" illustrations. The lessons start from scratch and cover every skill a top artist needs. Finally, the famous artists developed a wonderful way to give each student personal correction and advice all through his training.

Albert Dorne is not surprised by the success of his students. "The art field is growing. We keep getting calls from all over the country, asking us for practical well-trained students who can step into full-time or part-time art jobs."

Famous Artists Talent Test

To find others with art talent worth developing, the famous artists created a 12-page talent test. Thousands paid $1 for this test, but now the School offers it free and will grade it free. If you show talent on the test, you will be eligible for training by the School. No obligation. Simply mail coupon. It might be your first step to an exciting, well-paid career in art.

America's 12 Most Famous Artists

Norman Rockwell	Fred Ludekens
Jon Whitcomb	Ben Stahl
Al Parker	Robert Fawcett
Stevan Dohanos	Austin Briggs
Dong Kingman	Harold Von Schmidt
Peter Helck	Albert Dorne

FAMOUS ARTISTS SCHOOLS
Studio 5386 Westport, Conn.

I would like to find out whether I have art talent worth developing. Please send me, without obligation, your Famous Artists Talent Test.

Mr.
Mrs. .... Age ....
Miss (please print)

Address ....

City .... Zone ....

County .... State ....

IND.
THE
Fantastic
Four
10¢
APPROVED BY THE COMICS CODE AUTHORITY
MC
2
JAN.
THEY HAD TAKEN A DEADLY OATH TO DESTROY THE FANTASTIC FOUR!!
THEY WERE MERCILESS! THEY WERE INHUMAN! THEY HAD POWERS FAR GREATER THAN EARTHMEN! THEY WERE
"SKRULLS FROM OUTER SPACE!"

THE FANTASTIC FOUR is published by CANAM PUBLISHERS SALES CORP. OFFICE OF PUBLICATION: 655 MADISON AVENUE, NEW YORK, N.Y. Published bi-monthly. Copyright 1961 by CANAM PUBLISHERS SALES CORP., 655 Madison Avenue, New York, N.Y. Vol. 1 No. 2, JANUARY 1962 issue. Price 10c per copy. Subscription rate $1.45 for 12 issues including postage. No similarity between any of the names, characters, persons, and/or institutions appearing in this magazine with those of any living or dead person or institution is intended, and any such similarity which may exist is purely coincidental. Printed in the U.S.A. by The Eastern Color Printing Co., Waterbury 20, Conn.

THE
FANTASTIC FOUR
MEET THE SKRULLS FROM OUTER SPACE!
WHAT IS HAPPENING HERE ?? WHAT IS THE THING DOING, SWIMMING MILES OFF-SHORE TOWARDS A LONELY TEXAS TOWER? WHY DO HIS EYES GLEAM WITH A SINISTER, CRAFTY LIGHT? SILENTLY, POWER-FULLY, HE SWIMS CLOSER-- CLOSER-- HIDDEN BY THE DEEPENING TWILIGHT!
Stan Lee + J. Kirby
W-457
UNSEEN, UNSUSPECTED, HE SWIMS TOWARDS ONE OF THE TOWER'S MIGHTY SUPPORT POSTS...
AND THEN...
1

LIKE A FALLEN GIANT, THE MIGHTY STRUCTURE CRUMBLES AND SLOWLY SINKS INTO THE SEA!
THE BOATS! GET TO THE BOATS!
LUCKY WE ALL GOT AWAY WITH OUR LIVES!
BUT WHAT CAUSED IT? WAS IT A DEPTH CHARGE?
LOOK! SWIMMING AWAY! IT...IT'S THE THING! HE DID IT! THE THING WRECKED THE TOWER!
MEANWHILE, MANY MILES AWAY, IN ONE OF AMERICA'S MOST EXPENSIVE JEWELRY STORES...
WE DON'T USUALLY TAKE THIS GEM OUT OF THE VAULT TO SHOW PEOPLE, MISS STORM! IT'S WORTH ALMOST TEN MILLION DOLLARS! BUT FOR YOU, I CAN MAKE AN EXCEPTION!
YES, IT IS JUST WHAT I'VE BEEN LOOKING FOR!
IT-- IT IS?
I MUST ADMIT I NEVER REALLY EXPECTED ANYONE TO BUY SUCH AN EXPENSIVE GEM!
BUY?
I DON'T INTEND TO BUY IT!
SHE--SHE'S GONE!
GUARDS! GUARDS!!

SHE MUST BE HERE, SIR! NO ONE WENT PAST US AT THE DOOR!
YOU FOOLS! OF COURSE SHE WENT PAST YOU!
THAT WAS SUSAN STORM--THE INVISIBLE GIRL!
HOW IN BLAZES CAN WE EVER CATCH HER?
AND IN THE MIDWEST, WE ARE ABOUT TO WITNESS ANOTHER FANTASTIC EVENT, DURING THE DEDICATION OF A GIGANTIC NEW MONUMENT...
THIS PRICELESS STATUE TOOK FIVE YEARS TO CARVE OUT OF SOLID MARBLE!
AND NOW...
LOOK! IN THE SKY!
IT'S THE HUMAN TORCH!
HE'S GOING TO--OH, NO! NO!!
HIS BLAZING BODY COMPLETELY MELTED THE STATUE!
HE--HE'S FLYING OFF--LAUGHING!
BUT ONE FINAL DEED YET REMAINS TO BE DONE--AT A POWER PLANT! IN THE HEART OF THE CITY, A WORKMAN STARES AS HE SEES...
THAT ARM!! IT CAN ONLY BELONG TO MISTER FANTASTIC!
HE'S SWITCHING OFF ALL THE POWER IN THE CITY!!
IT IS DONE! THE CITY HAS BEEN PLUNGED INTO UTTER DARKNESS!
CAN WE BELIEVE OUR STARTLED EYES? IS IT POSSIBLE THAT THE FANTASTIC FOUR HAVE REALLY PERPETRATED THOSE CRIMINAL ACTS? OR IS THERE MORE TO THIS THAN MEETS THE EYE??
3

WE HAVE DONE OUR WORK WELL! WE HAVE SUCCEEDED!
YES! BY NOW THE ENTIRE NATION IS HUNTING THE FANTASTIC FOUR!
THE ORDER IS OUT-- SHOOT ON SIGHT! THERE WILL BE NO PLACE TO HIDE!
I'VE BEEN WONDERING --HOW DID YOU ALL ACCOMPLISH YOUR FEATS?
ALTHOUGH THE ARMY THINKS IT WAS DONE BY BRUTE STRENGTH, I SECRETLY DEMOLISHED THE WATER TOWER BY MEANS OF THIS CONCEALED ELECTRONIC DETONATOR!
AS FOR ME, I QUICKLY CHANGED MY SIZE TO ONLY A FEW INCHES TALL-- BUT EVERYONE THOUGHT I HAD BECOME INVISIBLE!
MY TASK WAS AN EASY ONE! WITH THIS POWERED ANTI-GRAVITY GEAR AND A LOW VELOCITY THERMAL BOMB, I REALLY SEEMED TO BE A FLYING, FLAMING HUMAN!
AS FOR ME, I NEEDED NO SPECIAL DEVICES! FOR IT'S AN EASY MATTER FOR ME TO ALTER MY BODY IN ANY WAY I DESIRE!
JUST AS IT IS EASY FOR ALL OF US TO DO SO!
WHICH IS WHY THE UNSUSPECTING EARTHMEN WILL NEVER KNOW THAT WE SKRULLS HAVE IMPERSONATED THEIR FAMOUS FANTASTIC FOUR!
NOW, ALL THAT REMAINS IS FOR THE EARTHLINGS THEMSELVES TO HUNT DOWN AND DESTROY THE FANTASTIC FOUR!
AND ONCE THE FANTASTIC FOUR ARE SLAIN, NO POWER ON EARTH CAN STOP THE SKRULL INVASION!
EVEN NOW, OUR MOTHER SHIP HOVERS UNSEEN, ABOVE EARTH'S ATMOSPHERE, WAITING FOR OUR SIGNAL TO LAUNCH THE ATTACK!
AND THUS WE LEARN THE SECRETS OF THE INCREDIBLE FEATS WE HAVE SEEN! ABOVE US, THE SKRULLS FROM OUTER SPACE HAVE TURNED ALL EARTH AGAINST THE FANTASTIC FOUR!
DAILY GLOBE
FANTASTIC FOUR DECLARED PUBLIC ENEMIES
HUNT WIDENS FOR MEMBERS OF STRANGE GROUP...
DAILY BUGLE
DRAGNET OUT FOR FANTASTIC FOUR!
SHOOT TO KILL!
4

WHILE MILES AWAY, IN AN ISOLATED HUNTING LODGE, THE MOST UNUSUAL HUMANS ON EARTH LEARN WHAT HAS HAPPENED...
...THE FANTASTIC FOUR HAVE BECOME THE MOST DANGEROUS MENACE WE HAVE EVER FACED! THEY MUST BE FOUND! THEY MUST BE PUNISHED!
TURN THAT RADIO OFF! WE HAVE TO THINK!
IT IS OBVIOUS THAT SOME FOUR-SOME IS IMPERSON-ATING US! BUT HOW? WHY?
BUT, REED, HOW COULD ANY HUMANS IMPERSONATE US? NO ONE ELSE HAS OUR POWERS!
AW, I'M NOT WORRIED! REED WILL FIGURE OUT WHAT TO DO, AND THEN WE'LL TAKE CARE OF THEM, I'LL BET!
BAH! WHILE THE THREE OF YOU BEAT YOUR GUMS, THE WHOLE COUNTRY IS HUNTING US AS THOUGH WE'RE FOUR MONSTERS!
WELL, MAYBE THEY'RE RIGHT! MAYBE I AM A MONSTER! I LOOK LIKE ONE--AND SOMETIMES I FEEL LIKE ONE!
BUT NOBODY'S CATCHIN' ME WITHOUT A FIGHT! IF THEY SAY I'M A MENACE, I'LL BE A MENACE! I'LL SHOW 'EM ALL!
THAT'S WHAT I'LL DO TO ANYONE WHO GETS IN MY WAY!
REED! STOP HIM! HE'S GOING MAD!
CRASH!
EASY, THING, EASY! WE CAN'T FIGHT THE WHOLE HUMAN RACE!
FIRST, WE'VE GOT TO FIND OUT WHAT'S BEHIND THIS PLAN TO DISCREDIT US!

CONTINUED AFTER NEXT PAGE...

Training for Big Pay MADE SIMPLE!

A quick new way to get into Auto Mechanics

30 JOB EXPERIENCE PROJECTS

. . . to help you bridge the gap between theory and practice—to lead you from lessons to engines in easy stages

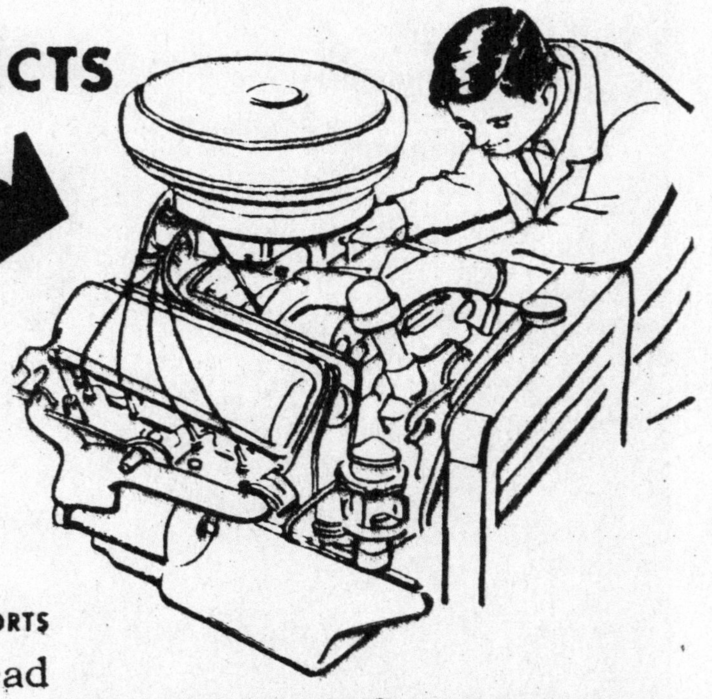

"Good Auto Industry Jobs Go Begging"

—A FAMOUS CHICAGO NEWSPAPER REPORTS

If you are worried about a layoff, low pay, or dim prospects, read this information printed in a Chicago newspaper: "Unemployment may be a national problem, but the troubles in segments of the auto industry are exactly the opposite. Jobs are going begging. Good jobs. Ones paying well and offering better-than-expected freedom from layoffs. There are perhaps 300,000 openings to be filled in cities and towns across the country . . ."

Learn by practicing at home

A well-known auto executive says that 250,000 more auto mechanics are needed. "We know of one manufacturer alone who needs nearly 60,000 mechanics for its dealerships," he adds. Obviously, *now* is the time to train for a better job, high pay, steady work! Train at home in spare time for a bright future as an auto mechanic. Learn by practicing the easy CTI way. It's fast too.

You get instruments and tools

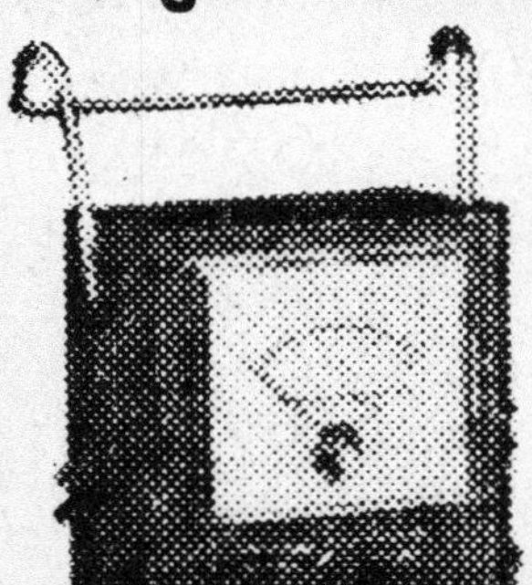

THE PORTABLE VISO-ANALYZER

Another CTI "first". Called "the most versatile of all trouble-shooting instruments" by a leading trade magazine. You will use it to detect failures in the electrical system. A great time and work saver.

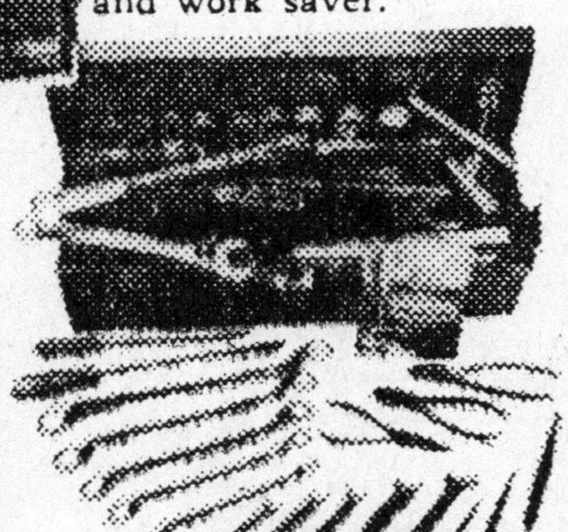

MECHANIC'S TOOLS

socket set and tray included

ENGINE TUNE-UP KIT

Compression Tester, Vacuum Gauge and Fuel Pump Tester, Ignition Timing Light, portable steel case.

Get experience as you train

As part of its practical training program, CTI sends you 30 Job Experience Projects. These exclusive projects make it easy for you to make the transition from lessons to repairs. You learn by practicing, gain skill in the use of tools and test instruments, acquire useful experience that builds your confidence. CTI shop projects do away with low-pay apprenticeship—get you into the top pay bracket much more quickly.

Go in business—Earn more money

America needs 25,000 more auto repair shops! There are opportunities in almost any community to go in business for yourself, gain independence, earn more money than ever. Many CTI graduates own their shops—and most of them started in their back yards.

Diesel or Body-Fender instruction

Diesel or Body-Fender instruction is provided by CTI in addition to the complete course in Auto Mechanics. No extra charge for this training. Only CTI offers you this generous choice.

So practical that many earn cash soon after they start

Many CTI students begin fixing cars after a few lessons. They earn extra money—which helps pay tuition, buys extra equipment. At the same time, these students become skillful and experienced in the use of tools and instruments. All this is a result of CTI's *practical* home study lessons. And now, in addition, you get 30 Job Experience Projects.

Proof that CTI training works

Letters from students prove value of CTI training. Read these unsolicited testimonials: "Am now a senior auto mechanic. Made $800 during training." —*Ronald Wharton, Md.* "Started a small business in my garage. Now have two part-time helpers."—*John Reed, Cal.* "Am proud I finished course. Have two job offers."—*Barden Vance, Ind.* "Am working as a mechanic and earn twice what I used to. Made $25 a week as I trained."—*Jerome Slowik, Ill.* "Have three job offers. Made $170 as a student." —*Willie Cooper, Fla.* "Have started my own tune-up and brake shop. Am earning about $50 a week more than before." —*G. Guntz, Cal.* You can do as well.

First get the facts—Then decide

Imagine—over 250,000 jobs waiting for auto mechanics! Isn't it worth your while to look into your opportunities? Just mail coupon. No obligation.

CLIP COUPON BEFORE YOU TURN PAGE— BE SURE TO MAIL TODAY— *FACTS FREE!*

COMMERCIAL TRADES INSTITUTE
1400 GREENLEAF AVENUE
CHICAGO 26, ILLINOIS — DEPT. A-171

Send me your opportunity booklet, Make Big Money in Auto Mechanics. Also, Sample Lessons. Both FREE.

Name ____________ Age ______
Address ____________
City ____________ Zone ______ State ______

COMMERCIAL TRADES INSTITUTE · CHICAGO 26, ILLINOIS

A Non-Profit Organization • Accredited by National Home Study Council

PART 2
PRISONER OF THE SKRULLS
EVEN AS THE FANTASTIC FOUR PONDER THEIR NEXT MOVE, GRIM, SILENT FIGURES STEALTHILY CREEP TOWARD THEIR CABIN-- LIKE A HORDE OF AVENGING WRAITHS!
V-457
THE FIRST THING WE MUST DO IS LEARN WHO IS IMPERSONATING US!
AND WHY!
AND THEN WE'LL PULVERIZE 'EM!
ATTENTION!! FANTASTIC FOUR!! WE HAVE YOU SURROUNDED!
COME OUT WITH YOUR HANDS UP, OR WE'LL FIRE!
A
7

HAH!! THEY'RE NOT AS TOUGH AS EVERYONE SAYS!
ONE FALSE MOVE AND WE'LL SHOOT!
RELAX, SOLDIER! WE DON'T PLAN TO FIGHT THE WHOLE U.S. ARMY!
LESS THAN AN HOUR LATER, AT A FEDERAL PRISON...
YOU'LL EACH BE IN A SPECIALLY-CONSTRUCTED PRIVATE CELL!
EVEN YOUR STRANGE TALENTS WON'T BE ABLE TO FREE YOU FROM HERE!
SO, THEY DON'T THINK WE CAN ESCAPE?
THEY THINK OUR POWERS AREN'T STRONG ENOUGH...
WELL, THEY MAY BE RIGHT...
...BUT I DOUBT IT!
THEY PUT ME IN A SPECIAL ASBESTOS ROOM, SO THAT MY FLAME CAN'T DO ANY DAMAGE!
BUT THEY OVERLOOKED ONE THING...
I KNOW THAT ANY ROOM, NO MATTER HOW TIGHTLY SEALED, MUST HAVE AT LEAST ONE AIR VENT!
AND I'VE FOUND IT!
8

EVERY INCH OF THIS CELL IS MADE OF THICK BATTLE-SHIP STEEL!
THEY'RE NOT TAKIN' ANY CHANCES WITH ME!
BUT ANYTHING WILL GIVE IF YOU HAMMER AT IT LONG ENOUGH...
BAM!
...IN THE EXACT SAME PLACE WITH ENOUGH FORCE!
BAM!
AND FORCE IS ONE THING I'VE GOT PLENTY OF!
BAM!
THE CELL IS COMPLETELY EMPTY!
THEY'RE AFRAID I MIGHT MAKE A WEAPON OF ANY ARTICLES I FIND!
BUT I NEED NO SPECIAL WEAPONS! MY BODY IS WEAPON ENOUGH!
ALL I NEED DO IS HAVE MY SENSITIVE FINGERS PROBE EVERY INCH OF FLOOR AND WALL...
...UNTIL I FIND ONE SMALL IMPERFECTION, NO MATTER HOW TINY! A LOOSE RIVET... A TINY CRACK... ANYTHING!
LATER, AT THE INVISIBLE GIRL'S CELL...
HERE'S YOUR DINNER, MISS STORM!
WH-WHERE IS SHE??
MP
MP
HEY!! WHA--?
SOMETHING JUST PUSHED PAST US!
FWEEETT!
9

AND AT THAT MOMENT, ALL PANDEMONIUM BREAKS LOOSE...
THAT ONE SMALL AIR VENT WAS ALL I NEEDED TO BURST INTO FLAMES! AND NOW...
EVEN STEEL WILL SHATTER IF YOU POUND AT IT LONG ENOUGH! AND I NEVER GET TIRED!
ONE SIDE, SOLDIER BOYS, BEFORE I TRAMPLE ON YA!
JUST WHAT I WAS LOOKING FOR...
...A LOOSE RIVET!
THIS ELASTIC BODY OF MINE IS A BLESSING IN DISGUISE! NO CELL CAN HOLD ME FOR LONG!
YOU! HALT!
THEY SPOTTED ME! NOW IT'S UP TO THE TORCH!
QUICK! GRAB THAT WHIRLYBIRD OVER THERE! I'LL HOLD 'EM OFF TILL YOU'RE AIRBORNE!
I KNEW WE COULD DO IT!
BAH! I'D RATHER STAY AND FIGHT!
WE DID IT!... WE'RE FREE!
YES, BUT--FOR HOW LONG?

NOT LONG AFTERWARDS, AT ONE OF THE FANTASTIC FOUR'S MANY SECRET APARTMENT HIDEOUTS...
IT'S OBVIOUS THAT OUR FIRST STEP IS TO SET A TRAP--TO CATCH THE FOUR MYSTERIOUS CHARACTERS WHO ARE IMPERSON-ATING US!
I GUESS I'M THE BEST ONE TO DO THAT, REED!
YOU??
I DON'T BELIEVE IN SENDIN' A KID TO DO A MAN'S JOB! IF ANYONE SETS TRAPS, IT'LL BE ME!
AW, SHUT UP AND LET US THINK, WILL YA?
KNOCK IT OFF, YOU TWO! I'VE GOT AN IDEA! TAKE A LOOK AT TODAY'S NEWSPAPER!
DAILY GLOBE
NEW ROCKET TO BE TESTED
HEY! I GOT IT! OUR FOUR IMITATORS MAY GET CONFUSED IF ONE OF US TRIES TO SABOTAGE THAT ROCKET SITE! THEY MAY THINK IT'S ONE OF THEM, AND REVEAL THEMSELVES!
I'LL LEAVE RIGHT AWAY!
WHO SAID YOU WERE GONNA TACKLE THAT JOB?
I SAID SO!
ANY OBJECTIONS?
UGHH!
FLAME OFF, TORCH! AND BACK AWAY, THING! THIS IS NO TIME TO BE FIGHTING AMONG OURSELVES!
IF HE EVER LOSES THAT FLAME OF HIS, I'LL--
11

THING, I UNDERSTAND HOW BITTER YOU ARE--AND I KNOW YOU HAVE EVERY RIGHT TO BE BITTER!! BUT WE'LL JUST DESTROY OURSELVES IF WE KEEP AT EACH OTHER'S THROATS THIS WAY! DON'T YOU SEE?
I SEE...
...AND SOMETIMES... I THINK I'D BE BETTER OFF -- THE WORLD WOULD BE BETTER OFF -- IF I WERE DESTROYED!
AW, FORGET IT, THING! I'M NOT HOLDIN' ANY GRUDGES!
LISTEN, GANG! I'LL ATTACK THAT ROCKET AND HOPE THAT OUR IMITATORS WILL ATTACK ME! THEN WATCH FOR MY SIGNAL!
AND SO, A SHORT TIME LATER...
CLEAR THE FIELD!
EVERYTHING IS IN READINESS!
WHA--WHAT'S THAT FLASH IN THE SKY?
WHERE?
OVER THERE!
MELTING THROUGH THAT UNFINISHED LAUNCHING PLATFORM OUGHT TO DO THE TRICK!
IT'S THE HUMAN TORCH! HE'S ATTACKING OUR LAUNCHING SITE!
HE'S TOO FAST-- TOO LOW! OUR GUNS CAN'T TRACK HIM!
12

WITHIN SECONDS, THE HUMAN TORCH COMES FROM BEHIND A CONCEALING HANGAR, SNAPS OFF HIS FLAME, AND...
IT'S NOW OR NEVER! IF THOSE IMITATORS ARE ANY-WHERES AROUND--
THERE HE IS!
TORCH! QUICK! INTO THE CAR!
KNOWING HE IS TAKING HIS LIFE INTO HIS HANDS, JOHNNY STORM ENTERS THE WAITING CAR AND SEES...
IF I DIDN'T KNOW BETTER, I'D SWEAR YOU WERE SUSAN STORM AND REED RICHARDS, TWO OF THE FANTASTIC FOUR!
WELL, THAT'S WHO WE'RE SUPPOSED TO BE, ISN'T IT?
MINUTES LATER, AT THE ALIENS' HEADQUARTERS...
YOU FOOLS! WHY DID YOU BRING HIM? HE IS THE REAL HUMAN TORCH!
BUT WE THOUGHT--
YOU THOUGHT WHAT I WANTED YOU TO THINK!
NOW THAT YOU SEE WE ARE NOT OF YOUR PLANET EARTH, YOU CAN NOT LEAVE HERE ALIVE!
MISTER, NO MATTER WHAT PLANET YOU'RE FROM, I'M STILL GONNA BE TOO HOT FOR YOU TO HANDLE!
STOP HIM! HE HAS A FLARE GUN!
TOO LATE!
THERE!! NOW WHEN THE OTHERS SEE MY SIGNAL, YOU'LL WISH YOU HAD STAYED WHERE YOU CAME FROM!
4

CONTINUED AFTER NEXT PAGE...

SPECIAL OFFER TO READERS OF THIS MAGAZINE

New ACCORDIONS—SAVE up to 1/2

off retail prices of comparable accordions—DIRECT IMPORTER-TO-YOU!

TRADE-INS WELCOMED

Small Down Payment
BUY ON E-Z TERMS

5-DAY FREE TRIAL

OVER 30 MODELS for STUDENTS TEACHERS PROFES-SIONALS

WORLD'S LARGEST ACCORDION DEALER brings you these sensational values! Prices slashed on all our fine Italian-made accordions! Play the most popular instrument of all. **Have fun, be a leader!** Choose over 30 newest models that lead the world in superb tone and breath-taking beauty. All latest improvements and features. Buy direct from the importer. **You save up to 50%** off retail prices of comparable accordions. Small down payment; pay the balance on easiest terms. Big trade-in allowance. Try before you buy on FREE 5-DAY NO RISK PLAN. Complete satisfaction assured!

FREE BONUS GIFTS for promptness...

- Easy-to-play music
- Music Stand
- Name in chrome letters
- Deluxe Case
- Music Portfolio
- Plus Other Valuable Gifts

LIFETIME GUARANTEE

Your A. C. A. Accordion is guaranteed against original defects in workmanship and materials for the life of the instrument. Parts and labor free. Rush coupon for big new Color Catalogs and low Importer-to-You Prices . . . FREE. No obligation. Write!

Accordion Corporation of America
Dept. MV-121, 2003 W. Chicago Ave., Chicago 22, Ill.

FREE! GET COLOR CATALOG and Importer-to-You Prices

Accordion Corporation of America, Dept. MV-121
2003 W. Chicago Ave., Chicago 22, Ill.
Send Free Color Catalogs and Importer-to-You Prices.

NAME..

ADDRESS......................................

CITY.......................ZONE.... STATE........

REWARD

$2,000.00

FOR THIS COIN!

Illustrated: 1804 silver dollar — 19,000 minted, only 12 accounted for—where are the rest?

FOR CERTAIN COINS WE PAY UP TO:	
Pennies Before 1919	9,000.00
Silver Dollars Before 1936	8,000.00
Nickles Before 1945	6,000.00
Dimes Before 1946	5,000.00
Half Dollars Before 1947	4,500.00
Quarters Before 1941	3,500.00
Half Cents Before 1910	3,500.00
Lincoln Pennies Before 1940	200.00

Stop spending pocket change worth hundreds of dollars. New large illustrated catalogue lists the actual price we will pay for all United States Coins. Certain half cent coins are worth up to $3,500.00 for Canadian Coins. Our valuable Coin Book may reward you many thousands of dollars. Coins do not have to be old to be valuable. Thousands of dollars have been paid for coins dated as recently as 1940 to 1956. It's easy to learn the rare dates and to identify rare coins in your possession with our new 1961 catalogue. A fortune may be waiting for you. Millions of Dollars have been paid for rare coins. Don't sell your valuable coins for less than they are worth! Hold on to your coins until you obtain our catalogue. Send $1.00 for newest Coin Catalogue to: **BEST VALUES CO., COIN DEPT 208 403 MARKET ST. Newark, New Jersey.**

MAIL MONEY-SAVING NO-RISK FREE TRIAL COUPON NOW!

BEST VALUES CO., COIN DEPT. 208
403 Market St.
Newark, New Jersey

Rush your Latest Large Coin Catalogue listing the actual prices you will pay for United States Coins. I enclose $1. Send Postage Prepaid.

Name..

Address......................................

City..........................State..........

THE FANTASTIC FOUR
FIGHT BACK!
LET GO OF THAT WEAPON!
WHEW! NOW I KNOW HOW THE OLD INDIAN FIGHTERS FELT WHEN THE CAVALRY ARRIVED!
NEVER THOUGHT WE'D TRACK YA DOWN, DID YA??
V-457
I MUST ESCAPE!... MUST WARN THE OTHERS!
TSK! TSK! DON'T YOU KNOW IT'S IMPOLITE TO RUSH PAST A LADY?
ALL RIGHT, PLAYMATES, THAT WRAPS IT UP! ONE WRONG MOVE FROM ANY OF YOU AND IT'LL BE YOUR LOSS!
NO WONDER OUR LEADERS DARE NOT INVADE EARTH UNTIL THE FANTASTIC FOUR ARE STOPPED!
15

NOW GIVE US THE WHOLE STORY, FAST! WHERE ARE YOU FROM? WHAT IS YOUR MISSION?... TALK!!
NO! WE WILL NEVER TELL YOU ANYTHING!
LET ME AT 'EM! I'LL MAKE 'EM TALK! JUST WATCH ME!
NO, THING! NO!
REED!! HELP ME!
EASY, THING-- EASY!! YOU DON'T KNOW YOUR OWN STRENGTH! YOU'LL KILL THEM! LET US HANDLE IT!
THEY'VE MADE US OUTCASTS! TURNED ALL EARTH AGAINST US! THEY'VE GOT TO PAY FOR THAT!!
HEAR THAT? THIS IS YOUR LAST CHANCE! TALK, OR I'LL TURN THE THING LOOSE ON YOU!
NO! NO! KEEP THAT MONSTER FROM US! WE'LL TELL YOU WHAT YOU WANT TO KNOW!
WE SKRULLS HAVE AN INVASION FLEET WAITING ABOVE YOUR ATMOSPHERE-- BUT BEFORE WE ATTACK EARTH, OUR LEADERS WANTED TO BE SURE THAT THE FANTASTIC FOUR WOULD BE UNABLE TO FIGHT US!
...FOR WE KNOW OF YOUR DREAD POWERS!
HMM-- LOOKS LIKE A STALEMATE! WE'VE GOT THE FOUR OF THEM, BUT THERE IS STILL A MIGHTY INVASION FLEET MENACING EARTH!
WE MUST DESTROY THAT FLEET SOME-HOW-- OR EARTH WILL NEVER BE SAFE!
BUT HOW CAN THE FOUR OF US HOPE TO STOP A WHOLE INVASION?
THERE IS ONLY ONE THING TO DO...
THEY MASQUERADED AS US!...
NOW WE MUST POSE AS THEM!!
16

MINUTES LATER, THE FOUR DEFEATED SKRULLS REVEAL THE SECRET OF THEIR HIDDEN SPACE SHIP! AND, WITH A SILENT PRAYER, THE FANTASTIC FOUR HEAD INTO-- WHAT??
IT LOOKS LIKE AN INNOCENT WATER TOWER ATOP THIS BUILDING!
LOOK!! ABOVE US! THE MOTHER SHIP!
IT'S GIGANTIC! IT'S THE SIZE OF AN EARTH CITY!!
FINALLY, THE SHIPS MAKE CONTACT!
SO! YOU HAVE RETURNED! IS YOUR MISSION ACCOMPLISHED?
ARE THE FANTASTIC FOUR DEAD OR IMPRISONED?
SHALL I SIGNAL THE INVASION?
THERE CAN BE NO INVASION! THE FANTASTIC FOUR CANNOT BE BEATEN!
NO!! IT CAN'T BE! IT CAN'T!
EARTH'S DEFENSES CAN DEFEAT US!
I MUST HAVE PROOF! DO YOU HEAR? GIVE ME PROOF!!
HERE ARE ACTUAL PHOTOS OF WHAT WE WOULD FACE IF WE INVADE EARTH!
17

THOSE ARE SOME OF EARTH'S MOST POWERFUL WARRIORS!
I PRAY HE DOESN'T SUSPECT THAT THEY'RE ACTUALLY CLIPPED FROM "STRANGE TALES" AND "JOURNEY INTO MYSTERY"!
...AND EARTH HAS THOUSANDS OF THOSE HIDDEN SPACE MINES WHICH WOULD DESTROY ANY INVADING ARMY!
NOT TO MENTION AN ARMY OF GIANT MONSTROUS INSECTS READY TO CRUSH ANY ALIEN INVASION!
INCREDIBLE!! UNBELIEVABLE! WE'VE GOT TO LEAVE THIS GALAXY AT ONCE, BEFORE THOSE TERRIFYING CREATURES DISCOVER US!
IF YOU HADN'T WARNED ME IN TIME, WE WOULD SURELY HAVE ALL BEEN SLAIN!
QUICKLY! UNMASK AND JOIN US AS WE LEAVE THIS ACCURSED PLANET FOREVER!
NO! WE MUST STAY BEHIND AND REMOVE ALL EVIDENCE OF OUR PRESENCE ON EARTH! WE SHALL SACRIFICE OURSELVES SO THAT YOU WILL BE SAFE!
NEVER IN OUR HISTORY HAS THERE BEEN SO NOBLE A DEED! TAKE THIS HIGHEST AWARD OF YOUR BRAVERY!
WHEW! YOU DON'T KNOW THE HALF OF IT, BROTHER!
18

MOMENTS LATER, THE MIGHTY STAR SHIP LEAVES OUR ATMOSPHERE -- FOREVER!!
THERE THEY GO! EARTH IS SAFE!
AND HERE WE GO, DRIFTING BACK TO THE SURFACE!
LOOK!! WE'RE HEADING BACK INTO THE RADIATION BELT AGAIN! IT MADE A MONSTER OF ME ONCE-- WHAT FURTHER HARM WILL IT DO TO ME THIS TIME?
EASY, FELLA! WE'VE GOT TO PASS THROUGH IT! THERE'S NO OTHER WAY!
NO!! I WON'T!! NO! ARGHHH!!!! NOT AGAIN!! OHH-- WE'RE IN IT! WE'RE IN THE RADIATION BELT!!
THE THING-- SAVAGE, POWERFUL, A JUGGERNAUT OF DESTRUCTION, COWERS LIKE A FRIGHTENED CHILD AS THE SPACESHIP PLUNGES THROUGH THE MYSTERIOUS COSMIC BELT!! AND THEN -- IT HAPPENS!!
I'M CHANGING AGAIN! I KNOW IT! I--I CAN FEEL IT!!
CHANGING.... CHANGING...
... INTO WHAT?!?
BUT, AT THAT SPLIT-SECOND...
HANG ON! WE'VE LANDED!
19

THE FANTASTIC FOUR...
CAPTURED!
STEPPING OUT OF THE NOW-MOTIONLESS SHIP, FOUR PAIRS OF EYES ARE BLINDED BY THE GLARE OF GIANT FLOOD-LIGHTS!
V-457
KEEP THOSE LIGHTS ON 'EM, MEN!
WE'VE BEEN WAITING FOR THE FOUR OF YOU!
CHIEF, BEFORE YOU TRY TO ARREST US, LET ME TELL YOU THE TRUE STORY OF--
SAVE IT, REED! I'VE GOT A JOB TO DO AND I'M DOING IT!
DON'T KID YOURSELF! YOU CAN'T HOLD US! I CAN SMASH ALL OF YOU SINGLE-HANDED! YOU KNOW WHO I AM, DON'T YOU?
NEVER SAW YOU BEFORE, MISTER--BUT I'M LOCKING YOU UP WITH THE OTHERS!
NEVER SAW ME BEFORE? WHO YOU KIDDIN', MISTER?
THERE AIN'T ANYBODY ON EARTH DOESN'T KNOW THE THING WHEN THEY SEE 'IM!
BEN!! LOOK AT YOURSELF! LOOK!
20

WHA--?? LET'S HAVE YOUR MIRROR!! I'LL--HEY!! I'M NOT A MONSTER ANY MORE!! I'M A MAN AGAIN!!
OH, BEN, I'M SO HAPPY FOR YOU!
MY FACE--MY HANDS! THEY'RE HUMAN! HUMAN!!!!
WAIT!! WHA--WHAT'S HAPPENING?
OH, NO!! NOT AGAIN!
DON'T LET IT HAPPEN AGAIN--DON'T--DON'T--
I SHOULD HAVE KNOWN! IT COULDN'T BE--IT WAS JUST A JOKE!! YEAH--A REAL FUNNY JOKE!
BEN, DON'T LOSE HOPE! YOU BECAME NORMAL FOR THOSE FEW SECONDS! THAT MIGHT MEAN THE POWER OF THE COSMIC RAYS IS GROWING WEAKER! SOMEDAY YOU MAY TURN NORMAL AGAIN--FOR-- --GOOD!
SHE'S RIGHT, PAL! THAT WAS JUST A START!
LOOK! I DON'T KNOW WHAT YOU'RE TRYING TO PULL, BUT IT WON'T WORK! YOU'RE ALL UNDER ARREST!
CHIEF, BEFORE YOU DO ANYTHING ELSE, TAKE US TO MY APARTMENT! I PROMISE IT WILL EXPLAIN EVERYTHING THAT'S HAPPENED!
21

AND SO, WITH SIRENS BLARING, THE ARMED MOTORCADE SPEEDS TOWARD ITS DESTINATION...
THOSE CRIMES WERE NOT COMMITTED BY THE FANTASTIC FOUR, CHIEF! IT WAS A QUARTET OF ALIENS IMPERSONATING US!!
SURE, REED, SURE! AND I STILL BELIEVE IN SANTA CLAUS, TOO!
AT THE APARTMENT, THE POLICE CONFIDENTLY OPEN THE DOOR--AND ARE MET BY...
HOLY HANNAH!! THAT THING WAS NEVER SPAWNED ON EARTH!
SHUT THE DOOR AGAIN! HURRY!
I CAN'T! IT'S TOO LATE!
OUTA THE WAY, WEAKLINGS! LET ME HANDLE THIS!
HERE COMES ANOTHER ONE-- MORE GRUESOME THAN THE FIRST!
OPEN FIRE!!
BULLETS WILL NEVER STOP THOSE CREATURES!
MEBBE NOT--BUT I KNOW SOMETHING THAT WILL!
FLAME ON!!
LOOK!! THE TORCH IS DRIVING IT BACK!
IT'S COWERING FROM THE INTENSE HEAT!!
22

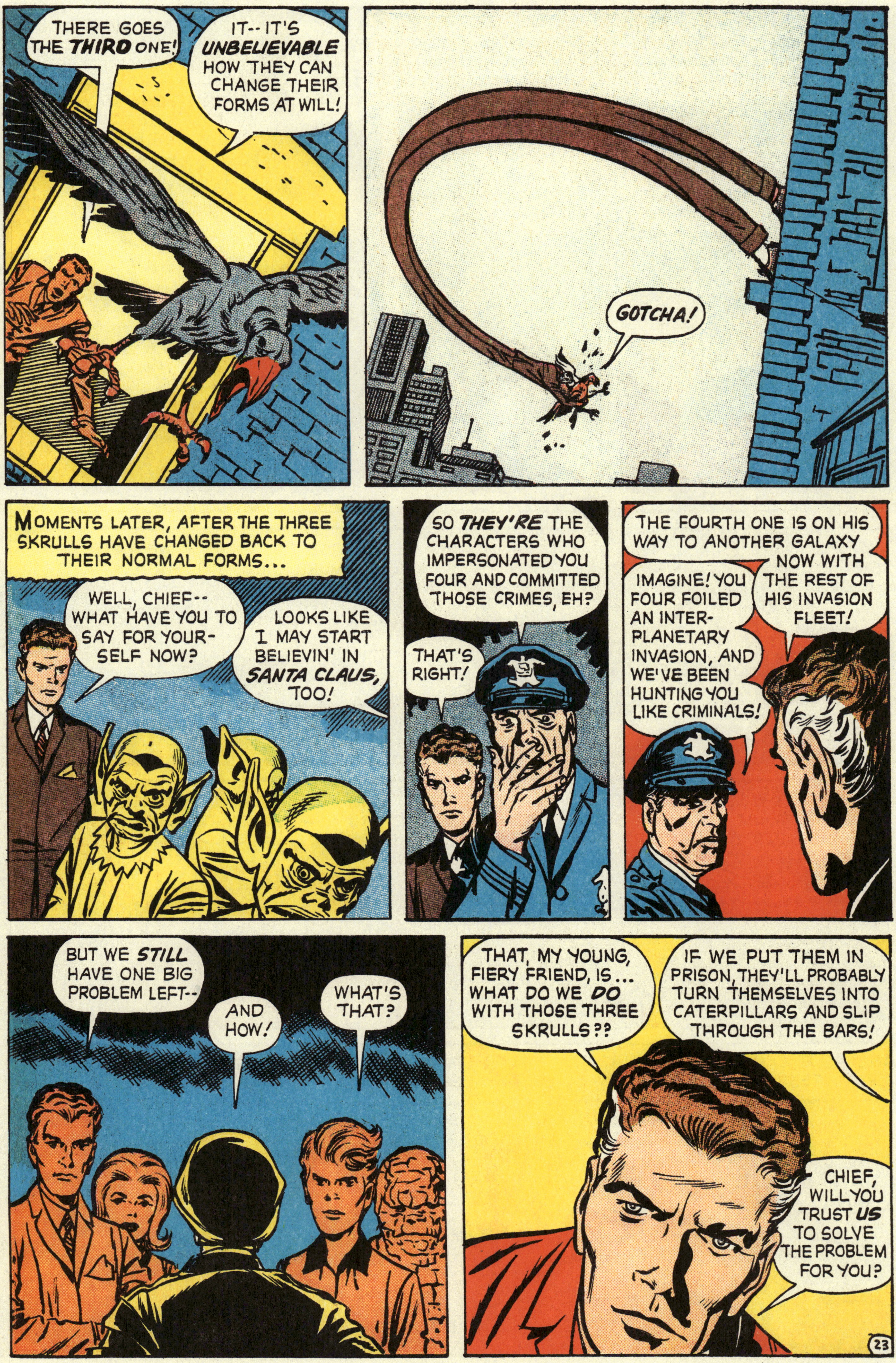
THERE GOES THE THIRD ONE!
IT-- IT'S UNBELIEVABLE HOW THEY CAN CHANGE THEIR FORMS AT WILL!
GOTCHA!
MOMENTS LATER, AFTER THE THREE SKRULLS HAVE CHANGED BACK TO THEIR NORMAL FORMS...
WELL, CHIEF-- WHAT HAVE YOU TO SAY FOR YOURSELF NOW?
LOOKS LIKE I MAY START BELIEVIN' IN SANTA CLAUS, TOO!
SO THEY'RE THE CHARACTERS WHO IMPERSONATED YOU FOUR AND COMMITTED THOSE CRIMES, EH?
THAT'S RIGHT!
THE FOURTH ONE IS ON HIS WAY TO ANOTHER GALAXY NOW WITH THE REST OF HIS INVASION FLEET!
IMAGINE! YOU FOUR FOILED AN INTER-PLANETARY INVASION, AND WE'VE BEEN HUNTING YOU LIKE CRIMINALS!
BUT WE STILL HAVE ONE BIG PROBLEM LEFT--
AND HOW!
WHAT'S THAT?
THAT, MY YOUNG, FIERY FRIEND, IS... WHAT DO WE DO WITH THOSE THREE SKRULLS??
IF WE PUT THEM IN PRISON, THEY'LL PROBABLY TURN THEMSELVES INTO CATERPILLARS AND SLIP THROUGH THE BARS!
CHIEF, WILL YOU TRUST US TO SOLVE THE PROBLEM FOR YOU?
23

MY BOY, AFTER WHAT I'VE SEEN TODAY, I'D TRUST YOU FOUR WITH ANYTHING!... GOOD LUCK TO YOU, LAD!
THANK YOU, CHIEF! YOU WON'T REGRET YOUR DECISION!
I GUESS THIS MEANS THE FANTASTIC FOUR WON'T BE HUNTED ANY MORE, EH, CHIEF?
HUNTED?? IF THE PUBLIC KNEW WHAT WE KNEW, THEY'D GET A MEDAL!
WHAT WILL WE DO WITH THEM, REED?
NO MATTER WHAT WE DO, THEY CAN ALWAYS CHANGE THEIR FORM AND ESCAPE!
THERE'S ONE WAY WE CAN BE CERTAIN THEY WON'T ESCAPE!
NO! NO! DON'T KILL US! DON'T!
WE PROMISE TO CAUSE NO MORE HARM! WE'LL LIVE AMONG YOU IN PEACE! WE SWEAR IT!
WE HATE BEING SKRULLS! WE'D RATHER BE ANYTHING ELSE!
SO BE IT! I WILL TELL YOU WHAT TO CHANGE INTO!
...AND I WILL HYNOTIZE YOU SO THAT YOU WILL FORGET YOUR PREVIOUS IDENTITIES! YOU WILL REMAIN WHAT YOU BECOME-- FOR AS LONG AS YOU LIVE!
WILL WE HAVE A PEACEFUL EXISTENCE?
PROMISE WE'LL BE CONTENTED!
AND SO IT CAME TO PASS THAT THE THREE CAPTIVE SKRULLS BECAME THE MOST CONTENTED CREATURES ON EARTH--AS THEY GRAZED PEACEFULLY OUT IN THE PASTURE...
MOOO!!
SO ENDS THE MENACE OF THE SKRULLS!
YEAH, BUT I'VE GOT A FEELING THERE'S EVEN WORSE TROUBLE AHEAD!
HEY, THING--HOW COME YOU'RE SUCH AN OPTIMIST?
The END

DON'T MISS "AMAZING ADULT FANTASY" COMICS--ON SALE NOW!

STAMP COLLECTING OUTFIT
A packet of stamps from all parts of world. A package of stamp hinges; perforation gauge and millimeter scale; watermark detector. Everything ONLY 10c to approval buyers.
LORRAINE W. BROWN, Dept. 10, Marion, Mich.

1c Thousands of beautiful stamps at only 1c each—why pay more when you can get the best for less. Write today for approvals.
PENNY STAMP SERVICE
Orange California

½ OFF ½ OFF ½ OFF
Our BARGAIN APPROVALS are sold at 50% off Scott's Catalogue Prices . . .
MAKE US PROVE IT!
CATALINA STAMPS, Box 206, Avalon, Calif.

BETTER U.S. APPROVALS
To introduce our BETTER U.S. APPROVALS we offer 15 of the most wanted U.S. stamps, including a Columbian, Bi-Cents, Army-Navy, Famous American, Airs and other Commems, for only 10c.
OCEAN STAMPS, BOX 64-D, BROOKLYN 29, N.Y.

111 DIF. BONANZA 10¢
Includes Complete Red Cross Set, Triangle, Scout, Fr. So. Antartica, Singapore, Hungary Street Scenes, etc. Only 10¢ with Approvals.
FAIRWAY — Box 65-C — Garden Grove, Calif.

SPUTNIKS - ROCKETS - SPACE STAMPS
10 different ONLY 10¢ to introduce our sparkling approval selections of animals, flowers, sports, pictorials and space issues.
CAMBRIA STAMPS, Box 2205, Anaheim, Calif.

25 DIFF. CHINA 10¢
BIG Value ONLY 10c to Approval Buyers.
EXTRA! We give our regular customers a 56,000 Space Album after certain purchases.
WEST COAST STAMPS, Box 2187-X, Santa Ana, Calif.

UNITED NATIONS
First stamp issue, considered to be one of the world's most attractive sets. Pictures UN Bldg, Emblem etc. Only 10c with approvals.
WALTER WELLES
Box 1246-MG, Church St. Sta., N.Y.C. 8

CHINA STAMPS 10¢
Packet of Hard-To-Get China Stamps Only 10c to new prospective customers from our foreign approvals True-Value Service, Box 2098-E Santa Ana, Calif.

LOOK — GIANT PHILIPPINE
stamp, plus New Zealand, Cuba and others. Only 5c with U.S. or foreign approvals.
Earl Thompson, 5448 Odell St., St. Louis 9, Mo.

105 DISSIMILAR British Colony stamps for only **10¢** with approvals.
CROWN STAMP COMPANY Virgil616Ontario

107 DISTINCT British Colonial stamps for only **10¢.** with approvals.
LINCOLN STAMP CO. St. Catharines416Ont.

103 DIVERSIFIED British Empire stamps for only **10¢** with approvals.
NIAGARA STAMP CO. St. Catharines516Ont.

American Historical Collection!! Enormous George Washington beauty, F. D. Roosevelt DIAMOND, Giant Abe Lincoln USA Flag commemorative, plus Midget soldier, Latin Orchid issue, Old IFNI overprint, etc. 10¢ with approvals. **Roseland Stamps, Spring Lake 19A, Mich.**

225 STAMPS FOR ONLY 10¢
THIS MAMMOTH VALUE INCLUDES STAMPS WORTH UP TO 25c! ALSO APPROVALS. WRITE TODAY!
MYSTIC STAMP CO Camden 3, New York

Yoshie Imanami

I CAN PARALYZE A 200-LB. ATTACKER WITH JUST ONE FINGER! Yet I weigh only 93 lbs.! YOU TOO can protect yourself with my SECRET Oriental System of Yubiwaza.

Girls, these days it isn't safe to be alone even during daylight—let alone coming home at night on dark streets. Mugging and other kinds of attacks can do more harm than the loss of mere money. Yet—although I'm under 5 feet and weigh only 93 lbs.—I don't have a bit of fear—day or night! That's because my forefathers in Japan always passed along to each generation the secrets of Yubiwaza—the amazing system of ONE-FINGER DEFENSE. With Yubiwaza, I've subdued huge bullies almost twice my size and weight . . . I've made rough characters cry out for help themselves . . . and I've left muggers suffering in pain on the ground! And I've done all this just by placing a single finger on the right spot of my attacker's body!
Simply press your finger on one of the vital spots shown in this Yubiwaza System and your attacker may lose consciousness . . . or become paralyzed—completely unable to move. He releases his grip on you instantly—becomes helpless himself! I've revealed every secret of the ONE-FINGER SELF-DEFENSE SYSTEM in my book, Yubiwaza. I guarantee you can protect yourself as easily and surely as I have done—or your money back! Now you can walk home at night unafraid, with the knowledge no harm can come to you as long as you know YUBIWAZA. My system is profusely illustrated with LIVE ACTION photos of me demonstrating each secret. My system can be used by any man as well—so why not order an extra copy for your favorite man! For my complete instructions, send only 99c plus 26c postage (Total: $1.25). YUBIWAZA, c/o Precise, Dept. Y-2, **Box 322, Lenox Hill Sta., New York, N.Y.**

ONLY 99c

1001 THINGS YOU CAN GET FREE Gifts • Samples Books • Stamps Etc. **50¢**
THINGS FREE • P.O. BOX 1225 • NEWARK 1, N. J.

POEMS WANTED for musical setting and recording. Send poems. Free Examination.
AMERICA'S LARGEST SONG STUDIO
FIVE STAR MUSIC MASTERS, 92 BEACON BLDG., BOSTON, MASS.

1847, First USA Rariety!! Goliath foreign beauty shows Ben Franklin in this outstanding issue!! Plus Congo Freedom stamp, unused ½ inch midget stamp freak, real Cigar issue, Icy Greenland, Free China Bomer, airmail giant, etc., only 10c with approvals. **Capital Stamp Co., Ferrysburg 19D, Mich.**

World's Best Magic Tricks Revealed
BE A MAGICIAN! Learn the secrets of great magicians like Houdini, Thurston, etc. Learn how to do over 200 different tricks with coins, cards, rope, etc. Amaze and mystify your friends. Nothing else to buy. **50¢**
MAGIC TRICKS • P.O. BOX 1225 • NEWARK 1, N. J.

POEMS WANTED
For musical setting. Send your Poems today for Free Examination. Any subject. Immediate consideration.
CROWN MUSIC CO., 49-MC W. 32 St., New York 1

DRAW The First Day!

Anything you want to draw is automatically seen on paper thru amazing new invention. "Magic Art Reproducer." Then easily follow lines of "picture image" with pencil. Also reduces or enlarges. Free 10 Day Trial! Pay postman on delivery $1.98 plus postage. Or send $1.98 and we pay postage. Money Back Guarantee.
NORTON Dept. 607, 296 Broadway, N.Y.C.

55 "FDR" & POPE TRIANGLES! Lot 55 DIFFERENT has FDR Diamond. "Pope" Triangle. Greenland. Angola Map. Rhodesia etc. Catalogs $1.15—ALL only 5c with Approvals. LONGHORN STAMP CO. Box 3068. Ellwood Sta. Lubbock, Tex.

GIGANTIC COLLECTION FREE!
Includes Triangles, Early United States — Animals — Commemoratives — British Colonies —High Value Pictorials, etc. Complete Collection plus Big Illustrated Magazine all free. Send 5c for postage.
GRAY STAMP CO., Dept. MC, Toronto, Canada

Let me show you

HOW TO SPEAK AND WRITE LIKE A COLLEGE GRADUATE

I have helped thousands of men and women who have not had college training in English to become effective speakers, writers, and conversationalists. With my new C. I. METHOD, you can stop making mistakes, build up your vocabulary, speed up your reading, develop writing skill, learn the "secrets" of conversation. You don't have to go back to school. Takes only 15 minutes a day at home. Costs little. 32-page booklet mailed FREE upon request. Send me a card or letter TODAY!
Don Bolander, Career Institute
Dept. E-9412, 30 E. Adams St., Chicago 3, Illinois
Please mail me your **FREE** 32-page booklet on English.
Name
Address
City Zone State

SPECIAL! OLD U. S.
Famous Americans, Flags, Presidents, Commemoratives, Airmails 10c with approvals Plus Surprise Packet. **10¢**
METROPOLITAN STAMPS
Box 312T, Jackson Heights, N. Y.

Add SUPER MUSCLES The Fastest Quickest Way to CHEST, Wrist, Arms, Back!
Speedy Results seen in 10 Days or Money Refunded!

Costs only 99c for the easiest, quickest way to make your back alive with amazing power packed muscles and make your body packed full of still smooth muscles. Now you can quickly have biceps and forearms bulging with muscles that put dynamite in your hands and fists. You can quickly have a body so powerful it will dramatically obey your every command.
Here is the new way to pack layer upon layer of muscle—right where you may need it most. Try the new Super Karate Super Fast Muscle Builder Way to develop a body that commands attention and respect wherever you go—whether you are fat or skinny—short or tall—old or young.
Send only 99c plus 26c postage and handling—Total $1.25 Cash, Check, or M. O. and your Super Karate Super Fast Muscle Builder will be rushed to you in plain wrapper by return mail. The quicker you start the quicker you'll have the pounds of SOLID MUSCLE you want. Send $1.25 now to Home Gym Co., Dept. G 1, **Box 322, Lenox Hill Sta., New York 21, N. Y.**

ONLY 99c

Test your talent!

Contest Prize: $495.00 Scholarship in Commercial Art

Draw your choice of any one of these heads—the boxer, the girl or the inspector. Make your drawing any size except like a tracing. Use pencil. Everyone who enters contest gets a free estimate of his talent. Winner receives the complete course in advertising art, illustrating, cartooning and painting taught by world's largest home study art school, Art Instruction, Inc.

Try for this free art course! The school is an accredited member of National Home Study Council. Students are taught, individually, by professional artists. Purpose of contest: to uncover hidden talent. Entries for January 1962 contest due by January 31. None returned. Amateurs only. Our students not eligible. Winner notified. Here's a contest you will enjoy, if you like to draw. Copy at least one of these heads and mail it to the school.

Use 1 coupon—
then pass this page
on to a friend.

1. AI/ART INSTRUCTION, INC.
Studio 11941 • 500 South 4th St., Minneapolis 15, Minn.
Please enter my drawing in your draw-a-head contest.
(PLEASE PRINT)
Name ______
Occupation ______ AGE ______
Address ______ Apt. ______
City ______ Zone ______
County ______ State ______

2. AI/ART INSTRUCTION, INC.
Studio 11941 • 500 South 4th St., Minneapolis 15, Minn.
Please enter my drawing in your draw-a-head contest.
(PLEASE PRINT)
Name ______
Occupation ______ AGE ______
Address ______ Apt. ______
City ______ Zone ______
County ______ State ______

3. AI/ART INSTRUCTION, INC.
Studio 11941 • 500 South 4th St., Minneapolis 15, Minn.
Please enter my drawing in your draw-a-head contest.
(PLEASE PRINT)
Name ______
Occupation ______ AGE ______
Address ______ Apt. ______
City ______ Zone ______
County ______ State ______

ANNOUNCING
THE ALL-NEW
DAISY
B•B GUN
"SPITTIN' IMAGE"
of the GREAT MODEL 94 WINCHESTER
. . . RIFLE THAT WON THE GOLDEN WEST!
Here's the new kind of B • B Gun you want for that first or second Daisy—Model 1894 Lever-Matic! Looks, loads, cocks, aims like famous Model 94 Winchester. Real "Spittin' Image" features: slim-line carbine barrels, bands . . 2-way lever cocking . . side-loading and "safety" hammer. Own this accurate force-feed 40 shot style repeater; full 38". At sport, hardware, department stores. Model 1894 only . .
$12.95
NEW 2-WAY COCKING
'Lever-Matic' gun lever cocks half-way on a forward motion—completes on return motion.
NEW SIDE LOAD PORT
B•Bs are quickly, easily loaded into port on right side of 1894's receiver plate. Fun to load!
NEW SAFETY
Gun won't fire unless hammer "thumb-cocked." Also fun using as a "clicker" gun!
NEW SIGHTS
Rear sight adjustable; front sight blade type; dependable and accurate aiming.
Rush post card now for Free Daisy B•B Gun Catalog picturing amazing new "1894" and other Daisys priced at only $5.95 to $14.95.
ASK DAD . . . HE HAD A
IT'S A DAISY B•B GUN
PRICES HIGHER IN CANADA
PRICES SUBJECT TO CHANGE WITHOUT NOTICE
Also NEW!
JUMBO
B•B TUBE
First and only Jumbo Tube of 500 B•Bs! More for your money. Ask stores for Daisy's Jumbo "530" Tube only
25¢
Per Tube!
DAISY MANUFACTURING COMPANY, DEPT. 1491, ROGERS, ARKANSAS, U.S.A.
75 Years of Quality Leisure-Time Products

IND.
12¢
THE Fantastic Four
APPROVED BY THE COMICS CODE AUTHORITY
MC
3 MAR.
THE GREATEST COMIC MAGAZINE IN THE WORLD!!
IN THIS GREAT, COLLECTORS'-ITEM ISSUE, YOU WILL SEE, FOR THE FIRST TIME: THE AMAZING FANTASTI-CAR, THE COLORFUL NEW FANTASTIC FOUR COSTUMES, AND OTHER STARTLING SURPRISES!
ALSO, LEARN THE SECRET OF THE FANTASTIC FOUR'S SKYSCRAPER HIDE-OUT!!

NEW DISCOVERY IN HYPNOTISM

shows how to hypnotize in 30 seconds!

Yes, an amazing new method has been developed to bring on quick, easy induction of the hypnotic trance. Now, for the first time, you too can benefit from this recent discovery in hypnotic induction.

QUICK RESULTS

Want to hypnotize your friends? Your club members? HOW TO HYPNOTIZE is a remarkable primer that shows you just how to master the latest improved induction methods. The author, a widely experienced hypnotist and consultant, gives you the exact positions to take, the precise phraseology, all the steps necessary to hypnotize even the most difficult subjects.

EXCLUSIVELY in How to HYPNOTIZE

ENTIRELY NEW METHOD

Until recently the process of hypnotic induction was largely based on trial and error methods which succeeded mainly with subjects who were highly susceptible to hypnosis in the first place. The truth is that these highly susceptible subjects make up a very small percentage of the population. That is why amateurs and beginning hypnotists have so often been disappointed in their attempts at trance induction. Now, however, recent scientific research has developed ENTIRELY NEW METHODS that are not only sure fire in their results but quick and easy to achieve! For the first time, these new methods are presented in HOW TO HYPNOTIZE in language that you can easily and successfully follow on the very first reading!

SHOWS YOU STEP BY STEP

This book — which has been acclaimed by doctors and psychologists — is guaranteed to give you all the know-how necessary to induce the trance state in others. It not only explains the latest discoveries in hypnotic induction, but it shows step by step, move by move, exactly how to bring on the trance; how to transform the trance into deeper and still deeper states; and how to terminate the trance quickly and effectively without any dangers whatsoever. You are even given alternative methods, so that you can actually chose the one that suits you best.

USED BY DOCTORS
The book that is being used by doctors and psychologists to learn hypnotic induction is now available to you

$1.98 FOR ONLY

Photographically Illustrated
40 photographic illustrations show how you can achieve trance induction in as little as 30 seconds!

FREE 10-DAY OFFER

FREE 10-day examination of this book is offered to you if you mail us coupon today. If not delighted with results return it within 10 days for a full refund of the purchase price.

FREE 10-DAY OFFER
Mail Coupon Today

GUARANTEE
This guarantees you that HOW TO HYPNOTIZE will show you how to induce the trance, or your purchase price will be refunded upon return of the book.
Signed, BOND BOOK

Bond Book Co., Dept. HM-192
43 W. 61st Street, New York 23, N.Y.

Send How to Hypnotize for 10 day Free trial. My purchase price will be promptly refunded if I'm not satisfied.

☐ Send C.O.D. I'll pay postman $1.98 plus postage.
☐ I enclose $1.98. Bond Book pays postage.

NAME ____________________
ADDRESS ____________________
CITY ____________ ZONE ____ STATE ____________

THE FANTASTIC FOUR is published by CANAM PUBLISHERS SALES CORP. OFFICE OF PUBLICATION: 655 MADISON AVENUE, NEW YORK, N.Y. Published bi-monthly. Copyright 1961 by CANAM PUBLISHERS SALES CORP., 655 Madison Avenue, New York, N.Y. Vol. 1 No. 3, MARCH 1962 issue. Price 10c per copy. Subscription rate $1.70 for 12 issues including postage. No similarity between any of the names, characters, persons, and/or institutions appearing in this magazine with those of any living or dead person or institution is intended, and any such similarity which may exist is purely coincidental. Printed in the U.S.A. by The Eastern Color Printing Co., Waterbury 20, Conn.

THE FANTASTIC FOUR, in...
THE MENACE OF THE MIRACLE MAN
CAN EVEN THE FANTASTIC FOUR DEFEAT A MAN WHO PERFORMS... MIRACLES???
AH! FROM MY VANTAGE POINT UP HERE, I SEE THAT WE HAVE FOUR CELEBRITIES IN OUR AUDIENCE!! LET ME INTRODUCE THEM TO YOU...
Stan Lee + J. KIRBY
CHAPTER 1
LOOK! THE MIRACLE MAN IS ACTUALLY FLOATING IN THE AIR!!
HOW DOES HE DO IT?? THERE ARE NO WIRES... NOTHING!! HE REALLY DOES WORK MIRACLES!
HE--HE CAN DO ANYTHING!
V-563
THE FIRST IS REED RICHARDS, BETTER KNOWN AS MISTER FANTASTIC!!
AND NEXT TO HIM, FULLY VISIBLE, IT SEEMS, IS THE SO-CALLED INVISIBLE GIRL!
ON HER LEFT WE FIND... THE THING! DON'T BE BASHFUL, THING! LET US LOOK AT YOU!
GET THAT SPOT-LIGHT OFF ME!!
AND THE YOUNGEST MEMBER OF THE FANTASTIC FOUR... KNOWN TO THE WORLD AS THE HUMAN TORCH!
1

THERE YOU HAVE THE FANTASTIC FOUR!! THEY ARE SUPPOSED TO BE THE MOST POWERFUL, MOST AMAZING QUARTET IN HISTORY!! BUT, I SAY TO YOU...
...BAH!!
NEXT TO MY POWER, THEY ARE NOTHING!
CAN THEY BECOME ALL-POWERFUL GIANTS AT WILL??
LOOK!!
IT--IT'S IMPOSSIBLE!
CAN THEY CHANGE THE COMPOSITION OF THEIR BODIES TO ANYTHING THEY WISH? CAN THEY TURN THEMSELVES INTO WATER, METAL, OR EVEN ...GAS!!
WE MUST BE DREAMING!
IT'S MAD! INSANE!
WILL THE POWER OF THE ELEMENTS DO THEIR BIDDING? CAN THEY CONTROL THE STORM? THE THUNDER? THE LIGHTNING?
HA HA HA HA
THE FANTASTIC FOUR!! I SNEER AT THEIR PUNY POWERS! I MOCK THEIR CHILDISH FEATS!
THING! WAIT!!
LEGGO!! THAT'S THE LAST STRAW!!
LET ME AT 'IM! I'LL WIPE THAT GRIN OFF HIS OILY FACE!! LET ME AT 'IM!
2

AH, I WAS HOPING ONE OF YOU WOULD ACCEPT MY FRIENDLY CHALLENGE!
STEP RIGHT UP, THING! LET US HAVE A LITTLE TEST OF STRENGTH!
YOUR OVERRATED BRUTE FORCE AGAINST MY MIRACULOUS POWERS!! THIS WILL BE A DEFEAT YOU SHALL NEVER FORGET! PICK ANY ONE OF THESE TWO TREE TRUNKS... THEY ARE BOTH THE SAME SIZE AND WEIGHT!
I'LL TAKE THIS ONE, LOUDMOUTH! NOW WHAT?
NOW... TRY TO SHATTER IT!!
YA THINK I CAN'T, HUH??
POW
JUST WATCH THIS!!
UGH!! MMMPFF!! THERE!! THERE--I-I-DID IT!
CRASH!
ALL RIGHT, SMART GUY IT'S YOUR TURN!
AH, SO IT IS! BUT YOU'LL FORGIVE ME IF I DO NOT EXHAUST MYSELF, AS YOU DID!
FOR ME, THE POWER OF ONE FINGER IS QUITE ENOUGH!
!

IT'S A TRICK! IT'S GOTTA BE A TRICK!! NOBODY IS THAT POWERFUL!!
YOU LUMBERING FOOL!! WHAT DO YOU KNOW OF MY MIRACULOUS POWER??! YOU, WITH ALL YOUR ANIMAL STRENGTH, COULD NOT HURT ME WITH YOUR HARDEST BLOW!
OH NO?? TRY THIS ON FOR SIZE!!
CERTAINLY, IF IT WILL SERVE TO CONVINCE YOU!
IT AIN'T POSSIBLE! I COULDA SMASHED THRU A STONE WALL WITH THAT PUNCH! LET ME AT 'IM AGAIN...
AND SO I CONCLUDE MY PERFORM-ANCE!
REED!! STOP HIM! HE'S GOING BERSERK!
HOLD IT, THING! THAT'S ENOUGH!
MINUTES LATER, IN THEIR AIR-POWERED FANTASTICAR, FOUR MYSTIFIED FIGURES APPROACH THEIR SECRET HEADQUARTERS...
YOU'VE BEEN SO SILENT, REED! WHAT ARE YOU THINKING?
I'M THINKING THAT IT IS FORTUNATE FOR US, AND FOR THE WORLD, THAT THE MIRACLE MAN IS NOT A CRIMINAL! FOR, IF HE WERE...
...HE MIGHT BE THE ONE FOE WE COULD NOT DEFEAT!!
BUT LITTLE DOES MR. FANTASTIC REALIZE HOW PROPHETIC HIS WORDS ARE! FOR, AT THAT VERY MOMENT, BACKSTAGE...
THE TIME HAS COME FOR ME TO THROW OFF MY MASK OF RESPECTABILITY!!
NOW THAT I HAVE DEMONSTRATED MY POW-ERS TO THE WORLD, IT IS TIME FOR THE MIRACLE MAN TO... STRIKE!
4

BUT I NEED A BOLD, BREATH-TAKING FEAT TO STRIKE FEAR INTO THE HEART OF THE PUBLIC!
...SOMETHING TO MAKE THEM REALIZE THAT THE HUMAN RACE IS POWER-LESS AGAINST ME!
WAIT!! THERE! IN FRONT OF THE THEATRE BELOW!! THAT'S MY ANSWER! THAT MONSTER STATUE ON EXHIBIT!
BIJOU
THE MONSTER FROM MARS
I SHALL PERFORM THE IMPOSSIBLE!! I SHALL BRING THAT HUGE, MONSTER STATUE TO LIFE, AS MY UNCONQUERABLE SLAVE!
AND SO, THE GROUNDWORK IS LAID FOR THE MOST AMAZING BATTLE OF ALL TIME...
SET THE CONTROLS ON AUTOMATIC, THING... WE'RE HOME!
I'LL NEVER STOP BEING IMPRESSED BY THE WAY THE FANTASTICAR LANDS ITSELF!
ONLY REED COULD HAVE DESIGNED THIS ROOF TO WORK LIKE AN AIRCRAFT CARRIER'S DECK!
AND NONE OF THE TENANTS SUSPECT THAT WE OWN THE ENTIRE TOWER OF THIS BUILDING!
CUT-AWAY DIAGRAM OF THE FANTASTIC FOUR'S SECRET HEADQUARTERS...
OBSERVATORY
SAVE THIS FOR FUTURE REFERENCE.
ANTI-VIBRATION WALL
FANTASTICAR HANGAR
FANTASTI-COPTER HANGAR
POGO ORBIT PLANE HANGAR
PHOTO ANALYSIS ROOM
LONG-RANGE PASSENGER MISSILE... CAN REACH ANY PART OF THE WORLD IN MINUTES.
HIDDEN ELEVATOR
MISSILE MONITORING ROOM
MISSILE READY ROOM
PROJECTION ROOM
CONFERENCE ROOM
GIANT MAP ROOM
LAUNCH PAD
LIVING QUARTERS AND LABORATORIES ON FLOORS BELOW
5

CHAPTER II
"THE MONSTER LIVES!"
STAN LEE & J. KIRBY
BIJOU
THE MONSTER FROM MARS!
NOW SHOWING
GUESS I'LL SEE WHAT'S DOIN' ON TV TONIGHT, REED!
HEY!! THIS IS KEEN! THEY'RE TELEVISING THE WORLD PREMIERE OF "THE MONSTER FROM MARS!"
THAT HUGE EXHIBIT OF THE MONSTER ON DISPLAY OUTSIDE THE THEATRE MUST HAVE COST A SMALL FORTUNE!
6

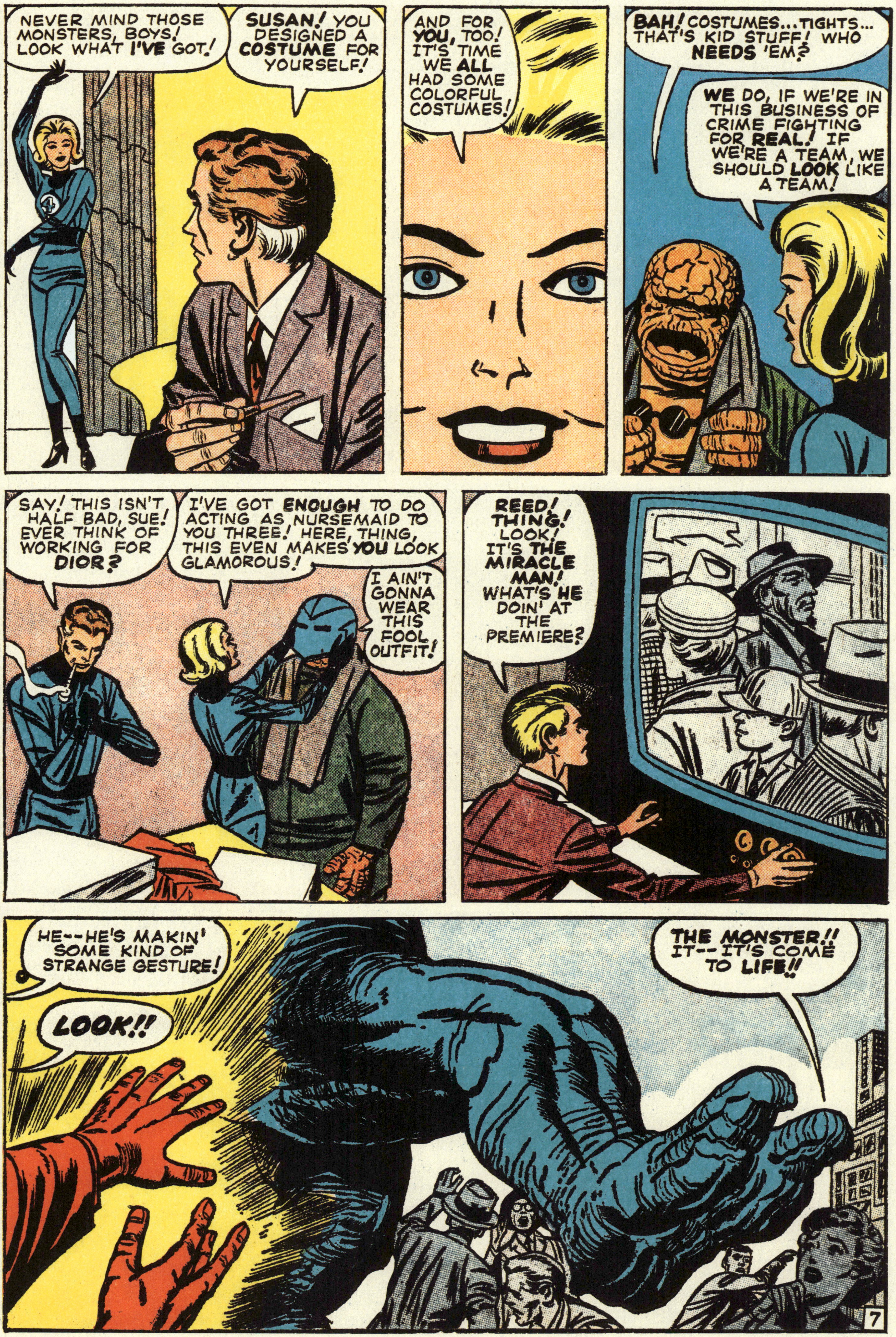
NEVER MIND THOSE MONSTERS, BOYS! LOOK WHAT I'VE GOT!
SUSAN! YOU DESIGNED A COSTUME FOR YOURSELF!
AND FOR YOU, TOO! IT'S TIME WE ALL HAD SOME COLORFUL COSTUMES!
BAH! COSTUMES... TIGHTS... THAT'S KID STUFF! WHO NEEDS 'EM?
WE DO, IF WE'RE IN THIS BUSINESS OF CRIME FIGHTING FOR REAL! IF WE'RE A TEAM, WE SHOULD LOOK LIKE A TEAM!
SAY! THIS ISN'T HALF BAD, SUE! EVER THINK OF WORKING FOR DIOR?
I'VE GOT ENOUGH TO DO ACTING AS NURSEMAID TO YOU THREE! HERE, THING, THIS EVEN MAKES YOU LOOK GLAMOROUS!
I AIN'T GONNA WEAR THIS FOOL OUTFIT!
REED! THING! LOOK! IT'S THE MIRACLE MAN! WHAT'S HE DOIN' AT THE PREMIERE?
HE--HE'S MAKIN' SOME KIND OF STRANGE GESTURE!
LOOK!!
THE MONSTER!! IT--IT'S COME TO LIFE!!
7

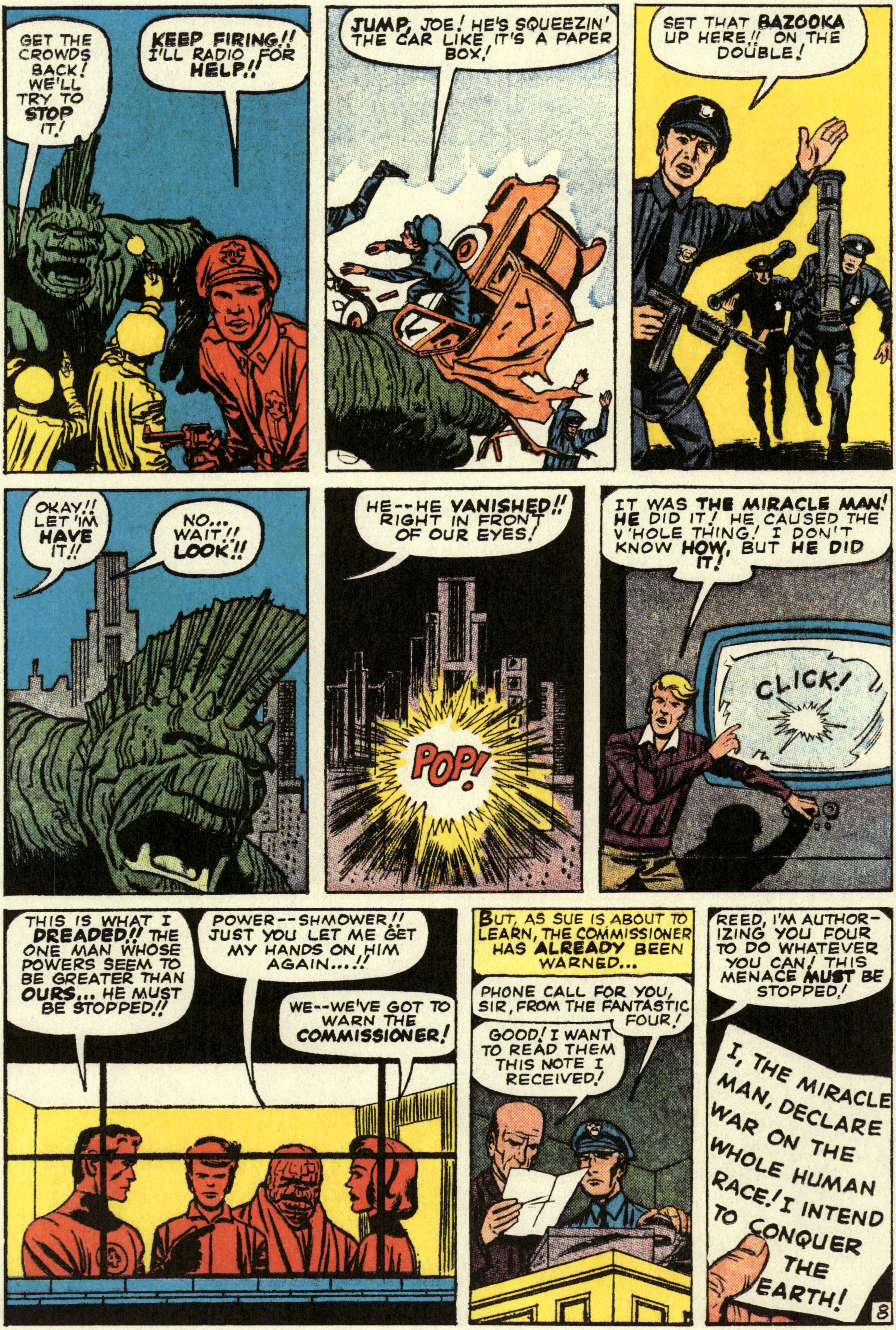
GET THE CROWDS BACK! WE'LL TRY TO STOP IT!
KEEP FIRING!! I'LL RADIO FOR HELP!!
JUMP, JOE! HE'S SQUEEZIN' THE CAR LIKE IT'S A PAPER BOX!
SET THAT BAZOOKA UP HERE!! ON THE DOUBLE!
OKAY!! LET 'IM HAVE IT!!
NO... WAIT!! LOOK!!
HE--HE VANISHED!! RIGHT IN FRONT OF OUR EYES!
POP!
IT WAS THE MIRACLE MAN! HE DID IT! HE CAUSED THE WHOLE THING! I DON'T KNOW HOW, BUT HE DID IT!
CLICK!
THIS IS WHAT I DREADED!! THE ONE MAN WHOSE POWERS SEEM TO BE GREATER THAN OURS... HE MUST BE STOPPED!!
POWER--SHMOWER!! JUST YOU LET ME GET MY HANDS ON HIM AGAIN...!!
WE--WE'VE GOT TO WARN THE COMMISSIONER!
BUT, AS SUE IS ABOUT TO LEARN, THE COMMISSIONER HAS ALREADY BEEN WARNED...
PHONE CALL FOR YOU, SIR, FROM THE FANTASTIC FOUR!
GOOD! I WANT TO READ THEM THIS NOTE I RECEIVED!
REED, I'M AUTHORIZING YOU FOUR TO DO WHATEVER YOU CAN! THIS MENACE MUST BE STOPPED!
I, THE MIRACLE MAN, DECLARE WAR ON THE WHOLE HUMAN RACE! I INTEND TO CONQUER THE EARTH!
8

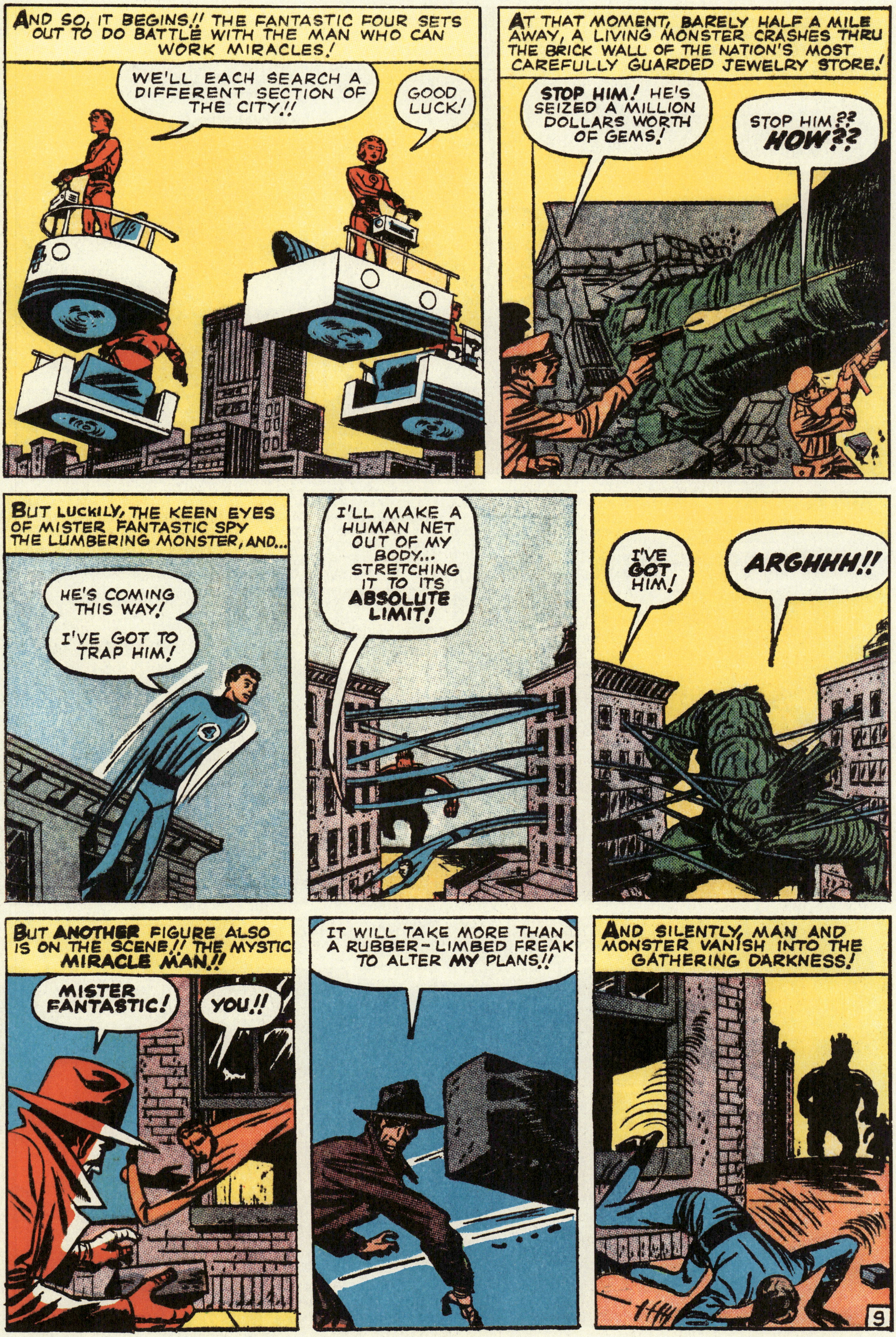
AND SO, IT BEGINS!! THE FANTASTIC FOUR SETS OUT TO DO BATTLE WITH THE MAN WHO CAN WORK MIRACLES!
WE'LL EACH SEARCH A DIFFERENT SECTION OF THE CITY!!
GOOD LUCK!
AT THAT MOMENT, BARELY HALF A MILE AWAY, A LIVING MONSTER CRASHES THRU THE BRICK WALL OF THE NATION'S MOST CAREFULLY GUARDED JEWELRY STORE!
STOP HIM! HE'S SEIZED A MILLION DOLLARS WORTH OF GEMS!
STOP HIM?? HOW??
BUT LUCKILY, THE KEEN EYES OF MISTER FANTASTIC SPY THE LUMBERING MONSTER, AND...
HE'S COMING THIS WAY!
I'VE GOT TO TRAP HIM!
I'LL MAKE A HUMAN NET OUT OF MY BODY... STRETCHING IT TO ITS ABSOLUTE LIMIT!
I'VE GOT HIM!
ARGHHH!!
BUT ANOTHER FIGURE ALSO IS ON THE SCENE!! THE MYSTIC MIRACLE MAN!!
MISTER FANTASTIC!
YOU!!
IT WILL TAKE MORE THAN A RUBBER-LIMBED FREAK TO ALTER MY PLANS!!
AND SILENTLY, MAN AND MONSTER VANISH INTO THE GATHERING DARKNESS!
9

CONTINUED AFTER NEXT PAGE..

Great NEW Idea from CTI

...to help you get and hold a fine job (or start a business of your own) in *Air Conditioning and Refrigeration!*

Here Is Your "Training Shop"

REAR VIEW

Move up to a better job, higher pay, steady work. Install and repair air conditioners and refrigerators in homes, office buildings, shopping centers, factories, autos. Air conditioning is one of America's two fastest-growing industries. Over 150 million units are in use, and nearly 8 million units more are produced annually. It's an uncrowded field for mechanics and technicians. There are more jobs and fewer qualified applicants. Industry leaders report that *20,000 men must be trained each year* to fill new job openings. Train yourself at home for higher income, more security. It's easy, it's fast when you enroll with CTI. For complete information, *fill out and mail coupon below, for three valuable free booklets.* No obligation.

FRONT VIEW

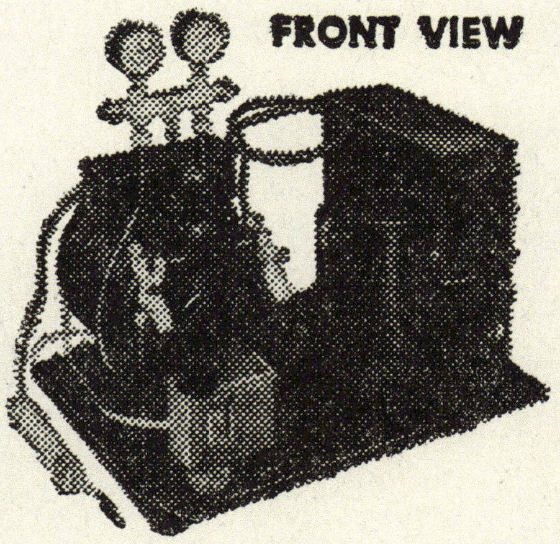

EXCLUSIVE CTI FEATURE!

25 KITS—20 SHOP PROJECTS

Illustrated above is a view of the new CTI condensing unit, fully assembled. This is a commercial-type, heavy-duty, ¼ h.p. unit. You build it from 25 kits of parts (and with tools) that CTI sends without extra cost. In addition, CTI includes 20 Shop Projects, which simulate the kind of problems you are likely to encounter in the field. After assembling your condenser, you may then build an air conditioner, freezer, refrigerator or milk cooler.

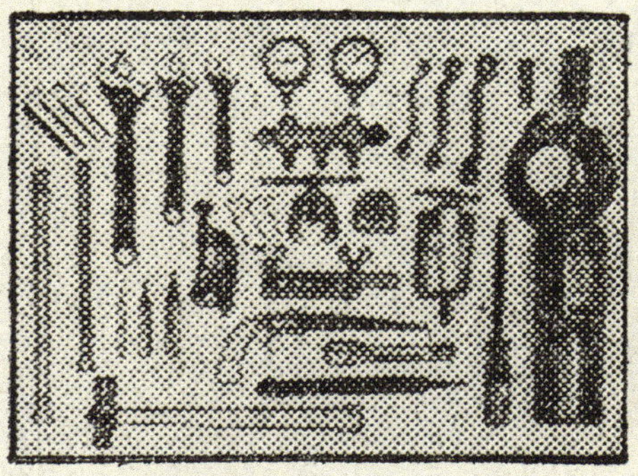

Tools Are Included

You receive wrenches, tube flaring tools, hammer, tubing, fittings, gauges and many other items used by the experienced mechanic. Everything is of professional quality. Best of all, CTI trains you to use tools with speed and skill.

You learn by practicing with operating equipment

Thousands once learned this rewarding craft just by completing home study lessons. But CTI goes a step farther—and an important step it is! CTI also sends you 25 kits of tools and parts. You build these parts into an operating unit. It's a practical method because *you get experience as you train.*

Go in Business

Because air conditioning and refrigeration is expanding so rapidly all over the nation, opportunities to go in business are plentiful. Many CTI graduates have accomplished this high aim. Start in a small way, from your own home, and gradually expand. In time you may wish to add a sales division. Manufacturers offer attractive franchises, including merchandising aids, to ambitious, qualified men.

Earn Cash in Spare Time

Soon after enrolling, many CTI students earn money in spare time. Some handle servicing on a monthly fee basis for food stores, restaurants, taverns and office buildings. Many work part time at local dealers. Quite a number of CTI students have a full-time business going by the time they graduate. CTI kit training gives you the practice and experience you need to step from lesson study to actual field work.

3 FREE BOOKLETS

Get complete information—read it—and then decide. The facts are free. Mail coupon for 3 opportunity booklets. Act today.

MAIL COUPON TODAY

COMMERCIAL TRADES INSTITUTE
1400 GREENLEAF AVENUE .DEPT. R-2
CHICAGO 26, ILLINOIS

Send me your 3 free booklets: Success in Air Conditioning & Refrigeration; Proof from Graduates; and Lesson Samples.

NAME________________________ AGE______

ADDRESS________________________________

CITY______________ ZONE______ STATE______

CTI

PROOF FROM GRADUATES

CTI has prepared a fascinating, new booklet called "Proof from Graduates." In their own words, CTI graduates tell you how training has helped them to better jobs, higher pay, or a business of their own. Send coupon for your copy.

COMMERCIAL TRADES INSTITUTE CHICAGO 26, ILLINOIS

A Non-Profit Organization • Accredited by National Home Study Council

CHAPTER III
"THE FLAME THAT DIED!"
Stan Lee J. Kirby
THING!! LOOK!! IT'S THE TORCH!
HE'S FOUND THE MONSTER!
V-563
THAT MEANS ONE THING...
YEAH! THE MIRACLE MAN MUST BE THERE, TOO! LET'S GO!
YOU STAY HIDDEN, SUE, IN CASE WE NEED YOU!
AS FOR ME, I'M GETTIN' OUTTA THIS MONKEY SUIT SO I CAN MOVE!
11

BUT, BEFORE THE ENRAGED THING CAN REACH THE SCENE...
ATTA BOY! YOU GOT ME!
BUT I'VE GOT NEWS FOR YOU...
YOU'RE ABOUT TO LEARN SOMETHING ABOUT THE HUMAN TORCH...
...I'M JUST TOO HOT TO HANDLE!
HE WAS NOTHING BUT WOOD AND PLASTER!! HOW DID THE MIRACLE MAN MAKE HIM MOVE?? HOW??!
WE CAN'T TAKE ANY CHANCES WITH THAT FLAMING MENACE FLYING AROUND! BRING HIM DOWN, MEN!
HOLD YOUR FIRE, YOU FOOLS!! IT'S THE HUMAN TORCH! HE JUST SAVED OUR ATOMIC TANK!
BUT THERE IS ONE WHO DOES NOT HOLD HIS FIRE....!!
THIS WILL STOP THAT BLAZING NUISANCE!
UGH!! CH--CHEMICAL FOAM!
MY FLAME'S GOING OUT!! IF ONLY...THE OTHERS...WILL BE... IN TIME...
TORCH!!
THE MIRACLE MAN DID IT, THING!! GET HIM... GET HIM!!
12

CONTINUED AFTER NEXT PAGE..

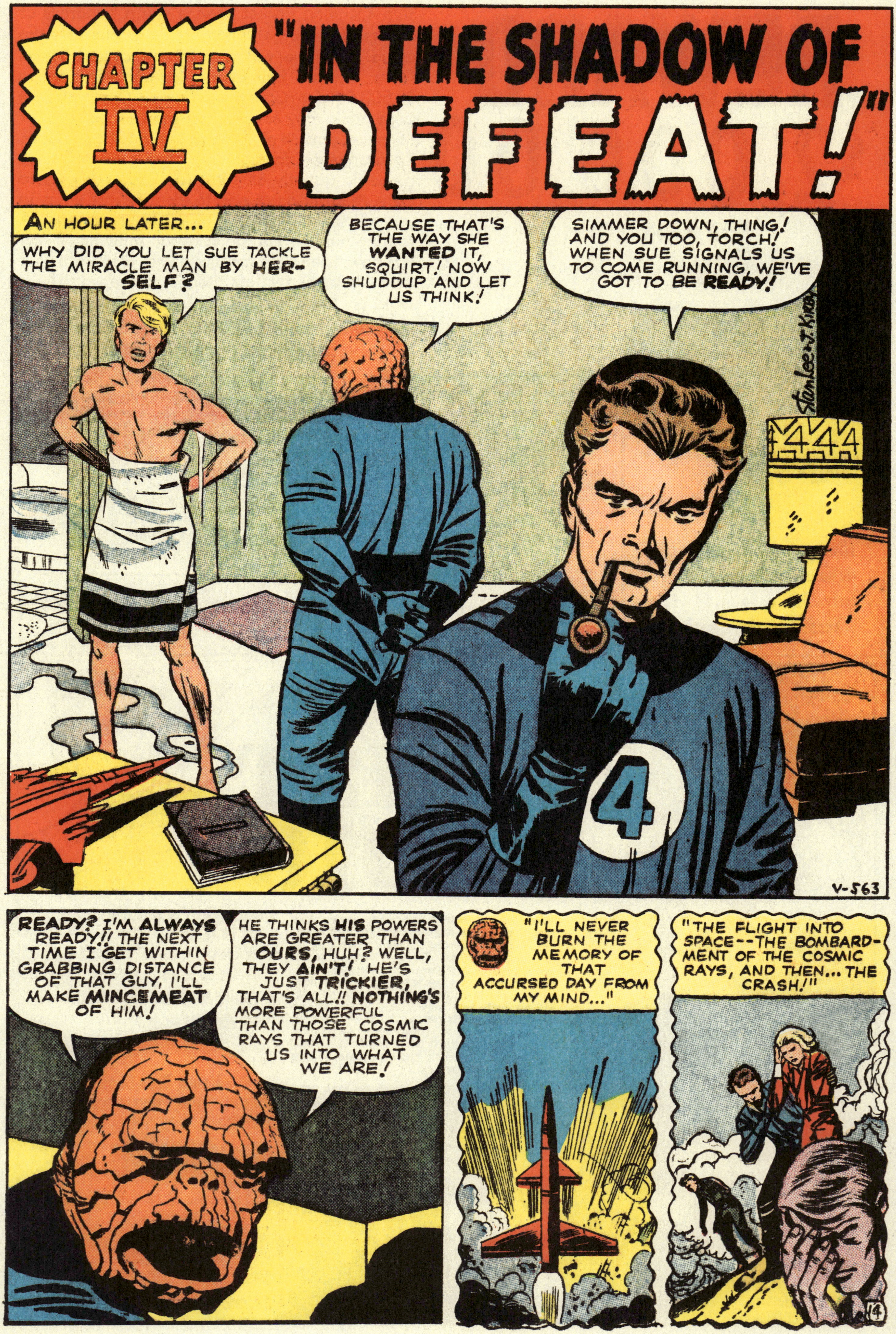
CHAPTER IV
"IN THE SHADOW OF DEFEAT!"
AN HOUR LATER...
WHY DID YOU LET SUE TACKLE THE MIRACLE MAN BY HER-SELF?
BECAUSE THAT'S THE WAY SHE WANTED IT, SQUIRT! NOW SHUDDUP AND LET US THINK!
SIMMER DOWN, THING! AND YOU TOO, TORCH! WHEN SUE SIGNALS US TO COME RUNNING, WE'VE GOT TO BE READY!
Stan Lee-J. Kirby
V-563
READY? I'M ALWAYS READY!! THE NEXT TIME I GET WITHIN GRABBING DISTANCE OF THAT GUY, I'LL MAKE MINCEMEAT OF HIM!
HE THINKS HIS POWERS ARE GREATER THAN OURS, HUH? WELL, THEY AIN'T! HE'S JUST TRICKIER, THAT'S ALL!! NOTHING'S MORE POWERFUL THAN THOSE COSMIC RAYS THAT TURNED US INTO WHAT WE ARE!
"I'LL NEVER BURN THE MEMORY OF THAT ACCURSED DAY FROM MY MIND..."
"THE FLIGHT INTO SPACE--THE BOMBARD-MENT OF THE COSMIC RAYS, AND THEN... THE CRASH!"
14

"I'LL NEVER FORGET SEEING SUSAN GROW INVISIBLE RIGHT BEFORE MY EYES!"
"OR THE LOOK ON ALL YOUR FACES AS I TALKED TO YOU, WHILE I WAS STILL BEN GRIMM..."
"...BEFORE I BEGAN TO... CHANGE..."
"...INTO THE THING!"
"AND HOW ABOUT YOU, REED? HOW DID YOU FEEL WHEN, DURING OUR BATTLE, YOU REALIZED YOU HAD CHANGED, TOO?"
"...YOUR LIMBS HAD TURNED TO ELASTIC! YOU COULD MOLD THEM INTO ANY SHAPE!"
"BUT THE MOST UNCANNY THING OF ALL WAS SEEING JOHNNY'S BODY TURN TO LIVING FLAME!"
"BEING LIGHTER THAN AIR, AS HE BLAZED LIKE A HUMAN TORCH, HE WAS ACTUALLY ABLE TO FLY! GRAVITY MEANT NOTHING TO HIM!"
"THAT'S WHEN WE DECIDED THAT OUR DESTINIES WERE ALL ENTWINED, AND SO WE DECIDED TO REMAIN TOGETHER, AS THE FANTASTIC FOUR!"
FATE HAS BEEN GOOD TO US, BEN! WE'VE BEEN ABLE TO USE OUR POWERS TO HELP MANKIND... TO FIGHT EVIL AND INJUSTICE!
SURE! IT'S BEEN GREAT FOR YOU! BUT WHAT ABOUT ME! I'M JUST A WALKIN' FRIGHT! AN UGLY, GRUESOME THING!
15

BUT YOU ONCE CHANGED TO YOUR NORMAL SELF FOR A FEW MINUTES! IT MIGHT HAPPEN AGAIN... FOR A LONGER TIME!
BAH! I DON'T WANT TO BE NORMAL FOR A FEW MINUTES! I WANT TO BE BEN GRIMM AGAIN! I WANT SUE TO LOOK AT ME THE WAY SHE LOOKS AT YOU!
MY SISTER?? DON'T KID YOURSELF, THING! SHE WOULDN'T GO FOR YOU IF YOU LOOKED LIKE ROCK HUDSON!!
WHY, YOU CRUMMY BRAT!! I'LL TEACH YOU TO LAUGH AT ME!
HEY, YOU BIG APE! I WAS ONLY KIDDIN'! LOOK OUT!
DON'T!!
ALL RIGHT! IF IT'S A FIGHT YOU WANT...
FLAME OFF, BLAST YA! FIGHT LIKE A MAN!
SURE, IF YOU USE YOUR INHUMAN STRENGTH, THAT'S OKAY! BUT IF I USE MY FLAME, YOU DON'T LIKE IT! I'M LEAVIN'! I'M SICK OF LOOKIN' AT YOUR UGLY FACE! YOU GIVE ME A SWIFT PAIN!
GO ON... GET OUT... WHILE YOU STILL CAN!
WHY CAN'T YOU CONTROL YOURSELF, THING? WHY MUST WE ALWAYS FIGHT AMONG OURSELVES? WHAT'S WRONG WITH US?
ALL I GOTTA DO IS LOOK IN THE MIRROR TO ANSWER THAT ONE, BROTHER!! AW, THE HECK WITH IT! WHERE'S SUE? WHEN IS SHE GONNA SIGNAL US??
16

EVEN AS THE THING WONDERS ABOUT THE INVISIBLE GIRL'S WHEREABOUTS, WE PICK UP HER TRAIL AS THE ATOMIC TANK ENTERS AN AUTO JUNKYARD AT THE EDGE OF TOWN!
WITHIN MINUTES I'LL HAVE THIS TANK SO WELL-HIDDEN THAT IT WILL NEVER BE FOUND!
THE MIRACLE MAN IS COVERING THE TANK OVER WITH THE SHELLS OF OLD WRECKED AUTOS!
NOW IF I CAN JUST ALERT THE OTHERS BEFORE HE SUSPECTS I'M HERE!
BUT SUDDENLY, DISASTER STRIKES FROM AN UNEXPECTED SOURCE...
A DOG! HE HAS CAUGHT MY SCENT!
RRRWOOFF!
WHAT IS IT, BOY? WHY ARE YOU GROWLING? NOBODY IS THERE!
GRRR!
WAIT!! A DOG NEVER GROWLS FOR NO REASON! SOMEONE MUST BE THERE! AND IF I CAN'T SEE ANYONE, IT CAN ONLY MEAN ONE THING...
TOO BAD, INVISIBLE GIRL!! IT WON'T WORK! I KNOW YOU'RE THERE!
BECOME VISIBLE! THE MIRACLE MAN COMMANDS YOU!!
AHHH! THAT'S MORE LIKE IT!
AND NOW, YOU MUST OBEY ME!! I AM YOUR MASTER!!
SIGNAL THE OTHER MEMBERS OF THE FANTASTIC FOUR!! I SHALL DEFEAT THEM FOREVER, HERE AND NOW!!
17

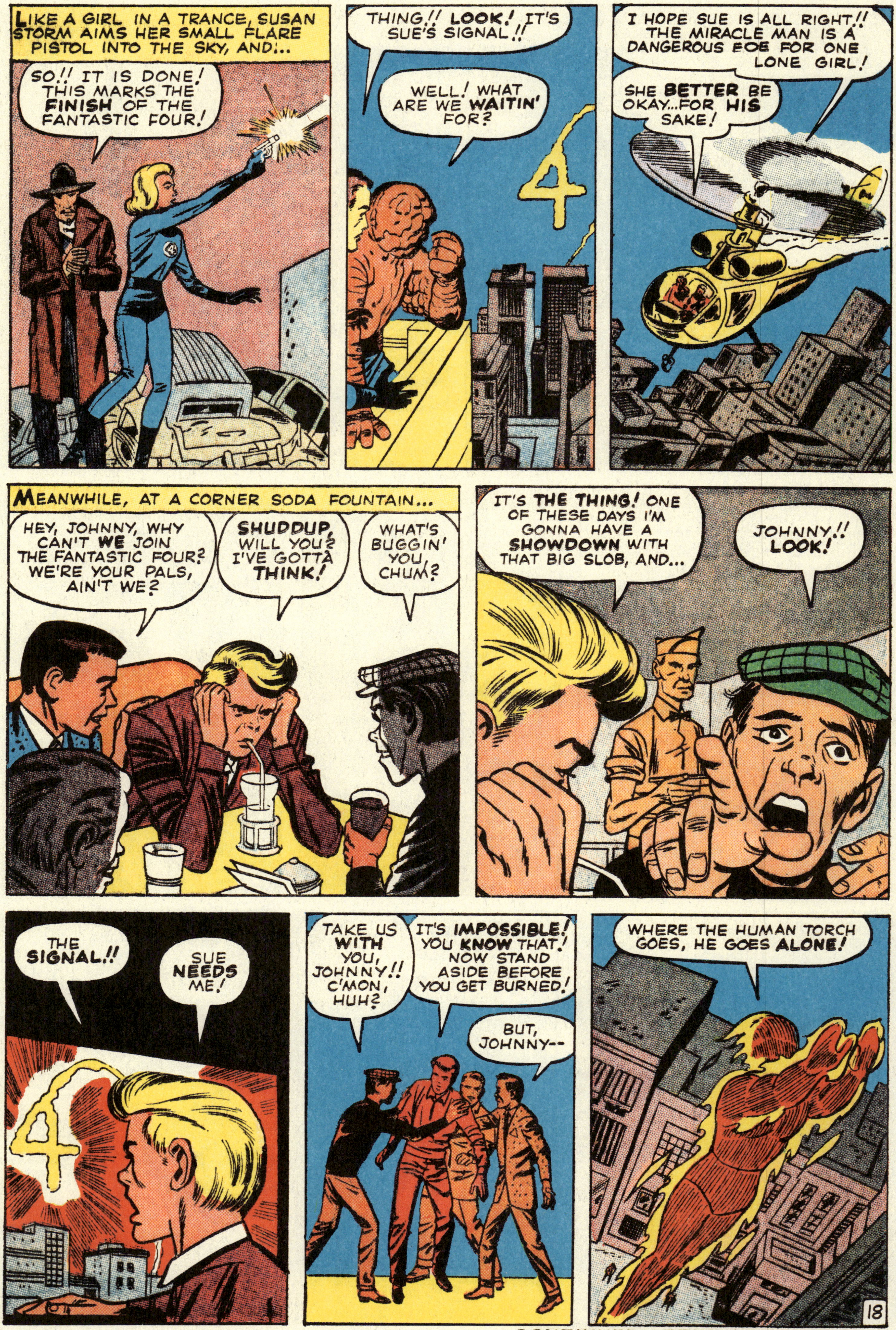

CONTINUED AFTER NEXT PAGE...

BOYS — 12 or older —

Here's a swell way to MAKE $1 to $5 WEEKLY and Win Dandy FREE PRIZES Too!

over 30,000 boys **SELL GRIT** *"America's Greatest Family Newspaper"* IN SPARE TIME

Besides getting lots of spending money and winning prizes, selling GRIT gives boys valuable business training which helps them to become successful men.

GRIT will help you get started in a profitable business of your own. We send you complete, easy to understand selling instructions. You pay *only* for the papers you sell until you know how many to order.

GRIT sells for 15c
YOU MAKE 5¢ PROFIT
on every copy you sell

—win these and many other prizes too.

MAIL THIS COUPON
← *Today*
in an envelope or pasted on a post card

GRIT PUBLISHING CO., Williamsport, Pa.

Send my first bundle of papers, selling helps and prize offers. MC2-2

Name ....

Are You a Boy? ..... Age ..... Date Born .... Year ....

In Care of ....

Street and No. .... R. F. D. ....

Post Office .... State ....

Print Your Last Name Plainly Here

TRANSISTOR RADIO

• All Assembled And Ready To Play

ONLY $9.98 • Complete With Aerial, Earphone, and Carrying Case

Here is a beautiful, imported transistor radio with two transistors at a price that all you kids can afford. Fully assembled—nothing to build—nothing to complete, this handsome radio plays beautifully with true quality reception brought in by its sensational aerial that lets the whole gang enjoy good listening of music, sports, or any top radio program, because your calibrated tuning dial aids you in bringing in stations bright and clear.

Listen Anytime—Anywhere

You can always enjoy this sensational transistor radio wherever you are, because it also has a personal earphone that lets you tune in your favorite program with complete privacy...put the plug in and only you can hear...pull the earplug out and everyone hears.

So Handy—Can Be Taken Anywhere

No longer is there a need to carry expensive, heavy, battery type radios that are bulky and need constant replacement. And this compact beauty weighs less than 1 lb.

Here's All You Get

When you order your transistor radio, with its calibrated tuning dial, it comes to you complete with its own carrying case, aerial and private earphone...there is nothing else to build...nothing left to put together. It's ready to play. So don't delay! Simply fill out the order blank. The complete price for the transistor radio with carrying case, aerial, and private listening earphone is only $ 9.98

30 Day Free Trial

Order now on a 30 Day Free Trial. If you are not 100% delighted, then simply return it for prompt refund of full purchase price. Because of the sensational low price of the transistor radio, we are forced to ask for an additional 36¢ shipping charge.

Money Back Guarantee

Honor House Products Corp. **Dept. CK-19**
Lynbrook, N.Y.

Rush me my transistor radio with private earphone and carrying case. I understand if I am not 100% delighted, I may return it after 30 Day Free Trial for prompt refund of full purchase price.

☐ I enclose $ 9.98 plus 36¢ shipping charge.

☐ Send C.O.D. I enclose $1 deposit. Balance on delivery plus C.O.D. and shipping charges.

Name..

Address..

CHAPTER V
"THE FINAL CHALLENGE!"
FATE WORKS IN MYSTERIOUS WAYS! WHO WOULD EVER DREAM THAT THE MOST POWERFUL FOES IN ALL THE WORLD WOULD HAVE THEIR LAST BATTLE IN A LONELY JUNK-YARD AT THE EDGE OF TOWN?!
YOUR MONSTER IS DESTROYED, MIRACLE MAN, AND NOW WE'VE FOUND YOU! THIS TIME YOU WON'T GET AWAY!
GET AWAY? YOU FOOLS! IT'S YOU WHO ARE TRAPPED! I'M ABOUT TO DESTROY YOU ALL!
IF YOU THINK YOU'RE SCARIN' US WITH THAT OVERGROWN KEY, MISTER, YOU GOT ANOTHER THINK COMIN'!!
Stan Lee + J. Kirby
C'MON, REED, WHAT ARE WE WAITIN' FOR? LET'S PULVERIZE HIM!
HOLD IT, THING! THERE'S MORE TO THAT KEY THAN MEETS THE EYE!
YOU ARE VERY PERCEPTIVE, MISTER FANTASTIC!! TOO BAD YOU ARE ABOUT TO DIE!
THIS IS MORE THAN JUST AN OVERSIZED KEY...
...BEFORE YOUR VERY EYES, I CAN MAKE IT CHANGE INTO...
A MACHINE GUN!!!
9

AND NOW, FAREWELL! ...TO YOU ALL!
NOT SO FAST, MISTER...
I'LL SHOW YOU A LITTLE QUICK-CHANGE TRICK, TOO!
EVER TRY TO HIT A BOUNCING RUBBER BALL??
REED CAN'T DODGE THOSE DUM-DUMS FOREVER! I GOTTA DO SOMETHING!!
LIKE A LUMBERING DREADNAUGHT, THE MIGHTY THING RACES BETWEEN MR. FANTASTIC AND THE DEADLY SHELLS, LETTING HIS OWN INCREDIBLY STRONG BODY ABSORB THE FULL IMPACT OF THE BULLETS UNTIL...
UGH!! OOOFF--
AT LAST! HE'S OUTTA AMMO!
THING! YOU SAVED ME!
BIG DEAL!! YOU BETTER MOVE, BROTHER, BEFORE LAUGHING BOY GETS AWAY WITH SUE AGAIN!
BUT BEFORE THE EXHAUSTED MR. FANTASTIC, OR THE BATTERED THING CAN ACT, THE MIRACLE MAN REACHES THE ATOMIC TANK, AND...
HE'S ESCAPING!
20

REED! THING! WAIT!! I SAW THE MIRACLE MAN CUT THE DRIVE CABLE OF YOUR COPTER! IT'S DEATH TO USE IT!
THE TORCH!
ABOUT TIME YOU GOT HERE, JUNIOR!
QUICK! WE CAN STILL FOLLOW HIM IN ONE OF THESE ANTIQUE RACING CARS WHICH ARE STORED HERE BETWEEN EXHIBITIONS!!
HECK! I CAN FLY FASTER THAN THAT HEAP!
WELL, WHY DON'T YOU, LOUD-MOUTH?
35
BECAUSE THIS IS MORE FUN! WHEEEE!
CAN'T YOU EVER BE SERIOUS, BRAT? DIDJA FORGET THAT YOUR OWN SISTER IS THE MIRACLE MAN'S PRISONER?
35
LOOK OUT!!
HE HIT A TIRE!
WE'RE GONNA CRASH!
NOT IF I CAN HELP IT!!
HANG ON!!
35
HURRY UP AND CATCH HIM, WILL YOU?!! I CAN'T TAKE MUCH MORE OF THIS!
GRAB THE WHEEL, THING! I'LL FINISH THIS MY WAY!
35
TORCH, WAIT! WATCH OUT FOR SUE, YOU FOOL!!

BUT THE HUMAN TORCH CAUSES NO HARM TO THE ATOMIC TANK! INSTEAD, HE INCREASES HIS FLAME UNTIL IT BECOMES A BLAZING FLASH IN FRONT OF THE TANK... A FLASH WHICH TEMPORARILY BLINDS THE MIRACLE MAN!
I-I CAN'T SEE!!
AND, MINUTES LATER...
MY EYES--MY EYES--
YOU'LL BE OKAY, BUSTER!! BUT IF YOU'VE HARMED MY SISTER...
HE DID IT!! THE TORCH DID IT!!
AND NOW IT'S MY TURN!!
I'VE BEEN WAITING FOR THIS FOR A LONG TIME...
HOLD IT, THING!!
YOU CAN'T DO IT!! YOU'LL KILL HIM!
HIS POWER IS GONE! HE'LL NEVER HURT ANYONE AGAIN! THE LAW CAN HANDLE HIM NOW!
HUH?? BUT HOW-- HOW DO YOU KNOW?
I'LL EXPLAIN LATER! FIRST, I WANT YOU TO BRING SUE OUT OF HER TRANCE!
DO AS I SAY, OR I'LL TURN YOU OVER TO THE THING!
I-I'LL DO IT!
YOU ARE YOURSELF AGAIN, SUSAN STORM!
SNAP

HE IS NO MIRACLE MAN! HE HAS NO MAGIC POWERS! HE IS MERELY A CLEVER HYPNOTIST, A MASTER OF MASS ILLUSION! THE MONSTER NEVER REALLY MOVED--HE HYPNOTIZED US INTO THINKING IT DID!
HE DIDN'T REALLY SPLIT THAT LOG ON STAGE WITH ONE FINGER... HE MADE EVERYONE THINK HE DID! AND THE SAME FOR ALL HIS SUPPOSEDLY MIRACULOUS FEATS!
HOW--HOW DID YOU GUESS?
BECAUSE A TRUE MIRACLE MAN WOULD NOT HAVE NEEDED TO STEAL JEWELS... HE COULD HAVE CONJURED UP ALL THE WEALTH IN THE WORLD! A MIRACLE MAN WOULD NOT HAVE NEEDED TO FLEE FROM US... YOU COULD HAVE SIMPLY VANISHED... OR CAUSED US TO DISAPPEAR, FOREVER!
BUT NOW, YOUR HYPNOTIC POWER IS GONE, DUE TO TORCH'S ALMOST BLINDING FLASH!
WAIT A MINUTE, REED!! ARE YOU TRYIN' TO GIVE THAT FLAMING JUVENILE DELINQUENT THE CREDIT FOR THIS CAPER??
OH, PLEASE! DON'T START ARGUING AMONG YOURSELVES AGAIN!! I--I JUST CAN'T STAND ANY MORE!
RELAX, SIS! THEY'RE NOT GONNA ARGUE ABOUT ME ANY MORE! I HAD ALL THE BOSSIN' AROUND I CAN TAKE! I'M CUTTIN' OUT OF THIS COMBO, RIGHT NOW!
BUT YOU CAN'T QUIT US, JOHNNY!
AW, LET HIM GO! HE'S MORE TROUBLE THAN HE'S WORTH!
TORCH!! COME BACK! PLEASE!!
IT'S TOO LATE, SUE!
OH, REED, WHAT WILL BECOME OF HIM?
IT'S NOT HIM I'M WORRIED ABOUT...
...IT'S MANKIND! FOR WHAT WILL WE DO--
WHAT CAN WE DO, IF... IF HE SHOULD TURN AGAINST US?!!
NEXT ISSUE, THE SUSPENSE MOUNTS UNBEARABLY AS THE TORCH STRIKES BACK! AND DON'T BE SURPRISED TO SEE ANOTHER GREAT CHARACTER WHOM YOU DEMANDED WE BRING BACK! ALL IN THE NEXT WONDERFUL ISSUE!
23
THE END

THE FANTASTIC FOUR
PIN-UP PAGE
JOHNNY STORM
THE HUMAN TORCH!
V-364

FANTASTIC FOUR FAN PAGE

DEAR EDITOR:

I think the Fantastic Four will become a great success. The Thing and the Torch are very new and different. I would also like to know what the name of your artist is.

Alan Weiss
Pardee Place
Las Vegas, Nevada

It'll *become* a success?? What do you think it is NOW? Chicken liver?? Considering that our artist signs the name JACK KIRBY on everything he can get his greedy little fingers on, I think we can safely claim that that's his name!

4.

DEAR EDITOR:

The best thing about the comic is the character conflicts. It's nice to see a group of super-heroes who aren't unnaturally buddy-buddy. The cover of #1 was pretty poor, it didn't stand out. I wish the name of Mr. Fantastic were different. It sounds too much like Mr. Clean.

Rick Wood
Ames St.
Cambridge, Mass.

Rick, no two fans ever seem to agree on what cover is best. Same thing applies to characters' names. So, let's hear from you other readers. What type of covers do YOU prefer, and how do you feel about the name Mr. Fantastic? (We'll bet at least ONE joker writes that he'd prefer Mr. Clean!)

4.

DEAR EDITOR:

You've got a heckuva nerve making a doll like Susan Storm invisible!

Unsigned
Dallas
Texas

Listen, Unsigned, with wolves like YOU around, she's a lot better off that way!

4.

DEAR EDITOR:

Before I started to write this letter, I read The Fantastic Four over 50 times! So then I decided to tell you what I thought of it. It is GREAT, WONDERFUL, FANTASTIC, BREATH-TAKING and STUPENDOUS, to say the least!

My biggest request is for more of the Human Torch in action.

George Paul
Park Ave.
Hoboken, N.J.

No WONDER you thought the mag was great, George, after reading it fifty times, brother, you've been BRAINWASHED! As for seeing more of the Torch, you've got a treat coming in the next issue!

4.

DEAR EDITOR:

Just finshed reading Fantastic Four and must admit to being disappointed. I expect better things from the team of Lee-Kirby. Jack is capable of better art work, and the Thing ought to revert to human form at will as his teammates do. The story also suffers from "Creeping Monsterism" to paraphrase Jean Shepard, that has dominated most, if not all, of your comics for some time.

Bill Sarill
Colorado Street
Boston, Mass.

See how fair we are? We print the knocks as well as the boosts! (The next time anyone around this office opens another one of Bill's letters, he's thru!!) As for the Thing reverting to human form, it's not that easy, pal. If you don't believe us, take a dose of cosmic rays yourself and see what happens!

4.

DEAR EDITOR:

Are you the same one who also puts out STRANGE TALES, TALES TO ASTONISH, JOURNEY INTO MYSTERY, TALES OF SUSPENSE, AMAZING ADULT FANTASY, and a lot of Westerns like KID COLT, OUTLAW, and teen-age titles like PATSY WAKER? If so, how do you do it?

S. Brodsky
Brooklyn
New York

With great difficulty!

P.S.—We've just noticed something . . . unlike many other collections of letters in different mags, our fans all seem to write well, and intelligently. We assume this denotes that our readers are a cut above average, and that's the way we like 'em!

Address your letters to:
THE EDITOR
FANTASTIC FOUR
THIRD FLOOR
655 MADISON AVENUE
NEW YORK 21, N. Y.

IMPORTANT NOTE:
We receive so much mail that it is utterly impossible to engage in correspondence with any readers. As many letters as possible will be answered on this page each issue. Please do not ask us to write to you personally.

For a Successful Career in Radio Television Electronics

N.R.I. Trained These Men

"I am a senior Electronics instructor in the service school of Sikorsky Division of United Aircraft. NRI training helped me qualify for this position." JOSEPH W. SENIA, Stratford, Conn.

"After graduating I was a shipboard radio operator. At present I am chief engineer of Station WARA. The NRI Course was a wonderful foundation." R. D. ARNOLD, Attleboro, Mass.

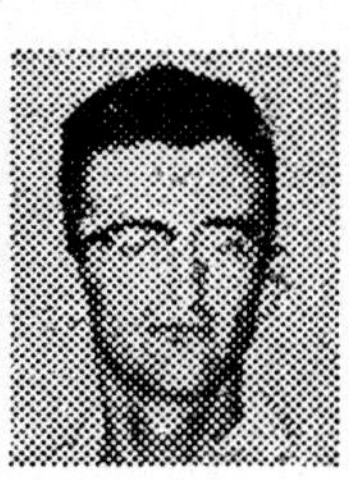

"When I graduated I was working in a textile factory trying to make ends meet. Now I own one of the most modern Television-Radio Service shops in this section." A. C. TAYLOR, Glasgow, Ky.

FAST GROWING FIELD OFFERS YOU HIGH PAY—PRESTIGE—BRIGHT FUTURE

Better than average jobs with bright futures are waiting for men in Electronics . . . jobs for which YOU could qualify through NRI training. Train at home in your spare time, while you hold your present job. Earn higher pay, enjoy greater prestige in jobs with TV and Radio Stations, in industrial plants, or in a business of your own selling, installing and servicing Radio and TV sets.

Train With The Leader

For 45 years, NRI has featured the best Radio-TV Electronics training for beginners —for men without previous experience. Throughout the U.S. and Canada, successful NRI graduates are proof that it's practical to train at home, in your spare time, at your own pace. NRI supplies this training at low cost because it is the oldest and largest home-study Radio-TV Electronics school. In every respect, the Electronics field is a profitable one for the ambitious man. And the NRI "learn-by-doing" method is the practical way for you to get into this exciting field quickly.

Earn While You Learn

Soon after enrolling, NRI shows you how to earn extra money in your spare time repairing sets. Many start profitable businesses this way. Others get good jobs within a year. Take the first step to a successful new career NOW. Mail coupon for descriptive catalog. National Radio Institute, Washington 16, D. C.

Without Extra Charge NRI Sends Equipment You Need to Get Practical Experience

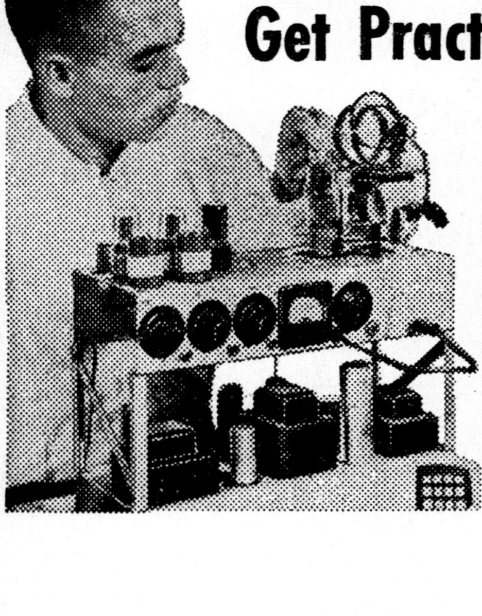

NRI training is based on "learn-by-doing" methods tested and approved by leading educators. Special NRI kits give you actual experience—bringing to life the things you study. Build radio, voltmeter, transmitter, TV set, other valuable equipment to keep and use in your new, higher-paying, brighter career. Free Catalog shows all equipment you get, opportunities in field, success stories of graduates. 60-day trial enrollment plan. Easy terms. Mail coupon NOW.

FREE 64-PAGE CATALOG

MAIL THIS COUPON TODAY

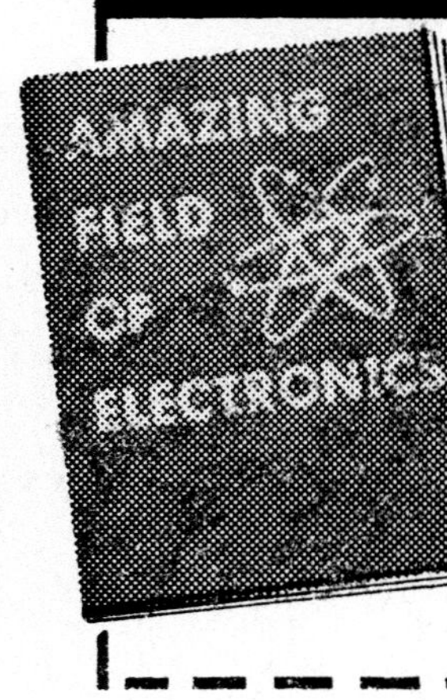

NATIONAL RADIO INSTITUTE
Washington 16, D.C. 2BM1

Send me catalog and information FREE. (No representative will call. Please print.)

Name________________________Age___

Address________________________

City____________Zone___State______

ACCREDITED MEMBER NATIONAL HOME STUDY COUNCIL

MASON
NEW KIND OF SHOE WILL FILL YOUR POCKETS WITH CASH!
SEND COUPON FOR MY FREE OUTFIT!
Make Money! Just 8 Easy Orders a Day Bring You Up to $960 a Month!
From the moment you step into Mason's revolutionary new Ripple Sole shoes, things start to happen. People stop you on the street . . . want to know where they can buy this amazingly different kind of shoe. And there are plenty of good reasons why you'll sell Mason Ripple Sole Shoes on sight. First, they are so different. No one has ever seen anything like 'em! These are the shoes that give shock-reducing gliding action . . . forward thrust . . . to every step you take. More comfortable, because they feature Mason's famous Air Cushion innersoles. Every-one wants 'em!
But Ripple Sole shoes are only one of many exciting new features in the powerful Selling Outfit I'll send you FREE! Using this outfit in the way I'll show you, you can earn as much as $960 EXTRA monthly on just 8 easy orders a day! I'll set you up in a "Shoe Store Business" you can run from home. You'll have no expenses. You'll never have to invest one cent. Yet you keep 100% of the profit! No wonder James Kelly of Ohio made $93.55 selling Mason Nationally-Advertised shoes—in a single evening! No wonder C. Tuttle averages $80 a week! It's easy, with our way of selling shoes. You need no experience. We carry the stock. We ship the shoes. All you do is show the styles, take orders! You get cash, prizes, bonuses!
210 Fast-Selling Styles To Send Your Profits Soaring!
It's easy for you to make money fast, with so many new ideas like the Ripple Sole, amazing Shu-lok laceless shoe—plus dozens of time-tested, popularity-proven staple items like water-shedding Sylflex shoes, sturdy, comfortable, long-wearing work shoes, steel-toe safety shoes, others! Mason shoes sell fast! They're nationally Advertised in magazines read by thousands of people daily! Sell to friends, neighbors folks where you work. Top men make up to $10 an hour—from their very first hour!
Best "Shoe Store Business" in Town!
You feature foamy-soft Air Cushion innersoles . . . sturdy steel shanks . . . Nylon stitching . . . special work soles of Neoprene, Cork, Cushion Neoprene Crepe. Customers "repeat" time after time—profits pour in as long as you care to earn cash! And Mason Shoes are never sold by stores—so folks must buy from YOU. You run the best "shoe store business" in town, because you draw on a selection of over a quarter million pairs of top-quality shoes in sizes from 2 to 15 . . . widths all the way from extra-narrow AAAA to extra-wide EEEE! No need to substitute . . . your customers get the size and width they need, in the style they want!
Here's How You Can START IMMEDIATELY!
Send no money—now or later. Simply fill out and mail the coupon below, and we'll rush you FREE Starting Business Outfit worth up to $960 EXTRA MONTHLY CASH PROFIT to you! You'll get Kit featuring 210 quick-selling dress, sport, work shoe styles for men and women . . . foolproof Measuring Equipment . . . How-To-Make-BIG-MONEY Booklet . . . EVERYTHING you need to start making loads of extra cash from your first hour. Act today, because Mason's amazing Ripple Sole Shoe is new—exciting—in big demand! Rush coupon Now!
MASON SHOE MFG., CO.
Chippewa Falls, Wisconsin (Since 1904)
Dept. H-79
WORKERS WANT MASON ON-THE-JOB SHOES! NOW THEY CAN BUY THEM FROM YOU!
YOUR SURE SOURCE OF EXTRA INCOME!
Wherever you go, working people are eager prospects for famous Mason Air Cushion extra-comfort on-the-job shoes. That's why so many Mason Shoe Counselors multiply earnings with quantity orders, by specializing in shoe needs of policemen, postmen, factory workers, nurses, waitresses, service station men! We furnish sales aids . . . show you how to get the orders. Don't delay—mail coupon for your FREE Starting Outfit today!
RUSH MY FREE OUTFIT!
Mr. Ned Mason, Dept. H-79
Mason Shoe Mfg. Co., Chippewa Falls, Wisconsin
You bet I want to earn as much as $960 EXTRA MONTHLY CASH by showing your new Ripple Sole Shoe and 209 other proven moneymakers! Rush EVERYTHING I need—FREE and postpaid—to start making extra cash at once!
Name
PLEASE PRINT
Address
Town
State

IND.
THE WORLD'S GREATEST COMIC MAGAZINE!
APPROVED BY THE COMICS CODE AUTHORITY
12¢
THE Fantastic Four
4 MAY
MC
STOP HIM! IF THE SUB-MARINER REACHES THE WATER, HE'LL BECOME INVINCIBLE!
"THE COMING OF THE SUB-MARINER!"

THE FANTASTIC FOUR is published by CANAM PUBLISHERS SALES CORP. OFFICE OF PUBLICATION: 655 MADISON AVENUE, NEW YORK, N.Y. Published bi-monthly. Vol. 1 No. 4, MAY 1962 issue. Price 12c per copy. Subscription rate $1.70 for 12 issues including postage. Printed in the U.S.A. by The Eastern Color Printing Co., Waterbury 20, Conn.

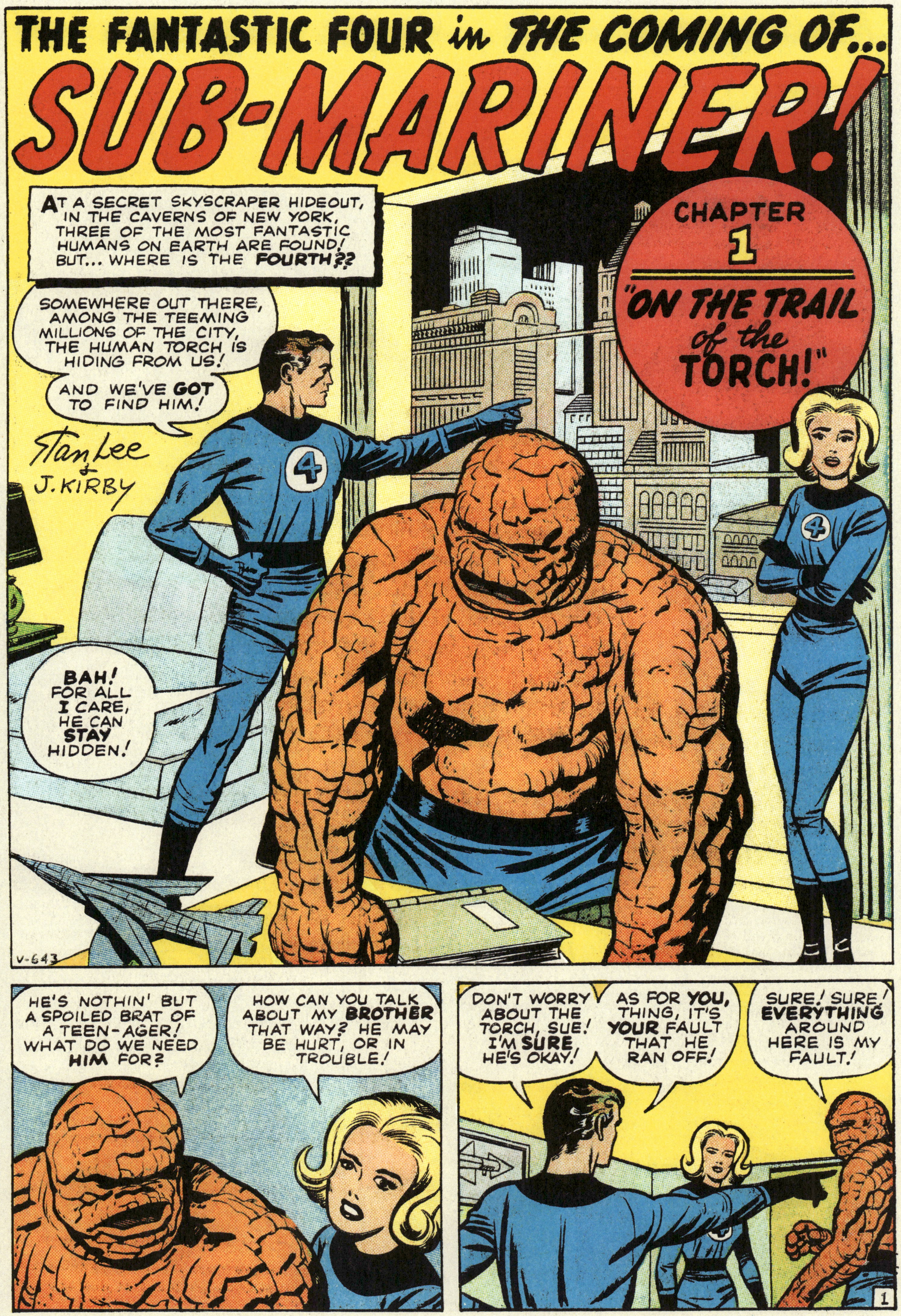
THE FANTASTIC FOUR in THE COMING OF...
SUB-MARINER!
AT A SECRET SKYSCRAPER HIDEOUT, IN THE CAVERNS OF NEW YORK, THREE OF THE MOST FANTASTIC HUMANS ON EARTH ARE FOUND! BUT... WHERE IS THE FOURTH??
CHAPTER 1
"ON THE TRAIL of the TORCH!"
SOMEWHERE OUT THERE, AMONG THE TEEMING MILLIONS OF THE CITY, THE HUMAN TORCH IS HIDING FROM US!
AND WE'VE GOT TO FIND HIM!
Stan Lee & J. KIRBY
BAH! FOR ALL I CARE, HE CAN STAY HIDDEN!
V-643
HE'S NOTHIN' BUT A SPOILED BRAT OF A TEEN-AGER! WHAT DO WE NEED HIM FOR?
HOW CAN YOU TALK ABOUT MY BROTHER THAT WAY? HE MAY BE HURT, OR IN TROUBLE!
DON'T WORRY ABOUT THE TORCH, SUE! I'M SURE HE'S OKAY!
AS FOR YOU, THING, IT'S YOUR FAULT THAT HE RAN OFF!
SURE! SURE! EVERYTHING AROUND HERE IS MY FAULT!
1

"BUT IT IS YOUR FAULT, THING! YOUR FAULT THAT THE TORCH IS HIDING OUT FROM US, AS WELL AS FROM THE POLICE AND THE ARMY!
"REMEMBER HOW HE TACKLED THE MONSTER WHICH THE MIRACLE MAN HAD BROUGHT TO LIFE?* HE WAS ONE OF US, THEN!
(*SEE "FANTASTIC FOUR" #3 MARCH)
"SINGLE-HANDED, HE FOUGHT THE ENORMOUS CREATURE...
"--AND SINGLE-HANDED HE DEFEATED HIM!!
"FINALLY, THANKS TO THE TORCH, OUR ATOMIC CANNON WAS RETURNED SAFELY TO THE ARMY! EVERYONE WAS HAPPY ABOUT IT, THING, BUT NOT YOU!
"NO! YOU WERE JEALOUS OF THE TORCH'S ACHIEVEMENT, AND SO YOU PICKED AN ARGUMENT WITH HIM--AN ARGUMENT WHICH MADE HIM WANT TO DESERT ALL OF US!"
I'M THRU WITH THE FANTASTIC FOUR, UNDERSTAND? THRU!
TORCH! WAIT!!
WELL, WE'RE NOT GOING TO LET IT END THAT WAY!! WE'RE GOING TO FIND THAT BOY!! AND THAT MEANS YOU TOO, THING!!
YOU BET IT MEANS ME! AND WHEN I DO FIND 'IM, I'LL TEACH HIM TO RUN OFF ON US THAT WAY!
OH, REED! IF HE HARMS THE TORCH--
EASY, SUE! HE WON'T HURT HIM! I SWEAR IT!
2
THE HULK IS COMING!

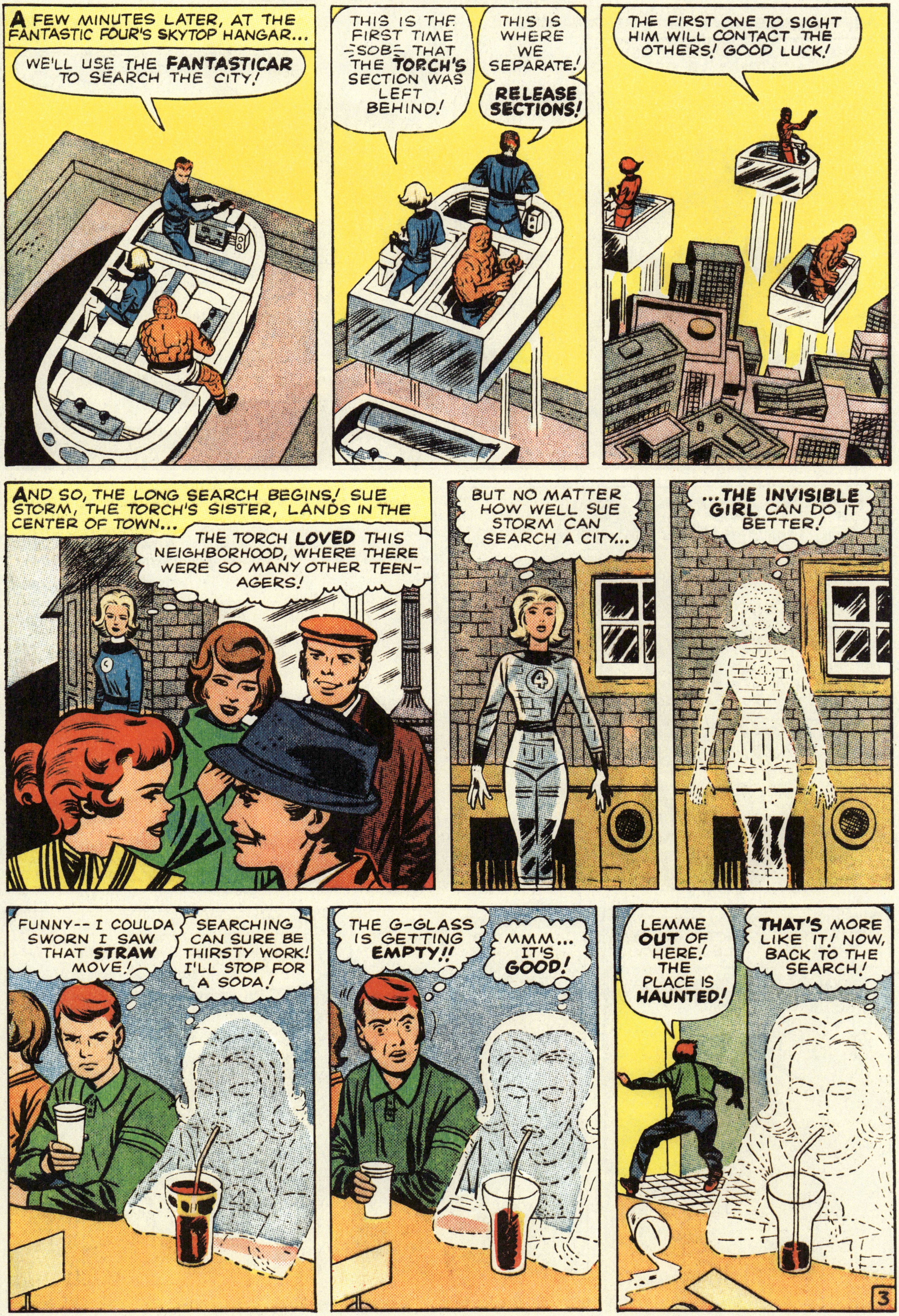
A FEW MINUTES LATER, AT THE FANTASTIC FOUR'S SKYTOP HANGAR...
WE'LL USE THE FANTASTICAR TO SEARCH THE CITY!
THIS IS THE FIRST TIME -SOB- THAT THE TORCH'S SECTION WAS LEFT BEHIND!
THIS IS WHERE WE SEPARATE! RELEASE SECTIONS!
THE FIRST ONE TO SIGHT HIM WILL CONTACT THE OTHERS! GOOD LUCK!
AND SO, THE LONG SEARCH BEGINS! SUE STORM, THE TORCH'S SISTER, LANDS IN THE CENTER OF TOWN...
THE TORCH LOVED THIS NEIGHBORHOOD, WHERE THERE WERE SO MANY OTHER TEEN-AGERS!
BUT NO MATTER HOW WELL SUE STORM CAN SEARCH A CITY...
...THE INVISIBLE GIRL CAN DO IT BETTER!
FUNNY-- I COULDA SWORN I SAW THAT STRAW MOVE!
SEARCHING CAN SURE BE THIRSTY WORK! I'LL STOP FOR A SODA!
THE G-GLASS IS GETTING EMPTY!!
MMM... IT'S GOOD!
LEMME OUT OF HERE! THE PLACE IS HAUNTED!
THAT'S MORE LIKE IT! NOW, BACK TO THE SEARCH!

MEANWHILE, WHAT OF MISTER FANTASTIC?
THERE ARE SOME CYCLISTS! PERHAPS THEY'VE SEEN THE TORCH!
ULP!!
ONLY WAY TO FIND OUT IS TO ASK THEM!
M-MISTER FANTASTIC!! GEE!! I--I NEVER KNEW YOU WERE FOR REAL!
I'M REAL ENOUGH, SON! BUT IF YOU DON'T KNOW WHERE JOHNNY STORM IS, I'VE NO MORE TIME TO WASTE WITH YOU!
WOW!! MR. FANTASTIC HIMSELF LIFTED ME RIGHT OFF MY CYCLE!! WAIT'LL I TELL THE GANG! WILL I BE A BIG MAN!!
I'VE GOT TO KEEP TRYING! SOONER OR LATER I'LL FIND SOME TEEN-AGER WHO'S SEEN HIM!
BUT LITTLE DOES MISTER FANTASTIC SUSPECT THAT LESS THAN ONE MILE AWAY...
ATTA BOY, JOHNNY! YOU'RE GETTIN' IT!
SWANSON'S GARAGE
WOW! NOBODY CAN MODIFY AN ENGINE LIKE YOU, JOHNNY!
AW, YOU'RE ONLY SAYIN' THAT 'CAUSE IT'S TRUE!
BOY! JUST THINK! THE WHOLE COUNTRY'S LOOKING FOR THE HUMAN TORCH!!
AND HE'S RIGHT HERE WITH US, WORKING ON OUR SPORTS CAR ENGINES!!
4

I'VE GOTTA DO A LITTLE WELDING BEFORE I CAN FIX THOSE GASKETS!
SO, HERE GOES!
FLAME ON!
HEY, GANG! DIG THAT!
THIS BEATS A WELDING IRON ANY DAY!
AND IF THERE'S A REAL BIG WELDING JOB TO DO...
NOTICE HOW I CAN CONTROL MY FLAME? BY NOT MOVING, IT DOESN'T GO NEAR THE GASOLINE!
BUT, AT THAT VERY MOMENT, OUTSIDE THE GARAGE...
BEFORE I KNOCK MYSELF OUT SEARCH-ING THE WHOLE CITY, I'LL PLAY A HUNCH!
THAT BRAT USED TO HANG AROUND HERE, FIDDLIN' WITH HOT RODS, EVERY CHANCE HE GOT!
HEY!! I CAN FEEL THE HEAT! HE'S INSIDE!
THE THING!!
YOU'RE BLAMED RIGHT IT'S THE THING, TORCH!! AND NOW I'LL TEACH YOU WHAT HAPPENS TO DESERTERS!
AND YOUR FLAME DOESN'T SCARE ME NOW! I KNOW YOU CAN'T MOVE WHILE YOU'RE BURNING, BECAUSE THERE'S GASOLINE ALL OVER HERE! ONE SPARK AND YOUR PALS ARE DONE FOR!
5

CHAPTER 2 ENTER THE SUB-MARINER!

WHAT IS THE HULK??

AS THE THING SINKS TO HIS KNEES IN HELPLESS RAGE, JOHNNY STORM REACHES THE OUTSKIRTS OF-- THE BOWERY!
THIS IS ONE PLACE WHERE NOBODY'LL FIND ME! I'LL JUST LOSE MYSELF AMONG ALL THE OTHER HUMAN DERELICTS HERE!
SAM'S MARKET
MIGHT AS WELL FIND A PLACE TO SACK DOWN FOR THE NIGHT! I GUESS THIS ONE IS NO WORSE THAN THE OTHERS!
MENS HOTEL 25
A FEW MINUTES LATER...
WELL, IT'S NOT THE WALDORF, BUT IT'LL KEEP ME SAFELY HIDDEN WHILE I PLAN MY NEXT MOVE!
SAY! LOOK AT THIS OLD, BEAT-UP COMIC MAG! IT'S FROM THE 1940's!!
RULES
THE SUB-MARINER!!
I REMEMBER SIS TALKING ABOUT HIM ONCE! HE USED TO BE THE WORLD'S MOST UNUSUAL CHARACTER!
SUB-MARINER
YEAH, JUST LIKE SIS SAID, HE COULD LIVE UNDERWATER, AND WAS AS STRONG AS TEN MEN!
I WONDER WHAT EVER HAPPENED TO HIM? HE WAS SUPPOSED TO BE IMMORTAL!
READIN' ABOUT SUB-MARINER, HUH?
WE GOT A STUMBLE-BUM RIGHT HERE WHO'S AS STRONG AS THAT JOKER WAS SUPPOSED TO BE!
HEY, OLD MAN-- WAKE UP!
YOU WOULDN'T THINK IT TO LOOK AT THAT OLD BUM, BUT JUST WAIT!
HUH?? WHAT--?

C'MON, OLD MAN! WE GOT US A NEW TENANT! SHOW HIM WHAT YA CAN DO!
GO 'WAY... I WANNA SLEEP! LEMME BE!
WHY DON'T YOU LEAVE THE OLD FELLA ALONE? HE'S PROBABLY TIRED!
HE'S NEVER TOO TIRED TO SHOW HOW STRONG HE IS, ARE YA, OLD MAN?
COME ON, YA MANGY BUM, TEAR THIS PHONE BOOK IN HALF! TEAR IT, I SAID!
POW
GO AWAY, YOU PUNY FLEA!
ALL RIGHT, BOYS-- LET'S TEACH 'IM A LITTLE LITTLE LESSON!
GET 'IM!!
YAY!! I BEEN SPOILIN' FOR A GOOD FIGHT!
I SAID...
POW
GO AWAY...
WHAM!
...ALL OF YOU!!
BAM

CONTINUED AFTER NEXT PAGE...

AMAZING LOW PRICE ONLY

$6.98

8MM MOTION PICTURE PROJECTOR

FULLY ELECTRIC AUTOMATIC REWIND

You will be thrilled and delighted with this motion picture projector that will bring to life 8 MM color or black and white movies right in your own home. Imported and mass produced using special skills, this sturdy projector is useful and practical without being fancy, and that's why this price is possible. Yes, now home movies are a luxury you can afford. Take all the movies you want without worrying about the cost of a projector. You'll show movies to friends and relatives, hold parties and so much more.

PORTABLE AND FULLY EQUIPPED

This sensational 8 MM projector is fully electric and powered by standard batteries. There are no plugs or connections to get out of order and it's portable . . . can be used indoors or out. Projector with automatic rewind, motor and light switch and screen, all yours for the unbelievable price of $6.98 plus 63¢ shipping charges.

10 Day Free Trial

Don't Delay! Order now. If you are not 100% delighted, then simply return it for prompt refund of full purchase price. Only $6.98 plus 63¢ shipping charges.

FEATURES

- Fully Electric
- Automatic Rewind
- Motor and Light Switch
- Projects Both Color and Black and White 8MM Movie Film
- Complete With Screen
- Sturdy Construction

Honor House Prod. Corp. Dept. BP-59
Lynbrook, N.Y.

Rush me my fully electric 8 MM motion picture projector with automatic rewind, motor and light switch and screen at once. I understand that if I am not 100% delighted, I may return it for prompt refund of full purchase price.

☐ I enclose $6.98 and 63¢ shipping charges. Same Guarantee.

☐ Send C.O.D. I will pay postman on delivery plus C.O.D. and shipping charges.

Name..........

Address..........

COMPLETE 4 PIECE MATCHED SET OF LUGGAGE

Unbelievably Priced at ONLY **$2.98**

Yes, that price is correct . . . Only $2.98 for the complete 4 piece set. Not $2.98 each, but $2.98 complete for all 4 pieces. And, there is nothing else to buy . . . no extras, no additions. Its modern appearance and wide-stitched simulated leatherette material will amaze you with its good looks.

IMPORTED AND MASS PRODUCED TO MAKE THIS PRICE POSSIBLE

This tremendous bargain is possible only through the use of pressed chipboard. This wonderfully versatile material bends around three sides and is bonded by sturdy wide stitching to the overlapping closing. Snap locks and handles are riveted in place. The big one has extra metal stripping for strength and long wear. Inside has laminated modern design print. Each piece fits inside the next larger which saves your storage space and makes our shipping easier.

NOT FANCY LUGGAGE — BUT USEFUL, PRACTICAL

You will be thrilled and delighted with the many, many uses you will find for this set. It will make a marvelous gift and your thoughtfulness will be appreciated for such a long time. Lightweight. It avoids the silly situation where the luggage weighs more than the clothing carried. When this offer was first made to us by the overseas company we couldn't believe our ears, but we were delighted when we saw it just a few days ago—and you will be too. Each piece serves a specific purpose such as vanity and cosmetic case (8"), personal Valet (10"), overnight case (12") or family size (14").

Remember, the complete price for all 4 matched pieces of luggage is only $2.98. Because of its size, we are forced to ask for an additional 63c shipping charge. Note: Due to the Federal Law, there is a 10% excise tax on all purchases of luggage. This Federal tax (30c in this instance) is turned over directly by us to the Government. We merely act as agents and in no way, benefit. Kindly add this 30c to your purchase price when ordering.

MONEY BACK GUARANTEE

10 Day Free Trial

Simply fill in the coupon and when your 4 piece matching set of luggage arrives, pay the postman only $2.98 plus C.O.D., shipping charges and excise tax. Then, even use them for 10 full days, and if you are not 100% delighted then simply return them for your full purchase price refund.

HONOR HOUSE PRODUCTS CORP. Dept. CV-51
Lynbrook, N. Y.

Rush my matching 4-piece set of luggage at once. I understand if I am not 100% delighted I may return it for prompt refund of full purchase price.

☐ I enclose $2.98 plus 63c shipping charges and 30c Federal excise tax. Same Money Back Guarantee.

Send C.O.D. I will pay postman on delivery plus C.O.D., shipping charges and excise tax.

Name ______

Address ______

CHAPTER 3
LET THE WORLD BEWARE!
Stan Lee & J. Kirby
AT THE VERY MOMENT THAT JOHNNY STORM MAKES HIS INCREDIBLE DISCOVERY, THE OTHER MEMBERS OF THE FANTASTIC FOUR ARE CONTINUING THEIR STRANGE SEARCH...
ARE YOU SURE YOU'VE SEEN NO TRACE OF A FLAMING TEEN-AGER BLAZING THRU THE SKY?
HOLY SMOKE! I R-READ ABOUT YOU GUYS, BUT I NEVER DREAMT YOU REALLY EXISTED!
V-643
PERHAPS SOMEONE MIGHT CATCH A GLIMPSE OF HIM FROM A PASSING TRAIN!
...AND IF YOU SEE ANY TRACE OF THE TORCH, REMEMBER--CONTACT THE FANTASTIC FOUR!
MISTER, THE FIRST GUY I'LL CONTACT WILL BE MY EYE DOCTOR!
11

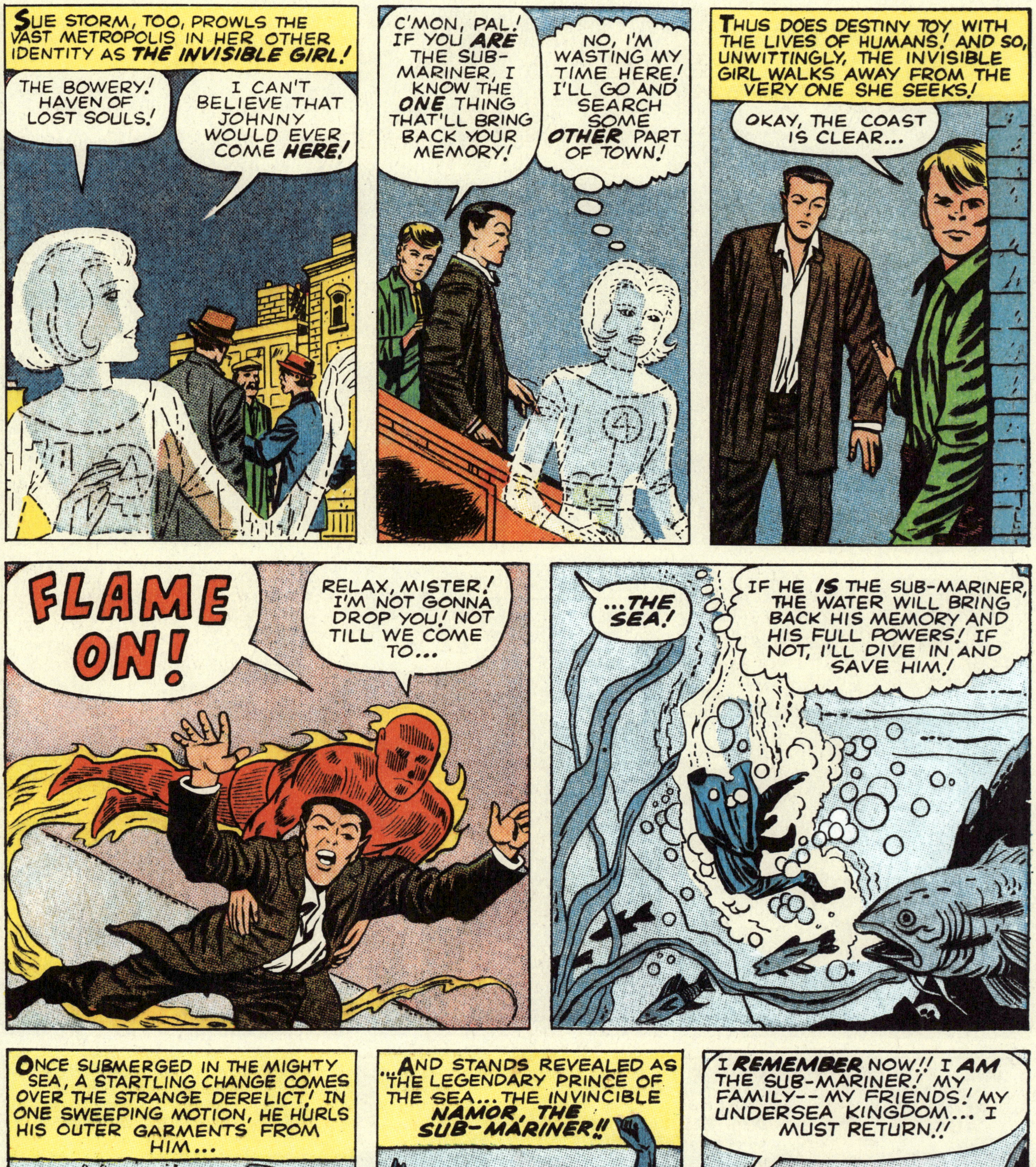

WHAT IS THE HULK??

CONTINUED AFTER NEXT PAGE...

Learn Radio-Television Electronics
by Practicing at Home in Your Spare Time
WITHOUT EXTRA CHARGE NRI provides special kits that bring to life things you study. Makes learning easy, interesting, fast. All equipment yours to keep.
Fast Growth Offers You High Pay, Prestige, Bright Future
From Radio-TV Servicing and Broadcasting to missile launching sites like Cape Canaveral, NRI graduates share in the gigantic Electronics industry. Interesting jobs await you in studios, on ships and planes, in your own business. Mail coupon today for NRI catalog.
Many NRI graduates help build, install, operate and service automated electronic equipment for the new "Space Age" we live in—equipment used in offices, factories, the military. Others have important jobs as inspectors, laboratory technicans, etc., or hold essential civilian posts with the Government and Armed Forces.
J. M. SMITH President
If you check the classified advertisements in your local newspaper, you will see more job opportunities for men with Electronics training than for any other category. These are better than average jobs, with bright futures . . . jobs for which YOU could qualify through NRI training. Thousands of men like yourself—most of them without a high school diploma—earn good money, enjoy greater prestige in TV and Radio broadcasting, in industrial plants making Electronic equipment or in businesses of their own.
Train With The Leader
Throughout the U.S. and Canada, successful NRI graduates are proof that it's practical to train at home, in your spare time, at your own pace. Keep your present job while training. For 45 years, NRI has featured the best Radio-TV Electroncis training for beginners—for men without previous experience. NRI supplies training at low cost because it is the oldest and largest home-study school of its kind. You will find the Electronics field a profitable one for the ambitious man. The NRI "learn-by-doing" method is the most practical way for you to get into this exciting field quickly.
NRI Trained These Men
I was working in a textile factory trying to make ends meet. Now I own one of the most modern service shops in this section. ARGIE C. TAYLOR, Glasgow, Ky.
After graduating I was a shipboard radio operator. Now I am chief engineer at Station WARA. NRI was a wonderful foundation. RAYMOND D. ARNOLD, Attleboro, Mass.
Thanks to NRI I am in a top position with the Federal Aviation Agency in the Navaids Electronic Section. JOE DUCKWORTH, Fort Worth. Texas.
Four months after starting your course I left my job in a hardware store to work at Raytheon Manufacturing. Now I am an engineering assistant in Microwave Power Tube Research and Development Laboratory. LEONARD BLOOM, Newton Centre, Mass.
Start Soon to Earn More
NRI training can bring prompt financial return. Soon after enrolling, NRI shows you how to earn $10, $15 and more a week extra fixing sets in your spare time. This can lead to a profitable Radio-TV business of your own. Others have found good paying jobs within a year after enrolling.
Mail the coupon below TODAY for our FREE CATALOG. It tells in words and pictures about the amazing field of Electronics. Read success stories. See the equipment you get. Find out about the NRI 60-day free trial enrollment offer and convenient monthly terms. National Radio Institute. Washington 16, D. C.
GET 64 PAGE CATALOG FREE
MAIL THIS COUPON NOW
The Amazing Field of Electronics
National Radio Institute
Washington 16, D.C.
2DM1
Send me full information without cost or obligation. No representative will call. (Please print.)
Name....................Age..........
Address....................
City....................Zone.....State..........
ACCREDITED MEMBER NATIONAL HOME STUDY COUNCIL

CHAPTER 4
SUB-MARINER'S REVENGE!
NO SOONER DOES NAMOR UTTER THOSE FATEFUL WORDS, THAN THE THREE OTHER MEMBERS OF THE MIGHTY FOURSOME, BACK AT THEIR HEADQUARTERS AGAIN, PLANNING THEIR NEXT MOVE, SEE...
LOOK!!
A FLARE!! IT MUST BE THE TORCH! LET'S GO!!
HURRY!! HE MUST BE IN DANGER! IT'S THE EMERGENCY SIGNAL!!
Stan Lee + J. KIRBY
AND, IN THE STREETS BELOW, ALL EYES TURN SKYWARD, AS THEY BEHOLD THE MOST DRAMATIC, MOST EXCITING SECRET SYMBOL OF ALL!!
IT CAME FROM THE WATERFRONT! I KNEW HE'D NEED US! THAT BRAT CAN'T STAY OUTTA TROUBLE WITHOUT US!
FASTER, REED! FASTER!
EASY, SUE! WE'RE ALMOST THERE!
14

THERE HE IS!
HE'S ALRIGHT! THANK HEAVENS! HE'S ALRIGHT!
WHAT'S THE IDEA SCARIN' US THAT WAY? YOU KNOW THAT FLARE IS ONLY TO BE USED IN EMERGENCIES!
QUIET, THING!
THIS IS AN EMERGENCY, YOU BIG APE!
DO YOU THINK I'D HAVE CALLED YOU IF IT WASN'T IMPORTANT? I NEVER WANTED TO SEE ANY OF YOU AGAIN! BUT WE'RE GONNA NEED EACH OTHER NOW!! THE SUB-MARINER IS BACK! AND HE'S OUT TO DESTROY THE WHOLE HUMAN RACE!
THE SUB-MARINER!!
I THOUGHT HE HAD DIED LONG AGO! NOBODY'S HEARD OF HIM FOR YEARS!
HE'S ALIVE, ALL RIGHT! AND HE'S MORE DANGEROUS THAN EVER!
BAH! WHO'S WORRIED? NOTHING HUMAN CAN STAND UP TO THE THING!
THAT'S THE SCARY PART, MISTER! HE ISN'T HUMAN!
NO, NAMOR, PRINCE OF THE SEA, ISN'T QUITE HUMAN--FOR HIS RACE WAS OLD WHEN THE STARS WERE YOUNG! AND, MANY FATHOMS BELOW...
I'LL UNLEASH A MONSTER SUCH AS MANKIND HAS NEVER DREAMED OF!
THERE HE IS!! STILL SLUMBERING--AS HE HAS DONE FOR AGES!! THE LARGEST LIVING THING IN ALL THE WORLD... THE DEADLY GIGANTO!
ONLY ONE THING CAN AROUSE HIM...THIS TRUMPET-HORN WHICH MY ANCESTORS BURIED HERE CENTURIES AGO!

HEARING THE EERIE, UNDERSEA BLAST, WITH ONE EARTH-SHAKING SHRUG, THE UNDERSEA BEHEMOTH SHAKES OFF THE SLEEP OF AGES, AND...
I'VE DONE IT! I'VE AWAKENED THE MONSTER! NOW NOTHING CAN STOP HIM!
HE'LL FOLLOW THE TRUMPET-HORN WHEREVER IT LEADS...
AND, IN THE HANDS OF SUB-MARINER, IT LEADS TO-- THE SURFACE WORLD!
FOR THE LOVE OF HEAVEN... LOOK !!
MINDLESSLY, THE GIGANTIC CREATURE SPLINTERS THE OLD TRAMP STEAMER, AS THE CREW ESCAPES TO SOUND THE ALARM...
WE--WE ARE TOO SMALL FOR HIM TO NOTICE!
I'VE GOT THE EMERGENCY RADIO WORKING, SIR!
AND, WITHIN SECONDS...
I KNOW IT SOUNDS IMPOSSIBLE, BUT...
NOWADAYS, NOTHING IS IMPOSSIBLE!
THEY SAID IT'S HEADED TOWARDS NEW YORK!
FOR THE FIRST TIME IN HISTORY, THE INCREDIBLE ORDER IS GIVEN... EVACUATE NEW YORK!
DON'T PANIC!! JUST KEEP MOVING!
HURRY! HURRY!
AND, THRU THE NOW-SILENT CANYONS OF THE DESERTED CITY, THE NATION'S MOST POWERFUL WEAPONS ARE BROUGHT INTO POSITION!
HERE IT COMES!

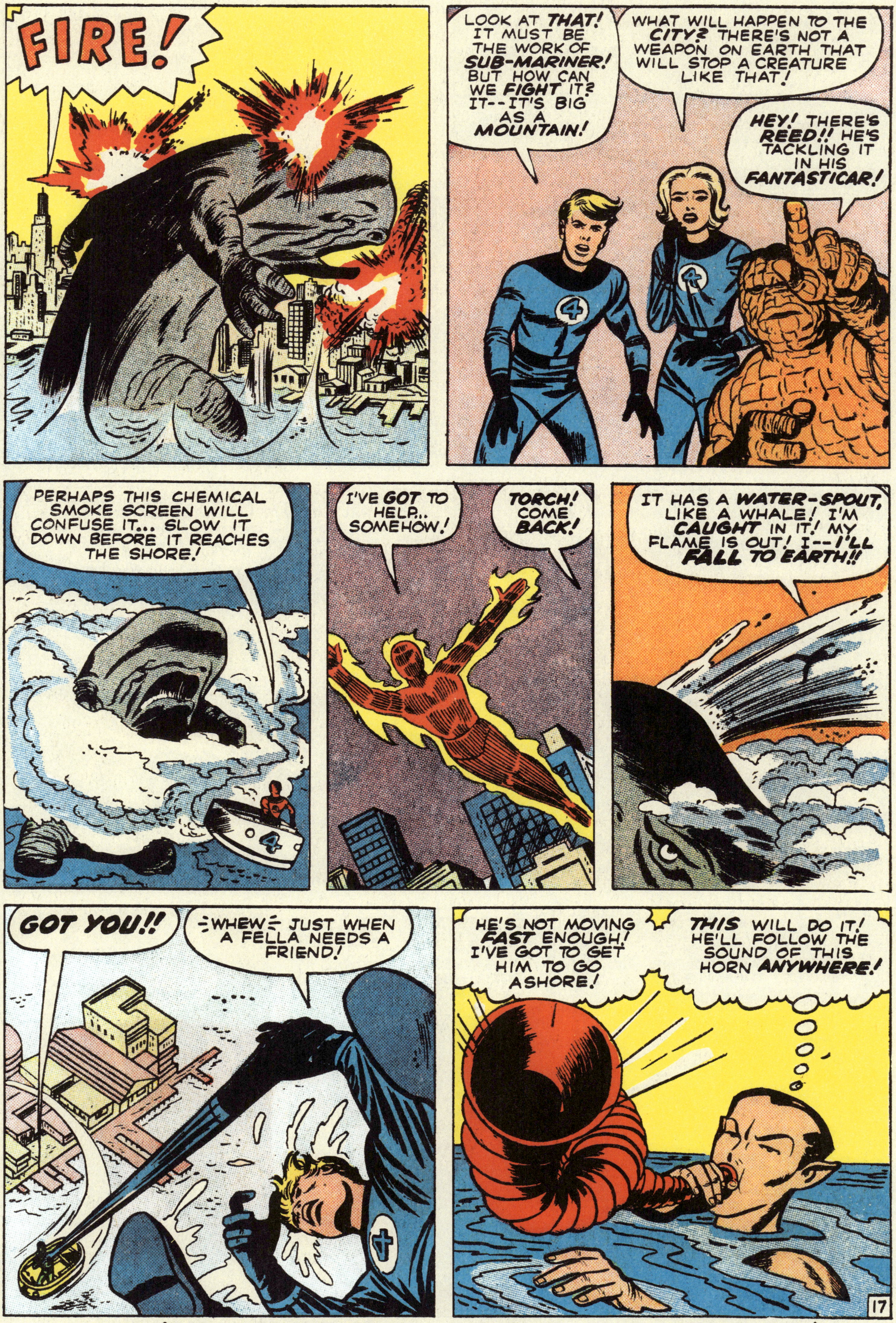

YOU'VE NEVER SEEN ANYONE LIKE THE HULK!

CONTINUED AFTER NEXT PAGE...

"I'll give you the keys to this brand new car..." just 30 short days from now!

Just 4 orders daily for my super comfort shoes will make the down payment for you . . . and you can easily pay the balance with the profits I'll show you how to make!

At last . . . even in your spare time . . . you can start a business that makes money fast—so fast it can put you in a 1962 car of your choice in one short month! Here's how: At our expense, we'll set you up in a profitable Mason "Shoe Store" business. You need no previous experience . . . don't invest a dime! James Kelly tried our offer — made $93.55 in just one evening's friendly work! Yes, everyone wants exciting, Nationally Advertised Mason Shoes. That's why you pocket steady cash profits, enjoy easy repeat sales, BIG money . . . PLUS monthly bonus checks and rich prizes!

YOUR OWN BUSINESS!

It's easy, because you run this "Store" from home. Just show the hundreds of Mason Shoe and Jacket styles to friends, relatives, people at work . . . and take their orders! It's so *convenient* for your customers! You have no inventory — no overhead expenses — you keep 100% of the profit.

230 DIFFERENT STYLES

Mason Shoes SELL FAST!

You'll offer over 230 styles for men and women . . . featuring foamy soft *air-cushion* innersoles . . . every shoe so comfortable they almost sell themselves for dress, work, sport wear. You'll have no problem fitting people, because you draw on our stock of over 250,000 pairs . . . sizes from 2½ to 15, widths from AAAA to EEEE. Your customers are delighted. Remember, Mason Shoes aren't sold by stores . . . folks must buy these Nationally Advertised Shoes from you.

MASON SHOE MFG. CO. Dept. H-80 Chippewa Falls, Wis.

FREE SELLING KIT!

The moment we receive the coupon below, we'll rush your complete Business Outfit FREE and postpaid! You'll receive a powerful Outfit showing the full Mason line *in color;* a dramatic 10-second Air Cushion demonstrator; "how-to-make-money" Booklet; special measuring board; National ad reprints . . . Good-Will Gifts . . . *everything* you need to start making *big money* your very first hour!

START SELLING NOW!

Stop *dreaming* about that new car . . . now you can *own* it by rushing this coupon to us at once! Just 4 easy orders a day will easily *give* you enough profit *in one month* to make the down payment—and your profits in this exciting business should soon pay for the car and many other luxuries besides!

RUSH MY FREE OUTFIT!

MR. NED MASON, Dept. H-80
Mason Shoe Manufacturing Company
Chippewa Falls, Wisconsin

Send my FREE Business Outfit Today! I want to start a profitable shoe business and earn up to $480 a month . . . and *more*, so I can start driving my own brand new 1962 car SOON!

Name ....
PLEASE PRINT
Address ....
Town .... State ....

5 CENTS PROFIT YOURS ON EVERY COPY SOLD.

30,000 Boys Selling Each Week Know

It's Fun
It's Easy

You Can Make $1 to $5 Every Week in a Few Hours

Fellows!

Earn all the spending money you want. GRIT is popular in 900,000 homes. It is easy to sell. You get FREE PRIZES in addition to the money you make. You also gain valuable business experience to help you become a successful man. I'll be glad to help you get started in this business of your own.

Pay only for copies sold until you know how many to order. Papers will be sent immediately.

START NOW EARNING BIG CASH PROFITS AND FREE PRIZES

Print Name and Address Below

If You Are a Boy 12 Years Old or Older

MAIL THIS TODAY

In an Envelope or Pasted on a Post Card

GRIT PUBLISHING CO., Williamsport, Pa.

Send my first bundle of papers, selling helps and prize offers. MC4-2

Name ....
Are You a Boy? .... Age .... Date Born .... Year ....
In Care of ....
Street and No. .... R. F. D. ....
Post Office .... State ....
Print Your Last Name Plainly Here

CHAPTER 5
"RETURN TO THE DEEP!"
Stan Lee & J. KIRBY
SLOWLY, WARILY, KNOWING THAT EACH STEP MIGHT BE HIS LAST, THE THING STALKS DEEPER AND DEEPER INSIDE THE GIGANTIC SEA CREATURE...
V-643
...PAST THE LONG-SINCE FORGOTTEN REMAINS OF ANCIENT VESSELS...OCEAN CRAFT WHICH HAD FALLEN VICTIM TO GIGANTO, LONG AGES AGO!
AND THEN, SUDDENLY...
YEOW! I SHOULDA GUESSED! A GIANT LIKE HIM WOULD BE APT TO SWALLOW LOTS OF UNDERSEA MONSTERS ALIVE!
AND HERE'S ONE OF 'EM!
19

AND, AS THE TIMING ELEMENT OF THE DEADLY BOMB TICKS ON...
WELL, I'VE FOUGHT EVERYTHING ELSE IN MY TIME, SO...
TICK TICK TICK TICK
I MIGHT AS WELL TACKLE YOU, TOO!
THAT DOES IT!
BUT NOW, I'VE ONLY SECONDS TO SPARE! IF HIS MOUTH IS SHUT NOW, I'M A GONER!
TICK TICK TICK TICK TICK TICK TICK TICK TICK
MADE IT!! -UGH-
BOOOM
HE DID IT!! THE MONSTER IS DEAD!
HE SAVED THE CITY! PERHAPS THE WORLD!
EASY! DON'T DROP HIM, JOHNNY! THE SHOCK MUST HAVE KNOCKED HIM OUT!!
I DIDN'T THINK ANYTHING COULD STUN THE BIG GORILLA!
AH--HE'S COMING TO NOW!
I HATE TO SAY IT, THING... BUT, I'M PROUD OF YOU!
BIG DEAL! THAT, AND A DIME, WILL GET ME A CUP OF COFFEE!
QUIET, YOU TWO! WHO'S THAT?
YOU'LL FIND OUT SOON ENOUGH WHO I AM! THE WHOLE WORLD WILL KNOW THE SUB-MARINER!!
YOU HAVEN'T BEATEN ME YET! AS LONG AS I HAVE THIS HORN, I CAN SUMMON COUNTLESS OTHER SEA MONSTERS TO ATTACK YOU!

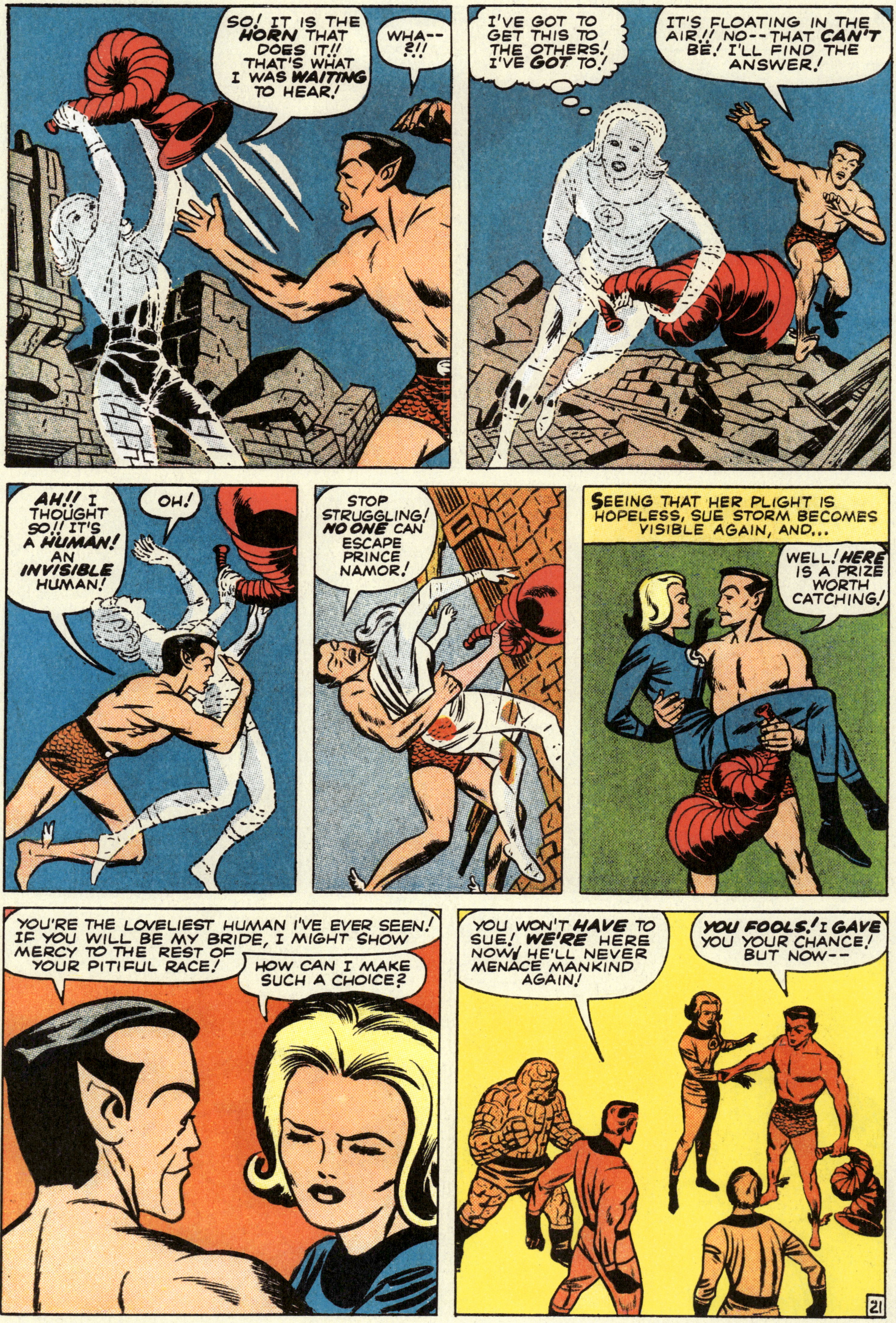
SO! IT IS THE HORN THAT DOES IT!! THAT'S WHAT I WAS WAITING TO HEAR!
WHA-- ?!!
I'VE GOT TO GET THIS TO THE OTHERS! I'VE GOT TO!
IT'S FLOATING IN THE AIR!! NO--THAT CAN'T BE! I'LL FIND THE ANSWER!
AH!! I THOUGHT SO!! IT'S A HUMAN! AN INVISIBLE HUMAN!
OH!
STOP STRUGGLING! NO ONE CAN ESCAPE PRINCE NAMOR!
SEEING THAT HER PLIGHT IS HOPELESS, SUE STORM BECOMES VISIBLE AGAIN, AND...
WELL! HERE IS A PRIZE WORTH CATCHING!
YOU'RE THE LOVELIEST HUMAN I'VE EVER SEEN! IF YOU WILL BE MY BRIDE, I MIGHT SHOW MERCY TO THE REST OF YOUR PITIFUL RACE!
HOW CAN I MAKE SUCH A CHOICE?
YOU WON'T HAVE TO SUE! WE'RE HERE NOW! HE'LL NEVER MENACE MANKIND AGAIN!
YOU FOOLS! I GAVE YOU YOUR CHANCE! BUT NOW--
21

NOW I'LL HAVE THE GIRL, AND MY REVENGE!! THE NEXT TIME I BLOW THIS HORN, I SHALL UNLEASH A HORDE OF UNDERSEA MONSTERS SUCH AS MANKIND NEVER DREAMT OF!!
"HELPLESS BEFORE THE INVINCIBLE ATTACK, YOU HUMANS WILL BE DRIVEN OUT OF YOUR CITIES... UNTIL YOU RETURN TO THE CAVES IN WHICH YOUR ANCESTORS DWELLED! THIS IS MY PROPHECY!"
HE MEANS IT!! HE--HE MIGHT DO IT! WE CAN'T TAKE THE CHANCE!
NO, PRINCE NAMOR, YOU MUSTN'T!! I-I'LL DO ANYTHING--I'LL BECOME YOUR BRIDE!
ONE LIFE SUCH AS MINE DOESN'T MATTER--BUT HUMANITY MUST BE SPARED!
YOU SPEAK AS THOUGH YOU ARE SACRIFICING YOURSELF!
DON'T YOU REALIZE WHAT AN HONOR I OFFER YOU!?? YOU CAN BECOME PRINCESS NAMORA, BRIDE OF THE SUB-MARINER!! CO-RULER OF EARTH!
THIS HAS GONE FAR ENOUGH!
SOMEBODY'S GOTTA SHOW NAMOR THAT HE CAN'T DEFEAT MANKIND SINGLE-HANDED!
LET ME TACKLE 'IM! I CAN'T WAIT TO GET MY HANDS ON THAT BIG-TALKIN' FISHMAN!
BUT, HAVING REGAINED HIS FULL STRENGTH AGAIN, THE UNDERSEA MONARCH SCATTERS HIS ASTONISHED ATTACKERS LIKE TENPINS!
BACK, YOU CLODS! NONE MAY STRIKE THE IMPERIAL PERSON OF NAMOR, THE SUB-MARINER!
22

YOU'VE NEVER SEEN ANYONE LIKE THE HULK!

THE HULK IS COMING!

Address YOUR letters to:
THE EDITOR
FANTASTIC FOUR
THIRD FLOOR
655 MADISON AVE.
NEW YORK 21, N. Y.

FANTASTIC FAN PAGE 4

DEAR EDITOR:

I've got to hand it to you. It takes a lot of guts to write "The Greatest Comic Magazine in the World" on the cover of a mag. But, in your case, the risk paid off, because I don't think any comic reader can doubt it. The Fantastic Four has everything! Great art, terrific characters, and a more adult approach to the stories than any other mag I've read (except "Amazing Adult Fantasy," which is yours too, I understand). You are definitely starting a new trend in comics — stories about characters who act like real people, not just lily-white do-gooders who would insult the average reader's intelligence. Keep it up and I'm your fan for life!

Len Blake
Los Angeles
California

What a letter! If we had any sense, we'd end this section right now, while we're ahead. But, we've got more space to fill, so here goes . . .

DEAR EDITOR:

I thought I'd seen everything, but when you showed the Thing putting on his new costume and grumbling: "Bah! Costumes — that's kid stuff! Who needs 'em? I ain't gonna wear this fool outfit!" I nearly flipped! At last I've found a magazine with characters which are different! They're unpredictable, and unforgettable! If you don't make the Fantastic Four a monthly, I'll shoot myself!

Anthony Gonzales
Mexico City
Mexico

We've been thinking about making the F.F. a monthly, Tony. All we need now are a few extra pair of hands and a new work day with 48 hours in it! But, if we can find a way to do it, let the competition beware!

DEAR EDITOR:

Are you kidding?? What kind of super-characters are these? They're always fighting among themselves! They have the same jealousies and personality clashes as real people! Have you flipped your lids?? Do you think comic mag readers are intelligent enough to appreciate all that good writing jazz? If you want my opinion — you're darn right!

S. Goldberg
Forest Hills
New York

Whew! You had us worried there for a minute, S. G.! But it seems that we ARE right, for in just a short time the Fantastic Four has become the most talked-about comic mag in the country! Now, if only people will stop talking about it and start buying it . . .

DEAR EDITOR:

Big deal! So you finally hit a winner with the Fantastic Four! Now, what are you going to do for an encore??

Shirley Howard
Chicago
Illinois

That's easy, Shirl! We can always come up with new titles like The Fantastic Five, The Fantastic Six, etc. — As long as we don't run out of numbers!

DEAR EDITOR:

In your second issue, in the Skrulls From Outer Space yarn, when Susan Storm holds the stolen gem and becomes invisible, the gem becomes invisible too! Explain *that!*

Bruce Fogel
Oak Park
Michigan

Tell you what — let's make a CONTEST out of it! We'll give $5.00 to the reader who sends in the best explanation. (How's that for getting off the hook, pal??)

DEAR EDITOR:

How about biogs of Stan Lee and Jack Kirby? And don't tell me that the Fantastic Four are real people, but Lee and Kirby are imaginary!

Jim Moony
Hollywood
California

We're real enough, Jimmy boy! But everytime Kirby poses for a picture, the camera lens breaks! And whenever Lee starts to write about himself, he uses the word "I" and "Me" so much that the typewriter quits! However, we may yield to public demand in the future. (Some demand! One grubby little post card!)

DEAR EDITOR:

My favorite Fantastic Four character is The Human Torch!! Why don't you have a whole book just about him?

Unsigned
Fall River
Massachusetts

Maybe we will, Unsigned. But first, we'd like to know what our other fans (both of them) think. So let us know, huh? Which is your favorite character? And don't be wise-guys and tell us Millie the Model and Patsy Walker!

It's impossible for us to answer your letters personally. So, watch this space for your answer. It may take years, but what else have you got to do??

START YOUR OWN BUSINESS!
ORDERS
ELECTRICAL APPLIANCE REPAIRING
SECURITY — INDEPENDENCE
WORK SHORT HOURS
There are millions of electrical equipment units in daily use . . . in factories, homes, office buildings and on farms. Skilled electrical technicians are needed to keep this equipment in good running condition. Learn at home in spare time.
You can now BE TRAINED to fill this BIG NEED . . . a need that grows day by day because of new electrical inventions for home and factory.
If you are mechanically inclined, can hold and use tools, we can give you the training and time-saving kits that will enable you to . . . Command More Money at Work . . . A Better Paying Job Elsewhere . . . Or A Business Of Your Own!
The ELECTRONIC KIT, a multi-purpose trouble detector, and other valuable Shop Method Training is sent to you! All instruction material is written in simple, easy-to-understand language, chock full of hundreds of detailed photos and drawings. Used by servicemen the country over.
We show you how to quickly locate the trouble, how to fix it and what to charge. ALSO, how to solicit business and keep business coming to you.
Get Full Facts on how you can get this training at home in your spare time and pay for it out of your earnings while learning!
FREE BOOK
On America's fastest growing Industry
IN YOUR OWN KITCHEN, BASEMENT, OR GARAGE
You don't need elaborate fixtures or expensive equipment to be a successful repairman. Work as many hours as you wish. The Electrical Appliance Technician is his own boss!
$5.00 - $6.00 HOUR
often charged for making ordinary repairs. We show you how to repair refrigerators, vacuum cleaners, washing machines, motors, etc., etc.
AGE IS NO BARRIER
Nor is a minor physical handicap. Work is light, pleasant and PROFITABLE.
EARN WHILE YOU LEARN!
Only had your course a few short weeks and have already made $800.00. Going to quit my job paying $250.00 straight salary to operate my own business.—J. D. S., St. Louis, Mo.
I work day times at the shipyard and after 4:00 P. M. I operate from my cellar and garage. I average $10.00 to $15.00 clear every day.—Walter Hanhy, Brockton, Mass.
SEND COUPON TODAY
WORKING KIT FURNISHED
CHRISTY TRADES SCHOOL, Dept. A-171
3214 W. Lawrence Ave., Chicago 25, Ill.
Gentlemen:
Please rush me your FREE ILLUSTRATED BOOK about Electrical Appliance Servicing, facts on your Electronic Kit and Special form for paying later from earnings while learning.
NAME Age
ADDRESS
CITY Zone State

UNION

Test Your Talent!

CONTEST PRIZE: *$495.00 Scholarship in Commercial Art*

CONFEDERATE

Draw either one of these Civil War soldiers. Make your drawing any size except like a tracing. Use pencil. Everyone who enters the contest gets a professional estimate of his talent. Winner receives the complete course in commercial art that is taught by Art Instruction, Inc., now the world's largest home study art school.

Try for this free art course—professional training in advertising art, illustrating, cartooning and painting. Each student is taught, individually, by artists with commercial art experience. Art textbooks, illustrated in color, and step-by-step lesson assignments cover the entire course. Study of art fundamentals is followed by specialized work of the student's choice. Art Instruction, Inc. is an accredited member of the National Home Study Council.

Purpose of contest: to uncover talent with promise. Entries for November 1961 contest due by November 30. None returned. Amateurs only. Our students not eligible. Winner notified. Does an art career appeal to you? Start on your entry today.

*Use **1** coupon—then pass this page on to a friend.*

1. ART INSTRUCTION, INC.
Studio 8941 • 500 South 4th St., Minneapolis 15, Minn.
Please enter my drawing in your draw-a-head contest. (PLEASE PRINT)
Name ____
Occupation ____ AGE ____
Address ____ Apt. ____
City ____ Zone ____
County ____ State ____

2. ART INSTRUCTION, INC.
Studio 8941 • 500 South 4th St., Minneapolis 15, Minn.
Please enter my drawing in your draw-a-head contest. (PLEASE PRINT)
Name ____
Occupation ____ AGE ____
Address ____ Apt. ____
City ____ Zone ____
County ____ State ____

3. ART INSTRUCTION, INC.
Studio 8941 • 500 South 4th St., Minneapolis 15, Minn.
Please enter my drawing in your draw-a-head contest. (PLEASE PRINT)
Name ____
Occupation ____ AGE ____
Address ____ Apt. ____
City ____ Zone ____
County ____ State ____

IND.
THE WORLD'S GREATEST COMIC MAGAZINE!
APPROVED BY THE COMICS CODE AUTHORITY
12¢
THE Fantastic Four
MC
5 JULY
"MEET... DOCTOR DOOM!"
WITH A TURN OF THIS DIAL, I SHALL DESTROY THE FOUR OF YOU, FOREVER!!
AIR
I'VE GOT TO REACH HIM! HE'S DRAINING THE AIR OUT OF THE ROOM! I CAN'T BREATHE! MY--MY STRENGTH IS EBBING!
AIR!! I GOTTA HAVE AIR!
MY FLAME IS DYING WITHOUT OXYGEN! I'M HELPLESS!
I MUST GET IN TO SAVE THEM! BUT HOW? HOW??

THE FANTASTIC FOUR is published by CANAM PUBLISHERS SALES CORP. OFFICE OF PUBLICATION: 655 MADISON AVENUE, NEW YORK, N.Y. Published bi-monthly. Copyright 1962 by CANAM PUBLISHERS SALES CORP., 655 Madison Avenue, New York, N. Y. Vol. 1 No. 5, JULY 1962 issue. Price 12c per copy. Subscription rate $1.70 for 12 issues including postage. No similarity between any of the names, characters, persons, and/or institutions appearing in this magazine with those of any living or dead person or institution is intended, and any such similarity which may exist is purely coincidental. Printed in the U.S.A. by The Eastern Color Printing Co., Waterbury 20, Conn.

THE FANTASTIC FOUR, IN...
"PRISONERS OF
DOCTOR DOOM!"
THE FANTASTIC FOUR!! HAH! LITTLE DO THEY DREAM THEY ARE NAUGHT BUT PAWNS IN THE HANDS OF DOCTOR DOOM!
DEMONS
PART 1
Stan Lee & J. Kirby
SCIENCE AND SORCERY
V-235
BUT NOW IT IS TIME TO LET THE FANTASTIC FOUR FEEL MY MIGHT!
--FOR OF ALL THE HUMANS ON EARTH, ONLY I HAVE THE POWER TO DEFEAT THEM!
1

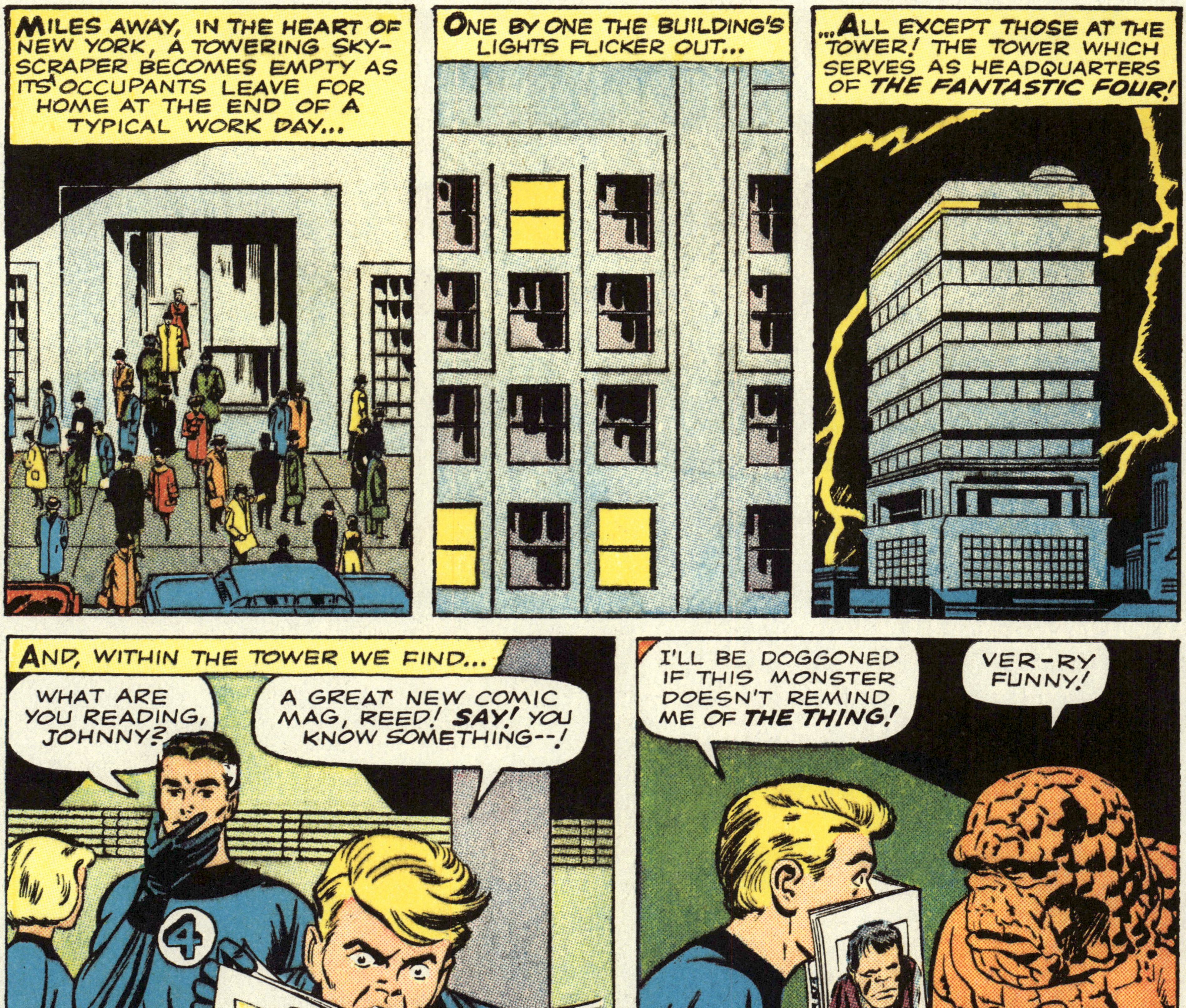
MILES AWAY, IN THE HEART OF NEW YORK, A TOWERING SKY-SCRAPER BECOMES EMPTY AS ITS OCCUPANTS LEAVE FOR HOME AT THE END OF A TYPICAL WORK DAY...
ONE BY ONE THE BUILDING'S LIGHTS FLICKER OUT...
...ALL EXCEPT THOSE AT THE TOWER! THE TOWER WHICH SERVES AS HEADQUARTERS OF THE FANTASTIC FOUR!
AND, WITHIN THE TOWER WE FIND...
WHAT ARE YOU READING, JOHNNY?
A GREAT NEW COMIC MAG, REED! SAY! YOU KNOW SOMETHING--!
HULK
I'LL BE DOGGONED IF THIS MONSTER DOESN'T REMIND ME OF THE THING!
VER-RY FUNNY!
GIMME THAT MAG, SQUIRT! I'LL TEACH YA TO COMPARE ME TO A COMIC BOOK MONSTER!
HEY!
HULK
IF YOU WANT IT SO BAD, I'LL WARM IT UP FOR YOU, BIG MAN!
OWW!
COME BACK HERE!
COME 'N GET ME!
2

YOU'RE DURNED RIGHT I'LL GET YOU, TORCH! AND WHEN I DO--
STOP HIM, REED!
THING! KNOCK IT OFF!!
THIS WILL COOL YOU OFF, KID BROTHER!
AW, SUE! I WAS JUST HAVING A LITTLE FUN!
FUN? YOU TWO WON'T BE SATISFIED TILL YOU'VE PULVERIZED EACH OTHER!
WHAT'S THE MATTER WITH THE FOUR OF US? WHENEVER WE'RE NOT FIGHTING SOME MENACE TO MANKIND, WE END UP FIGHTING AMONG OURSELVES!
SKIP THE LECTURE, PAL! I'M A BIG BOY NOW!
REED! WHAT HAPPENED?? THE LIGHTS ALL WENT OUT!
IMPOSSIBLE! WE HAVE OUR OWN GENERATOR HERE!
IT MUST HAVE BEEN AFFECTED BY SOME MORE POWERFUL FORCE! BUT-- WHAT?
FOR THE ANSWER, LET US LOOK UP AT THE SKY, OUTSIDE THE TOWER!
SOON I WILL HAVE THEM TRAPPED AND COMPLETELY AT MY MERCY!
NOTHING CAN ESCAPE MY LITTLE WEB!
NOT EVEN THE FANTASTIC FOUR!
3

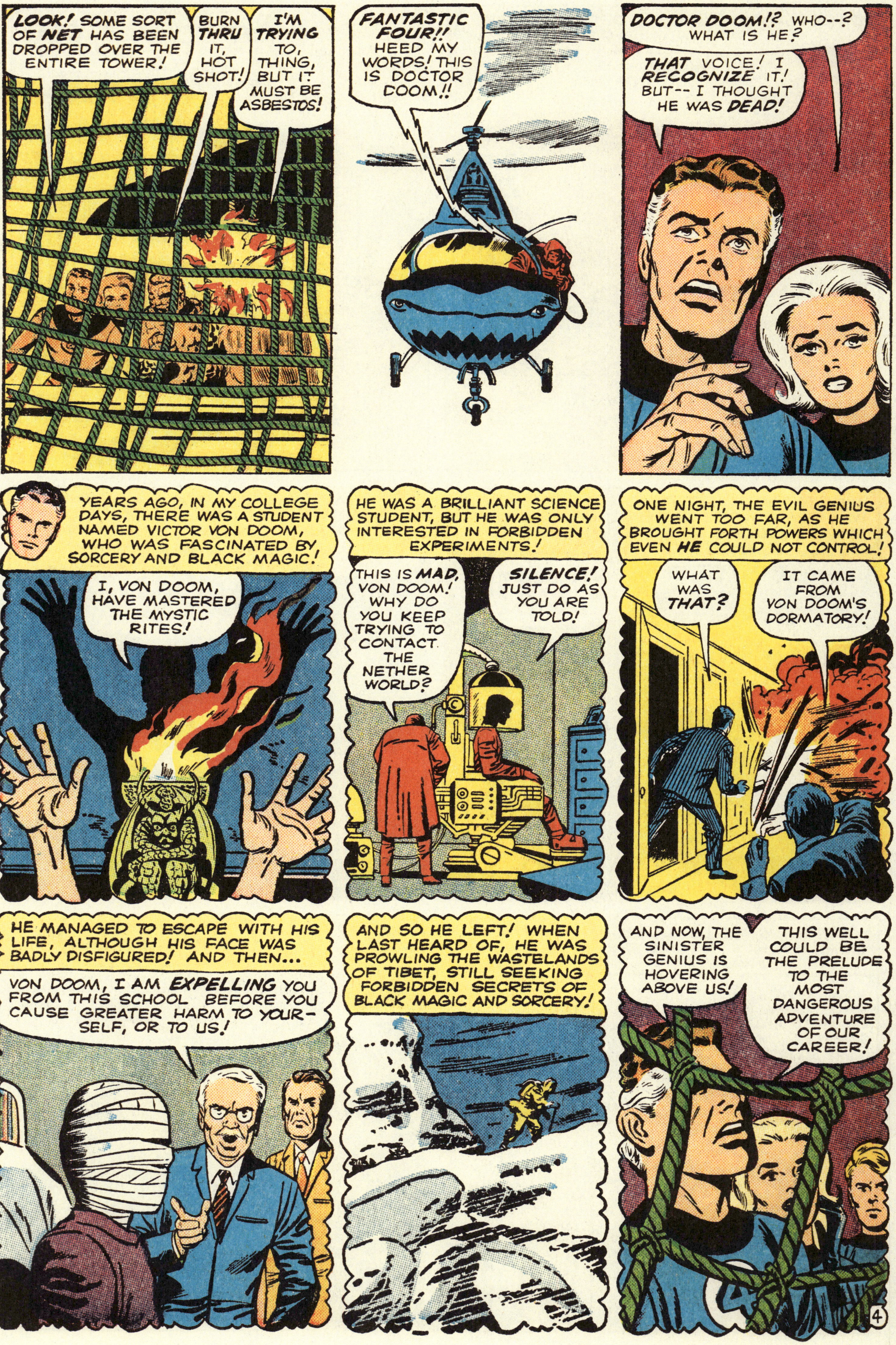
LOOK! SOME SORT OF NET HAS BEEN DROPPED OVER THE ENTIRE TOWER!
BURN THRU IT, HOT SHOT!
I'M TRYING TO, THING, BUT IT MUST BE ASBESTOS!
FANTASTIC FOUR!! HEED MY WORDS! THIS IS DOCTOR DOOM!!
DOCTOR DOOM!? WHO--? WHAT IS HE?
THAT VOICE! I RECOGNIZE IT! BUT-- I THOUGHT HE WAS DEAD!
YEARS AGO, IN MY COLLEGE DAYS, THERE WAS A STUDENT NAMED VICTOR VON DOOM, WHO WAS FASCINATED BY SORCERY AND BLACK MAGIC!
I, VON DOOM, HAVE MASTERED THE MYSTIC RITES!
HE WAS A BRILLIANT SCIENCE STUDENT, BUT HE WAS ONLY INTERESTED IN FORBIDDEN EXPERIMENTS!
THIS IS MAD, VON DOOM! WHY DO YOU KEEP TRYING TO CONTACT THE NETHER WORLD?
SILENCE! JUST DO AS YOU ARE TOLD!
ONE NIGHT, THE EVIL GENIUS WENT TOO FAR, AS HE BROUGHT FORTH POWERS WHICH EVEN HE COULD NOT CONTROL!
WHAT WAS THAT?
IT CAME FROM VON DOOM'S DORMATORY!
HE MANAGED TO ESCAPE WITH HIS LIFE, ALTHOUGH HIS FACE WAS BADLY DISFIGURED! AND THEN...
VON DOOM, I AM EXPELLING YOU FROM THIS SCHOOL BEFORE YOU CAUSE GREATER HARM TO YOURSELF, OR TO US!
AND SO HE LEFT! WHEN LAST HEARD OF, HE WAS PROWLING THE WASTELANDS OF TIBET, STILL SEEKING FORBIDDEN SECRETS OF BLACK MAGIC AND SORCERY!
AND NOW, THE SINISTER GENIUS IS HOVERING ABOVE US!
THIS WELL COULD BE THE PRELUDE TO THE MOST DANGEROUS ADVENTURE OF OUR CAREER!
4

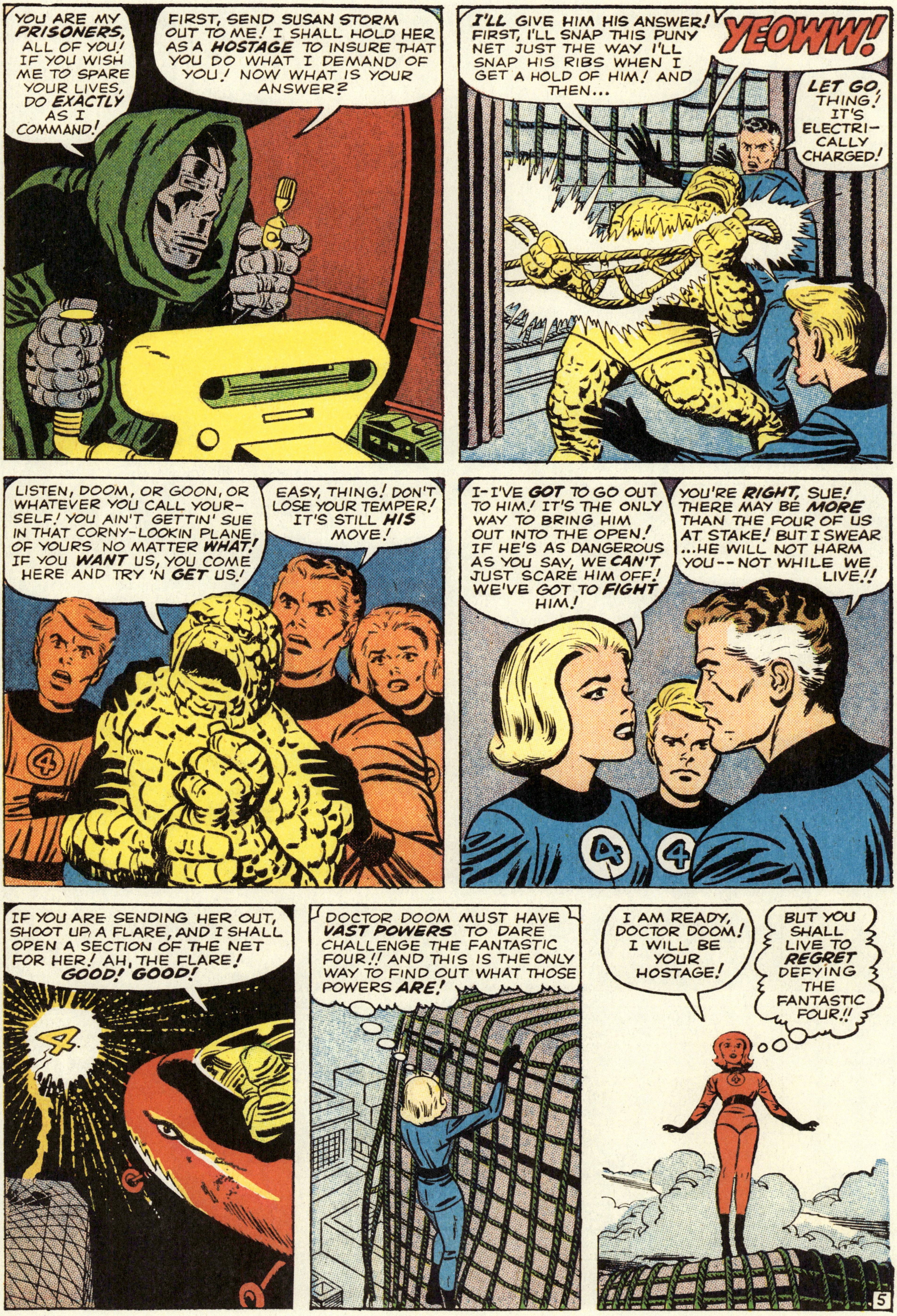
YOU ARE MY PRISONERS, ALL OF YOU! IF YOU WISH ME TO SPARE YOUR LIVES, DO EXACTLY AS I COMMAND!
FIRST, SEND SUSAN STORM OUT TO ME! I SHALL HOLD HER AS A HOSTAGE TO INSURE THAT YOU DO WHAT I DEMAND OF YOU! NOW WHAT IS YOUR ANSWER?
I'LL GIVE HIM HIS ANSWER! FIRST, I'LL SNAP THIS PUNY NET JUST THE WAY I'LL SNAP HIS RIBS WHEN I GET A HOLD OF HIM! AND THEN...
YEOWW!
LET GO, THING! IT'S ELECTRI-CALLY CHARGED!
LISTEN, DOOM, OR GOON, OR WHATEVER YOU CALL YOUR-SELF! YOU AIN'T GETTIN' SUE IN THAT CORNY-LOOKIN PLANE OF YOURS NO MATTER WHAT! IF YOU WANT US, YOU COME HERE AND TRY 'N GET US!
EASY, THING! DON'T LOSE YOUR TEMPER! IT'S STILL HIS MOVE!
I-I'VE GOT TO GO OUT TO HIM! IT'S THE ONLY WAY TO BRING HIM OUT INTO THE OPEN! IF HE'S AS DANGEROUS AS YOU SAY, WE CAN'T JUST SCARE HIM OFF! WE'VE GOT TO FIGHT HIM!
YOU'RE RIGHT, SUE! THERE MAY BE MORE THAN THE FOUR OF US AT STAKE! BUT I SWEAR ...HE WILL NOT HARM YOU--NOT WHILE WE LIVE!!
IF YOU ARE SENDING HER OUT, SHOOT UP A FLARE, AND I SHALL OPEN A SECTION OF THE NET FOR HER! AH, THE FLARE! GOOD! GOOD!
4
DOCTOR DOOM MUST HAVE VAST POWERS TO DARE CHALLENGE THE FANTASTIC FOUR!! AND THIS IS THE ONLY WAY TO FIND OUT WHAT THOSE POWERS ARE!
I AM READY, DOCTOR DOOM! I WILL BE YOUR HOSTAGE!
BUT YOU SHALL LIVE TO REGRET DEFYING THE FANTASTIC FOUR!!

PART 2
"BACK TO THE PAST!"
Stan Lee & J. Kirby
HE'S TAKING SUE ABOARD HIS SHIP!
LISTEN! HE'S SPEAKING TO US AGAIN!
NOW THAT THE INVISIBLE GIRL IS MY HOSTAGE, I SHALL GIVE YOU YOUR ORDERS! FIRST, I WANT YOU ALL TO BOARD MY PLANE, AND YOU MUST SWEAR YOU WILL NOT ATTACK ME!
V-735
IF YOU AGREE, FIRE YOUR FLARE GUN AGAIN!
GIMME THAT GUN! WE'RE GOIN' ON HIS PLANE! WE'RE NOT LETTIN' HIM GET AWAY FROM US!
REED, WHAT IF DOCTOR DOOM TRIES TO KILL US WHEN WE BOARD HIS PLANE?
EASY, JOHNNY! HE WANTS MORE THAN OUR DEATH! THIS IS PART OF SOME STRANGE MASTER PLAN, AND WE MUST SEE IT THRU!
6

AH! THEY AGREE TO BOARD MY SHIP, AS I PLANNED THEY WOULD! I KNEW MISTER FANTASTIC COULD NOT RESIST TRYING TO LEARN WHAT MY MISSION IS!
ONE FLIP OF A SWITCH AND THEY WILL BE MINE!
HOLY SMOKE, REED! THIS DOCTOR DOOM CHARACTER MUST BE A REAL WIZARD AT INVENTING THINGS!
I TOLD YOU HE IS AN EVIL GENIUS! WE MUST NEVER UNDERESTIMATE HIM!
SO FAR MY PLAN IS WORKING WITHOUT A HITCH!
THEN, WITH A SUDDEN, UNEXPECTED SURGE OF ROCKET POWER THE HELICOPTER BLAZES THRU THE SKY AT ALMOST UNBELIEVABLE SPEED!
WE WILL REACH MY CASTLE STRONGHOLD WITHIN MINUTES!
AND NOW, MY RELUCTANT PASSENGERS, WELCOME TO THE HOME OF DOCTOR DOOM!
IT--IT'S A REGULAR FORTRESS!
7

MINUTES LATER...
WELL, WHAT ARE WE WAITIN' FOR? LET'S RUSH 'IM!
WE CAN'T, THING! WE PROMISED NOT TO ATTACK HIM TILL WE HEAR HIM OUT!
YOU ARE WISE TO RESTRAIN YOURSELVES! FAST THOUGH YOU MAY BE, MY LITTLE PET HERE IS FASTER!
NOW THAT WE ARE ALL TOGETHER, I HAVE A MISSION FOR YOU TO PERFORM FOR ME! IF YOU CARRY IT OUT SUCCESSFULLY, YOU WILL ALL BE REWARDED! IF NOT, I HAVE A HOSTAGE!
TALK FAST, MISTER! WHAT IS THE MISSION?
I HAVE SUCCESSFULLY DEVELOPED THE MOST INCREDIBLE INVENTION OF THE AGE... AN ACTUAL TIME TRAVEL DEVICE! AND I WANT YOU TO GO CENTURIES INTO THE PAST AND OBTAIN THE LEGENDARY TREASURE OF BLACKBEARD FOR ME!
HE--HE MEANS IT!!
WHY DON'T YOU GO GET THAT TREASURE YOURSELF?
I CANNOT! I MUST REMAIN HERE TO OPERATE THE MACHINE!
WELL, SHALL WE DO IT?
GOSH! A CHANCE TO ACTUALLY VISIT THE PAST! WHO COULD REFUSE?
I COULD! WHAT IF HE DOESN'T BRING US BACK?
I WANT THAT TREASURE! I SHALL BRING YOU BACK!
DESPITE HIS OTHER FAULTS, DOOM IS NOT A LIAR! HE WILL KEEP HIS WORD!
HE'D BETTER!
DOOM, IF WE DON'T RETURN... SWEAR YOU WILL SET SUE FREE!
DONE! I ONLY NEEDED HER TO LURE YOU HERE!
AND NOW, I SHALL SEND YOU BACK... HUNDREDS OF YEARS INTO THE PAST! YOU WILL HAVE FORTY-EIGHT HOURS TO BRING ME BLACKBEARD'S TREASURE CHEST! DO NOT FAIL!
LOOK! WHAT'S THAT BUTTON HE'S PRESSING?
8

IT'S THE TIME TRAVEL MACHINE!
WE WERE STANDING ON IT ALL THE TIME!
REED! JOHNNY! THING! BE CAREFUL!! PLEASE... BE CAREFUL!!
THEY'RE GONE!
YES! GONE TO BRING ME THE GEMS WHICH, UNKNOWN TO THEM, WILL MAKE DOCTOR DOOM RULER OF EARTH!
-GASP- IT WORKED!! LOOK! LOOK WHERE WE ARE!
WE'VE GOT TO MOVE FAST! WE'VE ONLY GOT FORTY-EIGHT HOURS!
THE FIRST THING WE NEED ARE SOME CLOTHES! WE'RE MUCH TOO CONSPICUOUS IN OUR COSTUMES!
I STOLE THESE CLOTHES, YE SWAB! THEY'RE MINE!
YE MISERABLE SEA DOG! YE SWORE TO DIVIDE THE BOOTY WITH ME!
I SAY THEY'RE MINE! WANNA MAKE SOME-THINGOUT OF IT??
FLEE!! 'TIS A DEMON!
PERFECT! A WHOLE BUNDLE OF SUITS AND BOOTS!
9

THIS IS KEEN! I FEEL LIKE ERROL FLYNN!
LET ME DISGUISE YOU TOO, THING! A FAKE BEARD, HAT, AND EYE PATCH SHOULD DO THE TRICK!
TAKE IT EASY, BUB! I DON'T WANNA SUFFOCATE IN THIS OUTFIT!
ALMOST FINISHED!
THERE! YOU LOOK REAL NATURAL!
SAY! THIS FEELS PRETTY GOOD!
AHOY, MATEY! LET'S SEE IF WE CAN DATE ONE OF THESE PRETTY BARMAIDS! HEH HEH!
KNOCK IT OFF, THING! WE'VE STILL GOT TO FIND BLACKBEARD AND FIGURE OUT A WAY TO GET HIS TREASURE!
METHINKS THOSE THREE STRANGERS WOULD LIKE TO JOIN MY CREW, WENCH!
FEED THEM SOME GROG TO PUT THEM TO SLEEP! BE QUICK AT IT, LASS!
REFRESH YOURSELF, MASTER!
SAY! THE SERVICE HERE IS PRETTY GOOD!
MOMENTS LATER...
GOSH, I'M--SLEEPY! HOW ABOUT YOU, THING? AND-- REED-- ≷YAWN≶
IT IS DONE! NOW TO CARRY THEM TO OUR SHIP, AND SET SAIL! WHEN THEY AWAKE, THEY WILL BE PART OF OUR PIRATE CREW!
10

PART 3
"ON THE TRAIL OF BLACKBEARD"
STAN LEE • J. KIRBY
V-735
HOURS LATER, THE THING IS FIRST TO AWAKEN...
...SLOWLY, SILENTLY, HE LOOKS ABOUT HIM...
...ONLY TO FIND THAT THEY ARE LOCKED IN THE MUSTY HOLD OF A PIRATE SHIP!
11

WHILE UP ON DECK...
WAKEN THE PRISONERS! PUT THEM TO WORK! MOVE, YOU SWABS!
SINCE WHEN DO YOU GIVE ORDERS HERE, MISTER SPLINY! I'M AS FIT TO COMMAND AS ANY!
I'LL SHOW YE WHO GIVES THE ORDERS, YE MISERABLE LUBBER!
YAH!
ALL RIGHT, BOYS--YOUR LITTLE GAME IS OVER NOW!!
WHO DARES--? URRP!
I DARE!!
BIT OFF A LITTLE MORE THAN YOU CAN CHEW, HUH?? COME 'N GET IT, PLAYMATES!
Y'KNOW, JOHNNY, I FEEL SORRY FOR THOSE PIRATES! THEY'RE ONLY A DOZEN OF 'EM AGAINST THE THING!
YEAH! HE'S GOT 'EM OUTNUMBERED!
LOOK OUT!
BAM!
THAT WASN'T VERY SOCIABLE, SAILOR!
12

MUTINEERS, BE YE? I'LL GIVE YE A TASTE OF ME BLADE!
WANNA BET?
?
FLAME ON!
IT IS SORCERY! YE BE ENCHANTED!
THAT'S AS GOOD A NAME FOR IT AS ANY, MISTER!
BACK! STAY BACK! IT IS DEATH TO DEFY THE MIRACULOUS ONES!
NOW THAT'S MORE LIKE IT!!
SUDDENLY...
WE ARE ATTACKED!
BOOM!
IT'S ANOTHER PIRATE SHIP! MEBBE IT'S BLACKBEARD!
SHE'S LOADED WITH TREASURE! IT COULD BE BLACK-BEARD!
THING! TORCH! GET READY FOR THE FIGHT OF OUR LIVES!
ALL RIGHT, YOU SWABS! THAT MEANS YOU, TOO! WE'RE ALL IN THIS TOGETHER! GET ME??
AYE AYE, MIGHTY ONE!

STEP ASIDE, GENTS! I'LL SOFTEN 'EM UP A BIT FIRST!
THE YOUTH IS MAD!
FLAME ON!
StanLee + J. KIRBY
BATTLE!
PART 4
AVAST!! WE ARE ATTACKED BY A FLAMING DEMON!
V-735
14

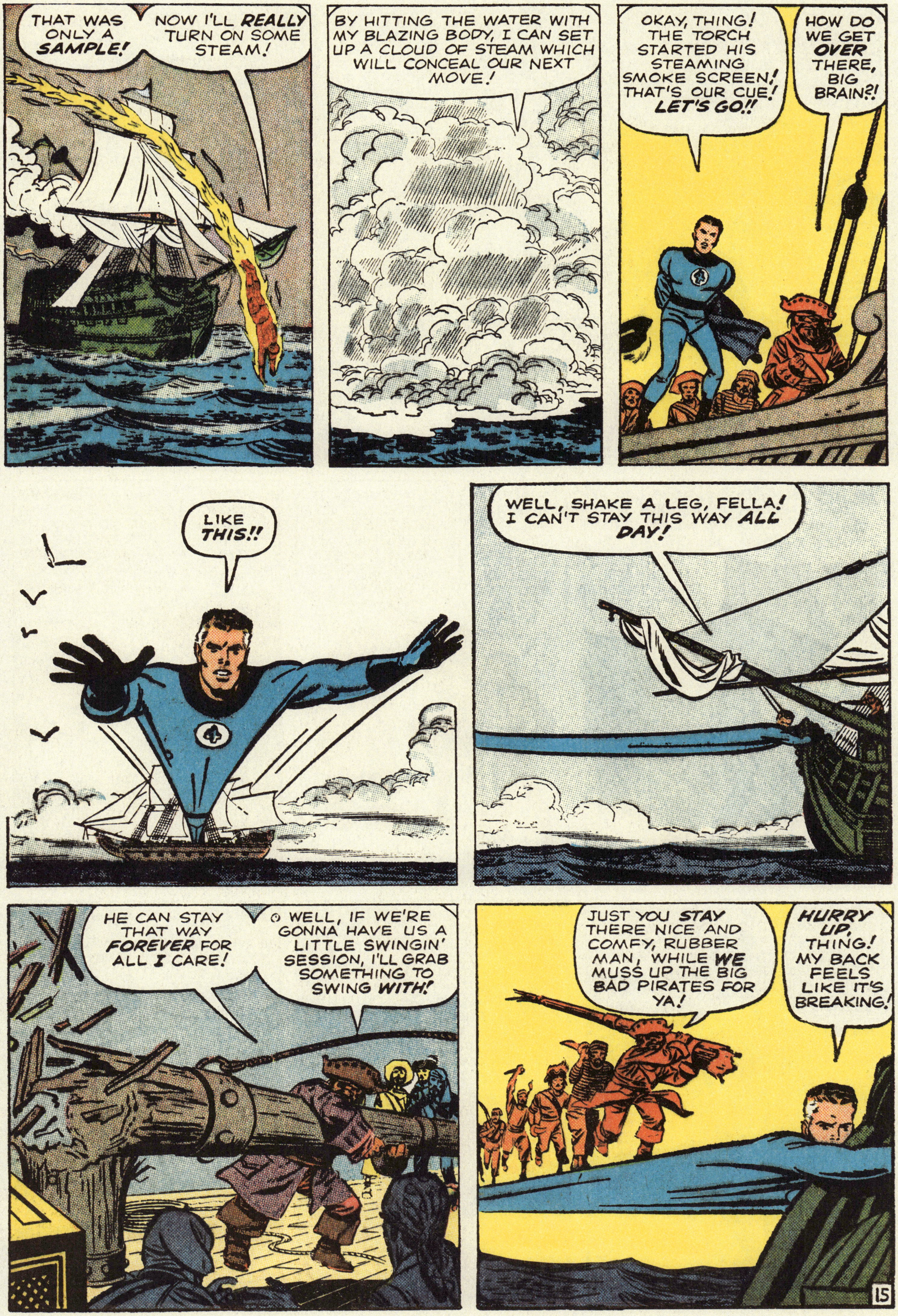
THAT WAS ONLY A SAMPLE!
NOW I'LL REALLY TURN ON SOME STEAM!
BY HITTING THE WATER WITH MY BLAZING BODY, I CAN SET UP A CLOUD OF STEAM WHICH WILL CONCEAL OUR NEXT MOVE!
OKAY, THING! THE TORCH STARTED HIS STEAMING SMOKE SCREEN! THAT'S OUR CUE! LET'S GO!!
HOW DO WE GET OVER THERE, BIG BRAIN?!
LIKE THIS!!
WELL, SHAKE A LEG, FELLA! I CAN'T STAY THIS WAY ALL DAY!
HE CAN STAY THAT WAY FOREVER FOR ALL I CARE!
WELL, IF WE'RE GONNA HAVE US A LITTLE SWINGIN' SESSION, I'LL GRAB SOMETHING TO SWING WITH!
JUST YOU STAY THERE NICE AND COMFY, RUBBER MAN, WHILE WE MUSS UP THE BIG BAD PIRATES FOR YA!
HURRY UP, THING! MY BACK FEELS LIKE IT'S BREAKING!
15

YAHOO! GO GET 'EM, BOYS!
FOLLOW THE BLACK-BEARDED ONE! ATTACK!
THEY FIGHT LIKE DEMONS POSSESSED! WE HAVE NO CHANCE!
AND, BRIEF MINUTES LATER...
HOORAY FOR THE MIGHTY BEARDED ONE!
HOORAY FOR BLACKBEARD!
HAIL BLACK-BEARD! SCOURGE OF THE SEVEN SEAS!
BLACKBEARD?? BUT THEY'RE TALKING ABOUT THE THING!
GOOD LORD!! I SEE IT NOW! THE THING IS BLACKBEARD! HE CAME BACK TO THE PAST TO FIND ...HIMSELF!
THEN THIS TREASURE WHICH WE JUST FOUND IN THE HOLD BELONGS TO US NOW!
OR, ACTUALLY IT BELONGS TO BLACKBEARD... FOR THE MEN HAVE CHOSEN HIM AS THEIR LEADER!
WOW! LOOK AT THIS STUFF!
THIS IS TERRIF! WE COME TO THE PAST TO FIND THE TREASURE OF BLACKBEARD ...AND IT TURNS OUT TO BE OURS!
SORRY, MEN, BUT IT WON'T BE OURS! WE'LL DIVIDE IT AMONG THE MEN! IF DOCTOR DOOM WANTED IT, THERE MUST BE SOME DANGEROUS POWER WHICH IT POSSESSES, AND WE'VE GOT TO SEE THAT HE NEVER GETS IT!
INSTEAD, WE'LL LOAD THIS CHEST WITH WORTHLESS CHAINS FOR DOCTOR DOOM! FOR, NOW THAT WE FULFILLED OUR PROMISE TO DOOM, WE CAN RETURN TO OUR OWN AGE!
WE KEPT OUR WORD! WE ARE BRINGING HIM BLACKBEARD'S TREASURE CHEST!
FOR WE NEVER PROMISED TO BRING THE TREASURE ITSELF!

YOU TWO CAN GO BACK IF YOU WANNA! AS FOR ME, I LIKE IT HERE!
REED! HE ACTUALLY ENJOYS BEING BLACKBEARD!
BUT HE CAN'T REMAIN HERE IN THE PAST!
WHY CAN'T I STAY? THE FUTURE HOLDS NOTHING FOR ME! IN THE TWENTIETH CENTURY I'M NOTHIN' BUT A MONSTER... A FREAK!
BUT HERE I'M SOMEBODY! I'M A LEADER OF MEN! I'M A CAPTAIN! I'M THE GUY WHO STARTED THE LEGEND OF BLACKBEARD! THE KIDS WILL READ ABOUT ME IN SCHOOL SOME DAY! I AIN'T GIVIN' THIS UP ...NEVER!
AND I'LL MAKE SURE YOU TWO DON'T TRY TO TAKE ME BACK! TIE 'EM UP, MEN-- FAST!
DON'T BE SCARED OF THE TORCH! HE'S STILL SOAKIN' WET! HE CAN'T FLAME ON YET!
THAT'S IT! WRAP A SAIL AROUND MR. FANTASTIC! IT WON'T DO HIM ANY GOOD TO STRETCH IF HE'S GOT NO PLACE TO STRETCH OUT OF!
NOW PUT 'EM OVER THE SIDE IN A LIFE BOAT! BY THE TIME THEY GET FREE, WE'LL HAVE LOST OURSELVES IN THE FOG!! THEY'LL NEVER FIND US AGAIN!
THING! DON'T DO IT!! DON'T CUT YOURSELF OFF FROM US! YOU MUSTN'T! YOU'LL REGRET IT SOME DAY!! DON'T DO IT!!
AT THAT VERY MOMENT, AS THOUGH IN ECHO TO THE TORCH'S WORDS...
AHOY, ALL HANDS!! TWISTER AHEAD!
17

THE GALE IS FREEING ME!! I CAN MOVE AGAIN! TORCH! WHERE ARE YOU??
OVER HERE, REED!! WE--WE'RE BEING WASHED OVERBOARD!! REED!! HELP!!
SECONDS LATER, AS SUDDENLY AS IT HAD APPEARED, THE FURY OF THE STORM BLOWS ITSELF OUT TO SEA...
REED!! THING!! HELP!!
EASY, LAD! I SEE YOU! HANG ON!
C-CAN'T STAY AFLOAT MUCH LONGER...
GOSH, REED... I-- I WAS ALMOST DONE FOR!
YOU'RE ALRIGHT NOW, TORCH! BUT WE'VE GOT TO FIND THE THING! IT'S ALMOST TIME FOR DOCTOR DOOM TO BRING US BACK!
THERE HE IS... WASHED ASHORE!
HIS DISGUISE MUST HAVE BEEN BLOWN OFF BY THE STORM!
DON'T SAY IT, RUBBER MAN! I KNOW! I WAS A FOOL! I MUSTA GOT CARRIED AWAY BY BEING ACCEPTED--AS A NORMAL MAN--EVEN IF IT WAS ONLY BY A BAND OF CUT-THROAT PIRATES! I--I JUST LOST MY DUMB HEAD FOR AWHILE!
WE'RE IN LUCK, REED! HERE'S THE PIRATE CHEST! IT WAS WASHED ASHORE, ALSO!
BUT NOW, HOW IS DOCTOR DOOM GONNA GET US BACK TO THE PRESENT?
AT THAT INSTANT, ACROSS THE GULF OF CENTURIES, A HAND ACTIVATES AN ATOMIC POWER CIRCUIT, AND...
THEY HAVE HAD ENOUGH TIME TO OBTAIN THE GEMS OF BLACKBEARD FOR ME! AND IF THEY FAILED, THEY WILL DIE!
18

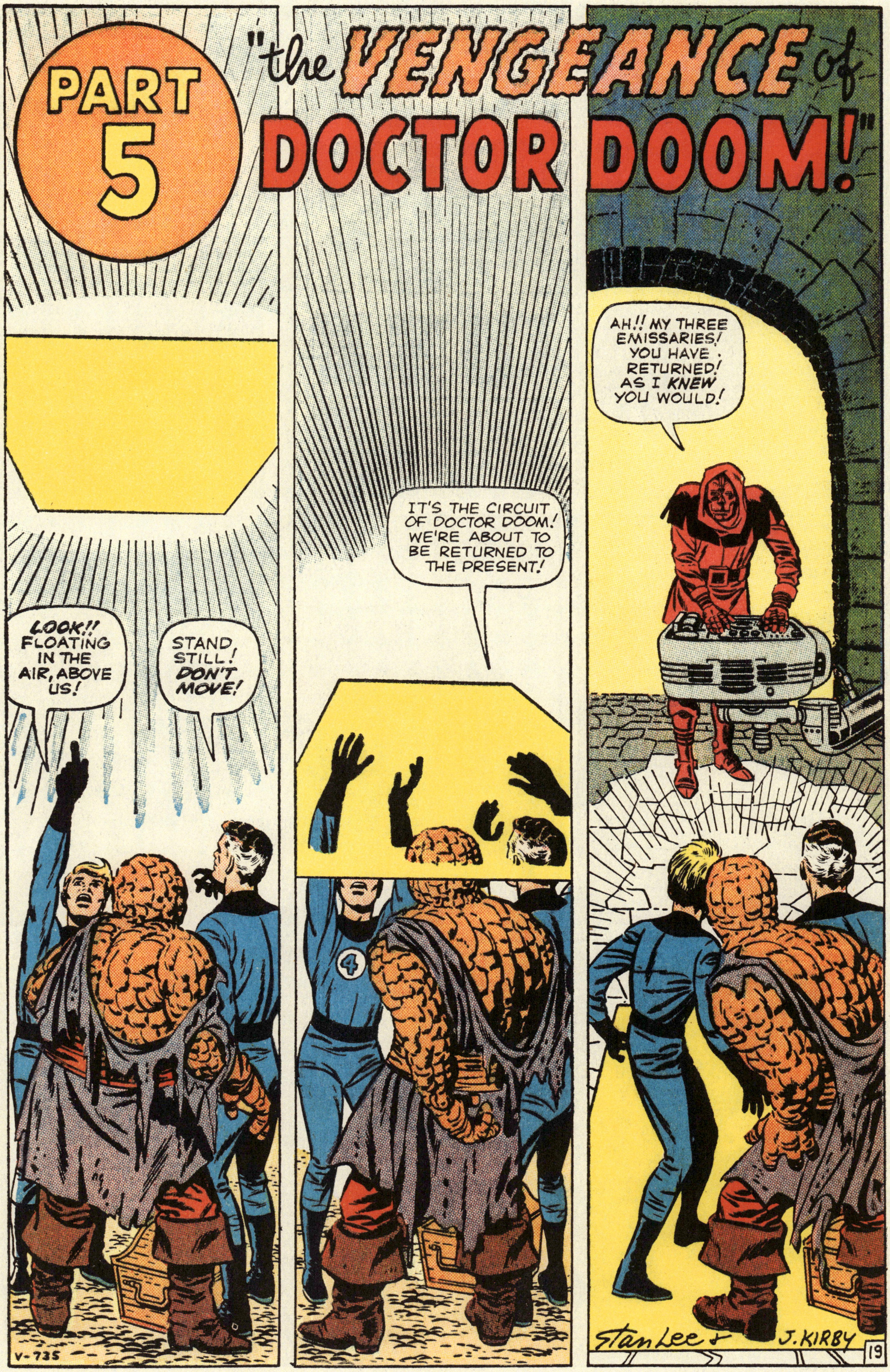

PART 5
"the VENGEANCE of DOCTOR DOOM!"
LOOK!! FLOATING IN THE AIR, ABOVE US!
STAND STILL! DON'T MOVE!
IT'S THE CIRCUIT OF DOCTOR DOOM! WE'RE ABOUT TO BE RETURNED TO THE PRESENT!
AH!! MY THREE EMISSARIES! YOU HAVE RETURNED! AS I KNEW YOU WOULD!
Stan Lee & J. KIRBY
V-735
19

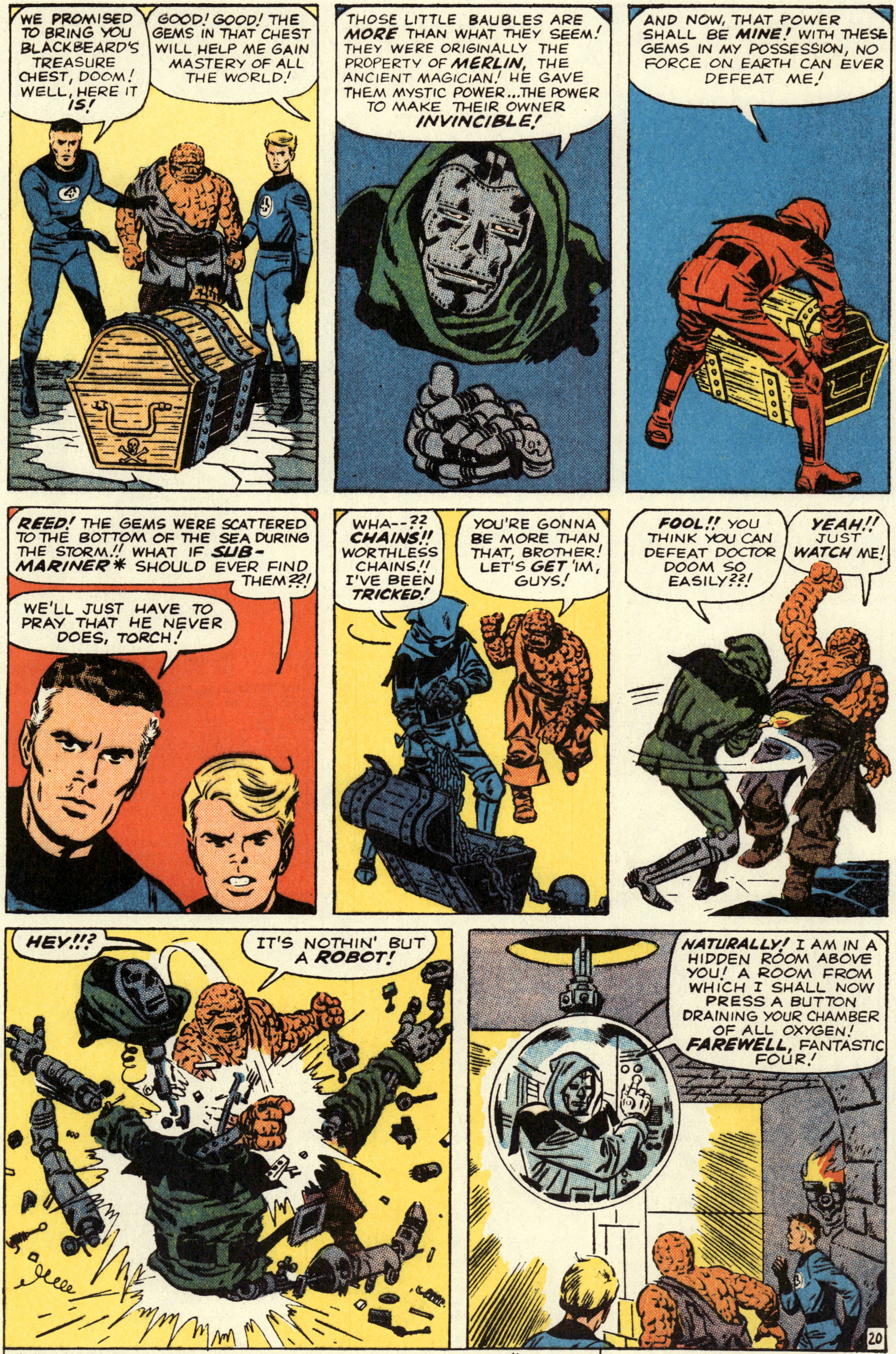

* "SUB-MARINER"!.. SEE FANTASTIC FOUR, ISSUE #4, MAY

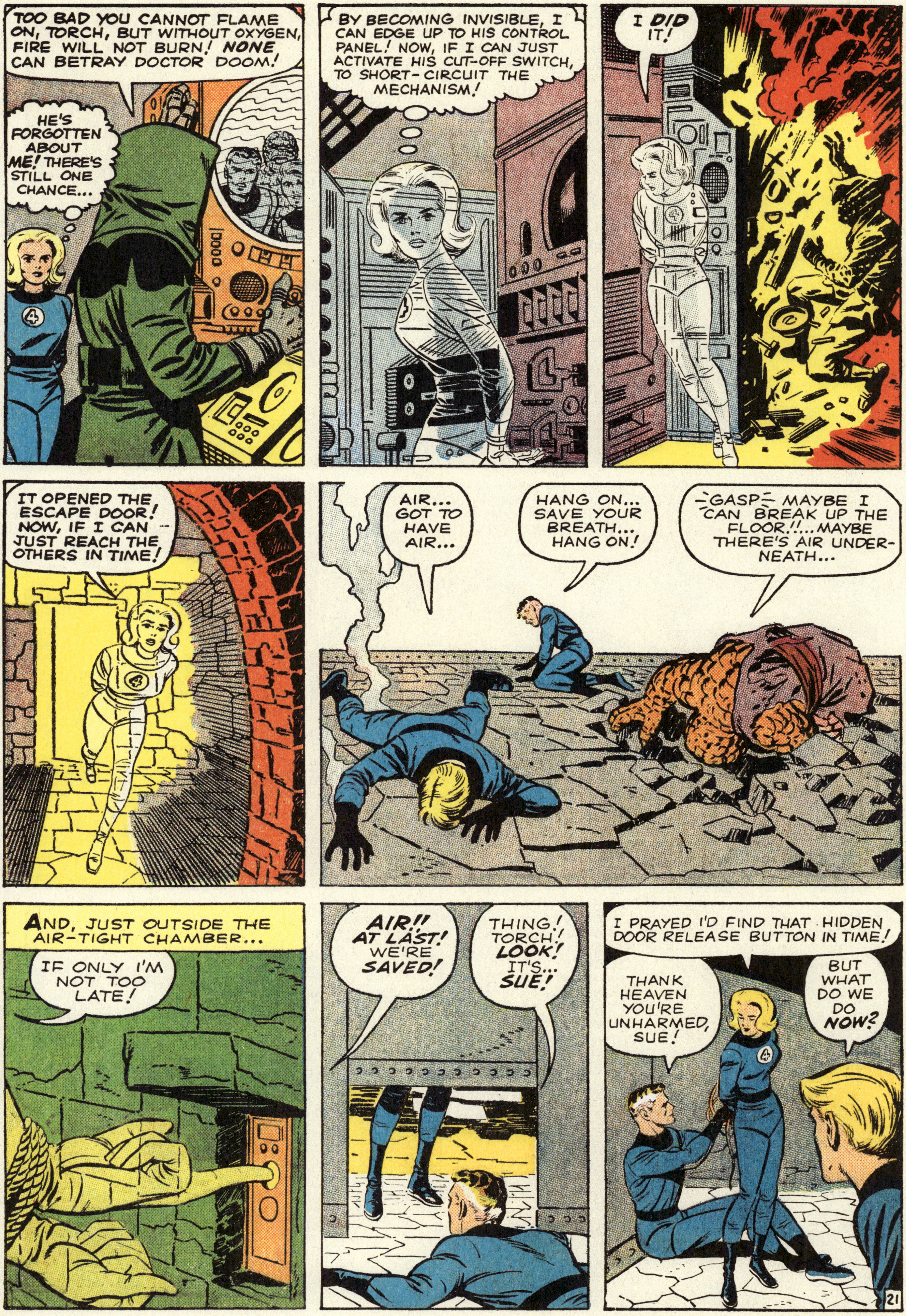
TOO BAD YOU CANNOT FLAME ON, TORCH, BUT WITHOUT OXYGEN, FIRE WILL NOT BURN! NONE CAN BETRAY DOCTOR DOOM!
HE'S FORGOTTEN ABOUT ME! THERE'S STILL ONE CHANCE...
BY BECOMING INVISIBLE, I CAN EDGE UP TO HIS CONTROL PANEL! NOW, IF I CAN JUST ACTIVATE HIS CUT-OFF SWITCH, TO SHORT-CIRCUIT THE MECHANISM!
I DID IT!
IT OPENED THE ESCAPE DOOR! NOW, IF I CAN JUST REACH THE OTHERS IN TIME!
AIR... GOT TO HAVE AIR...
HANG ON... SAVE YOUR BREATH... HANG ON!
-GASP- MAYBE I CAN BREAK UP THE FLOOR!!... MAYBE THERE'S AIR UNDERNEATH...
AND, JUST OUTSIDE THE AIR-TIGHT CHAMBER...
IF ONLY I'M NOT TOO LATE!
AIR!! AT LAST! WE'RE SAVED!
THING! TORCH! LOOK! IT'S... SUE!
I PRAYED I'D FIND THAT HIDDEN DOOR RELEASE BUTTON IN TIME!
THANK HEAVEN YOU'RE UNHARMED, SUE!
BUT WHAT DO WE DO NOW?
21

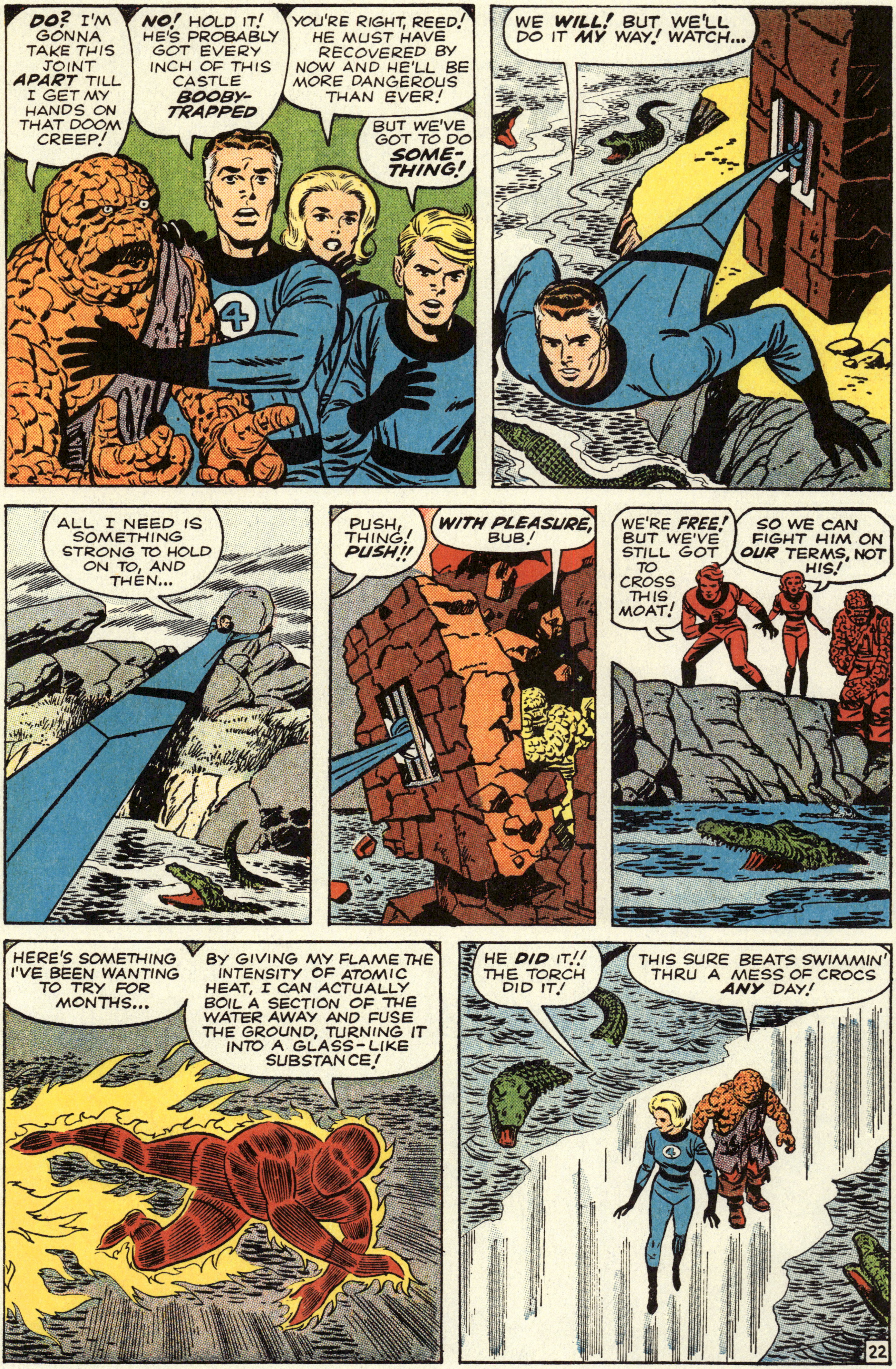
DO? I'M GONNA TAKE THIS JOINT APART TILL I GET MY HANDS ON THAT DOOM CREEP!
NO! HOLD IT! HE'S PROBABLY GOT EVERY INCH OF THIS CASTLE BOOBY-TRAPPED
YOU'RE RIGHT, REED! HE MUST HAVE RECOVERED BY NOW AND HE'LL BE MORE DANGEROUS THAN EVER!
BUT WE'VE GOT TO DO SOME-THING!
WE WILL! BUT WE'LL DO IT MY WAY! WATCH...
ALL I NEED IS SOMETHING STRONG TO HOLD ON TO, AND THEN...
PUSH, THING! PUSH!!
WITH PLEASURE, BUB!
WE'RE FREE! BUT WE'VE STILL GOT TO CROSS THIS MOAT!
SO WE CAN FIGHT HIM ON OUR TERMS, NOT HIS!
HERE'S SOMETHING I'VE BEEN WANTING TO TRY FOR MONTHS...
BY GIVING MY FLAME THE INTENSITY OF ATOMIC HEAT, I CAN ACTUALLY BOIL A SECTION OF THE WATER AWAY AND FUSE THE GROUND, TURNING IT INTO A GLASS-LIKE SUBSTANCE!
HE DID IT!! THE TORCH DID IT!
THIS SURE BEATS SWIMMIN' THRU A MESS OF CROCS ANY DAY!
22

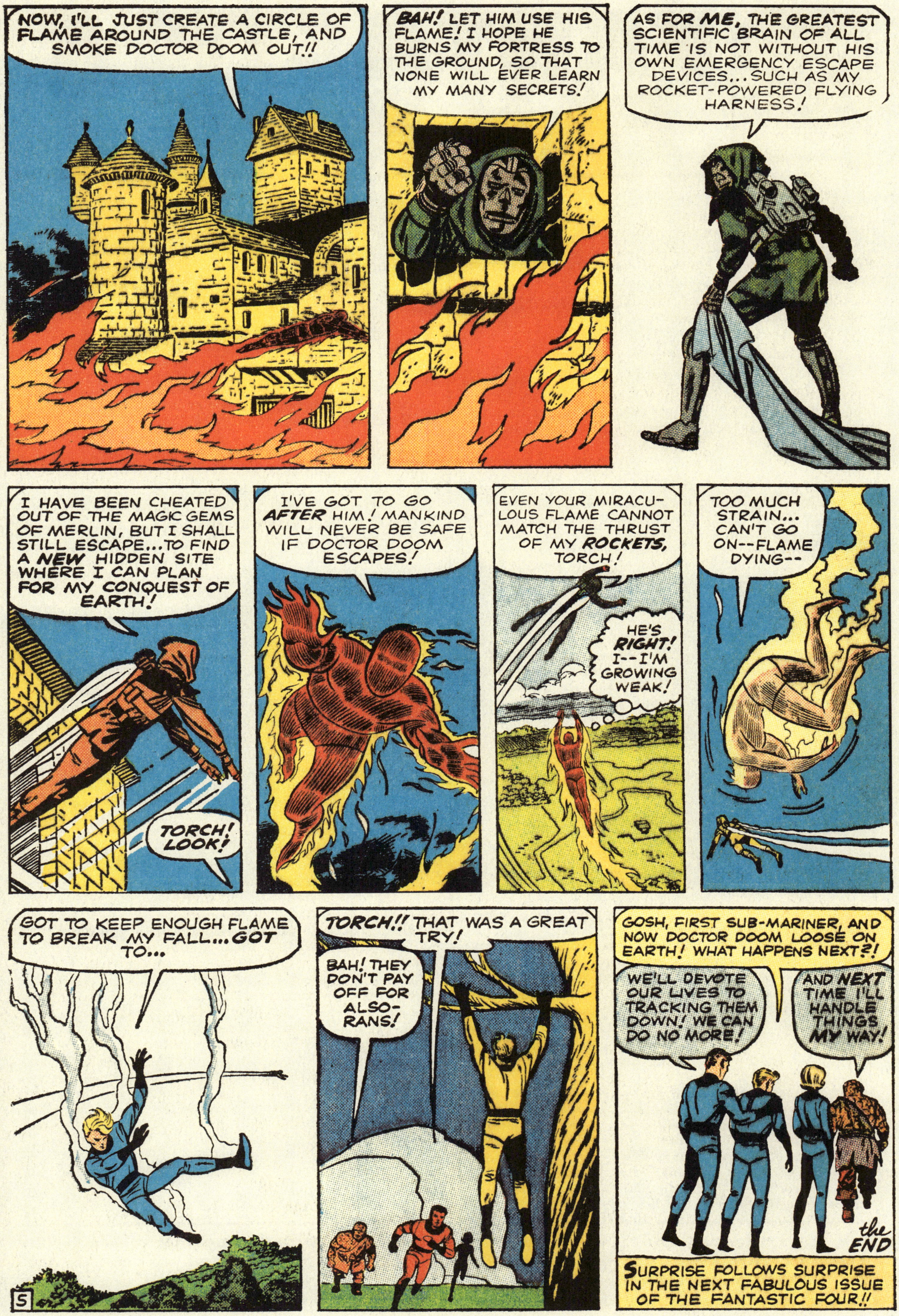

NOW, I'LL JUST CREATE A CIRCLE OF FLAME AROUND THE CASTLE, AND SMOKE DOCTOR DOOM OUT!!
BAH! LET HIM USE HIS FLAME! I HOPE HE BURNS MY FORTRESS TO THE GROUND, SO THAT NONE WILL EVER LEARN MY MANY SECRETS!
AS FOR ME, THE GREATEST SCIENTIFIC BRAIN OF ALL TIME IS NOT WITHOUT HIS OWN EMERGENCY ESCAPE DEVICES... SUCH AS MY ROCKET-POWERED FLYING HARNESS!
I HAVE BEEN CHEATED OUT OF THE MAGIC GEMS OF MERLIN, BUT I SHALL STILL ESCAPE... TO FIND A NEW HIDDEN SITE WHERE I CAN PLAN FOR MY CONQUEST OF EARTH!
TORCH! LOOK!
I'VE GOT TO GO AFTER HIM! MANKIND WILL NEVER BE SAFE IF DOCTOR DOOM ESCAPES!
EVEN YOUR MIRACULOUS FLAME CANNOT MATCH THE THRUST OF MY ROCKETS, TORCH!
HE'S RIGHT! I--I'M GROWING WEAK!
TOO MUCH STRAIN... CAN'T GO ON--FLAME DYING--
GOT TO KEEP ENOUGH FLAME TO BREAK MY FALL... GOT TO...
5
TORCH!! THAT WAS A GREAT TRY!
BAH! THEY DON'T PAY OFF FOR ALSO-RANS!
GOSH, FIRST SUB-MARINER, AND NOW DOCTOR DOOM LOOSE ON EARTH! WHAT HAPPENS NEXT?!
WE'LL DEVOTE OUR LIVES TO TRACKING THEM DOWN! WE CAN DO NO MORE!
AND NEXT TIME I'LL HANDLE THINGS MY WAY!
the END
SURPRISE FOLLOWS SURPRISE IN THE NEXT FABULOUS ISSUE OF THE FANTASTIC FOUR!!

Address YOUR letters to:
THE EDITOR
FANTASTIC FOUR
THIRD FLOOR
655 MADISON AVE.
NEW YORK 21, N. Y.

FANTASTIC FAN PAGE 4

DEAR EDITOR:
. . . FF #3 was excellent! The feud angle made it all the better though, particularly the ending. The continuity in FF is all that could possibly be asked. I've just subscribed to FF for two years – I hope it runs much much longer than that.

Roy Thomas
Sullivan, Mo.

So do we, Roy, so de we!

DEAR EDITOR:
. . . Bill Sarill states that the Thing ought to revert to human form at will. Why? The Thing's inability to look human is unique and without it the FF would be just a league of super-heroes. Instead of the name "Mr. Fantastic" how about "Mr. Elastic"?

Mike Randall
Atchison, Kansas

Thanks, Mike. Now let's get some more opinions.

DEAR EDITOR:
. . . Why does everybody know who their human identities are? Shouldn't they be kept secret?

Rick McGuire
Parsons, Kansas

Maybe so, Rick, but how do you keep a flaming teenager, a four-story skyscraper hideout with a built-in rocket launcher, etc. a secret? Besides, remember us saying in an earlier issue that we wanted our stories to be different, and perhaps a bit more logical?

DEAR EDITOR:
The FF is fantastic, wonderful, and amazing! But how about more action with Invisible Girl?

Scotty Smith
Anchorage, Alaska

How do you MEAN that, bub? Anyhow, we'll have a talk with Sue and tell her to ham it up a bit more, okay? That is, if we can FIND her!

DEAR EDITOR:
I have just read "The Menace of the Miracle Man" and it was terrific. But, when I turned to your letters page, I was sorrow stricken. This insult was entirely uncalled for. The only reason fans write is because they feel they have become personal friends with the editors. I will continue to read your mag, but I won't enjoy it as much as previously.

William J. Marcolongo
Philadelphia, Pa.

Aw, Bill, don't be mad! The only reason we mention that we can't answer letters personally is so that you WON'T be offended if you receive no letter. Surely you can understand that we don't have time to answer dozens of letters daily and still edit magazines! Of course, we could always have some office boy answer them and sign our name, but we don't believe in kidding the reader. Dig?

DEAR EDITOR:
While the third issue of FF was the best yet, I think your covers are too crowded. Also, I'd like to read longer letters on the Fan Pg. And keep your sense of humor bottled up, too. And please, no more monsters. Now here's what I do like: The new costumes, the skyscraper hideout, the Fantasticar. Also, the rivalry between characters is excellent, as is the fact that no member has a secret identity. The Human Torch is your strongest character – so original. And I'd like a new name for Mr. Fantastic.

Roger Mann
Minneapolis, Minn.

No comment yet, pal. We're still trying to decide if you're for us or agin' us!

DEAR EDITOR:
How about having a 25¢ comic of the FF? It's great!

Harold McIntosh
Marblehead, Mass.

Can't do it yet, Hal, but tell you what – if you wanna pay 25¢ for the mag now, be our guest. The dealers will love you!

DEAR EDITOR:
Why has the thing four fingers instead of five? It's a terrific mag and gets better each issue. My friends and I have a FF Fan Club.

Cruz Jiminez
Ft. Riley, Kansas

Lots of readers have asked about the Thing's fingers. What bugs US is: if you don't question a man becoming a monster, a boy turning into flame, a human body stretching at will, then WHY does everyone object to one itsy-bitsy missing finger? Anyway, by way of explanation, we'll take the easy way out and blame it on the cosmic rays! And, good luck with your club, Cruz. Where do we apply?

DEAR EDITOR:
. . . The FF is interesting and different than any other comic mag. But I'd like to request that the Thing be able to become human at will.

William Frazier
Mt. Sterling, Ky.

YOU'D like to request it? What do you think the THING would like? Well, mebbe some day . . .

DEAR EDITOR:
You boast on your cover "The Greatest Comic Magazine in the World." Good for you. And the way you answer some of those wiseacres does my heart good. I've just about HAD it with nice, polite editors making excuses for goody-goody comic heroes! I like your unusual and true-to-life personal conflicts among the four – hope you retain that realism. And I like the name Mr. Fantastic. Glad you didn't call him Stretch-O, Elastic Man, Capt. Rubber, or some such junk. I like the Thing, the full-length stories, etc. BUT, on the cover of FF #3 the Torch had two left hands!

Ronn Foss
Suisun, Calif.

But he DID have five fingers on each, huh Ronn?

Well, that's it for now. We're learning a lot from your letters. We've learned that you do like the name "MR. FANTASTIC" and that you don't like it. You do like the Thing and you don't like him. Well, we can't please everyone, but we're sure gonna try. Keep your letters coming, don't get too angry at us, and always face front!

NOW ON SALE!
APPROVED BY THE COMICS CODE AUTHORITY
12¢
THE INCREDIBLE HULK
MC
1 MAY
THE STRANGEST MAN OF ALL TIME!!
IS HE MAN OR MONSTER
OR...
IS HE BOTH
FANTASY AS YOU LIKE IT!
NEED WE SAY MORE?

IND.
THE WORLD'S GREATEST COMIC MAGAZINE!
APPROVED BY THE COMICS CODE AUTHORITY
12¢
THE Fantastic Four
MC
6 SEPT.
HAVE THE FANTASTIC FOUR AT LAST MET THEIR MATCH WHEN MIGHTY SUB-MARINER AND EVIL DOCTOR DOOM TEAM UP?? DON'T MISS "the DIABOLICAL DUO JOIN FORCES!"
THE TIME HAS COME, SUB-MARINER! DESTROY THE FANTASTIC FOUR!
NO MATTER WHAT POWERS YOU BOTH HAVE, WE SHALL DEFEAT YOU! THE FANTASTIC FOUR SWEAR IT!

THE FANTASTIC FOUR is published by CANAM PUBLISHERS SALES CORP. OFFICE OF PUBLICATION: 655 MADISON AVENUE, NEW YORK, N.Y. Published monthly. Copyright 1962 by CANAM PUBLISHERS SALES CORP., 655 Madison Avenue, New York, N. Y. Vol. 1 No. 6, SEPT. 1962 issue. Price 12c per copy. Subscription rate $1.75 for 12 issues including postage. No similarity between any of the names, characters, persons, and/or institutions appearing in this magazine with those of any living or dead person or institution is intended, and any such similarity which may exist is purely coincidental. Printed in the U.S.A. by The Eastern Color Printing Co., Waterbury 20, Conn.

THE FANTASTIC FOUR in
by... Stan Lee + J. KIRBY
"CAPTIVES of the DEADLY DUO!"
IT'S THE HUMAN TORCH! HEADING FOR THE FANTASTIC FOUR'S SKYSCRAPER HEADQUARTERS !!!
PART 1
AYERS
THE TORCH!! A LIVING LEGEND! --AND I THOUGHT I'D NEVER SEE HIM WITH MY OWN EYES!
WE CAN'T BE CERTAIN... NOT FROM THIS DISTANCE! IT MAY JUST BE SOME NATURAL PHENOMENON!
I'VE SEEN THAT "NATURAL PHENOMENON" IN ACTION BEFORE -- AND HIS THREE PARTNERS, TOO!
Y-835
1

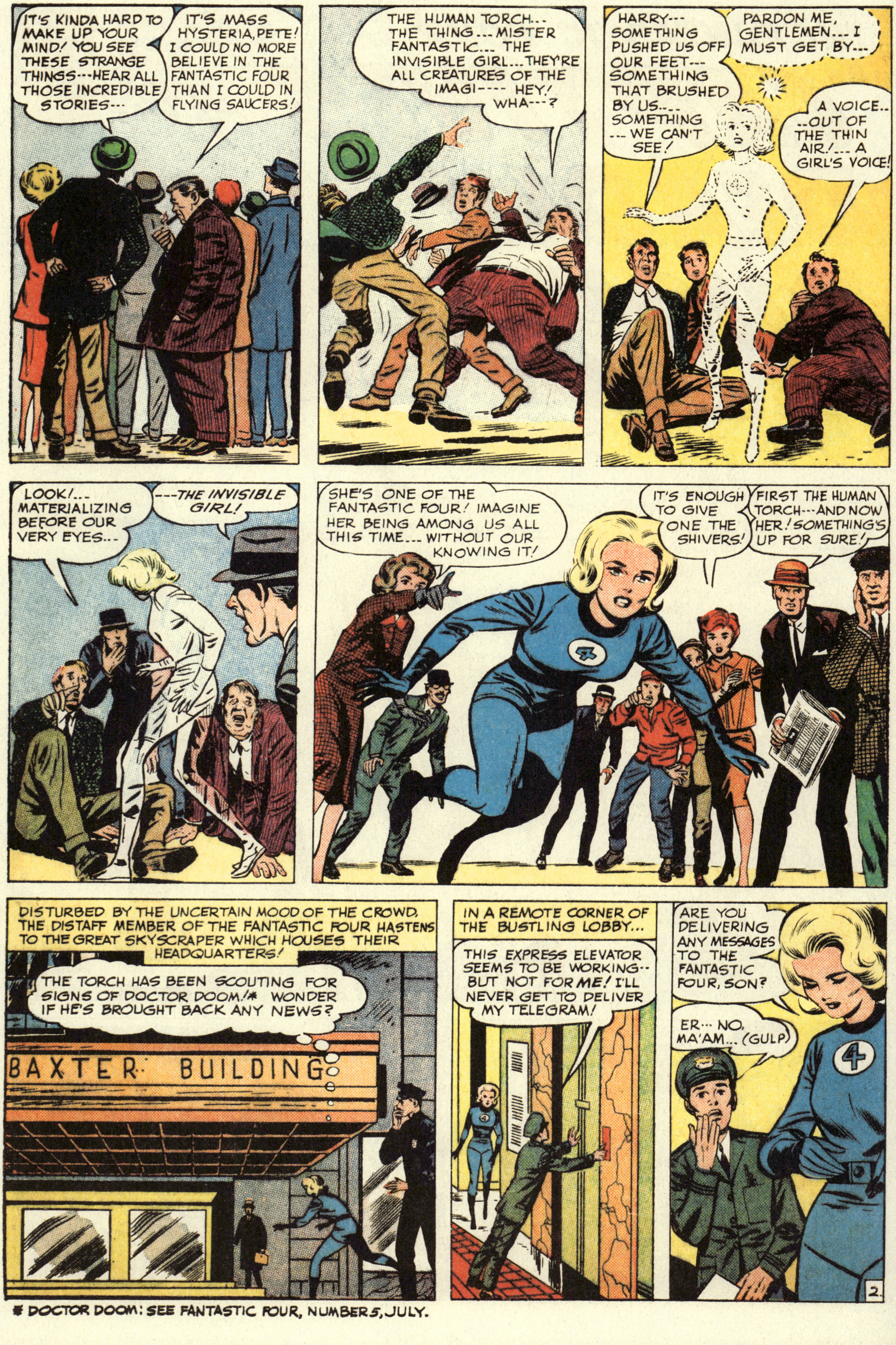

IT'S KINDA HARD TO MAKE UP YOUR MIND! YOU SEE THESE STRANGE THINGS---HEAR ALL THOSE INCREDIBLE STORIES---
IT'S MASS HYSTERIA, PETE! I COULD NO MORE BELIEVE IN THE FANTASTIC FOUR THAN I COULD IN FLYING SAUCERS!
THE HUMAN TORCH... THE THING... MISTER FANTASTIC... THE INVISIBLE GIRL... THEY'RE ALL CREATURES OF THE IMAGI---- HEY! WHA---?
HARRY--- SOMETHING PUSHED US OFF OUR FEET--- SOMETHING THAT BRUSHED BY US--- SOMETHING --- WE CAN'T SEE!
PARDON ME, GENTLEMEN... I MUST GET BY---
A VOICE.. ..OUT OF THE THIN AIR!... A GIRL'S VOICE!
LOOK!... MATERIALIZING BEFORE OUR VERY EYES...
---THE INVISIBLE GIRL!
SHE'S ONE OF THE FANTASTIC FOUR! IMAGINE HER BEING AMONG US ALL THIS TIME... WITHOUT OUR KNOWING IT!
IT'S ENOUGH TO GIVE ONE THE SHIVERS!
FIRST THE HUMAN TORCH---AND NOW HER! SOMETHING'S UP FOR SURE!
DISTURBED BY THE UNCERTAIN MOOD OF THE CROWD, THE DISTAFF MEMBER OF THE FANTASTIC FOUR HASTENS TO THE GREAT SKYSCRAPER WHICH HOUSES THEIR HEADQUARTERS!
THE TORCH HAS BEEN SCOUTING FOR SIGNS OF DOCTOR DOOM!* WONDER IF HE'S BROUGHT BACK ANY NEWS?
BAXTER BUILDING
IN A REMOTE CORNER OF THE BUSTLING LOBBY...
THIS EXPRESS ELEVATOR SEEMS TO BE WORKING-- BUT NOT FOR ME! I'LL NEVER GET TO DELIVER MY TELEGRAM!
ARE YOU DELIVERING ANY MESSAGES TO THE FANTASTIC FOUR, SON?
ER... NO, MA'AM... (GULP)
2
* DOCTOR DOOM: SEE FANTASTIC FOUR, NUMBER 5, JULY.

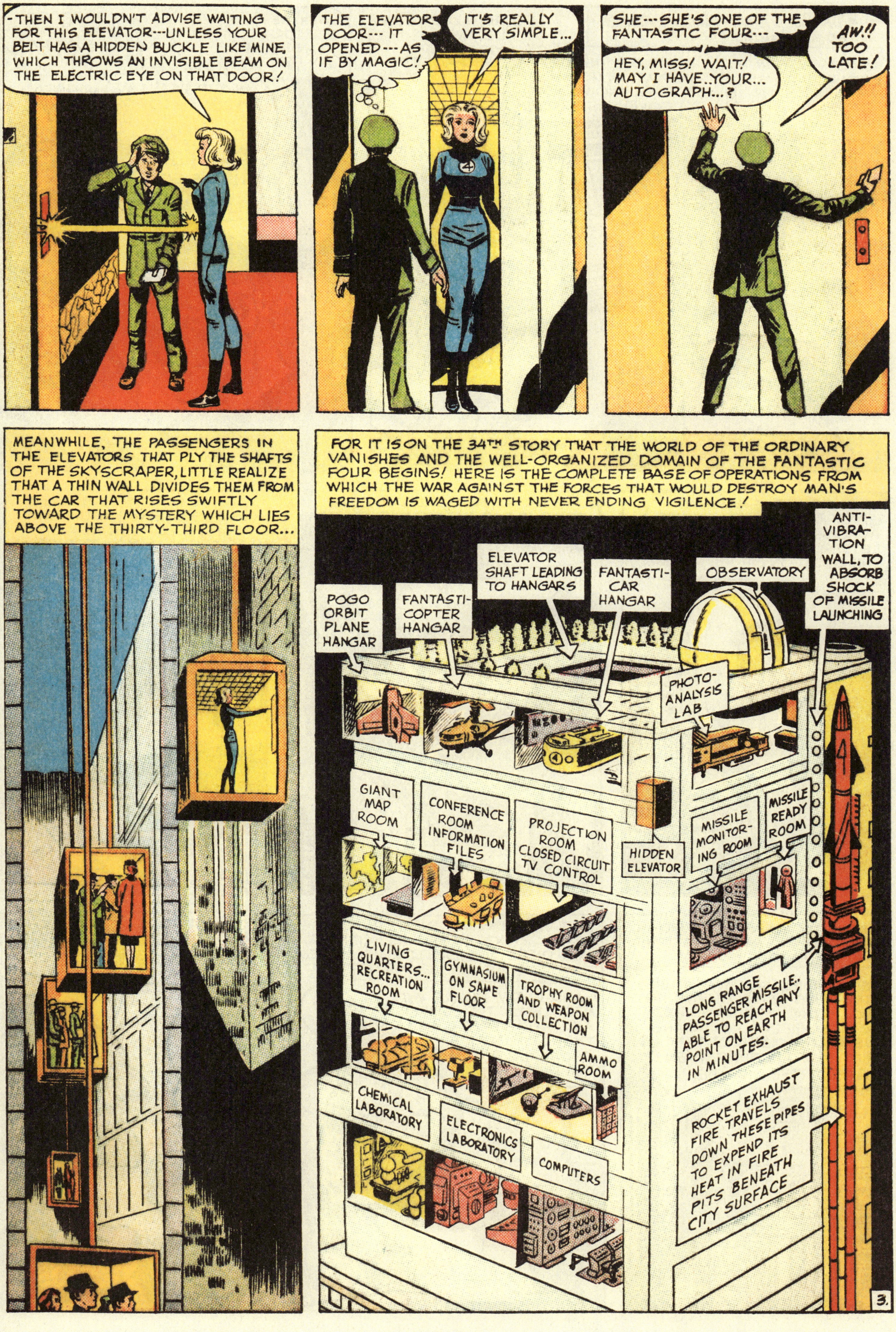

-THEN I WOULDN'T ADVISE WAITING FOR THIS ELEVATOR---UNLESS YOUR BELT HAS A HIDDEN BUCKLE LIKE MINE, WHICH THROWS AN INVISIBLE BEAM ON THE ELECTRIC EYE ON THAT DOOR!
THE ELEVATOR DOOR--- IT OPENED---AS IF BY MAGIC!
IT'S REALLY VERY SIMPLE...
SHE---SHE'S ONE OF THE FANTASTIC FOUR---
HEY, MISS! WAIT! MAY I HAVE..YOUR... AUTOGRAPH...?
AW!! TOO LATE!
MEANWHILE, THE PASSENGERS IN THE ELEVATORS THAT PLY THE SHAFTS OF THE SKYSCRAPER, LITTLE REALIZE THAT A THIN WALL DIVIDES THEM FROM THE CAR THAT RISES SWIFTLY TOWARD THE MYSTERY WHICH LIES ABOVE THE THIRTY-THIRD FLOOR...
FOR IT IS ON THE 34TH STORY THAT THE WORLD OF THE ORDINARY VANISHES AND THE WELL-ORGANIZED DOMAIN OF THE FANTASTIC FOUR BEGINS! HERE IS THE COMPLETE BASE OF OPERATIONS FROM WHICH THE WAR AGAINST THE FORCES THAT WOULD DESTROY MAN'S FREEDOM IS WAGED WITH NEVER ENDING VIGILENCE!
POGO ORBIT PLANE HANGAR
FANTASTI-COPTER HANGAR
ELEVATOR SHAFT LEADING TO HANGARS
FANTASTI-CAR HANGAR
OBSERVATORY
ANTI-VIBRA-TION WALL, TO ABSORB SHOCK OF MISSILE LAUNCHING
PHOTO-ANALYSIS LAB
GIANT MAP ROOM
CONFERENCE ROOM INFORMATION FILES
PROJECTION ROOM CLOSED CIRCUIT TV CONTROL
HIDDEN ELEVATOR
MISSILE MONITOR-ING ROOM
MISSILE READY ROOM
LIVING QUARTERS... RECREATION ROOM
GYMNASIUM ON SAME FLOOR
TROPHY ROOM AND WEAPON COLLECTION
AMMO ROOM
LONG RANGE PASSENGER MISSILE. ABLE TO REACH ANY POINT ON EARTH IN MINUTES.
CHEMICAL LABORATORY
ELECTRONICS LABORATORY
COMPUTERS
ROCKET EXHAUST FIRE TRAVELS DOWN THESE PIPES TO EXPEND ITS HEAT IN FIRE PITS BENEATH CITY SURFACE

THE INVISIBLE GIRL FINALLY EMERGES IN THE RECREATION ROOM...
TORCH! I WAS IN THE CROWD THAT WAS WATCHING YOUR RETURN... HAVE YOU...?
NOTHING TO REPORT ON DOCTOR DOOM! HE SURE KNOWS HOW TO COVER HIS TRACKS!
SURE! WHO COULDN'T HIDE FROM A HOT-HEADED TEEN-AGER? I'LL BET I COULD FIND HIM!
UNTIL WE KNOW WHAT DOCTOR DOOM IS UP TO, NONE OF US CAN FEEL SAFE!
DON'T WORRY SIS! WHATEVER HE DOES-- WE'LL BE READY FOR 'IM!
IN THE MEANTIME WE HAVE A LOT OF MAIL TO CATCH UP WITH! HERE'S ANOTHER LETTER FROM THAT LITTLE BOY WHO'S HOSPITALIZED...
IN FACT HE'S AT HARMON GENERAL HOSPITAL, RIGHT ACROSS THE STREET! THIS LETTER GIVES HIS FLOOR AND THE LOCATION OF HIS ROOM! SAY...
...WON'T HE BE TICKLED IF I JUST DROP IN FOR A VISIT, UNEXPECTEDLY! IT'LL SURE GIVE HIM SOMETHING TO TALK ABOUT WITH HIS FELLOW "SHUT-INS!"
WHA--? I-I MUST BE SEEING THINGS! B-BUT NO! IT--IT'S MISTER FANTASTIC... IN PERSON!
I THOUGHT YOU MIGHT LIKE A CHAT, TOMMY!
HAPPILY, THE YOUNGSTER BUBBLES OVER, THROWING MANY QUESTIONS AT HIS FAMOUS GUEST!
WELL--THE REASON MY COSTUME STRETCHES TO ANY LENGTH THAT I DO, IS THAT IT IS WOVEN FROM CHEMICAL FIBERS CONTAINING UNSTABLE MOLECULES THAT SHIFT IN STRUCTURE WHEN I AFFECT THE CHANGE!
BUT THE GENERAL PUBLIC IS MADE UP OF CRITICS AS WELL AS FRIENDS... AND THERE ARE CHALLENGES AS WELL AS QUESTIONS!
"--AND IF THE THING WILL MEET US ON THE CORNER OF ASHBY AND MAIN STREET, WE'LL KNOCK THAT CHIP OFF HIS SHOULDER AND MAKE HIM LIKE IT! SIGNED--"
"...THE YANCY STREET GANG!" I'VE HEARD FROM THOSE MEALY-MOUTHED BRAGGARTS BEFORE! THEY GET THEIR KICKS OUT OF TRYIN' TO RILE ME!
WELL, ARE YOU GONNA ANSWER THEM, THING?
4.

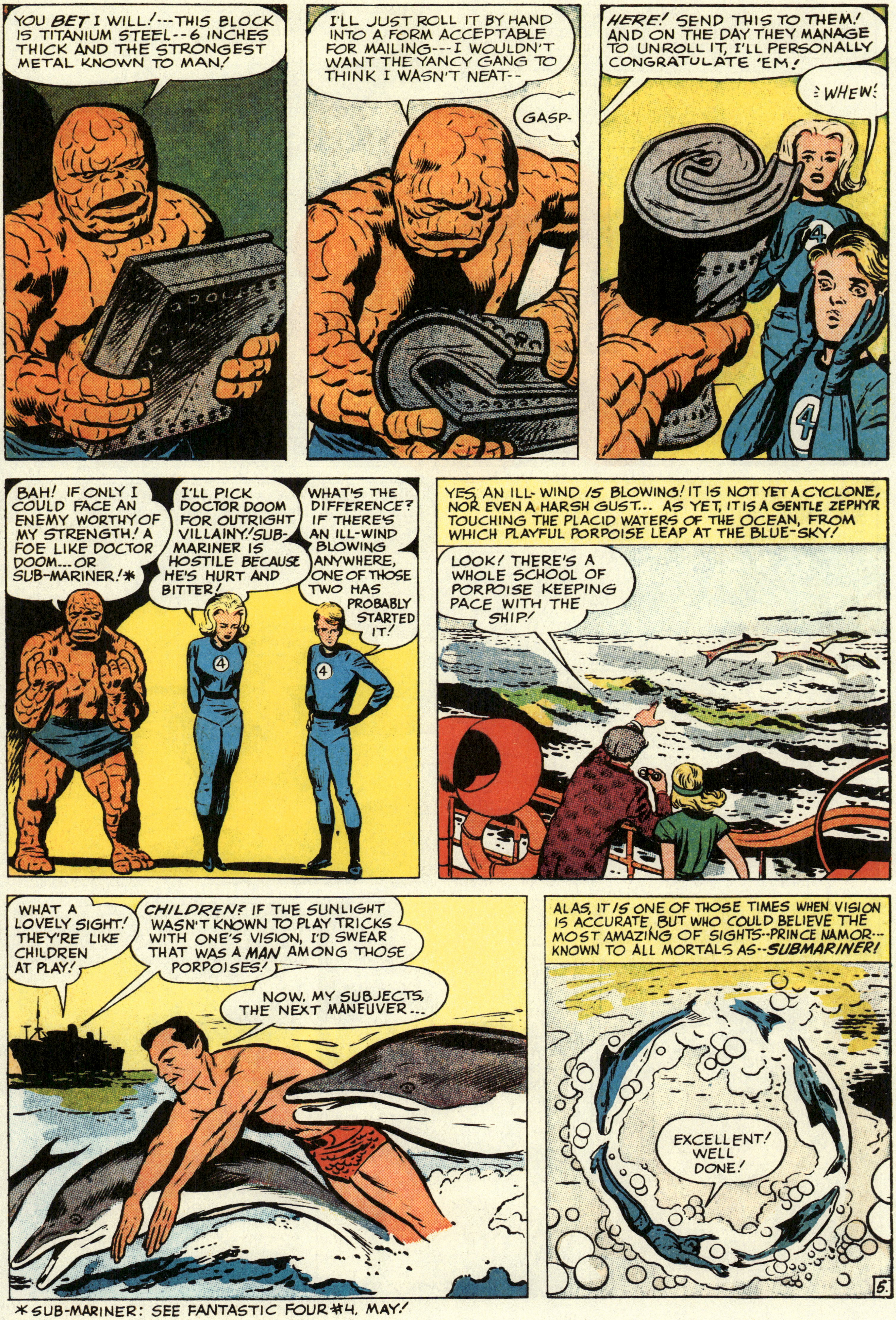

*SUB-MARINER: SEE FANTASTIC FOUR #4, MAY!

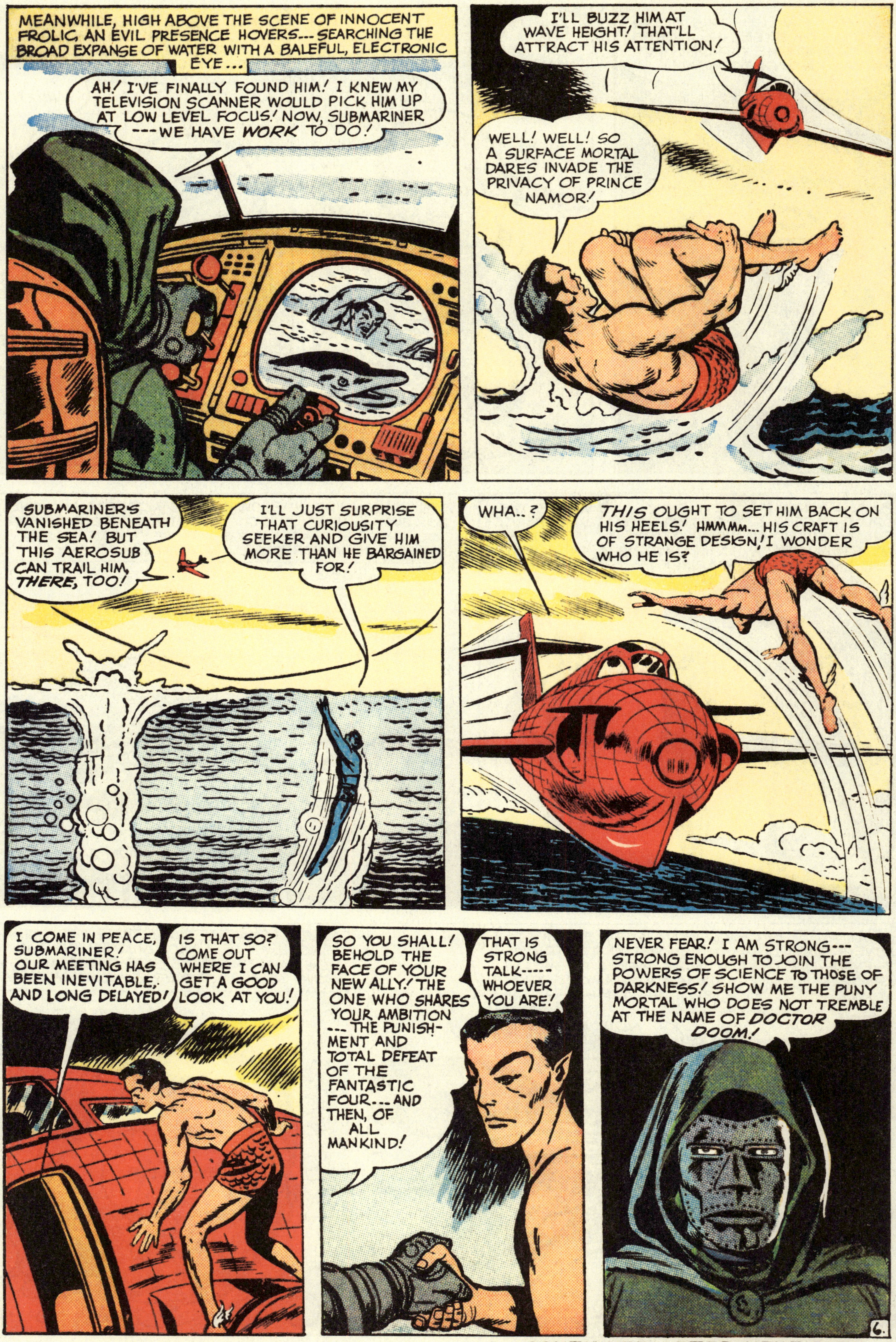

CONTINUED AFTER NEXT PAGE...

FANTASTIC FOUR in
Stan Lee + J. Kirby
"WHEN SUPER-MENACES UNITE"
PART 2
EAGER FOR A PARLEY, DOCTOR DOOM FOLDS BACK THE WINGS OF HIS AERO SUB AND NOSES IT INTO THE DEPTHS OF THE SEA, AS SUBMARINER DARTS THROUGH THE COLD GREEN SHADOWS OF HIS DOMAIN!
V-835
THEY MOVE ACROSS SUBMERGED CANYONS AND VALLEYS, OVER THE RUINS OF A ONCE PROUD CITY WHERE A VANISHED RACE ONCE LIVED IN HARMONY--GHOST VOICES THAT ONCE HAILED SUBMARINER AS PRINCE NAMOR!
SUBMARINER FINALLY LEADS DOCTOR DOOM TO HIS NEW QUARTERS, A LARGE, DOMED VILLA IN A FIELD OF SWAYING UNDERSEA VEGETATION! THE AIRLOCK OPENS TO ADMIT THEM...
7.

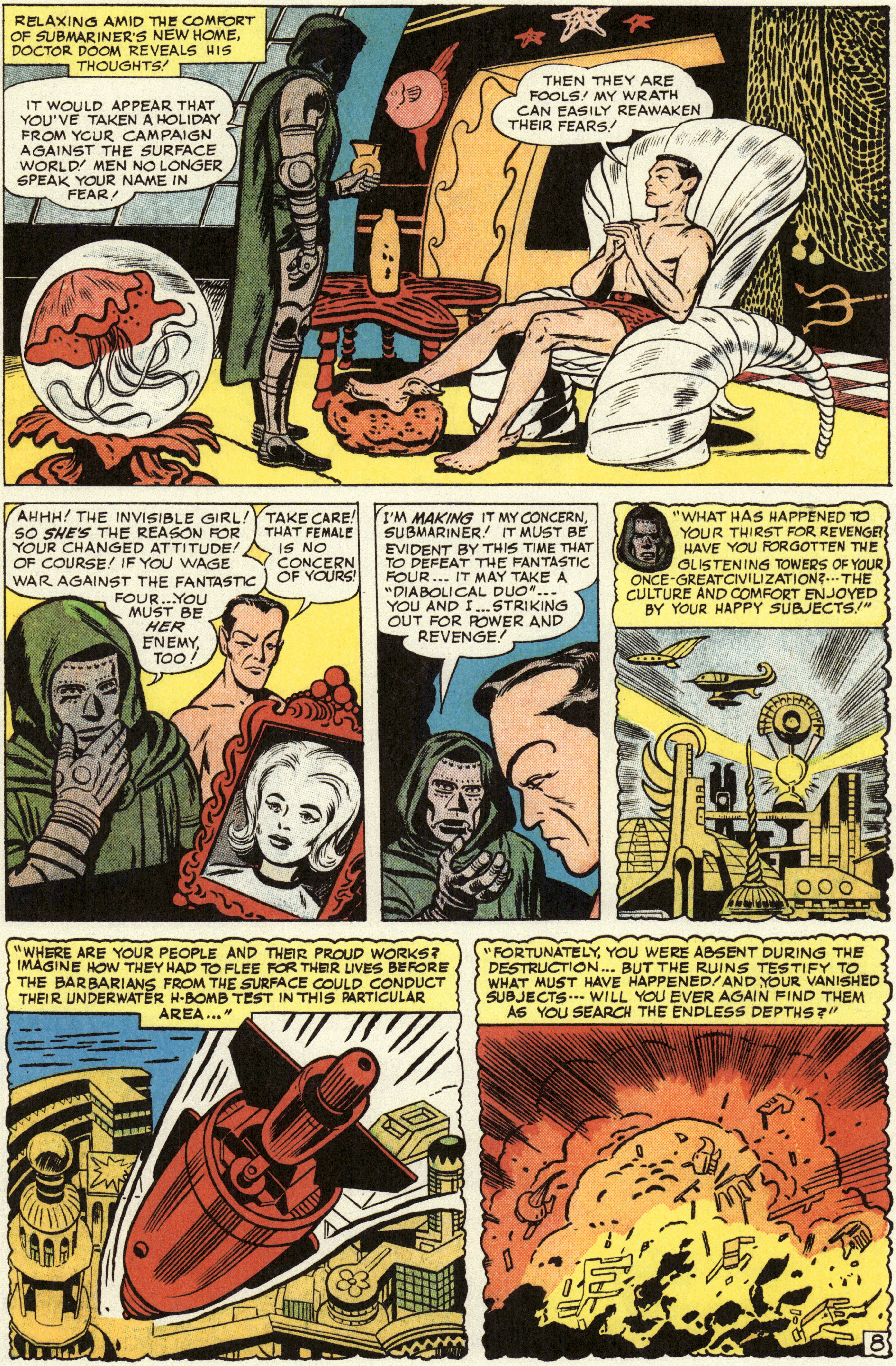

RELAXING AMID THE COMFORT OF SUBMARINER'S NEW HOME, DOCTOR DOOM REVEALS HIS THOUGHTS!
IT WOULD APPEAR THAT YOU'VE TAKEN A HOLIDAY FROM YOUR CAMPAIGN AGAINST THE SURFACE WORLD! MEN NO LONGER SPEAK YOUR NAME IN FEAR!
THEN THEY ARE FOOLS! MY WRATH CAN EASILY REAWAKEN THEIR FEARS!
AHHH! THE INVISIBLE GIRL! SO SHE'S THE REASON FOR YOUR CHANGED ATTITUDE! OF COURSE! IF YOU WAGE WAR AGAINST THE FANTASTIC FOUR...YOU MUST BE HER ENEMY, TOO!
TAKE CARE! THAT FEMALE IS NO CONCERN OF YOURS!
I'M MAKING IT MY CONCERN, SUBMARINER! IT MUST BE EVIDENT BY THIS TIME THAT TO DEFEAT THE FANTASTIC FOUR... IT MAY TAKE A "DIABOLICAL DUO"... YOU AND I... STRIKING OUT FOR POWER AND REVENGE!
"WHAT HAS HAPPENED TO YOUR THIRST FOR REVENGE? HAVE YOU FORGOTTEN THE GLISTENING TOWERS OF YOUR ONCE-GREAT CIVILIZATION?... THE CULTURE AND COMFORT ENJOYED BY YOUR HAPPY SUBJECTS!"
"WHERE ARE YOUR PEOPLE AND THEIR PROUD WORKS? IMAGINE HOW THEY HAD TO FLEE FOR THEIR LIVES BEFORE THE BARBARIANS FROM THE SURFACE COULD CONDUCT THEIR UNDERWATER H-BOMB TEST IN THIS PARTICULAR AREA..."
"FORTUNATELY, YOU WERE ABSENT DURING THE DESTRUCTION... BUT THE RUINS TESTIFY TO WHAT MUST HAVE HAPPENED! AND YOUR VANISHED SUBJECTS... WILL YOU EVER AGAIN FIND THEM AS YOU SEARCH THE ENDLESS DEPTHS?"
8

IMAGINE-- YOUR GREAT AND PROUD PEOPLE--- STRUGGLING FOR THOUSANDS OF YEARS, DEFEATING ALL THE TERRORS OF THE DEEP TO BUILD A CIVILIZATION SUPERB AND BEAUTIFUL... YES, BEAUTIFUL AND GLOWING WITH LIFE--- UNTIL THAT LAST TERRIFYING MOMENT--- WHEN THAT MONSTER OF A BOMB LODGED IN THE MIDST OF THAT BEAUTY---
GONE! ALL THAT GLORIOUS HISTORY GONE IN ONE BRIEF INSTANT!.. REPLACED BY AN UGLY CRATER IN THE OCEAN FLOOR.. LITTERED WITH FUSED MASONRY AND BITTER MEMORIES THAT CRY OUT... REVENGE! REVENGE!!
REVENGE UPON THE SURFACE WORLD WHICH DID THIS IN ITS IGNORANCE! REVENGE UPON HUMANITY'S DEFENDERS! DEATH TO THE FANTASTIC FOUR!
I... I.. I CANNOT HARM THE GIRL! BUT I WILL AID YOU IN DEFEATING THE OTHERS!
VERY WELL THEN! I AGREE! BUT BEFORE I TELL YOU OF MY PLAN, LET ME DEMONSTRATE THE POWER OF MY MAGNETIC BRAINCHILDREN!
I CALL THIS CYLINDER A "GRABBER"! AT A TOUCH OF THIS CONTROL KNOB, I CAN LAUNCH IT IN ANY DIRECTION! OBSERVE!
TRAVELING ON ITS MAGNETIC BEAM, THE GRABBER SWIFTLY, TIRELESSLY COVERS VAST DISTANCES OF THE UNDERSEA KINGDOM...
AS IF IT HAD A WILL OF ITS OWN, THE GRABBER ZEROES IN ON THE HEAD OF A HUGE PAGAN IDOL, MIRED FOR CENTURIES IN THE OOZE OF THE SEA BOTTOM...
THE HUGE MASS BEGINS TO STIR, TREMBLING IN THE PULL OF A TITANIC, UNSEEN FORCE! SLOWLY, IT IS LIFTED FROM THE STRONG GRIP OF ITS AGE OLD PRISON...
THEN, WITH ONE SUDDEN, FRIGHTFUL YANK, THE MAMMOTH IDOL'S HEAD BREAKS FREE AND DRIFTS LIKE A FEATHER ON THE MAGNETIC CURRENT TRAVELLED BY THE GRABBER!

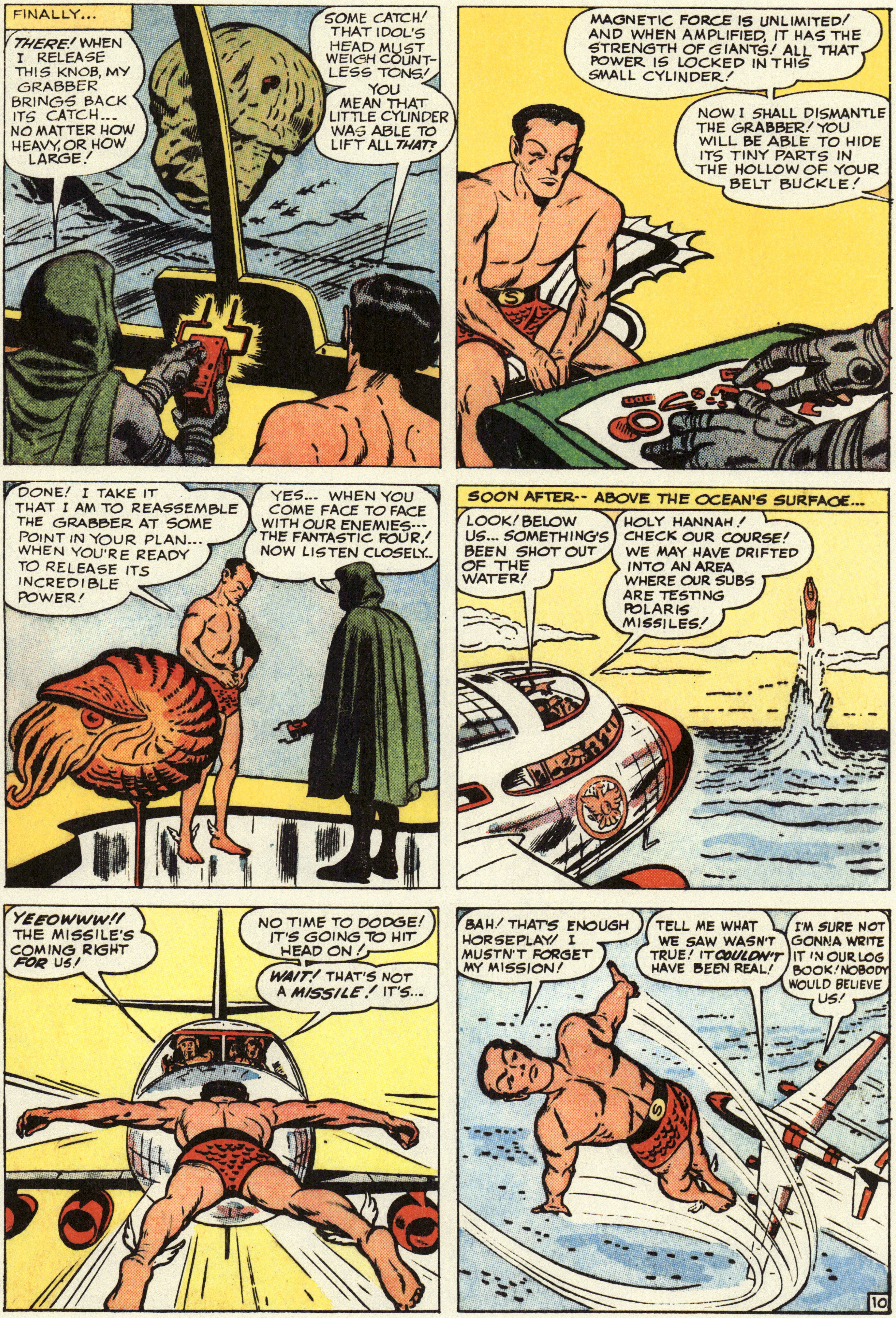
FINALLY...
THERE! WHEN I RELEASE THIS KNOB, MY GRABBER BRINGS BACK ITS CATCH... NO MATTER HOW HEAVY, OR HOW LARGE!
SOME CATCH! THAT IDOL'S HEAD MUST WEIGH COUNTLESS TONS! YOU MEAN THAT LITTLE CYLINDER WAS ABLE TO LIFT ALL THAT?
MAGNETIC FORCE IS UNLIMITED! AND WHEN AMPLIFIED, IT HAS THE STRENGTH OF GIANTS! ALL THAT POWER IS LOCKED IN THIS SMALL CYLINDER!
NOW I SHALL DISMANTLE THE GRABBER! YOU WILL BE ABLE TO HIDE ITS TINY PARTS IN THE HOLLOW OF YOUR BELT BUCKLE!
DONE! I TAKE IT THAT I AM TO REASSEMBLE THE GRABBER AT SOME POINT IN YOUR PLAN... WHEN YOU'RE READY TO RELEASE ITS INCREDIBLE POWER!
YES... WHEN YOU COME FACE TO FACE WITH OUR ENEMIES--- THE FANTASTIC FOUR! NOW LISTEN CLOSELY...
SOON AFTER-- ABOVE THE OCEAN'S SURFACE...
LOOK! BELOW US... SOMETHING'S BEEN SHOT OUT OF THE WATER!
HOLY HANNAH! CHECK OUR COURSE! WE MAY HAVE DRIFTED INTO AN AREA WHERE OUR SUBS ARE TESTING POLARIS MISSILES!
YEEOWWW!! THE MISSILE'S COMING RIGHT FOR US!
NO TIME TO DODGE! IT'S GOING TO HIT HEAD ON!
WAIT! THAT'S NOT A MISSILE! IT'S...
BAH! THAT'S ENOUGH HORSEPLAY! I MUSTN'T FORGET MY MISSION!
TELL ME WHAT WE SAW WASN'T TRUE! IT COULDN'T HAVE BEEN REAL!
I'M SURE NOT GONNA WRITE IT IN OUR LOG BOOK! NOBODY WOULD BELIEVE US!
10

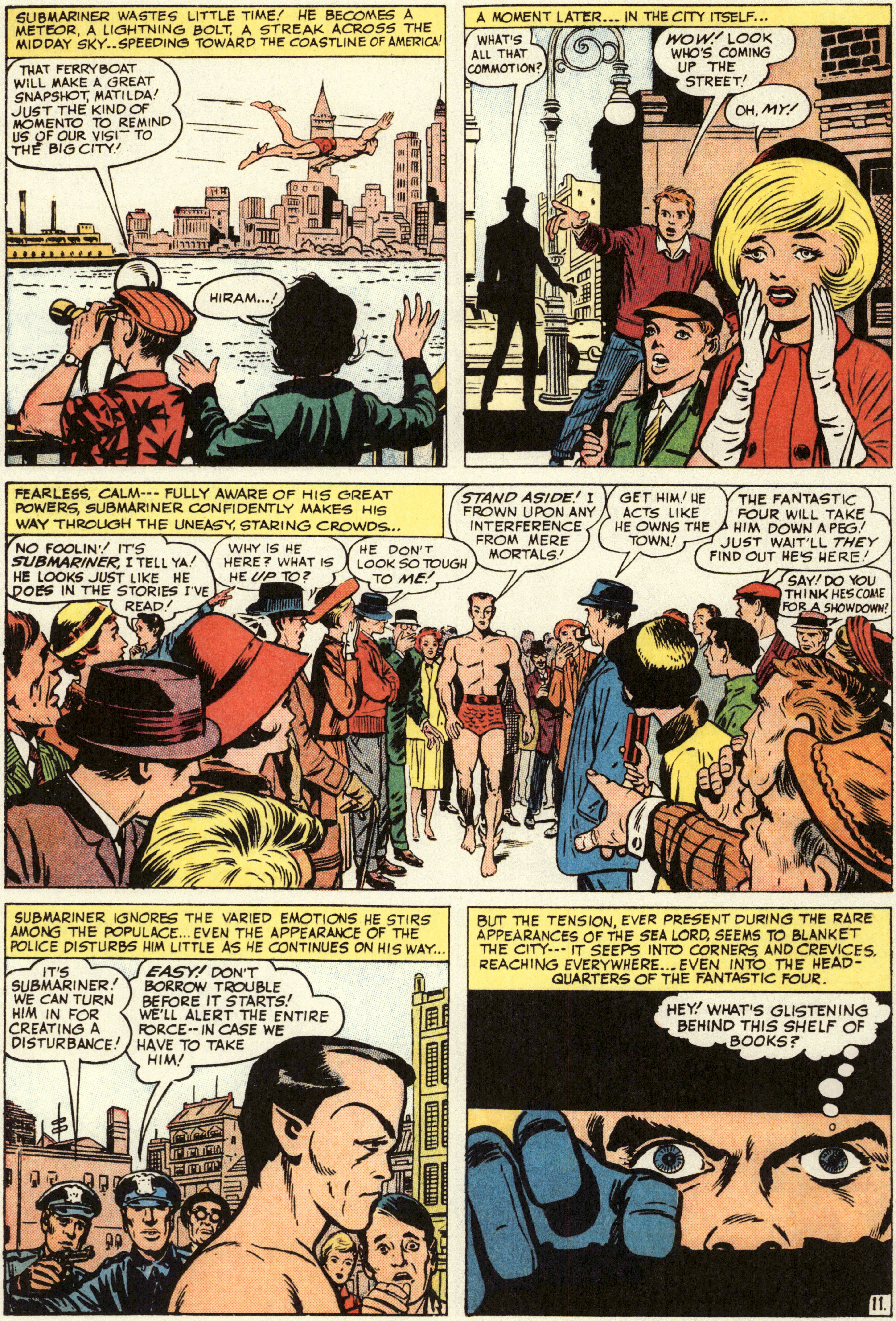

SUBMARINER WASTES LITTLE TIME! HE BECOMES A METEOR, A LIGHTNING BOLT, A STREAK ACROSS THE MIDDAY SKY.. SPEEDING TOWARD THE COASTLINE OF AMERICA!
THAT FERRYBOAT WILL MAKE A GREAT SNAPSHOT, MATILDA! JUST THE KIND OF MOMENTO TO REMIND US OF OUR VISIT TO THE BIG CITY!
HIRAM...!
A MOMENT LATER... IN THE CITY ITSELF...
WHAT'S ALL THAT COMMOTION?
WOW! LOOK WHO'S COMING UP THE STREET!
OH, MY!
FEARLESS, CALM--- FULLY AWARE OF HIS GREAT POWERS, SUBMARINER CONFIDENTLY MAKES HIS WAY THROUGH THE UNEASY, STARING CROWDS...
NO FOOLIN'! IT'S SUBMARINER, I TELL YA! HE LOOKS JUST LIKE HE DOES IN THE STORIES I'VE READ!
WHY IS HE HERE? WHAT IS HE UP TO?
HE DON'T LOOK SO TOUGH TO ME!
STAND ASIDE! I FROWN UPON ANY INTERFERENCE FROM MERE MORTALS!
GET HIM! HE ACTS LIKE HE OWNS THE TOWN!
THE FANTASTIC FOUR WILL TAKE HIM DOWN A PEG! JUST WAIT'LL THEY FIND OUT HE'S HERE!
SAY! DO YOU THINK HE'S COME FOR A SHOWDOWN?
SUBMARINER IGNORES THE VARIED EMOTIONS HE STIRS AMONG THE POPULACE... EVEN THE APPEARANCE OF THE POLICE DISTURBS HIM LITTLE AS HE CONTINUES ON HIS WAY...
IT'S SUBMARINER! WE CAN TURN HIM IN FOR CREATING A DISTURBANCE!
EASY! DON'T BORROW TROUBLE BEFORE IT STARTS! WE'LL ALERT THE ENTIRE FORCE-- IN CASE WE HAVE TO TAKE HIM!
BUT THE TENSION, EVER PRESENT DURING THE RARE APPEARANCES OF THE SEA LORD, SEEMS TO BLANKET THE CITY--- IT SEEPS INTO CORNERS AND CREVICES, REACHING EVERYWHERE... EVEN INTO THE HEAD-QUARTERS OF THE FANTASTIC FOUR.
HEY! WHAT'S GLISTENING BEHIND THIS SHELF OF BOOKS?
11.

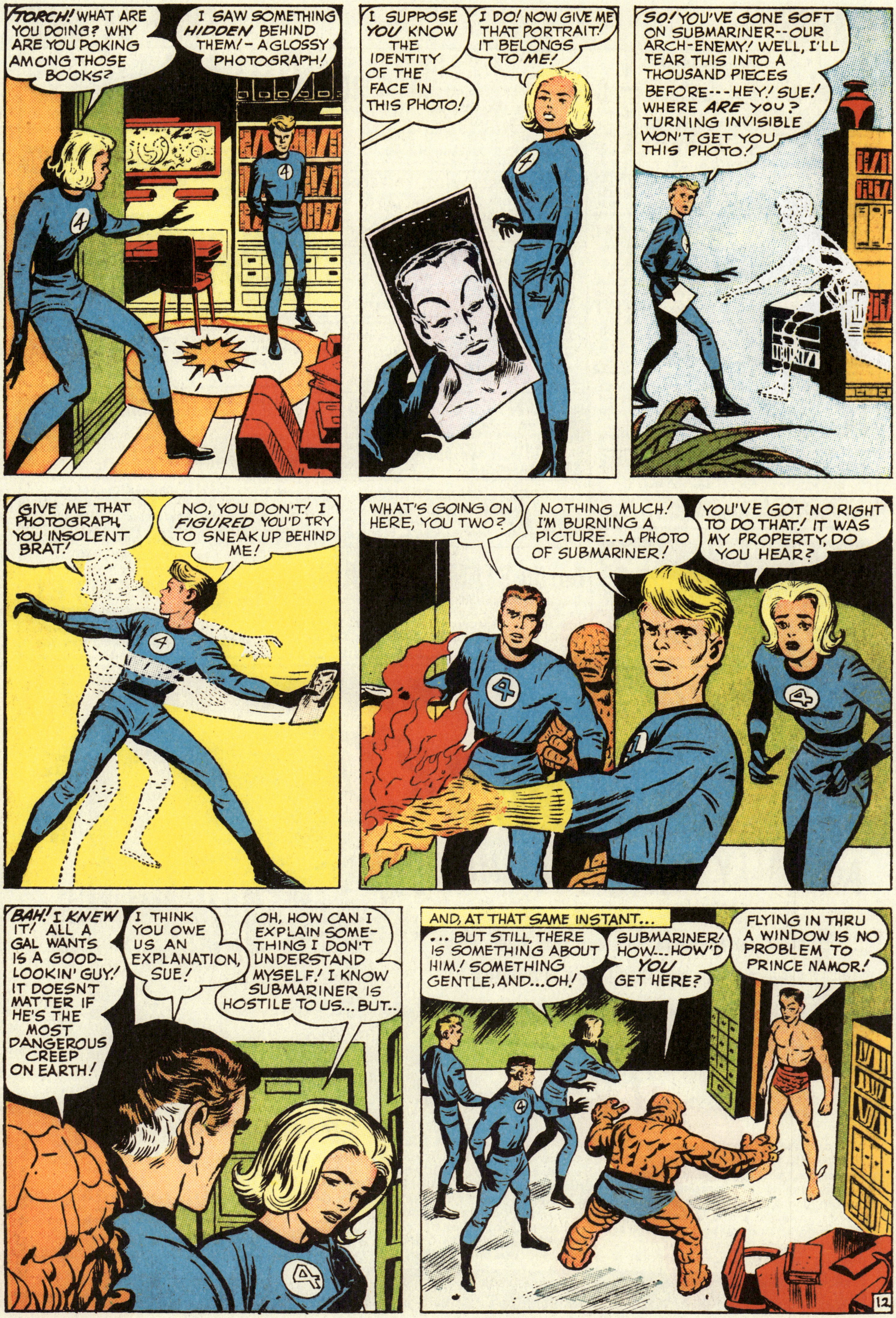
TORCH! WHAT ARE YOU DOING? WHY ARE YOU POKING AMONG THOSE BOOKS?
I SAW SOMETHING HIDDEN BEHIND THEM! - A GLOSSY PHOTOGRAPH!
I SUPPOSE YOU KNOW THE IDENTITY OF THE FACE IN THIS PHOTO!
I DO! NOW GIVE ME THAT PORTRAIT! IT BELONGS TO ME!
SO! YOU'VE GONE SOFT ON SUBMARINER--OUR ARCH-ENEMY! WELL, I'LL TEAR THIS INTO A THOUSAND PIECES BEFORE---HEY! SUE! WHERE ARE YOU? TURNING INVISIBLE WON'T GET YOU THIS PHOTO!
GIVE ME THAT PHOTOGRAPH, YOU INSOLENT BRAT!
NO, YOU DON'T! I FIGURED YOU'D TRY TO SNEAK UP BEHIND ME!
WHAT'S GOING ON HERE, YOU TWO?
NOTHING MUCH! I'M BURNING A PICTURE---A PHOTO OF SUBMARINER!
YOU'VE GOT NO RIGHT TO DO THAT! IT WAS MY PROPERTY, DO YOU HEAR?
BAH! I KNEW IT! ALL A GAL WANTS IS A GOOD-LOOKIN' GUY! IT DOESN'T MATTER IF HE'S THE MOST DANGEROUS CREEP ON EARTH!
I THINK YOU OWE US AN EXPLANATION, SUE!
OH, HOW CAN I EXPLAIN SOMETHING I DON'T UNDERSTAND MYSELF! I KNOW SUBMARINER IS HOSTILE TO US... BUT..
AND, AT THAT SAME INSTANT...
... BUT STILL, THERE IS SOMETHING ABOUT HIM! SOMETHING GENTLE, AND...OH!
SUBMARINER! HOW...HOW'D YOU GET HERE?
FLYING IN THRU A WINDOW IS NO PROBLEM TO PRINCE NAMOR!
12

STAMPS

SHOP BY MAIL

1c APPROVAL HEADQUARTERS 1/2 C
Be wise, earn premiums while buying many stamps at 1/2 price . . . Send for trial approval selection and full details.
FAIRWAY STAMPS, Box 65-M, Garden Grove, Calif.

BETTER U.S. APPROVALS
To introduce our BETTER U.S. APPROVALS we offer 15 of the most wanted U.S. stamps, including a Columbian, Bi-Cents, Army-Navy, Famous American, Airs and other Commems. for only 10¢.
OCEAN STAMPS, BOX 64-D, BROOKLYN 29, N.Y.

1/2 OFF 1/2 OFF 1/2 OFF
Our BARGAIN APPROVALS are sold at 50% off Scott's Catalogue Prices . . .
MAKE US PROVE IT!
CATALINA STAMPS, Box 206, Avalon, Calif.

STAMP COLLECTING OUTFIT
A packet of stamps from all parts of world. A package of stamp hinges; perforation gauge and millimeter scale; watermark detector. Everything ONLY 10c to approval buyers.
LORRAINE W. BROWN, Dept. 10, Marion, Mich.

1c Thousands of beautiful stamps at only 1c each—why pay more when you can get the best for less. Write today for approvals.
PENNY STAMP SERVICE
Orange California

25 DIFF. CHINA 10¢
BIG Value ONLY 10c to Approval Buyers.
EXTRA! We give our regular customers a 56,000 Space Album, after certain purchases.
WEST COAST STAMPS, Box 2187-X, Santa Ana, Calif.

225 STAMPS FOR ONLY 10¢
THIS MAMMOTH VALUE INCLUDES STAMPS WORTH UP TO 25c! ALSO APPROVALS. WRITE TODAY!
MYSTIC STAMP CO Camden 3, New York

SPECIAL! OLD U. S.
Famous Americans, Flags, Presidents, Commemoratives, Airmails 10c with approvals **10¢**
Plus Surprise Packet.
METROPOLITAN STAMPS
Box 312T, Jackson Heights, N. Y.

307 WORLDWIDE DIFFERENT stamps all for only **25¢** with approvals.
NIAGARA STAMP CO. St. Catharines216Ont.

STAMP JUNGLE including Zabu, Kookaburra, Koalabear, Kangaroo, Rhinoceros, **10¢.** Approvals.
CROWN STAMP COMPANY Virgil316Ontario

25 DIFFERENT LARGE American Commemoratives for just **10¢** with approvals.
LINCOLN STAMP CO. St. Catharines116Ont.

UNITED NATIONS
First stamp issue, considered to be one of the world's most attractive sets. Pictures UN Bldg. Emblem etc. Only 10c with approvals.
WALTER WELLES
Box 1246-MG, Church St. Sta., N.Y.C. 8

LOOK — GIANT PHILIPPINE
stamp, plus New Zealand, Cuba and others. Only 5c with U.S. or foreign approvals.
Earl Thompson, 5448 Odell St., St. Louis 9, Mo.

***Terrific* STAMP BARGAIN!**
Israel–Iceland–San Marino–plus triangle set–Plus Anti-gua–Borneo–Virgin–Scouts–Congo–Russia–Plus large stamp book–all 4 offers free. Send 10c for mailing cost.
EMPIRE STAMP CORP., Dept. MC, Toronto, Canada

POEMS WANTED for musical setting and recording. Send poems Free Examination.
AMERICA'S LARGEST SONG STUDIO
FIVE STAR MUSIC MASTERS, 92 BEACON BLDG., BOSTON, MASS.

World's Best Magic Tricks Revealed
BE A MAGICIAN! Learn the secrets of great magicians like Houdini, Thurston, etc. Learn how to do over 200 different tricks with coins, cards, rope, etc. Amaze and mystify your friends. Nothing else to buy. **50¢**
MAGIC TRICKS • P. O. BOX 1225 • NEWARK 1, N. J

1001 THINGS YOU CAN GET FREE 50¢ Gifts • Samples Books • Stamps Etc.
THINGS FREE • P.O. BOX 1225 • NEWARK 1, N. J.

WILL ROGERS AIR! HELICOPTER TRIANGLE!! Plus Monte Carlo Dove Triangle! Stamp printed in Solid Gold! New York Empire State Bldg. airmail, lovely Congo Orchids in full colors, etc., 10c with approvals. Sunny Stamps Service, Apopka 19A Florida.

Fantastic Fish Triangles!! Valuable "Ben Franklin" on CANAL ZONE!! Flaming bi-colored Volcano Triangle!! Lovely Olympics Triangle!! Plus Icy Greenland, Weird Wild Beast issue & others. 10¢ with approvals.
Roseland Stamps, Spring Lake 19, Mich.

Holy Stamp Depicting Christ & Cross!! Plus Triangle Discus Thrower, enormous multi-colored Spanish Diamond issue, wonderful MAP COLLECTION from Timor, Macao & Angola. EXTRA! Brilliant Flag set, etc., only 10c with approvals.
Capital Stamp Co., Ferrysburg 19C, Mich.

POEMS WANTED For musical setting. Send your Poems today for Free Examination. Any subject. Immediate consideration.
CROWN MUSIC CO., 49-MC W. 32 St., New York 1

'SWINGINGEST' WAY TO SAVE!

JUKE BOX BANK

ACTUALLY PLAYS REAL MUSIC

- Full-Color Miniature Juke Box That Really Plays
- Takes Pennies, Nickels, Dimes and Quarters
- Fool-Proof Mechanism—Requires No Batteries
- All-Metal Construction—Built To Last

All For Only $1.98 ppd.

Who said saving money is no fun? Now, with this amazing new JUKE BOX BANK, you'll save every coin you can get your hands on. Your friends and relatives will add to your savings, too. Because *everyone* wants to hear this tiny juke box play over and over again. It's just like a full-size juke box in every detail. You just drop in any size coin, from a penny on up to a quarter. Instantly, a tiny record starts to spin . . . and out comes the music. What's more, it's completely mechanical . . . requires no batteries or electricity. Built of sturdy metal to last for years. Order your JUKE BOX BANK today. It's the "swingingest" new way to save . . . yet costs only $1.98 ppd.

MEDFORD PRODUCTS, Dep' O Box 39, Bethpage N Y

MAIL COUPON TODAY

Medford Products, Dept. MCB
P. O. Box 39
Bethpage, N. Y.

Please rush me ____ JUKE BOX BANKS at $1.98 each, ppd. I enclose $________ cash, check or M.O. I understand that if I am not completely delighted, my money will be refunded.

Name________________
Street________________
City__________ Zone____ State______

FANTASTIC FOUR in
PART 3
"WHEN FRIENDS FALL OUT!"
WAIT! WE'VE GOT TO KEEP OUR TEMPERS! LET HIM SPEAK HIS PIECE!
I WON'T GIVE HIM THE CHANCE! I'LL... I'LL PULVERIZE THAT HUMAN FISH INTO DRY DUST! LET ME AT HIM!
NO! IF SUBMARINER MEANT US HARM, HE WOULDN'T HAVE WALKED IN AMONG US THIS WAY...
THE GIRL IS RIGHT! MY MISSION IS ONE OF PEACE!
Stan Lee + J. KIRBY
V-835
WELL, I DON'T BELIEVE HIM! STAND AWAY FROM HIM, SUE! I'LL SEE TO IT THAT HE DOESN'T ESCAPE US AGAIN!
A CIRCLE OF FLAME!
V-835
NO! NO! YOU CAN'T DO THIS! YOU MUST HEAR HIM OUT! WHY, HE'S NOT EVEN TRYING TO DEFEND HIMSELF!
HE'S TOO ANGRY TO LISTEN TO REASON! YOU'D BEST STAY OUT OF THE WAY! I DO NOT FEAR THE TORCH!

WAIT.. !!
PRINCE NAMOR FEARS NOTHING ON THIS PLANET! LET HIM DO HIS WORST!
WE'LL SEE HOW BRAVE YOU ARE, MISTER BIG TALK! I THINK I'LL SOFTEN UP YOUR STEEL NERVES BEFORE I REALLY GO TO WORK ON YOU!
THE HUMAN TORCH BURNS A CIRCLE OF FIRE INTO THE FLOOR AROUND SUBMARINER! AND WHEN IT'S COMPLETED...
JUST THE KIND OF CHILDISH PRANK I'D EXPECT FROM YOU!
YOU WON'T THINK SO IN ONE SECOND !!
SUDDENLY, THE FLOOR GIVES WAY BENEATH SUBMARINER'S FEET AS THE FLAMING CIRCLE FALLS INTO THE ROOM BELOW!
WELL, YOU CAN SEE I DID NOT FALL THROUGH! YOU FORGOT I HAVE THE POWER TO DEFY GRAVITY!
BUT, UNLIKE YOU, MY POWER DOES NOT FADE, EVEN AS YOUR FLAME BEGINS TO FADE NOW!
AND INDEED, BEFORE THE HUMAN TORCH CAN ACT, HIS WHITE HOT FLAME LOSES ITS CONSISTENCY AND BEGINS TO COOL---UNTIL---
MY FLAME HAS RUN ITS TIME LIMIT! I'M CHANGING BACK TO HUMAN FORM! I'VE FAILED! ...FAILED!
FATE HAS GIVEN YOU A REPRIEVE, SUBMARINER! ...NOW SPEAK... OR GIVE BATTLE!
I'VE COME TO SEEK YOUR TRUST! YOU SEE, MINE IS A LONELY KINGDOM... AND A LASTING FRIENDSHIP MAY PROVE OF MORE VALUE THAN ANY FLEETING TASTE OF REVENGE !!
VERY IMPRESSIVE, SUBMARINER, ONLY I'M NOT INCLINED TO SHAKE YOUR HAND TOO READILY! HOW DO WE KNOW IT'S NOT A PLOT? HOW DO WE KNOW YOU HAVEN'T SET A TRAP?
YEAH! YOU'D BETTER DO SOME FAST CHECKING, PAL! I'LL KEEP AN EYE ON HIM!
OH, PLEASE LISTEN TO HIM! CAN'T YOU SEE HE'S SINCERE?
I'M STILL FOR CHECKING! COME ON, TORCH! WE CAN LOOK IN ON EVERY ROOM BY CLOSED CIRCUIT TELEVISION!
WE CAN FIND OUT SOON ENOUGH IF HE'S SET ANY TRAPS IN HERE!
14.

LOBBY
MISSILE LAUNCH AREA
CONFERENCE ROOM
CHEMISTRY LAB
ELECTRONICS LAB
MAP STUDY
OBSERVATORY
PROJECTION ROOM--- ALL CLEAR!
ROOF LANDING STRIP... RIGHT CORNER--- ALL CLEAR!
I DON'T GET IT! WE'VE SCANNED EVERY CORNER OF OUR BASE OF OPERATIONS WITHOUT FINDING ONE BOOBY TRAP! NOTHING SEEMS AMISS! YET, I CAN'T GET RID OF THE FEELING THAT SUBMARINER'S BEEN UP TO NO GOOD!
LUCKILY THE WORKING DAY IS OVER! THE REST OF THE BUILDING IS EMPTY! WE CAN CHECK THAT OUT, TOO!
WELL, MY SUSPICIOUS FRIEND-- DOES MY PRESENCE HERE PASS YOUR RIGID INSPECTION?
I'M NOT SATISFIED YET, SUBMARINER! STAY WHERE YOU ARE! I'M COMING BACK TO ASK A FEW MORE QUESTIONS!
WELL, YOU'LL JUST HAVE TO WAIT FOR THE TIME BEING! I'M ON A HOLIDAY---AND I'VE DECIDED TO TAKE THIS CHARMING YOUNG LADY ON A TOUR OF THE CITY...
LIBRARY
SUBMARINER'S FLIPPANT MOOD SUDDENLY VANISHES AS A LOUD TREMOR SHAKES THE ENTIRE BUILDING!
CRACK
SLOWLY, SMOOTHLY THE GREAT SKYSCRAPER BEGINS TO RISE FREE OF ITS FOUNDATION... BEGINS TO RISE ABOVE THE NOW-DESERTED STREETS...
THE BUILDING... IT'S RISING INTO THE AIR!
WE'RE GOING HIGHER-- FASTER--
THIS IS YOUR DOING, SUBMARINER! YOU CAN STOP THIS!
I CAN'T, YOU FOOLS! I PLANTED THE TRAP... BUT IT'S BEEN TRIGGERED BY DOCTOR DOOM!
15.

SO LIFE-LIKE . . .
YOU'LL EXPECT IT TO HISS!
GIANT 10-FOOT
INFLATABLE
BOA-CONSTRICTOR
This green and black giant is a full 10-feet long! As thick around as your arm! When you hold it up, it wiggles like a real snake! Put it down and instantly, automatically, it coils itself up! You can even wrap it around your body! And that's not all. Take it with you when you go swimming . . . it will keep you afloat. For sun-bathing, use it coiled up, as a pillow. Makes a great decoration for your room, too! Giant 10-feet-long Boa-Constrictor is made of heavy leak-resistant rubber. Inflates in a jiffy . . . deflates just as quickly for storage. And it costs only $2.98. Rush coupon today!
• Giant Size! 10 feet long! As thick around as your arm!
• Actually coils itself up—automatically!
• Heavy, leak-resistant rubber . . . not cheap plastic!
ONLY
$2.98
MEDFORD PRODUCTS, Dept. MCG-10A
P.O. Box 39
Bethpage, N.Y.
Yes! Rush me my giant-size, 10-foot-long inflatable Boa-Constrictor. Enclosed is $2.98 in .... cash, ... check, ... M.O. I understand that if I am not delighted, my money will be promptly refunded.
Name........
Address........
City........ Zone........ State........
MEDFORD PRODUCTS, Dept. MCG-10A P.O. Box 39, BETHPAGE, N. Y.

$AVE HUNDREDS OF DOLLAR$...
THIS NEW, MAGIC WAY!
SEE HOW IT WORKS:
Put In A Coin
Close The Drawer
Like Magic, It's Gone!
AMAZING CHEST-O BANK
... is more than a bank! It's actually a magic trick that will have your family, friends and neighbors waiting in line to put in their money—just to see how it works. But only you know the secret ... and only you have the key to get out the money and buy the things you've always wanted. What's more, the CHEST-O BANK is a beautiful addition to your room ... because it's an accurate scale model of a $35,000 genuine antique colonial chest-on-chest. And it's made to last ... high-pressure molded of grained cherrywood polystyrene with a steel vault-type back and gleaming nickel-plated key. Best of all, it costs only $1.98 postpaid. And if you don't get back twice that amount within the first 10 days you own it, just send it back and we'll refund every penny of your money. Order your CHEST-O BANK today.
MAIL COUPON TODAY
Medford Products, Dept. MCG-10
P.O. Box 39, Bethpage, N.Y.
Please rush me ______ CHEST-O BANK(S) at $1.98 each, ppd. I am enclosing $______ in cash, check or M.O. (No C.O.D.) I understand that if I am not amazed and delighted, I can return it within 10 days for a full refund.
Name______
Address______
City______ Zone___ State______
ONLY $1.98 ppd.
Size: 6¼" high x 3¼" wide
MEDFORD PRODUCTS, Dept. MCG-10, Box 39, Bethpage, N.Y.

THE FANTASTIC FOUR
in "TRAPPED!"
PART 4
Stan Lee + J. Kirby
WE'RE NOW THOUSANDS OF FEET ABOVE THE CITY, AND GOING HIGHER! AT THIS RATE WE'VE ONLY MINUTES LEFT BEFORE WE REACH THE UPPER ATMOSPHERE!
WHAT HAS DOCTOR DOOM TO DO WITH THIS, SUBMARINER?
THE DOUBLE-CROSSING DOG IS IN A ROCKET PLANE ABOVE, PULLING THIS BUILDING INTO SPACE!
V-835
BUT HOW-? HOW IS HE DOING IT?
THERE IS A CONTROL PANEL IN HIS PLANE ATTRACTING A MAGNETIC "GRABBER" WHICH I PLANTED IN A DARK CORNER OF THE BASEMENT!
THEN OUR ONLY HOPE OF EVER GETTING DOWN IS TO SEIZE CONTROL OF THAT PLANE!
THE AIR'S GETTING MIGHTY THIN! WE'LL PERISH FROM LACK OF OXYGEN BEFORE WE CAN TAKE ANY ACTION!
16

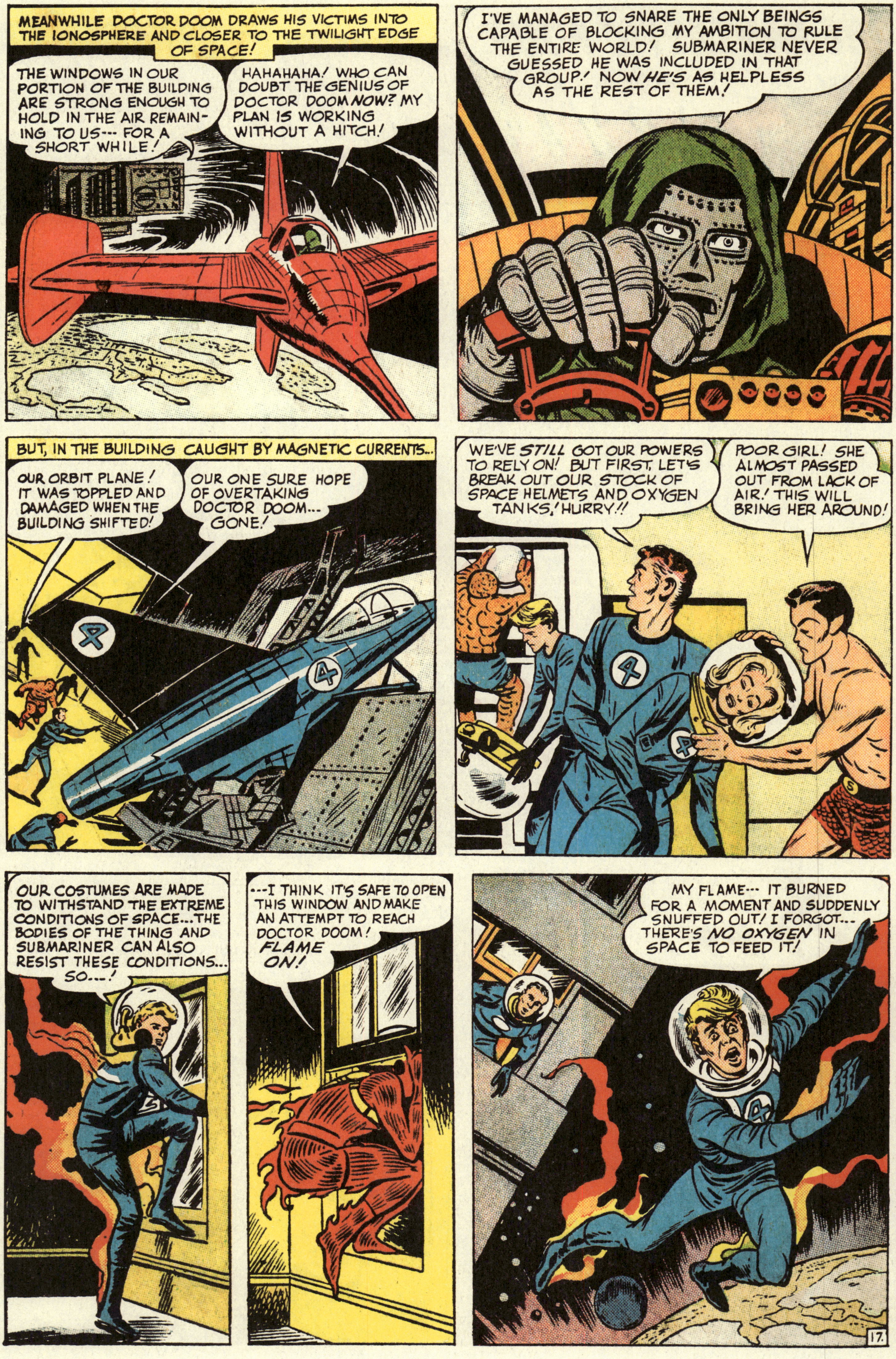
MEANWHILE DOCTOR DOOM DRAWS HIS VICTIMS INTO THE IONOSPHERE AND CLOSER TO THE TWILIGHT EDGE OF SPACE!
THE WINDOWS IN OUR PORTION OF THE BUILDING ARE STRONG ENOUGH TO HOLD IN THE AIR REMAINING TO US--- FOR A SHORT WHILE!
HAHAHAHA! WHO CAN DOUBT THE GENIUS OF DOCTOR DOOM NOW? MY PLAN IS WORKING WITHOUT A HITCH!
I'VE MANAGED TO SNARE THE ONLY BEINGS CAPABLE OF BLOCKING MY AMBITION TO RULE THE ENTIRE WORLD! SUBMARINER NEVER GUESSED HE WAS INCLUDED IN THAT GROUP! NOW HE'S AS HELPLESS AS THE REST OF THEM!
BUT, IN THE BUILDING CAUGHT BY MAGNETIC CURRENTS...
OUR ORBIT PLANE! IT WAS TOPPLED AND DAMAGED WHEN THE BUILDING SHIFTED!
OUR ONE SURE HOPE OF OVERTAKING DOCTOR DOOM... GONE!
WE'VE STILL GOT OUR POWERS TO RELY ON! BUT FIRST, LET'S BREAK OUT OUR STOCK OF SPACE HELMETS AND OXYGEN TANKS, HURRY!!
POOR GIRL! SHE ALMOST PASSED OUT FROM LACK OF AIR! THIS WILL BRING HER AROUND!
OUR COSTUMES ARE MADE TO WITHSTAND THE EXTREME CONDITIONS OF SPACE...THE BODIES OF THE THING AND SUBMARINER CAN ALSO RESIST THESE CONDITIONS... SO...!
---I THINK IT'S SAFE TO OPEN THIS WINDOW AND MAKE AN ATTEMPT TO REACH DOCTOR DOOM! FLAME ON!
MY FLAME--- IT BURNED FOR A MOMENT AND SUDDENLY SNUFFED OUT! I FORGOT... THERE'S NO OXYGEN IN SPACE TO FEED IT!
17.

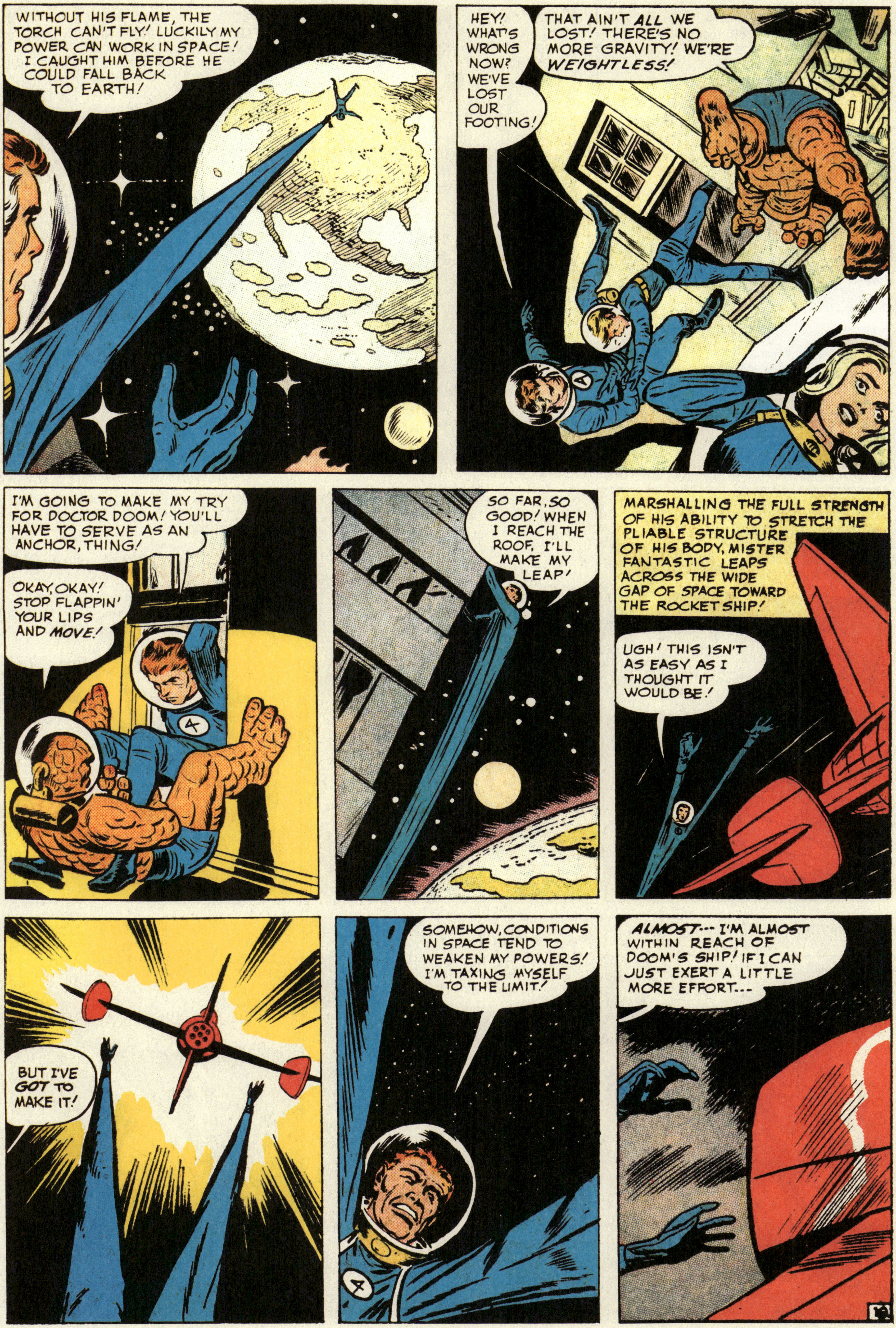

WITHOUT HIS FLAME, THE TORCH CAN'T FLY! LUCKILY MY POWER CAN WORK IN SPACE! I CAUGHT HIM BEFORE HE COULD FALL BACK TO EARTH!
HEY! WHAT'S WRONG NOW? WE'VE LOST OUR FOOTING!
THAT AIN'T ALL WE LOST! THERE'S NO MORE GRAVITY! WE'RE WEIGHTLESS!
I'M GOING TO MAKE MY TRY FOR DOCTOR DOOM! YOU'LL HAVE TO SERVE AS AN ANCHOR, THING!
OKAY, OKAY! STOP FLAPPIN' YOUR LIPS AND MOVE!
SO FAR, SO GOOD! WHEN I REACH THE ROOF, I'LL MAKE MY LEAP!
MARSHALLING THE FULL STRENGTH OF HIS ABILITY TO STRETCH THE PLIABLE STRUCTURE OF HIS BODY, MISTER FANTASTIC LEAPS ACROSS THE WIDE GAP OF SPACE TOWARD THE ROCKET SHIP!
UGH! THIS ISN'T AS EASY AS I THOUGHT IT WOULD BE!
BUT I'VE GOT TO MAKE IT!
SOMEHOW, CONDITIONS IN SPACE TEND TO WEAKEN MY POWERS! I'M TAXING MYSELF TO THE LIMIT!
ALMOST--- I'M ALMOST WITHIN REACH OF DOOM'S SHIP! IF I CAN JUST EXERT A LITTLE MORE EFFORT...

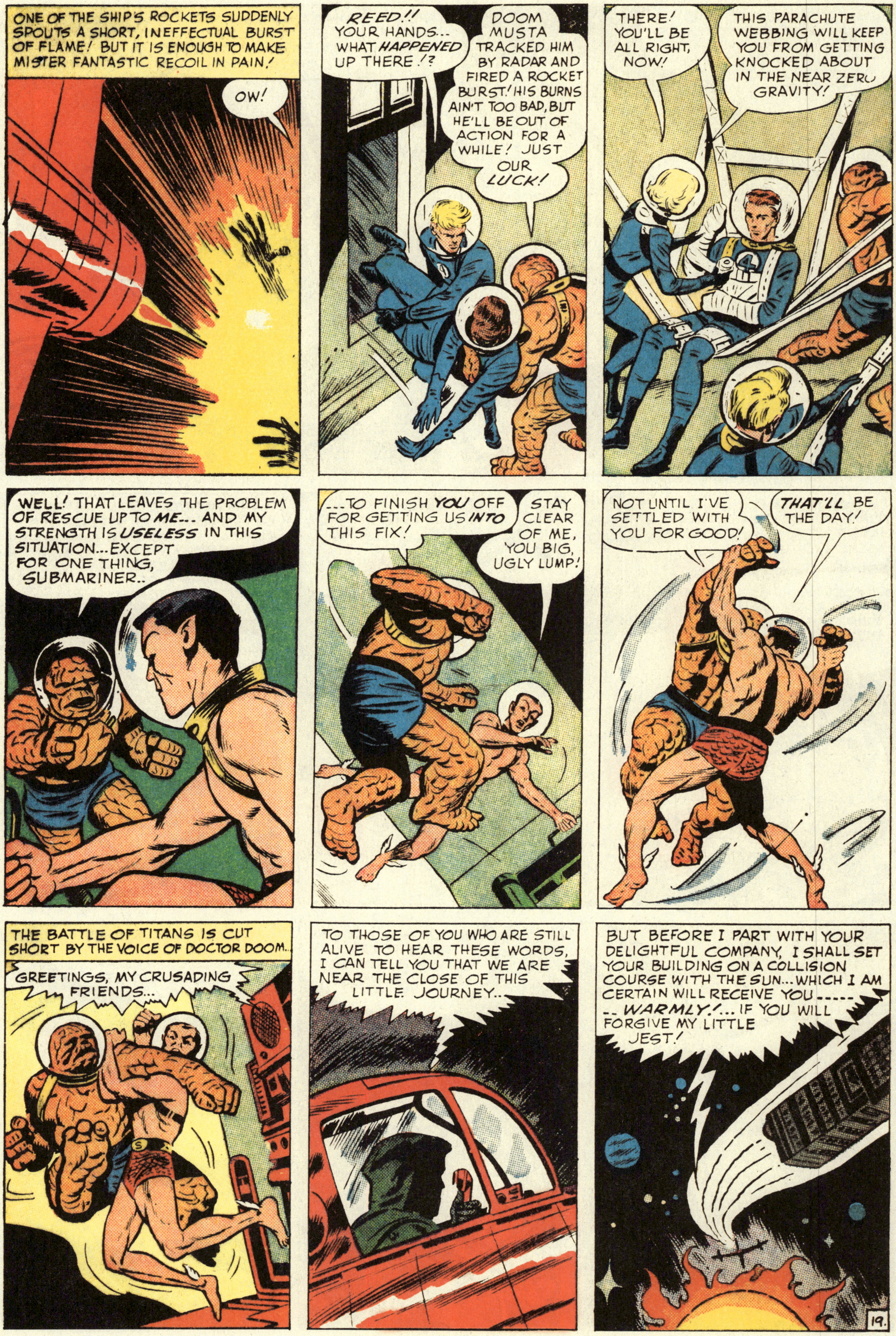

ONE OF THE SHIP'S ROCKETS SUDDENLY SPOUTS A SHORT, INEFFECTUAL BURST OF FLAME! BUT IT IS ENOUGH TO MAKE MISTER FANTASTIC RECOIL IN PAIN!
OW!
REED!! YOUR HANDS... WHAT HAPPENED UP THERE!?
DOOM MUSTA TRACKED HIM BY RADAR AND FIRED A ROCKET BURST! HIS BURNS AIN'T TOO BAD, BUT HE'LL BE OUT OF ACTION FOR A WHILE! JUST OUR LUCK!
THERE! YOU'LL BE ALL RIGHT, NOW!
THIS PARACHUTE WEBBING WILL KEEP YOU FROM GETTING KNOCKED ABOUT IN THE NEAR ZERO GRAVITY!
WELL! THAT LEAVES THE PROBLEM OF RESCUE UP TO ME... AND MY STRENGTH IS USELESS IN THIS SITUATION...EXCEPT FOR ONE THING, SUBMARINER..
...TO FINISH YOU OFF FOR GETTING US INTO THIS FIX!
STAY CLEAR OF ME, YOU BIG, UGLY LUMP!
NOT UNTIL I'VE SETTLED WITH YOU FOR GOOD!
THAT'LL BE THE DAY!
THE BATTLE OF TITANS IS CUT SHORT BY THE VOICE OF DOCTOR DOOM..
GREETINGS, MY CRUSADING FRIENDS...
TO THOSE OF YOU WHO ARE STILL ALIVE TO HEAR THESE WORDS, I CAN TELL YOU THAT WE ARE NEAR THE CLOSE OF THIS LITTLE JOURNEY..
BUT BEFORE I PART WITH YOUR DELIGHTFUL COMPANY, I SHALL SET YOUR BUILDING ON A COLLISION COURSE WITH THE SUN... WHICH I AM CERTAIN WILL RECEIVE YOU ----- WARMLY!... IF YOU WILL FORGIVE MY LITTLE JEST!
19.

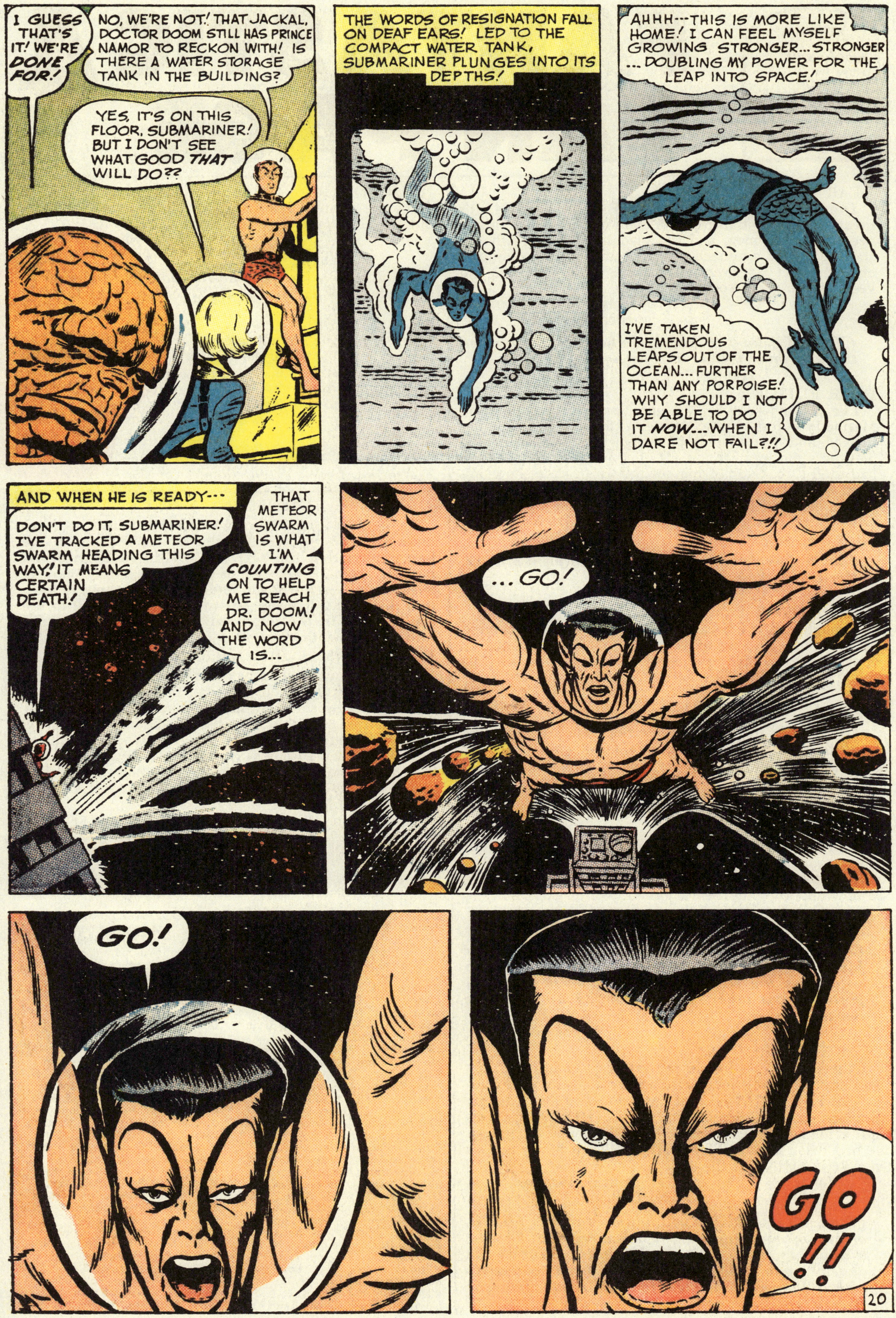
I GUESS THAT'S IT! WE'RE DONE FOR!
NO, WE'RE NOT! THAT JACKAL, DOCTOR DOOM STILL HAS PRINCE NAMOR TO RECKON WITH! IS THERE A WATER STORAGE TANK IN THE BUILDING?
YES, IT'S ON THIS FLOOR, SUBMARINER! BUT I DON'T SEE WHAT GOOD THAT WILL DO??
THE WORDS OF RESIGNATION FALL ON DEAF EARS! LED TO THE COMPACT WATER TANK, SUBMARINER PLUNGES INTO ITS DEPTHS!
AHHH---THIS IS MORE LIKE HOME! I CAN FEEL MYSELF GROWING STRONGER... STRONGER ... DOUBLING MY POWER FOR THE LEAP INTO SPACE!
I'VE TAKEN TREMENDOUS LEAPS OUT OF THE OCEAN... FURTHER THAN ANY PORPOISE! WHY SHOULD I NOT BE ABLE TO DO IT NOW... WHEN I DARE NOT FAIL?!!
AND WHEN HE IS READY---
DON'T DO IT, SUBMARINER! I'VE TRACKED A METEOR SWARM HEADING THIS WAY! IT MEANS CERTAIN DEATH!
THAT METEOR SWARM IS WHAT I'M COUNTING ON TO HELP ME REACH DR. DOOM! AND NOW THE WORD IS...
...GO!
GO!
GO !!
20

Address YOUR letters to:
THE EDITOR
FANTASTIC FOUR
THIRD FLOOR
655 MADISON AVE.
NEW YORK 21, N. Y.

FANTASTIC FAN PAGE 4

DEAR EDITOR:
I've just read a copy of THE FANTASTIC #4. It's great! There's nothing like it! This was the first time I ever read your mag, and I'm glad I did! You really are starting a new approach toward comic mags, where the characters act like every day people. Congratulations and keep up the good work!

Gregory Christiano
Bronx 65, N. Y.

(What WE want to know is, where were you when the first three issues were on sale, Greg?)

DEAR EDITOR:
I've just finished FF #4 and your treatment of Sub Mariner was just terrible! Namor's kingdom had been destroyed, and if you would put yourself in his place, you'd feel the same way HE did. If anything, you should have had the FF make up to him for the wrong-doings precipitated against him, instead of making him out to be a human monster! I'll bet you don't dare print this!

Marlene Du Vall
Lansing, Mich.

(Aw, it doesn't take much courage to print a letter, Marlene.)

DEAR EDITOR:
I bought FF #4 because of the Sub Mariner featured on the cover. I'll keep buying it if you keep the quality of the stories as high as this issue. How about a 64-page comic for two bits with Torch, Namor, Thing, etc.?

Lawrence Crilly
Elizabeth, New Jersey

(A number of readers have requested a 25¢ issue of FF. At present, we're afraid the quality of the mag might suffer if we try too many pages at once, but we will keep it in mind, and we may have a surprise for you after a while.)

DEAR EDITOR:
I am real happy to see that you listen to your readers, as for example giving the FF costumes. Well, as you probably know by now, all the characters are very popular, so how about giving them all their own magazines?

Harry Fitch
Rochester

(We aim to please, Harry. Don't you, or any of our fans, dare miss the OCT. issue of STRANGE TALES — it stars the HUMAN TORCH! We'll keep you posted about other changes coming up in future issues.)

DEAR EDITOR:
I think the FF is one of the greatest comic magazines ever printed. Here's an idea for a story. I'm sure your readers like THE THING as much as I do. How about a story in which you have Ben Grimm (THE THING) turn back into a human for a full issue with the same strength as he had when he was THE THING? Then he turns back into THE THING at the end!

Donald Murphres
Calhoun, Georgia

(We can't reveal what will happen to THE THING, or any of our characters in advance, Don, because it would spoil the element of surprise. But you can depend upon it that we will try to keep coming up with unexpected angles for ALL our fantastic friends!)

DEAR EDITOR:
It's the greatest! But I think Susan Storm ought to be thrown out. She never does anything.

Martin Ross
N. Y. 65, N. Y.

(Well, this is the first anti-Invisible Girl letter we've received! What do the REST of you fans think?)

DEAR EDITOR:
First, you give the whole comic mag business a shot in the arm with the sensational FF, and then, before we can even catch our breath, you come out with THE HULK, which promises to give the FF some stiff competition! What ELSE do you guys have up your sleeves?

Leon Foster
Alberta, Canada

(A couple of very tired arms from writing and drawing, Leon . . . but thanks for the kind words.)

IMPORTANT NOTE:

In issue #4 of THE FANTASTIC FOUR, we announced a $5.00 prize for the reader sending in the best explanation for THE INVISIBLE GIRL'S disappearing gem. Well, we received so many correct answers, all well-written and carefully thought out, that the only fair thing was to award the $5.00 to the fan sending in the letter which we received FIRST! And so, the winner is:

Jonathan Latham, 1011 Nichols Drive, Raleigh, N. C.

Jonathan's winning answer told that it was NOT Susan Storm who disappeared, but one of the Skrulls impersonating her by shrinking in size. The gem vanished by being carried away, unseen, by the minute-sized Skrull.

Many letters which we later received also contained the correct answer. Inasmuch as we cannot send $5.00 to all the writers, we're doing the next best thing and printing their names below. Thanks and congratulations to all of you sharp-eyed fans.

(P.S. This page is being set in type on March 14, 1962. So, the names which follow are those received up to this date.)

Michael Snell, Milford, Mass.
Paul Ward, Roslindale, Mass.
Joseph Reynolds, Jerseyville, Ill.
David Crall, Dodge City, Kans.
Sandra Schupp, Syosset, N. Y.
Craig Miller, Cedar Rapids, Iowa
G. Reagle Jr., Des Plaines, Ill.
K. Koenigs, Milwaukee 18, Wis.
J. Zielinski, Elmwood Pk., Ill.
Al Kracalik, Des Plaines, Ill.
Dana Riell, Brooklyn 36, N. Y.
John Davis, N. Y. 28, N. Y.
Bob Holman, Salt Lake City, Utah
Rita Townsend, Gallup, N. Mex.
Jim Brewster, Wilkes-Barre, Pa.
Marven Bland, Baltimore, Md.
Rodney Grey, Los Angeles, Calif.
Harry Beatty, Massapequa, N. Y.
Jose Nieves, N. Y. 29, N. Y.
Frank Schillig, Cherry Valley, N. J.
Charles Rockyvich, Phoenix, Ariz.
T. Baganz, Sturgeon Bay, Wis.
Edward Glover, Louisville, Ky.
John Creeley, New Rochelle, N. Y.
M. Liberatore. Ashland, Mass.
Roger Choate, Houston, Tex.
G. Lamont Brownell, Phila., Pa.
M. Madden, Jeffersonville, Ind.
Bob Williamson, Gretna, La.
Michael Fallis, Salem, Mass.
Richard Hoffman, Chicago 18, Ill.
Billy Sequino. Warren, R. I.
William Wiehe, York, Pa.
Kevin Breen, Buffalo, N. Y.
Richard Silver, Paramus, N. J.
Lewis Strasburg, Orem, Utah
Chris Fuller, Mayville, Wis.
Dennis Stephens, Wapello, Iowa
Paul Carr, Drexel Hill, Pa.
Eugene Zielinski, Chicago 14, Ill.
Danny Peterson, Salinas, Calif.
Dennis Day, Clarksville, Ind.
M. Greenfield, Bloomingdale, O.
Charles Mammano, Hazlet, N. J.
Gerald Adair, Philadelphia, Pa.
Robert Stevenson, Medford, Ore.
Chris Bennett, Amarillo, Tex.
S. Howard, Cleveland, Ohio
Don Jarvis, Garden City, Mich.
L. Behrns, Colorado Spgs., Colo.
E. Giannattasio, Massa., Pk., N. Y.
Kenneth Peters, Baltimore, Md.
S. Champagne, Penacook, N. H.
Mike Sisson, Topeka, Kans.
M. Dorobis, Jersey City 5, N. J.
Ronald Vigil, Vallejo, Calif.
Carmen Martinez, N. Y. 9, N. Y.
Peter Ortiz,, N. Y. 9, N. Y.
M. Russell, Wappingers Falls, N.Y.
Danny Turner, Miami, Fla.
J. Martin, Bowling Green, Ky.
W. Nielsen, Port Arthur, Tex.
Paul Hill, Portsmouth, N. H.
S. Perrin, Santa Barbara, Calif.
Dennis Fiegl, Buffalo 6. N. Y.
B. Stanis, Waterbury, Conn.
B. Carrothers, New Phila., Ohio
George Paul, Hoboken, N. J.
R. De Bruyn, Buffalo 13, N. Y.
Dan Eiler, Newton Falls, Ohio
Bill Hall, Winston-Salem, N. C.
Daryl Anderson, Atlanta, Ga.

THE FANTASTIC FOUR
PART 5
"THE END...OR THE BEGINNING?"
Stan Lee + J. Kirby
IT WORKED! I WAS ABLE TO LEAP FROM ONE PASSING METEOR TO THE OTHER, UNTIL NOW...
V-835
...NOW FOR THE RECKONING!
BUT SUDDENLY, AT THE FLIP OF A CONTROL LEVER FROM INSIDE THE AMAZING SHIP, AN ALL-POWERFUL BAND OF MAGNETISM PINS PRINCE NAMOR TO THE STEEL HULL OF THE CABIN!
UGH!! CAN'T MOVE!
21.

UNABLE TO RISE, SUBMARINER'S POWERFUL FISTS EXERT TREMENDOUS PRESSURE ON THE FUSILAGE BENEATH HIM!
THIS MAGNETIC FORCE MAY KEEP ME FROM GETTING UP... BUT IT CAN'T STOP ME FROM GOING DOWN!
THE THICK METAL BUCKLES AND GROANS... UNTIL SUBMARINER'S ARMS CRASH THROUGH INTO THE SHIP'S INTERIOR!
WHEN THE AIR RUSHES OUT, THE HULL BENEATH SUBMARINER COLLAPSES, AND CARRIES HIM DOWN WITH IT!
NOW IF I CAN ONLY BREAK INTO THE PILOT'S CABIN BEFORE DOCTOR DOOM MAKES HIS NEXT MOVE! I'M SURE HE KNOWS I'M IN THE SHIP!
SUDDENLY, A THOUSAND GREAT HAMMER-BLOWS OF ELECTRICITY SMASH INTO THE SEA MONARCH, HURLING HIM BACK INTO THE DARKNESS.
CRACK
MEANWHILE, ON THE OTHER SIDE OF THE STEEL WALL, DOCTOR DOOM LISTENS FOR SOUNDS OF MOVEMENT...
I DON'T HEAR A THING! THAT'S THE END OF SUBMARINER! HIS ATTEMPT TO STOP ME WAS THE LAST!
VOLTS
NOW, ALL I HAVE TO DO IS PUSH DOWN THIS LEVER AND BREAK CONTACT WITH THE BUILDING! SLOWLY BUT SURELY IT WILL SPIRAL INTO THE SUN.. TAKING WITH IT THE REST OF MY ENEMIES!
OWWW!! I-I CAN'T TOUCH ANYTHING! THE WHOLE CABIN IS CHARGED WITH ELECTRICITY!
22.

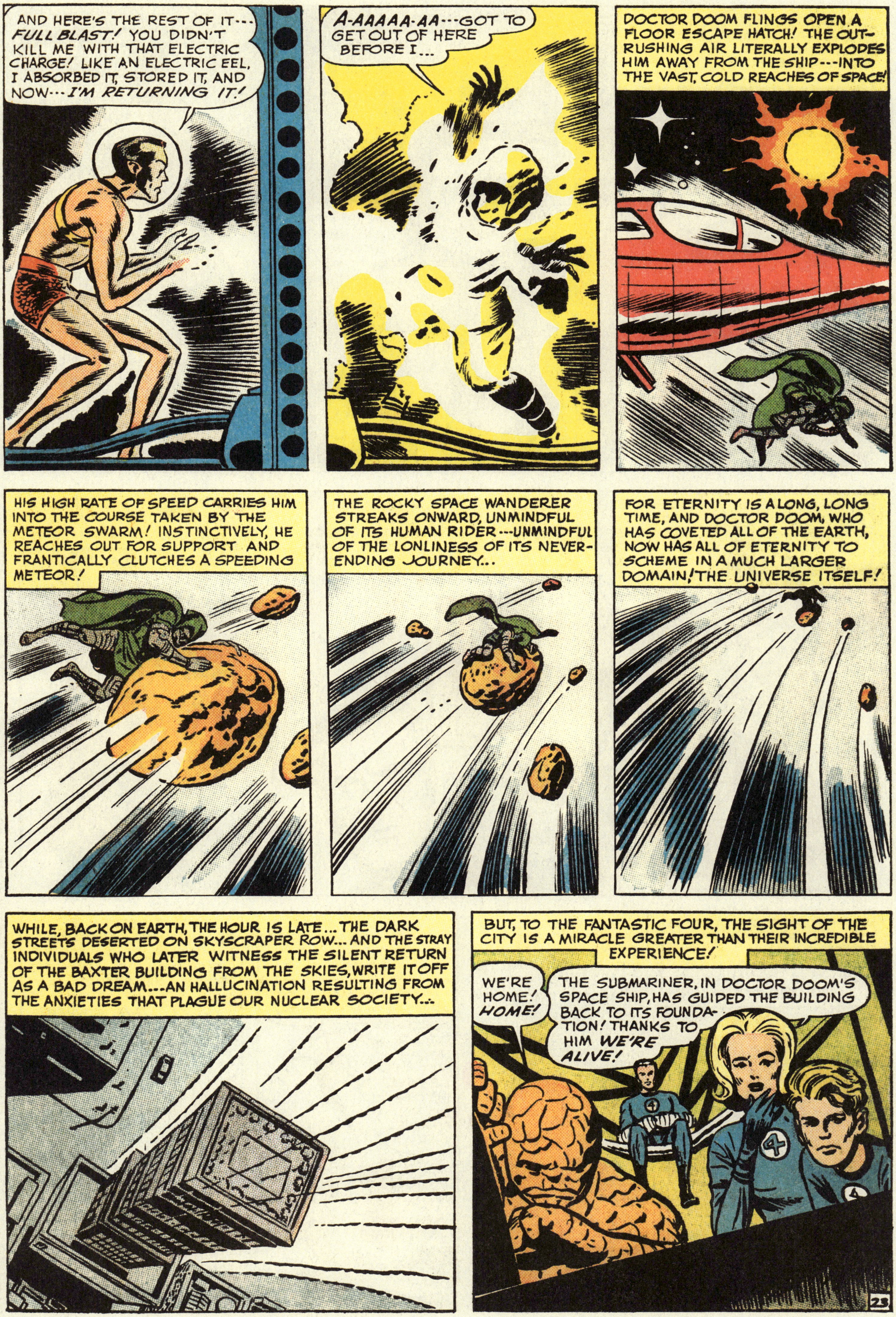

AND HERE'S THE REST OF IT--- FULL BLAST! YOU DIDN'T KILL ME WITH THAT ELECTRIC CHARGE! LIKE AN ELECTRIC EEL, I ABSORBED IT, STORED IT, AND NOW--- I'M RETURNING IT!
A-AAAAA-AA---GOT TO GET OUT OF HERE BEFORE I...
DOCTOR DOOM FLINGS OPEN A FLOOR ESCAPE HATCH! THE OUT-RUSHING AIR LITERALLY EXPLODES HIM AWAY FROM THE SHIP---INTO THE VAST, COLD REACHES OF SPACE!
HIS HIGH RATE OF SPEED CARRIES HIM INTO THE COURSE TAKEN BY THE METEOR SWARM! INSTINCTIVELY, HE REACHES OUT FOR SUPPORT AND FRANTICALLY CLUTCHES A SPEEDING METEOR!
THE ROCKY SPACE WANDERER STREAKS ONWARD, UNMINDFUL OF ITS HUMAN RIDER---UNMINDFUL OF THE LONLINESS OF ITS NEVER-ENDING JOURNEY...
FOR ETERNITY IS A LONG, LONG TIME, AND DOCTOR DOOM, WHO HAS COVETED ALL OF THE EARTH, NOW HAS ALL OF ETERNITY TO SCHEME IN A MUCH LARGER DOMAIN! THE UNIVERSE ITSELF!
WHILE, BACK ON EARTH, THE HOUR IS LATE... THE DARK STREETS DESERTED ON SKYSCRAPER ROW... AND THE STRAY INDIVIDUALS WHO LATER WITNESS THE SILENT RETURN OF THE BAXTER BUILDING FROM THE SKIES, WRITE IT OFF AS A BAD DREAM...AN HALLUCINATION RESULTING FROM THE ANXIETIES THAT PLAGUE OUR NUCLEAR SOCIETY...
BUT, TO THE FANTASTIC FOUR, THE SIGHT OF THE CITY IS A MIRACLE GREATER THAN THEIR INCREDIBLE EXPERIENCE!
WE'RE HOME! HOME!
THE SUBMARINER, IN DOCTOR DOOM'S SPACE SHIP, HAS GUIDED THE BUILDING BACK TO ITS FOUNDATION! THANKS TO HIM WE'RE ALIVE!
23

HOW DO YOU THANK AN ENEMY? SUBMARINER'S SOMEWHERE ABOVE US IN THAT CONFOUNDED SHIP.. ...AND IF I COULD REACH HIM...I STILL DON'T KNOW IF I'D SHAKE HIS HAND OR TRY TO SMASH HIM!
OH, HE ISN'T OUR ENEMY! I JUST KNOW IT! HE'S SO FULL OF PAIN AND BITTERNESS, THAT IT BLINDS HIS BETTER INSTINCTS! SUBMARINER NEEDS TIME... TIME TO HEAL!
AT THAT MOMENT...
I FOUND IT! I FOUND THAT GRABBER GADGET JUST WHERE SUBMARINER SAID HE PLANTED IT!
WE'D BETTER REMOVE IT! IT'S DANGEROUS AS LONG AS IT REMAINS ACTIVE!
YEAH! IT'S LIKE LIVING WITH A LIVE BOMB!
AND SOON AFTER, IN THE BUILDING BASEMENT!
THERE IT IS! CONCEIVED BY DOCTOR DOOM...AND DELIVERED BY A MIS-GUIDED PRINCE NAMOR!
YOU MEAN THAT THING?? THAT THING LIFTED THE ENTIRE BUILDING! IT'S NO BIGGER THAN A TINCAN!
UGH! TALK ABOUT POWER! WE CAN'T BUDGE THIS THING!
YOU FORGET THAT IT HARNESSES THE STRENGTH OF A TITANIC NATURAL FORCE!
DOCTOR DOOM WAS AN EVIL GENIUS... BUT A GENIUS, NEVERTHELESS! WHAT A TRAGEDY THAT HIS GREAT MENTAL ABILITIES PRODUCED SUCH MIRACLES FOR SINISTER PURPOSES!
AS FOR SUB-MARINER, WHO KNOWS WHAT HIS FUTURE HOLDS FOR HIM?
LOOK OUT!
THE GADGET DETACHED ITSELF! IT'S FLYING AWAY!
IT'S TOO LATE TO STOP IT!
AS IF POSSESSED BY A WILL OF ITS OWN, THE GRABBER STREAKS ACROSS THE CITY WITH THE SPEED OF LIGHT-- UNTIL IT IS LOST TO SIGHT OVER THE OCEAN!
24
SOMETIME LATER, IN A REMOTE LATITUDE, THE CYLINDER HOMES IN ON THE SPACE SHIP PILOTED BY SUBMARINER...
THEN, WHEN IT IS INSIDE THE SHIP, PRINCE NAMOR SENDS THE VEHICLE INTO A SPIN AND HURTLES FROM IT!
THE SEA WILL MAKE A FIT RESTING PLACE FOR THE WORKS OF DOCTOR DOOM! THEY WILL LIE WHERE THEY CAN DO NO FURTHER HARM!
SO SHALL I RETURN TO THE SEA! PERHAPS SOMEDAY WHEN I AM NO LONGER HAUNTED BY BITTER MEMORIES OF MY LOST PEOPLE, I MAY RETURN...BUT UNTIL THEN, THIS IS WHERE I BELONG! IN THE SEA WHICH IS MY HOME!
NEXT ISSUE: DON'T MISS THE MOST STARTLING FANTASTIC FOUR ADVENTURE OF ALL! WATCH FOR IT!!

THE END–

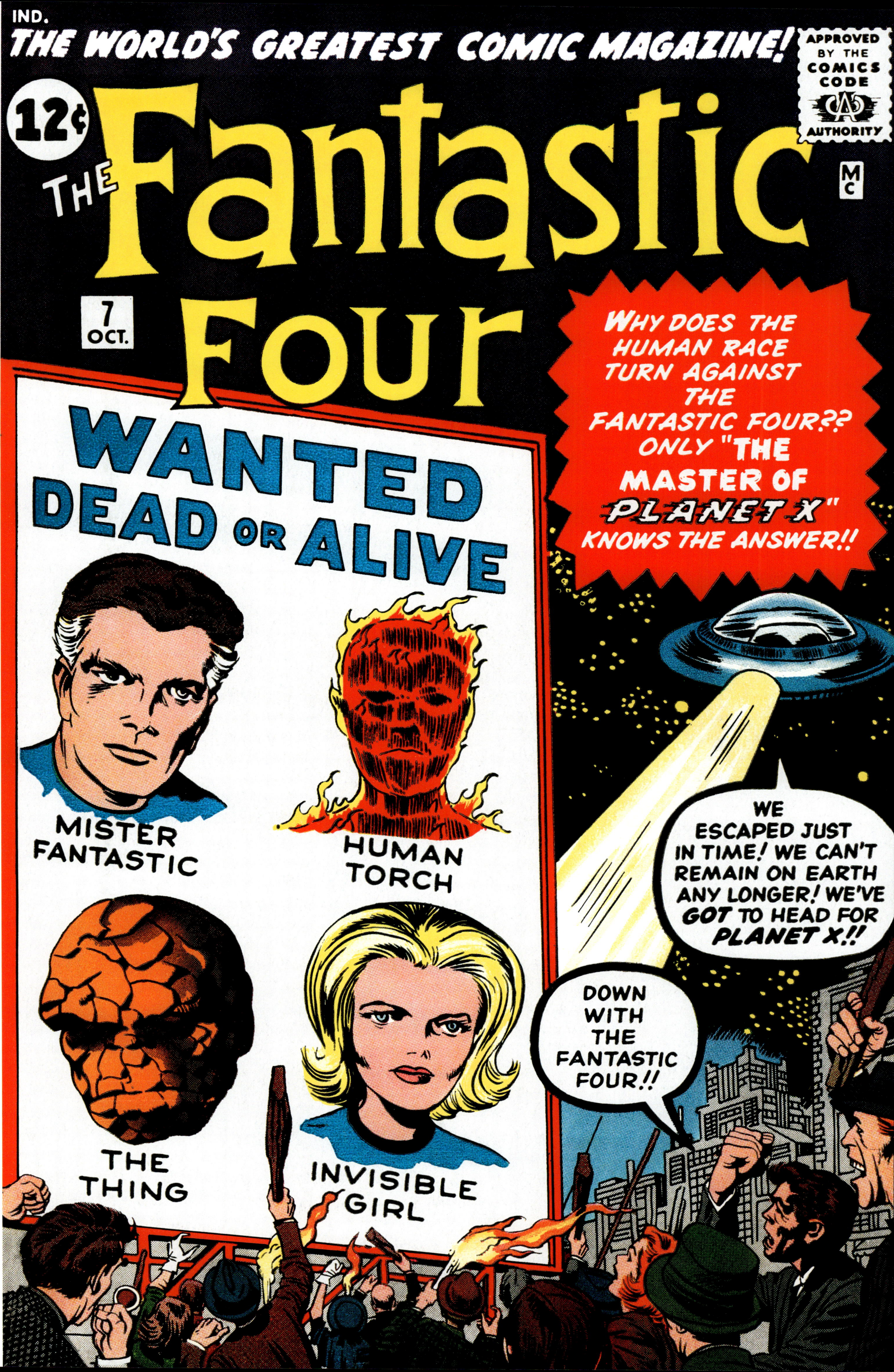
IND.
THE WORLD'S GREATEST COMIC MAGAZINE!
APPROVED BY THE COMICS CODE AUTHORITY
12¢
THE Fantastic Four
MC
7 OCT.
WHY DOES THE HUMAN RACE TURN AGAINST THE FANTASTIC FOUR?? ONLY "THE MASTER OF PLANET X" KNOWS THE ANSWER!!
WANTED DEAD OR ALIVE
MISTER FANTASTIC
HUMAN TORCH
THE THING
INVISIBLE GIRL
WE ESCAPED JUST IN TIME! WE CAN'T REMAIN ON EARTH ANY LONGER! WE'VE GOT TO HEAD FOR PLANET X!!
DOWN WITH THE FANTASTIC FOUR!!

THE FANTASTIC FOUR is published by CANAM PUBLISHERS SALES CORP. OFFICE OF PUBLICATION: 655 MADISON AVENUE, NEW YORK, N.Y. Published monthly. Copyright 1962 by CANAM PUBLISHERS SALES CORP., 655 Madison Avenue, New York, N. Y. Vol. 1 No. 7, OCTOBER 1962 issue. Price 12c per copy. Subscription rate $1.75 for 12 issues including postage. Foreign subscription $3.25 in American funds. No similarity between any of the names, characters, persons, and/or institutions appearing in this magazine with those of any living or dead person or institution is intended, and any such similarity which may exist is purely coincidental. Printed in the U.S.A. by The Eastern Color Printing Co., Waterbury 20, Conn.

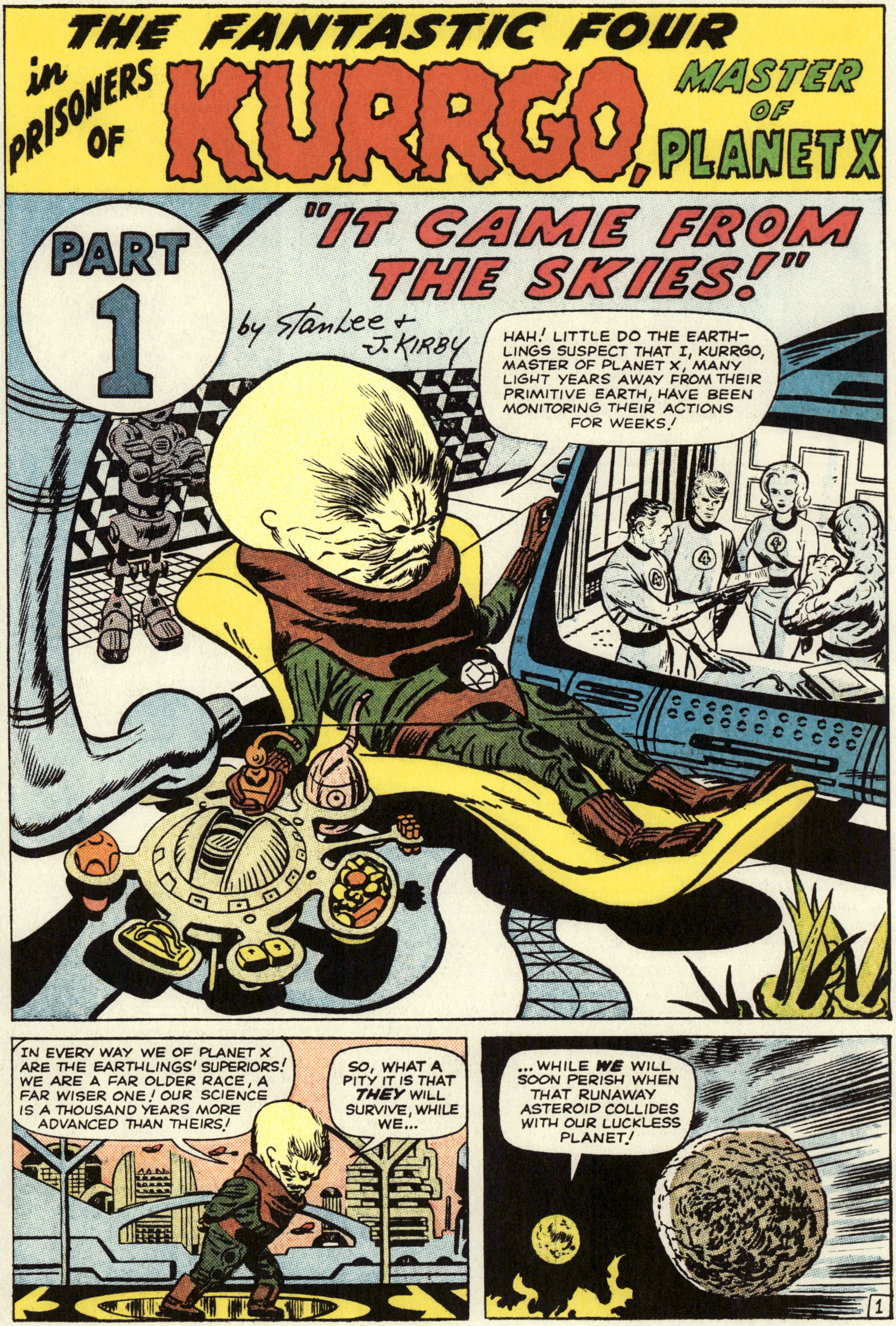
THE FANTASTIC FOUR
in PRISONERS OF
KURRGO,
MASTER OF PLANET X
PART 1
"IT CAME FROM THE SKIES!"
by Stan Lee + J. Kirby
HAH! LITTLE DO THE EARTHLINGS SUSPECT THAT I, KURRGO, MASTER OF PLANET X, MANY LIGHT YEARS AWAY FROM THEIR PRIMITIVE EARTH, HAVE BEEN MONITORING THEIR ACTIONS FOR WEEKS!
IN EVERY WAY WE OF PLANET X ARE THE EARTHLINGS' SUPERIORS! WE ARE A FAR OLDER RACE, A FAR WISER ONE! OUR SCIENCE IS A THOUSAND YEARS MORE ADVANCED THAN THEIRS!
SO, WHAT A PITY IT IS THAT THEY WILL SURVIVE, WHILE WE...
...WHILE WE WILL SOON PERISH WHEN THAT RUNAWAY ASTEROID COLLIDES WITH OUR LUCKLESS PLANET!

OH, KURRGO, MY LORD! IF ONLY WE HAD ENOUGH SPACE SHIPS TO ENABLE US TO FLEE OUR PLANET BEFORE THE HOLOCAUST!
FOOL! YOU KNOW WE HAVE ONLY TWO SPACE SHIPS ON PLANET X! FOR WE HAVE NEVER CARED FOR SPACE TRAVEL!
BUT ONE OF THOSE SHIPS IS EVEN NOW BLAZING TOWARDS EARTH... TOWARDS THE ONLY FOUR CREATURES IN ALL THE UNIVERSE WHO MIGHT FIND A WAY TO SAVE US!
"PILOTED BY MY OWN PERSONAL ROBOT, THE SHIP MUST LAND ON EARTH AND CAPTURE THE FANTASTIC FOUR! THEN, THEY ARE TO BE BROUGHT TO PLANET X, AS MY PRISONERS!"
MEANWHILE, COUNTLESS LIGHT YEARS AWAY, LITTLE DREAMING OF THE ADVENTURE FATE HAS IN STORE FOR THEM, WE FIND THE FANTASTIC FOUR IN THEIR SKYSCRAPER HEADQUARTERS...
WE HAVEN'T MUCH TIME! WE'RE DUE TO APPEAR IN WASHINGTON LATER, TO ATTEND A GOVERNMENT DINNER IN OUR HONOR!
AW, WHO NEEDS IT, REED? I'M NOT EVEN HUNGRY!
SUCH SHORT NOTICE! I HAVEN'T GOT A THING TO WEAR!
BAH! IT'S JUST A WASTE OF TIME! I AIN'T GOIN'!
"THE THING'S RIGHT, REED! HECK, WE'RE NO SPEECH-MAKERS! IMAGINE WHAT WOULD HAPPEN IF I HAVE TO TRY TO SAY SOMETHING CLEVER--!"
THAT REMINDS ME OF A JOKE I HEARD ABOUT TWO BEATNIKS...
...OR, EH, AH, MAYBE YOU'VE ALREADY HEARD IT...?
"I'D PROBABLY GET ALL TENSE AND NERVOUS, AND THE THE NEXT THING WE KNOW, IT WOULD BE JUST MY LUCK TO BURST INTO FLAME!"
THAT'S FOOLISH AND YOU KNOW IT, TORCH! NOW, DOES ANYONE ELSE HAVE A BEEF?
YOU BET!
"CAN YA IMAGINE HOW I'D LOOK IN FRONT OF ALL THOSE CONGRESSMEN AT A BIG STATE DINNER? THEY'D THINK I WAS NUTTY IF I KEPT ALL BUNDLED UP, BUT I'D SCARE 'EM TO DEATH IF I TOOK MY HAT AND COAT OFF!"
2

"AND THEN, WHAT IF THOSE WISE-GUY PHOTOGRAPHERS TRY FOR SOME PICTURES OF ME??"
HOW ABOUT A SHOT OF YOU WITH THE SENATOR, THING?
WHAT'S THE BIG IDEA?!!
GOOD HEAVENS! WHAT AN OGRE!
"YOU KNOW MY TEMPER! IN A COUPLE OF SECONDS, I'D START TEARIN' THE JOINT APART! AND I'M JUST THE GUY TO DO IT, TOO!"
NO SIREE! I DON'T WANT ANY PART OF THAT FANCY PANTS DINNER!
HOW ABOUT YOU, SUE?
OH, REED, I-I'M AFRAID TO GO!
"I'M NOT USED TO MEETING ALL THOSE IMPORTANT PEOPLE!"
MY DEAH, SAY HELLO TO MADAME AMBASSADOR...
CHARMED, I'M SURE!
"I'M LIABLE TO GET SO FLUSTERED THAT BEFORE I KNOW IT, I MIGHT VANISH IN FRONT OF THEIR EYES! IF THAT EVER HAPPENED, I'D SIMPLY DIE OF EMBARRASSMENT!"
ALL RIGHT, I'VE HEARD ALL YOUR SILLY LITTLE EXCUSES, AND I'M SURE YOU FEEL BETTER NOW THAT YOU'VE SAID THEM! SO, LET'S START GETTING READY NOW, AND LET'S END ALL THIS NONSENSE! YOU KNOW WE CAN'T REFUSE A REQUEST FROM CONGRESS!
NOW GO GET DRESSED, TORCH!
DO YOU HAVETA DO EVERYTHING HE TELLS YA, SQUIRT?
SURE! I'M NOT A STUBBORN OX LIKE SOME GUYS I KNOW!
CALL ME A STUBBORN OX, WILL HE? I'LL TEACH THAT FLAMING FOOL!
3

HEY!
WHO'S THE WISE GUY ??!
WHAT'SAMATTER, HOT HEAD! DID I MAKE THINGS TOO WARM FOR YA??
HISSSSSSS
MEANWHILE, UNAWARE OF THE THING'S HASTY ACTION...
REED! WHAT'S WRONG?
I DON'T KNOW, SUE! IT CAN'T BE A FIRE-- THIS WHOLE BUILDING IS FIREPROOF!
I'D BETTER SLITHER IN THERE AND CHECK THE VENTILATING UNITS!
THAT'S FUNNY! EVERYTHING IS IN PERFECT WORKING ORDER!
LISTEN, REED! THAT SHOUTING --IT SOUNDS LIKE THE TORCH!
AND THE THING ISN'T HERE! I SHOULD HAVE GUESSED!
THINK YOU'RE PRETTY CLEVER, DON'T YOU? I OUGHTTA--
AW, CLAM UP! I JUST WANTED TO START A LITTLE RUCKUS SO I WOULDN'T HAVE TO GO TO THAT BLAMED DINNER!
THING, STOP FEELING SO SORRY FOR YOURSELF!
HOW DO YOU THINK I FEEL! I'M IN THE MIDDLE OF A NEW ROCKET FUEL EXPERIMENT WHICH IS ALMOST REACHING FRUITION, AND I'VE GOT TO INTERRUPT IT ALSO!
BIG DEAL! WE ALREADY GOT ROCKET FUEL, HAVEN'T WE?!
4

BUT LET US LEAVE THE FANTASTIC FOUR TO THEIR BICKERING FOR A MOMENT AND WATCH A NEW, STRANGE FORM ENTER EARTH'S ATMOSPHERE! THE FORM OF A STAR SHIP FROM OUTER SPACE! AND, AT THE VERY INSTANT THAT WE NOTICE IT, ONE OF AMERICA'S NEW EYE-IN-THE-SKY SATELLITES ALSO FLASHES THE WORD TO COMMAND HEADQUARTERS BELOW...
WHAT, IS IT?? AN ATTACK BY THE REDS?
NO EARTH NATION EVER BUILT A A SHIP LIKE THAT!
IT--IT SOUNDS INCREDIBLE --BUT IT CAN ONLY COME FROM-- OUTER SPACE!
MINUTES LATER, ATOP A NEW YORK SKYSCRAPER...
C'MON, THING, CHEER UP! YOU MIGHT EVEN ENJOY THE DINNER!
SURE--SURE! I JUST LOVE TO HAVE PEOPLE GAPIN' AT ME AND LAUGHIN' BEHIND MY BACK!
HEY! WHAT'S THAT?
IT'S SOMETHING IN THE SKY!
SOUNDS LIKE A NEW TYPE OF JET!
WHERE? I DON'T SEE ANYTHING!
OVER THERE! WOW! LOOK AT 'ER GO! MUST BE A NEW MISSILE TEST!
WELL, WE'VE GOT NO TIME FOR RUBBER-NECKING! WE'RE DUE IN WASHINGTON NOW!
WE'VE GOT AN AUDIENCE BELOW!
I'D LIKE TO TRADE PLACES WITH 'EM! THEY DON'T HAVE TO GO TO A DULL DINNER!
LOOK! IT'S THE FANTASTIC FOUR IN THEIR FANTASTI-CAR!

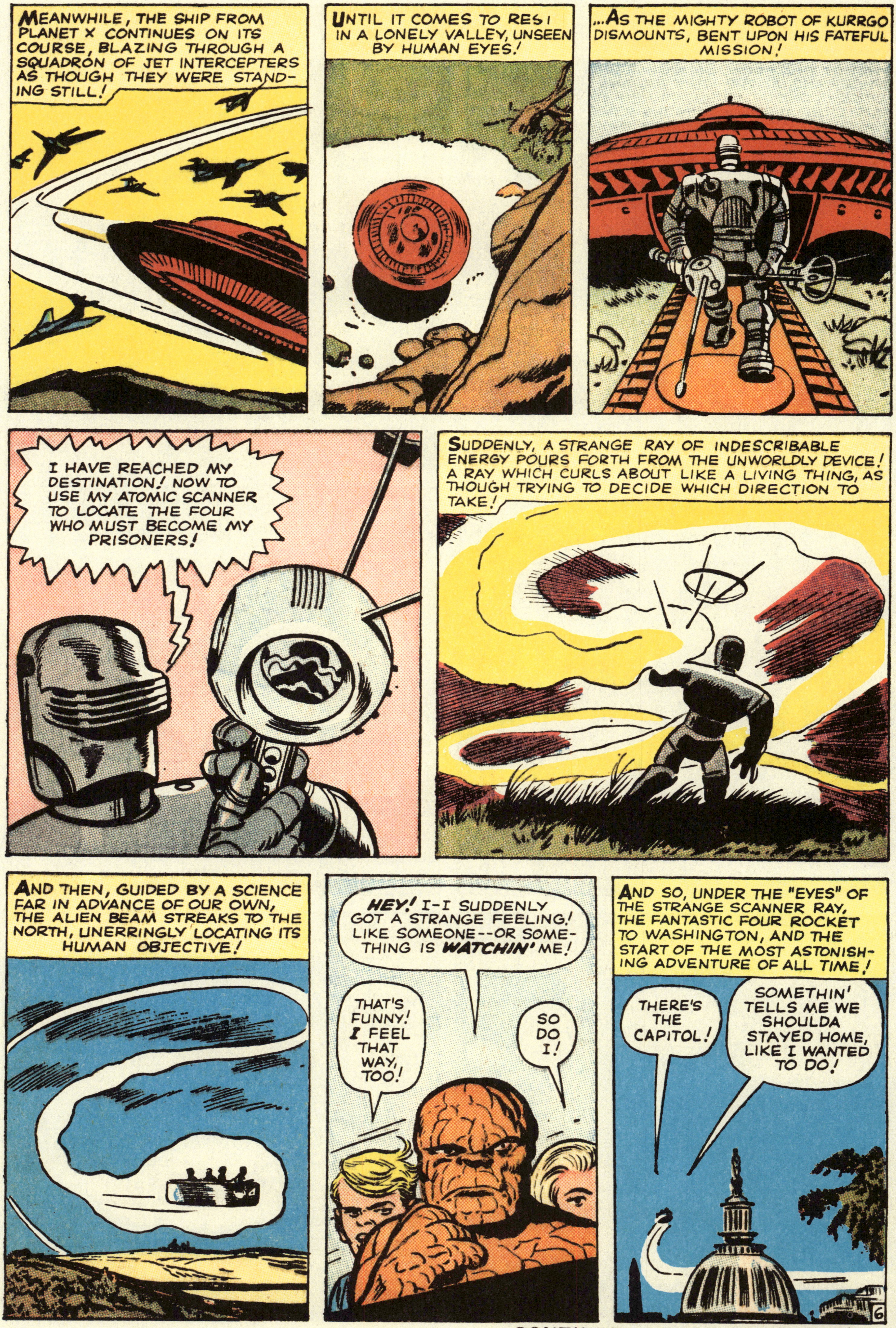

CONTINUED AFTER NEXT PAGE...

NOW! OWN AND OPERATE YOUR OWN SCALE MODEL . . .
ELECTRIC MONORAIL
NEWEST MIRACLE of MODERN ENGINEERING!
It's the talk of the engineering world! The new, fabulous MONORAIL . . . designed for the 1962 World's Fair! And now, you can own and operate your own scale model ELECTRIC MONORAIL. See it zip around, over the ground, suspended on a single metal rail. Control it yourself on its own full-color scenic layout. Send it speeding across the countryside over cross-roads . . . past lakes, amusement parks, stores and houses. Stop it at the station . . . start it up again . . . you're the boss! You'll have hours of fun, and be the envy of every other kid in the neighborhood! Your MONORAIL'S powerful motor is driven by a single, inexpensive flashlight battery. All-metal construction means it's built to last. Order today . . . the complete set is only $2.98. And you get your money back if not delighted.
COMPLETE! NOTHING ELSE TO BUY!
YOU GET:
★ Scale Model Electric Monorail
★ Special Curved Monorail Track
★ 8 Bridge-Type Track Supports
★ Full Color Folding Scenic Layout
All for Only $2.98
MEDFORD PRODUCTS, Dept. MCG9A Box 39, Bethpage, N.Y.
RUSH COUPON TODAY!
Medford Products, Dept. MCG9A
Box 39, Bethpage, N.Y.
Please rush me my ELECTRIC MONORAIL, complete with track, track supports and full-color scenic layout. Enclosed is check or M.O. for $2.98 (No. C.O.D.) I understand that if I am not delighted, my money will be refunded.
Name
Address
City Zone State
NOT 3, NOT 6, NOT 9, NOT 12, BUT . . .
14 NEW SENSATIONAL TRICKS
A MILLION LAUGHS,
ALL FOR ONLY $1
Now, be the life of EVERY party . . . amaze and amuse your family and friends . . . with this giant collection of 14, yes 14 mystifying, mirth-producing gags and tricks. It's the most amazing collection of guaranteed laugh-getters ever assembled . . . a giant box of shocks and surprises you'll use over and over again. Every trick is easy for you to pull, when you know its secret. You would be willing to pay as much as $1.00 each for some of these unforgettable party tricks, yet you can now get ALL 14 for only $1.00 . . . a super-colossal value! Order today . . . be the center of attention tomorrow!
Rush Coupon Today . . . Money Back Guarantee!
MEDFORD PRODUCTS BOX 39 BETHPAGE, N. Y.
Here's what you get For only $1.00
Nail Thru Finger
Mystery Calculater
Invisible Ink
Wonder Voice Thrower
Suckers Card Trick
Fake Firecracker
Auto & Hat Nail
Trick Animals
Pyramid Puzzle
Trick Safety Pin
Dragnet Mystery
Magic Snakes
Snapping Chewing Gum
Imitation Lit Cigarette
and many others
MEDFORD PRODUCTS, Dept. MCG-9
P.O. Box 39, Bethpage, N. Y.
Yes, rush me ___ sets of 14 sensational party tricks, for only $1.00 per set. I enclose $___ in cash, check or money order plus 25c postage & handling. I understand that if I am not amazed and delighted, my money will be promptly refunded.
Name
Address
City Zone State

THE FANTASTIC FOUR
PART 2
OUTLAWED!
WELL, I GUESS THIS ISN'T SO BAD, REED! AT LEAST NOBODY ASKED ME TO MAKE A SPEECH!
I SUPPOSE THESE NERVE-WRACKING CEREMONIES ARE THE PRICE WE MUST PAY FOR FAME!
GET THAT BLASTED CAMERA OUT OF MY EAR, MAC, OR I'LL WRAP IT AROUND YOUR FAT HEAD!
V-835
MR. FANTASTIC, AS LEADER OF THE FANTASTIC FOUR, WILL YOU ACCEPT THIS TROPHY AS A SYMBOL OF THE GRATITUDE OF YOUR FELLOW COUNTRYMEN?
WE ARE HONORED, SIR!
BUT, EVEN AS THE CEREMONY CONTINUES, THE STRANGE SPACE SHIP NOISELESSLY ROCKETS OVER THE NATION'S CAPITOL AT A SPEED SO GREAT THAT NONE CAN SEE IT!
THOSE I SEEK ARE DIRECTLY BELOW! IT IS NOW TIME TO ACT!
Stan Lee + J. Kirby
7

MY MASTER, THE MIGHTY KURRGO, ORDERED ME TO ACTIVATE THE HOSTILITY RAY AS I FLY OVER MY QUARRY! AND SO...
RREEEEEEEE
SUDDENLY, FROM THE UN-EARTHLY STAR SHIP, A STRANGE, PIERCING HUM ISSUES FORTH, BLANKETING THE CITY WITH ITS EERIE VIBRATIONS!
HHMMMMMMMMMMMM
NO PLACE IN THE NATION'S CAPITOL IS SAFE FROM THE SUBSONIC HUM...
HERE'S YOUR DINNER, DARLING!
MMMMM
THANKS, HONEY!
MMMMMMMMMM
DON'T YOU "HONEY" ME, YOU CREEP!
EVERYWHERE IN THE CITY, THE STORY IS THE SAME...
HERE, SIR-- LET ME HELP YOU UP!
THANK YOU, YOUNG MAN! YOU'RE VERY KIND!
MMMMMMMMMMMMM
TAKE YOUR FILTHY HANDS OFF ME, YOU CRUMMY BUM!
AND, AT THE TESTIMONIAL DINNER FOR THE FANTASTIC FOUR...
...AND NOW, I'D LIKE TO SAY A FEW FINAL WORDS IN PRAISE OF THIS WONDERFUL PATRIOTIC FOURSOME TO WHOM OUR NATION OWES SO MUCH!
POUR IT ON, BUB! WE CAN STAND IT AS LONG AS YOU CAN!
MMMMMMMMM....
IT'S TIME THE PUBLIC AWOKE TO THE FACT THAT THE FOUR OF YOU ARE THE WORST MENACES EVER TO THREATEN THIS LAND!
!

SUDDENLY, BEFORE THE ASTONISHED FOURSOME KNOW WHAT HAS HAPPENED, THE ADMIRING CROWD OF WELL-WISHERS TURNS INTO A SAVAGE, HATE-FILLED RIOTING MOB!
DOWN WITH THE FANTASTIC FOUR!
DRIVE THEM OUT OF THE COUNTRY!
EVERYONE'S GONE MAD!
REED! WHAT IS IT? WHAT'S HAPPENED ??
I DON'T KNOW, KID! BUT UNTIL WE FIND OUT, WE'VE GOT TO RUN FOR SAFETY!
THEY ACTED AS THOUGH THEY WANTED TO DESTROY US!
I AIN'T MUCH GOOD AT HAND-SHAKES, BUT FIGHTIN'! THAT'S SOMETHIN' I CAN UNDER-STAND!
THERE THEY GO! DON'T LET THEM GET AWAY!
AFTER THEM!
CALL THE POLICE! THE MILITIA! GET THE FANTASTIC FOUR!
FLAME ON!
EASY, BOYS! I DON'T WANNA HURT ANY-BODY, BUT LET US PASS OR ELSE IT'S GONNA GET AWFUL HOT AROUND HERE!
WE CAN'T TACKLE HIM WITH-OUT ASBESTOS SUITS!
WE'RE SURROUNDED! QUICK, SUE--TURN INVISIBLE WHILE I KEEP THE TROOPS BUSY!
BUT HOW WILL YOU GET AWAY, REED??
JUST WATCH ME!
OOOF!
SHE'S OVER HERE! I GOT HER!
NO! SHE'S HERE! I GOT HER!
SORRY, BOYS!
9

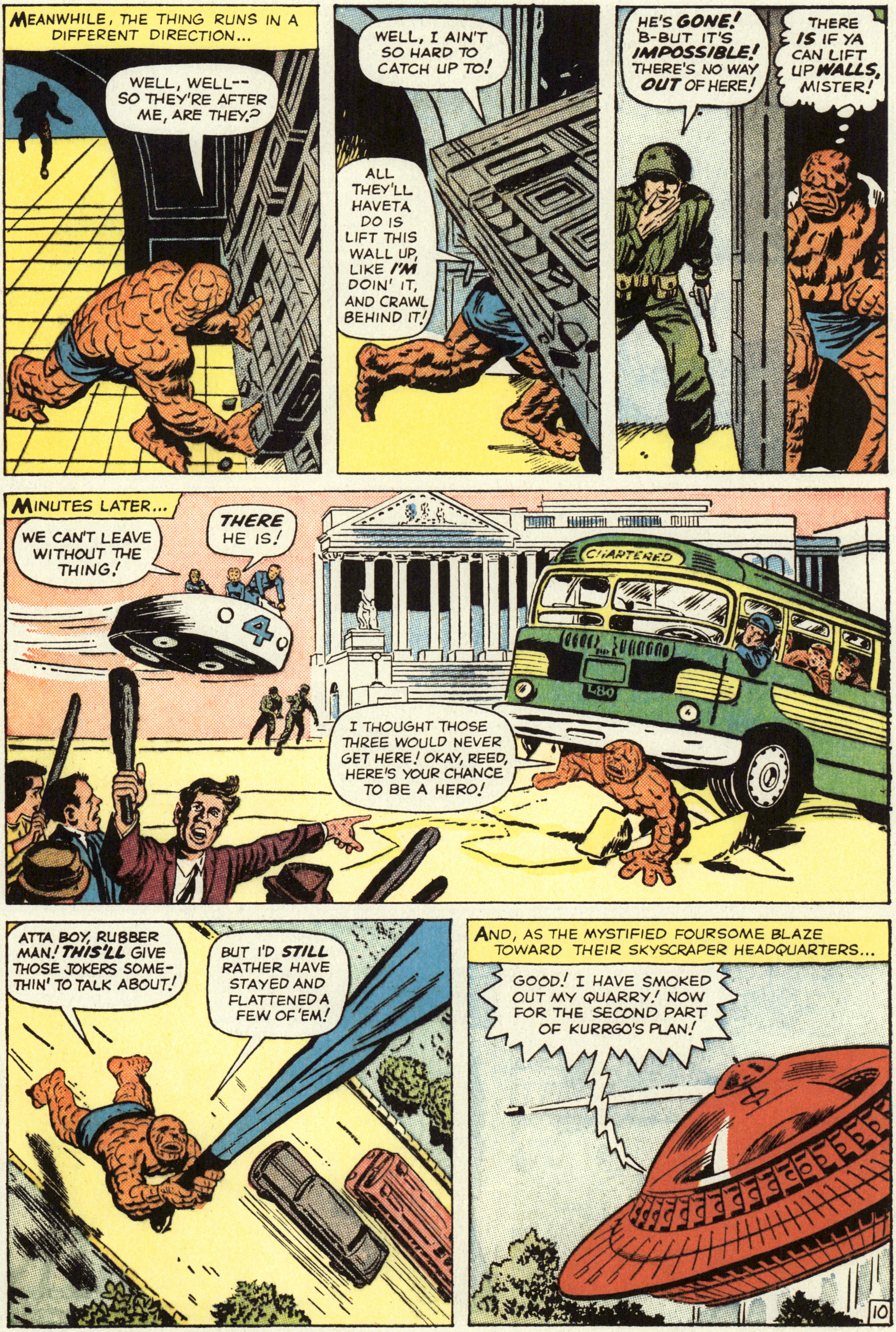
MEANWHILE, THE THING RUNS IN A DIFFERENT DIRECTION...
WELL, WELL-- SO THEY'RE AFTER ME, ARE THEY?
WELL, I AIN'T SO HARD TO CATCH UP TO!
ALL THEY'LL HAVETA DO IS LIFT THIS WALL UP, LIKE I'M DOIN' IT, AND CRAWL BEHIND IT!
HE'S GONE! B-BUT IT'S IMPOSSIBLE! THERE'S NO WAY OUT OF HERE!
THERE IS IF YA CAN LIFT UP WALLS, MISTER!
MINUTES LATER...
WE CAN'T LEAVE WITHOUT THE THING!
THERE HE IS!
CHARTERED
I THOUGHT THOSE THREE WOULD NEVER GET HERE! OKAY, REED, HERE'S YOUR CHANCE TO BE A HERO!
ATTA BOY, RUBBER MAN! THIS'LL GIVE THOSE JOKERS SOME-THIN' TO TALK ABOUT!
BUT I'D STILL RATHER HAVE STAYED AND FLATTENED A FEW OF 'EM!
AND, AS THE MYSTIFIED FOURSOME BLAZE TOWARD THEIR SKYSCRAPER HEADQUARTERS...
GOOD! I HAVE SMOKED OUT MY QUARRY! NOW FOR THE SECOND PART OF KURRGO'S PLAN!
10

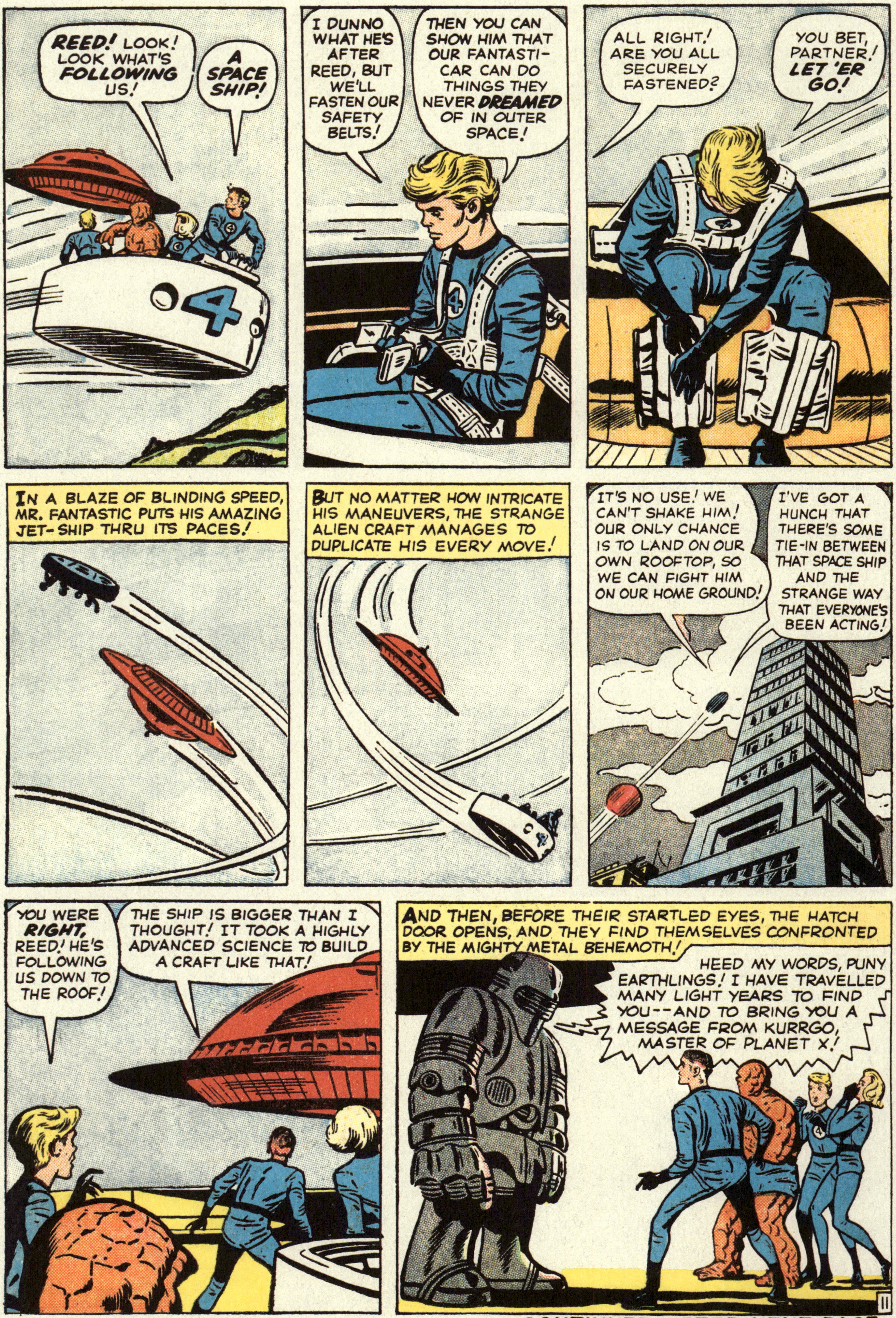

CONTINUED AFTER NEXT PAGE.

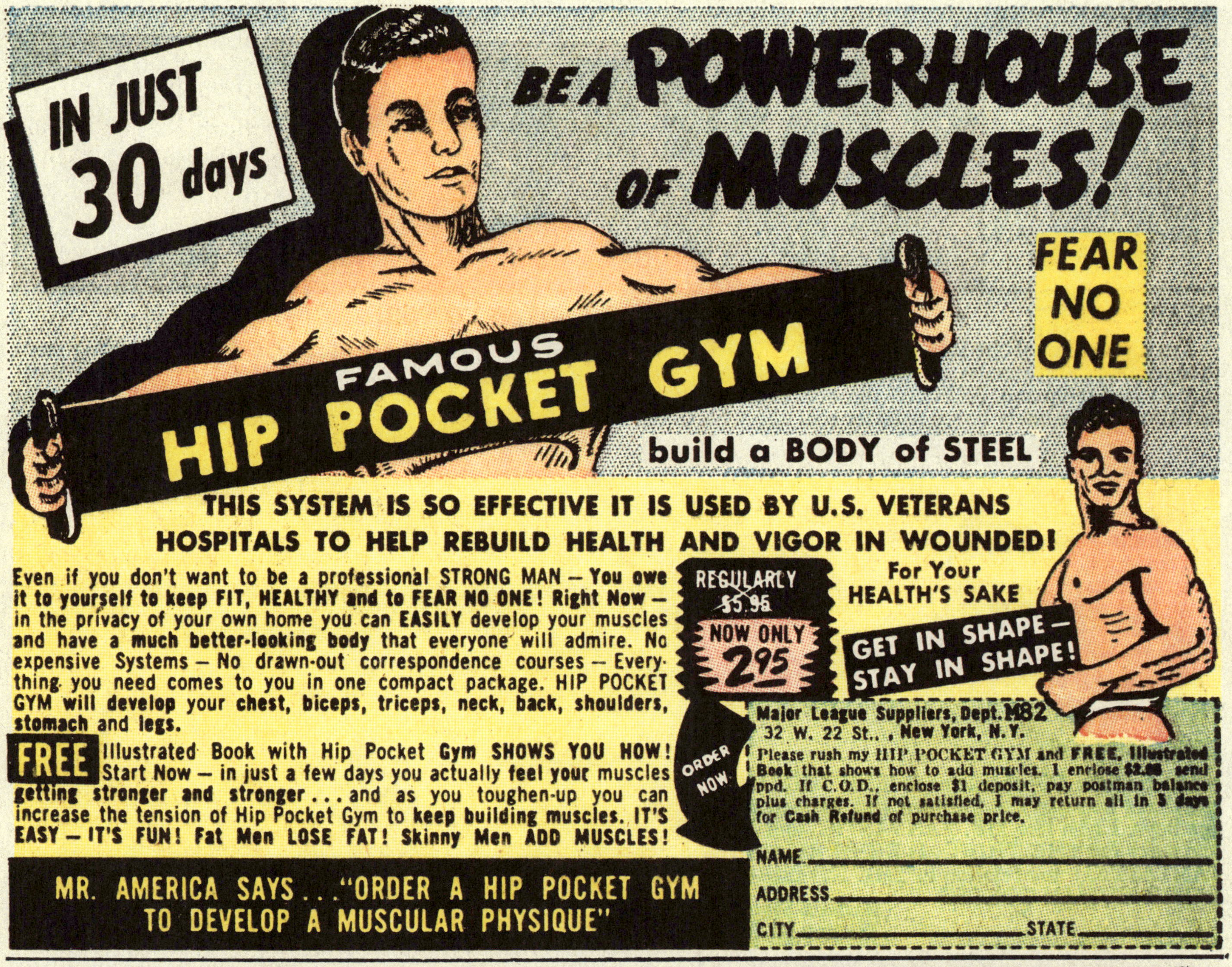
IN JUST 30 days
BE A POWERHOUSE OF MUSCLES!
FEAR NO ONE
FAMOUS HIP POCKET GYM
build a BODY of STEEL
THIS SYSTEM IS SO EFFECTIVE IT IS USED BY U.S. VETERANS HOSPITALS TO HELP REBUILD HEALTH AND VIGOR IN WOUNDED!
Even if you don't want to be a professional STRONG MAN — You owe it to yourself to keep FIT, HEALTHY and to FEAR NO ONE! Right Now — in the privacy of your own home you can EASILY develop your muscles and have a much better-looking body that everyone will admire. No expensive Systems — No drawn-out correspondence courses — Everything you need comes to you in one compact package. HIP POCKET GYM will develop your chest, biceps, triceps, neck, back, shoulders, stomach and legs.
FREE Illustrated Book with Hip Pocket Gym SHOWS YOU HOW! Start Now — in just a few days you actually feel your muscles getting stronger and stronger . . . and as you toughen-up you can increase the tension of Hip Pocket Gym to keep building muscles. IT'S EASY — IT'S FUN! Fat Men LOSE FAT! Skinny Men ADD MUSCLES!
REGULARLY $5.95
NOW ONLY 2.95
ORDER NOW
For Your HEALTH'S SAKE
GET IN SHAPE — STAY IN SHAPE!
Major League Suppliers, Dept. M82
32 W. 22 St., , New York, N.Y.
Please rush my HIP POCKET GYM and FREE, Illustrated Book that shows how to add muscles. I enclose send ppd. If C.O.D., enclose $1 deposit, pay postman balance plus charges. If not satisfied, I may return all in 5 days for Cash Refund of purchase price.
NAME
ADDRESS
CITY STATE
MR. AMERICA SAYS . . . "ORDER A HIP POCKET GYM TO DEVELOP A MUSCULAR PHYSIQUE"

LOOK! Boys Wanted TO SELL GRIT
SPENDING MONEY! PRIZES!
5 CENTS PROFIT YOURS ON EVERY COPY SOLD.
30,000 Boys Selling Each Week Know
It's Fun It's Easy
You Can Make $1 to $5 Every Week in a Few Hours
START NOW EARNING BIG CASH PROFITS AND FREE PRIZES
Fellows!
Earn all the spending money you want. GRIT is popular in 900,000 homes. It is easy to sell. You get FREE PRIZES in addition to the money you make. You also gain valuable business experience to help you become a successful man. I'll be glad to help you get started in this business of your own.
Pay only for copies sold until you know how many to order. Papers will be sent immediately.
Print Name and Address Below
If You Are a Boy 12 Years Old or Older
MAIL THIS TODAY
In an Envelope or Pasted on a Post Card
GRIT PUBLISHING CO., Williamsport, Pa.
Send my first bundle of papers, selling helps and prize offers. MC8-2
Name
Are You a Boy? .... Age .... Date Born .... Year ....
In Care of
Street and No. .... R. F. D. ....
Post Office .... State ....
Print Your Last Name Plainly Here

THE FANTASTIC FOUR in
PART 3
"BOUND FOR PLANET X!"
BEHOLD! THIS IS A SCENE ON YOUR EARTH STREET! OBSERVE HOW THE CROWDS ARE RIOTING! IT IS YOU THEY WOULD SEIZE!
REED! THIS IS NO TIME TO STUDY NEW GADGETS! WHAT MADE SOCIETY SUDDENLY TURN AGAINST US?? AND WHAT ARE WE GOING TO DO ABOUT IT!??
A PORTABLE SELF-CONTAINED TV RECEIVER! AMAZING!!
Stan Lee + J. KIRBY
12

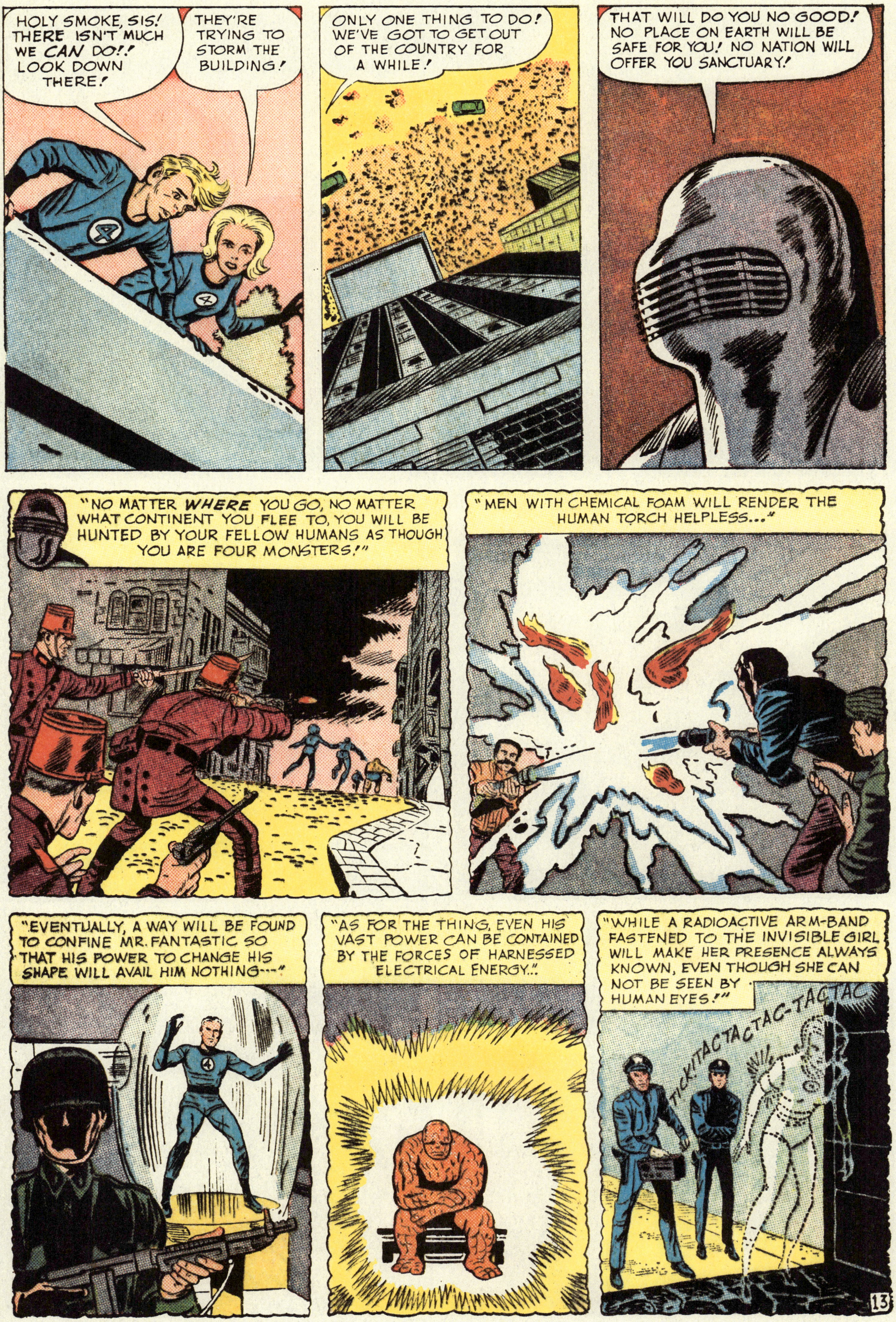

HOLY SMOKE, SIS! THERE ISN'T MUCH WE CAN DO!! LOOK DOWN THERE!
THEY'RE TRYING TO STORM THE BUILDING!
ONLY ONE THING TO DO! WE'VE GOT TO GET OUT OF THE COUNTRY FOR A WHILE!
THAT WILL DO YOU NO GOOD! NO PLACE ON EARTH WILL BE SAFE FOR YOU! NO NATION WILL OFFER YOU SANCTUARY!
"NO MATTER WHERE YOU GO, NO MATTER WHAT CONTINENT YOU FLEE TO, YOU WILL BE HUNTED BY YOUR FELLOW HUMANS AS THOUGH YOU ARE FOUR MONSTERS!"
"MEN WITH CHEMICAL FOAM WILL RENDER THE HUMAN TORCH HELPLESS..."
"EVENTUALLY, A WAY WILL BE FOUND TO CONFINE MR. FANTASTIC SO THAT HIS POWER TO CHANGE HIS SHAPE WILL AVAIL HIM NOTHING---"
"AS FOR THE THING, EVEN HIS VAST POWER CAN BE CONTAINED BY THE FORCES OF HARNESSED ELECTRICAL ENERGY..."
"WHILE A RADIOACTIVE ARM-BAND FASTENED TO THE INVISIBLE GIRL WILL MAKE HER PRESENCE ALWAYS KNOWN, EVEN THOUGH SHE CAN NOT BE SEEN BY HUMAN EYES!"
TICK-TACTAC-TAC-TACTAC
13

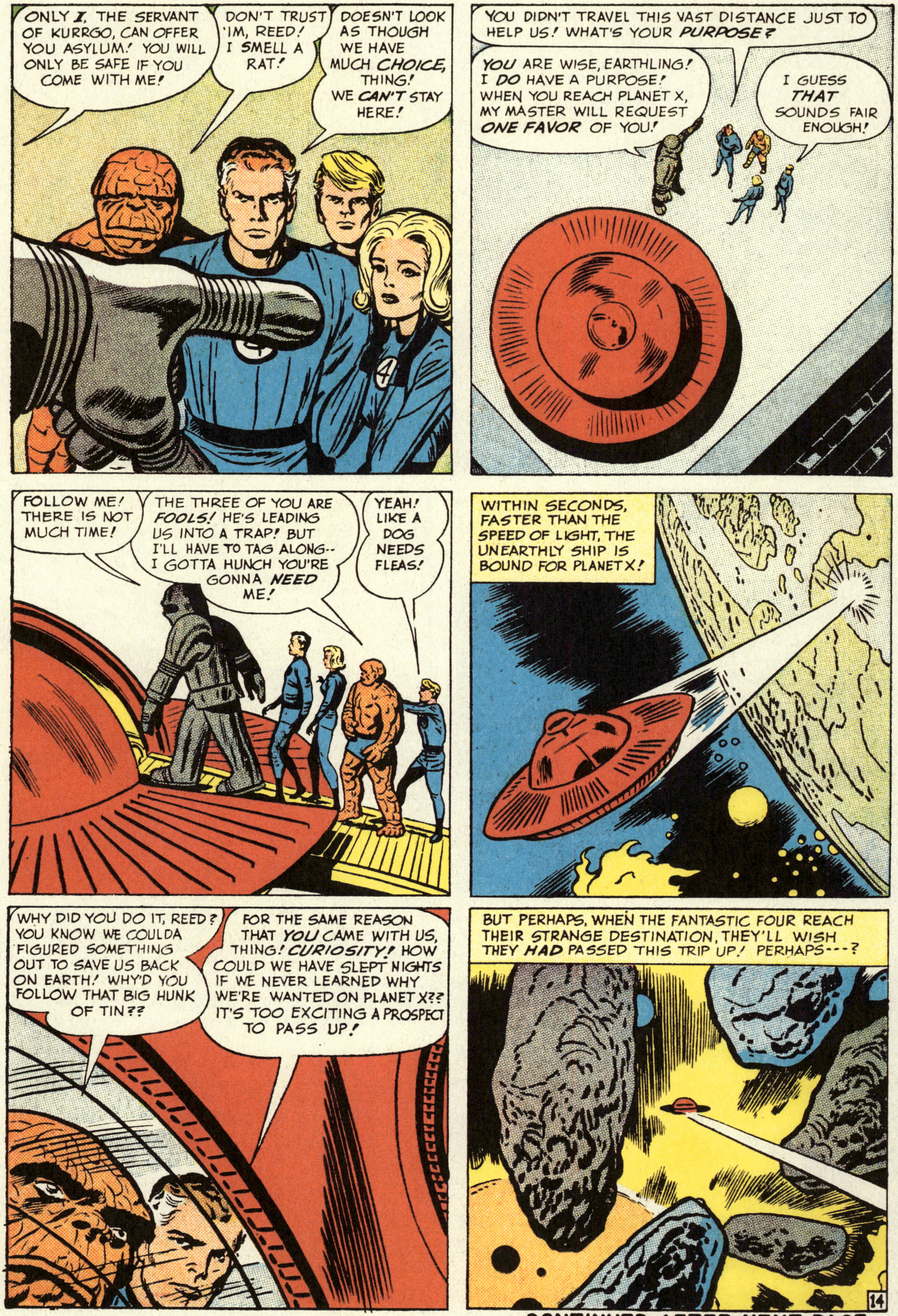

CONTINUED AFTER NEXT PAGE...

STAMPS

SHOP BY MAIL

STAMP COLLECTING OUTFIT
A packet of stamps from all parts of world. A package of stamp hinges; perforation gauge and millimeter scale; watermark detector. Everything ONLY 10c to approval buyers.
LORRAINE W. BROWN, Dept. 10, Marion, Mich.

1c Thousands of beautiful stamps at only 1c each—why pay more when you can get the best for less. Write today for approvals.
PENNY STAMP SERVICE
Orange California

BETTER U.S. APPROVALS
To introduce our BETTER U.S. APPROVALS we offer 15 of the most wanted U.S. stamps, including a Columbian, Bi-Cents, Army-Navy, Famous American, Airs and other Commems. for only 10c.
OCEAN STAMPS, BOX 64-D, BROOKLYN 29, N.Y.

1/2 OFF OUR APPROVALS are sold at 50% of Scott Catalogue prices. MAKE US PROVE IT!
CATALINA STAMPS, Dept. C Orange, California

25 DIFF. CHINA 10¢
BIG Value ONLY 10c to Approval Buyers. EXTRA! We give our regular customers a 56,000 Space Album after certain purchases.
WEST COAST STAMPS, Box 2187-X, Santa Ana, Calif.

WEIRD DIAMOND SHAPE COFFEE STAMPS
Lovely Flower Triangle! First American big commemorative. Greenland, Idol Dancer, etc. 10¢ with approvals. Capital Stamp Co., Ferrysburg 19 Mich.

BIG STAMP JUNGLE 10¢
With Approvals. Zabu, kookaburra, lion, koalabear, rhinoceros and many others.
Watermark Detector FREE
CROWN STAMP CO, VIRGIL 316, ONT.

WORLD - WIDE STAMPS ! !
100 diff. stamps of World FREE to approval service applicants 5¢. 8 diff. Mint Space Stamps for 25¢.
SPRUCELAND C2, 115 State St., Spgfld 3, Mass.

$5 SPECIAL STAMP OFFER! 10¢
Amazing offer to introduce our better U.S approvals Get 2 different $5.00 U.S. stamps PLUS 20 more hi-values, air mails, commemoratives, etc. Send only 10¢ for this splendid value. Send your dime TODAY to
IRWIN STAMP CO. - Box 11 - BROOKLYN 30, N. Y.

GIGANTIC COLLECTION FREE!
Includes Triangles, Early United States – Animals – Commemoratives – British Colonies –High Value Pictorials, etc. Complete Collection plus Big Illustrated Magazine, all free. Send 5c for postage.
GRAY STAMP CO., Dept. MC, Toronto, Canada

American Historical Collection!! Enormous George Washington beauty, F. D. Roosevelt DIAMOND, Giant Abe Lincoln USA Flag commemorative, plus Midget soldier, Latin Orchid issue, Old IFNI overprint, etc. 10¢ with approvals. **Roseland Stamps, Spring Lake 19A, Mich.**

55 "FDR" & POPE TRIANGLE!! Lot 55 DIFFERENT has FDR Diamond, "Pope" Triangle, Greenland, Angola Map, Rhodesia etc. Catalogs $1.15—ALL only 5c with Approvals.
LONGHORN STAMP CO., Box 3068, Ellwood Sta. Lubbock, Tex.

FABULOUS AMERICAN SET
Flag Set, National Park Set, and Presidential Set value up to $5. Send 10c for 15 of the above Stamps plus full particulars and Approvals.
MAXIM STAMP CO., Dept. MC
145 Nassau St., New York 38, N. Y.

DRESSES 24c
Shoes 39c • Men's Suits $4.95
Trousers $1.20. Better used clothing.
Write for FREE Catalog
TRANSWORLD, Dept. 143-A
162 Christopher Ave., Brooklyn 12, N. Y.

POEMS WANTED for musical setting and recording. Send poems Free Examination.
AMERICA'S LARGEST SONG STUDIO
FIVE STAR MUSIC MASTERS, 92 BEACON BLDG., BOSTON, MASS

250 WAYS TO MAKE LOTS OF MONEY AT HOME SEND 50c FOR LIST
"SPARE CASH" • P.O. BOX 1225 • NEWARK 1, N. J.

103 DIFF. BRITISH EMPIRE 10c
From Britain's farflung Colonies
Genuine Catalog value over $2.00.
100% Satisfaction Guaranteed — approvals.
LINCOLN STAMP CO., St. Catharines 416, Ont.

LOOK — GIANT PHILIPPINE
stamp, plus New Zealand, Cuba and others. Only 5c with U.S. or foreign approvals.
Earl Thompson, 5448 Odell St., St. Louis 9, Mo.

GHANA
7 Different beautiful Ghana Commemoratives valued at more than 60¢ — just 10¢ to all those requesting our famous approvals.
VIKING, GREAT NECK 13, N. Y.

WILL ROGERS AIR! HELICOPTER TRIANGLE!! Plus Monte Carlo Dove Triangle! Stamp printed in Solid Gold! New York Empire State Bldg. airmail, lovely Congo Orchids in full colors, etc., 10c with approvals. Sunny Stamps Service, Apopka 19A, Florida.

TERRIFIC TRIANGLES!!
Frightful Fish, Sports, Volcanoes TRIANGLES, also African Flowers, weird Angola Map, tri-colored Flag, etc. to approval buyers for 4c postage.
POTOMAC STAMP COMPANY
Dept. 7 Washington 15, D. C.

MAYFLOWER STAMP ALBUM 10c
487 Illustrations, 64 pages
To introduce our approvals.
NIAGARA STAMP CO., St. Catharines 716, Ont.

POEMS WANTED
For musical setting. Send your Poems today for Free Examination. Any subject. Immediate consideration.
CROWN MUSIC CO., 49-MC W. 32 St., New York 1

1000 TRICKS 25c AMAZE!... ENTERTAIN! HAVE FUN! START NOW!
BIG EXCITING MAGIC & FUN CATALOG! 160 PAGES!
Tricks, Jokes, Magic, Illusions, Secrets! Puzzles, Stunts, etc. World famous! Rush name, address & only 25c.
FREE CARD TRICK GIVEN with Each Catalog!
HOUSE OF 1000 MYSTERIES
Dept. MC8-62 Trumbull Conn.

225 STAMPS FOR ONLY 10¢
THIS MAMMOTH VALUE INCLUDES STAMPS WORTH UP TO 25c! ALSO APPROVALS. WRITE TODAY!
MYSTIC STAMP CO Camden 3 New York

PHOTO BARGAINS

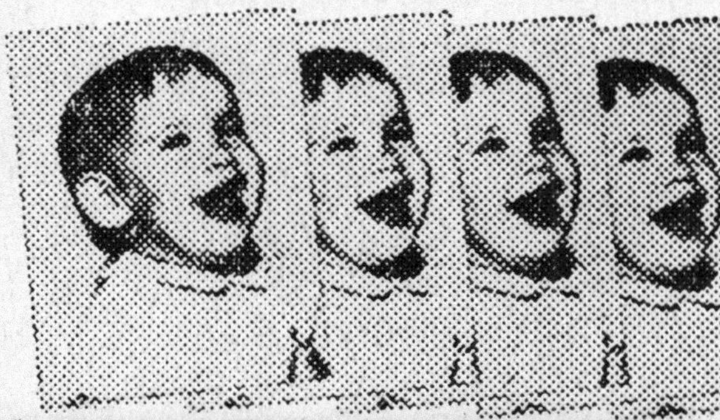

ONLY 1.00 YOUR CHOICE
2 8x10 ENLARGEMENTS (1 Colored in Oil)
or
4 5x7 ENLARGEMENTS (1 Colored in Oil)
or
25 WALLET PHOTOS (plus FREE 5x7 Enl.)
Lovely reproductions of your favorite photo on finest quality double weight portrait paper. Send any size photo, snapshot, or negative (returned unharmed). Add 25¢ for postage and handling.
QUALITY VALUES
2 East Avenue, Studio 669 A, Larchmont, N.Y.

SONG IDEAS WANTED
s/a Songwriters, with publisher contacts, want song ideas. SHARE ROYALTIES. NO FEES. Send poems:
SONGWRITERS' ASSOCIATES
Studio 19, 1650 Broadway, New York 19, N. Y.

1001 THINGS YOU CAN GET FREE 50¢ Gifts • Samples Books • Stamps Etc.
THINGS FREE • P.O. BOX 1225 • NEWARK 1, N. J.

INSIGNIA 40 for $1.00
ARMY • NAVY • MARINE
Includes 40 Different Shoulder Emblems, Ratings, Chevrons, Q-Bars, Medals, Ribbons, Collar Insignia, etc. ORDER NOW! Send $1.00 for 40 or $5.00 for 250. NO DUPLICATES —ALL DIFFERENT
EMBLEM SALES CO. Dept. 1000
P.O. Box 167, Madison Sq. Sta., N.Y. 10

AUTOMATIC REPEATING MAGIC WATER PISTOL
Aim at One Person — Shoot Water at Someone Else!
ONLY 95¢ POST PAID (NO COD's) MONEY BACK GUARANTEE

TURN KNOB TO SHOOT WATER RIGHT OR LEFT
Naranjo & Company, P.O. Box 134, Kew Gardens, N.Y.

NEW— POCKET SIZE INVENTION HELPS HYPNOTIZE YOURSELF or OTHERS IN MINUTES!

MUST WORK OR MONEY BACK!
Hold the HYPNO-COIN in front of the person you want to hypnotize. Gently vibrate the plastic lense. This sets a whirling hypnotic pattern into motion that is so fascinating, it captures and holds your subject's gaze. Now give your hypnotic suggestions! Get this amazing hypnotic aid complete with a FREE revealing booklet of secrets and instructions that tell you what to say and do, how to command and re-hypnotize with the snap of a finger, how to thrill and amaze them with hypnotic stunts, etc. Get the COIN, Booklet and Stand for Self Hypnosis – only $1.00 ppd. Sent in a plain wrapper. Money back if not delighted!
HYPNOTIC-AIDS • Dept. A83, 1133 Broadway, N.Y.C. 10
$1.00 Name.................... Address....................

THE FANTASTIC FOUR in
PART 4
"TWENTY FOUR HOURS TILL ZERO!"
Stan Lee + J. Kirby
FINALLY, AFTER HOURS OF VOYAGING THRU SPACE, THE WHIRLING STARSHIP REACHES PLANET X! THEN, A HATCH SLOWLY OPENS AND BEFORE THEY KNOW IT, THE FANTASTIC QUARTET FIND THEMSELVES FLOATING TOWARDS THE SURFACE... DESCENDING GENTLY ON AN INVISIBLE BEAM OF ANTI-GRAVITY MATTER!
15

AND FINALLY...
WOW!! WHATTA RIDE!
LOOK OUT BELOW!
THIS ANTI-GRAV RAY MAY BE TERRIFIC, BUT I STILL PREFER ELEVATORS!
MY MISSION IS ENDED, MASTER! I HAVE BROUGHT THE FANTASTIC FOUR!
GOOD!
SO THAT'S KURRGO, THE MASTER OF PLANET X, EH? PUNY-LOOKIN' SHRIMP, AIN'T HE?
QUIET, THING! WHY HAVE YOU SUMMONED US TO YOUR PLANET, KURRGO?
YOU SHALL LEARN THE ANSWER SOON ENOUGH, EARTHLING!
WE OF PLANET X ARE YOUR SUPERIORS IN MANY WAYS! WE HAVE DEVELOPED ANTI-GRAVITY! WE HAVE LEARNED THE SECRET OF STAR TRAVEL! BUT THERE IS YET ONE PROBLEM WE HAVE NOT SOLVED!
AND WHAT IS THAT?
"THE PROBLEM OF HOW TO SAVE OUR PLANET FROM TOTAL DESTRUCTION! ALREADY, IN THE COASTLANDS, THE TIDES GROW UNCONTROLLABLY HIGH!"
"THRU OUT OUR PLANET THE LAND IS IN A STATE OF UPHEAVAL, AS VOLCANOS AND ERUPTIONS THREATEN OUR ENTIRE POPULATION!"
"DRIVEN BY FEAR AND PANIC, OUR PEOPLE ARE TURNING AGAINST EACH OTHER! SOON, NOTHING WILL BE ABLE TO STOP THE RIOTS... ...NOTHING EXCEPT THE DOOM WHICH IS HURTLING TOWARDS US!"
16

THERE! THERE IS OUR PROBLEM! A RUNAWAY PLANET, STREAKING THRU THE SKIES---ABOUT TO STRIKE PLANET X!
AND IF YOU, WITH ALL YOUR WIZARDRY AND POWERS, CANNOT FIND A WAY TO SAVE US THEN WE WILL PERISH-- ---TOGETHER!
REED! WHAT CAN WE DO?? THERE'S NO WAY TO STOP A RACING PLANET
I KNEW WE SHOULDN'T COME! BUT NOBODY'D LISTEN TO ME!
WE --WE'RE ALL DOOMED !!
WAIT!..WHY CAN'T EVERYONE ESCAPE IN SPACE SHIPS?
BECAUSE, ALTHO' WE HAVE THE SECRET OF SPACE TRAVEL, WE HAVE NEVER CARED TO VISIT OTHER WORLDS! AND SO, ONLY TWO LARGE SHIPS HAVE BEEN BUILT! WHAT GOOD ARE THEY, WHEN THE POPULATION OF PLANET X IS... FIVE BILLION INHABITANTS??!
WELL, BIG BRAIN! YOU GOT US INTO THIS! WHAT DO WE DO NOW??
I DON'T KNOW, THING! BUT THIS IS NO TIME FOR SQUABBLING! WE'VE ALL GOT TO THINK!
THINK--MY EYE! LET'S GET THAT WALKIN' HUNKA TIN TO TAKE US BACK TO EARTH---PRONTO!
NO! HE IS MY SERVANT! HE TAKES ORDERS FROM NONE BUT KURRGO!
OH YEAH?? WELL, WE'LL SEE ABOUT THAT!
FOOL! HE IS MADE OF THE STRONGEST SUBSTANCE IN THE UNIVERSE!
OWWWW...!!
HE--- WASN'T KIDDIN'!
SUDDENLY AT A COMMAND FROM KURRGO, THE SILENT ROBOT GRASP THE THING'S ACHING ARM AND HURLS HIM ACROSS THE CHAMBER, AS THOUGH HIS FOE WERE WEIGHTLESS!
EVEN YOUR STRENGTH IS NO MATCH FOR THOSE WHO HAVE MASTERED GRAVITY!
17

NOBODY DOES THAT TO THE THING -- NOBODY!!
FLAME ON!
REACH ALL YOU WANT TO, TIN MAN! YOU'LL FIND THAT I'M TOO HOT TO HANDLE!
I'M GONNA DO SOMETHING I'VE ALWAYS BEEN AFRAID TO TRY BEFORE!
BY INCREASING MY FLAME TO FEVER PITCH, I CAN ATTAIN THE GREATEST HEAT IN THE UNIVERSE!
I CAN MATCH THE FIERY BLAZE OF AN EXPLODING STAR ...A SUPER NOVA!!
NO, TORCH-- --NO!!.. DON'T DO IT!!
IT'S TOO MUCH POWER! YOU WON'T BE ABLE TO CONTROL IT! STOP, TORCH!!
IT'S NO USE! HE CAN'T EVEN HEAR ME!
GET BACK--- ALL OF YOU! I'LL STOP HIM!
HE'LL HAVE TO STOP WHEN HE SEES ME!
TORCH, DON'T!
AND NOW, I'LL---SUE! NO!! GOT TO TURN! CAN'T HURT SUE!!
WHEW! THAT WAS A CLOSE ONE, KID! YOU ALMOST BLEW US ALL UP!
IDIOTS! DON'T WASTE PRECIOUS MINUTES! EVERY SECOND BRINGS US CLOSER TO DESTRUCTION! YOU MUST FIND A WAY TO SAVE PLANET X-- IN 24 HOURS!
18.

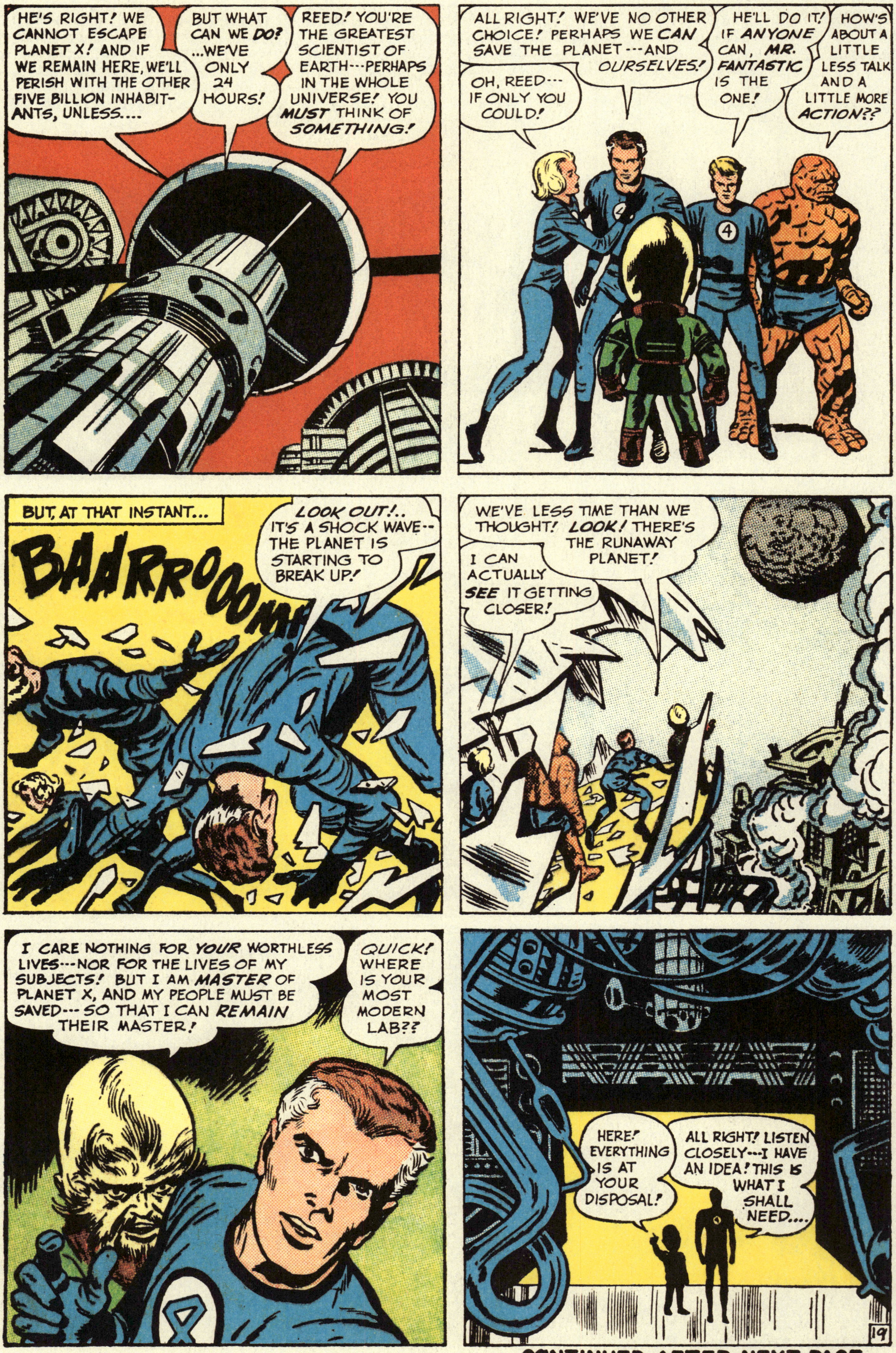

CONTINUED AFTER NEXT PAGE...

Address YOUR letters to:
THE EDITOR
FANTASTIC FOUR
THIRD FLOOR
655 MADISON AVE.
NEW YORK 21, N. Y.

FANTASTIC 4 FAN PAGE

DEAR EDITOR:

I'm a great fan of the FANTASTIC FOUR and think it is tops! One thing puzzles me, though—Was THE THING just as bad-tempered BEFORE the accident, or did the radiation which made him a monster also affect his brain?

Warren Jacobs
Yonkers, N. Y.

Good question, Warren. Actually, before Ben Grimm became THE THING, he was a rough and ready jet pilot, hot-tempered but good-natured, always ready for a laugh or a challenge. In fact, before telling you more about him, an idea hit us. Perhaps we will, in a future issue, devote part of story to the lives of the Fantastic Four BEFORE they got their strange powers. How about it, fans?

DEAR EDITOR:

My favorite FF character is THE HUMAN TORCH, but that's because I'm fourteen and happen to like teenage boys. I also like MR. FANTASTIC, and I sometimes feel sorry for THE THING. Is REED RICHARDS (MR. FANTASTIC) any relation to THE INVISIBLE GIRL — or THE HUMAN TORCH?

Barbara Stock
Pontiac 18, Mich.

Many readers have written to ask what the FANTASTIC FOUR's relationship with each other is. Apparently many of you missed our first issue, so to briefly explain: THE HUMAN TORCH and THE INVISIBLE GIRL (Johnny and Sue) are brother and sister. MR. FANTASTIC (Reed) had been a good friend of Sue's, and THE THING (Ben) was the pilot they hired to fly them on their ill-fated space voyage.

DEAR EDITOR:

I like your mag, but let's watch it, huh! In chapter three of FF #5, you show MR. FANTASTIC stretching up to kayo a pirate. They didn't make rubberized clothes in those days, you know!

Alan Carlson
Cadillac, Mich.

Oops!

DEAR EDITOR:

Good show! I am of course referring to FF #5! Jack Kirby's illustrating shows definite improvement. The cover was especially excellent, as were the battle scenes on the pirate ship. HUMAN TORCH is unmistakably your best character; he is certainly deserving of his own mag, as a reader recently suggested. As for THE THING conflict, I feel he (or "it"?) should remain basically the same as he is because this unique character adds color to the group, which makes it comparable to no other. The name MR. FANTASTIC is too egotistical, yet "Mr. Elastic" would be even more ridiculous.

Melvin Herbers
Elyria, Ohio

Regarding the TORCH, Mel, and all you other readers who have clamored for Johnny to appear in another magazine, don't miss STRANGE TALES #101, on sale now. You've got a pleasant surprise in store for you!

DEAR EDITOR:

Much as I like even numbers, I think adding one more member to the FANTASTIC FOUR wouldn't hurt. Besides, "Fantastic Five" sounds just as good — even better. He could be a scientific genius and assist MR. FANTASTIC, or a wizard who uses magic to fight crime — or perhaps an alien from space. What do you think?

Sal Anzaldi
Pompton Plains, N. J.

Why stop with just five, Sal? Why not the "Fantastic Six", or "Ten" or "Eighty-Three"?? Well, as usual, we'll leave it up to the fans. We're sure our other readers have some very definite opinions on this earth-shaking subject!

DEAR EDITOR:

As an English schoolboy reading THE FANTASTIC FOUR for the first time, may I say how intrigued I am with it! I have been thrilled with the story about SUB-MARINER, and hope I will miss none of the future copies so that I may keep up to date with this smashing magazine.

John Davidson
Newcastle-on-Tyne 3,
England

How ABOUT that?!! We may ask for a State Department subsidy for building up good will! Many thanks, John — we hope you'll continue to enjoy the adventures of your American cousins!

DEAR EDITOR:

Congratulations to "The World's Greatest Comic"! It is the most original, most exciting, most realistic, most surprising comic in the universe! We like the way the FF are always reading comics! (Showing their high mentality!) The costumes are great! One bad thing though — The FANTASTICAR looks like a bathtub! Why not call it the "Fantastitub"? Having the THING able to change back to human at will would be ridiculous! Some readers think it's a good idea, but we think it's ECHH! We'll keep buying FF till you stop printing them!

P.S. Your wisecracks are also ECHH!

Rusty and Larry Bush
Forest Hills 75, N. Y.

We had a dandy crack to answer your letter with, Bushes, but we won't! Satisfied?

THAT WRAPS IT UP FOR THIS ISH, FANS! BY THE WAY, WE THOUGHT OF A GREAT WAY TO GET REVENGE ON ANYONE WHO MIGHT WRITE US A TOO-CRITICAL LETTER! WE'LL SPELL HIS NAME WRONG WHEN WE PRINT IT! OH, THE POWER WE EDITORS HAVE!

PART 5
THE FANTASTIC FOUR in "the END of PLANET X!"
Stan Lee + J. Kirby
WITH SUPPLIES HASTILY BROUGHT BY KURRGO'S ROBOTS, AND THE HELP OF HIS SUPERHUMAN PARTNERS, MR. FANTASTIC UNDERTAKES THE MOST DRAMATIC RACE AGAINST TIME OF HIS CAREER, AS HE FRANTICALLY CONSTRUCTS ONE OF THE MOST ASTONISHING DEVICES OF ALL TIME!
HURRY, TORCH! I NEED THAT CASTING!
JUST ANOTHER FEW SECONDS, REED, AND I'LL HAVE IT ALL WELDED!
WE'VE GOT TO FINISH IN TIME! WE'VE SIMPLY GOT TO!
HEY! WHERE DO YOU WANT THIS BLAMED THING? I CAN'T HOLD IT ALL DAY!
AYERS
V-895
20

ONLY A FEW HOURS REMAINING, EARTHLING!
YOU'RE JUST IN TIME, KURRGO --I'VE FINISHED!
HERE IS THE THING THAT WILL SAVE US ALL! THIS VIAL IS FILLED WITH REDUCING GAS!
REDUCING GAS??! WHAT NONSENSE IS THAT??
THE EARTHLING HAS ASKED US TO VOLUNTEER --SO THAT HE MAY DEMONSTRATE!
WATCH, KURRGO-- AND YOU'LL SEE WHAT "NONSENSE" THIS IS!
STRIKING THE WALL BEHIND THE TWO VOLUNTEERS, THE VIAL OF GAS SHATTERS!
WITHIN SECONDS, THE TWO CREATURES FROM PLANET X ARE ENVELOPED IN THE THICK SWIRLING MISTS, UNTIL...
THEY- THEY'RE GONE!
NO, KURRGO! NOT GONE!
THEY'VE MERELY BEEN REDUCED IN SIZE! REDUCED A THOUSANDFOLD!
IT- IT IS INCREDIBLE! BUT OF WHAT USE ARE SUCH ELABORATE PARLOR TRICKS?? HOW WILL THIS SAVE PLANET X???
21

"DON'T YOU SEE? MY REDUCING GAS CAN BE FIRED BY PROJECTILES TO EVERY PART OF PLANET X, WHERE IT WILL INSTANTLY SPREAD, COVERING THE ENTIRE SURFACE OF YOUR WORLD!"
"WITHIN SECONDS, EVERYONE WHOM THE GAS TOUCHES WILL BE REDUCED A THOUSANDFOLD! THIS MEANS THAT ALL FIVE BILLION OF YOUR PEOPLE WILL BE ABLE TO FIT INTO ONE SPACE SHIP! EVERYONE ON PLANET X WILL FIND SAFETY AS YOU FLY TO ANOTHER WORLD!"
"AND, UPON LANDING ON ANY NEW PLANET OF YOUR CHOOSING, YOU NEED ONLY RELEASE ANOTHER GAS PROJECTILE WHICH WILL CONTAIN THE ANTIDOTE TO THE SHRINKING GAS!"
"THEN, AS THE PEOPLE LEAVE THE SHIP AND WALK THRU THE MISTS OF THE ANTIDOTE GAS, THEY WILL SPEEDILY RESUME THEIR NORMAL SIZE! YOUR PROBLEM IS SOLVED!"
I NEVER THOUGHT YOU'D DO IT, PAL! I GOTTA HAND IT TO YOU!
C'MON, REED! WE'VE NO TIME FOR TALK! LET'S GET OUTTA HERE OURSELVES!
YES! WHERE IS OUR ESCAPE ROCKET?
YOU ARE FREE TO RETURN TO EARTH IN OUR SECOND ROCKET! GO, WHILE THERE STILL IS TIME!
HURRY! IT LOOKS AS THOUGH WE'RE NOT A MINUTE TOO SOON!
22

BUT, EVEN AS THE FANTASTIC FOURSOME RACES TO THE WAITING SPACESHIP, PLANET X BEGINS TO WRITHE IN ITS FINAL DEATH THROES!
LOOK OUT!
WE'LL BE CRUSHED BY THAT BOULDER!
NOBODY'S GETTIN' CRUSHED WHILE I'M AROUND!
THIS IS WHAT I WOULDA DONE TO THAT WALKIN' HUNK OF TIN, IF HE DIDN'T HAVE GRAVITY ON HIS SIDE!
LOOK! HOW CAN WE CROSS THAT CHASM TO REACH THE SHIP?
IF WE DON'T GET THERE SOON, WE'LL BE DOOMED ALONG WITH PLANET X!
ONLY ONE THING TO DO! LET'S HOPE I CAN STRETCH FAR ENOUGH!
YOU DID IT! LET'S GO!
THANK GOODNESS!
WITHIN SECONDS, THE HUMANS REACH THE SHIP AND BLAST OFF FROM THE DOOMED PLANET!
WHILE FAR BELOW, MR. FANTASTIC'S MASTER PLAN IS PUT INTO EFFECT IMMEDIATELY! REDUCING PROJECTILES ARE FIRED TO EVERY SECTION OF THE PLANET!
BOOM! BOOM!
23

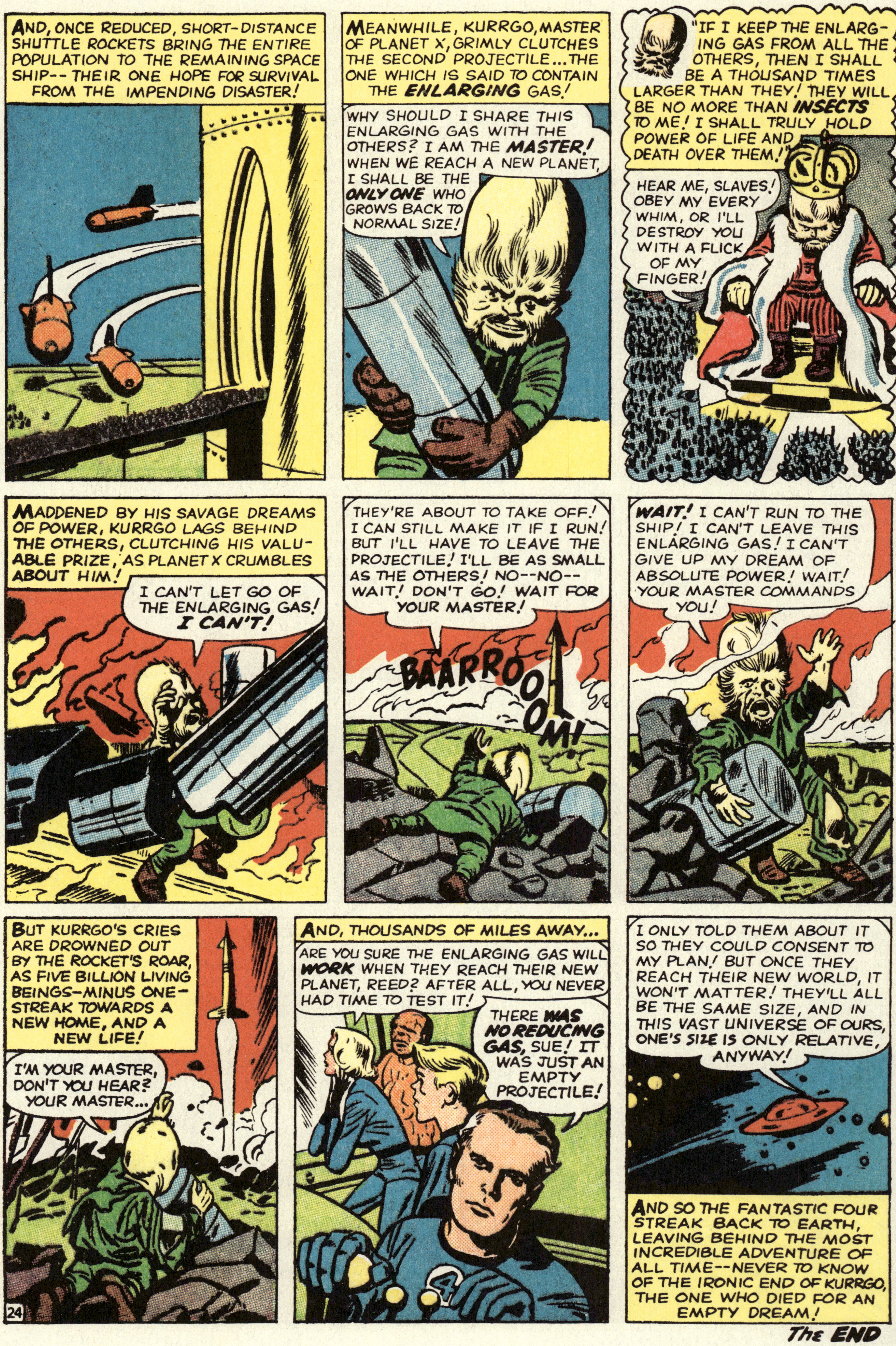

AND, ONCE REDUCED, SHORT-DISTANCE SHUTTLE ROCKETS BRING THE ENTIRE POPULATION TO THE REMAINING SPACE SHIP-- THEIR ONE HOPE FOR SURVIVAL FROM THE IMPENDING DISASTER!
MEANWHILE, KURRGO, MASTER OF PLANET X, GRIMLY CLUTCHES THE SECOND PROJECTILE ... THE ONE WHICH IS SAID TO CONTAIN THE ENLARGING GAS!
WHY SHOULD I SHARE THIS ENLARGING GAS WITH THE OTHERS? I AM THE MASTER! WHEN WE REACH A NEW PLANET, I SHALL BE THE ONLY ONE WHO GROWS BACK TO NORMAL SIZE!
"IF I KEEP THE ENLARGING GAS FROM ALL THE OTHERS, THEN I SHALL BE A THOUSAND TIMES LARGER THAN THEY! THEY WILL BE NO MORE THAN INSECTS TO ME! I SHALL TRULY HOLD POWER OF LIFE AND DEATH OVER THEM!"
HEAR ME, SLAVES! OBEY MY EVERY WHIM, OR I'LL DESTROY YOU WITH A FLICK OF MY FINGER!
MADDENED BY HIS SAVAGE DREAMS OF POWER, KURRGO LAGS BEHIND THE OTHERS, CLUTCHING HIS VALUABLE PRIZE, AS PLANET X CRUMBLES ABOUT HIM!
I CAN'T LET GO OF THE ENLARGING GAS! I CAN'T!
THEY'RE ABOUT TO TAKE OFF! I CAN STILL MAKE IT IF I RUN! BUT I'LL HAVE TO LEAVE THE PROJECTILE! I'LL BE AS SMALL AS THE OTHERS! NO--NO-- WAIT! DON'T GO! WAIT FOR YOUR MASTER!
BAARROOOOM!
WAIT! I CAN'T RUN TO THE SHIP! I CAN'T LEAVE THIS ENLARGING GAS! I CAN'T GIVE UP MY DREAM OF ABSOLUTE POWER! WAIT! YOUR MASTER COMMANDS YOU!
BUT KURRGO'S CRIES ARE DROWNED OUT BY THE ROCKET'S ROAR, AS FIVE BILLION LIVING BEINGS--MINUS ONE--STREAK TOWARDS A NEW HOME, AND A NEW LIFE!
I'M YOUR MASTER, DON'T YOU HEAR? YOUR MASTER...
AND, THOUSANDS OF MILES AWAY...
ARE YOU SURE THE ENLARGING GAS WILL WORK WHEN THEY REACH THEIR NEW PLANET, REED? AFTER ALL, YOU NEVER HAD TIME TO TEST IT!
THERE WAS NO REDUCING GAS, SUE! IT WAS JUST AN EMPTY PROJECTILE!
I ONLY TOLD THEM ABOUT IT SO THEY COULD CONSENT TO MY PLAN! BUT ONCE THEY REACH THEIR NEW WORLD, IT WON'T MATTER! THEY'LL ALL BE THE SAME SIZE, AND IN THIS VAST UNIVERSE OF OURS, ONE'S SIZE IS ONLY RELATIVE, ANYWAY!
AND SO THE FANTASTIC FOUR STREAK BACK TO EARTH, LEAVING BEHIND THE MOST INCREDIBLE ADVENTURE OF ALL TIME--NEVER TO KNOW OF THE IRONIC END OF KURRGO, THE ONE WHO DIED FOR AN EMPTY DREAM!
24
The END

THE WORLD'S GREATEST MOLDER OF HANDSOME HE-MEN and CHAMPS out of WEAKLINGS says

SKINNY OR FAT, 15, 20, 30 OR 40 YEARS OF AGE I'LL BUILD YOU INTO A NEW ATHLETIC MIGHTY-MUSCLED ALL-MALE HE-MAN

in 10 THRILLING MINUTES a day, as I have done to MILLIONS in 35 YEARS."

YOU can now get FREE!

ALL these 5 famous PICTURE-PACKED STRENGTH-TEST COURSES to Make YOU a SUPER-MAN.
(formerly $5.00 each)
Now FREE to you if you mail coupon AT ONCE! LAST CHANCE!

BEN REBHUHN
20 years Directing Head of the most famous and largest home-training body building institute in the world, through which millions of youths and men applied for training, of which countless were changed from skinny and fat weaklings into streamlined heroic he-men.

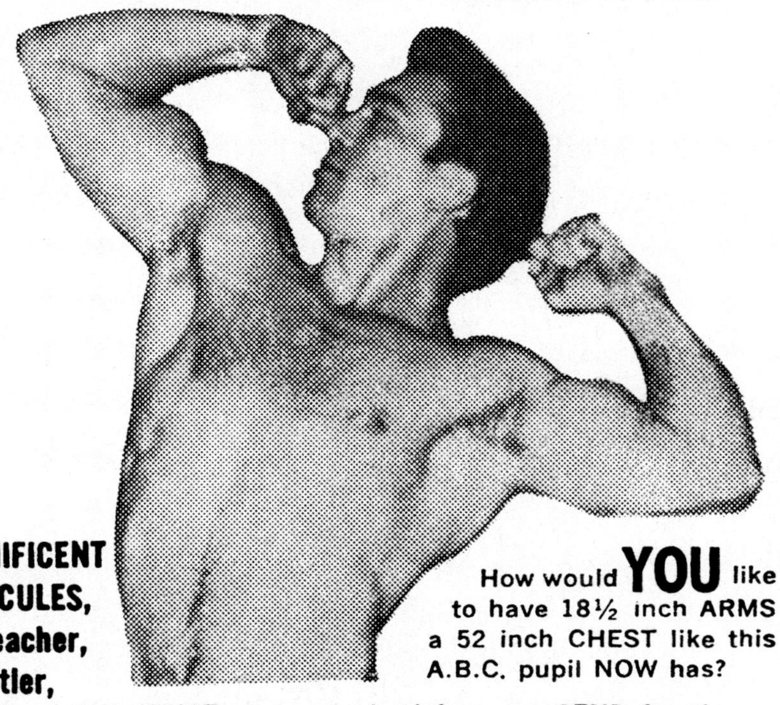

This now MAGNIFICENT MODERN HERCULES, 26 year old teacher, William Butler,

How would YOU like to have 18½ inch ARMS a 52 inch CHEST like this A.B.C. pupil NOW has?

says to YOU, "No matter WHAT your age, I advise you, SEND for the A.B.C. WONDER PICTURE COURSES at once.

Under the World's GREATEST BODY-BUILDER, I now have 18½" ARMS, a 52" CHEST; my STRENGTH has greatly improved. So have my sports. I have won titles like 'Mr. Virginia', 'Mr. State Y.M.C.', etc.

"NO MATTER WHAT YOUR AGE I'll show you, by my quick, easy SECRETS

How to GAIN OR LOSE UP TO 50 LBS. FAST

like my pupils here did and THOUSANDS do now."

17 YEAR OLD SILLS

"I GAINED 60 LBS. OF SHAPELY MIGHTY MUSCLES.

BEFORE mailing coupon, I was a 125 lb. 6 ft. skinny weakling,"

says JOHN SILL.

"I LOST 30 LBS. OF DANGEROUS UGLY FAT 4 INCHES OFF MY WAIST!

28 year old Felipe Mendoza

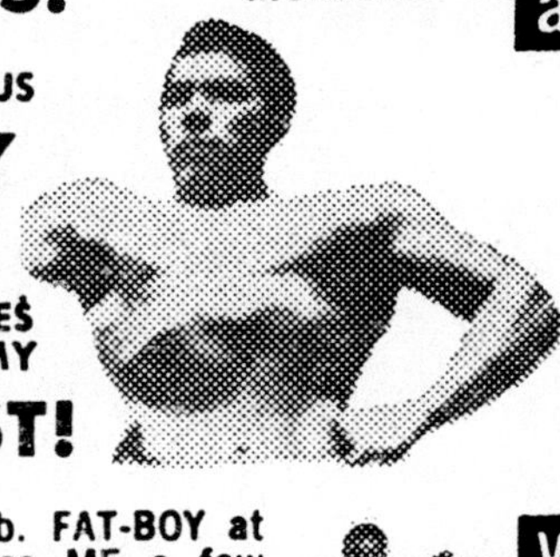

"That 220 lb. FAT-BOY at the right was ME a few short weeks ago."

A.B.C. streamlined my body, made me a new man
my 47" chest
my 32" waist
15" difference
attracts admiration at the beach.

YOU can add 7 inches to your CHEST 3½ inches to each ARM and the rest in proportion just as I did.

YOU can WIN the 18" tall SILVER TROPHY with name on it, A GOLD MEDAL, $100, as I did."

45 year old FATHER and 18 year old SON — now Pals — train A.B.C. way together!

"Both gained pounds of powerful muscles. Advise all you fathers and sons to send for the A B C courses without foolish delay."
—LARRY CAMPBELL

YOU become A WINNER in ALL you do like these and MILLIONS of my pupils!

YOU become A STAR in ANY SPORT! YOU fear NO MAN or BULLY!

YOU can soon be a HERO of MEN like Butler is and an IDOL of WOMEN in a few weeks!

Yes! In just 10 THRILLING MINUTES a day, in the SECRECY of YOUR OWN ROOM at home, MY RAPID-FIRE, EASY as ABC FAMOUS PICTURE METHODS will start building you THE VERY FIRST NIGHT. I'll show you How to Mold 16 INCH ARMS of MIGHT, a big, deep 45 INCH CHEST housing TIRELESS LUNGS, WIDE MANLY SHOULDERS — a BROAD BRAWNY BACK, tapering to a SLENDER WAIST with punch-proof STOMACH MUSCLES, LEGS of RUNNING POWER.

WOMEN always say, "I just adore A.B.C. ALL-MALE HE-MEN".

NO! I don't care now skinny or flabby you are now. if you're in your teens, twenties, thirties or forties, I'll show you in just 10 thrilling minutes in your home, how you can make yourself over by the easy, quick method I turned myself from wreck to a tower of strength and endurance. of others into all-male he-men!

YES! You'll ADD INCHES of MIGHTY MUSCLES to your ARMS, deepen your CHEST, broaden your BACK and SHOULDERS. From HEAD to HEELS you'll gain SIZE, POWER, LIGHTNING SPEED, ENDURANCE. You'll become a SUCCESSFUL HE-MAN in LOOKS and ACTS — a WINNER in EVERYTHING — athletics, business, studies.

BEFORE mailing coupon this A.B.C. pupil was this 90 lb. skeleton. Gained 70 lbs. Made football team.

"I'm proud of you now, Tony"

You wouldn't give me a tumble before I gained 28 A.B.C. lbs.

Pascarella

AMERICAN BODY BUILDING CLUB, Dept. MA-28 GREAT NECK, NEW YORK

Mail me FREE all 5 WORLD FAMOUS STRENGTH TEST COURSES, including PHOTO BOOK of FAMOUS STRONG MEN, once weaklings, now famous Strong Men, and How to Become one of Them.

☐ I enclose 10c for mailing and handling.
I am under no other obligation.
I'm checking everything I need to give me the kind of body I want.
☐ I want to gain .... lbs. (fill in). ☐ Triple my strength.
☐ I want to streamline my body, get rid of flabby fat.
☐ I want to add inches of muscle to my ☐ ARMS ☐ CHEST ☐ SHOULDERS ☐ POWERFUL LEGS ☐ SLIM WAIST
☐ I want to become a winning athlete. ☐ I want new pep.

NAME..AGE..........
DO NOT MAIL COUPON IF UNDER 14 YEARS OF AGE.
ADDRESS..
CITY.................... ZONE...... STATE..................

FREE
Sports, Self-defense, Strong-man Stunts Courses Apparatus. Let me know how to get these FREE!

AMERICAN BODY BUILDING CLUB, Dept. MA-28 GREAT NECK, NEW YORK

IND.
THE WORLD'S GREATEST COMIC MAGAZINE!
APPROVED BY THE COMICS CODE AUTHORITY
12¢
THE Fantastic Four
MC
8 NOV.
OBEY ME, MY PUPPETS! FOR MY WILL IS YOUR WILL! YOU SHALL NEVER ESCAPE YOUR NEW MASTER!
I CAN'T HELP MYSELF! THE PUPPET-MASTER IS MAKING ME ATTACK THE OTHERS!
DON'T, THING! WE MUSTN'T LET HIM CONTROL US!
"PRISONERS OF THE PUPPET-MASTER!"

THE FANTASTIC FOUR is published by CANAM PUBLISHERS SALES CORP. OFFICE OF PUBLICATION: 655 MADISON AVENUE, NEW YORK, N.Y. Published monthly. Copyright 1962 by CANAM PUBLISHERS SALES CORP., 655 Madison Avenue, New York, N.Y. Vol. 1 No 8, NOVEMBER, 1962 issue. Price 12¢ per copy. Subscription rate $1.75 for 12 issues including postage. Foreign subscription $3.25 in American funds. No similarity between any of the names, characters, persons, and/or institutions appearing in this magazine with those of any living or dead person is intended, and any such similarity which may exist is purely coincidental. Printed in the U.S.A. by The Eastern Color Printing Co., Waterbury 20, Conn.

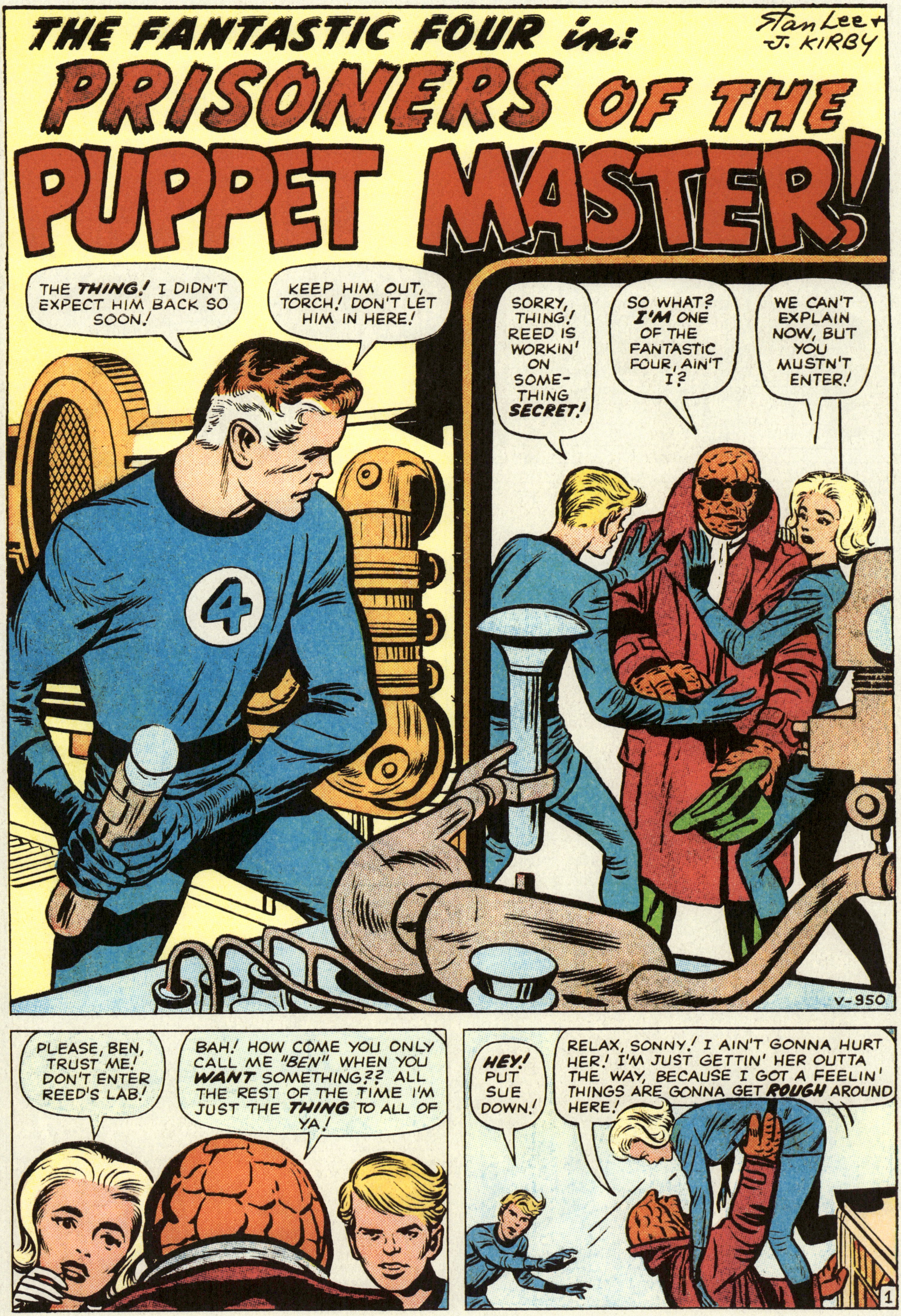
THE FANTASTIC FOUR in:
PRISONERS OF THE PUPPET MASTER!
Stan Lee + J. KIRBY
THE THING! I DIDN'T EXPECT HIM BACK SO SOON!
KEEP HIM OUT, TORCH! DON'T LET HIM IN HERE!
SORRY, THING! REED IS WORKIN' ON SOME-THING SECRET!
SO WHAT? I'M ONE OF THE FANTASTIC FOUR, AIN'T I?
WE CAN'T EXPLAIN NOW, BUT YOU MUSTN'T ENTER!
V-950
PLEASE, BEN, TRUST ME! DON'T ENTER REED'S LAB!
BAH! HOW COME YOU ONLY CALL ME "BEN" WHEN YOU WANT SOMETHING?? ALL THE REST OF THE TIME I'M JUST THE THING TO ALL OF YA!
HEY! PUT SUE DOWN!
RELAX, SONNY! I AIN'T GONNA HURT HER! I'M JUST GETTIN' HER OUTTA THE WAY, BECAUSE I GOT A FEELIN' THINGS ARE GONNA GET ROUGH AROUND HERE!
1

OKAY NOW! I'M GONNA TEACH YOU AND THAT WALKIN' RUBBER-BAND NOT TO TRY TO KEEP SECRETS FROM ME!
THING, WAIT! YOU DON'T UNDER-STAND!
I UNDERSTAND PLENTY! I'M THRU BEIN' A PATSY FOR YOU TWO GRAND-STANDERS!
YOU'RE REAL BUDDY-BUDDY WITH ME WHEN YOU NEED MY MUSCLE-- BUT WHENEVER SOMETHING IM-PORTANT COMES ALONG, I AIN'T GOOD ENOUGH TO BE TOLD ABOUT IT!
WELL, NOW THERE'S BE SOME CHANGES AROUND HERE!
LISTEN, YOU BIG LUMP OF LARD--DON'T TRY TO SCARE ME! HERE, SEE WHAT YOU'R STRENGTH CAN DO AGAINST MY ROMAN CANDLE PUNCH!
LOOK OUT, JUNIOR! THAT'S HOT!
IF YOU THINK THAT'S HOT, I'LL JUST CIRCLE YOU WITH THIS RING OF FIRE UNTIL YOU CAN COOL OFF!
SONNY, THAT FLAME OF YOURS DON'T BURN FOREVER--AND WHEN IT DIES DOWN, I'M GONNA MAKE MINCE-MEAT OUTTA YA!
KNOCK IT OFF, BOTH OF YOU! HERE, THING, I'LL DOUSE THAT FLAME FOR YOU!
BOY! REED'S GETTIN' TO BE "MR. KILLJOY OF 1962"!
HUSH, JOHNNY! HE'S ONLY TRYING TO HELP!
NOW LOOK, THING--I CAN EXPLAIN WHY I DIDN'T WANT YOU IN MY LAB...
STOW IT, CHUM! I'M FED UP TO HERE WITH YOUR SMOOTH TALK!
2

I'M CUTTIN' OUT OF THIS COMBO, AS OF NOW! THE FANTASTIC FOUR CAN GO TO BLAZES FOR ALL I CARE!
THING, WAIT! YOU'RE MAKING A BIG MISTAKE!
REED! WHAT WILL WE DO?
IT'S A PUZZLEMENT, SUE! BEN IS ONE HARD-HEADED GUY!
YOU'D BETTER FOLLOW HIM--INVISIBLY! YOUR COSTUME WOULD ATTRACT TOO MUCH ATTENTION!
AND SO:
BEN, YOU CAN'T WALK OUT LIKE THIS! WE NEED YOU!
SURE! THAT'S WHY YOU TREAT ME LIKE DRACULA'S BROTHER! SORRY, LADY! I AIN'T BUYIN'!
HEY! WHAT GIVES!
I DUNNO! LOOK AT THAT BIG CLOWN TALKIN' TO HIMSELF!
NOW GET LOST, SISTER! SAVE THAT SOB STUFF FOR REED! HE EATS IT UP!
HEY, MAC, YOU SOME KINDA NUT OR SOMETHIN'?
WHO WANTS TO KNOW?
WE DO, FATSO!
HOW ABOUT INTRODUCIN' US TO THE LADY YOU WERE TALKIN' TO??
YEAH! WHAT WAS SHE? A GREMLIN, OR ONE OF THE GOOD FAIRIES? HAW HAW!
I'LL BET YOU'VE NEVER BEEN KICKED BY A GREMLIN BEFORE, WISE-GUY!
H-HOLY SMOKE! HE WENT FLYIN'-- ALL OF A SUDDEN! WHA-WHAT'S GOIN' ON??
WHILE YOU TRY TO FIGURE IT OUT, BIG MOUTH, HERE'S A LAMP POST YOU CAN LEAN AGAINST! I'LL EVEN WRAP IT AROUND YA SO YOU DON'T FALL ON YOUR UGLY FACE LIKE HE DID!
THING! FORGET ABOUT THEM! LOOK! UP THERE!
WHERE?
3

ON THE BRIDGE! THAT MAN! HE'LL BE KILLED!
I HAVE TO CLIMB TO THE TOP, BUT I DON'T KNOW WHY!
HE'S TOO FAR AWAY! THERE'S NO WAY FOR US TO STOP HIM!
BUT PERHAPS MR. FANTASTIC, OR THE TORCH CAN DO SOMETHING!
A SPLIT-SECOND LATER, THE MOST DRAMATIC SIGHT IN THE CITY APPEARS IN THE SKY! THE CALL TO ACTION OF THE MOST COLORFUL TEAM OF ADVENTURERS THE WORLD HAS EVER KNOWN! THE AWE-INSPIRING FLARE SIGNAL OF THE FANTASTIC FOUR!
4
LOOK, REED! OUR SIGNAL! IT MUST BE FROM SUE!
THE FLARE IS HOVERING OVER THE BRIDGE TOWER! THERE'S SOME-ONE UP THERE!
HE'S ABOUT TO JUMP! IF I CAN ONLY-- UGH! NO-- IT'S TOO FAR!
CAN'T MAKE IT! IT'S UP TO YOU, TORCH!

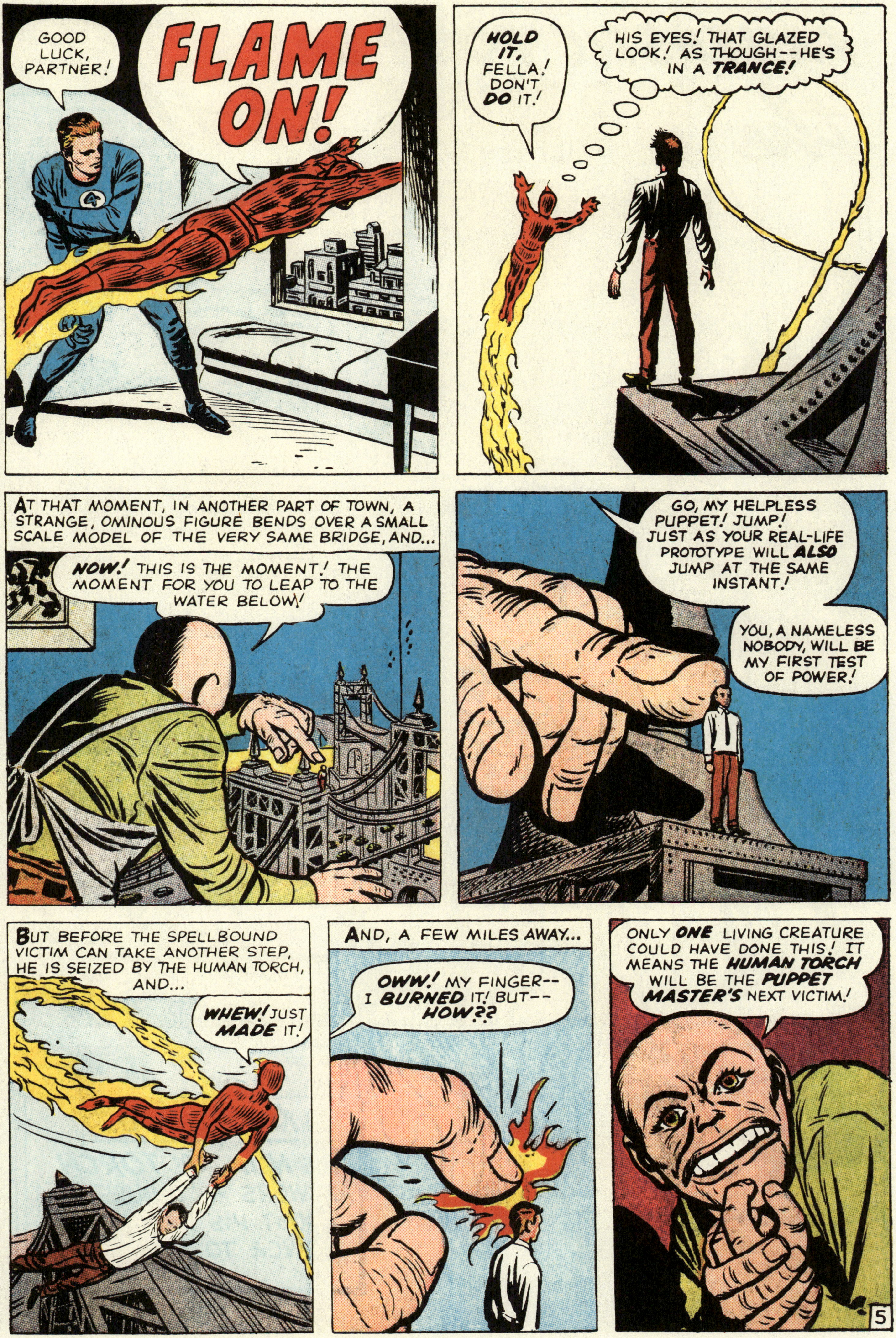
GOOD LUCK, PARTNER!
FLAME ON!
HOLD IT, FELLA! DON'T DO IT!
HIS EYES! THAT GLAZED LOOK! AS THOUGH--HE'S IN A TRANCE!
AT THAT MOMENT, IN ANOTHER PART OF TOWN, A STRANGE, OMINOUS FIGURE BENDS OVER A SMALL SCALE MODEL OF THE VERY SAME BRIDGE, AND...
NOW! THIS IS THE MOMENT! THE MOMENT FOR YOU TO LEAP TO THE WATER BELOW!
GO, MY HELPLESS PUPPET! JUMP! JUST AS YOUR REAL-LIFE PROTOTYPE WILL ALSO JUMP AT THE SAME INSTANT!
YOU, A NAMELESS NOBODY, WILL BE MY FIRST TEST OF POWER!
BUT BEFORE THE SPELLBOUND VICTIM CAN TAKE ANOTHER STEP, HE IS SEIZED BY THE HUMAN TORCH, AND...
WHEW! JUST MADE IT!
AND, A FEW MILES AWAY...
OWW! MY FINGER-- I BURNED IT! BUT-- HOW??
ONLY ONE LIVING CREATURE COULD HAVE DONE THIS! IT MEANS THE HUMAN TORCH WILL BE THE PUPPET MASTER'S NEXT VICTIM!
5

Stan Lee & J. Kirby
FANTASTIC FOUR in "the HANDS of the PUPPET MAKER"
PART 2
FATHER! I HEARD YOU CRY OUT! WHAT IS WRONG?
V-950
NOTHING, ALICIA! IT IS NO CONCERN OF YOURS!
I HAVE **WORK** TO DO! RETURN TO YOUR ROOM! AND I HAVE TOLD YOU NEVER TO CALL ME "FATHER"! I AM ONLY YOUR **STEP-FATHER!** DO YOU UNDERSTAND?
Y-YES!
6

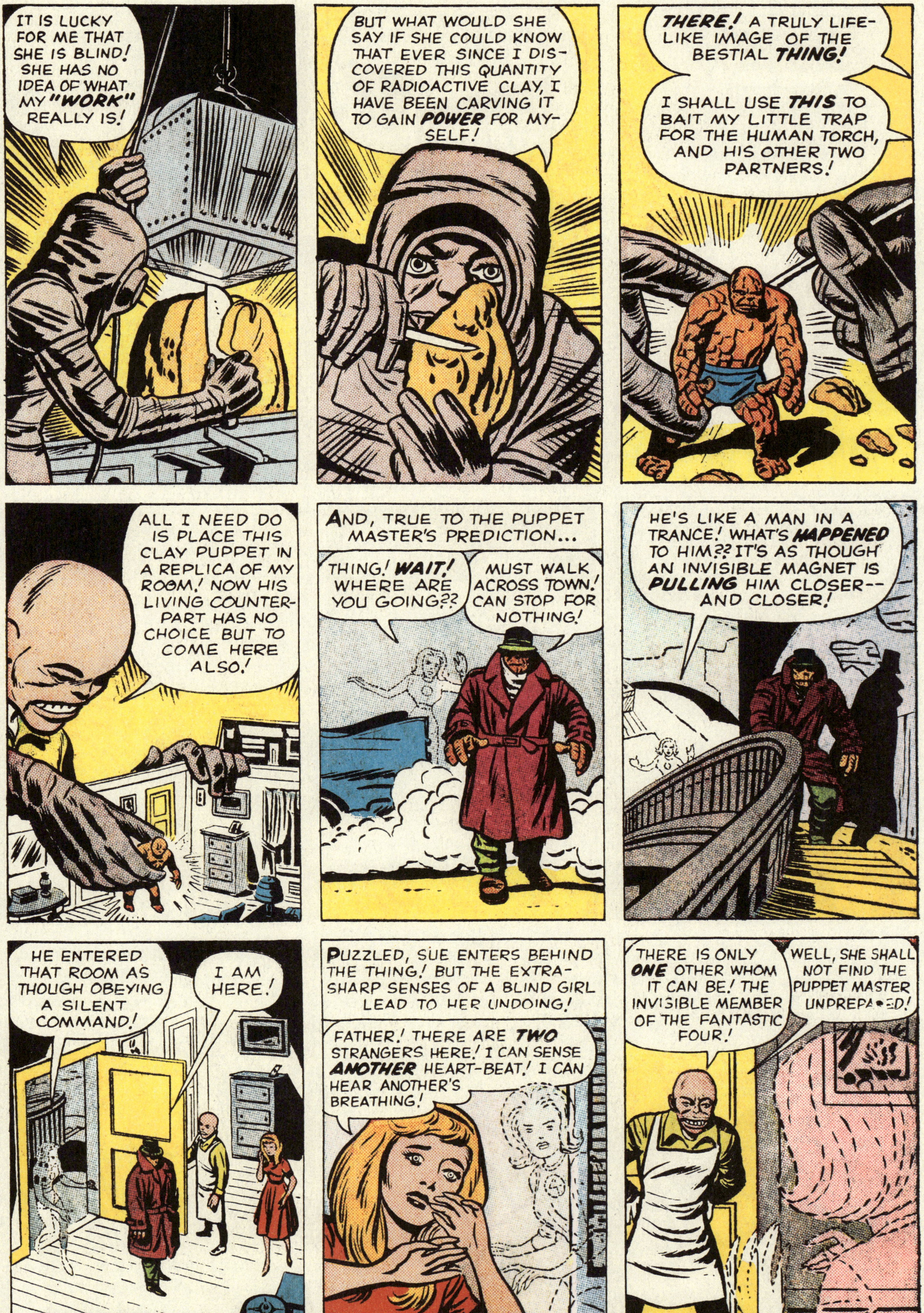
IT IS LUCKY FOR ME THAT SHE IS BLIND! SHE HAS NO IDEA OF WHAT MY "WORK" REALLY IS!
BUT WHAT WOULD SHE SAY IF SHE COULD KNOW THAT EVER SINCE I DISCOVERED THIS QUANTITY OF RADIOACTIVE CLAY, I HAVE BEEN CARVING IT TO GAIN POWER FOR MYSELF!
THERE! A TRULY LIFE-LIKE IMAGE OF THE BESTIAL THING!
I SHALL USE THIS TO BAIT MY LITTLE TRAP FOR THE HUMAN TORCH, AND HIS OTHER TWO PARTNERS!
ALL I NEED DO IS PLACE THIS CLAY PUPPET IN A REPLICA OF MY ROOM! NOW HIS LIVING COUNTERPART HAS NO CHOICE BUT TO COME HERE ALSO!
AND, TRUE TO THE PUPPET MASTER'S PREDICTION...
THING! WAIT! WHERE ARE YOU GOING??
MUST WALK ACROSS TOWN! CAN STOP FOR NOTHING!
HE'S LIKE A MAN IN A TRANCE! WHAT'S HAPPENED TO HIM?? IT'S AS THOUGH AN INVISIBLE MAGNET IS PULLING HIM CLOSER-- AND CLOSER!
HE ENTERED THAT ROOM AS THOUGH OBEYING A SILENT COMMAND!
I AM HERE!
PUZZLED, SUE ENTERS BEHIND THE THING! BUT THE EXTRA-SHARP SENSES OF A BLIND GIRL LEAD TO HER UNDOING!
FATHER! THERE ARE TWO STRANGERS HERE! I CAN SENSE ANOTHER HEART-BEAT! I CAN HEAR ANOTHER'S BREATHING!
THERE IS ONLY ONE OTHER WHOM IT CAN BE! THE INVISIBLE MEMBER OF THE FANTASTIC FOUR!
WELL, SHE SHALL NOT FIND THE PUPPET MASTER UNPREPA•ED!
7

FIRST, THE THREE OF US SHALL DON **GAS MASKS!**
THE REST IS CHILDISHLY SIMPLE!
ETHER
THAT ODOR-- IT-IT'S **ETHER!**
I'VE GOT TO GET AIR! THE WINDOW ...IF ONLY--NO --NO USE--IT'S LOCKED!
THING! DON'T JUST **STAND** THERE! HELP ME! WHAT'S **WRONG** WITH YOU?? WHAT HAS HE **DONE** TO YOU?? ANSWER ME--
--ANSWER ME--
ONCE SHE FALLS ASLEEP, SUE STORM IS NO LONGER ABLE TO CONTROL HER AMAZING POWER OF INVISIBILITY, AND...
SO **THIS** IS THE INVISIBLE GIRL!
I HOPE THE **OTHERS** WILL BE EQUALLY EASY TO DEFEAT!
SHE LOOKS REMARKABLY LIKE **YOU,** ALICIA! IN FACT... THAT GIVES ME AN **IDEA!**
MINUTES LATER...
FASHIONING A UNIFORM LIKE HERS, AND A BLONDE WIG FOR YOU ARE **CHILD'S PLAY** FOR THE PUPPET MASTER!
THERE! IT IS **DONE!**

AND NOW, ALICIA, WHILE OUR UNINVITED GUEST SLEEPS, YOU WILL TAKE HER PLACE! YOU WILL PLAY A HARMLESS LITTLE PRANK FOR ME!
A LITTLE PRANK? BUT WHAT, FATHER?
DO NOT QUESTION ME! JUST OBEY!
THIS MAN--HIS FACE FEELS STRONG AND POWERFUL! AND YET, I CAN SENSE A GENTLENESS TO HIM--THERE IS SOMETHING TRAGIC--SOMETHING SENSITIVE!
ENOUGH OF YOUR PRATTLE! STAND BACK! I WANT TO TEST HIS STRENGTH!
I HAVE PUT A STEEL HAMMER IN HIS HAND...
AND NOW, AT MY COMMAND...
PERFECT! HE HAS NO WILL BUT MY WILL! NO BRAIN BUT MY BRAIN!
GO WITH HIM, ALICIA! SAY NOTHING, BUT DO NOT LEAVE HIS SIDE!
THIS IS ALL SO STRANGE! I DO NOT UNDERSTAND!
BUT I MUST DO AS I AM TOLD!
AND WHEN THEY PLAY OUT THEIR LITTLE ACT, I SHALL PROVE MY POWER IN ANOTHER WAY! I SHALL USE A NEW PUPPET ...THE PERSONAL TRUSTEE OF THE WARDEN OF STATE PRISON!

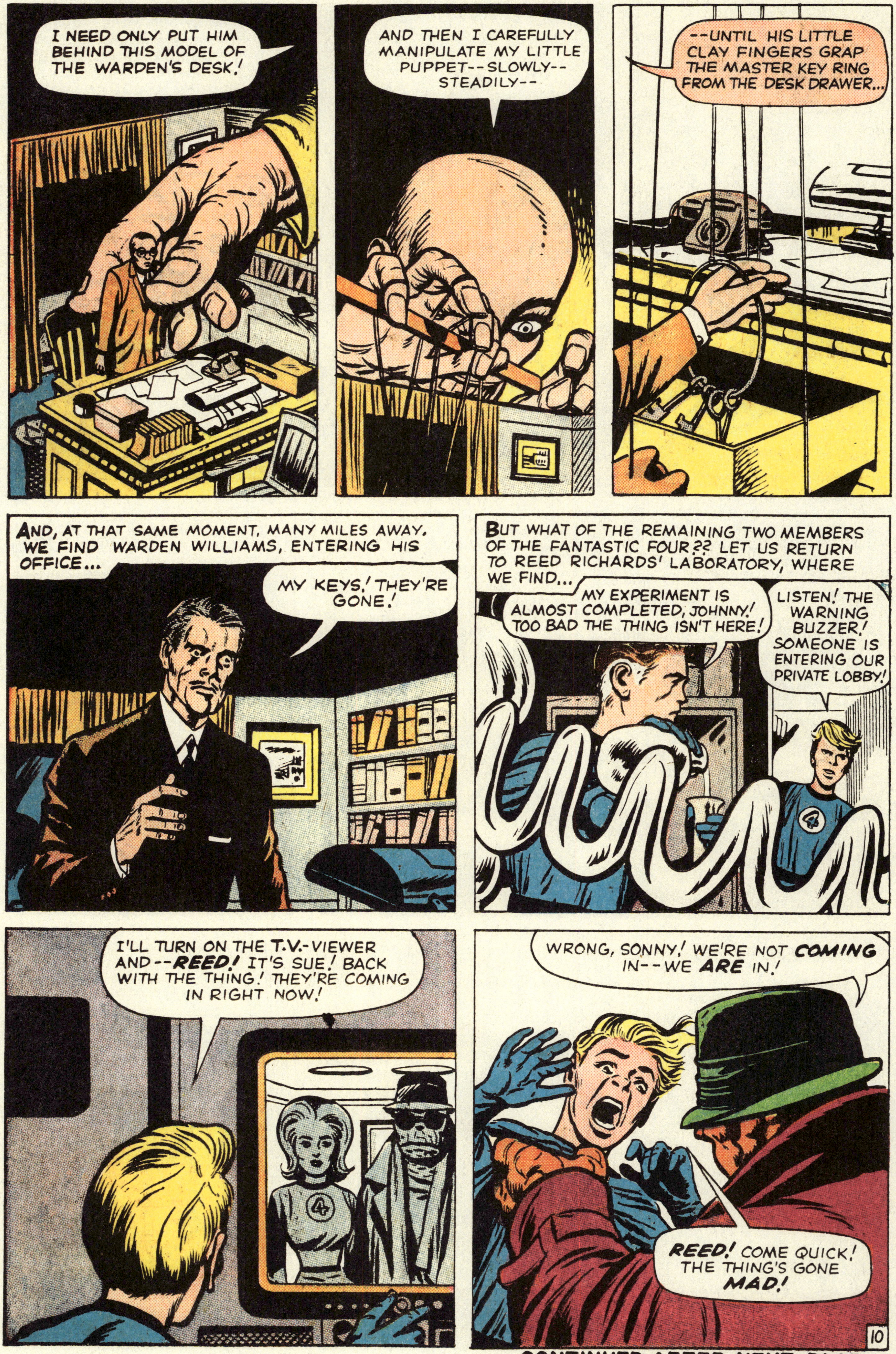

CONTINUED AFTER NEXT PAGE...

Important News for the man who needs a GOOD JOB, MORE MONEY AND GREATER SECURITY

1. **Air Conditioning and Refrigeration offers better opportunities in a growing *uncrowded* field**
2. **CTI provides proven Home Training which lets you *learn by practicing* with real equipment**

Why worry about a poor-pay or unsteady job when the blessings of a big-money career in Air Conditioning and Refrigeration are within your reach? This fast-growing industry needs 20,000 newly-trained mechanics each year. It is pleading for skilled men who can install the 8 million air conditioners, refrigerators and freezers that are produced annually . . . and service the 150 million units already in use. Send for complete information on how you can qualify for a full-time, top-pay job in a dynamic, uncrowded field!

CTI Home Training Is Easy—Fast—Proven

CTI Home Training is prepared so that even a man of limited education, who has been out of school for years, can understand it. The lessons are written in simple English, and many illustrations are used to explain operating principles. Training kits of parts and tools are provided so that the student can develop his skill and acquire practical experience. CTI instructors are efficient and courteous. The student gets personalized training as well as extra help if he needs it.

Why Many Students Earn Cash as They Train

A CTI student spends a considerable part of his time training with kits we send. The 20 field-type projects provide him with experience. Due to the practical nature of this exclusive training, many students soon do repair work in spare time for profit. They make calls on their own, or develop servicing arrangements with local distributors and contractors. Their earnings often pay the cost of tuition before graduation.

How to Start a Business of Your Own

Once a student begins to do part-time servicing, he actually puts himself in his own business. Some students make contracts with owners of food stores, restaurants, and air conditioned buildings to handle servicing on a monthly fee basis. An impressive number of CTI students follow this success pattern—have a prosperous business under way by the time they graduate. Air Conditioning and Refrigeration is well suited for starting out on a modest basis, with very little capital, and then expanding as service calls increase.

Letters Prove Value of CTI Training

We want to send you a fascinating booklet called *Proof from Graduates*. In their own words, men who have earned diplomas record their successes. Better jobs, higher pay, self-employment, confidence—these are a few of the rewards of a sound training program carried to fulfillment. We'll rush this testimonials booklet, along with other factual information, as soon as we hear from you.

CTI

COMMERCIAL TRADES INSTITUTE CHICAGO 26, ILLINOIS

A Non-Profit Organization • Accredited by National Home Study Council

Only CTI sends parts to build a refrigerating unit. You get 25 kits, which also include mechanic's tools. During this practical phase of your training, you complete 20 job projects similar to what you will encounter in the field. If you wish, you may build your condenser into an air conditioner, freezer, refrigerator or milk cooler. The advantages of CTI Home Training are clear: You learn the interesting way—by practicing. You develop your skill, acquire experience, gain confidence.

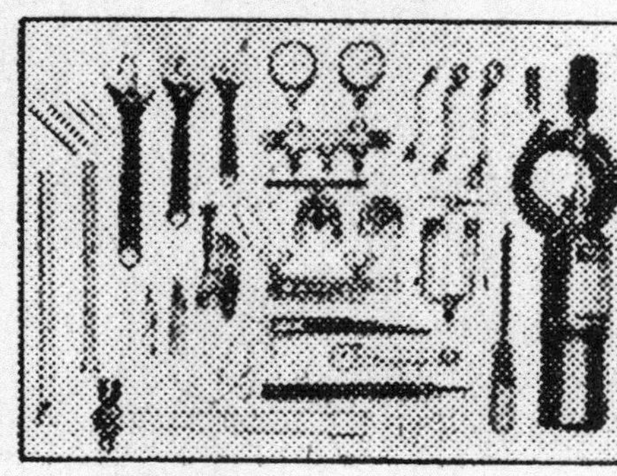

Opportunities Are Great for a Fresh Start

Whether you are a young man looking for a field with bright prospects, or a mature person who is stuck in a job with no future, you will find the breaks you need in Air Conditioning and Refrigeration. During the past 12 years, the production of air conditioners increased by 400%—a growth matched by just one other industry! Despite this growth, the industry is said to be in its infancy, because only 8% of all American homes are air conditioned. Auto air conditioning is big business, too—Nearly 600,000 units installed annually!

If you are looking for a fresh start in life, consider Air Conditioning and Refrigeration. No industry is growing faster. The pay scale, working conditions, and the 20,000 new jobs that open each year are unique attractions indeed. Send for free information at once.

COMMERCIAL TRADES INSTITUTE
1400 GREENLEAF AVENUE
CHICAGO 26, ILLINOIS **DEPT. R-945**

Please send me your three free booklets: Success in Air Conditioning and Refrigeration, Proof from Graduates, and Lesson Samples. No obligation.

Name________________ Age_____
Address________________
City__________ Zone_____ State_____

THE FANTASTIC FOUR in
"THE Lady AND THE MONSTER!"
Stan Lee + J. KIRBY
PART 3
REED--I CAN'T FLAME ON YET! USED TOO MUCH FLAME DURING THE PAST HOUR! IT'S UP TO YOU NOW! YOU'VE GOT TO STOP HIM!
V-950
NO! I CAN TELL BY HIS EYES--HIS EXPRESSION! SOMETHING'S HAPPENED TO HIM! HE DOESN'T KNOW WHAT HE'S DOING!
ONLY ONE THING TO DO! IF I CAN LURE HIM INTO THE LAB!
11

I DID IT! HE CRASHED RIGHT INTO THE CHEMICAL VIAL, AS I HOPED HE WOULD!
NOW TO SEE IF THE POTION WORKS!
AS THE COOL LIQUID TOUCHES HIS MIGHTY FRAME, THE THING SEEMS TO SUDDENLY GO LIMP! SLOWLY HE SAGS TO THE FLOOR, DRENCHED BY THE STRANGE FORMULA, UNTIL...
OHHH, MY HEAD!
WHA-WHAT HAPPENED??
MY FACE! IT-IT'S HUMAN AGAIN! I'M BEN GRIMM AGAIN! I'M--ME!
AND, WITH THE CHANGE IN BEN GRIMM, THE POWER OF THE PUPPET MASTER ENDS, AND THE SPELL IS OVER!
REED--HOW DID IT HAPPEN? HOW?
IT WAS THIS CHEMICAL! THIS IS WHAT I WAS WORKING ON IN THE LAB! I DIDN'T WANT YOU TO KNOW ABOUT IT, IN CASE IT FAILED! YOU'VE HAD SO MANY DISAPPOINTMENTS, I DIDN'T WANT YOU TO SUFFER ANOTHER ONE, UNTIL I WAS SURE!
YOU WERE DOING IT FOR ME! AND ALL THE TIME I THOUGHT YOU HATED ME! THOUGHT YOU WERE SCHEMING AGAINST ME! REED, I-I FEEL LIKE--
STOW IT, PARTNER! YOU HAD EVERY RIGHT TO BLOW YOUR TOP! BUT NOW, WE'VE STILL GOT A JOB CUT OUT FOR US!
12

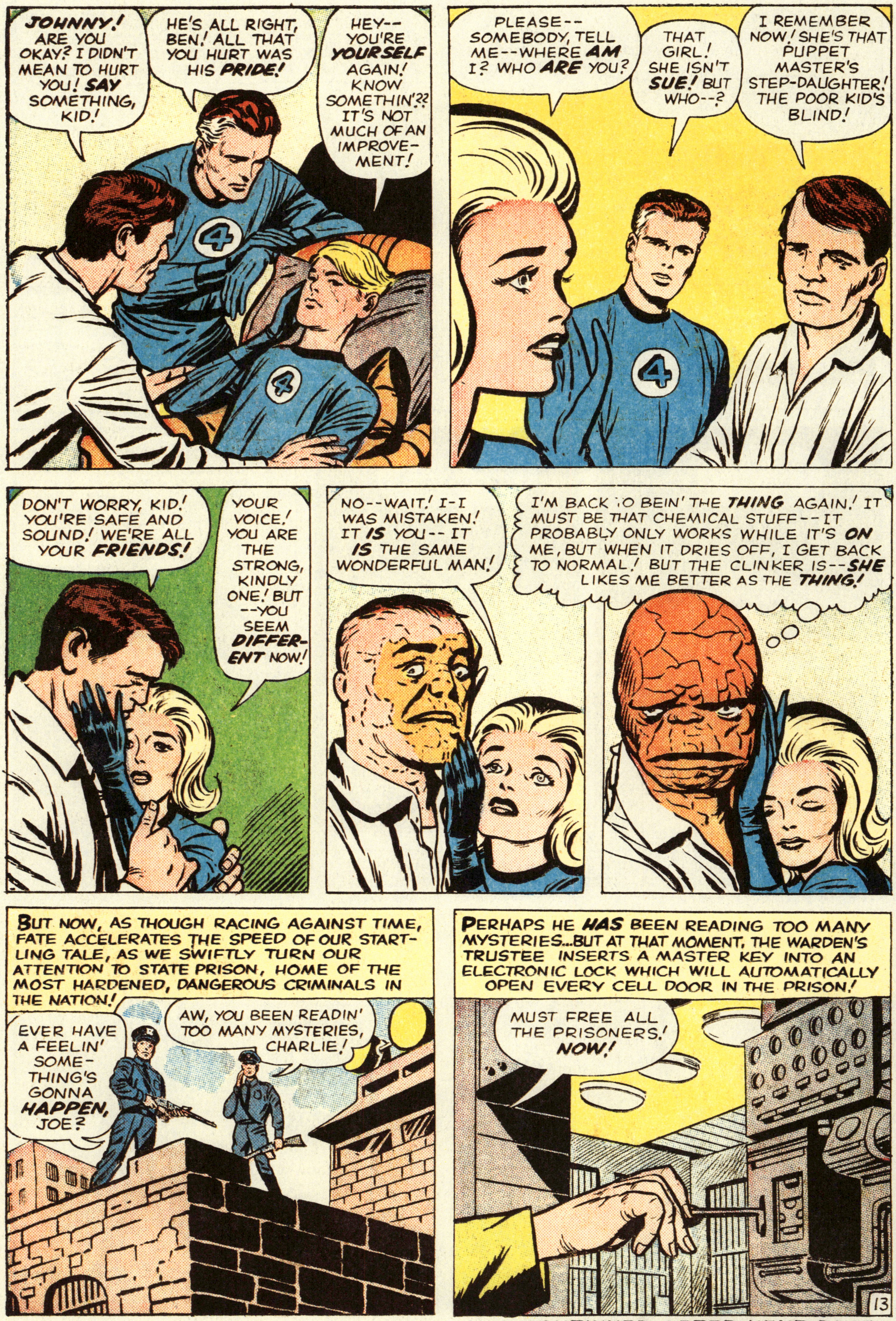

CONTINUED AFTER NEXT PAGE..

1001 THINGS THAT YOU CAN GET FREE
SAMPLE
GIFT
BOOKS
SAMPLE
Copyright 1962 Jetco Advertising
This List Tell You Where To Send For Free Samples, Books, Foreign Stamps & Coins, Etc.
Imagine! They're yours for the asking—hundreds of $$$ worth of free offers and giveaway items by writing to different manufacturers, associations, government agencies, etc. This list tells you where to write for the FREE ITEMS—such as Free Gifts, Free Products, Samples, Informative Books, Maps, Show Tickets, Foreign Stamps & Coins, Toys, Films, Posters, etc.
FREE
Complete List For Only 69¢
Plus 6c postage and handling. Total of 75c
PARTY BOOK
SPECIAL OFFER!
Work At Home - Over 100 Proven Money-Making Ideas
Be your own boss! Earn money in your spare time! $25 - $50 weekly possible in your own business. Folder describes ideas and tells what to do!
50¢
Get Both Valuable Lists — FOR ONLY $1.00 POST PAID
Introductory offer saves you money. Hurry—offer limited!
THINGS FREE • P.O. BOX 1225-MC • NEWARK 1, NEW JERSEY

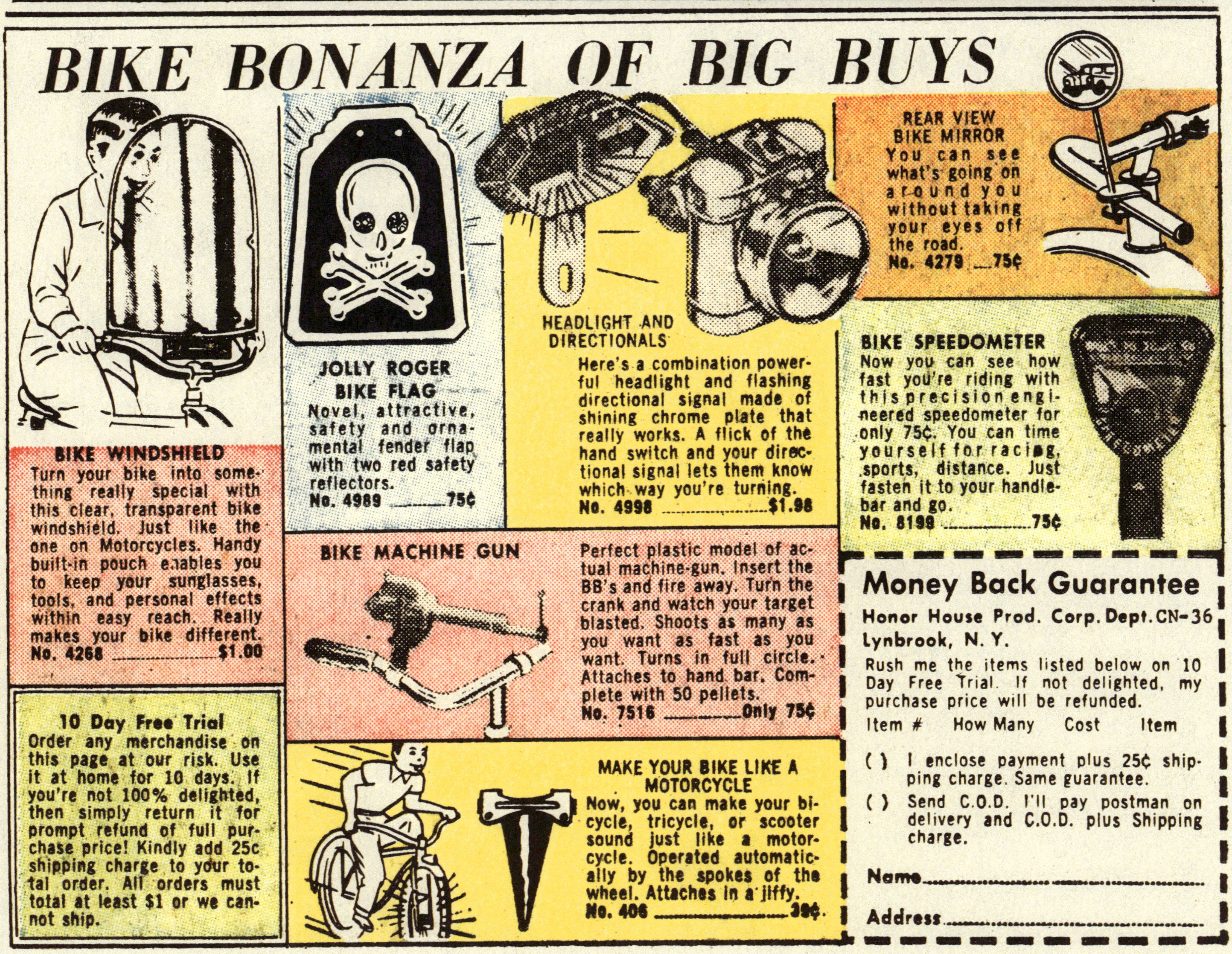

BIKE BONANZA OF BIG BUYS
REAR VIEW BIKE MIRROR
You can see what's going on around you without taking your eyes off the road.
No. 4279 ....75¢
JOLLY ROGER BIKE FLAG
Novel, attractive, safety and ornamental fender flap with two red safety reflectors.
No. 4989 ....75¢
HEADLIGHT AND DIRECTIONALS
Here's a combination powerful headlight and flashing directional signal made of shining chrome plate that really works. A flick of the hand switch and your directional signal lets them know which way you're turning.
No. 4998 ....$1.98
BIKE SPEEDOMETER
Now you can see how fast you're riding with this precision engineered speedometer for only 75¢. You can time yourself for racing, sports, distance. Just fasten it to your handlebar and go.
No. 8199 ....75¢
BIKE WINDSHIELD
Turn your bike into something really special with this clear, transparent bike windshield. Just like the one on Motorcycles. Handy built-in pouch enables you to keep your sunglasses, tools, and personal effects within easy reach. Really makes your bike different.
No. 4268 ....$1.00
BIKE MACHINE GUN
Perfect plastic model of actual machine-gun. Insert the BB's and fire away. Turn the crank and watch your target blasted. Shoots as many as you want as fast as you want. Turns in full circle. Attaches to hand bar. Complete with 50 pellets.
No. 7516 ....Only 75¢
Money Back Guarantee
Honor House Prod. Corp. Dept. CN-36
Lynbrook, N. Y.
Rush me the items listed below on 10 Day Free Trial. If not delighted, my purchase price will be refunded.
Item # How Many Cost Item
( ) I enclose payment plus 25¢ shipping charge. Same guarantee.
( ) Send C.O.D. I'll pay postman on delivery and C.O.D. plus Shipping charge.
Name..........
Address..........
10 Day Free Trial
Order any merchandise on this page at our risk. Use it at home for 10 days. If you're not 100% delighted, then simply return it for prompt refund of full purchase price! Kindly add 25c shipping charge to your total order. All orders must total at least $1 or we cannot ship.
MAKE YOUR BIKE LIKE A MOTORCYCLE
Now, you can make your bicycle, tricycle, or scooter sound just like a motorcycle. Operated automatically by the spokes of the wheel. Attaches in a jiffy.
No. 406 ....39¢

FANTASTIC FOUR in
"FACE-TO-FACE with the PUPPET MASTER!"
Stan Lee + J. KIRBY
PART 4
CELL BLOCK 2
KIRBY AYERS
THE PUPPET MASTER IS SO ENGROSSED IN MANIPULATING A JAIL-BREAK, THAT THIS IS MY CHANCE TO ESCAPE!
CREAK
V-950
HE-HE HEARD ME!
WHO OPENED THE DOOR? THE GIRL! SHE'S GONE!
14

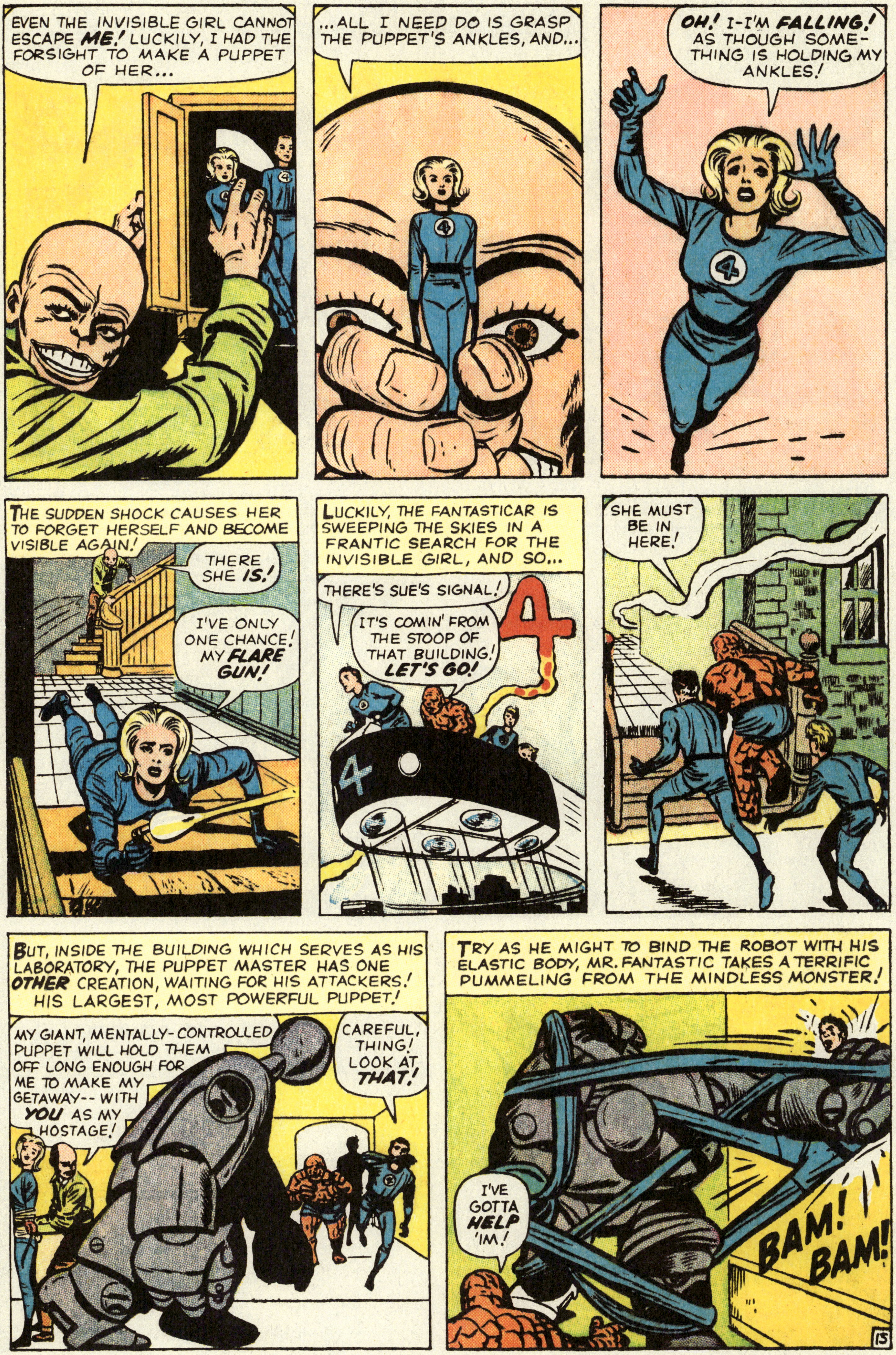
EVEN THE INVISIBLE GIRL CANNOT ESCAPE ME! LUCKILY, I HAD THE FORSIGHT TO MAKE A PUPPET OF HER...
...ALL I NEED DO IS GRASP THE PUPPET'S ANKLES, AND...
OH! I-I'M FALLING! AS THOUGH SOMETHING IS HOLDING MY ANKLES!
THE SUDDEN SHOCK CAUSES HER TO FORGET HERSELF AND BECOME VISIBLE AGAIN!
THERE SHE IS!
I'VE ONLY ONE CHANCE! MY FLARE GUN!
LUCKILY, THE FANTASTICAR IS SWEEPING THE SKIES IN A FRANTIC SEARCH FOR THE INVISIBLE GIRL, AND SO...
THERE'S SUE'S SIGNAL!
IT'S COMIN' FROM THE STOOP OF THAT BUILDING! LET'S GO!
4
SHE MUST BE IN HERE!
BUT, INSIDE THE BUILDING WHICH SERVES AS HIS LABORATORY, THE PUPPET MASTER HAS ONE OTHER CREATION, WAITING FOR HIS ATTACKERS! HIS LARGEST, MOST POWERFUL PUPPET!
MY GIANT, MENTALLY-CONTROLLED PUPPET WILL HOLD THEM OFF LONG ENOUGH FOR ME TO MAKE MY GETAWAY-- WITH YOU AS MY HOSTAGE!
CAREFUL, THING! LOOK AT THAT!
TRY AS HE MIGHT TO BIND THE ROBOT WITH HIS ELASTIC BODY, MR. FANTASTIC TAKES A TERRIFIC PUMMELING FROM THE MINDLESS MONSTER!
I'VE GOTTA HELP 'IM!
BAM! BAM!
15

TRY TO GIVE ME A BEAR HUG, WILL YA? WELL, HERE'S SOMETHIN' YOU AIN'T GONNA LIKE!
POW
GOOD WORK, THING! I CAN SEE YOU DON'T NEED ANY HELP FROM ME!
I NEVER DID, HOT-STUFF!
SUDDENLY, THE TORCH FLAMES OFF AS HE EXCLAIMS...
HEY! WHERE'S THE PUPPET MASTER?? AND SUE??
BUT THE AMAZING THREESOME ARRIVE SCANT SECONDS TOO LATE...
HAH! EVEN YOU CANNOT CATCH MY WINGED FLYING HORSE--MY GREATEST PUPPET OF ALL!
WHA--???
I WOULDN'T BET ON IT, MISTER!
BAH, TAKE THE GIRL! I HAVE NO FURTHER USE FOR HER!
THE TORCH IS AFTER ME! BUT HE DOESN'T SUSPECT THAT MY FLYING STEED IS JET-POWERED!
I CAN'T GET NEAR 'IM! HE'S TOO FAST FOR ME!
16

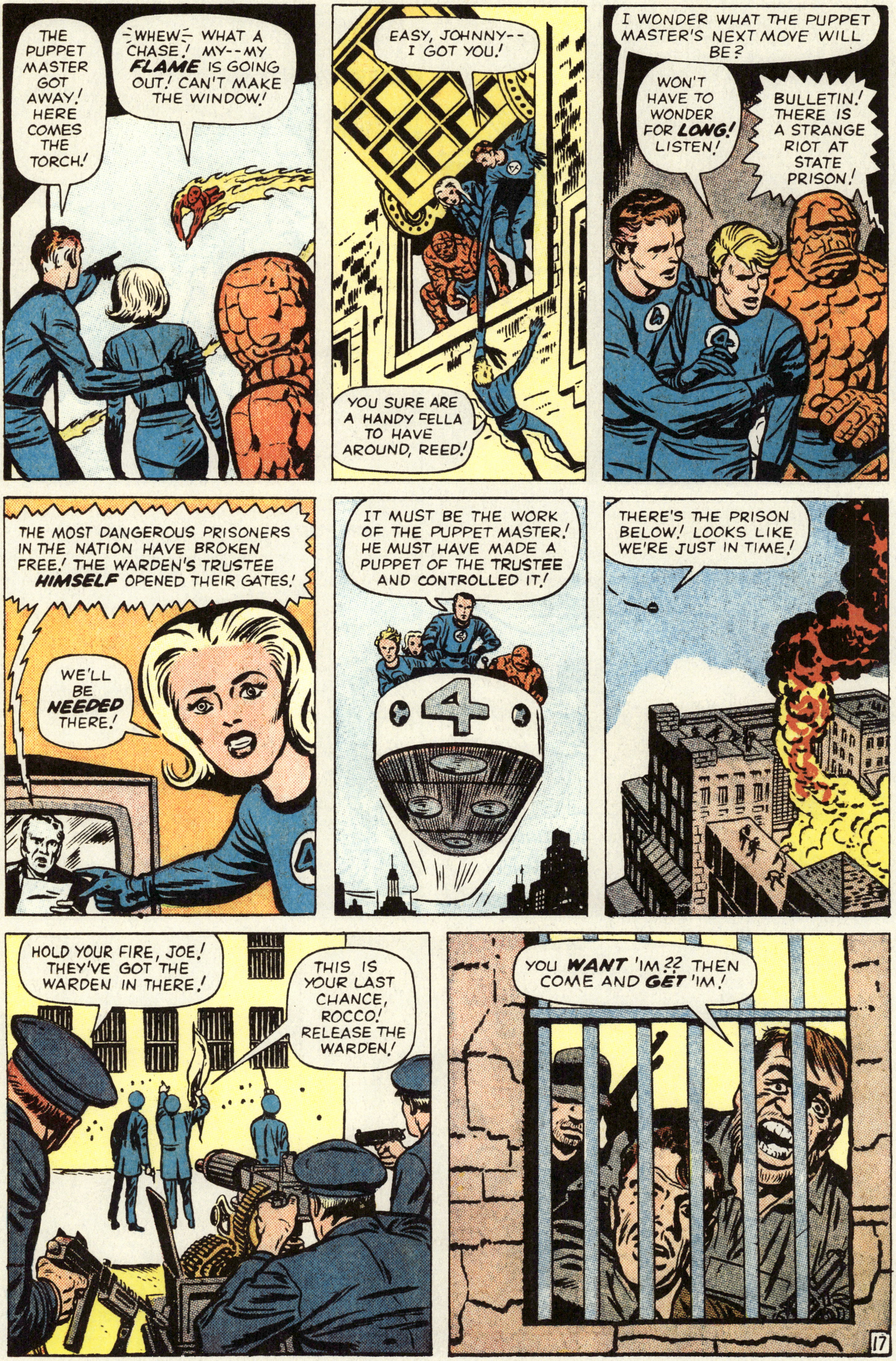

THE PUPPET MASTER GOT AWAY! HERE COMES THE TORCH!
-WHEW- WHAT A CHASE! MY--MY FLAME IS GOING OUT! CAN'T MAKE THE WINDOW!
EASY, JOHNNY-- I GOT YOU!
YOU SURE ARE A HANDY FELLA TO HAVE AROUND, REED!
I WONDER WHAT THE PUPPET MASTER'S NEXT MOVE WILL BE?
WON'T HAVE TO WONDER FOR LONG! LISTEN!
BULLETIN! THERE IS A STRANGE RIOT AT STATE PRISON!
THE MOST DANGEROUS PRISONERS IN THE NATION HAVE BROKEN FREE! THE WARDEN'S TRUSTEE HIMSELF OPENED THEIR GATES!
WE'LL BE NEEDED THERE!
IT MUST BE THE WORK OF THE PUPPET MASTER! HE MUST HAVE MADE A PUPPET OF THE TRUSTEE AND CONTROLLED IT!
4
THERE'S THE PRISON BELOW! LOOKS LIKE WE'RE JUST IN TIME!
HOLD YOUR FIRE, JOE! THEY'VE GOT THE WARDEN IN THERE!
THIS IS YOUR LAST CHANCE, ROCCO! RELEASE THE WARDEN!
YOU WANT 'IM?? THEN COME AND GET 'IM!
17

CONTINUED AFTER NEXT PAGE...

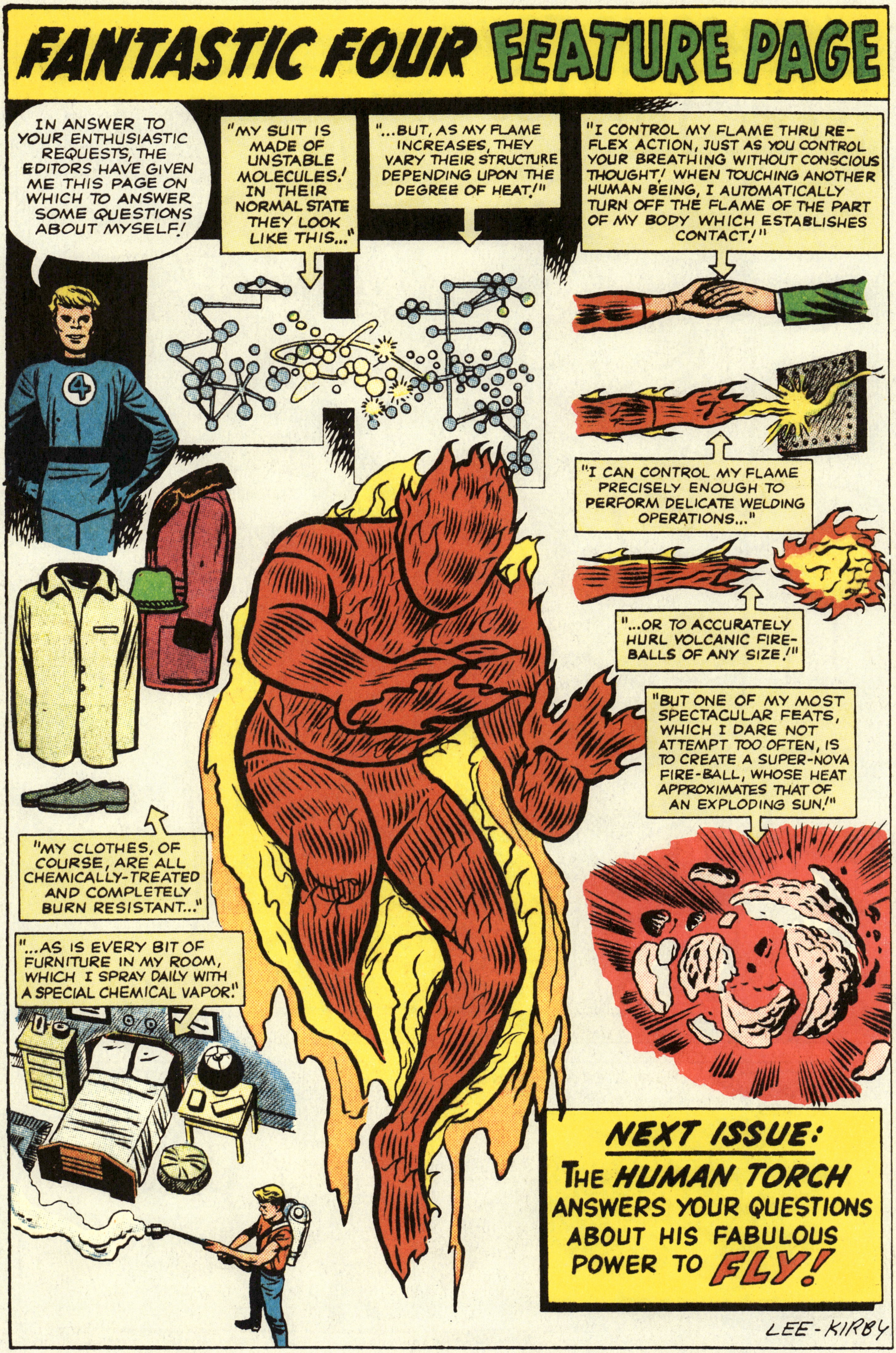
FANTASTIC FOUR FEATURE PAGE
IN ANSWER TO YOUR ENTHUSIASTIC REQUESTS, THE EDITORS HAVE GIVEN ME THIS PAGE ON WHICH TO ANSWER SOME QUESTIONS ABOUT MYSELF!
"MY SUIT IS MADE OF UNSTABLE MOLECULES! IN THEIR NORMAL STATE THEY LOOK LIKE THIS..."
"...BUT, AS MY FLAME INCREASES, THEY VARY THEIR STRUCTURE DEPENDING UPON THE DEGREE OF HEAT!"
"I CONTROL MY FLAME THRU RE-FLEX ACTION, JUST AS YOU CONTROL YOUR BREATHING WITHOUT CONSCIOUS THOUGHT! WHEN TOUCHING ANOTHER HUMAN BEING, I AUTOMATICALLY TURN OFF THE FLAME OF THE PART OF MY BODY WHICH ESTABLISHES CONTACT!"
"I CAN CONTROL MY FLAME PRECISELY ENOUGH TO PERFORM DELICATE WELDING OPERATIONS..."
"...OR TO ACCURATELY HURL VOLCANIC FIRE-BALLS OF ANY SIZE!"
"BUT ONE OF MY MOST SPECTACULAR FEATS, WHICH I DARE NOT ATTEMPT TOO OFTEN, IS TO CREATE A SUPER-NOVA FIRE-BALL, WHOSE HEAT APPROXIMATES THAT OF AN EXPLODING SUN!"
"MY CLOTHES, OF COURSE, ARE ALL CHEMICALLY-TREATED AND COMPLETELY BURN RESISTANT..."
"...AS IS EVERY BIT OF FURNITURE IN MY ROOM, WHICH I SPRAY DAILY WITH A SPECIAL CHEMICAL VAPOR!"
NEXT ISSUE:
THE HUMAN TORCH ANSWERS YOUR QUESTIONS ABOUT HIS FABULOUS POWER TO FLY!
LEE-KIRBY

Stan Lee & J. Kirby
FANTASTIC FOUR in
DEATH OF A PUPPET!
PART 5
HEY! THE WALL'S CAVIN' IN!
THING! WHAT ARE YOU DOING?
JUST WATCH AND SEE, PAL!
SUFFERIN' SNAKES-- WHAT'S THAT??!
V-950
HEY--DON'T! LEGGO!
S'MATTER? YA WANT OUT, DON'T YA?
HERE! HAVE A FREE RIDE, COMPLIMENTS OF THE THING!
GANGWAY!
19

HEY! WHA--?
WHUMP!
STRRRIKE! RIGHT SMACK DAB INTO THE SAND PILE!
IT'LL TAKE 'EM A COUPLE OF SECONDS TO CATCH THEIR BREATH AGAIN!
JUST ENOUGH TIME FOR ME TO WRAP THESE IRON CELL DOORS TOGETHER, AND...
..CORRAL THE WHOLE KABOODLE OF 'EM!
WHAM!
BUT, UNKNOWN TO THE THING, THERE ARE STILL OTHER FREED CONVICTS WHO HAVE SEIZED AUTOMATIC WEAPONS!
LET'S GET THAT BIG FREAK AND MOW 'IM DOWN!
YEAH!
BUT THEY HAVE RECKONED WITHOUT THE AMAZING MR. FANTASTIC!
THE ELASTICITY OF MY BODY WILL ENABLE ME TO ABSORB THE SHELLS, AND THEN...
...BY SNAPPING MYSELF IN THE OTHER DIRECTION, I CAN FIRE THEM BACK LIKE A SLING-SHOT!
THWANG!
20

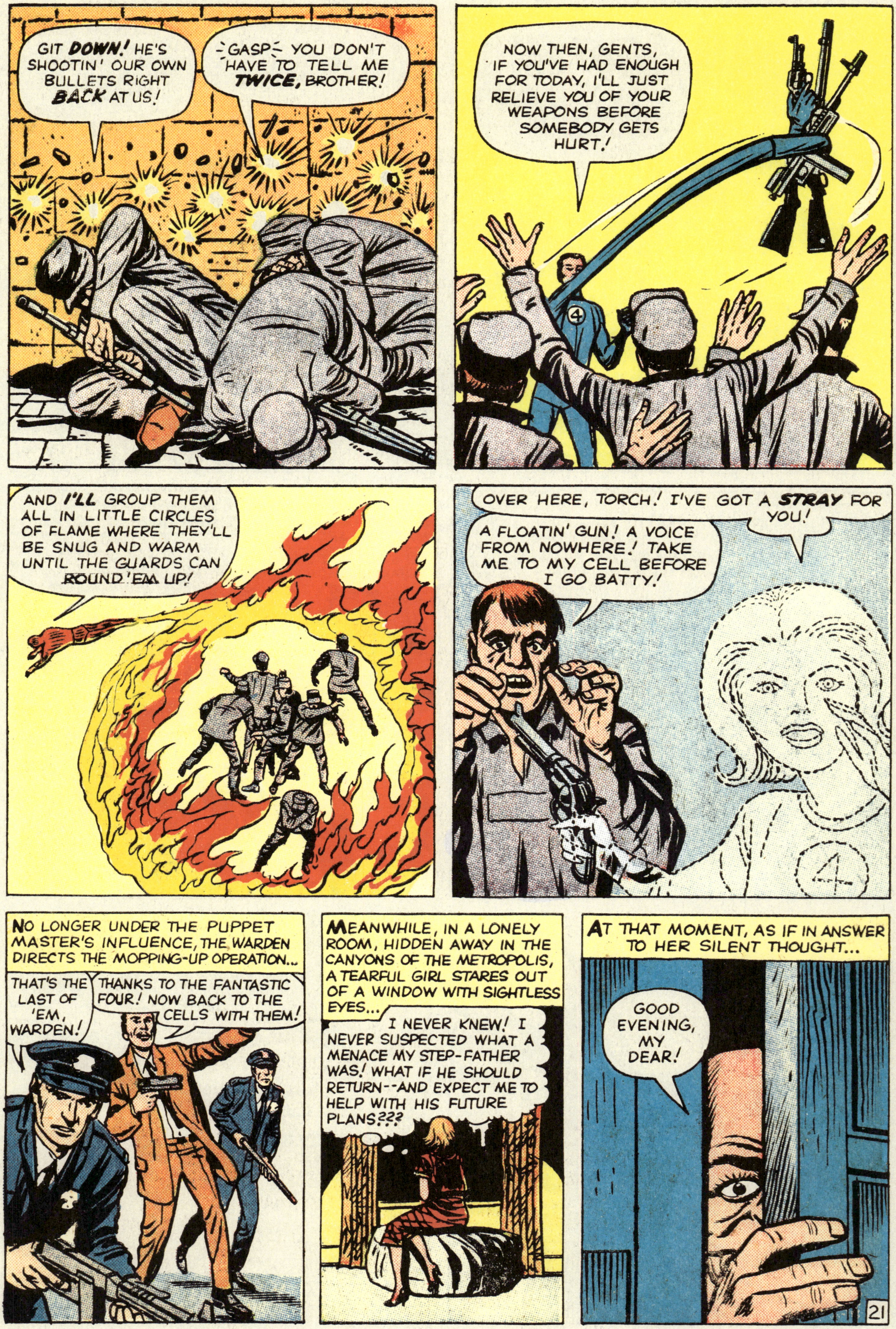
GIT DOWN! HE'S SHOOTIN' OUR OWN BULLETS RIGHT BACK AT US!
-GASP- YOU DON'T HAVE TO TELL ME TWICE, BROTHER!
NOW THEN, GENTS, IF YOU'VE HAD ENOUGH FOR TODAY, I'LL JUST RELIEVE YOU OF YOUR WEAPONS BEFORE SOMEBODY GETS HURT!
AND I'LL GROUP THEM ALL IN LITTLE CIRCLES OF FLAME WHERE THEY'LL BE SNUG AND WARM UNTIL THE GUARDS CAN ROUND 'EM UP!
OVER HERE, TORCH! I'VE GOT A STRAY FOR YOU!
A FLOATIN' GUN! A VOICE FROM NOWHERE! TAKE ME TO MY CELL BEFORE I GO BATTY!
NO LONGER UNDER THE PUPPET MASTER'S INFLUENCE, THE WARDEN DIRECTS THE MOPPING-UP OPERATION...
THAT'S THE LAST OF 'EM, WARDEN!
THANKS TO THE FANTASTIC FOUR! NOW BACK TO THE CELLS WITH THEM!
MEANWHILE, IN A LONELY ROOM, HIDDEN AWAY IN THE CANYONS OF THE METROPOLIS, A TEARFUL GIRL STARES OUT OF A WINDOW WITH SIGHTLESS EYES...
I NEVER KNEW! I NEVER SUSPECTED WHAT A MENACE MY STEP-FATHER WAS! WHAT IF HE SHOULD RETURN--AND EXPECT ME TO HELP WITH HIS FUTURE PLANS???
AT THAT MOMENT, AS IF IN ANSWER TO HER SILENT THOUGHT...
GOOD EVENING, MY DEAR!
21

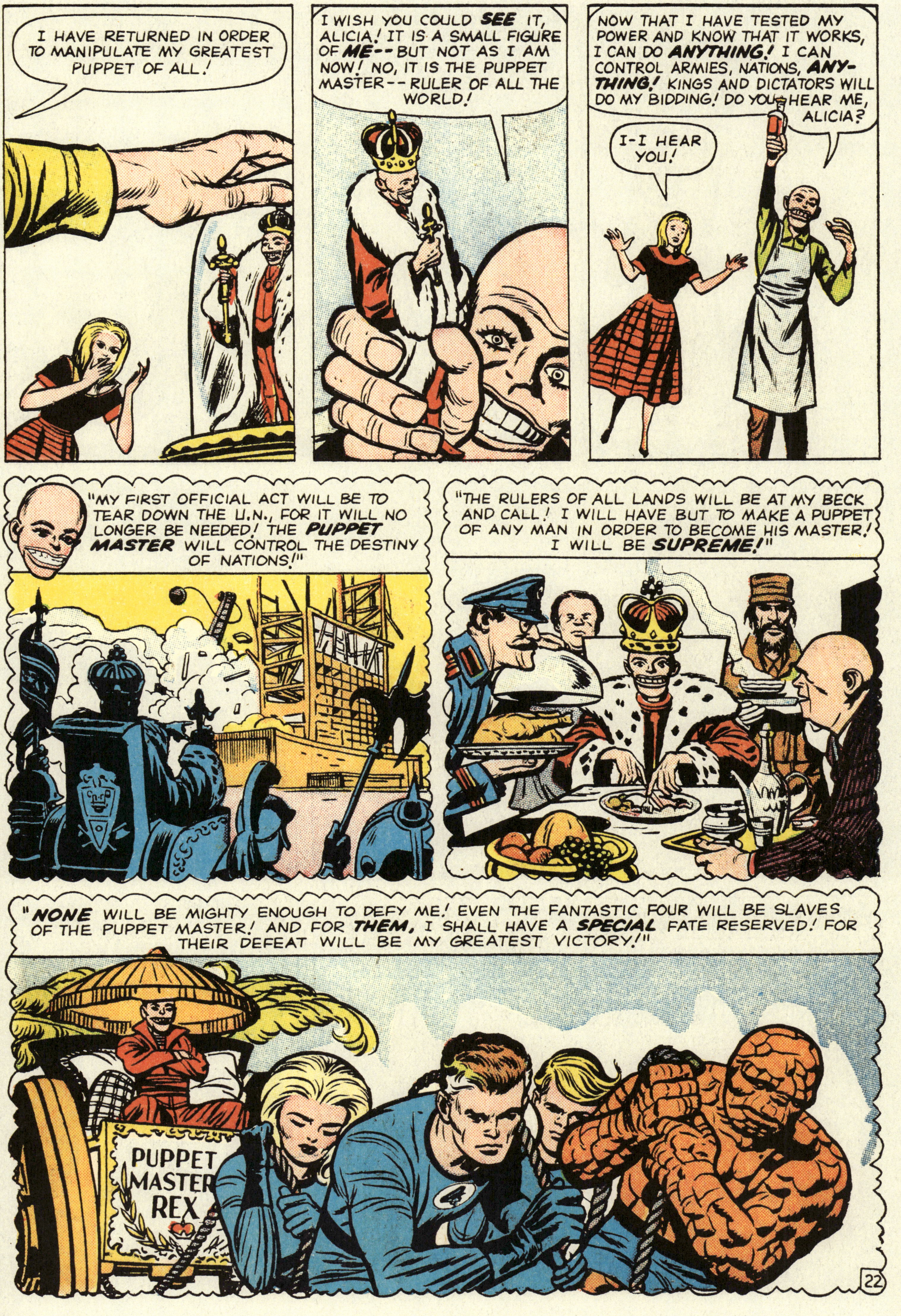
I HAVE RETURNED IN ORDER TO MANIPULATE MY GREATEST PUPPET OF ALL!
I WISH YOU COULD SEE IT, ALICIA! IT IS A SMALL FIGURE OF ME-- BUT NOT AS I AM NOW! NO, IT IS THE PUPPET MASTER-- RULER OF ALL THE WORLD!
NOW THAT I HAVE TESTED MY POWER AND KNOW THAT IT WORKS, I CAN DO ANYTHING! I CAN CONTROL ARMIES, NATIONS, ANYTHING! KINGS AND DICTATORS WILL DO MY BIDDING! DO YOU HEAR ME, ALICIA?
I-I HEAR YOU!
"MY FIRST OFFICIAL ACT WILL BE TO TEAR DOWN THE U.N., FOR IT WILL NO LONGER BE NEEDED! THE PUPPET MASTER WILL CONTROL THE DESTINY OF NATIONS!"
"THE RULERS OF ALL LANDS WILL BE AT MY BECK AND CALL! I WILL HAVE BUT TO MAKE A PUPPET OF ANY MAN IN ORDER TO BECOME HIS MASTER! I WILL BE SUPREME!"
"NONE WILL BE MIGHTY ENOUGH TO DEFY ME! EVEN THE FANTASTIC FOUR WILL BE SLAVES OF THE PUPPET MASTER! AND FOR THEM, I SHALL HAVE A SPECIAL FATE RESERVED! FOR THEIR DEFEAT WILL BE MY GREATEST VICTORY!"
PUPPET MASTER REX
22

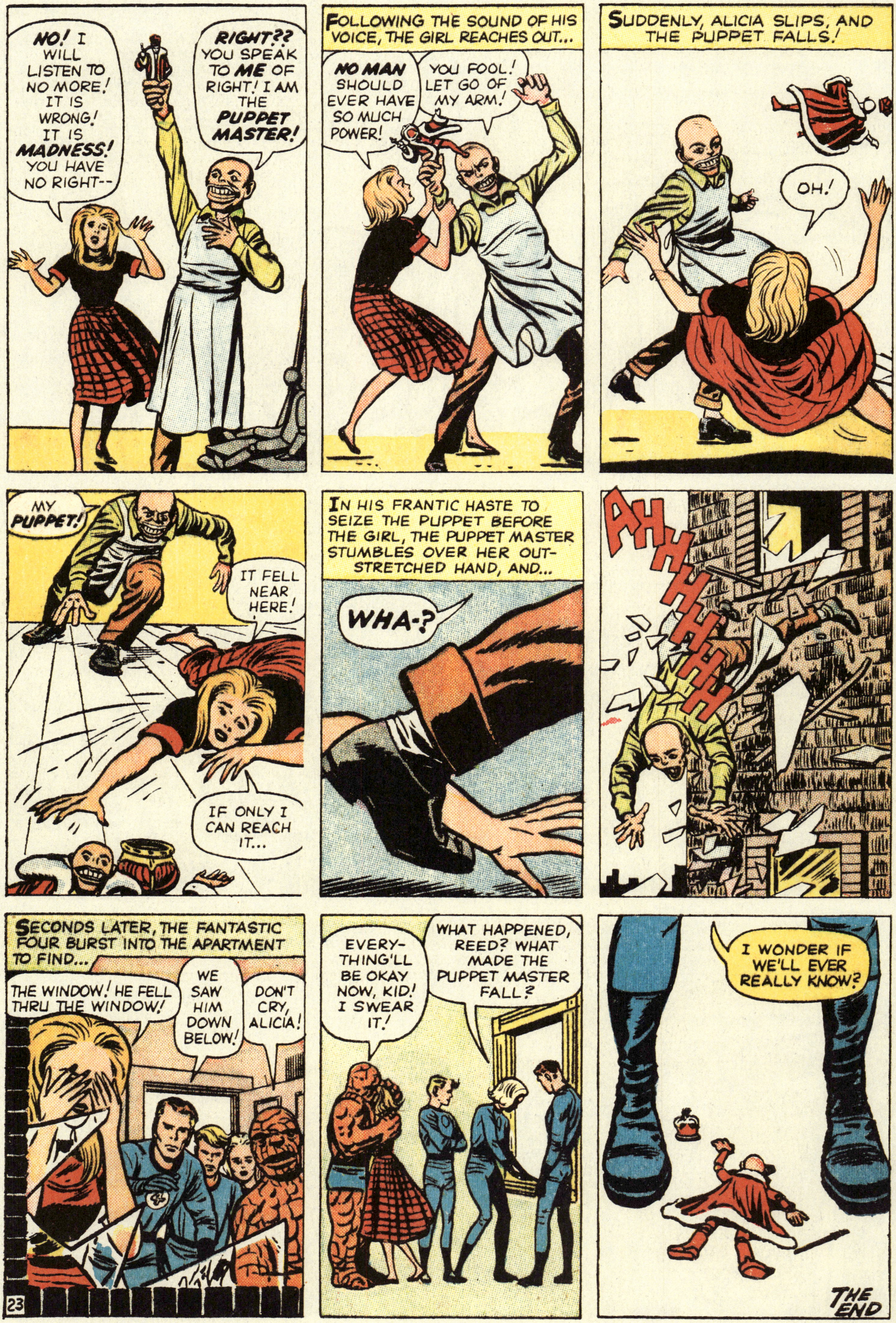
NO! I WILL LISTEN TO NO MORE! IT IS WRONG! IT IS MADNESS! YOU HAVE NO RIGHT--
RIGHT?? YOU SPEAK TO ME OF RIGHT! I AM THE PUPPET MASTER!
FOLLOWING THE SOUND OF HIS VOICE, THE GIRL REACHES OUT...
NO MAN SHOULD EVER HAVE SO MUCH POWER!
YOU FOOL! LET GO OF MY ARM!
SUDDENLY, ALICIA SLIPS, AND THE PUPPET FALLS!
OH!
MY PUPPET!
IT FELL NEAR HERE!
IF ONLY I CAN REACH IT...
IN HIS FRANTIC HASTE TO SEIZE THE PUPPET BEFORE THE GIRL, THE PUPPET MASTER STUMBLES OVER HER OUT-STRETCHED HAND, AND...
WHA-?
AHHHHHHH
SECONDS LATER, THE FANTASTIC FOUR BURST INTO THE APARTMENT TO FIND...
THE WINDOW! HE FELL THRU THE WINDOW!
WE SAW HIM DOWN BELOW!
DON'T CRY, ALICIA!
EVERY-THING'LL BE OKAY NOW, KID! I SWEAR IT!
WHAT HAPPENED, REED? WHAT MADE THE PUPPET MASTER FALL?
I WONDER IF WE'LL EVER REALLY KNOW?
THE END
23

Address YOUR letters to:
THE EDITOR
FANTASTIC FOUR
THIRD FLOOR
655 MADISON AVE.
NEW YORK 21, N. Y.

FANTASTIC FAN PAGE 4

DEAR EDITOR:
I've just finished reading FF #6 and all I can say is "WOW!" It's the greatest issue of the greatest magazine in the world! The idea of Sub-Mariner teaming up with Dr. Doom was a stroke of genius! And the characterization —I actually feel I KNOW Sub-Mariner, that's how REAL he seems—as do all your characters! You guys are the greatest!

H. Steinhill
Manila, Philippines

DEAR EDITOR:
I think your mag is stupendous and all that jazz, but being a girl and reading the FANTASTIC FOUR everybody thinks I'm odd! How can I convince my friends that FF isn't meant only for boys—or is it? One other thing—how did the FF meet? Or did I miss a copy?

Cynthia Moore
Cape Cod, Mass.

Cynthia honey, WE like to think that it's the people who DON'T read FF that are odd! As for how they met, we'll keep summarizing their origin from time to time to let you new readers catch up.

DEAR EDITOR:
The FF is the most realistic mag yet! But I have a few criticisms about it: 1) Mr. Fantastic could have a better name. 2) Please don't play the "black magic" theme very often. 3) When the FF team addresses The Thing, I think they should call him something else besides "Thing." All in all, your mag is great, but how does the Torch fly?

Don Henrehan, Jr.
West Islip, N. Y.

By actual count, Don, most readers seem to like the name Mr. Fantastic. As for the black magic "theme" as you call it, we'll try not to overdo it. But tell us, what would YOU call the Thing? (Inasmuch as his real name is Ben Grimm, "Ben" would seem to be the logical appellation, but we sometimes fear that new readers wouldn't know why he is being called Ben unless we constantly explain it. See the things editors have to worry about?) The Torch flies because he's lighter than air and is propelled by the energy of his flame.

DEAR EDITOR:
You people should be shot! On account of you I'm becoming a hoarder! You make it impossible to throw away an FF mag. Each issue has something that makes me want to save it and re-read it over and over again. Take #6 for example. That diagram of the FF's skyscraper headquarters was a knockout! Each time I look at it I seem to find something new. It's worth the price of the magazine by itself! And the fight in the sky—man, it's too much! You'll have to stop publishing, or find me a bigger closet!

Frederick Foster
Tucson, Ariz.

DEAR EDITOR:
Who does Martin Ross think he is? In your #6 issue he wrote a letter saying that Susan Storm ought to be thrown out because she never does anything! If you ever throw that doll out, I want to know where you throw her, because I'm making a bee-line for the place! Take it from me . . . don't change anything about your mag, and especially your characters.

Angry Artie Starr
Miami, Fla.

DEAR EDITOR:
The characters in the FF seem so real to me, that I've been trying to decide who should play their roles when they get into the movies. (And it better be SOON.) Here is my list of selections—I'd be interested in seeing what other fans think. MR. FANTASTIC: Gregory Peck. HUMAN TORCH: Troy Donahue. THE THING: Steeve Reeves (With make-up on, of course). INVISIBLE GIRL: Tuesday Weld. What do YOU think?

H. Sher
Brooklyn, N. Y.

Say, it looks like this might be fun, H.! We'll print the suggestions which our other fans send us in a future issue of FF.

DEAR EDITOR:
Here's what I think of your magazine: I LIKE: The name "Mr. Fantastic," your sense of humor, the fact that the Thing can't change into human form, the feud between the Torch and the Thing, your covers, the costumes, the hideout, the Fantasticar, the idea of no secret identities, and the idea of four fingers for The Thing. I DON'T LIKE: The way Mr. Fantastic always swears that he won't let anything happen!

Paul J. Batchie
Austin Road, Mahopac

DEAR EDITOR:
I've noticed that ever since the great success of the Fantastic Four, some of your so-called competitors are using characters who stretch like Mr. Fantastic in lots of their mags. I don't think it's fair. What can you do about it?

Joe Dinnis
Indianapolis, Ind.

Nothing, Joe, except revel in the knowledge that imitation is the sincerest form of flattery!

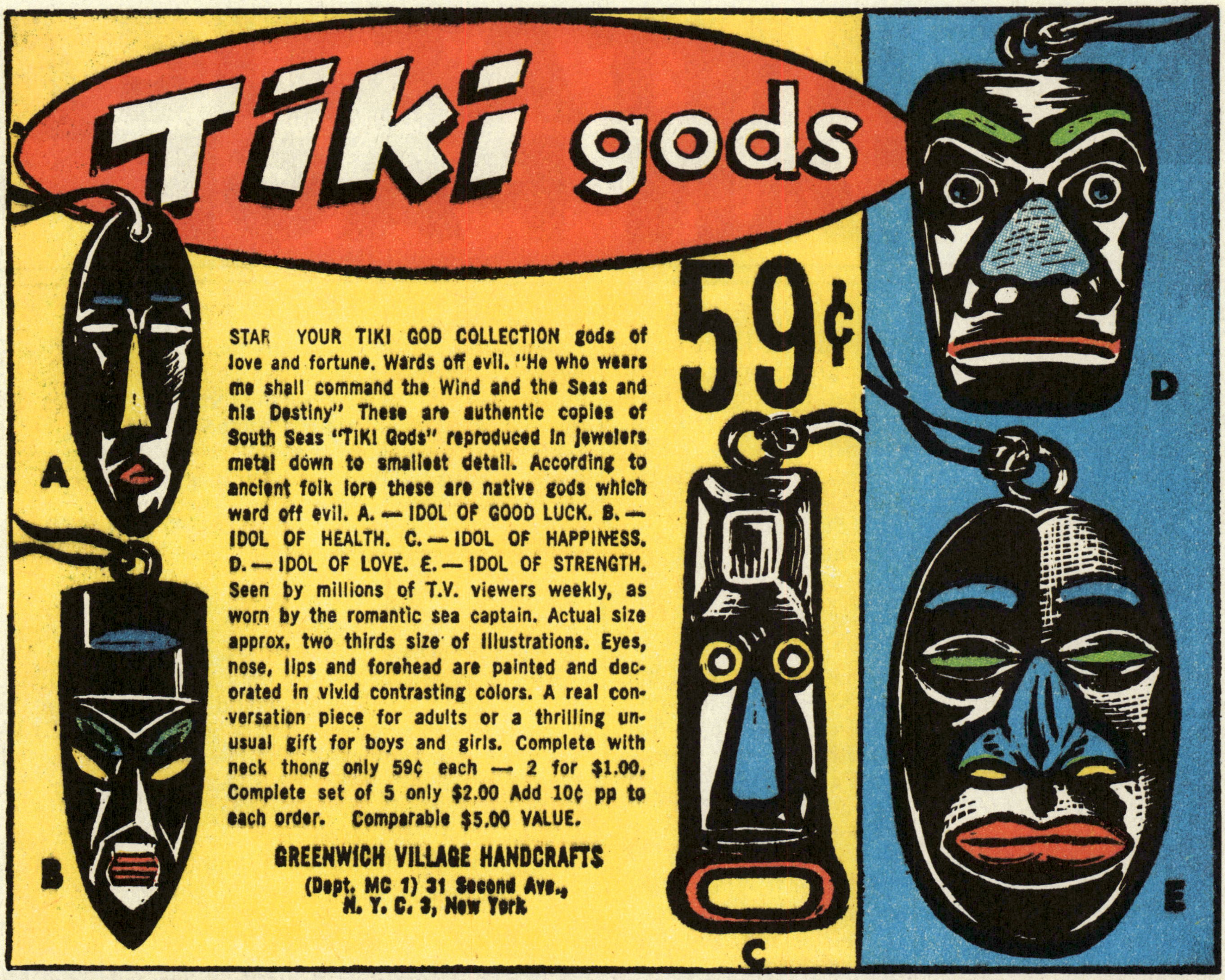

TiKi gods
59¢
STAR YOUR TIKI GOD COLLECTION gods of love and fortune. Wards off evil. "He who wears me shall command the Wind and the Seas and his Destiny" These are authentic copies of South Seas "TIKI Gods" reproduced in jewelers metal down to smallest detail. According to ancient folk lore these are native gods which ward off evil. A. — IDOL OF GOOD LUCK. B. — IDOL OF HEALTH. C. — IDOL OF HAPPINESS. D. — IDOL OF LOVE. E. — IDOL OF STRENGTH. Seen by millions of T.V. viewers weekly, as worn by the romantic sea captain. Actual size approx. two thirds size of illustrations. Eyes, nose, lips and forehead are painted and decorated in vivid contrasting colors. A real conversation piece for adults or a thrilling unusual gift for boys and girls. Complete with neck thong only 59¢ each — 2 for $1.00. Complete set of 5 only $2.00 Add 10¢ pp to each order. Comparable $5.00 VALUE.
GREENWICH VILLAGE HANDCRAFTS
(Dept. MC 1) 31 Second Ave.,
N. Y. C. 3, New York
A
B
C
D
E

REVERSIBLE AUTO SEAT COVERS
MADE OF FLEXTON — SERVICE GAUGE PLASTIC FOR LONG WEAR
• Waterproof. Easy to attach to seats for good fit. Roomy and neat. Elastic shirring and reinforced overlap side grips insure over-all seat coverage. Will dress up your car's interior and give protection to seat upholstery. Whisk off mud, oil, sand, grime with a damp rag for bright as new appearance. Sewn with nylon thread for long wear and durability.
ORDER FROM MANUFACTURER AND SAVE!
Choice of split or front seat styles only $2.98 each. Complete set for Front & Rear only $5.00. Specify make of car and seat style with each order. Save Money and buy a set today.
RUSH ORDER TODAY!
10 day Money Back Guarantee!
STYLE #400
Snake-Zebra Design—Printed Plastic can be used on either side. Gives snappy, distinctive dress up appearance. Front or Rear Seat only $2.98
STYLE #500
Leopard Cowhide design on Printed Flexton Plastic. Leopard on one side, Cowhide on the other. Either side gives beauty to your car's seats. Never gets dirty for it cleans with a whisk of a damp cloth. Front or Rear. $2.98
NOVEL MFG. Dept.—LC-1
33 Second Ave., New York 3, N. Y..
Please send me seat covers I have marked. I can try for 10 days and return for refund of purchase price if I am not satisfied. I will add 25¢ Postage on prepaid orders. On C.O.D. orders I'll send $2. deposit.
☐ Zebra-Snake Design, Reversible
☐ Leopard Cowhide Design, Reversible
☐ Split Seat $2.98 ☐ Solid Seat $2.98
☐ Set (Front & Rear) $5.00
☐ I enclose payment ☐ Send C.O.D.
Name
Address
City Zone State

STOP — THINK

Why buy stamps from others, when we reward your purchases with your choice of—all volumes Scott's International Albums, Scott's 1962 Catalogues, even Master Global Albums, Absolutely FREE when you buy our sensational Foreign Approvals (no U.S.). References or parents' consent required. Write to
BARGAIN STAMP SERVICE
REDLANDS 5 CALIFORNIA

STAMP COLLECTING OUTFIT

A packet of stamps from all parts of world. A package of stamp hinges; perforation gauge and millimeter scale; watermark detector. Everything ONLY 10c to approval buyers.
LORRAINE W. BROWN, Dept. 10, Marion, Mich.

1c

Thousands of beautiful stamps at only 1c each—why pay more when you can get the best for less. Write today for approvals.
PENNY STAMP SERVICE
Orange California

BETTER U.S. APPROVALS

To introduce our BETTER U.S. APPROVALS we offer 15 of the most wanted U.S. stamps, including a Columbian, Bi-Cents, Army-Navy, Famous American, Airs and other Commems. for only 10c.
OCEAN STAMPS, BOX 64-D, BROOKLYN 29, N.Y.

1/2 OUR APPROVALS OFF

are sold at 50% of Scott Catalogue prices.
MAKE US PROVE IT!
CATALINA STAMPS, Dept. C Orange, California

111 DIF. BONANZA 10¢

Includes Complete Red Cross Set, Triangle, Scout, Fr. So. Antartica, Singapore, Hungary Street Scenes, etc. Only 10¢ with Approvals.
FAIRWAY — Box 65-C — Garden Grove, Calif.

$5.00 FOR 10¢

Rare ORIENTAL COLLECTION Cataloging over $5.00 Only 10¢ when you buy our Foreign Approvals. PLUS valuable Albums — other FREE GIFTS.
COAST STAMPS, 1609 So. Park Santa Ana, Calif.

$5 SPECIAL STAMP OFFER! 10¢

Amazing offer to introduce our better U.S. approvals. Get 2 different $5.00 U.S. stamps PLUS 20 more hi-values, air mails, commemoratives, etc. Send only 10¢ for this splendid value. Send your dime TODAY to:
IRWIN STAMP CO. - Box 11 - BROOKLYN 30, N.Y.

Fantastic Fish Triangles!! Valuable "Ben Franklin" on CANAL ZONE!! Flaming bi-colored Volcano Triangle!! Lovely Olympics Triangle!! Plus Icy Greenland, Weird Wild Beast issue & others. 10¢ with approvals.
Roseland Stamps, Spring Lake 19, Mich.

STAMP JUNGLE including Zabu, Kookaburra, Koalabear, Kangaroo, Rhinoceros, **10¢**. Approvals.
CROWN STAMP COMPANY Virgil316Ontario

Terrific STAMP BARGAIN!

Israel–Iceland–San Marino–plus triangle set–Plus Antigua–Borneo–Virgin–Scouts–Congo–Russia–Plus large stamp book–all 4 offers free. Send 10c for mailing cost.
EMPIRE STAMP CORP., Dept. MC, Toronto, Canada

55 "FDR" & POPE TRIANGLE!! Lot 55 DIFFERENT has FDR Diamond, "Pope" Triangle, Greenland, Angola Map, Rhodesia etc. Catalogs $1.15—ALL only 5c with Approvals.
LONGHORN STAMP CO., Box 3068, Ellwood Sta. Lubbock, Tex.

100 YEAR OLD U.S.STAMPS

OURS is really the only firm capable of sending "On Approval" ALL U. S. Stamps including ALL U. S. Commemoratives, besides All Foreign Sets and Singles, All Roosevelts, Coronations etc. Try our SUPERIOR Approvals. Send 10¢ for Special Bargain of 50 diff. U. S. and Stamp Literature
GLOBUS STAMP CO., NEW YORK 10, N. Y., Dept. 323

.177 CAL. ROSCO AIR RIFLE $6.95 ppd.

SHOOTS PELLETS

BREAK ACTION

This high powered sportsman's air rifle is terrific for target practice, shooting rodents, small game, etc. Shoots .177 pellets accurately, powerfully. To load and activate mechanism, simply break barrel. Steel barrel with front & rear sights, beautiful walnut stock. (Regularly $14.95) NOW ONLY $6.95 including FREE can of 200 pellets. Additional can of 200 pellets . . . 50¢. Send cash, check or M.O. Satisfaction guaranteed.
SEAPORT TRADERS, INC.
1221 S. Grand, Dept. MC G6, Los Angeles 15, Calif.

POEMS WANTED

For musical setting. Send your Poems today for Free Examination. Any subject. Immediate consideration.
CROWN MUSIC CO., 49-MC W. 32 St., New York 1

"OLD GLORY" IN FLAMING COLORS!!! USA Flag giant beauty from Honduras! Enormous UNITED NATIONS Mexican Stamp! Plus Strange Gorilla issue, Duke of Windsor' Morocco, lovely Macao Flowers, Wild Buffalo stamp & others, 10c with approvals. Sunny Stamps Service, Apopka 19, Fla.

TERRIFIC TRIANGLES!! Frightful Fish, Sports, Volcanoes TRIANGLES, also African Flowers, weird Angola Map, tri-colored Flag, etc. to approval buyers for 4c postage.
POTOMAC STAMP COMPANY
Dept. 7 Washington 15, D. C.

25 DIFFERENT LARGE American Commemoratives for just **10¢** with approvals.
LINCOLN STAMP CO. St. Catharines116Ont.

1847, First USA Rariety!! Goliath foreign beauty shows Ben Franklin in this outstanding issue!! Plus Congo Freedom stamp, unused 1/2 inch midget stamp freak, real Cigar issue, Icy Greenland, Free China Bomer, airmail giant, etc., only 10c with approvals. **Capital Stamp Co., Ferrysburg 19D, Mich.**

307 WORLDWIDE DIFFERENT stamps all for only **25¢** with approvals.
NIAGARA STAMP CO. St. Catharines216Ont.

LOOK — GIANT PHILIPPINE
stamp, plus New Zealand, Cuba and others. Only 5c with U.S. or foreign approvals.
Earl Thompson, 5448 Odell St., St. Louis 9, Mo.

You save more than money with U.S. Savings Bonds

225 STAMPS FOR ONLY 10¢

THIS MAMMOTH VALUE INCLUDES STAMPS WORTH UP TO 25c! ALSO APPROVALS. WRITE TODAY!
MYSTIC STAMP CO Camden 3, New York

SPECIAL! OLD U.S.
Famous Americans, Flags, Presidents, Commemoratives, Airmails 10c with approvals Plus Surprise Packet. **10¢**
METROPOLITAN STAMPS
Box 312T, Jackson Heights, N. Y.

STOP STOOPING!

with amazing, new Pi Peer Shoulder Brace

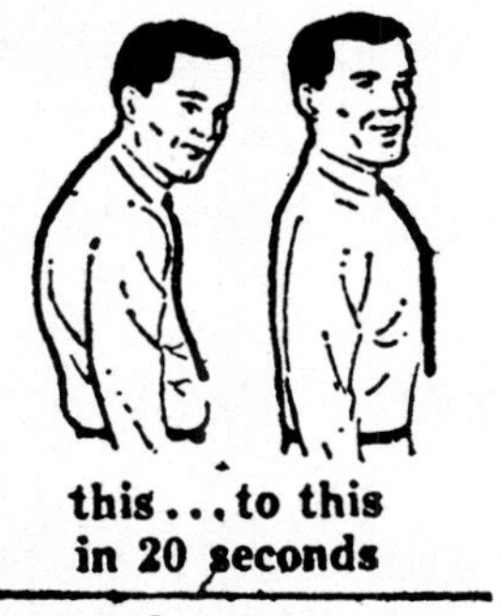

Corrects posture instantly, comfortably. Scientific design provides even, distributed support for sagging shoulders. Improves appearance, gives you a wonderful new feeling of confidence. Slips on in seconds. No fitting. Made of highest quality ventilated-for-comfort 3-ply cushioned material. Arm bands softly padded for maximum comfort. Lightweight, cool. FOR MEN AND WOMEN. Can't be detected under light clothing. Give measurement around chest. Only $4.95. Sent postpaid except on COD's. Money-back guarantee if returned postpaid in 30 days.

Piper Brace Co. • Dept. M42H
811 Wyandotte • Kansas City 5, Mo.

COIN COLLECTORS!

Foreign Coin — Banknote — Checklist and price list FREE for 5¢ postage to approval service applicants only. Indian Cents 2 diff. for 25¢.
SPRUCELAND C1, 115 State St, Spgfld 3, Mass.

BASEBALL CARDS 4¢ EACH

Order by number—50¢ minimum order
7 series, $2.75 each—Full set, 7 series $18.00.
Send 25¢ for price list of all types of cards.
CARD COLLECTORS CO., Box 293B, Franklin Sq. N. Y.

POEMS

WANTED for musical setting and recording. Send poems Free Examination.
AMERICA'S LARGEST SONG STUDIO
FIVE STAR MUSIC MASTERS, 92 BEACON BLDG., BOSTON, MASS.

4 LIVE COLOR CHANGING CHAMELEONS

PREPAID $1.00
Send 25¢ For Complete Snake and Other Reptile Price List.
LOUISIANA BIOLOGICAL CENTER
BOX 336,
NORCO, LOUISIANA

INDIAN WAR BONNET KIT

All parts and illustrated instructions to make an authentic Indian Chief's War Bonnet. You will also receive FREE, our 52 page illustrated catalog. All for ONLY $3.00 postpaid (no C.O.D.) Satisfaction guaranteed or money back. Send your $3.00 today to
CHIEF GREY OWL, 150 Beaver Rd., Jamaica 33, N.Y.

1000 TRICKS 25c

AMAZE!... ENTERTAIN! HAVE FUN! START NOW!

BIG EXCITING MAGIC & FUN CATALOG! 160 PAGES!
Tricks, Jokes, Magic, Illusions, Secrets! Puzzles, Stunts, etc. World famous! Rush name, address & only 25c.

FREE CARD TRICK GIVEN with Each Catalog!
HOUSE OF 1000 MYSTERIES
Dept. MC6-62 Trumbull Conn.

INSIGNIA 40 for $1.00

ARMY • NAVY • MARINE

Includes 40 Different Shoulder Emblems, Ratings, Chevrons, Q-Bars, Medals, Ribbons, Collar Insignia, etc. ORDER NOW! Send $1.00 for 40 or $5.00 for 250. NO DUPLICATES —ALL DIFFERENT
EMBLEM SALES CO. Dept. 1000
P.O. Box 167, Madison Sq. Sta., N.Y. 10

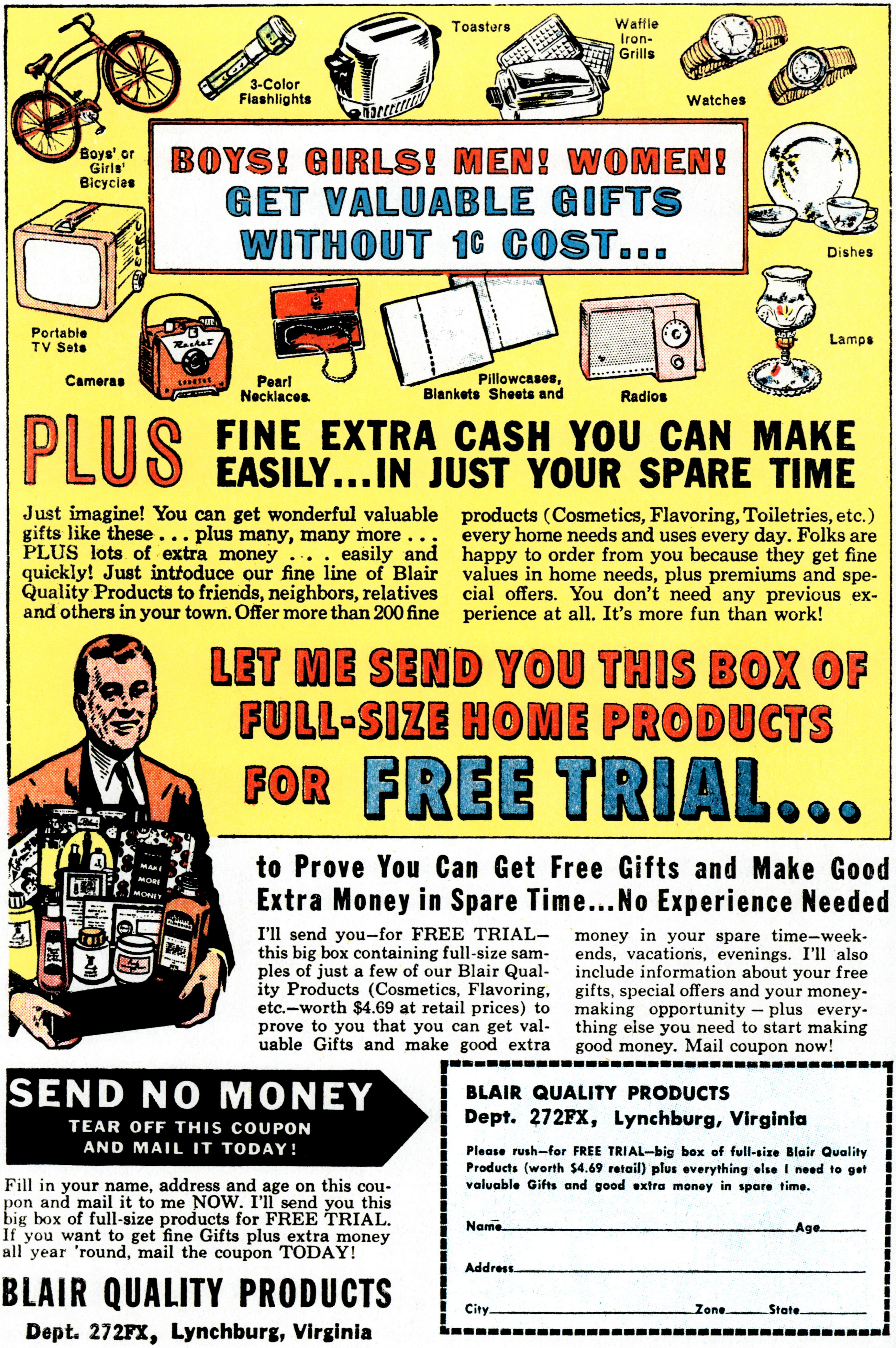

Toasters
Waffle Iron-Grills
3-Color Flashlights
Watches
Boys' or Girls' Bicycles
BOYS! GIRLS! MEN! WOMEN!
GET VALUABLE GIFTS
WITHOUT 1¢ COST...
Dishes
Portable TV Sets
Lamps
Cameras
Pearl Necklaces
Pillowcases, Blankets Sheets and
Radios
PLUS FINE EXTRA CASH YOU CAN MAKE EASILY...IN JUST YOUR SPARE TIME
Just imagine! You can get wonderful valuable gifts like these . . . plus many, many more . . . PLUS lots of extra money . . . easily and quickly! Just introduce our fine line of Blair Quality Products to friends, neighbors, relatives and others in your town. Offer more than 200 fine products (Cosmetics, Flavoring, Toiletries, etc.) every home needs and uses every day. Folks are happy to order from you because they get fine values in home needs, plus premiums and special offers. You don't need any previous experience at all. It's more fun than work!
LET ME SEND YOU THIS BOX OF FULL-SIZE HOME PRODUCTS FOR FREE TRIAL...
MAKE MORE MONEY
to Prove You Can Get Free Gifts and Make Good Extra Money in Spare Time...No Experience Needed
I'll send you—for FREE TRIAL—this big box containing full-size samples of just a few of our Blair Quality Products (Cosmetics, Flavoring, etc.—worth $4.69 at retail prices) to prove to you that you can get valuable Gifts and make good extra money in your spare time—weekends, vacations, evenings. I'll also include information about your free gifts, special offers and your money-making opportunity — plus everything else you need to start making good money. Mail coupon now!
SEND NO MONEY
TEAR OFF THIS COUPON AND MAIL IT TODAY!
Fill in your name, address and age on this coupon and mail it to me NOW. I'll send you this big box of full-size products for FREE TRIAL. If you want to get fine Gifts plus extra money all year 'round, mail the coupon TODAY!
BLAIR QUALITY PRODUCTS
Dept. 272FX, Lynchburg, Virginia
BLAIR QUALITY PRODUCTS
Dept. 272FX, Lynchburg, Virginia
Please rush—for FREE TRIAL—big box of full-size Blair Quality Products (worth $4.69 retail) plus everything else I need to get valuable Gifts and good extra money in spare time.
Name Age
Address
City Zone State

IND.
THE WORLD'S GREATEST COMIC MAGAZINE!
APPROVED BY THE COMICS CODE AUTHORITY
12¢
THE Fantastic Four
MC
9 DEC.
LITTLE DO THEY DREAM THAT THEY WILL SOON BE AT THE MERCY OF THE SUB-MARINER!
WHAT HAPPENS TO COMIC MAGAZINE HEROES WHEN THEY CAN'T PAY THEIR BILLS AND HAVE NO PLACE TO TURN? DON'T MISS THE NEWEST AND MOST ORIGINAL TALE OF ALL... "THE END OF THE FANTASTIC FOUR!"
FANTASTIC FOUR EVICTED FROM BUILDING!
5 TOWER FLOORS FOR RENT!
HEROES ONE MINUTE--BUMS THE NEXT!! HOW DID IT HAPPEN TO US??!

SKINNY OR FAT, 15, 20, 30 OR 40 YEARS OF AGE

Just RUSH me your LAST CHANCE COUPON below with YOUR NAME and ADDRESS ON IT and I'll show YOU absolutely FREE

How to GAIN UP TO 50 LBS. OF MIGHTY MUSCLES!

And Become a REAL HE-MAN like MANY THOUSANDS of My Pupils in 10 Minutes of FUN a Day

Are YOU SKINNY like I was?

a sickly skeleton who developed a streamlined physique and great physical endurance.

American Body building Club president

BEN REBHUHN

at 50 years of age. A brilliant UNIVERSITY EDUCATOR,

authority on creating a HEALTHY MIND in a HEALTHY BODY,

says Dr. Winfield Scott Pugh, Commander U.S. Navy Medical Corps.

Yes! I'll Show You By My Quick, Easy Methods How To

ADD POWERFUL NEW INCHES OF MUSCLES around YOUR ARMS, CHEST, LEGS, etc.

How to IMPROVE YOUR HE-MAN LOOKS 100%.

How to BECOME A WINNING ATHLETE IN ALL POPULAR SPORTS.
How to BEAT ANY BULLY.
How to DO FEATS of STRENGTH.
How to be a WINNER in EVERYTHING YOU TACKLE.

YES! Your Success Story Can Soon be like John Sill and thousands of my pupils. Think of it — a skinny weakling like you became a MAGNIFICENT MR. MUSCLES — won a BIG SILVER TROPHY, his name, accomplishments engraved on it and $100. A few weeks before, everybody picked on John, too weak to fight for his rights. TODAY everybody admires John's movie star build, he-man STRENGTH, his mighty ARMS, heroic CHEST, slender WAIST, rock-like TORSO, broad manly BACK, wide military SHOULDERS, new popularity with the BOYS and GIRLS. His winning drive in ALL SPORTS, his energy at work and studies.

NO! I don't care how skinny or flabby you are, if you are in your teens, twenties or thirties, I'll show you in just 10 thrilling minutes a day in your home, you can make yourself over by the easy, quick method I turned myself from a wreck to a tower of strength and endurance.

YES! YOU'LL ADD INCH upon INCH of MIGHTY MUSCLES to YOUR ARMS, YOU'LL DEEPEN YOUR CHEST, BROADEN YOUR BACK and SHOULDERS. From HEAD to HEELS you'll gain SIZE, POWER, LIGHTNING SPEED, ENDURANCE. You'll become the SUCCESSFUL HE-MAN IN LOOKS and ACTS — a WINNER in EVERYTHING, athletics, business, studies.

I GAINED 60 LBS. OF SHAPELY MIGHTY MUSCLES

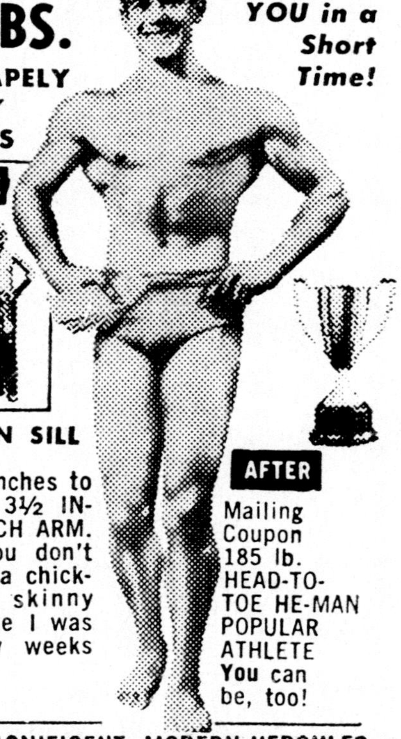

This Can Be YOU in a Short Time!

BEFORE Mailing Coupon I was a 125 lb. 6 ft. skinny weakling

says JOHN SILL

I added 7 inches to MY CHEST, 3½ INCHES to EACH ARM. No, Pal! You don't have to be a chicken-chested skinny weakling like I was only a few weeks ago.

AFTER Mailing Coupon 185 lb. HEAD-TO-TOE HE-MAN POPULAR ATHLETE You can be, too!

This now MAGNIFICENT, MODERN HERCULES, 26 yr. old teacher, Wm. Butler,

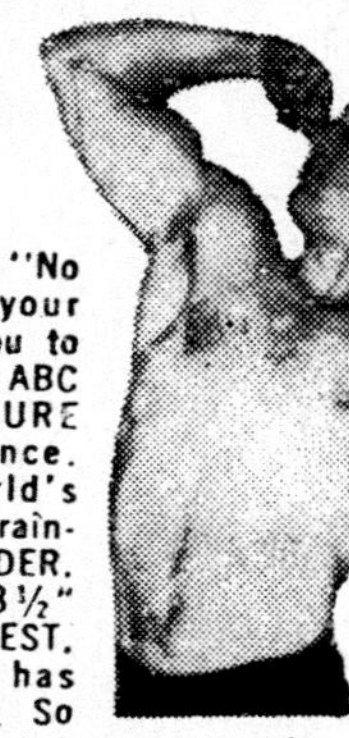

says to YOU. "No matter WHAT your age, I advise you to SEND for the ABC WONDER PICTURE COURSES at once. Under the World's greatest home training BODY BUILDER. I now have 18½" ARMS, a 52" CHEST, my STRENGTH has greatly improved. So have my sports. I have won titles like "Mr. Virginian," "Mr. State Y.M.C.A.," etc.

How would **YOU** like to have 18½ inch ARMS, a 52 inch CHEST like this ABC pupil NOW HAS?

I BROKE A WORLD'S STRENGTH RECORD!

JIM NORMAN became Athlete of the Year. Lifted the front End of a 2700 lb. Car. Quit being a bag-of-bones weakling like I was. In 10 minutes of fun a day, A.B.C. CAN DO FOR YOU ALL HE DID FOR ME! I gained 25 TERRIFIC LBS. of HANDSOME POWER-PACKED MUSCLES.

BEFORE — AFTER mailing coupon below— like you do NOW.

DEVELOP YOUR 520 MUSCLES BY THE GREATEST METHOD!

Friend, I traveled the world, studying every secret to PERFECTLY develop your body. My "5-Way Progressive Natural Power Method" is TESTED-PROVED by hundreds of thousands LIKE YOU! SAVE YEARS, hundreds of DOLLARS! Do as movie stars, champions — John Sill, Jim Norman, Tony Pascarella — did! Mail coupon NOW!

Pick the kind of BODY YOU WANT
Check ALL Your Needs —

WIN A BIG Silver Trophy and $100 IN CASH

MAIL THE COUPON TO ME NOW and I'll Send You FREE these 5 AMAZING PICTURE-PACKED TEST COURSES (before it is too late) as John Sill and the others did

PLUS BOOK OF PHOTOS OF FAMOUS STRONG MEN ONCE WEAK LIKE YOU

MILLIONS were sold at $1.00. Send for them ALL FREE. Mail Coupon BEFORE IT IS TOO LATE!

AMERICAN BODY BUILDING CLUB, Dept. MA-211, GREAT NECK, NEW YORK

Mail me FREE all 5 WORLD FAMOUS STRENGTH TEST COURSES, including PHOTO BOOK of FAMOUS STRONG MEN, once weaklings, now famous Strong Men, and How to Become one of Them.

☐ I enclose 10c for mailing and handling.
I am under no other obligation.
I'm checking everything I need to give me the kind of body I want.
☐ I want to gain ....lbs. (fill in). ☐ Triple my strength.
☐ I want to streamline my body, get rid of flabby fat.
☐ I want to add inches of muscle to my ☐ ARMS ☐ CHEST ☐ SHOULDERS ☐ POWERFUL LEGS ☐ SLIM WAIST
☐ I want to become a winning athlete. ☐ I want new pep.

NAME...AGE..........
DO NOT MAIL COUPON IF UNDER 14 YEARS OF AGE.
ADDRESS...
CITY..............................ZONE.......STATE..............

FREE Sports, Self-defense, Strong-man Stunts Courses Apparatus. Let me know how to get these FREE!

THE FANTASTIC FOUR is published by CANAM PUBLISHERS SALES CORP. OFFICE OF PUBLICATION: 655 MADISON AVENUE, NEW YORK, N.Y. Published monthly. Copyright 1962 by CANAM PUBLISHERS SALES CORP., 655 Madison Avenue, New York, N.Y. Vol. 1 No. 9; DECEMBER, 1962 issue. Price 12¢ per copy. Subscription rate $1.75 for 12 issues including postage. Foreign subscription $3.25 in American funds. No similarity between any of the names, characters, persons, and/or institutions appearing in this magazine with those of any living or dead person is intended, and any such similarity which may exist is purely coincidental. Printed in the U.S.A. by The Eastern Color Printing Co., Waterbury 20, Conn.

THE END OF THE FANTASTIC FOUR!
IN A HIDDEN CHAMBER, FAR UNDER THE SEA, PRINCE NAMOR, THE AMAZING SUB-MARINER TUNES INTO A TV NEWSCAST FROM THE SURFACE WORLD, AND HEARS A STARTLING ANNOUNCEMENT...
BULLETIN! THE WORLD-FAMOUS FANTASTIC FOUR ARE BANKRUPT! THEY HAVE ANNOUNCED PLANS TO DISSOLVE THEIR PARTNERSHIP AND SELL ALL THEIR POSSESSIONS IN ORDER TO PAY THEIR DEBTS!
WHAT'S THAT??
SCRIPT.... STAN LEE
ART....... JACK KIRBY
INKING.... DICK AYERS
LETTERING.. ART SIMEK
V-995
THE FANTASTIC FOUR ARE ABOUT TO SPLIT UP, EH?
NOW ISN'T THAT MIGHTY INTERESTING!
SO THEY'RE PENNILESS, ARE THEY? WELL, THIS MAY JUST BE THE OPPORTUNITY I'VE BEEN WAITING FOR!
1

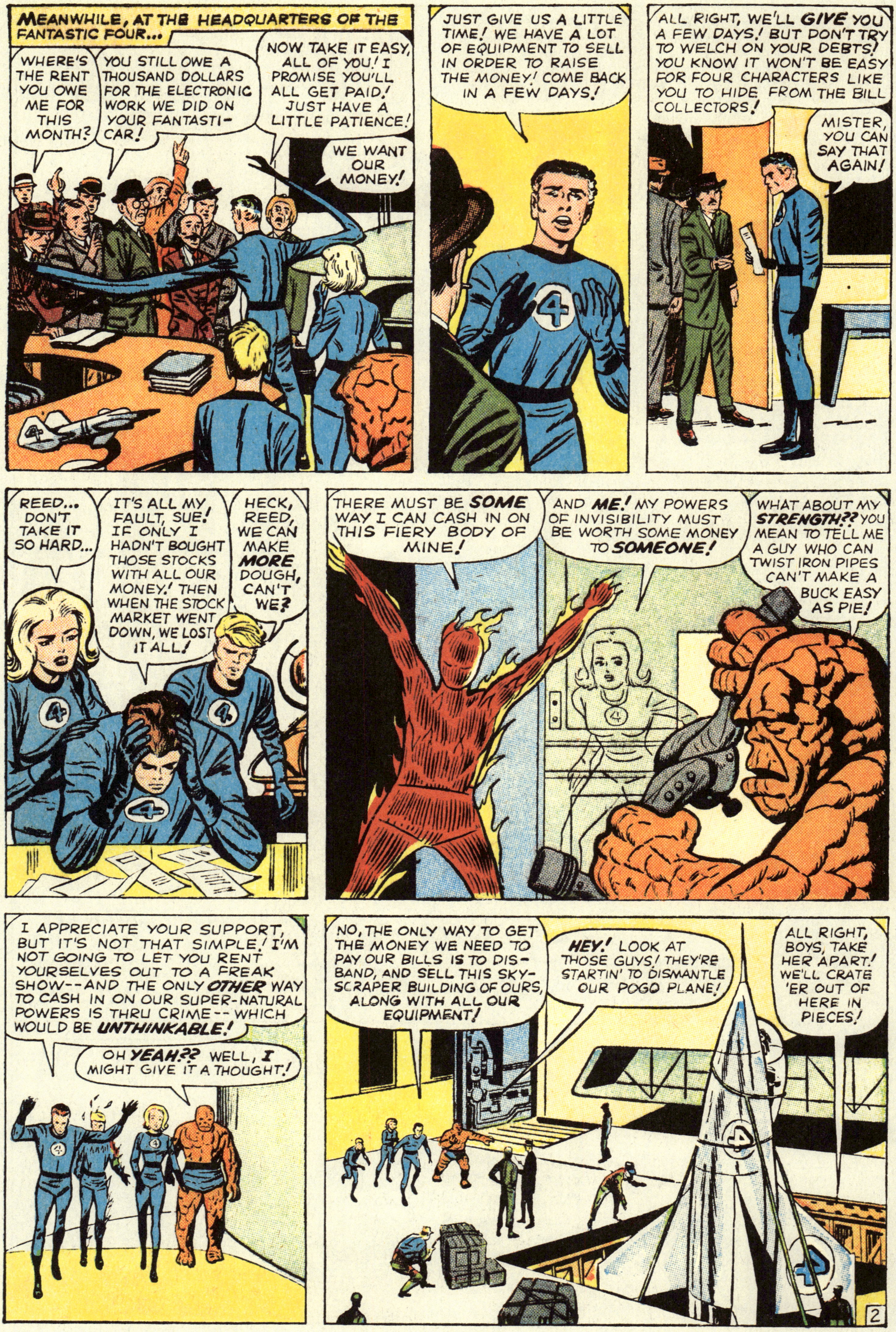
MEANWHILE, AT THE HEADQUARTERS OF THE FANTASTIC FOUR...
WHERE'S THE RENT YOU OWE ME FOR THIS MONTH?
YOU STILL OWE A THOUSAND DOLLARS FOR THE ELECTRONIC WORK WE DID ON YOUR FANTASTI-CAR!
NOW TAKE IT EASY, ALL OF YOU! I PROMISE YOU'LL ALL GET PAID! JUST HAVE A LITTLE PATIENCE!
WE WANT OUR MONEY!
JUST GIVE US A LITTLE TIME! WE HAVE A LOT OF EQUIPMENT TO SELL IN ORDER TO RAISE THE MONEY! COME BACK IN A FEW DAYS!
ALL RIGHT, WE'LL GIVE YOU A FEW DAYS! BUT DON'T TRY TO WELCH ON YOUR DEBTS! YOU KNOW IT WON'T BE EASY FOR FOUR CHARACTERS LIKE YOU TO HIDE FROM THE BILL COLLECTORS!
MISTER, YOU CAN SAY THAT AGAIN!
REED... DON'T TAKE IT SO HARD...
IT'S ALL MY FAULT, SUE! IF ONLY I HADN'T BOUGHT THOSE STOCKS WITH ALL OUR MONEY! THEN WHEN THE STOCK MARKET WENT DOWN, WE LOST IT ALL!
HECK, REED, WE CAN MAKE MORE DOUGH, CAN'T WE?
THERE MUST BE SOME WAY I CAN CASH IN ON THIS FIERY BODY OF MINE!
AND ME! MY POWERS OF INVISIBILITY MUST BE WORTH SOME MONEY TO SOMEONE!
WHAT ABOUT MY STRENGTH?? YOU MEAN TO TELL ME A GUY WHO CAN TWIST IRON PIPES CAN'T MAKE A BUCK EASY AS PIE!
I APPRECIATE YOUR SUPPORT, BUT IT'S NOT THAT SIMPLE! I'M NOT GOING TO LET YOU RENT YOURSELVES OUT TO A FREAK SHOW--AND THE ONLY OTHER WAY TO CASH IN ON OUR SUPER-NATURAL POWERS IS THRU CRIME--WHICH WOULD BE UNTHINKABLE!
OH YEAH?? WELL, I MIGHT GIVE IT A THOUGHT!
NO, THE ONLY WAY TO GET THE MONEY WE NEED TO PAY OUR BILLS IS TO DISBAND, AND SELL THIS SKY-SCRAPER BUILDING OF OURS, ALONG WITH ALL OUR EQUIPMENT!
HEY! LOOK AT THOSE GUYS! THEY'RE STARTIN' TO DISMANTLE OUR POGO PLANE!
ALL RIGHT, BOYS, TAKE HER APART! WE'LL CRATE 'ER OUT OF HERE IN PIECES!
2

LEGGO OF MY PLANE, YOU CRUMBS! I OUGHTTA PULVERIZE YA FOR THAT!
THING! KNOCK IT OFF! I **SOLD** THE PLANE TO THEM! I **HAD** TO! WE'RE GETTING A GOOD PRICE FOR IT!
NO PRICE IS GOOD ENOUGH FOR ALL THE WORK WE PUT INTO **DESIGNIN'** THAT SHIP!
I KNOW HOW YOU FEEL, THING--BUT WE'VE **GOTTA** SELL THE PLANE--AND EVERYTHING ELSE, TOO!
OKAY, OKAY, I'M COOLED OFF NOW! JUST LEAVE ME ALONE! THAT'S ALL --LEAVE ME ALONE!
I-I NEVER THOUGHT I'D SEE THE DAY WHEN WE'D LOSE ALL OF REED'S WONDERFUL INVENTIONS!
4
SOME ROTTEN MANAGER **YOU** WERE, RUBBER-MAN! YOU MADE A **FORTUNE** BY SELLING PATENTS ON ALL YOUR INVENTIONS --ENOUGH DOUGH TO KEEP US GOING FOR YEARS-- BUT YOU HADDA BE A BIG SHOT AND INVEST IT ALL IN STOCKS! YOU LUNKHEAD!
TAKE IT EASY, THING! YOU CAN RIDE A MAN JUST SO FAR-- AND HE'LL FINALLY **BREAK!** I'M **WARNING** YOU!
BAH! MAYBE IT'S BETTER THIS WAY! THOSE THREE DO-GOODERS WERE BEGINNIN' TO CRAMP MY STYLE! I CAN PROBABLY MAKE OUT BETTER ON MY OWN! TAXI! HEY, **TAXI!**
SAY, YOU'RE THE **THING,** AIN'T YOU? SORRY, PAL, YOU AIN'T RIDIN' **THIS** CAB! I HEARD HOW THE FOUR OF YOU ARE FLAT BROKE! I DON'T WANNA BE HUNG UP FOR NO TAXI BILL!
SO! YOU DON'T WANT ME FOR A PASSENGER, EH? WELL, I'M **THRU** TAKIN' GUFF FROM CREEPS LIKE YOU!
HEY! LET ME DOWN! NO! **STOP! HALLLP!**

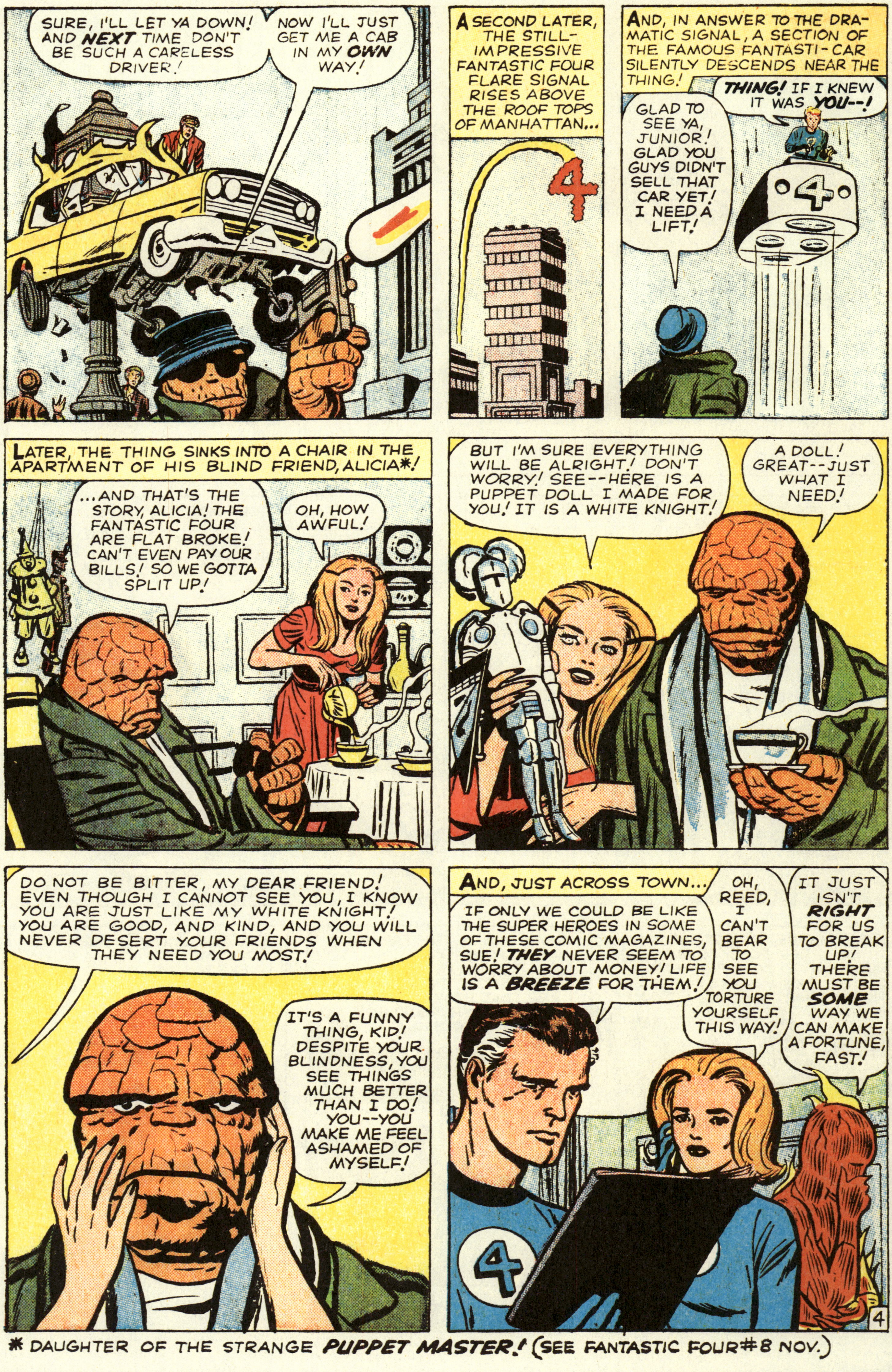
SURE, I'LL LET YA DOWN! AND NEXT TIME DON'T BE SUCH A CARELESS DRIVER!
NOW I'LL JUST GET ME A CAB IN MY OWN WAY!
A SECOND LATER, THE STILL-IMPRESSIVE FANTASTIC FOUR FLARE SIGNAL RISES ABOVE THE ROOF TOPS OF MANHATTAN...
AND, IN ANSWER TO THE DRAMATIC SIGNAL, A SECTION OF THE FAMOUS FANTASTI-CAR SILENTLY DESCENDS NEAR THE THING!
THING! IF I KNEW IT WAS YOU--!
GLAD TO SEE YA, JUNIOR! GLAD YOU GUYS DIDN'T SELL THAT CAR YET! I NEED A LIFT!
LATER, THE THING SINKS INTO A CHAIR IN THE APARTMENT OF HIS BLIND FRIEND, ALICIA*!
...AND THAT'S THE STORY, ALICIA! THE FANTASTIC FOUR ARE FLAT BROKE! CAN'T EVEN PAY OUR BILLS! SO WE GOTTA SPLIT UP!
OH, HOW AWFUL!
BUT I'M SURE EVERYTHING WILL BE ALRIGHT! DON'T WORRY! SEE--HERE IS A PUPPET DOLL I MADE FOR YOU! IT IS A WHITE KNIGHT!
A DOLL! GREAT--JUST WHAT I NEED!
DO NOT BE BITTER, MY DEAR FRIEND! EVEN THOUGH I CANNOT SEE YOU, I KNOW YOU ARE JUST LIKE MY WHITE KNIGHT! YOU ARE GOOD, AND KIND, AND YOU WILL NEVER DESERT YOUR FRIENDS WHEN THEY NEED YOU MOST!
IT'S A FUNNY THING, KID! DESPITE YOUR BLINDNESS, YOU SEE THINGS MUCH BETTER THAN I DO! YOU--YOU MAKE ME FEEL ASHAMED OF MYSELF!
AND, JUST ACROSS TOWN...
IF ONLY WE COULD BE LIKE THE SUPER HEROES IN SOME OF THESE COMIC MAGAZINES, SUE! THEY NEVER SEEM TO WORRY ABOUT MONEY! LIFE IS A BREEZE FOR THEM!
OH, REED, I CAN'T BEAR TO SEE YOU TORTURE YOURSELF THIS WAY!
IT JUST ISN'T RIGHT FOR US TO BREAK UP! THERE MUST BE SOME WAY WE CAN MAKE A FORTUNE, FAST!
4
* DAUGHTER OF THE STRANGE PUPPET MASTER! (SEE FANTASTIC FOUR #8 NOV.)

JOHNNY DOESN'T UNDERSTAND THAT IT TAKES MONEY TO RUN AN OUTFIT LIKE OURS! THERE'S THE UPKEEP ON OUR PLANES, EQUIPMENT, ELECTRONIC DEVICES... SAY, WHAT IS THIS TELEGRAM?
NEVER MIND MY TIP, TORCH! I FIGGER YOU GUYS NEED THE DOUGH MORE THAN ME!
IT'S LIKE A MIRACLE! AN OFFER FROM S.M. STUDIOS --IN HOLLYWOOD! ONE MILLION DOLLARS CASH TO US IF WE'LL STAR IN A MOVIE!
OH, REED--
THAT'S GREAT!
BUT WHAT ABOUT THE THING? YOU KNOW HOW HE FEELS ABOUT MAKING A SPECTACLE OF HIMSELF! HE HATES TO HAVE PEOPLE STARE AT HIM!
YOU AIN'T JUST FLAPPIN' YOUR LIPS, MISTER!
BUT I JUST FOUND OUT I'M A WHITE KNIGHT-- AND US WHITE KNIGHTS DON'T DESERT THEIR COMPANIONS IN ARMS! I'M WITH YA, GANG!
I DON'T KNOW WHAT YOU'RE TALKING ABOUT, BUT WELCOME BACK-- PARTNER!
WATCH IT, YA BIG APE! YOU'RE EVEN MORE DANGEROUS WHEN YOU'RE BEIN' FRIENDLY!
IT'S AGREED, THEN? WE STAY TOGETHER AND GO TO HOLLYWOOD TO MAKE THE PICTURE!
AND THE MILLION DOLLARS WE RECEIVE WILL PAY ALL OUR BILLS AND GIVE US A FRESH START!
BUT NEXT TIME I'LL HANDLE THE MONEY!
YAY! IT'S JUST LIKE OLD TIMES AGAIN!
THERE'S JUST ONE LITTLE DETAIL-- HOW DO WE GET TO HOLLYWOOD?
THAT'S RIGHT! WE'RE BROKE--AND IT'S EXPENSIVE TO TRAVEL CROSS-COUNTRY!
I GUESS THERE'S ONLY ONE THING TO DO...
I'LL STAY OUT OF SIGHT BACK HERE, SO I DON'T SCARE ANYONE AWAY!
SOMEONE'LL STOP SOONER OR LATER!
DON'T BE EMBARRASSED! WE'LL ALL LAUGH ABOUT THIS ONE DAY!
I HOPE SO!

PART 2
SUB-MARINER GIVES THE ORDERS!
A FEW DAYS, AND MANY WEARY MILES LATER, AT THE NEWLY-FORMED S.M. STUDIOS IS HOLLYWOOD, CALIFORNIA...
SM -STUDIOS-
SO THIS IS HOLLYWOOD!
ISN'T IT THRILLING ?!
THIS AIN'T SO BAD! SOME OF THOSE JOKERS ARE ALMOST AS FUNNY-LOOKING AS ME!
V-995
GOSH! WITH ALL THE CELEBRITIES AROUND HERE, NOBODY'S EVEN NOTICING US!
LET'S BE GLAD THEY AREN'T! NEXT THING FOR US TO DO IS FIND OUT WHERE WE'RE SUPPOSED TO REPORT TO!
SAY, CURLY, WHERE'S THE HEAD OFFICE OF THIS JOINT?
R-RIGHT B-BEHIND YOU!!!
6

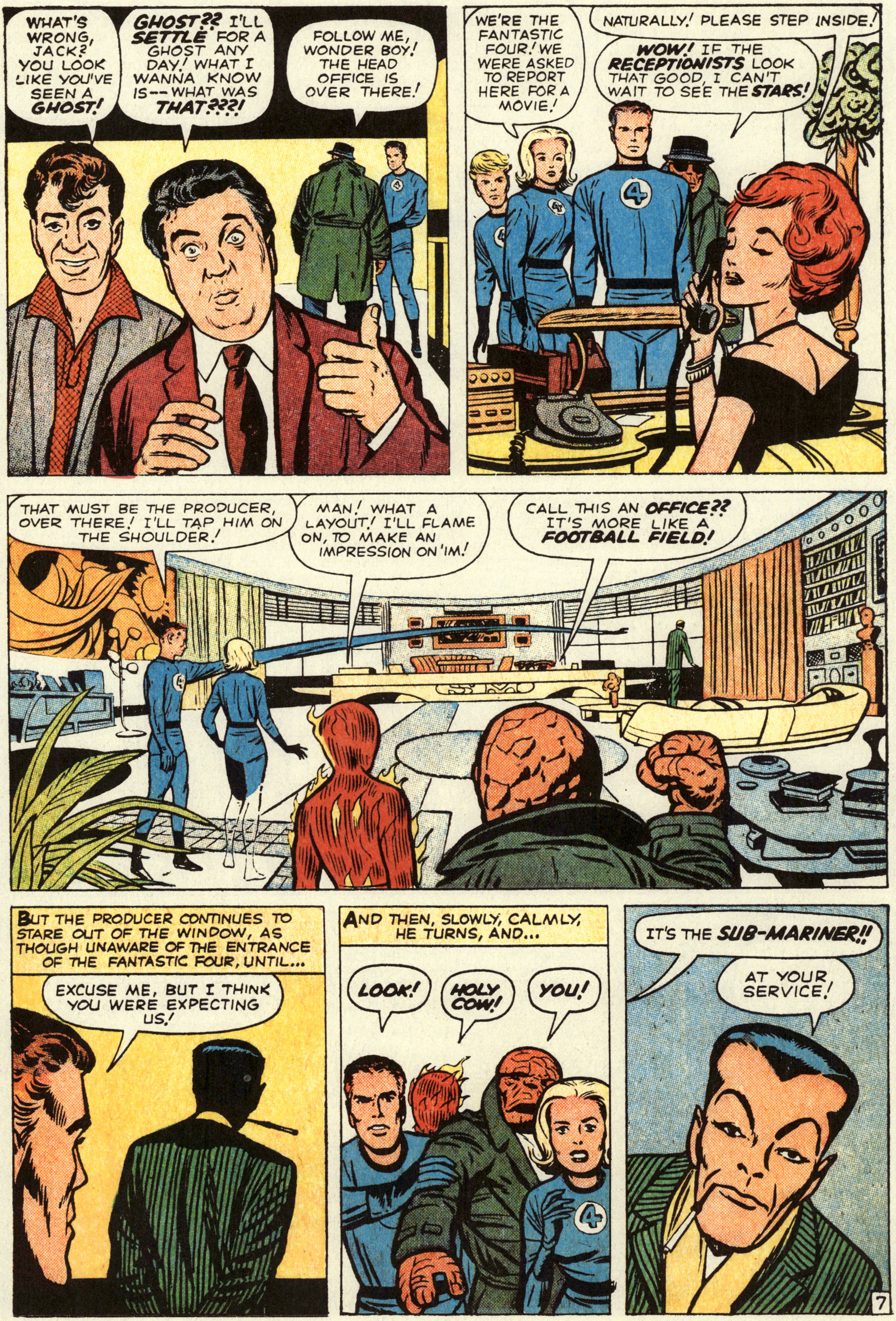
WHAT'S WRONG, JACK? YOU LOOK LIKE YOU'VE SEEN A GHOST!
GHOST?? I'LL SETTLE FOR A GHOST ANY DAY! WHAT I WANNA KNOW IS--WHAT WAS THAT???!
FOLLOW ME, WONDER BOY! THE HEAD OFFICE IS OVER THERE!
WE'RE THE FANTASTIC FOUR! WE WERE ASKED TO REPORT HERE FOR A MOVIE!
NATURALLY! PLEASE STEP INSIDE!
WOW! IF THE RECEPTIONISTS LOOK THAT GOOD, I CAN'T WAIT TO SEE THE STARS!
THAT MUST BE THE PRODUCER, OVER THERE! I'LL TAP HIM ON THE SHOULDER!
MAN! WHAT A LAYOUT! I'LL FLAME ON, TO MAKE AN IMPRESSION ON 'IM!
CALL THIS AN OFFICE?? IT'S MORE LIKE A FOOTBALL FIELD!
BUT THE PRODUCER CONTINUES TO STARE OUT OF THE WINDOW, AS THOUGH UNAWARE OF THE ENTRANCE OF THE FANTASTIC FOUR, UNTIL...
EXCUSE ME, BUT I THINK YOU WERE EXPECTING US!
AND THEN, SLOWLY, CALMLY, HE TURNS, AND...
LOOK!
HOLY COW!
YOU!
IT'S THE SUB-MARINER!!
AT YOUR SERVICE!
7

YOU NEED NOT LOOK SO SURPRISED! MY OFFER OF A MILLION DOLLARS WAS GENUINE ENOUGH! YOU SEE, ALL THE WEALTH OF THE SEA IS MINE!
"FOR YEARS, I HAVE COLLECTED TREASURE FROM WRECKED SUNKEN SHIPS--PIRATE GALLEONS AND OTHERS CARRYING ALL SORTS OF PRICELESS CARGO!"
"AGES AGO, MY ANCESTORS WITNESSED THE BURYING OF COUNTLESS HORDES OF STOLEN TREASURE... AND EACH GENERATION OF UNDERSEA PEOPLE HANDED THE LOCATIONS DOWN TO EACH FOLLOWING GENERATION!"
SO, OUT OF BOREDOM, I BOUGHT THIS STUDIO AND DECIDED TO FILM A MOVIE ABOUT MY FORMER ARCH-FOES! NOW HERE--HERE IS PART PAYMENT OF THE SUM I PROMISED YOU!
THE MONEY LOOKS GENUINE ENOUGH--AND WE'RE NOT IN A POSITION TO BE TOO PARTICULAR ABOUT WHO WE WORK FOR!
HE-HE'S SO MASTERFUL--SO CONFIDENT!
THE WHOLE THING STILL SMELLS FISHY TO ME... BUT I SURE LIKE THE FEEL OF THESE GREENBACKS IN MY MITT!
A SHORT TIME LATER...
NAMOR SAID WE WERE TO REPORT FOR WORK MONDAY, WHICH GIVES US TIME TO MAKE OURSELVES LOOK A BIT MORE PRESENTABLE!
FIRST THING I'M DOIN' WITH MY DOUGH IS BUYIN' A SNAZZY SPORTS CAR!
AND SO...
THANKS FOR THE LIFT, HANDSOME, BUT WHY WON'T YOU TELL US YOUR NAME?
ARE YOU AN ACTOR? YOU MUST BE, WITH A CAR LIKE THIS!
WAIT'LL WE GET OUT IN THE COUNTRY AND I'LL SHOW YOU WHAT THIS BABY CAN DO!
CAREFUL! THE ROAD IS UNPAVED UP AHEAD!
DON'T LET THAT WORRY YOU! I'LL PAVE IT FOR YOU IN A FLASH! NOTHING LIKE A FIREBALL TO FUSE THE GROUND AND MAKE IT SMOOTH!
8

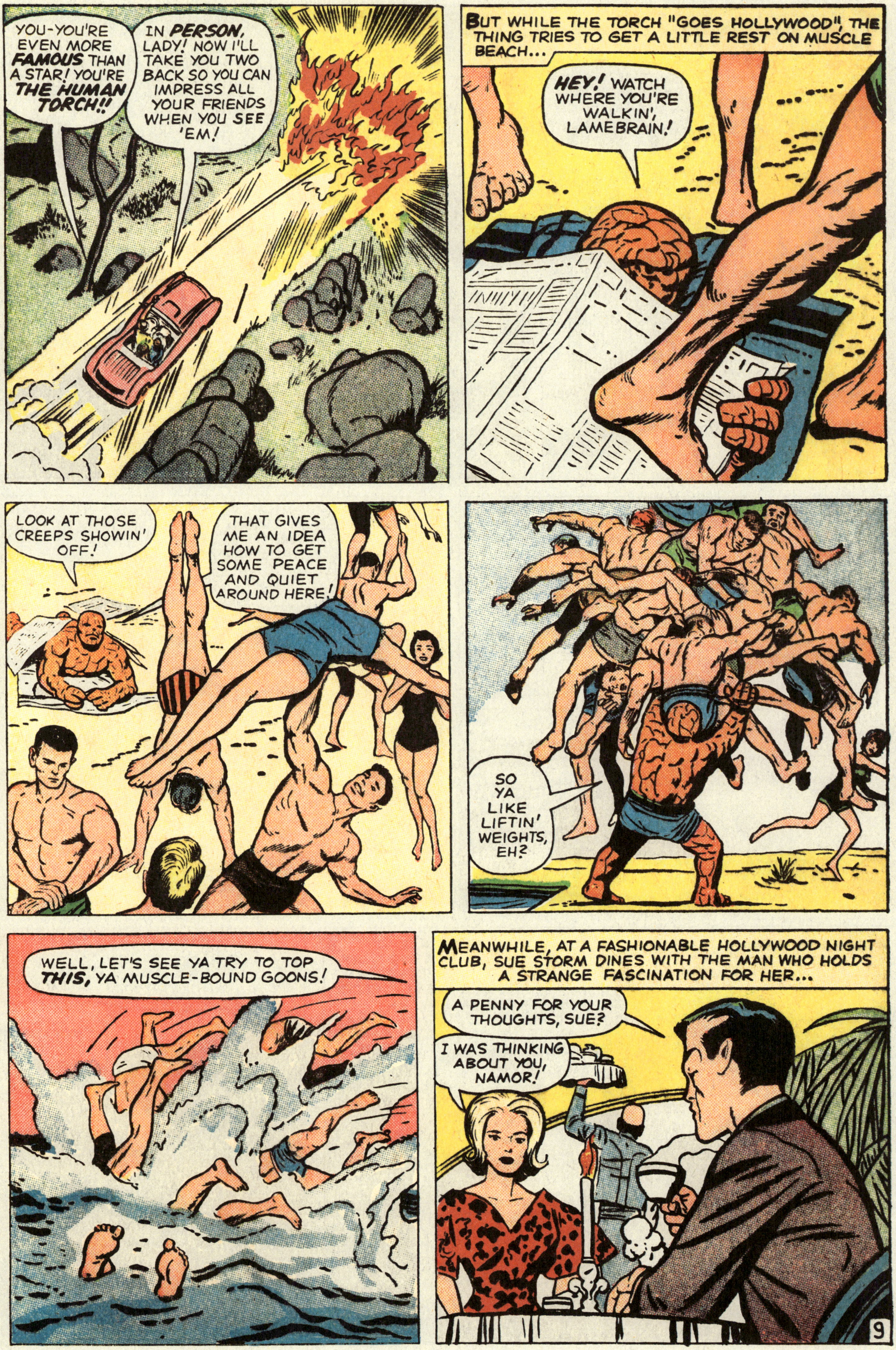
YOU-YOU'RE EVEN MORE FAMOUS THAN A STAR! YOU'RE THE HUMAN TORCH!!
IN PERSON, LADY! NOW I'LL TAKE YOU TWO BACK SO YOU CAN IMPRESS ALL YOUR FRIENDS WHEN YOU SEE 'EM!
BUT WHILE THE TORCH "GOES HOLLYWOOD", THE THING TRIES TO GET A LITTLE REST ON MUSCLE BEACH...
HEY! WATCH WHERE YOU'RE WALKIN', LAMEBRAIN!
LOOK AT THOSE CREEPS SHOWIN' OFF!
THAT GIVES ME AN IDEA HOW TO GET SOME PEACE AND QUIET AROUND HERE!
SO YA LIKE LIFTIN' WEIGHTS, EH?
WELL, LET'S SEE YA TRY TO TOP THIS, YA MUSCLE-BOUND GOONS!
MEANWHILE, AT A FASHIONABLE HOLLYWOOD NIGHT CLUB, SUE STORM DINES WITH THE MAN WHO HOLDS A STRANGE FASCINATION FOR HER...
A PENNY FOR YOUR THOUGHTS, SUE?
I WAS THINKING ABOUT YOU, NAMOR!
9

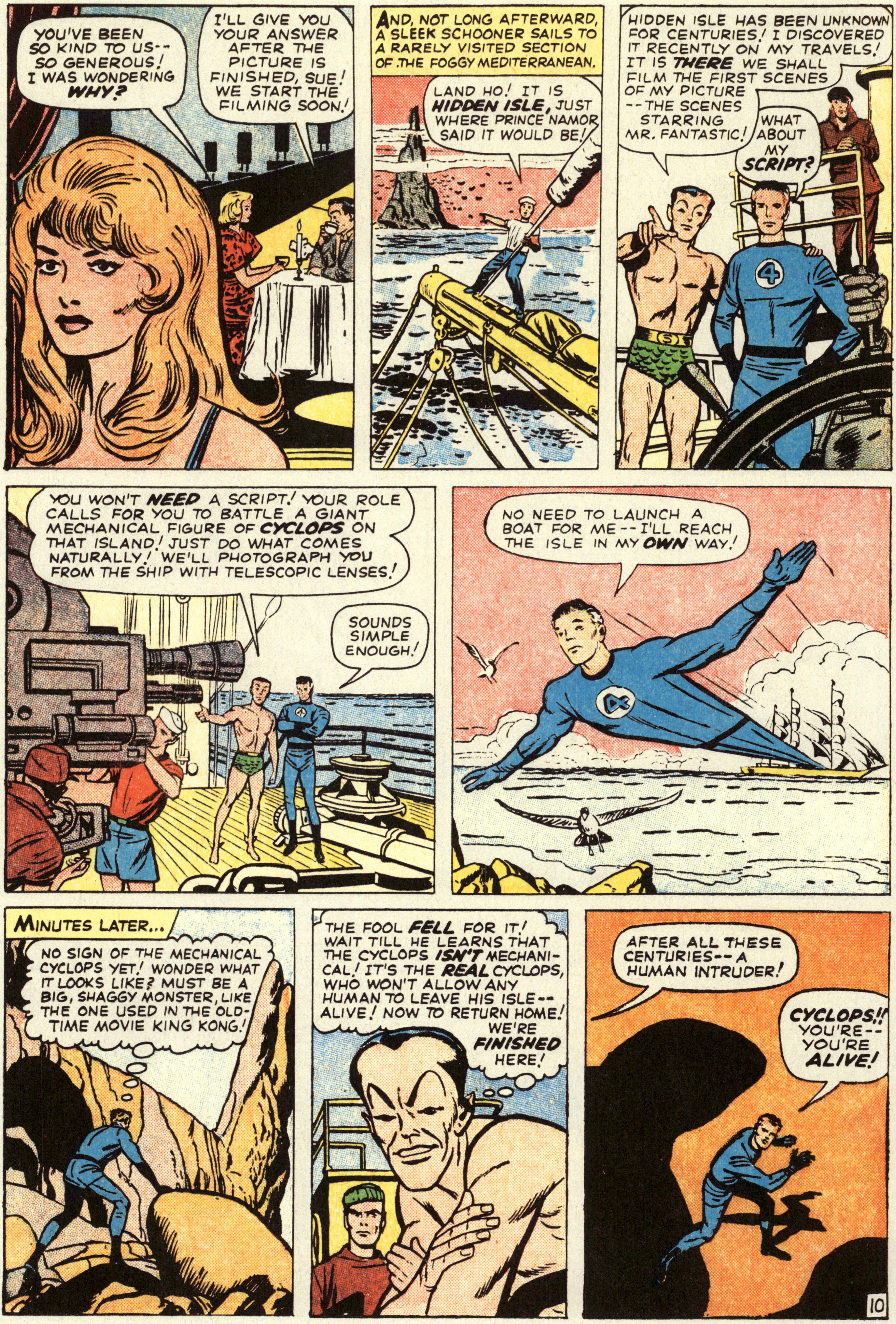

YOU'VE BEEN SO KIND TO US-- SO GENEROUS! I WAS WONDERING WHY?
I'LL GIVE YOU YOUR ANSWER AFTER THE PICTURE IS FINISHED, SUE! WE START THE FILMING SOON!
AND, NOT LONG AFTERWARD, A SLEEK SCHOONER SAILS TO A RARELY VISITED SECTION OF THE FOGGY MEDITERRANEAN.
LAND HO! IT IS HIDDEN ISLE, JUST WHERE PRINCE NAMOR SAID IT WOULD BE!
HIDDEN ISLE HAS BEEN UNKNOWN FOR CENTURIES! I DISCOVERED IT RECENTLY ON MY TRAVELS! IT IS THERE WE SHALL FILM THE FIRST SCENES OF MY PICTURE --THE SCENES STARRING MR. FANTASTIC!
WHAT ABOUT MY SCRIPT?
YOU WON'T NEED A SCRIPT! YOUR ROLE CALLS FOR YOU TO BATTLE A GIANT MECHANICAL FIGURE OF CYCLOPS ON THAT ISLAND! JUST DO WHAT COMES NATURALLY! WE'LL PHOTOGRAPH YOU FROM THE SHIP WITH TELESCOPIC LENSES!
SOUNDS SIMPLE ENOUGH!
NO NEED TO LAUNCH A BOAT FOR ME--I'LL REACH THE ISLE IN MY OWN WAY!
MINUTES LATER...
NO SIGN OF THE MECHANICAL CYCLOPS YET! WONDER WHAT IT LOOKS LIKE? MUST BE A BIG, SHAGGY MONSTER, LIKE THE ONE USED IN THE OLD-TIME MOVIE KING KONG!
THE FOOL FELL FOR IT! WAIT TILL HE LEARNS THAT THE CYCLOPS ISN'T MECHANICAL! IT'S THE REAL CYCLOPS, WHO WON'T ALLOW ANY HUMAN TO LEAVE HIS ISLE--ALIVE! NOW TO RETURN HOME! WE'RE FINISHED HERE!
AFTER ALL THESE CENTURIES-- A HUMAN INTRUDER!
CYCLOPS!! YOU'RE-- YOU'RE ALIVE!
10

PART 3
"THE FURY OF Mr. FANTASTIC"
OF COURSE I LIVE! I AM IMMORTAL! BUT YOU, LOWLY HUMAN, ARE NOT!
SUB-MARINER TRICKED ME! I'VE BLUNDERED INTO A TRAP!
NAMOR ORDERED ME TO KEEP YOU PRISONER ON THIS ISLE! BUT I HAVE NO USE FOR PRISONERS!
NO TIME TO DODGE!
CRASH!
11

SECONDS LATER, AFTER THE DUST HAS CLEARED...
ONE THING NAMOR FORGOT TO TELL YOU-- THE REASON THEY CALL ME MR. FANTASTIC!
RUN, PUNY HUMAN! RUN TILL YOU DROP! THERE IS NO ESCAPE FROM HIDDEN ISLE! SOONER OR LATER I SHALL CRUSH YOU!
WELL, DON'T JUST STAND THERE! IF YOU'RE GONNA THROW THAT THING, THEN THROW IT!
THOSE WILL BE THE LAST WORDS YOU'LL EVER UTTER!
I HOPED YOU'D DO THAT! AND NOW...
IT'S MY TURN!
THE FANTASTIC BODY OF REED RICHARDS ABSORBS THE BOLDER'S IMPACT, AND THEN HURLS IT BACK TOWARDS THE ASTONISHED GIANT!
YOU ARE MORE THAN HUMAN! BUT STILL NO MATCH FOR CYCLOPS!
MY STRENGTH IS TOO GREAT! NOTHING YOU CAN DO WILL STOP ME!
THE DINOSAURS WERE STRONG, TOO--BUT LOOK WHAT HAPPENED TO THEM!
12

CONTINUED AFTER NEXT PAGE...

PART 4
"the FLAME of BATTLE"
FLAME ON!
I-I DON'T UNDERSTAND! THEY--THEY DON'T SEEM THE LEAST BIT AWED!
YOU WASTE YOUR TIME! FLAME MEANS NOTHING TO US! SEIZE HIM!
V-995
I'D BETTER TAKE TO THE AIR WHILE I THINK THIS OUT! I'VE HEARD OF A STRANGE TRIBE WHICH IS IMMUNE TO FIRE! THEY MUST BE THAT TRIBE!
WHY DIDN'T SUB-MARINER WARN ME? AND--WHERE IS HIS PLANE? WHY ISN'T HE FILMING THIS?
FOLLOW HIM FROM THE GROUND! PRINCE NAMOR SAID THAT HIS FLAME DIES DOWN SOONER OR LATER--THEN HE WILL BE OUR PRISONER!
14

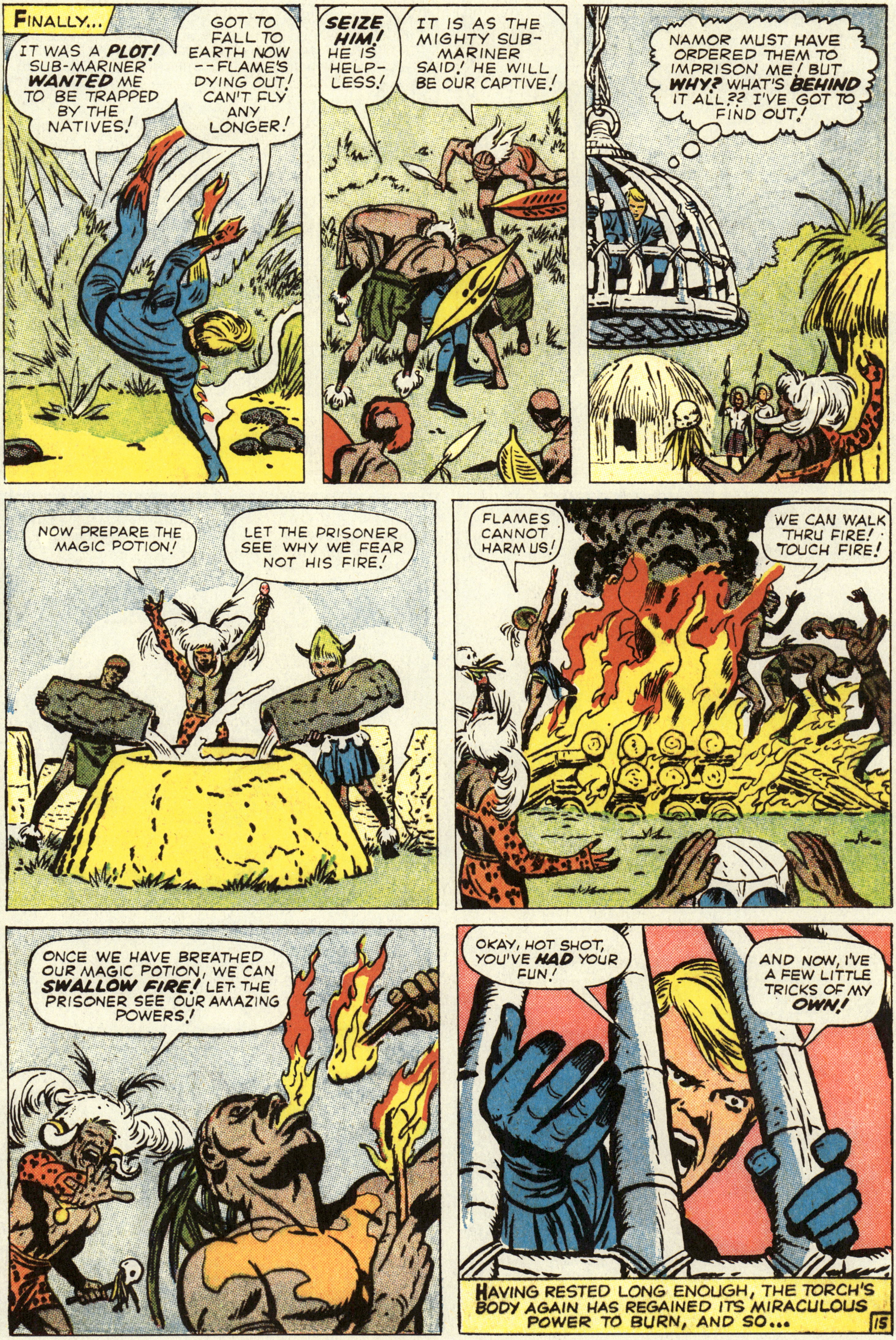

FINALLY...
IT WAS A PLOT! SUB-MARINER WANTED ME TO BE TRAPPED BY THE NATIVES!
GOT TO FALL TO EARTH NOW --FLAME'S DYING OUT! CAN'T FLY ANY LONGER!
SEIZE HIM! HE IS HELP-LESS!
IT IS AS THE MIGHTY SUB-MARINER SAID! HE WILL BE OUR CAPTIVE!
NAMOR MUST HAVE ORDERED THEM TO IMPRISON ME! BUT WHY? WHAT'S BEHIND IT ALL?? I'VE GOT TO FIND OUT!
NOW PREPARE THE MAGIC POTION!
LET THE PRISONER SEE WHY WE FEAR NOT HIS FIRE!
FLAMES CANNOT HARM US!
WE CAN WALK THRU FIRE! TOUCH FIRE!
ONCE WE HAVE BREATHED OUR MAGIC POTION, WE CAN SWALLOW FIRE! LET THE PRISONER SEE OUR AMAZING POWERS!
OKAY, HOT SHOT, YOU'VE HAD YOUR FUN!
AND NOW, I'VE A FEW LITTLE TRICKS OF MY OWN!
HAVING RESTED LONG ENOUGH, THE TORCH'S BODY AGAIN HAS REGAINED ITS MIRACULOUS POWER TO BURN, AND SO...
15

IT'LL TAKE MORE THAN A BAMBOO CAGE TO HOLD ME WHEN I USE MY NITRO-FLAME!
FLAME ON!
AND EVEN IF YOUR SPEARS ARE TIPPED IN A POTION WHICH WILL HARM MY FLAMING BODY, FIRST YOU HAVETA FIGURE OUT WHICH OF THESE FLAMING IMAGES I CAN CREATE IS THE REAL ME!
AND BY THE TIME YOU SPOT ME, I'LL BE WELL OUT OF RANGE OF THOSE PEA-PICKERS OF YOURS!
YOU WILL NOT ESCAPE! WHEN YOUR FLAME DIES, WE WILL AGAIN SEIZE YOU-- BUT NEXT TIME WE SLAY YOU ON SIGHT!
THAT'S WHERE HE'S WRONG! THERE AIN'T GONNA BE A NEXT TIME!
NOT IF THAT VOLCANO I SEE YONDER HAS A SPARK OF LIFE STILL LEFT IN IT!
I'M IN LUCK! IT'S BEEN SMOLDERING FOR YEARS! ALL IT'LL TAKE NOW IS ONE WELL-AIMED FIRE-BALL, LIKE THIS!
16

SUDDENLY, AS THE FIREBALL REACHES ITS GLOWING CENTER, THE SLUMBERING VOLCANO ERUPTS WITH A MIND-STAGGERING EXPLOSION!
THOSE FIRE-EATERS MAY NOT FEAR FLAME, BUT THERE IS ONE THING EVEN THEY CANNOT STAND UP TO...
...AND THAT IS-- A SEA OF MOLTEN LAVA!
THE NATIVES ESCAPED ...BUT THE LAVA DESTROYED THEIR MAGIC POTIONS! THEY WON'T DARE BATTLE ME NOW--THEY'VE LOST THEIR IMMUNITY TO FLAME!
BUT NOW I'VE GOT TO HEAD FOR THE STATES, AND A SHOWDOWN WITH THAT SCHEMING, DOUBLE-DEALING SUB-MARINER!
MEANWHILE, LET US JOIN PRINCE NAMOR ONCE MORE...
WHILE MY CAMERA CREWS FILM MR. FANTASTIC AND THE TORCH ON LOCATION, THING, WE'LL SHOOT OUR BIG FIGHT SCENE RIGHT HERE ON THE HOLLYWOOD BEACH!
OUR BIG FIGHT SCENE?? ARE YOU KIDDIN', FISH-MAN? WHAT MAKES YOU THINK YOU COULD GIVE ME A BATTLE?
I'M GLAD YOU ASKED ME!
SUDDENLY, WITH UNBELIEVABLE SPEED AND STRENGTH, NAMOR STRIKES!
HERE'S THE FIRST PART OF YOUR ANSWER, YOU WALKING GARGOYLE!

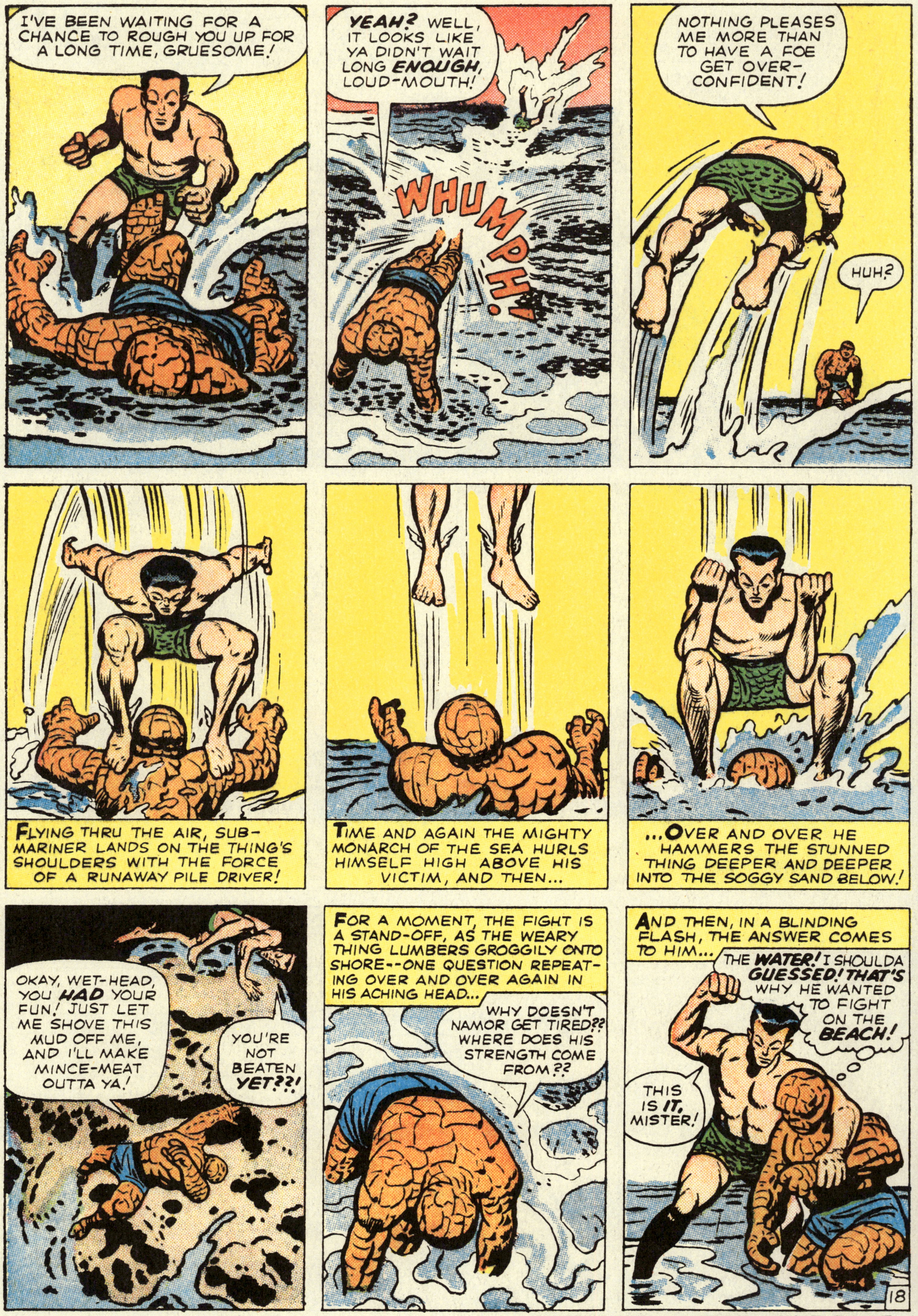

CONTINUED AFTER NEXT PAGE..

Address YOUR letters to:
THE EDITOR
FANTASTIC FOUR
THIRD FLOOR
655 MADISON AVE.
NEW YORK 21, N. Y.

FANTASTIC FAN PAGE 4

DEAR EDITOR:
I would like to know how the Human Torch can see thru the flames in his eyes?
Dennis Smith
Weskan, Kansas

The same way you can see underwater when you're swimming if you open your eyes in the water. The Torch's eyes are as accustomed to seeing thru flame as yours could become to seeing thru water.

DEAR EDITOR:
The best feature of the FF is the handling of the characters which gives each one his own personality. The inside conflict between members of the FF plays an important part in keeping up the quality. Until the appearance of Sub-Mariner, you had too many monsters, but the stories have improved greatly. The Sept. issue was the best ever published. With proper understanding, Namor could be set right and made into a top rate super hero. Any chance of the FF becoming the Fantastic Five, or Six by adding Spider-Man or Thor to the roll call? If you had all six, plus Namor, you'd have a wonderful and unique combination of unusual powers and conflicts and human interest. You'd also have a heck of a time finding worthy foes for such a team. Congrats to Lee and Kirby and everyone else responsible for the FF.
Buddy Saunders
Arlington, Texas

Thanks, Buddy. We'll see what the other fans think of your suggestions. If anyone wants to change it to the Fantastic Hundred, we quit!

DEAR EDITOR:
— One favor I'd like to ask of your staff and yourself: Why not start a FF fan club? I think it would go over real big because your mag is becoming the most talked about publication in our town!
Leroy Auston
Jacksonville, Texas

Many readers have asked about FF fan clubs — and many have written to say they've already started them in their neighborhoods. Tell you what — why not start your own chapter, send us its membership roll and name of officers, and when we get enough info about the various clubs, we'll devote a page or two to them in a future ish. If the demand seems great enough we will then organize the chapters on a national basis. Okay?

DEAR EDITOR:
Just read the latest tremendous issue of "The World's Greatest Comic Magazine" and I'm writing to tell you that the boast on the cover is proven twice-over on the pages within. Lee and Kirby's other heroes, Ant-Man and Thor are great too. Thanks again for all the wonderful mags you put out.
Mike Tuohey
Detroit, Mich.

It's a funny thing. We get almost as much mail mentioning Thor, The Hulk, Ant-Man, and our other super characters as we do mentioning the FF — I guess you fans follow all the mags and you seem to feel that the FF Mag is sort of the headquarters, or clearing house for the others. Well, we're glad you feel that way and hope the letters will continue to pour in.

DEAR EDITOR:
I have tried to hold back for months but can't do it. My hatred of your mags has caused me to write. Your letters column is stupid with asinine replies to only laudatory letters. Artwork is horrible. Your heroes are lilly-lilly with obvious faking of emotions. When you're dealing with human emotions, you have to be serious about it. The so-called heroes who act like "real people" (if so, I pity the human race) are fighting the greatest menace to mankind in each story. And they're too good to be realistic.
Paul Gambaccini
Westport, Conn.

Well, like Paul says, we only print the flattering letters, huh?

DEAR EDITOR:
Although you guys have the greatest comic, you sure make dandy mistakes. In #7 I saw the biggest mistakes in comic mag history. Right at the end of your story Mr. Fantastic said: "There was no reducing gas." He was *supposed* to say "Enlarging gas!" Naturally, it happened at the most important part of the story! But I'm not letting you off there! What happened when the FF returned to earth? Why weren't the people on earth still mad at them? Mistakes! Mistakes! Actually, I like your mag so much, I've just subscribed for two years!
Richard Berry
Haskell, N. J.

Wow! If we claim to have the world's greatest comic mag, it probably follows that we'll have the world's greatest mistakes too! You're right, Dick, and so are the hundreds of other fans who wrote in to correct us. It was just one of those things we always fear will happen. Stan Lee missed the mistake! Jack Kirby missed it! Dick Ayers, our inker, missed it! The letterer, proof-reader, and various kibitzers around the office all missed it too! I guess it proves our fans are sharper-eyed than anybody. As for the humans not still being angry when the FF returned to earth — that's simple. Once Kurrgo's robot left earth, the effect of the hostility ray wore off and things returned to normal. Does that get us off the hook?

DEAR EDITOR:
The only thing I can say about the FF is—Fantastic! Your only fault is your letters page. You don't have enough space to get really good letters. Should be at least 2 pages. Otherwise, the FF is one of the most perfect comics in history!
Harold Smith
New Orleans 19, La.

Many, many fans have desired more space to be devoted to our fan mail and pan mail. But here's the problem — our mags each have 32 pages, of which 7 pages are devoted to ads. (Don't tell us to drop the ads — we need 'em! They help us pay for the best stories and art we can buy!) That leaves 25 pages. Having one pin-up page and one letters page leaves us only 23 pages on which to print stories which we'd like to devote a hundred pages to. So, you be the judge — we'll take a vote — one page less for the FF stories? Or leave everything as is? As always, you, our readers, really edit this mag!

NOW BEFORE CLOSING, WE JUST WANT TO MENTION, IN ANSWER TO MANY REQUESTS, WE WILL HAVE A SPECIAL PIN-UP PAGE OF SUE STORM, THE GORGEOUS INVISIBLE GIRL, NEXT ISSUE. SEE YOU THEN!

VENGEANCE IS OURS!
PART 5
NO, YOU DON'T, FISH-MAN! BEFORE WE DO ANYTHING ELSE, I'M GONNA DRAG YOU 'WAY UP ON SHORE, AWAY FROM THE WATER!
NO! YOU CAN'T! IF-IF I EVER GET MY ARMS LOOSE, I'LL FINISH YOU FOR GOOD NOW! YOU CAN'T DRAG PRINCE NAMOR OUT OF THE SEA THIS WAY! NO!
DESPITE THE SUPER-HUMAN EFFORTS OF THE STEEL-MUSCLED SUB-MARINER, THE RAMPAGING THING MAKES ONE LAST HERCULEAN EFFORT AS HE EXERTS EVERY LAST OUNCE OF HIS UNBELIEVABLE STRENGTH TO REMOVE NAMOR FROM THE SOURCE OF HIS POWER!
V-995
UNTIL, FINALLY...
STOP SQUIRMING, SONNY! THIS'LL ONLY HURT FOR A MINUTE!
YOU COWARD! YOU WOULDN'T DARE LET ME REMAIN IN THE SURF!
THEN SUDDENLY, AS A HEAVY THUNDER-STORM DARKENS THE HEAVENS, THE THING IS STRUCK, FULL-FORCE, BY A SUPER-CHARGED BOLT OF LIGHTNING!
19

SHAKING THE COBWEBS FROM HIS BRAIN, NAMOR WATCHES AS THE THING REELS DIZZILY, BUT STILL REMAINS STANDING...
BY THE TRIDENT OF DAVY JONES! WHAT DOES IT TAKE TO KNOCK YOU OUT??!!
THE THING HAS ABSORBED A SHOCK WHICH WOULD HAVE BEEN FATAL TO ANY LESSER MAN, BUT IT HAS A STRANGE EFFECT ON NAMOR'S HULKING FOE...
THERE, IN THE GATHERING DARKNESS, THE MYSTERIOUS POWER OF THE ELECTRICAL CHARGE CAUSES THE THING TO CHANGE ONCE AGAIN...
AND, WITHIN SECONDS, THE THING GIVES WAY TO HUSKY, HANDSOME, UNCOMPREHENDING BEN GRIMM!
BUT, IN THE DARKNESS, STILL WEAKENED FROM THE POUNDING HE SUFFERED AT THE HANDS OF THE THING, SUB-MARINER IS UNAWARE OF THE CHANGE, AS HE THROWS ONE LAST, PILE-DRIVING BLOW AT THE SHADOWY FIGURE WHO STANDS BEFORE HIM!
IF THIS DOESN'T STOP HIM, I'M LICKED! CAN'T FIGHT--ANY MORE--
UGH!
I DID IT! I DEFEATED THE THING! I'VE BEATEN THEM ALL! I'VE WON--WON!
SLOWLY, NAMOR STUMBLES AWAY, WAITING FOR THE ALMOST LIMITLESS STRENGTH TO RETURN TO HIS MORE-THAN-HUMAN BODY--NOT SUSPECTING THAT HIS VICTORY IS NOT QUITE AS COMPLETE AS HE WOULD HAVE WISHED IT TO BE!
AND THEN, MINUTES LATER, AT THE OFFICES OF S. N. PRODUCTIONS...
NAMOR! YOU'RE BACK! BUT WHERE ARE THE OTHERS?
WHAT DOES IT MATTER?! FORGET ABOUT THEM! YOU ARE LOOKING AT THE MAN WHO TRIUMPHED OVER THEM ALL!
20

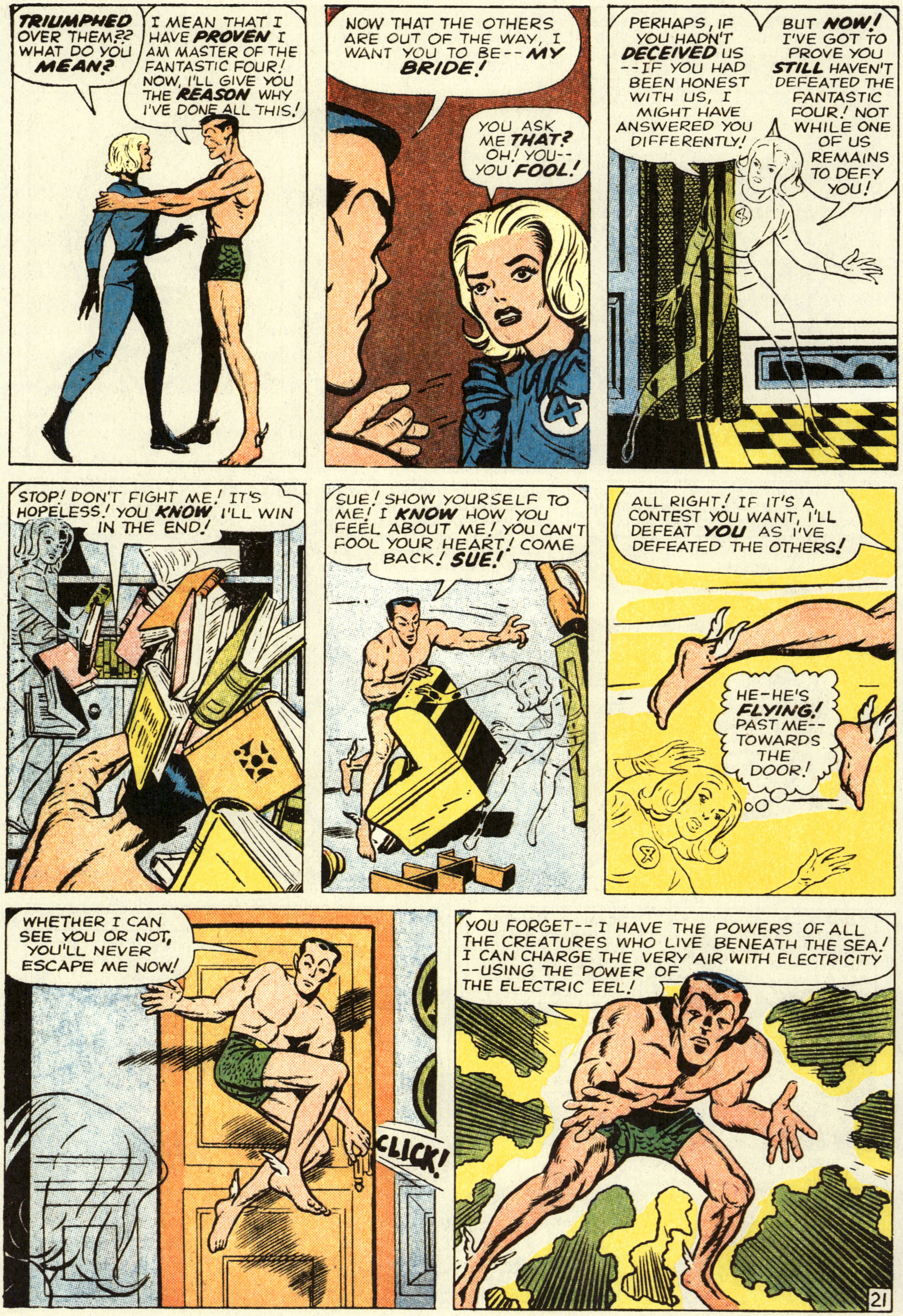

TRIUMPHED OVER THEM?? WHAT DO YOU MEAN?
I MEAN THAT I HAVE PROVEN I AM MASTER OF THE FANTASTIC FOUR! NOW, I'LL GIVE YOU THE REASON WHY I'VE DONE ALL THIS!
NOW THAT THE OTHERS ARE OUT OF THE WAY, I WANT YOU TO BE--MY BRIDE!
YOU ASK ME THAT? OH! YOU-- YOU FOOL!
PERHAPS, IF YOU HADN'T DECEIVED US --IF YOU HAD BEEN HONEST WITH US, I MIGHT HAVE ANSWERED YOU DIFFERENTLY!
BUT NOW! I'VE GOT TO PROVE YOU STILL HAVEN'T DEFEATED THE FANTASTIC FOUR! NOT WHILE ONE OF US REMAINS TO DEFY YOU!
STOP! DON'T FIGHT ME! IT'S HOPELESS! YOU KNOW I'LL WIN IN THE END!
SUE! SHOW YOURSELF TO ME! I KNOW HOW YOU FEEL ABOUT ME! YOU CAN'T FOOL YOUR HEART! COME BACK! SUE!
ALL RIGHT! IF IT'S A CONTEST YOU WANT, I'LL DEFEAT YOU AS I'VE DEFEATED THE OTHERS!
HE-HE'S FLYING! PAST ME-- TOWARDS THE DOOR!
WHETHER I CAN SEE YOU OR NOT, YOU'LL NEVER ESCAPE ME NOW!
CLICK!
YOU FORGET-- I HAVE THE POWERS OF ALL THE CREATURES WHO LIVE BENEATH THE SEA! I CAN CHARGE THE VERY AIR WITH ELECTRICITY --USING THE POWER OF THE ELECTRIC EEL!
21

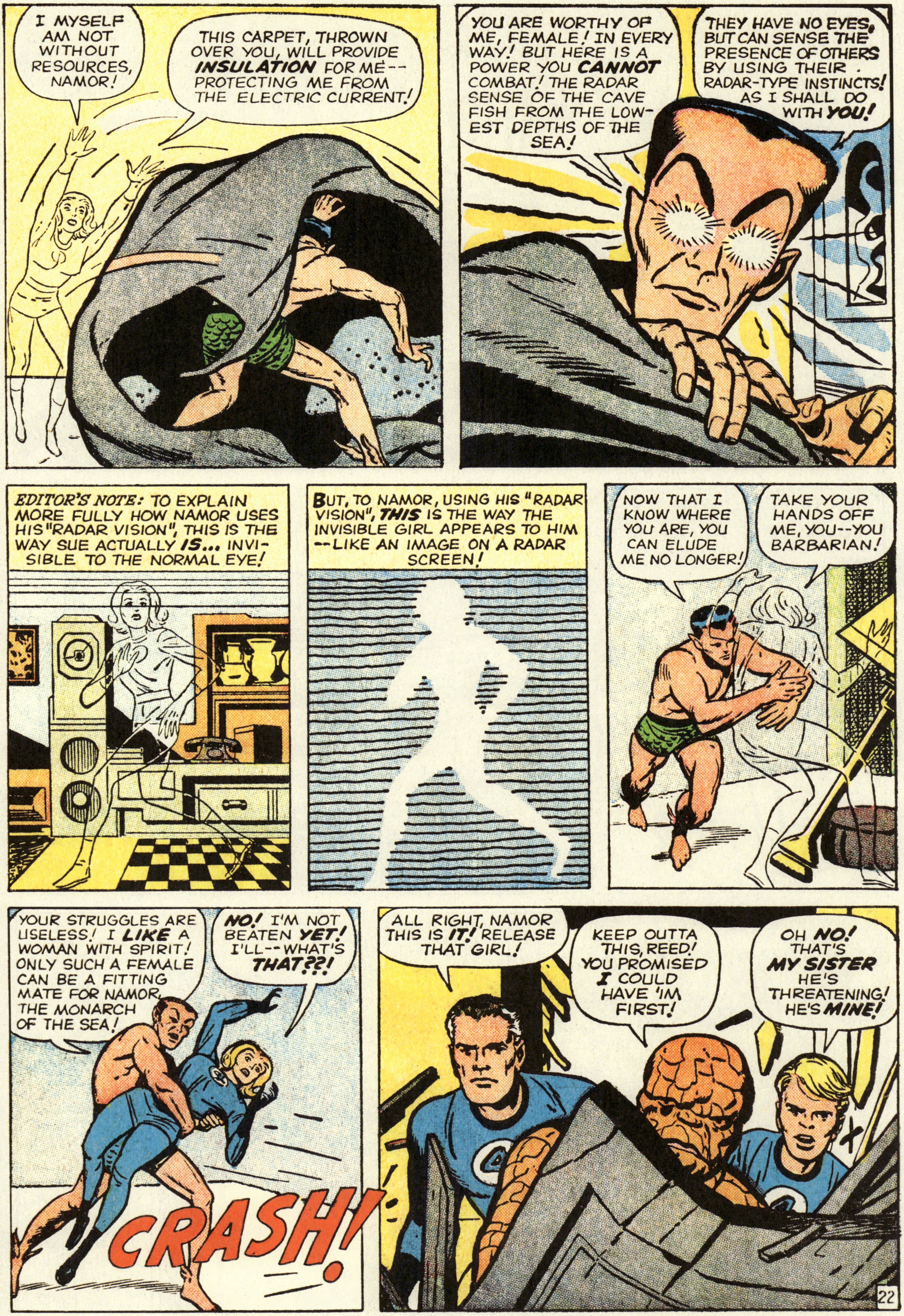
I MYSELF AM NOT WITHOUT RESOURCES, NAMOR!
THIS CARPET, THROWN OVER YOU, WILL PROVIDE **INSULATION** FOR ME-- PROTECTING ME FROM THE ELECTRIC CURRENT!
YOU ARE WORTHY OF ME, FEMALE! IN EVERY WAY! BUT HERE IS A POWER YOU **CANNOT** COMBAT! THE RADAR SENSE OF THE CAVE FISH FROM THE LOWEST DEPTHS OF THE SEA!
THEY HAVE **NO EYES**, BUT CAN SENSE THE PRESENCE OF OTHERS BY USING THEIR RADAR-TYPE INSTINCTS! AS I SHALL DO WITH **YOU!**
EDITOR'S NOTE: TO EXPLAIN MORE FULLY HOW NAMOR USES HIS "RADAR VISION", THIS IS THE WAY SUE ACTUALLY **IS...** INVISIBLE TO THE NORMAL EYE!
BUT, TO NAMOR, USING HIS "RADAR VISION", **THIS** IS THE WAY THE INVISIBLE GIRL APPEARS TO HIM --LIKE AN IMAGE ON A RADAR SCREEN!
NOW THAT I KNOW WHERE YOU ARE, YOU CAN ELUDE ME NO LONGER!
TAKE YOUR HANDS OFF ME, YOU--YOU BARBARIAN!
YOUR STRUGGLES ARE USELESS! I **LIKE** A WOMAN WITH SPIRIT! ONLY SUCH A FEMALE CAN BE A FITTING MATE FOR NAMOR, THE MONARCH OF THE SEA!
NO! I'M NOT BEATEN **YET!** I'LL--WHAT'S **THAT??!**
CRASH!
ALL RIGHT, NAMOR THIS IS **IT!** RELEASE THAT GIRL!
KEEP OUTTA THIS, REED! YOU PROMISED **I** COULD HAVE 'IM FIRST!
OH **NO!** THAT'S **MY SISTER** HE'S THREATENING! HE'S **MINE!**

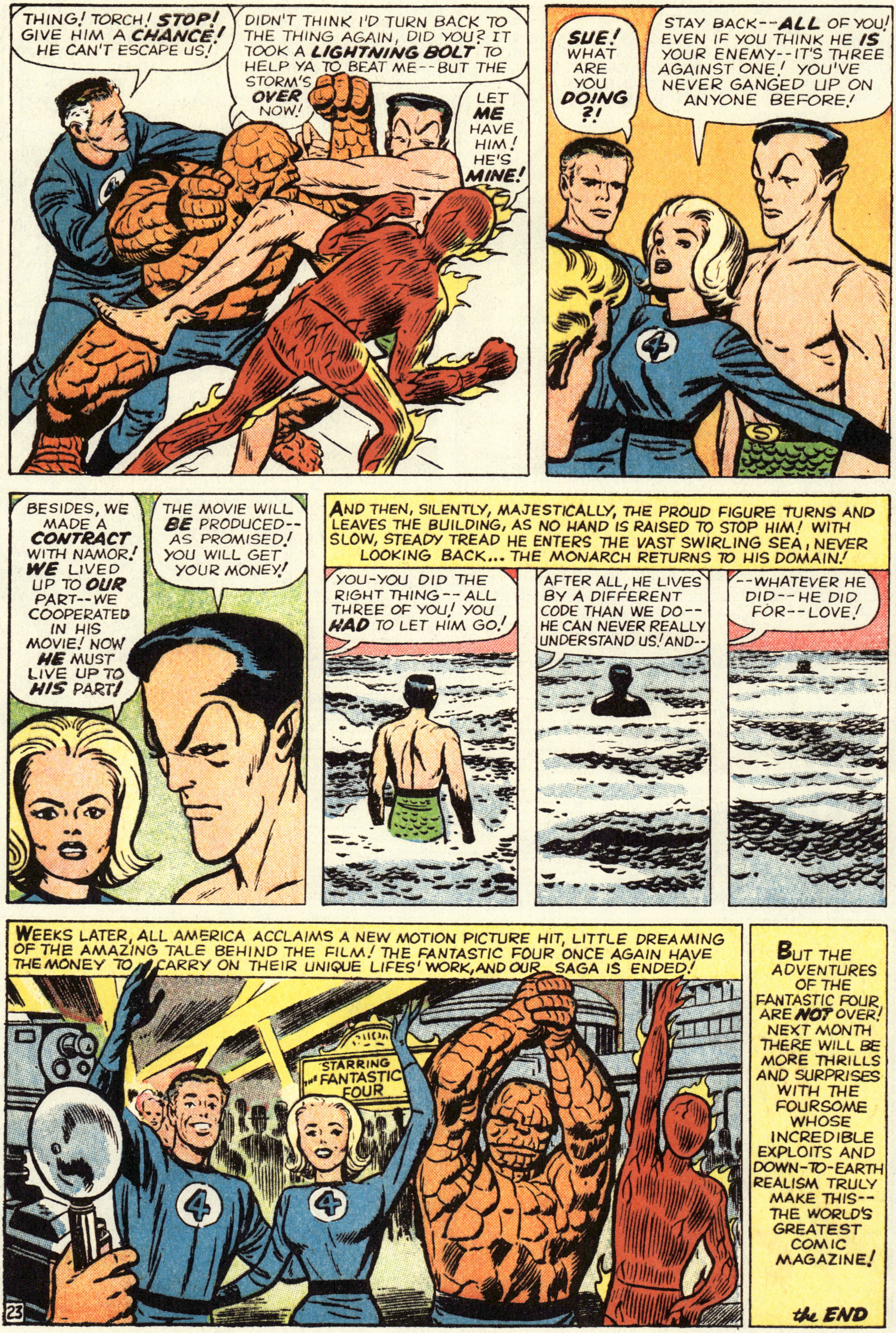
THING! TORCH! STOP! GIVE HIM A CHANCE! HE CAN'T ESCAPE US!
DIDN'T THINK I'D TURN BACK TO THE THING AGAIN, DID YOU? IT TOOK A LIGHTNING BOLT TO HELP YA TO BEAT ME--BUT THE STORM'S OVER NOW!
LET ME HAVE HIM! HE'S MINE!
SUE! WHAT ARE YOU DOING ?!
STAY BACK--ALL OF YOU! EVEN IF YOU THINK HE IS YOUR ENEMY--IT'S THREE AGAINST ONE! YOU'VE NEVER GANGED UP ON ANYONE BEFORE!
BESIDES, WE MADE A CONTRACT WITH NAMOR! WE LIVED UP TO OUR PART--WE COOPERATED IN HIS MOVIE! NOW HE MUST LIVE UP TO HIS PART!
THE MOVIE WILL BE PRODUCED--AS PROMISED! YOU WILL GET YOUR MONEY!
AND THEN, SILENTLY, MAJESTICALLY, THE PROUD FIGURE TURNS AND LEAVES THE BUILDING, AS NO HAND IS RAISED TO STOP HIM! WITH SLOW, STEADY TREAD HE ENTERS THE VAST SWIRLING SEA, NEVER LOOKING BACK... THE MONARCH RETURNS TO HIS DOMAIN!
YOU-YOU DID THE RIGHT THING--ALL THREE OF YOU! YOU HAD TO LET HIM GO!
AFTER ALL, HE LIVES BY A DIFFERENT CODE THAN WE DO--HE CAN NEVER REALLY UNDERSTAND US! AND--
--WHATEVER HE DID--HE DID FOR--LOVE!
WEEKS LATER, ALL AMERICA ACCLAIMS A NEW MOTION PICTURE HIT, LITTLE DREAMING OF THE AMAZING TALE BEHIND THE FILM! THE FANTASTIC FOUR ONCE AGAIN HAVE THE MONEY TO CARRY ON THEIR UNIQUE LIFES' WORK, AND OUR SAGA IS ENDED!
STARRING THE FANTASTIC FOUR
BUT THE ADVENTURES OF THE FANTASTIC FOUR ARE NOT OVER! NEXT MONTH THERE WILL BE MORE THRILLS AND SURPRISES WITH THE FOURSOME WHOSE INCREDIBLE EXPLOITS AND DOWN-TO-EARTH REALISM TRULY MAKE THIS--THE WORLD'S GREATEST COMIC MAGAZINE!
23
the END

HOW THE HUMAN TORCH FLIES!
A FANTASTIC FOUR FEATURE PAGE!
LAST ISSUE, I PROMISED TO EXPLAIN MY METHOD OF FLYING! AND SO...
...BASICALLY, MY POWER OF FLIGHT COMES FROM MY INTENSE FLAME WHICH AFFECTS THE MOLECULES OF MY BODY SO THAT THEY BECOME LIGHTER THAN AIR, CAUSING ME TO BE ABLE TO RISE AND SOAR!
MY BIGGEST ENEMY IS WATER! SO I CAREFULLY STUDY WEATHER MAPS TO LEARN WHERE RAIN IS APT TO FALL! THEN I AVOID THOSE AREAS WHENEVER POSSIBLE!
AT LEAST ONCE A WEEK, I TEST MY MANEUVERABILITY BY FLYING THRU A PRACTICE COURSE WHICH REED DESIGNED FOR ME!
I CONSTANTLY TRAIN MYSELF TO BE OBSERVANT, SO THAT I CAN BE OF USE TO THE FANTASTIC FOUR BY SPOTTING PEOPLE AND PLACES FROM MY VANTAGE POINT OVERHEAD!
MY MAXIMUM SPEED IS CAPABLE OF CREATING A SONIC BOOM... SO I MUST BE CAREFUL NOT TO ATTAIN THAT SPEED WHEN FLYING OVER DENSELY POPULATED AREAS!
CRACK!
MY WEAKNESS IS THE FACT THAT MY FLAME BURNS FOR ONLY A LIMITED PERIOD OF TIME! THE BRIGHTER IT BURNS, AND THE FASTER I FLY, THE SOONER IT IS EXTINGUISHED! SO, I DARE NOT BLAZE TOO BRIGHTLY, OR FLY TOO FAST UNTIL I HAVE MADE SURE I WON'T NEED MY FLAME FOR TOO LONG A TIME!
Stan Lee + J. KIRBY

THROW YOUR VOICE
Throw your voice into trunks, behind doors, everywhere. Instrument fits in your mouth and out of sight. Fool teacher, friends and family. Free book on "How to Become a Ventriloquist."
No. 2137.....25¢
Ventro & Book
SILENT DOG WHISTLE
This whistle can't be heard by human ears, but Rover can hear it half a mile away. Your dog will understand that this whistle is for him alone. Be amazed how quickly he responds.
No. 3701 . . . . . . $1.00
MUSICAL JUKE BOX BANK
Drop in a coin and the turntable revolves to a lilting melody ... just like the modern juke box that youngsters adore. Makes saving a pleasure—money mounts up. Made of sturdy metal. 4½"x4".
No. 2005.... $1.50
DRAW OR PAINT ANYTHING IN ONE MINUTE
Amazing new art reproducer actually reflects any indoor or outdoor scene you wish to draw on any paper. Simply follow the line of your picture image, and presto! A beautiful drawing is yours.
No. 3306 ...... $1.98
SEE BEHIND GLASSES
A specially treated pair of sunglasses with secret mirrors that enable you to see behind you, without anyone knowing your watching. Really comes in handy at times.
3030 75¢
JIU JITSU
YOU, TOO, CAN BE TOUGH
Master Jui Jitsu and you'll win any fight. This book gives all the grips, blocks, etc which are so effective in counterattack. FREE book on how to perform strong man stunts also included.
NO. 224 . ... 1.00
SURPRISE PACKAGE
Are you willing to take a chance? We won't tell you what you get, but because you're willing to gamble, we'll give you more than your money's worth.
Only 50¢
No. 678.... ......
AMAZING MINIATURE RADIO
This tiny, feather weight radio operates without batteries, without tubes, but brings you years of listening pleasure. There's nothing to wear out, nothing to replace.
No. 3644 $4.98
TREASURE CHEST OF FUN
TRANSISTOR RADIO KIT
This amazing radio kit contains all the components to construct a powerful, highly efficient instrument. It operates 1,000 hours on 2 junior pen light batteries and is simple to construct. Full instructions and all parts are included for you to build your own private transistor radio.
No. 2131 .... $5.98
KRAZY KRAX
Apply this to the television screen and it appears that the glass is cracked.
No. 3333...60c
OH DEAR! MORE EXPENSE!
THE PERFECT T-V GAG!
BANK VAULT WITH ALARM
Bank vault has combination type lock that gives an alarm when opened. Protects valuables and possessions. Frighten off would be invaders of your privacy. Excellent for storing money, valuables, prizes.
No. 2113 .... $1.49
BIKE WINDSHIELD
Turn your bike into something really special with this clear, transparent bike windshield. Just like the one on Motorcycles. Handy built-in pouch enables you to keep your sunglasses, tools, and personal effects within easy reach. Really makes your bike different.
No. 4268 ....$1.00
MINIATURE SECRET CAMERA
1.25
EXPLODING HAND GRENADE
This menacing hand grenade looks and works just like a real one. All you do is pull the pin, throw the grenade, and watch the fun as the caps explode. It's harmless.
2109 .... 75¢
INSECT COLLECTING KIT
Complete equipment for making perfect safe, insect specimens. SET includes efficient net for catching insect, "killing jar", forceps, magnifying glass, mounting pins, preserving strips, identification labels, etc. Full instructions are included,
No. 2117 .... 1.00
Sorry, but we cannot ship orders totalling less than $1.00"
Kindly add 15¢ for postage and handling to all orders
BIKE SPEEDOMETER
Now you can see how fast you're riding with this precision engineered speedometer for only 75¢. You can time yourself for racing, sports, distance. Just fasten it to your handlebar and go.
No. 8199 .... 75¢
HONOR HOUSE PROD. CORP., Dept. GK-58 LYNBROOK, N.Y.
Rush me the items listed below. If I am not 100% satisfied, I may return any part of of my purchase after 10 days Free Trial for full refund of purchase price.
ITEM - NAME OF ITEM HOW MANY TOTAL PRICE
☐ I enclose .... in full payment. Same guarantee.
☐ Send C.O.D. I will pay postman on delivery plus postage.
Name..
Address..
CANADIAN FRIENDS: For quick service, send orders directly to:
NEW YORK IMPORTS BOX 121 DOWNSVIEW, TORONTO
AMAZING NEW SPACE PHONE SET — 2 WAY . . SENDS . . . RECEIVES
You can talk back and forth between houses, from room to room, and from secret hiding places, because it's portable - no electric wires - no batteries.
No. 3104 ....69¢
ATOMIC SMOKE BOMB
Just light one and watch the column of thick, white smoke rise to the ceiling, mushrooming into a dense cloud, just like an A-Bomb.
No. 971........................20¢

STAMP COLLECTING OUTFIT
A packet of stamps from all parts of world. A package of stamp hinges; perforation gauge and millimeter scale; watermark detector. Everything ONLY 10c to approval buyers.
LORRAINE W. BROWN, Dept. 10, Marion, Mich.

1c
Thousands of beautiful stamps at only 1c each—why pay more when you can get the best for less. Write today for approvals.
PENNY STAMP SERVICE
Orange California

BETTER U.S. APPROVALS
To introduce our BETTER U.S. APPROVALS we offer 15 of the most wanted U.S. stamps, including a Columbian, Bi-Cents, Army-Navy, Famous American, Airs and other Commems. for only 10c.
OCEAN STAMPS, BOX 64-D, BROOKLYN 29, N.Y.

1/2 OFF
OUR APPROVALS are sold at 50% of Scott Catalogue prices. MAKE US PROVE IT!
CATALINA STAMPS, Dept. C Orange, California

111 DIF. BONANZA 10¢
Includes Complete Red Cross Set, Triangle, Scout, Fr. So. Antartica, Singapore, Hungary Street Scenes, etc. Only 10¢ with Approvals.
FAIRWAY — Box 65-C — Garden Grove, Calif.

25 DIFF. CHINA 10¢
BIG Value ONLY 10c to Approval Buyers.
EXTRA! We give our regular customers a 56,000 Space Album after certain purchases.
WEST COAST STAMPS, Box 2187-X, Santa Ana, Calif.

LOOK — GIANT PHILIPPINE
stamp, plus New Zealand, Cuba and others. Only 5c with U.S. or foreign approvals.
Earl Thompson, 5448 Odell St., St. Louis 9, Mo.

25 LARGE U.S. COMMEMS
Only 10c with approval bargains. Perforation gauge sent FREE.
LINCOLN STAMP CO., St. Catharines 116, Ont.

"OLD GLORY" IN FLAMING COLORS!!! USA Flag giant beauty from Honduras! Enormous UNITED NATIONS Mexican Stamp! Plus Strange Gorilla issue, Duke of Windsor' Morocco, lovely Macao Flowers, Wild Buffalo stamp & others, 10c with approvals. Sunny Stamps Service, Apopka 19, Fla.

Terrific STAMP BARGAIN!
Israel-Iceland-San Marino-plus triangle set-Plus Antigua-Borneo-Virgin-Scouts-Congo-Russia-Plus large stamp book-all 4 offers free. Send 10c for mailing cost.
EMPIRE STAMP CORP., Dept. MC, Toronto, Canada

$5 SPECIAL STAMP OFFER! 10¢
Amazing offer to introduce our better U.S. approvals. Get 2 different $5.00 U.S. stamps PLUS 20 more hi values, air mails, commemoratives, etc. Send only 10¢ for this splendid value. Send your dime TODAY to:
IRWIN STAMP CO. - Box 11 BROOKLYN 30, N. Y.

Holy Stamp Depicting Christ & Cross!! Plus Triangle Discus Thrower, enormous multi-colored Balkans Diamond issue, wonderful MAP COLLECTION from Timor, Macao & Angola. EXTRA! Brilliant Flag set, etc., only 10c with approvals. Capital Stamp Co., Ferrysburg 19C Mich.

103 DIFF. BRITISH EMPIRE 10c
From Britain's farflung Colonies
Genuine Catalog value over $2.00.
100% Satisfaction Guaranteed — approvals.
CROWN STAMP CO., VIRGIL 616, ONT.

FABULOUS AMERICAN SET
Flag Set, National Park Set, and Presidential Set value up to $5. Send 10c for 15 of the above Stamps plus full particulars and Approvals.
MAXIM STAMP CO., Dept. MC
145 Nassau St., New York 38, N. Y.

BE TALLER
New scientific method will add inches to your present height, even after maturity. Results positively guaranteed. Send for FREE literature and information.
Height Increase Institute Dept. MC 1
G.P.O. Box 1902, N. Y. 1, N. Y.

POEMS
WANTED for musical setting and recording. Send poems Free Examination.
AMERICA'S LARGEST SONG STUDIO
FIVE STAR MUSIC MASTERS, 92 BEACON BLDG., BOSTON, MASS.

COIN COLLECTORS!
Foreign Coin — Banknote — Checklist and price list FREE for 5¢ postage to approval service applicants only. Indian Cents 2 diff. for 35¢.
SPRUCELAND C3, 115 State St, Spgfld 3, Mass.

TERRIFIC TRIANGLES!!
Frightful Fish, Sports, Volcanoes TRIANGLES, also African Flowers, weird Angola Map, tri-colored Flag, etc. to approval buyers for 4c postage.
POTOMAC STAMP COMPANY
Dept. 7 Washington 15, D. C.

307 WORLD ALL DIFFERENT 25c
XTRA Special introductory offer
Actual Scott value over $6.00
Approvals. Satisfaction guaranteed.
NIAGARA STAMP CO., St. Catharines 216, Ont.

Fantastic Fish Triangles!! Valuable "Ben Franklin" on CANAL ZONE!! Flaming bi-colored Volcano Triangle!! Lovely Olympics Triangle!! Plus Icy Greenland, Weird Wild Beast issue & others. 10¢ with approvals. Roseland Stamps, Spring Lake 19, Mich.

55 "FDR" & POPE TRIANGLE!!
Lot 55 DIFFERENT has FDR Diamond, "Pope" Triangle, Greenland, Angola Map, Rhodesia etc. Catalogs $1.15—ALL only 5c with Approvals.
LONGHORN STAMP CO., Box 3068, Ellwood Sta. Lubbock, Tex.

POEMS WANTED
For musical setting. Send your Poems today for Free Examination. Any subject. Immediate consideration.
CROWN MUSIC CO., 49-MC W. 32 St., New York 1

225 STAMPS FOR ONLY 10¢
THIS MAMMOTH VALUE INCLUDES STAMPS WORTH UP TO 25c! ALSO APPROVALS. WRITE TODAY!
MYSTIC STAMP CO Camden 3, New York

INSIGNIA 40 for $1.00
ARMY · NAVY · MARINE
Includes 40 Different Shoulder Emblems, Ratings, Chevrons, Q-Bars, Medals, Ribbons, Collar Insignia, etc. ORDER NOW! Send $1.00 for 40 or $5.00 for 250. NO DUPLICATES —ALL DIFFERENT
EMBLEM SALES CO. Dept. 1000
P.O. Box 167, Madison Sq. Sta., N.Y. 10

DRESSES 24c
Shoes 39c • Men's Suits $4.95
Trousers $1.20. Better used clothing.
Write for FREE Catalog
TRANSWORLD, Dept. 143-B
162 Christopher Ave., Brooklyn 12, N. Y.

SEW LEATHER
AND TOUGH MATERIALS EASILY

COMPLETE, EASY-TO-USE, HEAVY DUTY STITCHER KIT IN ONE COMPACT TOOL

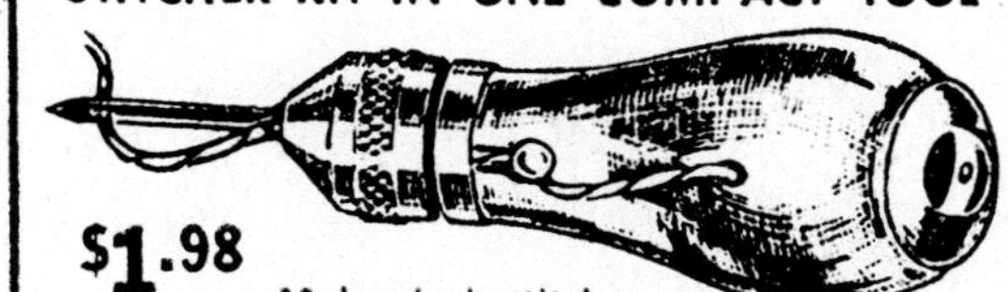

$1.98 Postpaid
Makes lock-stitches like a machine

Save money with HEAVY-DUTY STITCHER. It's easy to sew or repair anything made of Leather, Canvas, Nylon, Plastic, other heavy materials. Quick "push pull" action makes firm, even lock-stitches like a machine. Gets into hard-to-get-at-places. Just the tool needed for repairing Luggage, Footwear, Convertible Tops, Awnings, Seat Covers, Sportsgear, Rugs, Saddlery, etc. Comes complete with 3 different needles (fine, heavy, curved) and bobbin of strong waxed thread (10 yds.) all self-contained in HEAVY-DUTY STITCHER. Easy-to-follow directions included. Extra needles and thread always available. Send $1.98 money order or check and we pay postage. If C.O.D. $1.98 plus postage. Money back guarantee.
SPORTSMAN'S POST, Dept. A-431
366 Madison Avenue, New York 17

SONG IDEAS
WANTED
S/A Songwriters, with publisher contacts, want song ideas. SHARE ROYALTIES. NO FEES. Send poems:
SONGWRITERS' ASSOCIATES
Studio 19, 1650 Broadway, New York 19, N. Y.

FREE 5 x 7 PORTRAIT ENLARGEMENT

30 WALLET PHOTOS $1 plus 25c handling & postage
beautifully printed on PROFESSIONAL paper, size 2½ x 3½. Send any negative, photo or snapshot (returned unharmed) with $1.25 and receive 30 wallet photos (60 for $2.00) plus FREE 5 x 7 enlargement. If not satisfied money refunded
SEAGEE, 2 Allen St., Dept. 2E N.Y. 2, N.Y.

NEW— POCKET SIZE INVENTION HELPS HYPNOTIZE YOURSELF or OTHERS IN MINUTES!

MUST WORK OR MONEY BACK!
Hold the HYPNO-COIN in front of the person you want to hypnotize. Gently vibrate the plastic lense. This sets a whirling hypnotic pattern into motion that is so fascinating, it captures and holds your subject's gaze. Now give your hypnotic suggestions! Get this amazing hypnotic aid complete with a FREE revealing booklet of secrets and instructions that tell you what to say and do, how to command and re-hypnotize with the snap of a finger, how to thrill and amaze them with hypnotic stunts, etc. Get the COIN, Booklet and Stand for Self Hypnosis — only $1.00 ppd. Sent in a plain wrapper. Money back if not delighted!
HYPNOTIC-AIDS • Dept. A84 1133 Broadway, N.Y.C. 10
$1.00 Name..... Address.....

1000 MAGIC TRICKS • 25¢

MAGIC IS FUN!
Amaze, mystify, entertain with 1000 great new magic tricks. Easier than you think! Make money in spare time. Rush name, address and 25¢ for Big 160 Page Catalog of Tricks, Gags, Jokes, Mysteries, Illusions, etc. All illustrated. No skill needed. World's best 25¢ offer.
EVEN HOUDINI WOULD LIKE THIS!
HOUSE OF 1000 MYSTERIES
DEPT. MC10-62 • TRUMBULL, CONN.

IND.
THE WORLD'S GREATEST COMIC MAGAZINE!
APPROVED BY THE COMICS CODE AUTHORITY
12¢
THE Fantastic Four
MC
HOLD YOUR BREATH!! HERE IS... "THE RETURN OF DOCTOR DOOM!"
10 JAN.
HOW'S THIS FOR A TWIST, JACK? WE'VE GOT DOCTOR DOOM AS ONE OF THE FANTASTIC FOUR!!
...AND MISTER FANTASTIC HIMSELF IS THE VILLAIN!! OUR FANS OUGHTTA FLIP OVER THIS YARN!!
IN THIS EPIC ISSUE: SURPRISE FOLLOWS SURPRISE AS YOU ACTUALLY MEET LEE AND KIRBY IN THE STORY!! PLUS: A GORGEOUS PIN-UP OF THE INVISIBLE GIRL!
4

THE FANTASTIC FOUR is published by CANAM PUBLISHERS SALES CORP. OFFICE OF PUBLICATION: 655 MADISON AVENUE, NEW YORK, N.Y. Published monthly. Copyright 1962 by CANAM PUBLISHERS SALES CORP., 655 Madison Avenue, New York, N.Y. Vol. 1 No. 10, JANUARY, 1963 issue. Price 12¢ per copy. Subscription rate $1.75 for 12 issues including postage. Foreign subscription $3.25 in American funds. No similarity between any of the names, characters, persons, and/or institutions appearing in this magazine with those of any living or dead person is intended, and any such similarity which may exist is purely coincidental. Printed in U.S.A. by The Eastern Color Printing Co., Waterbury 20, Conn.

SCRIPT: STAN LEE • PENCILLING: JACK KIRBY INKING: DICK AYERS

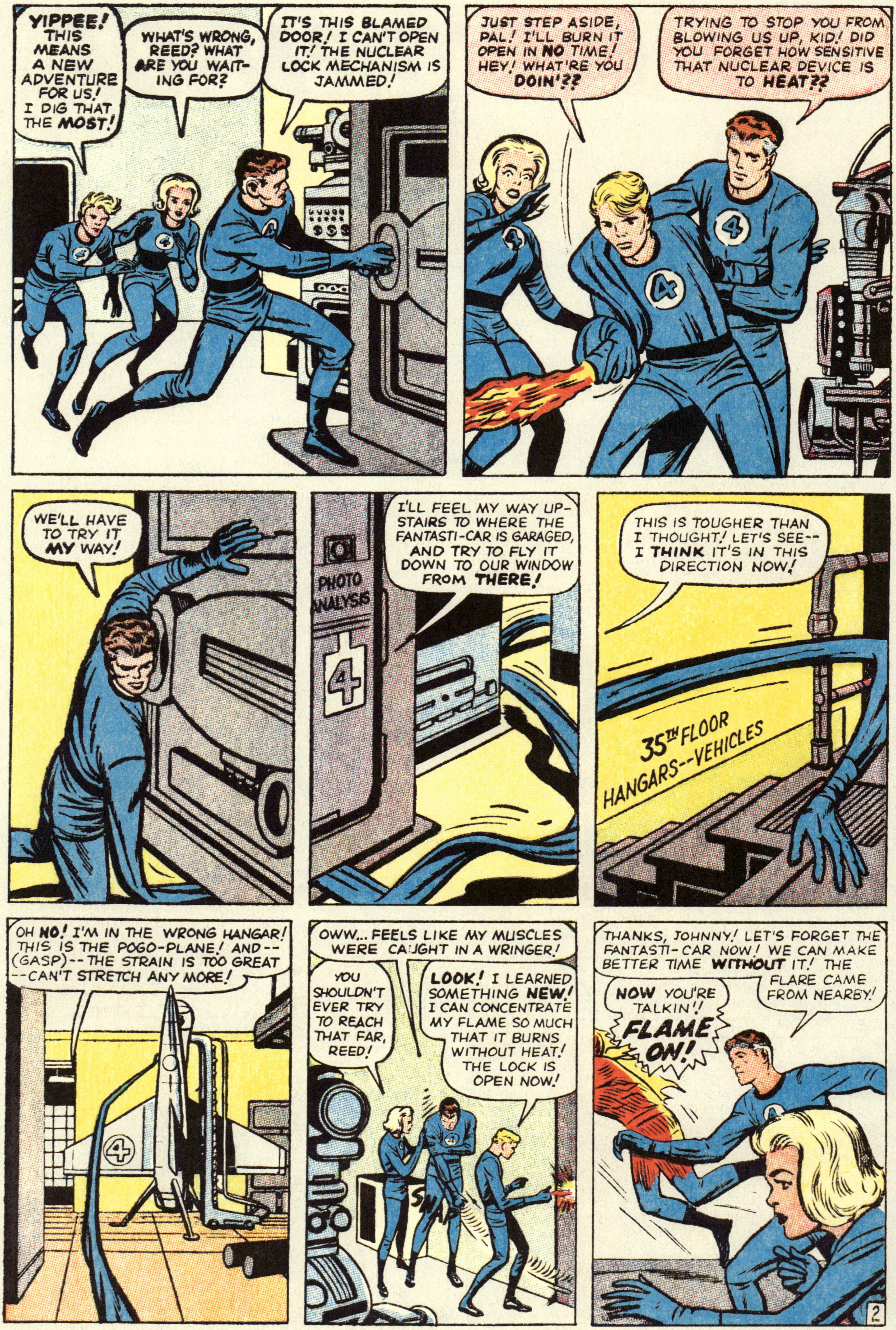

YIPPEE! THIS MEANS A NEW ADVENTURE FOR US! I DIG THAT THE MOST!
WHAT'S WRONG, REED? WHAT ARE YOU WAITING FOR?
IT'S THIS BLAMED DOOR! I CAN'T OPEN IT! THE NUCLEAR LOCK MECHANISM IS JAMMED!
JUST STEP ASIDE, PAL! I'LL BURN IT OPEN IN NO TIME! HEY! WHAT'RE YOU DOIN'??
TRYING TO STOP YOU FROM BLOWING US UP, KID! DID YOU FORGET HOW SENSITIVE THAT NUCLEAR DEVICE IS TO HEAT??
WE'LL HAVE TO TRY IT MY WAY!
PHOTO ANALYSIS
4
I'LL FEEL MY WAY UPSTAIRS TO WHERE THE FANTASTI-CAR IS GARAGED, AND TRY TO FLY IT DOWN TO OUR WINDOW FROM THERE!
THIS IS TOUGHER THAN I THOUGHT! LET'S SEE-- I THINK IT'S IN THIS DIRECTION NOW!
35TH FLOOR HANGARS--VEHICLES
OH NO! I'M IN THE WRONG HANGAR! THIS IS THE POGO-PLANE! AND-- (GASP)-- THE STRAIN IS TOO GREAT --CAN'T STRETCH ANY MORE!
OWW... FEELS LIKE MY MUSCLES WERE CAUGHT IN A WRINGER!
YOU SHOULDN'T EVER TRY TO REACH THAT FAR, REED!
LOOK! I LEARNED SOMETHING NEW! I CAN CONCENTRATE MY FLAME SO MUCH THAT IT BURNS WITHOUT HEAT! THE LOCK IS OPEN NOW!
SNAP
THANKS, JOHNNY! LET'S FORGET THE FANTASTI-CAR NOW! WE CAN MAKE BETTER TIME WITHOUT IT! THE FLARE CAME FROM NEARBY!
NOW YOU'RE TALKIN'! FLAME ON!
2

THE FLARE CAME FROM AROUND THE CORNER! THE THING MUST BE VISITING HIS GIRL FRIEND, ALICIA! GANGWAY, FOLKS--I'M IN A HURRY!
LOOK OUT! IT'S THE HUMAN TORCH!
THAT YOUNG SHOW-OFF SHOULD BE TAUGHT A LESSON BEFORE HE HURTS SOMEBODY!
HEY! THERE'S MR. FANTASTIC! LET'S GET HIS AUTOGRAPH!
I WANT A PIECE OF HIS UNIFORM, FOR A MEMENTO!
ISN'T HE HANDSOME! COME HERE, YOU ADORABLE THING!
WHEW! THANK HEAVENS FOR MY STRETCHING POWERS!
WELL, WELL! IF IT AIN'T THE FAMOUS INVISIBLE GIRL! SO THIS IS WHAT YA LOOK LIKE! MMM-- YOU SHOULDN'T EVER TURN INVISIBLE, DOLL!
HOW'S ABOUT A SMILE FOR ONE OF YOUR FANS??
JUST WAIT'LL I TELL 'EM DOWN AT THE POOL ROOM THAT I MET THE INVIS-- HEY! WHAT THE--??!
GET LOST, REPULSIVE!
AND NOW TO GET TO ALICIA'S APARTMENT! THAT MUST BE WHERE THE THING--
WHAT'S WRONG WITH THAT DRIVER?? IS HE TRYING TO HIT ME??
OH! I FORGOT! I'M INVISIBLE! HE DOESN'T SEE ME!
I'VE GOT TO TURN VISIBLE --NOW!
HOLY SMOKE! WHERE'D THAT GAL COME FROM??
WHEW! HE JUST MISSED ME!
SCREEEEEEEEEEE!
HONEST, OFFICER--IT WASN'T MY FAULT!
I KNOW-- I KNOW! I SAW HER, TOO!
3

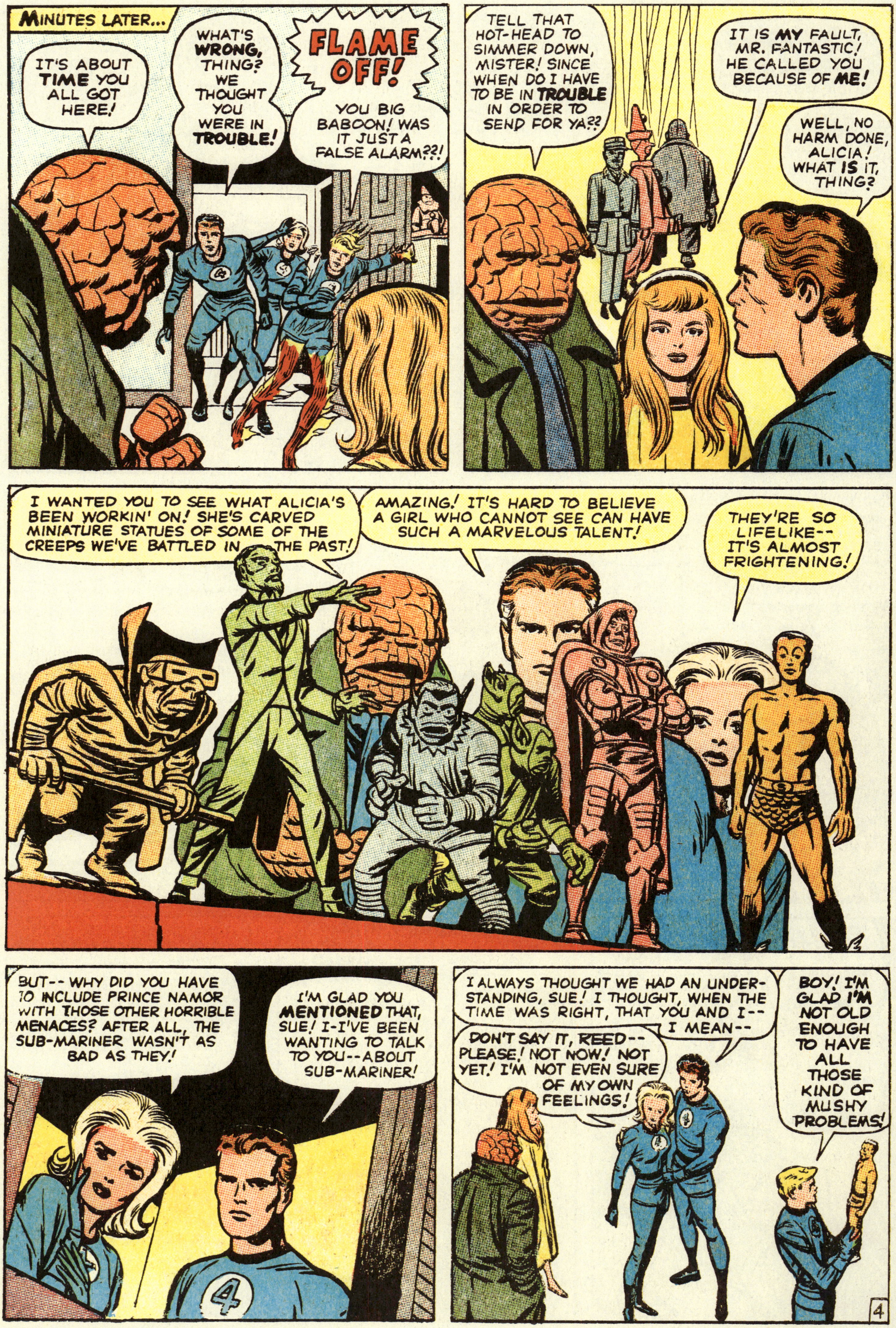
MINUTES LATER...
IT'S ABOUT TIME YOU ALL GOT HERE!
WHAT'S WRONG, THING? WE THOUGHT YOU WERE IN TROUBLE!
FLAME OFF!
YOU BIG BABOON! WAS IT JUST A FALSE ALARM??!
TELL THAT HOT-HEAD TO SIMMER DOWN, MISTER! SINCE WHEN DO I HAVE TO BE IN TROUBLE IN ORDER TO SEND FOR YA??
IT IS MY FAULT, MR. FANTASTIC! HE CALLED YOU BECAUSE OF ME!
WELL, NO HARM DONE, ALICIA! WHAT IS IT, THING?
I WANTED YOU TO SEE WHAT ALICIA'S BEEN WORKIN' ON! SHE'S CARVED MINIATURE STATUES OF SOME OF THE CREEPS WE'VE BATTLED IN THE PAST!
AMAZING! IT'S HARD TO BELIEVE A GIRL WHO CANNOT SEE CAN HAVE SUCH A MARVELOUS TALENT!
THEY'RE SO LIFELIKE-- IT'S ALMOST FRIGHTENING!
BUT-- WHY DID YOU HAVE TO INCLUDE PRINCE NAMOR WITH THOSE OTHER HORRIBLE MENACES? AFTER ALL, THE SUB-MARINER WASN'T AS BAD AS THEY!
I'M GLAD YOU MENTIONED THAT, SUE! I-I'VE BEEN WANTING TO TALK TO YOU--ABOUT SUB-MARINER!
I ALWAYS THOUGHT WE HAD AN UNDERSTANDING, SUE! I THOUGHT, WHEN THE TIME WAS RIGHT, THAT YOU AND I-- I MEAN--
DON'T SAY IT, REED-- PLEASE! NOT NOW! NOT YET! I'M NOT EVEN SURE OF MY OWN FEELINGS!
BOY! I'M GLAD I'M NOT OLD ENOUGH TO HAVE ALL THOSE KIND OF MUSHY PROBLEMS!
4

* SEE **FANTASTIC FOUR** #6 "THE DIABOLICAL DUO JOIN FORCES!"

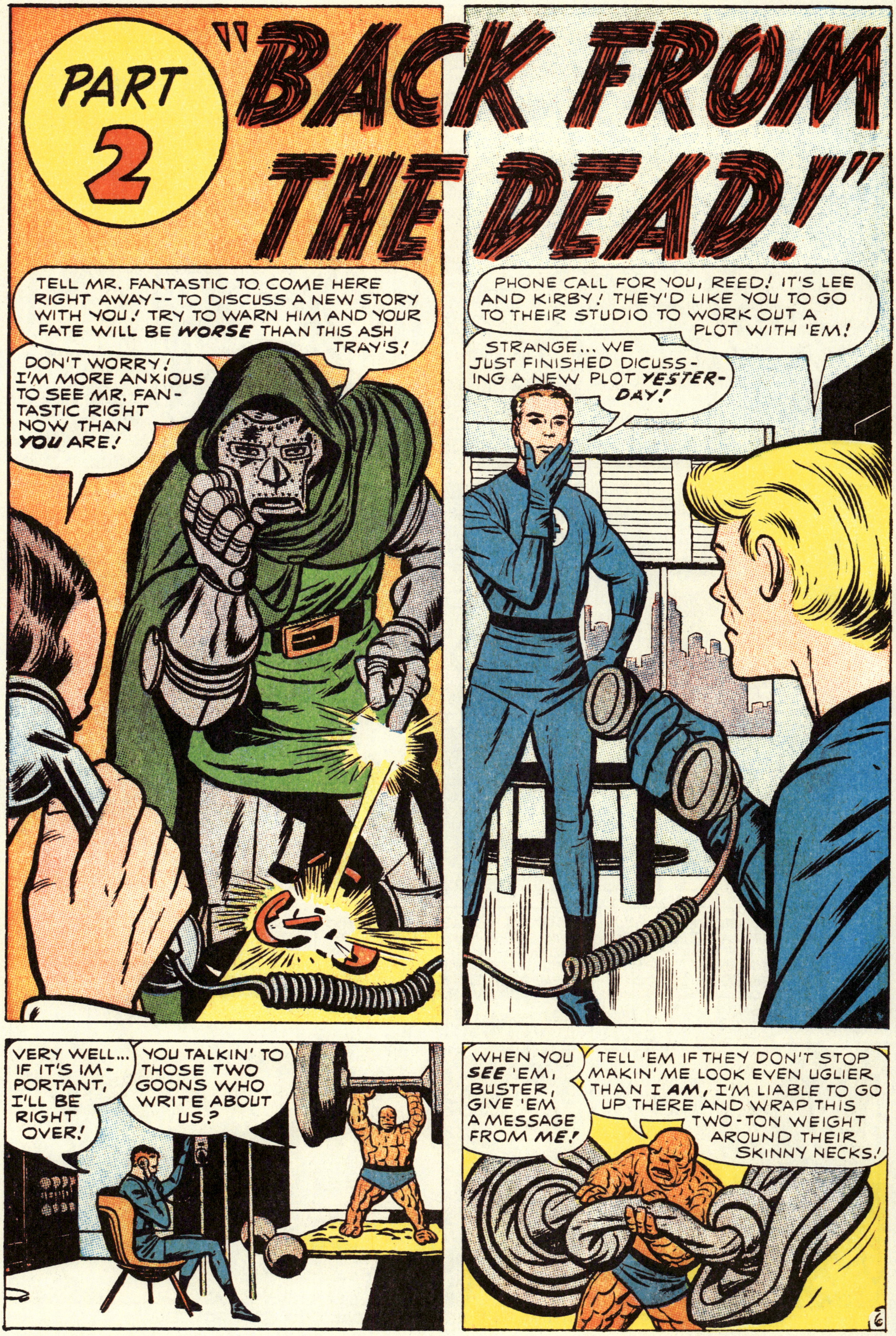
PART 2
"BACK FROM THE DEAD!"
TELL MR. FANTASTIC TO COME HERE RIGHT AWAY-- TO DISCUSS A NEW STORY WITH YOU! TRY TO WARN HIM AND YOUR FATE WILL BE WORSE THAN THIS ASH TRAY'S!
DON'T WORRY! I'M MORE ANXIOUS TO SEE MR. FANTASTIC RIGHT NOW THAN YOU ARE!
PHONE CALL FOR YOU, REED! IT'S LEE AND KIRBY! THEY'D LIKE YOU TO GO TO THEIR STUDIO TO WORK OUT A PLOT WITH 'EM!
STRANGE... WE JUST FINISHED DICUSSING A NEW PLOT YESTERDAY!
VERY WELL... IF IT'S IMPORTANT, I'LL BE RIGHT OVER!
YOU TALKIN' TO THOSE TWO GOONS WHO WRITE ABOUT US?
WHEN YOU SEE 'EM, BUSTER, GIVE 'EM A MESSAGE FROM ME!
TELL 'EM IF THEY DON'T STOP MAKIN' ME LOOK EVEN UGLIER THAN I AM, I'M LIABLE TO GO UP THERE AND WRAP THIS TWO-TON WEIGHT AROUND THEIR SKINNY NECKS!
6

SIMMER DOWN, THING! TELL ME, WHAT MAKES YOU SO BAD-TEMPERED ALL THE TIME?
YOU KIDDIN', REED? THIS IS HIS GOOD-NATURED MOOD! USUALLY HE'S EVEN MORE UNBEARABLE!
VE-RY FUNNY, TWERP! WHO WRITES YOUR GAGS, THE LOCAL UNDERTAKER?
WELL, I'LL GO AND SEE WHAT LEE AND KIRBY WANT AND THEN-- HEY! LEGGO! STOP STRETCHING MY CLOTHES, YOU TWO! C'MON-- STOP IT!
AW, DON'T BE A SOURPUSS, PARTNER! WE JUST WANT TO MAKE SURE YOU REMEMBERED TO WEAR YOUR STRETCH-SUIT, IN CASE YOU NEED IT!
WHAT ARE YA COMPLAININ' ABOUT, RUBBER FACE? WE CAN'T MAKE YOUR CLOTHES LOOK ANY WORSE!
MEANWHILE, ACROSS TOWN FROM THE SCENE OF FRIENDLY HORSEPLAY, WE FIND...
DOOM, YOU'RE A FOOL IF YOU THINK YOU CAN DEFEAT THE FANTASTIC FOUR!
THEY BEAT YOU IN THE PAST, AND THEY'LL DO IT AGAIN!
SILENCE! THERE IS THE BUZZER! ANSWER IT!
WHAT'S THAT? REED RICHARDS IS OUTSIDE? YES-- I'M EXPECTING HIM! SHOW HIM IN!
AH! MY MOMENT IS AT HAND! NOW STEP ASIDE-- QUICKLY!
HELLO, FELLAS! I--
UGH!
LEE AND KIRBY
MY "SLEEPING GAS" WILL KEEP HIM HELPLESS TILL I AWAKEN HIM!
I HAVE GIVEN YOU A CARD WITH MY ADDRESS! CALL THE OTHER THREE AND TELL THEM I SHALL WAIT FOR THEM THERE!
THEY WILL GALLANTLY RUSH TO SAVE THEIR LEADER--AND THAT WILL BE THEIR UNDOING!
NOW, I SHALL LEAVE AS I ARRIVED--BY MEANS OF THE MYSTIC SCIENCE KNOWN ONLY TO DR. DOOM! FAREWELL-- FOR NOW!
7

GULP! IT-- IT ISN'T POS-SIBLE!
JACKSON, WITH A GUY LIKE DOOM, ANTHING IS POSSI-BLE! HE SEEMED SO CONFIDENT--I HOPE THE FANTASTIC FOUR CAN DEFEAT HIM!
AND, A FEW HOURS LATER, AT THE SECRET LABORA-TORY OF THE MASTER MENACE...
AWAKE, REED RICHARDS! I COMMAND YOU!
DOCTOR DOOM! BUT HOW??
I BROUGHT YOU HERE BY MEANS OF MY MENTAL-TELEPORTER! I ONLY HAVE TO THINK OF A PLACE, AND I CAN BE THERE!
IN A WAY, YOU ARE RESPONSIBLE FOR MY OBTAINING THIS DEVICE--AS WELL AS THE OTHER MARVELS I POS-SESS! LET ME EXPLAIN!
"YOU MAY REMEMBER MONTHS AGO...YOU THOUGHT YOU HAD SEEN THE LAST OF ME AS I WAS CARRIED INTO SPACE ON A SPEEDING METEOR! BUT FORTUNE WAS WITH ME! BEFORE VERY LONG, I WAS SIGHTED BY BEINGS FROM ANOTHER GALAXY!..
"THEY CALLED THEMSELVES THE OVOIDS, AND THEIR SCIENCE AND CULTURE WERE A MILLION YEARS AHEAD OF OURS!"
WELCOME TO OUR SHIP, EARTHMAN!
"MY FIRST THOUGHT WAS TO PROTECT MY-SELF FROM THEM--BUT I LEARNED IT WAS NOT NECESSARY!"
STAY BACK! COME ANY CLOSER AND I'LL FIRE!
PUT AWAY YOUR PUNY WEAPON, MORTAL! WE MEAN YOU NO HARM!
IF WE WISHED TO INJURE YOU, WE COULD DO IT BY THE POWER OF THOUGHT ALONE!
SEE HOW WE CAN MOVE OBJECTS OF ANY WEIGHT, AS EASILY AS YOU BLINK YOUR EYE!
IF I COULD STEAL SOME OF THEIR POWERS... LEARN THEIR SECRETS... THE WORLD WOULD BE MINE!
8

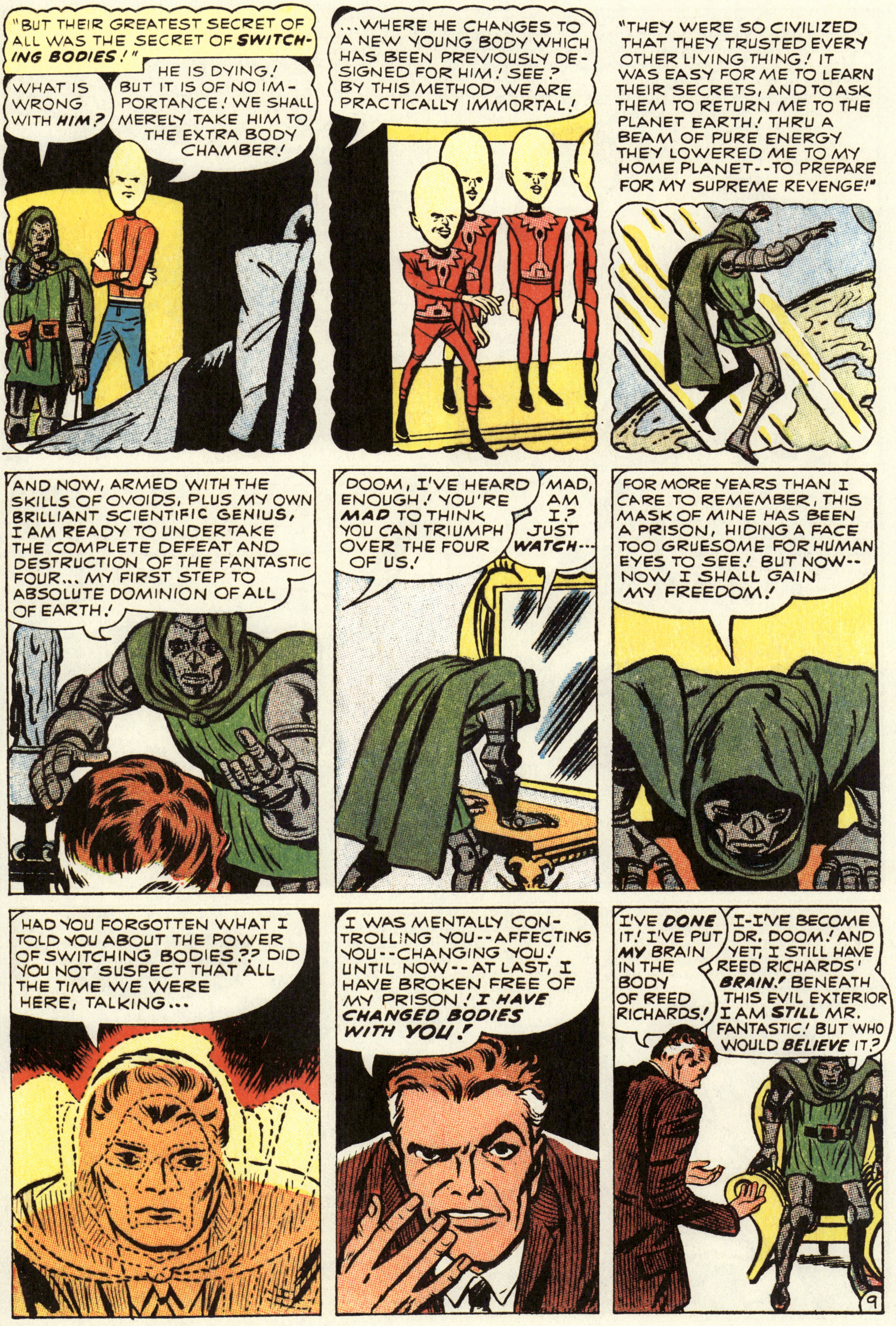
"BUT THEIR GREATEST SECRET OF ALL WAS THE SECRET OF **SWITCHING BODIES**!"
WHAT IS WRONG WITH **HIM**?
HE IS DYING! BUT IT IS OF NO IMPORTANCE! WE SHALL MERELY TAKE HIM TO THE EXTRA BODY CHAMBER!
...WHERE HE CHANGES TO A NEW YOUNG BODY WHICH HAS BEEN PREVIOUSLY DESIGNED FOR HIM! SEE? BY THIS METHOD WE ARE PRACTICALLY IMMORTAL!
"THEY WERE SO CIVILIZED THAT THEY TRUSTED EVERY OTHER LIVING THING! IT WAS EASY FOR ME TO LEARN THEIR SECRETS, AND TO ASK THEM TO RETURN ME TO THE PLANET EARTH! THRU A BEAM OF PURE ENERGY THEY LOWERED ME TO MY HOME PLANET--TO PREPARE FOR MY SUPREME REVENGE!"
AND NOW, ARMED WITH THE SKILLS OF OVOIDS, PLUS MY OWN BRILLIANT SCIENTIFIC GENIUS, I AM READY TO UNDERTAKE THE COMPLETE DEFEAT AND DESTRUCTION OF THE FANTASTIC FOUR... MY FIRST STEP TO ABSOLUTE DOMINION OF ALL OF EARTH!
DOOM, I'VE HEARD ENOUGH! YOU'RE **MAD** TO THINK YOU CAN TRIUMPH OVER THE FOUR OF US!
MAD, AM I? JUST **WATCH**...
FOR MORE YEARS THAN I CARE TO REMEMBER, THIS MASK OF MINE HAS BEEN A PRISON, HIDING A FACE TOO GRUESOME FOR HUMAN EYES TO SEE! BUT NOW-- NOW I SHALL GAIN MY FREEDOM!
HAD YOU FORGOTTEN WHAT I TOLD YOU ABOUT THE POWER OF SWITCHING BODIES?? DID YOU NOT SUSPECT THAT ALL THE TIME WE WERE HERE, TALKING...
I WAS MENTALLY CONTROLLING YOU--AFFECTING YOU--CHANGING YOU! UNTIL NOW--AT LAST, I HAVE BROKEN FREE OF MY PRISON! **I HAVE CHANGED BODIES WITH YOU!**
I'VE **DONE** IT! I'VE PUT **MY** BRAIN IN THE BODY OF REED RICHARDS!
I-I'VE BECOME DR. DOOM! AND YET, I STILL HAVE REED RICHARDS' **BRAIN**! BENEATH THIS EVIL EXTERIOR I AM **STILL** MR. FANTASTIC! BUT WHO WOULD **BELIEVE** IT?
9

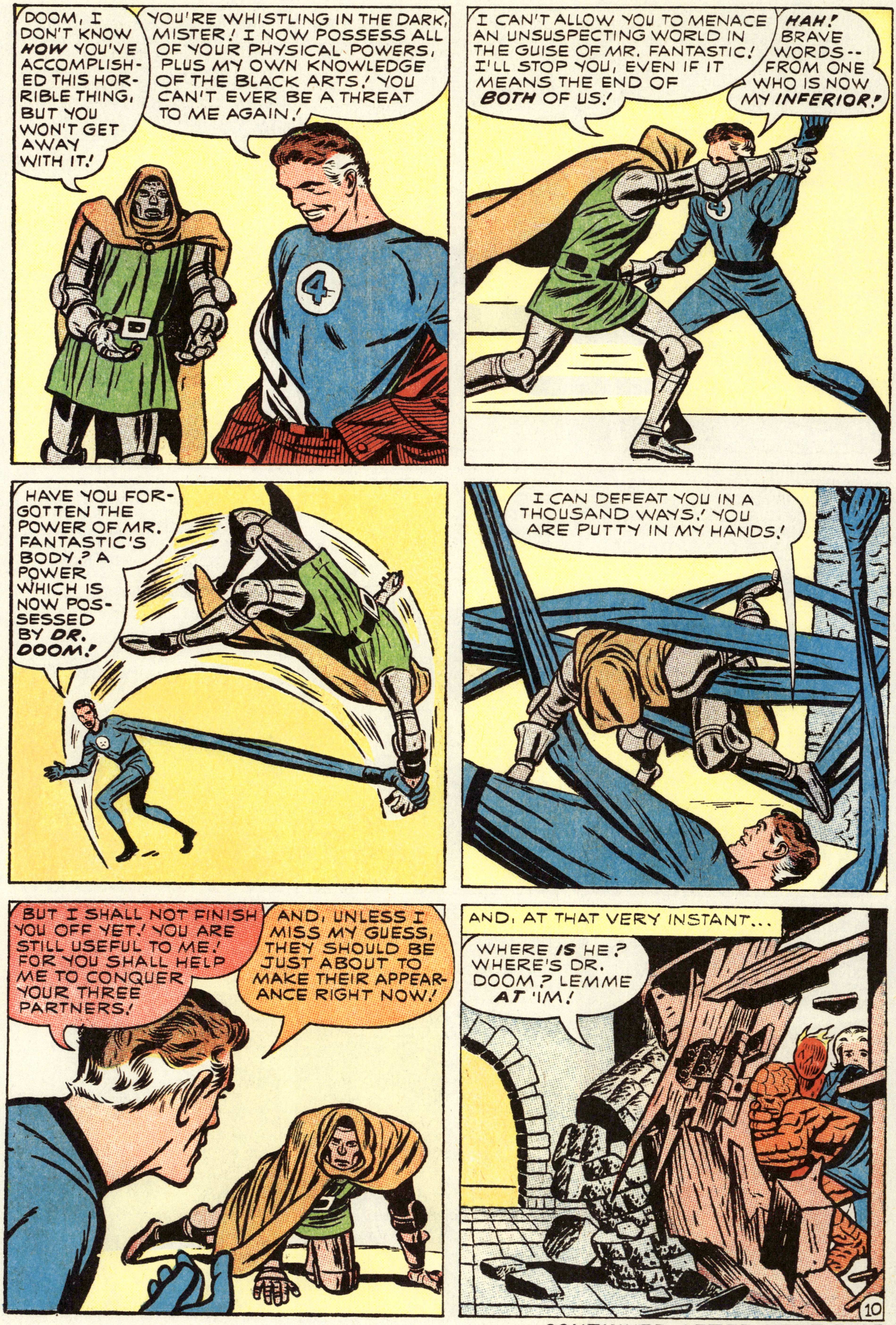

CONTINUED AFTER NEXT PAGE

TIKI gods
HAND PAINTED—VIVID COLORS
3 DIMENSIONAL—JEWELLERS METAL!
59¢
Start your TIKI GOD collection now. These are authentic copies of HEATHEN IDOLS which have been worshipped for centuries by South Sea Islanders. According to ancient native folklore, "HE WHO WEARS ME SHALL COMMAND THE WIND AND THE SEAS AND HIS DESTINY". (only ⅔ actual size)
NOW—you too, can wear a TIKI ON A THONG. Millions of TV viewers have each week seen the TIKI GOOD LUCK CHARM worn by the romantic Sea Captain. Reproduced in Jewellers Metal. These GODS are authentic—copied down to the smallest detail. Eyes—Nose—Mouth are HAND PAINTED by skilled artists in bright BARBARIC COLORS! A most unusual conversation piece for adults. A Thrilling Unusual Gift for boys and girls. Nationally sold at leading department stores and jewellers for $1.00-$1.98 each.
NOW ONLY 59¢ each—2 for $1.00! Save money—buy the complete set of 5 TIKI GODS—a comparable $10.00 value—NOW ONLY $2.00 (A—IDOL OF LOVE), (B—IDOL OF GOOD LUCK), (C—IDOL OF JOY AND HAPPINESS), (D—IDOL OF STRENGTH AND POWER), (E—IDOL OF WITCHCRAFT). Add 10¢ Parcel Post to each order. All orders shipped immediately. Money-back if not delighted.
(Send for our free catalog)
GREENWICH VILLAGE HANDCRAFTS
Dept. T-4317 31 Second Ave., New York 3, N.Y.
A
B
C 1
D
E
UGLY BLACKHEADS OUT in Seconds with VACUTEX
FELLOWS! GIRLS! Keep Skin Clear and Clean!
I WONDER WHY WE'RE NOT POPULAR SIS?
ASK YOUR FRIEND TOM
TOM, WHY DON'T SIS AND I GET INVITED TO PROMS AND PARTIES
FRANKLY, JIM ITS THOSE UGLY BLACKHEADS
AREN'T YOU GLAD WE HEARD ABOUT VACUTEX
BLACKHEADS "PET HATE"
Say Men, Girls In Choosing Date
What a "black mark" is the blackhead . . . according to men and girls popular enough to be choosy about dates! Because blackheads ARE ugly! Blackheads ARE grimy! They DON'T look good in close-ups!
So can you blame the fellow who says, "Sure, I meet lots of girls who look cute at first glance. But if, on that second glance, I see dingy blackheads, it's good night!"
Or can you blame the girl who confesses, "I hate to go out with that fellow who has blackheads." But you—are YOUR ears burning?
Extract every blackhead with a SAFE extractor. Don't use finger nails. Don't squeeze. That may mean infection, injured tissues, a marred skin.
ACTUAL LENGTH 3½"
New! SCIENTIFIC VACUUM ACTION!
VACUTEX is painless . . . safe . . . fast! In seconds you are rid of those ugly blackheads that make your skin look grimy and dingy . . . give others such a wrong impression. VACUTEX creates gentle vacuum pressure around the blackhead and extracts it—quickly!—without injury to tender skin tissues. No painful squeezing! No dangerous infection from germy fingers. You'll be delighted by your instantly improved appearance. Others will notice your clearer, cleaner skin! Try VACUTEX—now!
No Squeezing
No Infection
No Injury to Skin Tissues
Just place VACUTEX over blackhead — release extractor—and blackhead's out!
10 DAY TRIAL OFFER
If not thrilled to be rid of embarrassing hated blackheads this new quick way—return VACUTEX in 10 days and get money back.
10 DAY TRIAL GUARANTEE
BALLCO PRODUCTS CO. Dept. 26
735 East State St., Westport, Conn.
☐ Enclosed find $1 plus 25¢ to cover postage and handling.
My money will be refunded if I am not delighted.
NAME
ADDRESS
SORRY, NO C.O.D.

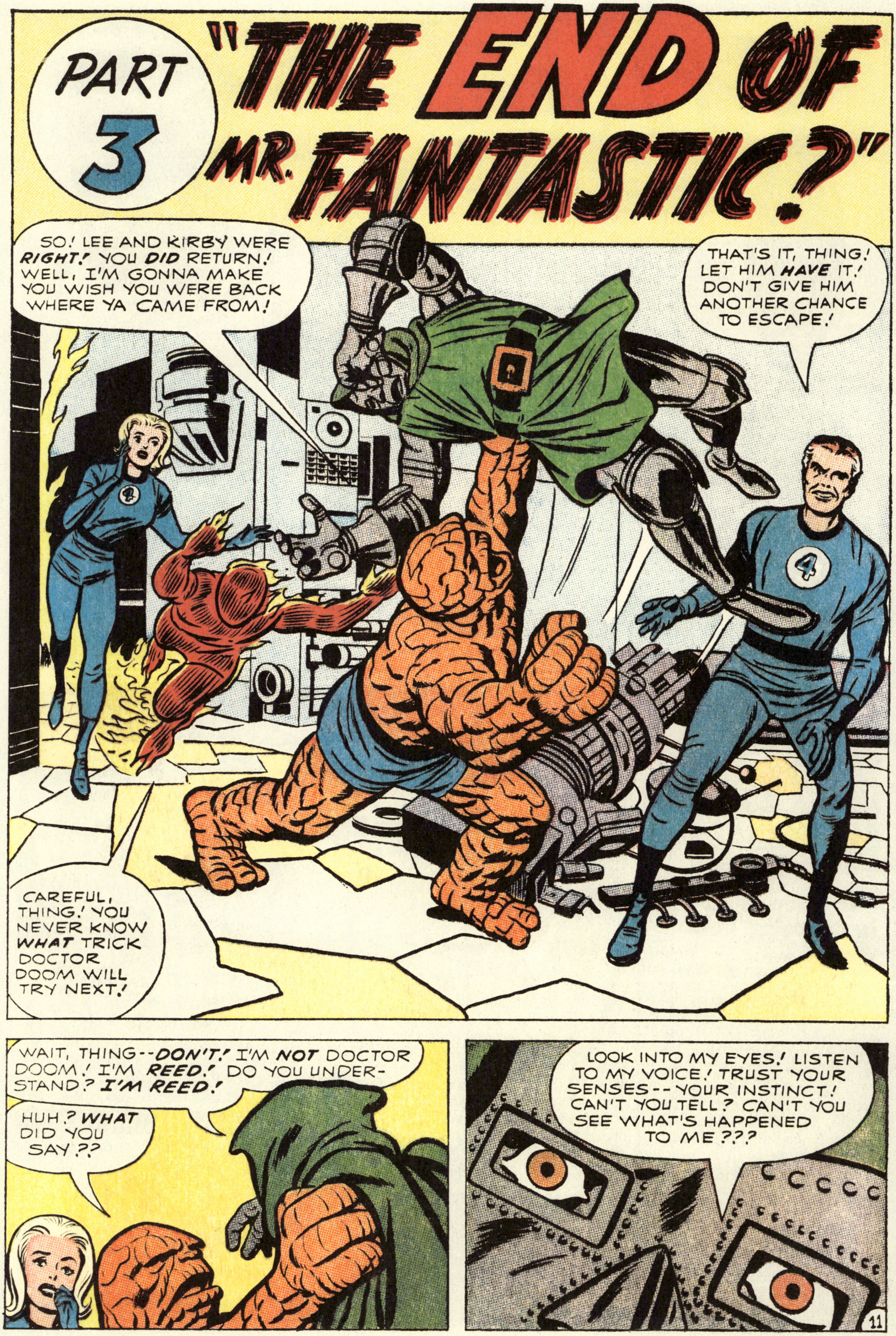
PART 3
"THE END OF MR. FANTASTIC?"
SO! LEE AND KIRBY WERE RIGHT! YOU DID RETURN! WELL, I'M GONNA MAKE YOU WISH YOU WERE BACK WHERE YA CAME FROM!
THAT'S IT, THING! LET HIM HAVE IT! DON'T GIVE HIM ANOTHER CHANCE TO ESCAPE!
CAREFUL, THING! YOU NEVER KNOW WHAT TRICK DOCTOR DOOM WILL TRY NEXT!
WAIT, THING--DON'T! I'M NOT DOCTOR DOOM! I'M REED! DO YOU UNDERSTAND? I'M REED!
HUH? WHAT DID YOU SAY??
LOOK INTO MY EYES! LISTEN TO MY VOICE! TRUST YOUR SENSES--YOUR INSTINCT! CAN'T YOU TELL? CAN'T YOU SEE WHAT'S HAPPENED TO ME???
11

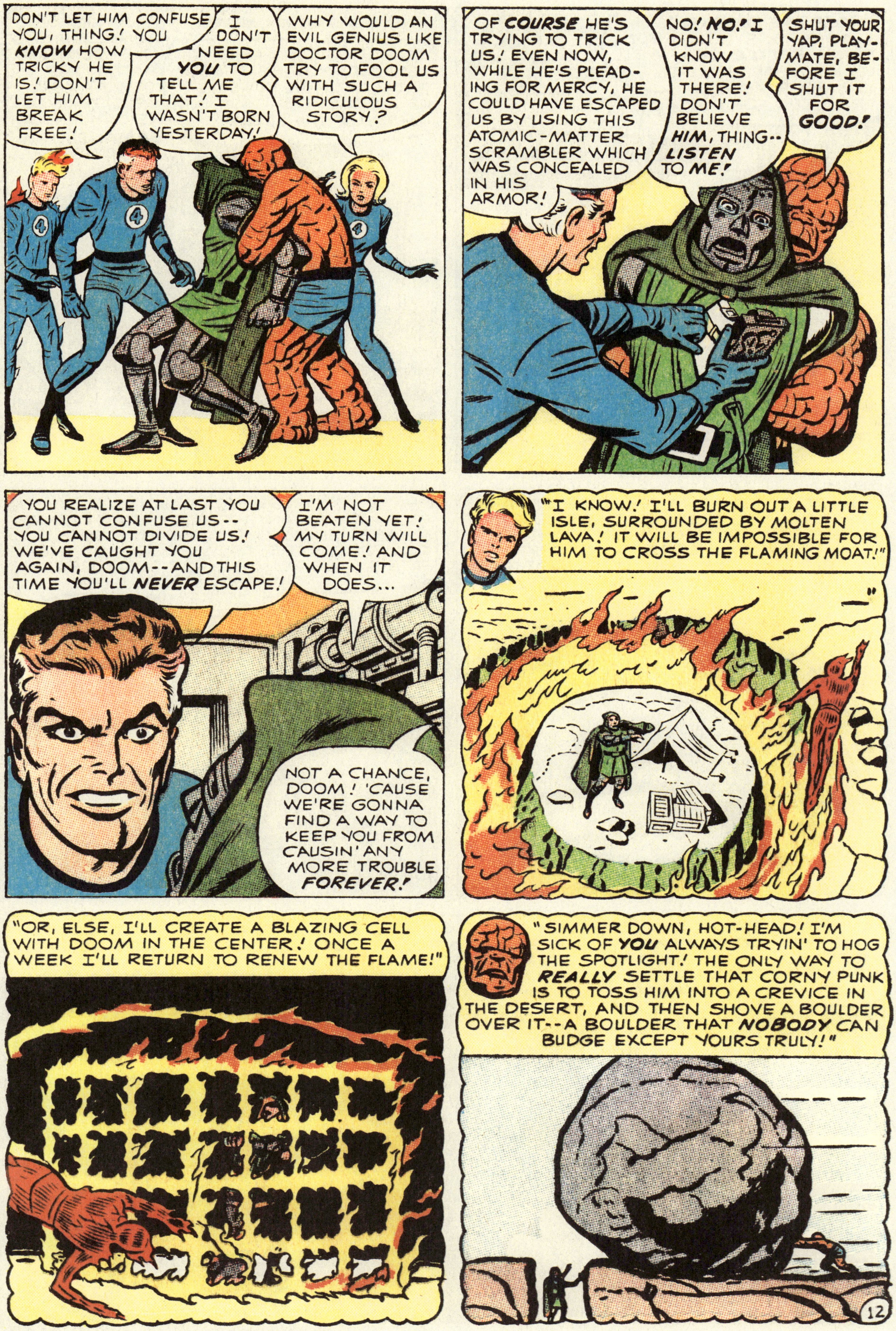

DON'T LET HIM CONFUSE YOU, THING! YOU KNOW HOW TRICKY HE IS! DON'T LET HIM BREAK FREE!
I DON'T NEED YOU TO TELL ME THAT! I WASN'T BORN YESTERDAY!
WHY WOULD AN EVIL GENIUS LIKE DOCTOR DOOM TRY TO FOOL US WITH SUCH A RIDICULOUS STORY?
OF COURSE HE'S TRYING TO TRICK US! EVEN NOW, WHILE HE'S PLEADING FOR MERCY, HE COULD HAVE ESCAPED US BY USING THIS ATOMIC-MATTER SCRAMBLER WHICH WAS CONCEALED IN HIS ARMOR!
NO! NO! I DIDN'T KNOW IT WAS THERE! DON'T BELIEVE HIM, THING-- LISTEN TO ME!
SHUT YOUR YAP, PLAYMATE, BEFORE I SHUT IT FOR GOOD!
YOU REALIZE AT LAST YOU CANNOT CONFUSE US-- YOU CANNOT DIVIDE US! WE'VE CAUGHT YOU AGAIN, DOOM--AND THIS TIME YOU'LL NEVER ESCAPE!
I'M NOT BEATEN YET! MY TURN WILL COME! AND WHEN IT DOES...
NOT A CHANCE, DOOM! 'CAUSE WE'RE GONNA FIND A WAY TO KEEP YOU FROM CAUSIN' ANY MORE TROUBLE FOREVER!
"I KNOW! I'LL BURN OUT A LITTLE ISLE, SURROUNDED BY MOLTEN LAVA! IT WILL BE IMPOSSIBLE FOR HIM TO CROSS THE FLAMING MOAT!"
"OR, ELSE, I'LL CREATE A BLAZING CELL WITH DOOM IN THE CENTER! ONCE A WEEK I'LL RETURN TO RENEW THE FLAME!"
"SIMMER DOWN, HOT-HEAD! I'M SICK OF YOU ALWAYS TRYIN' TO HOG THE SPOTLIGHT! THE ONLY WAY TO REALLY SETTLE THAT CORNY PUNK IS TO TOSS HIM INTO A CREVICE IN THE DESERT, AND THEN SHOVE A BOULDER OVER IT--A BOULDER THAT NOBODY CAN BUDGE EXCEPT YOURS TRULY!"
12

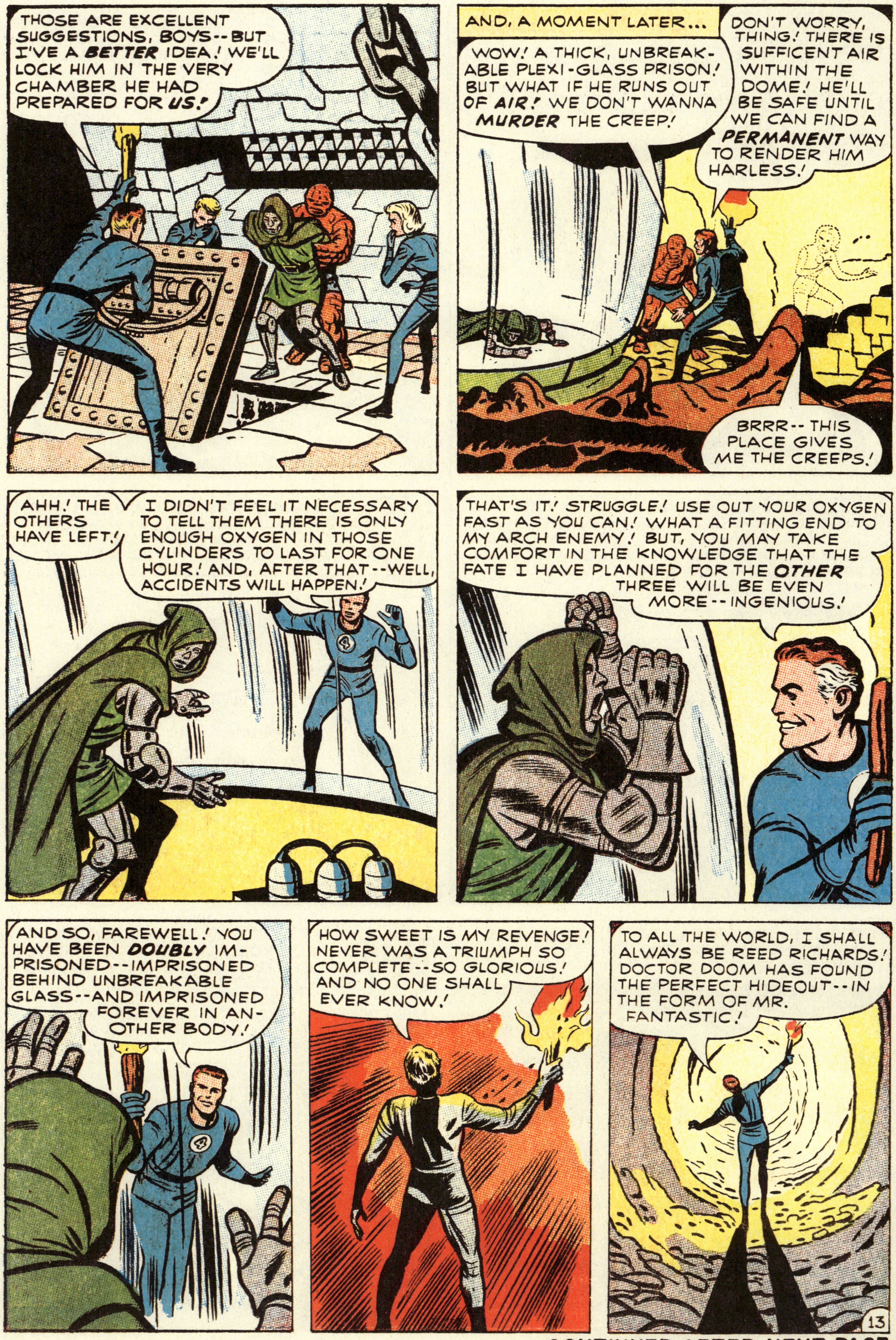

CONTINUED AFTER NEXT PAGE

REWARD $9,985.50

FOR THIS COIN!

ILLUSTRATED: 1804 Silver Dollar, 19,000 Minted, only 12 accounted for—where are the rest?

$500,000.00 SEARCH FOR RARE COINS!

Stop spending valuable coins worth hundreds of dollars. New 1963 catalogue lists hundreds of coins we want to buy and gives the price range we will pay for these United States Coins. Certain half cent coins are worth up to $3,500.00 for Canadian Coins. Our valuable Coin Book may reward you many thousands of dollars. Coins do not have to be old to be valuable. Thousands of dollars have been paid for coins dated as recently as 1940 to 1956. Now you too can learn the rare dates and how to identify rare coins in your possession with our new 1963 catalogue. A fortune may be waiting for you. Millions of Dollars have been paid for rare coins. Don't sell your valuable coins for less than they are worth! Hold on to your coins until you obtain our catalogue. Send $1.00 for newest Coin Catalogue to:
BEST VALUES CO., Coin Dept. A-306
285 MARKET ST., Newark, New Jersey.

MAIL MONEY-SAVING NO-RISK FREE TRIAL COUPON NOW!
My purchase price will be promptly refunded if I'm not satisfied.

FOR CERTAIN COINS WE PAY UP TO

CERTAIN	
Gold Coins Before 1929.	$10,000.00
Pennies Before 1919.	9,000.00
Silver Dollars Before 1936.	8,000.00
Nickels Before 1945.	6,000.00
Dimes Before 1946.	5,000.00
Half Dollars Before 1947.	4,500.00
Quarters Before 1941.	3,500.00
Half Cents Before 1910.	3,500.00
Lincoln Pennies Before 1940.	200.00

BEST VALUES CO., COIN DEPT. A-306
285 Market St.
Newark, New Jersey
Rush your Latest 1963 Coin Catalogue listing the actual price range you will pay for United States Coins listed in the catalogue. I enclose $1. Send Postage Prepaid.

Name ....
Address ....
City .... Zone....
State ....

NEW FLY THIS EXCITING GIANT 7 FOOT WINDHOOKER!

BE FIRST IN YOUR NEIGHBORHOOD TO ENJOY THIS SENSATIONAL SPORT FOR MEN and BOYS!

When you hook the wind with this giant kite . . . be ready for the kind of thrill fishermen get when they hook into a crazy fighting marlin. This is no toy . . . this is a 7 foot giant that will thrill and excite the most adventurous sportsmen. Compete with your friends for record high flying . . . for diving and maneuvering . . . for diving at targets . . . for dueling with other kites. You can assemble it in about 20 minutes. You get everything . . . heavy gauge plastic vinyl, rigid belly section, expandable steel struts, 200 ft. of cable cord, and cord feeder, simple instructions and exciting flying hints—and all for only $2.98 ppd. or 2 for $5.00. Money back if not delighted. Order this sensational Windhooker now. No C.O.D.

YOUR MONEY BACK IF NOT DELIGHTED

$2.98 ppd.
2 for $5.00

Grayson Products
Dept. W-1, 210 Fifth Ave., N. Y. 10, N. Y.
I enclose $____ Send ____ Windhookers
Name________
Address________
City________ State________

PART 4
"NO PLACE TO TURN!"
A SHORT TIME LATER, AT THE FANTASTIC FOUR'S HEADQUATERS...
SAY, WHAT'S GOIN' ON, SUE? WHERE'D YOU GET THE TOY ANIMALS?
THEY'RE NOT TOYS, JOHNNY! INCREDIBLE AS IT SEEMS, THEY'RE ALIVE! THEY RAN OUT WHEN WE OPENED REED'S LAB DOOR!
I DON'T GET IT! WHAT NEW EXPERI-MENT IS HE WORKIN' ON NOW? AND HOW DOES IT TIE UP TO THIS NEWSPAPER HEADLINE??
DAILY BULLETIN
ZOO
NIMALS
ISSING
WELL, WE'D BETTER ROUND 'EM UP AND RETURN 'EM TO THE LAB BEFORE REED GETS BACK!
YES! YOU KNOW HOW ANGRY HE GETS IF ANYONE INTER-FERES WITH HIS WORK!
BIG DEAL! SO WHAT'LL HE DO TO ME--SLAP MY WRIST??! COME HERE, YA PESTY CRITTER!
14

WELL, WHAT'S GOING **ON** HERE?
IT'S OKAY, REED! THESE LITTLE ANIMALS GOT LOOSE, AND WE'RE TRYIN' TO PUT 'EM BACK!
LOOKS TO ME LIKE **YOU'RE** THE ONE WITH THE EXPLAININ' TO DO, BUDDY!
HMMM, I SUPPOSE YOU'RE RIGHT! YOU WANT TO KNOW **WHERE** THESE TINY CREATURES **CAME** FROM, EH?
BLAMED **RIGHT** WE DO! AND IF **YOU'RE** THE JOKER WHO STOLE 'EM FROM THE ZOO, THEN THAT MAKES OL' HOLIER-THAN-THOU REED AS MUCH A LAW-BREAKER AS ANYONE ELSE!
DAILY
ZOO ANIMA MISSIN
WAIT! DON'T CONDEMN ME UNTIL YOU'VE HEARD MY MOTIVES! I DID IT ONLY FOR **YOU!** LOOK, DO YOU SEE THIS LITTLE DEVICE? IT IS MY NEW REDUCING RAY!
RE-DUCING RAY?? BUT-- **WHY?**
ALL RIGHT, SISTER! YOU'RE **ASKING** FOR IT! I'LL COME UP WITH A STORY THAT WILL HAVE THE THREE OF YOU **BEGGING** ME--TO SEAL YOUR OWN DOOM!
I DEVELOPED THAT RAY TO HELP ME **INCREASE** YOUR OWN POWERS! IT MAY BE HARD FOR YOU TO UNDERSTAND, SO...
LET ME GIVE YOU A LITTLE EXAMPLE...
"AS YOU KNOW, AGES AGO THE DINOSAURS WERE THE LORDS OF EARTH! BUT, UNFORTUNATELY FOR THEM, THEIR BODIES GREW TOO LARGE WHILE THEIR BRAINS REMAINED THE SAME--UNTIL THEY SIMPLY GREW THEMSELVES OUT OF EXISTENCE!"
"BUT, WHAT IF THEY HAVE BEEN **SMALLER?** IF THEIR BODIES HAD BEEN A FRACTION OF THEIR NATURAL SIZE, THEN THEIR **BRAINS** WOULD HAVE BEEN MUCH LARGER BY COMPARISON! TODAY, THE DINOSAURS MIGHT **STILL** BE THE RULERS OF EARTH!"
15

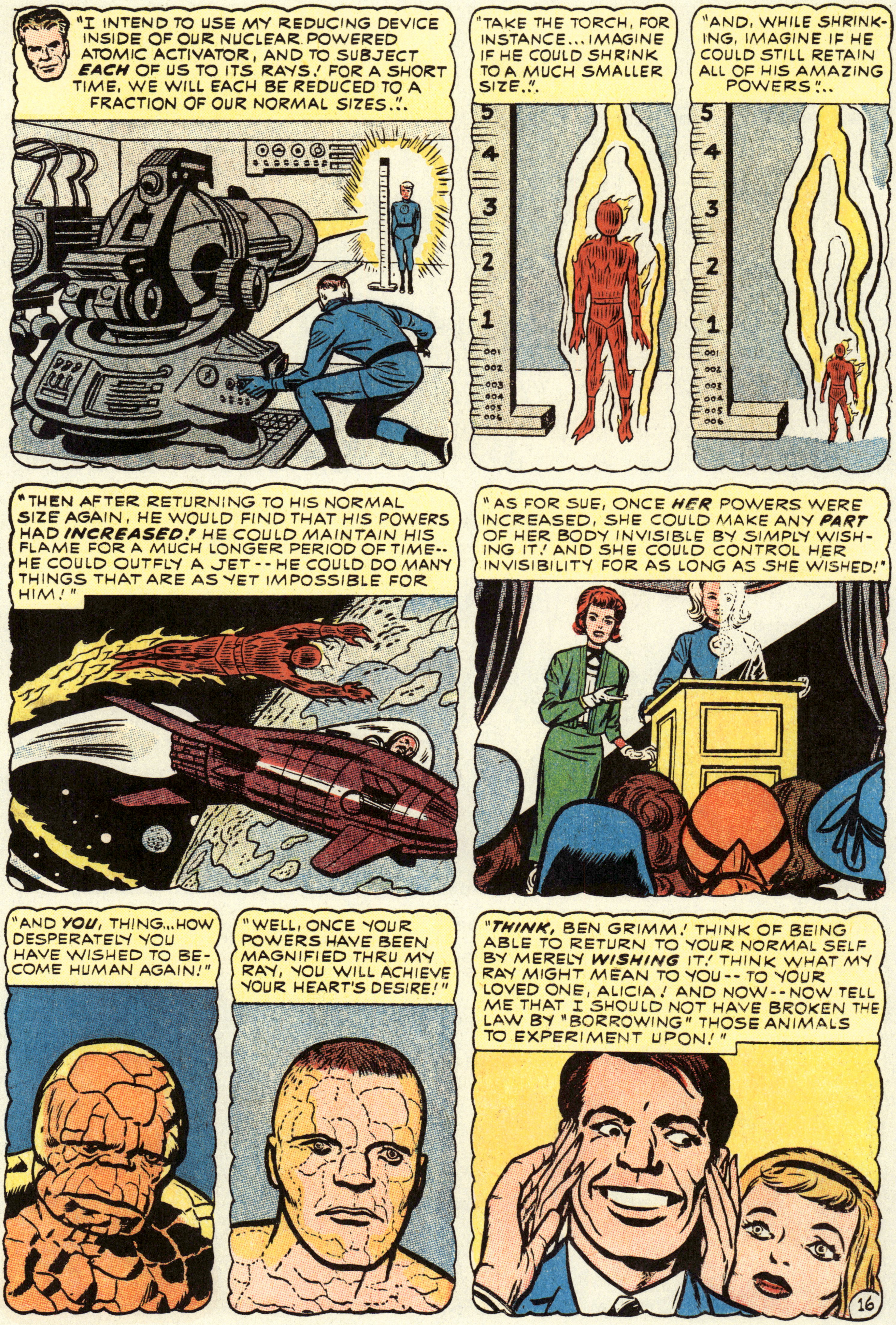
"I INTEND TO USE MY REDUCING DEVICE INSIDE OF OUR NUCLEAR POWERED ATOMIC ACTIVATOR, AND TO SUBJECT EACH OF US TO ITS RAYS! FOR A SHORT TIME, WE WILL EACH BE REDUCED TO A FRACTION OF OUR NORMAL SIZES..."
"TAKE THE TORCH, FOR INSTANCE... IMAGINE IF HE COULD SHRINK TO A MUCH SMALLER SIZE..."
5
4
3
2
1
"AND, WHILE SHRINKING, IMAGINE IF HE COULD STILL RETAIN ALL OF HIS AMAZING POWERS"...
5
4
3
2
1
"THEN AFTER RETURNING TO HIS NORMAL SIZE AGAIN, HE WOULD FIND THAT HIS POWERS HAD INCREASED! HE COULD MAINTAIN HIS FLAME FOR A MUCH LONGER PERIOD OF TIME-- HE COULD OUTFLY A JET -- HE COULD DO MANY THINGS THAT ARE AS YET IMPOSSIBLE FOR HIM!"
"AS FOR SUE, ONCE HER POWERS WERE INCREASED, SHE COULD MAKE ANY PART OF HER BODY INVISIBLE BY SIMPLY WISHING IT! AND SHE COULD CONTROL HER INVISIBILITY FOR AS LONG AS SHE WISHED!"
"AND YOU, THING...HOW DESPERATELY YOU HAVE WISHED TO BECOME HUMAN AGAIN!"
"WELL, ONCE YOUR POWERS HAVE BEEN MAGNIFIED THRU MY RAY, YOU WILL ACHIEVE YOUR HEART'S DESIRE!"
"THINK, BEN GRIMM! THINK OF BEING ABLE TO RETURN TO YOUR NORMAL SELF BY MERELY WISHING IT! THINK WHAT MY RAY MIGHT MEAN TO YOU -- TO YOUR LOVED ONE, ALICIA! AND NOW -- NOW TELL ME THAT I SHOULD NOT HAVE BROKEN THE LAW BY "BORROWING" THOSE ANIMALS TO EXPERIMENT UPON!"

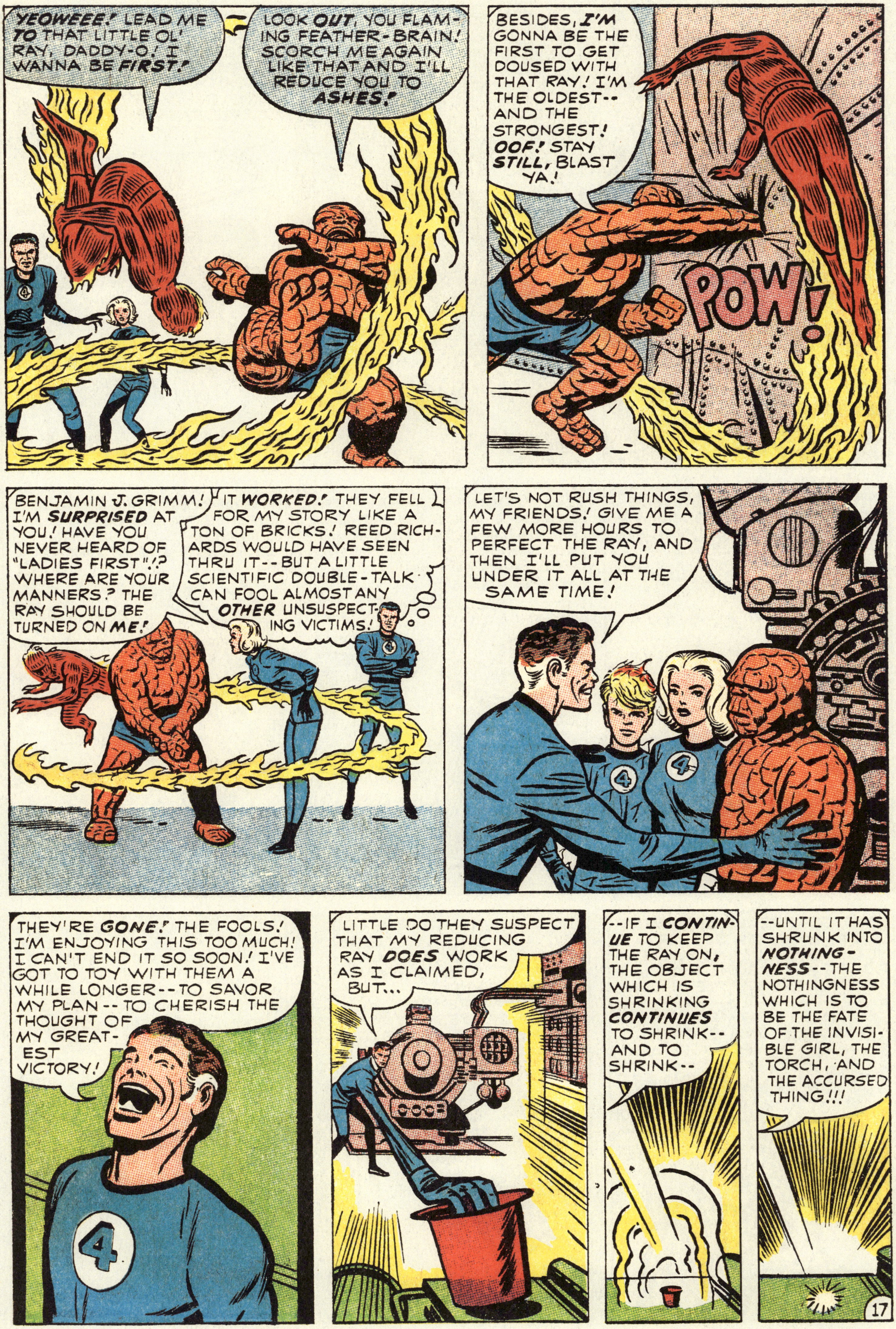
YEOWEEE! LEAD ME TO THAT LITTLE OL' RAY, DADDY-O! I WANNA BE FIRST!
LOOK OUT, YOU FLAMING FEATHER-BRAIN! SCORCH ME AGAIN LIKE THAT AND I'LL REDUCE YOU TO ASHES!
BESIDES, I'M GONNA BE THE FIRST TO GET DOUSED WITH THAT RAY! I'M THE OLDEST-- AND THE STRONGEST! OOF! STAY STILL, BLAST YA!
POW!
BENJAMIN J. GRIMM! I'M SURPRISED AT YOU! HAVE YOU NEVER HEARD OF "LADIES FIRST"!? WHERE ARE YOUR MANNERS? THE RAY SHOULD BE TURNED ON ME!
IT WORKED! THEY FELL FOR MY STORY LIKE A TON OF BRICKS! REED RICHARDS WOULD HAVE SEEN THRU IT--BUT A LITTLE SCIENTIFIC DOUBLE-TALK CAN FOOL ALMOST ANY OTHER UNSUSPECTING VICTIMS!
LET'S NOT RUSH THINGS, MY FRIENDS! GIVE ME A FEW MORE HOURS TO PERFECT THE RAY, AND THEN I'LL PUT YOU UNDER IT ALL AT THE SAME TIME!
THEY'RE GONE! THE FOOLS! I'M ENJOYING THIS TOO MUCH! I CAN'T END IT SO SOON! I'VE GOT TO TOY WITH THEM A WHILE LONGER--TO SAVOR MY PLAN--TO CHERISH THE THOUGHT OF MY GREATEST VICTORY!
LITTLE DO THEY SUSPECT THAT MY REDUCING RAY DOES WORK AS I CLAIMED, BUT...
--IF I CONTINUE TO KEEP THE RAY ON, THE OBJECT WHICH IS SHRINKING CONTINUES TO SHRINK--AND TO SHRINK--
--UNTIL IT HAS SHRUNK INTO NOTHINGNESS--THE NOTHINGNESS WHICH IS TO BE THE FATE OF THE INVISIBLE GIRL, THE TORCH, AND THE ACCURSED THING!!!
17

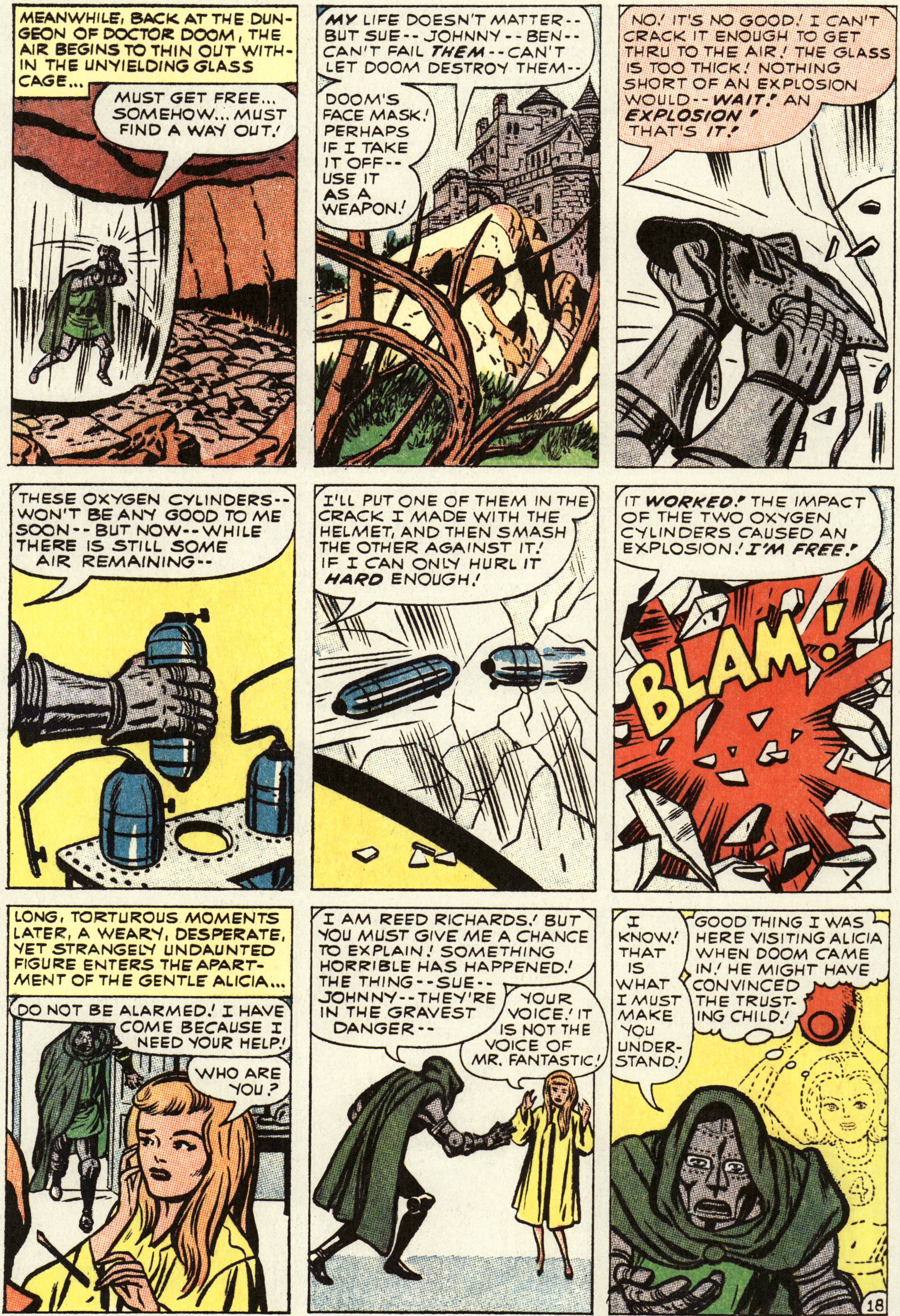

CONTINUED AFTER NEXT PAGE...

THE FANTASTIC FOUR
PIN-UP PAGE
SUE STORM, The Glamorous INVISIBLE GIRL
IN ANSWER TO MANY REQUESTS, NOTE THE DETAILS IN THE CONTROL PANEL OF SUE'S SECTION OF THE FABULOUS FANTASTI-CAR!
1962
Love and Kisses to my Wonderful Fans—
Sue

PART 5
"THE REAL DOCTOR DOOM!"
THERE! LUCKY I STRUCK A VULNERABLE SPOT! OH, ALICIA--IF I HADN'T BEEN HERE TO TELL YOU THE GOOD NEWS ABOUT REED'S RAY, I SHUDDER TO THINK WHAT MIGHT HAVE HAPPENED! I-I'D BETTER CALL THE OTHERS RIGHT AWAY!
WHAT HAPPENED, SUE? I HEARD THE SOUND OF A MUFFLED BLOW--WAS IT--COULD IT HAVE BEEN THE AWESOME DOCTOR DOOM??
HELLO, OPERATOR--GET ME THE FANTASTIC FOUR'S HEADQUARTERS--HURRY!
STRANGE! BENEATH THIS COLD STEEL I CAN FEEL A WARMTH OF SPIRIT--OF KINDNESS...
I DON'T UNDERSTAND! HOW CAN THAT BE DR. DOOM? THERE'S AN AURA OF GOODNESS ABOUT HIM...OF NOBILITY!
ALICIA! YOU DON'T KNOW WHAT YOU'RE SAYING! YOU'RE TALKING ABOUT THE MOST SINISTER, THE MOST RUTHLESS MENACE ON EARTH! HE IS THE MOST DANGEROUS HUMAN OF ALL TIME!

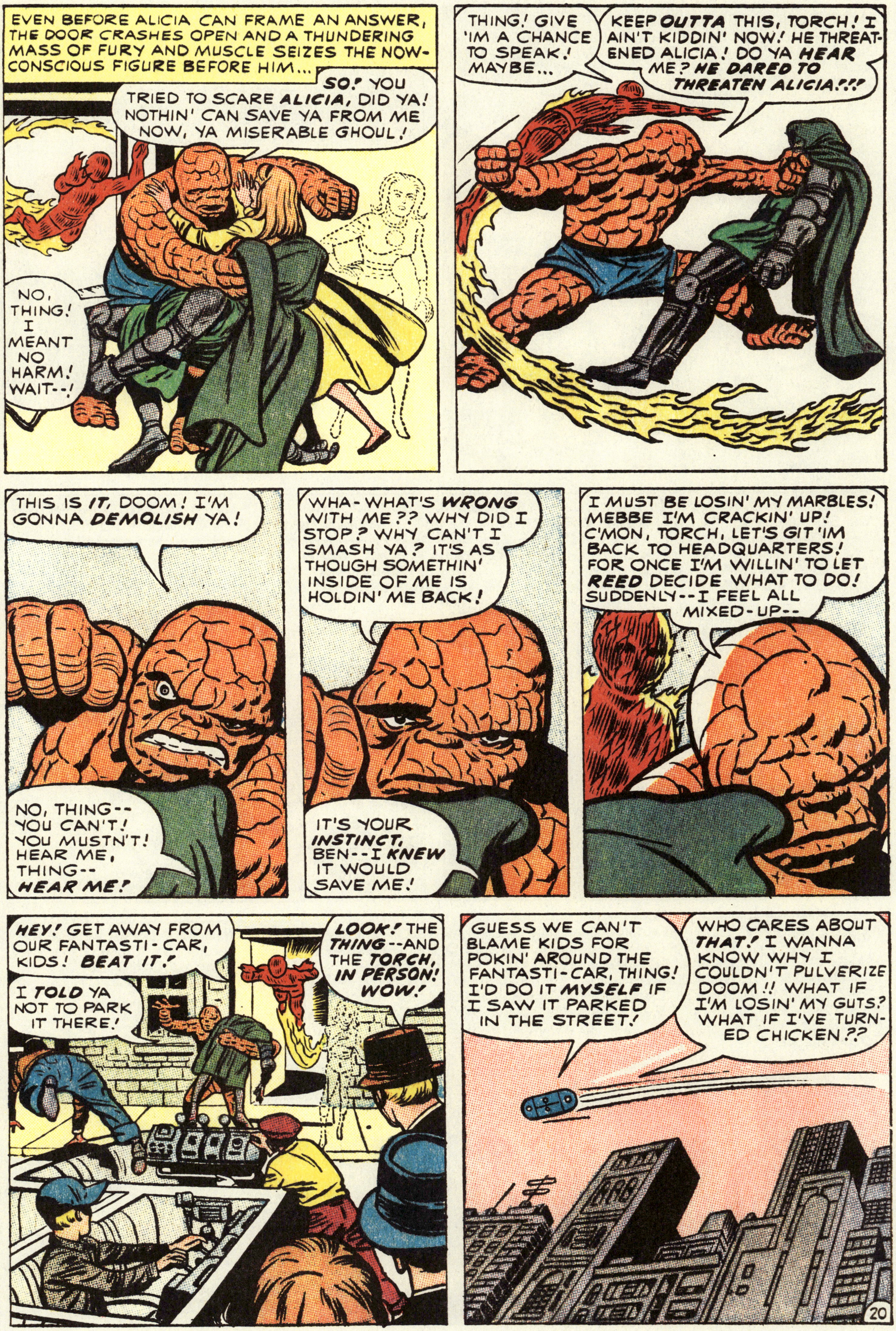
EVEN BEFORE ALICIA CAN FRAME AN ANSWER, THE DOOR CRASHES OPEN AND A THUNDERING MASS OF FURY AND MUSCLE SEIZES THE NOW-CONSCIOUS FIGURE BEFORE HIM...
SO! YOU TRIED TO SCARE ALICIA, DID YA! NOTHIN' CAN SAVE YA FROM ME NOW, YA MISERABLE GHOUL!
NO, THING! I MEANT NO HARM! WAIT--!
THING! GIVE 'IM A CHANCE TO SPEAK! MAYBE...
KEEP OUTTA THIS, TORCH! I AIN'T KIDDIN' NOW! HE THREATENED ALICIA! DO YA HEAR ME? HE DARED TO THREATEN ALICIA!?!
THIS IS IT, DOOM! I'M GONNA DEMOLISH YA!
NO, THING-- YOU CAN'T! YOU MUSTN'T! HEAR ME, THING-- HEAR ME!
WHA- WHAT'S WRONG WITH ME?? WHY DID I STOP? WHY CAN'T I SMASH YA? IT'S AS THOUGH SOMETHIN' INSIDE OF ME IS HOLDIN' ME BACK!
IT'S YOUR INSTINCT, BEN--I KNEW IT WOULD SAVE ME!
I MUST BE LOSIN' MY MARBLES! MEBBE I'M CRACKIN' UP! C'MON, TORCH, LET'S GIT 'IM BACK TO HEADQUARTERS! FOR ONCE I'M WILLIN' TO LET REED DECIDE WHAT TO DO! SUDDENLY--I FEEL ALL MIXED-UP--
HEY! GET AWAY FROM OUR FANTASTI-CAR, KIDS! BEAT IT!
I TOLD YA NOT TO PARK IT THERE!
LOOK! THE THING--AND THE TORCH, IN PERSON! WOW!
GUESS WE CAN'T BLAME KIDS FOR POKIN' AROUND THE FANTASTI-CAR, THING! I'D DO IT MYSELF IF I SAW IT PARKED IN THE STREET!
WHO CARES ABOUT THAT! I WANNA KNOW WHY I COULDN'T PULVERIZE DOOM!! WHAT IF I'M LOSIN' MY GUTS? WHAT IF I'VE TURNED CHICKEN??
20

AND SO...
BLAST THE LUCK! HOW DID RICHARDS ESCAPE?? I'VE GOT TO MOVE FAST NOW!
REED, WE BROUGHT DOCTOR DOOM HERE, SO YOU COULD TELL US WHAT TO DO WITH HIM!
NO--NO! DON'T ASK HIM! NOT HIM! HOW CAN I CONVINCE YOU?? THERE MUST BE SOME WAY!
THERE! I PUT ELECTRONIC COIL ROPES ON HIS WRISTS! THEY'LL KEEP HIM HARMLESS FOR AWHILE! NOW LET'S GET TO THE RAY! ONCE I'VE INCREASED YOUR POWERS, YOU'LL BE BETTER ABLE TO DEAL WITH DR. DOOM!
CAN'T WASTE A SECOND! I'VE GOT TO DISPOSE OF THESE THREE WHILE RICHARDS IS HELPLESS!
THAT'S IT, SUE! NOW YOU STAND NEXT TO HER, TORCH--AND YOU TOO, THING! THIS IS A GREAT MOMENT FOR US!
THEY'LL NEVER KNOW HOW GREAT! IN A FEW SECONDS I'LL BE RID OF THEM FOREVER! AND THEN I CAN FINISH MR. FANTASTIC OFF AT MY LEISURE!
BUT, AT THAT INSTANT, A DESPERATE FIGURE HURLS HIMSELF INTO THE ROOM...
DON'T DO IT! DON'T LET HIM TRAIN THAT RAY ON YOU! BELIEVE WHAT YOU WANT ABOUT ME, BUT DON'T TRUST HIM! HE'LL DESTROY YOU!
STAY BACK, YOU MEDDLING FOOL! BACK, I SAY!
NOW I KNOW WHAT'S BEEN BUGGIN' ME! IT SOUNDS CRAZY BUT REED SOMEHOW DON'T SOUND LIKE REED!
I'VE BEEN THINKING THE SAME THING! LET ME HANDLE THIS, THING! I'VE GOT AN IDEA!
"THERE ARE SOME CONSTRUCTION MEN EXCAVATING A BUILDING FOUNDATION ON THE STREET BELOW! BY CONTROLLING MY HEAT, I CAN WARM UP THE PARTICLES IN THE AIR HERE ENOUGH TO CAUSE A HEAT MIRAGE"...
...MAKING THE DYNAMITE'S REFLECTION SEEM TO BE RIGHT IN THIS ROOM! STAND BACK, THING--AND WATCH!
21

DYNAMITE! ABOUT TO GO OFF!
GOT TO PULL THE FUSE BEFORE SUE AND THE OTHERS ARE INJURED!
DYNAMITE! I'LL SAVE MYSELF BY SLITHERING UP THIS VENT!
HEY! WHERE ARE YOU GOIN'?!
COME BACK HERE, BUSTER! YOU GOT A HEAP OF EXPLAININ' TO DO!
NO! LET GO, YOU FOOL! ARE YOU MAD?!
BROTHER, YOU DON'T KNOW HOW MAD! CRAZY AS IT IS, I BELIEVE THAT YOU AND REED SWITCHED BODIES...
YEAH! MY TRICK WORKED! I KNEW THAT THE REAL DOCTOR DOOM WOULD TRY TO SAVE HIS OWN WORTHLESS HIDE, WHILE THE REAL MR. FANTASTIC WOULD TRY TO SAVE THE REST OF US!
YOU - YOU KNOW ??!!
AND, AT THAT SPLIT-SECOND, UNDER THE STAGGERING SHOCK OF LEARNING THAT HIS INCREDIBLE SCHEME HAS BEEN EXPOSED, DR. DOOM UNTHINKINGLY RELAXES HIS MENTAL CONTROL OVER THE TWO BODIES, AND IN FRONT OF EVERYONE'S STARTLED EYES, THE AWESOME CHANGE TAKES PLACE ONCE MORE!
WHAT HAVE I DONE?! I-I'M MYSELF AGAIN! I'VE FAILED! I'VE BEEN DEFEATED -- BY THE ACCURSED FANTASTIC FOUR!
STOP! STAY BACK! ALL OF YOU! I'M STILL DR. DOOM! YOU'LL NEVER BRING ME TO JUSTICE, DO YOU HEAR! I'LL FIND A WAY TO BEAT YOU YET!
BACK, I SAY! NONE MAY LAY A HAND ON DR. DOOM! I STILL HAVE ONE MORE ACE I CAN PLAY!

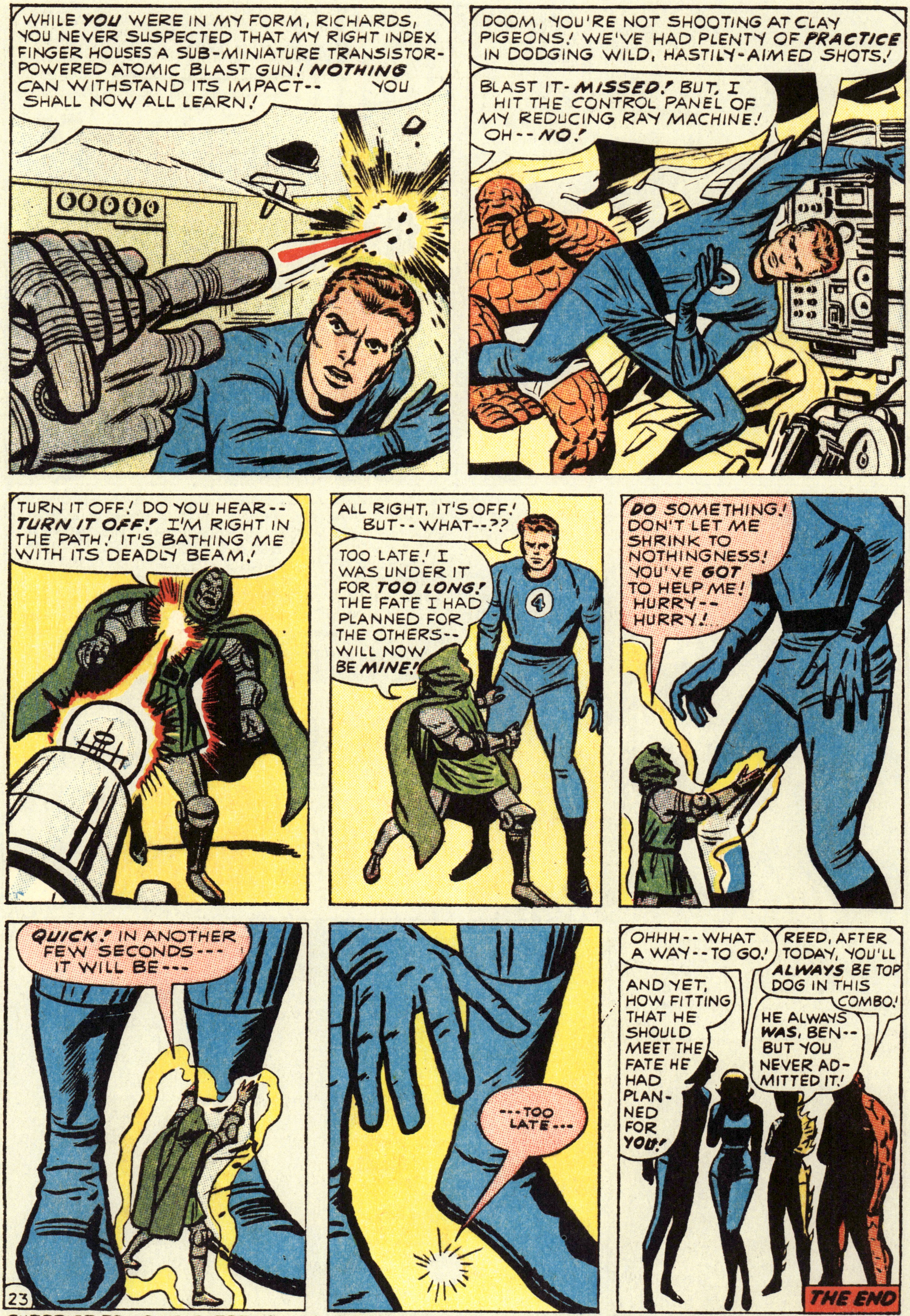

SURPRISE FOLLOWS SURPRISE IN OUR NEXT GREAT ISSUE! MORE THRILLING DETAILS ABOUT THE ***ORIGIN*** OF THE F.F.! A SPECIAL PIN-UP OF ***SUB-MARINER!*** AND--MEET ***THE IMPOSSIBLE MAN!*** RESERVE YOUR COPY TODAY!-- Stan + Jack

Address YOUR letters to:
LEE and KIRBY
FANTASTIC FOUR
THIRD FLOOR
655 MADISON AVE.
NEW YORK 21, N. Y.

FANTASTIC FOUR FAN PAGE

Hi, fans and friends! Look—enough of that "Dear Editor" jazz from now on! Jack Kirby and Stan Lee (that's us!) read every letter personally, and we like to feel that we know you and that you know us! So we changed the salutations in the following letters to show you how much friendlier they sound our way! Also we have a lot of announcements to make this month—but we'll hold them off till after the next letter....

DEAR STAN AND JACK:

In ish #7, on page 11 you have the Fantasti-car flying upside-down when chased by a flying saucer! Since the Fantasti-car is propelled by powerful fans on the bottom, it seems impossible for it to fly in this manner! Anyway, keep up the great work!

David Santiago
San Jose, Calif.

Dave has a good point BUT the Fantasti-car's great speed gives it enough momentum to maintain its trajectory while turning over, until it can regain its normal flying position with its air jets on the bottom.

ANNOUNCEMENT #1: In answer to literally HUNDREDS of requests, we will have a TWO-PAGE fan mail section starting with our next issue!

DEAR STAN:

I'm sure that by now every reader and his mother-in-law has written in to tell you that you are a complete nut! Why? Mainly because in STRANGE TALES #101 you had the audacity to say that no one knows that Johnny is the Torch! Every bona fide FF reader knows that is no secret! Well, don't despair! I have risen from my stack of comics to defend you! As you no doubt know, you were the first to do away with those foolish comic idiosyncrasies known as "secret identities." Of course, everyone loved this and FF became a smash hit. Then, you decide to put your best character, the Human Torch, in STRANGE TALES. Something in the process got mixed up and you said he had a—should I say it?—secret identity! Well, that lone story showed how foolish that business is, like the time Johnny had to make a false Torch! NOW the reader really appreciates that the FF are "secret identityless!" One other point, please print some longer letters. Short letters don't allow the full expression of the reader, and are not as enjoyable.

Steve Stern
Oceanside, N. Y.

Many readers have written to call our attention to the Torch's secret identity fluff also, Steve! We did our best to straighten the whole thing out satisfactorily (we hope) in STRANGE TALES #106, which will go on sale Dec. 10th. See if you approve of the way we tried to wiggle out of our king-sized error.

DEAR EDITORS OF THE GREATEST COMIC MAG:

(NOTE: That's ONE salutation we won't change—Stan and Jack) Your comics are the best I've ever read. At one time I had all seven FF's, but when I returned from summer camp I discovered that someone had swiped issues #1 and #2. So, if any fan is willing to sell either one or both for 35¢ apiece, I will gladly buy them. Please print my complete address.

Rob Sansing
3507 Firestone Blvd.
Pensacola, Florida

And that brings us to ANNOUNCEMENT #2: We have been beseiged with requests for back issues of FF. Unfortunately, our supply of copies from #1 to #9 is completely exhausted. If anyone has a large supply to sell, we would be glad to print his name and address in this column for the benefit of our readers. But, in the meantime, to avoid disappointment, we suggest you reserve your issues in advance at your local magazine stand.

DEAR STAN AND JACK:

How long has it been since you were told FF is the world's greatest comic? Pretty often, huh? Well, it is and it has been for the past seven issues, and here's why: ISSUE #1: You introduced a completely original team of super-heroes. ISSUE #2: You developed their personalities realistically. ISSUE #3: You gave them a fabulous headquarters, costumes, and assorted gimmicks. ISSUE #4: You gave us Sub-Mariner, the greatest off-beat villain ever. ISSUE #5: You topped Sub Mariner with Doctor Doom! ISSUE #6: You united those two villains and best of all, you became a monthly mag. ISSUE #7: For the first time in my memory, you had a team of heroes hated by the human race! But now, my question is: Can you produce another seven or more, just as original, just as well-written and well-drawn? Or will you fade into oblivion? Here's hoping you and the Hulk, Thor, Antman, and Spiderman stick around for a long time.

Lee Cohen
Skokie, Ill.

Thanks Lee—and now, the remainder of our announcements: Spiderman, who last appeared in AMAZING FANTASY #15, has made no new appearances for a few months, because we waited to see what the fans thought of him. Well, your reaction has been terrific, and so we are launching a new series of Spiderman tales which will go on sale the beginning of December. More details next ish.

Here are the results of some polls taken from your letters: Some issues back a reader suggested eliminating the Invisible Girl from FF. You fans were definite in your reaction. Eight letters favored dropping Sue Storm, BUT 639 demanded that she remain one of the team! The vote with regard to adding new members to the FF is still a close one. So far, 422 readers have asked for new members, while 486 favor keeping the original four with no new additions—except for guest star appearances.

DEAR STAN AND JACK:

I have a comic fan club organized and we publish a fanzine each month in which we discuss new comics that come out, and old ones, etc. Would you ask any interested readers to contact me?

G. B. Love
9875 S.W. 212th Street
Miami 57, Florida

And that brings us to our FINAL announcement—we cannot stem the tide of demands to have the FF meet THE HULK! And so, in a future issue of FF we think you will find one of the most unusual and thought-provoking tales of all, as the FF and THE HULK come face to face! Watch for it! See you next month!—Stan & Jack.

HERE'S SOMETHING YOU'VE ALWAYS WANTED!
STORYLAND SERIES
OF EXCITING SUBJECTS FOR ALL AGES, IN FULL COLOR
• ORBITAL FLIGHTS • TRAVEL • SCIENCE • STORIES
—at lowest prices ever offered!
14 FULL COLOR TRANSPARENCIES $1.00 POSTPAID
MADE ON GENUINE EASTMAN COLOR FILM
PLUS STURDY PLASTIC
MAGIC VIEWER
Here's an opportunity for you to develop a complete 35 MM library IN FULL COLOR. Choose those subjects you prefer — be the envy of all your friends. Extra cards, consisting of 14 colorful transparencies, with individual captions, cost only 50¢ each . . . minimum order 2 for $1.00. Check those titles you want and get set for many hours of pleasure.
Send for free booklet of listings and titles.
AT YOUR DEALER'S — OR ORDER DIRECTLY FROM US
For the Family
TRAVEL TOUR BARGAIN-PAKS
SEE THE WORLD VIA 40 FULL COLOR 2" x 2" SLIDES
$10 VALUE —ONLY $3.95
SELECT LOCALE YOU WANT —CHOICE OF 50 TOURS
CHECK THE SET YOU WANT ($1.00 INCL. VIEWER)
ADDITIONAL SUBJECTS ONLY 50¢ EACH
Story of Fire
The Land of Oz
The Nightingale
Johnny Appleseed
Make a Puppet, Part 1
Make a Puppet, Part 2
Shadow Play is Fun
Animals in the Zoo
Daniel Boone
Pinocchio
Jack and Beanstalk
Indian Life
What Will Weather Be
Calendar Tells When
How We Tell Time
Happy Halloween
Can You Make Change?
What's in the Atom
Force Called Gravity
Rocket to the Moon
Through the Microscope
How Rivers Are Formed
The Story of Early Man
How Color TV Works
The Work of the Blood
Man from the Dim Past
A Man-Made Moon
The Amazing Ben Franklin
Birth of Nat'l. Anthem
How We Elect Presidents
Christopher Columbus
Adventures of Marco Polo
Alaska—Our 49th State
UNIVERSAL COLOR SLIDES CO.
428-A East 89th Street
New York 28, N. Y.
Enclosed please find $________. Send me all subjects checked.
Name
Address
City ______ Zone ____ State ____

New ACCORDIONS—SAVE up to 1/2
off retail prices of comparable accordions—DIRECT IMPORTER-TO-YOU!
TRADE-INS WELCOMED
Small Down Payment
BUY ON E-Z TERMS
5-DAY FREE TRIAL
OVER 30 MODELS for STUDENTS TEACHERS PROFESSIONALS
WORLD'S LARGEST ACCORDION DEALER brings you these sensational values! Prices slashed on all our fine Italian-made accordions! Play the most popular instrument of all. Have fun, be a leader! Choose over 30 newest models that lead the world in superb tone and breath-taking beauty. All latest improvements and features. Buy direct from the importer. You save up to 50% off retail prices of comparable accordions. Small down payment; pay the balance on easiest terms. Big trade-in allowance. Try before you buy on FREE 5-DAY NO RISK PLAN. Complete satisfaction assured!
LIFETIME GUARANTEE
Your A. C. A. Accordion is guaranteed against original defects in workmanship and materials for the life of the instrument. Parts and labor free. Rush coupon for big new Color Catalogs and low Importer-to-You Prices . . . FREE. No obligation. Write!
FREE BONUS GIFTS for promptness...
• Easy-to-play music
• Music Stand
• Name in chrome letters
• Deluxe Case
• Music Portfolio
Plus Other Valuable Gifts
Accordion Corporation of America
Dept. MV-102, 2003 W. Chicago Ave., Chicago 22, Ill.
FREE! GET COLOR CATALOG and Importer-to-You Prices
Accordion Corporation of America, Dept. MV-102
2003 W. Chicago Ave., Chicago 22, Ill.
Send Free Color Catalogs and Importer-to-You Prices.
NAME
ADDRESS
CITY ______ ZONE ___ STATE ______

HEY KIDS
BE A WHEEL IN THE NEIGHBORHOOD WITH THE NEW
IT'S NEW, IT'S FUN, IT'S SAFER
YOU CAN NOW DRIVE YOUR BIKE LIKE A CAR . . . NO MORE OLD FASHIONED HANDLE BARS
It's safer. No more bars to poke and hurt you.
Perrywheel®
YOU CAN INSTALL IT YOURSELF. IT'S EASY!
CONSTRUCTION
Plastic guard, chrome rim and bar
Sizes—Bike . . . 14″
Tricycle . . . 11″
Color—Red or White
RUSH!!! MAIL IN TODAY
PERRY SAFETY WHEEL CORP., Dept. 101
6226 So. Western Ave., L.A. 47, California
Please Send Perrywheel
SIZE COLOR PRICE
☐ 14″ Size for Bike ☐ R ☐ W 3.98
☐ 11″ Size for Tricycle ☐ R ☐ W 3.69
Name
Address
City State
SEND $3.00 DOWN FOR C.O.D. ORDERS

KISSING DOLLS!
ONLY 50c Complete Set
THEY JUST CAN'T STAY APART!
These adorable imported 3 dimensional dolls rush together to kiss as soon as they are placed near each other. Great fun for kids 6 to 60.
They change positions, move and turn their heads. 3 inches tall, unbreakable, and life like color that actually looks alive! Self-operating, nothing to get out of order. A wonderful value at our price of only 50¢ per set. Supply is limited, rush your order now.
MALCO CO., Dept. 198-M
117 Utterby Road, Malverne, N. Y.
Please send me .... sets of Kissing Dolls.
☐ 1 set for 50¢ ☐ 2 sets for $1.00
☐ 3 sets for $1.50
Limit 3 sets to a customer.
I enclose ☐ cash ☐ check ☐ money order
Sorry, No C.O.D.'s
Name
Address
City Zone State

BOYS, GIRLS, MEN, WOMEN

IF YOU KNOW JUST 20 PEOPLE...

YOU CAN MAKE AT LEAST $50.00 -MORE LIKELY $100.00 to $200.00 IN YOUR SPARE TIME!

Get These 2 Assortments ON APPROVAL

YULETIDE CHARM ASS'T. *(top)* is a tremendous value! 21 beautiful, sparkling cards glowing and glistening with old-fashioned Christmas cheer!

REGAL LUSTRE ASS'T. *(bottom)* . . . 21 magnificent cards on lustrous Kromekote paper, enriched with gold bronzing and sparkling decorations. Sells on sight!

Everyone You Know Needs Christmas Cards and Everyone Loves Wallace Brown Cards

Do you know 20 people? Of course you do! Add up a half-dozen relatives, perhaps 5 neighbors, the butcher, the baker, the milkman, the grocer, your dentist, several friends and other tradespeople—and you've probably got a lot more than 20. So what are you waiting for? These folks alone can bring you in at least $50.00, probably $100.00 to $200.00 extra money in just a few hours spare time. And this is just a start! Almost *everyone* you know needs Christmas Cards, and when you show them the spectacular nationally famous 1962 Wallace Brown Line of Cards and Gift Items—it's love at first sight. They'll snap up 2, 3, 6 or more Christmas Card Boxes right on the spot. Keep up to 50¢ of every dollar you take in! This is the fun way of making money because it's so easy. We send you samples that do the selling for you. And, besides making money you'll save money on your own personal Christmas Cards, Gifts, Wrappings, etc. See for yourself without risking a penny. Mail coupon, you'll be glad you did!

GET FREE CATALOG, TOO!

–Send Coupon Below

Be first in your neighborhood to cash in on this easy way to extra money with the 1962 Wallace Brown Line of Christmas Cards and Gift Items. Mail coupon this minute! You'll get 2 Christmas Card Assortments on approval. And FREE Samples of Name-Imprinted Personal Christmas Cards. Plus FREE full-color catalog showing lots more money-makers, including many Christmas Assortments, Everyday Greeting Card Assortments, Decorated Stationery, Gift Wrappings, Novelty Gifts, etc. Everything you need to start making money at once—and we show you how.

FREE Samples of Popular-Priced, Name-Imprinted PERSONAL CHRISTMAS CARDS

Thrill your friends and neighbors and make even MORE MONEY for yourself with exquisite, custom-designed NAME-IMPRINTED Christmas Cards at amazingly low prices. A large variety of exclusive, original designs for folks who want the finest quality in Personalized Christmas Cards at prices everybody can afford. They sell just by being shown. It's easy, too, because . . . *we ship direct to your customers and we pay the postage.* You have no bother, no trouble and no wasted time making deliveries. Send the coupon right away for your FREE Samples of the 4 Great New Lines of these fast-selling Personalized Christmas Cards!

ORGANIZATIONS:

Churches, clubs, veterans' auxiliaries, etc. can now add hundreds of dollars to their treasuries with these fast sellers. Give organization name on coupon for Fund-Raising Plan. Mail coupon NOW!

Wallace Brown, Inc. 11 East 26th St., Dept. D-134 New York 10, New York

SEND NO MONEY Paste Coupon on postcard or mail in envelope

WALLACE BROWN, INC., 11 East 26th St. Dept. D-134 New York 10, N.Y.

Send 2 Christmas Card Assortments on approval, plus FREE Samples of Name-Imprinted Personal Christmas Cards, FREE full-color Catalog, and details of simple money-making plan.

Name____________________

Address____________________

City & Zone______________ State________

If writing for an organization, give its name____________________

IND.
THE WORLD'S GREATEST COMIC MAGAZINE!
APPROVED BY THE COMICS CODE AUTHORITY
12¢
THE Fantastic FOUR
MC
11 FEB.
WHAT'S GOING ON HERE? WHY IS THE FANTASTIC FOUR BACKING AWAY HELPLESSLY FROM... "THE IMPOSSIBLE MAN" ?????
DON'T MISS THIS GREAT OFF-BEAT COLLECTORS' ITEM ISSUE!
Also: YOU REQUESTED... "A DAY WITH THE FANTASTIC FOUR!"
FEATURING NEVER-BEFORE-REVEALED FACTS ABOUT THE F.F.'s PAST AND PRESENT!

SHOP BY MAIL

STAMPS

THE FANTASTIC FOUR is published by CANAM PUBLISHERS SALES CORP. OFFICE OF PUBLICATION: 655 MADISON AVENUE, NEW YORK, N.Y. Published monthly. Copyright 1962 by CANAM PUBLISHERS SALES CORP., 655 Madison Avenue, New York, N.Y. Vol. 1 No. 11 FEBRUARY, 1963 issue. Price 12¢ per copy. Subscription rate $1.75 for 12 issues including postage. Foreign subscription $3.25 in American funds. No similarity between any of the names, characters, persons, and/or institutions appearing in this magazine with those of any living or dead person is intended, and any such similarity which may exist is purely coincidental. Printed in U.S.A. by The Eastern Color Printing Co., Waterbury 20, Conn.

SPECIAL BONUS TO OUR READERS!
Presenting: THE TYPE OF STORY MOST REQUESTED BY YOUR LETTERS AND POST CARDS...
A VISIT WITH the FANTASTIC FOUR
SAY, FELLA, WHAT'S EVERYONE STANDIN' ON LINE FOR?
GET WITH IT, PEANUT! THIS IS THE DAY THE NEW FANTASTIC FOUR COMES OUT!
HEY! COME ON-- KEEP THAT LINE MOVIN'!
HMMM, LOOKS AS THOUGH WE'LL HAVE TO WAIT OUR TURN TO GET THE LATEST ISSUE!
OH, LET'S JUST COME BACK LATER, REED!
I TOLD YA WE SHOULDA GOTTEN HERE SOONER!
WHAT'S THE BIG DEAL? WE KNOW HOW THE STORIES END!
FANTASTIC FAN PAGE 4
HEY, CHARLIE, LOOK! I JUST GOT THE LATEST COPY! AND MY LETTER'S ON THE FAN PAGE!
SCRIPT: STAN LEE • ART: JACK KIRBY • INKING: DICK AYERS • LETTERING: ART SIMEK
X-72

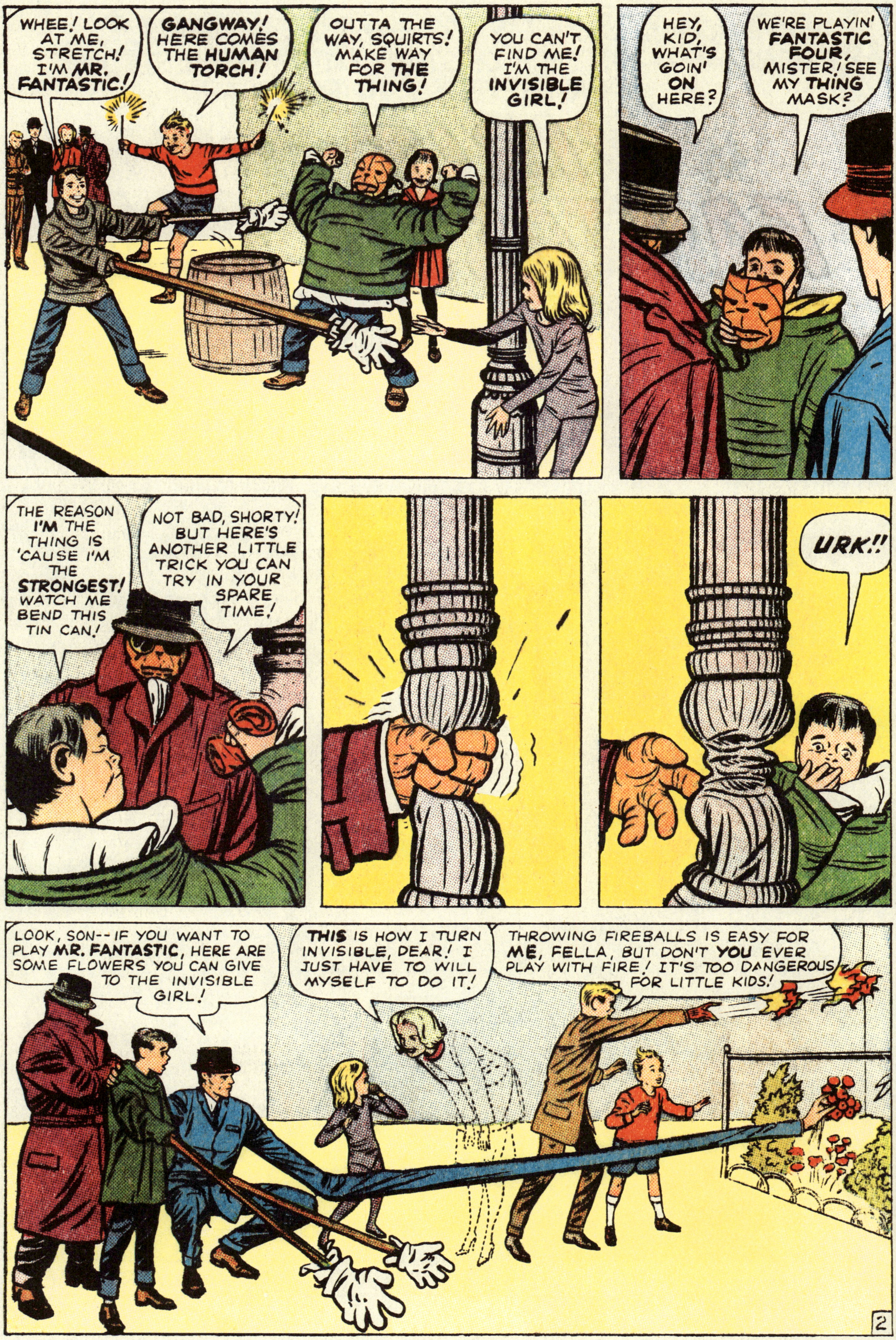
WHEE! LOOK AT ME, STRETCH! I'M MR. FANTASTIC!
GANGWAY! HERE COMES THE HUMAN TORCH!
OUTTA THE WAY, SQUIRTS! MAKE WAY FOR THE THING!
YOU CAN'T FIND ME! I'M THE INVISIBLE GIRL!
HEY, KID, WHAT'S GOIN' ON HERE?
WE'RE PLAYIN' FANTASTIC FOUR, MISTER! SEE MY THING MASK?
THE REASON I'M THE THING IS 'CAUSE I'M THE STRONGEST! WATCH ME BEND THIS TIN CAN!
NOT BAD, SHORTY! BUT HERE'S ANOTHER LITTLE TRICK YOU CAN TRY IN YOUR SPARE TIME!
URK!!
LOOK, SON-- IF YOU WANT TO PLAY MR. FANTASTIC, HERE ARE SOME FLOWERS YOU CAN GIVE TO THE INVISIBLE GIRL!
THIS IS HOW I TURN INVISIBLE, DEAR! I JUST HAVE TO WILL MYSELF TO DO IT!
THROWING FIREBALLS IS EASY FOR ME, FELLA, BUT DON'T YOU EVER PLAY WITH FIRE! IT'S TOO DANGEROUS FOR LITTLE KIDS!
2

GOSH! DO YOU KNOW WHO THEY WERE?!!
THEY WERE SO CLOSE I COULDA REACHED OUT 'N TOUCHED 'EM!
SO LONG, YOUNGSTERS! IT WAS NICE MEETING YOU!
I GUESS THEY'LL HAVE SOMETHING TO TALK ABOUT FOR A WHILE!
SURE-- THEY'LL TELL HOW THEY MET FOUR FREAKS IN THE STREET!
AW, CHEER UP, THING! IT ISN'T-- SAY! LOOK WHO'S HERE!
THIS DAD-BURNED MAIL SACK GETS HEAVIER EVERY DAY! BLASTED FAN LETTERS!
IT'S MR. LUMPKIN, WITH OUR DAILY MAIL DELIVERY! WHY DON'T ONE OF YOU BOYS GIVE HIM A HAND?
WHATCHA GRIPIN' ABOUT, LUMPY? IT AIN'T SO HEAVY!
MY! COULD WE USE YOU IN THE POST OFFICE DEPARTMENT, MR. THING!
BY THE WAY, MR. RICHARDS, ARE YOU LOOKIN' TO HIRE ANY NEW MEMBERS FOR YOUR GROUP? I HAVEN'T EXACTLY GOT ANY SUPER POWERS, BUT I CAN WIGGLE MY EARS REAL GOOD, AND--
WE'RE ALL FILLED UP RIGHT NOW, LUMPY, BUT WE'LL KEEP YOU IN MIND, OLD TIMER!
C'MON, SUE, LET'S OPEN THE ELEVATOR DOOR AND GO UPSTAIRS! IT'S GONNA TAKE FOREVER TO GET THRU ALL THAT FAN MAIL!
DON'T BE IMPATIENT, LITTLE BROTHER! I'VE GOT TO DO THIS BY THE NUMBERS!
FIRST, I'LL SLIDE THE HIDDEN PANEL ASIDE ON MY BELT TO ACTIVATE THE ELECTRONIC BEAM!
AW, COME OFF IT, SIS! YOU'RE BEGINNIN' TO SOUND LIKE A MAD SCIENTIST ON THE LATE SHOW!
DON'T BE DISRESPECTFUL TO YOUR ELDERS, JOHNNY BOY!
OKAY, "GRAN'MA" !!
3

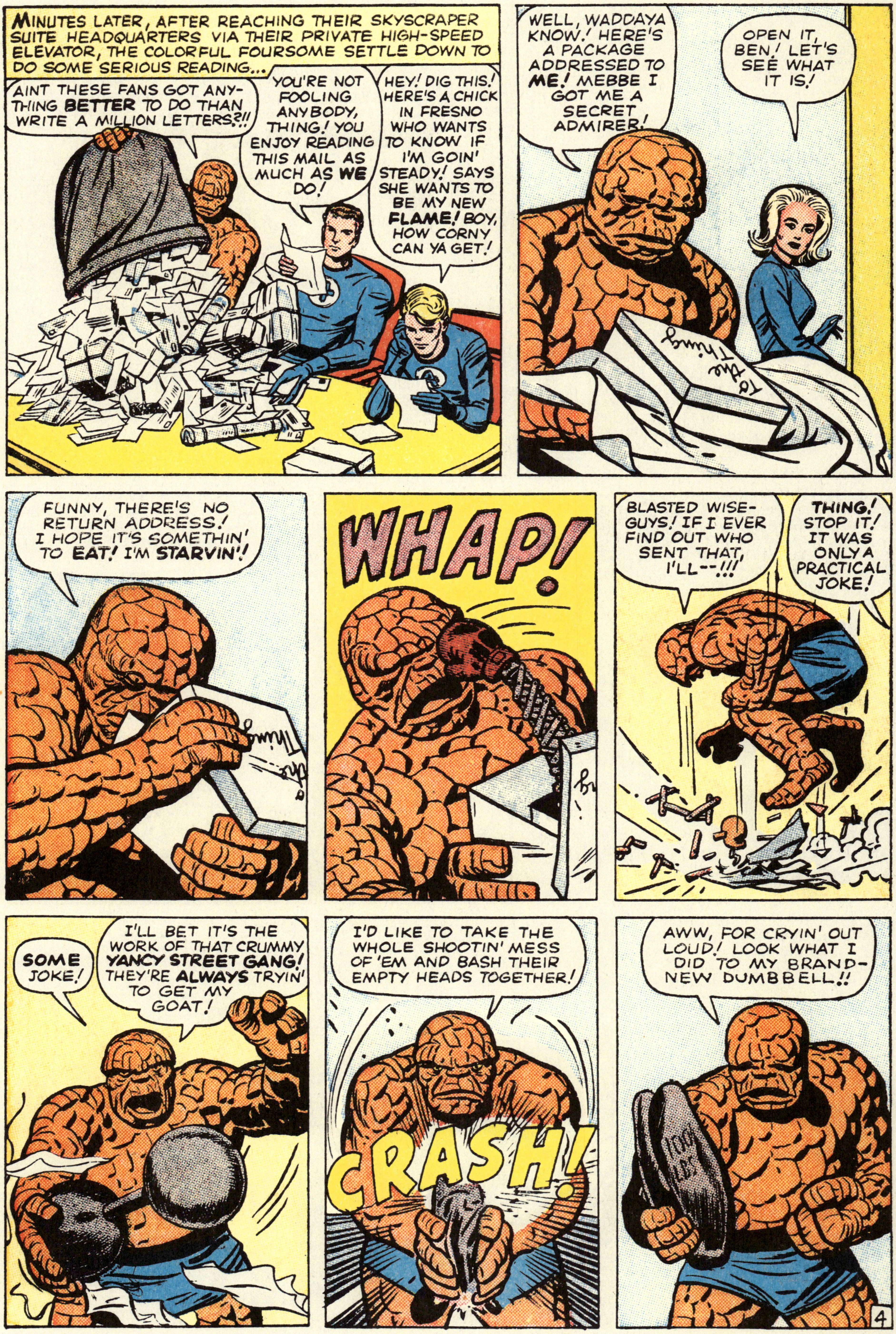
MINUTES LATER, AFTER REACHING THEIR SKYSCRAPER SUITE HEADQUARTERS VIA THEIR PRIVATE HIGH-SPEED ELEVATOR, THE COLORFUL FOURSOME SETTLE DOWN TO DO SOME SERIOUS READING...
AINT THESE FANS GOT ANYTHING BETTER TO DO THAN WRITE A MILLION LETTERS?!!
YOU'RE NOT FOOLING ANYBODY, THING! YOU ENJOY READING THIS MAIL AS MUCH AS WE DO!
HEY! DIG THIS! HERE'S A CHICK IN FRESNO WHO WANTS TO KNOW IF I'M GOIN' STEADY! SAYS SHE WANTS TO BE MY NEW FLAME! BOY, HOW CORNY CAN YA GET!
WELL, WADDAYA KNOW! HERE'S A PACKAGE ADDRESSED TO ME! MEBBE I GOT ME A SECRET ADMIRER!
OPEN IT, BEN! LET'S SEE WHAT IT IS!
FUNNY, THERE'S NO RETURN ADDRESS! I HOPE IT'S SOMETHIN' TO EAT! I'M STARVIN'!
WHAP!
BLASTED WISE-GUYS! IF I EVER FIND OUT WHO SENT THAT, I'LL--!!!
THING! STOP IT! IT WAS ONLY A PRACTICAL JOKE!
SOME JOKE!
I'LL BET IT'S THE WORK OF THAT CRUMMY YANCY STREET GANG! THEY'RE ALWAYS TRYIN' TO GET MY GOAT!
I'D LIKE TO TAKE THE WHOLE SHOOTIN' MESS OF 'EM AND BASH THEIR EMPTY HEADS TOGETHER!
CRASH!
AWW, FOR CRYIN' OUT LOUD! LOOK WHAT I DID TO MY BRAND-NEW DUMBBELL!!
4

DON'T BLOW YOUR STACK, OLD PAL! HERE, HOLD OUT YOUR HAND --I'VE **GOT** SOMETHING FOR YOU!
KNOCK IT OFF, REED! I AINT IN THE MOOD TO PLAY GAMES NOW!
IT'S NO GAME, BEN! IT'S THE LATEST VERSION OF A NEW SERUM I'VE BEEN WORKING ON FOR YOU!
NUTS! I'M **SICK** OF BEIN' A GUINEA PIG FOR YOU! **NONE** OF THESE THINGS EVER WORK RIGHT!
BUT THIS FORMULA IS **DIFFERENT,** BEN! IT MAY LAST **LONGER** THAN THE OTHERS!
HEY! LOOK HOW **FAST** IT'S WORKIN'! I-I'M TURNIN' INTO A NORMAL MAN AGAIN! I CAN **FEEL** IT!
WELCOME BACK TO THE HUMAN RACE, PARTNER!
REED--DO YOU--DO YOU THINK THAT **THIS** TIME THE CHANGE'LL BE **PERMANENT!**
WE'LL HAVE TO WAIT AND SEE!
OH, BEN, YOU'RE A REAL LIVING DOLL AGAIN! MMMMM **MMM!**
WHO AM **I** TO DISAGREE?
POOR BEN! IF HE CHANGES BACK TO THE THING AGAIN, I DON'T WANNA BE AROUND TO SEE IT!
THE CONVERSATION'S GETTIN' TOO MUSHY, GANG! I'M CUTTIN' OUT FOR A WHILE!
WAIT A MINUTE, JUNIOR! WHAT ABOUT ALL THAT UNFINISHED FAN MAIL?
AW, I'LL READ IT LATER! I'M GONNA GET DOWN TO THE GARAGE AND FOOL AROUND WITH MY NEW TR-4!
POF!
OKAY, KID! SEE YOU LATER!

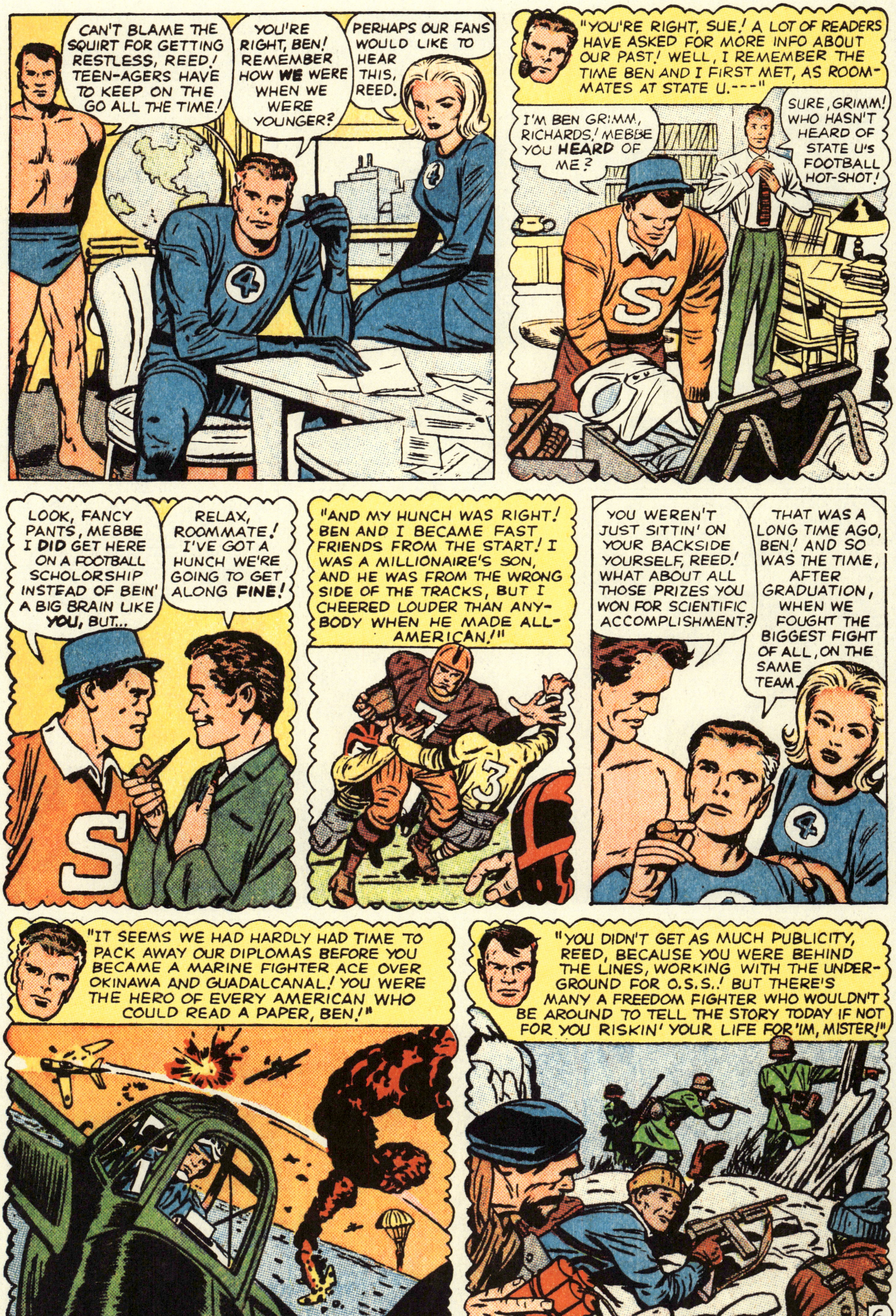

CAN'T BLAME THE SQUIRT FOR GETTING RESTLESS, REED! TEEN-AGERS HAVE TO KEEP ON THE GO ALL THE TIME!
YOU'RE RIGHT, BEN! REMEMBER HOW WE WERE WHEN WE WERE YOUNGER?
PERHAPS OUR FANS WOULD LIKE TO HEAR THIS, REED.
"YOU'RE RIGHT, SUE! A LOT OF READERS HAVE ASKED FOR MORE INFO ABOUT OUR PAST! WELL, I REMEMBER THE TIME BEN AND I FIRST MET, AS ROOM-MATES AT STATE U.---"
I'M BEN GRIMM, RICHARDS! MEBBE YOU HEARD OF ME?
SURE, GRIMM! WHO HASN'T HEARD OF STATE U's FOOTBALL HOT-SHOT!
LOOK, FANCY PANTS, MEBBE I DID GET HERE ON A FOOTBALL SCHOLORSHIP INSTEAD OF BEIN' A BIG BRAIN LIKE YOU, BUT...
RELAX, ROOMMATE! I'VE GOT A HUNCH WE'RE GOING TO GET ALONG FINE!
"AND MY HUNCH WAS RIGHT! BEN AND I BECAME FAST FRIENDS FROM THE START! I WAS A MILLIONAIRE'S SON, AND HE WAS FROM THE WRONG SIDE OF THE TRACKS, BUT I CHEERED LOUDER THAN ANY-BODY WHEN HE MADE ALL-AMERICAN!"
YOU WEREN'T JUST SITTIN' ON YOUR BACKSIDE YOURSELF, REED! WHAT ABOUT ALL THOSE PRIZES YOU WON FOR SCIENTIFIC ACCOMPLISHMENT?
THAT WAS A LONG TIME AGO, BEN! AND SO WAS THE TIME, AFTER GRADUATION, WHEN WE FOUGHT THE BIGGEST FIGHT OF ALL, ON THE SAME TEAM.
"IT SEEMS WE HAD HARDLY HAD TIME TO PACK AWAY OUR DIPLOMAS BEFORE YOU BECAME A MARINE FIGHTER ACE OVER OKINAWA AND GUADALCANAL! YOU WERE THE HERO OF EVERY AMERICAN WHO COULD READ A PAPER, BEN!"
"YOU DIDN'T GET AS MUCH PUBLICITY, REED, BECAUSE YOU WERE BEHIND THE LINES, WORKING WITH THE UNDER-GROUND FOR O.S.S.! BUT THERE'S MANY A FREEDOM FIGHTER WHO WOULDN'T BE AROUND TO TELL THE STORY TODAY IF NOT FOR YOU RISKIN' YOUR LIFE FOR 'IM, MISTER!"
6

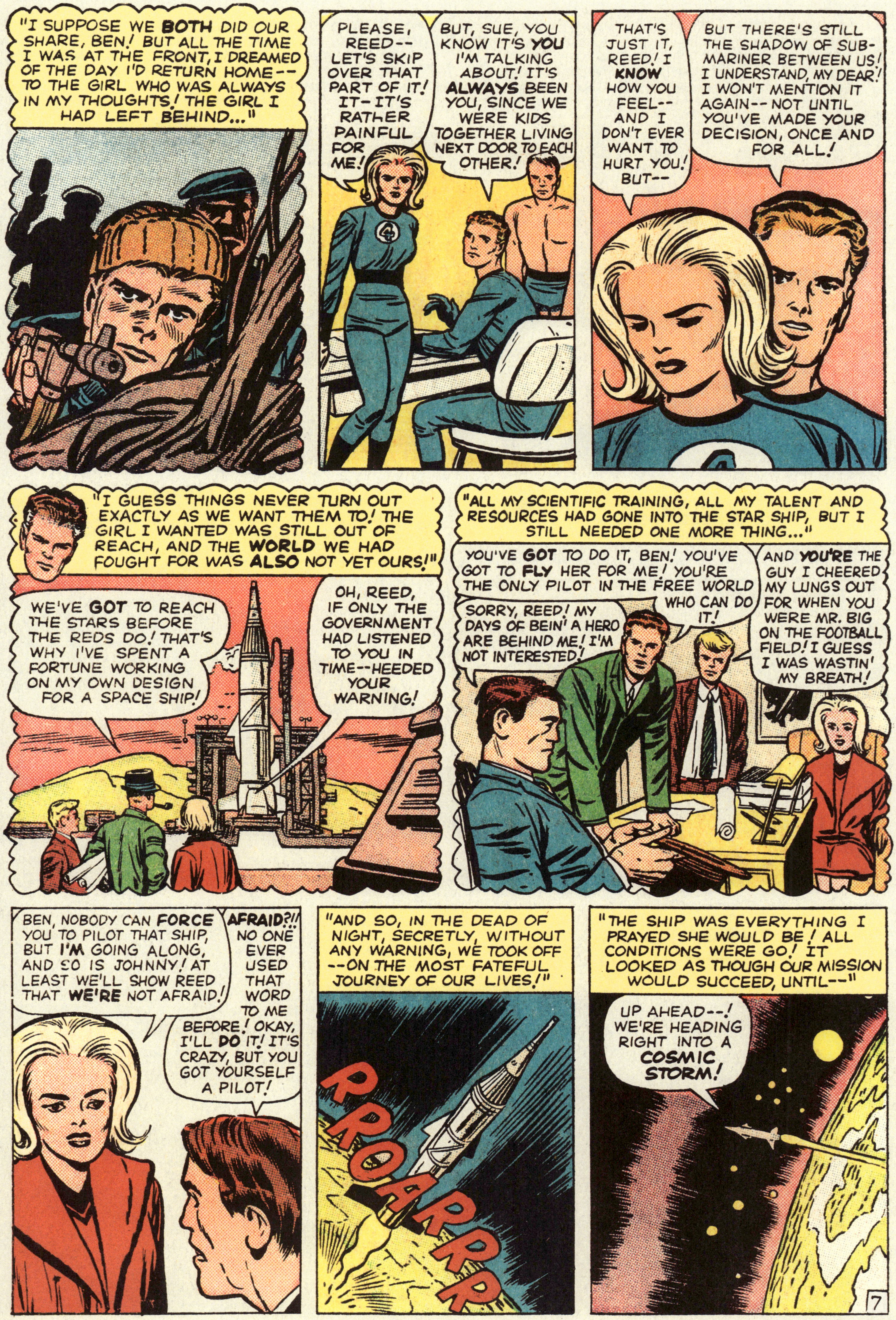

"I SUPPOSE WE BOTH DID OUR SHARE, BEN! BUT ALL THE TIME I WAS AT THE FRONT, I DREAMED OF THE DAY I'D RETURN HOME-- TO THE GIRL WHO WAS ALWAYS IN MY THOUGHTS! THE GIRL I HAD LEFT BEHIND..."
PLEASE, REED-- LET'S SKIP OVER THAT PART OF IT! IT--IT'S RATHER PAINFUL FOR ME!
BUT, SUE, YOU KNOW IT'S YOU I'M TALKING ABOUT! IT'S ALWAYS BEEN YOU, SINCE WE WERE KIDS TOGETHER LIVING NEXT DOOR TO EACH OTHER!
THAT'S JUST IT, REED! I KNOW HOW YOU FEEL-- AND I DON'T EVER WANT TO HURT YOU! BUT--
BUT THERE'S STILL THE SHADOW OF SUB-MARINER BETWEEN US! I UNDERSTAND, MY DEAR! I WON'T MENTION IT AGAIN-- NOT UNTIL YOU'VE MADE YOUR DECISION, ONCE AND FOR ALL!
"I GUESS THINGS NEVER TURN OUT EXACTLY AS WE WANT THEM TO! THE GIRL I WANTED WAS STILL OUT OF REACH, AND THE WORLD WE HAD FOUGHT FOR WAS ALSO NOT YET OURS!"
WE'VE GOT TO REACH THE STARS BEFORE THE REDS DO! THAT'S WHY I'VE SPENT A FORTUNE WORKING ON MY OWN DESIGN FOR A SPACE SHIP!
OH, REED, IF ONLY THE GOVERNMENT HAD LISTENED TO YOU IN TIME--HEEDED YOUR WARNING!
"ALL MY SCIENTIFIC TRAINING, ALL MY TALENT AND RESOURCES HAD GONE INTO THE STAR SHIP, BUT I STILL NEEDED ONE MORE THING..."
YOU'VE GOT TO DO IT, BEN! YOU'VE GOT TO FLY HER FOR ME! YOU'RE THE ONLY PILOT IN THE FREE WORLD WHO CAN DO IT!
SORRY, REED! MY DAYS OF BEIN' A HERO ARE BEHIND ME! I'M NOT INTERESTED!
AND YOU'RE THE GUY I CHEERED MY LUNGS OUT FOR WHEN YOU WERE MR. BIG ON THE FOOTBALL FIELD! I GUESS I WAS WASTIN' MY BREATH!
BEN, NOBODY CAN FORCE YOU TO PILOT THAT SHIP, BUT I'M GOING ALONG, AND SO IS JOHNNY! AT LEAST WE'LL SHOW REED THAT WE'RE NOT AFRAID!
AFRAID?!! NO ONE EVER USED THAT WORD TO ME BEFORE! OKAY, I'LL DO IT! IT'S CRAZY, BUT YOU GOT YOURSELF A PILOT!
"AND SO, IN THE DEAD OF NIGHT, SECRETLY, WITHOUT ANY WARNING, WE TOOK OFF --ON THE MOST FATEFUL JOURNEY OF OUR LIVES!"
RROARRR
"THE SHIP WAS EVERYTHING I PRAYED SHE WOULD BE! ALL CONDITIONS WERE GO! IT LOOKED AS THOUGH OUR MISSION WOULD SUCCEED, UNTIL--"
UP AHEAD--! WE'RE HEADING RIGHT INTO A COSMIC STORM!
7

"COSMIC STORM! THE MYSTERIOUS, DREADED SPACE MENACE WHICH NO HUMANS HAD EVER FACED BEFORE! IT BUFFETED OUR SHIP ABOUT LIKE A FEATHER IN A HURRICANE-- BUT IT DID FAR WORSE THAN THAT..."
"SILENTLY, INVISIBLY, INEXORABLY, THE STRANGE COSMIC RAYS POURED IN THRU THE SHIP, STRIKING ALL OF US WITH A POWER AND A FORCE UNEQUALLED BY ANYTHING IN THE KNOWN UNIVERSE!"
"THE REST WAS LIKE A NIGHTMARE! ONLY BEN'S SUPERB SKILL ENABLED US TO SURVIVE A CRASH LANDING BACK ON EARTH--A LANDING WHICH WAS THE BEGINNING OF THE STRANGEST SAGA WE'VE EVER KNOWN!"
THANK HEAVENS WE'RE ALIVE! WE'RE ALL ALIVE!
"YES, WE WERE ALIVE-- AND MORE THAN JUST ALIVE! MUCH MUCH MORE!"
WHA-WHAT'S HAPPENING TO ME?
I'M CHANGING! I'M TURNING INTO--INTO--
--A THING!
"AND WILL WE EVER FORGET THAT FIRST SIGHT OF JOHNNY, BURSTING INTO LIVING FLAME...?"
JOHNNY! YOUR BODY--IT'S A BLAZE OF FIRE!
I'M A HUMAN TORCH!
I'M LIGHTER THAN AIR!
I CAN FLY!
I CAN DO ANYTHING!

"AND THEN WE SAW SUE TURN INVISIBLE, FADING AWAY IN FRONT OF OUR EYES!"
REED! WHAT'S HAPPENING TO ME??
YOU'RE VANISHING!
WE'VE ALL BEEN AFFECTED BY THE COSMIC RAYS! ALL OF US!
I-I'M AFRAID TO TRY TO GUESS WHAT FANTASTIC CHANGE WILL HAPPEN TO YOU, REED!
"WELL, WE ALL KNOW WHAT HAPPENED TO ME! AND THE WORLD FIRST LEARNED OF IT WHEN I USED MY STRETCHING POWER TO SIGNAL A PASSING JET TO COME AND RESCUE US!"
HE SEES ME!
WE'VE COME A LONG WAY SINCE THOSE EARLY DAYS... AND HAD MANY ALMOST UNBELIEVABLE ADVENTURES!
BUT THEY WERE YOUR ADVENTURES --THE THREE OF YOU-- MUCH MORE THAN MINE!
SUE! WHAT ARE YOU TALKING ABOUT? WHAT DO YOU MEAN?
I-I HADN'T WANTED TO MENTION IT, REED, BUT I'VE GOTTEN SOME LETTERS LATELY --SOME DISTURBING LETTERS!
YOU?? I CAN'T BELIEVE IT! LET US SEE 'EM, SUE!
THERE! A NUMBER OF READERS HAVE SAID THAT I DON'T CONTRIBUTE ENOUGH TO YOU... YOU'D BE --BETTER OFF WITHOUT ME! AND PERHAPS THEY'RE-- RIGHT!
SHE'S NOT EXAGGERATING, BEN! LOOK!
I NEVER EXPECTED ANYTHING LIKE THIS!
WELL, IT'S TIME TO SET THE RECORD STRAIGHT-- HERE AND NOW!
TAKE IT EASY, PAL! THE KIDS DIDN'T MEAN ANY HARM-- THEY JUST DON'T UNDERSTAND!
9

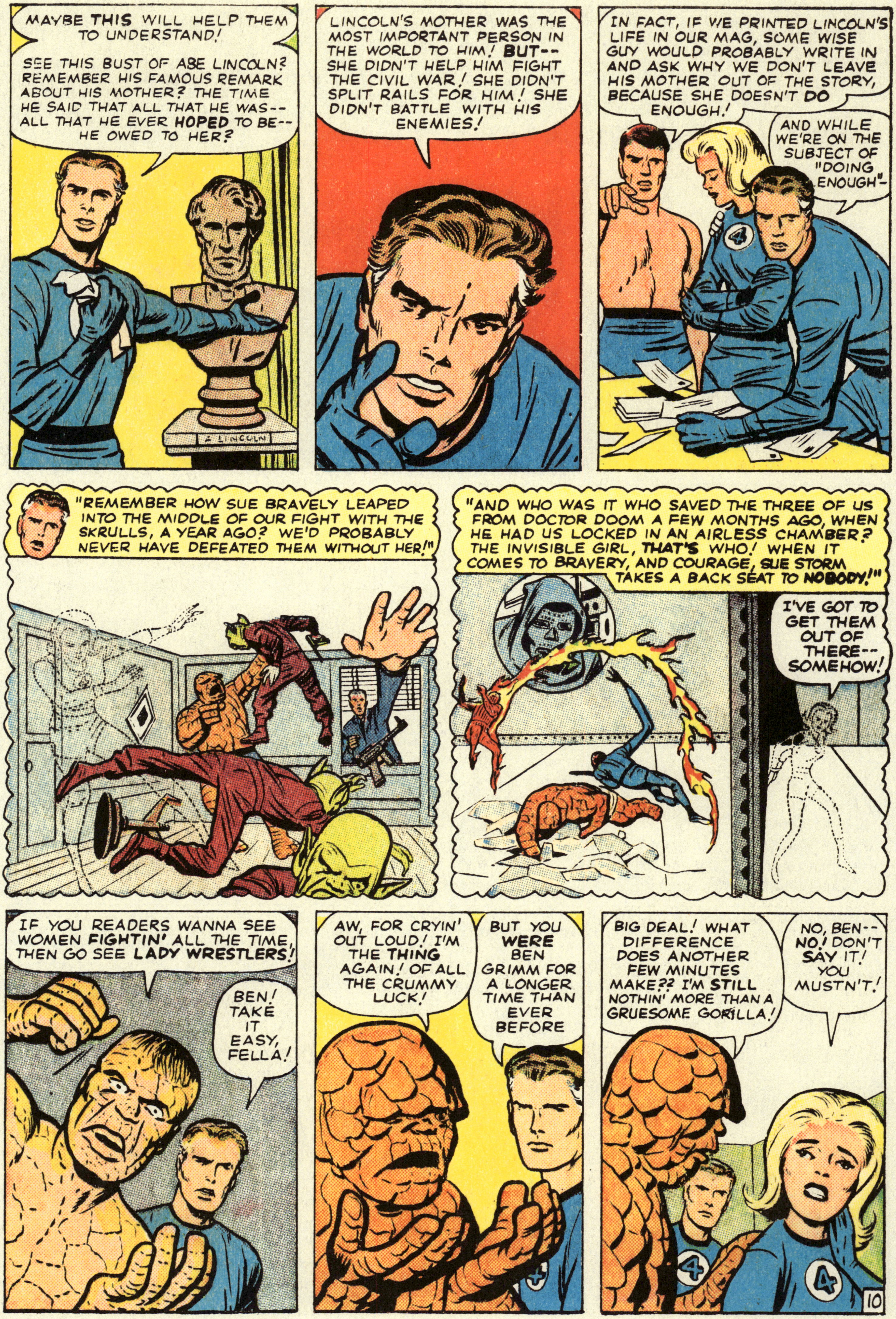
MAYBE THIS WILL HELP THEM TO UNDERSTAND!
SEE THIS BUST OF ABE LINCOLN? REMEMBER HIS FAMOUS REMARK ABOUT HIS MOTHER? THE TIME HE SAID THAT ALL THAT HE WAS-- ALL THAT HE EVER HOPED TO BE-- HE OWED TO HER?
A. LINCOLN
LINCOLN'S MOTHER WAS THE MOST IMPORTANT PERSON IN THE WORLD TO HIM! BUT-- SHE DIDN'T HELP HIM FIGHT THE CIVIL WAR! SHE DIDN'T SPLIT RAILS FOR HIM! SHE DIDN'T BATTLE WITH HIS ENEMIES!
IN FACT, IF WE PRINTED LINCOLN'S LIFE IN OUR MAG, SOME WISE GUY WOULD PROBABLY WRITE IN AND ASK WHY WE DON'T LEAVE HIS MOTHER OUT OF THE STORY, BECAUSE SHE DOESN'T DO ENOUGH!
AND WHILE WE'RE ON THE SUBJECT OF "DOING ENOUGH"--
"REMEMBER HOW SUE BRAVELY LEAPED INTO THE MIDDLE OF OUR FIGHT WITH THE SKRULLS, A YEAR AGO? WE'D PROBABLY NEVER HAVE DEFEATED THEM WITHOUT HER!"
"AND WHO WAS IT WHO SAVED THE THREE OF US FROM DOCTOR DOOM A FEW MONTHS AGO, WHEN HE HAD US LOCKED IN AN AIRLESS CHAMBER? THE INVISIBLE GIRL, THAT'S WHO! WHEN IT COMES TO BRAVERY, AND COURAGE, SUE STORM TAKES A BACK SEAT TO NOBODY!"
I'VE GOT TO GET THEM OUT OF THERE-- SOMEHOW!
IF YOU READERS WANNA SEE WOMEN FIGHTIN' ALL THE TIME, THEN GO SEE LADY WRESTLERS!
BEN! TAKE IT EASY, FELLA!
AW, FOR CRYIN' OUT LOUD! I'M THE THING AGAIN! OF ALL THE CRUMMY LUCK!
BUT YOU WERE BEN GRIMM FOR A LONGER TIME THAN EVER BEFORE
BIG DEAL! WHAT DIFFERENCE DOES ANOTHER FEW MINUTES MAKE?? I'M STILL NOTHIN' MORE THAN A GRUESOME GORILLA!
NO, BEN-- NO! DON'T SAY IT! YOU MUSTN'T!
10

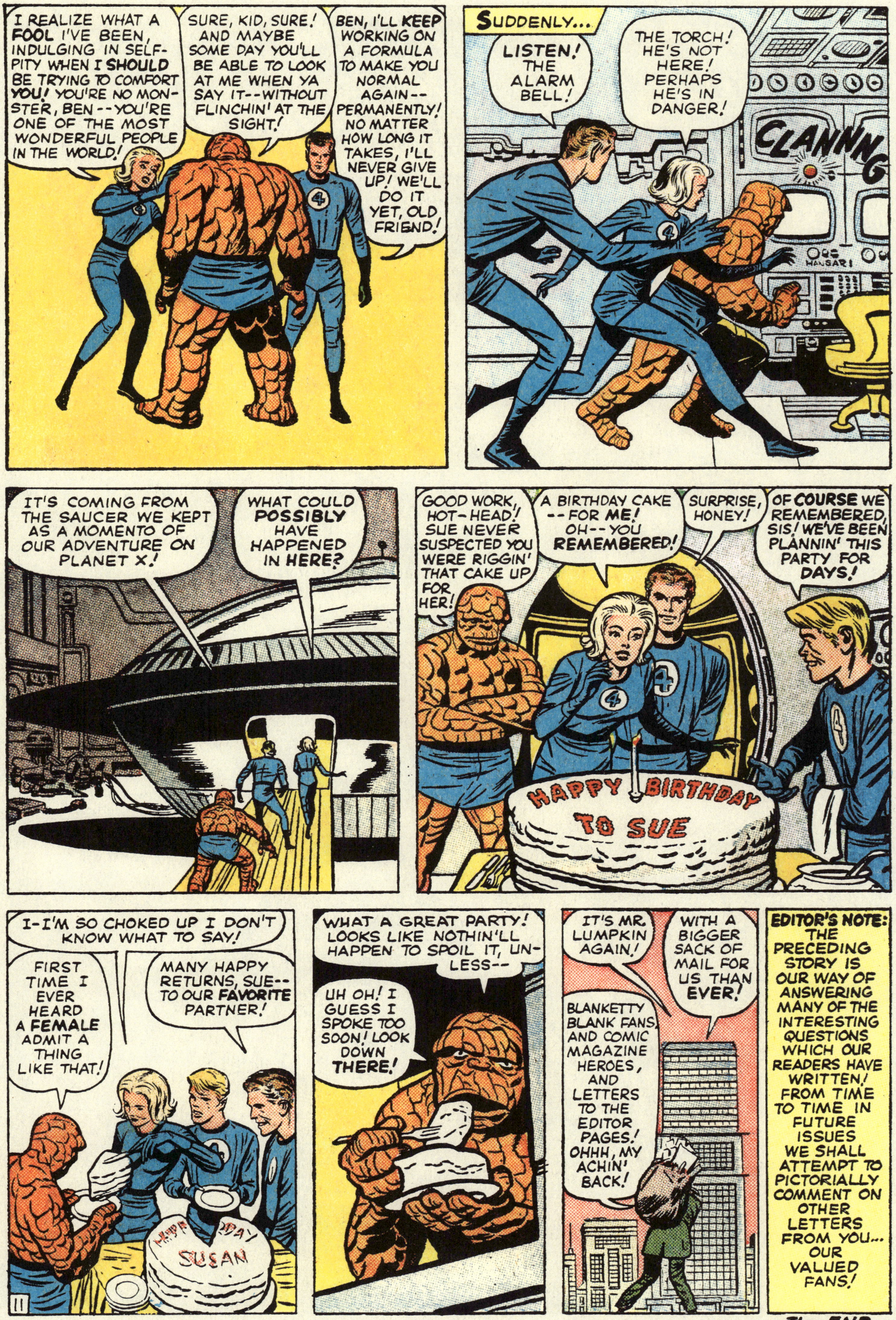
I REALIZE WHAT A FOOL I'VE BEEN, INDULGING IN SELF-PITY WHEN I SHOULD BE TRYING TO COMFORT YOU! YOU'RE NO MONSTER, BEN--YOU'RE ONE OF THE MOST WONDERFUL PEOPLE IN THE WORLD!
SURE, KID, SURE! AND MAYBE SOME DAY YOU'LL BE ABLE TO LOOK AT ME WHEN YA SAY IT--WITHOUT FLINCHIN' AT THE SIGHT!
BEN, I'LL KEEP WORKING ON A FORMULA TO MAKE YOU NORMAL AGAIN--PERMANENTLY! NO MATTER HOW LONG IT TAKES, I'LL NEVER GIVE UP! WE'LL DO IT YET, OLD FRIEND!
SUDDENLY...
LISTEN! THE ALARM BELL!
THE TORCH! HE'S NOT HERE! PERHAPS HE'S IN DANGER!
CLANNNG
IT'S COMING FROM THE SAUCER WE KEPT AS A MOMENTO OF OUR ADVENTURE ON PLANET X!
WHAT COULD POSSIBLY HAVE HAPPENED IN HERE?
GOOD WORK, HOT-HEAD! SUE NEVER SUSPECTED YOU WERE RIGGIN' THAT CAKE UP FOR HER!
A BIRTHDAY CAKE --FOR ME! OH--YOU REMEMBERED!
SURPRISE, HONEY!
OF COURSE WE REMEMBERED, SIS! WE'VE BEEN PLANNIN' THIS PARTY FOR DAYS!
HAPPY BIRTHDAY TO SUE
I-I'M SO CHOKED UP I DON'T KNOW WHAT TO SAY!
FIRST TIME I EVER HEARD A FEMALE ADMIT A THING LIKE THAT!
MANY HAPPY RETURNS, SUE--TO OUR FAVORITE PARTNER!
SUSAN
11
WHAT A GREAT PARTY! LOOKS LIKE NOTHIN'LL HAPPEN TO SPOIL IT, UNLESS--
UH OH! I GUESS I SPOKE TOO SOON! LOOK DOWN THERE!
IT'S MR. LUMPKIN AGAIN!
WITH A BIGGER SACK OF MAIL FOR US THAN EVER!
BLANKETTY BLANK FANS AND COMIC MAGAZINE HEROES, AND LETTERS TO THE EDITOR PAGES! OHHH, MY ACHIN' BACK!
EDITOR'S NOTE: THE PRECEDING STORY IS OUR WAY OF ANSWERING MANY OF THE INTERESTING QUESTIONS WHICH OUR READERS HAVE WRITTEN! FROM TIME TO TIME IN FUTURE ISSUES WE SHALL ATTEMPT TO PICTORIALLY COMMENT ON OTHER LETTERS FROM YOU... OUR VALUED FANS!
The END

AT LAST THE FANTASTIC FOUR MEET A FOE WHOSE POWER IS EVEN GREATER THAN THEIRS!! HERE IS:
THE IMPOSSIBLE MAN
HE'S THE MOST DANGEROUS CREATURE IN THE GALAXY!
IF WE CAN'T CLOBBER HIM... WHO CAN?
HE EVEN LAUGHS AT MY FLAME!
HE LOOKS SO HUMOROUS-- HOW CAN HE BE SUCH A MENACE?
STORY: STAN LEE
ART: JACK KIRBY
INKING: DICK AYERS
LETTERING: ART SIMEK
X-73
1

MANY STRANGE THINGS CAN HAPPEN IN HOBO JUNGLES, BUT WE FEEL SAFE IN SAYING THAT THIS IS THE STRANGEST...
HOLY MACKERAL!
WH-WHERE'D YOU COME FROM?
THE PLANET POPPUP, IN THE TENTH GALAXY! WHERE ELSE?
THAT SETTLES IT! I'LL NEVER DRINK NUTHIN' STRONGER THAN MILK AGAIN!
I AM RAVENOUSLY HUNGRY AFTER MY LONG JOURNEY! MAY I SHARE YOUR FOOD?
LISTEN, CORNBALL, WE'RE LEGITIMATE HOBOES, AND WE DON'T LIKE FREE-LOADERS, NO MATTER WHERE THEY COME FROM!
YEAH! IF YA WANNA EAT, YOU GOTTA PAY FOR IT! WITH NICE COLD CASH!
CASH? WHAT A STRANGE WORD! WHAT IS CASH?
SAY, ARE YOU TRYIN' TO PULL OUR LEG, PIN-HEAD?
CASH IS WHAT THEY KEEP IN BANKS, MISTER! JUST GO TO A BANK AND ASK FOR SOME! THEY LOVE TO GIVE IT AWAY!
MANY THANKS! I'LL DO JUST THAT!
SUCH A FRIENDLY PLANET! I THINK I'M GOING TO LIKE IT HERE!
POP!
SSSSSSWISSSSH
EDITOR'S NOTE: BY NOW, YOU'RE PROBABLY THINKING THAT STAN AND JACK HAVE FLIPPED THEIR LIDS! BUT WAIT--THINGS MAY GET EVEN WHACKIER!
SALUTATIONS, MISTER BANKER! I HAVE COME FOR SOME CASH SO THAT I MAY BUY FOOD!
GOOD GRIEF! HOW DID YOU GET IN HERE?? THE VAULT IS STILL LOCKED!
THE SAME WAY ANYBODY WOULD GET IN, OF COURSE! I MADE MYSELF SMALL ENOUGH TO CRAWL UNDER THE DOOR! LIKE THIS!
POP!
GET A DOCTOR! I'M GOING MAD!
THAT MUST BE WHAT CASH IS! I'D BETTER TAKE ENOUGH OF IT! I EXPECT TO BE HERE FOR A WHILE!
POP!
LOOK! MR. HOWELL WASN'T HYSTERICAL! THERE IS A KOOKIE CHARACTER TRYIN' TO ROB THE BANK!
DROP THAT DOUGH AND REACH, MISTER--OR WE'LL START BLASTIN'!
2

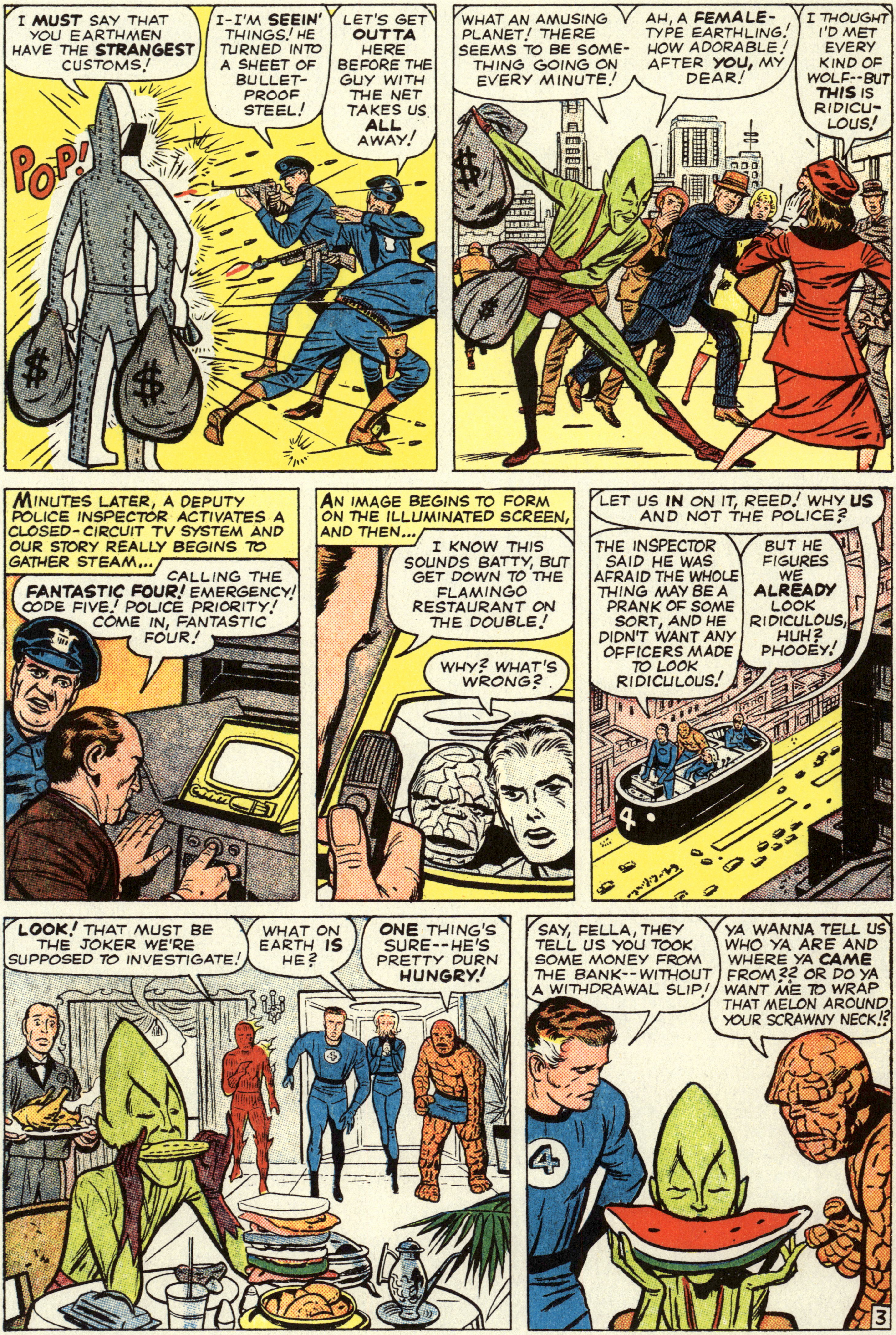

I MUST SAY THAT YOU EARTHMEN HAVE THE STRANGEST CUSTOMS!
I-I'M SEEIN' THINGS! HE TURNED INTO A SHEET OF BULLET-PROOF STEEL!
LET'S GET OUTTA HERE BEFORE THE GUY WITH THE NET TAKES US ALL AWAY!
POP!
WHAT AN AMUSING PLANET! THERE SEEMS TO BE SOMETHING GOING ON EVERY MINUTE!
AH, A FEMALE-TYPE EARTHLING! HOW ADORABLE! AFTER YOU, MY DEAR!
I THOUGHT I'D MET EVERY KIND OF WOLF--BUT THIS IS RIDICULOUS!
MINUTES LATER, A DEPUTY POLICE INSPECTOR ACTIVATES A CLOSED-CIRCUIT TV SYSTEM AND OUR STORY REALLY BEGINS TO GATHER STEAM...
CALLING THE FANTASTIC FOUR! EMERGENCY! CODE FIVE! POLICE PRIORITY! COME IN, FANTASTIC FOUR!
AN IMAGE BEGINS TO FORM ON THE ILLUMINATED SCREEN, AND THEN...
I KNOW THIS SOUNDS BATTY, BUT GET DOWN TO THE FLAMINGO RESTAURANT ON THE DOUBLE!
WHY? WHAT'S WRONG?
LET US IN ON IT, REED! WHY US AND NOT THE POLICE?
THE INSPECTOR SAID HE WAS AFRAID THE WHOLE THING MAY BE A PRANK OF SOME SORT, AND HE DIDN'T WANT ANY OFFICERS MADE TO LOOK RIDICULOUS!
BUT HE FIGURES WE ALREADY LOOK RIDICULOUS, HUH? PHOOEY!
LOOK! THAT MUST BE THE JOKER WE'RE SUPPOSED TO INVESTIGATE!
WHAT ON EARTH IS HE?
ONE THING'S SURE--HE'S PRETTY DURN HUNGRY!
SAY, FELLA, THEY TELL US YOU TOOK SOME MONEY FROM THE BANK--WITHOUT A WITHDRAWAL SLIP!
YA WANNA TELL US WHO YA ARE AND WHERE YA CAME FROM?? OR DO YA WANT ME TO WRAP THAT MELON AROUND YOUR SCRAWNY NECK!?
3

"MAY I COMPLIMENT YOU EARTHLINGS ON YOUR COLORFUL LANGUAGE! BUT, TO ANSWER YOUR QUESTION, I COME FROM THE PLANET POPPUP! IT'S A CHARMING WORLD, BUT ONE GETS BORED WITH ALL THE DANGERS ON POPPUP--WHICH IS WHY I DECIDED TO TAKE A VACATION--TO EARTH!"
"ON POPPUP, OUR EVOLUTIONARY PROCESSES ARE SO SWIFT, THAT WE CAN CHANGE OURSELVES INTO ANYTHING, IN ORDER TO SURVIVE THE MENACES WHICH CONSTANTLY ATTACK US!"
THAT URRPO-FISH WILL BREAK HIS TEETH IF HE TRIES TO BITE ME NOW!
POP!
IT'S ALMOST UNBELIEVABLE! HERE ON EARTH, IT TAKES AGES FOR THE SMALLEST EVOLUTIONARY CHANGE, SUCH AS MANKIND GAINING THE POWER TO WALK ERECT! BUT ON HIS HOME PLANET, THEY SEEM ABLE TO CHANGE INTO ANYTHING, IN A SPLIT-SECOND! THAT IS--IF WE CAN BELIEVE HIM!
I BELIEVE 'IM! I BELIEVE 'IM!
"BUT I'M PROBABLY BORING YOU WITH THESE DETAILS! EVERYONE KNOWS HOW WE POPPUPIANS CAN TURN OURSELVES INTO ANYTHING, JUST BY THINKING OF IT! IN FACT, THE WAY I REACHED YOUR FRIENDLY PLANET WAS BY BECOMING A SELF-POWERED SPACE SHIP!"
IF YOU'RE TRYIN' TO MAKE FOOLS OF US, WALNUT-HEAD, I'M GONNA MOP UP THE PLACE WITH YA!
HOLD IT, THING! FIRST, LET'S EXPLAIN SOME OF OUR EARTH CUSTOMS TO HIM--SUCH AS THE FACT THAT YOU CAN'T JUST TAKE MONEY OUT OF A BANK!
REALLY? THEN WHY DIDN'T THEY STOP ME?
BROTHER, YOU'RE JUST BEGGIN' FOR IT! NOW RELAX--IT'LL ONLY HURT A MINUTE!
CAREFUL, MY EXCITABLE FRIEND! YOU'RE LIABLE TO FIND ME A BIT THORNY!
YEOW!
POP!
HEY, THAT WASN'T FUNNY! I'LL SETTLE THAT LITTLE WISE-GUY'S HASH ONCE AND FOR ALL!
FLAME ON!
4

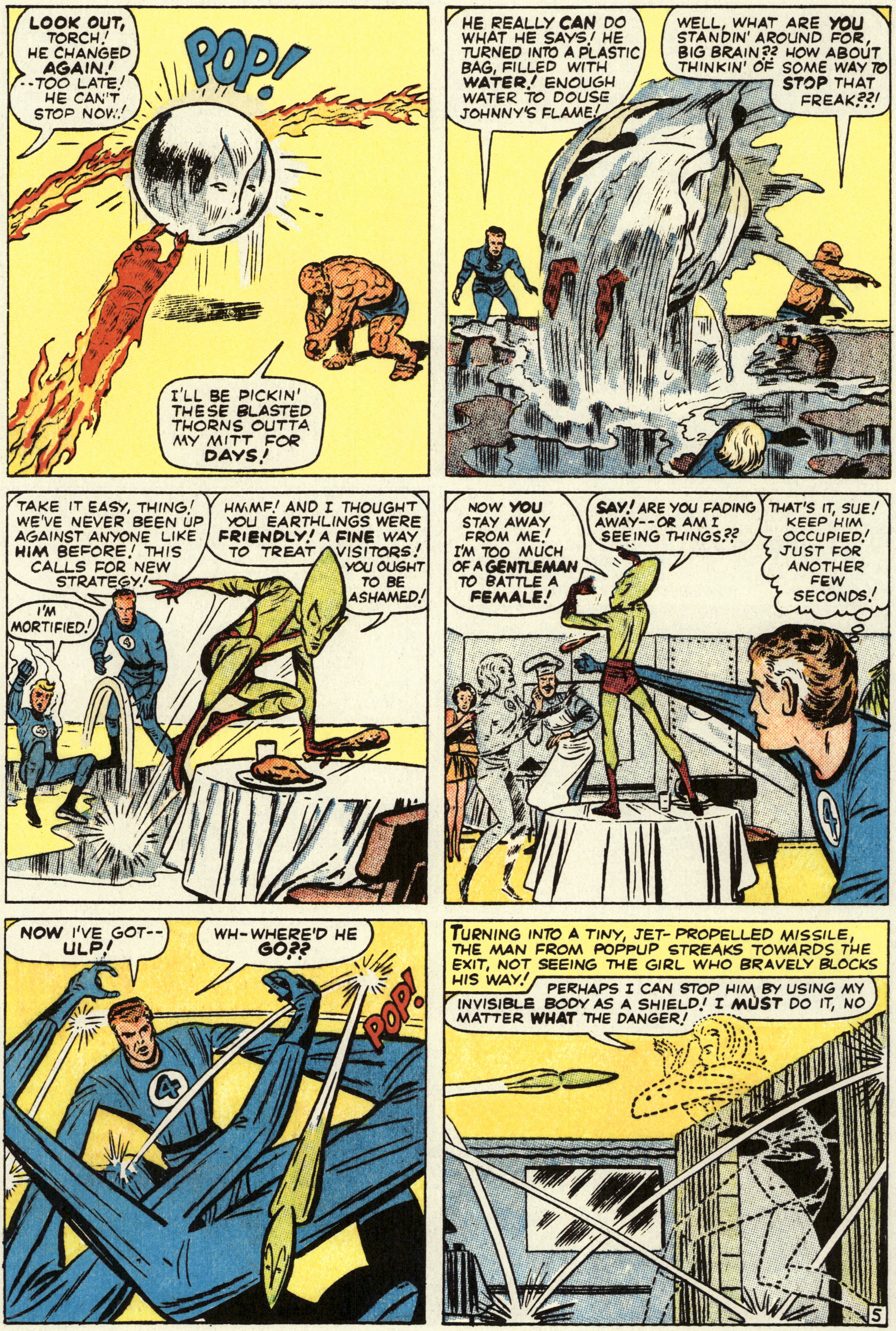
LOOK OUT, TORCH! HE CHANGED AGAIN! --TOO LATE! HE CAN'T STOP NOW..!
POP!
I'LL BE PICKIN' THESE BLASTED THORNS OUTTA MY MITT FOR DAYS!
HE REALLY CAN DO WHAT HE SAYS! HE TURNED INTO A PLASTIC BAG, FILLED WITH WATER! ENOUGH WATER TO DOUSE JOHNNY'S FLAME!
WELL, WHAT ARE YOU STANDIN' AROUND FOR, BIG BRAIN?? HOW ABOUT THINKIN' OF SOME WAY TO STOP THAT FREAK??!
TAKE IT EASY, THING! WE'VE NEVER BEEN UP AGAINST ANYONE LIKE HIM BEFORE! THIS CALLS FOR NEW STRATEGY!
HMMF! AND I THOUGHT YOU EARTHLINGS WERE FRIENDLY! A FINE WAY TO TREAT VISITORS! YOU OUGHT TO BE ASHAMED!
I'M MORTIFIED!
NOW YOU STAY AWAY FROM ME! I'M TOO MUCH OF A GENTLEMAN TO BATTLE A FEMALE!
SAY! ARE YOU FADING AWAY--OR AM I SEEING THINGS??
THAT'S IT, SUE! KEEP HIM OCCUPIED! JUST FOR ANOTHER FEW SECONDS!
NOW I'VE GOT-- ULP!
WH-WHERE'D HE GO??
POP!
TURNING INTO A TINY, JET-PROPELLED MISSILE, THE MAN FROM POPPUP STREAKS TOWARDS THE EXIT, NOT SEEING THE GIRL WHO BRAVELY BLOCKS HIS WAY!
PERHAPS I CAN STOP HIM BY USING MY INVISIBLE BODY AS A SHIELD! I MUST DO IT, NO MATTER WHAT THE DANGER!
5

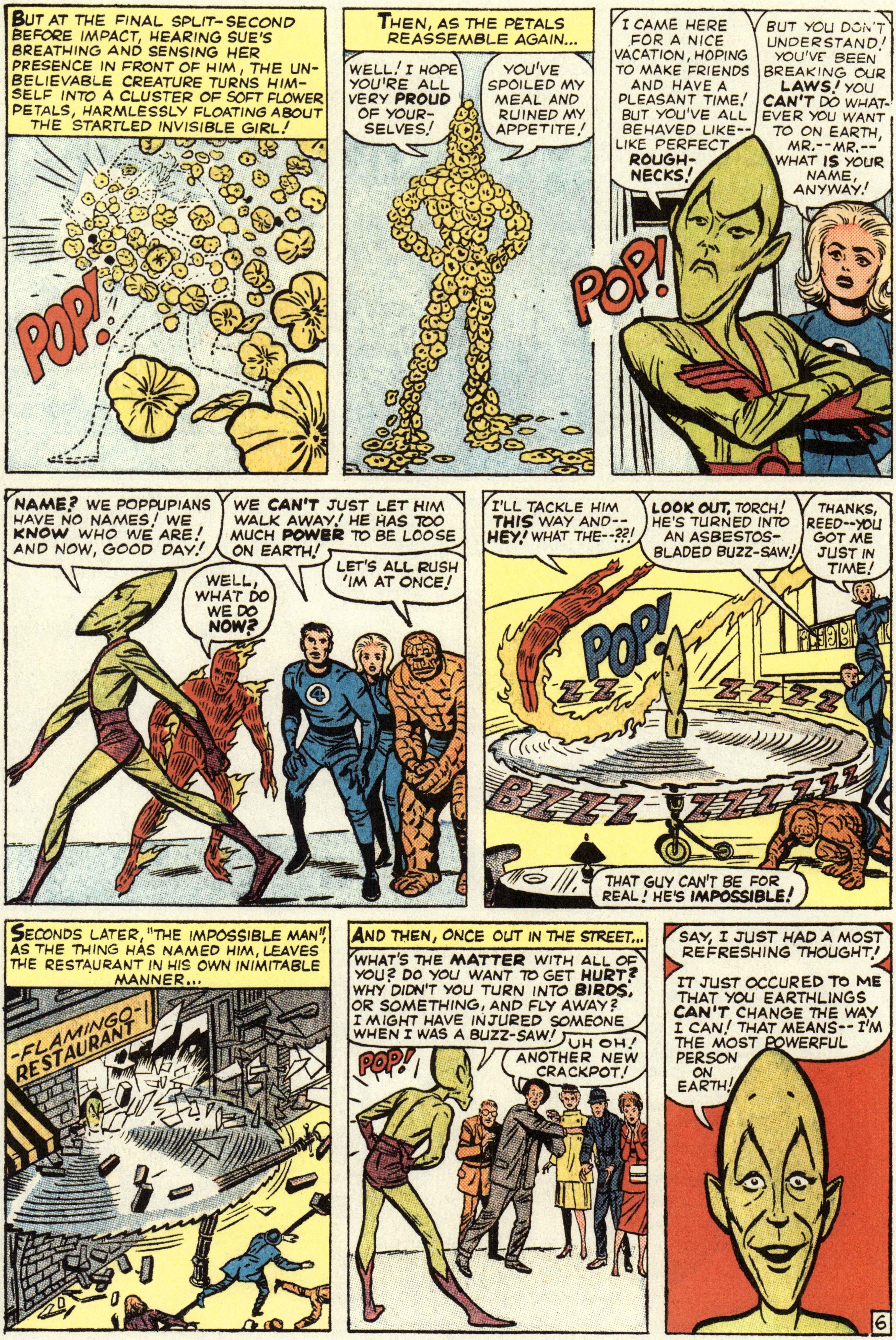
BUT AT THE FINAL SPLIT-SECOND BEFORE IMPACT, HEARING SUE'S BREATHING AND SENSING HER PRESENCE IN FRONT OF HIM, THE UNBELIEVABLE CREATURE TURNS HIMSELF INTO A CLUSTER OF SOFT FLOWER PETALS, HARMLESSLY FLOATING ABOUT THE STARTLED INVISIBLE GIRL!
POP!
THEN, AS THE PETALS REASSEMBLE AGAIN...
WELL! I HOPE YOU'RE ALL VERY PROUD OF YOURSELVES!
YOU'VE SPOILED MY MEAL AND RUINED MY APPETITE!
I CAME HERE FOR A NICE VACATION, HOPING TO MAKE FRIENDS AND HAVE A PLEASANT TIME! BUT YOU'VE ALL BEHAVED LIKE--LIKE PERFECT ROUGHNECKS!
BUT YOU DON'T UNDERSTAND! YOU'VE BEEN BREAKING OUR LAWS! YOU CAN'T DO WHATEVER YOU WANT TO ON EARTH, MR.--MR.--WHAT IS YOUR NAME, ANYWAY!
POP!
NAME? WE POPPUPIANS HAVE NO NAMES! WE KNOW WHO WE ARE! AND NOW, GOOD DAY!
WE CAN'T JUST LET HIM WALK AWAY! HE HAS TOO MUCH POWER TO BE LOOSE ON EARTH!
WELL, WHAT DO WE DO NOW?
LET'S ALL RUSH 'IM AT ONCE!
I'LL TACKLE HIM THIS WAY AND--HEY! WHAT THE--??!
LOOK OUT, TORCH! HE'S TURNED INTO AN ASBESTOS-BLADED BUZZ-SAW!
THANKS, REED--YOU GOT ME JUST IN TIME!
POP!
ZZZ
ZZZZZ
BZZZZ ZZZZZZZ
THAT GUY CAN'T BE FOR REAL! HE'S IMPOSSIBLE!
SECONDS LATER, "THE IMPOSSIBLE MAN"! AS THE THING HAS NAMED HIM, LEAVES THE RESTAURANT IN HIS OWN INIMITABLE MANNER...
-FLAMINGO-RESTAURANT
AND THEN, ONCE OUT IN THE STREET...
WHAT'S THE MATTER WITH ALL OF YOU? DO YOU WANT TO GET HURT? WHY DIDN'T YOU TURN INTO BIRDS, OR SOMETHING, AND FLY AWAY? I MIGHT HAVE INJURED SOMEONE WHEN I WAS A BUZZ-SAW!
POP!
UH OH! ANOTHER NEW CRACKPOT!
SAY, I JUST HAD A MOST REFRESHING THOUGHT!
IT JUST OCCURED TO ME THAT YOU EARTHLINGS CAN'T CHANGE THE WAY I CAN! THAT MEANS--I'M THE MOST POWERFUL PERSON ON EARTH!
6

THIS VACATION OF MINE IS GOING TO BE EVEN MORE FUN THAN I THOUGHT! I CAN DO ANYTHING I WANT TO!
WOULD YOU MIND GETTING OUT OF THIS VEHICLE? I WOULD LIKE TO DRIVE IT FOR A WHILE!
GOWAN BACK TO THE MASQUERADE, CHARLIE! I GOT NO TIME TO PLAY GAMES!
TAXI
MY NAME ISN'T CHARLIE!
POP!
GANGWAY!
I JUST QUIT THE HACKIN' BUSINESS!
NO WONDER HE WAS RELUCTANT TO LEAVE THE CAB! THIS IS MOST DELICIOUS SPORT!
FASTER, HOTSHOT! I SEE 'IM! STEP ON IT BEFORE HE TURNS INTO A MACKERAL OR SOMETHIN'!
WE MUSTN'T LOSE HIM THIS TIME, BEN! BE CAREFUL!
4
TAXI
CAREFUL? YA NEVER BECOME A COMIC BOOK HERO BY BEIN' CAREFUL!
OH! IT'S ONE OF THE KILLJOYS AGAIN!
OKAY, LAUGHING BOY --END OF THE LINE!
RRR
RRRRRRRR
RRRRR

NOW WE GOT A LITTLE SQUARIN' UP TO DO, SONNY!
HOLD IT, THING! BRUTE FORCE WON'T SETTLE HIM!
WE'VE GOT TO USE STRATEGY!
I WAS AFRAID OF THAT! HE'S CHANGED AGAIN! HE'S BECOME ONE OF THE HEAVIEST SUBSTANCES IN THE GALAXY!
WHO? A SKINNY RUNT LIKE HIM? HEY--YOU'RE RIGHT! I CAN HARDLY BUDGE 'IM!
LOOK! SOMEONE MUST HAVE SENT FOR THE NATIONAL GUARD!
POP!
STEP ASIDE, ALL FOUR OF YOU! THE GOVERNOR ORDERED US TO HANDLE THAT CHARACTER ONCE AND FOR ALL!
ALTHOUGH I CAN'T FIGGER OUT WHY HE SENT A WHOLE REGIMENT TO TAKE ONE LITTLE SQUIRT LIKE HIM INTO CUSTODY!
LISTEN TO ME, CAPTAIN! THIS "LITTLE SQUIRT", AS YOU CALL HIM, IS THE MOST DANGEROUS LIVING CREATURE ON EARTH! YOUR WEAPONS AND YOUR MEN WILL BE POWERLESS AGAINST HIM!
BROTHER, YOU BEEN WORKIN' TOO HARD! YOU'VE POPPED YOUR CORK!
THIS IS THE BEST VACATION I'VE EVER HAD!
THERE'S SOME NEW ACTIVITY GOING ON EVERY MINUTE!
I'M GOING TO RECOMMEND EARTH TO THE POPPUP TOURIST BUREAU!
HEY! WHERE'RE YOU GOIN'?
NOWHERE! I'M STAYING RIGHT HERE!
WHERE'D THAT BOMB COME FROM?? TAKE COVER! DISPERSE!
TICK
TICK TICK TICK
TICK
POP!
8

I DON'T KNOW WHAT YOU'RE UP TO...
...BUT YOU'RE NOT GETTING AWAY WITH IT WHILE I CAN STOP YOU!
TICK TICK TICK TICK TICK
THERE! I'LL TOSS YOU UP INTO THE SUB-STRATOSPHERE!
WHEEE! THANKS! THIS IS FUN!
BUT NOW I WANT TO COME DOWN TO EARTH AGAIN...
SO I'LL JUST EXPLODE INTO A ZILLION PIECES!
BARROOM!
AND RE-FORM MYSELF WITH WINGS, SO I GLIDE DOWN IN YOUR NICE SOFT ATMOSPHERE!
LOOK, HERE I AM! DON'T WORRY--I'M ALL RIGHT! SEE? I'M UP HERE!
HE'S COMING BACK AGAIN!
WITH ALL HIS POWERS THERE'S NO WAY TO STOP HIM!
LET ME TRY! I'VE GOT AN IDEA!
FLAME ON!
BOY! JUST GIVE ME ANOTHER CRACK AT 'IM!
BY FLYING AROUND IN CIRCLES THIS WAY I'LL SET UP A HYPNOTIC PATTERN WHICH MAY MAKE HIM LOSE CONSCIOUSNESS!
IT WORKED! HE'S PLUMMETING TO EARTH --OUT OF CONTROL!

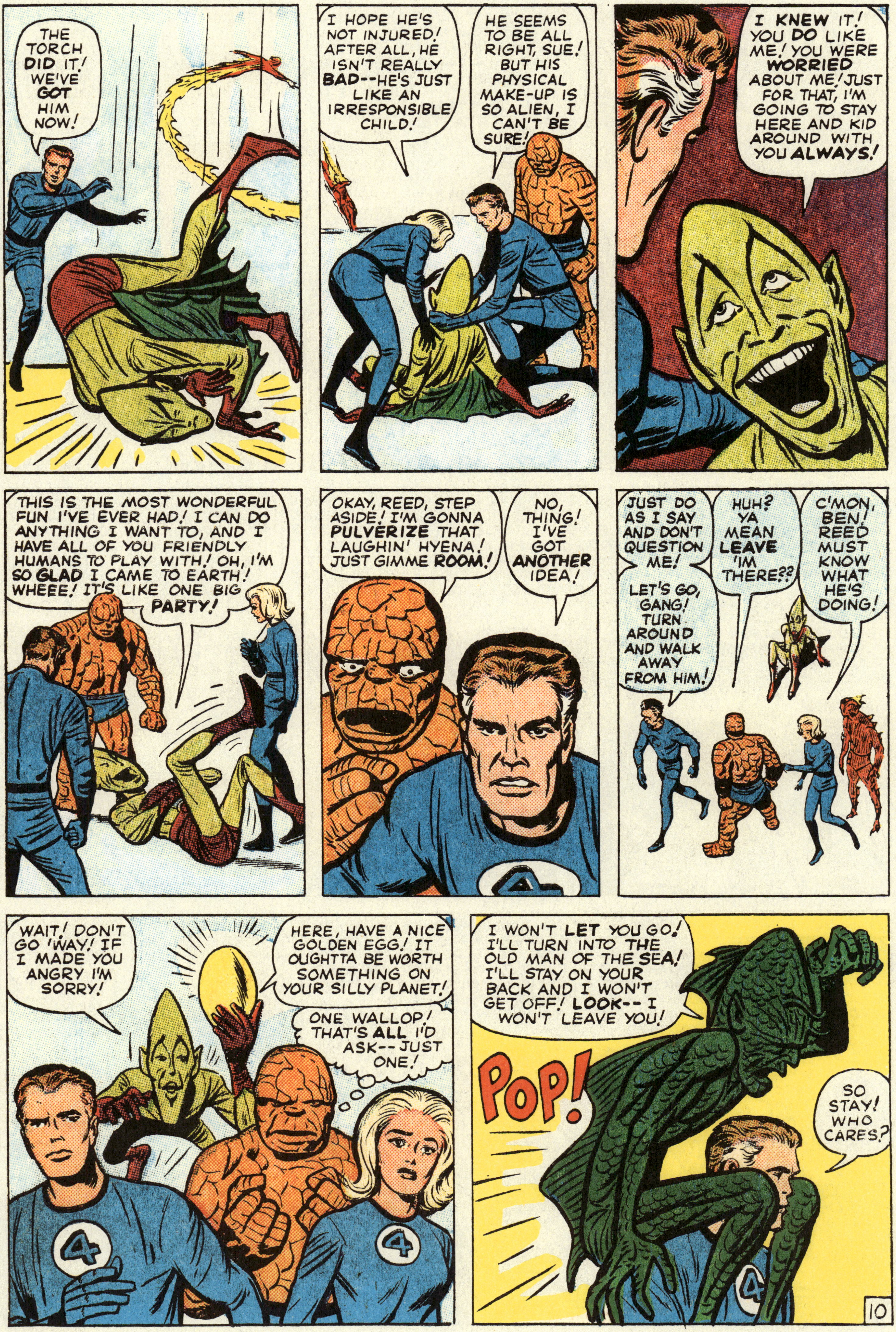

THE TORCH DID IT! WE'VE GOT HIM NOW!
I HOPE HE'S NOT INJURED! AFTER ALL, HE ISN'T REALLY BAD--HE'S JUST LIKE AN IRRESPONSIBLE CHILD!
HE SEEMS TO BE ALL RIGHT, SUE! BUT HIS PHYSICAL MAKE-UP IS SO ALIEN, I CAN'T BE SURE!
I KNEW IT! YOU DO LIKE ME! YOU WERE WORRIED ABOUT ME! JUST FOR THAT, I'M GOING TO STAY HERE AND KID AROUND WITH YOU ALWAYS!
THIS IS THE MOST WONDERFUL FUN I'VE EVER HAD! I CAN DO ANYTHING I WANT TO, AND I HAVE ALL OF YOU FRIENDLY HUMANS TO PLAY WITH! OH, I'M SO GLAD I CAME TO EARTH! WHEEE! IT'S LIKE ONE BIG PARTY!
OKAY, REED, STEP ASIDE! I'M GONNA PULVERIZE THAT LAUGHIN' HYENA! JUST GIMME ROOM!
NO, THING! I'VE GOT ANOTHER IDEA!
JUST DO AS I SAY AND DON'T QUESTION ME!
LET'S GO, GANG! TURN AROUND AND WALK AWAY FROM HIM!
HUH? YA MEAN LEAVE 'IM THERE??
C'MON, BEN! REED MUST KNOW WHAT HE'S DOING!
WAIT! DON'T GO 'WAY! IF I MADE YOU ANGRY I'M SORRY!
HERE, HAVE A NICE GOLDEN EGG! IT OUGHTTA BE WORTH SOMETHING ON YOUR SILLY PLANET!
ONE WALLOP! THAT'S ALL I'D ASK-- JUST ONE!
I WON'T LET YOU GO! I'LL TURN INTO THE OLD MAN OF THE SEA! I'LL STAY ON YOUR BACK AND I WON'T GET OFF! LOOK-- I WON'T LEAVE YOU!
POP!
SO STAY! WHO CARES?
10

YOU'RE ALL A BUNCH OF SOREHEADS, THAT'S WHAT YOU ARE!
POP!
I KNEW HE'D LEAVE IF I IGNORED HIM!
BUT HE'S STILL FREE TO MENACE THE REST OF EARTH! NOW WHAT DO WE DO?
NOTHING! WE WON'T EVEN TRY TO FIGHT HIM! LET HIM DO WHATEVER HE WANTS TO!
HEY, IS THAT MISTER FANTASTIC TALKIN'??
I CAN'T BELIEVE IT! IS HE TURNIN' CHICKEN?? IS HE SCARED OF THE IMPOSSIBLE MAN?
LISTEN, EVERYBODY! THERE'S NO USE IN FIGHTING THE IMPOSSIBLE MAN! LET HIM HAVE HIS OWN WAY! IGNORE HIM! DON'T FIGHT HIM! THAT IS WHAT I SHALL RECOMMEND TO THE POLICE OF EVERY STATE IN THE NATION!
NEVER THOUGHT REED RICHARDS WOULD TURN YELLOW!
ME NEITHER!
AND, IN THE DAYS THAT FOLLOW, ALTHOUGH BEWILDERED BY HIS APPARANT SURRENDER, PEOPLE EVERYWHERE TAKE MR. FANTASTIC'S ADVICE...
THAT CREEPY PINHEAD IS RUININ' OUR WHOLE TV SHOW!
JUST LET HIM ALONE! THE WORD IS OUT FROM UPSTAIRS TO IGNORE THE IMPOSSIBLE MAN!
LOOK AT ME, FELLAS! LOOK WHAT I'M DOING!
I STOLE THIS SILLY LITTLE AIRPLANE AND CRASHED IT RIGHT NEAR THOSE POLICEMEN! WHY DON'T THEY TRY TO PUNISH ME?
WHAT'S NEW, MIKE?
NOTHIN' MUCH, JOE! IT'S BEEN A PRETTY QUIET DAY SO FAR!
C'MON, KILLER! NEVER MIND YOUR OPPONENT! TRY TO KNOCK ME OUT! PLEASE --TRY TO FIGHT ME!
IT'LL BE A NICE DAY TODAY IF IT DON'T RAIN, HUH?
YEAH, KILLER!
AND, NOT LONG AFTERWARDS...
LOOK! THERE HE IS! WHAT'S WRONG WITH HIM?
THE ONE THING I HOPED WOULD BE WRONG ...HE'S BORED SICK!
BAH! WHAT A BUNCH OF DEAD-HEADS ON THIS PLANET! AND I THOUGHT I WAS GONNA HAVE A LOT OF FUN! PHOOEY!
11
I'M GONNA FIND ME ANOTHER PLANET WHERE A FELLA CAN HAVE SOME FUN! EARTH IS TOO DULL! I'M NEVER GONNA COME BACK--AND I'LL TELL ALL THE OTHER POPPUPIANS TO STAY AWAY, TOO!
EARTH WILL NEVER GET OUR TOURIST BUSINESS! NO SIREE!
POP!
YOU WERE RIGHT, REED! HE'S GONE--FOREVER!
WHAT LUCK FOR US!
I STILL WISH I COULDA CLOBBERED 'IM FIRST!
HE WAS BEATEN BY THE ONE THING HE COULDN'T FIGHT--SHEER BOREDOM!
AND THAT WRAPS UP OUR CHANGE-OF-PACE ISSUE FOR NOW! HOPE YOU LIKED IT! NEXT MONTH, IT'S BACK TO NORMAL AGAIN WITH A SURPRISE-PACKED FULL-LENGTH THRILLER--THE FANTASTIC FOUR MEET--THE HULK! DON'T MISS IT!
THE END

THE FANTASTIC FOUR
PIN-UP PAGE
PRINCE NAMOR, THE MIGHTY SUBMARINER!
FOSSIL FISH, OF SPECIES THOUGHT TO BE EXTINCT FOR MILLIONS OF YEARS--VANQUISHED BY SUBMARINER IN UNCHARTERED DEEPS!
MAP OF UNDERSEA EARTH
PROW OF VESSEL FOUND BY SUBMARINER IN UNCHARTERED SUNKEN ATLANTIS!
LARGEST PEARL IN EXISTENCE--BLASTED LOOSE BY SUBMARINER FROM 30 FOOT CLAM!

Address YOUR letters to:
LEE and KIRBY
FANTASTIC FOUR
THIRD FLOOR
655 MADISON AVE.
NEW YORK 21, N. Y.

FANTASTIC FAN PAGE 4

X-74

Dear Stan and Jack:

Do you mind telling us who wrote the story for FF #8? It was probably the greatest one we've ever seen. The only mistake was in the art department. The Puppet Master's teeth were a little too big for him. Otherwise the story was terrif! Also, we agree with Angry Artie Star that if you throw out Sue Storm tell us where you throw her because we'll make a beeline for that place, too. We also agree that the FF should be in the movies. So count this letter as a vote in favor.

James Barnhill & Larry Berry
2813 Malta Place
Las Vegas, Nevada

Thanks, guys. But you must be the only two readers left who don't know that Stan Lee writes the stories and Jack Kirby draws them. As for the FF being in the movies, many, many fans have written enthusiastically to agree with H. Sher's idea. In fact, in a future issue, we'll print some of the many suggestions for casting which we're received, as soon as we can sort them all out.

Dear Stan and Jack:

I believe congratulations are in order. The FF have been in existence for over a year. It has been an interesting year. Twelve months ago I purchased a new comic book which styled itself "The World's Greatest Comic Magazine." It was not, however, this modest declaration which drew me to the book, but rather the sight of the Human Torch. The first and second issues did little to support your boast. You were not even the best comic of your type. I was about ready to abandon you when issue #3 came out. In that issue, you began to show some style. With the appearance of Sub-Mariner in #4 you began to pick up speed. The creation of Dr. Doom in #5 was another inspiration. To boot, your principles have taken on definite form. The four of them began their lives as mannikins mouthing pious platitudes. They have matured into warm, vibrant personalities, each with his own strength and weaknesses. They are, in short, human, yet credibly more than human. The Torch-Thing feud has been handled well, and I hope to see it continued. I've noticed, however, that the Thing seems to be learning to control his temper. This, too, I think is good. He seems to do more good when his brute strength is directed by a cool head then when, as in the early issues, he goes on destructive rampages. Under the head of complaints, I have only one. It concerns the Invisible Girl. Now let me make it plain that I don't want her eliminated. She has too much potential for that. My complaint is that her potential is seldom utilized. I object chiefly to the fact that in eight tries, she has been captured by four of the villains. I think she would make a better action character than a hostage. In summation, I cannot say you've fulfilled your claim to being "The World's Greatest Comic Magazine," but you've done much towards correcting your early flaws. I am confident that a poll of comic readers would rank you in the top ten. Such progress in so short a time should be commended. One more thing before closing: I agree wholeheartedly with Comrade Sher that the FF would do well in the movies. I'm also in general agreement with his "casting." Gregory Peck, Troy Donahue and Tuesday Weld would do well as Mr. Fantastic, Human Torch, and Invisible Girl. For the Thing, however, I would recommend Lon Chaney, Jr. rather than Steve Reeves.

Larry Tucker
1707 Lucile
Wichita Falls, Texas

Heck, Larry, it would look silly to change our slogan to "ALMOST The World's Greatest Comic Magazine"! Besides, after reading your letter, the Thing tells us not to worry. He says you're probably just one of the Yancy Street Boys!

Dear Stan and Jack:

I think the FF are the best super-hero group ever made! I say they should be on TV! I don't care who plays the roles, but they should be on. Mr. Fantastic's name is okay —so is the Thing's. Don't dare get rid of Invisible Girl! Please re-publish the first issue for those of us who missed it. How come in the FF mag they all live in a big city, but in STRANGE TALES, the Torch and Sue live in a small town called Centerville? What gives? Anyway, you have easily the best comic mag ever printed. By the way, how long can the Torch keep his flame on? Have the Thing change to Ben Grimm more often. And thanks for a great mag.

Billy Rintz
1024 S. Oak Street
Hillsboro, Illinois

Let's quickly answer Billy's letter point by point: Thanks. So do we. Okay. We won't. Maybe someday. They don't all LIVE in the skyscraper—that's just their headquarters. Thanks. No definite time—depends on his physical condition and on how long he had his flame on the previous time. Okay. You're welcome. (Whew!)

Hey, you guys,

What happened? The last issue I have is #5, and now I pick up #8! This proves that the FF is the greatest! If a fella isn't careful, they're sold out before he can get a copy. Around here the closest place to buy comics is the drugstore. New shipments come in on Tuesdays, and I've been going for my copy on Thursday, so by the time I got there they were gone. Luckily, I went on Tuesday last time and I got a copy! I'd like to know if I could get #6? I've heard a lot about it and wondered if I could somehow get that famous issue from you. (No one wants to trade for it.) And now for my big question—What happened to the Thing's boots? He wore them in #4!

Kurt Dagenais
141 Second St.
East Providence 14, Rhode Island

Sorry, Kurt, as we mentioned in a previous issue, we have no back numbers for sale. BUT perhaps one of our other readers will notice your letter and come to the rescue. As for the Thing's boots, it looks as though he just got tired of wearing them. He probably figured that when a guy looks the way HE does, no one will notice whether he's barefoot or not.

Dear Stan and Jack:

Thanks a million. You have brought enjoyment back to comic books for me. I have been reading all different types of mags for about eight years now and have been bored stiff. After the first year or two, every story I read was practically the same with a few minor changes and I found myself buying them purely from habit. Every new comic hero seems to be a duplicate of another with an extra power or so added. That is, all except the FF. I must admit, I first started to buy your mag from habit, but every time I read one of them I derived more and more pleasure from it. Finally, after reading #8 I turned to the front and read it over again and again and again. I used to throw comics away before, but from now on I'm saving every FF I can get my greedy little hands on. One request: If anything comes of the fondness which Alicia showed for the Thing, don't let it dangle on and on like other mags do. And now, every time I get bored, I'll just open one of your books and escape to a world of wonderful realistic fantasy.

William Paul
112 O'Grady Street
Fall River, Mass.

Thanks, Bill—and we'll do likewise with your letter.

Dear Stan and Jack:

DeaHow old are Mr. Fantastic, The Thing, Invisible Girl, and the Human Torch? My cousins and I play Fantastic Four all the time.

Betty Dille
Indianapolis, Indiana

Mr. Fantastic and Ben Grimm are both in their late thirties, having graduated college when they were very young. Sue Storm is in her twenties, and Johnny was just seventeen. (We can't tell Sue's EXACT age because, being a female, she'd never talk to us again!)

Dear Stan and Jack:

I think that the FF is the best comic mag ever to hit the newsstands! I like the Torch because of his weird powers, and besides that, my name is Johnny Storm. The FF has a personality all of its own, and is different from the other crime fighters. I think that the FF Feature Page in #8 was the most!

Johnny Storm
San Pedro, California

Tell us, Johnny, would the Torch STILL be your favorite if your name was Ben Grimm?

Dear Stan and Jack:

The Human Torch is a sensation! It made a hit with all my friends overnight. PLEASE DON'T KILL IT! We are getting a bunch of signatures ready to send in to save the Torch also.

David Lancaster
(President of
SAVE THE TORCH DRIVE)
3717 Sprindale
Fort Worth, Texas

Huh? Who said anything about killing the Torch? We're all for saving the Torch, but tell us, Dave—save him from WHAT?

Dear Stan and Jack:

I just can't help myself. I'm constantly writing to you in congratulation of something or other. This time it's ish #9. First of all, the story was created on a sound premise. What other characters in the long history of comics ever had money worries? As I opened the book, my eyes came to rest on a tiny block containing the names of the writer, artist, inker, and letterer. I was glad to see Dick Ayers and Art Simek get the credit they deserve. The return of Sub-Mariner struck a responsive chord, although I think he would be a better hero than a villain. Your human touches such as Reed's losing the money in stocks, the Thing upset about the whole mess, and the hitch-hiking scene (which was worth the price of the whole book), added greatly to the characters and personalities of the FF. Could you keep Alicia around as one of the Thing's only friends? She is a strong character and would add just that much more to the mag. Why—WHY does some joker with no imagination suggest that Thor, or Ant-Man, or Spider Man join the FF? If these fans would stop and think a minute, they'd realize that one of those other heroes would steal the show. I'm kind of a writer myself and I realize that a hero by himself has to have a certain number of gimmicks or powers to sell magazines. A prime example is the Human Torch. When he made his debut in STRANGE TALES, extra powers had to be created for him. *(What powers?—ed.)* Thor, because he is a lone hero, is as powerful as the whole FF, but in a different way. Such a hero would hog most of the action. The same goes for Namor and the Hulk. The group was created as the Fantastic Four, and it would be best to leave them that way. By the way—Kong-gratulations! (That's king-sized congrats!) Many happy returns on your birthday. As of ish #8, the FF is a year old! May you have a thousand more! One parting note: I was glad to see such stars as Jim Arness, Amanda Blake, Bing Crosby, Bob Hope, etc featured in #9. It added to the realism of the fabulous foursome. Many thanks for a year of the greatest magazine in the world. P.S.: I have a complete collection of your great mags!

Sherman Howard
3776 E. 154th Street
Cleveland 28, Ohio

Sherm, it took us so long to READ your letter, that we've no time left to ANSWER it! But we appreciate your carefully considered comments, and we're sure our fans will, too.

Well, that wraps it up for this ish! Hope you enjoyed our new, expanded two-page fan section. And remember, next issue the F.F. come face to face with THE HULK in a story which we feel will be considered a comic classic for years to come. See you then.

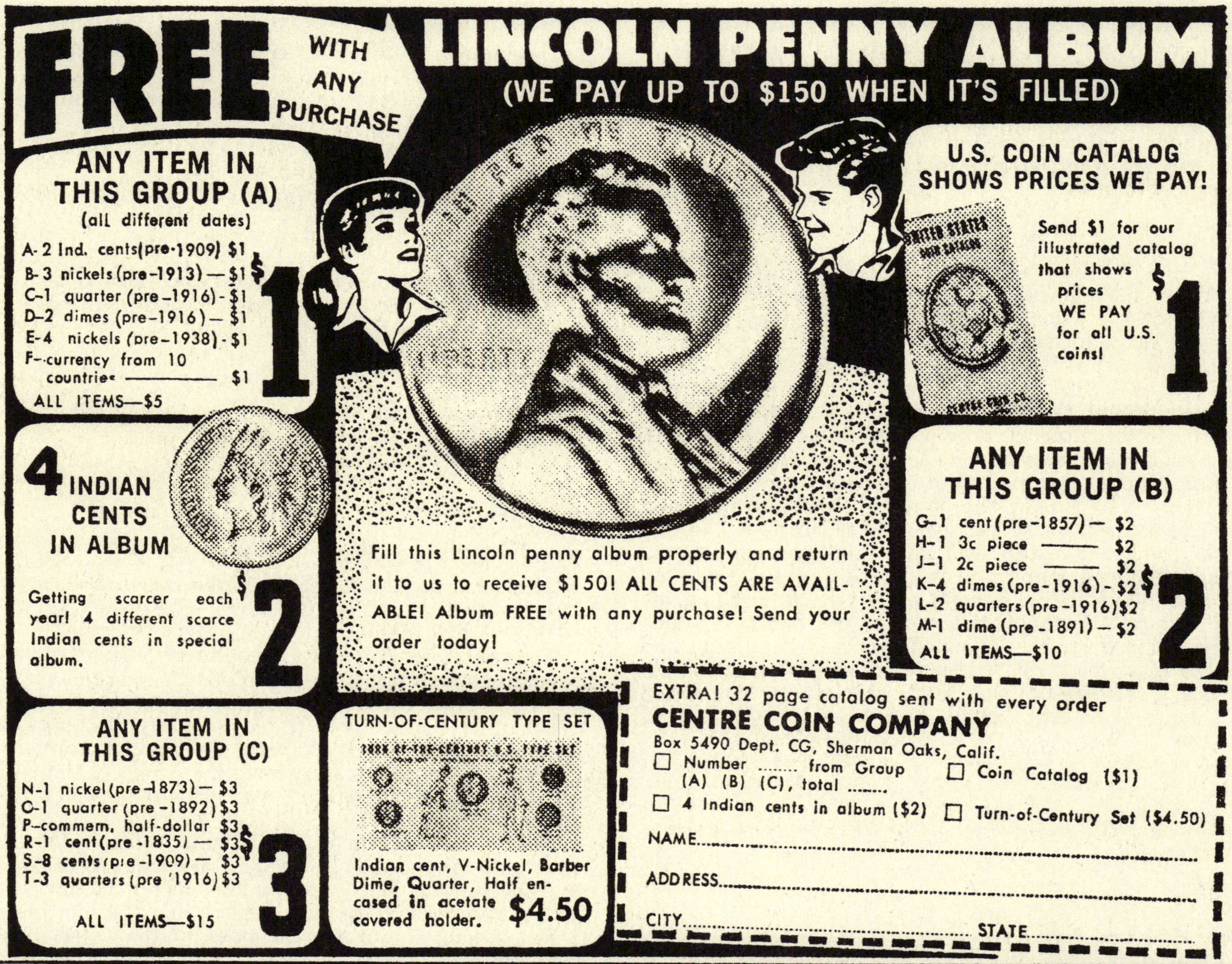
FREE
WITH ANY PURCHASE
LINCOLN PENNY ALBUM
(WE PAY UP TO $150 WHEN IT'S FILLED)
ANY ITEM IN THIS GROUP (A)
(all different dates)
A-2 Ind. cents(pre-1909) $1
B-3 nickels (pre-1913) — $1
C-1 quarter (pre-1916) - $1
D-2 dimes (pre-1916) — $1
E-4 nickels (pre-1938) - $1
F-currency from 10 countries — $1
ALL ITEMS—$5
$1
U.S. COIN CATALOG SHOWS PRICES WE PAY!
Send $1 for our illustrated catalog that shows prices WE PAY for all U.S. coins!
$1
4 INDIAN CENTS IN ALBUM
Getting scarcer each year! 4 different scarce Indian cents in special album.
$2
Fill this Lincoln penny album properly and return it to us to receive $150! ALL CENTS ARE AVAILABLE! Album FREE with any purchase! Send your order today!
ANY ITEM IN THIS GROUP (B)
G-1 cent (pre-1857) — $2
H-1 3c piece — $2
J-1 2c piece — $2
K-4 dimes (pre-1916) - $2
L-2 quarters (pre-1916) $2
M-1 dime (pre-1891) — $2
ALL ITEMS—$10
$2
ANY ITEM IN THIS GROUP (C)
N-1 nickel (pre-1873) — $3
C-1 quarter (pre-1892) $3
P-commem. half-dollar $3
R-1 cent (pre-1835) — $3
S-8 cents (pre-1909) — $3
T-3 quarters (pre 1916) $3
ALL ITEMS—$15
$3
TURN-OF-CENTURY TYPE SET
Indian cent, V-Nickel, Barber Dime, Quarter, Half encased in acetate covered holder.
$4.50
EXTRA! 32 page catalog sent with every order
CENTRE COIN COMPANY
Box 5490 Dept. CG, Sherman Oaks, Calif.
☐ Number .... from Group (A) (B) (C), total ....
☐ Coin Catalog ($1)
☐ 4 Indian cents in album ($2)
☐ Turn-of-Century Set ($4.50)
NAME
ADDRESS
CITY
STATE

RECORD YOUR VOICE AT HOME
ONLY $6.98
FUN FOR THE WHOLE FAMILY
FEATURES:
• Handy Portable Carrying Case
• Cuts Actual Records
• Records at 33⅓, 45, or 78
• Sing, Tell Jokes, Record
MAKE YOUR OWN RECORDS ANYWHERE
Kids, now you can cut your own records at home. Sing, tell jokes, record secret conversations, speeches, take off your favorite shows and music, and it's all ready to play back instantly. Put your voice on records, or a pals, or Mom & Dad's and then play it back at home, parties, gatherings, or wherever your family and friends gather.
IT'S FUN — IT'S REVOLUTIONARY IT'S ELECTRONIC
You receive complete recording equipment, including recording arm and head, microphone, tracking disc, cutting needles, and full supply of blank records. It all attaches to your phonograph, and you're all set to record what you like, where you like and when you like. Takes only 30 seconds, and anyone can operate it. Records at 33⅓, 45 or 78 R.P.M.'s Only $6.98 plus 45¢ shipping charges. Additional blank recording disks are available from us at $3.00 per package of 12.
10 DAY FREE TRIAL
Don't delay! Order now! Use this exciting recorder for parties, gatherings, recording sessions and just plain fun for 10 full days. Test it in your own home, and if you're not 100% delighted, simply return for prompt refund of the full purchase price. Only $6.98 plus 45¢ shipping charges.
MONEY BACK GUARANTEE
Honor House Products Corp. Dept. RL-99
Lynbrook, New York
Rush my Voice Recorder at once. If I am not 100% delighted after 10 day free trial, I may return the merchandise for prompt refund of full purchase price.
☐ I enclose $6.98 plus 45¢ shipping charges.
☐ Send C.O.D. I will pay postman on delivery plus shipping charges.
Name
Address

GROG GROWS OWN TAIL
PLANT TAIL OUTSIDE AND IT GROWS LIKE MAD INTO A BEAUTIFUL SHADE TREE! Grog, amazing prehistoric monster, comes with half-a-tail. In a few days the tail starts growing. It grows, grows, g-r-o-w-s. Remove the tail from Grog's body and plant it outside and it springs quickly into a flowering, fragrant shade tree. Then Grog grows another tail. Remove the tail again and he grows another, and another . . . endlessly. Only $1 plus 25c postage. Satisfaction or money back.
$1.00
MONEY BACK GUARANTEE
Please include 25c postage and handling.
WESTERN WORLD PRODUCTS, Dept. 3
2611 Tilden Ave., Los Angeles 64, Calif.
I am enclosing cash, check or money order for $1 plus 25c postage for which please send me my grog. I understand if I am not satisfied my money will be returned.
(PLEASE PRINT PLAINLY)
Name
Address
City Zone State

BOYS
12 or older
MAKE $1 to $5 WEEKLY
IN YOUR SPARE TIME
5¢ PROFIT on every GRIT you sell.
Win FREE PRIZES, Like These, Too
GRIT
Sell GRIT
"America's Greatest Family Newspaper"
Enjoyed by 900,000 Families Every Week
Over 30,000 boys, 12 or older, sell GRIT every week in a few hours of their spare time — make lots of spending money — win prizes — get valuable business training.
GRIT WILL HELP YOU GET STARTED in a profitable business of your own. We will send you papers and easy-to-understand selling instructions.
You pay only for the papers you sell until you know how many to order. GRIT sells for 15c a copy. You keep 5c and send GRIT 10c for each paper you sell.
If you are a boy — 12 or older
Grab This Great Opportunity!
SEND THE COUPON NOW
in an envelope or pasted on a postcard
GRIT PUBLISHING CO., Williamsport, Pa.
NC 83
Send my first bundle of papers, selling helps and prize offers.
Name
Are You a Boy? Age Date Born Year
In Care of
Street and No. R. F. D.
Post Office State
Print Your Last Name Plainly Here

Curious Coins! Odd Paper Money!

CATALOG PRICE 75¢—BUT YOURS

FREE to get names for our mailing list

SEND for this valuable packet of odd and curious coins and paper money – an exciting introduction to fast growing hobby! You'll find money from Formosa (Free China – our ally), East Africa, Austria, Turkey, etc. Catalog price 75¢ –but yours FREE on this special offer!

JOIN THIS FUN RIGHT AWAY

Get your FREE packet of coins and money – plus $100,000 in Confederate "money" as your bonus – together with lists of popular coins available, and other interesting offers on approval. Just send coupon now, with 10¢ to help cover shipping, to:

LITTLETON COIN CO., Dept. MC-8
Littleton, New Hampshire

MAIL TODAY FOR FREE COINS AND MONEY

LITTLETON COIN CO., Dept. MC-8
Littleton, New Hampshire

Please rush me FREE packet of coins and money – together with $100,000 replica Confederate money . . . lists of popular coins available . . . and other interesting offers on approval. Enclosed is 10¢ to cover shipping.

Name...
(Please Print Plainly)

Address...

City.............................Zone.....State.......

Also FREE $100,000 CONFEDERATE BILL

This lots-of-fun actual replica is yours for promptness while the supply lasts.

INSTANT LIVE SEA ANIMALS

just add water . . . you've got INSTANT LIFE

ONLY $1.00

It's true. Now, right before your eyes — in just 24-72 hours — a happy troupe of hundreds of playful tumbling sea-monkeys (exotic Saskatchewan Brine Shrimp) that are more fun than a sea full of seals. Amaze both children and adults as you watch the comic antics of these fantastic underwater sea clowns. Day and night you'll see them chase each other in a playful game of hide and seek. The loser gets caught by the tail and is spun in a dizzy circle. See the "showoffs" turn somersaults under water . . . see the ticklish ones scratch each others' backs. Watch them cavort singly or glide gracefully in formation creating your own underwater circus.

MIRACLE OF LIFE

Right before your eyes these genuine live sea animals burst forth from "magic" powder eggs which will remain alive as long as eight years. You can raise an entire troupe in an ordinary glass jar using just tap water. It's so easy . . . just empty the package into a jar or fish bowl, add water and you have created "instant life." You can have a whole sea brood to give as gifts or sell if you wish.

SEE THEM OBEY YOUR SILENT COMMANDS

Darken the room and watch them follow a flashlight or candle beam forwards, backwards, sideways or around like a pack of happy kids playing follow the leader. Order now.

SEE THEM CHANGE COLOR

Mail this coupon and we'll send you 3 colors of sea-monkeys — white, pink and red. These are their natural colors. Yet, with a drop of vegetable food dye in their water, you can change the color of these little sea monkeys as often as you wish. Make them green, blue, purple, yellow or any other hue or shade without harming them. This dye will enable you to see their internal organs and how their life processes function.

MONEY BACK GUARANTEE

BARGAIN CO. (Dept. MCR) 101 East 32nd St., New York.
Rush me my "magic" eggs for hatching my live sea animals at once. I understand if I am not 100% delighted, I may return it for prompt refund of my purchase price.

☐ I enclose $1.00 plus 25c shipping charge for one order.

☐ SAVE 50c. I enclose $2.00. Send double order for hatching two live sea circuses.

Name________________

Address________________

City________ Zone____ State________

IND.
THE WORLD'S GREATEST COMIC MAGAZINE!
APPROVED BY THE COMICS CODE AUTHORITY
12¢
THE Fantastic FOUR
MC
12 MAR.
AT LAST!!! the FANTASTIC FOUR meet THE HULK!
THE HULK IS NEARBY! I CAN FEEL IT!
ANOTHER SECOND AND I'LL DESTROY THEM ALL!!
A BOOK-LENGTH EPIC!! NEED WE SAY MORE?!!!

THE FANTASTIC FOUR is published by CANAM PUBLISHERS SALES CORP. OFFICE OF PUBLICATION: 655 MADISON AVENUE, NEW YORK, N.Y. Published monthly. Copyright 1962 by CANAM PUBLISHERS SALES CORP., 655 Madison Avenue, New York, N.Y. Vol. 1 No. 12, MARCH, 1963 issue. Price 12¢ per copy. Subscription rate $1.75 for 12 issues including postage. Foreign subscription $3.25 in American funds. No similarity between any of the names, characters, persons, and/or institutions appearing in this magazine with those of any living or dead person is intended, and any such similarity which may exist is purely coincidental. Printed in U.S.A. by The Eastern Color Printing Co., Waterbury 20, Conn.

THE INCREDIBLE HULK
YOU ARE ABOUT TO WITNESS, IN VIVID DETAIL, ALL THE SPELLBINDING EVENTS WHICH WILL LEAD UP TO THE EXPLOSIVE MOMENT WHEN THE FANTASTIC FOUR WILL MEET...
AS A WELL-DRESSED, SOPHISTICATED AUDIENCE LEAVES THE CITY SYMPHONY AUDITORIUM, NONE SUSPECT THE FAMOUS FIGURE WHO IS IN THEIR MIDST!
OH, BEN... WASN'T BEETHOVEN'S FIFTH THE MOST BEAUTIFUL SYMPHONY YOU'VE EVER HEARD?
IF YOU SAY SO, KID! PERSONALLY, I GET MY KICKS FROM LOW-DOWN NEW ORLEANS JAZZ!
SCRIPT.......... STAN LEE
ART............. JACK KIRBY
INKING........ DICK AYERS
LETTERING ... ART SIMEK
X-101
LOOK, MY DEAR! A COMPANY OF INFANTRYMEN! HERE IN NEW YORK!
HEY!
LOOK OUT WHO YOU'RE POKIN'!
1

DON'T RAISE YOUR VOICE TO ME, MY GOOD MAN! I WAS MERELY TRYING TO SEE THOSE TROOPS, AND--ULP! A--A MONSTER!
OH, NOW YOU'RE INSULTIN' ME ALSO, HUH?
BEN--WHAT ARE YOU DOING?!!
HERE! YA WANNA SEE THE SOLDIER BOYS?? TAKE A GOOD LOOK!
DID YOU SEE THAT CHARACTER LIFT THAT GUY UP LIKE HE WAS A FEATHER??
AND HE PUT HIM DOWN AGAIN GENTLE AS A LAMB!
HEY! HE'S STRONG ENOUGH TO BE THE ONE WE'RE LOOKIN' FOR!
SURROUND HIM!
DON'T LET 'IM GET AWAY!
BEN! WHAT IS IT? WHAT'S HAPPENING?
STAY BACK, ALICIA--I'LL HANDLE IT!
CAREFUL OF THE GIRL--IT LOOKS LIKE SHE'S BLIND!
HOLY HANNAH! HE TORE THAT HYDRANT CLEAN OUT OF THE STREET!
ARE YOU GUYS ALL NUTS??!
LET'S RUSH 'IM!
BRUSHING HIS ATTACKER CARELESSLY ASIDE, THE MIGHTY THING HURLS HIMSELF UPON THE POWERFUL JET OF WATER, CAUSING IT TO SPRAY IN ALL DIRECTIONS WITH CONCENTRATED FORCE, SCATTERING THE NEARBY TROOPS!
MAYBE THIS'LL COOL YOU GUYS OFF!
QUICK! NAIL HIM WITH THAT SPECIALLY PREPARED BAZOOKA--POINT BLANK RANGE!
NOW! WHILE HE'S IN THE OPEN!
2

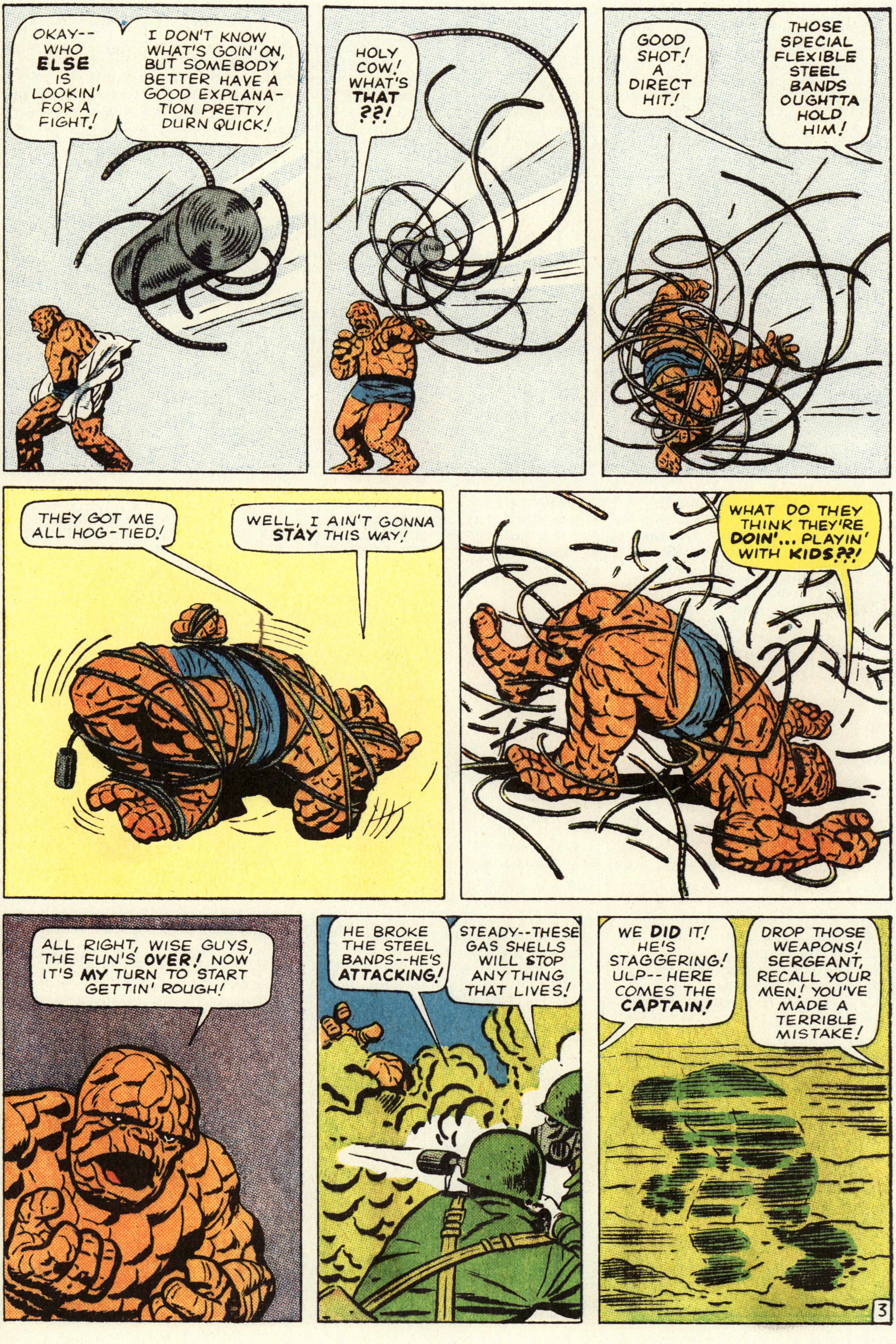
OKAY-- WHO ELSE IS LOOKIN' FOR A FIGHT!
I DON'T KNOW WHAT'S GOIN' ON, BUT SOMEBODY BETTER HAVE A GOOD EXPLANATION PRETTY DURN QUICK!
HOLY COW! WHAT'S THAT ??!
GOOD SHOT! A DIRECT HIT!
THOSE SPECIAL FLEXIBLE STEEL BANDS OUGHTTA HOLD HIM!
THEY GOT ME ALL HOG-TIED!
WELL, I AIN'T GONNA STAY THIS WAY!
WHAT DO THEY THINK THEY'RE DOIN'... PLAYIN' WITH KIDS??!
ALL RIGHT, WISE GUYS, THE FUN'S OVER! NOW IT'S MY TURN TO START GETTIN' ROUGH!
HE BROKE THE STEEL BANDS--HE'S ATTACKING!
STEADY--THESE GAS SHELLS WILL STOP ANYTHING THAT LIVES!
WE DID IT! HE'S STAGGERING! ULP--HERE COMES THE CAPTAIN!
DROP THOSE WEAPONS! SERGEANT, RECALL YOUR MEN! YOU'VE MADE A TERRIBLE MISTAKE!
3

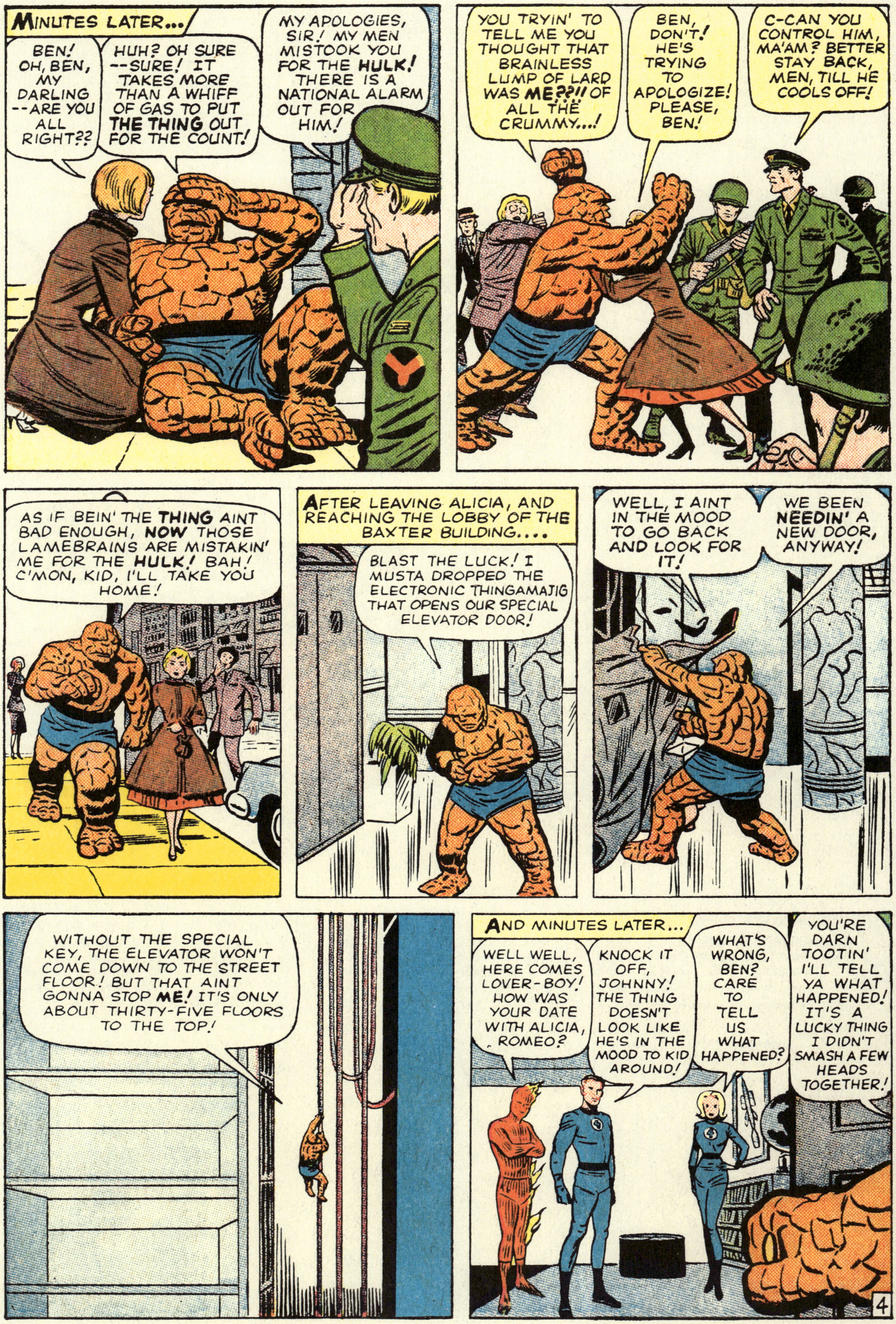

MINUTES LATER...
BEN! OH, BEN, MY DARLING --ARE YOU ALL RIGHT??
HUH? OH SURE --SURE! IT TAKES MORE THAN A WHIFF OF GAS TO PUT THE THING OUT FOR THE COUNT!
MY APOLOGIES, SIR! MY MEN MISTOOK YOU FOR THE HULK! THERE IS A NATIONAL ALARM OUT FOR HIM!
YOU TRYIN' TO TELL ME YOU THOUGHT THAT BRAINLESS LUMP OF LARD WAS ME??!! OF ALL THE CRUMMY...!
BEN, DON'T! HE'S TRYING TO APOLOGIZE! PLEASE, BEN!
C-CAN YOU CONTROL HIM, MA'AM? BETTER STAY BACK, MEN, TILL HE COOLS OFF!
AS IF BEIN' THE THING AINT BAD ENOUGH, NOW THOSE LAMEBRAINS ARE MISTAKIN' ME FOR THE HULK! BAH! C'MON, KID, I'LL TAKE YOU HOME!
AFTER LEAVING ALICIA, AND REACHING THE LOBBY OF THE BAXTER BUILDING....
BLAST THE LUCK! I MUSTA DROPPED THE ELECTRONIC THINGAMAJIG THAT OPENS OUR SPECIAL ELEVATOR DOOR!
WELL, I AINT IN THE MOOD TO GO BACK AND LOOK FOR IT!
WE BEEN NEEDIN' A NEW DOOR, ANYWAY!
WITHOUT THE SPECIAL KEY, THE ELEVATOR WON'T COME DOWN TO THE STREET FLOOR! BUT THAT AINT GONNA STOP ME! IT'S ONLY ABOUT THIRTY-FIVE FLOORS TO THE TOP!
AND MINUTES LATER...
WELL WELL, HERE COMES LOVER-BOY! HOW WAS YOUR DATE WITH ALICIA, ROMEO?
KNOCK IT OFF, JOHNNY! THE THING DOESN'T LOOK LIKE HE'S IN THE MOOD TO KID AROUND!
WHAT'S WRONG, BEN? CARE TO TELL US WHAT HAPPENED?
YOU'RE DARN TOOTIN' I'LL TELL YA WHAT HAPPENED! IT'S A LUCKY THING I DIDN'T SMASH A FEW HEADS TOGETHER!
4

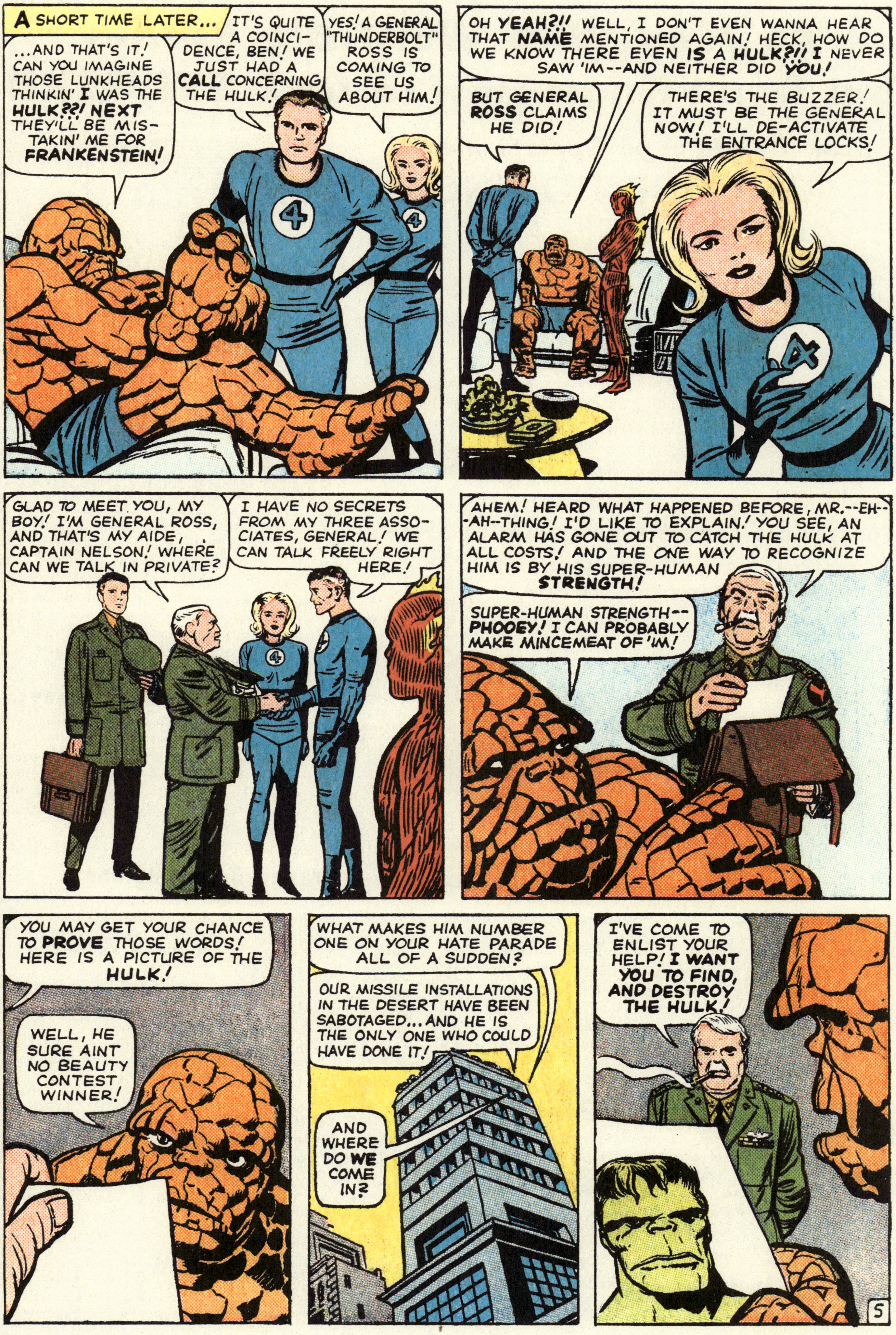

A SHORT TIME LATER...
...AND THAT'S IT! CAN YOU IMAGINE THOSE LUNKHEADS THINKIN' I WAS THE HULK??! NEXT THEY'LL BE MIS-TAKIN' ME FOR FRANKENSTEIN!
IT'S QUITE A COINCI-DENCE, BEN! WE JUST HAD A CALL CONCERNING THE HULK!
YES! A GENERAL "THUNDERBOLT" ROSS IS COMING TO SEE US ABOUT HIM!
OH YEAH?!! WELL, I DON'T EVEN WANNA HEAR THAT NAME MENTIONED AGAIN! HECK, HOW DO WE KNOW THERE EVEN IS A HULK?!! I NEVER SAW 'IM--AND NEITHER DID YOU!
BUT GENERAL ROSS CLAIMS HE DID!
THERE'S THE BUZZER! IT MUST BE THE GENERAL NOW! I'LL DE-ACTIVATE THE ENTRANCE LOCKS!
GLAD TO MEET YOU, MY BOY! I'M GENERAL ROSS, AND THAT'S MY AIDE, CAPTAIN NELSON! WHERE CAN WE TALK IN PRIVATE?
I HAVE NO SECRETS FROM MY THREE ASSO-CIATES, GENERAL! WE CAN TALK FREELY RIGHT HERE!
AHEM! HEARD WHAT HAPPENED BEFORE, MR.--EH--AH--THING! I'D LIKE TO EXPLAIN! YOU SEE, AN ALARM HAS GONE OUT TO CATCH THE HULK AT ALL COSTS! AND THE ONE WAY TO RECOGNIZE HIM IS BY HIS SUPER-HUMAN STRENGTH!
SUPER-HUMAN STRENGTH--PHOOEY! I CAN PROBABLY MAKE MINCEMEAT OF 'IM!
YOU MAY GET YOUR CHANCE TO PROVE THOSE WORDS! HERE IS A PICTURE OF THE HULK!
WELL, HE SURE AINT NO BEAUTY CONTEST WINNER!
WHAT MAKES HIM NUMBER ONE ON YOUR HATE PARADE ALL OF A SUDDEN?
OUR MISSILE INSTALLATIONS IN THE DESERT HAVE BEEN SABOTAGED... AND HE IS THE ONLY ONE WHO COULD HAVE DONE IT!
AND WHERE DO WE COME IN?
I'VE COME TO ENLIST YOUR HELP! I WANT YOU TO FIND, AND DESTROY THE HULK!
5

PART 2
MISSION: STOP THE HULK!
THESE ARE THE MOST RECENT RECORDED MOVING PICTURES OF THE HULK HIMSELF! THEY WERE TAKEN BY AN AUTOMATIC CAMERA PLACED IN THE SIGHTING DEVICE OF A SPECIAL CANNON!
WELL, I GUESS WE'RE LOOKING AT PROOF POSITIVE THAT HE DOES EXIST!
AND THIS IS THE CANNON, THREE SECONDS LATER, AFTER THE HULK FINISHED HIS SAVAGE ONSLAUGHT! ONLY THE FILM CARTRIDGE REMAINED INTACT!
HOLD IT, SIR! SUE! WHERE IS SHE?
RIGHT HERE, REED! FORGIVE ME! THE--THE SIGHT OF THAT MONSTER UNNERVED ME SO THAT I LOST CONTROL OF MY VISIBILITY POWER!
6

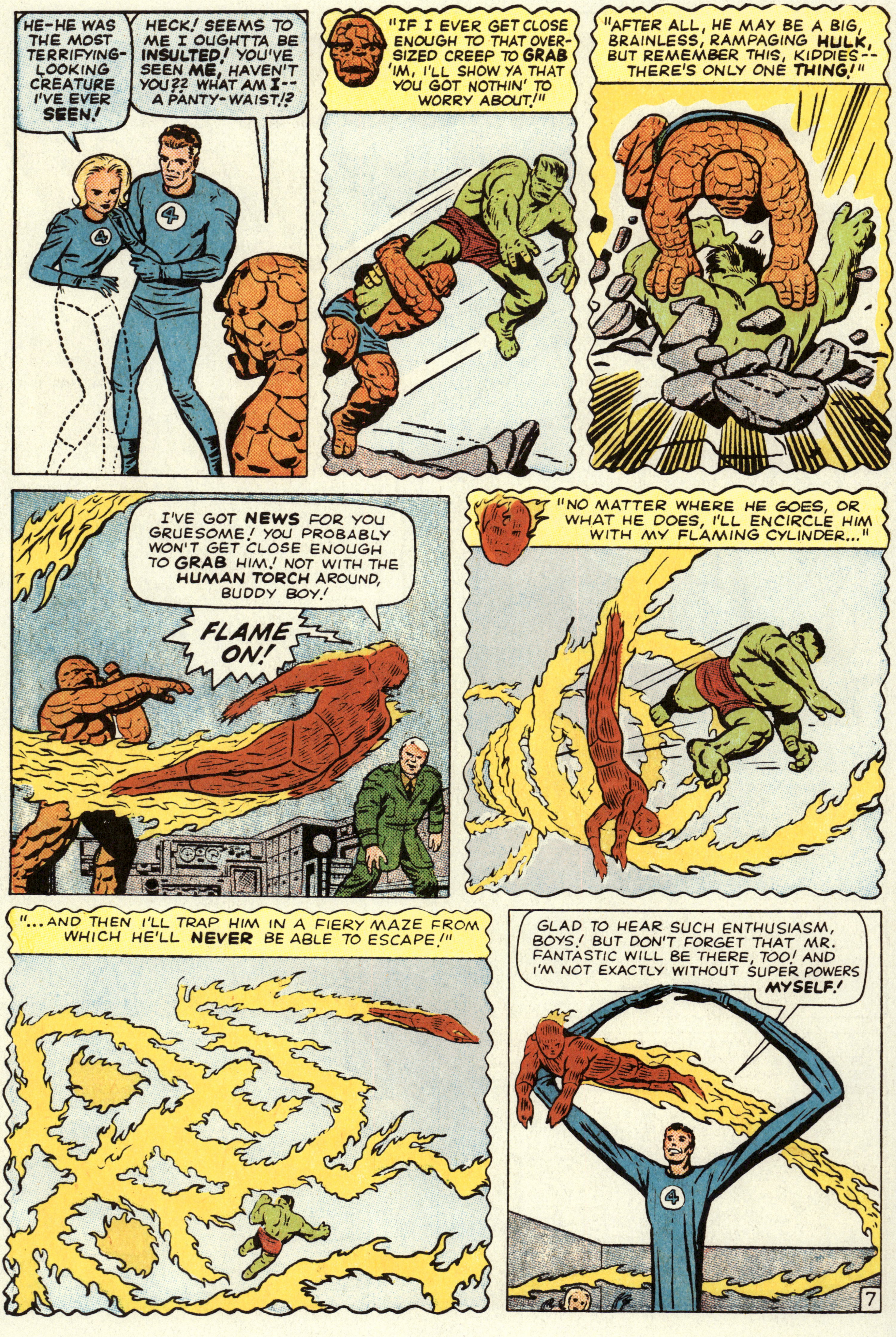
HE-HE WAS THE MOST TERRIFYING-LOOKING CREATURE I'VE EVER SEEN!
HECK! SEEMS TO ME I OUGHTTA BE INSULTED! YOU'VE SEEN ME, HAVEN'T YOU?? WHAT AM I-- A PANTY-WAIST!?
"IF I EVER GET CLOSE ENOUGH TO THAT OVER-SIZED CREEP TO GRAB 'IM, I'LL SHOW YA THAT YOU GOT NOTHIN' TO WORRY ABOUT!"
"AFTER ALL, HE MAY BE A BIG, BRAINLESS, RAMPAGING HULK, BUT REMEMBER THIS, KIDDIES-- THERE'S ONLY ONE THING!"
I'VE GOT NEWS FOR YOU GRUESOME! YOU PROBABLY WON'T GET CLOSE ENOUGH TO GRAB HIM! NOT WITH THE HUMAN TORCH AROUND, BUDDY BOY!
FLAME ON!
"NO MATTER WHERE HE GOES, OR WHAT HE DOES, I'LL ENCIRCLE HIM WITH MY FLAMING CYLINDER..."
"...AND THEN I'LL TRAP HIM IN A FIERY MAZE FROM WHICH HE'LL NEVER BE ABLE TO ESCAPE!"
GLAD TO HEAR SUCH ENTHUSIASM, BOYS! BUT DON'T FORGET THAT MR. FANTASTIC WILL BE THERE, TOO! AND I'M NOT EXACTLY WITHOUT SUPER POWERS MYSELF!
7

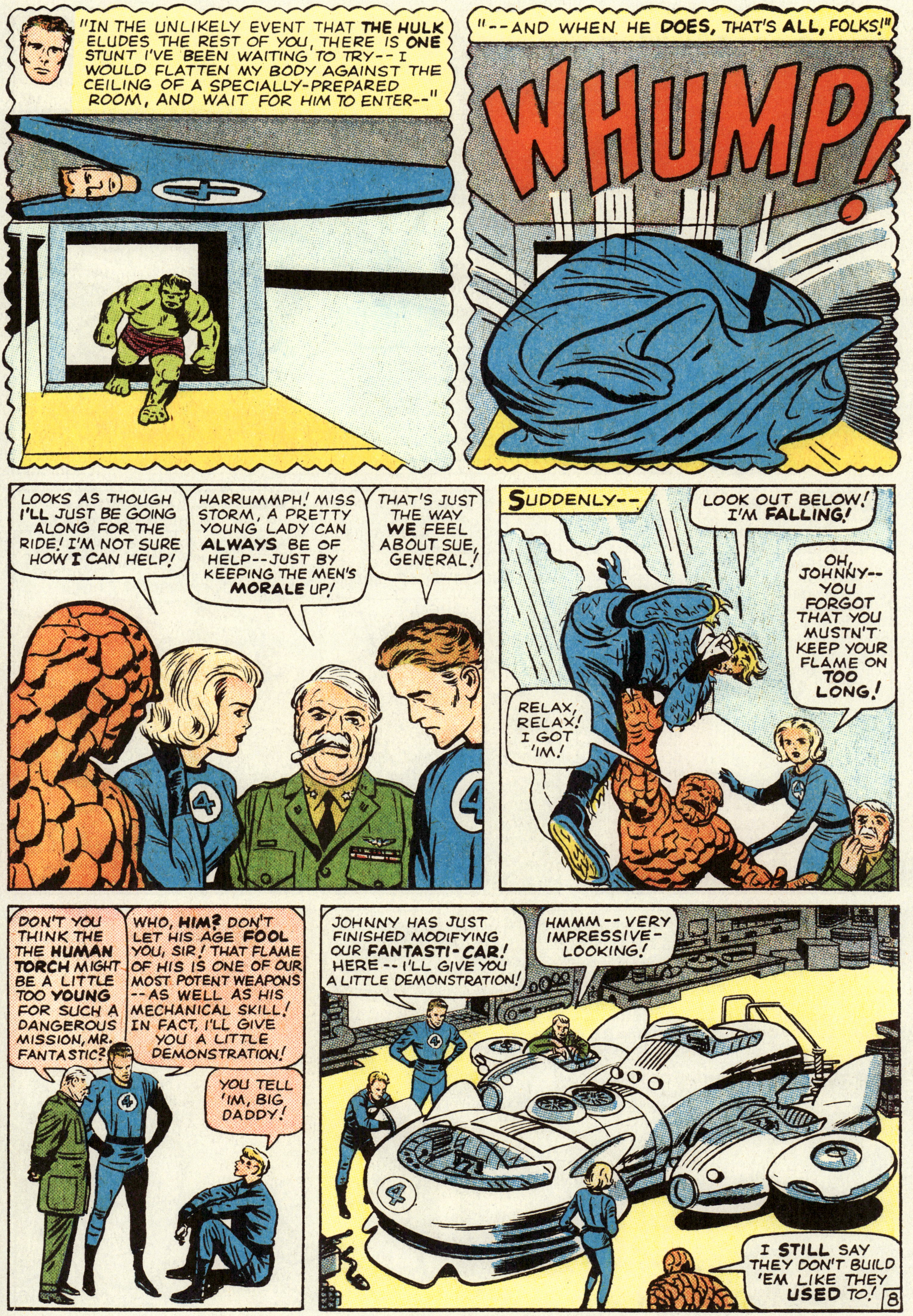
"IN THE UNLIKELY EVENT THAT THE HULK ELUDES THE REST OF YOU, THERE IS ONE STUNT I'VE BEEN WAITING TO TRY-- I WOULD FLATTEN MY BODY AGAINST THE CEILING OF A SPECIALLY-PREPARED ROOM, AND WAIT FOR HIM TO ENTER--"
"--AND WHEN HE DOES, THAT'S ALL, FOLKS!"
WHUMP!
LOOKS AS THOUGH I'LL JUST BE GOING ALONG FOR THE RIDE! I'M NOT SURE HOW I CAN HELP!
HARRUMMPH! MISS STORM, A PRETTY YOUNG LADY CAN ALWAYS BE OF HELP--JUST BY KEEPING THE MEN'S MORALE UP!
THAT'S JUST THE WAY WE FEEL ABOUT SUE, GENERAL!
SUDDENLY--
LOOK OUT BELOW! I'M FALLING!
OH, JOHNNY-- YOU FORGOT THAT YOU MUSTN'T KEEP YOUR FLAME ON TOO LONG!
RELAX, RELAX! I GOT 'IM!
DON'T YOU THINK THE THE HUMAN TORCH MIGHT BE A LITTLE TOO YOUNG FOR SUCH A DANGEROUS MISSION, MR. FANTASTIC?
WHO, HIM? DON'T LET HIS AGE FOOL YOU, SIR! THAT FLAME OF HIS IS ONE OF OUR MOST POTENT WEAPONS --AS WELL AS HIS MECHANICAL SKILL! IN FACT, I'LL GIVE YOU A LITTLE DEMONSTRATION!
YOU TELL 'IM, BIG DADDY!
JOHNNY HAS JUST FINISHED MODIFYING OUR FANTASTI-CAR! HERE -- I'LL GIVE YOU A LITTLE DEMONSTRATION!
HMMM -- VERY IMPRESSIVE-LOOKING!
I STILL SAY THEY DON'T BUILD 'EM LIKE THEY USED TO!
8

A NUMBER OF OUR FANS THRUOUT THE COUNTRY HAD WRITTEN TO US SAYING THE FANTASTI-CAR LOOKED TOO MUCH LIKE A FLYING BATHTUB! AND JOHNNNY AGREED WITH THEM!
TELL ME MORE ABOUT THIS THING --WHAT'S HER TOP SPEED? HER CRUISING RANGE?
TOP SPEED'S A SECRET, GENERAL-- BUT IT'S FASTER THAN YOU'D SUSPECT! AS FOR HER CRUISING RANGE, WE'VE EXTENDED IT TO BETTER THAN THREE THOUSAND MILES--ENOUGH TO TAKE US CLEAR ACROSS THE U.S.A.!
STOP YAKKIN' AND SHOW THE BRASS HOW ALL FOUR SECTIONS CAN DISENGAGE AND FLY SEPARATELY! AND REMEMBER, THAT WAS MY IDEA!
AS A MATTER OF FACT, WHY DON'T WE USE THE FANTASTI-CAR NOW TO FLY TO THE MISSILE AREA? WE CAN TAKE YOU WITH US, GENERAL!
AND SO, A FEW HOURS LATER...
THOSE JET PROPS UNDER EACH SMALL WING REALLY HOLD THIS SHIP UP SMOOTHLY!
UH OH! HERE'S SOMETHING YOU HADN'T COUNTED ON --A RAIN STORM!
WE'VE PREPARED FOR THAT TOO, SIR! AT THE FLICK OF A BUTTON, THE WINDSHIELD ROLLS OVER AND FORMS A TRANSPARENT WATERPROOF AND BULLETPROOF SHIELD!
I'VE GOT TO TELL ARMY ORDNANCE ABOUT THIS!
LATER* AT A LARGE MISSILE BASE IN THE SOUTHWEST...
THERE'S AN EXAMPLE OF THE HULK'S WORK! PROJECT 34, ANTI-GRAV MISSILE, WRECKED!
BUT HOW CAN YOU BE SURE THE HULK DID IT?
LOOK AT THAT TANGLED STEEL! NO ONE ELSE HAS THE STRENGTH TO DO THAT!
*EXACT FLYING TIME WITHHELD AT REQUEST OF REED RICHARDS!
IMMEDIATELY UPON LANDING, GENERAL ROSS CALLS A HIGH-LEVEL CONFERENCE...
GENTLEMEN, THIS IS REED RICHARDS, KNOWN AS MR. FANTASTIC, REPRESENTING THE FANTASTIC FOUR!
I'M DR. BRUCE BANNER, CIVILIAN SCIENTIFIC EXEC AT THIS BASE! THIS IS MY ASSISTANT, DR. KARL KORT, AND MY YOUNG HELPER, RICK JONES!
EVERY MINUTE COUNTS, GENERAL! HOW DOES THE FANTASTIC FOUR PROPOSE TO CATCH THE HULK?
HI!
THAT'S THE KIND OF TALK I LIKE! ACTION TALK! LET'S PLAN OUR CAMPAIGN!
BUT, GENERAL, I STILL MAINTAIN THAT THE HULK IS NOT OUR MAN! ALL OUR MISSILE APPARATUS WAS DESTROYED FROM THE INSIDE OUT! I'M CONVINCED A RAMPAGING CREATURE LIKE THE HULK WOULD HAVE TORN THE DEVICES FROM THE OUTSIDE IN!
9

BANNER, I'VE TOLD YOU OUR MISSION IS TO CATCH THE HULK! WE'LL LISTEN TO YOUR THEORIES AFTER HE'S PUT OUT OF ACTION! NOW YOU AND MR. FANTASTIC START PUTTING YOUR HEADS TOGETHER!
IT'LL BE A PLEASURE TO WORK WITH YOU, DR. BANNER! I'VE LONG BEEN AN ADMIRER OF YOUR ATOMIC RESEARCH!
I'M HIGHLY FLATTERED THAT THE MOST BRILLIANT SCIENTIFIC BRAIN OF OUR TIME SHOULD SAY THAT TO ME!
WELL, YOU GENTLEMEN WON'T BE NEEDING ME FOR A WHILE! I'LL GET BACK TO MY WORK!
HEY, SHORTY, HOW MUCH LONGER THEY GONNA KEEP US COOLIN' OUR HEELS OUT HERE?
GASP! WHA- WHAT ARE YOU??!
S'MATTER-- AINT YOU NEVER SEEN A THING BEFORE??
I'M GETTIN' FED UP WITH GUYS DOIN' DOUBLE-TAKES EVERY TIME THEY SEE ME!
LOOK AT 'IM GO! I THINK YOU SCARED THE POOR GUY OUTTA A YEAR'S GROWTH, THING!
AND HE CAN'T SPARE IT!
HEY--HE DROPPED HIS WALLET!
RELAX, BIG FELLA! I'LL GET IT FOR HIM!
I'VE BEEN WANTING TO TRY THIS FLAMING LASSO TRICK SINCE I DREAMED IT UP!
NOT BAD, EH? AND I DIDN'T EVEN SINGE THE LEATHER!
I AINT IN THE MOOD FOR TRICKS! THEY CAN'T KEEP ME WAITIN' OUT HERE ANY LONGER!
OKAY, SOLDIER BOYS! READY OR NOT, HERE I COME!
THING! DON'T! IT'S A PRIVATE MEETING!
EASY WITH THAT CHOPPER, SARGE! WE'RE ON YOUR TEAM!
THING! WHAT ARE YOU DOING?? HAVE YOU LOST YOUR SENSES?!!
10

An Amazing Invention—"Magic Art Reproducer"

DRAW THE FIRST DAY

NO LESSONS! NO TALENT!

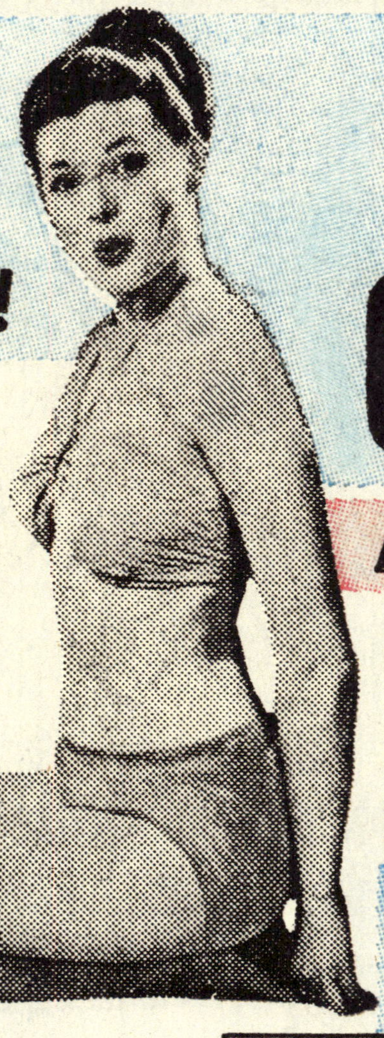

Even if You CAN'T DRAW A STRAIGHT LINE

You Can Draw Your Family, Friends, Anything From REAL LIFE—Like An Artist... Even if You CAN'T DRAW A Straight Line!

Anyone can Draw With This Amazing New Invention—Instantly!

De Luxe Model Complete for only

—With extra high power, extra clear and sharp "reproducer" unit.

$1.98

A New Hobby Gives You A Brand New Interest!

Yes, anyone from 5 to 80 can draw or sketch or paint anything now... the very first time you use the "Magic Art Reproducer" like a professional artist—no matter how "hopeless" you think you are! An unlimited variety and amount of drawings can be made. Art is admired and respected by everyone. Most hobbies are expensive, but drawing costs very little. just some inexpensive paper, pencils, crayons, or paint. No costly upkeep. nothing to wear out, no parts to replace. It automatically reproduces anything you want to draw on any sheet of paper. Then easily and quickly follow the lines of the "picture image" with your pencil ... and you have an accurate original drawing that anyone would think an artist had done. No guesswork, no judging sizes and shapes! Reproduces black and white and actual colors for paintings.

Also makes drawing larger or smaller as you wish.

Anyone can use it on any desk, table, board, etc.—indoors or outdoors! Light and compact to be taken wherever you wish. No other lessons or practice or talent needed! You'll be proud to frame your original drawings for a more distinctive touch to your home. Give them to friends as gifts that are "different," appreciated.

Have fun! Be popular! Everyone will ask you to draw them. You'll be in demand! After a short time, you may find you can draw well without the "Magic Art Reproducer" because you have developed a "knack" and feeling artists have—which may lead to a good paying art career.

FREE!

"How to Easily Draw Artists' Models"

This valuable illustrated guide is yours free with order of "Magic Art Reproducer." Packed with pictures showing all the basic poses of artists' models with simple instruction for beginners of art. Includes guidance on anatomy, techniques and figure action.

SEND NO MONEY! Free 10-Day Trial!

Just send name and address. Pay postman on delivery $1.98 plus postage. Or send only $1.98 with order and we pay postage. You must be convinced that you can draw anything like an artist, or return merchandise after 10-day trial and your money will be refunded.

NORTON PRODUCTS Dept. 833, 296 Broadway New York 7, N. Y.

ALSO EXCELLENT FOR EVERY OTHER TYPE OF DRAWING AND HOBBY!

Create Your Own Design for All Hobbies! Reproduce on anything.

Copy all cartoons, comics.

Outdoor Scenes, landscapes, buildings

Copy photos, portraits of family, friends, etc.

Still life, vases, bowls of fruit, lamps, furniture, all objects.

Copy blueprints, plans.

FREE 10-DAY TRIAL COUPON

NORTON PRODUCTS, Dept. 833
296 Broadway, New York 7, N. Y.

Rush my "Magic Art Reproducer" plus FREE illustrated guide "*How to Easily Draw Artists' Models.*" I will pay postman on delivery only $1.98 plus postage. I must be convinced that I can draw anything like an artist. or I can return merchandise after 10-day trial and get my money back.

Name________________

Address________________

City & Zone________ State________

☐ Check here if you wish to save postage by sending only $1.98 with coupon. Same Money Back Guarantee!

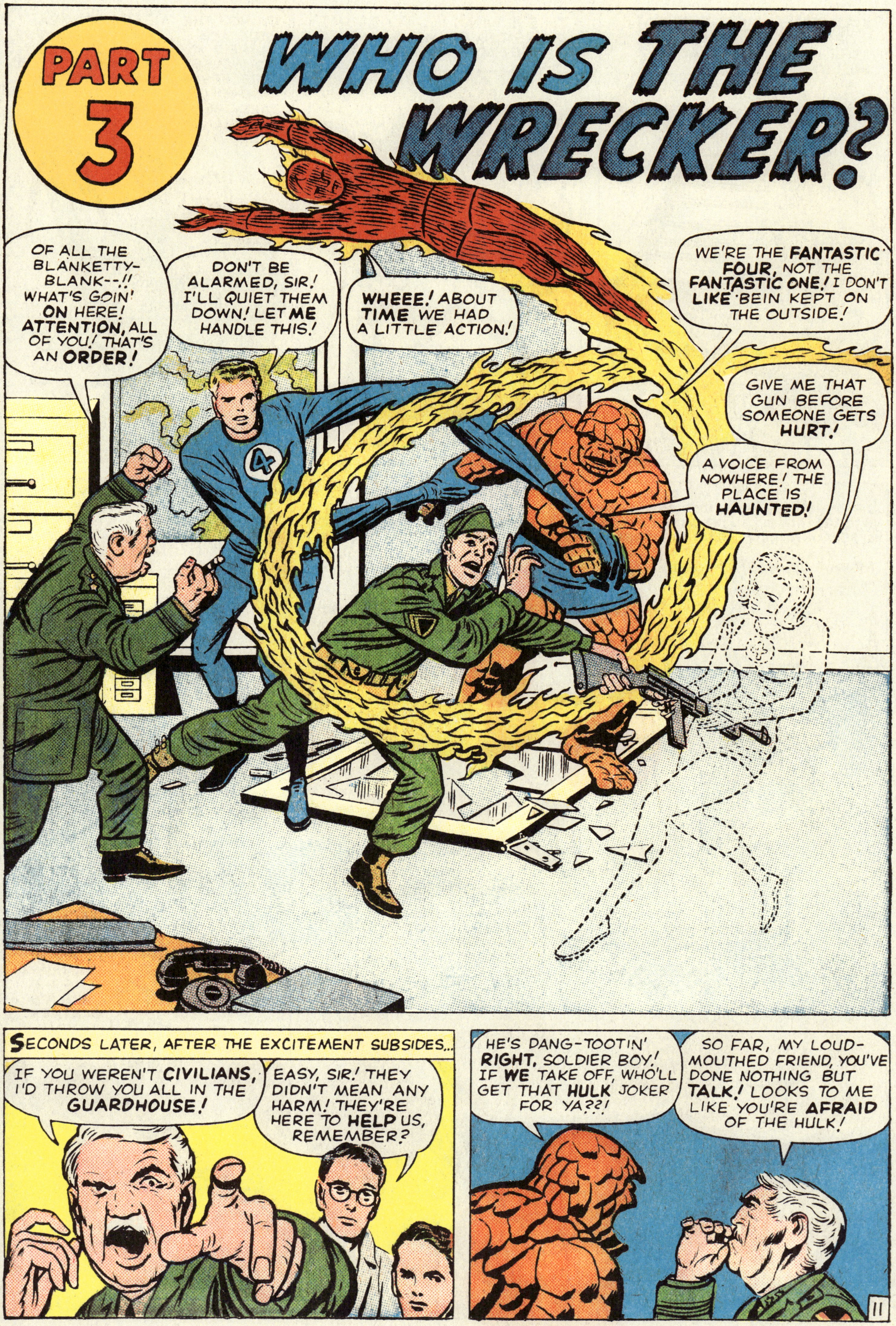
PART 3
WHO IS THE WRECKER?
OF ALL THE BLANKETTY-BLANK--!! WHAT'S GOIN' ON HERE! ATTENTION, ALL OF YOU! THAT'S AN ORDER!
DON'T BE ALARMED, SIR! I'LL QUIET THEM DOWN! LET ME HANDLE THIS!
WHEEE! ABOUT TIME WE HAD A LITTLE ACTION!
WE'RE THE FANTASTIC FOUR, NOT THE FANTASTIC ONE! I DON'T LIKE BEIN KEPT ON THE OUTSIDE!
GIVE ME THAT GUN BEFORE SOMEONE GETS HURT!
A VOICE FROM NOWHERE! THE PLACE IS HAUNTED!
SECONDS LATER, AFTER THE EXCITEMENT SUBSIDES...
IF YOU WEREN'T CIVILIANS, I'D THROW YOU ALL IN THE GUARDHOUSE!
EASY, SIR! THEY DIDN'T MEAN ANY HARM! THEY'RE HERE TO HELP US, REMEMBER?
HE'S DANG-TOOTIN' RIGHT, SOLDIER BOY! IF WE TAKE OFF, WHO'LL GET THAT HULK JOKER FOR YA??!
SO FAR, MY LOUD-MOUTHED FRIEND, YOU'VE DONE NOTHING BUT TALK! LOOKS TO ME LIKE YOU'RE AFRAID OF THE HULK!
11

AFRAID OF THE HULK, AM I ??
I'LL SHOW YA WHO'S AFRAID OF WHAT!!!
THIS IS WHAT I'LL DO TO THAT OVERSIZED CRUMB-BUM WHEN I GET MY HANDS ON 'IM!
RRRRRRIIP!
OH NO! THE BIG APE RUINED MY BOUND SET OF TELEPHONE BOOKS! OF ALL THE--!!!
EASY, GENERAL! WE'LL REIMBURSE YOU FOR THEM! BUT YOU'VE GOT TO WATCH WHAT YOU SAY TO THE THING!
A FINE KETTLE OF FISH THIS IS! I'VE HIRED MYSELF A BUNCH OF BLASTED PRIMA DONNAS!
MR. FANTASTIC, ANYTHING I CAN DO TO HELP YOU FIND THE WRECKER, LET ME KNOW!
THE WRECKER?
THAT'S OUR NAME FOR THE SABOTEUR!
STRANGE--DR. BANNER AND RICK SEEM SO SURE THAT THE HULK ISN'T THE GUILTY ONE!
TOO BAD WE CAN'T TELL THEM WHY WE'RE SO SURE THE HULK IS INNOCENT, EH, RICK?
YES, DOC!
HEY, RICK--I'VE GOT A WALLET FOR YOU TO RETURN TO SOMEONE!
WATCH WHAT YOU'RE DOIN', TORCH!
HAH! FOOLED YOU, HUH? YOU THOUGHT YOU'D BURN YOURSELF --BUT I DOUSED THE FLAME IN MY HANDS!
BOY! YOU'RE JUST A BARREL OF LAUGHS, AINT YA?
DON'T BLAME YOU FOR BEIN' IMPRESSED, SON!
LOOK AT HIM GREEN WITH ENVY! TRYIN' NOT TO ADMIT HE'S OVERWHELMED BY ME!
HE WOULDN'T BE SO SWELL-HEADED IF HE KNEW I WAS THE HULK'S PARTNER!
12

LATER, UNSEEN BY THE OTHERS, RICK JONES AND BRUCE BANNER ENTER A SECRET, UNDERWATER TUNNEL, KNOWN ONLY TO THEMSELVES...
RICK, IT'S GOING TO BE UP TO US TO FIND THE WRECKER! I CAN'T CONVINCE THE OTHERS THAT THE HULK IS INNOCENT!
GOSH, DOC, IF ONLY YOU COULD TAKE THE FANTASTIC FOUR INTO YOUR CONFIDENCE!
THEN, AT DR. BANNER'S PRIVATE LAB...
HERE IT IS, RICK-- A SCALE MODEL OF MY GREATEST WORK, PROJECT 34, WHICH THE WRECKER DESTROYED!
WHAT'S IT SUPPOSED TO DO, DOC?
"PLACED IN THE CENTER OF A CITY, IT WOULD EMIT ELECTRO-MAGNETIC WAVES, BLANKETING THE AREA..."
"...MAKING ANY U.S. CITY COMPLETELY INVULNERABLE TO ENEMY MISSILES OR ROCKETS! ONCE I PERFECT IT, IT WILL BE THE PERFECT DEFENSE IN A NUCLEAR AGE!"
BUT THE WRECKER, WHOEVER HE IS, IS TRYING TO STOP MY WORK! AND HE HAS CLEVERLY MANAGED TO MAKE GENERAL ROSS THINK THE HULK IS BEHIND THE SABOTAGE!
BY THE WAY, THE TORCH GAVE ME THIS WALLET TO RETURN TO KARL KORT! I'LL TAKE IT TO HIM!
I SURE HOPE THE HULK DOESN'T APPEAR WHILE THE FANTASTIC FOUR ARE HERE! THEY MIGHT BE TOO MUCH EVEN FOR HIM TO HANDLE!
SAY! WHAT'S THIS CARD STICKIN' OUT OF KORT'S WALLET? IT LOOKS LIKE...
IT IS! IT'S A MEMBERSHIP CARD IN A SUBVERSIVE COMMUNIST-FRONT ORGANIZATION!
THAT MEANS-- KARL KORT MUST BE-- A RED!
I'VE GOTTA TELL THE HULK! HE'LL KNOW WHAT TO--
YOU'RE NOT TELLING ANYONE, YOU LITTLE SNOOP!
SO YOU'RE IN LEAGUE WITH THE HULK, ARE YOU?? WELL, WELL! NOW I'LL BE ABLE TO DESTROY HIM AS WELL AS BANNER'S PROJECT 34!
YOU-- YOU'RE THE WRECKER!
13

PART 4
"the HULK AT LAST!"
THING! GET OUT OF THERE! THAT ROCKET SLED ISN'T READY FOR TESTING YET! IT HAS SOME BUGS WE HAVEN'T BEEN ABLE TO IRON OUT!
RELAX, NAPOLEON! WE JUST IRONED 'EM OUT FOR YA! BESIDES, I ALWAYS WANTED TO RIDE ON ONE THESE KIDDIE-CARS!
I NOTICED THE SLED HERE, GENERAL, AND I SAW WHAT THE PROBLEM WAS! I THINK WE'VE GOT IT LICKED FOR YOU! ANYWAY, WE'LL KNOW IN A MOMENT!
ROCKET SLED X2A-17
ALL CONDITIONS ARE "GO", REED! WHENEVER BEN IS READY!
I CHECKED ALL THE RAILS AND WELDED A FEW WEAK SPOTS! LET 'ER RIP!
HOLY COW! THAT ROCKET SLED WASN'T SUPPOSED TO BE OPERATIONAL FOR AT LEAST TWO WEEKS!
THAT WAS BEFORE MR. FANTASTIC GOT HERE! HE STRAIGHTENED OUT THOSE ELECTRONIC CIRCUITS LIKE THEY WERE NOTHIN'!
WEEEEEOOOOOOO!
-GULP- THE THING'S GOT HER UP TO FIFTY G's!
IT'S IMPOSSIBLE! NOTHING CAN STAND THAT PRESSURE AND NOT BE FLATTENED LIKE A PANCAKE!
YOU KIDDIN'? I CAN SEE HIM LAUGHING AND -- AND HE SEEMS TO BE WHISTLING!

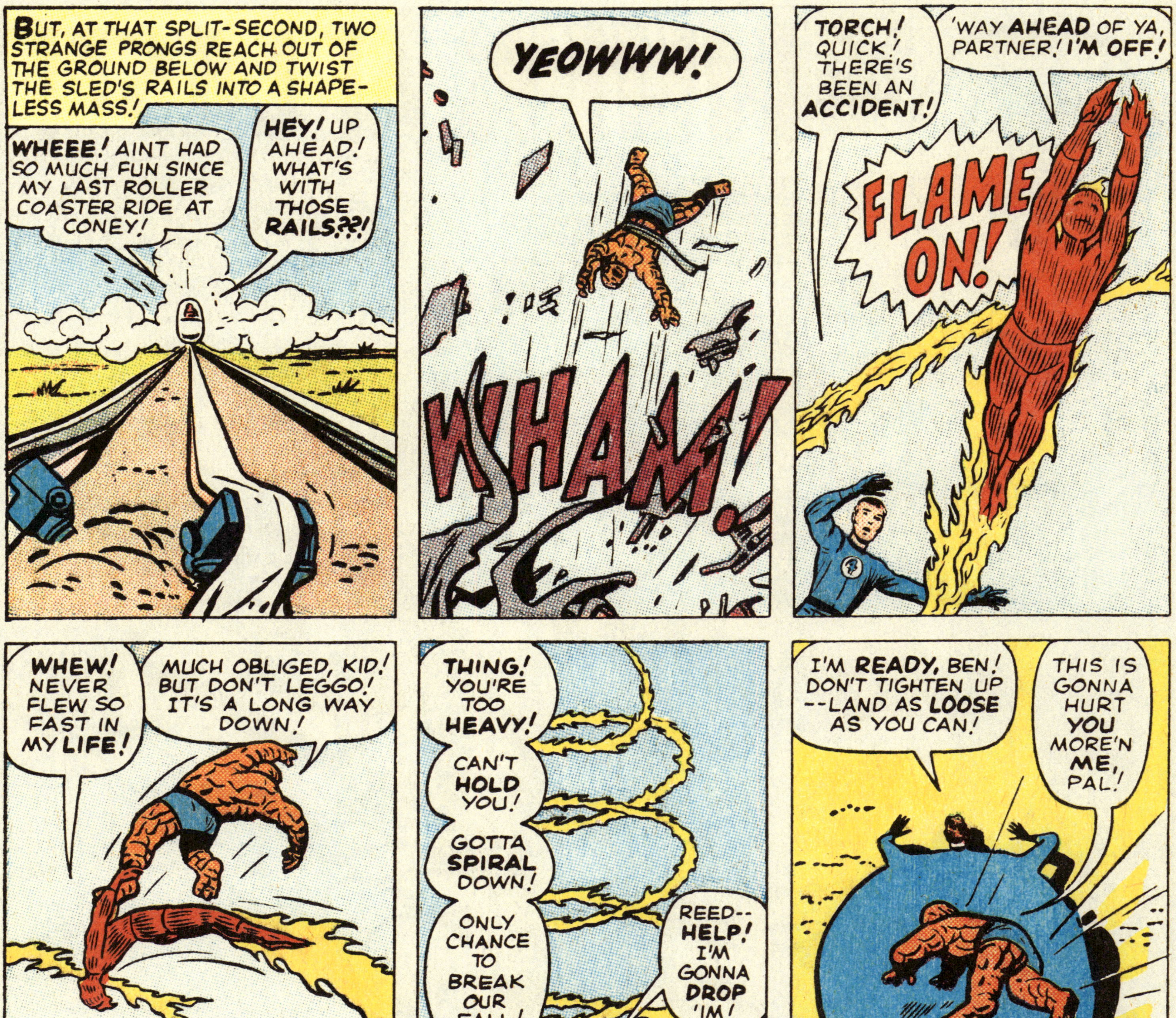

BUT, AT THAT SPLIT-SECOND, TWO STRANGE PRONGS REACH OUT OF THE GROUND BELOW AND TWIST THE SLED'S RAILS INTO A SHAPELESS MASS!
WHEEE! AINT HAD SO MUCH FUN SINCE MY LAST ROLLER COASTER RIDE AT CONEY!
HEY! UP AHEAD! WHAT'S WITH THOSE RAILS??!
YEOWWW!
WHAM!
TORCH! QUICK! THERE'S BEEN AN ACCIDENT!
'WAY AHEAD OF YA, PARTNER! I'M OFF!
FLAME ON!
WHEW! NEVER FLEW SO FAST IN MY LIFE!
MUCH OBLIGED, KID! BUT DON'T LEGGO! IT'S A LONG WAY DOWN!
THING! YOU'RE TOO HEAVY!
CAN'T HOLD YOU!
GOTTA SPIRAL DOWN!
ONLY CHANCE TO BREAK OUR FALL!
REED-- HELP! I'M GONNA DROP 'IM!
I'M READY, BEN! DON'T TIGHTEN UP --LAND AS LOOSE AS YOU CAN!
THIS IS GONNA HURT YOU MORE'N ME, PAL!
SECONDS LATER...
OKAY, BIG FELLA! EVERYTHING'S UNDER CONTROL!
BUT YOU MEN WRECKED OUR ROCKET SLED!
YOU'RE BATTY! IT WAS SABOTAGED, BUB! THE THING SAW IT!
LOOK-- HERE COMES DOCTOR BANNER! HE SEEMS UPSET!
I NEED YOUR HELP! RICK JONES IS GONE! I'M AFRAID THE WRECKER GOT HIM!
WE WERE LOOKING FOR YOU, TOO! SOMEONE JUST SABOTAGED THE ROCKET SLED!
WHAT'S ALL THIS "WRECKER" JAZZ! IT'S THE HULK, AND WE KNOW IT!

NO ONE BUT THAT BLASTED HULK COULDA BEEN STRONG ENOUGH TO TWIST THOSE ROCKET SLED TRACKS! AND WHEN I GET AHOLD OF HIM....!
NO! IT ISN'T THE HULK, IT'S THE WRECKER! AND IF YOU DON'T GIVE UP THE CASE, HE'LL HARM RICK!
DR. BANNER, I DON'T UNDERSTAND! HOW DO YOU KNOW? WHAT PROOF DO YOU HAVE?
NONE! YOU'VE JUST GOT TO BELIEVE ME! HOW-- HOW CAN I CONVINCE YOU??!
WE CAN'T GIVE UP A TASK JUST ON YOUR SAY SO!
WAIT! I KNOW YOU HAVE MORE TO TELL US! WHY WON'T YOU SPEAK? WHAT ARE YOU HIDING?
IT'S NO USE! HOW CAN I EXPECT THEM TO BELIEVE ME, WHEN I CAN'T TELL THEM THE WHOLE TRUTH??
Y'KNOW SOMETHIN'? I DON'T TRUST THAT GUY!
ME NEITHER!
I DIDN'T DARE SHOW THEM THIS NOTE I FOUND NEAR WHERE RICK DISAPPEARED! BUT I JUST CAN'T IGNORE IT!
TO THE HULK! RICK JONES IS MY PRISONER! UNLESS YOU DRIVE THE FANTASTIC FOUR FROM THIS AREA, YOU WILL NEVER SEE HIM AGAIN! the WRECKER
MINUTES LATER, IN HIS HIDDEN, UNDERGROUND LAB, KNOWN ONLY TO DR. BANNER AND RICK JONES...
THERE'S NO WAY THAT I CAN MAKE THE FANTASTIC FOUR LEAVE THIS AREA!
DRAMATICALLY, THE SCIENTIST REMOVES HIS CLOTHES AND STANDS UPON A SENSITIVE, AWESOME DEVICE OF HIS OWN DESIGN...
IT IS TIME FOR ME TO AGAIN ACTIVATE THE ONLY MACHINE ON EARTH WHICH CAN DUPLICATE THE INCREDIBLE GAMMA RAYS OF MY GAMMA BOMB!
BZZZT
FOR, ALTHOUGH BRUCE BANNER CANNOT COPE WITH THE WRECKER, OR THE FANTASTIC FOUR...
--THERE IS ONE WHO CAN--
--AND IT IS TIME FOR THE HULK TO AGAIN WALK THE EARTH!
16

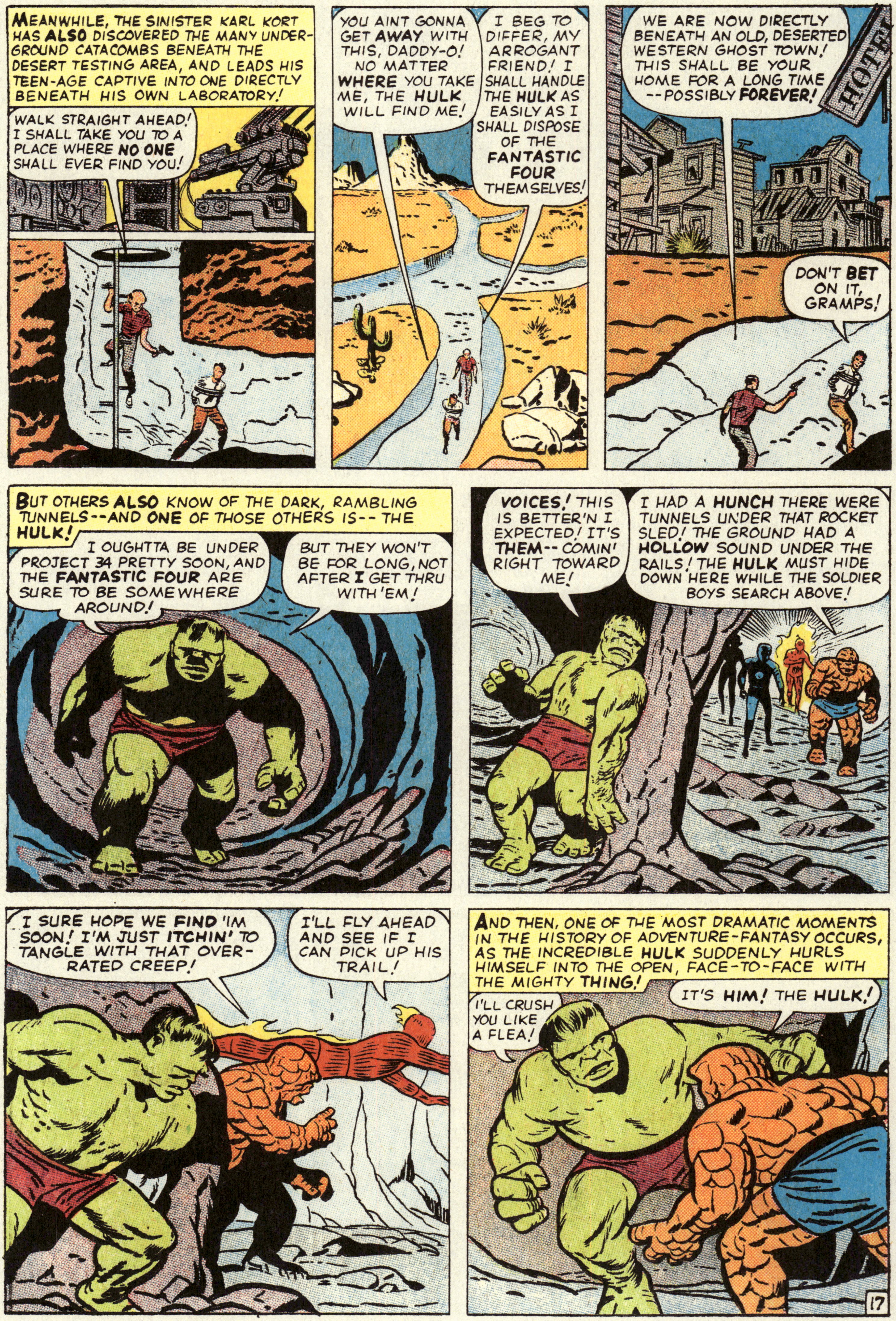
MEANWHILE, THE SINISTER KARL KORT HAS ALSO DISCOVERED THE MANY UNDER-GROUND CATACOMBS BENEATH THE DESERT TESTING AREA, AND LEADS HIS TEEN-AGE CAPTIVE INTO ONE DIRECTLY BENEATH HIS OWN LABORATORY!
WALK STRAIGHT AHEAD! I SHALL TAKE YOU TO A PLACE WHERE NO ONE SHALL EVER FIND YOU!
YOU AINT GONNA GET AWAY WITH THIS, DADDY-O! NO MATTER WHERE YOU TAKE ME, THE HULK WILL FIND ME!
I BEG TO DIFFER, MY ARROGANT FRIEND! I SHALL HANDLE THE HULK AS EASILY AS I SHALL DISPOSE OF THE FANTASTIC FOUR THEMSELVES!
WE ARE NOW DIRECTLY BENEATH AN OLD, DESERTED WESTERN GHOST TOWN! THIS SHALL BE YOUR HOME FOR A LONG TIME --POSSIBLY FOREVER!
HOTE
DON'T BET ON IT, GRAMPS!
BUT OTHERS ALSO KNOW OF THE DARK, RAMBLING TUNNELS--AND ONE OF THOSE OTHERS IS-- THE HULK!
I OUGHTTA BE UNDER PROJECT 34 PRETTY SOON, AND THE FANTASTIC FOUR ARE SURE TO BE SOMEWHERE AROUND!
BUT THEY WON'T BE FOR LONG, NOT AFTER I GET THRU WITH 'EM!
VOICES! THIS IS BETTER'N I EXPECTED! IT'S THEM-- COMIN' RIGHT TOWARD ME!
I HAD A HUNCH THERE WERE TUNNELS UNDER THAT ROCKET SLED! THE GROUND HAD A HOLLOW SOUND UNDER THE RAILS! THE HULK MUST HIDE DOWN HERE WHILE THE SOLDIER BOYS SEARCH ABOVE!
I SURE HOPE WE FIND 'IM SOON! I'M JUST ITCHIN' TO TANGLE WITH THAT OVER-RATED CREEP!
I'LL FLY AHEAD AND SEE IF I CAN PICK UP HIS TRAIL!
AND THEN, ONE OF THE MOST DRAMATIC MOMENTS IN THE HISTORY OF ADVENTURE-FANTASY OCCURS, AS THE INCREDIBLE HULK SUDDENLY HURLS HIMSELF INTO THE OPEN, FACE-TO-FACE WITH THE MIGHTY THING!
I'LL CRUSH YOU LIKE A FLEA!
IT'S HIM! THE HULK!
17

HAVING THE ADVANTAGE OF SURPRISE, THE HULK GETS IN THE FIRST BLOW, A THUNDERING LEFT WHICH COULD FELL A BULL ELEPHANT! BUT THE THING IS MERELY TOPPLED OFF BALANCE FOR A SECOND...
ARGHHH! IT'S LIKE HITTING A STONE WALL!
POW!
HE'S STRONGER THAN I THOUGHT! I'LL HAVE TO--
WHAT'S THIS?? ANOTHER OF THE FANTASTIC FOUR! THE FLAMING ONE!
SO! WE FOUND YOU AT LAST, HUH?!
MOVING WITH UNBELIEVABLE SPEED FOR ONE SO HUGE, THE HULK SCOOPS UP A SMALL MOUNTAIN OF SAND AND EARTH, COVERING THE STARTLED TORCH WITH IT AND DOUSING HIS FLAME AT THE SAME TIME!
NO TIME TO WASTE! MUST BEAT YOU FAST! MUST FIND RICK!
NOW TO FIND THE LAST TWO MEMBERS OF THE FANTASTIC FOUR AND FINISH THEM OFF!
MAYBE THEY'VE REACHED THE SURFACE BY NOW!
FIRST, I'LL MAKE SURE THAT THE THING AND THE TORCH STAY BELOW FOR A WHILE!
BUT NO MATTER HOW DENSELY PACKED A PORTION OF EARTH MAY BE, IT CAN NEVER STOP THE UNBELIEVABLY PLIABLE LIMBS OF MR. FANTASTIC FROM FINDING THEIR WAY THRU!
THE HULK IS JUST AHEAD OF ME! I CAN HEAR HIS THUNDEROUS STRIDES!
GOT YOU!

BUT EVEN MR. FANTASTIC IS NO MATCH FOR THE HULK'S PONDEROUS STRENGTH, AS THE ENRAGED CREATURE BREAKS LOOSE OF REED'S TWISTING-VINE GRIP, AND GOES ON A SEEMINGLY MAD RAMPAGE!
NICE DIGGIN, THING! I KNEW THE HULK COULDN'T KEEP YOU DOWN FOR LONG!
THEY'VE ALL GOTTEN FREE! BUT I'LL STOP 'EM WITH THIS!
BARKER HOUSE
LOOK OUT! HE'S GOING TO HURL THAT WOODEN FRAME HOUSE AT US!
DON'T WORRY ABOUT HIM, KID! THIS TIME HE AINT TAKIN' ME BY SURPRISE!
GUESS AGAIN, BUSTER! THOSE CORNY STUNTS DON'T IMPRESS THE THING!
WHAM!
CAN'T SAVE RICK UNLESS I GET RID OF THE FANTASTIC FOUR!
BUT THEY'RE TOO POWERFUL TO BEAT ALL AT ONCE! GOT TO SEPARATE 'EM!
I'LL LEAP INTO THE AIR AND FLATTEN THE THING FIRST, IN A POWER DIVE!
NO YOU DON'T, BROTHER! THIS TIME I'VE GOT YOU!
YEAH? WELL, WATCH THIS--
LIKE A LIVING TORNADO, THE HULK SPINS HIMSELF AROUND, CAUSING MR. FANTASTIC TO UNWIND HIS BODY BEFORE THE IRRESISTABLE POWER OF THE INCREDIBLE CREATURE!
BUT, EVEN AS THEY LAND, A FLAMING, FLASHING, FURIOUS FIGURE HURTLES TOWARDS HIS MIGHTY FOE!
EVEN YOU CAN'T STOP ME NOW, HULK!

BUT THE HULK HAS ONE MORE POWER HE CAN USE--ONE WHICH NEVER FAILS TO STOP THOSE WHO DO NOT EXPECT IT!
BRACE YOURSELF FOR A LITTLE SURPRISE, YOU FLAMING BRAT!
SO MIGHTY ARE HIS ARMS, THAT WHEN HE CLAPS HIS HANDS TOGETHER WITH FULL FORCE, IT HAS THE EFFECT OF A SUPERSONIC BOOM SHOCK WAVE!
HERE'S A LITTLE LULLABY FROM ME TO YOU!
WHOOOM
HA! THAT'LL KEEP 'EM OUTTA ACTION FOR A WHILE!
BUT WHERE'S THE FOURTH ONE? WHERE'S THE THING?
RIGHT HERE, GRUESOME! THERE AINT A SOUND YOU CAN LISTEN TO THAT I CAN'T HANDLE ALSO!
WELL, WELL! SO THE BIG BAD HULK IS THROWIN' THINGS, HUH? THAT AINT GONNA HELP YOU NOW!
ANYONE CAN FIGHT WITH HIS MOUTH! BUT WHEN I GET MY HANDS ON YOU...
AND SO THE TWO HUMAN BEHEMOTHS MEET HEAD-ON, AS THE VERY EARTH BENEATH THEIR FEET TREMBLES FROM THE IMPACT!
I BEEN LOOKIN' FORWARD TO THIS FOR A LONG LONG TIME!
NOW I'VE GOT YOU!
CRASSHH
SLOWLY, INEXORABLY, THE LARGER HULK LIFTS THE RAGING THING OFF HIS FEET, AS THE MIND-STAGGERING BATTLE REACHES ITS FINAL CLIMAX! BUT THEN--AT THAT INSTANT--A STRANGE, ATOM-POWERED RAY SHOOTS OUT FROM THE TUNNEL BELOW, AND...
DON'T MOVE, MISTER! MY PILE-DRIVER PUNCH IS COMIN' RIGHT AT YA!
I'LL SMASH YOU TO THE GROUND LIKE A PANCAKE! I'LL-- UGHHHH!
20

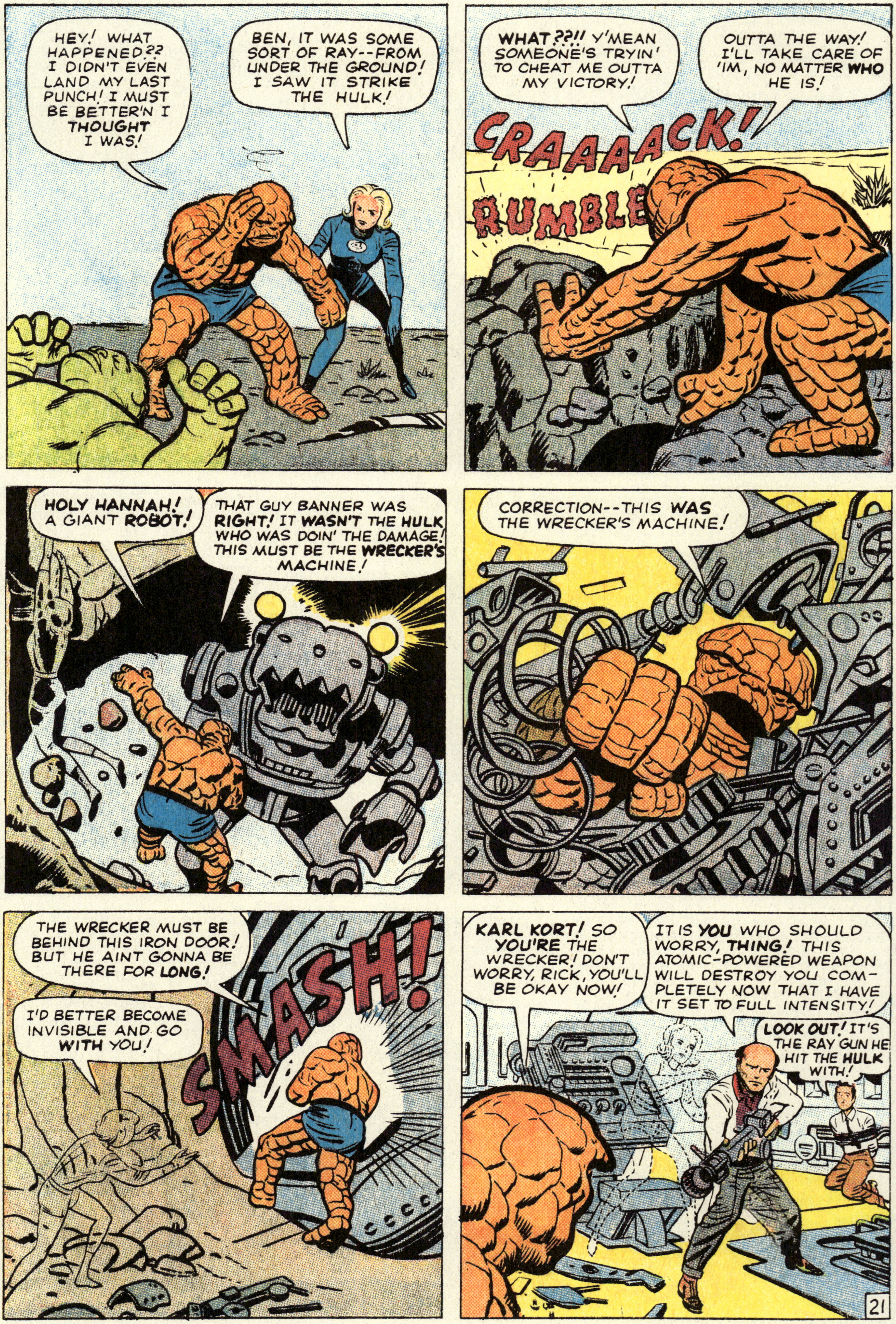
HEY! WHAT HAPPENED?? I DIDN'T EVEN LAND MY LAST PUNCH! I MUST BE BETTER'N I THOUGHT I WAS!
BEN, IT WAS SOME SORT OF RAY--FROM UNDER THE GROUND! I SAW IT STRIKE THE HULK!
WHAT??!! Y'MEAN SOMEONE'S TRYIN' TO CHEAT ME OUTTA MY VICTORY!
OUTTA THE WAY! I'LL TAKE CARE OF 'IM, NO MATTER WHO HE IS!
CRAAAACK!
RUMBLE
HOLY HANNAH! A GIANT ROBOT!
THAT GUY BANNER WAS RIGHT! IT WASN'T THE HULK WHO WAS DOIN' THE DAMAGE! THIS MUST BE THE WRECKER'S MACHINE!
CORRECTION--THIS WAS THE WRECKER'S MACHINE!
THE WRECKER MUST BE BEHIND THIS IRON DOOR! BUT HE AINT GONNA BE THERE FOR LONG!
I'D BETTER BECOME INVISIBLE AND GO WITH YOU!
SMASH!
KARL KORT! SO YOU'RE THE WRECKER! DON'T WORRY, RICK, YOU'LL BE OKAY NOW!
IT IS YOU WHO SHOULD WORRY, THING! THIS ATOMIC-POWERED WEAPON WILL DESTROY YOU COMPLETELY NOW THAT I HAVE IT SET TO FULL INTENSITY!
LOOK OUT! IT'S THE RAY GUN HE HIT THE HULK WITH!
21

WELL, HE'LL NEVER AIM THAT HORRIBLE DEVICE AT ANOTHER LIVING BEING!
WHA--? WHAT HAPPENED?
BZZZT
BUSTER, WHAT HAPPENED AINT NOTHIN' TO WHAT'S GONNA HAPPEN TO YOU!
DON'T HURT HIM, BEN! THE GENERAL WILL WANT HIM FOR QUESTIONING!
ROTTEN, LOW-DOWN SPY! I'D LIKE JUST TWO MINUTES ALONE WITH 'IM!
Y'KNOW SOMETHIN', THING? YOU'RE A PRETTY RIGHT GUY AFTER ALL!
THERE THEY ARE, REED!
WE FOUND THE ROBOT YOU SMASHED, THING! SO WE FIGURED--SAY! WHAT ARE YOU DOING WITH DOCTOR KORT?
DOCTOR, HA! MEET THE WRECKER, KIDDIES!
SO! YOU WERE THE ONE SABOTAGING BRUCE BANNER'S CITY DEFENSE RAY! I SUPPOSE IT WAS EASY FOR YOU TO THROW THE BLAME ON THE HULK, BY USING THAT MONSTROUS ROBOT OF YOURS!
SURE! EVERY-ONE FIGGERED NOBODY BUT THE HULK COULD DO THAT MUCH DAMAGE! 'CEPTIN' ME, OF COURSE!
BUT--WHERE IS THE HULK?
EVEN AS SUE SPEAKS, THE INCREDIBLE HULK'S MIGHTY BODY RECOVERS FROM THE EFFECTS OF THE SPY'S RAY GUN, AND...
CAN HEAR 'EM TALKING--UNDER MY FEET! CAUGHT THE WRECKER! RICK IS SAFE!
WITH ONE GIGANTIC LEAP, THE MIGHTIEST LEGS ON EARTH SEND THE HULK SOARING UPWARD...
STILL WEAK FROM RAY--NO REASON TO HANG AROUND--GOTTA CHANGE BACK TO BRUCE BANNER--
DON'T WANT THING TO FIND ME TILL I GET MY FULL STRENGTH BACK! WOULDN'T STAND A CHANCE AGAINST 'IM NOW!

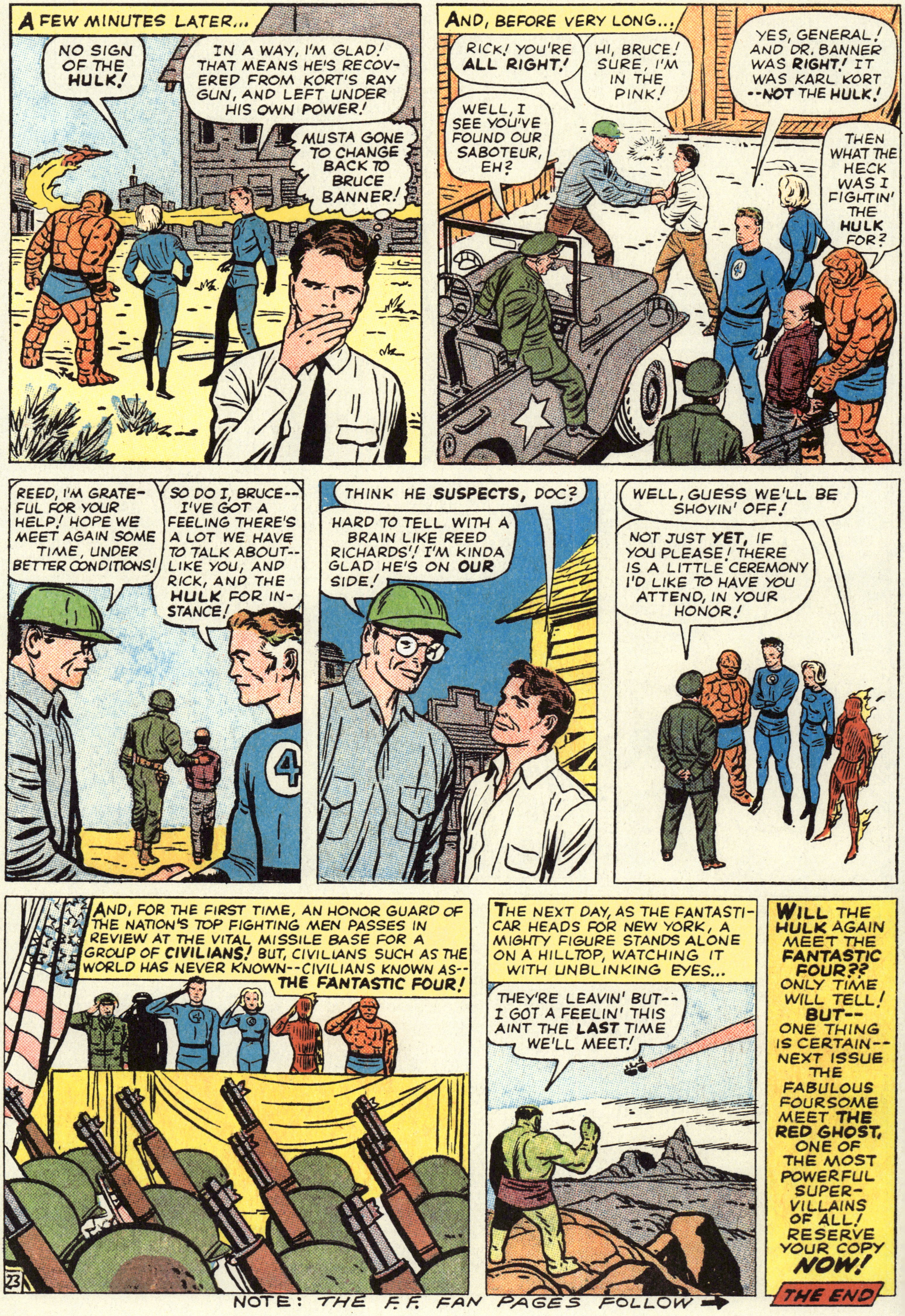

A FEW MINUTES LATER...
NO SIGN OF THE HULK!
IN A WAY, I'M GLAD! THAT MEANS HE'S RECOVERED FROM KORT'S RAY GUN, AND LEFT UNDER HIS OWN POWER!
MUSTA GONE TO CHANGE BACK TO BRUCE BANNER!
AND, BEFORE VERY LONG...
RICK! YOU'RE ALL RIGHT!
HI, BRUCE! SURE, I'M IN THE PINK!
WELL, I SEE YOU'VE FOUND OUR SABOTEUR, EH?
YES, GENERAL! AND DR. BANNER WAS RIGHT! IT WAS KARL KORT --NOT THE HULK!
THEN WHAT THE HECK WAS I FIGHTIN' THE HULK FOR?
REED, I'M GRATEFUL FOR YOUR HELP! HOPE WE MEET AGAIN SOME TIME, UNDER BETTER CONDITIONS!
SO DO I, BRUCE-- I'VE GOT A FEELING THERE'S A LOT WE HAVE TO TALK ABOUT-- LIKE YOU, AND RICK, AND THE HULK FOR INSTANCE!
THINK HE SUSPECTS, DOC?
HARD TO TELL WITH A BRAIN LIKE REED RICHARDS'! I'M KINDA GLAD HE'S ON OUR SIDE!
WELL, GUESS WE'LL BE SHOVIN' OFF!
NOT JUST YET, IF YOU PLEASE! THERE IS A LITTLE CEREMONY I'D LIKE TO HAVE YOU ATTEND, IN YOUR HONOR!
AND, FOR THE FIRST TIME, AN HONOR GUARD OF THE NATION'S TOP FIGHTING MEN PASSES IN REVIEW AT THE VITAL MISSILE BASE FOR A GROUP OF CIVILIANS! BUT, CIVILIANS SUCH AS THE WORLD HAS NEVER KNOWN--CIVILIANS KNOWN AS-- THE FANTASTIC FOUR!
THE NEXT DAY, AS THE FANTASTI-CAR HEADS FOR NEW YORK, A MIGHTY FIGURE STANDS ALONE ON A HILLTOP, WATCHING IT WITH UNBLINKING EYES...
THEY'RE LEAVIN' BUT-- I GOT A FEELIN' THIS AINT THE LAST TIME WE'LL MEET!
WILL THE HULK AGAIN MEET THE FANTASTIC FOUR?? ONLY TIME WILL TELL! BUT-- ONE THING IS CERTAIN-- NEXT ISSUE THE FABULOUS FOURSOME MEET THE RED GHOST, ONE OF THE MOST POWERFUL SUPER-VILLAINS OF ALL! RESERVE YOUR COPY NOW!
THE END
23
NOTE: THE F.F. FAN PAGES FOLLOW

Address YOUR letters to:
LEE and KIRBY
FANTASTIC FOUR
THIRD FLOOR
655 MADISON AVE.
NEW YORK 21, N. Y.

FANTASTIC FAN PAGE 4

Dear Stan and Jack:

Issue Number 9 was your usual best, which is darn good. This tale carried an intriguing title, "The End of the Fantastic Four," and one that sort of had you going. The thing that made this story was the reappearance of the Sub-Mariner. These Sub-Mariner-Four tales are masterpieces and this is due to the clash in personalities. One, at first glance, would look at Namor as a rival of the Four, but at second glance you see things differently. It was probably summed up in what Sue Storm said, "After all, he lives by a different code than we do — he can never really understand us! And — whatever he did — he did for — love." Artwise, you come off pretty well. If you stick to the way you've drawn the Thing in this issue, especially the overflowing eyebrows as in pages 3 and 4, you would have an almost perfect looking (as far as I'm concerned) Thing. The only complaints I have artwise run thusly: 1) You can't draw the Torch. I especially dislike the way the Torch looks when he's standing still. Besides looking bad, it doesn't seem right. Here you've said that his flame burns for only a limited period of time, and then you have him using up this limited period of time just standing around. And 2) it may seem silly but — you can't draw human-looking feet. Maybe it's because you're so used to drawing the huge-toed Thing and the Hulk, but improvement would be appreciated. Thanks for your time and your great publication. Regards.

Tommy Jones
622 Plater
Aberdeen, Maryland

Stan is answering this one. Jack is in a corner learning to draw feet. The reason the TORCH flames on occasionally when he's just standing around is that his flame is somewhat like a battery — it must be charged once in a while. If it isn't used every so often, it might not ignite when he needs it.

Dear Stan and Jack:

In answer to so many requests for back issues of FF, Tales to Astonish, Strange Tales, Hulk, etc., please send me your complete "want" list, as I have a small stock of the FF group. Submit your highest bid and you may beat a straight sale price so as to be sure to obtain a desired issue. All my issues are in fine to mint condition. All issues will be mailed flat. Best o' luck, Stan and Jack, and may your sales be many.

Dean Newman
P.O. Box 855
Bard, California

We don't publish "want" lists, but we ARE printing your letter, Dean, in case some of our fans might want to contact you.

Dear Stan and Jack:

I think, . . . No, I *know* the FF is the greatest magazine on the market! When I read the letter from PAUL GAMBACCINI I could have kicked that x!!-*/? in the seat! Imagine! Saying the FF is stupid, the artwork horrible, etc.! He must be a KOOK not to love the FF on sight! I have read every printed issue of FF, and I wouldn't trade any of them for 100 of any other magazine! As for that PAUL WHAT'S HIS NAME?, if he hates your magazine, nobody is forcing him to read it. Please don't add, subtract, divide, or multiply the FF's or change the characters or their dispositions. I love the idea of a FF T.V. series as mentioned in a previous issue. I wish you turned out an issue a week, but I suppose it is hard to write such wonderful stories. My favorite FF characters are in this order: 1. Johnny Storm, 2. Susan Storm, 3. Mr. Fantastic, 4. The Thing.

Please, please print this letter; include everything stated so we can show every kook in the world like that Paul, that FF is the world's greatest magazine, and in case anyone wants to argue with me, send their complaints to Marsha Cox, Route 5, Nampa, Idaho.

Marsha Cox
Nampa, Idaho

Thanks, Marsha, we appreciate your enthusiasm. Hope we don't later learn that you're just a wily stamp collector!

Dear Stan and Jack:

Have had the latest issues of Fantastic Four, Strange Tales, Journey Into Mystery, and The Incredible Hulk for some time, and it is time for me to throw my two-bits worth into the ring. FF #9 . . . very, very good. I don't see Reed Richards losing his shirt on a bunch of stocks (after all, if he'd invested in the blue chip stocks he still would have had an appreciable amount of money coming in), but otherwise it was a fine story. Sub-Mariner's scheme was intriguing and Invisible Girl-Namor battles were great, but I'd have liked to have seen Torch and Mr. Fantastic battle the Sea Monarch. There were some discrepancies in the layout of S.M. Studios. After all, the personalities shown all belong to various and sundry studios, and despite Namor's wealth, he couldn't have gotten them out from under their contracts. Also, Bing Crosby and Jackie Gleason were barely recognizable and I have yet to figure out who it was that was talking to Gleason after Jackie talked to the Thing. Oh yes, why'd the FF have to hitch-hike? Torch could have flown, and Mr. Fantastic could easily have covered the distance with "mile at a time" strides. Talking about Mr. Fantastic, he should use his abilities more. He could have scouted that island thoroughly by standing in one spot and stretching up to get an aerial view. I realize that Mr. F. probably isn't used to his fabulous powers, but don't you think he would have realized the possibilities by now? Regarding Dr. Doom in FF #10: I like both Namor and Doom, but how about some other villains? Mole Man should be making a return about now. Also, Miracle Man could escape, find (I don't know how) the Skrulls, and hypnotise them into going back into their original state and working for him. The possibilities of those shape-changing outer space types never were realized in FF #2.

Steve Perrin
4420 Meadowlark Lane
Santa Barbara, California

The only way to handle a letter like this is to devote a whole issue to answering it! But — not for

a few years! Besides, mebbe some of our readers would like to answer a few of Steve's comments?

Dear Stan and Jack:

I've been reading the Fantastic Four ever since it came out, and I'd like to say it's great! It's original, highly entertaining, and realistic. Here's my opinion of your characters: Mr. Fantastic: Reed Richards is the ideal type of hero to lead such an organization. I think his name should remain the same. Maybe the name 'Mr. Fantastic' is too egotistical, but it gives the magazine that extra touch. He is my favorite character. The Thing: I think the conflict between Ben Grimm and his fellow members gives the mag another touch not often used in a comic magazine. I'm also glad that Ben can't turn back to a human at will. Reed's formula (in "Prisoners of the Puppet Master"), although at first I thought it was going to ruin the mag, actually made me an even-more-ardent fan, because of its limitations. However, he looks different now. Compare him in issues 1 and 8, and see how the art changed. The Invisible Girl: Susan Storm ought to play a more important part in your stories. As for M. Ross's suggestions about kicking her out because she never does anything, he can like it or lump it for all I care. I think Reed should go out for her more than he has been doing. The Human Torch: Great! I like the way Johnny's flame sometimes dies out when in flight, and the way he can make it do whatever he wants it to do. I think he got what he deserved in the story about the "Puppet Master" and believe me, he deserved it! As for Alicia, I hope she at least becomes an honorary member. I agreed with H. Sher about who should play the heroes (and heroine) in the movies. And I picked out stars to play the villains. They are: The Moleman, Peter Lorre (with Makeup); Dr. Doom, Boris Karloff; Sub-Mariner, Johnny Weismuller; The Puppet Master, Yul Brynner, with a little makeup. This is too long to print, I know, but thanks for listening.

Steve Utley
Trenton, New Jersey

Too long to print? Not a chance! Why do you think we increased this section to two pages?

Dear Stan and Jack:

Never have I seen a truer title than "THE END OF THE FANTASTIC FOUR!" I love the F4, I have every issue, and love every issue. But #9 was kind of silly. The idea of heroes going bankrupt is ridiculous! Fans read comics because the heroes in them *act* like comic book heroes, and not like real-life people. For Heaven's sake, don't ruin the FANTASTIC FOUR! They've come along so well, and now to have a plot like the "END OF THE FANTASTIC FOUR!" Your best bet would be to have startling adventures – see if your other readers agree. I also think SUB-MARINER should become a hero, SPIDERMAN should join to make it THE FANTASTIC FIVE, and TORCH should get his own book. One last "thing"– the reason the F4 fight is because of THE THING. Get rid of him!

Fred Bronson
11620 Port Road
Culver City, California

Every super-villain we've had has tried to get rid of the THING — and you expect US to do it? We can't even get rid of an annoying rattle in our radiator!

Dear Stan and Jack:

I've but one comment to make regarding your magazine, which is: "IT STINKS." That is if you don't like great stories, original and unique characters, and wholesome entertainment. As for the controversy about the THING, I believe he should be kept as is, except that Reed might invent a serum that would change him back to Ben Grimm for limited periods of time. As for adding more members, definitely not. Ditto for evicting Sue Storm, alias INVISIBLE GIRL. This would only serve to detract from the FF's originality and uniqueness. I find no words which describe "The End of the Fantastic Four." However, you overdid the beginning. Surely some rich philanthropist or some organization would realize the importance of the Fantastic Four and contribute something to their cause. Also, at the end of the story Namor states, "The movie will be produced – as promised." How could it be, when in the chapter entitled, "The Fury of Mr. Fantastic" Namor states, ". . . Now to return home. We're finished here." The same goes for the HUMAN TORCH episode. Keep up the good work.

David Zeltzer
23861 Rennsselaer
Oak Park, Michigan

When Namor said the movie would be produced, he then hired new writers and legitimate cameramen and they produced it. But — that's another story.

Dear Stan and Jack:

Once I asked you for FF #1. Of course you didn't have it. Now I wish you would publish my full name and address. I will give anyone 50¢ for that issue *if* no pages are missing or anything is wrong with it. Aloha!

Edward Corbett
145 Sanford Street
Glens Falls, New York

P.S. Compliments to the world's greatest comic magazine.

Hey! If we knew they'd be worth so much, we'd have charged 50¢ each OURSELVES!

Dear Stan and Jack:

Oboy, was *Fantastic Four* #9 ever great! The idea of a super-hero team going broke is almost heresy by conventional comic book standards, but it's such off-the-beaten-path-stories as the *End of the Fantastic Four* that makes yours the greatest mag going. You guys aren't afraid to place your characters in human situations, and the constant by-play between the Thing and Human Torch and Susan and Sub-Mariner is so true to life that it makes other pseudo-dramatic comics look pretty sick. I suppose – to be realistic – I should find some word of criticism (negative, that is) to say about your comic, but I can't. Having followed Mr. Kirby's wonderful art since the '40's, I can truthfully say that you couldn't have gotten a better artist to do *FF*. He has a way with costume heroes that has been mastered by few other artists in the medium and, also, his highly original renditions of monsters with gaping jaws and cracked hides make the Thing, at once, a figure of awe and sympathy. This is *art* – no question about it. The superior and imaginative scripts by Mr. Lee further insure that when the day comes that comics are accorded their rightful place in the Arts, along with music, painting, and drama, the *Fantastic Four* magazine will be held up as the best example of this. Thanks for many hours of entertainment.

Landon Chesney
1955 Harle Avenue
Cleveland, Tennessee

Landon, old pal, if you ever run for president, let us know!

IMPORTANT NOTE: The FANTASTIC FOUR make a guest appearance in the new AMAZING SPIDER-MAN Comics, #1, on sale December 10th. DON'T MISS IT!

104
KINGS' Knights
ONLY $1.49 postpaid
Here's What You Get:
• 4 Kings on horseback with swords
• 12 Knights in armor on horseback with Pikes
• 12 Knights on horseback with Banners
• 4 Buglers afoot
• 12 Knights on horseback with battle axes
• 20 Footsoldiers with Maces and side swords
• 20 Footsoldiers with swords and shields
• 20 Footsoldiers with long bows
A GLORIOUS SET OF PLASTIC TOYS EVERY CHILD WILL BE PLEASED TO OWN!
Comes in two separate armies . . . the BLACK KNIGHTS and the WHITE KNIGHTS! Form your own battle lines! Every fight a delight! Fun for everyone in the family
Comes in Treasure Chest box in which to store your toys away! You must be satisfied or your money refunded in full!
104 Kings Knights ,Dept. G
Carle Place, L. I., N. Y.
No C.O.D.'s
Gentlemen:
I am enclosing $1.49 for each set of Knights. Kindly rush these to me. If not satisfied, I may return them for full refund.
PRINT NAME
ADDRESS
CITY
STATE
Canadian and Foreign orders: send $1.98 International Postal Money Order with order.

MY SECRET NEW DYNAFLEX METHOD

CAN BUILD YOU A MAGNIFICENT NEW HE-MAN-MUSCLED BODY IN JUST TEN MINUTES A DAY—with absolutely NO weights—NO bar-bells—NO EXERCISE AT ALL!

Yes! If the girls LAUGH at you now when you take off your shirt—they'll be breaking down the doors to get dates with you—once they've seen the rugged DYNAFLEX BODY I can give you! I'll build you a tough brutal massive body—shoulders clad with solid inches of he-man BRAWN. I'll give you bulging biceps, trip-hammer fists, power-packed legs, and a chest that will have you popping the buttons off your shirt with pride! (—says MIKE MARVEL, "Builder of Champion Bodies")

ARE YOU WEAK, ALWAYS TIRED, LACK PEP?

Whether you're thin and scrawny, or sagging with unsightly fat—my secret DYNAFLEX method will cram pep, vigor and red-blooded vitality into your puny, exhausted body. Once DYNAFLEX makes you a two-fisted dynamo of manly beauty, rippling with power, glowing with magnetic sex-appeal—you'll be bursting with get-up-and-go. Man, you'll be really ALIVE—tingling with zest and rip-roaring energy—for the first time in years!

PROOF!

"I tried two other systems, before my buddy told me about DYNAFLEX. It *really* works—and how! I've put two inches of solid muscle on my biceps, three inches on my chest. It's like magic!"
L. C., New York City

"I never thought you could build terrific muscles without exercises or weights. Started DYNAFLEX two weeks ago, and am building a *great* physique."
E. G., Detroit, Mich.

"DYNAFLEX is the best yet. Only three weeks, and I have more dates than I can handle! I am telling all my pals about DYNAFLEX." F. S., Chicago, Ill.

ARE YOU ASHAMED OF YOUR BODY NOW?

Pal—do YOURSELF a favor! Take a good long look in a mirror. Do you see a puny, starved body—scrawny arms—bony shoulders—a flabby stomach and skinny legs? Do girls laugh and fellows grin when you take off your shirt?

BELIEVE IT OR NOT—I can add solid pounds of rippling, steely he-man MEAT to your build. I can take those skeleton arms and PACK EVERY INCH with explosive virile MAN-MUSCLE. I can take that caved-in chest and build on six rugged inches of strong sleek MAN-SIZED BRAWN. I can clothe your skinny frame with GIANT RIPPLING DYNAFLEX MUSCLES that will have the girls gasping with awe and admiration! And with NO tiring excreise, NO high-priced bar-bells or gym equipment!

Or is your problem a body sagging with soft rolls of unhealthy, unhandsome FAT? Puny muscles — sagging stomach — bloated face — arms heavy with layers of BLUBBER? Are you ASHAMED to go to the beach and let them see your "FAT-MAN PHYSIQUE"?

If so, wake up fella! THIS IS IT! I will peel off that fat and give you a lean virile DYNAFLEX BODY, armored with a sheath of hard tough handsome muscle. I can build you into a healthy, streamlined HERCULES—bursting with dynamic manly strength. I'll give you a taut rock-hard midsection—legs muscled like coiled steel springs. I can pack solid DYNAMITE into your fists and give you a rugged handsome build brim-full of the magnetic SUPER-BODY SEX-APPEAL girls are hungry for. And with NO starvation diets—NO fatiguing calisthenics—NO expensive health-foods!

HOW DYNAFLEX BUILDS BEAUTIFUL BODIES

DYNAFLEX is the modern miracle of body-building. It takes no tiresome exercises, "crash" diets, protein foods, and no weights or bar-bells. DYNAFLEX is the amazing discovery of a West German Doctor whose research into the Science of Strength found a thrilling new way to build GIANT BRAWNY MUSCLES in ten minutes a day. With DYNAFLEX you "flex" each muscle once—in a certain way—that is more effective than if you exercised that muscle 20, 30, even 100 times the old-fashioned way. With DYNAFLEX you get bigger results in ten minutes than after hours of grunting and groaning, hefting heavy weights.

DYNAFLEX coaxes each muscle in your body to bring out its round, steely fullness and satiny symmetery. DYNAFLEX packs that muscle with glowing vibrant new strength and energy—FAST. In ten minutes a day I can cover your bony frame with healthy rippling muscle—give you a deep, powerful chest — solid shoulders and iron wrists—tough, slim midsection—and trim, steel-spring legs — simply thru "DYNA-FLEXING" each muscle once a day!

There's nothing wrong with the bar-bell and weight-lifting method . . . but why bother? Why waste time and money, why sweat and strain your way to a streamlined symmetrical SAMSON-STRONG BODY—when you can do it better—bigger—faster—easier with the DYNAFLEX SECRET?

STRONG-MAN SEX-APPEAL ATTRACTS GIRLS

Be honest. Down deep you KNOW you envy the boy with the virile, magnificent build. Every man and boy secretly desires a broad brawny back, a solid man-muscled chest, handsome he-man shoulders, arms rippling with tough, steely sinews, a narrow waist, slim hips and springy, power-packed legs. Girls go for a fellow with TWO-FISTED BIG MUSCLE SEX-APPEAL . . . and they only laugh at skinny guys or "fatso's".

Let me give you a glowing new body, brimming over with energy and irresistible inches of solid muscle on your chest—he-man appeal. I can build three inches of beef and brawn on your shoulders. I will mold you a handsome super-body of terrific strength, give you a crushing grip, legs crammed with steel springs. A lean taut rock-solid punch-proof midsection. Pack your body with energy and thrilling stamina that will have girls falling at your feet.

GIVE ME TEN MINUTES A DAY —THAT'S ALL!

After DYNAFLEX, you'll be able to roll up your sleeves and take off your shirt and, for the first time in your life, you'll be PROUD of your manly build. Yes, pal, say goodbye to your weak, flabby frame—get ready for adventure and romance with a solid physique that glows and vibrates with virile he-man appeal. You'll be really proud to have people see your MAGNIFICENT HE-MAN-MUSCLES at the beach or gym. And, when the fellows stare with envy and jealousy—when the girls crowd around to squeeze your iron biceps or touch your bulging brawny chest—when they ask in amazement HOW you did it—tell them about the Magic Secret of DYNAFLEX!

Your Pal,
MIKE MARVEL
"Builder of Champion Bodies"

YOU PAY ONLY 1.98 COMPLETE NOTHING ELSE TO BUY

Mike Marvel System, DEPT. 63, 285 Market St., Newark, N.J.

FREE! 'SECRETS OF ATTRACTING GIRLS'!

Fellows! Mail the coupon now, and receive Mike Marvel's FREE GIFT to you, this exciting and informative book. Discover a secret method for developing a new, almost MAGNETIC way of attracting the girls. At parties, dances, at the beach—you will have the girls clustering around you breathlessly, while the guys watch enviously. "What does HE have that WE don't?" they will say. The answer is in this exciting new book, your GIFT from Mike Marvel. Fill out and mail the coupon NOW!

Outside USA: Send International Money Order or cash. Great Britain: $1.98 is about 15 shillings. For air mail delivery, send 1 pound.

MAIL MONEY-SAVING NO-RISK FREE TRIAL COUPON NOW!

Check as many of the boxes you want HERE — Complete System $1.98.

- ☐ Lose fat, be trim and solid
- ☐ Build deep brawny chest, bulging with vigorous strength
- ☐ Lose fat, be trim, strong, handsome
- ☐ Mold mighty back, broad beefy shoulders
- ☐ Build muscle on skinny wrists and arms
- ☐ Develop crushing grip, two-fisted punch-power

MIKE MARVEL System. Dept. 63
285 Market St.,
Newark, N.J.

Okay, Mike! Here's $1.98. Send me your COMPLETE (nothing else to buy later) body-building course. I want to use your new secret of DYNAFLEX, to win a HERCULES HE-MAN BODY in just ten minutes a day. Rush my copies of the DYNAFLEX SYSTEM and my free gift book "Secrets of Attracting Girls" on your money-back guarantee, in plain wrappers. If I don't develop a splendid physique and become more popular with girls you will refund my money in full.

NAME .... AGE ....

ADDRESS ....

CITY .... ZONE ...... STATE ......
(Please Print!)

IND.
THE WORLD'S GREATEST COMIC MAGAZINE!
APPROVED BY THE COMICS CODE AUTHORITY
12¢
THE Fantastic Four
MC
13 APR.
ENOUGH FANTASY AND SUPER-CHARACTERS TO FILL 3 MAGAZINES! ONE OF THE MOST FANTASTIC TALES OF ALL...
MYSTERY ON THE MOON!!!
MORE THAN TWO HUNDRED THOUSAND MILES FROM EARTH, THE FANTASTIC FOUR FACE THE MENACE OF...
"THE RED GHOST!"
ALSO......IN THIS SPELLBINDING TALE YOU WILL MEET THE MOST DRAMATIC BEING OF ALL TIME! THE MYSTERIOUS WATCHER!
WHO IS HE? WHAT IS HE?

THE FANTASTIC FOUR is published by CANAM PUBLISHERS SALES CORP. OFFICE OF PUBLICATION: 655 MADISON AVENUE, NEW YORK, N.Y. Published monthly. Copyright 1962 by CANAM PUBLISHERS SALES CORP., 655 Madison Avenue, New York, N.Y. Vol. 1 No. 13, APRIL, 1963 issue. Price 12¢ per copy. Subscription rate $1.75 for 12 issues including postage. Foreign subscription $3.25 in American funds. No similarity between any of the names, characters, persons, and/or institutions appearing in this magazine with those of any living or dead person is intended, and any such similarity which may exist is purely coincidental. Printed in U.S.A. by The Eastern Color Printing Co., Waterbury 20, Conn.

THE FANTASTIC FOUR, versus
THE RED GHOST
AND HIS INDESCRIBABLE SUPER-APES!
TWILIGHT IN NEW YORK! AT THE SKYSCRAPER HEADQUARTERS OF AMERICA'S GREATEST SUPER-HEROES ALL IS QUIET, UNTIL SUDDENLY, UNEXPECTEDLY, THE STILLNESS IS SHATTERED BY A PULSE-STOPPING EXPLOSION FROM THE LAB OF MR. FANTASTIC!
SUFFERIN' CATS! LOOK AT REED'S LAB! WHAT HAPPENED ??
SOMETHING MUST HAVE GONE WRONG WITH HIS EXPERIMENT, JOHNNY! BUT--BUT WHERE IS HE??
YOU TWO STAY BACK! I'LL SHOVE THAT JUNK ASIDE AND SEE IF HE'S UNDER IT!
STORY......STAN LEE
ART........JACK KIRBY
INKING.....S. DITKO
LETTERING..ART SIMEK
X-138
REED! WHERE ARE YA, GUY??
STOP TRYIN' TO WORRY US, YOU BLASTED ANIMATED RUBBER BAND! REED! SAY SOMETHING!
WATCH OUT, BEN! MAYBE I CAN FIND 'IM! I'LL FLY OVER THE WRECKAGE!
STOP TALKIN' AND MOVE, HOT-HEAD! HE MUST BE PINNED UNDER SOME OF THAT DEBRIS!
1

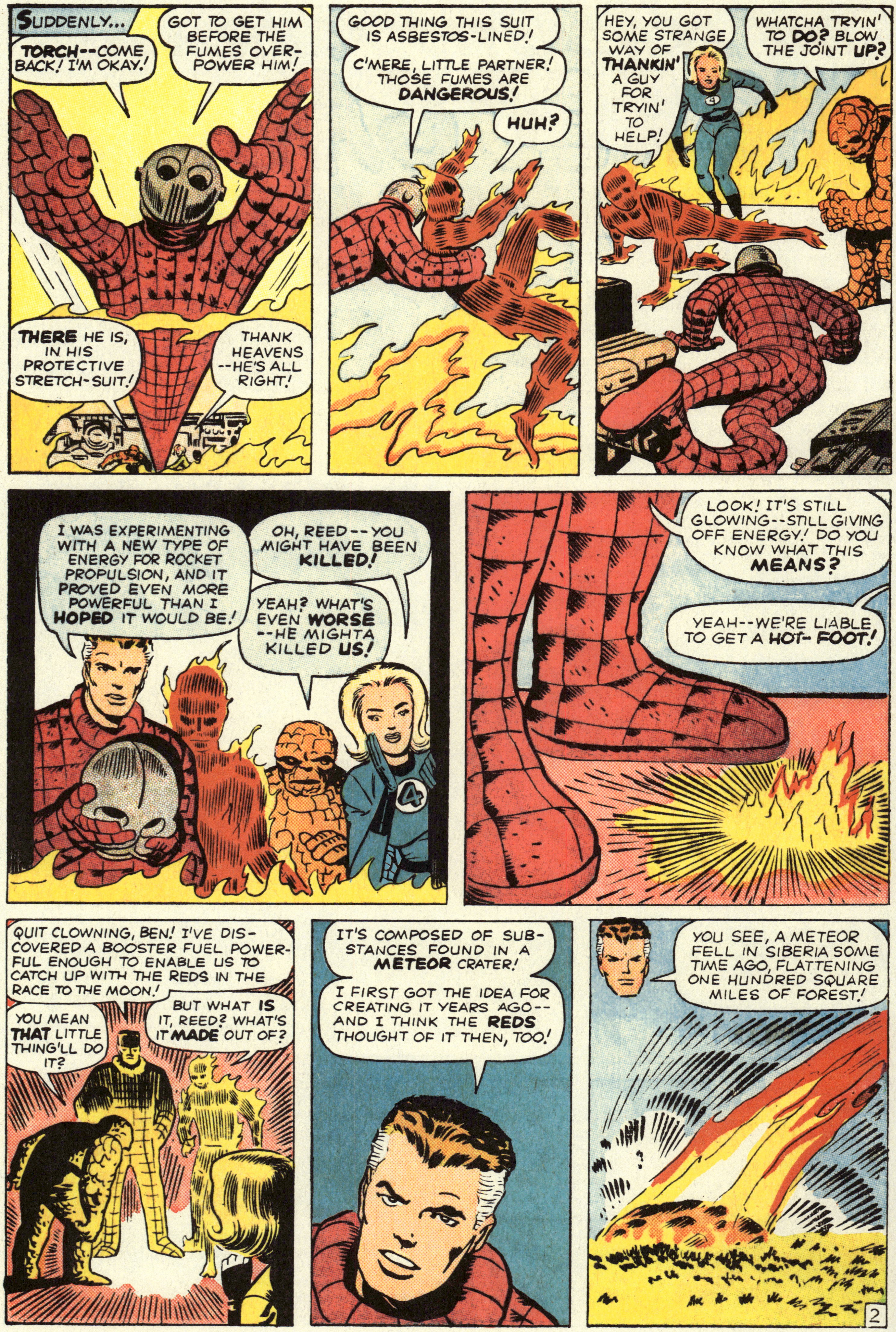
SUDDENLY...
TORCH--COME BACK! I'M OKAY!
GOT TO GET HIM BEFORE THE FUMES OVER-POWER HIM!
THERE HE IS, IN HIS PROTECTIVE STRETCH-SUIT!
THANK HEAVENS --HE'S ALL RIGHT!
GOOD THING THIS SUIT IS ASBESTOS-LINED!
C'MERE, LITTLE PARTNER! THOSE FUMES ARE DANGEROUS!
HUH?
HEY, YOU GOT SOME STRANGE WAY OF THANKIN' A GUY FOR TRYIN' TO HELP!
WHATCHA TRYIN' TO DO? BLOW THE JOINT UP?
I WAS EXPERIMENTING WITH A NEW TYPE OF ENERGY FOR ROCKET PROPULSION, AND IT PROVED EVEN MORE POWERFUL THAN I HOPED IT WOULD BE!
OH, REED--YOU MIGHT HAVE BEEN KILLED!
YEAH? WHAT'S EVEN WORSE --HE MIGHTA KILLED US!
LOOK! IT'S STILL GLOWING--STILL GIVING OFF ENERGY! DO YOU KNOW WHAT THIS MEANS?
YEAH--WE'RE LIABLE TO GET A HOT-FOOT!
QUIT CLOWNING, BEN! I'VE DISCOVERED A BOOSTER FUEL POWERFUL ENOUGH TO ENABLE US TO CATCH UP WITH THE REDS IN THE RACE TO THE MOON!
YOU MEAN THAT LITTLE THING'LL DO IT?
BUT WHAT IS IT, REED? WHAT'S IT MADE OUT OF?
IT'S COMPOSED OF SUBSTANCES FOUND IN A METEOR CRATER!
I FIRST GOT THE IDEA FOR CREATING IT YEARS AGO--AND I THINK THE REDS THOUGHT OF IT THEN, TOO!
YOU SEE, A METEOR FELL IN SIBERIA SOME TIME AGO, FLATTENING ONE HUNDRED SQUARE MILES OF FOREST!
2

"I HAVE LONG SUSPECTED THAT THEY DEVELOPED THEIR POWERFUL ROCKET THRUST BY UTILIZING THE ENERGY OF THE BURNED-OUT METEOR! SO, I RECENTLY EXPLORED AN AMERICAN METEOR CRATER IN ARIZONA, TO SATISFY MYSELF!"
"I BROUGHT PIECES OF METEORITE BACK TO THE LAB WITH ME, FOR INTENSIVE STUDY! AND THEN I DISCOVERED IT--!"
I WAS RIGHT! THERE IS LIMITLESS ENERGY CONTAINED WITHIN THIS FRAGMENT FROM OUTER SPACE!
AND NOW, I'VE FOUND A WAY TO HARNESS THAT ENERGY! ALL I HAVE TO DO IS EXPOSE THIS IRON BAR TO THE CORRECT RADIATION...
--AND IT WILL FURNISH THE POWER TO SEND A HUGE ROCKET STRAIGHT TO THE MOON!
THIS MEANS AMERICA MAY WIN THE SPACE RACE!
BY NEXT WEEK, AS SOON AS I'VE FINISHED CONVERTING OUR EXPERIMENTAL ROCKET, THAT'S WHERE I'LL BE-- IN THE MYSTERIOUS BLUE AREA OF THE MOON!
JUST ONE CHICKEN-SCRATCHIN' MINUTE THERE, PAL! WADDAYA MEAN WHERE YOU'LL BE??!
SPACE COORDINATE
THIS IS THE FANTASTIC FOUR, NOT A SOLO ACT! WE'RE GOIN' WITH YA!
NO! NO! IT'S TOO DANGEROUS--TOO UNTESTED! I CAN'T ASK YOU TO RISK YOUR LIVES WITH ME!
BUT YOU MIGHT NEED US, REED!
YOU'RE OUT-VOTED, BOSS-MAN! YOU'RE STUCK WITH US!
TROUBLE WITH YOU IS, WE'VE LET YOU BOSS US AROUND SO MUCH...
...THAT YOU'RE BEGINNIN' TO THINK YOU CAN GET ALONG WITHOUT US!
BEN, CUT IT OUT! DON'T--
BUT WE GOT A BIG INVESTMENT IN YOU! WE AINT GONNA LET YOU GO SOMEWHERE ALONE WHERE YOU MIGHT HURT YOUR ADORABLE SELF!
DO YOU GET THE MESSAGE, MISTER?
I READ YOU LOUD AND CLEAR, LITTLE FRIEND! YOU WIN! WE'LL ALL GO TOGETHER!
3

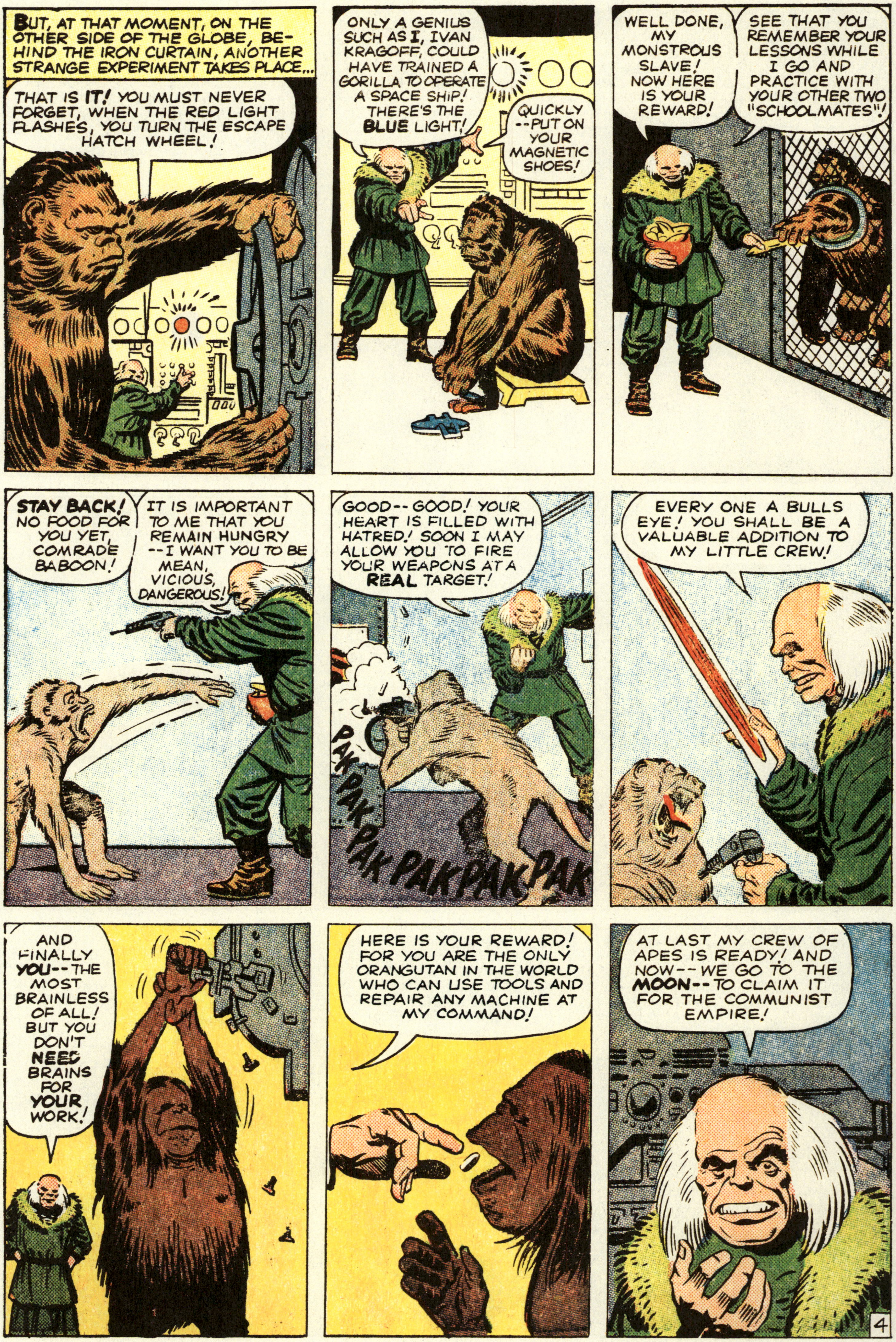
BUT, AT THAT MOMENT, ON THE OTHER SIDE OF THE GLOBE, BEHIND THE IRON CURTAIN, ANOTHER STRANGE EXPERIMENT TAKES PLACE...
THAT IS IT! YOU MUST NEVER FORGET, WHEN THE RED LIGHT FLASHES, YOU TURN THE ESCAPE HATCH WHEEL!
ONLY A GENIUS SUCH AS I, IVAN KRAGOFF, COULD HAVE TRAINED A GORILLA TO OPERATE A SPACE SHIP! THERE'S THE BLUE LIGHT!
QUICKLY --PUT ON YOUR MAGNETIC SHOES!
WELL DONE, MY MONSTROUS SLAVE! NOW HERE IS YOUR REWARD!
SEE THAT YOU REMEMBER YOUR LESSONS WHILE I GO AND PRACTICE WITH YOUR OTHER TWO "SCHOOLMATES"!
STAY BACK! NO FOOD FOR YOU YET, COMRADE BABOON!
IT IS IMPORTANT TO ME THAT YOU REMAIN HUNGRY --I WANT YOU TO BE MEAN, VICIOUS, DANGEROUS!
GOOD--GOOD! YOUR HEART IS FILLED WITH HATRED! SOON I MAY ALLOW YOU TO FIRE YOUR WEAPONS AT A REAL TARGET!
PAK PAK PAK PAK PAK PAK
EVERY ONE A BULLS EYE! YOU SHALL BE A VALUABLE ADDITION TO MY LITTLE CREW!
AND FINALLY YOU--THE MOST BRAINLESS OF ALL! BUT YOU DON'T NEED BRAINS FOR YOUR WORK!
HERE IS YOUR REWARD! FOR YOU ARE THE ONLY ORANGUTAN IN THE WORLD WHO CAN USE TOOLS AND REPAIR ANY MACHINE AT MY COMMAND!
AT LAST MY CREW OF APES IS READY! AND NOW--WE GO TO THE MOON--TO CLAIM IT FOR THE COMMUNIST EMPIRE!
4

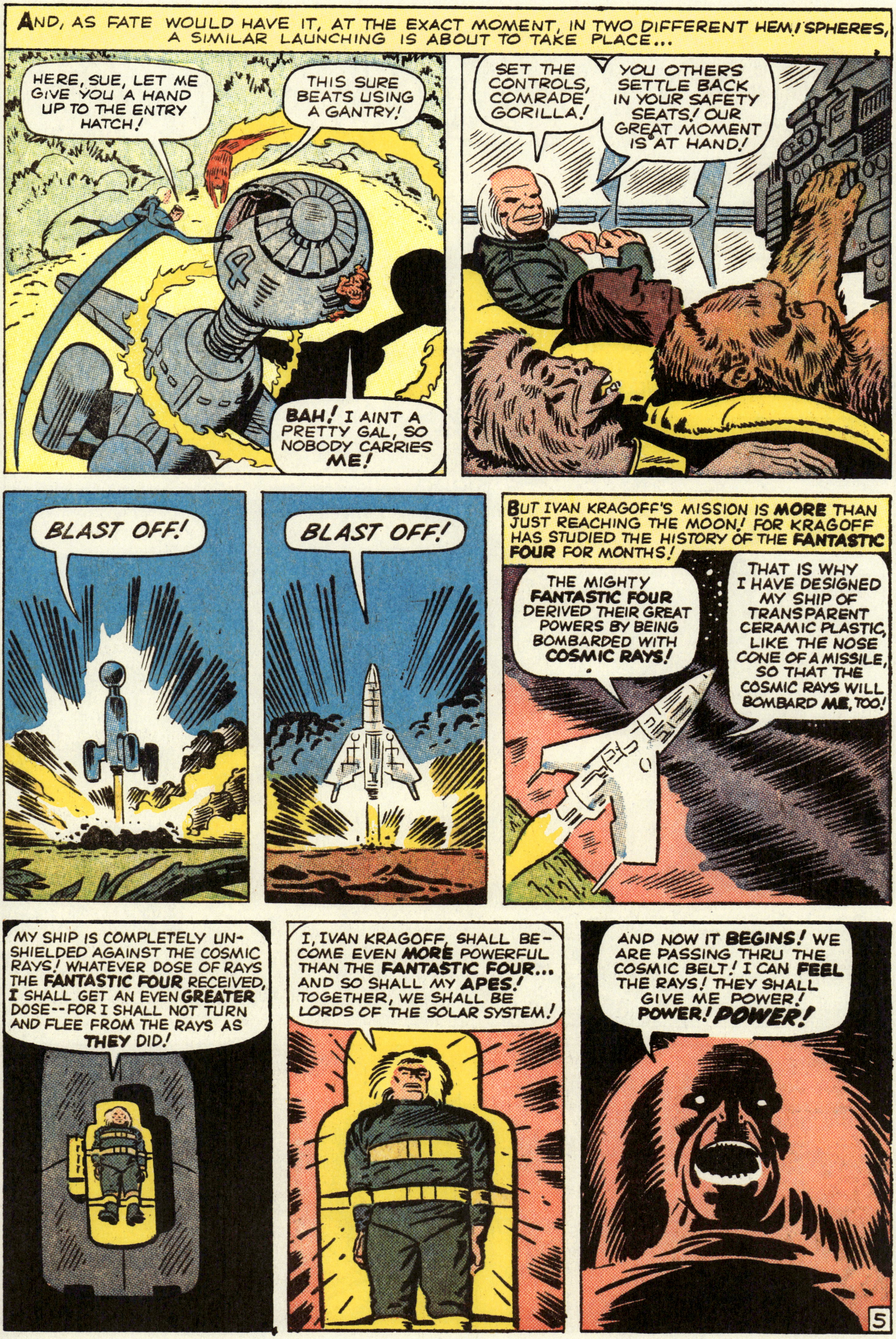
AND, AS FATE WOULD HAVE IT, AT THE EXACT MOMENT, IN TWO DIFFERENT HEMISPHERES, A SIMILAR LAUNCHING IS ABOUT TO TAKE PLACE...
HERE, SUE, LET ME GIVE YOU A HAND UP TO THE ENTRY HATCH!
THIS SURE BEATS USING A GANTRY!
BAH! I AINT A PRETTY GAL, SO NOBODY CARRIES ME!
SET THE CONTROLS, COMRADE GORILLA!
YOU OTHERS SETTLE BACK IN YOUR SAFETY SEATS! OUR GREAT MOMENT IS AT HAND!
BLAST OFF!
BLAST OFF!
BUT IVAN KRAGOFF'S MISSION IS MORE THAN JUST REACHING THE MOON! FOR KRAGOFF HAS STUDIED THE HISTORY OF THE FANTASTIC FOUR FOR MONTHS!
THE MIGHTY FANTASTIC FOUR DERIVED THEIR GREAT POWERS BY BEING BOMBARDED WITH COSMIC RAYS!
THAT IS WHY I HAVE DESIGNED MY SHIP OF TRANSPARENT CERAMIC PLASTIC, LIKE THE NOSE CONE OF A MISSILE, SO THAT THE COSMIC RAYS WILL BOMBARD ME, TOO!
MY SHIP IS COMPLETELY UN-SHIELDED AGAINST THE COSMIC RAYS! WHATEVER DOSE OF RAYS THE FANTASTIC FOUR RECEIVED, I SHALL GET AN EVEN GREATER DOSE--FOR I SHALL NOT TURN AND FLEE FROM THE RAYS AS THEY DID!
I, IVAN KRAGOFF, SHALL BE-COME EVEN MORE POWERFUL THAN THE FANTASTIC FOUR... AND SO SHALL MY APES! TOGETHER, WE SHALL BE LORDS OF THE SOLAR SYSTEM!
AND NOW IT BEGINS! WE ARE PASSING THRU THE COSMIC BELT! I CAN FEEL THE RAYS! THEY SHALL GIVE ME POWER! POWER! POWER!
5

PART 2
MENACE on the MOON!
MEANWHILE IN THE AMERICAN SHIP, SAFELY SHIELDED AGAINST THE MYSTERIOUS COSMIC RAYS...
GOT NO TIME TO LOOK AT ANYTHING NOW! I'M ENJOYIN' THIS FREE FALL! WHEEE--IT'S LIKE FLOATIN' ON A CLOUD!
LOOK! OFF IN THE DISTANCE! THERE'S ANOTHER SPACE SHIP!
IT HAS A COMMUNIST INSIGNIA! BUT THEY HAVE ANNOUNCED NO SPACE SHOTS! I DON'T UNDERSTAND!
THIS'LL GIVE ME A CHANCE TO USE THAT NEW ATMO-WEB SUIT YOU DESIGNED FOR ME, REED!
YOU MEAN YOU WANT TO FLY OUT AND INVESTIGATE THE SHIP?
SURE! THIS CHEMICAL TUXEDO RELEASES AN ARTIFICIAL ATMOSPHERE AROUND ME, ALLOWING ME TO FLAME ON IN AIRLESS SPACE! IT'LL BE A GASSER!
HERE GOES!
6

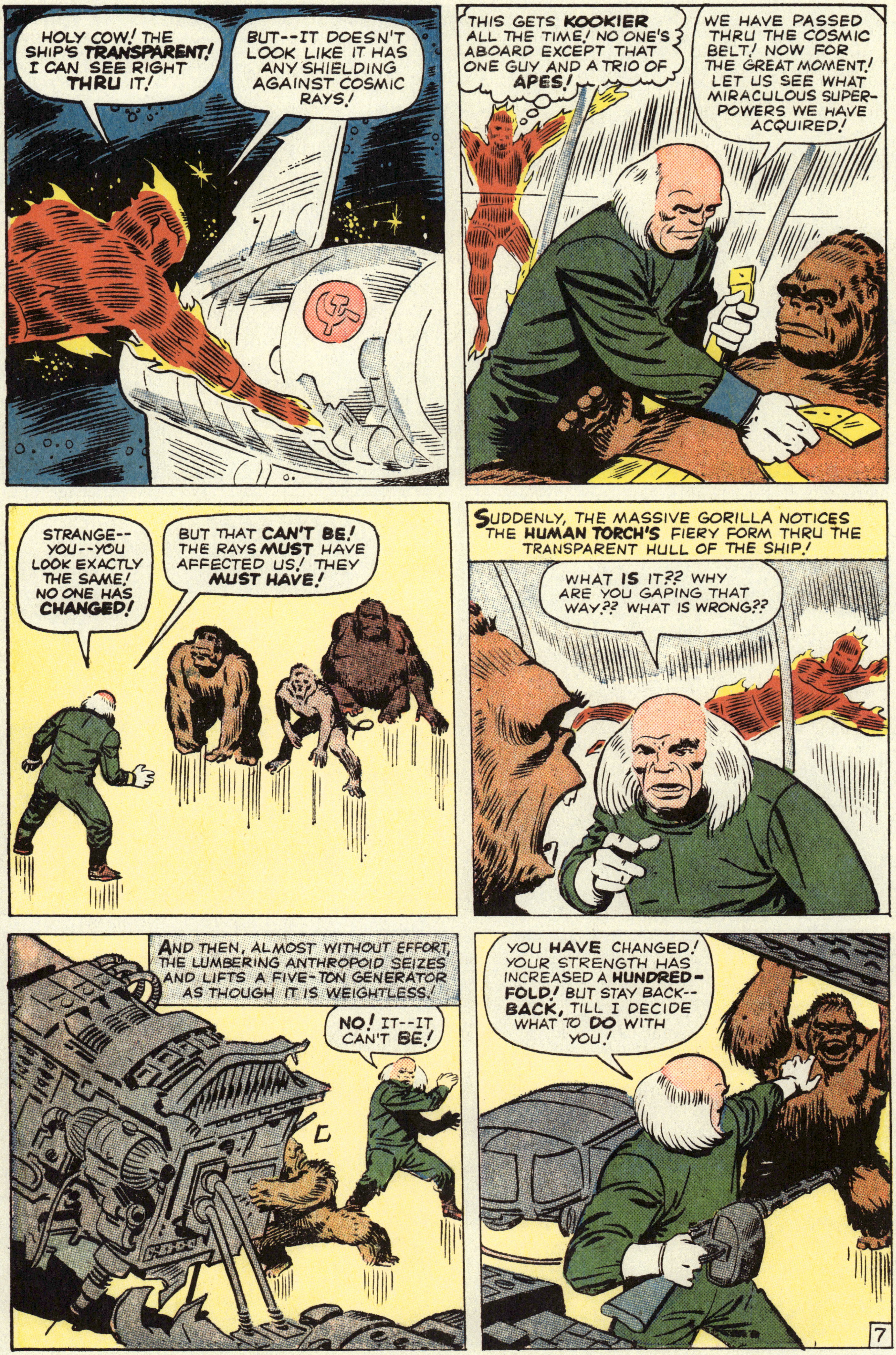
HOLY COW! THE SHIP'S TRANSPARENT! I CAN SEE RIGHT THRU IT!
BUT--IT DOESN'T LOOK LIKE IT HAS ANY SHIELDING AGAINST COSMIC RAYS!
THIS GETS KOOKIER ALL THE TIME! NO ONE'S ABOARD EXCEPT THAT ONE GUY AND A TRIO OF APES!
WE HAVE PASSED THRU THE COSMIC BELT! NOW FOR THE GREAT MOMENT! LET US SEE WHAT MIRACULOUS SUPER-POWERS WE HAVE ACQUIRED!
STRANGE-- YOU--YOU LOOK EXACTLY THE SAME! NO ONE HAS CHANGED!
BUT THAT CAN'T BE! THE RAYS MUST HAVE AFFECTED US! THEY MUST HAVE!
SUDDENLY, THE MASSIVE GORILLA NOTICES THE HUMAN TORCH'S FIERY FORM THRU THE TRANSPARENT HULL OF THE SHIP!
WHAT IS IT?? WHY ARE YOU GAPING THAT WAY?? WHAT IS WRONG??
AND THEN, ALMOST WITHOUT EFFORT, THE LUMBERING ANTHROPOID SEIZES AND LIFTS A FIVE-TON GENERATOR AS THOUGH IT IS WEIGHTLESS!
NO! IT--IT CAN'T BE!
YOU HAVE CHANGED! YOUR STRENGTH HAS INCREASED A HUNDRED-FOLD! BUT STAY BACK-- BACK, TILL I DECIDE WHAT TO DO WITH YOU!
7

THIS GUN WILL KEEP YOU AT BAY TILL--WAIT! THE GUN--WHAT'S HAPPENING TO IT??!
IT'S CHANGING! IT'S ALTERING ITS FORM! IT'S TURNING INTO--
--THE BABOON! HE TOO WAS AFFECTED BY THE COSMIC RAYS! HE NOW HAS THE POWER TO CHANGE HIS SHAPE--TO TURN INTO A COPY OF ANYTHING!
IT IS MORE THAN I DARED HOPE FOR! BUT WHAT ABOUT THE ORANGUTAN --AND ME??
THEN, AT THAT MOMENT, IVAN KRAGOFF ALSO NOTICES THE HUMAN TORCH...
THERE IS SOMEONE OUT THERE! THAT IS WHAT EXCITED THE GORILLA BEFORE!
...AND THE ORANGUTAN SEES THE TORCH, TOO!
WUUUMMMMMMMMMMM
WHAT ARE YOU DOING? YOUR ARM--MAGNETIC RAYS ARE COMING FROM IT! YOU--YOU'VE BECOME MAGNETIZED SOMEHOW!
BY POINTING HIS RIGHT ARM AT THE FIGURE OUTSIDE, THE ORANGUTAN REPELLED HIM, JUST AS A DE-POLARIZED MAGNET WOULD REPEL A SHEET OF TIN!
GOT TO MAKE IT BACK TO THE SHIP! GOT TO TELL THE OTHERS!
THEY'VE GOT TO BE WARNED! WE'RE RACING TO THE MOON WITH A COMMUNIST AND THREE SUPER APES--AND THE FOUR OF THEM MAY BE EVEN MORE POWERFUL THAN WE ARE!
4
8

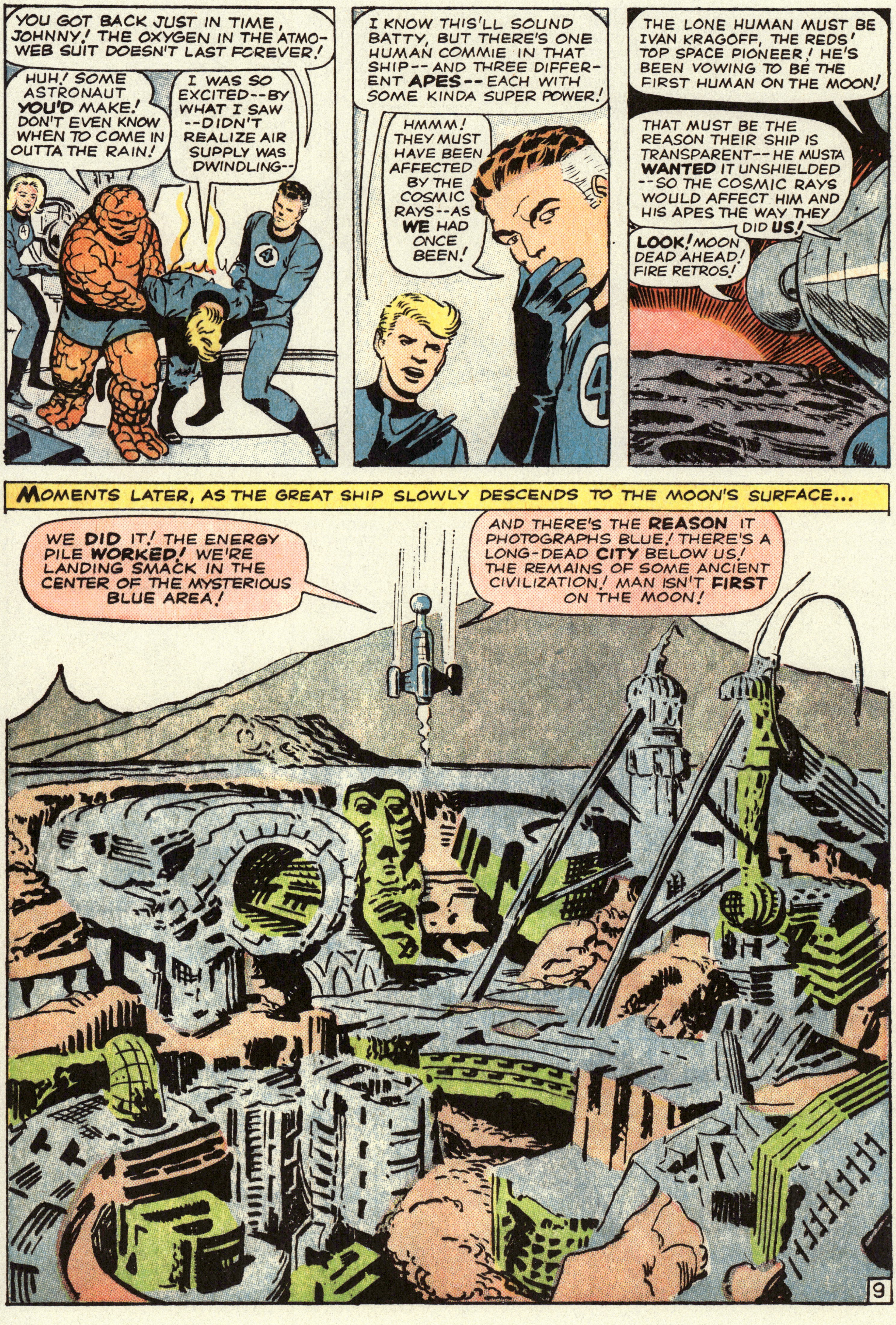

YOU GOT BACK JUST IN TIME, JOHNNY! THE OXYGEN IN THE ATMO-WEB SUIT DOESN'T LAST FOREVER!
HUH! SOME ASTRONAUT YOU'D MAKE! DON'T EVEN KNOW WHEN TO COME IN OUTTA THE RAIN!
I WAS SO EXCITED--BY WHAT I SAW --DIDN'T REALIZE AIR SUPPLY WAS DWINDLING--
I KNOW THIS'LL SOUND BATTY, BUT THERE'S ONE HUMAN COMMIE IN THAT SHIP--AND THREE DIFFERENT APES--EACH WITH SOME KINDA SUPER POWER!
HMMM! THEY MUST HAVE BEEN AFFECTED BY THE COSMIC RAYS--AS WE HAD ONCE BEEN!
THE LONE HUMAN MUST BE IVAN KRAGOFF, THE REDS' TOP SPACE PIONEER! HE'S BEEN VOWING TO BE THE FIRST HUMAN ON THE MOON!
THAT MUST BE THE REASON THEIR SHIP IS TRANSPARENT--HE MUSTA WANTED IT UNSHIELDED --SO THE COSMIC RAYS WOULD AFFECT HIM AND HIS APES THE WAY THEY DID US!
LOOK! MOON DEAD AHEAD! FIRE RETROS!
MOMENTS LATER, AS THE GREAT SHIP SLOWLY DESCENDS TO THE MOON'S SURFACE...
WE DID IT! THE ENERGY PILE WORKED! WE'RE LANDING SMACK IN THE CENTER OF THE MYSTERIOUS BLUE AREA!
AND THERE'S THE REASON IT PHOTOGRAPHS BLUE! THERE'S A LONG-DEAD CITY BELOW US! THE REMAINS OF SOME ANCIENT CIVILIZATION! MAN ISN'T FIRST ON THE MOON!
9

REED! THERE'S AIR HERE! WE WON'T NEED MASKS!
YIPPEE! I CAN FLAME ON! I CAN FLY!
THE ATMOSPHERE EXTENDS FOR MILES! IT MUST HAVE BEEN CREATED BY THE RACE THAT BUILT THIS CITY!
BUT WE'VE FORGOTTEN ABOUT THE OTHER SHIP! LET ME STRETCH UP AND LOOK AROUND! IT MUST ALSO HAVE LANDED BY NOW!
HEY, LOOK AT THIS! IT'S SOME KIND OF AN ULTRA-MODERN HOUSE!
AND IT LOOKS AS THOUGH SOME-ONE'S LIVING IN IT! IT'S NOT IN RUINS LIKE THE REST OF THE PLACE!
WE'D BETTER INVESTIGATE IT! C'MON, SUE, I'LL GIVE YOU A LIFT!
HEY! WAIT FOR ME! HOLD ON!
FOR CRYIN' OUT LOUD! LOOKS LIKE I JUST CAME ALONG FOR THE RIDE!
THE ONLY TIME ANYONE NOTICES ME IS WHEN THEY NEED A HUNK OF MUSCLE TO SAVE THEM!
I MUST BE LOSIN' MY MARBLES! COULDA SWORN I SAW THAT ROCK MOVE! AW, I'LL JUST KICK THE BLAMED THING OUTA MY WAY...
HEY! WHAT THE HECK--!
FOR THE LUVVA PETE! IT TURNED INTO A BABOON!
THERE'S MORE OF 'EM! THEY MUST BE THE THREE APES THE TORCH SAW!
LEGGO, BLAST YA! TAKE YOUR HAIRY PAWS OFF ME BEFORE I SMASH YOUR EMPTY HEADS TOGETHER!
10

ENOUGH, MY PETS! NOW LEAVE THE GROTESQUE AMERICAN TO ME!
YOU HAVE SEEN BUT A FRACTION OF OUR POWER! NOW YOU WILL FACE THE MOST UNBEATABLE FOE OF ALL AS YOU ARE DEFEATED BY THE RED GHOST!
"RED GHOST??" WHAT DO YOU THINK YOU'RE DOIN'-- SCARIN' A KID?
I'LL SHOW YA HOW WORRIED I AM ABOUT-- HEY!! WHA--?
HAH! NOW YOU KNOW! THIS IS THE POWER I GOT FROM THE COSMIC RAYS!
I CAN MAKE MY BODY UNSOLID-- LIKE A GHOST'S!! AND YOU CANNOT HURT THAT WHICH YOU CANNOT TOUCH!
SO WHAT? IF YOUR BODY IS AS UNSOLID AS A GHOST'S, THEN YOU CAN'T DO ANY HARM TO ANYBODY EITHER!!
THAT, MY UGLY ENEMY, IS WHERE YOU ARE WRONG!
THRU MENTAL CONTROL, I CAN WILL ANY PART OF MY BODY TO BECOME SOLID INSTANTLY! SOLID ENOUGH TO GRASP THIS CLUB, FOR INSTANCE!
BUT THEN, SUDDENLY--
ENOUGH! PUT DOWN THAT WEAPON! THE WATCHER COMMANDS YOU!
THE THING, THE RED GHOST, AND THE THREE SUPER-APES STARE IN AMAZEMENT AT THE ONE WHO SEEMS TO HAVE APPEARED FROM OUT OF NOWHERE! THEN, AS THE SUPER-APES START TO MOVE FORWARD, THEY ARE FORCED BACK BY WAVES OF SHEER, IRRESISTABLE ENERGY!
11

PART 3
"THE WATCHER APPEARS!"
SUDDENLY, BEFORE THE THING CAN MAKE ANOTHER MOVE, THE THREE APES ARE WHISKED AWAY FROM HIM BY AN INVISIBLE FORCE, AND PLACED INTO UNBREAKABLE GLOBULES OF SHIMMERING SYNTHO-MATTER! AND THEN, A STRANGE, RICH VOICE RINGS OUT...
CEASE THIS USELESS CONFLICT! THE WATCHER COMMANDS YOU!
FOR CRYIN' OUT LOUD! WHAT'S GOIN' ON HERE??! HOW'D THE APES GET INTO THOSE FLOATING GLOBES?? AND WHO--WHO IS THAT??
X-138
IT SHALL ALL BE EXPLAINED, IN DUE TIME! BUT FIRST...
...I MUST BRING BOTH OPPOSING FORCES TOGETHER! COME FROM YOUR PLACE OF CONCEALMENT, IVAN KRAGOFF!
12

AND THEN, SLOWLY, QUIETLY, THE WATCHER SPEAKS...
HEAR MY WORDS, YOU OF EARTH! I COME FROM A WORLD SO FAR FROM HERE THAT YOU DO NOT EVEN SUSPECT ITS EXISTENCE! OUR ENTIRE HOME PLANET IS ONE VAST GIGANTIC COMPUTER!
"MY PEOPLE ROAM THE ENTIRE KNOWN UNIVERSE, WATCHING, OBSERVING OTHER WORLDS! WE HAVE SEEN PLANETS WHERE LIFE EVOLVED FROM SEAS OF MOLTEN METAL....!"
"WE HAVE WITNESSED THE DEATH OF WORLDS WHICH WERE OLDER THAN YOUR ENTIRE GALAXY--!"
"AND, WORST OF ALL, WE HAVE SEEN ONCE-NOBLE RACES TURN SAVAGE AND WARLIKE WITH THE PASSING OF TIME! A FATE WHICH YOUR OWN FOOLISH BREED SEEMS HEADED FOR! BUT, DURING ALL THE AGES, WE HAVE DONE NOTHING BUT WATCH-- NEVER HAVE WE INTERFERED! NEVER HAVE WE MADE OUR PRESENCE KNOWN!"
BUT NOW, I HAVE BROKEN THE SILENCE OF CENTURIES, IN ORDER TO SAVE YOUR PEOPLE FROM SAVAGERY!
YOU DARE THINK YOU CAN STOP THE COMMUNIST MARCH OF CONQUEST!?!
SHUDDUP! LET 'IM FINISH!
SOONER OR LATER, BOTH YOUR NATIONS MAY ENGAGE IN A WAR WHICH MIGHT DEVASTATE YOUR ENTIRE PLANET! THAT IS NOT MY CONCERN!
BUT NOW YOU BRING YOUR CONFLICT TO THE MOON -- TO MY DOMAIN! I WILL TOLERATE NO LARGE SCALE WAR HERE! INSTEAD--YOU AND ONLY YOU, SHALL FIGHT IT OUT! I HAVE SPOKEN!
LOOK!! HE--HE IS FADING AWAY!

WELL, IF WE'RE GONNA SETTLE THIS THING BETWEEN US, THERE'S NO TIME LIKE THE PRESENT, MAC!
FOOL! THERE IS NO WAY YOU CAN HARM ME! YOU CANNOT EVEN TOUCH ME! I SHALL DEFEAT YOU ALL!
BUT, AT THAT INSTANT, UNAWARE OF WHAT HAS TRANSPIRED OVER THE HORIZON, MR. FANTASTIC, GROPING FOR THE THING, FINDS HIM!
COME BACK, TORCH! I FOUND HIM! I'VE GOT THE THING!
HEY! WHAT THE--?? LEGGO!
WHERE HAVE YOU BEEN, BEN?? WE WERE LOOKING ALL OVER FOR YOU! EASY, BOY--YOU'RE CRUSHING MY ARM!
WE WANT TO SHOW YOU THE STRANGE HOUSE WE FOUND! SOMEONE MUST BE STILL LIVING IN IT!
YEAH, YEAH-- I KNOW! IT'S THE WATCHER!
THE WATCHER? WHAT DO YOU MEAN?
I'LL EXPLAIN LATER! IT AINT GONNA BE EASY!
HERE, THIS IS THE PLACE! WHAT DO YOU MAKE OF IT??
THIS HOUSE IS NOTHIN'-- WAIT'LL YOU SEE THE WATCHER HIMSELF! HE CAN DO ANYTHING! HE WANTS US TO FIGHT IT OUT WITH THAT COMMIE FOR CONTROL OF THE MOON!
LOOK! THAT MUST BE HIM INSIDE THE GLASS DOME!
AND THEN, SLOWLY, THE WATCHER BECOMES VISIBLE TO THE FANTASTIC FOUR, AS HE STANDS IN HIS GREAT CHAMBER, USING HIS VAST POWERS TO MANIPULATE THE VERY FABRIC OF SPACE AND TIME ITSELF!
AND NOW, I SHALL BRING BOTH WARRING FACTIONS TOGETHER, IN A VAST SECLUDED COMBAT AREA, HERE UPON THE MOON!
NO SOONER HAS THE THOUGHT PASSED THE WATCHER'S MIND, THEN THE FANTASTIC FOUR FIND THEMSELVES SWEPT UPWARD IN A WHIRLPOOL OF SHIMMERING ENERGY!
A FLOATING, SPINNING WHIRLPOOL WHICH BRINGS THEM TO A HUNDRED-MILES WIDE CHASM ON THE MOON'S SURFACE -- AND THE MOST CRUCIAL BATTLE OF THEIR CAREER!
14

PART 4
"DUEL IN THE DEAD CITY!"
WE'RE INSIDE AN ENORMOUS DEAD CITY! AND THERE IS STILL ENOUGH ATMOSPHERE LEFT TO ENABLE US TO BREATHE FREELY!
BREATHIN'S THE LEAST OF OUR WORRIES, SISTER! THE WATCHER MUST HAVE PUT THAT COMMIE AND THOSE BLASTED APES HERE SOMEWHERE TOO! AND THEY'VE ALL GOT SUPER POWERS THAT CAN MATCH OURS!
THAT'S NEVER BOTHERED US BEFORE! IF THAT RED WANTS A FIGHT, I FIGGER THE FANTASTIC FOUR ARE JUST THE ONES TO GIVE IT TO 'IM!
THIS IS WRONG! WHY SHOULD WE BATTLE KRAGOFF? WHY CAN'T WE LEAVE OUR DIFFERENCES BEHIND US? THIS IS THE FIRST STEP TO THE STARS-- AND WE SHOULD ALL MAKE THAT TRIP TOGETHER--AS FELLOW EARTHMEN!
X-138
THAT'S A REAL NOBLE THOUGHT, GALAHAD, BUT I GOT NEWS FOR YA--KRAGOFF AINT GONNA BUY IT!! NOT WHEN HE THINKS HIM AND THOSE APES ARE STRONG ENOUGH TO LICK US AND CLAIM THE MOON FOR THE COMMIES!
BEN, NOBODY IS STRONG ENOUGH TO DEFEAT A FREE PEOPLE! DON'T EVER FORGET THAT!
THAT HORRIBLE MAN --AND THOSE DEADLY BEASTS--THEY MIGHT BE WATCHING US AT THIS VERY MOMENT--WAITING TO STRIKE!
15

THE FEMALE IS RIGHT! AND YOU, TORCH, SHALL BE MY FIRST VICTIM! YOU CANNOT FLAME ON IF MY FREEZE-GUN COVERS YOU WITH A COATING OF ICE!!
DUCK, TORCH!! IF THAT SUBSTANCE HITS YOU-- ARGHHH--
A TRULY NOBLE GESTURE! YOU HAVE SACRIFICED YOURSELF FOR THE FLAMING ONE! BUT NOW I CAN SEIZE THE HELPLESS FEMALE AND HOLD HER HOSTAGE!
HE'S GOT SUE! BUT NOT FOR LONG!
YOU'N ME ARE ALWAYS CLAMORIN' FOR ACTION, HOT-HEAD! WELL, HERE'S OUR CHANCE! LET'S GO!
BETTER KEEP OUTTA MY WAY THERE!
NO GIBBERIN' BABOON IS GONNA STOP THE HUMAN TORCH!
BUT THE TORCH MEETS HIS FIRST SET-BACK WHEN, AT A COMMAND FROM THE RED GHOST--
--THE FAST-MOVING SUPER-APE TURNS HIMSELF INTO--A MASS OF THICK ASBESTOS, SMOTHERING THE TORCH'S FLAME WITHIN HIS DEADLY EMBRACE!
AND, AS THE THING RUSHES TO JOHNNY'S SIDE, THE RED GHOST BARKS OUT ANOTHER ORDER, AND THE SECOND SUPER-APE LEAPS INTO THE FRAY! A TON OF FIGHTING FURY SPRINGS AT THE THING, IN THE FORM OF A MADDENED GORILLA, WHOSE NORMAL BRUTAL STRENGTH HAS BEEN INCREASED A HUNDRED-FOLD BY THE AWESOME COSMIC RAYS!
OOOFF--!!
THOSE BLASTED RAYS MADE HIM STRONGER THAN ME! HE TOSSED ME LIKE I WAS NOTHIN'!! WE REALLY GOT A FIGHT ON OUR HANDS!
16

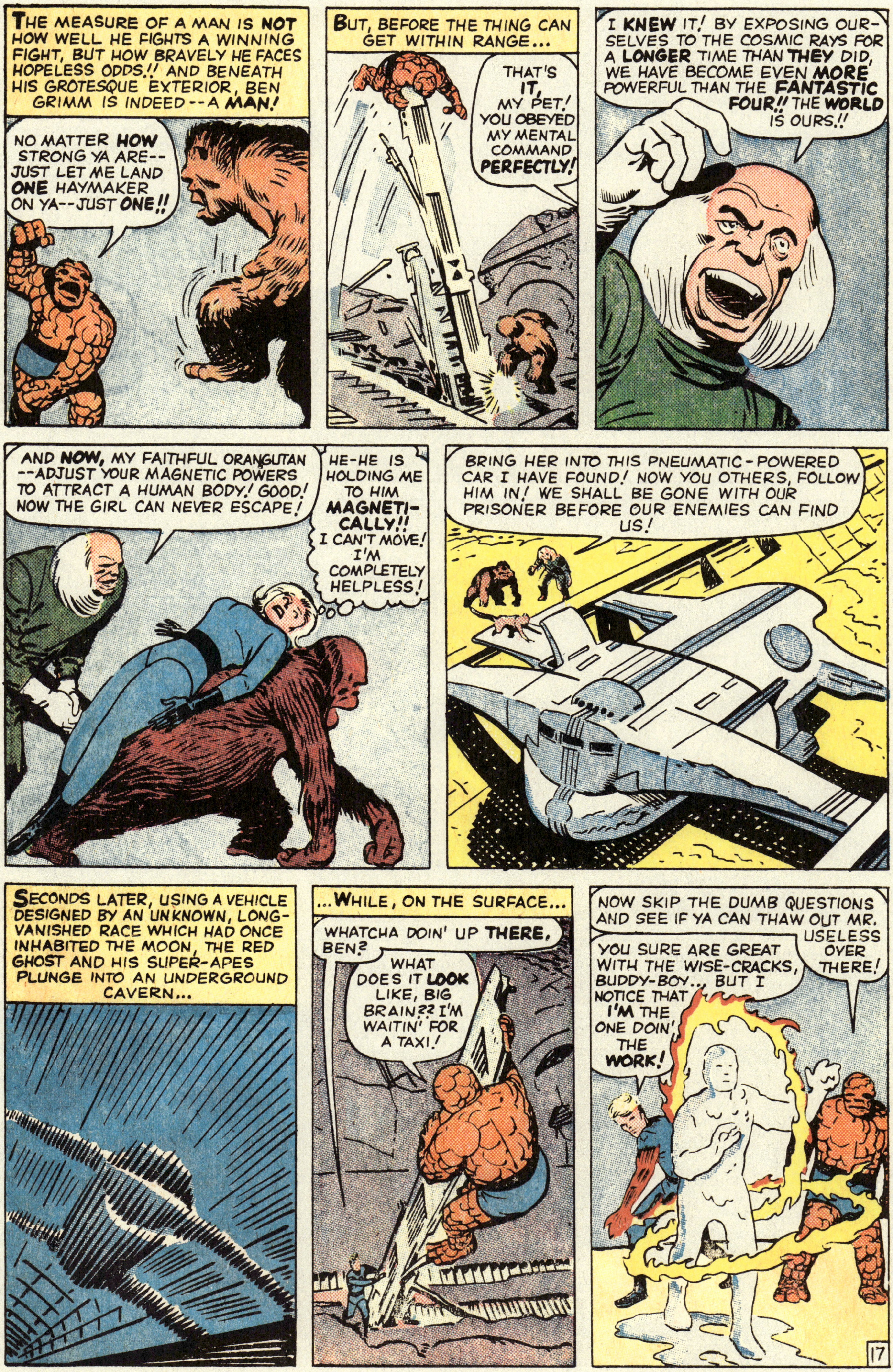
THE MEASURE OF A MAN IS NOT HOW WELL HE FIGHTS A WINNING FIGHT, BUT HOW BRAVELY HE FACES HOPELESS ODDS!! AND BENEATH HIS GROTESQUE EXTERIOR, BEN GRIMM IS INDEED--A MAN!
NO MATTER HOW STRONG YA ARE--JUST LET ME LAND ONE HAYMAKER ON YA--JUST ONE!!
BUT, BEFORE THE THING CAN GET WITHIN RANGE...
THAT'S IT, MY PET! YOU OBEYED MY MENTAL COMMAND PERFECTLY!
I KNEW IT! BY EXPOSING OURSELVES TO THE COSMIC RAYS FOR A LONGER TIME THAN THEY DID, WE HAVE BECOME EVEN MORE POWERFUL THAN THE FANTASTIC FOUR!! THE WORLD IS OURS!!
AND NOW, MY FAITHFUL ORANGUTAN --ADJUST YOUR MAGNETIC POWERS TO ATTRACT A HUMAN BODY! GOOD! NOW THE GIRL CAN NEVER ESCAPE!
HE-HE IS HOLDING ME TO HIM MAGNETICALLY!! I CAN'T MOVE! I'M COMPLETELY HELPLESS!
BRING HER INTO THIS PNEUMATIC-POWERED CAR I HAVE FOUND! NOW YOU OTHERS, FOLLOW HIM IN! WE SHALL BE GONE WITH OUR PRISONER BEFORE OUR ENEMIES CAN FIND US!
SECONDS LATER, USING A VEHICLE DESIGNED BY AN UNKNOWN, LONG-VANISHED RACE WHICH HAD ONCE INHABITED THE MOON, THE RED GHOST AND HIS SUPER-APES PLUNGE INTO AN UNDERGROUND CAVERN...
...WHILE, ON THE SURFACE...
WHATCHA DOIN' UP THERE, BEN?
WHAT DOES IT LOOK LIKE, BIG BRAIN?? I'M WAITIN' FOR A TAXI!
NOW SKIP THE DUMB QUESTIONS AND SEE IF YA CAN THAW OUT MR. USELESS OVER THERE!
YOU SURE ARE GREAT WITH THE WISE-CRACKS, BUDDY-BOY.. BUT I NOTICE THAT I'M THE ONE DOIN' THE WORK!
17

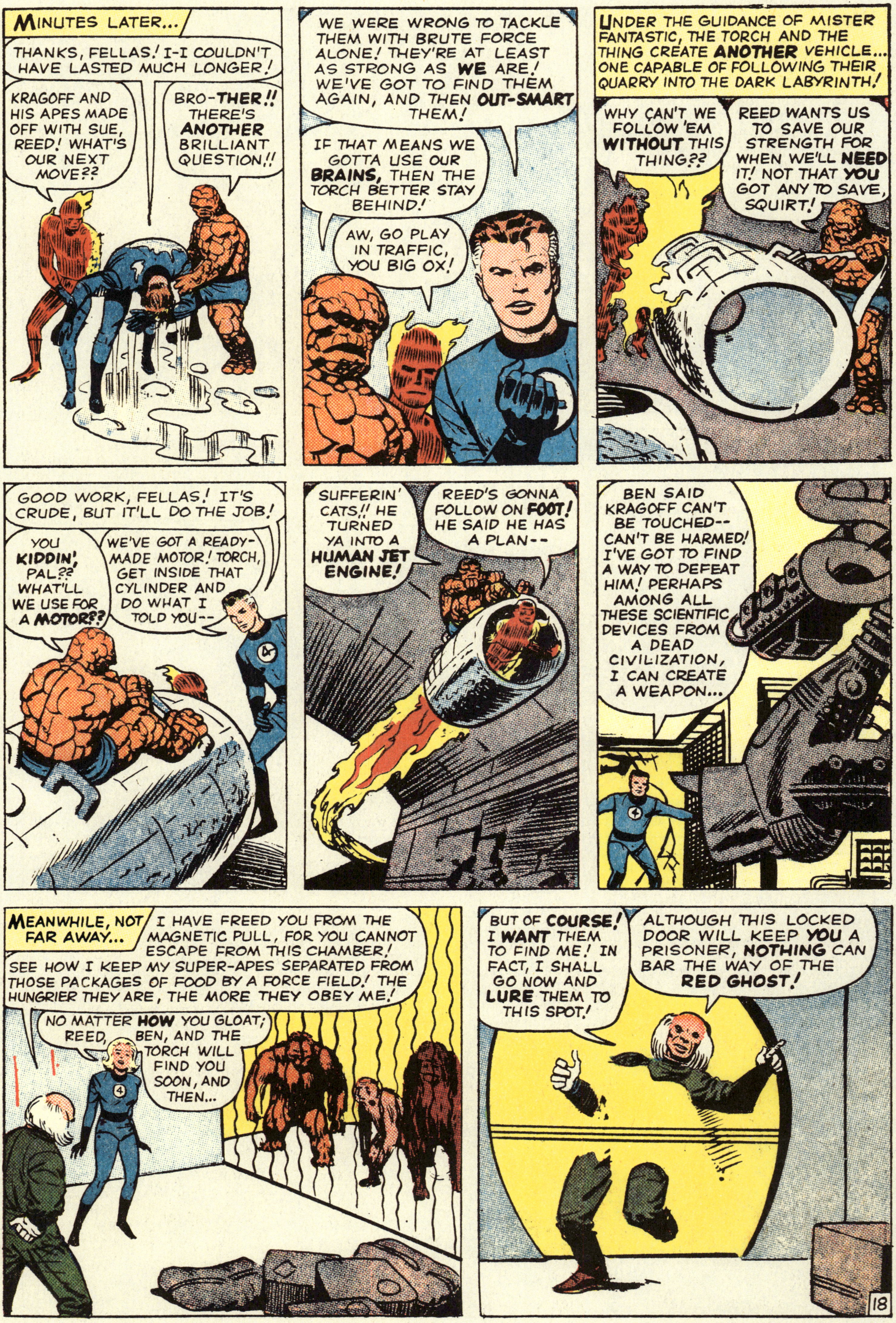
MINUTES LATER...
THANKS, FELLAS! I-I COULDN'T HAVE LASTED MUCH LONGER!
KRAGOFF AND HIS APES MADE OFF WITH SUE, REED! WHAT'S OUR NEXT MOVE??
BRO-THER!! THERE'S ANOTHER BRILLIANT QUESTION!!
WE WERE WRONG TO TACKLE THEM WITH BRUTE FORCE ALONE! THEY'RE AT LEAST AS STRONG AS WE ARE! WE'VE GOT TO FIND THEM AGAIN, AND THEN OUT-SMART THEM!
IF THAT MEANS WE GOTTA USE OUR BRAINS, THEN THE TORCH BETTER STAY BEHIND!
AW, GO PLAY IN TRAFFIC, YOU BIG OX!
UNDER THE GUIDANCE OF MISTER FANTASTIC, THE TORCH AND THE THING CREATE ANOTHER VEHICLE... ONE CAPABLE OF FOLLOWING THEIR QUARRY INTO THE DARK LABYRINTH!
WHY CAN'T WE FOLLOW 'EM WITHOUT THIS THING??
REED WANTS US TO SAVE OUR STRENGTH FOR WHEN WE'LL NEED IT! NOT THAT YOU GOT ANY TO SAVE, SQUIRT!
GOOD WORK, FELLAS! IT'S CRUDE, BUT IT'LL DO THE JOB!
YOU KIDDIN', PAL?? WHAT'LL WE USE FOR A MOTOR??
WE'VE GOT A READY-MADE MOTOR! TORCH, GET INSIDE THAT CYLINDER AND DO WHAT I TOLD YOU--
SUFFERIN' CATS!! HE TURNED YA INTO A HUMAN JET ENGINE!
REED'S GONNA FOLLOW ON FOOT! HE SAID HE HAS A PLAN--
BEN SAID KRAGOFF CAN'T BE TOUCHED-- CAN'T BE HARMED! I'VE GOT TO FIND A WAY TO DEFEAT HIM! PERHAPS AMONG ALL THESE SCIENTIFIC DEVICES FROM A DEAD CIVILIZATION, I CAN CREATE A WEAPON...
MEANWHILE, NOT FAR AWAY...
I HAVE FREED YOU FROM THE MAGNETIC PULL, FOR YOU CANNOT ESCAPE FROM THIS CHAMBER! SEE HOW I KEEP MY SUPER-APES SEPARATED FROM THOSE PACKAGES OF FOOD BY A FORCE FIELD! THE HUNGRIER THEY ARE, THE MORE THEY OBEY ME!
NO MATTER HOW YOU GLOAT; REED, BEN, AND THE TORCH WILL FIND YOU SOON, AND THEN...
BUT OF COURSE! I WANT THEM TO FIND ME! IN FACT, I SHALL GO NOW AND LURE THEM TO THIS SPOT!
ALTHOUGH THIS LOCKED DOOR WILL KEEP YOU A PRISONER, NOTHING CAN BAR THE WAY OF THE RED GHOST!
18

IF I COULD ONLY FIND A WAY TO ELIMINATE THIS FORCE FIELD-- TO FREE THE SUPER-APES! I WOULD TAKE MY CHANCES WITH THEM, RATHER THAN THE RED GHOST, FOR THEY ARE LIKE THE COMMUNIST MASSES, INNOCENTLY ENSLAVED BY THEIR EVIL LEADERS!
KRAGOFF HAS HAD MORE TIME THAN WE TO EXPLORE THE MYSTERIES OF THE DEAD CITY! BEING ABLE TO GO THRU WALLS, HE COULD INSPECT EVERYTHING HE DESIRED! BUT THERE MUST BE A WAY TO CONTROL THE FORCE FIELD HE DISCOVERED! IF ONLY-- WAIT! HERE IT IS--THIS MASTER CABLE!
I'VE BROKEN THE CIRCUIT! THE APES WILL BE FREE!
JUST AS I EXPECTED! THEY'RE SO RAVENOUSLY HUNGRY THAT THEY DON'T EVEN NOTICE ME IN THEIR FRANTIC ATTEMPT TO GET THE FOOD WHICH KRAGOFF HAD LEFT ON THE OTHER SIDE OF THE FORCE SCREEN!
IT'S LUCKY FOR ME, BECAUSE TURNING INVISIBLE WOULDN'T SAVE ME FROM THEM! THEIR SENSE OF SMELL COULD DETECT ME AS EASILY AS THEIR EYES!
AND NOW, NO LONGER UNDER THE RED GHOST'S MENTAL CONTROL, THEY WANT THEIR FREEDOM! I HOPED THEY WOULD USE THEIR STRENGTH TO BREAK THE DOOR DOWN!
AT THE SAME TIME, UNAWARE OF WHAT HAS TRANSPIRED BEHIND HIM...
THERE HE IS, TORCH! HE JUST CAME OUTTA THAT WALL!
THEY SEE ME! MY PLAN IS STILL WORKING PERFECTLY!
NOW TO QUICKLY RETURN BACK THRU THE WALL! THE TORCH WILL UNDOUBTEDLY BURN THRU THE STONE TO GET TO ME--
--AND, AS SOON AS HE APPEARS, THIS ALL-POWERFUL DISINTEGRATOR RAY WHICH I WAS FORTUNATE ENOUGH TO DISCOVER HERE, WILL DISPOSE OF HIM, AND THE THING, FOREVER!
AND, UNAWARE OF THE DEADLY DANGER AWAITING HIM BEHIND THE CAVERN WALL, THE HUMAN TORCH USES HIS FANTASTIC FLAME TO MELT HIS WAY TO THE RED GHOST!
19

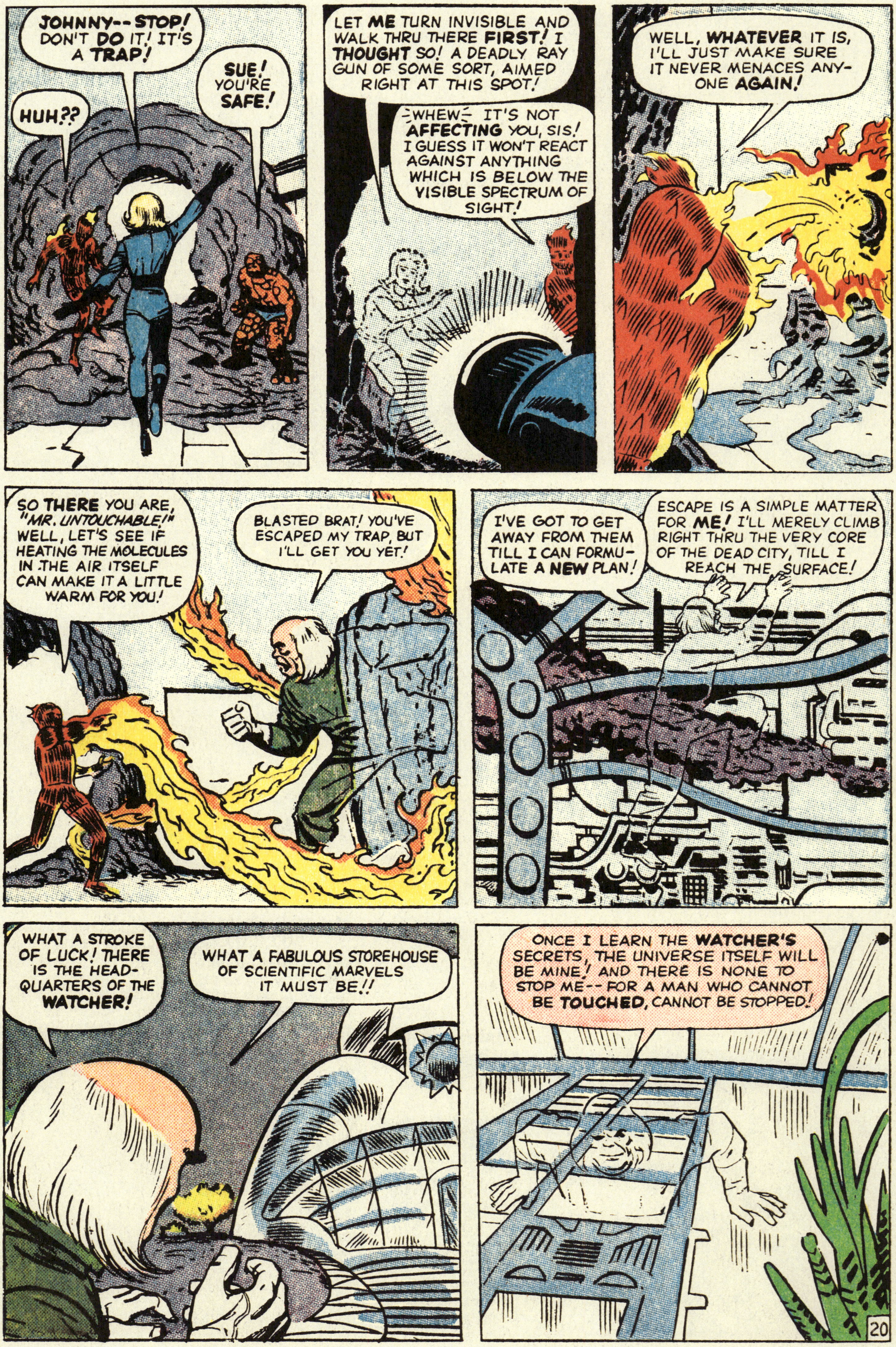
JOHNNY-- STOP! DON'T DO IT! IT'S A TRAP!
HUH??
SUE! YOU'RE SAFE!
LET ME TURN INVISIBLE AND WALK THRU THERE FIRST! I THOUGHT SO! A DEADLY RAY GUN OF SOME SORT, AIMED RIGHT AT THIS SPOT!
-WHEW- IT'S NOT AFFECTING YOU, SIS! I GUESS IT WON'T REACT AGAINST ANYTHING WHICH IS BELOW THE VISIBLE SPECTRUM OF SIGHT!
WELL, WHATEVER IT IS, I'LL JUST MAKE SURE IT NEVER MENACES ANY-ONE AGAIN!
SO THERE YOU ARE, "MR. UNTOUCHABLE!" WELL, LET'S SEE IF HEATING THE MOLECULES IN THE AIR ITSELF CAN MAKE IT A LITTLE WARM FOR YOU!
BLASTED BRAT! YOU'VE ESCAPED MY TRAP, BUT I'LL GET YOU YET!
I'VE GOT TO GET AWAY FROM THEM TILL I CAN FORMU-LATE A NEW PLAN!
ESCAPE IS A SIMPLE MATTER FOR ME! I'LL MERELY CLIMB RIGHT THRU THE VERY CORE OF THE DEAD CITY, TILL I REACH THE SURFACE!
WHAT A STROKE OF LUCK! THERE IS THE HEAD-QUARTERS OF THE WATCHER!
WHAT A FABULOUS STOREHOUSE OF SCIENTIFIC MARVELS IT MUST BE!!
ONCE I LEARN THE WATCHER'S SECRETS, THE UNIVERSE ITSELF WILL BE MINE! AND THERE IS NONE TO STOP ME-- FOR A MAN WHO CANNOT BE TOUCHED, CANNOT BE STOPPED!

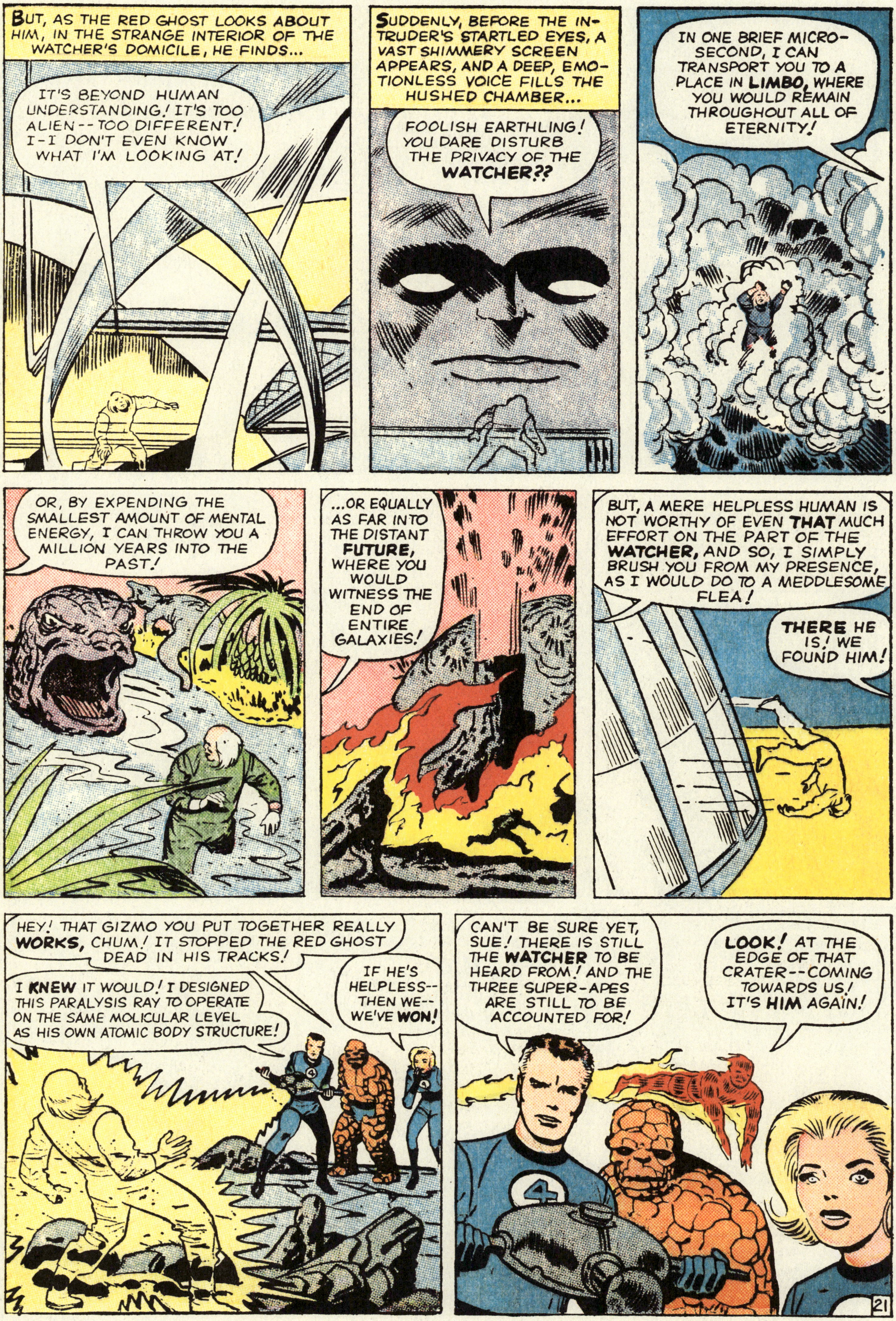

BUT, AS THE RED GHOST LOOKS ABOUT HIM, IN THE STRANGE INTERIOR OF THE WATCHER'S DOMICILE, HE FINDS...
IT'S BEYOND HUMAN UNDERSTANDING! IT'S TOO ALIEN--TOO DIFFERENT! I-I DON'T EVEN KNOW WHAT I'M LOOKING AT!
SUDDENLY, BEFORE THE INTRUDER'S STARTLED EYES, A VAST SHIMMERY SCREEN APPEARS, AND A DEEP, EMOTIONLESS VOICE FILLS THE HUSHED CHAMBER...
FOOLISH EARTHLING! YOU DARE DISTURB THE PRIVACY OF THE WATCHER??
IN ONE BRIEF MICRO-SECOND, I CAN TRANSPORT YOU TO A PLACE IN LIMBO, WHERE YOU WOULD REMAIN THROUGHOUT ALL OF ETERNITY!
OR, BY EXPENDING THE SMALLEST AMOUNT OF MENTAL ENERGY, I CAN THROW YOU A MILLION YEARS INTO THE PAST!
...OR EQUALLY AS FAR INTO THE DISTANT FUTURE, WHERE YOU WOULD WITNESS THE END OF ENTIRE GALAXIES!
BUT, A MERE HELPLESS HUMAN IS NOT WORTHY OF EVEN THAT MUCH EFFORT ON THE PART OF THE WATCHER, AND SO, I SIMPLY BRUSH YOU FROM MY PRESENCE, AS I WOULD DO TO A MEDDLESOME FLEA!
THERE HE IS! WE FOUND HIM!
HEY! THAT GIZMO YOU PUT TOGETHER REALLY WORKS, CHUM! IT STOPPED THE RED GHOST DEAD IN HIS TRACKS!
I KNEW IT WOULD! I DESIGNED THIS PARALYSIS RAY TO OPERATE ON THE SAME MOLICULAR LEVEL AS HIS OWN ATOMIC BODY STRUCTURE!
IF HE'S HELPLESS--THEN WE--WE'VE WON!
CAN'T BE SURE YET, SUE! THERE IS STILL THE WATCHER TO BE HEARD FROM! AND THE THREE SUPER-APES ARE STILL TO BE ACCOUNTED FOR!
LOOK! AT THE EDGE OF THAT CRATER--COMING TOWARDS US! IT'S HIM AGAIN!

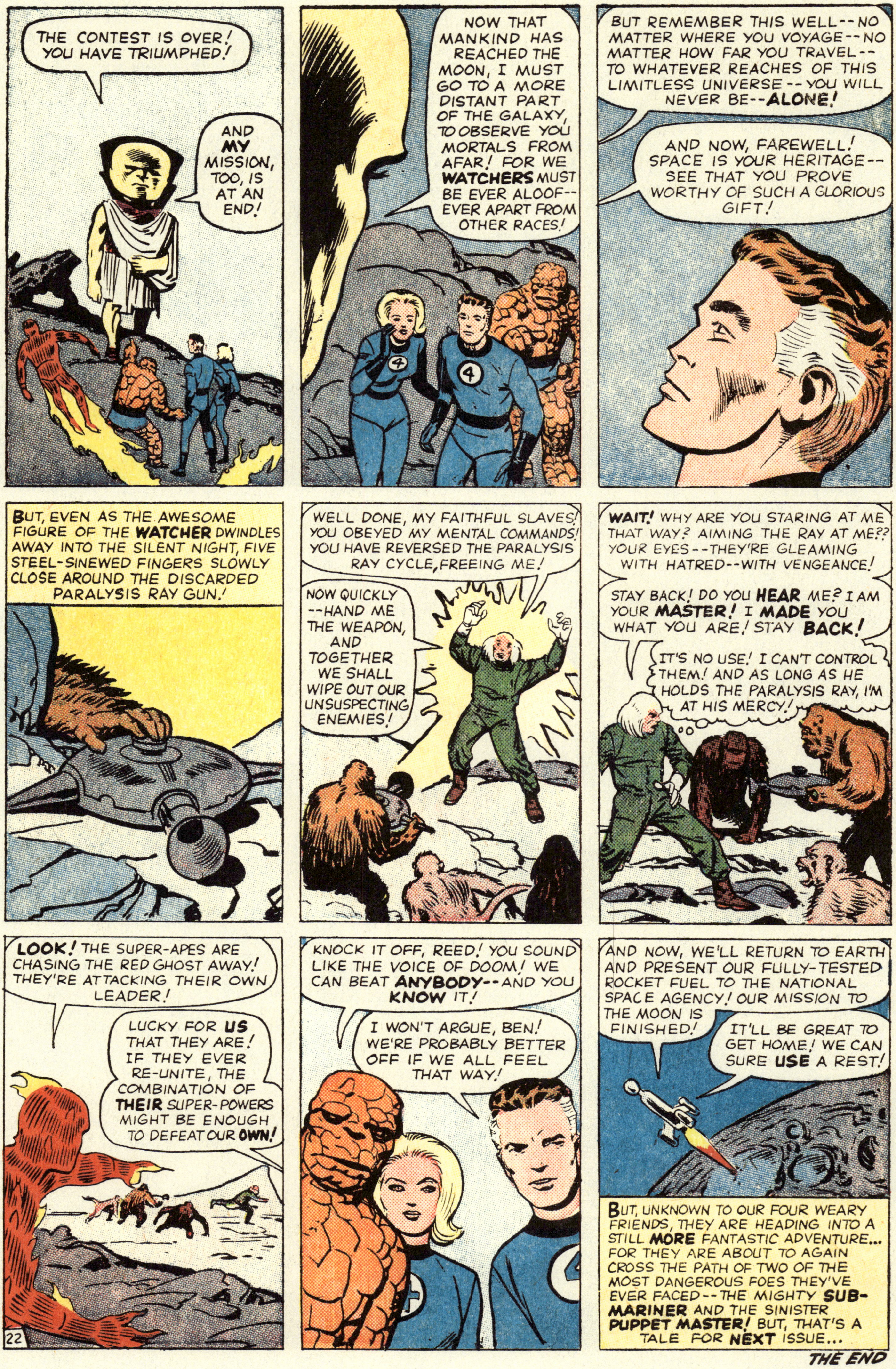
THE CONTEST IS OVER! YOU HAVE TRIUMPHED!
AND MY MISSION, TOO, IS AT AN END!
NOW THAT MANKIND HAS REACHED THE MOON, I MUST GO TO A MORE DISTANT PART OF THE GALAXY, TO OBSERVE YOU MORTALS FROM AFAR! FOR WE WATCHERS MUST BE EVER ALOOF-- EVER APART FROM OTHER RACES!
BUT REMEMBER THIS WELL--NO MATTER WHERE YOU VOYAGE--NO MATTER HOW FAR YOU TRAVEL-- TO WHATEVER REACHES OF THIS LIMITLESS UNIVERSE--YOU WILL NEVER BE--ALONE!
AND NOW, FAREWELL! SPACE IS YOUR HERITAGE-- SEE THAT YOU PROVE WORTHY OF SUCH A GLORIOUS GIFT!
BUT, EVEN AS THE AWESOME FIGURE OF THE WATCHER DWINDLES AWAY INTO THE SILENT NIGHT, FIVE STEEL-SINEWED FINGERS SLOWLY CLOSE AROUND THE DISCARDED PARALYSIS RAY GUN!
WELL DONE, MY FAITHFUL SLAVES! YOU OBEYED MY MENTAL COMMANDS! YOU HAVE REVERSED THE PARALYSIS RAY CYCLE, FREEING ME!
NOW QUICKLY --HAND ME THE WEAPON, AND TOGETHER WE SHALL WIPE OUT OUR UNSUSPECTING ENEMIES!
WAIT! WHY ARE YOU STARING AT ME THAT WAY? AIMING THE RAY AT ME?? YOUR EYES--THEY'RE GLEAMING WITH HATRED--WITH VENGEANCE!
STAY BACK! DO YOU HEAR ME? I AM YOUR MASTER! I MADE YOU WHAT YOU ARE! STAY BACK!
IT'S NO USE! I CAN'T CONTROL THEM! AND AS LONG AS HE HOLDS THE PARALYSIS RAY, I'M AT HIS MERCY!
LOOK! THE SUPER-APES ARE CHASING THE RED GHOST AWAY! THEY'RE ATTACKING THEIR OWN LEADER!
LUCKY FOR US THAT THEY ARE! IF THEY EVER RE-UNITE, THE COMBINATION OF THEIR SUPER-POWERS MIGHT BE ENOUGH TO DEFEAT OUR OWN!
22
KNOCK IT OFF, REED! YOU SOUND LIKE THE VOICE OF DOOM! WE CAN BEAT ANYBODY--AND YOU KNOW IT!
I WON'T ARGUE, BEN! WE'RE PROBABLY BETTER OFF IF WE ALL FEEL THAT WAY!
AND NOW, WE'LL RETURN TO EARTH AND PRESENT OUR FULLY-TESTED ROCKET FUEL TO THE NATIONAL SPACE AGENCY! OUR MISSION TO THE MOON IS FINISHED!
IT'LL BE GREAT TO GET HOME! WE CAN SURE USE A REST!
BUT, UNKNOWN TO OUR FOUR WEARY FRIENDS, THEY ARE HEADING INTO A STILL MORE FANTASTIC ADVENTURE... FOR THEY ARE ABOUT TO AGAIN CROSS THE PATH OF TWO OF THE MOST DANGEROUS FOES THEY'VE EVER FACED--THE MIGHTY SUB-MARINER AND THE SINISTER PUPPET MASTER! BUT, THAT'S A TALE FOR NEXT ISSUE...
THE END

Address YOUR letters to:
LEE and KIRBY
FANTASTIC FOUR
THIRD FLOOR
655 MADISON AVE.
NEW YORK 21, N. Y.

FANTASTIC FAN PAGE 4

Dear Stan and Jack:

I have sent numerous postcards to you, but now I think I should give you a complete record of my views. I hope you enjoy reading it as I did writing it. The artwork has improved greatly since issue #1, but I feel you can do better. Your artwork in #6 was below par. As far as covers go, #10 was startling, but not as good as others. #1 was terrible, as was #2, and the cover for #1 was too far from the story. All of your covers are unique, and . . . well . . . I guess generally fantastic, to use my favorite superlative. Stan, your writing cannot be topped although #1 and #2 were, as in the artwork, below par, far below! Your organization in #3 was just what you needed. Costumes were excellent, not too frilly, but still good-looking. The skyscraper headquarters was striking, and I loved your diagrams in #3 and #6, especially #6. I wish you would use the pogo-plane, copter, and missile more often. Now a member analysis: Invisible Girl is not all-important to the team, but I vote to keep her. You need a woman in the group. The Thing is striking because he doesn't resemble anything I have ever seen. Human Torch is of course your best character, and I love him in *Strange Tales.* Keep his saucy character. Mr Fantastic is perfect for the leader. Don't play him down too much because of the Torch. Also, I hope to see more romantic ties between him and Sue, maybe even marriage. But don't let the Sub-Mariner butt in, I beg of you. Doctor Doom is the greatest villain of all time. I expect to see much more of him. At first I thought Sub-Mariner could be rehabilitated, but what can you do after having been a villain for three issues?! I hope you get a new Puppet-Master, but not too soon, maybe in issue #15, or #16. You have got to bring back Moleman, possibly in league with Doctor Doom. It would be interesting to see how you would handle a villain whom you created in your first and worst issue. I would like to end with this: Your well-known claim of "The World's Greatest Comic Magazine" is truly correct and is no idle boast, so good luck, and Auf Wiedersehn!

Frederic Johnson
608 Summit St.
Rockford, Illinois

WHEW! We were better off when you were using postcards! But thanks for the comments, Fred.

Dear Stan and Jack:

How come Alicia could carve out statues when she is blind; how would she know what they look like?? Also, is Dr. Doom a robot?

Kenny Glenn
835 9th St.
Douglas, Arizona

ALICIA is gifted with sensitive fingers, just like many famous blind musicians. As for DR. DOOM, no, he is not a robot. Perhaps we'll be seeing more of him in the future.

Dear Stan and Jack:

In issue #10, you made a little boo-boo. On page 6, Doctor Doom is shown destroying an ashtray with his sub-miniature transistor-powered atomic blast gun which is, in this picture, housed in his *left* index finger. On page 23, he is shown shooting the same gun at Mr. Fantastic – and the caption says that the gun is in his right index finger! Should you omit such small mistakes, 99% of the critiques written you would be favorable ones. Don't get me wrong! It's just that little improvements would make your great magazine even better!

Harold Echtinaw, Jr.
808 E.M.L. Ave.
Kalamazoo, Michigan

We stand corrected, Hal—although why couldn't there be a TWO-GUN villain??

Dear Stan and Jack:

I would like to comment on Paul Gambaccini's panning letter which you printed in #9, as I agree with parts of it. It's obvious that his letter was written in anger and is rather one sided. Although your letter column is a little (a little? A lot!) stacked in your favor, your replies are not "asinine;" it's just that your humor (?) takes some getting used to. Artwork *is* pretty bad but if Mr. Gambaccini would look at #6 (which was inked by Steve Ditko, I think) he will have to admit Kirby's artwork has some good points which are heightened by the superb inking. Paul's probably the first guy to criticize the character conflicts. The characters act like real people would in such situations (for instance, *you'd* be grouchy if you looked like the Thing!). The light touch is necessary to keep the pathos of being changed into a freak from being *too* depressing. It also makes the story much more entertaining. The story plots are pretty stupid at times (the "Puppet-Master" story was really a dud except for the introduction of Alicia). Paul's last sentence ("They are too good to be realistic.") is puzzling. What does he mean, "good?" If he means "goody-goody," I disagree for obvious reasons. Most super-heroes are much more "goody-goody," although I see in Reed, a parody of the typical super-hero. His level-headed, unfailing judgment looks ridiculous when he is surrounded by more realistic characters. Some comments of my own: I think it was inconsistent with previous stories to have Sub-Mariner acting like a full villain in #9, and the stories are better when some of the reader's sympathy is with him. Otherwise, that was a really great story. I really got a kick out of Thing's fight with Sub-Mariner.

Robert Ford
Philadelphia, Pennsylvania

Hey, Bob, speak of the devil — look who our next letter is from!

Dear Editor:

FANTASTIC FOUR has greatly improved, but that's no reason it shouldn't be improved more. The cover of #10 is the best yet, and I have a feeling that you used one of those techniques to get it that way. "Return of Dr. Doom" was very good, but keep him away now! He's gone! He is an AWFUL villain; nothing special to him at all. I'm glad you're lengthening the letter page. Good for you! However, this "Dear Stan and Jack" stuff doesn't seem right; not respectful enough. I mean, you walk up to somebody and say, "Hiya, Kirby!" or, "How ya doin', Stan?" when you've never met him before?????!? Anyway, here are my suggestions: (We've only got room to print *some* – S. & J.) 1) Give HUMAN TORCH his own comic. He's great, no doubt about it. Sure, I know we get him monthly in STRANGE TALES, but that's not enough. 2) PLEASE eliminate those thick borderlines of the word balloons. They are hideous! 3) PLEASE ELIMINATE those five-page stories in your comics. Either make them one tale, or devote the space to THOR, ANT-MAN, etc. You see, I don't buy JOURNEY INTO MYSTERY or TALES TO ASTONISH because of these little stories.

4) None of these giant ant-eaters from Guafa, or insect kings from Zorda. O.K.? 5) Give SUB-MARINER his own magazine. 6)PLEASE eliminate those pin-up pages and text stories! They waste space! 7) Please don't print many of those silly "boo-boo" letters. 8) Let's have more human foes like SUB-MARINER and PASTE-POT-PETE!?!? 9) How about individual comics for ANT-MAN and THOR? (P.S. From the poses in FF #10, you'd think the faces of Lee and Kirby are as bad as Doctor Doom's! How about letting us *see* them, even if it is torture.)

Paul Gambaccini
8 Elizabeth Drive
Westport, Conn.

After the way you pick on our stories, which we think are great, we'd be afraid to show you our faces, which are probably NOT so great!

Dear Stan and Jack:
First of all, I would like to compliment you on issue #10. The first three pages, with the exception of a few panels, were really unnecessary. But it is places such as these that give a certain touch to your characters. I would like to see more of Dr. Doom. Now to go on to part two of my letter. I think the FF should be left exactly as they are. Keep Sue Storm, and the others exactly as they are. Which now brings me to the concluding part of my letter. I see that some fans want some old FF's. Well, I'm your man. Down here in Portsmouth, there is a back-issue store which sells old comics for 6¢. Send me your name, address, comic preferences, and a list of the ones you have. Be sure to include statements such as, "I only like *Tales to Astonish* after Ant-Man came out." I'll try to get the comics for you. Cost is only 6¢ and postage.

Paul Weinstein
2714 Gilbert Ave.
Portsmouth, Ohio

Thanks, Paul. Judging by the number of requests for back-numbers which WE receive, we imagine you'll hear from quite a lot of readers.

Dear Stan and Jack:
In FF #10, you show Johnny Storm (The Torch) saying, "I can concentrate my flame so much that it burns without heat!" He then burned through the lock. What's wrong with you guys? Don't you know that it's the heat that does the burning in a flame. Even if it would be possible to produce a flame without heat, its useful function would be to produce light. In other words, it's the *heat* in a flame that enables it to burn anything. Take away the heat, and you take away its ability to burn anything. Get the point?

Wayne Orlicki
1942 6th Ave.
San Diego 1, California

Nice try, Wayne, but didja ever hear of INFRA-RED rays? You can burn with them without heat. Much of the electrical cooking in large restaurants today is done without heat. If this keeps up, they may stop teaching Boy Scouts how to rub sticks together!

Dear Stan and Jack:
Well, it looks about time for me to eat crow! About three issues ago, my letter was published, and in that letter I commented on having Sue Storm "canned," to coin a term. Well, after having read, *A Day With The Fantastic Four*, in FF #11, and seeing the part where Sue goes to pieces, I realize what a mistake I made. I guess my mind slipped back to the days of the old time serials, and the damsels in distress. You know, it's the same way in life as it is in comics. You tend to think little of someone because you don't understand them or what they stand for. In closing, I ask that Lee and Kirby convey my deepest apologies to Sue . . . and tell her that from now on, she's a friend of mine.

Sincerely yours,
Marty Ross
2819 Schley Ave.
New York 65, N. Y.

You and a million other guys, Marty! But thanks for the thought!

Dear Stan and Jack:
FANTASTIC FOUR #9 was by far the best issue of this mag yet! I thought for sure you couldn't top the last ish . . . but you did — and undoubtedly will continue to top yourselves every issue (I hope!). Just can't get over the 21 *stupendous* SUB-MARINER vs. THING fight panels. Which reminds me . . . I've noticed other companies give out free original art and story scripts for the best letters they receive . . . and I think *you*, who have the best of art and plot should also give us readers something we can be proud of the rest of our lives. (Besides the next issue of the fabulous quartet.) How 'bout it? I just got FF #10 and . . . HOLY COW! DOC DOOM AGAIN!? And you guys in it too!? What more could a reader ask for 12¢?? One complaint: no face views of L&K. Glad to see you giving credits to your staff. A couple questions — Who inked FF #5?? The artwork in that issue surpassed anything you did before or have done yet. Whoever did it brought out sharp details, and brought out the best work of Jack Kirby's pencils ever done by anyone. You editors can*not* make a mistake. You try to give us readers what we clamor for, and if you fail with one way, you try another. Torch's having a secret identity was no error . . . you thought it was what we would like to see . . . it wasn't. Then you made amends in STRANGE TALES #106. *ONE LAST THING:* We fans let you know we liked the realism of your characters . . . but beware! Real people do DIE.

Your until Niagara Falls,
Mike Tuohey
16857 Sunderland
Detroit 19, Michigan

We aren't able to give out original scripts or art at this time, but hope to sometime in the future. Ish #5 was inked by an old friend of ours, Joe Sinnott, who has his own script in JRNY. INTO MYSTERY, #90 MARCH and will be seen more often in our future issues. As for real people dying — that's ONE thing you can't blame on us!

SPECIAL ANNOUNCEMENTS SECTION:

- **Once again we want to thank the hundreds of loyal fans whose interesting letters can't be printed due to lack of space. Please rest assured that either Stan, or Jack, or both read each and every one personally, and are tremendously grateful for your interest and support.**
- **Final result of our "ADD NEW CHARACTERS" poll: The count is three-to-one AGAINST adding any new members to the FF. But most readers would like to see frequent guest appearances by our other super-heroes. Will do.**
- **IRON-MAN, now appearing monthly in TALES OF SUSPENSE, is another star in our growing line of off-beat super-heroes. Treat yourself to a copy. Also, have you seen the new AMAZING SPIDER-MAN yet? We have a hunch you'll like him.**
- **Finally, the next ish of FF features — SUB-MARINER! If you don't reserve your copy at your dealer's NOW, don't say we didn't warn you!**

12¢
the AMAZING SPIDER-MAN
1 MAR.
THE FANTASTIC FOUR THINK I'M TRAPPED! BUT THEY DON'T SUSPECT MY REAL POWER!
2 GREAT FEATURE-LENGTH SPIDER-MAN THRILLERS!
EXTRA ADDED ATTRACTION: SPIDER-MAN MEETS THE FANTASTIC FOU
"the CHAMELEON STRIKES
NOW ON SALE!
12¢
TALES OF SUSPENSE
39 MAR.
WHO? OR WHAT, IS THE NEWEST, MOST BREATH-TAKING, MOST SENSATIONAL SUPER-HERO OF ALL...?
WHO?
WHO?
WHO?
"IRON MAN!"
HE LIVES! HE WALKS! HE CONQUERS!
FROM THE TALENTED BULL-PEN WHERE THE FANTASTIC FOUR, SPIDER-MAN, THOR AND YOUR OTHER FAVORITE SUPER-HEROES
DON'T MISS 'EM!

Make $5.00 to $20.00 a Week EXTRA operating this
"SATURDAY MORNING Shoe STORE"
We Furnish Everything FREE!
Make extra money next week end! Just visit with friends, relatives and neighbors on Saturday mornings and show them how they'll "walk on air" in Mason comfort shoes! Many a man sells 2, 3, 4 or 6 pairs of Mason shoes on Saturday mornings alone —without "knocking himself out"—and makes as much as $5 to $20 or more extra for 2 or 3 hours of his time. You keep all of your profits! We furnish you a FREE selling outfit containing everything you need to start making money right away. We carry the stock for you and ship the shoes for you—your profit is clear. You never invest a cent. And think what you'll save on your own shoes, too!
Here's Why You'll Make Money!
You'll take orders for over 230 different shoe styles for dress, sport or work, for men and women—a far greater selection than any neighborhood store can possibly stock. And you can fit almost anyone! You'll draw from our 300,000 pair stock with sizes ranging from 2½ to 15, widths AAAA to EEEE! You'll feature exclusive Velvet-eez shoes with foamy-soft air-cushion innersoles that let you "walk on air." You show many other exclusive features... Ripple Sole Shoes, Oil-Resistant Work Shoes, Magic Closure Shoes, colorful styles for women—a line that's far beyond the reach of any store. That's why EVERYBODY is your prospect. And because Mason Shoes are never sold through stores, folks must buy from you!
Don't Invest a Cent! We Give You FREE SELLING OUTFIT!
Fill out and mail coupon below. We'll rush you your FREE Selling Outfit. Kit features 230 fast-selling shoe styles, plus foolproof measuring equipment—and "How To Make Extra Money" booklet. Send no money now or later. Just rush the coupon for your FREE Selling Outfit . . . enjoy some extra money next Saturday!
RUSH STARTING OUTFIT
MR. VICTOR MASON
Mason Shoe Mfg. Company, Dept. H-655, Chippewa Falls, Wis.
Dear Victor: Please rush FREE and postpaid my Starting Shoe Business Outfit with EVERYTHING I need to start making extra cash Saturday mornings.
Name
(PLEASE PRINT)
Address
Town
State
MASON
SHOE MFG. CO., Dept. H-655
Chippewa Falls, Wisconsin

IND.
THE WORLD'S GREATEST COMIC MAGAZINE!
APPROVED BY THE COMICS CODE AUTHORITY
The Fantastic Four
14 MAY
MARVEL COMICS GROUP 12¢
HOW MUCH ACTION, HOW MUCH DRAMA DO YOU CRAVE?? BE ON HAND WHEN... "the SUB-MARINER STRIKES!"
AT LAST WE MEET AGAIN!! BUT THIS TIME... ON MY TERMS!!
UNDERSEA MONARCH VERSUS AMERICA'S GREATEST SUPER-HEROES!
PLUS THE SURPRISE RETURN OF ANOTHER FORMER VILLAIN!

THE FANTASTIC FOUR is published by CANAM PUBLISHERS SALES CORP. OFFICE OF PUBLICATION: 655 MADISON AVENUE, NEW YORK, N.Y. Published monthly. Copyright 1963 by CANAM PUBLISHERS SALES CORP., 655 Madison Avenue, New York, N.Y. Vol. 1 No. 14, MAY, 1963 issue. Price 12¢ per copy. Subscription rate $1.75 for 12 issues including postage. Foreign substription $3.25 in American funds. No similarity between any of the names, characters, persons, and/or institutions appearing in this magazine with those of any living or dead person is intended, and any such similarity which may exist is purely coincidental. Printed in U.S.A. by The Eastern Color Printing Co., Waterbury 20, Conn.

ONCE AGAIN, THE FANTASTIC FOUR FACE THE THREAT OF:
SUB-MARINER, and "THE MERCILESS PUPPET MASTER"
PART 1
HAVING DEFEATED THE RED GHOST ON THE MOON LAST ISSUE, THE WORLD'S MOST POPULAR SUPER-HERO TEAM HEADS FOR HOME AND NEW ADVENTURE!
SCRIPT........STAN LEE
ART...........JACK KIRBY
INKING.......DICK AYERS
LETTERING..ART SIMEK
MOVE, BUTTERFINGERS! I'LL TAKE OVER THE CONTROLS NOW! IT'S ALMOST TIME TO LAND THIS CRATE!
I'M GRABBIN' FORTY WINKS! WAKE ME WHEN WE'VE LANDED!
OKAY, PARTNER! BUT THE WAY I DESIGNED THIS BIRD, SHE CAN PRACTICALLY LAND BY HERSELF!
WE'VE JUST RECEIVED RADIO LANDING CLEARANCE!
X-144
WONDER IF WE'LL RECEIVE MUCH OF AN OVATION WHEN WE LAND, REED?
AS THE FIRST EARTHMEN TO RETURN FROM A ROUND TRIP TO THE MOON? YOU CAN BET ON IT, LADY!
ALL AIR TRAFFIC HALTED WITHIN THOUSAND-MILE PERIMETER! FANTASTIC FOUR--LAND AT WILL!
HERE THEY COME!
THEY MADE IT! THEY REALLY MADE IT!
1

AS THE MIGHTY MOON-SHIP PREPARES TO LAND, EXCITEMENT REACHES A FEVER PITCH ALL OVER THE EARTH, AND ESPECIALLY IN THE FREE WORLD! AT NEW YORK'S GIGANTIC IDLEWILD AIRPORT, ALL EYES SCAN THE BLUE SKY ABOVE, UNTIL FINALLY...
THERE'S THE SHIP, CHARLIE! ROLL 'EM!
GOT 'ER! CLEAR AS A BELL!
LOOK AT HER GLIDING IN-- SMOOTH AS SILK!
HARD TO BELIEVE SHE'S THE BRAINCHILD OF ONLY ONE MAN! BUT I GUESS WHEN THAT MAN IS REED RICHARDS, IT COULD BE!
IT'S THEM ALL RIGHT!
SEE THE NUMBER FOUR ON THE TAIL!
JUST THINK-- THIS SCENE IS BEING TRANSMITTED BY TELESTAR TO EVERY PART OF THE GLOBE!
EMERGENCY VEHICLES, STAND BY! ROLL THAT TRUCK OVER HERE! MOVE!
TV
4
GOOD WORK, THING! IT'S A PERFECT LANDING!
WELL, WHAT DID YOU EXPECT? IT'S MY JOB, AINT IT?
AND THEN, AS THE GREAT SHIP FINALLY COMES TO REST...
LOOK AT THAT TURNOUT! WE'LL BE MOBBED!
FIRST GUY WHO ASKS ME TO MAKE SPEECH GETS A FAT LIP!
YOU CAN'T BLAME PEOPLE FOR BEING EXCITED, BEN!
4
2

-ULP- WHAT A MOB! MAYBE IF I FLAME OFF, I CAN LOSE MYSELF IN THE CROWD!
SURE, WITH A MILLION CAMERAS ON YOU, AND WEARIN' THAT BRIGHT BLUE GET-UP, YOU'RE GONNA LOSE YOURSELF! WHAT DO YOU USE FOR A BRAIN, SQUIRT?
LOOK! THERE HE IS! IT'S MR. FANTASTIC!
SARGE--HELP! I CAN'T HOLD THESE NUTTY FEMALES BACK!
I'D DIE FOR A LOCK OF HIS HAIR!
NOW, GIRLS--TAKE IT EASY! LET'S NOT LOSE OUR DIGNITY!
THAT VOICE! THOSE EYES! THOSE SHOULDERS! HE'S TOO MUCH!
MISTER FANTASTIC FAN CLUB
CLAYVILLE CHAPTER
TWO RIVAL FAN CLUBS FIGHTIN' OVER MR. FANTASTIC! WHAT A SHOT!
WE SAW HIM FIRST!
FLASH!
HE'S OURS!
MEANWHILE, AT EVERY BIG EVENT, THERE IS ALWAYS SOMEONE WHO TRIES TO CASH IN ON THE PUBLICITY...
--AND MY FEARLESS WRESTLER, THE GOLDEN ANGEL, CHALLENGES THE THING TO MEET HIM IN A FIGHT TO THE FINISH! DID YOU GET ALL THAT, BOYS?
OF ALL THE CRUMMY CORNBALLS....!
SO YOU'RE THE GOLDEN ANGEL, HUH?
?
WELL, I AIN'T GONNA WRESTLE YOU! AND YOU KNOW WHY?
'CAUSE YOU'RE SO BIG AND TOUGH THAT I'M SHAKIN' IN MY ITTY BITTY BOOTS, THAT'S WHY!
SUE STORM, TOO, HAS HER PROBLEMS...
BUT YOU CAN'T TURN DOWN A CHANCE LIKE THIS! A LIFETIME HOLLYWOOD CONTRACT!
DON'T LISTEN TO HIM! I'M PREPARED TO PAY YOU A FORTUNE TO ENDORSE OUR DEODORANT ON TV!

WHERE DID SHE GO?
SHE MUST HAVE TURNED INVISIBLE!
SOME PEOPLE JUST HAVE NO GRATITUDE!
AT THAT MOMENT, HIGH OVER THE AIRPORT, A STRANGE, WARM-AIR FUNNEL SUDDENLY APPEARS, HOVERING OVER SUE, REED, AND THE THING...
ONLY ONE WAY TO GET MY LI'L PARTNERS AWAY FROM THAT MOB!
I'VE BEEN WAITING FOR A CHANCE TO TRY THIS LITTLE GIMMICK! THE WHIRLING WARM AIR FORMS A SUCTION IN A VACUUM, AND THEN...
REED! BEN! WHAT'S HAPPEN-ING?
WE'RE BEING DRAWN UP INTO THIS WARM AIR FUNNEL BY THE TORCH! AND JUST IN TIME, TOO!
AWW, I DIDN'T EVEN GET A CHANCE TO CLOBBER ANYBODY BACK THERE IN THE MOB!
HI, GROUP! I THOUGHT YOU'D NEVER GET HERE!
AFTER CATCHING THEIR BREATH, THE COLORFUL FOURSOME HEADS FOR THEIR SKYSCRAPER SUITE VIA THEIR PRIVATE ROOFTOP ELEVATOR!
I DON'T KNOW WHETHER I OUGHTTA THANK YOU, OR PASTE YOU ONE, HOT-HEAD!
WHY DON'T YOU GO GET A JOB AS A FOOD TESTER IN A POISON FACTORY?!
FINALLY, UPON REACHING THEIR INNER SANCTUM...
AHHH, THIS IS THE LIFE! WAKE ME UP AT CHRISTMAS! NEXT CHRISTMAS!
HMMM, I THINK I'D BETTER DO A LITTLE HOUSE-CLEANING!
JUST SO LONG AS YOU DO IT SILENTLY!
4

BUT, A FEW HOURS LATER, AFTER A GOOD REST, THINGS ARE BACK TO NORMAL AGAIN WITH THE FANTASTIC FOUR...
THERE! THAT FINISHES MY SCIENTIFIC REPORT TO N.A.S.A. ABOUT OUR NEW ROCKET FUEL!
NOW I'LL FIND SUE AND ASK HER TO TYPE IT UP SO THAT WE CAN DISPATCH IT TO WASHINGTON VIA SPECIAL COURIER!
HMMM, THERE SHE IS, OPERATING MY NEW EXPERIMENTAL "ROVING-EYE" TV APPARATUS! SHE'S GOT IT FOCUSED ON THE BOTTOM OF THE SEA!
SO THERE YOU ARE, SUE! I'VE BEEN LOOKING FOR YOU!
OH! REED! YOU--YOU STARTLED ME!
SHE BLANKED IT OUT IN ALARM! AND I'M SURE I KNOW WHY!
YOU'RE STILL THINKING ABOUT THE SUB-MARINER, AREN'T YOU, SUE? NO, DON'T ANSWER-- THERE'S NO NEED TO! SOMETIMES I WISH YOU COULD FIND HIM AGAIN, SO WE COULD SETTLE THINGS BETWEEN US, ONCE AND FOR ALL!
AND THEN, AFTER GIVING SUE THE REPORT TO TYPE...
STRANGE HOW NOBODY IS EVER REALLY MASTER OF HIS OWN FATE!
I'VE ALWAYS THOUGHT OF MYSELF AS BEING ABLE TO ACCOMPLISH ALMOST ANYTHING! WITH MY SCIENTIFIC TALENT, AND MY SUPER-FLEXIBLE BODY, IT SEEMED THAT NOTHING COULD EVER DEFEAT ME!
"NOTHING COULD OUTSMART ME--NO PROBLEM COULD LONG REMAIN UNSOLVED WHEN I PUT MY MIND TO IT! NO OBSTACLE COULD STOP ME IF I DIDN'T WISH TO BE STOPPED!"
"PERHAPS I ALLOWED MY-SELF TO GET TOO OVER-CONFIDENT, TOO CONVINCED OF MY OWN ABILITY TO ACCOMPLISH ANYTHING I SET MY MIND TO!"
FOR NOW, THOUGH THE WORLD KNOWS ME AS THE INVINCIBLE MISTER FANTASTIC, I AM UNABLE TO WIN MY MOST CHERISHED GOAL! I AM UNABLE TO COMPLETELY CONQUER THE HEART OF THE GIRL I LOVE!
5

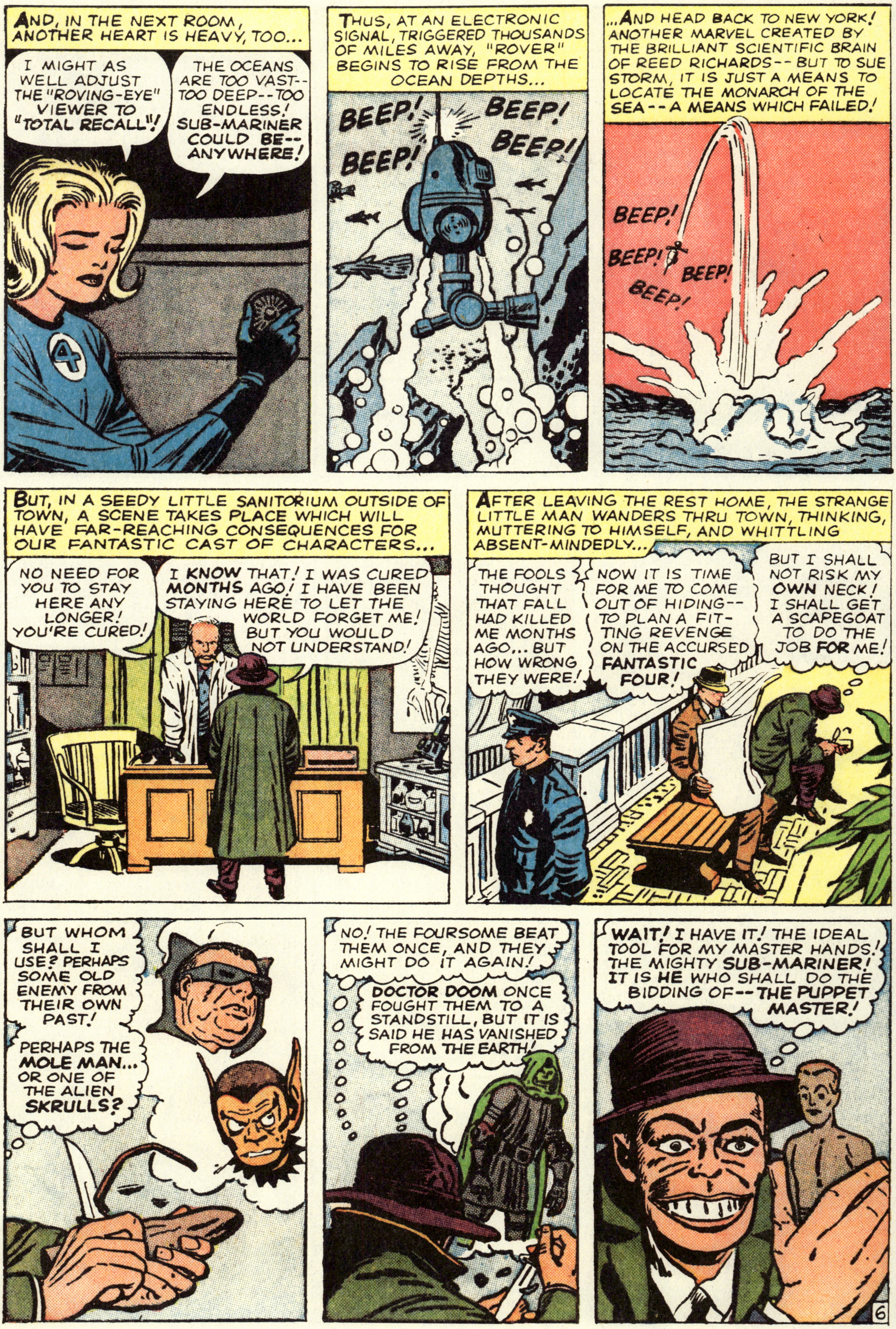

AND, IN THE NEXT ROOM, ANOTHER HEART IS HEAVY, TOO...
I MIGHT AS WELL ADJUST THE "ROVING-EYE" VIEWER TO "TOTAL RECALL"!
THE OCEANS ARE TOO VAST-- TOO DEEP--TOO ENDLESS! SUB-MARINER COULD BE-- ANYWHERE!
THUS, AT AN ELECTRONIC SIGNAL, TRIGGERED THOUSANDS OF MILES AWAY, "ROVER" BEGINS TO RISE FROM THE OCEAN DEPTHS...
BEEP! BEEP! BEEP! BEEP!
...AND HEAD BACK TO NEW YORK! ANOTHER MARVEL CREATED BY THE BRILLIANT SCIENTIFIC BRAIN OF REED RICHARDS-- BUT TO SUE STORM, IT IS JUST A MEANS TO LOCATE THE MONARCH OF THE SEA -- A MEANS WHICH FAILED!
BEEP! BEEP! BEEP! BEEP!
BUT, IN A SEEDY LITTLE SANITORIUM OUTSIDE OF TOWN, A SCENE TAKES PLACE WHICH WILL HAVE FAR-REACHING CONSEQUENCES FOR OUR FANTASTIC CAST OF CHARACTERS...
NO NEED FOR YOU TO STAY HERE ANY LONGER! YOU'RE CURED!
I KNOW THAT! I WAS CURED MONTHS AGO! I HAVE BEEN STAYING HERE TO LET THE WORLD FORGET ME! BUT YOU WOULD NOT UNDERSTAND!
AFTER LEAVING THE REST HOME, THE STRANGE LITTLE MAN WANDERS THRU TOWN, THINKING, MUTTERING TO HIMSELF, AND WHITTLING ABSENT-MINDEDLY...
THE FOOLS THOUGHT THAT FALL HAD KILLED ME MONTHS AGO... BUT HOW WRONG THEY WERE!
NOW IT IS TIME FOR ME TO COME OUT OF HIDING-- TO PLAN A FITTING REVENGE ON THE ACCURSED FANTASTIC FOUR!
BUT I SHALL NOT RISK MY OWN NECK! I SHALL GET A SCAPEGOAT TO DO THE JOB FOR ME!
BUT WHOM SHALL I USE? PERHAPS SOME OLD ENEMY FROM THEIR OWN PAST!
PERHAPS THE MOLE MAN... OR ONE OF THE ALIEN SKRULLS?
NO! THE FOURSOME BEAT THEM ONCE, AND THEY MIGHT DO IT AGAIN!
DOCTOR DOOM ONCE FOUGHT THEM TO A STANDSTILL, BUT IT IS SAID HE HAS VANISHED FROM THE EARTH!
WAIT! I HAVE IT! THE IDEAL TOOL FOR MY MASTER HANDS! THE MIGHTY SUB-MARINER! IT IS HE WHO SHALL DO THE BIDDING OF-- THE PUPPET MASTER!
6

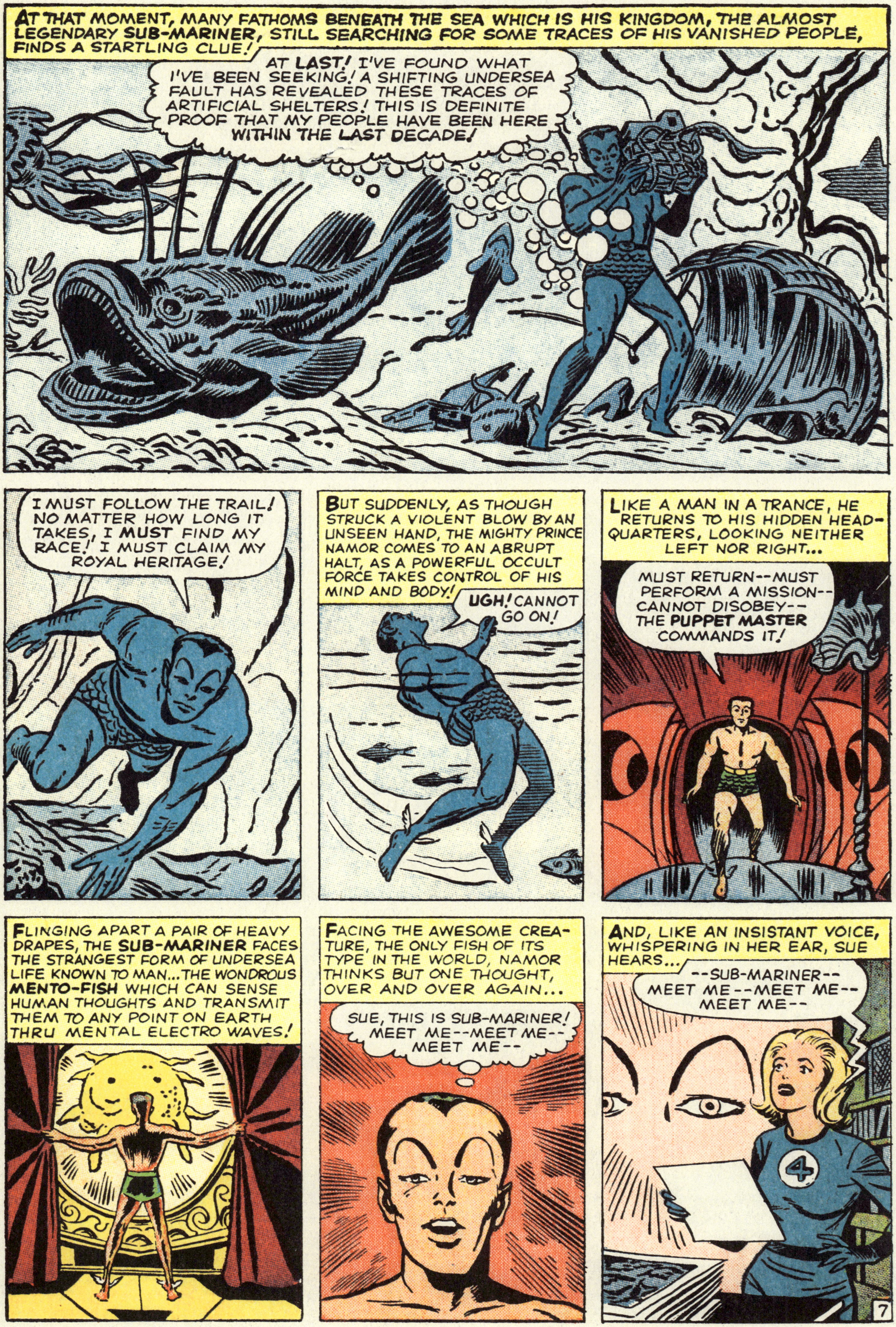

AT THAT MOMENT, MANY FATHOMS BENEATH THE SEA WHICH IS HIS KINGDOM, THE ALMOST LEGENDARY SUB-MARINER, STILL SEARCHING FOR SOME TRACES OF HIS VANISHED PEOPLE, FINDS A STARTLING CLUE!
AT LAST! I'VE FOUND WHAT I'VE BEEN SEEKING! A SHIFTING UNDERSEA FAULT HAS REVEALED THESE TRACES OF ARTIFICIAL SHELTERS! THIS IS DEFINITE PROOF THAT MY PEOPLE HAVE BEEN HERE WITHIN THE LAST DECADE!
I MUST FOLLOW THE TRAIL! NO MATTER HOW LONG IT TAKES, I MUST FIND MY RACE! I MUST CLAIM MY ROYAL HERITAGE!
BUT SUDDENLY, AS THOUGH STRUCK A VIOLENT BLOW BY AN UNSEEN HAND, THE MIGHTY PRINCE NAMOR COMES TO AN ABRUPT HALT, AS A POWERFUL OCCULT FORCE TAKES CONTROL OF HIS MIND AND BODY!
UGH! CANNOT GO ON!
LIKE A MAN IN A TRANCE, HE RETURNS TO HIS HIDDEN HEAD-QUARTERS, LOOKING NEITHER LEFT NOR RIGHT...
MUST RETURN--MUST PERFORM A MISSION--CANNOT DISOBEY--THE PUPPET MASTER COMMANDS IT!
FLINGING APART A PAIR OF HEAVY DRAPES, THE SUB-MARINER FACES THE STRANGEST FORM OF UNDERSEA LIFE KNOWN TO MAN...THE WONDROUS MENTO-FISH WHICH CAN SENSE HUMAN THOUGHTS AND TRANSMIT THEM TO ANY POINT ON EARTH THRU MENTAL ELECTRO WAVES!
FACING THE AWESOME CREATURE, THE ONLY FISH OF ITS TYPE IN THE WORLD, NAMOR THINKS BUT ONE THOUGHT, OVER AND OVER AGAIN...
SUE, THIS IS SUB-MARINER! MEET ME--MEET ME--MEET ME--
AND, LIKE AN INSISTANT VOICE, WHISPERING IN HER EAR, SUE HEARS...
--SUB-MARINER--MEET ME--MEET ME--MEET ME--
4
7

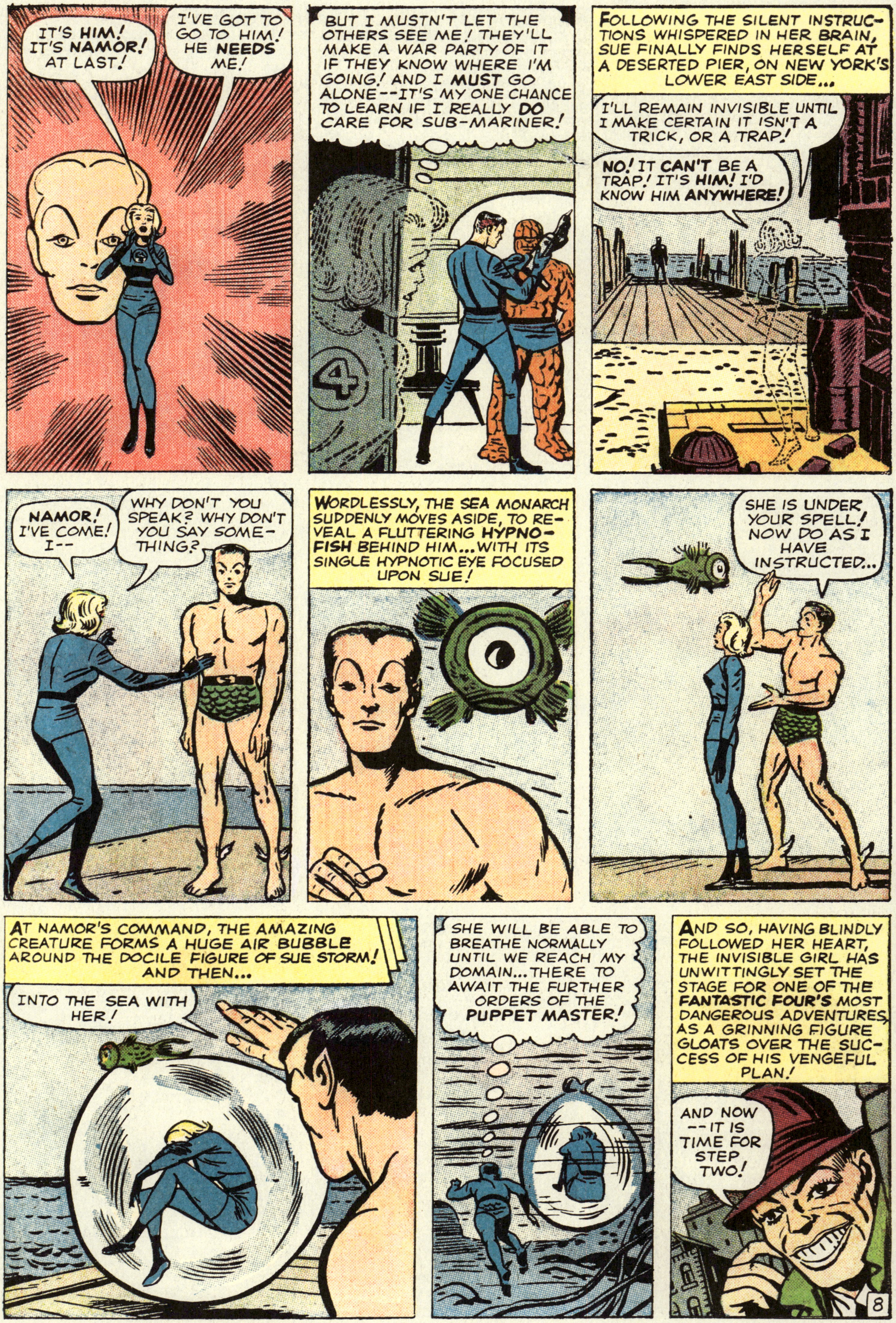

IT'S HIM! IT'S NAMOR! AT LAST!
I'VE GOT TO GO TO HIM! HE NEEDS ME!
BUT I MUSTN'T LET THE OTHERS SEE ME! THEY'LL MAKE A WAR PARTY OF IT IF THEY KNOW WHERE I'M GOING! AND I MUST GO ALONE--IT'S MY ONE CHANCE TO LEARN IF I REALLY DO CARE FOR SUB-MARINER!
FOLLOWING THE SILENT INSTRUCTIONS WHISPERED IN HER BRAIN, SUE FINALLY FINDS HERSELF AT A DESERTED PIER, ON NEW YORK'S LOWER EAST SIDE...
I'LL REMAIN INVISIBLE UNTIL I MAKE CERTAIN IT ISN'T A TRICK, OR A TRAP!
NO! IT CAN'T BE A TRAP! IT'S HIM! I'D KNOW HIM ANYWHERE!
NAMOR! I'VE COME! I--
WHY DON'T YOU SPEAK? WHY DON'T YOU SAY SOMETHING?
WORDLESSLY, THE SEA MONARCH SUDDENLY MOVES ASIDE, TO REVEAL A FLUTTERING HYPNO-FISH BEHIND HIM...WITH ITS SINGLE HYPNOTIC EYE FOCUSED UPON SUE!
SHE IS UNDER YOUR SPELL! NOW DO AS I HAVE INSTRUCTED...
AT NAMOR'S COMMAND, THE AMAZING CREATURE FORMS A HUGE AIR BUBBLE AROUND THE DOCILE FIGURE OF SUE STORM! AND THEN...
INTO THE SEA WITH HER!
SHE WILL BE ABLE TO BREATHE NORMALLY UNTIL WE REACH MY DOMAIN...THERE TO AWAIT THE FURTHER ORDERS OF THE PUPPET MASTER!
AND SO, HAVING BLINDLY FOLLOWED HER HEART, THE INVISIBLE GIRL HAS UNWITTINGLY SET THE STAGE FOR ONE OF THE FANTASTIC FOUR'S MOST DANGEROUS ADVENTURES, AS A GRINNING FIGURE GLOATS OVER THE SUCCESS OF HIS VENGEFUL PLAN!
AND NOW --IT IS TIME FOR STEP TWO!
8

BACK IN HIS HIDEOUT, THE PUPPET MASTER DONS A LEAD-LINED SUIT, AND...
AS LONG AS THIS RADIO-ACTIVE CLAY HOLDS OUT, I AM COMPLETE MASTER OF ANY LIVING CREATURE WHOSE FORM I MOLD INTO A PUPPET!
THEN, AFTER THE CLAY HAS BEEN TREATED AND COATED WITH A THIN FILM OF LEAD PAINT...
MY REVENGE WILL BE MUCH SWEETER IF I DO NOT MANIPULATE THE FANTASTIC FOUR! INSTEAD, I SHALL LEAVE THEM THEIR FREE WILL, WHILE THE SUB-MARINER, UNDER MY CONTROL, DEFEATS THEM!
AND, BACK AT THEIR SKYSCRAPER HEADQUARTERS, THE FANTASTIC FOUR ARE STILL UNAWARE OF THE DIRE DANGER WHICH AWAITS THEM...
HEY! HOW MUCH LONGER DO I HAVE TO HOLD THIS BLAMED THING?? IT FEELS LIKE IT WEIGHS TEN TONS!
IT DOES! THAT'S THE IDEA! I'M TRYING TO TEST, ONCE AND FOR ALL, EXACTLY WHAT THE LIMITS OF YOUR STRENGTH ARE!
WELL, TELL THAT BLAZING BRAT TO STOP PLAYIN' HIDE-AND-SEEK AROUND ME, OR I'LL SHOVE THIS OVER-SIZED TOOTHPICK DOWN HIS THROAT!
AW, I'M JUST TRYIN' TO SEE WHAT-- HEY! LOOK! LOOK WHO'S THERE!
IT'S THE SUB-MARINER! OUTTA MY WAY!
I'M 'WAY AHEAD OF YOU, PAL! HE'S MINE!
SCRUNTCH!
HEY! WHAT GIVES??? I WENT RIGHT THRU HIM!!!
YEAH? WELL I WON'T!
9

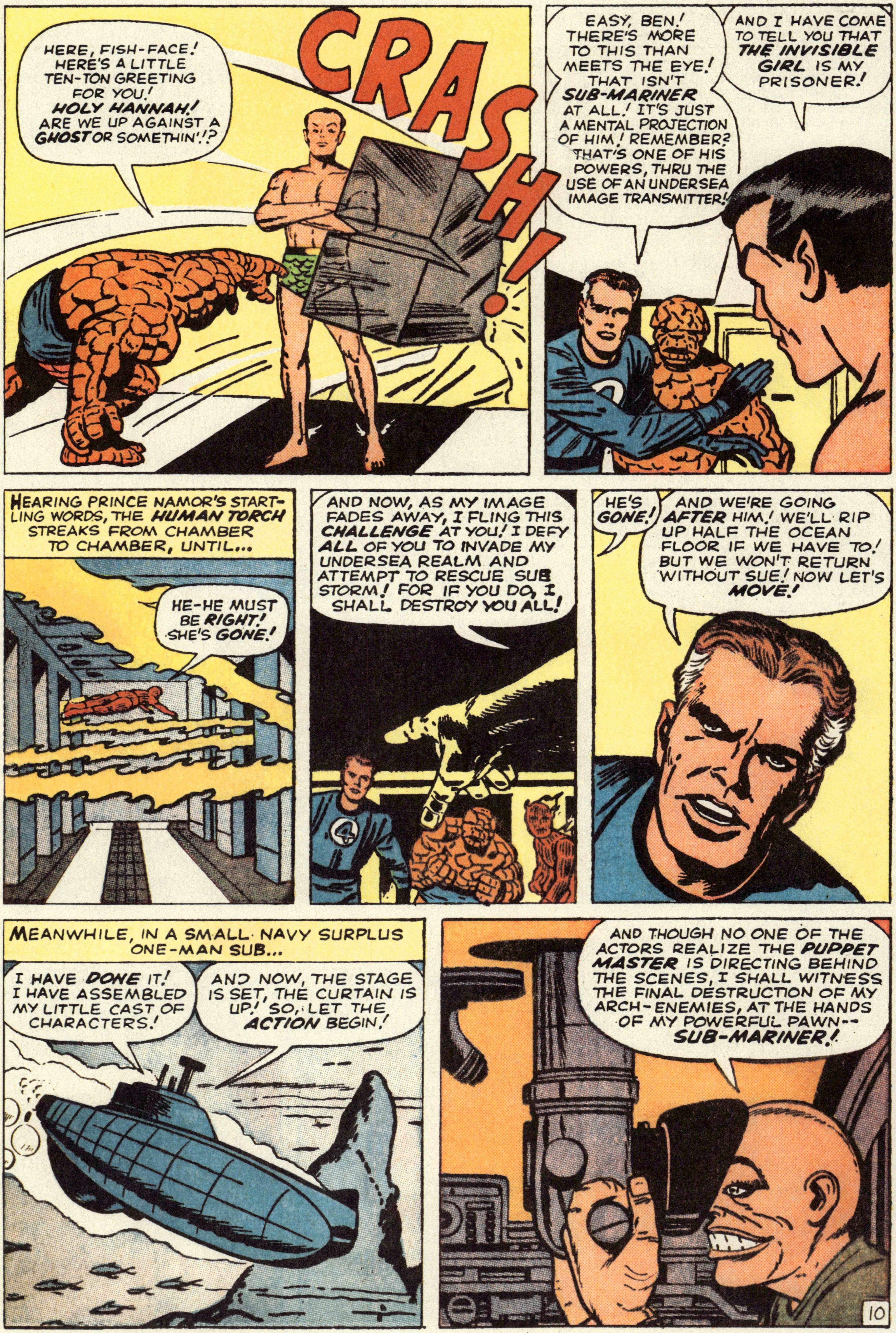

HERE, FISH-FACE! HERE'S A LITTLE TEN-TON GREETING FOR YOU! HOLY HANNAH! ARE WE UP AGAINST A GHOST OR SOMETHIN'!?
CRASH!
EASY, BEN! THERE'S MORE TO THIS THAN MEETS THE EYE! THAT ISN'T SUB-MARINER AT ALL! IT'S JUST A MENTAL PROJECTION OF HIM! REMEMBER? THAT'S ONE OF HIS POWERS, THRU THE USE OF AN UNDERSEA IMAGE TRANSMITTER!
AND I HAVE COME TO TELL YOU THAT THE INVISIBLE GIRL IS MY PRISONER!
HEARING PRINCE NAMOR'S STARTLING WORDS, THE HUMAN TORCH STREAKS FROM CHAMBER TO CHAMBER, UNTIL...
HE-HE MUST BE RIGHT! SHE'S GONE!
AND NOW, AS MY IMAGE FADES AWAY, I FLING THIS CHALLENGE AT YOU! I DEFY ALL OF YOU TO INVADE MY UNDERSEA REALM AND ATTEMPT TO RESCUE SUE STORM! FOR IF YOU DO, I SHALL DESTROY YOU ALL!
HE'S GONE!
AND WE'RE GOING AFTER HIM! WE'LL RIP UP HALF THE OCEAN FLOOR IF WE HAVE TO! BUT WE WON'T RETURN WITHOUT SUE! NOW LET'S MOVE!
MEANWHILE, IN A SMALL NAVY SURPLUS ONE-MAN SUB...
I HAVE DONE IT! I HAVE ASSEMBLED MY LITTLE CAST OF CHARACTERS!
AND NOW, THE STAGE IS SET, THE CURTAIN IS UP! SO, LET THE ACTION BEGIN!
AND THOUGH NO ONE OF THE ACTORS REALIZE THE PUPPET MASTER IS DIRECTING BEHIND THE SCENES, I SHALL WITNESS THE FINAL DESTRUCTION OF MY ARCH-ENEMIES, AT THE HANDS OF MY POWERFUL PAWN-- SUB-MARINER!

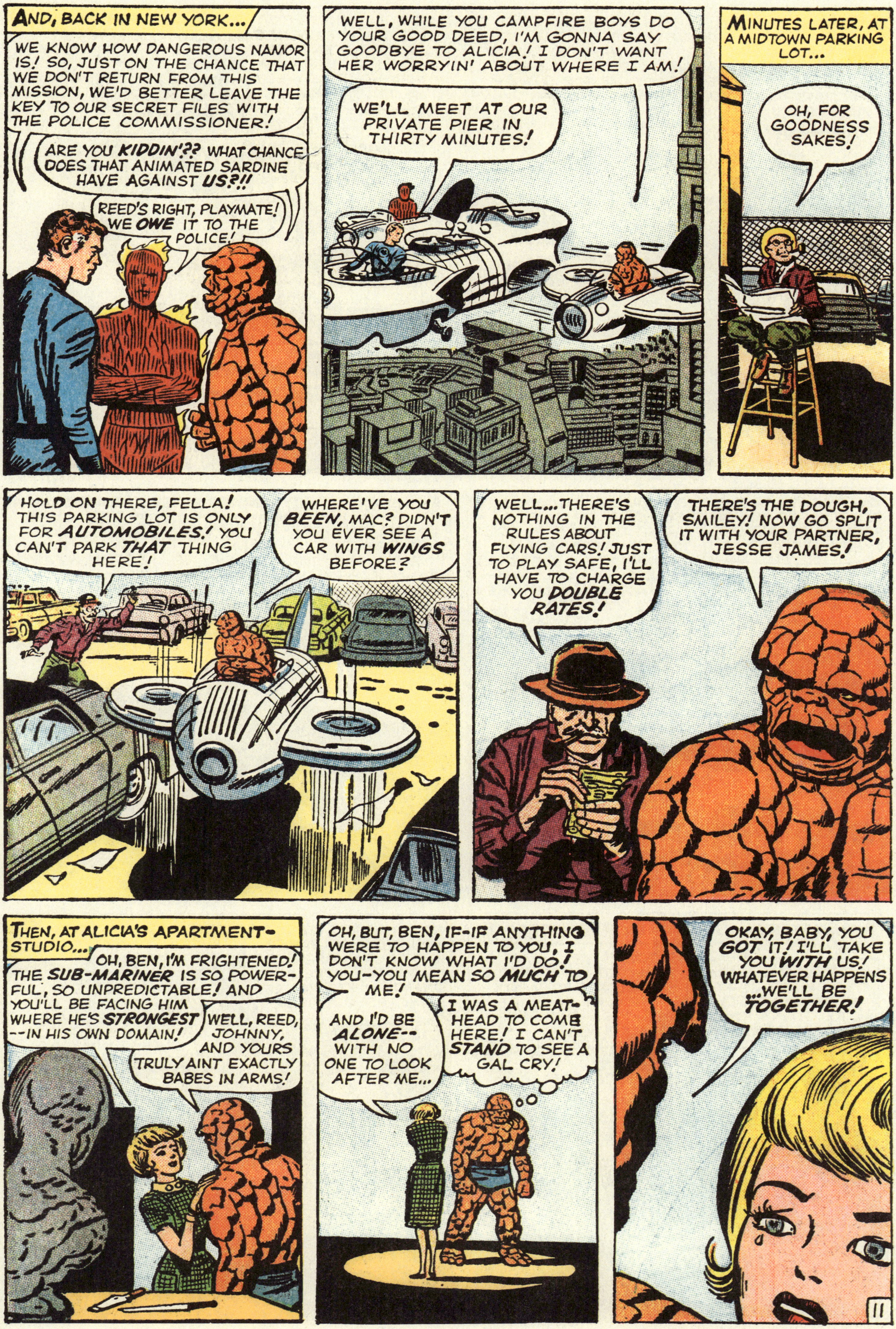
AND, BACK IN NEW YORK...
WE KNOW HOW DANGEROUS NAMOR IS! SO, JUST ON THE CHANCE THAT WE DON'T RETURN FROM THIS MISSION, WE'D BETTER LEAVE THE KEY TO OUR SECRET FILES WITH THE POLICE COMMISSIONER!
ARE YOU KIDDIN'?? WHAT CHANCE DOES THAT ANIMATED SARDINE HAVE AGAINST US?!!
REED'S RIGHT, PLAYMATE! WE OWE IT TO THE POLICE!
WELL, WHILE YOU CAMPFIRE BOYS DO YOUR GOOD DEED, I'M GONNA SAY GOODBYE TO ALICIA! I DON'T WANT HER WORRYIN' ABOUT WHERE I AM!
WE'LL MEET AT OUR PRIVATE PIER IN THIRTY MINUTES!
MINUTES LATER, AT A MIDTOWN PARKING LOT...
OH, FOR GOODNESS SAKES!
HOLD ON THERE, FELLA! THIS PARKING LOT IS ONLY FOR AUTOMOBILES! YOU CAN'T PARK THAT THING HERE!
WHERE'VE YOU BEEN, MAC? DIDN'T YOU EVER SEE A CAR WITH WINGS BEFORE?
WELL...THERE'S NOTHING IN THE RULES ABOUT FLYING CARS! JUST TO PLAY SAFE, I'LL HAVE TO CHARGE YOU DOUBLE RATES!
THERE'S THE DOUGH, SMILEY! NOW GO SPLIT IT WITH YOUR PARTNER, JESSE JAMES!
THEN, AT ALICIA'S APARTMENT-STUDIO...
OH, BEN, I'M FRIGHTENED! THE SUB-MARINER IS SO POWERFUL, SO UNPREDICTABLE! AND YOU'LL BE FACING HIM WHERE HE'S STRONGEST--IN HIS OWN DOMAIN!
WELL, REED, JOHNNY, AND YOURS TRULY AINT EXACTLY BABES IN ARMS!
OH, BUT, BEN, IF-IF ANYTHING WERE TO HAPPEN TO YOU, I DON'T KNOW WHAT I'D DO! YOU-YOU MEAN SO MUCH TO ME!
AND I'D BE ALONE--WITH NO ONE TO LOOK AFTER ME...
I WAS A MEAT-HEAD TO COME HERE! I CAN'T STAND TO SEE A GAL CRY!
OKAY, BABY, YOU GOT IT! I'LL TAKE YOU WITH US! WHATEVER HAPPENS ...WE'LL BE TOGETHER!
11

AND SO...
JUST A MINUTE, YOU! THAT'S MY JOB! I'LL BACK THAT CONTRAPTION OUT FOR YOU!
IN A PIG'S EYE YOU WILL! NOBODY HANDLES THAT LITTLE JOB BUT ME! BESIDES, YOU'RE WASTIN' TIME! YOU OUGHTTA BE OUT LOOKIN' FOR OTHER SUCKERS WHO YOU CAN OVER-CHARGE!
HERE, LAUGHING BOY! TO MAKE SURE I DON'T SCRAPE ANYBODY'S FENDERS WHEN I JET OUTTA HERE, I'LL JUST MOVE THESE OTHER HEAPS SAFELY OUTTA THE WAY!
DON'T! HOW'LL I EXPLAIN TO TO THEIR OWNERS?? CUT IT OUT! AWW, HAVE A HEART, WILL YA??!
THAT'LL TEACH THE OLD PIRATE NOT TO CHARGE DOUBLE FOR MY FANTASTI-CAR! I'M ALMOST SORRY I DIDN'T LEAVE THOSE JALOPIES PILED UP THERE, INSTEAD OF PUTTIN' 'EM BACK AGAIN AFTER HE GOT THE MESSAGE!
OH, BEN DEAR, IF ONLY YOU COULD LEARN TO CONTROL YOUR TEMPER!
NOT A CHANCE, HONEY! I GOT A REP TO LIVE UP TO! CAN'T DISAPPOINT MY PANTIN' PUBLIC!
AND, EXACTLY THIRTY MINUTES LATER...
ADMIRAL SAWYER WAS VERY COOPERATIVE, BEN! HE LENT US THIS EXPERIMENTAL BATHYSCAPH WITH NO QUESTIONS ASKED!
WELCOME, ABOARD, ALICIA! WE HAD A HUNCH BEN WOULD BE BRINGING YOU!
FOR THE LUVVA PETE! I WAS ALL SET FOR A KNOCK-DOWN ARGUMENT ABOUT WHY I CAN'T TAKE HER WITH ME! NOW ALL THE SPEECHES I PREPARED ARE WASTED!
NB 141
THEN, AFTER REACHING ONE OF THE DEEPEST OCEAN AREAS...
HEY, BIG BRAIN, HOW DO YOU KNOW WHAT PART OF THIS PUDDLE YOU'RE GONNA FIND THE SUB-MARINER IN?
I DON'T! WE'LL HAVE TO TAKE POT LUCK! BUT I SUSPECT HE INHABITS THE VERY DEEPEST REGIONS--SUCH AS THIS AREA!
BE ON GUARD, ALL OF YOU! SUB-MARINER IS PROBABLY OBSERVING OUR EVERY MOVE, THRU ONE OF HIS COUNTLESS UNDERSEA DEVICES!
YEAH? WELL, I'M JUST SHIVERIN' IN MY LITTLE PINK BOOTIES!
LET HIM OBSERVE ALL HE WANTS TO! WHEN WE FIND HIM, WE'LL MOP UP THE OCEAN FLOOR WITH HIM!
12

SUDDENLY, AS IF BY SOME SILENT COMMAND, THE ENTIRE SEA BEGINS TO GROW HOSTILE TO THE TINY BATHYSCAPH!
LOOK OUT! WE'RE BEING ATTACKED BY HUGE SHOOTING QUILLS FROM SOME SORT OF GIANT UNDERSEA PORCUPINE!
THOSE BARBS CAN'T HURT US -- BUT THIS IS ONLY THE BEGINNING!
HANG ON! SOMETHING'S CAUSED AN UNDER-WATER TORNADO!
IF IT KEEPS UP MUCH LONGER, THIS TUB'LL SHAKE ITSELF APART!
OPEN THE ESCAPE HATCH, REED! I CAN HELP WITH MY FLAME!
DON'T LET 'IM DO IT, REED! COME BACK, HOT-HEAD! YOU'LL DROWN OUT THERE! TORCH! WAIT--!
DON'T WORRY, THING! BY MAKING MY FLAME WHITE HOT, I CAN TEMPORARILY TURN THE WATER TO STEAM, DISPELLING THE SPINNING CURRENTS WHILE MY FLAME LASTS!
FLAME ON!
THERE! I DID IT! THE TORNADO'S STOPPED WHIRLING!
BUT IT DISSIPATED TOO MUCH OF MY FLAME! I'M COOLING OFF!
CAN'T HOLD MY BREATH MUCH LONGER! WATER PRESSURE BEGINNING TO CRUSH ME!
WELL, AT LEAST I SAVED THE OTHERS! NOW-- THEY'VE GOT TO FIND SUE -- GOT TO --
BUT SUDDENLY A STRONG, SUPPLE ARM REACHES OUT, AND SKILLFUL, SURE FINGERS FIND THEIR OBJECTIVE...
GOT HIM! NOW, IF I CAN JUST PULL HIM INTO THE ESCAPE HATCH BEFORE MY LUNGS BURST FROM LACK OF OXYGEN!
DRAGGING THE HELPLESS LAD TOWARDS HIM, INCH BY INCH, SECOND BY SECOND, THE DUO FINALLY REACH THE SAFETY OF THE BATHYSCAPH'S INTERIOR AGAIN...
YOU'LL BE OKAY AFTER A LITTLE REST!
SURE, UNLESS SUB-MARINER HAS ANY OTHER CUTE TRICKS TO SPRING ON US!
13

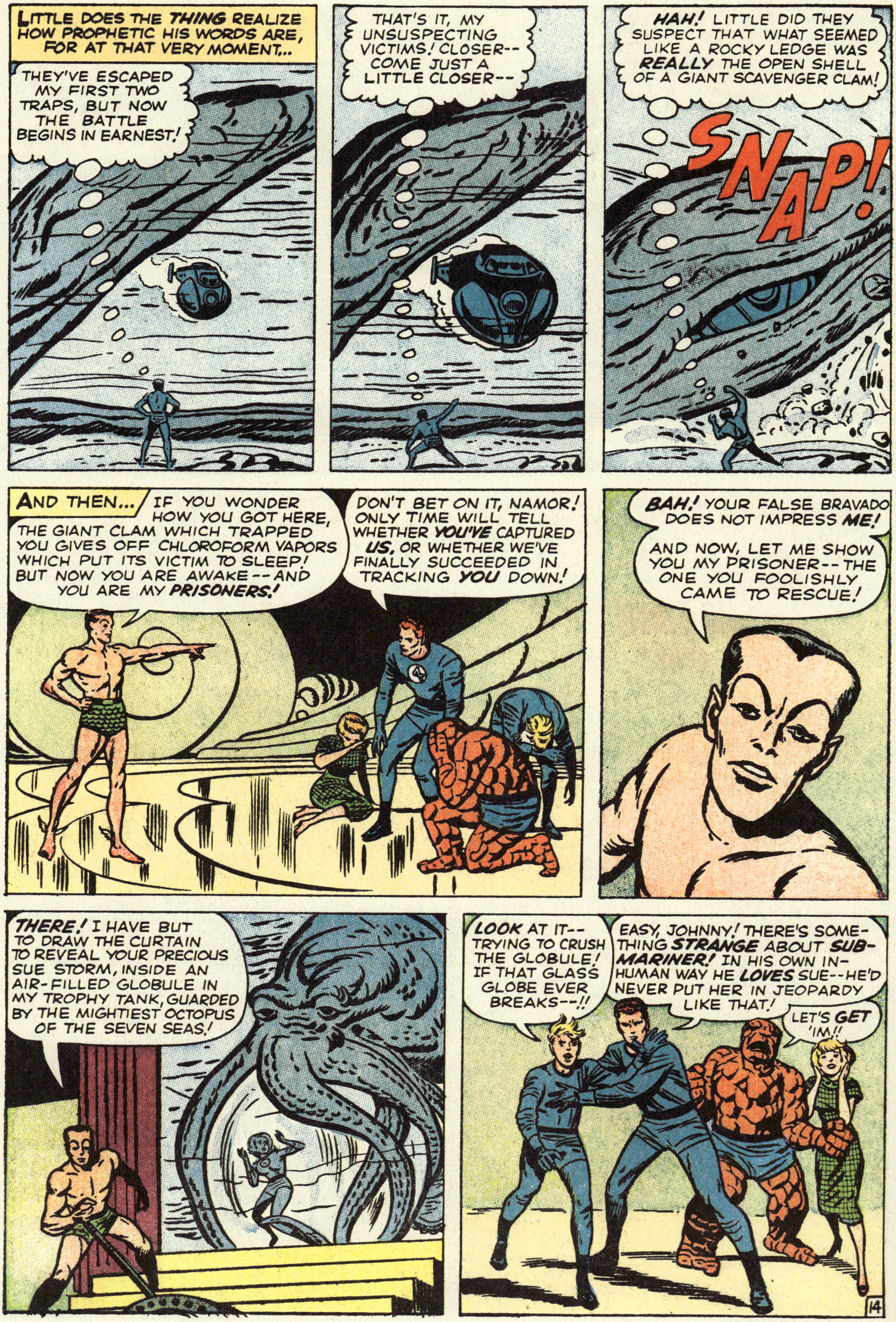

LITTLE DOES THE THING REALIZE HOW PROPHETIC HIS WORDS ARE, FOR AT THAT VERY MOMENT...
THEY'VE ESCAPED MY FIRST TWO TRAPS, BUT NOW THE BATTLE BEGINS IN EARNEST!
THAT'S IT, MY UNSUSPECTING VICTIMS! CLOSER-- COME JUST A LITTLE CLOSER--
HAH! LITTLE DID THEY SUSPECT THAT WHAT SEEMED LIKE A ROCKY LEDGE WAS REALLY THE OPEN SHELL OF A GIANT SCAVENGER CLAM!
SNAP!
AND THEN...
IF YOU WONDER HOW YOU GOT HERE, THE GIANT CLAM WHICH TRAPPED YOU GIVES OFF CHLOROFORM VAPORS WHICH PUT ITS VICTIM TO SLEEP! BUT NOW YOU ARE AWAKE--AND YOU ARE MY PRISONERS!
DON'T BET ON IT, NAMOR! ONLY TIME WILL TELL WHETHER YOU'VE CAPTURED US, OR WHETHER WE'VE FINALLY SUCCEEDED IN TRACKING YOU DOWN!
BAH! YOUR FALSE BRAVADO DOES NOT IMPRESS ME!
AND NOW, LET ME SHOW YOU MY PRISONER--THE ONE YOU FOOLISHLY CAME TO RESCUE!
THERE! I HAVE BUT TO DRAW THE CURTAIN TO REVEAL YOUR PRECIOUS SUE STORM, INSIDE AN AIR-FILLED GLOBULE IN MY TROPHY TANK, GUARDED BY THE MIGHTIEST OCTOPUS OF THE SEVEN SEAS!
LOOK AT IT-- TRYING TO CRUSH THE GLOBULE! IF THAT GLASS GLOBE EVER BREAKS--!!
EASY, JOHNNY! THERE'S SOMETHING STRANGE ABOUT SUB-MARINER! IN HIS OWN INHUMAN WAY HE LOVES SUE--HE'D NEVER PUT HER IN JEOPARDY LIKE THAT!
LET'S GET 'IM!!
14

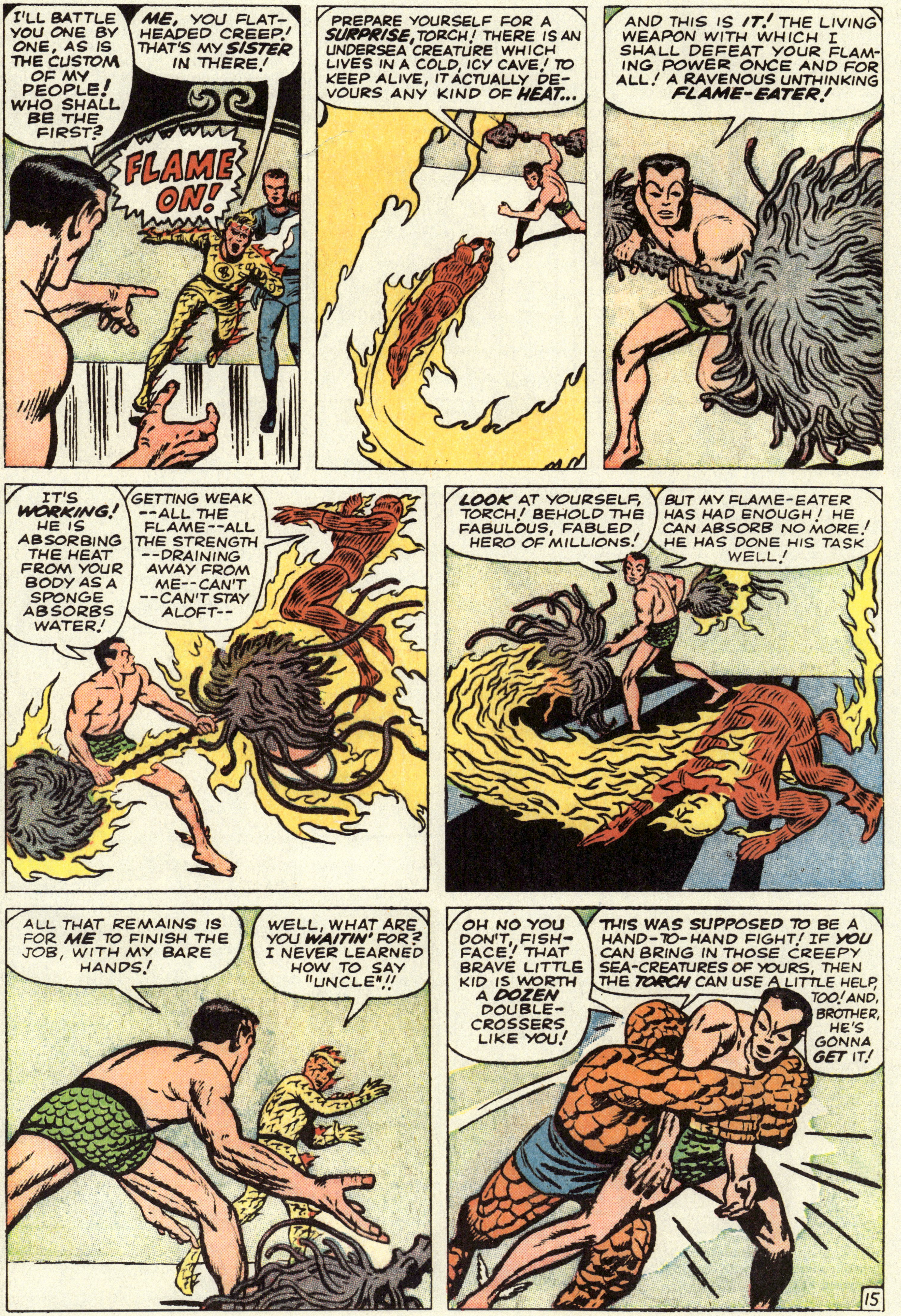
I'LL BATTLE YOU ONE BY ONE, AS IS THE CUSTOM OF MY PEOPLE! WHO SHALL BE THE FIRST?
ME, YOU FLAT-HEADED CREEP! THAT'S MY SISTER IN THERE!
FLAME ON!
PREPARE YOURSELF FOR A SURPRISE, TORCH! THERE IS AN UNDERSEA CREATURE WHICH LIVES IN A COLD, ICY CAVE! TO KEEP ALIVE, IT ACTUALLY DE-VOURS ANY KIND OF HEAT...
AND THIS IS IT! THE LIVING WEAPON WITH WHICH I SHALL DEFEAT YOUR FLAM-ING POWER ONCE AND FOR ALL! A RAVENOUS UNTHINKING FLAME-EATER!
IT'S WORKING! HE IS ABSORBING THE HEAT FROM YOUR BODY AS A SPONGE ABSORBS WATER!
GETTING WEAK --ALL THE FLAME--ALL THE STRENGTH --DRAINING AWAY FROM ME--CAN'T --CAN'T STAY ALOFT--
LOOK AT YOURSELF, TORCH! BEHOLD THE FABULOUS, FABLED HERO OF MILLIONS!
BUT MY FLAME-EATER HAS HAD ENOUGH! HE CAN ABSORB NO MORE! HE HAS DONE HIS TASK WELL!
ALL THAT REMAINS IS FOR ME TO FINISH THE JOB, WITH MY BARE HANDS!
WELL, WHAT ARE YOU WAITIN' FOR? I NEVER LEARNED HOW TO SAY "UNCLE"!!
OH NO YOU DON'T, FISH-FACE! THAT BRAVE LITTLE KID IS WORTH A DOZEN DOUBLE-CROSSERS LIKE YOU!
THIS WAS SUPPOSED TO BE A HAND-TO-HAND FIGHT! IF YOU CAN BRING IN THOSE CREEPY SEA-CREATURES OF YOURS, THEN THE TORCH CAN USE A LITTLE HELP, TOO! AND, BROTHER, HE'S GONNA GET IT!
15

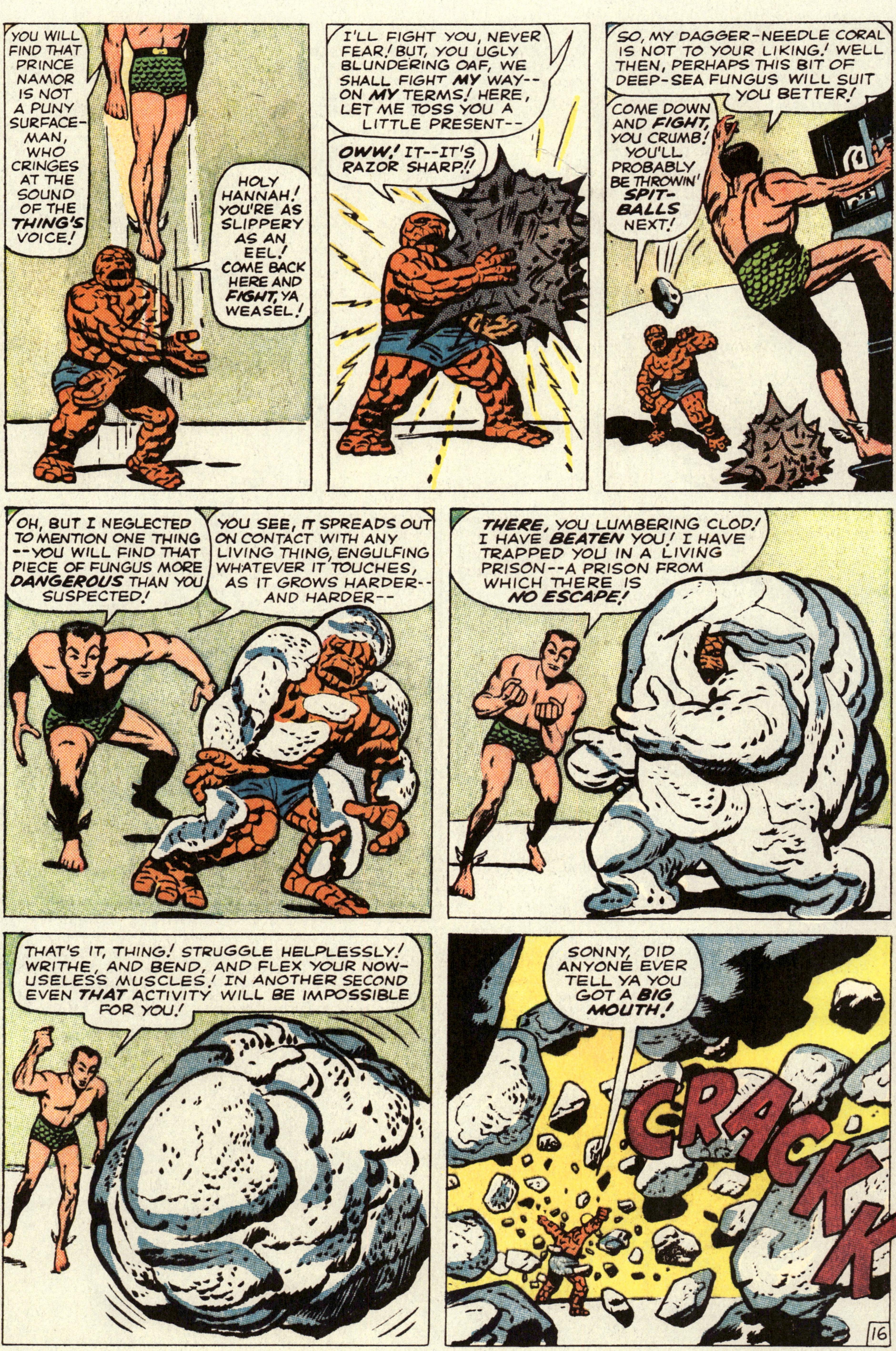

YOU WILL FIND THAT PRINCE NAMOR IS NOT A PUNY SURFACE-MAN, WHO CRINGES AT THE SOUND OF THE THING'S VOICE!
HOLY HANNAH! YOU'RE AS SLIPPERY AS AN EEL! COME BACK HERE AND FIGHT, YA WEASEL!
I'LL FIGHT YOU, NEVER FEAR! BUT, YOU UGLY BLUNDERING OAF, WE SHALL FIGHT MY WAY-- ON MY TERMS! HERE, LET ME TOSS YOU A LITTLE PRESENT--
OWW! IT--IT'S RAZOR SHARP!!
SO, MY DAGGER-NEEDLE CORAL IS NOT TO YOUR LIKING! WELL THEN, PERHAPS THIS BIT OF DEEP-SEA FUNGUS WILL SUIT YOU BETTER!
COME DOWN AND FIGHT, YOU CRUMB! YOU'LL PROBABLY BE THROWIN' SPIT-BALLS NEXT!
OH, BUT I NEGLECTED TO MENTION ONE THING --YOU WILL FIND THAT PIECE OF FUNGUS MORE DANGEROUS THAN YOU SUSPECTED!
YOU SEE, IT SPREADS OUT ON CONTACT WITH ANY LIVING THING, ENGULFING WHATEVER IT TOUCHES, AS IT GROWS HARDER-- AND HARDER--
THERE, YOU LUMBERING CLOD! I HAVE BEATEN YOU! I HAVE TRAPPED YOU IN A LIVING PRISON--A PRISON FROM WHICH THERE IS NO ESCAPE!
THAT'S IT, THING! STRUGGLE HELPLESSLY! WRITHE, AND BEND, AND FLEX YOUR NOW-USELESS MUSCLES! IN ANOTHER SECOND EVEN THAT ACTIVITY WILL BE IMPOSSIBLE FOR YOU!
SONNY, DID ANYONE EVER TELL YA YOU GOT A BIG MOUTH!
CRACKK

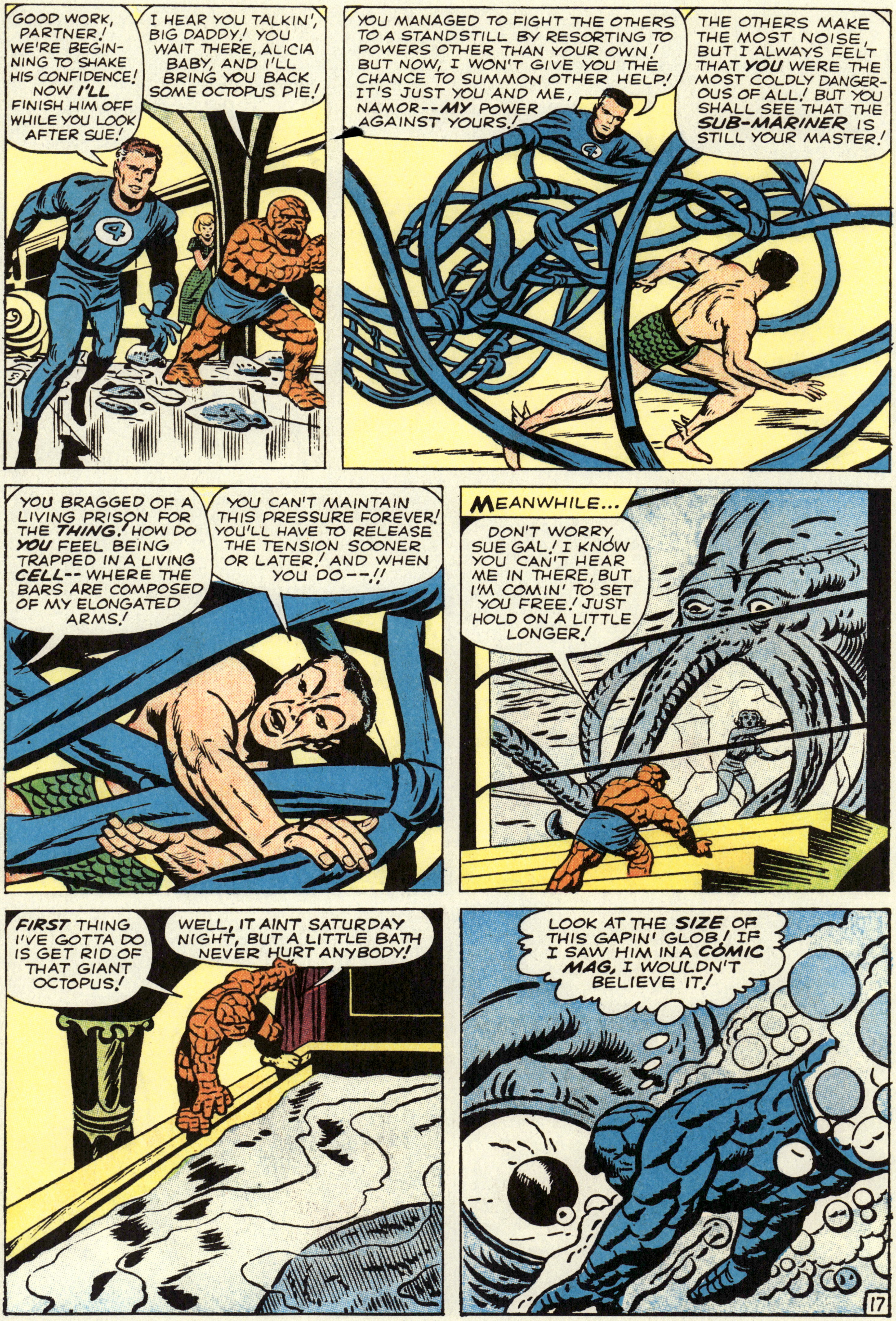
GOOD WORK, PARTNER! WE'RE BEGINNING TO SHAKE HIS CONFIDENCE! NOW I'LL FINISH HIM OFF WHILE YOU LOOK AFTER SUE!
I HEAR YOU TALKIN', BIG DADDY! YOU WAIT THERE, ALICIA BABY, AND I'LL BRING YOU BACK SOME OCTOPUS PIE!
YOU MANAGED TO FIGHT THE OTHERS TO A STANDSTILL BY RESORTING TO POWERS OTHER THAN YOUR OWN! BUT NOW, I WON'T GIVE YOU THE CHANCE TO SUMMON OTHER HELP! IT'S JUST YOU AND ME, NAMOR--MY POWER AGAINST YOURS!
THE OTHERS MAKE THE MOST NOISE, BUT I ALWAYS FELT THAT YOU WERE THE MOST COLDLY DANGEROUS OF ALL! BUT YOU SHALL SEE THAT THE SUB-MARINER IS STILL YOUR MASTER!
YOU BRAGGED OF A LIVING PRISON FOR THE THING! HOW DO YOU FEEL BEING TRAPPED IN A LIVING CELL-- WHERE THE BARS ARE COMPOSED OF MY ELONGATED ARMS!
YOU CAN'T MAINTAIN THIS PRESSURE FOREVER! YOU'LL HAVE TO RELEASE THE TENSION SOONER OR LATER! AND WHEN YOU DO--!!
MEANWHILE...
DON'T WORRY, SUE GAL! I KNOW YOU CAN'T HEAR ME IN THERE, BUT I'M COMIN' TO SET YOU FREE! JUST HOLD ON A LITTLE LONGER!
FIRST THING I'VE GOTTA DO IS GET RID OF THAT GIANT OCTOPUS!
WELL, IT AINT SATURDAY NIGHT, BUT A LITTLE BATH NEVER HURT ANYBODY!
LOOK AT THE SIZE OF THIS GAPIN' GLOB! IF I SAW HIM IN A COMIC MAG, I WOULDN'T BELIEVE IT!

SCORE ONE FOR OUR SIDE! HE TURNED AWAY FROM TRYIN' TO SHATTER THAT GLOBE, AND HE'S COMIN' AFTER ME!
I'LL JUST GRAB AHOLD OF THESE TENTACLES BEFORE HE KNOWS WHAT'S HAPPENIN'!!
HIS BRAIN IS SO SMALL THAT I'LL SWING HIM OUTTA HERE BEFORE HE CAN THINK OF TRYIN' TO BREAK MY HOLD!
OKAY, CUDDLES, HANG ON--YOU'RE GOIN' FOR A LITTLE RIDE!
THEN, AS THE MONSTROUS, UNTHINKING CREATURE GOES SKIMMING TOWARDS THE TOP OF NAMOR'S ENORMOUS DOMED HEADQUARTERS, THE THING RUSHES TO SUE STORM...
HOLD YOUR BREATH, SUE! I'LL HAVE YOU OUTTA HERE IN TWO SECONDS!
BRAVE KID! NOT A WHIMPER OUT OF HER! FIRST TIME I EVER SAW A FEMALE WHO COULD KEEP HER MOUTH SHUT SO LONG!
BUT, AS THE TRIUMPHANT THING CARRIES SUE TO SAFETY, ANOTHER PAIR OF EYES ARE FOCUSED ON THE TENSE SCENE...
THE FANTASTIC FOUR ARE MORE POWERFUL THAN I THOUGHT!
THIS WAS NOT THE WAY I PLANNED IT!
EVEN IN HIS OWN UNDERSEA LAIR, THE ACCURSED FOURSOME MAY SUCCEED IN DEFEATING THE SUB-MARINER!
NO LONGER CAN I LET THINGS TAKE THEIR NATURAL COURSE! NOW I MYSELF MUST TAKE A HAND! IT IS TIME FOR ME TO DESTROY THEM ALL!
18

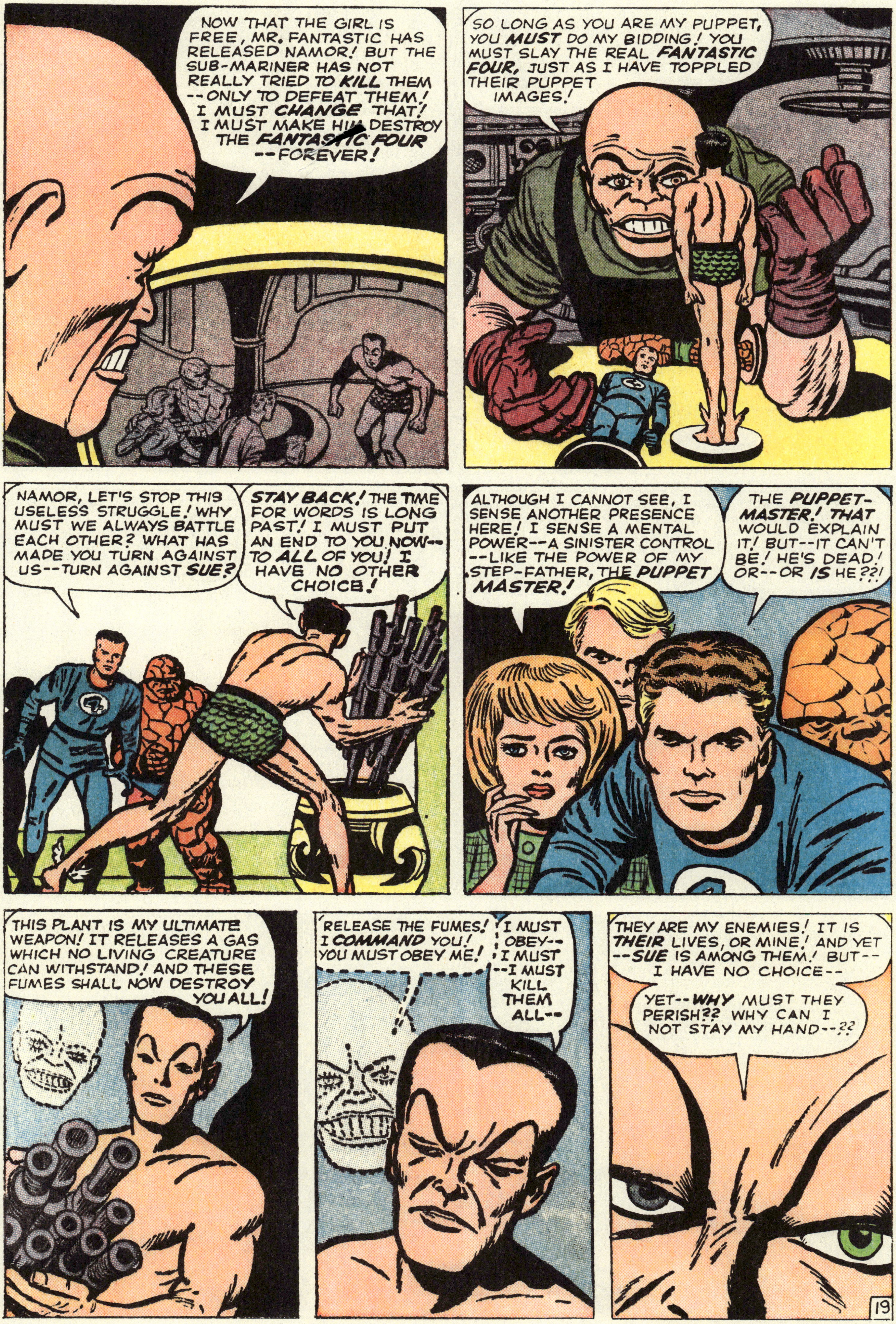
NOW THAT THE GIRL IS FREE, MR. FANTASTIC HAS RELEASED NAMOR! BUT THE SUB-MARINER HAS NOT REALLY TRIED TO KILL THEM --ONLY TO DEFEAT THEM! I MUST CHANGE THAT! I MUST MAKE HIM DESTROY THE FANTASTIC FOUR --FOREVER!
SO LONG AS YOU ARE MY PUPPET, YOU MUST DO MY BIDDING! YOU MUST SLAY THE REAL FANTASTIC FOUR, JUST AS I HAVE TOPPLED THEIR PUPPET IMAGES!
NAMOR, LET'S STOP THIS USELESS STRUGGLE! WHY MUST WE ALWAYS BATTLE EACH OTHER? WHAT HAS MADE YOU TURN AGAINST US--TURN AGAINST SUE?
STAY BACK! THE TIME FOR WORDS IS LONG PAST! I MUST PUT AN END TO YOU NOW-- TO ALL OF YOU! I HAVE NO OTHER CHOICE!
ALTHOUGH I CANNOT SEE, I SENSE ANOTHER PRESENCE HERE! I SENSE A MENTAL POWER--A SINISTER CONTROL --LIKE THE POWER OF MY STEP-FATHER, THE PUPPET MASTER!
THE PUPPET-MASTER! THAT WOULD EXPLAIN IT! BUT--IT CAN'T BE! HE'S DEAD! OR--OR IS HE??!
THIS PLANT IS MY ULTIMATE WEAPON! IT RELEASES A GAS WHICH NO LIVING CREATURE CAN WITHSTAND! AND THESE FUMES SHALL NOW DESTROY YOU ALL!
RELEASE THE FUMES! I COMMAND YOU! YOU MUST OBEY ME!
I MUST OBEY-- I MUST --I MUST KILL THEM ALL--
THEY ARE MY ENEMIES! IT IS THEIR LIVES, OR MINE! AND YET --SUE IS AMONG THEM! BUT-- I HAVE NO CHOICE--
YET--WHY MUST THEY PERISH?? WHY CAN I NOT STAY MY HAND--??
19

STAY BEHIND ME-- ALL OF YOU! WHATEVER'S COMIN', I'LL TAKE IT FIRST! I AINT SO EASY TO KILL, AND IT'LL GIVE YOU TIME TO ERASE THAT SLIMY WETHEAD ONCE AND FOR ALL!
THAT'S IT, THING! KEEP HIS ATTENTION ON YOU WHILE I TAKE A FEW PREVENTATIVE MEASURES!
NO! I CAN'T! I WON'T! I CAN'T MURDER THE --WHA--? WHAT HAPPENED?!!
I DIDN'T MEAN TO ACTIVATE THE FUMES!! HOW WERE THEY RELEASED?? WHAT IS ME??
BUT--YOU'RE STILL-- STILL STANDING! IT'S IMPOSSIBLE! NOTHING CAN SURVIVE THOSE LETHAL FUMES! NOT EVEN YOU!!
DID YOU THINK I WOULD BE UNPREPARED FOR SUCH A DEADLY THREAT?? I PLACED THESE FLEX-O-GEN PACKETS ON ALL OUR FACES BEFORE YOU STRUCK!
AND NOW, NAMOR, FOR THE FINAL RECKONING! YOU'RE TOO POWERFUL, TOO UNPREDICTABLE, TO BE ALLOWED TO MENACE MANKIND ANY LONGER!
ONE SIDE, SUE! WE GOT US SOME MOPPIN' UP TO DO!
I WANT HIM FIRST! JUST HIM AND ME --WITH NO CREEPY FISH HELPIN' HIM!
WAIT! ALL OF YOU-- STOP! YOU MUSTN'T! LISTEN TO ME!
HE DOESN'T KNOW WHAT HE'S DOING! HE ISN'T TO BLAME FOR WHAT'S HAPPENED! ALICIA WAS RIGHT! NAMOR IS UNDER SOME SORT OF A SPELL--UNDER SOME EVIL INFLUENCE! I KNOW IT!
STAND ASIDE! THEY DO NOT FRIGHTEN THE SUB-MARINER!
BUT, AT THAT FATEFUL MOMENT, THE GIANT OCTOPUS, WHICH HAD BEEN HURLED TO THE TOP OF NAMOR'S DOME BY THE RAMPAGING THING, SHATTERS THE THICK PLEXIGLASS SHELL IN AN AWESOME DISPLAY OF ALMOST LIMITLESS STRENGTH!

AND THEN, FREE ONCE MORE TO RAVAGE THE OCEAN DEPTHS, THE MIGHTY CREATURE, IN ITS UNCONTROLLABLE RAGE, SEEKS A NEW VICTIM TO ATTACK!
UP AHEAD! SOMETHING WAVERING-- TENTACLES REACHING TOWARDS ME--
OH NO--NO! IT'S THE BEAST--THE GIANT OCTOPUS! IT SEES ME! IT'S COMING TOWARDS THE SUB!
TOO LATE TO CHANGE COURSE! ONLY ONE CHANCE! I'VE GOT TO CONTROL IT! I'VE ONLY SECONDS IN WHICH TO MAKE A PUPPET OF THE DEADLY BRUTE!!
HE'S COMING CLOSER! BUT HE WON'T GET ME! I'LL HAVE HIM UNDER MY CONTROL BEFORE HE CAN TOUCH THE SHIP! NO ONE CAN DEFEAT THE PUPPET MASTER, AS LONG AS I HAVE MY RADIO-ACTIVE CLAY!
BUT, IN HIS FRANTIC HASTE, THE PUPPET MASTER OVERLOOKS ONE LITTLE DETAIL--A DETAIL WHICH MEANS THE DIFFERENCE BETWEEN VICTORY, OR DISASTER FOR HIM!
FOR THE SINISTER SCULPTOR FORGOT THAT YOU CANNOT CONTROL THE MIND OF A CREATURE WHICH IS ALMOST MINDLESS! AND SO...
NO! STAY BACK! BACK! I COMMAND YOU! IT'S NO USE! HE DOESN'T OBEY! HE'S TRYING TO CRUSH THE SUB--
AND, AT THAT SAME SPLIT-SECOND, SUB-MARINER SUDDENLY RECOILS, AS THOUGH HIS BRAIN HAS RECEIVED A VIOLENT SHOCK!
OHHH! MY HEAD! THE PRESSURE-- IT'S GONE!!
LOOK! SOMETHING'S HAPPENED TO NAMOR!
NO TIME FOR THAT NOW! THE WATER IS RUSHING IN THRU THAT GAPING HOLE ABOVE!
HEY! THE TORCH FIXED IT! HE WELDED IT TOGETHER AGAIN WITH HIS FLAME! SO YOU FINALLY PULLED YOUR OWN WEIGHT AROUND HERE, EH, SONNY BOY?!!
AW, KNOCK IT OFF, THING! YOU KNOW THAT IF I HAD MY OWN FAN CLUB, YOU'D BE THE FIRST ONE TO VOLUNTEER TO BE PRESIDENT!
21

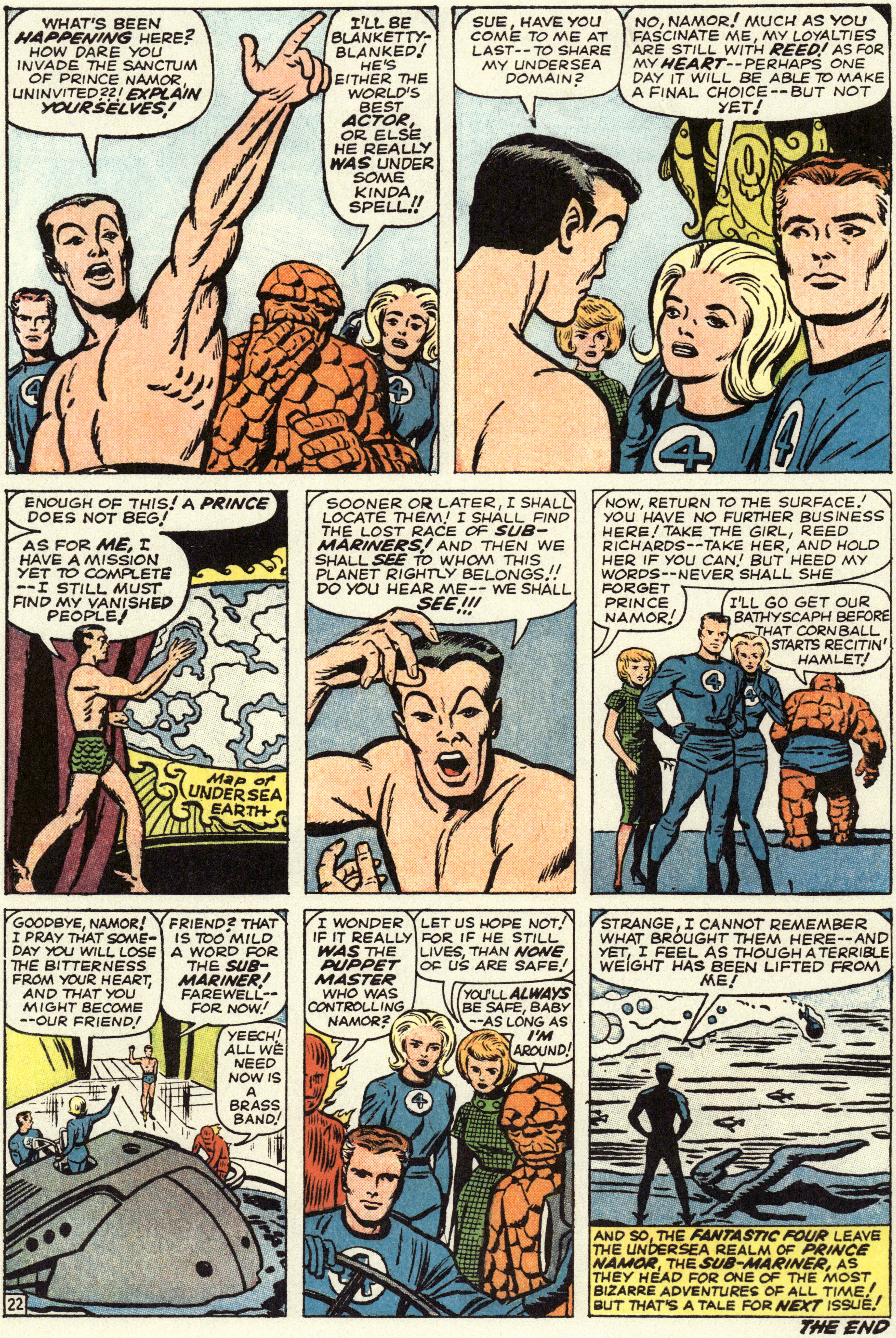
WHAT'S BEEN HAPPENING HERE? HOW DARE YOU INVADE THE SANCTUM OF PRINCE NAMOR, UNINVITED?? EXPLAIN YOURSELVES!
I'LL BE BLANKETTY-BLANKED! HE'S EITHER THE WORLD'S BEST ACTOR, OR ELSE HE REALLY WAS UNDER SOME KINDA SPELL!!
SUE, HAVE YOU COME TO ME AT LAST-- TO SHARE MY UNDERSEA DOMAIN?
NO, NAMOR! MUCH AS YOU FASCINATE ME, MY LOYALTIES ARE STILL WITH REED! AS FOR MY HEART--PERHAPS ONE DAY IT WILL BE ABLE TO MAKE A FINAL CHOICE--BUT NOT YET!
ENOUGH OF THIS! A PRINCE DOES NOT BEG!
AS FOR ME, I HAVE A MISSION YET TO COMPLETE --I STILL MUST FIND MY VANISHED PEOPLE!
Map of UNDERSEA EARTH
SOONER OR LATER, I SHALL LOCATE THEM! I SHALL FIND THE LOST RACE OF SUB-MARINERS! AND THEN WE SHALL SEE TO WHOM THIS PLANET RIGHTLY BELONGS!! DO YOU HEAR ME-- WE SHALL SEE!!!
NOW, RETURN TO THE SURFACE! YOU HAVE NO FURTHER BUSINESS HERE! TAKE THE GIRL, REED RICHARDS--TAKE HER, AND HOLD HER IF YOU CAN! BUT HEED MY WORDS--NEVER SHALL SHE FORGET PRINCE NAMOR!
I'LL GO GET OUR BATHYSCAPH BEFORE THAT CORNBALL STARTS RECITIN' HAMLET!
GOODBYE, NAMOR! I PRAY THAT SOME-DAY YOU WILL LOSE THE BITTERNESS FROM YOUR HEART, AND THAT YOU MIGHT BECOME --OUR FRIEND!
FRIEND? THAT IS TOO MILD A WORD FOR THE SUB-MARINER! FAREWELL-- FOR NOW!
YEECH! ALL WE NEED NOW IS A BRASS BAND!
22
I WONDER IF IT REALLY WAS THE PUPPET MASTER WHO WAS CONTROLLING NAMOR?
LET US HOPE NOT! FOR IF HE STILL LIVES, THAN NONE OF US ARE SAFE!
YOU'LL ALWAYS BE SAFE, BABY --AS LONG AS I'M AROUND!
STRANGE, I CANNOT REMEMBER WHAT BROUGHT THEM HERE--AND YET, I FEEL AS THOUGH A TERRIBLE WEIGHT HAS BEEN LIFTED FROM ME!
AND SO, THE FANTASTIC FOUR LEAVE THE UNDERSEA REALM OF PRINCE NAMOR, THE SUB-MARINER, AS THEY HEAD FOR ONE OF THE MOST BIZARRE ADVENTURES OF ALL TIME! BUT THAT'S A TALE FOR NEXT ISSUE!
THE END

Address YOUR letters to:
LEE and KIRBY
FANTASTIC FOUR
THIRD FLOOR
655 MADISON AVE.
NEW YORK 21, N. Y.

FANTASTIC FAN PAGE 4

Dear Stan and Jack:

We have formed a Fantastic Four fan club, and would like for you to send us ideas for some activities we can do at the meetings. At present at our meetings, we: first read our reports on the last adventure, then; make up a new adventure and *play* it. After that, our president, Mr. Fantastic, assigns parts of the adventure to each person. If you can, please send us materials to get going. Thank you.

Fantastically yours,
Stewart Scheifer, Secretary,
FF Fan Club
330 E. 173 St.
New York 57, N.Y.

Say, Stu, you ought to send US material — you seem to have more ideas than WE do! Actually we've heard from MANY friends who are starting F.F. fan clubs, and as soon as we can figure out what to do about it we're gonna devote some space to fan club doings in a future ish.

Dear Stan and Jack:

As an English major at the University of Texas, I would like to congratulate you on the high standards of literary excellence you've set in "The World's Greatest Comic Magazine." I love it! Sometimes the symbolism is too much for me – but that doesn't keep me from enjoying each exciting issue. Your mag is as good as the great comics of the early 50's. So keep up the good work. I can hardly wait for the next issue.

Bill Hauptman
Box 39
A-Bar Hotel
Austin, Texas

Bill, we'll REALLY know we've arrived when we hear that some English major wrote a term paper about the F.F., thereby winning a scholarship! But we won't hold our breaths waiting!

Dear Stan and Jack:

I may have missed out, but please inform me what happened to Dr. Doom's face, and why it is so horrible to look at? Also, how about a story concerning the Ant-Man, Thor, or Spider-Man meeting the FF. *And* I didn't know Dr. Doom, the Invisible Girl, or the Hulk could fly. On the cover of ish 10, you have all of them flying. Please explain!

David Languth
106 24th St.
Altoona, Pa.

Some day in the future, Dave, we'll do a nice long meaty story about what really happened to DOC DOOM'S face — so let's save it till then. As for the F.F. meeting some of our other superheroes – could be! But the gang on the cover of ish #10 WEREN'T flying – that's known as a symbolic drawing — a vignette — an impressionistic rendition — a surrealistic interpretation of — aw, heck! It would be easier to claim that they CAN fly!

Dear Stan and Jack:

I believe that Thing should be the head of the gang because he is the strongest guy in the gang. Now, what do you say?

Victor Phillips
410 North Hamilton
Indianapolis, Indiana

We'll say what we ALWAYS say! We'll pass the buck by asking you fans to VOTE on it! Anybody think someone other than Reed should head the F.F.?

Dear Stan and Jack:

I have compiled a list of what I think are the best stories, art, etc. of '62. This list does not include #1. Best story – *The End of the Fantastic Four.* Best artwork – issues #4 and #9. Most humorous story – #9 and #7. Most humorous panels – #'s 2-5, page 9, #9; panel #1, page 4, issue #9; panel #2, page 10, issue #2. Best all-round issue – #9, which in my opinion will never be equalled. Now for a couple of questions: In #2, the Thing says that he never gets tired, but in #9 when he fights the Sub-Mariner, he gets so tired that he can hardly stand. Also, in #1, the flare-gun shoots the words, "The Fantastic Four" into the air. Now all it shoots is the number "4." How come? In closing, I would like to give you my utmost congratulations – for yours is the only one that indeed deserves the title of "The World's Greatest Comic Magazine!"

Lee Whittlesey
320 West Johnson
Norman, Oklahoma

The THING never DID get tired until he fought the SUB-MARINER – but battling Prince Namor isn't exactly a rest cure! As for the flare gun, the F.F. saves a lot of smoke with each shot by only using one numeral — and, with the high price of smoke today, every little bit counts! Or, would you rather have the truth, Lee? We GOOFED again! So shoot us!

Dear Stan and Jack:

I like your comic mag a lot, but what I don't understand is who drives the Fantasticar when the four parts of it are together?

Jeffrey Roy Pontello
R. D. 6, Fairdale
Cambridge, Ohio

Usually Reed, although any of the four can handle it. Due to MR. FANTASTIC'S inventive genius, it's actually easier to handle than the average family car.

Dear Stan and Jack:

Sorry, but I don't agree that F. F. is the "World's Greatest Comic!" Matter of fact, the stories are often poorly written (perhaps you have too many irons in the fire, Stan!), the art, sloppy! What I can't understand is – why I like it!!! Being a collector-type, I have all 11 issues. All right, so I'm a nut!

Mark Savage
1104 W. 4th St.
Tyler, Texas

So you bought the first eleven issues? So we should have more nuts like you!

Dear Stan and Jack:

Now listen here. I just can't stand to hold back any longer. I've just read issue #11 of FF, and all I can say is that your magazine is unequaled, matchless, first class, rare, priceless, exquisite, choice, unobjectionable, and inestimably fine. The original creativity that you give is unheard of, truely making your mag the T.W.G.C.M. (The World's Greatest Comic Magazine.) Another thing. Anybody who wants to drop the Invisible Girl is nuts! She adds that special touch that makes your mag great. In issue #11, the ideas were stupendous! 'A Visit With the Fantastic Four' was a brand new idea never before thought of or dared. 'The Impossible Man' met all expectations and more. Congratulations, Stan Lee! Keep up the good work.

Kathleen McCoy
630 Central Ave.
Oildale, California

One thing we like, Kathy, is a fan with IMPECCABLE judgment and taste!

Dear Stan and Jack:

Your mag is truly the "World's Greatest Comic Book." As your issues went on, they got better in art and stories. I'd like to say that Prince Namor is a good villain, but he is very ugly (with long eyebrows and pointed ears). What

PLEASE TURN PAGE →

Sue sees in him is beyond me. Please have a ballot on Sue's marrying Reed. I vote yes all the way.

Joseph Shoemaker
27 Sunny Crest Rd.
Trumbull, Connecticut

Joey boy, there are SOME things that can't be settled by a vote!

Dear Stan and Jack:

When I first bought your magazine, I thought it was just another drop-in-the-bucket. But then I started to thumb through it — Boy, oh boy, what a mistake I'd made. This magazine has fine artwork, the characters have reality, and you seem to be able to weasel out of any error your readers say you make. But here's one you can't squirm out of: In #11, page 10, the Impossible Man turned into the Old Man of the Sea. Now, how could he do this when he's a stranger to the earth and knows nothing about us, Hmmm? Richard Eilts

109 Henderlong Pkwy.
Crown Point, Indiana

Simple, Dick! Where do you think the Old Man of the Sea CAME from? He was an alien TOO, from the Impossible Man's home planet! In fact, rumor hath it that they were second cousins.

Dear Stan and Jack:

In your recent story, 'The Return of Dr. Doom,' you show Reed Richards changing bodies with Dr. Doom. So when Reed Richards (as Dr. Doom) had Doom's body, he should have been able to get out of the airless chamber because he had Dr. Doom's brain! Explain this. And please, no wise cracks. Kevin Johnson

600 Pioneer Ave.
Tooele, Utah

Uh uh, Kevin! Nobody said anything about their changing BRAINS! They only swapped BODIES! They KEPT their own personalities, remember? And another thing — if you spent an hour a day, every day, reading fan mail, YOU'D feel like bustin' loose with a wise-crack once in a while yourself!

Dear Stan and Jack:

Nine issues ago, I sent you guys the best of luck with your F.F. Now I realize that you didn't need luck, but you got something three times as good, that something being the most inventive comic in the history of the business. Each issue of F.F. brought new surprises as well as carefully worked out plots and artwork. The villains are very unique indeed, and your human approach, although a bit overdone, is a revolutionary idea never before attempted in a comic mag. The Thing and his crazy humor never fail to break me up, even in the most tense situation. Mr. Fantastic seems a born leader, and the Torch — well, he's just terrific. Sue Storm — ooh-la-la. Enough said. One gripe, however. Other fans might lynch me for even bringing this up, but I think the covers on each issue are too cluttered with action. Well, now that I've got that off my chest, may I say don't let the stories get stale, and I'll be a fan for life.

Jim Broeker
4336 N. Lawndale
Chicago 18, Illinois

Jim, we couldn't let these mags get stale if we WANTED to — not with you wide-awake fans breathing down our necks every minute — bless you all!

Dear Stan and Jack:

Oboy, oboy, oboy, I found a goof in ish #11, where Mr. Fantastic was talking about Sue's being helpful with the Skrulls. In the picture, page 10, panel 4, you show her tripping a Skrull. The dotted outline of her is no doubt an outline of Sue in her uniform,— but the FF's didn't get their uniforms until the ish following the Skrull adventure. You made another goof on Sue's cake. First the cake said, "Happy Birthday to Sue," but in the next panel, it says, "Happy Birthday, Susan." So, two goofs — but they didn't effect how good this particular story was —"A Visit with the Fantastic Four." Enjoyed your new ish immensely."The Impossible Man" was great and so was the Pin-up Page. The main things I want to see are: an FF annual; a reprint of # 1: the FF in T.V. or movies. I love the "World's Greatest Comic Mag." Thanks a lot for it.

Arthur Davis, Jr.
2809 Avenham Ave.
Roanoke, Virginia

And thank YOU, A.D., for taking the time, etc. As far as all our mistakes are concerned, we make 'em while we're being real careful! Can you imagine if we ever get CARELESS??!

Dear Stan and Jack:

Issue #11 was one of the worst issues you've ever printed. The Fantastic Four hardly tried to stop the Impossible Man. It showed that the Four were no match for him — and the Impossible Man is a ridiculous villain. I would like to see Submariner come back in a future issue. And I have an idea as to how you can get Dr. Doom back. What if he were to shrink into an atom world, a world inside an atom. The people who inhabited that atom would have their own tiny world, and a race far ahead of us in scientific knowledge. They would enlarge Dr. Doom until he would be his normal size. With these two villains, you've really got the greatest mag.

Barry Goldstein
50 Ave. D
New York 9, N. Y.

And WITHOUT 'em I suppose we're just hamfat, eh? Oh well, to each his own!

HERE IT IS: SPECIAL ANNOUNCEMENT TIME!

- **We get many requests for letters pages in JOURNEY INTO MYSTERY, STRANGE TALES and TALES OF SUSPENSE! We'd LOVE to add 'em, honestly, but we simply can't! It takes HOURS to put together a letters page such as this one, because we take it very seriously. We read each letter, discuss it, and analyze it thoroughly before making our selection. We don't entrust the job to assistants, or sub-editors! But, how's this for an idea? Let's let our F.F. FAN PAGE be the melting pot for ALL our mags (except SPIDERMAN which will have its own letters page) and we'll print any exceptionally interesting letters about THOR, ANT-MAN, HUMAN TORCH, or IRON MAN on these pages.**
- **Have you noticed our new trade mark, on the upper left hand corner of the cover? ALL our mags will soon be sporting this handsome insignia. We kinda hope you'll make it a point to look for them, and better still, buy a few!**
- **Here's a little teaser: Nothing definite yet, but hundreds of you have written to request an F.F. ANNUAL. Well, we're working on it! More info later on.**
- **How would you you like to see a war story mag written and drawn in the same style as the F.F.? Well, we've GOT one for you — by Stan and Jack, called SGT. FURY And His HOWLING COMMANDOS! If you dig real battle action, solid characterization, and the MARVEL COMICS GROUP style of story-telling, then FURY is for you! Better reserve your copy at your dealer's now!**
- **NEXT ISSUE: We've cooked up a whiz-dinger of a super-villain, and get a load of this title: THE F.F. BATTLE "THE THINKER, AND HIS AWESOME ANDROID!" Like it or not, you've gotta admit we've got COURAGE! So reserve your copy now, and we'll see you next ish!**

WATCH FOR
THE GREATEST SYMBOLS IN COMICS!
MARVEL COMICS GROUP 12¢
"THE AMAZING SPIDER-MAN"
"ANT-MAN" APPEARING IN TALES TO ASTONISH
"THOR" APPEARING IN JOURNEY INTO MYSTERY
"IRON-MAN" APPEARING IN TALES OF SUSPENSE
"HUMAN TORCH" APPEARING IN STRANGE TALES + FANTASTIC FOUR
MANY OTHER STARS NOW ON SALE
PLUS
NEW SURPRISES ON OUR DRAWING BOARD, FROM THE HOUSE OF IDEAS!
MARVEL COMICS GROUP 12¢

GIVE ME JUST ONE EVENING and I'LL TEACH YOU TO HYPNOTIZE EASILY!

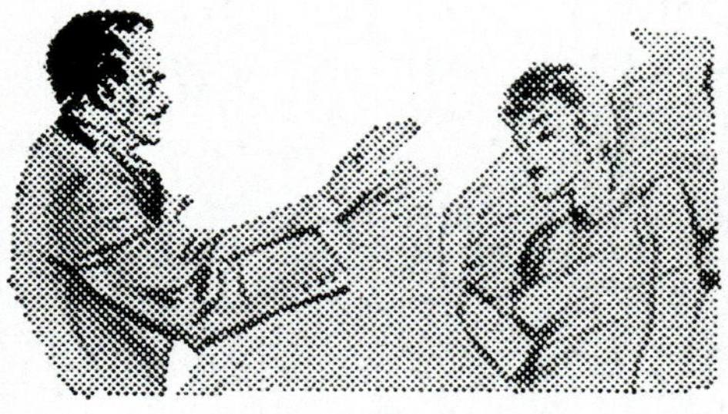

Hypnotize others quickly, safely---perform any known HYPNOTIC FEAT with EASE! Amaze friends-Exert your Hypnotic Power over others - Be POPULAR and WANTED!

YES, it's true! You can hypnotize anyone so EASILY and quickly you'll be amazed! And it doesn't take special talents or long months of study. The very first day you receive this miracle GUIDE TO HYPNOTISM you'll be able to perform wonders that will astound everyone. It's that SIMPLE.... WHEN YOU KNOW HOW.

Imagine the thrill of being able to EXERT YOUR POWER OVER OTHERS. You'll be the center of attraction at parties or work. You'll be able to make others do your bidding...perform and entertain with feats that have baffled millions for years. And you'll do these wonders with EASE. For, Hypnotism is no longer a secret miracle of science but a POWER anyone can exert over another..when you know how!

25 MIRACLE LESSONS

- HOW TO HYPNOTIZE — New Simple Technique
- HOW TO AWAKEN SUBJECT
- THE POST-HYPNOTIC SUGGESTION — How to make others do your bidding after they are awakened; hypnotiz - ing by telephone.
- HOW TO GAIN MAGNETIC NEW PERSONALITY
- MESMERISM — Quick technique for hypnotizing.
- MAGNETIC HEALING — How to stop pain. Much surgery is performed by Hypnotism.
- HOW TO HYPNOTIZE FOR MONEY
- CURING BAD HABITS — End sleeplessness, stop smoking, lose weight, etc.
- POWER OF SUGGESTION
- HYPNOTIZE YOURSELF
- MAGNETIC INFLUENCE — Control others.
- HYPNOTIZING CROWDS
- HOW TO ENTERTAIN
- MIND READING
- HYPNOTISM IN BUSINESS

and much, much more is covered!

Palmer-Jones Publishers. Dpt. 22
285 Market St., Newark, N. J.

SIMPLE SECRETS REVEALED AT LAST

For years the knowledge of how to produce hypnotic sleep has been so well guarded that only a few have mastered this art. But now the veil of secrecy has been lifted and the innermost SECRETS and techniques revealed for the first time. The fact is that Hypnotism is a scientific fact that anyone can learn. Once you know these secrets and methods you can bring about this strange and wonderful control that has only been used by doctors, psychiatrists and entertainers in the past. Yes, now this remarkable phenomena will be yours to use for pleasure, self-development and countless other benefits.

YOU CAN PERFORM ANY HYPNOTIC FEAT!

First, you must understand that what another person does with Hypnotism, you can also do. There isn't anything anyone has ever done with this art that you cannot do! YOU can make people cry, laugh, shout, stop smoking, recall childhood memories, act like an infant, make water taste like vinegar, get folks to sing, dance ... do a 1001 things they would never do when not UNDER YOUR POWER. And the most amazing thing of all is --- HOW EASY IT IS TO DO!

SO EASY TO MASTER!

Here at last is the most perfect, complete and easily-learned course on Hypnotism ever written. In three short, simple chapters you learn the hidden secrets of Hypnotism and how to work this scientific miracle. No long, technical, mumbo-jumbo explanations are given. The entire 25-lesson Guide to Hypnotism is written in plain, SIMPLE language that anyone can understand. After the third lesson you are able to begin performing countless techniques and powers clearly explained in the next 22 lessons. You'll learn how to cure bad habits in yourself and others, how to BUILD PERSONAL MAGNETISM, SLEEP without drugs, use Hypnotism to help STOP PAIN, stop smoking, BUILD WILL POWER, LOSE WEIGHT, IMPROVE YOUR MEMORY and so much more. And you'll learn how to MAKE MONEY with your new power by entertaining at parties, lodges, club meetings, etc. Truly, this knowledge will give you a New SURGE of CONFIDENCE and POWER unlike any you have ever known!

ACT, FEEL AND BE A NEW PERSON!

How often have you wished that you could EXERT a MAGNETIC POWER and INFLUENCE OVER OTHERS? Get people to respond to your every command..win respect, admiration and envy from both men and women! Well, DREAM NO LONGER. It's all possible through the secret, magnetic power of Hypnotism. You'll not only be MASTER OVER OTHERS but also yourself. You can BUILD A STRONG, MAGNETIC PERSONALITY through Self-Hypnotism. You use Mesmerism to READ the MINDS of others and Plant YOUR Thoughts in their minds. You can direct yourself to ACCOMPLISH anything, as easily as you can command others. You have the power to accomplish your innermost dreams.

25 Fact-Packed LESSONS TELL ALL!

Never before has such a Complete and authentic course on Hypnotism been available at such a low price. Doctors and students have PAID hundreds of DOLLARS for personal instruction in Hypnotism, when obtainable. Knowledge such as this can be worth THOUSANDS of DOLLARS to the user over the years. Yet, due to printing economies, large press runs and also by the elimination of correspondence costs, the complete 25-Lesson Guide To HYPNOTISM is yours for only $1.98. Yes, only $1.98 for the COMPLETE COURSE bound in book form. Certainly a tiny investment for so much!

• USE FOR 30 DAYS • WITHOUT OBLIGATION!

PROVE to Yourself that YOU CAN HYPNOTIZE ANYONE! Order the 25-Lesson Guide to Hypnotism today and put it to the test the very next evening. The first three chapters teach you the SECRET of Hypnotism and the 22 chapters that follow introduce you to many new WONDERS of this miraculous art. For the next 30 days as our guest, perform the WONDERS of Hypnotism among your friends, at home and at work. Then, if you don't feel it's the GREATEST VALUE you have ever received for $1.98--we don't want you to keep it. Just mail it back and the small payment you sent will be PROMPTLY refunded---no questions asked. You have nothing to lose -- amazing new POWERS TO GAIN! So order now!

CHECK HERE HYPNOTIC POWERS YOU WANT!

- ☐ INFLUENCE OTHERS
- ☐ SELF-HYPNOSIS
- ☐ CURE BAD HABITS
- ☐ LOSE WEIGHT
- ☐ STOP SMOKING
- ☐ PERFORM STUNTS, TRICKS
- ☐ DO MIND READING
- ☐ GAIN MAGNETIC PERSONALITY
- ☐ RELIEVE TENSION
- ☐ MAKE MONEY

MAIL NO-RISK FREE TRIAL COUPON!

PALMER-JONES PUBLISHERS, Dept. 22
285 Market Street, Newark, New Jersey

YES, Send me for 30-day HOME TRIAL the complete 25-Lesson GUIDE TO HYPNOTISM.

☐ I enclose $1.98 - payment in full - which will be refunded to me if I am not 100% delighted.

Name__________

Address__________

City__________ Zone____ State______

☐ I agree that I will not use this power for other than proper use.

IND.
THE WORLD'S GREATEST COMIC MAGAZINE!
APPROVED BY THE COMICS CODE AUTHORITY
THE Fantastic Four
15 JUNE
MARVEL COMICS GROUP 12¢
FEATURING... "THE MAD THINKER AND HIS AWESOME ANDROID!"
LET NONE OF THE FANTASTIC FOUR LEAVE ALIVE!! THE THINKER COMMANDS IT!
HE-HE'S TURNING OUR OWN WEAPONS AGAINST US!! WE HAVEN'T A CHANCE!
NOT ONLY HAS THE MAD THINKER TAKEN OVER THE FANTASTIC FOUR'S HEADQUARTERS, BUT HE'S BEATING THEM AT THEIR OWN GAME!
JUST WAIT! SOONER OR LATER...I'LL GET MY MITTS ON YOU!! JUST WAIT!!

THE FANTASTIC FOUR is published by CANAM PUBLISHERS SALES CORP. OFFICE OF PUBLICATION: 655 MADISON AVENUE, NEW YORK, N.Y. Published monthly. Copyright 1963 by CANAM PUBLISHERS SALES CORP., 655 Madison Avenue, New York, N.Y. Vol. 1 No. 15, JUNE, 1963 issue. Price 12¢ per copy. Subscription rate $1.75 for 12 issues including postage. Foreign substription $3.25 in American funds. No similarity between any of the names, characters, persons, and/or institutions appearing in this magazine with those of any living or dead person is intended, and any such similarity which may exist is purely coincidental. Printed in U.S.A. by The Eastern Color Printing Co., Waterbury 20, Conn.

THE FANTASTIC FOUR BATTLE...
the MAD THINKER
AND HIS
AWESOME ANDROID!
A BOOK-LENGTH SAGA!
THE ANDROID... NEITHER ANIMAL, NOR VEGETABLE, NOR MINERAL! WHAT IS IT?
SCRIPT.........STAN LEE
ART.............JACK KIRBY
INKING........DICK AYERS
LETTERING...ART SIMEK
X-191
AND NOW, READ ON...
1

YOU ARE NOW EXPERIENCING ONE OF THE MOST EXCITING MOMENTS IN MAGAZINE READING: THE START OF AN ALL-NEW FANTASTIC FOUR ADVENTURE! THIS IS NEW YORK, HOME OF THE FAMOUS BAXTER BUILDING, WHICH HOUSES THE FANTASTIC FOUR'S SKYSCRAPER HEADQUARTERS!
SUDDENLY, A LEAN, POWERFUL HAND FIRES A BRIGHT FLARE INTO THE EVENING SKY...
...AND OUR ADVENTURE INTO FANTASY BEGINS!
LOOK! THE RED ALERT SIGNAL OF THE FANTASTIC FOUR!
4
NOT FAR AWAY, IN A QUIET LANE IN CENTRAL PARK, WE FIND A TEEN-AGER AND HIS DATE...
OF COURSE I'M ANGRY, JOHNNY! DO YOU KNOW HOW MANY DATES YOU'VE BROKEN WITH ME??
AW, PEGGY, YOU KNOW I COULDN'T HELP IT! BUT I'M HERE NOW, AND THERE'S A MOON ABOVE, AND YOU SURE LOOK GORGEOUS...
OH, JOHNNY, HOW I'VE LONGED FOR THIS WONDERFUL MOMENT!
GREAT BALLS OF FIRE!! AT A TIME LIKE THIS!
4
SORRY, PEG, I'LL HAVE TO LEAVE YOU FOR A WHILE! HOPE YOU CAN DRIVE!
FLAME ON!
OH NO! NOT AGAIN!!
AND, IN A CHI-CHI BEAUTY PARLOR ON FIFTH AVENUE...
I JUST KNOW I'VE SEEN THAT GIRL SOMEWHERE!
AH, MISS STORM, NOW FOR THE SUPREME MOMENT! I, PERSONALLY, SHALL CREATE YOUR NEW HAIR-DO!
I HAVE CANCELLED ALL OTHER APPOINTMENTS SO THAT I COULD DEVOTE MYSELF ENTIRELY TO YOU TODAY!
REED'S SIGNAL! IT MEANS COME A'RUNNING, NO MATTER WHAT!
4
2

WAIT! YOU CAN'T DO THIS TO ME! I SHALL DESTROY MYSELF!
YOU AND ME BOTH, PIERRE! I'VE WAITED MONTHS FOR OUR APPOINT-MENT!
BETTER TURN INVISIBLE! I CAN'T RUN THRU THE STREETS WITH CURLERS IN MY HAIR!
AND WHAT OF THE GENTLE, GOOD-NATURED, PEACE-LOVING MEMBER OF THE FANTASTIC FOUR? AH, HERE HE IS--AS LOVABLE AND SHY AS EVER...
SEND ME A PICTURE LIKE THIS, WILL THEY?? WHEN I GET THRU WITH THAT CRUMMY YANCY STREET GANG, IT'LL TAKE A BLOTTER TO MOP 'EM UP!
TENTH AVE.
YANCY ST.
10TH A
THE THING IS A SISSY!
the YANCY STREET GANG
LOOK! THERE'S THE THING!
SO, THE UGLY LUMP GOT OUR LOVE-LETTER!
YOO-HOO, PRETTY BOY! HERE WE ARE!
WE'RE WAITIN' FOR YOU, FAT-HEAD!
IT'S THEM! ON THE ROOF!
DON'T GO 'WAY, CREEPS! I'LL TOSS YA A LITTLE BOUQUET!
CRIPES! JUST WHEN THE PARTY WAS GETTIN' STARTED!
4
WE KNEW IT! HE'S SCARED OF US!
WHERE YOU GOIN', THING--HOME TO GET HELP?
AWW, DID THE NICE LITTLE THING FORGET TO BRING HIS NURSEMAIDS! HAW HAW!
SO HELP ME--ONE OF THESE DAYS--ONE OF THESE DAYS--!!!
MINUTES LATER, AT THE FANTASTIC FOUR'S READY ROOM...
COME IN, BEN! WE'VE BEEN WAITING FOR YOU!
REED DIDN'T WANT TO EXPLAIN UNTIL WE WERE ALL TOGETHER!
WELL NOW, AINT THAT REAL NEIGHBORLY OF HIM!!
OKAY, NOW WHAT'S THIS ALL ABOUT, REED?
3

LOOKS TO ME LIKE RUBBER-FACE JUST LIKES TO SHOOT HIS LITTLE FLARE GUN! WHY DON'T YOU TAKE UP A NEW HOBBY -- LIKE PLAYIN' IN TRAFFIC??
YEAH! WHY THE RED ALERT? DOESN'T LOOK LIKE AN EMERGENCY TO ME!
SUPPOSE YOU BOTH BUTTON UP FOR A WHILE AND GIVE ME A CHANCE TO EXPLAIN!
I DIDN'T WANT TO INTERRUPT WHAT I WAS DOING ANY MORE THAN YOU DID!
I'M RIGHT IN THE MIDDLE OF A CRUCIAL EXPERIMENT WITH D. N. A., THE BASIC CELLS WHICH ARE THE BUILDING BLOCKS OF LIFE ITSELF!
I'VE ALREADY MANAGED TO CREATE A PRIMITIVE FORM OF ONE-CELLED LIFE WHICH LIVED FOR A FEW SECONDS!
DO YOU THINK I FEEL LIKE STOPPING NOW?
"BUT I RECEIVED AN URGENT CALL FROM THE CHIEF OF POLICE! HIS DEPARTMENT REPORTS THAT TOP MOBSTERS AND GANG LEADERS FROM ALL OVER THE COUNTRY ARE FLOCKING TO NEW YORK! THERE'S SOMETHING BIG IN THE WIND, AND HE WANTS US ALERTED!"
AND, EVEN AS MR. FANTASTIC SPEAKS...
IT'S EXACTLY 12:42 P.M.! THEY SHOULD BE ENTERING IN ONE AND ONE-HALF SECONDS!
ONE AND ONE-HALF SECONDS LATER...
OKAY, THINKER, HERE WE ARE!
START THE BALL ROLLIN'! IT AINT HEALTHY FOR US TO BE TOGETHER UNDER ONE ROOF!
AND NO FUNNY STUFF, SEE? WE GOT BOYS POSTED ALL AROUND THIS JOINT!
QUIET, YOU GUYS! THE THINKER IS THINKIN'!!
THESE ARE MY THOUGHTS: I HAVE SUMMONED YOU TO HELP ME FORM A GIGANTIC KINGDOM OF CRIME, WITH ME AS THE KING! FOR, WITH MY FABULOUS BRAIN, AND MY INFALLIBLE COMPUTING MACHINES, I CAN OUT-PLAN THE LAW AT EVERY TURN!
UNTIL THIS MOMENT, THE POLICE HAVE NOT EVEN DREAMT OF MY EXISTENCE! BUT I SHALL REMAIN HIDDEN NO LONGER! WITH YOU, THE MOST POWERFUL GANG LEADERS OF ALL, I SHALL DEVISE A FOOLPROOF PLAN TO CAPTURE AND TAKE CONTROL OF NEW YORK CITY ITSELF!!

"I WILL PROCLAIM NEW YORK AN INDEPENDENT NATION WITH ME AS ITS RULER! AND YOU SHALL BE MY CRIME-ENFORCEMENT OFFICERS! MY PLAN CANNOT FAIL, FOR I HAVE WORKED IT OUT TO THE LAST DETAIL ON MY COMPUTING MACHINES!"
"I SHALL EVEN APPOINT AMBASSADORS TO OTHER AMERICAN CITIES! I WILL SIGN TREATIES WITH THE REST OF AMERICA AND NEGOTIATE TRADE AND FOREIGN-AID PACTS!"
THESE ARE THE THINKER'S TERMS! YOU BETTER ACCEPT 'EM IF YOU DON'T WANT A WAR ON YOUR HANDS!
IT SOUNDS INTERESTING, THINKER! BUT YOU FORGOT ONE LITTLE DETAIL... YOU DON'T SUPPOSE THE FANTASTIC FOUR'LL BE TWIDDLIN' THEIR THUMBS WHILE ALL THIS IS GOIN' ON??
THE THINKER FORGETS NOTHING!
YEAH? WELL, IF ANYONE CAN BOOT YOU OUT FROM UNDER THAT CROWN YOU'RE COUNTIN' ON, MR. FANTASTIC'S THE GUY TO DO IT! NOBODY'S EVER BEATEN HIM YET!
AND THEN THERE'S THE HUMAN TORCH! NO MATTER HOW SMART YOU ARE, HE'LL FIND SOME WAY TO GIVE YOU THE HOTTEST THRONE IN HISTORY! I WOULDN'T WANNA MESS AROUND WITH HIM!
AND EVEN IF YOU PUT THEM OUT OF ACTION, DON'T FORGET THE INVISIBLE GIRL! WHAT'S TO STOP HER FROM SNEAKIN' UP ON YOU ANY TIME, UNSEEN, AND TAKIN' YOU BY SURPRISE?
THE WAY I SEE IT, YOU'LL BE LUCKY IF YOU'RE CAUGHT BY ONE OF THEM! BECAUSE I FIGURE IT WOULD BE A LOT BETTER THAN LETTIN' THE THING GET HIS PAWS ON YOU!
SILENCE, YOU INTELLECTUAL PIGMIES!! DON'T YOU THINK I'VE ALREADY PLANNED HOW TO GET THE FANTASTIC FOUR OUT OF THE WAY?? I NEVER OVERLOOK ANY DETAIL!
5

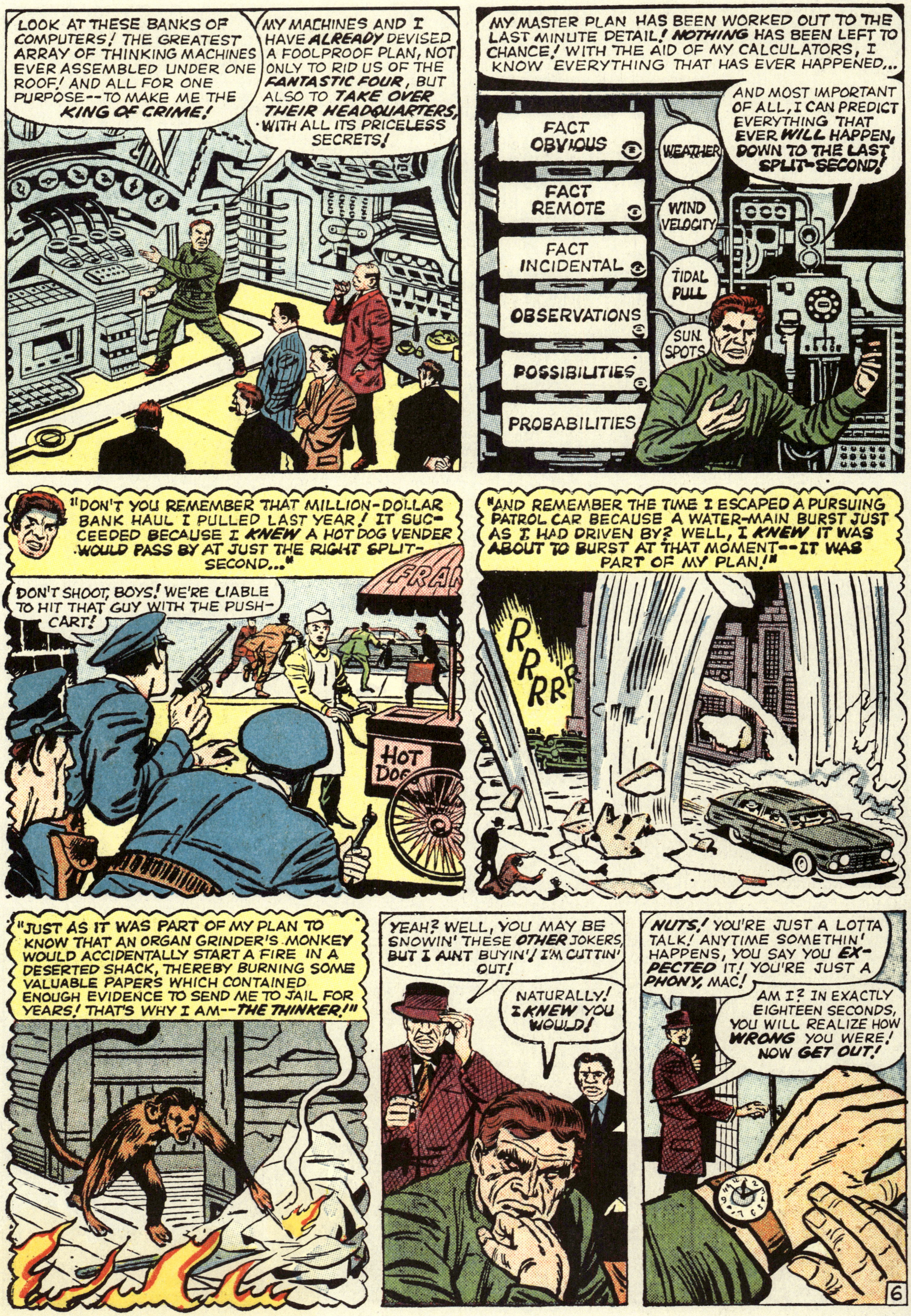

LOOK AT THESE BANKS OF COMPUTERS! THE GREATEST ARRAY OF THINKING MACHINES EVER ASSEMBLED UNDER ONE ROOF! AND ALL FOR ONE PURPOSE--TO MAKE ME THE KING OF CRIME!
MY MACHINES AND I HAVE ALREADY DEVISED A FOOLPROOF PLAN, NOT ONLY TO RID US OF THE FANTASTIC FOUR, BUT ALSO TO TAKE OVER THEIR HEADQUARTERS, WITH ALL ITS PRICELESS SECRETS!
MY MASTER PLAN HAS BEEN WORKED OUT TO THE LAST MINUTE DETAIL! NOTHING HAS BEEN LEFT TO CHANCE! WITH THE AID OF MY CALCULATORS, I KNOW EVERYTHING THAT HAS EVER HAPPENED...
AND MOST IMPORTANT OF ALL, I CAN PREDICT EVERYTHING THAT EVER WILL HAPPEN, DOWN TO THE LAST SPLIT-SECOND!
FACT OBVIOUS
FACT REMOTE
FACT INCIDENTAL
OBSERVATIONS
POSSIBILITIES
PROBABILITIES
WEATHER
WIND VELOCITY
TIDAL PULL
SUN SPOTS
"DON'T YOU REMEMBER THAT MILLION-DOLLAR BANK HAUL I PULLED LAST YEAR! IT SUCCEEDED BECAUSE I KNEW A HOT DOG VENDER WOULD PASS BY AT JUST THE RIGHT SPLIT-SECOND..."
DON'T SHOOT, BOYS! WE'RE LIABLE TO HIT THAT GUY WITH THE PUSH-CART!
HOT DOG
"AND REMEMBER THE TIME I ESCAPED A PURSUING PATROL CAR BECAUSE A WATER-MAIN BURST JUST AS I HAD DRIVEN BY? WELL, I KNEW IT WAS ABOUT TO BURST AT THAT MOMENT--IT WAS PART OF MY PLAN!"
RRRRR
"JUST AS IT WAS PART OF MY PLAN TO KNOW THAT AN ORGAN GRINDER'S MONKEY WOULD ACCIDENTALLY START A FIRE IN A DESERTED SHACK, THEREBY BURNING SOME VALUABLE PAPERS WHICH CONTAINED ENOUGH EVIDENCE TO SEND ME TO JAIL FOR YEARS! THAT'S WHY I AM--THE THINKER!"
YEAH? WELL, YOU MAY BE SNOWIN' THESE OTHER JOKERS, BUT I AINT BUYIN'! I'M CUTTIN' OUT!
NATURALLY! I KNEW YOU WOULD!
NUTS! YOU'RE JUST A LOTTA TALK! ANYTIME SOMETHIN' HAPPENS, YOU SAY YOU EXPECTED IT! YOU'RE JUST A PHONY, MAC!
AM I? IN EXACTLY EIGHTEEN SECONDS, YOU WILL REALIZE HOW WRONG YOU WERE! NOW GET OUT!
6

AND, EXACTLY EIGHTEEN SECONDS LATER...
WELL WELL! IF IT ISN'T BLACKIE SKARR! HOW NICE OF YOU TO WALK RIGHT INTO US THIS WAY!
THE FEDS!! I'M TRAPPED!
THE THINKER KNEW THIS WOULD HAPPEN! THOSE MACHINES OF HIS REALLY WORK! WHAT A CHUMP I WAS!
I TRUST YOU GENTLEMEN OBSERVED WHAT HAS JUST TRANSPIRED BELOW?
AND RIGHT TO THE SECOND, JUST LIKE YOU SAID! LOOKS LIKE YOU REALLY ARE ALL THAT YOU CLAIM TO BE, THINKER!
OKAY, THINKER, WE'RE WITH YA, ALL THE WAY! BUT HOW ARE YA GONNA HANDLE THE FANTASTIC FOUR??
I'VE BEEN WORKING ON THAT PROJECT FOR MONTHS! WATCH--
EACH MEMBER OF THE FANTASTIC FOUR IS A SEPARATE AND DISTINCT PROBLEM, AND I'VE FED MY COMPUTERS ALL THE AVAILABLE DATA ABOUT THEM! AFTER CAREFUL ANALYSIS, MY MACHINES AND I HAVE COME UP WITH THESE SOLUTIONS!
"PROBLEM ONE--THE HUMAN TORCH! I'VE ARRANGED FOR TWO MEN TO ARRIVE IN NEW YORK AT THIS VERY MOMENT! ACCORDING TO MY CALCULATIONS, THEY WILL DO OUR JOB FOR US..."
MIGHTY BIG TOWN, AINT IT, SHORTY?
YOU SAID IT, BONES!
THAR HE IS NOW, RIGHT ON TIME! HI, COUSIN JOHNNY!
COUSIN BONES! WELCOME TO NEW YORK!
MAN! HE SURE IS A CORKER, ISN'T HE? LOOK AT HIM FLAME AROUND UP THERE!
FLAME OFF!
I GOT YOUR TELEGRAM! WHAT'S THE TROUBLE, COUSIN?
IT'S MUH CIRCUS, COUSIN JOHNNY! ALL OF A SUDDEN BUSINESS HAS DROPPED OFF!
I NEED ME A REAL STAR ATTRACTION TO GET THE CROWDS BACK AGAIN--OR ELSE I'LL LOSE EVERYTHING! I WAS WONDERIN' ABOUT YOU, JOHNNY...?
GOSH! A CHANCE TO BE A CIRCUS STAR!! IF ONLY I COULD!!

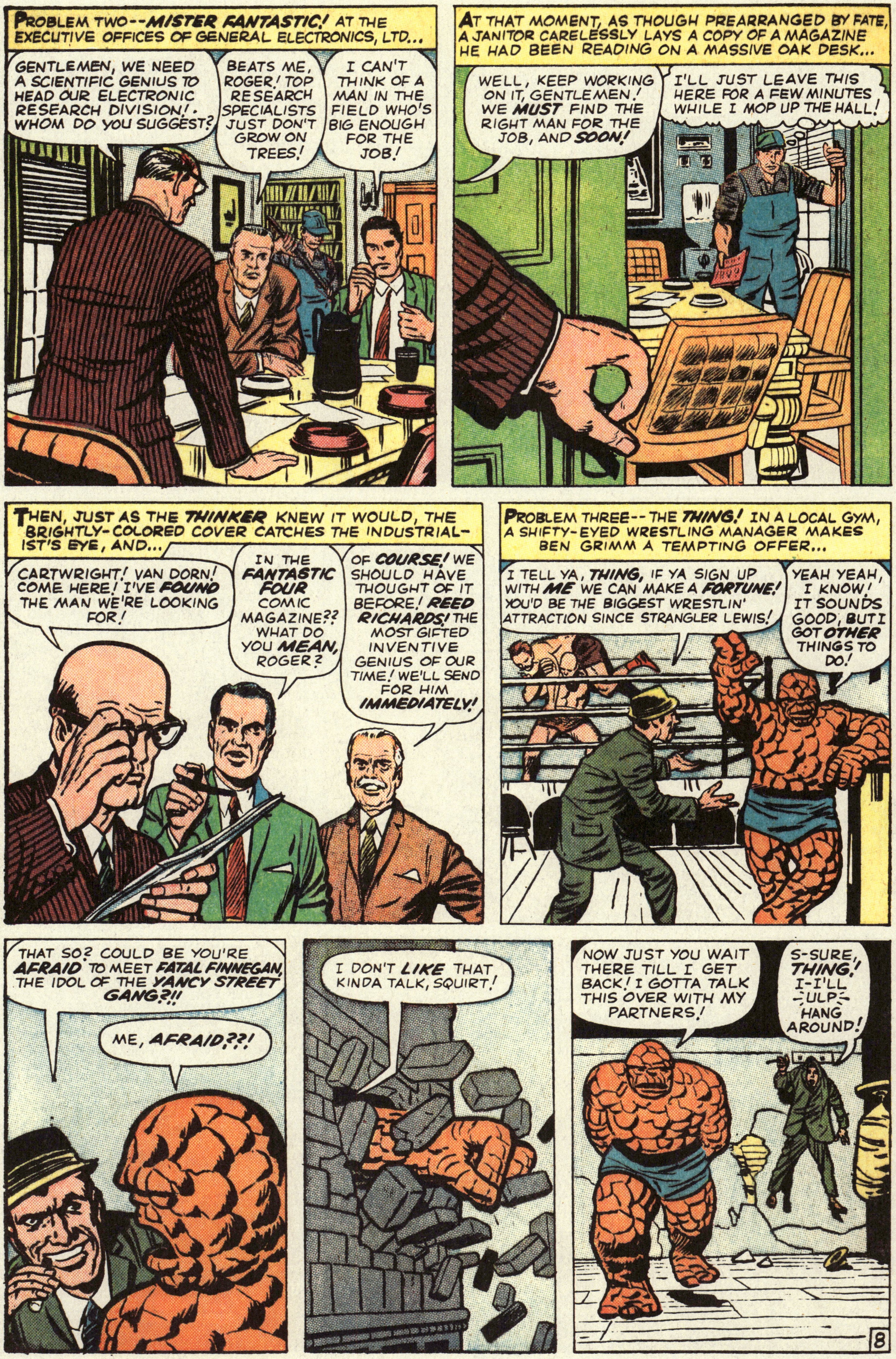
PROBLEM TWO--MISTER FANTASTIC! AT THE EXECUTIVE OFFICES OF GENERAL ELECTRONICS, LTD...
GENTLEMEN, WE NEED A SCIENTIFIC GENIUS TO HEAD OUR ELECTRONIC RESEARCH DIVISION! WHOM DO YOU SUGGEST?
BEATS ME, ROGER! TOP RESEARCH SPECIALISTS JUST DON'T GROW ON TREES!
I CAN'T THINK OF A MAN IN THE FIELD WHO'S BIG ENOUGH FOR THE JOB!
AT THAT MOMENT, AS THOUGH PREARRANGED BY FATE, A JANITOR CARELESSLY LAYS A COPY OF A MAGAZINE HE HAD BEEN READING ON A MASSIVE OAK DESK...
WELL, KEEP WORKING ON IT, GENTLEMEN! WE MUST FIND THE RIGHT MAN FOR THE JOB, AND SOON!
I'LL JUST LEAVE THIS HERE FOR A FEW MINUTES WHILE I MOP UP THE HALL!
THEN, JUST AS THE THINKER KNEW IT WOULD, THE BRIGHTLY-COLORED COVER CATCHES THE INDUSTRIALIST'S EYE, AND...
CARTWRIGHT! VAN DORN! COME HERE! I'VE FOUND THE MAN WE'RE LOOKING FOR!
IN THE FANTASTIC FOUR COMIC MAGAZINE?? WHAT DO YOU MEAN, ROGER?
OF COURSE! WE SHOULD HAVE THOUGHT OF IT BEFORE! REED RICHARDS! THE MOST GIFTED INVENTIVE GENIUS OF OUR TIME! WE'LL SEND FOR HIM IMMEDIATELY!
PROBLEM THREE-- THE THING! IN A LOCAL GYM, A SHIFTY-EYED WRESTLING MANAGER MAKES BEN GRIMM A TEMPTING OFFER...
I TELL YA, THING, IF YA SIGN UP WITH ME WE CAN MAKE A FORTUNE! YOU'D BE THE BIGGEST WRESTLIN' ATTRACTION SINCE STRANGLER LEWIS!
YEAH YEAH, I KNOW! IT SOUNDS GOOD, BUT I GOT OTHER THINGS TO DO!
THAT SO? COULD BE YOU'RE AFRAID TO MEET FATAL FINNEGAN, THE IDOL OF THE YANCY STREET GANG?!!
ME, AFRAID??!
I DON'T LIKE THAT KINDA TALK, SQUIRT!
NOW JUST YOU WAIT THERE TILL I GET BACK! I GOTTA TALK THIS OVER WITH MY PARTNERS!
S-SURE, THING! I-I'LL -ULP- HANG AROUND!
8

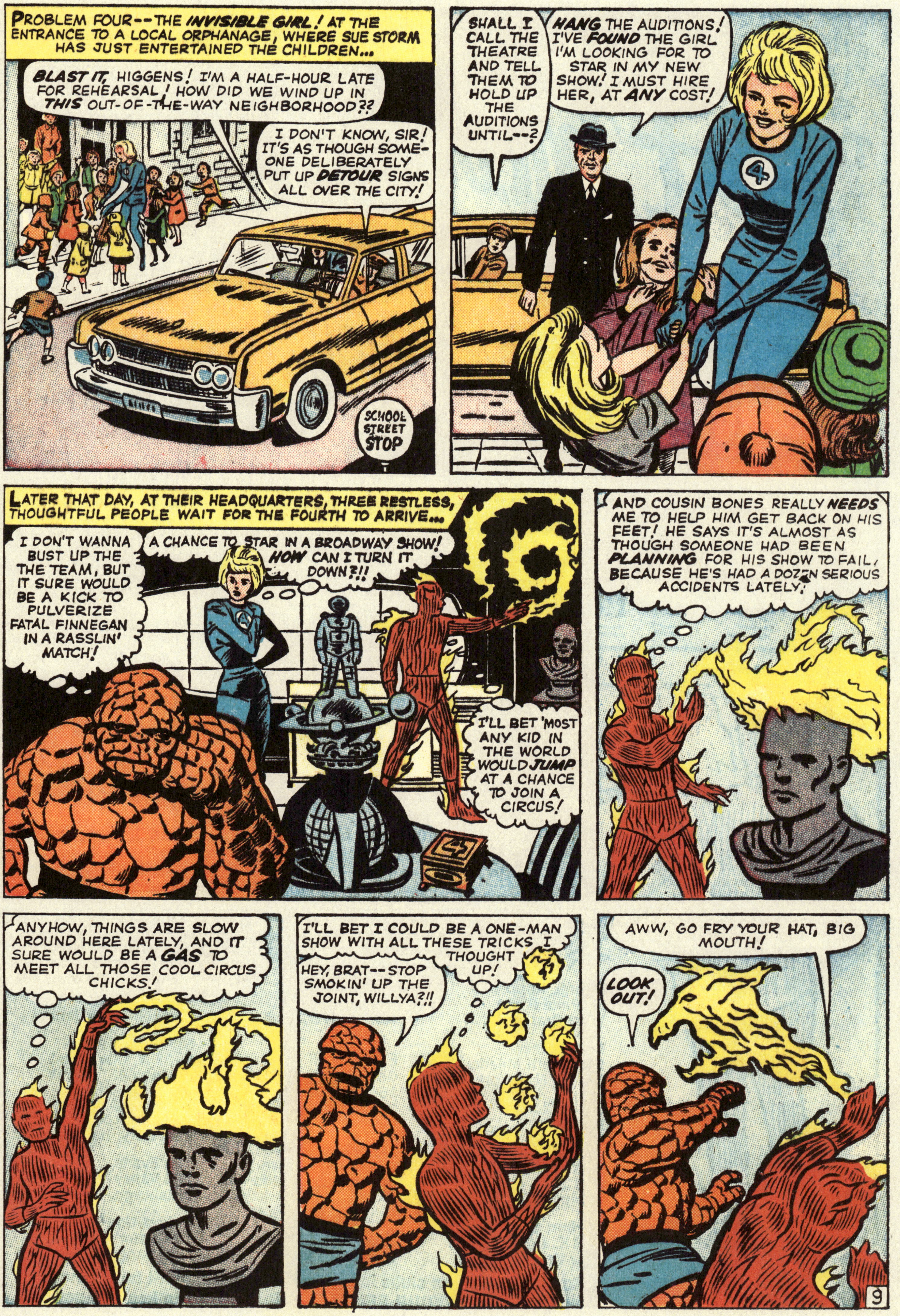
PROBLEM FOUR--THE INVISIBLE GIRL! AT THE ENTRANCE TO A LOCAL ORPHANAGE, WHERE SUE STORM HAS JUST ENTERTAINED THE CHILDREN...
BLAST IT, HIGGENS! I'M A HALF-HOUR LATE FOR REHEARSAL! HOW DID WE WIND UP IN THIS OUT-OF-THE-WAY NEIGHBORHOOD??
I DON'T KNOW, SIR! IT'S AS THOUGH SOME-ONE DELIBERATELY PUT UP DETOUR SIGNS ALL OVER THE CITY!
SCHOOL STREET STOP
SHALL I CALL THE THEATRE AND TELL THEM TO HOLD UP THE AUDITIONS UNTIL--?
HANG THE AUDITIONS! I'VE FOUND THE GIRL I'M LOOKING FOR TO STAR IN MY NEW SHOW! I MUST HIRE HER, AT ANY COST!
LATER THAT DAY, AT THEIR HEADQUARTERS, THREE RESTLESS, THOUGHTFUL PEOPLE WAIT FOR THE FOURTH TO ARRIVE...
I DON'T WANNA BUST UP THE THE TEAM, BUT IT SURE WOULD BE A KICK TO PULVERIZE FATAL FINNEGAN IN A RASSLIN' MATCH!
A CHANCE TO STAR IN A BROADWAY SHOW! HOW CAN I TURN IT DOWN?!!
I'LL BET 'MOST ANY KID IN THE WORLD WOULD JUMP AT A CHANCE TO JOIN A CIRCUS!
AND COUSIN BONES REALLY NEEDS ME TO HELP HIM GET BACK ON HIS FEET! HE SAYS IT'S ALMOST AS THOUGH SOMEONE HAD BEEN PLANNING FOR HIS SHOW TO FAIL, BECAUSE HE'S HAD A DOZEN SERIOUS ACCIDENTS LATELY!
ANYHOW, THINGS ARE SLOW AROUND HERE LATELY, AND IT SURE WOULD BE A GAS TO MEET ALL THOSE COOL CIRCUS CHICKS!
I'LL BET I COULD BE A ONE-MAN SHOW WITH ALL THESE TRICKS I THOUGHT UP!
HEY, BRAT--STOP SMOKIN' UP THE JOINT, WILLYA?!!
AWW, GO FRY YOUR HAT, BIG MOUTH!
LOOK OUT!
9

THAT DOES IT! I'M GONNA DOUSE THAT FLAME OF YOURS, AND THEN--
THING! TORCH! KNOCK IT OFF!
HECK, REED! THIS IS THE MOST FUN ANYONE'S HAD AROUND HERE FOR DAYS!
LET'S FACE IT, PAL! JOHNNY'S RIGHT! WE AINT CUT OUT FOR TWIDDLIN' OUR THUMBS! WE'RE ALL GETTIN' RESTLESS!
YES! PERHAPS WE ALL NEED A VACATION!
I WAS ABOUT TO SUGGEST THE SAME THING! MAYBE A TEMPORARY SEPARATION WOULD DO US ALL SOME GOOD!
THAT'S THE COOLEST! BUT WHAT ABOUT THOSE MOBSTERS HITTIN' NEW YORK, AND THE TROUBLE WE'RE SUPPOSED TO BE WATCHIN' FOR??
WE CAN ALWAYS RETURN TO HOME BASE IN A HURRY! I CAN BE REACHED AT GENERAL ELECTRONICS, IN NEW ENGLAND!
ME, I'LL BE TRAVELLIN' THRU THE SOUTH WITH THE BONES 'N BAILEY CIRCUS!
YOU'LL READ ABOUT ME IN THE PAPERS! I'M GONNA BE THE NEXT SENSATION OF THE GRUNT 'N GROAN CIRCUIT IN THE MIDWEST!
AND I'LL BE IN HOLLYWOOD, REHEARSING FOR MY VERY FIRST STARRING ROLE!
SIGH
AND SO, UNSUSPECTED BY THE FANTASTIC FOUR, ALL THE TINY DETAILS OF THE THINKER'S MASTER PLAN FALL NEATLY INTO PLACE! HE HAS WON THE FIRST ROUND OF A FIGHT WHICH THE COLORFUL QUARTET DOESN'T EVEN KNOW IT IS FIGHTING!
Y'KNOW SOMETHIN'? THIS IS THE FIRST TIME WE EVER BUSTED UP! IT'S A SPOOKY FEELIN'!
YOU'RE RIGHT, BEN!
AW, WE'LL GET TOGETHER AGAIN AFTER A WHILE!
AT LAST I CAN DRESS THE WAY I'VE ALWAYS WANTED TO!
NEVER THOUGHT I'D SAY THIS, SMALL FRY, BUT I'M GONNA MISS YOU!
SURE, YA BIG LUG! NOBODY ELSE WOULD PUT UP WITH YA! TAKE CARE OF YOURSELF, BIG FELLA!
FOR TWO CENTS I'D TRY TO GET 'EM TO CALL THE WHOLE THING OFF! NUTS! WHAT'S THE MATTER WITH ME! IT AINT THE END OF THE WORLD! EVERYBODY NEEDS A VACATION SOME TIME!
10

AND NOW, BACK TO THE MAN WHOSE METICULOUS PLANNING HAS BROUGHT ABOUT THE EVENTS YOU HAVE JUST WITNESSED! BACK TO --THE THINKER!
IT IS NOW EXACTLY THREE MINUTES AFTER FOUR! THEY SHOULD JUST BE LEAVING THEIR HEADQUARTERS AT THIS MOMENT!
OKAY, THINKER, LET'S SAY THEY ARE! SO WHAT GOOD DOES THAT DO US?
YEAH! WHAT'S OUR NEXT MOVE? HOW DO WE TAKE OVER THE CITY?
THE VERY FORCES OF NATURE HERSELF WILL HELP US! MY MACHINES HAVE CALCULATED THE COURSE OF AN APPROACHING METEOR, WHICH WILL STRIKE NEW YORK HARBOR IN EXACTLY FIFTEEN SECONDS!
I KNEW OF THIS IMPENDING EVENT WEEKS AGO, AND INCLUDED IT IN MY PLANS! IT WILL BE OUR SIGNAL TO STRIKE!
AT THE PRECISE SPLIT-SECOND PREDICTED BY THE THINKER, A HURTLING METEOR DOES INDEED PLUMMET INTO THE WATERS OUTSIDE OF NEW YORK'S LOWER BAY...
ALTHOUGH NO ONE IS INJURED, THE SHOCK OF IMPACT CAUSES A TEMPORARY PANIC AMONG THE POPULACE...
WHAT HAPPENED?? WHAT WAS THAT??!
MAYBE WE'RE BEING ATTACKED!! IT MUST BE WAR!
MINUTES LATER, AS THE SHOCK WEARS OFF, THE TRUTH IS LEARNED AND THE PANIC ENDS! BUT A NEW DANGER APPEARS! THE VIOLENT EARTH TREMOR HAS KNOCKED OUT ALL ELECTRIC POWER IN THE SPRAWLING CITY, AND CAUSED NUMEROUS SMALL FIRES AND EXPLOSIONS!
WOW! DID ONE LITTLE METEORITE DO ALL THAT??
LOOK! ALL THE STREET LIGHTS HAVE GONE OUT--AND THERE ARE FLAMES IN CENTRAL PARK!
IT'LL TAKE HOURS TO GET THINGS BACK TO NORMAL IN MIDTOWN NEW YORK!
AND, TAKING ADVANTAGE OF THE CONFUSION, THE THINKER AND HIS MEN INVADE THE NOW-DESERTED STRONGHOLD OF THE FANTASTIC FOUR!
YOU WERE RIGHT, THINKER! WITH THE ELECTRICITY KNOCKED OUT, NONE OF MR. FANTASTIC'S PROTECTIVE DEVICES ARE WORKIN'!
THIS IS THE ONLY TIME HIS HEADQUARTERS COULD BE BROKEN INTO, AND DUE TO MY FOOL-PROOF PLANNING, WE WERE ABLE TO CASH IN ON IT!
11

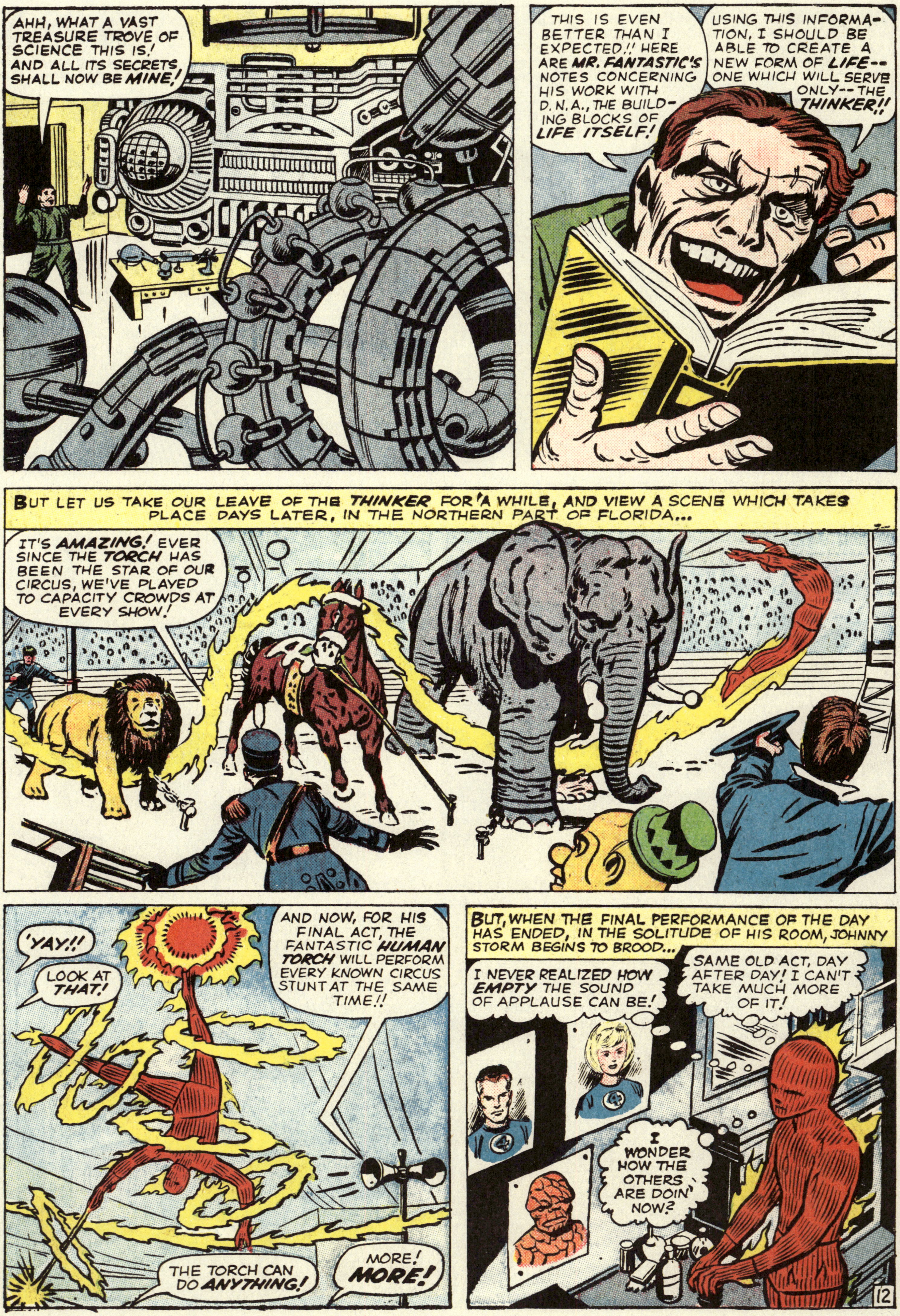
AHH, WHAT A VAST TREASURE TROVE OF SCIENCE THIS IS! AND ALL ITS SECRETS SHALL NOW BE MINE!
THIS IS EVEN BETTER THAN I EXPECTED!! HERE ARE MR. FANTASTIC'S NOTES CONCERNING HIS WORK WITH D.N.A., THE BUILDING BLOCKS OF LIFE ITSELF!
USING THIS INFORMATION, I SHOULD BE ABLE TO CREATE A NEW FORM OF LIFE -- ONE WHICH WILL SERVE ONLY -- THE THINKER!!
BUT LET US TAKE OUR LEAVE OF THE THINKER FOR A WHILE, AND VIEW A SCENE WHICH TAKES PLACE DAYS LATER, IN THE NORTHERN PART OF FLORIDA...
IT'S AMAZING! EVER SINCE THE TORCH HAS BEEN THE STAR OF OUR CIRCUS, WE'VE PLAYED TO CAPACITY CROWDS AT EVERY SHOW!
'YAY!!
LOOK AT THAT!
AND NOW, FOR HIS FINAL ACT, THE FANTASTIC HUMAN TORCH WILL PERFORM EVERY KNOWN CIRCUS STUNT AT THE SAME TIME!!
THE TORCH CAN DO ANYTHING!
MORE! MORE!
BUT, WHEN THE FINAL PERFORMANCE OF THE DAY HAS ENDED, IN THE SOLITUDE OF HIS ROOM, JOHNNY STORM BEGINS TO BROOD...
I NEVER REALIZED HOW EMPTY THE SOUND OF APPLAUSE CAN BE!
SAME OLD ACT, DAY AFTER DAY! I CAN'T TAKE MUCH MORE OF IT!
I WONDER HOW THE OTHERS ARE DOIN' NOW?
12

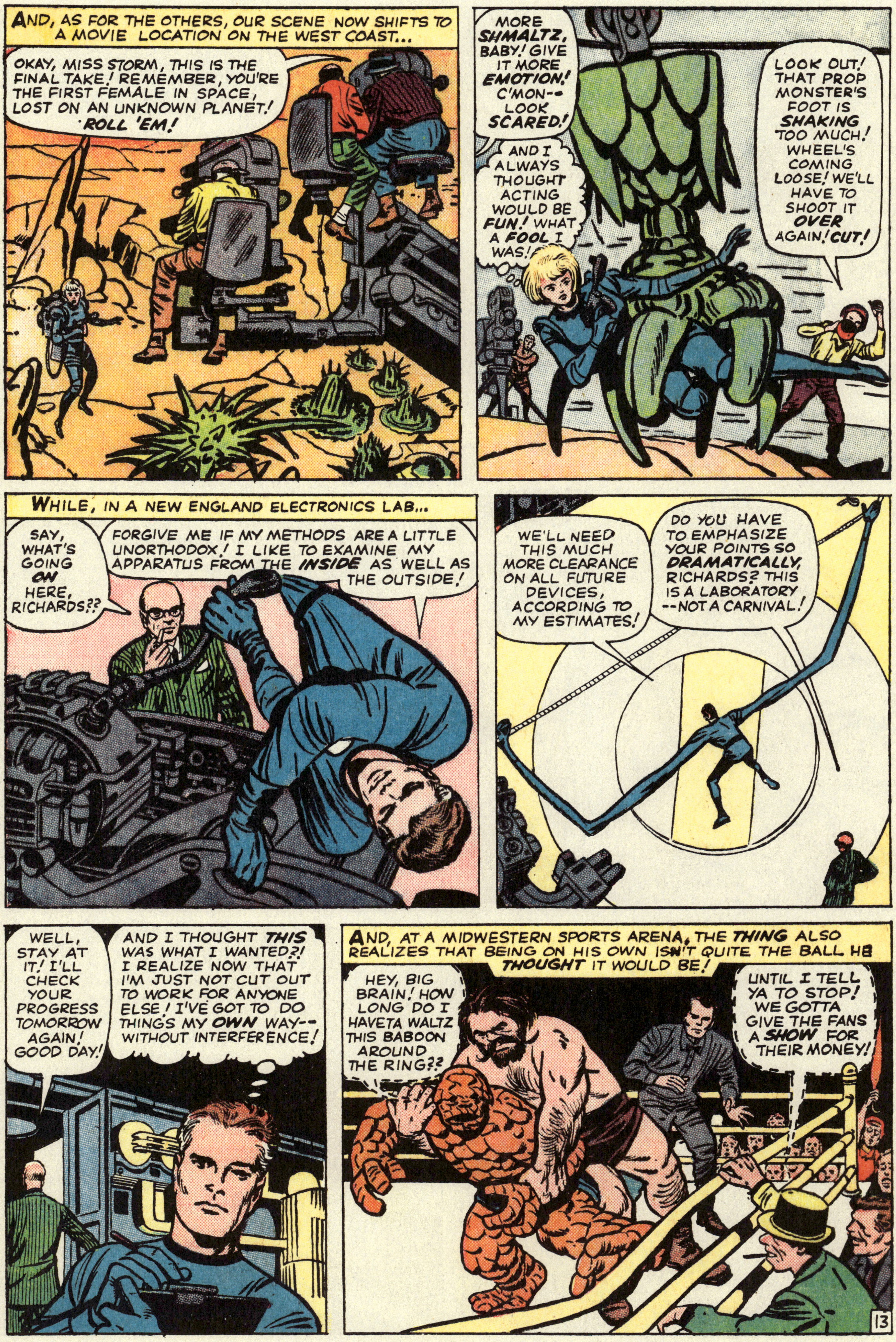
AND, AS FOR THE OTHERS, OUR SCENE NOW SHIFTS TO A MOVIE LOCATION ON THE WEST COAST...
OKAY, MISS STORM, THIS IS THE FINAL TAKE! REMEMBER, YOU'RE THE FIRST FEMALE IN SPACE, LOST ON AN UNKNOWN PLANET! ROLL 'EM!
MORE SHMALTZ, BABY! GIVE IT MORE EMOTION! C'MON-- LOOK SCARED!
AND I ALWAYS THOUGHT ACTING WOULD BE FUN! WHAT A FOOL I WAS!
LOOK OUT! THAT PROP MONSTER'S FOOT IS SHAKING TOO MUCH! WHEEL'S COMING LOOSE! WE'LL HAVE TO SHOOT IT OVER AGAIN! CUT!
WHILE, IN A NEW ENGLAND ELECTRONICS LAB...
SAY, WHAT'S GOING ON HERE, RICHARDS??
FORGIVE ME IF MY METHODS ARE A LITTLE UNORTHODOX! I LIKE TO EXAMINE MY APPARATUS FROM THE INSIDE AS WELL AS THE OUTSIDE!
WE'LL NEED THIS MUCH MORE CLEARANCE ON ALL FUTURE DEVICES, ACCORDING TO MY ESTIMATES!
DO YOU HAVE TO EMPHASIZE YOUR POINTS SO DRAMATICALLY, RICHARDS? THIS IS A LABORATORY --NOT A CARNIVAL!
WELL, STAY AT IT! I'LL CHECK YOUR PROGRESS TOMORROW AGAIN! GOOD DAY!
AND I THOUGHT THIS WAS WHAT I WANTED?! I REALIZE NOW THAT I'M JUST NOT CUT OUT TO WORK FOR ANYONE ELSE! I'VE GOT TO DO THINGS MY OWN WAY-- WITHOUT INTERFERENCE!
AND, AT A MIDWESTERN SPORTS ARENA, THE THING ALSO REALIZES THAT BEING ON HIS OWN ISN'T QUITE THE BALL HE THOUGHT IT WOULD BE!
HEY, BIG BRAIN! HOW LONG DO I HAVETA WALTZ THIS BABOON AROUND THE RING??
UNTIL I TELL YA TO STOP! WE GOTTA GIVE THE FANS A SHOW FOR THEIR MONEY!
13

HEY, UGLY, LOOK AT THAT BLONDE TOOTSIE IN THE FRONT ROW! AFTER I'M THRU WITH YOU UP HERE, I'M GONNA GO AND GET ME A DATE WITH THAT DOLL! VA VA VOOM!
YOU CRUMMY CREEP! THAT'S ALICIA! THAT'S MY GIRL YOU'RE TALKIN' ABOUT!
I'LL SHOW YA WHO'S GONNA DATE ALICIA!
HEY--STOP! CUT IT OUT! THIS AINT IN THE SCRIPT! HALLLP!
IF YOU STILL WANNA MEET ALICIA, AFTER YOU COME BACK FROM MY BOOMERANG THROW, THEN WE'LL TALK IT OVER!
ZOOOOOM!
HERE HE COMES!
NOW TO GIVE 'IM A NICE, WARM RECEPTION!
YOU CAN'T DO THIS TO ME! I DEMAND A RE-MATCH! I-I-GLOPP...
C'MON, KID! WE'RE GOIN' HOME! IF THAT'S WHAT WRESTLIN' IS, YOU CAN HAVE IT! ME, I'LL STICK TO TIDDLYWINKS!
DO NOT OPEN TILL XMAS
AND SO, THE COLORFUL QUARTET, AS THOUGH BY PREARRANGED SIGNAL, ALL RETURN TO THEIR HOME BASE, THE BUSTLING METROPOLIS OF NEW YORK, AT THE SAME TIME...
SO LONG, ALICIA! SEE YOU LATER!
BOY, AM I GLAD TO SEE YOU ALL AGAIN--EVEN YOU, BEN!
AND, AS THEY REACH THE MIGHTY BAXTER BUILDING...
I'VE GOT TO ADMIT IT FEELS WONDERFUL TO BE BACK IN HARNESS! IF YOU EVER HEAR ME KNOCK THESE UNIFORMS AGAIN, JUST--
HEY! LOOK! WHA-WHAT'S HAPPENED TO OUR HEADQUARTERS??!
THE WHOLE BUILDING HAS TURNED INTO A GIGANTIC CRYSTAL! BUT--HOW?? WHAT DOES IT MEAN??
14

IT'S INCREDIBLE! THE VERY ELEMENTS OF THE BUILDING THEMSELVES HAVE BEEN TRANSMUTED! THIS IS A NEW, UNKNOWN SUBSTANCE!
I CAN'T EVEN POKE A HOLE THRU IT! A THING LIKE THAT CAN GIVE A GUY A COMPLEX!
IT'S HEAT RESIS-TANT, TOO!
THIS MEANS WE'RE LOCKED OUT OF OUR OWN HEAD-QUARTERS!
I'LL PROBE FOR CRACKS --PERHAPS THERE'S A WEAK SPOT SOMEWHERE!
PHOOY! THAT'S TOO SLOW! MEBBE I CAN JUST DIG OUR WAY IN! I'LL BE THRU THIS CONCRETE SIDEWALK IN NO TIME!
THERE'S EVEN MORE TO THIS THAN MEETS THE EYE! LOOK AT ALL THE PASSERS-BY!
NO ONE SEEMS TO NOTICE WHAT'S HAPPENED TO THE BUILDING! THEY DON'T EVEN SEEM TO SEE IT!
SUDDENLY, THE FACE OF THE THINKER APPEARS, PROJECTED RIGHT THRU THE STRANGE, SHIMMERING CRYSTAL WALL!
NATURALLY NO ONE NOTICES! I HAVE AN ELECTRONIC HYPNO-RAY FIELD AROUND THIS ENTIRE BUILD-ING! I'VE BEEN EXPECTING YOU--FOR I AM THE THINKER!
THE THINKER?
I'VE MODIFIED MY HYPNO-RAY SO THAT ONLY YOU FOUR ARE AWARE OF MY PRESENCE! FOR YOU ARE TO BE MY GREATEST CONQUEST! ONCE I HAVE DE-FEATED THE FANTASTIC FOUR, NO POWER ON EARTH CAN STAND IN MY WAY!
GOOD GRIEF! ANOTHER POWER-MAD GENIUS FOR US TO CONTEND WITH!
TRUE! BUT I HAVE ONE ADVANTAGE! I HAVE THE USE OF MR. FANTASTIC'S SCIENTIFIC RE-SEARCH--RESEARCH WHICH WILL NOW BE TURNED AGAINST YOU!
LOOK! HE FADED AWAY! AND HE LEFT AN OPENING IN THE CRYSTAL FOR US TO ENTER THRU!
HE MEANS IT! HE WANTS US TO GET INSIDE AND FIGHT HIM! HE ACTUALLY THINKS HE CAN BEAT US!
WELL--WHAT ARE WE WAITIN' FOR??
I'LL JUST TOSS A SPEEDY BLUE-FLAME FIRE-BALL IN THERE, TO MAKE SURE THERE AREN'T ANY LITTLE TRAPS WAIT-ING FOR US!
15

GOOD THING YOU DID THAT, JOHNNY! HE HAD AN EXPLOSIVE DEVICE RIGGED UP!
WELL, IT'S NOT GONNA BOTHER US ANY MORE! SO LET'S GO AND GIVE THAT THINKER SOMETHIN' TO REALLY THINK ABOUT!
TORCHY, OL' PAL, YOU'RE BEGINNIN' TO SOUND LIKE ME! AND THAT'S PRETTY GOOD!
YOU KIDDIN'? IF I BELIEVED YOU, I'D NEVER OPEN MY MOUTH AGAIN!
WATCH YOURSELVES! NO TELLING WHAT LITTLE SURPRISES THE THINKER HAS FOR US!
HERE THEY COME! GET 'EM!
VIBRA-GUNS! MY OWN INVENTION! THE THINKER MUST HAVE FOUND THEM IN OUR ARSENAL!
TAKE COVER! TRY TO GET OUT OF RANGE! THE VIBRA-SOUND VIBRATIONS WILL SAP ALL THE STRENGTH FROM YOU UNTIL THEY RUN OUT OF POWER!
OH, REED! WE--WE CAN'T LET HIM BEAT US WITH YOUR OWN WEAPONS!
HAVE NO FEAR, BABY-- THE THING IS HERE! THIS'LL STOP THOSE RAYS!
HE-HE'S PULLIN' THOSE WALLS TOGETHER AS IF THEY'RE LACE CURTAINS!
I DON'T WANT NO PART OF HIM! LEMME OUT OF HERE!
THEY CAN'T GET THRU STEEL-- AND THAT'S JUST WHAT THESE SPECIAL WALLS ARE MADE OF!
IT IS NOW 3:43 P.M.! YOU HAVE PASSED YOUR FIRST TEST, AS I EXPECTED YOU WOULD! BUT YOU STILL HAVE TO GET TO THE 35TH FLOOR!
JUST SIT TIGHT, BROTHER! WE'LL GET THERE--YOU CAN BET ON IT!
HE DIDN'T THINK HE COULD STOP US BY SHUTTIN' OFF THE ELEVATORS, DID HE?
TAKE IT EASY, BEN! THAT'S MY SKIN YOU'RE HANGING ONTO!
COMPLAINTS! ALL I EVER GET IS COMPLAINTS!
REED! THE THINKER HAS HURLED SOME GAS CYLINDERS AT US!
IT'S NOT ORDINARY GAS, SUE! I CAN TELL BY THE ODOR--IT'S A FORMULA OF MY OWN!
WELL, DON'T KEEP US IN THE DARK, PARTNER! WHAT DOES IT DO??
16

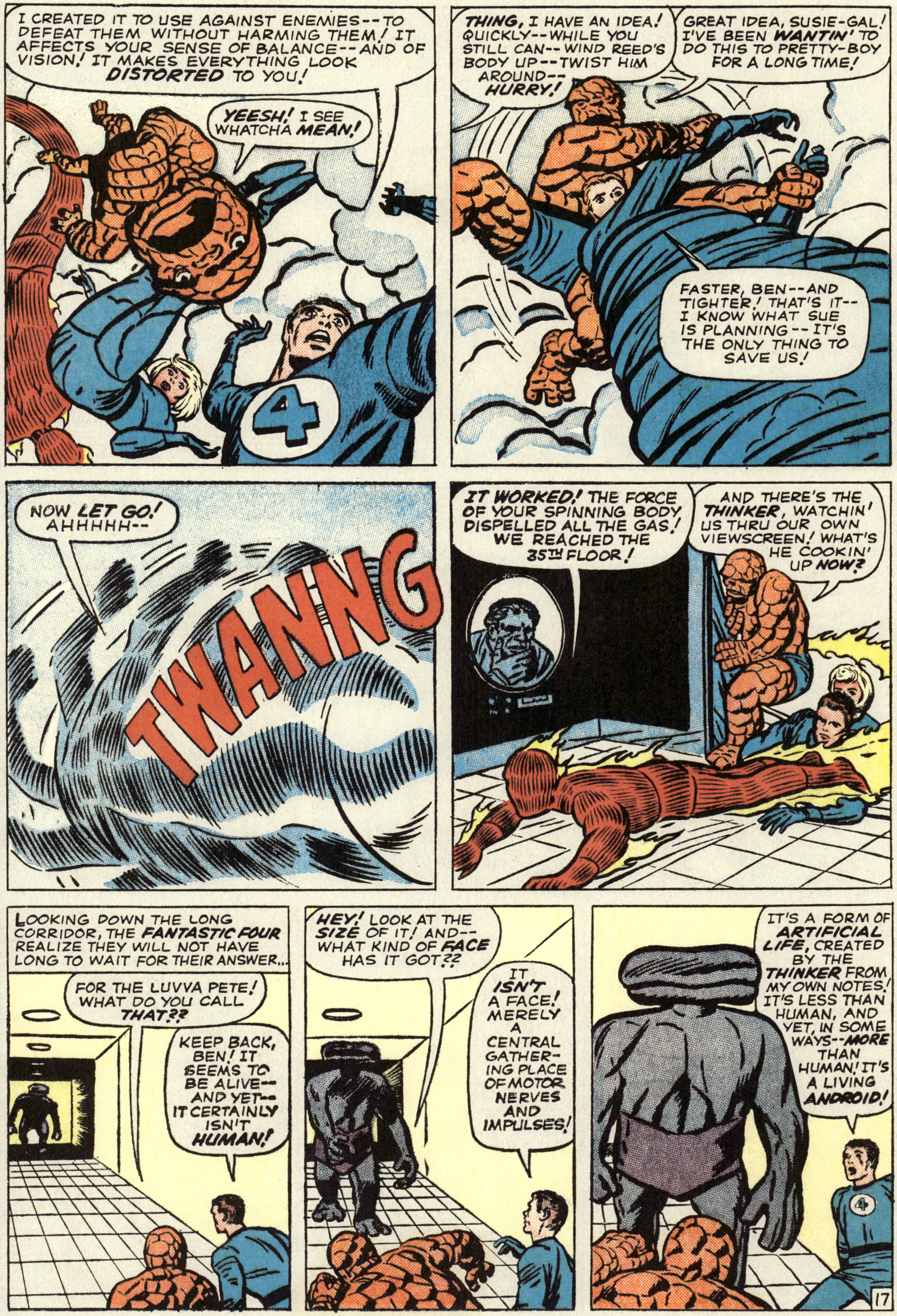

I CREATED IT TO USE AGAINST ENEMIES--TO DEFEAT THEM WITHOUT HARMING THEM! IT AFFECTS YOUR SENSE OF BALANCE--AND OF VISION! IT MAKES EVERYTHING LOOK DISTORTED TO YOU!
YEESH! I SEE WHATCHA MEAN!
THING, I HAVE AN IDEA! QUICKLY--WHILE YOU STILL CAN--WIND REED'S BODY UP--TWIST HIM AROUND--HURRY!
GREAT IDEA, SUSIE-GAL! I'VE BEEN WANTIN' TO DO THIS TO PRETTY-BOY FOR A LONG TIME!
FASTER, BEN--AND TIGHTER! THAT'S IT--I KNOW WHAT SUE IS PLANNING--IT'S THE ONLY THING TO SAVE US!
NOW LET GO! AHHHHH--
TWANNG
IT WORKED! THE FORCE OF YOUR SPINNING BODY DISPELLED ALL THE GAS! WE REACHED THE 35TH FLOOR!
AND THERE'S THE THINKER, WATCHIN' US THRU OUR OWN VIEWSCREEN! WHAT'S HE COOKIN' UP NOW?
LOOKING DOWN THE LONG CORRIDOR, THE FANTASTIC FOUR REALIZE THEY WILL NOT HAVE LONG TO WAIT FOR THEIR ANSWER...
FOR THE LUVVA PETE! WHAT DO YOU CALL THAT??
KEEP BACK, BEN! IT SEEMS TO BE ALIVE--AND YET--IT CERTAINLY ISN'T HUMAN!
HEY! LOOK AT THE SIZE OF IT! AND--WHAT KIND OF FACE HAS IT GOT??
IT ISN'T A FACE! MERELY A CENTRAL GATHERING PLACE OF MOTOR NERVES AND IMPULSES!
IT'S A FORM OF ARTIFICIAL LIFE, CREATED BY THE THINKER FROM MY OWN NOTES! IT'S LESS THAN HUMAN, AND YET, IN SOME WAYS--MORE THAN HUMAN! IT'S A LIVING ANDROID!
17

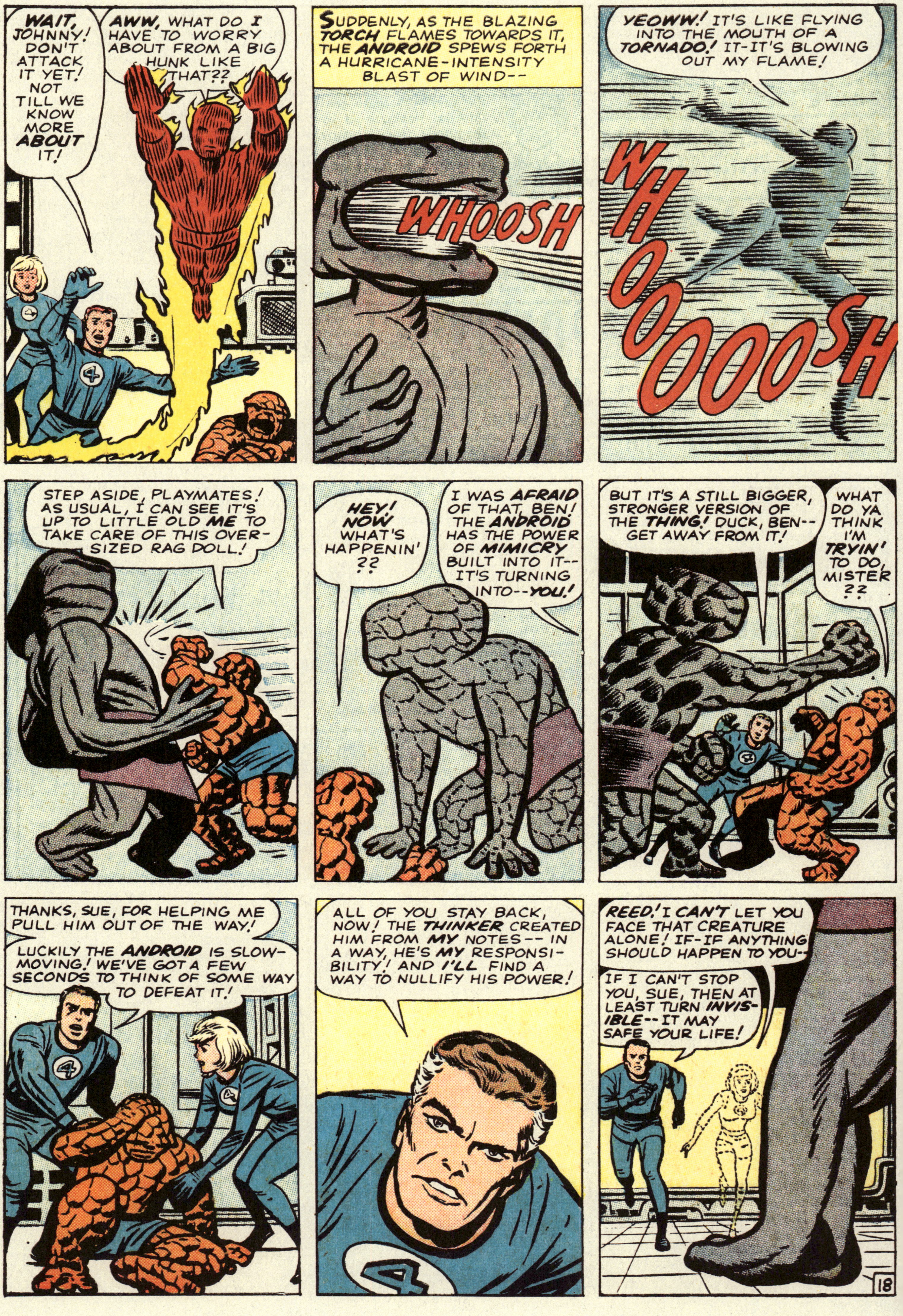

WAIT, JOHNNY! DON'T ATTACK IT YET! NOT TILL WE KNOW MORE ABOUT IT!
AWW, WHAT DO I HAVE TO WORRY ABOUT FROM A BIG HUNK LIKE THAT??
SUDDENLY, AS THE BLAZING TORCH FLAMES TOWARDS IT, THE ANDROID SPEWS FORTH A HURRICANE-INTENSITY BLAST OF WIND--
WHOOSH
YEOWW! IT'S LIKE FLYING INTO THE MOUTH OF A TORNADO! IT-IT'S BLOWING OUT MY FLAME!
WHOOOOOSH
STEP ASIDE, PLAYMATES! AS USUAL, I CAN SEE IT'S UP TO LITTLE OLD ME TO TAKE CARE OF THIS OVER-SIZED RAG DOLL!
HEY! NOW WHAT'S HAPPENIN' ??
I WAS AFRAID OF THAT, BEN! THE ANDROID HAS THE POWER OF MIMICRY BUILT INTO IT-- IT'S TURNING INTO--YOU!
BUT IT'S A STILL BIGGER, STRONGER VERSION OF THE THING! DUCK, BEN-- GET AWAY FROM IT!
WHAT DO YA THINK I'M TRYIN' TO DO, MISTER ??
THANKS, SUE, FOR HELPING ME PULL HIM OUT OF THE WAY!
LUCKILY THE ANDROID IS SLOW-MOVING! WE'VE GOT A FEW SECONDS TO THINK OF SOME WAY TO DEFEAT IT!
ALL OF YOU STAY BACK, NOW! THE THINKER CREATED HIM FROM MY NOTES-- IN A WAY, HE'S MY RESPONSIBILITY! AND I'LL FIND A WAY TO NULLIFY HIS POWER!
REED! I CAN'T LET YOU FACE THAT CREATURE ALONE! IF-IF ANYTHING SHOULD HAPPEN TO YOU--
IF I CAN'T STOP YOU, SUE, THEN AT LEAST TURN INVISIBLE-- IT MAY SAFE YOUR LIFE!
18

I'LL TRY TO KEEP HIM IMMOBILE AS LONG AS I CAN!
IF I REMEMBER MY NOTES CORRECTLY, HIS MOTOR NERVE TERMINAL IS ON HIS RIGHT SIDE, UNDER HIS ARM! YOU'VE GOT TO PRESS IT, SUE-- YOU MUSTN'T MISS! C-CAN'T HOLD HIM MUCH LONGER!
YOU DID IT, SUE! YOUR SENSITIVE TOUCH KNOCKED OUT THE ANDROID!
LUCKY FOR US THAT SUE WAS HERE! MY FINGERS ARE TOO BLUNT, YOU COULDN'T FREE YOURS LONG ENOUGH, AND THE ANDROID WOULDA SEEN THE TORCH AND KICKED 'IM AWAY!
IT IS ONE MINUTE TO FOUR! I CALCULATED THAT YOU WOULD BE HERE AT THIS SECOND IF YOU DEFEATED THE ANDROID! SO FAR, MY DEDUCTIONS HAVE BEEN PERFECT!
THAT CHARACTER SEEMS TO THINK THIS IS ONE BIG GAME HE'S PLAYIN'!!
WE'VE GOT YOUR MEN TRAPPED BEHIND A WALL OF STEEL DOWNSTAIRS, AND NOW WE'RE GONNA PUT THE KIBOSH ON YOU, TOO!
DID YOU EXPECT ME TO BE UNPREPARED FOR YOUR FLAME?? THE CHEMICAL IN THIS GUN, WHICH I TOOK FROM MR. FANTASTIC'S CABINET, WILL DOUSE YOUR FLAME--FOREVER!
YOU CALL YOURSELF THE THINKER! HUH--YOU'RE NOT SO MUCH! ALL YOUR WEAPONS AND POWERS ARE STOLEN FROM MR. FANTASTIC!
FOOL! ONLY SOMEONE AS BRILLIANT AS I WOULD HAVE BEEN ABLE TO OUTSMART YOUR LEADER!! WHO DO YOU THINK IT WAS WHO ARRANGED FOR ALL OF YOU TO LEAVE NEW YORK?
IT WAS ME! I ARRANGED EVERYTHING DOWN TO THE LAST DETAIL! AND NOW, AT LAST, I AM ARRANGING YOUR FINISH!
I HAVE A SEPARATE ANTI-MATTER SHELL ZEROED IN ON EACH OF YOU--AGAIN, THANKS TO MR. FANTASTIC WHO INVENTED THIS POTENT WEAPON!
AND SO, AT THIS SECOND, AT EXACTLY THE STROKE OF FOUR, JUST AS I HAD PLANNED, THE FANTASTIC FOUR WILL MEET THEIR--
MY GUN! THE SHELLS! WHA-WHAT HAS HAPPENED??
BZZZZZZZZT!
19

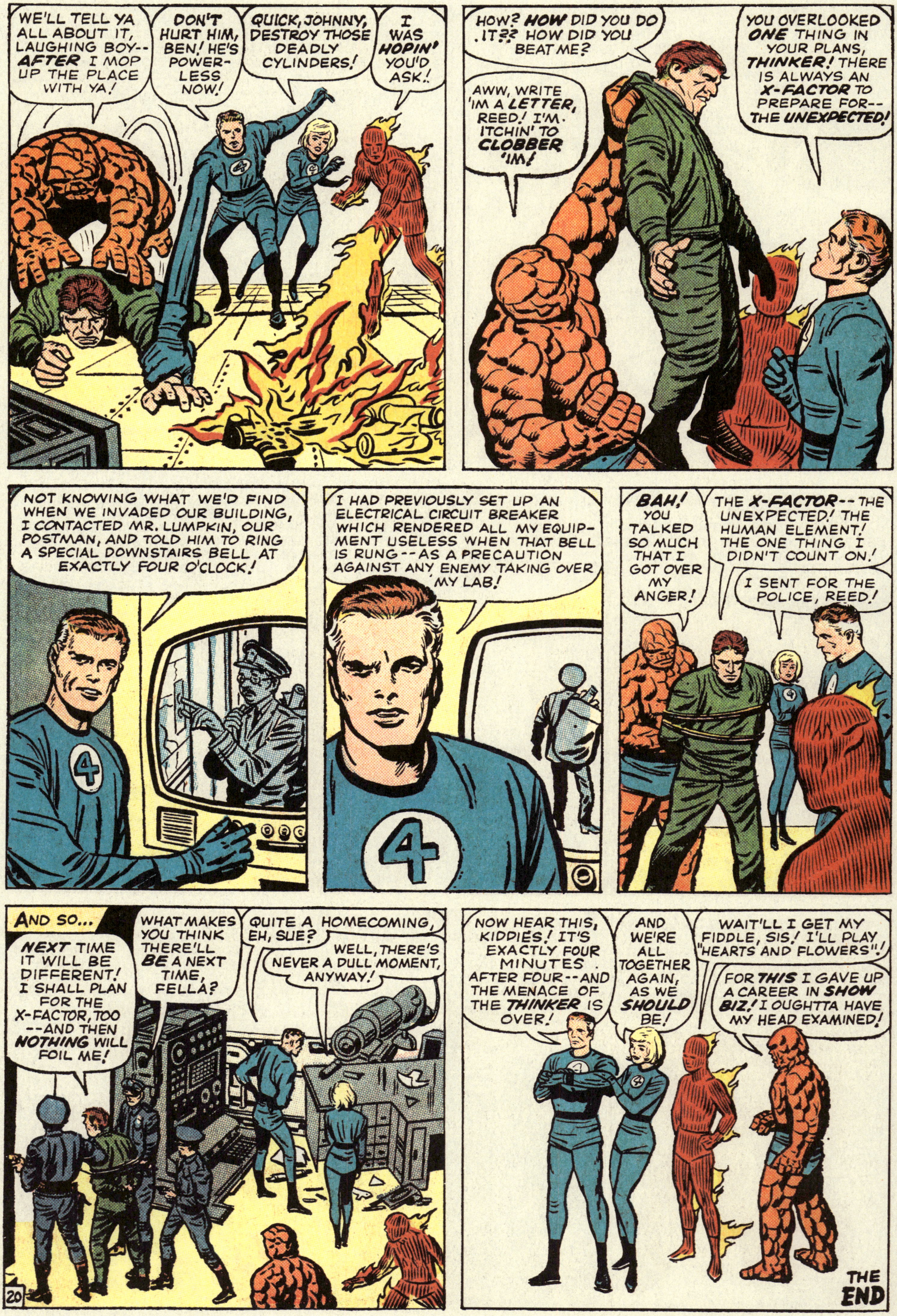

WE'LL TELL YA ALL ABOUT IT, LAUGHING BOY-- AFTER I MOP UP THE PLACE WITH YA!
DON'T HURT HIM, BEN! HE'S POWER-LESS NOW!
QUICK, JOHNNY, DESTROY THOSE DEADLY CYLINDERS!
I WAS HOPIN' YOU'D ASK!
HOW? HOW DID YOU DO IT?? HOW DID YOU BEAT ME?
AWW, WRITE 'IM A LETTER, REED! I'M ITCHIN' TO CLOBBER 'IM!
YOU OVERLOOKED ONE THING IN YOUR PLANS, THINKER! THERE IS ALWAYS AN X-FACTOR TO PREPARE FOR-- THE UNEXPECTED!
NOT KNOWING WHAT WE'D FIND WHEN WE INVADED OUR BUILDING, I CONTACTED MR. LUMPKIN, OUR POSTMAN, AND TOLD HIM TO RING A SPECIAL DOWNSTAIRS BELL AT EXACTLY FOUR O'CLOCK!
I HAD PREVIOUSLY SET UP AN ELECTRICAL CIRCUIT BREAKER WHICH RENDERED ALL MY EQUIP-MENT USELESS WHEN THAT BELL IS RUNG--AS A PRECAUTION AGAINST ANY ENEMY TAKING OVER MY LAB!
BAH! YOU TALKED SO MUCH THAT I GOT OVER MY ANGER!
THE X-FACTOR--THE UNEXPECTED! THE HUMAN ELEMENT! THE ONE THING I DIDN'T COUNT ON!
I SENT FOR THE POLICE, REED!
AND SO...
NEXT TIME IT WILL BE DIFFERENT! I SHALL PLAN FOR THE X-FACTOR, TOO --AND THEN NOTHING WILL FOIL ME!
WHAT MAKES YOU THINK THERE'LL BE A NEXT TIME, FELLA?
QUITE A HOMECOMING, EH, SUE?
WELL, THERE'S NEVER A DULL MOMENT, ANYWAY!
20
NOW HEAR THIS, KIDDIES! IT'S EXACTLY FOUR MINUTES AFTER FOUR--AND THE MENACE OF THE THINKER IS OVER!
AND WE'RE ALL TOGETHER AGAIN, AS WE SHOULD BE!
WAIT'LL I GET MY FIDDLE, SIS! I'LL PLAY "HEARTS AND FLOWERS"!
FOR THIS I GAVE UP A CAREER IN SHOW BIZ! I OUGHTTA HAVE MY HEAD EXAMINED!
THE END

THE FANTASTIC FOUR
PIN-UP Page
Sincerely,
Ben, Reed,
Sue, & Johnny-
-& Stan & JACK

SGT. FURY AND HIS HOWLING COMMANDOS
1 MAY
MARVEL COMICS GROUP 12¢
THINK YOU'VE READ WAR STORIES BEFORE? MISTER, WAIT TILL YOU SEE WHAT'S IN STORE FOR YOU HERE! IT'S ONLY THE GREATEST!
KEEP MOVIN', YOU LUNKHEADS!! NOBODY LIVES FOREVER! SO GIT THE LEAD OUT AND FOLLOW ME! WE GOT US A WAR TO WIN!
"SEVEN AGAINST THE NAZIS!"
ANOTHER BIG ONE FROM THE TALENTED TEAM THAT BRINGS YOU THE FAMOUS "FANTASTIC FOUR"
ACTION in the FANTASTIC FOUR STYLE
ON SALE NOW!!
ANOTHER WINNER FROM THE MARVEL COMIC GROUP

DON'T MISS
THE RETURN OF
DR. DOOM
IN THE NEXT GREATER-THAN-EVER ISSUE OF
FANTASTIC FOUR
RESERVE YOUR COPY TODAY!!

Address YOUR letters to:
LEE and KIRBY
FANTASTIC FOUR
THIRD FLOOR
655 MADISON AVE.
NEW YORK 21, N. Y.

FANTASTIC FAN PAGE 4

Dear Stan and Jack:

Thanks for 'A Visit with the Fantastic Four' in issue 11. It answered many of my questions about the FF's past. There is only one thing I don't understand: who is Sub-Mariner? Mr. Fantastic said that only the shadow of Sub-Mariner stood between him and the Invisible Girl. This doesn't make much sense when you don't know who Sub-Mariner *is*. But even without knowing the identity of Sub-Mariner, I think you've got the best of all the super-hero mags on sale.

Mary Hoffmann
858 11th St.
Santa Monica, California

"WHO IS SUB-MARINER?"!!! That's like saying "Who is Peter Pan?" (And sure enough, some wise-guy's gonna write to us asking: "Who IS Peter Pan?") Just keep reading the F.F., Mary, and sooner or later we have a hunch you'll be finding out quite a lot about ol' Subby!

Dear Stan and Jack:

As I sit here at my desk writing this letter, I find it hard to think up words that would satisfy the means of praising you. Which brings me to say that I have seen such magazines as *Journey Into Mystery, Strange Tales, Tales to Astonish,* and so forth turned from fantasy magazines into wonderful high quality super-hero comic books which, at the present, are contributing marvelously to the wonderful world of the comic book. Your new characters are about the best there ever were. *Amazing Fantasy,* now featuring the Spider-Man, is on its way to "fame and fortune" with this number one super-hero. Everything about him is terrific, especially his red and black costume which is magnificent for his type of character. As for the *Fantastic Four,* they're just-well, you might say, utterly fantastic! I could go into quite a bit of detail on my likes and dislikes concerning all of your characters, but this letter has only been a warm-hearted thank-you to the many creators behind the scenes of today's most action-packed comics.

Ronn Goff
729 Encanto Drive
Calexico, California

Ronn, let us take this opportunity to congratulate you on your good taste, judgment, and critical ability! Believe it or not, we agree with you!

Dear Stan and Jack:

In FF #9, the Thing is struck by a bolt of lightning during a thunderstorm, and is transformed into Ben Grimm, his human form (in other words, Thing is not human). So how, with no explanation, does he turn up in the next scene as Thing again? By the way, how does he manage to *waddle*, let alone walk, in his bulky body. Does Mr. Fantastic have an elastic limit? That is, will he always retain his original shape, no matter how far he is stretched? Can he be torn? Now, last question: Does the Torch ever perspire?

Reynolds M. Morris
Bellevue, Nebraska

Aw, come on, R.M.M., we don't go around asking personal questions about YOU! As for the THING, his big problem always has been (since his first contact with cosmic rays) that he cannot maintain his human form for very long. As for walking in his bulky body, he'd look even sillier SKIPPING all over the place. Yes, MR. FANTASTIC does have a stretchable limit, and we'll discuss it in greater detail in a future issue. As for the TORCH perspiring, we haven't got the nerve to ask him!

Dear Stan and Jack:

FF #12 was great! Of all of Stan's masterpieces, this was the classic of the year. The action shots were marvelous! Which shows that Jack's art is ever improving (is that possible?). I'm glad you dropped the feature page. To me it was always in the way, and having 23 pg. stories and a two-page letter column is worth having the feature page dropped (I'm sure all fans will agree) any day! The ending (where Reed and Dr. Banner were talking) was great!!! More of the Hulk and the Thing!!!

Michael "Mickey" Martin
1620 Deerwood Dr.
West Sacramento, California

Now we're embarrassed! We'll be bringing back the feature page from time to time — but how can we explain it to Mickey?

Dear Stan and Jack:

I have just finished reading FF #12, and all I can say is WOW! I've been wanting to see the Hulk meet the Thing ever since you started publishing these two characters. Having read the mag, I natch read the letter column. As for F. Bronson, he can go to *!!*- for all I care. Why, the Thing is your best character. Underneath that gruff exterior beats a heart of gold. I also agree with Steve Utley. Besides, I think that the relationship between Torch and Thing is improving. Well, thanks for listening.

Fred Gibbons
608 E. 6th Street
Mt. Vernon, Indiana

You're welcome, Freddy-boy! Thanks for writing!

Dear Stan and Jack:

Ordinarily I enjoy your scripts and find them remarkably fresh and original for a comic book; however, you need to do quite a bit more character development than was done in 'A Visit with the Fantastic Four' in issue #11. It is altogether unbelievable that characters of the complexity of the 1962 fantastic group should have emerged from the stereotypes you portrayed. Granted, you were being quite brief, but even so, couldn't Ben Grimm have possessed more than muscles and bravura? And Reed Richards would be more plausible if he were not intelligence personified. Can't they be more human beings, and less mere foils to each other? There is also one question in my mind regarding the story per se: how is it possible that one man could have enough money to build a starship when all authorities assure us that only a nation could afford it? Finally, isn't it slightly ridiculous for even a wealthy scientist-to-be to smoke a pipe at 17 or 18?

Ginger Church
#2562 IWU
Denton, Texas

You sure can't please everybody! Almost every one of the hundreds of letters we received were wildly enthusiastic about "A Visit With The FANTASTIC FOUR" — except Ginger's! But the thing we really got a kick out of was Ginger's comment about Reed smoking a pipe at the age of 17 or 18. It was only because he couldn't find his bubble gum, honey!

CONTINUED—

Dear Stan and Jack:

Good job! I'm talking about the *Fantastic Four* #11 featuring the 'Impossible Man.' It was one of the wildest, wackiest, and probably the worst story you have printed since issue #2. Conflicting statements? I think not. For several months your stories have been getting better and better. Each month we have been wondering, "Can they do it again?" "Get an even better tale next time?" Obviously you couldn't keep it up forever. So with this one issue all the tension is released. 'A Visit With the Fantastic Four' gave us many new facts about the characters—very good. 'The Impossible Man' by itself was not worthy of being printed; it's too off-beat. But coming behind the great stories you have published month after month, it was perfect. Now I'm calm again and waiting to get back on the track with #12.

Roger Mann
Minneapolis, Minnesota

Boy! Talk about a left-handed compliment! Well, anyway, as long as we're still friends, Rog. . .

Dear Stan and Jack:

Why does the Thing want to be normal again? As the Thing he is a hero, but as Ben Grimm he is just a test pilot. I know that being a test pilot must be exciting, but as the Thing he must have even more exciting adventures.

Ricky Phillips
1107 South Kiger
Independence, Missouri

We never thought of it that way, Ricky! Wonder how the rest of our readers feel? Would you rather remain as THE THING, or Ben Grimm?

Dear Stan and Jack:

Latest issue of FF (#11) one of the best yet. It truly is an "off-beat collectors' item isue," as the cover blurb claims. One thing I liked on the cover was the drawing of the heads of the Fantastic Four. Perfect! Might I suggest that they be added to the masthead permanently, Mr. Fantastic and the Thing on the left, and Human Torch and Invisible Girl on the right. The Thing continues to be, to me, the best of the Fantastic Four, and one of my all-time comic-book favorites, though I rather dislike the idea of a serum which occasionally turns him back to Ben Grimm. I especially liked the "Visit with the Fantastic Four" feature and, with thousands of others, I'm sure, wait for more. Best parts: first, the answer to fans who don't like the Invisible Girl ("Go see lady wrestlers!") although I feel myself that she ought to suddenly obtain the power to walk through objects as well; and second, but hardly less, the part where the Thing ruined his dumbbell in anger at the Yancy Street Gang. The Yancy Street Gang, with this issue, joins Pete's mother-in-law on the "September Bride" television program as one of the great "unseen" characters of all time. I hope you do not under any circumstances at any time yield to the temptation to show any of them – let them remain nefariously in the background to annoy the Thing for reasons left obscure. Please? "The Impossible Man" was a great yarn, too, reminding me a little (but not enough to spoil it for me by any means) of the science-fiction novel, *Martians Go Home*, of a few years ago. I hope he *does* return to earth sometime, this time *not* to be driven away by ignoring so that the Four must think up a new stunt. Or *could* they? Personally, I'd like an issue in which he decides to annoy earth's crimefighters, including the Four, Ant-Man, Thor, Spiderman (Perhaps), and maybe even the Hulk and Namor for good measure. As to your letter column, I would *love* to see the Four on T.V., but I realize that has about as large a chance as the proverbial snowball. Handled well, I think adults would really dig it, besides just us comic-book-loving souls. The Thing, in particular, has a real appeal, especially now that he's abandoned his boots.

Roy Thomas
307 Greensferry Rd.
Jackson, Mo.

Thanks for the comments, Roy. Glad we don't pay for these letters by the word.

Dear Stan and Jack:

I am not going off half-cocked and this is not a crank letter, however, I am going to try to belittle your characters for a reason that will be unmistakable later. Now to go through your complete list of heros in the order of my reading them. First the Fantastic Four will be my object. What good would Mr. Fantastic be if all he could find to chase were petty hold-up men and purse snatchers? Why should he exert himself by stopping their getaways??? Why should the Thing wear himself out with juvenile delinquents?? Hardly any reason. Who would like the Human Torch if all he did was melt down crooks' getaway cars? Very few. If the Invisible girl only followed crooks to their hideouts and then called the cops, she wouldn't have many fans, would she? If the Hulk hadn't armies and spies to fight, no fans, right? Thor's smashing in walls for a police raid would result in extinction. What else? Spiderman catching falling kids in his web wouldn't last too long, huh? Even the Ant-Man replacing wire taps—can you enjoy that? Forget it. So, instead of "Super-heros can do anything," your motto seems to be, "Super-heros are only as good as their villains." Just keep up the good work!

Bob Kennedy
871 Warwick Lane
Glendale 22, Missouri

We're not sure we understand Bob's point, but wouldn't this be a dull world if everything was nice and simple?

Dear Stan and Jack:

FANTASTIC FOUR #11 was the greatest!!! The first story was very good because it told about their past. But the second story was obviously the better of the two. It was the funniest I have ever read! I nearly died laughing at the panic this creature from the planet POPPUP caused. WOW! Some of the crazy things that were said were wild!! For instance, when the THING said, "Ya don't get to be a comic book hero by being careful." Please fellas, stick to science fiction stories in the future. I wouldn't want to see humor magazines run out of business. By the way, the pin-up of Sub-Mariner was superb!!!

Jerry Smith
915 W. Pierson
Phoenix 13, Arizona

Thanks, Jerry, for those kind words. But don't worry — we're sure THE NEW YORKER and MAD aren't worrying too much about us putting them out of business!

SPECIAL ANNOUNCEMENTS SECTION:

- **Many, many of you fabulous fans have written offering to pay various amounts of money for back issues. Also, some of you have written offering to SELL back issues. Unfortunately, we simply don't have the room to print these items, BUT — we have learned of a fan mag called the COMICOLLECTOR, published by Ronn Foss, at 233 Benton Ct., Suisun, California. Ronn prints items about comics for sale or trade, and so we suggest that those of you who wish to buy, sell, or trade mags contact the COMICOLLECTOR.**
- **Yes, there WILL be a FANTASTIC FOUR ANNUAL! We're working on it now, and are doing our best to make it the biggest, most exciting, most fantastic two-bits' worth you've ever seen! We hope to have it on sale early in the summer. More about the F.F. Annual later.**
- **COMING NEXT: Wait'll you see the yarn we have for you next issue! Not one, but TWO widely-requested characters! That ol' villain's villain, DOCTOR DOOM, will be back for fun and games, and as an extra surprise, another guest appearance of a MARVEL COMICS GROUP hero — The Astonishing ANT MAN will be on hand also! Tell your magazine dealer to reserve your copy now — you won't want to miss the great F.F. #16!**

IN THE NEXT SENSATIONAL ISSUE OF FANTASTIC FOUR SEE...
The Ant Man
JOIN FORCES WITH AMERICAS GREATEST SUPER-HEROES AS THEY BATTLE...
DOCTOR
DOOM!

Hey, gang, how about THIS? It seems that
FANTASTIC FOUR FAN CLUBS
have been springing up all over the country! Many readers have written to us, asking where the nearest one is located which they can join. For the benefit of those interested, here is a partial list of some of the first FF FAN CLUBS . . . why not contact the one nearest you?
George Kopp, 10 Pillot Place, West Orange, N. J.
Lesley Reed, 519 South Meadow St., Ithaca, New York
Steve Clark, Rt. 2, Alvord, Texas
Steve Goddard, 183 S. W. 4th, Newport, Oregon
Herbert Silver, President, 330 E. 173 St., New York 57, N. Y.
Bobby Marshall, 20 Dover St., Tom's River, N. J.
Bill Mitchell, Grant Blackman, 1647 Boyce Drive, Norfolk, Virginia
Fantastic Four Fan Club, 5650 Camillia Ave., Sacramento, California
Mark Carey, 734 North 8th Ave., Upland, California
Donald Schank, Pres., 7 Glendale Dr., Freehold, New Jersey
Stuart Kaufman, 6127 N. Claremont, Chicago 45, Illinois
Billy Wampler, 3100 Liverpool Rd., East Gary, Indiana
Tim Evans, 744 Valley View Road, Pittsburgh (16) Penn.
Robert Unger, 19 Cumming St., New York 34, New York
More about our fan clubs in issues to come. But, until further notice, send us news of YOUR FF FAN CLUB activities to keep us posted.

THE WORLD'S GREATEST COMIC MAGAZINE!
APPROVED BY THE COMICS CODE AUTHORITY
Fantastic Four
16 JULY
MARVEL COMICS GROUP 12¢
IND.
THE RETURN OF DOCTOR DOOM! THE WORLD'S MOST AMAZING SUPER-VILLAIN!!
SPECIAL SURPRISE GUEST STAR: ANT-MAN
VISIT THE MYSTERIOUS MICRO-WORLD of DOCTOR DOOM!!

THE FANTASTIC FOUR is published by CANAM PUBLISHERS SALES CORP. OFFICE OF PUBLICATION: 655 MADISON AVENUE, NEW YORK, N.Y. Published monthly. Copyright 1963 by CANAM PUBLISHERS SALES CORP., 655 Madison Avenue, New York, N.Y. Vol. 1 No. 16, JULY, 1963 issue. Price 12¢ per copy. Subscription rate $1.75 for 12 issues including postage. Foreign subscription $3.25 in American funds. No similarity between any of the names, characters, persons, and/or institutions appearing in this magazine with those of any living or dead person is intended, and any such similarity which may exist is purely coincidental. Printed in U.S.A. by The Eastern Color Printing Co., Waterbury 20, Conn.

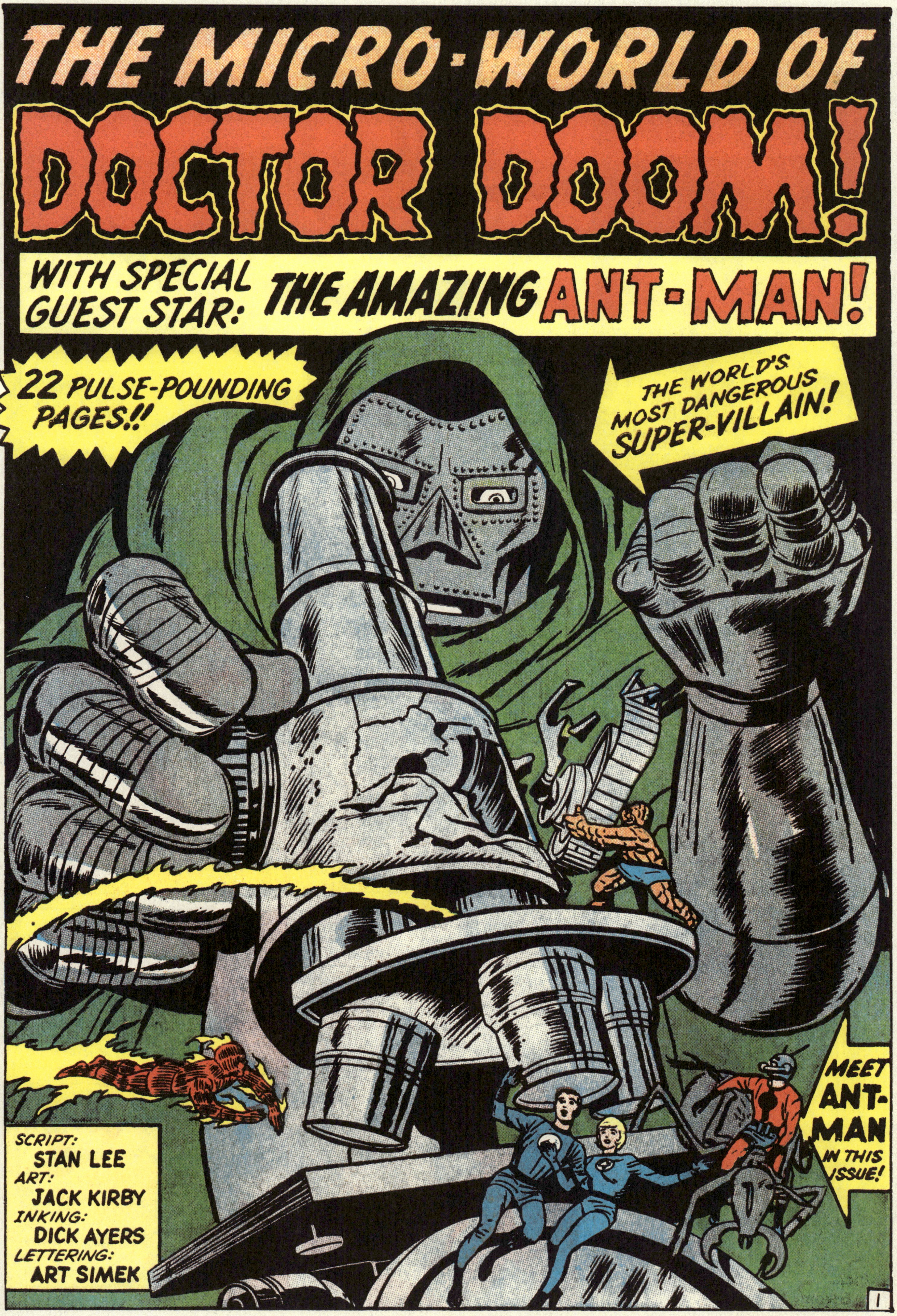
THE MICRO-WORLD OF
DOCTOR DOOM!
WITH SPECIAL GUEST STAR: THE AMAZING ANT-MAN!
22 PULSE-POUNDING PAGES!!
THE WORLD'S MOST DANGEROUS SUPER-VILLAIN!
MEET ANT-MAN IN THIS ISSUE!
SCRIPT: STAN LEE
ART: JACK KIRBY
INKING: DICK AYERS
LETTERING: ART SIMEK
1

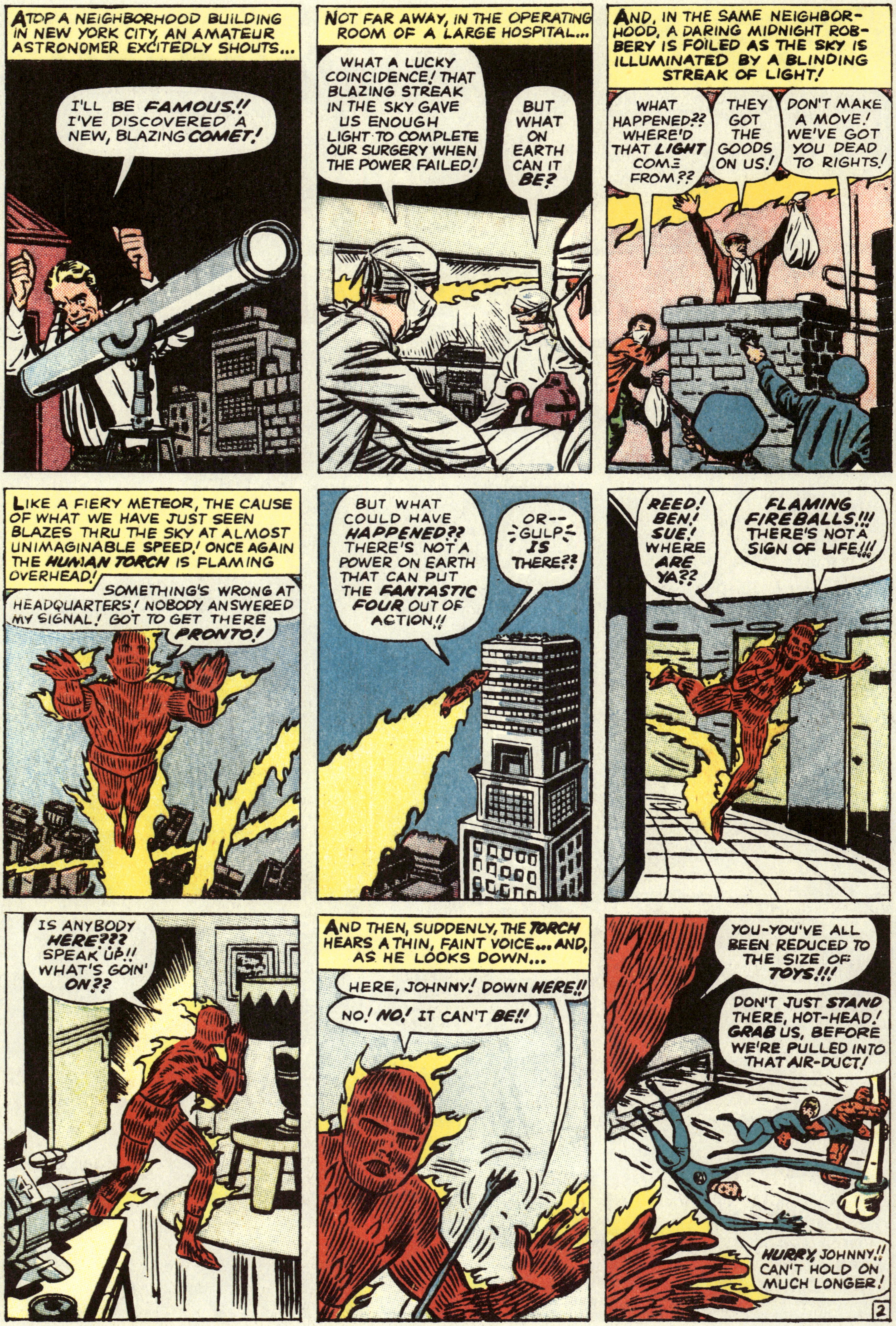

ATOP A NEIGHBORHOOD BUILDING IN NEW YORK CITY, AN AMATEUR ASTRONOMER EXCITEDLY SHOUTS...
I'LL BE FAMOUS!! I'VE DISCOVERED A NEW, BLAZING COMET!
NOT FAR AWAY, IN THE OPERATING ROOM OF A LARGE HOSPITAL...
WHAT A LUCKY COINCIDENCE! THAT BLAZING STREAK IN THE SKY GAVE US ENOUGH LIGHT TO COMPLETE OUR SURGERY WHEN THE POWER FAILED!
BUT WHAT ON EARTH CAN IT BE?
AND, IN THE SAME NEIGHBORHOOD, A DARING MIDNIGHT ROBBERY IS FOILED AS THE SKY IS ILLUMINATED BY A BLINDING STREAK OF LIGHT!
WHAT HAPPENED?? WHERE'D THAT LIGHT COME FROM??
THEY GOT THE GOODS ON US!
DON'T MAKE A MOVE! WE'VE GOT YOU DEAD TO RIGHTS!
LIKE A FIERY METEOR, THE CAUSE OF WHAT WE HAVE JUST SEEN BLAZES THRU THE SKY AT ALMOST UNIMAGINABLE SPEED! ONCE AGAIN THE HUMAN TORCH IS FLAMING OVERHEAD!
SOMETHING'S WRONG AT HEADQUARTERS! NOBODY ANSWERED MY SIGNAL! GOT TO GET THERE PRONTO!
BUT WHAT COULD HAVE HAPPENED?? THERE'S NOT A POWER ON EARTH THAT CAN PUT THE FANTASTIC FOUR OUT OF ACTION!!
OR-- GULP IS THERE??
REED! BEN! SUE! WHERE ARE YA??
FLAMING FIREBALLS!!! THERE'S NOT A SIGN OF LIFE!!!
IS ANYBODY HERE??? SPEAK UP!! WHAT'S GOIN' ON??
AND THEN, SUDDENLY, THE TORCH HEARS A THIN, FAINT VOICE... AND, AS HE LOOKS DOWN...
HERE, JOHNNY! DOWN HERE!!
NO! NO! IT CAN'T BE!!
YOU-YOU'VE ALL BEEN REDUCED TO THE SIZE OF TOYS!!!
DON'T JUST STAND THERE, HOT-HEAD! GRAB US, BEFORE WE'RE PULLED INTO THAT AIR-DUCT!
HURRY, JOHNNY!! CAN'T HOLD ON MUCH LONGER!
2

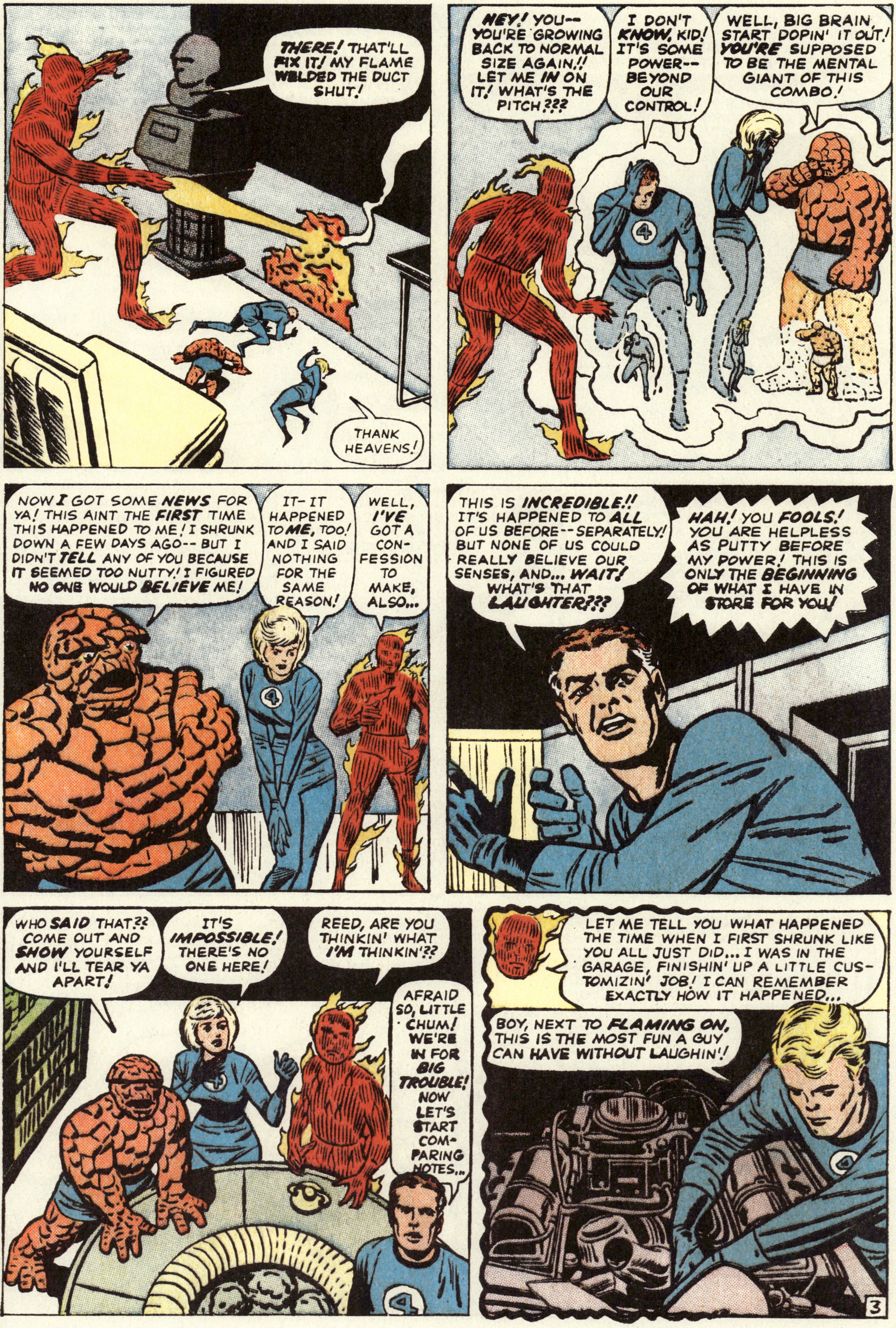
THERE! THAT'LL FIX IT! MY FLAME WELDED THE DUCT SHUT!
THANK HEAVENS!
HEY! YOU-- YOU'RE GROWING BACK TO NORMAL SIZE AGAIN!! LET ME IN ON IT! WHAT'S THE PITCH???
I DON'T KNOW, KID! IT'S SOME POWER-- BEYOND OUR CONTROL!
WELL, BIG BRAIN, START DOPIN' IT OUT! YOU'RE SUPPOSED TO BE THE MENTAL GIANT OF THIS COMBO!
NOW I GOT SOME NEWS FOR YA! THIS AINT THE FIRST TIME THIS HAPPENED TO ME! I SHRUNK DOWN A FEW DAYS AGO-- BUT I DIDN'T TELL ANY OF YOU BECAUSE IT SEEMED TOO NUTTY! I FIGURED NO ONE WOULD BELIEVE ME!
IT- IT HAPPENED TO ME, TOO! AND I SAID NOTHING FOR THE SAME REASON!
WELL, I'VE GOT A CONFESSION TO MAKE, ALSO...
THIS IS INCREDIBLE!! IT'S HAPPENED TO ALL OF US BEFORE-- SEPARATELY! BUT NONE OF US COULD REALLY BELIEVE OUR SENSES, AND... WAIT! WHAT'S THAT LAUGHTER???
HAH! YOU FOOLS! YOU ARE HELPLESS AS PUTTY BEFORE MY POWER! THIS IS ONLY THE BEGINNING OF WHAT I HAVE IN STORE FOR YOU!
WHO SAID THAT?? COME OUT AND SHOW YOURSELF AND I'LL TEAR YA APART!
IT'S IMPOSSIBLE! THERE'S NO ONE HERE!
REED, ARE YOU THINKIN' WHAT I'M THINKIN'??
AFRAID SO, LITTLE CHUM! WE'RE IN FOR BIG TROUBLE! NOW LET'S START COMPARING NOTES...
LET ME TELL YOU WHAT HAPPENED THE TIME WHEN I FIRST SHRUNK LIKE YOU ALL JUST DID... I WAS IN THE GARAGE, FINISHIN' UP A LITTLE CUSTOMIZIN' JOB! I CAN REMEMBER EXACTLY HOW IT HAPPENED...
BOY, NEXT TO FLAMING ON, THIS IS THE MOST FUN A GUY CAN HAVE WITHOUT LAUGHIN'!
3

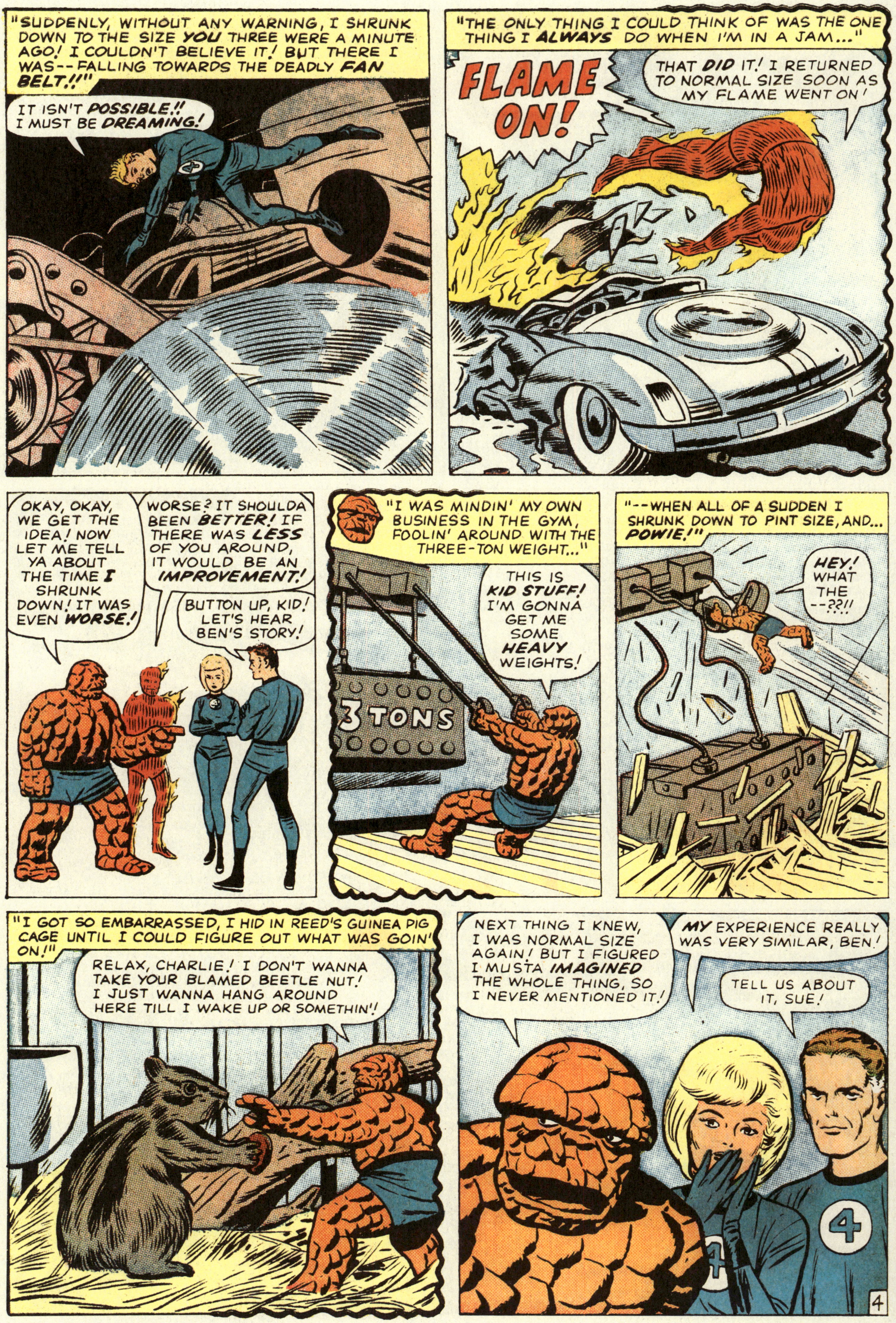
"SUDDENLY, WITHOUT ANY WARNING, I SHRUNK DOWN TO THE SIZE YOU THREE WERE A MINUTE AGO! I COULDN'T BELIEVE IT! BUT THERE I WAS--FALLING TOWARDS THE DEADLY FAN BELT!!"
IT ISN'T POSSIBLE!! I MUST BE DREAMING!
"THE ONLY THING I COULD THINK OF WAS THE ONE THING I ALWAYS DO WHEN I'M IN A JAM..."
FLAME ON!
THAT DID IT! I RETURNED TO NORMAL SIZE SOON AS MY FLAME WENT ON!
OKAY, OKAY, WE GET THE IDEA! NOW LET ME TELL YA ABOUT THE TIME I SHRUNK DOWN! IT WAS EVEN WORSE!
WORSE? IT SHOULDA BEEN BETTER! IF THERE WAS LESS OF YOU AROUND, IT WOULD BE AN IMPROVEMENT!
BUTTON UP, KID! LET'S HEAR BEN'S STORY!
"I WAS MINDIN' MY OWN BUSINESS IN THE GYM, FOOLIN' AROUND WITH THE THREE-TON WEIGHT..."
THIS IS KID STUFF! I'M GONNA GET ME SOME HEAVY WEIGHTS!
3 TONS
"--WHEN ALL OF A SUDDEN I SHRUNK DOWN TO PINT SIZE, AND... POWIE!"
HEY! WHAT THE --??!!
"I GOT SO EMBARRASSED, I HID IN REED'S GUINEA PIG CAGE UNTIL I COULD FIGURE OUT WHAT WAS GOIN' ON!"
RELAX, CHARLIE! I DON'T WANNA TAKE YOUR BLAMED BEETLE NUT! I JUST WANNA HANG AROUND HERE TILL I WAKE UP OR SOMETHIN'!
NEXT THING I KNEW, I WAS NORMAL SIZE AGAIN! BUT I FIGURED I MUSTA IMAGINED THE WHOLE THING, SO I NEVER MENTIONED IT!
MY EXPERIENCE REALLY WAS VERY SIMILAR, BEN!
TELL US ABOUT IT, SUE!
4

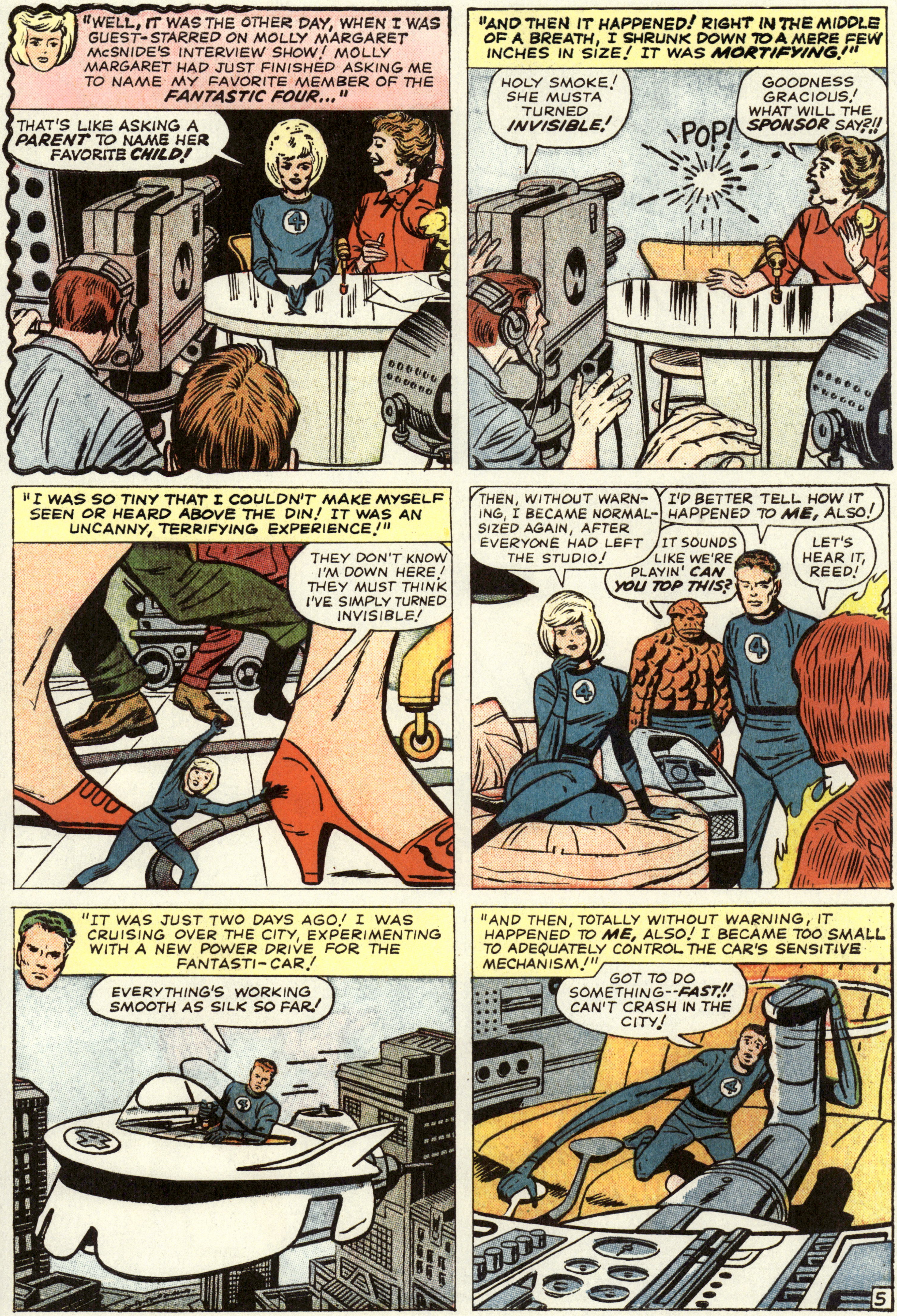
"WELL, IT WAS THE OTHER DAY, WHEN I WAS GUEST-STARRED ON MOLLY MARGARET McSNIDE'S INTERVIEW SHOW! MOLLY MARGARET HAD JUST FINISHED ASKING ME TO NAME MY FAVORITE MEMBER OF THE FANTASTIC FOUR..."
THAT'S LIKE ASKING A PARENT TO NAME HER FAVORITE CHILD!
"AND THEN IT HAPPENED! RIGHT IN THE MIDDLE OF A BREATH, I SHRUNK DOWN TO A MERE FEW INCHES IN SIZE! IT WAS MORTIFYING!"
HOLY SMOKE! SHE MUSTA TURNED INVISIBLE!
GOODNESS GRACIOUS! WHAT WILL THE SPONSOR SAY?!!
POP!
"I WAS SO TINY THAT I COULDN'T MAKE MYSELF SEEN OR HEARD ABOVE THE DIN! IT WAS AN UNCANNY, TERRIFYING EXPERIENCE!"
THEY DON'T KNOW I'M DOWN HERE! THEY MUST THINK I'VE SIMPLY TURNED INVISIBLE!
THEN, WITHOUT WARNING, I BECAME NORMAL-SIZED AGAIN, AFTER EVERYONE HAD LEFT THE STUDIO!
IT SOUNDS LIKE WE'RE PLAYIN' CAN YOU TOP THIS?
I'D BETTER TELL HOW IT HAPPENED TO ME, ALSO!
LET'S HEAR IT, REED!
"IT WAS JUST TWO DAYS AGO! I WAS CRUISING OVER THE CITY, EXPERIMENTING WITH A NEW POWER DRIVE FOR THE FANTASTI-CAR!
EVERYTHING'S WORKING SMOOTH AS SILK SO FAR!
"AND THEN, TOTALLY WITHOUT WARNING, IT HAPPENED TO ME, ALSO! I BECAME TOO SMALL TO ADEQUATELY CONTROL THE CAR'S SENSITIVE MECHANISM!"
GOT TO DO SOMETHING--FAST!! CAN'T CRASH IN THE CITY!
5

"WHETHER IT WAS LUCK, OR FATE, OR WHAT, I DON'T KNOW-- BUT I MANAGED TO AVOID A POWER DIVE AND PULLED HER NOSE UP JUST IN TIME!"
-WHEW!- THAT WAS CLOSE!
Y'KNOW, THERE'S ONE PERSON WHO MIGHT BE ABLE TO FIGURE OUT THE EXPLANATION FOR ALL THIS-- THE ASTONISHING ANT-MAN!!
WE HAVEN'T ANY IDEA OF HOW TO CONTACT HIM, REED! WE CAN'T EVEN BE SURE HE REALLY EXISTS!
ANT-MAN! SHMANT MAN! SINCE WHEN DO WE NEED HELP???
SINCE RIGHT NOW, BIG FELLA! THERE'S MORE TO THIS THAN WE CAN COPE WITH!
UNSEEN BY THE FANTASTIC FOUR, A TINY SOLDIER ANT HAD PICKED UP REED RICHARD'S MENTION OF THE NAME ANT-MAN, AND WAS EVEN NOW RELAYING THAT INFORMATION ACROSS TOWN...
CALLING ANT-MAN! CALLING--
FROM ANT TO ANT THE URGENT MESSAGE WAS REPEATED VIA THE SECRET COMMUNICATIONS NETWORK KNOWN ONLY TO ANT-MAN, UNTIL...
--ANT-MAN! CALLING ANT-MAN! CALLING ANT-MAN!--
--IN A HIDDEN LAB, CROWDED WITH HIGHLY SPECIALIZED CYBERNETIC EQUIPMENT, A HANDSOME, GRIM-FACED HELMETED MAN RECEIVES THE MESSAGE!
IT'S THE FANTASTIC FOUR! THEY NEED MY HELP!
ANT-MAN! WHAT IS IT? A NEW CASE?
I DON'T KNOW YET, WASP! REMAIN HERE AND WAIT FOR WORD FROM ME! I'VE GOT TO BECOME ANT-SIZED NOW AND VISIT THE FANTASTIC FOUR!
EDITOR'S NOTE
MEET THE WASP, ANT-MAN'S NEW PARTNER-IN-PERIL, STARTING WITH ISSUE #44 OF TALES TO ASTONISH!!

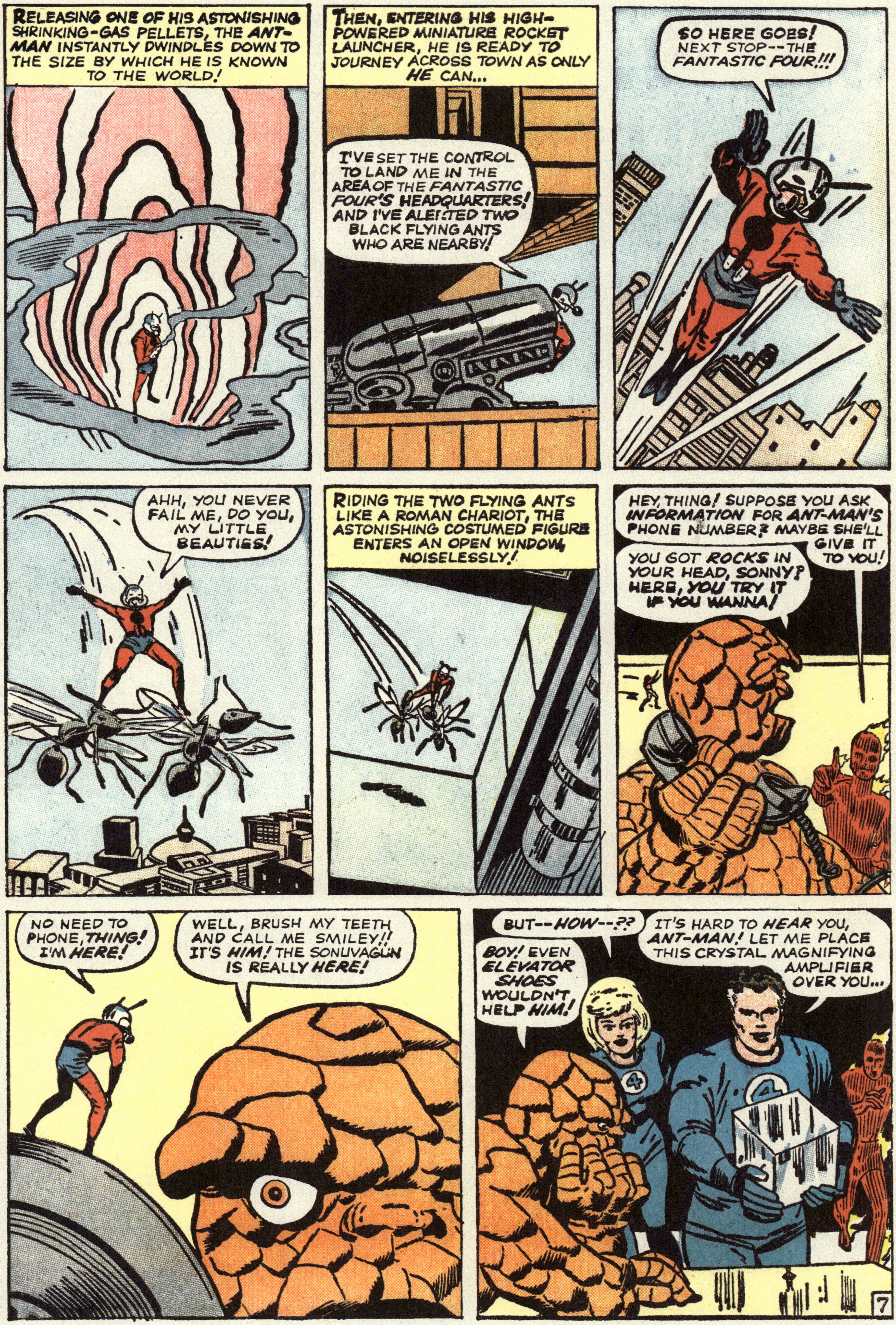

RELEASING ONE OF HIS ASTONISHING SHRINKING-GAS PELLETS, THE ANT-MAN INSTANTLY DWINDLES DOWN TO THE SIZE BY WHICH HE IS KNOWN TO THE WORLD!
THEN, ENTERING HIS HIGH-POWERED MINIATURE ROCKET LAUNCHER, HE IS READY TO JOURNEY ACROSS TOWN AS ONLY HE CAN...
I'VE SET THE CONTROL TO LAND ME IN THE AREA OF THE FANTASTIC FOUR'S HEADQUARTERS! AND I'VE ALERTED TWO BLACK FLYING ANTS WHO ARE NEARBY!
SO HERE GOES! NEXT STOP--THE FANTASTIC FOUR!!!
AHH, YOU NEVER FAIL ME, DO YOU, MY LITTLE BEAUTIES!
RIDING THE TWO FLYING ANTS LIKE A ROMAN CHARIOT, THE ASTONISHING COSTUMED FIGURE ENTERS AN OPEN WINDOW, NOISELESSLY!
HEY, THING! SUPPOSE YOU ASK INFORMATION FOR ANT-MAN'S PHONE NUMBER? MAYBE SHE'LL GIVE IT TO YOU!
YOU GOT ROCKS IN YOUR HEAD, SONNY? HERE, YOU TRY IT IF YOU WANNA!
NO NEED TO PHONE, THING! I'M HERE!
WELL, BRUSH MY TEETH AND CALL ME SMILEY!! IT'S HIM! THE SONUVAGUN IS REALLY HERE!
BUT--HOW--??
BOY! EVEN ELEVATOR SHOES WOULDN'T HELP HIM!
IT'S HARD TO HEAR YOU, ANT-MAN! LET ME PLACE THIS CRYSTAL MAGNIFYING AMPLIFIER OVER YOU...
7

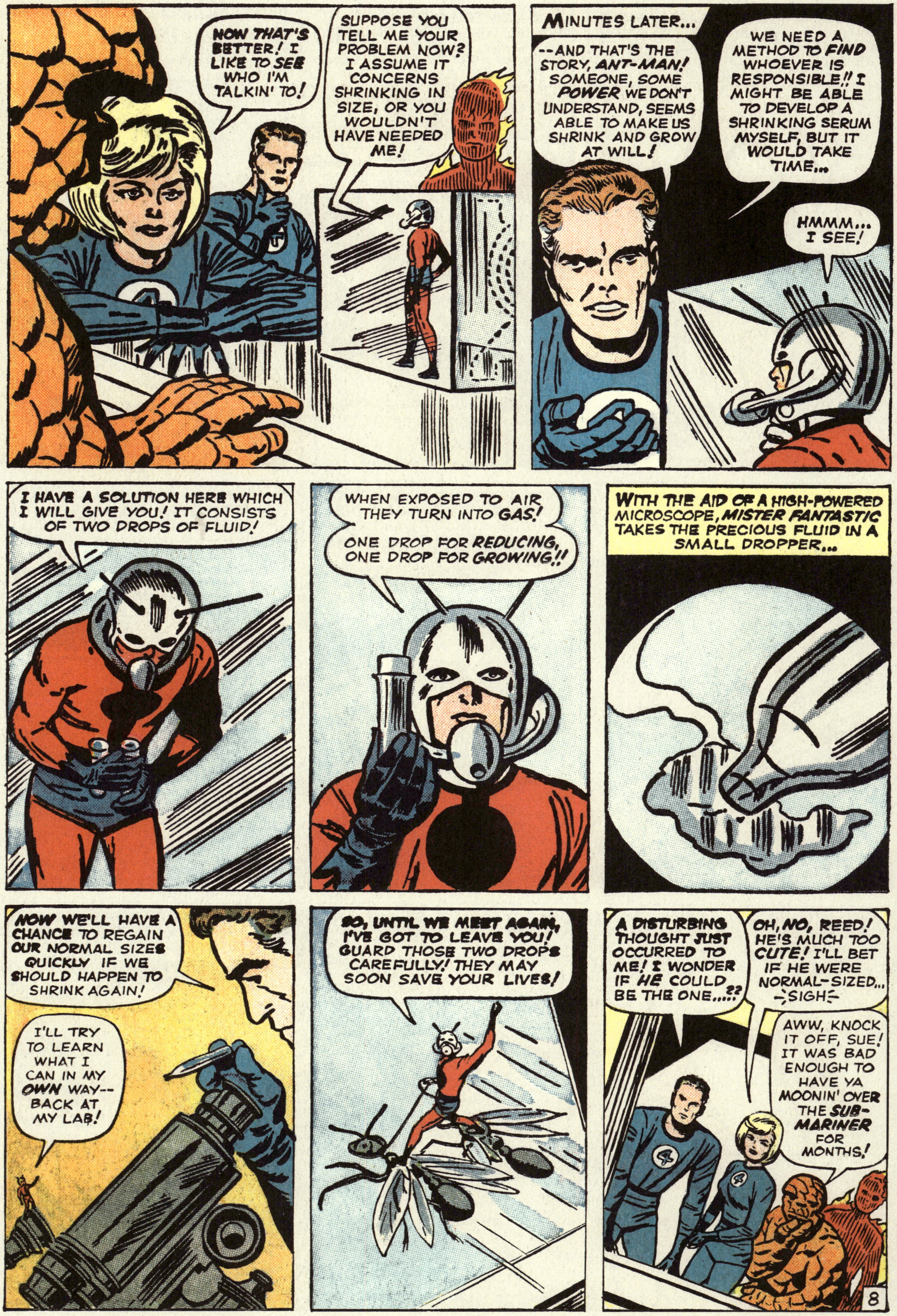

NOW THAT'S BETTER! I LIKE TO SEE WHO I'M TALKIN' TO!
SUPPOSE YOU TELL ME YOUR PROBLEM NOW? I ASSUME IT CONCERNS SHRINKING IN SIZE, OR YOU WOULDN'T HAVE NEEDED ME!
MINUTES LATER...
--AND THAT'S THE STORY, ANT-MAN! SOMEONE, SOME POWER WE DON'T UNDERSTAND, SEEMS ABLE TO MAKE US SHRINK AND GROW AT WILL!
WE NEED A METHOD TO FIND WHOEVER IS RESPONSIBLE!! I MIGHT BE ABLE TO DEVELOP A SHRINKING SERUM MYSELF, BUT IT WOULD TAKE TIME...
HMMM... I SEE!
I HAVE A SOLUTION HERE WHICH I WILL GIVE YOU! IT CONSISTS OF TWO DROPS OF FLUID!
WHEN EXPOSED TO AIR THEY TURN INTO GAS!
ONE DROP FOR REDUCING, ONE DROP FOR GROWING!!
WITH THE AID OF A HIGH-POWERED MICROSCOPE, MISTER FANTASTIC TAKES THE PRECIOUS FLUID IN A SMALL DROPPER...
NOW WE'LL HAVE A CHANCE TO REGAIN OUR NORMAL SIZES QUICKLY IF WE SHOULD HAPPEN TO SHRINK AGAIN!
I'LL TRY TO LEARN WHAT I CAN IN MY OWN WAY-- BACK AT MY LAB!
SO, UNTIL WE MEET AGAIN, I'VE GOT TO LEAVE YOU! GUARD THOSE TWO DROPS CAREFULLY! THEY MAY SOON SAVE YOUR LIVES!
A DISTURBING THOUGHT JUST OCCURRED TO ME! I WONDER IF HE COULD BE THE ONE....??
OH, NO, REED! HE'S MUCH TOO CUTE! I'LL BET IF HE WERE NORMAL-SIZED... -SIGH-
AWW, KNOCK IT OFF, SUE! IT WAS BAD ENOUGH TO HAVE YA MOONIN' OVER THE SUB-MARINER FOR MONTHS!

THE NEXT DAY, AT THE APARTMENT OF BEN GRIMM'S BLIND FRIEND, ALICIA...
HELLO, ALICIA DEAR! BEN, I'VE BEEN LOOKING FOR YOU! I'VE GOT SOMETHING--
CAN'T IT WAIT, PAL? I'M HELPIN' ALICIA WITH HER SPRING CLEANIN'...
I DON'T THINK YOU'LL WANT TO WAIT WITH THIS! I'VE BEEN WORKING ON A NEW SERUM TO MAKE YOU REVERT TO YOUR NORMAL FORM AGAIN, AND I WANT TO TRY OUT THE FIRST PHASE OF IT!
AWW, I'M SICK AND TIRED OF BEING A GUINEA PIG FOR YOU AND YOUR EXPERIMENTS! I AINT GONNA WASTE ANY MORE--HEY! STOP! CUT IT OUT! GLUBBB...
PTUI! IT TASTES LIKE DISH WATER! CAN'T YA EVEN USE SOME CHOCOLATE FLAVOR OR SOMETHIN'!
NEVER MIND THE TASTE, OLD FRIEND! LET'S WATCH THE RESULTS!
HEY! IT--IT'S STARTIN' TO BURN! I--I FEEL LIKE I'M CHOKIN'! WHAT DID YOU DO, POISON ME??
NO, YOU BIG APE! THAT MEANS IT'S WORKING!
WAIT TILL YOU SEE YOURSELF, BEN!! IT WON'T LAST, BECAUSE THIS IS JUST A PRELIMINARY FORMULA, BUT IT MEANS I'M ON THE RIGHT TRACK!
I-I DON'T FEEL LIKE THE THING ANY MORE!
LOOK OUT! CAN'T HOLD THE PIANO UP ANY MORE!! GANGWAY!
IT'S MY FAULT, BEN! I SHOULD HAVE REMINDED YOU TO PUT IT DOWN BEFORE I GAVE YOU THE FORMULA! BUT I WAS SO ANXIOUS...
BONNNG
OH, BEN! MY DARLING! ARE YOU HURT? WHY DO YOU FEEL SO DIFFERENT?? I--I LOVE YOU SO THAT I DON'T WANT YOU TO CHANGE! I DON'T EVER WANT ANYTHING TO CHANGE YOU!
IT'S ALL RIGHT, SUE BABY! I'M OKAY! AND NOTHIN'S EVER GONNA CHANGE FOR US! YOU CAN COUNT ON THAT, HONEY!
9

LOOK, REED, I APPRECIATE WHAT YOU'RE TRYIN' TO DO FOR ME, BUT NOTHIN' MAKES SENSE! I LOVE ALICIA, AND SHE LOVES ME BEST AS-- THE THING! SO WHY DON'T YOU FORGET ABOUT TRYIN' TO CHANGE ME BACK, AND WORK ON SOME WAY TO MAKE HER SEE AGAIN, INSTEAD?
PERHAPS YOU'RE RIGHT, BEN! I'LL--WAIT! LISTEN--WHAT'S THAT???
FLEE FOR YOUR LIVES! BEWARE OF DOCTOR DOOM! HE'S TRYING TO--- OHHH!! HELP!
A STRANGE GIRL'S VOICE! BUT-- FROM SO FAR AWAY! SO FAINT!
AND NOW, AS THE WEB OF FATE BEGINS TO TIGHTEN AROUND OUR COLORFUL CHARACTERS, LET US SWITCH OUR SCENE TO A TEEN-AGE PICNIC, WHERE WE FIND...
DO SOME TRICKS FOR US JOHNNY--PLEASE!
YEAH! C'MON, TORCHY, SHOW US WHAT YOU CAN DO!
WELL, SHYNESS WAS NEVER ONE OF MY BIG FAULTS!
HERE, I'LL SHOW YOU HOW TO GET THOSE WEINIES GRILLED IN RECORD TIME-- HOW'S THIS?!
WOWEEE!
AND HERE'S A LITTLE STUNT I PLAN TO PERFORM AT THE NEXT BIG GAME!
GO GLENVILLE HIGH
EVER SEE A FELLA TWIRL FLAMING LASSOES? WATCH!
FLAME ON!

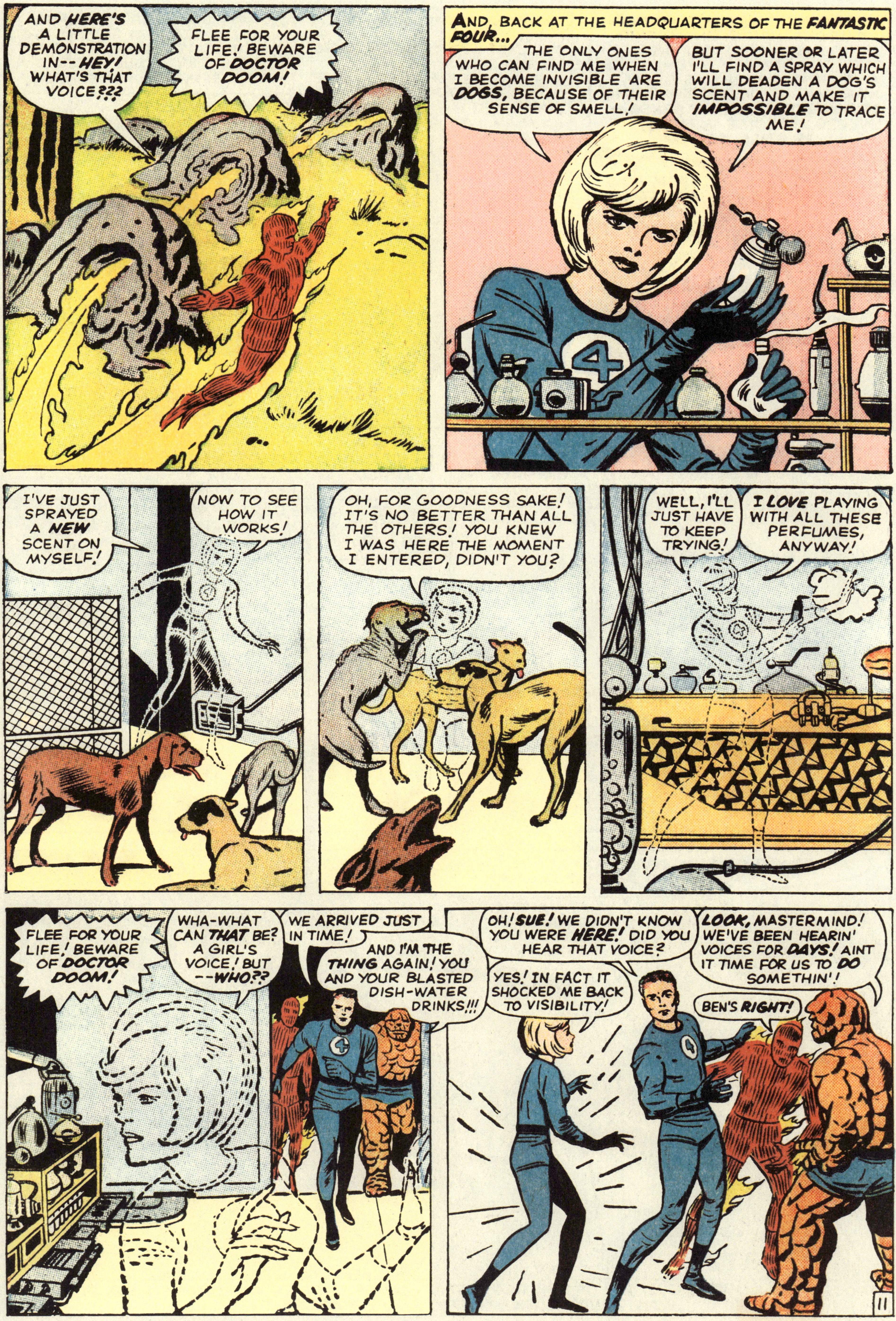
AND HERE'S A LITTLE DEMONSTRATION IN-- HEY! WHAT'S THAT VOICE???
FLEE FOR YOUR LIFE! BEWARE OF DOCTOR DOOM!
AND, BACK AT THE HEADQUARTERS OF THE FANTASTIC FOUR...
THE ONLY ONES WHO CAN FIND ME WHEN I BECOME INVISIBLE ARE DOGS, BECAUSE OF THEIR SENSE OF SMELL!
BUT SOONER OR LATER I'LL FIND A SPRAY WHICH WILL DEADEN A DOG'S SCENT AND MAKE IT IMPOSSIBLE TO TRACE ME!
I'VE JUST SPRAYED A NEW SCENT ON MYSELF!
NOW TO SEE HOW IT WORKS!
OH, FOR GOODNESS SAKE! IT'S NO BETTER THAN ALL THE OTHERS! YOU KNEW I WAS HERE THE MOMENT I ENTERED, DIDN'T YOU?
WELL, I'LL JUST HAVE TO KEEP TRYING!
I LOVE PLAYING WITH ALL THESE PERFUMES, ANYWAY!
FLEE FOR YOUR LIFE! BEWARE OF DOCTOR DOOM!
WHA-WHAT CAN THAT BE? A GIRL'S VOICE! BUT --WHO??
WE ARRIVED JUST IN TIME!
AND I'M THE THING AGAIN! YOU AND YOUR BLASTED DISH-WATER DRINKS!!!
OH! SUE! WE DIDN'T KNOW YOU WERE HERE! DID YOU HEAR THAT VOICE?
YES! IN FACT IT SHOCKED ME BACK TO VISIBILITY!
LOOK, MASTERMIND! WE'VE BEEN HEARIN' VOICES FOR DAYS! AINT IT TIME FOR US TO DO SOMETHIN'!
BEN'S RIGHT!

HERE'S WHAT WE KNOW SO FAR-- SOMEONE HAS BEEN CAUSING US TO SHRINK IN SIZE, THEN RETURN TO NORMAL! THEN, SOME MYSTERIOUS GIRL HAS BEEN WARNING US OF DOCTOR DOOM! IT DOESN'T MAKE ANY SENSE-- UNLESS, BY SOME MIRACLE, HE IS STILL ALIVE!
AWW, HOW COULD HE BE?
ONLY ONE WAY TO FIND OUT...
THE LAST WE SAW OF DR. DOOM, HE WAS SHRINKING INTO NOTHINGNESS!* WELL, WE'RE GOING AFTER HIM! I'VE PORTIONED THE ANT-MAN'S FORMULA INTO FOUR UNITS-- SO LET'S GO!
THAT'S WHAT I LIKE--ACTION!
SO FAST DOES THE COLORFUL QUARTET BEGIN TO SHRINK, THAT IT SEEMS AS THOUGH THEY ARE PLUNGING INTO THE VOTEX OF A MADLY SPINNING WHIRLPOOL!
WE'RE SHRINKING TOO FAST! QUICK--TAKE THE ENLARGING FORMULA, TO SLOW IT DOWN!!
GOTCHA, BOSS MAN!
AND FINALLY, THE SPINNING SLOWS DOWN-- THE VERTIGO STOPS, AND THE WORLD SEEMS TO TAKE SHAPE AROUND THEM...
WE'RE IN SOME SORT OF MICRO-WORLD-- A WORLD WHICH MIGHT FIT ON THE HEAD OF A PIN!
INDEED YOU ARE, MY DEAR! YOU ARE IN THE MICRO-WORLD OF DOCTOR DOOM!!!
WHAT HAVE I GOTTEN THE THREE OF YOU INTO!??
YOU WERE RIGHT! HE IS ALIVE!
*NOTE: THE COMPLETE STORY OF THE FANTASTIC FOUR'S LAST ENCOUNTER WITH DR. DOOM WAS TOLD IN FANTASTIC FOUR #10, SEPT.
12

YOUR ARRIVAL HERE IS NOT UNEXPECTED! I'VE BEEN WAITING FOR YOU TO SHOW UP!
YEAH?!! WELL, NOW THAT WE'RE HERE, I'M GONNA FINISH A JOB I STARTED A LONG TIME AGO! A JOB I SHOULDA FINISHED THEN!
BAH! YOU ARE BRAINLESS AS EVER! DID YOU THINK TO FIND ME UNPREPARED??
HOLY COW!! NOW WHAT??
HIS THRONE-- IT'S THE CONTROL CENTRAL FOR A BANK OF ELECTRONIC WEAPONS! HE JUST ACTIVATED ONE OF THEM!
IT'S ANOTHER SHRINKING RAY! HERE WE GO AGAIN!
SECONDS LATER...
AND NOW, MY HELPLESS FRIENDS, DO YOU STILL INTEND TO IMPETUOUSLY PIT YOUR PUNY POWERS AGAINST MY OWN??
BUT, BEFORE I DECIDE TO DISPOSE OF YOU, I SHALL TELL YOU A LITTLE STORY! I SUSPECT YOU WILL FIND IT INTERESTING!
IT IS THE STORY OF HOW I CAME HERE--AND HOW I BECAME RULER OF THIS WORLD!
"YOU WILL RECALL THAT I LAST TOOK LEAVE OF YOU IN A RATHER ABRUPT WAY, WHEN I WAS STRUCK BY THE SHRINKING RAY I HAD INTENDED TO DESTROY YOU WITH!"
13

"IT WAS THEN THAT I BEGAN MY DESCENT INTO THIS MICRO-WORLD, EVEN AS YOU JUST DID!"
"REACHING HERE, I FOUND MYSELF IN A PEACEFUL, PRIMITIVE, HAPPY WORLD! IT WAS ENOUGH TO MAKE MY BLOOD BOIL!"
THE FOOLS! THEY LIVE IN PEACE! THEY ARE CONTENTED AND HAPPY! BUT I'LL SOON PUT A STOP TO THAT!
"THE KING, AND PRINCESS PEARLA, WERE KINDLY TRUSTING SOULS! I MADE A SIMPLE TELESCOPE FOR THEM, AND IN RETURN I GAINED THEIR UNSUSPECTING TRUST AND CONFIDENCE!"
OUR NEW FRIEND IS TRULY A WIZARD! I SHALL MAKE HIM PERSONAL SCIENTIST TO THE CROWN!
"AS COURT SCIENTIST, I WAS ABLE TO SUPERVISE ALL SORTS OF CONSTRUCTION FOR MYSELF, MAKING WEAPONS AND DEVICES UNDREAMED OF IN THAT WORLD--OR IN YOURS!"
GOOD! FOLLOWING MY INSTRUCTIONS, YOU HAVE FORGED A MOLECULAR RAY APPARATUS, EVEN THOUGH AN OAF LIKE YOU DOESN'T COMPREHEND THE MEANING OF THE WORDS!
"MY NEW RAY HAD ONLY ONE PURPOSE--TO AFFECT THE SIZE OF LIVING BEINGS! THE FIRST TWO TO SAMPLE ITS POWER WERE THE KING, AND PRINCESS PEARLA!"
FROM THIS MOMENT ON, I AM RULER OF THIS WORLD, OR ELSE I SHALL SHRINK YOU TO ABSOLUTE NOTHINGNESS!
"NEXT, I CREATED A DEVICE ENABLING ME TO SEND MY VOICE AND MY RAY THRU THE INFINITE --TO REACH YOU, IN THE WORLD ABOVE! I PLAYED WITH YOU AS A CAT PLAYS WITH A MOUSE!"
BUT NOW, THE GAME HAS ENDED! YOU HAVE LOST-- AND YOU SHALL PAY THE PENALTY!
14

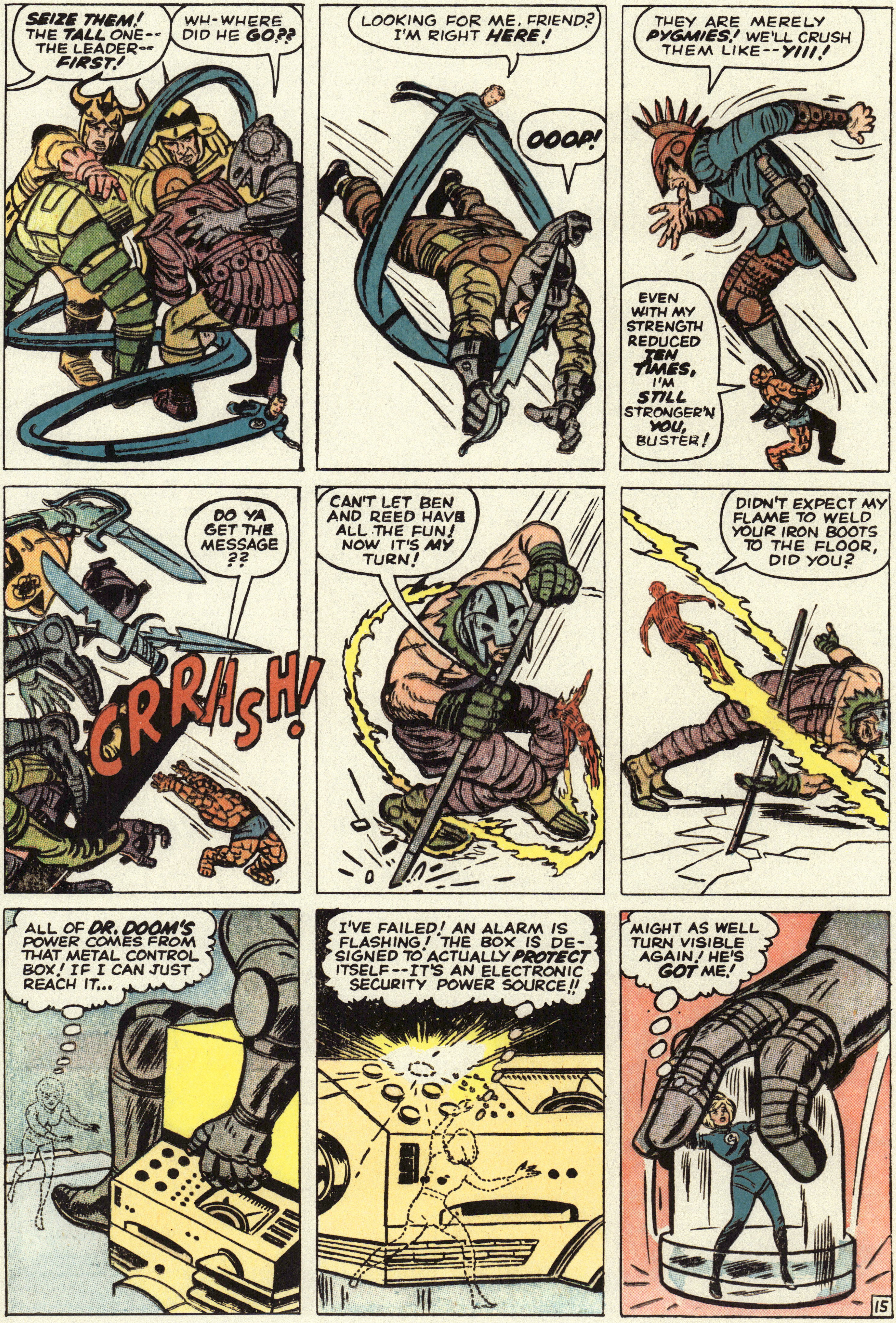
SEIZE THEM! THE TALL ONE-- THE LEADER-- FIRST!
WH-WHERE DID HE GO??
LOOKING FOR ME, FRIEND? I'M RIGHT HERE!
OOOF!
THEY ARE MERELY PYGMIES! WE'LL CRUSH THEM LIKE--YIII!
EVEN WITH MY STRENGTH REDUCED TEN TIMES, I'M STILL STRONGER'N YOU, BUSTER!
DO YA GET THE MESSAGE ??
CRRASH!
CAN'T LET BEN AND REED HAVE ALL THE FUN! NOW IT'S MY TURN!
DIDN'T EXPECT MY FLAME TO WELD YOUR IRON BOOTS TO THE FLOOR, DID YOU?
ALL OF DR. DOOM'S POWER COMES FROM THAT METAL CONTROL BOX! IF I CAN JUST REACH IT...
I'VE FAILED! AN ALARM IS FLASHING! THE BOX IS DESIGNED TO ACTUALLY PROTECT ITSELF--IT'S AN ELECTRONIC SECURITY POWER SOURCE!!
MIGHT AS WELL TURN VISIBLE AGAIN! HE'S GOT ME!
15

HERE SHE IS, MY HELPLESS FOES--THE **EX-INVISIBLE GIRL!** TRY TO SAVE HER **NOW!**
WE'RE JUST GONNA **DO** THAT LITTLE THING, YOU WALKIN' HUNK O' JUNK!
REALLY? IT MIGHT PROVE SOMEWHAT DIFFICULT TO SAVE **ANYONE** WHEN YOU YOURSELVES ARE **ASLEEP,** AS YOU **SHALL** BE IN TWO SECONDS, THANKS TO MY LITTLE SLEEP-INDUCING MIST!
FOR, YOU SEE, RICHARDS, GREAT A SCIENTIST AS **YOU** MAY BE, I, **DOCTOR DOOM,** AM BY FAR THE **GREATER!!**
LONG MINUTES LATER, THE **FANTASTIC FOUR** REGAIN CONSCIOUSNESS TO FIND THEMSELVES IMPRISONED IN A DANK DUNGEON, TOGETHER WITH THE CAPTIVE KING AND PRINCESS PEARLA...
HAVE TO WAKE UP --HAVE TO THINK! **DR. DOOM** MUST BE DEFEATED! FOR, IF **WE** FAIL, WHAT POWER ON EARTH --OR ON **THIS** WORLD CAN STOP HIM??
LOOKS LIKE WE'RE REALLY **LICKED** THIS TIME, REED! THE ODDS ARE ALL IN **DOOM'S** FAVOR!
YOU FOUR ARE FROM THE SAME WORLD AS **DR. DOOM,** THE TYRANT?
YEAH, YOUR MAJESTY-- BUT WE AINT **BRAGGIN'** ABOUT IT!
AS LONG AS **DOOM'S** TWISTED MIND KEEPS THINKING HE CAN OUT-SMART US, WE STILL HAVE A CHANCE! FIRST THING TO DO IS BREAK OUT OF **HERE!**
WE SEEM TO BE IN AN UNDERWATER DUNGEON! WE COULD USE THE **SUB-MARINER** AT A TIME LIKE THIS!
NO, **MISTER FANTASTIC,** THAT IS NOT **WATER** OUT THERE... IT IS DEADLY **ACID!!**
IT IS JUST ANOTHER DIABOLICAL JEST OF **DR. DOOM'S!** THOSE ARE **NOT** LIVING FISH OUT THERE...
THEY ARE, IN REALITY, METALLIC MECHANICAL SPIES WITH WHICH HE WATCHES EVERYTHING WE **DO** AND HEARS WHATEVER WE SAY!

DON'T YOU WORRY PRINCESS! WE'LL STILL MANAGE TO COME OUTTA THIS OKAY!
OH! THAT FLAME! IT'S SO-- FRIGHTENING!
HECK! I WOULDN'T SCARE A LIVING DOLL LIKE YOU!
FLAME OFF!
WHEN THINGS LOOK THE MOST HOPELESS FOR US, THAT'S WHEN OUR ENEMIES BETTER RUN FOR THE HILLS, CHICK!
AS FOR ME, THE HUMAN TORCH IS GONNA SEE TO IT THAT NOBODY HURTS ONE LITTLE FINGER-NAIL OF THAT DAINTY LITTLE HAND!
OHH...
C'MON, SQUIRT! LEAVE THE SPEECHES FOR TONY CURTIS! WE GOT WORK TO DO!
LEGGO, YA BIG OX! HAVEN'T YOU ANY ROMANCE IN YOUR SOUL??
WAIT A MINUTE! IT MUST HAVE BEEN YOUR VOICE WE HEARD, TRYING TO WARN US!
IT WAS! I KNEW HE WAS TRYING TO LURE YOU HERE -- SO I USED HIS RAY MACHINE A FEW TIMES WHEN HE WASN'T THERE!
"DR. DOOM WANTS ME TO MARRY HIM! BUT I DESPISE HIM! THAT IS WHY I AM HIS PRISONER, TOO! HE PLANS TO BETRAY THIS ENTIRE WORLD IF I REFUSE HIM! EVEN NOW HE IS CONTACTING THE PLANET TOK!"
"HE HAS OFFERED TOK A REWARD FOR JOINING HIM! YOU FOUR ARE TO BE THEIR REWARD -- AS SLAVES! EVEN NOW, THE TOK SHIP MUST BE LANDING..."
"THE TERRIBLE WARRIORS OF TOK ARE FEARED THRUOUT OUR UNIVERSE! THEY ARE HUGE, AND POWERFUL, COMING FROM A HEAVY PLANET WITH GRAVITY A DOZEN TIMES STRONGER THAN OURS! AND THEY ARE COMING FOR -- YOU!"

"THE LIZARD MEN OF TOK WILL MAKE YOU SERVE THEM AS LONG AS YOU LIVE! THEY'LL USE MR. FANTASTIC AS A BAILEY BRIDGE DURING THEIR INVASIONS..."
"AS FOR THE THING, THEY'LL EMPLOY HIS GREAT STRENGTH IN THEIR DIAMOND MINES, MAKING HIM DIG AND BURROW FOR THEM, UNTIL HE DROPS!"
"AND THE TORCH WILL BE FORCED TO HELP THE LIZARD MEN OF TOK ATTACK THEIR VICTIMS BY THE USE OF HIS FLAMING POWERS!"
"EVEN THE INVISIBLE GIRL WILL BE PRESSED INTO SERVICE, SPENDING THE REST OF HER DAYS AS A SCULLERY MAID, A DRUDGE FOR THE MERCILESS LIZARD MEN!"
--AND THERE IS NOTHING YOU CAN DO TO SAVE YOURSELVES! IT'S TOO LATE -SOB- TOO LATE FOR US ALL!
SAVE YOUR TEARS, PEARLA! DOCTOR DOOM HASN'T BEATEN US YET!
AND HE NEVER WILL, IF I EVER GET MY MITTS ON 'IM!
MEANWHILE, IN THE WORLD ABOVE, ANT-MAN RETURNS TO THE FANTASTIC FOUR'S LAB, TO FIND...
HMMM--BITS OF GLASS FROM MY REDUCING SERUM VIAL! THEY MUST HAVE SHRUNK TO ALMOST NOTHINGNESS, RIGHT AT THIS SPOT!
18

AND FOR ME, THE ONLY THING TO DO IS-- FOLLOW THEM!!!
SECONDS LATER, ANT-MAN LANDS IN THE MICRO-WORLD, WHERE HE FINDS HIMSELF THE SAME SIZE AS DOCTOR DOOM'S DEADLY GUARDS!
AN INTRUDER! SEIZE HIM!
UH OH-- TROUBLE!
WE NEED REINFORCE-MENTS! HIS STRENGTH IS--TOO MUCH--
HELP IS COMING! HOLD ON --UGH!
MORE GUARDS! COMING FROM EVERY DIRECTION! CAN'T FIGHT THEM ALL!
AND THEN, BEFORE HE CAN ATTEMPT TO ENLIST THE AID OF ANY INSECTS WHO MIGHT BE IN THE MICRO-WORLD, A BRUTAL FIST LASHES OUT, AND...
THERE! NOW TAKE HIM TO DOCTOR DOOM!
AH, ANOTHER DEFEATED INTRUDER FROM THE LARGER WORLD ABOVE, EH? GOOD! GOOD!
THE LIZARD MEN OF TOK WILL PAY ME WELL FOR SUCH HEALTHY SPECIMENS! THEY WILL BE ARRIVING VERY SOON NOW!
MEANWHILE...
I STILL WISH YOU'D LET ME POKE A HOLE THRU THAT WALL, REED!
IMPOSSIBLE, BEN! IF THOSE ACID WATERS RUSH IN, WE'RE FINISHED!
REED! I-I HAVE AN IDEA!
19

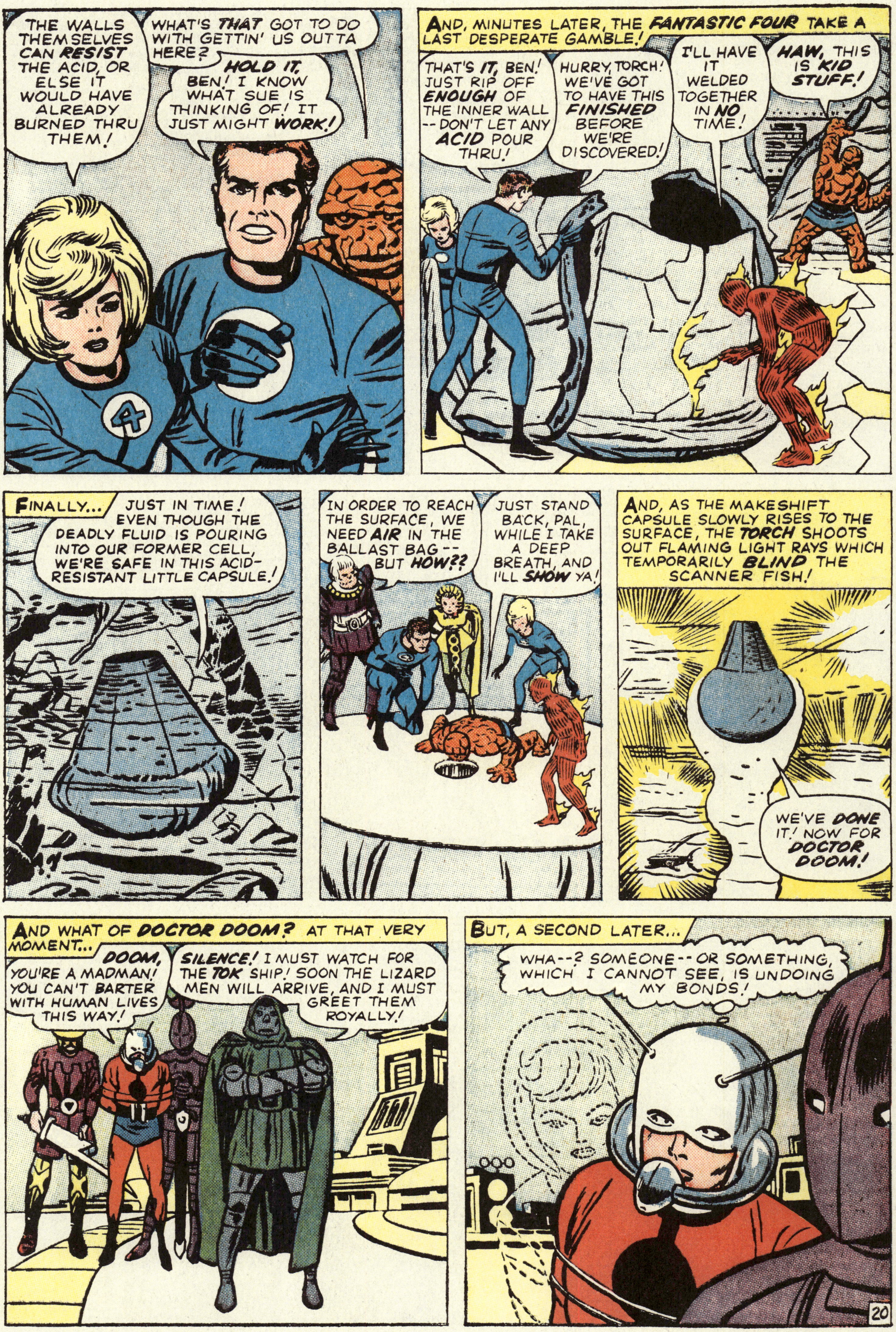
THE WALLS THEMSELVES CAN RESIST THE ACID, OR ELSE IT WOULD HAVE ALREADY BURNED THRU THEM!
WHAT'S THAT GOT TO DO WITH GETTIN' US OUTTA HERE?
HOLD IT, BEN! I KNOW WHAT SUE IS THINKING OF! IT JUST MIGHT WORK!
AND, MINUTES LATER, THE FANTASTIC FOUR TAKE A LAST DESPERATE GAMBLE!
THAT'S IT, BEN! JUST RIP OFF ENOUGH OF THE INNER WALL -- DON'T LET ANY ACID POUR THRU!
HURRY, TORCH! WE'VE GOT TO HAVE THIS FINISHED BEFORE WE'RE DISCOVERED!
I'LL HAVE IT WELDED TOGETHER IN NO TIME!
HAW, THIS IS KID STUFF!
FINALLY...
JUST IN TIME! EVEN THOUGH THE DEADLY FLUID IS POURING INTO OUR FORMER CELL, WE'RE SAFE IN THIS ACID-RESISTANT LITTLE CAPSULE!
IN ORDER TO REACH THE SURFACE, WE NEED AIR IN THE BALLAST BAG -- BUT HOW??
JUST STAND BACK, PAL, WHILE I TAKE A DEEP BREATH, AND I'LL SHOW YA!
AND, AS THE MAKESHIFT CAPSULE SLOWLY RISES TO THE SURFACE, THE TORCH SHOOTS OUT FLAMING LIGHT RAYS WHICH TEMPORARILY BLIND THE SCANNER FISH!
WE'VE DONE IT! NOW FOR DOCTOR DOOM!
AND WHAT OF DOCTOR DOOM? AT THAT VERY MOMENT...
DOOM, YOU'RE A MADMAN! YOU CAN'T BARTER WITH HUMAN LIVES THIS WAY!
SILENCE! I MUST WATCH FOR THE TOK SHIP! SOON THE LIZARD MEN WILL ARRIVE, AND I MUST GREET THEM ROYALLY!
BUT, A SECOND LATER...
WHA--? SOMEONE -- OR SOMETHING, WHICH I CANNOT SEE, IS UNDOING MY BONDS!
20

AND, WITHIN THE STRONGHOLD OF DOCTOR DOOM...
HURRY! WE'VE ALREADY STOOD IN FRONT OF DOOM'S ENLARGING RAY! NOW IT'S YOUR TURN!
HEY! SOMEONE SHOULDA WARNED ME! THIS THING TICKLES!
NOW LET'S GET A LITTLE ACTION AROUND HERE! FLAME ON!
WE'RE JUST IN TIME! I SEE A SHIP APPROACHING! IT MUST BE THE TOK INVADERS!
STAND BACK, PAL! THAT SHIP IS COMIN' IN LIKE A SPEEDBALL, AND I AINT HAD ANY BATTING PRACTICE TODAY!
FIRST, I'LL JUST GRAB THIS LITTLE CONTROL TOWER!
NEXT, I'LL TAKE A FEW PRACTICE SWINGS! AND NOW--
HOME RUN! THEY'LL NEVER COME BACK HERE AGAIN!
WHAM!
HEARING THE SOUND OF THE TREMENDOUS IMPACT OUTSIDE, THE ANT-MAN'S GUARDS RELAX THEIR VIGIL FOR A SECOND -- A MOVE WHICH IS THEIR UNDOING!
I WAS HOPING I'D GET A CHANCE TO TRY THIS AGAIN!
STOP HIM! STOP HIM!
STAND ASIDE, YOU FOOLS! I'LL FINISH HIM OFF, ONCE AND FOR ALL!
NOT WITH THAT GUN, YOU WON'T!
WHA--??

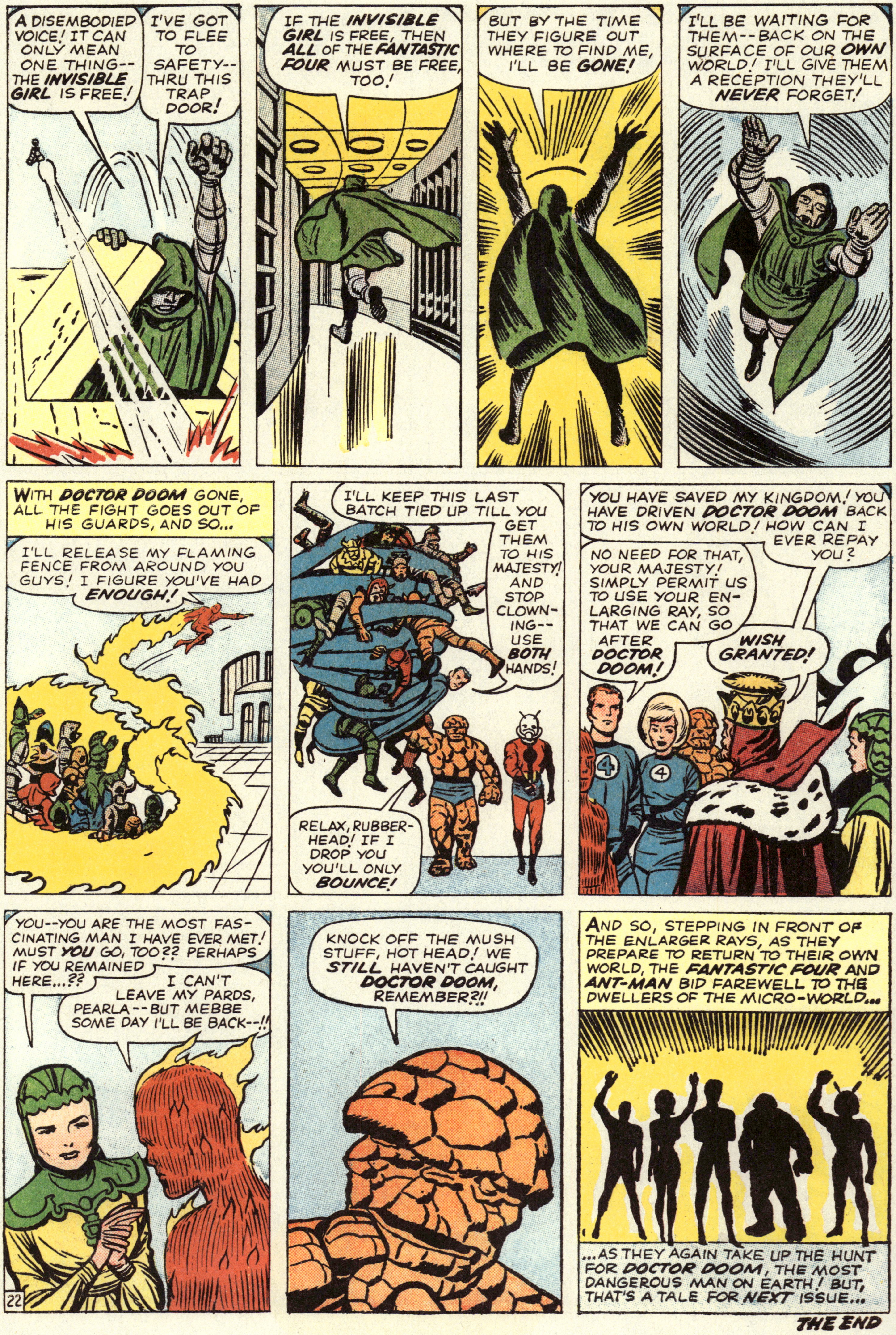
A DISEMBODIED VOICE! IT CAN ONLY MEAN ONE THING-- THE INVISIBLE GIRL IS FREE!
I'VE GOT TO FLEE TO SAFETY-- THRU THIS TRAP DOOR!
IF THE INVISIBLE GIRL IS FREE, THEN ALL OF THE FANTASTIC FOUR MUST BE FREE, TOO!
BUT BY THE TIME THEY FIGURE OUT WHERE TO FIND ME, I'LL BE GONE!
I'LL BE WAITING FOR THEM--BACK ON THE SURFACE OF OUR OWN WORLD! I'LL GIVE THEM A RECEPTION THEY'LL NEVER FORGET!
WITH DOCTOR DOOM GONE, ALL THE FIGHT GOES OUT OF HIS GUARDS, AND SO...
I'LL RELEASE MY FLAMING FENCE FROM AROUND YOU GUYS! I FIGURE YOU'VE HAD ENOUGH!
I'LL KEEP THIS LAST BATCH TIED UP TILL YOU GET THEM TO HIS MAJESTY! AND STOP CLOWNING--USE BOTH HANDS!
RELAX, RUBBER-HEAD! IF I DROP YOU YOU'LL ONLY BOUNCE!
YOU HAVE SAVED MY KINGDOM! YOU HAVE DRIVEN DOCTOR DOOM BACK TO HIS OWN WORLD! HOW CAN I EVER REPAY YOU?
NO NEED FOR THAT, YOUR MAJESTY! SIMPLY PERMIT US TO USE YOUR EN-LARGING RAY, SO THAT WE CAN GO AFTER DOCTOR DOOM!
WISH GRANTED!
YOU--YOU ARE THE MOST FAS-CINATING MAN I HAVE EVER MET! MUST YOU GO, TOO?? PERHAPS IF YOU REMAINED HERE...??
I CAN'T LEAVE MY PARDS, PEARLA--BUT MEBBE SOME DAY I'LL BE BACK--!!
22
KNOCK OFF THE MUSH STUFF, HOT HEAD! WE STILL HAVEN'T CAUGHT DOCTOR DOOM, REMEMBER?!!
AND SO, STEPPING IN FRONT OF THE ENLARGER RAYS, AS THEY PREPARE TO RETURN TO THEIR OWN WORLD, THE FANTASTIC FOUR AND ANT-MAN BID FAREWELL TO THE DWELLERS OF THE MICRO-WORLD...
...AS THEY AGAIN TAKE UP THE HUNT FOR DOCTOR DOOM, THE MOST DANGEROUS MAN ON EARTH! BUT, THAT'S A TALE FOR NEXT ISSUE...
THE END

Address YOUR letters to:
LEE and KIRBY
FANTASTIC FOUR
THIRD FLOOR
655 MADISON AVE.
NEW YORK 21, N. Y.

FANTASTIC FOUR FAN PAGE

Dear Stan and Jack:

I don't know how to start this letter off, so I'll just start in with the things I have to say: I have all the issues of the FF, and think they're great! Keep up the good work! I think the FF should meet *Thor*. It's meeting *Spider-Man* and the *Hulk* was so-so; you could have done better. And when *Spider-Man* entered through the window, he was captured by a capsule. In issue #5, the *Sub-Mariner* came through the window and the capsule didn't get him. What gives? A couple of issues ago, Dr. Doom was shrunk by his own weapon. Will we ever see him again? (Probably. All comic villains are born escape-artists.) I think the FF was better off not wearing costumes. The Invisible Girl and Mr. Fantastic should be in more action. I like the way Thing's "mad at the world," if you know what I mean. In the first two issues, you drew the Torch's flame somewhat differently than you do now. I liked it better the way you drew it in the first two issues. I think it would be interesting if somehow the FF's powers were sort of "mixed up." What I mean by this is this: What if: Sue were a "Thing," Johnny could turn invisible; Reed were a "Torch;" Ben would have Mr. Fantastic's power. Show more of the Impossible Man. Have more Pin-up pages. Your new character, "Iron Man," featured in *Tales of Suspense*, is pretty good.

Clifford Garber
25 Ocean Park
Lynn, Massachusetts

Know something, Cliff? You'd write a pretty good letter if you weren't so bashful about giving your opinions.

Dear Stan and Jack:

Unlike many of those who write, I can't say that I have read every issue of FF, but I still think that there are a few readers who are as dedicated to it as I. Take that Fred Bronson, for example—a steady reader since the first issue. What does he say? That fans read comics because the heroes don't act like real-life people, that's what. Of all the utter nonsense that I have ever heard that is the most ridiculous, and I'll give reasons to back that up. First of all, in order to enjoy almost any creative work (including comics), it is necessary to identify with some person. In music, for example, one should try to feel what the composer felt. In any of the media which tells a story, one should identify with at least one character. Otherwise, the story remains an empty shell, pretty to look at, but devoid of meaning. If a story relies upon either plot or character (and comic magazines are usually both), this is especially true. And now comes Fred Bronson, wanting to remove any shred of believability from your marvelous characters—an act which would make identification impossible. Secondly, the quality which makes yours the "world's greatest comic magazine" is precisely that your characters are true-to-life. To my knowledge, this trait is unique to you. In other respects you just barely maintain a moderately above-average rating. It is no accident that your best stories by far are those in which the personalities of the FF come through to play a main role in determining the outcome. I don't presume to know why most fans read most comics, but *this* fan reads *this* comic because its characters act like real-life people and not like comic book heroes. I apologize for such a lengthly letter, but I could not let such a point of view as Bronson's go unchallenged. If you're still with me after all this, thanks for listening.

Martha Beck
325 Dewey
Evanston, Illinois

We're with you, doll—all the way!

Dear Stan and Jack:

I must compliment you on your very GREAT comic magazine, 'The Fantastic Four.' It is by far the best I have ever seen (and I read almost all of them.) If this letter, or part of it, gets printed on your fan page, perhaps some of your critics will think that one such as I, who indulges in reading so-called 'light' material is a person of rather low intelligence. (Comic readers are held somewhat in scorn in some literary circles, you know.) I would like to say on my own behalf, that I do hold a completed college degree and that I also read other matter than comic magazines. I would like to say in your behalf that the entire magazine is worth all the praise it gets and even more, as the artwork, stories, and characters are of high quality.

Marya Rice
General Delivery
Main P. O.
Elizabeth, New Jersey

You're giving us such swelled heads, kid, that we may not sell any more copies of the FF to anyone unless they produce a diploma first!

Dear Stan and Jack:

I've tried putting off buying one or more titles, but in the first place, I can resist anything but temptation, and besides, I'm a collector and I'm mortally afraid of passing up anything for fear of its being sold out. *Thor* (Journey Into Mystery, #89) was so-so. For Thor that's pretty good, you know. Likewise the *Ant-Man* (Tales to Astonish, #41). The *Human Torch* (Strange Tales, #106) was pretty good, despite the fact that I kind of figured what the Torch was up to. *The Fantastic Four*, #12—Really good. You'll have to go some to outdo this issue. Since the *Hulk* has been running regularly in his own book, he doesn't seem so contrived as most of the antagonists the FF usually come up against. But I have to agree that Sue just doesn't get her share of the action. Shame on you for neglecting the poor girl! *The Amazing Spider-Man* #1! Buddy, you've got a real winner there in my book. I hope the younger readers agree, because I want to see this one *every* month! At least once!! And again, I'd like to plead with you to let Kirby loose—*just once*—give him lots of time and let him ink his own pencils. His tremendous talent manages to shine through anyway, but it's nothing compared to what he could do!

Phil Castora
Room 435, Russ Hotel
517-523 S. San Julian
Los Angeles, California

Let Kirby ink his own pencils?? Phil, we're trying to make sure he gets enough time just to PENCIL them!

Dear Stan and Jack:

I'm puzzled. When my parents were reading FF #11, they came to the pin-up of Sub-Mariner, and declared that Prince Namor was in comics before the *Fantastic Four.*

CONTINUED...

Perhaps you know something about this, and if you do, please give me the low-down.

Bill DeAndrew
56 Poningo St.
Port Chester, N. Y.

They're right, Bill! Years ago, in the Golden Age of Comics he was one of our biggest stars, and judging by the tremendous response we've had to his appearances, he well may be again!

Dear Stan and Jack:

Don't ever let anyone tell you that the FF are too impossible to exist *really*—or even in a comic. Every girl appears a little faint at times. And any teen-ager gets a little fired up, just as a grown man lets the beast in himself come out. Needless to say, a scientist must stretch a few points every now and then. So what's wrong if guys like Sue, Johnny, Ben and Reed do this in comics? It just proves that the FANTASTIC FOUR are a more believable group of super-heroes.

George Kitchen
1937 W. Pratt St.
Baltimore 23, Maryland

Pretty clever, George! We KNOW the F.F. exist! (At least, to US they do!) But the ones we're not sure about our READERS! We sometimes wonder if YOU guys and gals are for real!

Dear Stan and Jack:

I have been a fan of yours since the very first issue of the FF. I must admit that it has got something no other comic mag on the market has got. It has got a certain quality to it. Quality that has not been marred by the addition of ridiculous newcomers. Apparently you are the only current mag on the market that can refuse to cheapen their characters with Johnny-come lately's. I would like to say something about the so-called controversy over the *Thing*. In my opinion, the *Thing* is a part of your magazine that you cannot afford to do without. The personality you have provided him with is unique. The reason he is so essential is that he typifies the normal human being. He is not so perfect that he does not get mad and blow his top once in a while. I am saying this because in the recent issue #12, *FF Meets the Hulk*, I read some rather startling comments from Fred Bronson who wants to do away with the *Thing*. I just have one thing to say to Mr. Bronson. If he cannot stomach the conduct of the *Thing*, I suggest he watch 'Ding Dong School' every day on T.V. That way he would not have to put up with the dreadful language and ghastly conduct that has made the *Thing* an indispensable part of this superior comic magazine. Without the *Thing*, this magazine would be fairly easy to resist. As it is, it is practically impossible.

Gregg Smith
9543 Poole St.
La Jolla, California

Thanks, Gregg! We'll send DING DONG SCHOOL a bill for the plug tomorrow!

Dear Stan and Jack:

Since I am stating my personal wants (at the risk of making this sound like a letter to Santa Claus) I would rejoice at the sight of a mag which contains your super-heroes in single action (a good place for the Thing to meet the Yancy Street Gang), team-action (it would be interesting to see Ant-Man and Mr. Fantastic in conflict with The Chameleon and Paste-Pot Pete), and an occasional just plain science fiction story. You could also use this mag as a sounding board for your new super-heroes. Please put a letter column in *Tales to Astonish, Strange Tales, Journey Into Mystery,* and *Tales of Suspense*, or better yet, give Ant-Man, Thor, and possibly later Iron-Man their own magazines. Iron-Man has good potential, provided you do not give him too many transistorized gadgets. Perhaps a villain could find or steal one of his super-magnets and use it against him. There are almost unlimited possibilities provided he is not made too invulnerable. The Fantastic Four has always been my favorite mag. The art work in ish #13 was below par, although the plot was fairly good. I agree with Fredric Johnson in that the copter, pogo-plane and rocket should be used more. I doubt that you will get any more "flying bathtubs" complaints about the fantasticar, although I don't think Johnny modified it; instead, he built it anew. Now that you've modified it so greatly, for heaven's sake, don't be afraid to use it. The Red Ghost should return about issue #25. Perhaps he could team up with some of your other villains to battle the FF. I like the idea of teaming up two villains, especially when the villains are extremely different. I would enjoy seeing the Submariner in one or two stories as a complete hero. Thor is a very good character. He is best in combat against a super-villain, or at times, Loki. Loki is a good opponent, but don't use him every third issue. I like the idea of Odin saving Thor occasionally. Don't give Thor too many powers as this has ruined many a super hero. The powers displayed while combating the Stone Men and the Executioner are very good and they should not be multiplied. Spider-Man is an excellent hero although Steve's art work was a great deal better in *Amazing Fantasy*. Steve's drawing of the FF was horrid, (If someone slits my throat, we have a suspect.) Spider-Man should clear his name and keep himself out of the limelight. For the sake of fandom, don't make him into another *Hulk* in the sense that he becomes public enemy #1. I guess I've covered about everything in this letter. Good luck and keep up the good work. Yours til Dr. Doom rules the world . . .

Tom Dietz
141 E. Elm St.
Kent, Ohio

If you think that this is a long letter, you should see what we didn't print. Sure you wouldn't like to have two pages of story, and twenty of fan letters?

Dear Stan and Jack:

Boy, is my head spinning! Why, you ask? Well, over a year ago, you published the spectacular #1 issue of the FF. I thought you could never come out with any more of these unbelievable characters. Then you kept right on going strong and created the Mighty Thor, and at the same time, the Spider-Man. I could have done cartwheels. I tried to sit down for a breather, but you came out with the Astonishing Ant-Man and Iron-Man. Please don't create any more for a while or I'll have a nervous break-down. Here's hoping the FF, Ant-Man, Spider-Man, Thor, and Iron Man are published till my dying day—which I hope will be a long time from now.

David Singer
99 Herald St.
Rochester 21, N. Y.

Gosh—we haven't the heart to tell you about SGT. FURY AND THE HOWLING COMMANDOS, or about—but we'll leave that till next time!

SPECIAL ANNOUNCEMENTS SECTION:

- **Don't miss STRANGE TALES, #110 July, on sale the beginning of April. Besides the usual HUMAN TORCH feature thriller, you will find the first of a new series, featuring a new and different type of super-hero! His name's DR. STRANGE, and we can't wait to find out how you like him!**
- **Have you seen ANT-MAN'S beautiful new partner, THE WASP, in TALES TO ASTONISH yet?? We hear that SUE STORM is getting just a mite jealous — and when you see THE WASP, you'll soon see why!**
- **Next issue of FF will again feature DR. DOOM, in a super-thriller with a different twist! The THING has an important part to play in it, and we have a hunch you fans will really dig some of the unusual gimmicks and action! So, as we always say, do the smart thing — reserve your copy at your dealer's NOW!**
- **Thanks to all you fans who've writen to congratulate us on our new MARVEL COMICS GROUP name and cover trade mark. We're glad you like it, and promise to do our best to make sure that both you and we can be justly proud of it! That's it for now — see you next ish with the usual collection of thrills, spills, and chills!**

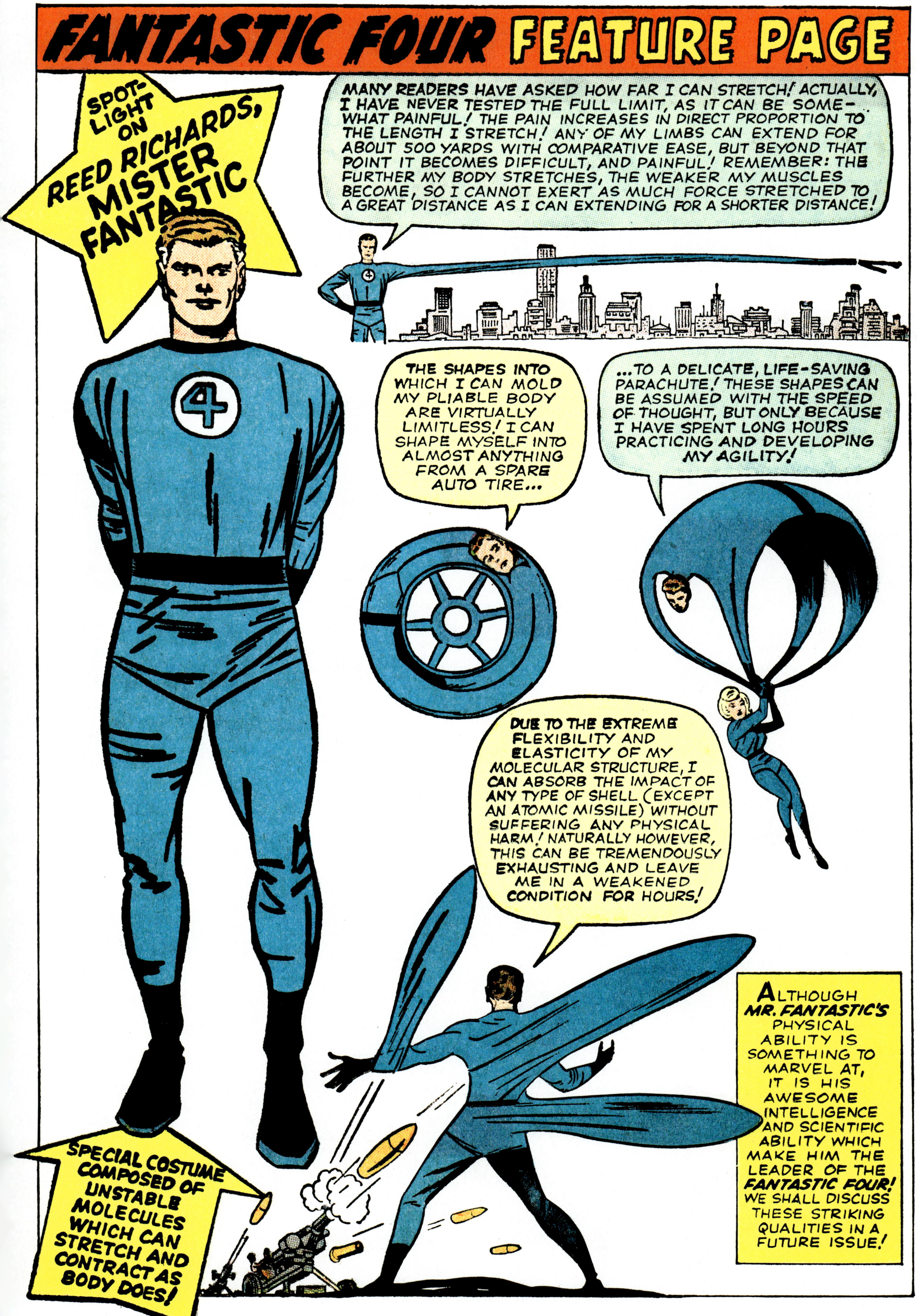
FANTASTIC FOUR FEATURE PAGE
SPOT-LIGHT ON REED RICHARDS, MISTER FANTASTIC
MANY READERS HAVE ASKED HOW FAR I CAN STRETCH! ACTUALLY, I HAVE NEVER TESTED THE FULL LIMIT, AS IT CAN BE SOME-WHAT PAINFUL! THE PAIN INCREASES IN DIRECT PROPORTION TO THE LENGTH I STRETCH! ANY OF MY LIMBS CAN EXTEND FOR ABOUT 500 YARDS WITH COMPARATIVE EASE, BUT BEYOND THAT POINT IT BECOMES DIFFICULT, AND PAINFUL! REMEMBER: THE FURTHER MY BODY STRETCHES, THE WEAKER MY MUSCLES BECOME, SO I CANNOT EXERT AS MUCH FORCE STRETCHED TO A GREAT DISTANCE AS I CAN EXTENDING FOR A SHORTER DISTANCE!
THE SHAPES INTO WHICH I CAN MOLD MY PLIABLE BODY ARE VIRTUALLY LIMITLESS! I CAN SHAPE MYSELF INTO ALMOST ANYTHING FROM A SPARE AUTO TIRE...
...TO A DELICATE, LIFE-SAVING PARACHUTE! THESE SHAPES CAN BE ASSUMED WITH THE SPEED OF THOUGHT, BUT ONLY BECAUSE I HAVE SPENT LONG HOURS PRACTICING AND DEVELOPING MY AGILITY!
DUE TO THE EXTREME FLEXIBILITY AND ELASTICITY OF MY MOLECULAR STRUCTURE, I CAN ABSORB THE IMPACT OF ANY TYPE OF SHELL (EXCEPT AN ATOMIC MISSILE) WITHOUT SUFFERING ANY PHYSICAL HARM! NATURALLY HOWEVER, THIS CAN BE TREMENDOUSLY EXHAUSTING AND LEAVE ME IN A WEAKENED CONDITION FOR HOURS!
SPECIAL COSTUME COMPOSED OF UNSTABLE MOLECULES WHICH CAN STRETCH AND CONTRACT AS BODY DOES!
ALTHOUGH MR. FANTASTIC'S PHYSICAL ABILITY IS SOMETHING TO MARVEL AT, IT IS HIS AWESOME INTELLIGENCE AND SCIENTIFIC ABILITY WHICH MAKE HIM THE LEADER OF THE FANTASTIC FOUR! WE SHALL DISCUSS THESE STRIKING QUALITIES IN A FUTURE ISSUE!

DO YOU WANT SPENDING MONEY?
Sell these popular Patriotic and Religious Mottoes
SEND US NO MONEY IN ADVANCE
Just write and ask us to send you 40 of these beautiful glittering mottoes which the public likes so well. Sell them easily and quickly to your friends and neighbors for only 35 each. At the end of 14 days send back, if you wish, all mottoes you have not sold, and send us only 25¢ for each you have sold. You keep all the rest of the money.
IF YOU SELL 25, YOU KEEP $2.50
IF YOU SELL 30, YOU KEEP $3.00
IF YOU SELL ALL 40 YOU KEEP $4.00
REMEMBER: No money is needed in advance. You take no risks. You can return all the mottoes you do not sell. You do not pay shipping costs or split your commission. You keep all the profit on each sale.
mother
God took the Sunshine from the Skies And made the Lovelight in your eyes; He gave you breath And with his Love made yours divine But best of all HE MADE YOU MINE
CHILD'S PRAYER
Now I Lay me down To Sleep. I pray the Lord my soul to keep. If I should Die before I Wake, I pray the Lord my soul to take
The Way Of The CROSS
HOME
Love one another AS I HAVE LOVED YOU
God Bless OUR HOME
WRITE FOR COMPLETE DETAILS TO
STEPHENS CREDIT SALES
Dept. R2 P. O. Box 1004
Nashville 3, Tennessee

THE WORLD'S GREATEST COMIC MAGAZINE!
APPROVED BY THE COMICS CODE AUTHORITY
IND.
Fantastic Four
17 AUG.
MARVEL COMICS GROUP 12¢
"IN THE CLUTCHES OF DOCTOR DOOM!"
CAN AMERICA'S MOST COLORFUL SUPER-COMBO ESCAPE FROM
THE MENACE OF THE MOVING BARS!
THE THREAT OF THE SWIRLING CEMENT!
THE PANIC OF THE DEADLY WHIRLWIND
THE PERIL OF THE ROOM WITHOUT A FLOOR!
MARVEL COMICS GROUP USHERS IN "THE MARVEL AGE OF COMICS!"

THE FANTASTIC FOUR is published by CANAM PUBLISHERS SALES CORP. OFFICE OF PUBLICATION: 655 MADISON AVENUE, NEW YORK, N.Y. Published monthly. Copyright 1963 by CANAM PUBLISHERS SALES CORP., 655 Madison Avenue, New York, N.Y. Vol. 1 No. 17, AUGUST, 1963 issue. Price 12¢ per copy. Subscription rate $1.75 for 12 issues including postage. Foreign subscription $3.25 in American funds. No similarity between any of the names, characters, persons, and/or institutions appearing in this magazine with those of any living or dead person is intended, and any such similarity which may exist is purely coincidental. Printed in U.S.A. by The Eastern Color Printing Co., Waterbury 20, Conn.

THE FABULOUS FANTASTIC FOUR...
STORY........STAN LEE
ART...........JACK KIRBY
INKING......DICK AYERS
LETTERING..ART SIMEK
"DEFEATED BY DOCTOR DOOM!"
HAPPY LANDINGS, ANT-MAN!
-SIGH- ISN'T HE THE CUTEST THING?!
I FEEL LIKE A MEATHEAD, WAVIN' TO SOMEONE THE SIZE OF A WORM!
LAST ISSUE, AIDED BY THE AMAZING ANT-MAN, THE FANTASTIC FOUR INVADED THE MICRO-WORLD OF DOCTOR DOOM, AND TRIUMPHED OVER THEIR ARCH-FOE! NOW, BACK HOME AGAIN, THEY BID ADIEU TO THEIR ANT-SIZED ALLY...
SO LONG, LITTLE PAL! YOU'RE A-OKAY IN OUR BOOK!
...AND SO BEGINS OUR NEW, EPIC TALE!
X-315
I'LL PUT AWAY THIS LITTLE LAUNCHING PLATFORM I BUILT FOR HIM! NEVER KNOW WHEN WE MIGHT NEED IT AGAIN!
WE COULD SURE USE A JOKER LIKE HIM IN OUR COMBO, EH, REED?
HE'D BE AN IMPROVEMENT OVER YOU, HOT-HEAD! WE WOULDN'T HAVETA KEEP A FIRE EXTINGUISHER HANDY WITH HIM AROUND!
WELL, WELL, YOU'RE TURNIN' INTO A REGULAR BOB HOPE!
ANT-MAN AND THE MIRISH
1

AW, KNOCK IT OFF, JUNIOR! I'M SO GLAD TO BE BACK TO MY NORMAL SIZE AGAIN THAT I AINT EVEN MAD AT YOU! THAT LITTLE TRIP TO DOCTOR DOOM'S MICRO-WORLD WASN'T EXACTLY MY IDEA OF A REST CURE! REMEMBER?
DO I REMEMBER? HECK, I'LL NEVER FORGET IT! WHEN OL' LAUGHING BOY REDUCED US TO THE SIZE OF TOYS, I THOUGHT WE WERE GONERS FOR SURE!
AND IF SUE AND REED HADN'T FIGURED OUT A WAY FOR US TO ESCAPE FROM THAT PRISON, SURROUNDED BY A SEA OF ACID, I GUESS I WOULDN'T BE SITTING HERE NOW, LOOKING AT YOUR 'UGH' FACE!
OH YEAH? YOU DIDN'T MIND LOOKIN' AT MY 'UGH FACE' WHEN I WAS MOPPIN' UP THE JOINT WITH DOOM'S LITTLE TIN SOLDIERS, DID YA? I'LL BET I LOOKED PRETTY GOOD TO YA THEN!
BUT DON'T FORGET, WHILE YOU TWO ARE SWAPPING PLATITUDES, DOCTOR DOOM MANAGED TO ESCAPE VIA THE ENLARGING RAY, AND HE'S FREE HERE ON EARTH AT THIS VERY MINUTE!
HIM? HE'S PROBABLY SHAKIN' IN HIS LITTLE BOOTIES RIGHT NOW, KNOWIN' THAT I'LL BE ON HIS TRAIL PRETTY SOON!
YOU KIDDIN'? HE'S PROBABLY LAUGHIN' HIMSELF TO DEATH!
ANYWAY, IT'S ABOUT TIME YOU TREATED ME WITH MORE RESPECT, BIG BOY! DON'T FORGET HOW THAT LIVIN' DOLL, PRINCESS PERLA, KNIGHTED ME BEFORE WE LEFT HER KINGDOM! YOU'RE LUCKY I DON'T MAKE YOU CALL ME "M'LORD"!
2

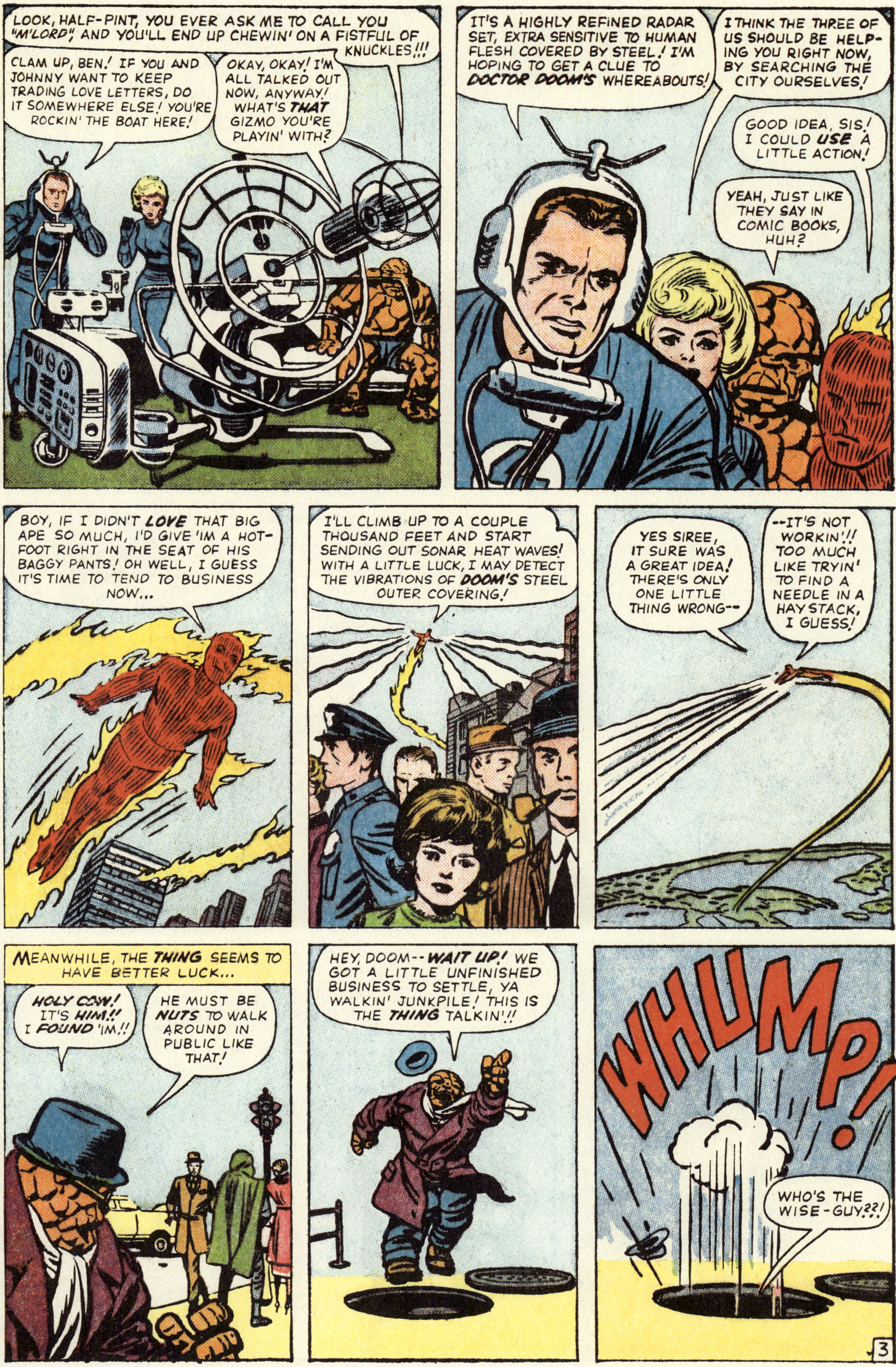
LOOK, HALF-PINT, YOU EVER ASK ME TO CALL YOU "M'LORD", AND YOU'LL END UP CHEWIN' ON A FISTFUL OF KNUCKLES!!!
CLAM UP, BEN! IF YOU AND JOHNNY WANT TO KEEP TRADING LOVE LETTERS, DO IT SOMEWHERE ELSE! YOU'RE ROCKIN' THE BOAT HERE!
OKAY, OKAY! I'M ALL TALKED OUT NOW, ANYWAY! WHAT'S THAT GIZMO YOU'RE PLAYIN' WITH?
IT'S A HIGHLY REFINED RADAR SET, EXTRA SENSITIVE TO HUMAN FLESH COVERED BY STEEL! I'M HOPING TO GET A CLUE TO DOCTOR DOOM'S WHEREABOUTS!
I THINK THE THREE OF US SHOULD BE HELPING YOU RIGHT NOW, BY SEARCHING THE CITY OURSELVES!
GOOD IDEA, SIS! I COULD USE A LITTLE ACTION!
YEAH, JUST LIKE THEY SAY IN COMIC BOOKS, HUH?
BOY, IF I DIDN'T LOVE THAT BIG APE SO MUCH, I'D GIVE 'IM A HOT-FOOT RIGHT IN THE SEAT OF HIS BAGGY PANTS! OH WELL, I GUESS IT'S TIME TO TEND TO BUSINESS NOW...
I'LL CLIMB UP TO A COUPLE THOUSAND FEET AND START SENDING OUT SONAR HEAT WAVES! WITH A LITTLE LUCK, I MAY DETECT THE VIBRATIONS OF DOOM'S STEEL OUTER COVERING!
YES SIREE, IT SURE WAS A GREAT IDEA! THERE'S ONLY ONE LITTLE THING WRONG--
--IT'S NOT WORKIN'!! TOO MUCH LIKE TRYIN' TO FIND A NEEDLE IN A HAYSTACK, I GUESS!
MEANWHILE, THE THING SEEMS TO HAVE BETTER LUCK...
HOLY COW! IT'S HIM!! I FOUND 'IM!!
HE MUST BE NUTS TO WALK AROUND IN PUBLIC LIKE THAT!
HEY, DOOM--WAIT UP! WE GOT A LITTLE UNFINISHED BUSINESS TO SETTLE, YA WALKIN' JUNKPILE! THIS IS THE THING TALKIN'!!
WHUMP!
WHO'S THE WISE-GUY??!
3

HOW THE *?#!!*?* DO I GET OUTTA HERE??!
LADY! LOOK OUT!
MY BRAKES ARE JAMMED!!
I AINT GOT TIME TO FIND THE RIGHT EXIT, SO I'LL JUST--
HEY! A GUY COULD GET A CHARLEY HORSE THIS WAY!!
OH! YOU-- YOU SAVED MY LIFE!
SURE, SURE! I'M JUST A BIG, FAT, HANDSOME HERO! NOW GET OUTTA THE WAY--I GOT THINGS TO DO!
WOW! IT'S THE THING! LOOK AT THAT BIG FELLA MOVE!
HE--HE'S SO GROTESQUE THAT HE'S ALMOST BEAUTIFUL!
HAH! I KNEW I'D CATCH UP TO 'IM! BOY, AM I GONNA ENJOY THIS!
HEY, BUSTER! TURN AROUND! I WANNA GAZE INTO YOUR BABY BLUES WHILE I MOP UP THE STREET WITH YA!
WHAT GIVES, MISTER?? YOU SOME KINDA FANATIC, OR SOMETHIN'??
I'LL BE A MONKEY'S UNCLE!! I BEEN ROBBED!!
TODAY AT THE BIJOU THEATER "WHEN KNIGHTS WERE BOLD!" SEE IT NOW!
AND, IN ANOTHER PART OF TOWN...
IF DOCTOR DOOM IS IN THE CITY, HE'LL BE SURE TO CONTACT SOME HARDENED CRIMINALS TO HELP HIM! SO, IF I INVISIBLY FOLLOW SOME UNDERWORLD TYPES, PERHAPS...
-GASP!- I WOULDN'T HAVE EXPECTED ANYTHING AS BLATANT AS THIS TO TAKE PLACE RIGHT OUT IN THE OPEN!
I THINK THIS IS WHAT YOU'VE BEEN WAITING FOR, MR. SPADE!
YEAH! LET ME HAVE IT, PROFESSOR, AND I'LL SEE IF IT'S THE ONE I WANT!
THIS SPECIAL ADAPTER IS WHAT WILL MAKE THE DIFFERENCE! NOTICE HOW SMOOTHLY IT FITS ON THE BARREL OF THE GUN! IT'S EASY TO HANDLE, AND NEVER MISSES!
4

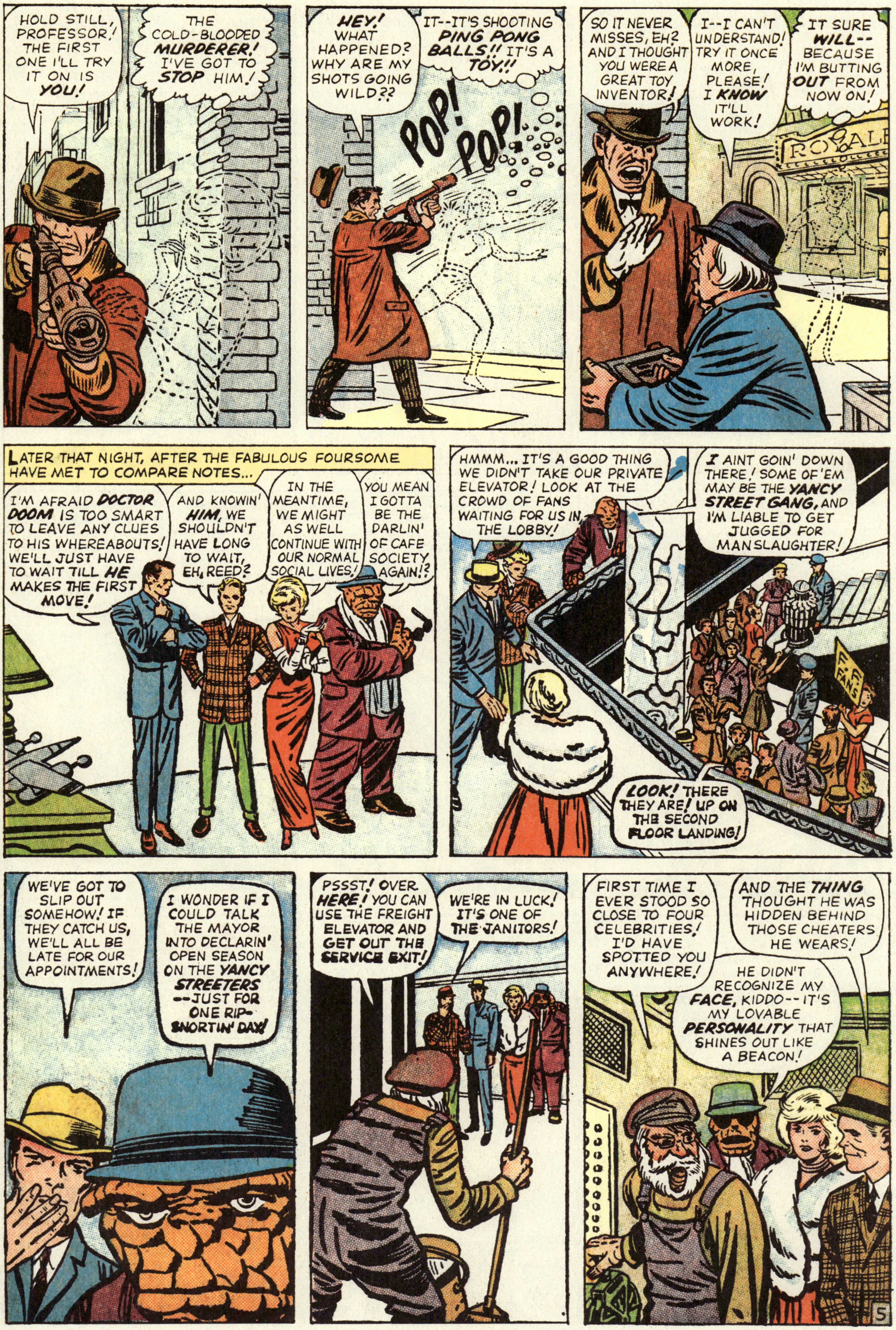

HOLD STILL, PROFESSOR! THE FIRST ONE I'LL TRY IT ON IS YOU!
THE COLD-BLOODED MURDERER! I'VE GOT TO STOP HIM!
HEY! WHAT HAPPENED? WHY ARE MY SHOTS GOING WILD??
IT--IT'S SHOOTING PING PONG BALLS!! IT'S A TOY!!
POP! POP!
SO IT NEVER MISSES, EH? AND I THOUGHT YOU WERE A GREAT TOY INVENTOR!
I--I CAN'T UNDERSTAND! TRY IT ONCE MORE, PLEASE! I KNOW IT'LL WORK!
IT SURE WILL-- BECAUSE I'M BUTTING OUT FROM NOW ON!
LATER THAT NIGHT, AFTER THE FABULOUS FOURSOME HAVE MET TO COMPARE NOTES...
I'M AFRAID DOCTOR DOOM IS TOO SMART TO LEAVE ANY CLUES TO HIS WHEREABOUTS! WE'LL JUST HAVE TO WAIT TILL HE MAKES THE FIRST MOVE!
AND KNOWIN' HIM, WE SHOULDN'T HAVE LONG TO WAIT, EH, REED?
IN THE MEANTIME, WE MIGHT AS WELL CONTINUE WITH OUR NORMAL SOCIAL LIVES!
YOU MEAN I GOTTA BE THE DARLIN' OF CAFE SOCIETY AGAIN!?
HMMM... IT'S A GOOD THING WE DIDN'T TAKE OUR PRIVATE ELEVATOR! LOOK AT THE CROWD OF FANS WAITING FOR US IN THE LOBBY!
I AINT GOIN' DOWN THERE! SOME OF 'EM MAY BE THE YANCY STREET GANG, AND I'M LIABLE TO GET JUGGED FOR MANSLAUGHTER!
F.F. FANS
LOOK! THERE THEY ARE! UP ON THE SECOND FLOOR LANDING!
WE'VE GOT TO SLIP OUT SOMEHOW! IF THEY CATCH US, WE'LL ALL BE LATE FOR OUR APPOINTMENTS!
I WONDER IF I COULD TALK THE MAYOR INTO DECLARIN' OPEN SEASON ON THE YANCY STREETERS --JUST FOR ONE RIP-SNORTIN' DAY!
PSSST! OVER HERE! YOU CAN USE THE FREIGHT ELEVATOR AND GET OUT THE SERVICE EXIT!
WE'RE IN LUCK! IT'S ONE OF THE JANITORS!
FIRST TIME I EVER STOOD SO CLOSE TO FOUR CELEBRITIES! I'D HAVE SPOTTED YOU ANYWHERE!
AND THE THING THOUGHT HE WAS HIDDEN BEHIND THOSE CHEATERS HE WEARS!
HE DIDN'T RECOGNIZE MY FACE, KIDDO-- IT'S MY LOVABLE PERSONALITY THAT SHINES OUT LIKE A BEACON!
5

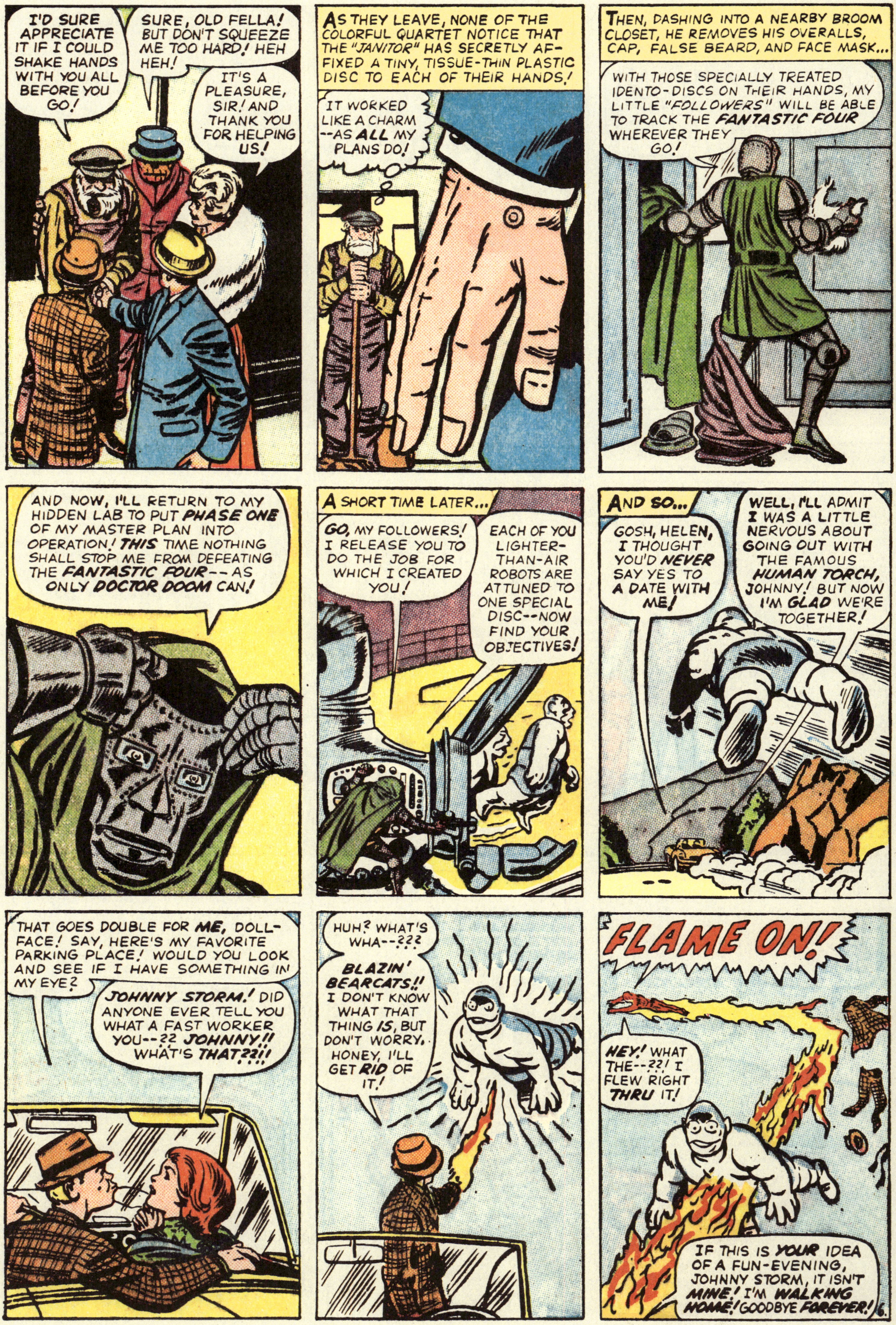

I'D SURE APPRECIATE IT IF I COULD SHAKE HANDS WITH YOU ALL BEFORE YOU GO!
SURE, OLD FELLA! BUT DON'T SQUEEZE ME TOO HARD! HEH HEH!
IT'S A PLEASURE, SIR! AND THANK YOU FOR HELPING US!
AS THEY LEAVE, NONE OF THE COLORFUL QUARTET NOTICE THAT THE "JANITOR" HAS SECRETLY AFFIXED A TINY, TISSUE-THIN PLASTIC DISC TO EACH OF THEIR HANDS!
IT WORKED LIKE A CHARM --AS ALL MY PLANS DO!
THEN, DASHING INTO A NEARBY BROOM CLOSET, HE REMOVES HIS OVERALLS, CAP, FALSE BEARD, AND FACE MASK...
WITH THOSE SPECIALLY TREATED IDENTO-DISCS ON THEIR HANDS, MY LITTLE "FOLLOWERS" WILL BE ABLE TO TRACK THE FANTASTIC FOUR WHEREVER THEY GO!
AND NOW, I'LL RETURN TO MY HIDDEN LAB TO PUT PHASE ONE OF MY MASTER PLAN INTO OPERATION! THIS TIME NOTHING SHALL STOP ME FROM DEFEATING THE FANTASTIC FOUR--AS ONLY DOCTOR DOOM CAN!
A SHORT TIME LATER...
GO, MY FOLLOWERS! I RELEASE YOU TO DO THE JOB FOR WHICH I CREATED YOU!
EACH OF YOU LIGHTER-THAN-AIR ROBOTS ARE ATTUNED TO ONE SPECIAL DISC--NOW FIND YOUR OBJECTIVES!
AND SO...
GOSH, HELEN, I THOUGHT YOU'D NEVER SAY YES TO A DATE WITH ME!
WELL, I'LL ADMIT I WAS A LITTLE NERVOUS ABOUT GOING OUT WITH THE FAMOUS HUMAN TORCH, JOHNNY! BUT NOW I'M GLAD WE'RE TOGETHER!
THAT GOES DOUBLE FOR ME, DOLL-FACE! SAY, HERE'S MY FAVORITE PARKING PLACE! WOULD YOU LOOK AND SEE IF I HAVE SOMETHING IN MY EYE?
JOHNNY STORM! DID ANYONE EVER TELL YOU WHAT A FAST WORKER YOU--?? JOHNNY!! WHAT'S THAT??!!
HUH? WHAT'S WHA--???
BLAZIN' BEARCATS!! I DON'T KNOW WHAT THAT THING IS, BUT DON'T WORRY, HONEY, I'LL GET RID OF IT!
FLAME ON!
HEY! WHAT THE--??! I FLEW RIGHT THRU IT!
IF THIS IS YOUR IDEA OF A FUN-EVENING, JOHNNY STORM, IT ISN'T MINE! I'M WALKING HOME! GOODBYE FOREVER!
6.

AND, AT THE SAME TIME, IN ANOTHER PLACE...
HA HA! BOY, AS IF THE THING ISN'T CONSPICU-OUS-LOOKING ENOUGH--
HE'S GOT HIS OWN PERSONAL FLOATING WATCH-DOG TRAILING AFTER HIM!
BEN, WHAT IS IT? WHY IS EVERY-ONE LAUGHING AT YOU?
I'LL TELL YA, LATER, ALICIA BABY! RIGHT NOW, I'M GONNA DEMOLISH ME A FLYIN' WISE-GUY!
TRY TO MAKE A LAUGHIN'-STOCK OUTTA THE THING, WILL YA?? WELL, THIS'LL TAKE THE WIND OUTTA YOUR SAILS!!!
HEY! I SLAMMED RIGHT THRU 'IM!! HE ISN'T EVEN SOLID!! HE'S SOME KINDA GHOST OR SOMETHIN'!!!
AS FOR SUE STORM, SHE HAS A MORE DECORATIVE FOLLOWER FOR HERSELF...
HOLD IT, MISS STORM! BEFORE WE SNAP YOU FOR THIS U.S. SAVINGS BOND POSTER, YOU'LL HAVE TO GET RID OF THAT THING ABOVE YOU!
GOOD HEAVENS! I DON'T KNOW WHAT IT IS, BUT I CAN'T SHAKE IT! IT FOLLOWS WHEREVER I GO!
THIS IS TERRIBLE! EVEN THOUGH I'VE TURNED INVISIBLE, IT'S STILL FOLLOWING ME! BUT HOW--WHY--??
AND, IN A DIGNIFIED LECTURE HALL, NOT FAR AWAY...
IT GIVES ME GREAT PLEASURE TO CONFER UPON REED RICHARDS THE HONORARY DEGREE OF DOCTOR OF--
ULP! WHAT ON EARTH IS THAT??!
DOCTOR RICHARDS!! WE ALL KNOW HOW BRILLIANT YOU ARE AT DEVISING COLORFUL SCIENTIFIC EFFECTS--BUT I HARDLY THINK THAT THIS IS THE PROPER TIME OR PLACE...
FORGIVE ME, SIR! I HAD NOTHING TO DO WITH--WITH WHAT-EVER THAT IS!!
WELL, LITTLE FRIEND, YOU RUINED MY EVENING, LOST ME AN HONORARY DEGREE, AND I STILL CAN'T LOSE YOU! BUT THAT'S ALL RIGHT--KEEP FOLLOWING TO MY LAB! I HAVE A HUNCH WHAT YOU ARE, AND WHO DESIGNED YOU!
IMPERIAL CAB

FINALLY, AT THE WORLD-FAMOUS HEADQUARTERS OF THE GREATEST SUPER-TEAM MANKIND HAS EVER KNOWN...
CALM DOWN, EVERYONE! I HAVE A LITTLE GADGET HERE WHICH WILL SOON TELL US WHAT WE WANT TO KNOW ABOUT THESE FLOATING "FOLLOWERS"!
ALL I WANNA KNOW IS HOW I CAN LAND JUST ONE HEALTHY PUNCH AT THAT FLYIN' FREAK ABOVE ME!
ME TOO! THE BLAMED THING RUINED A DATE I'VE BEEN PRO-MOTIN' FOR WEEKS!
THERE! I MODIFIED THIS ELECTRO-DETECTOR TO ZERO IN ON WHATEVER IS ATTRACTING THE "FOLLOWERS" TO US! SEE? IT'S POINTING AT MY WRIST!
BIG DEAL! WHATCHA TRYIN' TO PROVE?? THAT YA GOT ATTRACTIVE WRISTS??
OH HUSH, BEN! LET REED FINISH!
BEEEEEEELPPPPP!
HERE'S WHAT WE'VE BEEN SEEKING! THIS TINY PLASTIC DISC! LOOK AT YOUR WRISTS, TOO--I'LL WAGER YOU'VE EACH GOT ONE!
YOU'RE RIGHT! BUT WHAT DOES IT MEAN?
I KNEW THE "FOLLOWERS" WERE JUST INANIMATE THINGS WITH NO LIFE OF THEIR OWN! THEY HAD TO BE ATTRACTED BY SOMETHING--AND THESE LITTLE DISCS ACTED LIKE MAGNETS, KEEPING THEM WITH US!
YOU'RE RIGHT, BIG DADDY! I BRUSHED THAT BLAMED DISC OFF, AND LOOK--
IT'S FADIN' AWAY!
THEY WON'T BOTHER US ANY MORE! WITHOUT THE DISCS TO SUMMON THEM, THEY'LL SIMPLY FADE AWAY FOREVER!
WHAT LUNKHEADS WE WERE! THAT PHONY JANITOR MUSTA SLAPPED THOSE DISCS ON US WHEN HE WAS SHAKIN' OUR MITTS!
AND THAT MEANS HE MUST HAVE REALLY BEEN--DOCTOR DOOM!
THEN--FOR ALL WE KNOW, HE'S MONITORING OUR EVERY MOVEMENT RIGHT NOW WITH ONE OF THOSE DIABOLICAL MACHINES OF HIS!!
HOW RIGHT SHE IS!! BUT NOW THE FIRST PHASE OF MY PLAN IS ENDED! I ONLY INTENDED TO EMBARRASS AND CONFUSE THEM!
NOW I SHALL GO TO WORK WITH A VENGEANCE--AND MY FINAL PURPOSE SHALL BE--THEIR COMPLETE DESTRUCTION!
8

WHILE SPYING ON THE ACCURSED THING, I REALIZED THE ONE WAY I CAN DEFEAT THE HATED FOURSOME...
I SHALL STRIKE AT THEM THRU THEIR WEAKEST LINK--THE ONE WHOM THE THING LOVES--THE SIGHTLESS ALICIA!
ALTHOUGH MY BRAIN IS THE EQUAL OF REED RICHARDS' HIMSELF, I TOO HAVE HAD MY ONE WEAK SPOT...
I HAVE NEVER FULLY UNDERSTOOD OTHER HUMAN BEINGS! EVEN NOW, I CANNOT COMPREHEND HOW ONE AS LOVELY AS ALICIA CAN FEEL AFFECTION FOR THE GROTESQUE THING!!
HOW IRONIC IT IS THAT EVEN A GARGOYLE SUCH AS THE THING CAN FIND LOVE --EVEN HE CAN MINGLE WITH NORMAL PEOPLE!
AND YET, I--AND I ALONE, DARE NOT EXPOSE MY FACE TO THE VIEW OF OTHER HUMANS! I ALONE MUST HIDE LIKE A DARK WRAITH FROM THE SIGHT OF MY FELLOW MAN!
BUT I SHALL HAVE MY REVENGE --UPON THE ENTIRE HUMAN RACE--BEGINNING WITH THE FANTASTIC FOUR! AND STARTING-- NOW!
SUDDENLY, WITHOUT WARNING, AT THE FLICK OF A SWITCH FROM DOCTOR DOOM'S MASTER CONTROL PANEL, A STRANGE GRAPPLER RAY DRIFTS TO THE SPOT WHERE THE GENTLE ALICIA IS WALKING THRU THE STREET, AND THEN--
WHAT--IS HAPPENING TO ME??
I SEEM TO BE WALKING ON AIR!! I FEEL AS THOUGH I'M BEING LIFTED UPWARD--INTO THE SKY!! BUT IT'S IMPOSSIBLE! IT CANNOT BE!
HOWEVER, FEW THINGS ARE IMPOSSIBLE TO ONE WHO IS A MASTER OF SCIENCE... AND, SECONDS LATER, THE ASTONISHED GIRL PASSES THRU WHAT SEEMS TO BE A FLOATING CLOUD WHEN VIEWED FROM EARTH-- BUT IN REALITY, IS THE HIDING PLACE FOR DOCTOR DOOM'S INCREDIBLE FLOATING LABORATORY!
CLOSER--JUST A LITTLE CLOSER, AND MY TRAP WILL HAVE BEEN SPRUNG!
9

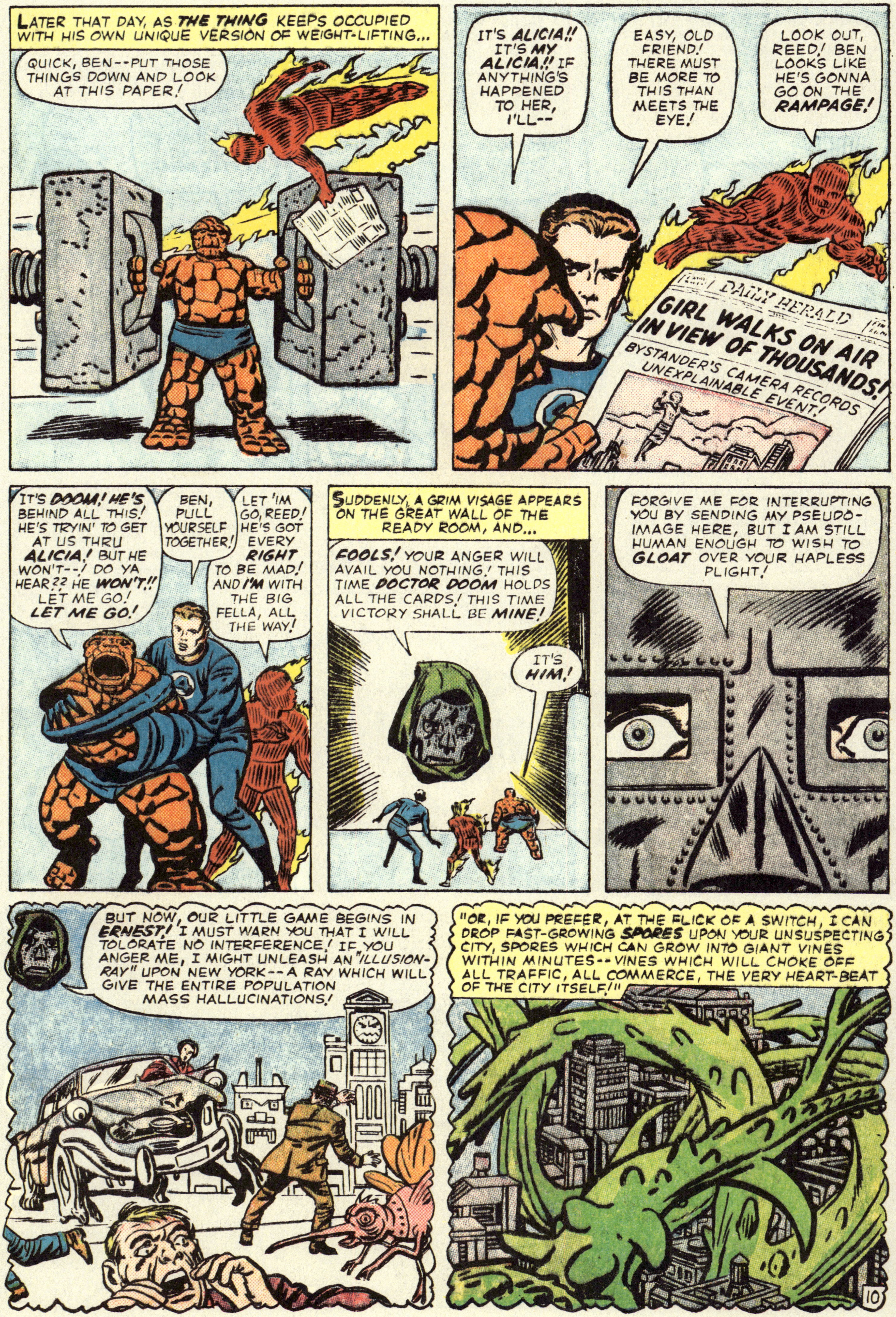
LATER THAT DAY, AS THE THING KEEPS OCCUPIED WITH HIS OWN UNIQUE VERSION OF WEIGHT-LIFTING...
QUICK, BEN--PUT THOSE THINGS DOWN AND LOOK AT THIS PAPER!
IT'S ALICIA!! IT'S MY ALICIA!! IF ANYTHING'S HAPPENED TO HER, I'LL--
EASY, OLD FRIEND! THERE MUST BE MORE TO THIS THAN MEETS THE EYE!
LOOK OUT, REED! BEN LOOKS LIKE HE'S GONNA GO ON THE RAMPAGE!
DAILY HERALD
GIRL WALKS ON AIR IN VIEW OF THOUSANDS!
BYSTANDER'S CAMERA RECORDS UNEXPLAINABLE EVENT!
IT'S DOOM! HE'S BEHIND ALL THIS! HE'S TRYIN' TO GET AT US THRU ALICIA! BUT HE WON'T--! DO YA HEAR?? HE WON'T!! LET ME GO! LET ME GO!
BEN, PULL YOURSELF TOGETHER!
LET 'IM GO, REED! HE'S GOT EVERY RIGHT TO BE MAD! AND I'M WITH THE BIG FELLA, ALL THE WAY!
SUDDENLY, A GRIM VISAGE APPEARS ON THE GREAT WALL OF THE READY ROOM, AND...
FOOLS! YOUR ANGER WILL AVAIL YOU NOTHING! THIS TIME DOCTOR DOOM HOLDS ALL THE CARDS! THIS TIME VICTORY SHALL BE MINE!
IT'S HIM!
FORGIVE ME FOR INTERRUPTING YOU BY SENDING MY PSEUDO-IMAGE HERE, BUT I AM STILL HUMAN ENOUGH TO WISH TO GLOAT OVER YOUR HAPLESS PLIGHT!
BUT NOW, OUR LITTLE GAME BEGINS IN ERNEST! I MUST WARN YOU THAT I WILL TOLORATE NO INTERFERENCE! IF YOU ANGER ME, I MIGHT UNLEASH AN "ILLUSION-RAY" UPON NEW YORK--A RAY WHICH WILL GIVE THE ENTIRE POPULATION MASS HALLUCINATIONS!
"OR, IF YOU PREFER, AT THE FLICK OF A SWITCH, I CAN DROP FAST-GROWING SPORES UPON YOUR UNSUSPECTING CITY, SPORES WHICH CAN GROW INTO GIANT VINES WITHIN MINUTES--VINES WHICH WILL CHOKE OFF ALL TRAFFIC, ALL COMMERCE, THE VERY HEART-BEAT OF THE CITY ITSELF!"
10

AND NEVER FORGET MY GREATEST THREAT--ALICIA IS NOW MY PRISONER! IF YOU WISH EVER TO SEE HER AGAIN, YOU MUST NOT DARE TO OPPOSE ME! THUS DO I RENDER THE FAMED FANTASTIC FOUR HELPLESS! THUS DOES DOCTOR DOOM BECOME THE MOST POWERFUL OF ALL!
WAIT! WHAT ABOUT ALICIA?? HEY--DON'T FADE AWAY--!!!
DOES HE REALLY THINK HE CAN THREATEN US?? DOES HE THINK ANYTHING WILL STOP ME FROM TRACKING HIM DOWN--FROM RIDDING THE WORLD OF THE THREAT HE POSES??
DON'T SAY THAT, REED! NOT WHILE ALICIA'S HIS PRISONER! YOU MUSTN'T CROSS HIM, DO YA HEAR?!! I WON'T LET YA!
BUT, BEN, DON'T YOU SEE? THIS IS WHAT HE WANTS!! TO TIE OUR HANDS! TO--UGH!
DON'T TRY TO SWEET-TALK ME INTO ANYTHING!! I AINT LETTIN' ALICIA COME TO HARM--NO MATTER WHAT!!
POW!
HA! I AM TRIUMPHANT EVEN BEYOND MY WILDEST HOPES! THEY ARE FIGHTING AMONGST THEMSELVES! SO, I SHALL LET THEM A WHILE LONGER--LET THEM TREMBLE AT MY NEXT MOVE--AS THE WORLD SHALL SOON TREMBLE!
FOR IT IS NOT MONEY I SEEK--NOT PERSONAL GAIN! WITH MY GENIUS, I CAN MAKE FORTUNES EASILY AS OTHERS MAKE PENNIES! NO, WHAT I CRAVE IS POWER! AND THAT IS WHAT I SHALL HAVE!
I SHALL SEND THIS SPECIALLY-PREPARED TAPE TO WASHINGTON, OUTLINING MY DEMANDS!
ACTUALLY, MY TERMS ARE MODEST FOR ONE AS POWERFUL AS I! ALL I INSIST UPON IS A POST IN THE PRESIDENT'S CABINET! IT IS ONLY FITTING THAT A MAN OF MY ABILITY HAVE AT LEAST CABINET RANK IN THE GOVERNMENT!
AND SO... NOT LONG AFTERWARDS...
IT'S ALMOST UNBELIEVABLE! HE ACTUALLY THREATENS US WITH WAR IF HIS TERMS ARE NOT MET!
THIS IS THE FIRST TIME IN HISTORY, SIR, THAT ONE MAN HAS THREATENED TO DECLARE WAR ON AN ENTIRE NATION!
NO MATTER WHAT WEAPONS HE MAY HAVE AT HIS DISPOSAL, WE CAN NEVER ALLOW THIS NATION TO BE DICTATATED TO BY ONE SINISTER MAN--NOT EVEN SO POWERFUL A MAN AS DOCTOR DOOM!
THERE IS ONLY ONE THING TO DO! WE MUST SHOW HIM THAT THE UNITED STATES CANNOT BE THREATENED BY ANYONE! WE MUST MOVE FORWARD AND PROCEED WITH GREAT VIGOR! AND NOW, GENTLEMEN, IF YOU'LL EXCUSE ME, IT'S CAROLINE'S BEDTIME!
11

THE NEXT DAY, NOT RECEIVING THE ANSWER HE DESIRED FROM THE WHITE HOUSE, DOCTOR DOOM BEGINS HIS ONE-MAN WAR! IN FACTORIES AND LABORATORIES ALL OVER THE COUNTRY--
SOMETHING'S WRONG WITH ALL THE ELECTRONIC MACHINES! THEY'VE GONE HAYWIRE!
BLINK BLINK
WEEEEOOOOOOOO
AMERICA'S DEFENSIVE MISSILES, GUIDED BY COMPLEX ELECTRONIC BRAINS, SUDDENLY GO OUT OF CONTROL...
IT'S AS THOUGH SOME EVIL GENIUS HAS TAMPERED WITH EVERY ELECTRICAL DEVICE IN THE NATION!
THE SAME THING IS HAPPENING TO EVERY MISSILE THRUOUT THE COUNTRY! IT'S UNCANNY!
WITHIN HOURS, EVERY MAN, WOMAN, AND CHILD IS AFFECTED, AS FACTORIES ARE SHUT DOWN DUE TO FAILURES IN MECHANICAL GUIDANCE CONTROLS AND AUTOMATED SAFETY DEVICES! ALMOST OVERNIGHT, THE MIGHTY INDUSTRIAL COMPLEX OF AMERICA SEEMS TO GRIND TO A HALT!
YOU GOTTA GET THOSE MACHINES FIXED!! WE WANT OUR JOBS BACK!!
CLOSED UNTIL FURTHER NOTICE
THE NEWS TRAVELS QUICKLY-- TO BEHIND THE IRON CURTAIN...
DA! IT IS THE BEST NEWS WE HAVE HEARD IN WEEKS!
SOON THE CAPITALISTIC COUNTRIES WILL BE HELPLESS BEFORE US!
STOP GLOATING, YOU NUMB-SKULLS! DOCTOR DOOM IS NOT DOING THIS FOR US! FOR ALL WE KNOW, HE MAY STRIKE HERE NEXT!
IF HE IS ABLE TO WRECK THE AMERICAN ELECTRONIC SYSTEM, WHY SHOULD HE NOT BE ABLE TO DO THE SAME TO OURS??
YOU ARE RIGHT, COMRADE K! I NEVER THOUGHT OF THAT!
DA! THAT IS WHY YOU WILL NEVER BE DICTATOR!
AND, IN NEW YORK, THE FANTASTIC FOUR RECEIVE A GRIM-FACED, BROODING VISITOR!
AND SO, THE JOINT CHIEFS OF STAFF FELT THAT INASMUCH AS YOU FOUR HAD BATTLED DR. DOOM IN THE PAST, AND DE-FEATED HIM, YOU MIGHT BE THE BEST CHOICE TO--
WE UNDERSTAND, COLONEL! WE'RE PREPARED TO DO WHAT-EVER IS NECESSARY!
SURE! WHATEVER DOOM CAN DO, MR. FANTASTIC CAN DO A HECKUVA LOT BETTER!
TALK, TALK, TALK, WHILE POOR ALICIA IS STILL HIS PRISONER!
AS A MATTER OF FACT, SIR, I HAVE ALREADY FORMULATED A PLAN OF ATTACK AGAINST OUR MUTUAL ENEMY!
OH? AND MAY I KNOW WHAT IT IS?
SORRY, COLONEL! IT WILL BE SAFER IF NOBODY BUT THE FOUR OF US KNOW ABOUT IT!
12

THEN, AFTER THE VISITOR FROM WASHINGTON HAS DEPARTED...
REED, I-I'M SORRY I BLEW UP YESTERDAY! BUT TELL ME-- IS THERE REALLY A PLAN?? IS THERE REALLY SOME WAY TO FIGHT THAT IRON-FACED SKUNK?? TELL ME!
THERE IS, OLD FRIEND! AND IT WILL BE MOSTLY UP TO YOU! LET ME EXPLAIN...
OH, REED, IF ONLY YOU COULD FIND A WAY!
WITH THE AID OF MY ELECTRO-SCANNER, I WAS RECENTLY ABLE TO DISCOVER DOCTOR DOOM'S HIDDEN HIDEAWAY!
THIS IS AN ULTRA-VIOLET RAY PHOTO I TOOK OF A STRANGE CLOUD WHICH HAD BEEN HOVERING OVER THE CITY-- LOOK WHAT IS WITHIN THE CLOUD!!
WE SHOULDA GUESSED! HE HAD TO BE SOMEWHERE CLOSE BY TO KEEP MONITORING US THE WAY HE DID!
BUT FINDING HIM WAS ONLY PART OF THE PROBLEM!
NOW I'LL SHOW YOU AN ENLARGEMENT OF A SECTION OF THAT PHOTO-- BLOWN UP ALMOST ONE THOUSAND TIMES ITS NORMAL SIZE!
HURRY, REED! WE'RE WASTIN' TIME!
BEN, IF I LET YOU RUSH TO ATTACK HIM, YOU'D BE A DEAD MAN WITHIN MINUTES! HE HAS THE MOST FOOL-PROOF DEFENSE AGAINST US EVER DEVISED!
SEE THAT?? THOSE ARE DISINTEGRATOR RAY GUNS-- JUST POISED AND READY FOR US!
AND THOSE FIGURES UP THERE-- WHAT IN SAM HILL ARE THEY???
THESE ARE THE MOST DIABOLICAL PARTS OF HIS TRAP! HIS "FOLLOWERS" DID MORE THAN JUST FOLLOW US BEFORE! THEY TRANSMITTED TO DOCTOR DOOM AN ACTUAL PRINTED CIRCUIT OF OUR ATOMIC AND MOLECULAR BODY STRUCTURE! SEE?
BUT SO WHAT??
13

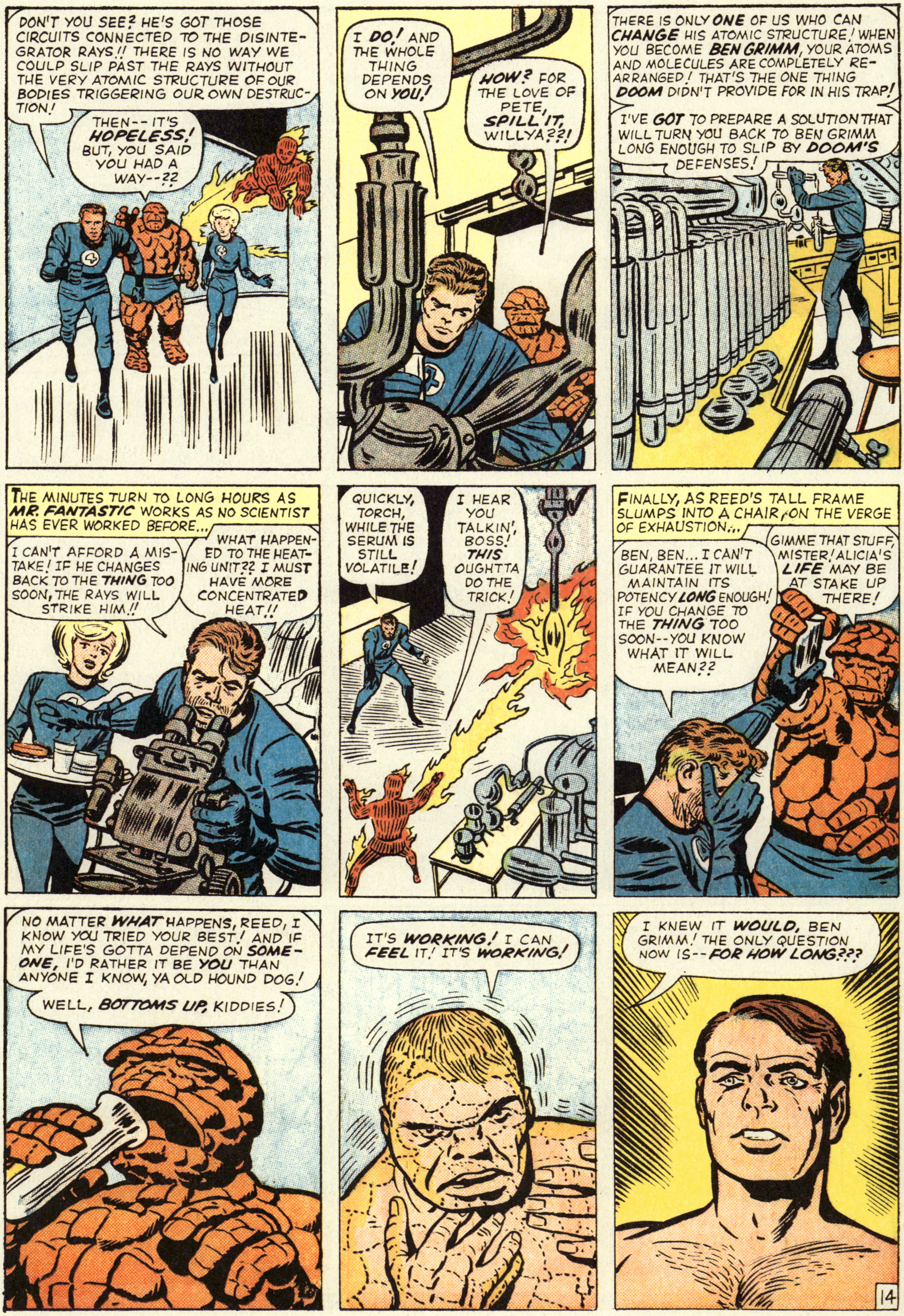
DON'T YOU SEE? HE'S GOT THOSE CIRCUITS CONNECTED TO THE DISINTEGRATOR RAYS!! THERE IS NO WAY WE COULD SLIP PAST THE RAYS WITHOUT THE VERY ATOMIC STRUCTURE OF OUR BODIES TRIGGERING OUR OWN DESTRUCTION!
THEN--IT'S HOPELESS! BUT, YOU SAID YOU HAD A WAY--??
I DO! AND THE WHOLE THING DEPENDS ON YOU!
HOW? FOR THE LOVE OF PETE, SPILL IT, WILLYA?? !
THERE IS ONLY ONE OF US WHO CAN CHANGE HIS ATOMIC STRUCTURE! WHEN YOU BECOME BEN GRIMM, YOUR ATOMS AND MOLECULES ARE COMPLETELY RE-ARRANGED! THAT'S THE ONE THING DOOM DIDN'T PROVIDE FOR IN HIS TRAP!
I'VE GOT TO PREPARE A SOLUTION THAT WILL TURN YOU BACK TO BEN GRIMM LONG ENOUGH TO SLIP BY DOOM'S DEFENSES!
THE MINUTES TURN TO LONG HOURS AS MR. FANTASTIC WORKS AS NO SCIENTIST HAS EVER WORKED BEFORE...
I CAN'T AFFORD A MISTAKE! IF HE CHANGES BACK TO THE THING TOO SOON, THE RAYS WILL STRIKE HIM!!
WHAT HAPPENED TO THE HEATING UNIT?? I MUST HAVE MORE CONCENTRATED HEAT!!
QUICKLY, TORCH, WHILE THE SERUM IS STILL VOLATILE!
I HEAR YOU TALKIN', BOSS! THIS OUGHTTA DO THE TRICK!
FINALLY, AS REED'S TALL FRAME SLUMPS INTO A CHAIR, ON THE VERGE OF EXHAUSTION...
BEN, BEN... I CAN'T GUARANTEE IT WILL MAINTAIN ITS POTENCY LONG ENOUGH! IF YOU CHANGE TO THE THING TOO SOON--YOU KNOW WHAT IT WILL MEAN??
GIMME THAT STUFF, MISTER! ALICIA'S LIFE MAY BE AT STAKE UP THERE!
NO MATTER WHAT HAPPENS, REED, I KNOW YOU TRIED YOUR BEST! AND IF MY LIFE'S GOTTA DEPEND ON SOMEONE, I'D RATHER IT BE YOU THAN ANYONE I KNOW, YA OLD HOUND DOG!
WELL, BOTTOMS UP, KIDDIES!
IT'S WORKING! I CAN FEEL IT! IT'S WORKING!
I KNEW IT WOULD, BEN GRIMM! THE ONLY QUESTION NOW IS--FOR HOW LONG???
14

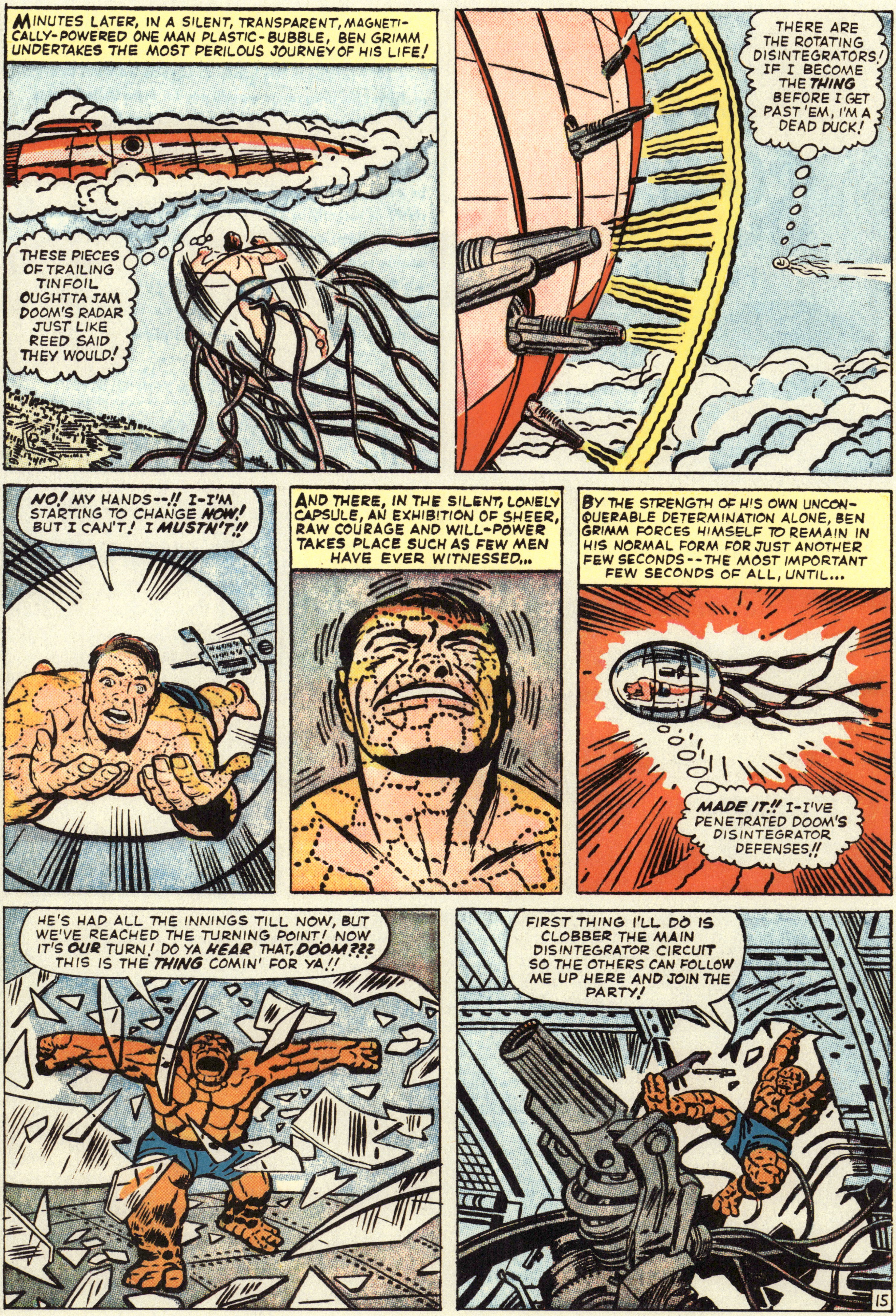
MINUTES LATER, IN A SILENT, TRANSPARENT, MAGNETICALLY-POWERED ONE MAN PLASTIC-BUBBLE, BEN GRIMM UNDERTAKES THE MOST PERILOUS JOURNEY OF HIS LIFE!
THESE PIECES OF TRAILING TINFOIL OUGHTTA JAM DOOM'S RADAR JUST LIKE REED SAID THEY WOULD!
THERE ARE THE ROTATING DISINTEGRATORS! IF I BECOME THE THING BEFORE I GET PAST 'EM, I'M A DEAD DUCK!
NO! MY HANDS--!! I-I'M STARTING TO CHANGE NOW! BUT I CAN'T! I MUSTN'T!!
AND THERE, IN THE SILENT, LONELY CAPSULE, AN EXHIBITION OF SHEER, RAW COURAGE AND WILL-POWER TAKES PLACE SUCH AS FEW MEN HAVE EVER WITNESSED...
BY THE STRENGTH OF HIS OWN UNCONQUERABLE DETERMINATION ALONE, BEN GRIMM FORCES HIMSELF TO REMAIN IN HIS NORMAL FORM FOR JUST ANOTHER FEW SECONDS--THE MOST IMPORTANT FEW SECONDS OF ALL, UNTIL...
MADE IT!! I-I'VE PENETRATED DOOM'S DISINTEGRATOR DEFENSES!!
HE'S HAD ALL THE INNINGS TILL NOW, BUT WE'VE REACHED THE TURNING POINT! NOW IT'S OUR TURN! DO YA HEAR THAT, DOOM??? THIS IS THE THING COMIN' FOR YA!!
FIRST THING I'LL DO IS CLOBBER THE MAIN DISINTEGRATOR CIRCUIT SO THE OTHERS CAN FOLLOW ME UP HERE AND JOIN THE PARTY!

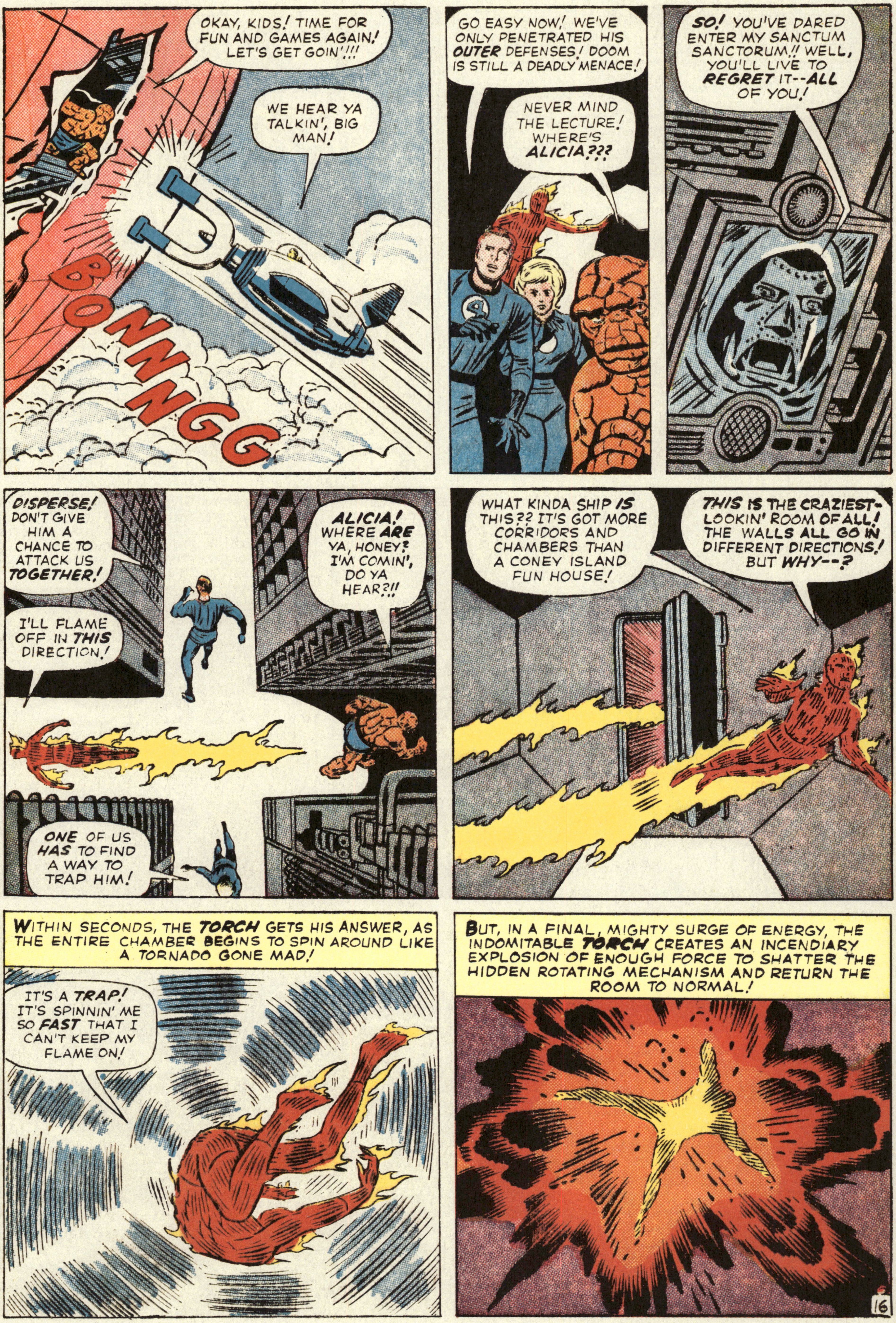
OKAY, KIDS! TIME FOR FUN AND GAMES AGAIN! LET'S GET GOIN'!!!
WE HEAR YA TALKIN', BIG MAN!
BONNNGG
GO EASY NOW! WE'VE ONLY PENETRATED HIS OUTER DEFENSES! DOOM IS STILL A DEADLY MENACE!
NEVER MIND THE LECTURE! WHERE'S ALICIA???
SO! YOU'VE DARED ENTER MY SANCTUM SANCTORUM!! WELL, YOU'LL LIVE TO REGRET IT--ALL OF YOU!
DISPERSE! DON'T GIVE HIM A CHANCE TO ATTACK US TOGETHER!
ALICIA! WHERE ARE YA, HONEY? I'M COMIN', DO YA HEAR?!!
I'LL FLAME OFF IN THIS DIRECTION!
ONE OF US HAS TO FIND A WAY TO TRAP HIM!
WHAT KINDA SHIP IS THIS?? IT'S GOT MORE CORRIDORS AND CHAMBERS THAN A CONEY ISLAND FUN HOUSE!
THIS IS THE CRAZIEST-LOOKIN' ROOM OF ALL! THE WALLS ALL GO IN DIFFERENT DIRECTIONS! BUT WHY--?
WITHIN SECONDS, THE TORCH GETS HIS ANSWER, AS THE ENTIRE CHAMBER BEGINS TO SPIN AROUND LIKE A TORNADO GONE MAD!
IT'S A TRAP! IT'S SPINNIN' ME SO FAST THAT I CAN'T KEEP MY FLAME ON!
BUT, IN A FINAL, MIGHTY SURGE OF ENERGY, THE INDOMITABLE TORCH CREATES AN INCENDIARY EXPLOSION OF ENOUGH FORCE TO SHATTER THE HIDDEN ROTATING MECHANISM AND RETURN THE ROOM TO NORMAL!
16

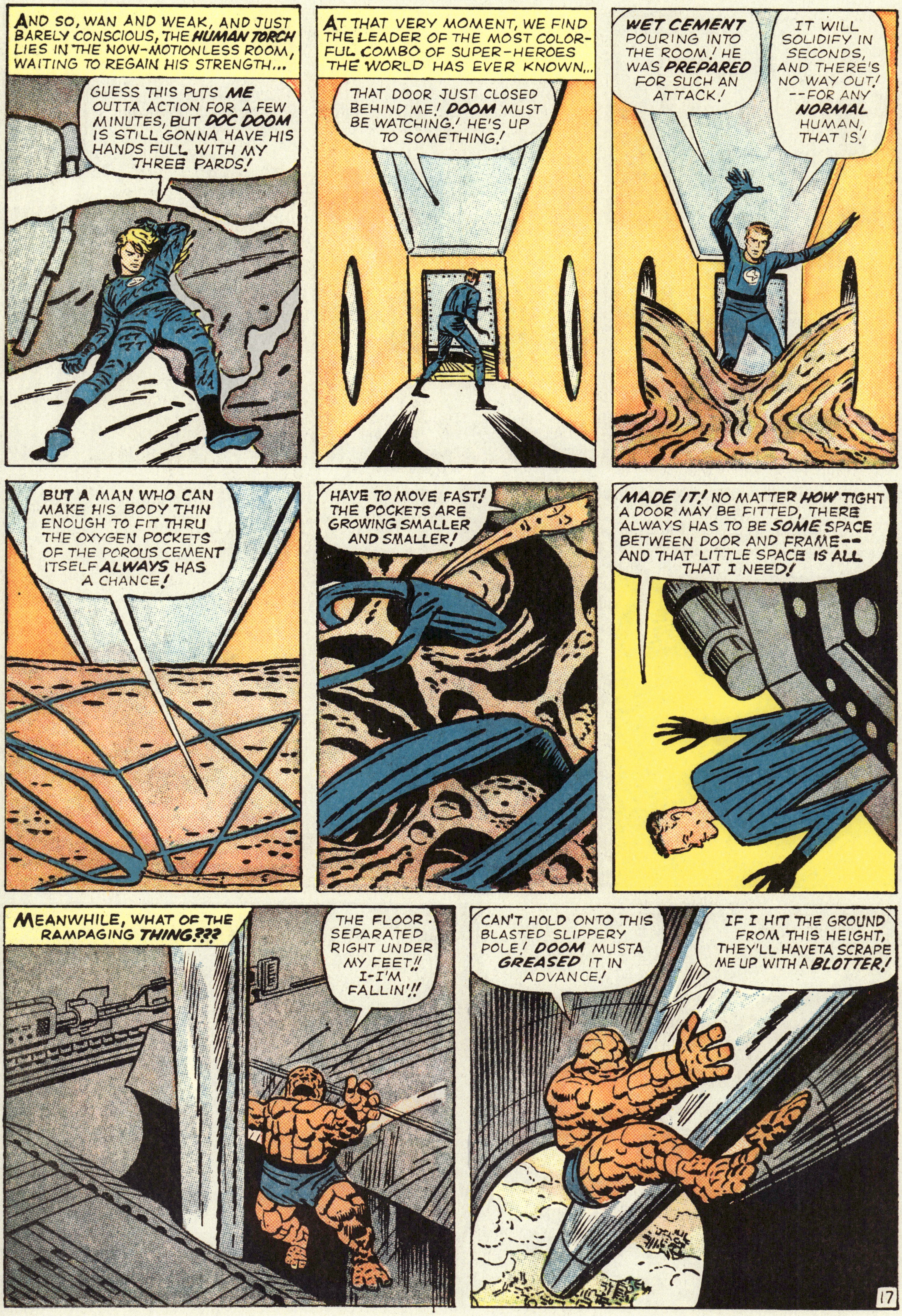
AND SO, WAN AND WEAK, AND JUST BARELY CONSCIOUS, THE HUMAN TORCH LIES IN THE NOW-MOTIONLESS ROOM, WAITING TO REGAIN HIS STRENGTH...
GUESS THIS PUTS ME OUTTA ACTION FOR A FEW MINUTES, BUT DOC DOOM IS STILL GONNA HAVE HIS HANDS FULL WITH MY THREE PARDS!
AT THAT VERY MOMENT, WE FIND THE LEADER OF THE MOST COLORFUL COMBO OF SUPER-HEROES THE WORLD HAS EVER KNOWN...
THAT DOOR JUST CLOSED BEHIND ME! DOOM MUST BE WATCHING! HE'S UP TO SOMETHING!
WET CEMENT POURING INTO THE ROOM! HE WAS PREPARED FOR SUCH AN ATTACK!
IT WILL SOLIDIFY IN SECONDS, AND THERE'S NO WAY OUT! --FOR ANY NORMAL HUMAN, THAT IS!
BUT A MAN WHO CAN MAKE HIS BODY THIN ENOUGH TO FIT THRU THE OXYGEN POCKETS OF THE POROUS CEMENT ITSELF ALWAYS HAS A CHANCE!
HAVE TO MOVE FAST! THE POCKETS ARE GROWING SMALLER AND SMALLER!
MADE IT! NO MATTER HOW TIGHT A DOOR MAY BE FITTED, THERE ALWAYS HAS TO BE SOME SPACE BETWEEN DOOR AND FRAME-- AND THAT LITTLE SPACE IS ALL THAT I NEED!
MEANWHILE, WHAT OF THE RAMPAGING THING???
THE FLOOR SEPARATED RIGHT UNDER MY FEET!! I-I'M FALLIN'!!
CAN'T HOLD ONTO THIS BLASTED SLIPPERY POLE! DOOM MUSTA GREASED IT IN ADVANCE!
IF I HIT THE GROUND FROM THIS HEIGHT, THEY'LL HAVETA SCRAPE ME UP WITH A BLOTTER!

BUT I CAN'T FALL!! ALICIA'S DEPENDIN' ON ME! I CAN'T FAIL HER!
I GOTTA HANG ON! I GOTTA!!
I DID IT-- GASP-! NOW-- IF I CAN JUST GET BACK UP--
THAT'S IT! JUST A LITTLE FURTHER! AND THEN--IT'LL BE DOCTOR DOOM AN' ME!
BUT, AT THAT VERY MOMENT, IN HIS HIDDEN VIEWING CHAMBER...
BAH! THAT ACCURSED FOURSOME HAS MORE LIVES THAN A PACK OF CATS!!
BUT EVEN THE FANTASTIC FOUR WILL NOT BE ABLE TO SURVIVE THE DREAD FURY OF MY HURTLING POWER SPHERES!
THERE THEY ARE NOW, TOGETHER AGAIN! I DO NOT SEE THE GIRL, BUT SHE IS UNIMPORTANT! ONCE MY POWER SPHERES HAVE DESTROYED THOSE, I CAN DISPOSE OF THE INVISIBLE GIRL AT MY LEISURE!
AH, MY GREATEST WEAPONS ARE WORKING PERFECTLY! ATTRACTED BY THEIR BODY HEAT, THE SPHERES ARE COMPLETELY ENCASING THE TRAPPED TRIO!
18

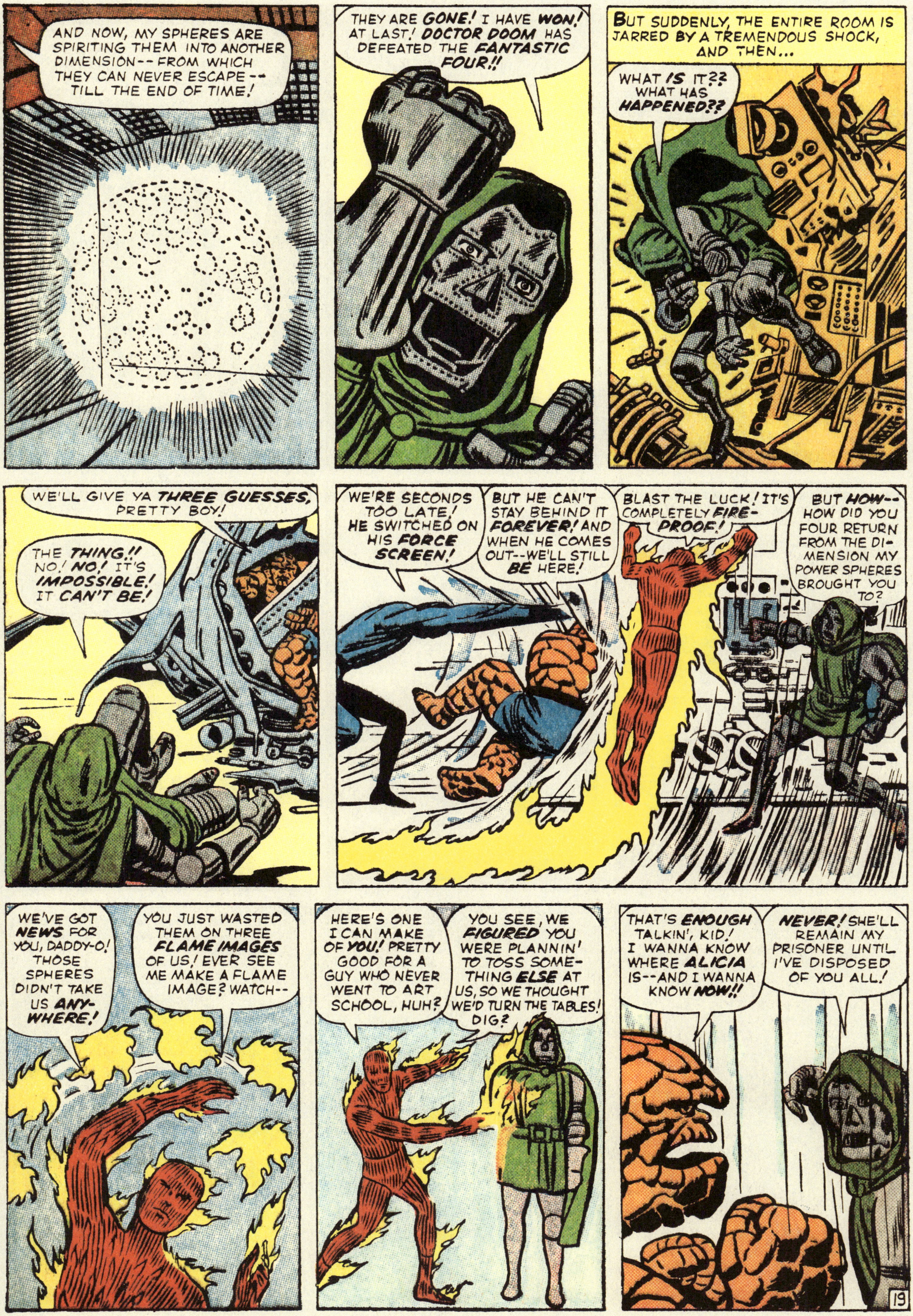
AND NOW, MY SPHERES ARE SPIRITING THEM INTO ANOTHER DIMENSION-- FROM WHICH THEY CAN NEVER ESCAPE -- TILL THE END OF TIME!
THEY ARE GONE! I HAVE WON! AT LAST! DOCTOR DOOM HAS DEFEATED THE FANTASTIC FOUR!!
BUT SUDDENLY, THE ENTIRE ROOM IS JARRED BY A TREMENDOUS SHOCK, AND THEN...
WHAT IS IT?? WHAT HAS HAPPENED??
WE'LL GIVE YA THREE GUESSES, PRETTY BOY!
THE THING!! NO! NO! IT'S IMPOSSIBLE! IT CAN'T BE!
WE'RE SECONDS TOO LATE! HE SWITCHED ON HIS FORCE SCREEN!
BUT HE CAN'T STAY BEHIND IT FOREVER! AND WHEN HE COMES OUT--WE'LL STILL BE HERE!
BLAST THE LUCK! IT'S COMPLETELY FIRE-PROOF!
BUT HOW-- HOW DID YOU FOUR RETURN FROM THE DIMENSION MY POWER SPHERES BROUGHT YOU TO?
WE'VE GOT NEWS FOR YOU, DADDY-O! THOSE SPHERES DIDN'T TAKE US ANYWHERE!
YOU JUST WASTED THEM ON THREE FLAME IMAGES OF US! EVER SEE ME MAKE A FLAME IMAGE? WATCH--
HERE'S ONE I CAN MAKE OF YOU! PRETTY GOOD FOR A GUY WHO NEVER WENT TO ART SCHOOL, HUH?
YOU SEE, WE FIGURED YOU WERE PLANNIN' TO TOSS SOMETHING ELSE AT US, SO WE THOUGHT WE'D TURN THE TABLES! DIG?
THAT'S ENOUGH TALKIN', KID! I WANNA KNOW WHERE ALICIA IS--AND I WANNA KNOW NOW!!
NEVER! SHE'LL REMAIN MY PRISONER UNTIL I'VE DISPOSED OF YOU ALL!
19

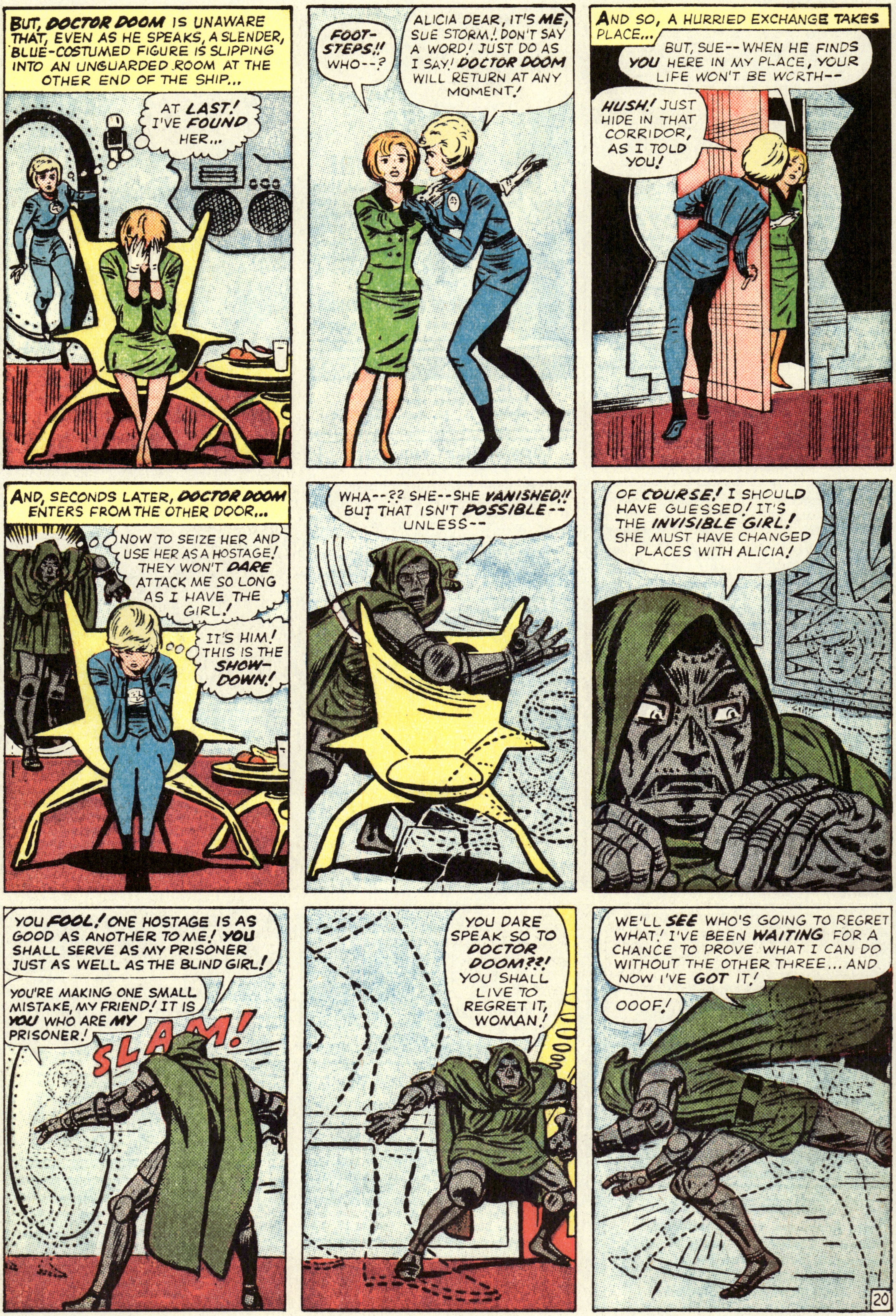
BUT, DOCTOR DOOM IS UNAWARE THAT, EVEN AS HE SPEAKS, A SLENDER, BLUE-COSTUMED FIGURE IS SLIPPING INTO AN UNGUARDED ROOM AT THE OTHER END OF THE SHIP...
AT LAST! I'VE FOUND HER...
FOOT-STEPS!! WHO--?
ALICIA DEAR, IT'S ME, SUE STORM! DON'T SAY A WORD! JUST DO AS I SAY! DOCTOR DOOM WILL RETURN AT ANY MOMENT!
AND SO, A HURRIED EXCHANGE TAKES PLACE...
BUT, SUE--WHEN HE FINDS YOU HERE IN MY PLACE, YOUR LIFE WON'T BE WORTH--
HUSH! JUST HIDE IN THAT CORRIDOR, AS I TOLD YOU!
AND, SECONDS LATER, DOCTOR DOOM ENTERS FROM THE OTHER DOOR...
NOW TO SEIZE HER AND USE HER AS A HOSTAGE! THEY WON'T DARE ATTACK ME SO LONG AS I HAVE THE GIRL!
IT'S HIM! THIS IS THE SHOW-DOWN!
WHA--?? SHE--SHE VANISHED!! BUT THAT ISN'T POSSIBLE--UNLESS--
OF COURSE! I SHOULD HAVE GUESSED! IT'S THE INVISIBLE GIRL! SHE MUST HAVE CHANGED PLACES WITH ALICIA!
YOU FOOL! ONE HOSTAGE IS AS GOOD AS ANOTHER TO ME! YOU SHALL SERVE AS MY PRISONER JUST AS WELL AS THE BLIND GIRL!
YOU'RE MAKING ONE SMALL MISTAKE, MY FRIEND! IT IS YOU WHO ARE MY PRISONER!
SLAM!
YOU DARE SPEAK SO TO DOCTOR DOOM??! YOU SHALL LIVE TO REGRET IT, WOMAN!
WE'LL SEE WHO'S GOING TO REGRET WHAT! I'VE BEEN WAITING FOR A CHANCE TO PROVE WHAT I CAN DO WITHOUT THE OTHER THREE... AND NOW I'VE GOT IT!
OOOF!

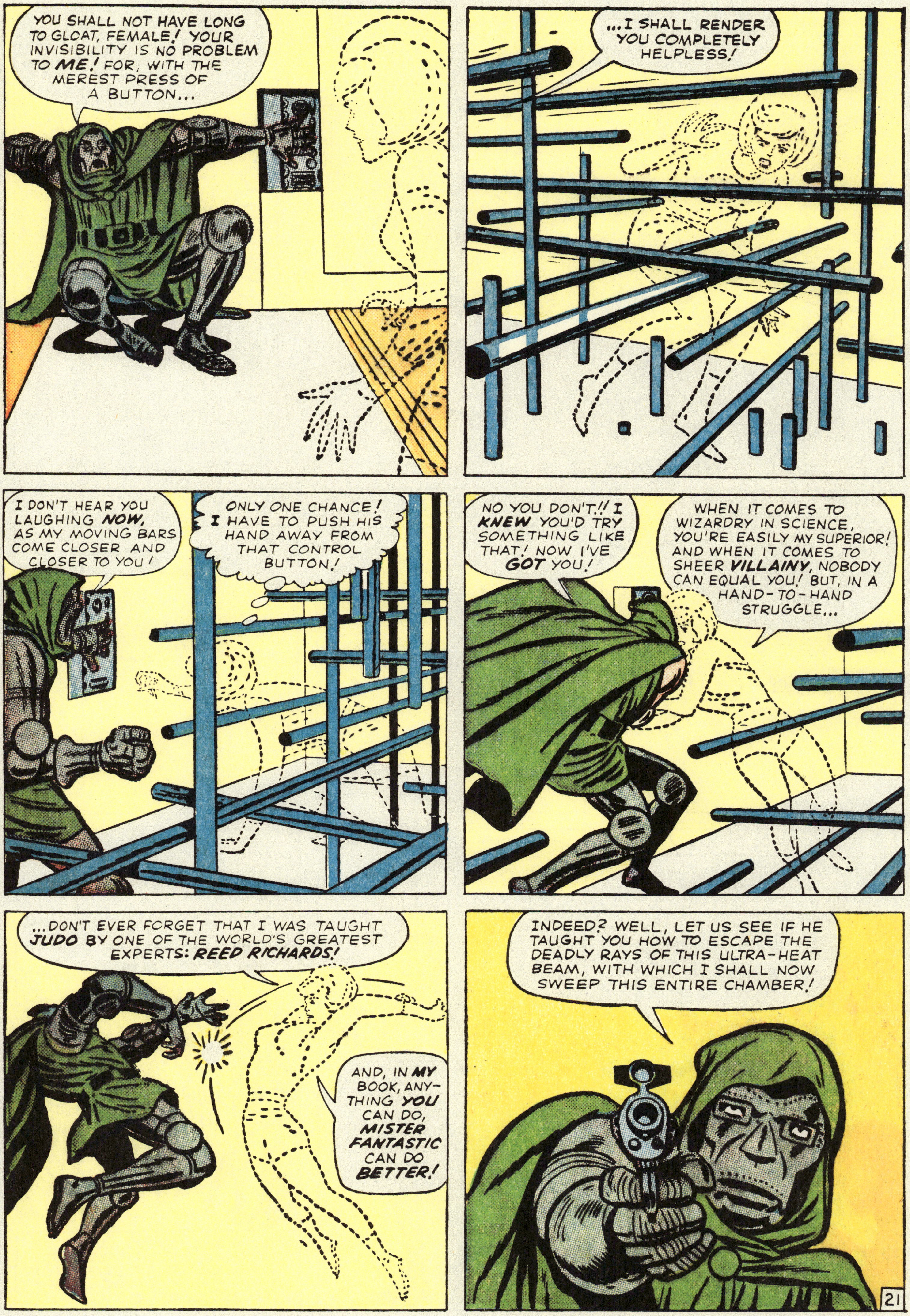
YOU SHALL NOT HAVE LONG TO GLOAT, FEMALE! YOUR INVISIBILITY IS NO PROBLEM TO ME! FOR, WITH THE MEREST PRESS OF A BUTTON...
...I SHALL RENDER YOU COMPLETELY HELPLESS!
I DON'T HEAR YOU LAUGHING NOW, AS MY MOVING BARS COME CLOSER AND CLOSER TO YOU!
ONLY ONE CHANCE! I HAVE TO PUSH HIS HAND AWAY FROM THAT CONTROL BUTTON!
NO YOU DON'T!! I KNEW YOU'D TRY SOMETHING LIKE THAT! NOW I'VE GOT YOU!
WHEN IT COMES TO WIZARDRY IN SCIENCE, YOU'RE EASILY MY SUPERIOR! AND WHEN IT COMES TO SHEER VILLAINY, NOBODY CAN EQUAL YOU! BUT, IN A HAND-TO-HAND STRUGGLE...
...DON'T EVER FORGET THAT I WAS TAUGHT JUDO BY ONE OF THE WORLD'S GREATEST EXPERTS: REED RICHARDS!
AND, IN MY BOOK, ANYTHING YOU CAN DO, MISTER FANTASTIC CAN DO BETTER!
INDEED? WELL, LET US SEE IF HE TAUGHT YOU HOW TO ESCAPE THE DEADLY RAYS OF THIS ULTRA-HEAT BEAM, WITH WHICH I SHALL NOW SWEEP THIS ENTIRE CHAMBER!
21

BUT, SUDDENLY...
BROTHER, YOUR CHAMBER-SWEEPIN' DAYS ARE OVER!
YOU--YOU FOUND ME--SO SOON??!
BUT I SHALL NEVER SUFFER THE HUMILIATION OF BEING CAPTURED BY THE LIKES OF YOU!!
COME BACK! YA CAN'T CHEAT ME OUTTA MY REVENGE THIS WAY!!
BEN! GET OUT OF THE WAY! I CAN STILL REACH OUT AND GRAB HIM--
BEN--NO! IT'S TOO LATE NOW!
SWIFTLY, SILENTLY, THE AWESOME FORM OF THE GREATEST MENACE OF OUR AGE PLUMMETS EARTHWARD... DOWN--DOWN--DOWN--UNTIL IT IS LOST FROM SIGHT IN THE BILLOWING CLOUDS BELOW!
A FEW SECONDS LATER...
BEN? MY DARLING--IT'S YOU! I KNOW IT IS!
ALICIA! I'M HERE, BABY! EVERYTHING'S OKAY NOW!
JOHNNY! SUE IS GONE! WE'VE GOT TO FIND HER!
DON'T WORRY, REED DEAR--YOU NEVER LOST ME!
SUE! YOU'RE ALL RIGHT! THAT MEANS OUR TRIUMPH IS COMPLETE!
SUE, DARLING--IF ANYTHING HAD HAPPENED TO YOU--
BENJAMIN GRIMM--STOP! YOU'RE MAKING MY HEAD SPIN!
THAT'S WHAT YOU DO TO ME, DOLL--EVERY TIME I LOOK AT YA!
YEESH! WHAT A LOT OF MUSH! I DON'T BLAME DOCTOR DOOM FOR JUMPIN'!!
BUT THE TORCH HASN'T MUCH TIME TO WORRY ABOUT THAT "MUSH", FOR NEXT ISSUE THE F.F. BATTLE A FOE WHO HAS ALL THE POWERS THEY HAVE--AND MORE! SEE YOU THEN!
the END

Address YOUR letters to:
LEE and KIRBY
FANTASTIC FOUR
THIRD FLOOR
655 MADISON AVE.
NEW YORK 21, N. Y.

FANTASTIC FAN PAGE 4

Dear Stan and Jack:

I've never written to you before and I'd like to say something about your book. Although people say that comics are for children, I must say that I am a 31 year-old child, 'cause I read them. I'm a stunt man and actor in the Frontier Cities of the old west, such as Carson City and Cimmaron City, play-acting for children. Last summer I got hold of one of the Fantastic Four comics that some child left behind after the show. I started reading it in spare time and actually enjoyed it, so I continued buying your comics. My personal opinion, and also that of some of the riders that work with me, is that it's a great book for a comic. I just got #12 of the *FF Meets the Hulk*, and that was great also.

Harry Warren
Silver Saddle Ranch
North Branch, New Jersey

A great book for a COMIC!!! Heck, Harry, we never claimed it was a great book for anything ELSE! But thanks for the thought, cowboy! Say — here's an idea: let's try to find out who is our OLDEST reader! So far, we have 31-year old Harry Warren. Who can top him?

Dear Stan and Jack:

I want you to know that I appreciate the fact that you are the only ones that have super-heros, none of which have protegees. Don't ever give them any. No one wants any Ant-Man, Jr., because that would cheapen Ant-Man. The circumstances that create a super-hero are unique, and when accidents like being bitten by a radioactive spider start happening twice, the whole mess becomes ridiculous. Last month was "Guest Appearance Month," so now we have "Guest Artist Month.' Steve Ditko inked the *Fantastic Four,* and also pencilled the *Hulk*. This is only the second time that Don Heck has drawn *Ant-Man* and *The Human Torch*. And Al Hartley illustrated *Thor*. What are you going to do next month?

Donald Markstein
2232 Wirth Pl.
New Orleans 15, La.

We don't know yet, but one thing you can bet on, Donald . . . there'll be SOMEBODY who'll pan us for it!

Dear Stan and Jack:

I got so sick of people saying in letters how bad the Invisible Girl is, how good the Human Torch is, etc., etc., that I decided to take a poll amongst my friends, relatives, neighbors, and so on. My goal was 100, but I got only 80 voters. Here are the results: Favorite Character: Human Torch — 38; Thing — 26; Mr. Fantastic — 13; Invisible Girl — 3. Should the Human Torch get his own magazine?: Yes — 51; No — 29. Should the Invisible Girl be kicked out?: Yes — 27; No — 53. Should a new character be added?: Yes — 71; No — 9. Who should the new character be?: Ant-Man — 27; Spider-Man — 26; Thor — 21; Hulk — 6.

Sebastian Stuart
101 Central Park West
N. Y. 23, N. Y.

What we wanna know is — how come only 80 voters? And MR. FANTASTIC demands a recount!

Dear Stan:

Just finished Fantastic Four #11 and 12 . . . Now I could waste time on superlatives — but I'm sure there are none I can use which some other fan hasn t used before me . . . but there's one thing I do wish to compliment you upon — and this is Stan Lee's "Komix Anti-Cliche League" which I think most fans don't appreciate. It takes a rare genius indeed to break all the fond, endearing, shining, *silly* little rules of komix . . . but I think it takes an even vaster genius to make a success of it . . . You, my friend, seem well in control of both forms of genius. The temptation is there — always to stick to the old, reliable "formulae" which have sold for umpteen writers before you and will probably sell for as many to come after you. However, I can sit back comfortably here and watch all these time-honored cliches come a-tumblin' down under the sharp, keen ax of Lee and Co., Inc. I see you strike out along unbroken trails with the *Thing and Spider-Man,* and *The Hulk,* and *Iron Man.* You imitate no one, and no one dares to imitate you! Now I ask you, if this isn't progress, what is it?? When the FF first came out, I bit my nails. I wanted to see the 'zine continue to exist, yet I was afraid that this brash young "upstart" had begun not only by biting the hand which fed it, but by biting arm, shoulders, and head as well. True, it violated cardinal rules. The first rule it violated was that Komix heros had to be epitomes of virtue — "Cripes!!," I thought, "the FF seem altogether too human to be fantasy heros! Migosh, they actually *quarrel* among themselves!" The next rule was that it was imperative that komix heros keep "secret" that (hoo-hah!) all-important "secret-identity"! This ended when it was found that Johnny Storm only *thought* he had a secret identity"! There, then, was no excuse for the FF's continuing success as a publication — yet, not only was it successful, but it has pushed even its strongest competitors so far into the background they can't even be counted as "competitors." If you get the point that I'm all for you, that's the only "point" I wish to make. Be watching you when I get back "stateside." Missed a lot of crucial issues over here — (but I don't believe I'm going to miss *too* many more!) Thanks for listening . . . Hope Jack learns to draw feet. May be a good idea to make him come to work barefoot in that New York snow so that he'll get the knack to drawing passably good feet — but don't tell him it's my idea. He may have Mafia connections . . . (and I'm in Italy).

SP/4 — Drury S. Moroz
RA 17465357
Cinc South Box 14
Navy 510. F.P.O.
New York, New York

Don't worry about Jack, pal. He's too busy counting his toes to bother anyone! As for Stan, he's going out to buy a larger hat!

Dear Stan and Jack:

I always read your mags and I think they are very exciting, but you make the most impossible things happen in them. Like the time the Fantastic Four met the 'Red Ghost' on the moon . . . I always thought that the moon had no gravity. How come the FF were not floating in space? In the same issue there was air on the moon. How come? Anyhow, it's still my favorite comic.

Peter Dovolas
9907 Larose
Montreal, P.Q.,
Canada

We were referring to a special "blue area" of the moon which had once been settled by another civilization. They had created an artificial gravity and atmosphere which still existed. There! That explanation is ambiguous enough to confuse almost anybody!

CONTINUED . . .

Dear Stan and Jack: (My resistance is useless)

"The Fantastic Four vs. the Red Ghost and His Indescribable Super Apes" (whew) is the best comic book story ever printed. For plot, characters, and parody, it canNOT be topped! I WOULD serve you fellows breakfast in bed, but your eating time is probably spent in making a great story for the next issue of FANTASTIC FOUR! Seriously, FF #13 was so good I nearly died from the prospects of having to wait for #14. The reasons are thusly: The cover was the best to come out of your company yet. However, I do have a few suggestions. First of all, the logo is bad — makes it look like a humor comic. Secondly, there's too much sensationalism and such stuff taking up space. "In this spellbinding tale, you will meet the most dramatic being . . ." Who cares? Who is he? Since you've already given us the name, I can be pretty assured that the name is the Watcher. Surprisingly enough, he *is* the most dramatic being of all time! 2) Art was amazing! Ditko's inking of Kirby's pencils are better than Ayer's on FF . . . the other way around on HULK. JK's version of TORCH was (Gracias a Dios!) improved tremendously since the first few pathetic issues. 3) Outrageous parody. That panel where MR. FANTASTIC made his sermon on the Reds and Americans both being earthmen ("This is wrong! Why can't we leave our differences behind us? We should be making this trip together.") Would have had me rolling in the chair, but for the fact that I was at the barber's at the time I read it. 4) Tremendous plot action. To thee, Stan Lee, all I can do is offer my greatest thanks! 5) Invisible Girl finally *did* something. Well, there were so many great things about the story that I can't list them all! All I can do is tell you that I bought *two* copies, and since #12 have subscribed to what is TRULY the "World's Greatest Comic Magazine." (Get me the smelling salts, Jack. I feel faint! — Are you kidding, Stan? I'm too shocked to move!) Next I have several hundred comments to make on FF #14, so I'll dig right in: First of all, congratulations on your new symbol. It's far more decorative than the cryptic "MC" which once hid in the farthest corner of the covers. I'm glad you reduced the logo, as it is one of the worst in comics history, making the FF sound like a humor mag (although it is the world's greatest *comic* magazine.) Kirby's art is getting much better. The story, 'The Merciless Puppet Master,' was badly named, as usual, but this didn't reflect the quality of the story. Puppet Master is one of your worst creations, but with Sub-Mariner he manages to become half-way decent. Nevertheless, I hope he doesn't escape from the digestive system of the giant octupus. Speaking of Sub-Mariner, I now recommend that he remain a villain; he's better this way than he ever possibly could be as a hero. I just love those side incidents in FF, and #14 didn't disappoint me. I nearly flipped from those scenes at the airport and SM's undersea sanctum! The parody and conflict in FF is WONDERFUL! Keep it up (not that you had any thoughts of discontinuing them, I hope)! And you're going to introduce an FF annual? Good Heavens, I hope this isn't the kind of grubby reprints that other companies are printing! If it's made of reprints, prepare to lose money . . . (IT ISN'T! . . . Ed.) Finally, I'd like to compliment you on the excellence of IRON MAN. I've raved before, but I'll rave again! IRON MAN is better than his predecessor, as well as three-quarters of the mush that cavorts through what is commonly called a comic magazine; naturally I'm not talking about FF! I hope these epistles don't bore you, but I feel compelled to talk whenever I read an FF . . . and once I've started talking, nobody stops me. So you finally converted me!

Paul Gambaccini
8 Elizabeth Drive
Westport, Connecticut

Glad we've converted you. P. G. But, now that we've got you, what do we DO with you?

Dear Stan, Jack, Steve, and all the rest —

MARVELous is the most fitting adjective for your group of comics . . . So far as I'm concerned, you have no competition, so I'll concentrate on comparison within your own ranks. After the fantastic handling by 'King' Kirby, THOR suffered a bit of a downfall in Al Hartley's hands. Tho' it's apparent he honestly tried hard to maintain Jack's marvelous flair, he couldn't help but fail — of course, this is my personal opinion; perhaps others are satisfied. The story of the Carbon Copy Man was Lee's usual par; fine. I for one enjoyed most the Ditko story in this ish, (Journey Into Mystery), and felt it conveyed a warm, wonderful message. I hope you continue with these off-beat incidents. IRONMAN's new — ah — what-would-you-call-it — it's not a uniform per se . . . Anyway; the yellow, simulating gold, is very fitting, as was the reason for the change. Don Heck really does wonders for Iron Man, as he does likewise with Ant Man. For my money, Heck's second only to Kirby and Ditko. FF #14 is nothing short of sensational; the combination of villains (tho' I'm glad you don't still exploit Namor as a pure do-badder) made for a unique conflict. The opening sequence of FF's landing was great realism! *Thing's* remark about a REP TO MAINTAIN FOR HIS PANTING PUBLIC was a master-stroke. SPIDER-MAN #2 is your own competition. Doubtless, he's your finest since the FF, due primarily to Steve's immaculate art and Stan's magnificent innovations. The visual 'spider-sense' (radiating black lines) is a superb touch, as are the night 'shots.' "Vulture" is surely a worthy nemesis. In my humble opinion, SM #2 is Ditko's finest art ever. My only kick is that Pete Parker looks more college-ish than a highschool student, but this is insignificant in the sheer enjoyment of the bulk of the art and plot. It goes without saying, Spider-Man is truly AMAZING. I could close by wishing long life to the MARVEL Comics Group, but I'm sure that the AMAZING Mr. Lee will see to that!

Ronn Foss
Wagon Wheels Apts. #5
Suisun, Calif.

Many thanks for your kind comments and generous praise, Ronn. If only the BOSS liked us as much as you do!

SPECIAL ANNOUNCEMENTS SECTION:

- **Okay, it's official! The first FANTASTIC FOUR *ANNUAL* goes on sale early in July! 72 unforgettable pages! 25¢! A 13-page reprint of the FF's origin, for the thousands who've requested it; but all the rest — BRAND-NEW, ORIGINAL STORIES AND ART! (Including the longest single fantasy epic ever presented in a comic mag!) Also, most of the questions you sent us are answered in this jam-packed swinging issue! NOW HEAR THIS: When the first printing is gone, that'll be ALL, brother! So if you've got nothing better to do with your 25¢, tell your dealer to reserve your copy NOW! Judging by the amount of requests we've had, they'll be sold out before the ink is dry! Dig?**

- **We've always believed in levelling with our fans. So, for those of you who've asked what happened to the HULK, here's the scoop: We decided to discontinue the mag because we felt we were spreading ourselves too thin! But, we got a BRING-BACK-THE-HULK petition from City College of N. Y.; Nome, Alaska; and places all over the free world! We honestly hadn't realized you were all so HULK-conscious! So, back he comes! We don't yet know where, when, or how, but be patient — mankind won't be Hulkless much longer!**

- **And, speaking of Annuals, here's another surprise . . . the STRANGE TALES *ANNUAL* goes on sale the middle of June, featuring the HUMAN TORCH and — who'da guessed it? SPIDERMAN!!! Just another minor masterpiece from MARVEL COMICS GROUP!**

- **Yes, we ARE planning new mags — new heroes — new villains! We hope we won't have too many lemons among them, but judging by the way you wonderful fans have received our mags so far, we think you and we are in for some fun and excitement in the months to come! So, till next ish, read our mags, read our competitors' mags, but READ! It's one of the greatest pleasures of all!**

FIRST, THE FANTASTIC FOUR!
And NOW, in the same inimitable style, by the same writer and artist... ANOTHER group of fabulous characters:
GET YOUR COPY TODAY!
SGT. FURY AND HIS HOWLING COMMANDOS
MARVEL COMICS GROUP 12¢
2 JULY
COMMANDOS, IT IS USELESS TO RESIST! YOU ARE "SEVEN DOOMED MEN!"
DON'T GIVE UP, YOU HOWLERS! WE'LL STILL LIVE TO HEAR THESE GOOSE STEPPIN' GOONS HOLLAR "UNCLE"!!
HEINEMUND CONCENTRATION CAMP
THE MARVEL COMICS GROUP USHERS IN THE MARVEL AGE OF COMICS!
X-322
BATTLE ACTION!! FIGHTING MEN!! AS ONLY THE MARVEL COMICS GROUP CAN PRESENT THEM!

THE WORLD'S GREATEST COMIC MAGAZINE!
APPROVED BY THE COMICS CODE AUTHORITY
Fantastic Four
18 SEPT.
MARVEL COMICS GROUP 12¢
HE HAS ALL THE POWERS OF THE FANTASTIC FOUR, PLUS STILL MORE! HOW CAN THEY EVER DEFEAT...
THE ALL-POWERFUL SUPER-SKRULL!

MY SECRET NEW DYNAFLEX METHOD

CAN BUILD YOU A MAGNIFICENT NEW HE-MAN-MUSCLED BODY IN JUST TEN MINUTES A DAY—with absolutely NO weights—NO bar-bells—NO EXERCISE AT ALL!

Yes! If the girls LAUGH at you now when you take off your shirt—they'll be breaking down the doors to get dates with you—once they've seen the rugged DYNAFLEX BODY I can give you! I'll build you a tough strong massive body—shoulders clad with solid inches of he-man BRAWN. I'll give you bulging biceps, trip-hammer fists, power-packed legs, and a chest that will have you popping the buttons off your shirt with pride! (—says MIKE MARVEL, "Builder of Champion Bodies")

"In my classes this same course of Instruction would cost $110.00."

Mike Marvel

ARE YOU WEAK, ALWAYS TIRED, LACK PEP?

Whether you're thin and scrawny, or sagging with unsightly fat—my secret DYNAFLEX method will cram pep, vigor and red-blooded vitality into your puny, exhausted body. Once DYNAFLEX makes you a two-fisted dynamo of manly beauty, rippling with power, glowing with magnetic sex-appeal—you'll be bursting with get-up-and-go. Man, you'll be really ALIVE—tingling with zest and rip-roaring energy—for the first time in years!

PROOF!

"I tried two other systems, before my buddy told me about DYNAFLEX. It *really* works—and how! I've put two inches of solid muscle on my biceps, three inches on my chest. It's like magic!"
L. C., New York City

"I never thought you could build terrific muscles without exercises or weights. Started DYNAFLEX two weeks ago, and am building a *great* physique."
E. G., Detroit, Mich.

"DYNAFLEX is the best yet. Only three weeks, and I have more dates than I can handle! I am telling all my pals about DYNAFLEX."
F. S., Chicago, Ill.

ARE YOU ASHAMED OF YOUR BODY NOW?

Pal—do YOURSELF a favor! Take a good long look in a mirror. Do you see a puny, starved body—scrawny arms—bony shoulders—a flabby stomach and skinny legs? Do girls laugh and fellows grin when you take off your shirt?

BELIEVE IT OR NOT—I can add solid pounds of rippling, steely he-man MEAT to your build. I can take those skeleton arms and PACK EVERY INCH with explosive virile MAN-MUSCLE. I can take that caved-in chest and build on six rugged inches of strong sleek MAN-SIZED BRAWN. I can clothe your skinny frame with GIANT RIPPLING DYNAFLEX MUSCLES that will have the girls gasping with awe and admiration! And with NO tiring exercise, NO high-priced bar-bells or gym equipment!

Or is your problem a body sagging with soft rolls of unhealthy, unhandsome FAT? Puny muscles — sagging stomach — bloated face — arms heavy with layers of BLUBBER? Are you ASHAMED to go to the beach and let them see your "FAT-MAN PHYSIQUE"?

If so, wake up fella! THIS IS IT! I will peel off that fat and give you a lean virile DYNAFLEX BODY, armored with a sheath of hard tough handsome muscle. I can build you into a healthy, streamlined HERCULES—bursting with dynamic manly strength. I'll give you a taut rock-hard midsection—legs muscled like coiled steel springs. I can pack solid DYNAMITE into your fists and give you a rugged handsome build brim-full of the magnetic Super-Body Appeal which girls admire. And with NO starvation diets NO fatiguing callisthenics—NO expensive health-foods!

HOW DYNAFLEX BUILDS BEAUTIFUL BODIES

DYNAFLEX is the modern miracle of body-building. It takes no tiresome exercises, "crash" diets, protein foods, and no weights or bar-bells. DYNAFLEX is the amazing discovery of a West German Doctor whose research into the Science of Strength found a thrilling new way to build GIANT BRAWNY MUSCLES in ten minutes a day. With DYNAFLEX you "flex" each muscle once—in a certain way—that is more effective than if you exercised that muscle 20, 30, even 100 times the old-fashioned way. With DYNAFLEX you get bigger results in ten minutes than after hours of grunting and groaning, hefting heavy weights. DYNAFLEX coaxes each muscle in your body to bring out its round, steely fullness and satiny symmetory. DYNAFLEX packs that muscle with glowing vibrant new strength and energy—FAST. In ten minutes a day I can cover your bony frame with healthy rippling muscle—give you a deep, powerful chest — solid shoulders and iron wrists—tough, slim midsection—and trim, steel-spring legs — simply thru "DYNA-FLEXING" each muscle once a day! There's nothing wrong with the bar-bell and weight-lifting method . . . but why bother? Why waste time and money, why sweat and strain your way to a streamlined symmetrical SAMSON-STRONG BODY — when you can do it better—bigger—faster—easier with the DYNAFLEX SECRET?

STRONG-MAN APPEAL ATTRACTS GIRLS

Be honest. Down deep you KNOW you envy the boy with the virile, magnificent build. Every man and boy secretly desires a broad brawny back, a solid man-muscled chest, handsome he-man shoulders, arms rippling with tough, steely sinews, a narrow waist, slim hips and springy, power-packed legs. Girls go for a fellow with TWO-FISTED BIG MUSCLE SEX-APPEAL . . . and they only laugh at skinny guys or "fatso's".

Let me give you a glowing new body, brimming over with energy and irresistible inches of solid muscle on your chest — he-man appeal. I can build three inches of beef and brawn on your shoulders. I will mold you a handsome super-body of terrific strength, give you a crushing grip, legs crammed with steel springs. A lean taut rock-solid punch-proof midsection. Pack your body with energy and thrilling stamina that will have girls falling at your feet.

GIVE ME TEN MINUTES A DAY —THAT'S ALL!

After DYNAFLEX, you'll be able to roll up your sleeves and take off your shirt and, for the first time in your life, you'll be PROUD of your manly build. Yes, pal, say goodbye to your weak, flabby frame—get ready for adventure and romance with a solid physique that glows and vibrates with virile he-man appeal. You'll be really proud to have people see your MAGNIFICENT HE-MAN-MUSCLES at the beach or gym. And, when the girls crowd around to admire your iron biceps and your bulging brawny chest—when they ask in amazement how you did it—tell them about the mag'c secret of DYNAFLEX!

Your Pal,
MIKE MARVEL
"Builder of Champion Bodies"

YOU PAY ONLY
1.98
COMPLETE
NOTHING ELSE TO BUY

Mike Marvel System, Dept. 281   285 Market St., Newark, N.J.

FREE! 'SECRETS OF ATTRACTING GIRLS'!

Fellows! Mail the coupon now, and receive Mike Marvel's FREE GIFT to you, this exciting and informative book. Discover a secret method for developing a new, almost MAGNETIC way of attracting the girls. At parties, dances, at the beach—you will have the girls clustering around you breathlessly, while the guys watch enviously. "What does HE have that WE don't?" they will say. The answer is in this exciting new book, your GIFT from Mike Marvel. Fill out and mail the coupon NOW!

Outside USA: Send International Money Order or cash. Great Britain: $1.98 is about 15 shillings. For air mail delivery, send 1 pound.

MAIL MONEY-SAVING NO-RISK FREE TRIAL COUPON NOW!

Check as many of the boxes you want HERE — Complete System $1.98.

- ☐ Lose fat, be trim and solid
- ☐ Build deep brawny chest, bulging with vigorous strength
- ☐ Lose fat, be trim, strong, handsome
- ☐ Mold mighty back, broad beefy shoulders
- ☐ Build muscle on skinny wrists and arms
- ☐ Develop crushing grip, two-fisted punch-power

MIKE MARVEL System, Dept. 281
285 MARKET STREET
NEWARK, NEW JERSEY

Okay, Mike! Here's $1.98. Send me your COMPLETE (nothing else to buy later) body-building course. I want to use your new secret of DYNAFLEX to win a HERCULES HE-MAN BODY in just ten minutes a day. Rush my copies of the DYNAFLEX SYSTEM and my free gift book "Secrets of Attracting Girls" on your money-back guarantee, in plain wrappers. If I don't develop a splendid physique and become more popular with girls you will refund my money in full.

NAME .... AGE......

ADDRESS ....

CITY .... ZONE .... STATE........
(Please Print!)

THE FANTASTIC FOUR is published by CANAM PUBLISHERS SALES CORP. OFFICE OF PUBLICATION: 655 MADISON AVENUE, NEW YORK, N.Y. Published monthly. Copyright 1963 by CANAM PUBLISHERS SALES CORP., 655 Madison Avenue, New York, N.Y. Vol. 1 No. 18, SEPTEMBER, 1963 issue. Price 12¢ per copy. Subscription rate $1.75 for 12 issues including postage. Foreign subscription $3.25 in American funds. No similarity between any of the names, characters, persons, and/or institutions appearing in this magazine with those of any living or dead person is intended, and any such similarity which may exist is purely coincidental. Printed in U.S.A. by The Eastern Color Printing Co., Waterbury 20, Conn.

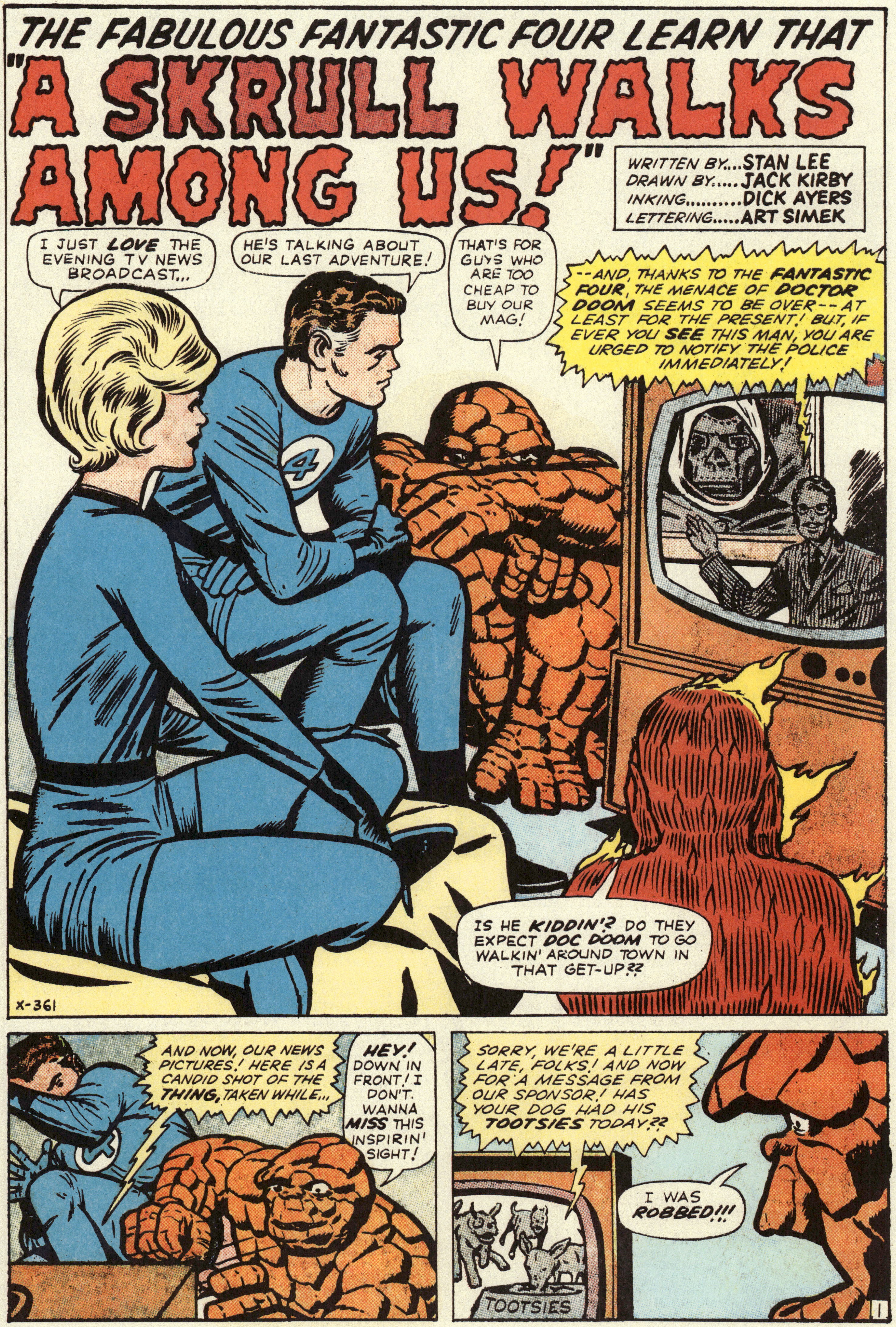
THE FABULOUS FANTASTIC FOUR LEARN THAT
"A SKRULL WALKS AMONG US!"
WRITTEN BY....STAN LEE
DRAWN BY.....JACK KIRBY
INKING.........DICK AYERS
LETTERING.....ART SIMEK
I JUST LOVE THE EVENING TV NEWS BROADCAST...
HE'S TALKING ABOUT OUR LAST ADVENTURE!
THAT'S FOR GUYS WHO ARE TOO CHEAP TO BUY OUR MAG!
--AND, THANKS TO THE FANTASTIC FOUR, THE MENACE OF DOCTOR DOOM SEEMS TO BE OVER-- AT LEAST FOR THE PRESENT! BUT, IF EVER YOU SEE THIS MAN, YOU ARE URGED TO NOTIFY THE POLICE IMMEDIATELY!
IS HE KIDDIN'? DO THEY EXPECT DOC DOOM TO GO WALKIN' AROUND TOWN IN THAT GET-UP??
X-361
AND NOW, OUR NEWS PICTURES! HERE IS A CANDID SHOT OF THE THING, TAKEN WHILE...
HEY! DOWN IN FRONT! I DON'T. WANNA MISS THIS INSPIRIN' SIGHT!
SORRY, WE'RE A LITTLE LATE, FOLKS! AND NOW FOR A MESSAGE FROM OUR SPONSOR! HAS YOUR DOG HAD HIS TOOTSIES TODAY??
I WAS ROBBED!!!
TOOTSIES
1

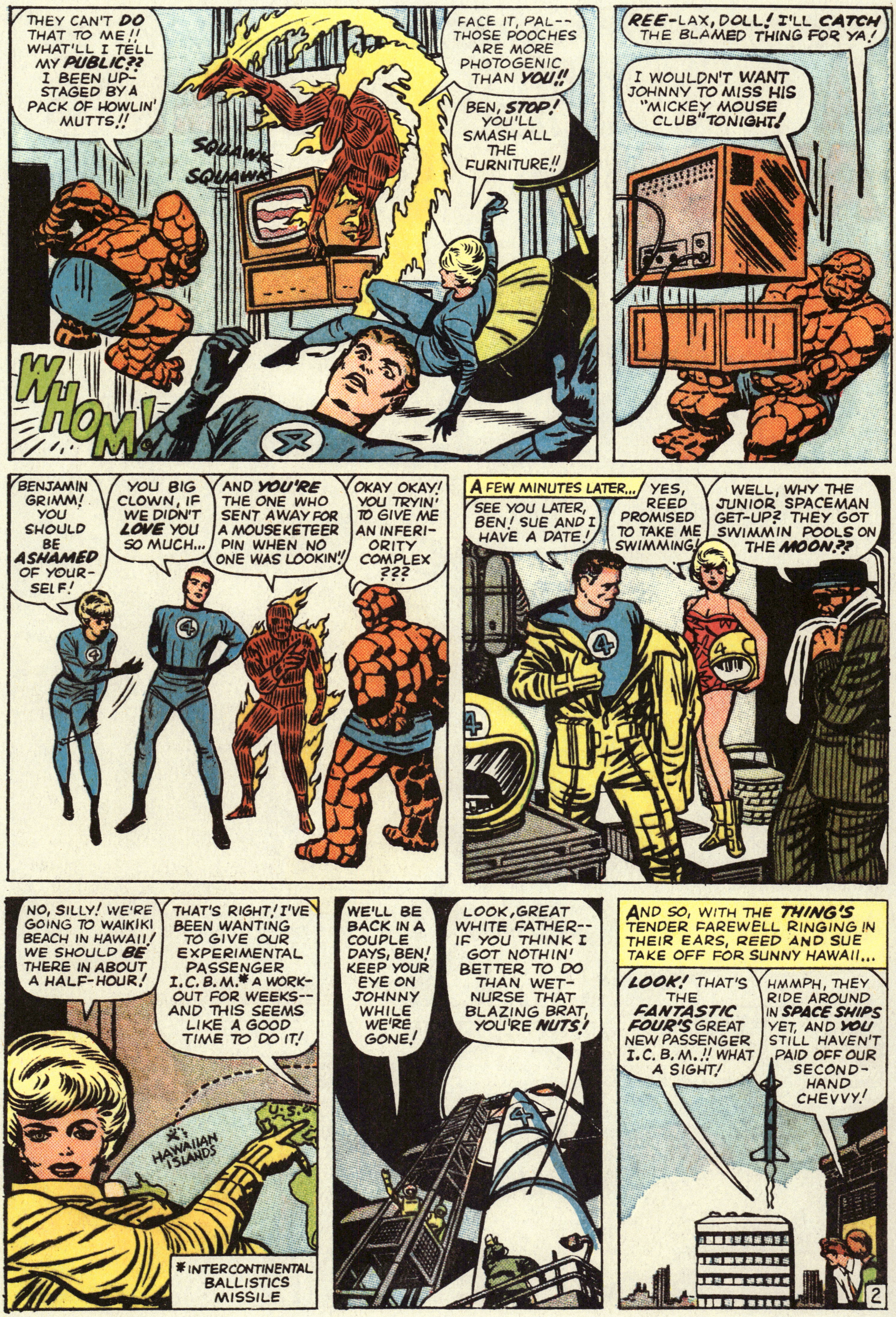
THEY CAN'T DO THAT TO ME!! WHAT'LL I TELL MY PUBLIC?? I BEEN UP-STAGED BY A PACK OF HOWLIN' MUTTS!!
FACE IT, PAL-- THOSE POOCHES ARE MORE PHOTOGENIC THAN YOU!!
BEN, STOP! YOU'LL SMASH ALL THE FURNITURE!!
SQUAWK SQUAWK
WHOM!
REE-LAX, DOLL! I'LL CATCH THE BLAMED THING FOR YA!
I WOULDN'T WANT JOHNNY TO MISS HIS "MICKEY MOUSE CLUB" TONIGHT!
BENJAMIN GRIMM! YOU SHOULD BE ASHAMED OF YOURSELF!
YOU BIG CLOWN, IF WE DIDN'T LOVE YOU SO MUCH...
AND YOU'RE THE ONE WHO SENT AWAY FOR A MOUSEKETEER PIN WHEN NO ONE WAS LOOKIN'!
OKAY OKAY! YOU TRYIN' TO GIVE ME AN INFERIORITY COMPLEX ???
A FEW MINUTES LATER...
SEE YOU LATER, BEN! SUE AND I HAVE A DATE!
YES, REED PROMISED TO TAKE ME SWIMMING!
WELL, WHY THE JUNIOR SPACEMAN GET-UP? THEY GOT SWIMMIN POOLS ON THE MOON??
NO, SILLY! WE'RE GOING TO WAIKIKI BEACH IN HAWAII! WE SHOULD BE THERE IN ABOUT A HALF-HOUR!
THAT'S RIGHT! I'VE BEEN WANTING TO GIVE OUR EXPERIMENTAL PASSENGER I.C.B.M.* A WORK-OUT FOR WEEKS-- AND THIS SEEMS LIKE A GOOD TIME TO DO IT!
U.S.
HAWAIIAN ISLANDS
*INTERCONTINENTAL BALLISTICS MISSILE
WE'LL BE BACK IN A COUPLE DAYS, BEN! KEEP YOUR EYE ON JOHNNY WHILE WE'RE GONE!
LOOK, GREAT WHITE FATHER-- IF YOU THINK I GOT NOTHIN' BETTER TO DO THAN WET-NURSE THAT BLAZING BRAT, YOU'RE NUTS!
AND SO, WITH THE THING'S TENDER FAREWELL RINGING IN THEIR EARS, REED AND SUE TAKE OFF FOR SUNNY HAWAII...
LOOK! THAT'S THE FANTASTIC FOUR'S GREAT NEW PASSENGER I.C.B.M.!! WHAT A SIGHT!
HMMPH, THEY RIDE AROUND IN SPACE SHIPS YET, AND YOU STILL HAVEN'T PAID OFF OUR SECOND-HAND CHEVVY!
2

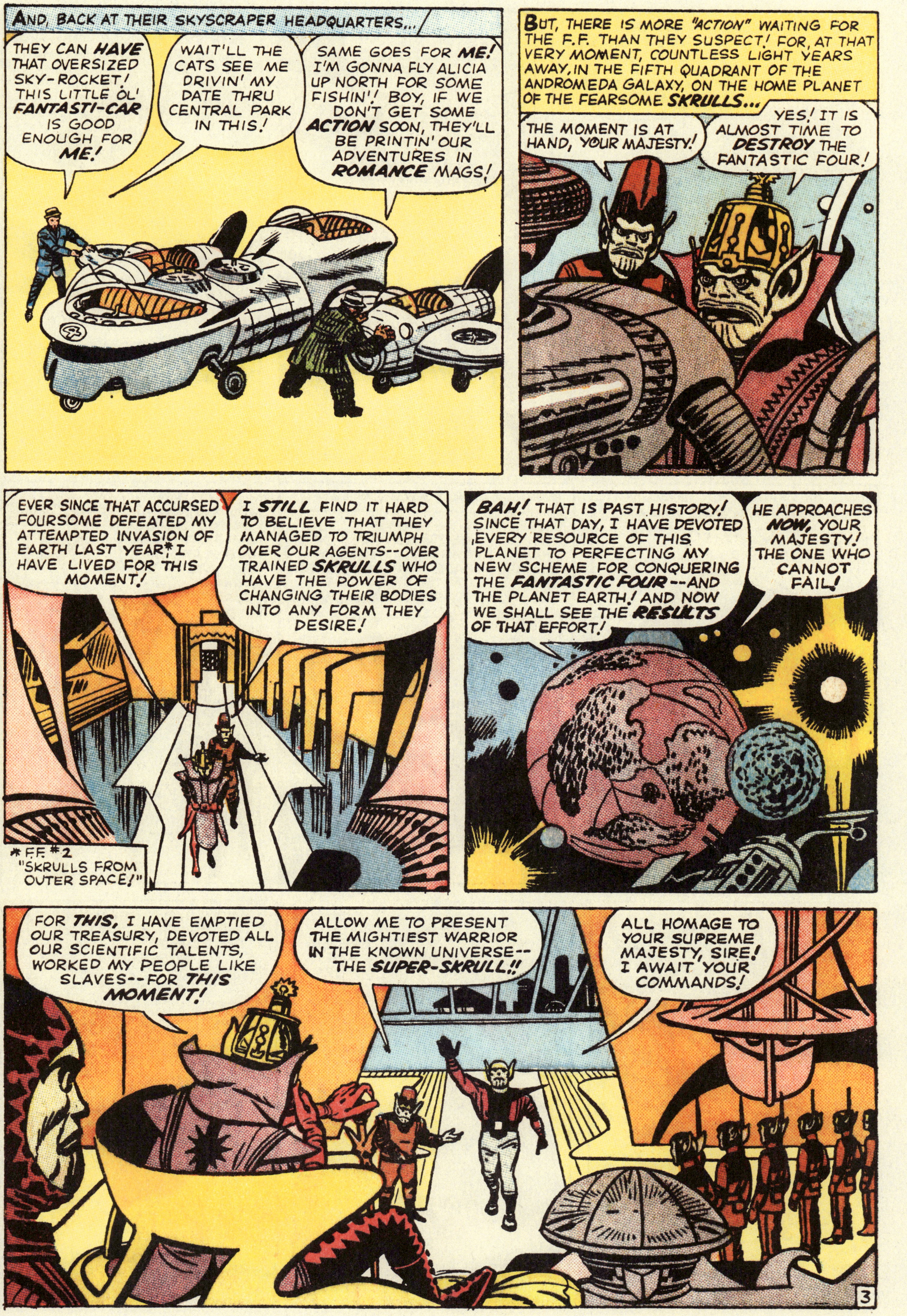

AND, BACK AT THEIR SKYSCRAPER HEADQUARTERS...
THEY CAN HAVE THAT OVERSIZED SKY-ROCKET! THIS LITTLE OL' FANTASTI-CAR IS GOOD ENOUGH FOR ME!
WAIT'LL THE CATS SEE ME DRIVIN' MY DATE THRU CENTRAL PARK IN THIS!
SAME GOES FOR ME! I'M GONNA FLY ALICIA UP NORTH FOR SOME FISHIN'! BOY, IF WE DON'T GET SOME ACTION SOON, THEY'LL BE PRINTIN' OUR ADVENTURES IN ROMANCE MAGS!
BUT, THERE IS MORE "ACTION" WAITING FOR THE F.F. THAN THEY SUSPECT! FOR, AT THAT VERY MOMENT, COUNTLESS LIGHT YEARS AWAY, IN THE FIFTH QUADRANT OF THE ANDROMEDA GALAXY, ON THE HOME PLANET OF THE FEARSOME SKRULLS...
THE MOMENT IS AT HAND, YOUR MAJESTY!
YES! IT IS ALMOST TIME TO DESTROY THE FANTASTIC FOUR!
EVER SINCE THAT ACCURSED FOURSOME DEFEATED MY ATTEMPTED INVASION OF EARTH LAST YEAR*, I HAVE LIVED FOR THIS MOMENT!
I STILL FIND IT HARD TO BELIEVE THAT THEY MANAGED TO TRIUMPH OVER OUR AGENTS--OVER TRAINED SKRULLS WHO HAVE THE POWER OF CHANGING THEIR BODIES INTO ANY FORM THEY DESIRE!
*F.F. #2 "SKRULLS FROM OUTER SPACE!"
BAH! THAT IS PAST HISTORY! SINCE THAT DAY, I HAVE DEVOTED EVERY RESOURCE OF THIS PLANET TO PERFECTING MY NEW SCHEME FOR CONQUERING THE FANTASTIC FOUR--AND THE PLANET EARTH! AND NOW WE SHALL SEE THE RESULTS OF THAT EFFORT!
HE APPROACHES NOW, YOUR MAJESTY! THE ONE WHO CANNOT FAIL!
FOR THIS, I HAVE EMPTIED OUR TREASURY, DEVOTED ALL OUR SCIENTIFIC TALENTS, WORKED MY PEOPLE LIKE SLAVES--FOR THIS MOMENT!
ALLOW ME TO PRESENT THE MIGHTIEST WARRIOR IN THE KNOWN UNIVERSE-- THE SUPER-SKRULL!!
ALL HOMAGE TO YOUR SUPREME MAJESTY, SIRE! I AWAIT YOUR COMMANDS!
3

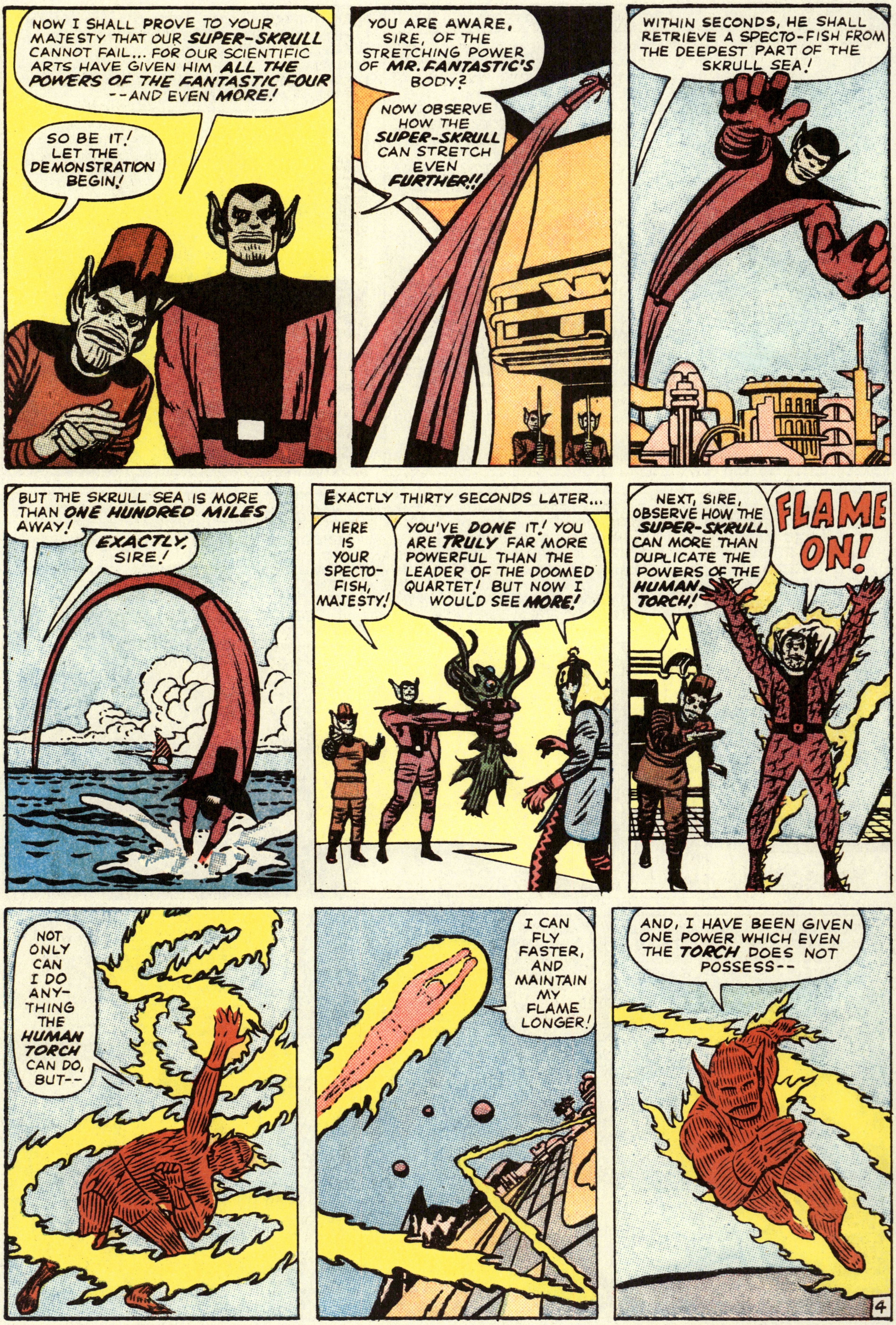

NOW I SHALL PROVE TO YOUR MAJESTY THAT OUR SUPER-SKRULL CANNOT FAIL... FOR OUR SCIENTIFIC ARTS HAVE GIVEN HIM ALL THE POWERS OF THE FANTASTIC FOUR --AND EVEN MORE!
SO BE IT! LET THE DEMONSTRATION BEGIN!
YOU ARE AWARE, SIRE, OF THE STRETCHING POWER OF MR. FANTASTIC'S BODY?
NOW OBSERVE HOW THE SUPER-SKRULL CAN STRETCH EVEN FURTHER!!
WITHIN SECONDS, HE SHALL RETRIEVE A SPECTO-FISH FROM THE DEEPEST PART OF THE SKRULL SEA!
BUT THE SKRULL SEA IS MORE THAN ONE HUNDRED MILES AWAY!
EXACTLY, SIRE!
EXACTLY THIRTY SECONDS LATER...
HERE IS YOUR SPECTO-FISH, MAJESTY!
YOU'VE DONE IT! YOU ARE TRULY FAR MORE POWERFUL THAN THE LEADER OF THE DOOMED QUARTET! BUT NOW I WOULD SEE MORE!
NEXT, SIRE, OBSERVE HOW THE SUPER-SKRULL CAN MORE THAN DUPLICATE THE POWERS OF THE HUMAN TORCH!
FLAME ON!
NOT ONLY CAN I DO ANY-THING THE HUMAN TORCH CAN DO, BUT--
I CAN FLY FASTER, AND MAINTAIN MY FLAME LONGER!
AND, I HAVE BEEN GIVEN ONE POWER WHICH EVEN THE TORCH DOES NOT POSSESS--

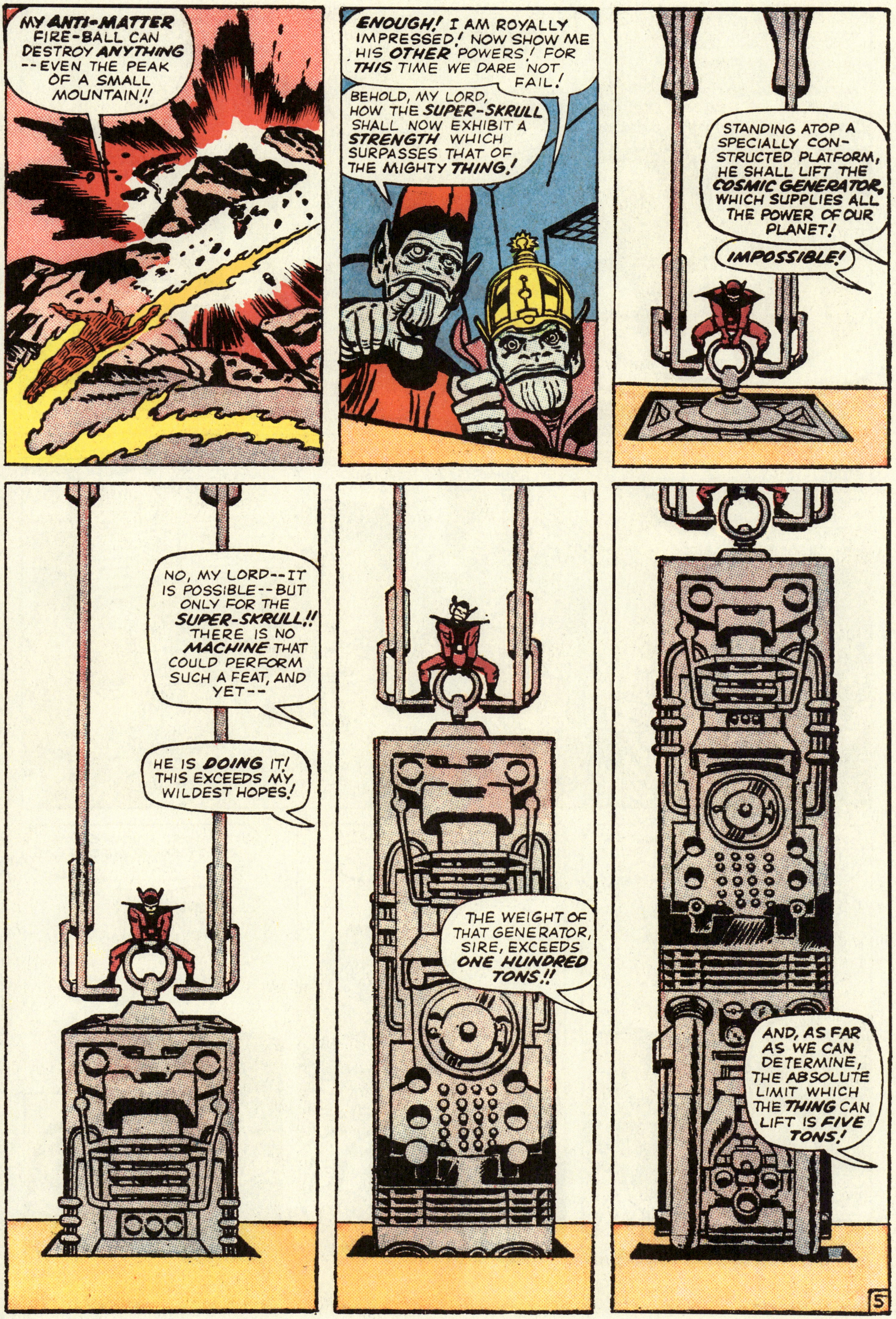
MY ANTI-MATTER FIRE-BALL CAN DESTROY ANYTHING --EVEN THE PEAK OF A SMALL MOUNTAIN!!
ENOUGH! I AM ROYALLY IMPRESSED! NOW SHOW ME HIS OTHER POWERS! FOR THIS TIME WE DARE NOT FAIL!
BEHOLD, MY LORD, HOW THE SUPER-SKRULL SHALL NOW EXHIBIT A STRENGTH WHICH SURPASSES THAT OF THE MIGHTY THING!
STANDING ATOP A SPECIALLY CONSTRUCTED PLATFORM, HE SHALL LIFT THE COSMIC GENERATOR, WHICH SUPPLIES ALL THE POWER OF OUR PLANET!
IMPOSSIBLE!
NO, MY LORD--IT IS POSSIBLE--BUT ONLY FOR THE SUPER-SKRULL!! THERE IS NO MACHINE THAT COULD PERFORM SUCH A FEAT, AND YET--
HE IS DOING IT! THIS EXCEEDS MY WILDEST HOPES!
THE WEIGHT OF THAT GENERATOR, SIRE, EXCEEDS ONE HUNDRED TONS!!
AND, AS FAR AS WE CAN DETERMINE, THE ABSOLUTE LIMIT WHICH THE THING CAN LIFT IS FIVE TONS!

BRING HIM TO ME! I MUST CONGRATULATE HIM! WHERE IS HE?
RIGHT IN FRONT OF YOU, SIRE!
IN FRONT OF ME?? YOU'RE MAD! I DO NOT SEE HIM!
BUT THAT IS MY FOURTH POWER, YOUR MAJESTY! THUS CAN I MATCH THE INVISIBLE GIRL!
MATCH HER? THIS IS NOT ENOUGH! YOU MUST OUT-DO HER! YOU MUST BE HER SUPERIOR!
HE DOES POSSESS ONE POWER WHICH SHE DOES NOT, SIRE! I SHALL DESCRIBE IT TO YOU LATER! BUT NOW...
IT IS TIME FOR ME TO EMBARK UPON MY MISSION! I SWEAR NEVER TO RETURN, MY LORD, UNTIL THE FANTASTIC FOUR ARE NO MORE--AND THE PLANET EARTH IS YOURS!
ONE WEEK LATER, AT A NEW YORK DEPARTMENT STORE, WE FIND THE FANTASTIC FOUR TOGETHER AGAIN, ON A SHOPPING TRIP...
I JUST ADORE SEEING THE NEW FASHIONS!
I THINK I'LL BROWSE AROUND THE BOOK DEPARTMENT!
BOY, IT MUST BE A GAS WORKIN' IN A PLACE WITH ALL THESE CHICKS!
CHICKS, SHMICKS! I'M GONNA GO BUY ME A BOWLIN' BALL!
YOU SURE THIS IS THE BIGGEST ONE YOU GOT, BUSTER? I AINT EXACTLY GOT SKINNY LITTLE FINGERS!
JUST TRY THAT ONE, SIR! IT WOULD EVEN FIT -HEH-HEH- A GORILLA!
OKAY, LAUGHIN' BOY, IF YOU SAY SO...
ULP
CRUNCH
YOU MUST KNOW SOME PRETTY SMALL GORILLAS, PAL!
I KNOW I SAW IT HAPPEN--BUT--
6

MEANWHILE, DESPITE ALL THEIR PRECAUTIONS, SOME WELL-MEANING, SHARP-EYED ADMIRERS RECOGNIZE SUE, REED, AND JOHNNY, AND--
YEESH! WOTTA RACKET! THEY MUST BE GIVIN' AWAY FREE SAMPLES OF SOMETHIN'!
LET ME THRU! LET ME THRU!
I CAN'T SEE! I WANT TO GET CLOSER!
DON'T PUSH! DON'T SHOVE! ONE AT A TIME! KEEP BACK, FOLKS --PLEASE!
I WAS FIRST! OUT OF MY WAY! WHERE'S THE MANAGER?
BEN! DON'T JUST STAND THERE! GET US OUT OF HERE!
FOR THE LUVVA PETE! IT'S YOU!
HANG ON, KIDDIES! I'LL GIVE YA A FREE RIDE!
BENJAMIN, YOU'RE A LIFE-SAVER!!
HECK, I WAS BEGINNIN' TO ENJOY IT!
OH DEAR! JUST WHEN I FOUND THE CUTEST NEGLIGEE ON SALE!
WHEW! LET'S GET OUT OF HERE BEFORE THEY FIND US AGAIN!
REED RICHARDS-- YOU'RE AN OLD SCAIRDY-CAT!
NAH! HE AINT SO OLD!
BOY! NEVER A DULL MOMENT!
BOYS! WAIT! LISTEN--
IT'S A SPECIAL BULLETIN COMIN' IN OVER THAT RADIO!
--AND TIMES SQUARE IS IN A STATE OF PANIC AND TURMOIL EVER SINCE THE ALIEN SPACE SHIP LANDED FIVE MINUTES AGO...
AN ALIEN SPACE SHIP-- IN TIMES SQUARE!!
IF THERE'S PANIC IN THE STREETS, THEN SOMETHING SERIOUS MUST BE WRONG!
NOW'S OUR CHANCE TO MAKE LIKE HEROES! WHAT'RE WE WAITIN' FOR?!!
7

UH OH! THE THUNDERIN' HERD FOUND US AGAIN! WELL, THIS IS NO TIME TO PLAY FOOTSIES WITH A BUNCH OF FRANTIC FANS!
FLAME ON!
SORRY, FOLKS! WE'VE GOT THINGS TO DO!
KEEP GOIN', JOHNNY-- I'M RIGHT BEHIND YOU!
MABEL! HOW CLUMSY CAN YOU BE!!?
I'LL LEAVE, TOO --IN MY OWN LITTLE WAY!
ZELDA! LOOK WHERE YOU'RE GOING, DEARIE!
AT THAT VERY MOMENT, TEN BLOCKS AWAY, IN THE HEART OF TIMES SQUARE...
I CLAIM THIS PLANET, AND ALL IT POSSESSES, IN THE NAME OF THE IMPERIAL SKRULL EMPIRE!
WHAT'S GOIN' ON?? WHAT'S HE ADVER-TISIN'?
NOTHIN', MAC! HE'S FOR REAL!
HE SURE IS! THREE WOMEN FAINTED ALREADY--
THE MILITIA OUGHTTA BE ARRIVIN' HERE ANY MINUTE!
8

I'LL PLANT MY BANNER TO MARK THE SPOT WHERE I LANDED, AND...
THE GROUND IS TOO HARD! IT WILL NOT PENETRATE!
BUT THAT IS NO PROBLEM TO THE SUPER-SKRULL!
L-LOOK! HE'S LIKE AN ALIEN HUMAN TORCH!
WITHIN MINUTES, AFTER THE SKRULL BANNER IS PLANTED--SEEING THAT THE AWESOME ALIEN HAS MADE NO HOSTILE MOVE-- THE MOOD OF THE CROWD CHANGES FROM FEAR AND PANIC TO STUNNED DISBELIEF...
I NEVER THOUGHT, IF AN ALIEN EVER LANDED, THAT IT WOULD BE LIKE THIS!
HE MUST THINK HE'S COLUMBUS OR SOMETHIN', PLANTING THAT NUTTY BANNER IN THE STREET!
YOU MAY ALL DISPERSE NOW, AND RETURN TO YOUR EVERY-DAY TASKS!
BEFORE LONG, I SHALL ISSUE THE FIRST IMPERIAL ORDERS FROM YOUR NEW PROVISIONAL SKRULL GOVERNMENT!
HE ACTUALLY SEEMS TO MEAN IT! HE THINKS HE HAS TAKEN POSSESSION OF THIS PLANET!
AW, WHY DOESN'T HE TAKE OFF THAT MASK AND GO BACK WHERE HE CAME FROM? WE GOT ENOUGH CRACKPOTS IN TOWN ALREADY!
YEAH! GET LOST, CREEP!
YOU DARE SPEAK THUS TO YOUR NEW MASTER??? BEGONE, BEFORE I FORGET HOW WEAK AND DEFENSELESS YOU ARE!
9

AND, IN THE HOME PLANET OF THE FIFTH QUADRANT OF THE ANDROMEDA GALAXY...
ALL GOES WELL, SIRE! OUR SUPER-SKRULL IS IN FULL COMMAND!
BAH! THAT IS CHILD'S PLAY! THE REAL TEST SHALL BE WHEN HE CONFRONTS THE FANTASTIC FOUR!
BEHOLD!! THE MOMENT IS AT HAND! EVEN NOW THE HUMAN TORCH APPROACHES!
QUICKLY, ADJUST THE FOCUS MORE CLEARLY! I HAVE WAITED MONTHS FOR THIS MOMENT! I DO NOT WANT TO MISS A THING!
FLAMIN' FIREBALLS!! IT'S A SKRULL--LIKE THE ONES WE FOUGHT A YEAR AGO!! BUT THIS ONE IS BIGGER--MORE DANGEROUS-LOOKIN' SOMEHOW!!
ALL RIGHT, PLAYMATE, THE PARTY'S OVER! WE LICKED YOU GUYS ONCE, AND WE'LL DO IT AGAIN!
THE HUMAN TORCH--AT LAST!
NOT THIS TIME, EARTHLING! THIS TIME YOU ARE FACING A SUPER SKRULL!!
FLAME ON!
I DON'T LIKE THE LOOKS OF THIS! THAT GUY IS LITERALLY FLYIN' RINGS AROUND ME!
ANYTHING YOU CAN DO, TORCH, I CAN DO BETTER!
FOR INSTANCE, I CAN FRY THE VERY AIR AROUND YOU, UNTIL IT TURNS INTO BLACK CARBON!
MY EYES!! I CAN'T SEE!
10

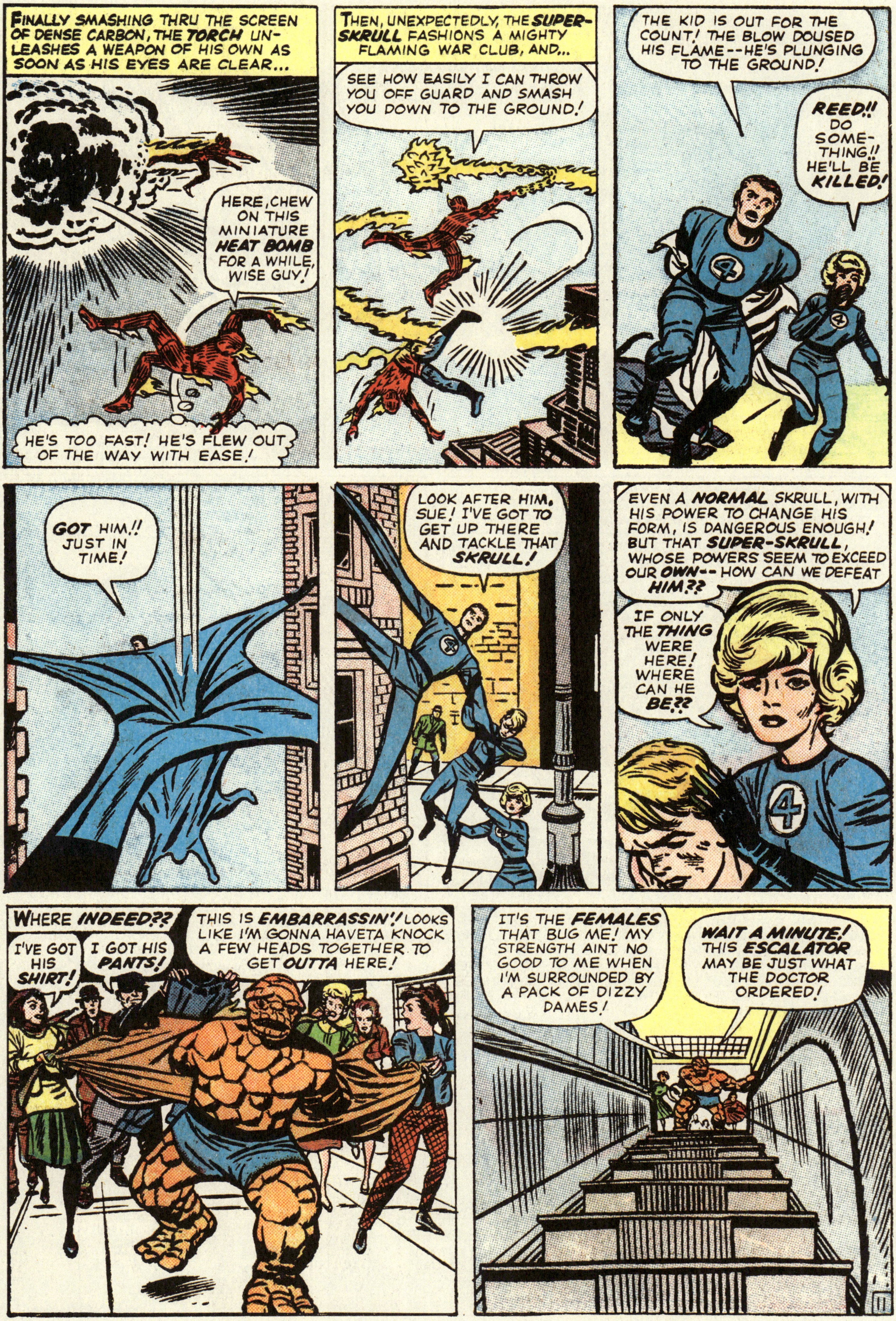
FINALLY SMASHING THRU THE SCREEN OF DENSE CARBON, THE TORCH UN-LEASHES A WEAPON OF HIS OWN AS SOON AS HIS EYES ARE CLEAR...
HERE, CHEW ON THIS MINIATURE HEAT BOMB FOR A WHILE, WISE GUY!
HE'S TOO FAST! HE'S FLEW OUT OF THE WAY WITH EASE!
THEN, UNEXPECTEDLY, THE SUPER-SKRULL FASHIONS A MIGHTY FLAMING WAR CLUB, AND...
SEE HOW EASILY I CAN THROW YOU OFF GUARD AND SMASH YOU DOWN TO THE GROUND!
THE KID IS OUT FOR THE COUNT! THE BLOW DOUSED HIS FLAME--HE'S PLUNGING TO THE GROUND!
REED!! DO SOME-THING!! HE'LL BE KILLED!
GOT HIM!! JUST IN TIME!
LOOK AFTER HIM, SUE! I'VE GOT TO GET UP THERE AND TACKLE THAT SKRULL!
EVEN A NORMAL SKRULL, WITH HIS POWER TO CHANGE HIS FORM, IS DANGEROUS ENOUGH! BUT THAT SUPER-SKRULL, WHOSE POWERS SEEM TO EXCEED OUR OWN-- HOW CAN WE DEFEAT HIM??
IF ONLY THE THING WERE HERE! WHERE CAN HE BE??
WHERE INDEED??
I'VE GOT HIS SHIRT!
I GOT HIS PANTS!
THIS IS EMBARRASSIN'! LOOKS LIKE I'M GONNA HAVETA KNOCK A FEW HEADS TOGETHER TO GET OUTTA HERE!
IT'S THE FEMALES THAT BUG ME! MY STRENGTH AINT NO GOOD TO ME WHEN I'M SURROUNDED BY A PACK OF DIZZY DAMES!
WAIT A MINUTE! THIS ESCALATOR MAY BE JUST WHAT THE DOCTOR ORDERED!
11

ALL I GOTTA DO IS FLATTEN IT OUT, LIKE THIS--
WOWEEEEEE! NOW LET'S SEE THOSE HOWLIN' HANNAHS FOLLOW ME!
I HOPE OL' KILLJOY REED HASN'T TAKEN CARE OF THAT ALIEN YET!
BUT, FOR ONCE THE THING HAS NOTHING TO WORRY ABOUT! IT LOOKS AS THOUGH THERE WILL BE PLENTY FOR HIM TO DO WHEN HE REACHES THE SCENE...
YOU ROTTEN MURDERER! YOU MIGHT HAVE CAUSED THE TORCH TO PLUNGE TO HIS DEATH!
EXACTLY, EARTHLING! JUST AS I SHALL DO WITH ALL FOUR OF YOU!
WE'LL SEE ABOUT THAT!! FIRST, I'LL WRAP YOU IN A HUMAN STRAIT-JACKET WHILE I TRY TO DECIDE WHAT TO DO WITH YOU!
BUT, WITHIN SECONDS, MISTER FANTASTIC LEARNS THAT THE SUPER-SKRULL'S POWER EXCEEDS THAT OF HIS OWN! FOR, ALTHOUGH COMPLETELY ENVELOPED, AND SEEMINGLY HELPLESS, HE BEGINS TO EXERT PRESSURE OF HIS OWN!
HE'S EXPANDING HIS OWN BODY! I CAN'T RESTRAIN HIM! HE'S GROWING BIGGER-- BIGGER--
IT'S UNBELIEVABLE!! NO MATTER HOW MUCH PRESSURE I EXERT, HE CONTINUES TO GROW LARGER!
CAN'T KEEP IT UP ANY LONGER!! --HE'S TOO POWERFUL!! STRAIN IS TOO GREAT--
12

FINALLY...
I--HAD TO LET GO!!
NOW DO YOU REALIZE HOW HELPLESS YOU ARE AGAINST ME? I AM MIGHTIER THAN ALL OF YOU!
FELLA, ON THIS PLANET, THAT'S ONLY CALLED "WINNING THE FIRST ROUND"!!
SUDDENLY, MR. FANTASTIC MOVES WITH THE SPEED OF THOUGHT...
LET'S SEE WHAT YOU CAN DO AGAINST A POWER BLOW FROM A HUMAN SLEDGE-HAMMER!
YOU'RE FAST! BUT NOT FAST ENOUGH FOR ME!
IN A SPLIT-SECOND, THE SUPER SKRULL'S ARM STRETCHES AN UNBELIEVABLE DISTANCE--TO THE MOUND OF LOOSE ROCKS ON THE PALISADES SHORE! THEN, GRASPING ONE IN HIS STEEL-LIKE FINGERS...
...HE MANAGES TO RETRIEVE IT IN TIME TO USE IT AS A SHIELD!
WHOOM!
13

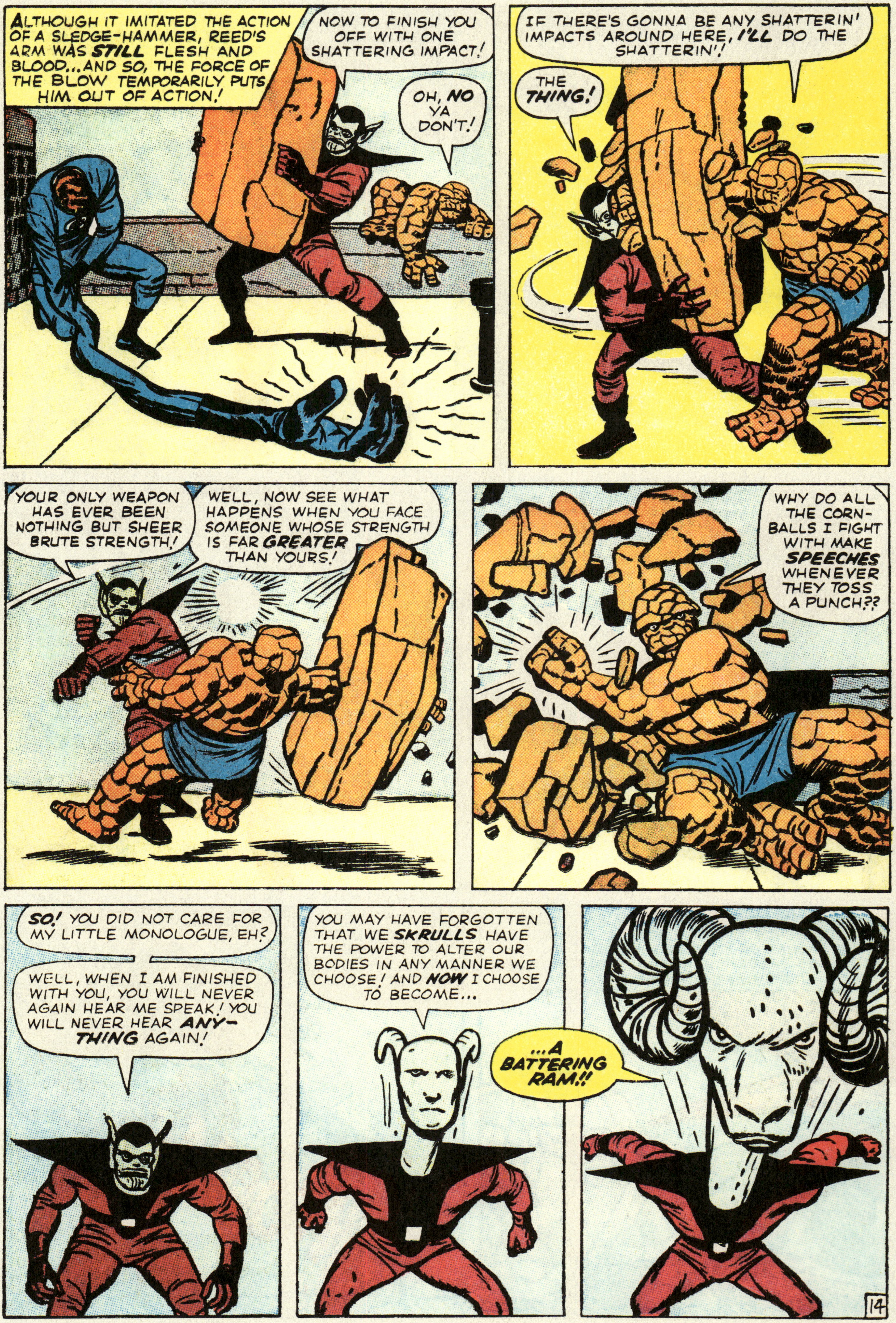
ALTHOUGH IT IMITATED THE ACTION OF A SLEDGE-HAMMER, REED'S ARM WAS STILL FLESH AND BLOOD... AND SO, THE FORCE OF THE BLOW TEMPORARILY PUTS HIM OUT OF ACTION!
NOW TO FINISH YOU OFF WITH ONE SHATTERING IMPACT!
OH, NO YA DON'T!
IF THERE'S GONNA BE ANY SHATTERIN' IMPACTS AROUND HERE, I'LL DO THE SHATTERIN'!
THE THING!
YOUR ONLY WEAPON HAS EVER BEEN NOTHING BUT SHEER BRUTE STRENGTH!
WELL, NOW SEE WHAT HAPPENS WHEN YOU FACE SOMEONE WHOSE STRENGTH IS FAR GREATER THAN YOURS!
WHY DO ALL THE CORN-BALLS I FIGHT WITH MAKE SPEECHES WHENEVER THEY TOSS A PUNCH??
SO! YOU DID NOT CARE FOR MY LITTLE MONOLOGUE, EH?
WELL, WHEN I AM FINISHED WITH YOU, YOU WILL NEVER AGAIN HEAR ME SPEAK! YOU WILL NEVER HEAR ANY-THING AGAIN!
YOU MAY HAVE FORGOTTEN THAT WE SKRULLS HAVE THE POWER TO ALTER OUR BODIES IN ANY MANNER WE CHOOSE! AND NOW I CHOOSE TO BECOME...
...A BATTERING RAM!!
14

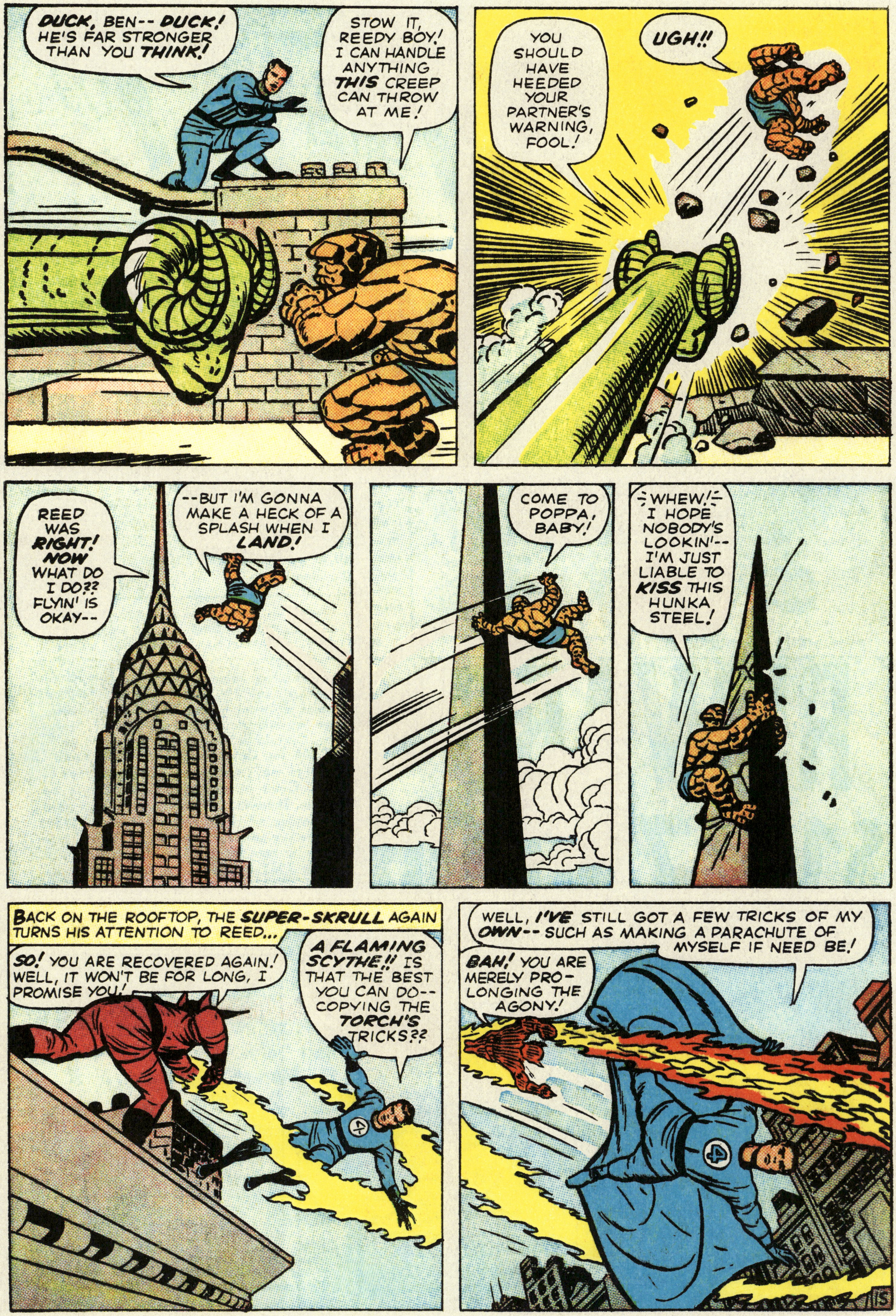
DUCK, BEN-- DUCK! HE'S FAR STRONGER THAN YOU THINK!
STOW IT, REEDY BOY! I CAN HANDLE ANYTHING THIS CREEP CAN THROW AT ME!
YOU SHOULD HAVE HEEDED YOUR PARTNER'S WARNING, FOOL!
UGH!!
REED WAS RIGHT! NOW WHAT DO I DO?? FLYIN' IS OKAY--
--BUT I'M GONNA MAKE A HECK OF A SPLASH WHEN I LAND!
COME TO POPPA, BABY!
WHEW! I HOPE NOBODY'S LOOKIN'-- I'M JUST LIABLE TO KISS THIS HUNKA STEEL!
BACK ON THE ROOFTOP, THE SUPER-SKRULL AGAIN TURNS HIS ATTENTION TO REED...
SO! YOU ARE RECOVERED AGAIN! WELL, IT WON'T BE FOR LONG, I PROMISE YOU!
A FLAMING SCYTHE!! IS THAT THE BEST YOU CAN DO-- COPYING THE TORCH'S TRICKS??
WELL, I'VE STILL GOT A FEW TRICKS OF MY OWN-- SUCH AS MAKING A PARACHUTE OF MYSELF IF NEED BE!
BAH! YOU ARE MERELY PROLONGING THE AGONY!
15

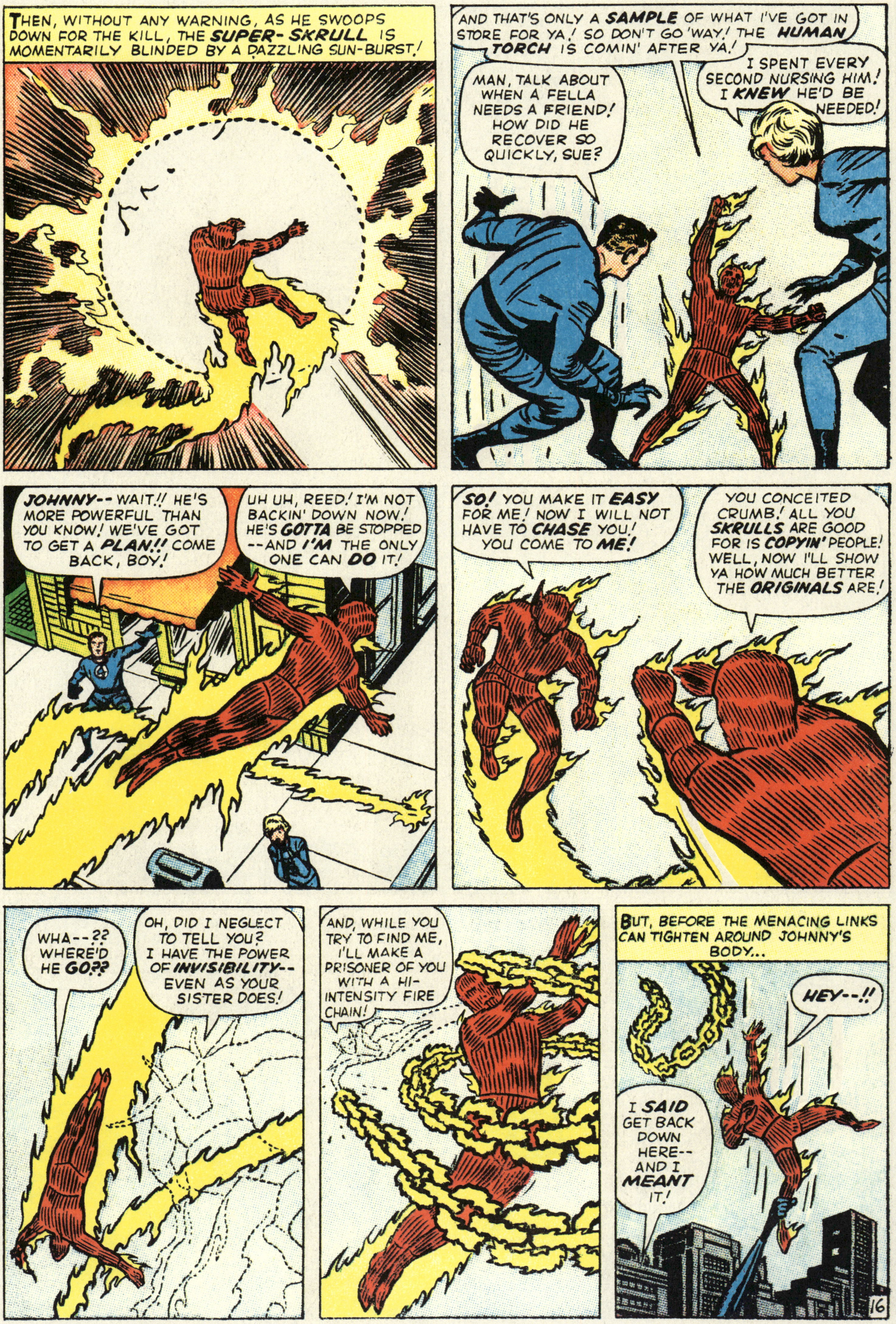
THEN, WITHOUT ANY WARNING, AS HE SWOOPS DOWN FOR THE KILL, THE SUPER-SKRULL IS MOMENTARILY BLINDED BY A DAZZLING SUN-BURST!
AND THAT'S ONLY A SAMPLE OF WHAT I'VE GOT IN STORE FOR YA! SO DON'T GO 'WAY! THE HUMAN TORCH IS COMIN' AFTER YA!
MAN, TALK ABOUT WHEN A FELLA NEEDS A FRIEND! HOW DID HE RECOVER SO QUICKLY, SUE?
I SPENT EVERY SECOND NURSING HIM! I KNEW HE'D BE NEEDED!
JOHNNY-- WAIT!! HE'S MORE POWERFUL THAN YOU KNOW! WE'VE GOT TO GET A PLAN!! COME BACK, BOY!
UH UH, REED! I'M NOT BACKIN' DOWN NOW! HE'S GOTTA BE STOPPED --AND I'M THE ONLY ONE CAN DO IT!
SO! YOU MAKE IT EASY FOR ME! NOW I WILL NOT HAVE TO CHASE YOU! YOU COME TO ME!
YOU CONCEITED CRUMB! ALL YOU SKRULLS ARE GOOD FOR IS COPYIN' PEOPLE! WELL, NOW I'LL SHOW YA HOW MUCH BETTER THE ORIGINALS ARE!
WHA--?? WHERE'D HE GO??
OH, DID I NEGLECT TO TELL YOU? I HAVE THE POWER OF INVISIBILITY-- EVEN AS YOUR SISTER DOES!
AND, WHILE YOU TRY TO FIND ME, I'LL MAKE A PRISONER OF YOU WITH A HI-INTENSITY FIRE CHAIN!
BUT, BEFORE THE MENACING LINKS CAN TIGHTEN AROUND JOHNNY'S BODY...
HEY--!!
I SAID GET BACK DOWN HERE-- AND I MEANT IT!
16

AWW, WHAT DID YOU DO THAT FOR? SAY! YOU BURNED YOURSELF ON MY LEG!
IT'LL BE ALL RIGHT, KID! I HAD TO DO IT! NONE OF US, ALONE, ARE A MATCH FOR THE SKRULL!
THIS IS TERRIBLE! I'VE NEVER FELT SO HELPLESS-- SO USELESS!
DON'T LET THAT BOTHER YOU, HONEY! WITH ALL OUR BLUSTER, WE HAVEN'T ACHIEVED ANY MORE THAN YOU! BUT--WHERE IS THE THING??
LOOK, REED! UP THERE!
THIS IS MIGHTY OBLIGIN' OF YOU GUYS! I WAS BEGINNIN' TO FEEL LIKE A GOL-DANGED WEATHER VANE UP THERE!
N.Y.C. POLICE
WHAT HAPPENED, SKINNY? DIDJA GET RID OF OUR LITTLE PLAYMATE YET?
NO, BEN! WE'VE GOT TO GET TO OUR HEAD-QUARTERS AND MAP OUT A PLAN OF ACTION!
HURRY! HE MADE HIMSELF INVISIBLE! HE MIGHT BE ANYWHERE!
I STILL THINK YOU SHOULDA LET ME SLUG IT OUT WITH 'IM!
SO! THEY ARE ATTEMPTING TO GAIN THE SAFETY OF THEIR HEAD-QUARTERS, EH?? WELL, THEY WILL FIND IT'S EASIER SAID THAN DONE!
HA! DID YOU THINK TO EVADE ME THAT EASILY??
MOVE!! ALL OF YOU! HE'S SHOOTING FIRE-ARROWS AT US!

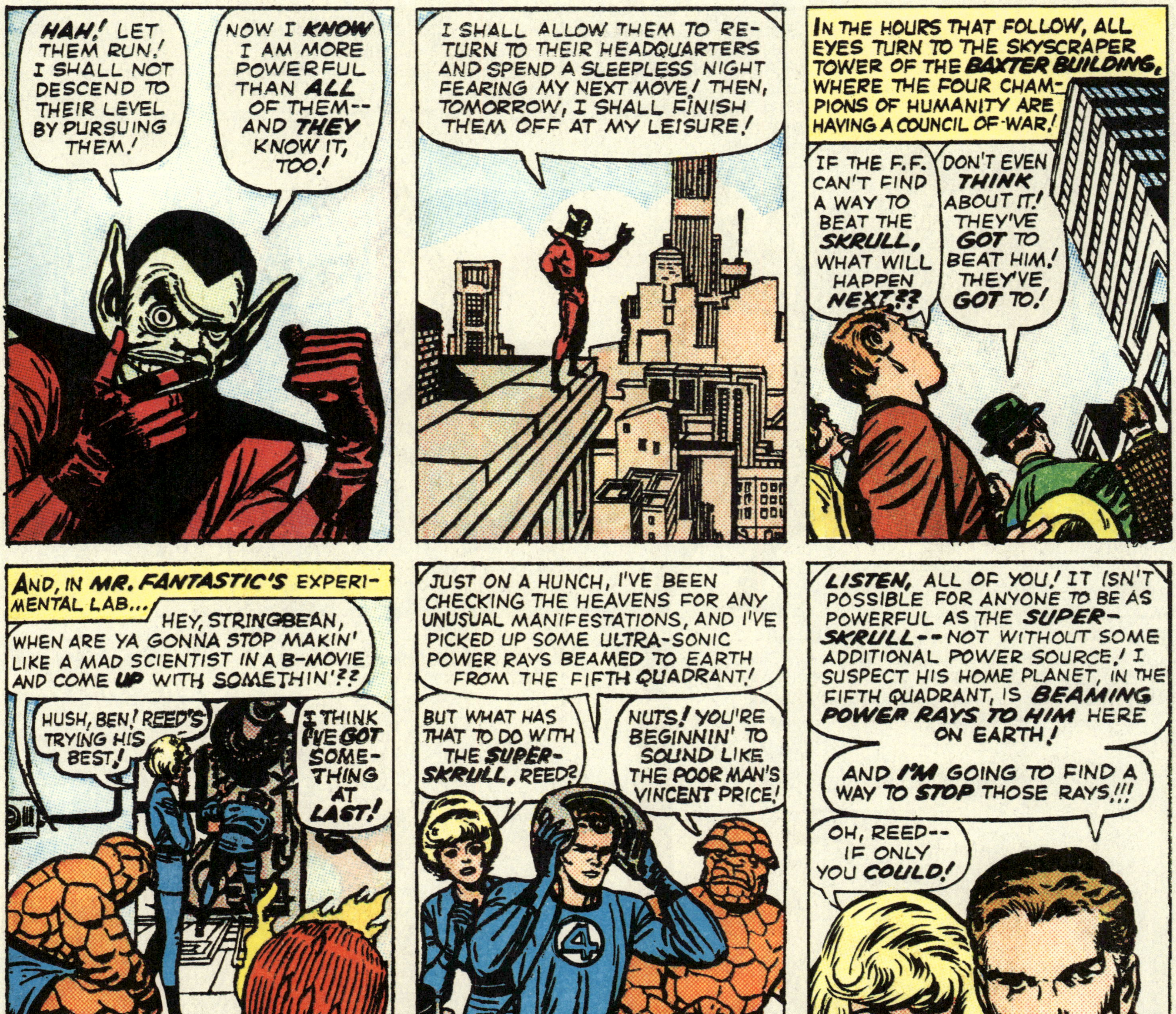
HAH! LET THEM RUN! I SHALL NOT DESCEND TO THEIR LEVEL BY PURSUING THEM!
NOW I KNOW I AM MORE POWERFUL THAN ALL OF THEM-- AND THEY KNOW IT, TOO!
I SHALL ALLOW THEM TO RETURN TO THEIR HEADQUARTERS AND SPEND A SLEEPLESS NIGHT FEARING MY NEXT MOVE! THEN, TOMORROW, I SHALL FINISH THEM OFF AT MY LEISURE!
IN THE HOURS THAT FOLLOW, ALL EYES TURN TO THE SKYSCRAPER TOWER OF THE BAXTER BUILDING, WHERE THE FOUR CHAMPIONS OF HUMANITY ARE HAVING A COUNCIL OF WAR!
IF THE F.F. CAN'T FIND A WAY TO BEAT THE SKRULL, WHAT WILL HAPPEN NEXT??
DON'T EVEN THINK ABOUT IT! THEY'VE GOT TO BEAT HIM! THEY'VE GOT TO!
AND, IN MR. FANTASTIC'S EXPERIMENTAL LAB...
HEY, STRINGBEAN, WHEN ARE YA GONNA STOP MAKIN' LIKE A MAD SCIENTIST IN A B-MOVIE AND COME UP WITH SOMETHIN'??
HUSH, BEN! REED'S TRYING HIS BEST!
I THINK I'VE GOT SOMETHING AT LAST!
JUST ON A HUNCH, I'VE BEEN CHECKING THE HEAVENS FOR ANY UNUSUAL MANIFESTATIONS, AND I'VE PICKED UP SOME ULTRA-SONIC POWER RAYS BEAMED TO EARTH FROM THE FIFTH QUADRANT!
BUT WHAT HAS THAT TO DO WITH THE SUPER-SKRULL, REED?
NUTS! YOU'RE BEGINNIN' TO SOUND LIKE THE POOR MAN'S VINCENT PRICE!
LISTEN, ALL OF YOU! IT ISN'T POSSIBLE FOR ANYONE TO BE AS POWERFUL AS THE SUPER-SKRULL-- NOT WITHOUT SOME ADDITIONAL POWER SOURCE! I SUSPECT HIS HOME PLANET, IN THE FIFTH QUADRANT, IS BEAMING POWER RAYS TO HIM HERE ON EARTH!
AND I'M GOING TO FIND A WAY TO STOP THOSE RAYS!!!
OH, REED-- IF ONLY YOU COULD!
SLOWLY, SILENTLY, THE LONG, TENSE MINUTES PASS, UNTIL FINALLY...
I'VE GOT IT! THIS TINY SUB-MINIATURIZED "JAMMER" WILL DO THE TRICK! ALL WE HAVE TO DO IS PUT IT ON THE SUPER-SKRULL!
WILL DO, BOSS MAN! LEMME HAVE IT!
SORRY, TORCH, YOU WOULDN'T HAVE A CHANCE TO GET CLOSE ENOUGH TO HIM! ONLY THE INVISIBLE GIRL CAN DO THE TRICK! ONCE SUE FASTENS THIS "JAMMER" ON THE SUPER-SKRUL', IT WILL STOP THE FLOW OF POWER-RAYS FROM HIS HOME PLANET, THEREBY WEAKENING HIM ENOUGH FOR US TO HANDLE HIM!
BUT WHAT IF YOU'RE WRONG, REED?? WHAT IF IT DOESN'T WORK?
THEN HE'LL APOLOGIZE, LOUD-MOUTH!
18

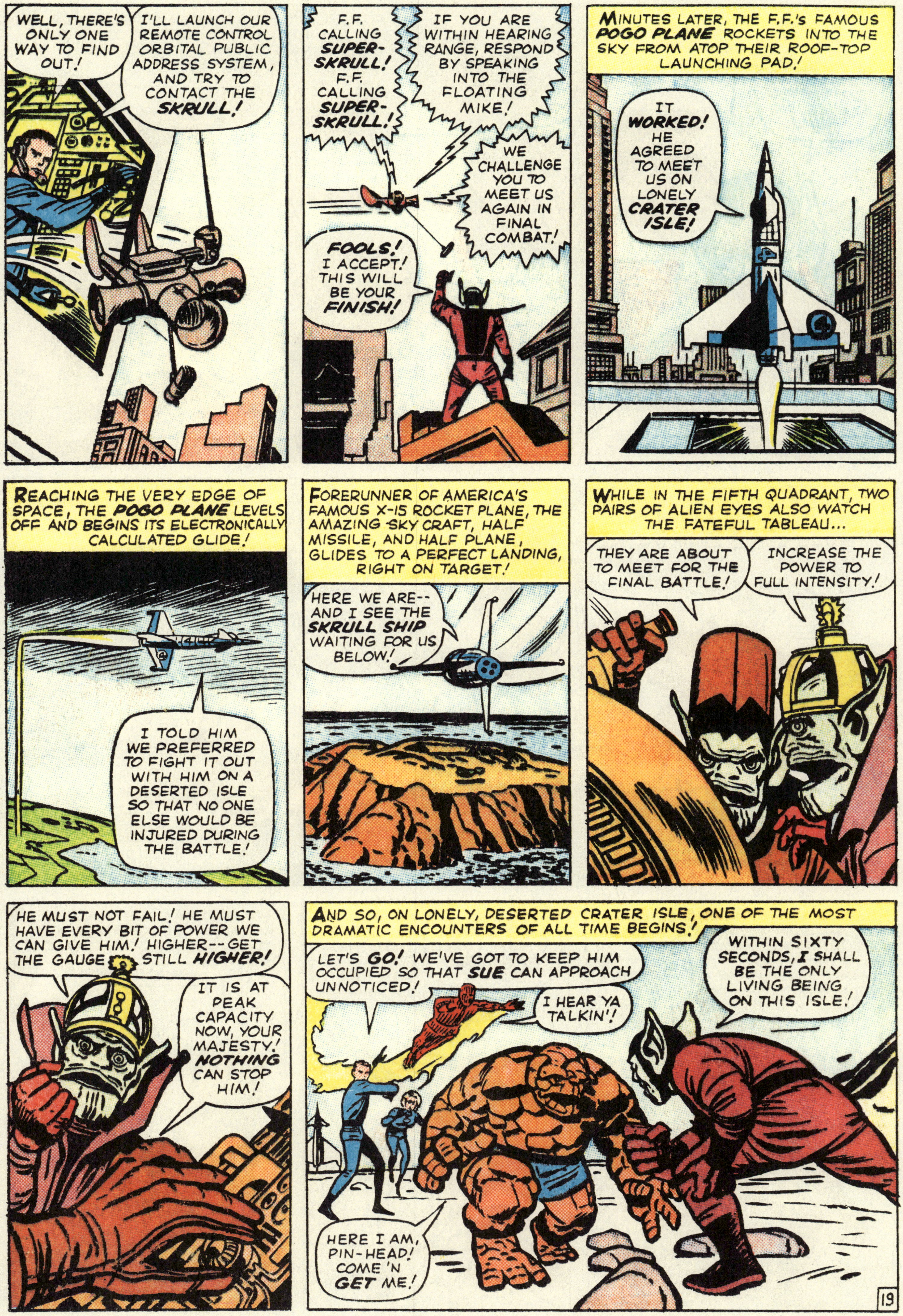

WELL, THERE'S ONLY ONE WAY TO FIND OUT!
I'LL LAUNCH OUR REMOTE CONTROL ORBITAL PUBLIC ADDRESS SYSTEM, AND TRY TO CONTACT THE SKRULL!
F.F. CALLING SUPER-SKRULL! F.F. CALLING SUPER-SKRULL!
IF YOU ARE WITHIN HEARING RANGE, RESPOND BY SPEAKING INTO THE FLOATING MIKE!
WE CHALLENGE YOU TO MEET US AGAIN IN FINAL COMBAT!
FOOLS! I ACCEPT! THIS WILL BE YOUR FINISH!
MINUTES LATER, THE F.F.'S FAMOUS POGO PLANE ROCKETS INTO THE SKY FROM ATOP THEIR ROOF-TOP LAUNCHING PAD!
IT WORKED! HE AGREED TO MEET US ON LONELY CRATER ISLE!
REACHING THE VERY EDGE OF SPACE, THE POGO PLANE LEVELS OFF AND BEGINS ITS ELECTRONICALLY CALCULATED GLIDE!
I TOLD HIM WE PREFERRED TO FIGHT IT OUT WITH HIM ON A DESERTED ISLE SO THAT NO ONE ELSE WOULD BE INJURED DURING THE BATTLE!
FORERUNNER OF AMERICA'S FAMOUS X-15 ROCKET PLANE, THE AMAZING SKY CRAFT, HALF MISSILE, AND HALF PLANE, GLIDES TO A PERFECT LANDING, RIGHT ON TARGET!
HERE WE ARE-- AND I SEE THE SKRULL SHIP WAITING FOR US BELOW!
WHILE IN THE FIFTH QUADRANT, TWO PAIRS OF ALIEN EYES ALSO WATCH THE FATEFUL TABLEAU...
THEY ARE ABOUT TO MEET FOR THE FINAL BATTLE!
INCREASE THE POWER TO FULL INTENSITY!
HE MUST NOT FAIL! HE MUST HAVE EVERY BIT OF POWER WE CAN GIVE HIM! HIGHER--GET THE GAUGE STILL HIGHER!
IT IS AT PEAK CAPACITY NOW, YOUR MAJESTY! NOTHING CAN STOP HIM!
AND SO, ON LONELY, DESERTED CRATER ISLE, ONE OF THE MOST DRAMATIC ENCOUNTERS OF ALL TIME BEGINS!
LET'S GO! WE'VE GOT TO KEEP HIM OCCUPIED SO THAT SUE CAN APPROACH UNNOTICED!
I HEAR YA TALKIN'!
WITHIN SIXTY SECONDS, I SHALL BE THE ONLY LIVING BEING ON THIS ISLE!
HERE I AM, PIN-HEAD! COME 'N GET ME!
19

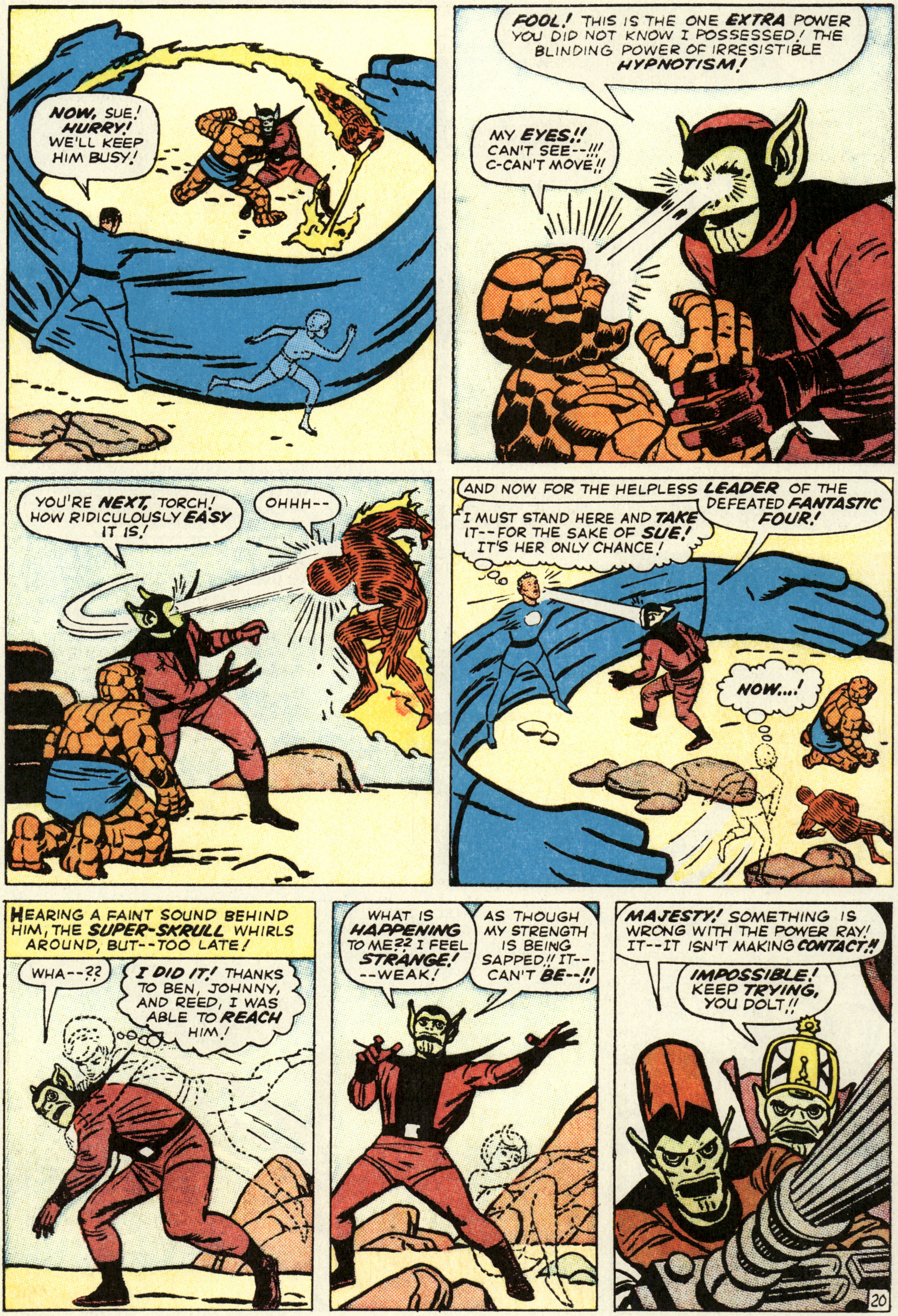
NOW, SUE! HURRY! WE'LL KEEP HIM BUSY!
FOOL! THIS IS THE ONE EXTRA POWER YOU DID NOT KNOW I POSSESSED! THE BLINDING POWER OF IRRESISTIBLE HYPNOTISM!
MY EYES!! CAN'T SEE--!!! C-CAN'T MOVE!!
YOU'RE NEXT, TORCH! HOW RIDICULOUSLY EASY IT IS!
OHHH--
AND NOW FOR THE HELPLESS LEADER OF THE DEFEATED FANTASTIC FOUR!
I MUST STAND HERE AND TAKE IT--FOR THE SAKE OF SUE! IT'S HER ONLY CHANCE!
NOW...!
HEARING A FAINT SOUND BEHIND HIM, THE SUPER-SKRULL WHIRLS AROUND, BUT--TOO LATE!
WHA--??
I DID IT! THANKS TO BEN, JOHNNY, AND REED, I WAS ABLE TO REACH HIM!
WHAT IS HAPPENING TO ME?? I FEEL STRANGE! --WEAK!
AS THOUGH MY STRENGTH IS BEING SAPPED!! IT--CAN'T BE--!!
MAJESTY! SOMETHING IS WRONG WITH THE POWER RAY! IT--IT ISN'T MAKING CONTACT!!
IMPOSSIBLE! KEEP TRYING, YOU DOLT!!
20

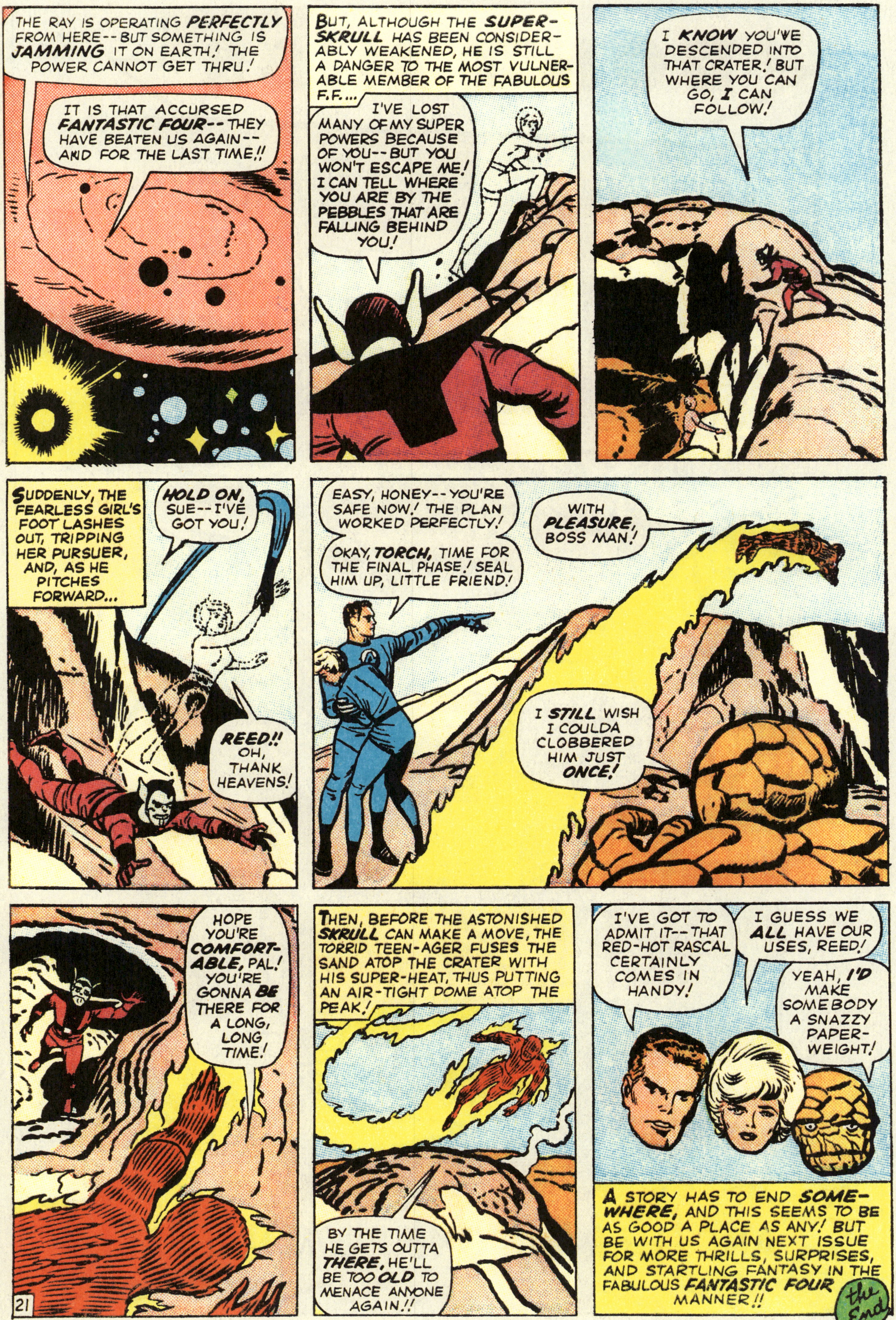
THE RAY IS OPERATING PERFECTLY FROM HERE--BUT SOMETHING IS JAMMING IT ON EARTH! THE POWER CANNOT GET THRU!
IT IS THAT ACCURSED FANTASTIC FOUR--THEY HAVE BEATEN US AGAIN--AND FOR THE LAST TIME!!
BUT, ALTHOUGH THE SUPER-SKRULL HAS BEEN CONSIDERABLY WEAKENED, HE IS STILL A DANGER TO THE MOST VULNERABLE MEMBER OF THE FABULOUS F.F....
I'VE LOST MANY OF MY SUPER POWERS BECAUSE OF YOU--BUT YOU WON'T ESCAPE ME! I CAN TELL WHERE YOU ARE BY THE PEBBLES THAT ARE FALLING BEHIND YOU!
I KNOW YOU'VE DESCENDED INTO THAT CRATER! BUT WHERE YOU CAN GO, I CAN FOLLOW!
SUDDENLY, THE FEARLESS GIRL'S FOOT LASHES OUT, TRIPPING HER PURSUER, AND, AS HE PITCHES FORWARD...
HOLD ON, SUE--I'VE GOT YOU!
REED!! OH, THANK HEAVENS!
EASY, HONEY--YOU'RE SAFE NOW! THE PLAN WORKED PERFECTLY!
OKAY, TORCH, TIME FOR THE FINAL PHASE! SEAL HIM UP, LITTLE FRIEND!
WITH PLEASURE, BOSS MAN!
I STILL WISH I COULDA CLOBBERED HIM JUST ONCE!
HOPE YOU'RE COMFORTABLE, PAL! YOU'RE GONNA BE THERE FOR A LONG, LONG TIME!
THEN, BEFORE THE ASTONISHED SKRULL CAN MAKE A MOVE, THE TORRID TEEN-AGER FUSES THE SAND ATOP THE CRATER WITH HIS SUPER-HEAT, THUS PUTTING AN AIR-TIGHT DOME ATOP THE PEAK!
BY THE TIME HE GETS OUTTA THERE, HE'LL BE TOO OLD TO MENACE ANYONE AGAIN!!
I'VE GOT TO ADMIT IT--THAT RED-HOT RASCAL CERTAINLY COMES IN HANDY!
I GUESS WE ALL HAVE OUR USES, REED!
YEAH, I'D MAKE SOMEBODY A SNAZZY PAPER-WEIGHT!
A STORY HAS TO END SOMEWHERE, AND THIS SEEMS TO BE AS GOOD A PLACE AS ANY! BUT BE WITH US AGAIN NEXT ISSUE FOR MORE THRILLS, SURPRISES, AND STARTLING FANTASY IN THE FABULOUS FANTASTIC FOUR MANNER!!
the End
21

DON'T MISS
THOR! ANT MAN! HULK! IRON MAN!
APPROVED BY THE COMICS CODE AUTHORITY
IND.
THE AVENGERS
1 SEPT.
MARVEL COMICS GROUP 12¢
EARTH'S MIGHTIEST SUPER-HEROES!
CAN THE COMBINED POWER OF THE AVENGERS DEFEAT THE SINISTER SPELLS OF LOKI, GOD OF EVIL?
LOKI! PREPARE FOR BATTLE!
THE AVENGERS... BAH! I'LL DESTROY YOU ALL!
SUPER-HEROES! SUPER-VILLAINS! SUPER-THRILLS! PRESENTED IN THE FABULOUS MARVEL MANNER!
ANOTHER BIG ONE FROM MARVEL!

Address YOUR letters to:
LEE and KIRBY
FANTASTIC FOUR
THIRD FLOOR
655 MADISON AVE.
NEW YORK 21, N. Y.

FANTASTIC 4 FAN PAGE

Dear Stan and Jack:

I should like to thank both of you sincerely for publishing your comic magazines. I am a senior in high school now, and I have rediscovered the world of my childhood through your comic magazines. I have been following your mags since about 1960, and your recent improvements are, excuse a miserable pun, "fantastic." With the Fantastic Four you brought the two greatest figures in comic book history to the public! I noticed that someone wrote to you asking that you remove the short stories from several of your books in order that the heros could have more room. I implore you not to lower the high standards which you have set for yourself and wind up with ordinary mags. Your shorts are great! (Don Heck's art is effective, as are Stan's and Steve Ditko's shorties) and many have messages to be conveyed. You accomplish your theme better than many prose writers I have encountered. Looking at your latest issues, I find that your trademark has changed again (you changed it once from Atlas to IND), this time to the *Marvel comics group*. It's perfect this way. I hope you realize that all your readers are not under twelve years of age. I know that many of my friends who haven't looked at a comic magazine for six or seven years are now anxiously awaiting every issue of the Marvel group (even the Westerns), and we are hoping that you won't let us down by throwing yourselves into a maelstrom of commerciality; that you will remember the tradition set down by the magazines of old, and continue your remarkable accomplishments.

Harold Silverman
1550 Northwood Drive
Cincinnati 37, Ohio

Many thanks, Hal. Sometmes we wonder whether all the extra effort that goes into our mags is worth while; but then we receive letters such as yours and we know the answer.

Dear Stan and Jack:

We have one of the oldest F4 Fan Clubs in the nation! We are a 53 member club, but are still looking for new members. If anyone would like to join, he may contact us at the address below. There will be no money involved at any stage of the process.

FF Fan Club, Baltimore Chapter
c/o Robert Allen Ellis
3308 Elmley Avenue
Baltimore 13, Maryland

We have received so many letters like Bob's that we realize the F4 Fan Club biz is getting bigger than we ever imagined! Unfortunately, we haven't space in the mag to list them all, but in the near future we'll try to send the chapters an F.F. newsletter. so keep sending us your notices with your lists of members.

Dear Stan and Jack:

Anxiously my fingers tore at the subscription folder which held the latest copy of the FF. Careful, so I wouldn't ruin what would of course be another great issue, I drew it out, and Voila! I embarked on another great adventure with the world's most unique comic book group! In this issue, you brought us lucky fans a new villain who is ripe for a comeback. Let's have more of that great mastermind of crime, The Thinker. I have to get all this praise I've got stored up for the FF off my mind! Any story that is sensational for another comic is an average story for Stan. And the art! I ask you, what are you supposed to say about a comic that is simply TERRIFIC? Great? Stupendous? Colossal? I give up. There is one thing I must complain about—the fact that none of your great westerns have gained any recognition in your letter column. Why not? I think they are the best westerns on sale, especially the Two-Gun Kid. Maybe you should give "Two-Gun" his own letter column and let this be the melting pot for your four western mags, like the FF is for your fantasy mags. And finally, I'd like to say that it was a good idea to give your company a name because it was pretty confusing without one. The symbol with the characters in the corner was a stroke of genius! May I ask who devised this great idea?

Paul B. Weinstein
2714 Gilbery Avenue
Portsmouth, Ohio

Steve Ditko dreamed up the idea, and we're sure glad he did.

Dear Stan and Jack:

Why don't you get some new villains? Your FF has been fighting villains of the past over and over again. For instance, the FF has fought Doctor Doom (whose face you so cleverly conceal, because if you tried to draw it you'd be afraid it wouldn't be ugly enough) four times. And worse yet, he has never been killed, even though he has been defeated every time. The Sub-Mariner has appeared four times also (not counting *Strange Tales*) and has not yet been beaten! As for the Puppet Master, how he could survive a fall of at LEAST three stories (back in the November 8th issue) I'll never know! Now to Sue Storm. How could a beautiful girl like her have a crush on the Sub-Mariner, a man (and I use the term loosely) with sixteen inch eyebrows, a trianguler-shaped head, gremlin-like ears, and a hairline like Satan's?

Dick Tedor
405 E. Sheridan Road
Lake Bluff, Illinois

But you still haven't told us, Dick—what's wrong with his looks?

Dear Stan and Jack:

Come on now! You have a good thing going and what do you do? You introduce an Ivan What's-his-name? What I mean is that issue #13 was very much under par!! Now that the Reds know that they can get cosmic powers, guess what's gonna happen? The Earth's gonna be run over by Super-Russians! You're always bragging that you're the world's best comic magazine. WELL, DON'T RUB IT IN! Your competitors are doing their best! (Bet I had you scared there for a minute). There is only one thing that bothers me . . . there are too many people swearing in your mags! *Ironman* swears he'll do this, and *Thor* swears he'll do that, and the villains swear all over the place!

Robert Caldwell
1726 Westchester Avenue
Peekskill, New York

Okay, Bob, we'll cut down on the swearing—we swear it!

Dear Stan and Jack:

I just finished reading your March issue of the Fantastic Four, and really thought it was great!!! I have been in the Army for 14 years now, and I never read a better comic book in my life! Keep up the good work!!

Sgt. R. Anderson
RA 19682472
733rd Med. Det.
APO 46, U.S. Forces
New York, New York

We'll try, Sarge! Wait'll you see what we have coming up in future issues!

CONTINUED . . .

Dear Stan and Jack:

The letter page of FF is no good. In other words, fans sometimes send letters in about mistakes in artwork, faults, etc. Must I go through an issue with a magnifying glass and find Johnny Storm's uniform green in one panel and blue in another in order to get my letter printed? Must you print some letters of people who don't like your magazine at all? Can't you print letters of people who ENJOY your magazine?

Steve Stough
225 West Lima Street
Findlay, Ohio

Sure we can, Steve. But while we're human enough to enjoy flattering mail, most fans would rather read controversial letters on these pages — letters they can argue about. We try to print all types, and always feel terribly bad about the hundreds of swell letters that we simply don't have room for.

Dear Stan and Jack:

I just bought your new comic, *Sargeant Fury and his Howling Commandos.* I don't really go for war stories, but I said if Marvel Comics is putting it out, it's worth a try—so I bought it and I love it! It's the best war story printed! Your Commandos are realistic, not like other war heroes in comics. All I can say is "Keep up the good work!"

Anthony Corda
61-44 148th Place
Flushing, New York

We're delighted with all the SGT. FURY mail we've received from FF fans! We weren't sure whether fantasy fans would enjoy war stories, but apparently the fact that they're written and drawn in the now-famous FF style has made the difference! Don't miss SGT. FURY's #3 ish — REED RICHARDS makes a brief appearance!

Dear Stan and Jack:

I have always thought Thor was your best single character and just recently, since the quality of the *Fantastic Four* stories has slipped, he's your best comic. And the thing about Thor is, he's not *just* good, he's great. The first time I met Thor, I was immediately taken by him. Though I missed his origin, I did see him beginning with *Journey Into Mystery* #84. There's just that something about him...From the very start when you depicted Dr. Blake making the change to Thor you had one extremely loyal fan. I was captured by his every movement; the way he swung his mighty hammer thrilled me to say the least. I especially enjoyed the way he swung, threw, and flew along with it. You could almost say I flew along with him. Then, with the introduction of Loki, you had me for life. As long as you feature, from time to time, a story with Loki doing battle against Thor, I'll always be reading this comic.

Tom Jones
622 Plater
Aberdeen, Maryland

Thanks, Tom. But what's this about the quality of the FF stories slipping? Judging by other letters we receive, we watch the mail each day for our Pulitzer prize!

Dear Stan and Jack:

I have read all of the FANTASTIC FOUR magazines and I really like the adventures that they have. I also read all the other stories like Spider-Man and Ant-Man. But there is just one thing wrong: NOT ENOUGH GIRLS. What I mean is that most of the characters are men. The adventures are great, but how about some good-looking girls in the stories? Why don't you have a girl that can help the FF instead of just being on the side like Alicia in #12? I don't want to tell you how to make a magazine, but I for one would rather look at girls than boys any day. These are all the comments that I will make right now, except that I always will be a fan of the FF.

Alan Wheeler
3070 Champion Street
Oakland 2, California

We've got NEWS for you, Al — the fourth member of the FF with the long blonde hair and pretty legs — she's no boy!

Dear Stan and Jack:

Ten, fifteen, twenty years from now, our sons and daughters will be collecting FANTASTIC FOUR just as we today seek out the old, original Sub-Mariner, Capt. America, etc. This is not a prediction... a year ago it may have been, but today, it's an undisputable fact substantiated by the overwhelming demand for back issues. Every single day, more and more new readers—future fans and collectors, are 'discovering' the fabulous, inimitable F4. Very soon I fear that the demand will exceed the supply of early (predominantly #'s 1 to 5) issues. For this reason, I hope that your F4 annual will contain reprints of 'the best from the past,' including the origin. Doubtless you are aware that you have virtually made comic history; never has there been... and I venture to guess, never again will there *be* illustrated heroes like the F4, and your companion characters. I, for one, am boundlessly grateful that you haven't even approached the stage of "milking them dry," but have truly FANTASTICALLY not only maintained your sublime standards, but increasingly never fail to continue improving characterizations with each fine issue. I cannot conceive *how* you do this ... it's a feat in itself to simply sustain interest at the high level you've achieved! What is greater than Greatness?? F4 #14 was tops, but #15 even tops it! To my way of thinking, you are your own enigma... your approach and technique for production defies analysis, so I shall content myself with enjoying the fruits of your labors.

Ronn Foss
Alter Ego-Comicollector
Wagon Wheels Apts., No. 5
Suisun, California

That's all for now! We're gonna rush out and buy a couple of new hats — two sizes bigger!

SPECIAL ANNOUNCEMENT SECTION.

- **It won't be much longer now! The FF ANNUAL goes on sale very soon! It contains facts about the FF's origin for those many new readers who've missed it, and a new type of feature in which you meet famous villains from earlier issues! But the really big excitement is the longest single, uninterrupted comic mag saga ever printed — in which SUB MARINER finds his lost race and declares war on mankind — and on the FF in particular!! Other features and surprises, too! Remember, there'll be no more when the first printing is sold out — so watch for it!**

- **Along the same lines, the STRANGE TALES ANNUAL features a whopping thriller starring HUMAN TORCH in the same story with SPIDER-MAN! See these two, colorful teen-age idols at their super-best in this big, jam-packed annual!**

- **Continuing our policy of making this the MARVEL AGE OF COMICS, we present two new super-hero mags which we feel are destined to become fantasy classics! THE AVENGERS, on sale in July, stars THOR, ANT-MAN, the HULK, and IRON MAN, all together in one book-length spectacular! And, on sale at the same time, is America's newest, most different group of super-heroes — the X-MEN! Who are they? What are they? Here's a hint — they're merely the GREATEST! Both mags by Stan and Jack, natch!**

- **Fred Bronson, of 11620 Port Road, Culver City, Cal., writes that his FF Fan Club will publish a small FF Club mag for club members. Members can receive the newsletter by sending a stamped, self-addressed envelope to Fred.**

- **But let's not forget about the LEADER in its field! Namely the FF! Our next ish will have the fabulous foursome taking a strange trip back thru time, to battle one of the most incredible foes of all! It's an action-packed thriller, with a few different twists, so watch for it! See you then!**

72 BIG PAGES
MARVEL COMICS GROUP USHERS IN THE MARVEL AGE OF COMICS!
72 BIG PAGES
Fantastic Four
ANNUAL
MARVEL COMICS GROUP 25¢
#1 1963
"THE UNDERSEA LEGIONS OF SUB-MARINER!"
AT LAST! SUB-MARINER FINDS HIS LONG-LOST RACE!
AND SO BEGINS THE MOST FANTASTIC BATTLE OF ALL TIME!
INSIDE THE PAGES OF THIS, THE WORLD'S GREATEST COMIC MAGAZINE!
SPIDER-MAN WAITS WITHIN THESE PAGES!!
Also: "THE ORIGIN OF THE FANTASTIC FOUR!" THE MOST REQUESTED SAGA EVER PRINTED!
And... DON'T MISS THE AWESOME "GALLERY OF VILLAINS!"
ANNUAL
72 BIG PAGES
STRANGE TALES
ANNUAL
MARVEL COMICS 25¢
#2 1963
THE AMAZING SPIDER-MAN
FACE-TO-FACE WITH...
THE HUMAN TORCH
EVEN YOU, TORCH, CANNOT ESCAPE FROM THE WEB OF SPIDER-MAN!
DON'T GET CALLOUSES FROM PATTING YOURSELF ON THE BACK, CHUM! I'M JUST GETTIN' STARTED!
THE LONG-AWAITED EPIC-LENGTH THRILLER IS ONLY ONE OF THE MANY WONDERFUL FEATURES WITHIN THESE UNFORGETTABLE PAGES!
THE MARVEL COMICS GROUP USHERS IN THE MARVEL AGE OF COMICS!
PLUS.... THE NEWEST, GREATEST, MOST ORIGINAL SUPER-TEAM EVER!
THE STRANGEST SUPER-HEROES OF ALL!
the X-MEN
APPROVED BY THE COMICS CODE AUTHORITY
SURE TO BE A SELL-OUT! RESERVE YOUR COPY TODAY!!

THE WORLD'S GREATEST COMIC MAGAZINE!
APPROVED BY THE COMICS CODE AUTHORITY
Fantastic Four
IND.
19 OCT.
MARVEL COMICS GROUP 12¢
"AT THE MERCY OF RAMA-TUT" THE PHAROAH FROM THE FUTURE!
I NEVER THOUGHT IT COULD HAPPEN! RAMA-TUT'S RAY GUN HAS MADE HELPLESS SLAVES OF THE FANTASTIC FOUR!
THERE, SUSAN STORM! THERE IS WHAT HAPPENS TO THOSE WHO DEFY ME--NO MATTER WHAT POWERS THEY POSSESS!

THE FANTASTIC FOUR is published by CANAM PUBLISHERS SALES CORP. OFFICE OF PUBLICATION: 655 MADISON AVENUE, NEW YORK, N.Y. Published monthly. Copyright 1963 by CANAM PUBLISHERS SALES CORP., 655 Madison Avenue, New York, N.Y. Vol. 1 No. 19, OCTOBER, 1963 issue. Price 12¢ per copy. Subscription rate $1.75 for 12 issues including postage. Foreign subscription $3.25 in American funds. No similarity between any of the names, characters, persons, and/or institutions appearing in this magazine with those of any living or dead person is intended, and any such similarity which may exist is purely coincidental. Printed in U.S.A. by The Eastern Color Printing Co., Waterbury 20, Conn.

The Fabulous FANTASTIC FOUR Find Themselves
"PRISONERS OF THE PHAROAH!"
WEAPONLESS! DEFENSELESS! TRAPPED IN THE LONG-DEAD MYSTERIOUS PAST, WITH ONLY THEIR OWN UNIQUE POWERS TO HELP THEM, THE FANTASTIC FOUR FACE THE MOST TOTALLY UNEXPECTED MENACE OF THEIR CAREER! SURPRISE FOLLOWS SURPRISE UNTIL YOU REACH THE MIND-STAGGERING CLIMAX WHICH AWAITS YOU WITHIN...
THOUGH YOU COME FROM THE DISTANT FUTURE, I KNOW ALL ABOUT YOU! AND I ALSO KNOW THAT ALL YOUR SUPER-POWERS ARE NO MATCH FOR MINE!
WRITTEN BY: STAN LEE
DRAWN BY: JACK KIRBY
INKING: DICK AYERS
LETTERING: S.ROSEN
1.

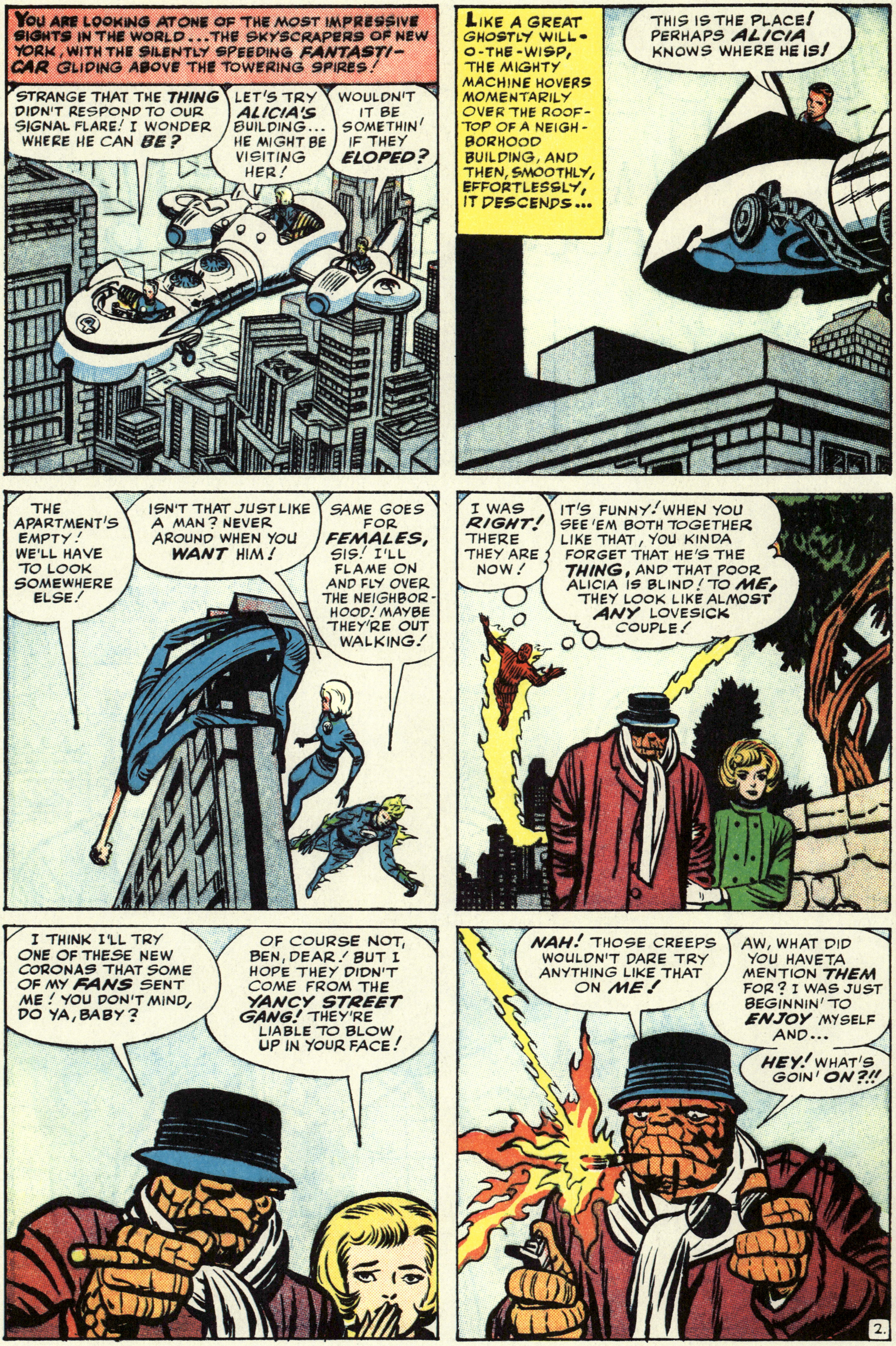
YOU ARE LOOKING AT ONE OF THE MOST IMPRESSIVE SIGHTS IN THE WORLD... THE SKYSCRAPERS OF NEW YORK, WITH THE SILENTLY SPEEDING FANTASTI-CAR GLIDING ABOVE THE TOWERING SPIRES!
STRANGE THAT THE THING DIDN'T RESPOND TO OUR SIGNAL FLARE! I WONDER WHERE HE CAN BE?
LET'S TRY ALICIA'S BUILDING... HE MIGHT BE VISITING HER!
WOULDN'T IT BE SOMETHIN' IF THEY ELOPED?
LIKE A GREAT GHOSTLY WILL-O-THE-WISP, THE MIGHTY MACHINE HOVERS MOMENTARILY OVER THE ROOF-TOP OF A NEIGHBORHOOD BUILDING, AND THEN, SMOOTHLY, EFFORTLESSLY, IT DESCENDS...
THIS IS THE PLACE! PERHAPS ALICIA KNOWS WHERE HE IS!
THE APARTMENT'S EMPTY! WE'LL HAVE TO LOOK SOMEWHERE ELSE!
ISN'T THAT JUST LIKE A MAN? NEVER AROUND WHEN YOU WANT HIM!
SAME GOES FOR FEMALES, SIS! I'LL FLAME ON AND FLY OVER THE NEIGHBORHOOD! MAYBE THEY'RE OUT WALKING!
I WAS RIGHT! THERE THEY ARE NOW!
IT'S FUNNY! WHEN YOU SEE 'EM BOTH TOGETHER LIKE THAT, YOU KINDA FORGET THAT HE'S THE THING, AND THAT POOR ALICIA IS BLIND! TO ME, THEY LOOK LIKE ALMOST ANY LOVESICK COUPLE!
I THINK I'LL TRY ONE OF THESE NEW CORONAS THAT SOME OF MY FANS SENT ME! YOU DON'T MIND, DO YA, BABY?
OF COURSE NOT, BEN, DEAR! BUT I HOPE THEY DIDN'T COME FROM THE YANCY STREET GANG! THEY'RE LIABLE TO BLOW UP IN YOUR FACE!
NAH! THOSE CREEPS WOULDN'T DARE TRY ANYTHING LIKE THAT ON ME!
AW, WHAT DID YOU HAVETA MENTION THEM FOR? I WAS JUST BEGINNIN' TO ENJOY MYSELF AND...
HEY! WHAT'S GOIN' ON?!!
2.

THE TORCH! YOU BLAMED PEST! YOU'RE GETTIN' AS BAD AS THOSE YANCY STREET CLOWNS!
BENJAMIN, DID ANYONE EVER TELL YOU YOU'RE BEAUTIFUL WHEN YOU'RE ANGRY?!!
NOW, CALM DOWN, ROMEO! I DON'T WANNA BREAK UP YOUR LITTLE BALCONY SCENE, BUT I'VE GOT A MESSAGE FOR YOU!
REED WANTS YOU TO REPORT BACK TO HEAD-QUARTERS, ON THE DOUBLE! AND BRING ALICIA WITH YOU!
ON MY DAY OFF? LOOK, SQUIRT, YOU TELL THAT BAG OF BONES NOT TO HOLD HIS BREATH WAITIN' FOR US!
NO, BEN! WE MUST GO! IT MIGHT BE SOMETHING IMPORTANT!
AND SO, A FEW MINUTES LATER...
ALL THE TESTS CHECK OUT PERFECTLY, REED! NOW IF ONLY BEN AND ALICIA WOULD GET HERE!
HERE THEY ARE NOW, SUE! COME IN, YOU TWO!
LISTEN, CURLY, YOU'VE GOT NO RIGHT TELLIN' ALICIA TO REPORT HERE WITH ME! SHE'S NOT A MEMBER OF THE FF! I THINK YOU'RE GETTIN' A NAPOLEON COMPLEX, PAL!
IT'S ALL RIGHT, BEN, DEAR! I ALWAYS ENJOY VISITING YOUR HEAD-QUARTERS!
NOW JUST TAKE THAT CHIP OFF YOUR SHOULDER FOR A MINUTE, OLD FRIEND, AND LET ME EXPLAIN! THIS HAPPENS TO CONCERN ALICIA...AS YOU BOTH WILL LEARN!
UH-OH! WHENEVER YOU USE THAT "OLD FRIEND" ROUTINE, IT MEANS LOOK OUT! BUT GO AHEAD! KEEP TALKIN'! I KNOW HOW YOU LOVE THE SOUND OF YOUR OWN VOICE!
IT STARTED YESTERDAY, BEN, WHEN SUE AND I WENT TO THE MUSEUM OF NATURAL HISTORY! I'VE BEEN DOING SOME RESEARCH ON EGYPTOLOGY, AND THERE WERE A FEW ELUSIVE FACTS I WANTED TO CHECK UP ON!
3.

IT'S STRANGE, SUE! THERE ARE A FEW YEARS OF ANCIENT EGYPTIAN HISTORY WHICH ARE COMPLETELY UNACCOUNTED FOR BY HISTORIANS! AS THOUGH THOSE YEARS JUST DIDN'T EXIST! I WONDER IF ...
HMMM! LOOK AT THIS!
"AND THEN I SAW IT! ALMOST HIDDEN AMONG THE COUNTLESS HIEROGLYPHICS ON DISPLAY... THE ONE LITTLE DETAIL WHICH MADE ME DECIDE TO CALL YOU AND ALICIA IMMEDIATELY!"
THE SIGNS ARE UNMISTAKEABLE, SUE! IT SHOWS A BLIND PHAROAH ... A VIAL CONTAINING A RADIOACTIVE HERB ... AND THEN, THE SAME PHAROAH, ABLE TO SEE AGAIN!
IT CAN MEAN ONLY ONE THING... AT A CERTAIN PERIOD IN EGYPTIAN HISTORY, ONE PHAROAH HAD FOUND A CURE FOR BLINDNESS! AND IT TOOK PLACE DURING THOSE STRANGELY MISSING YEARS!
IF YOU'RE SAYIN' WHAT I THINK YOU'RE SAYIN', REED, THEN THERE'S A CHANCE FOR ALICIA!
I HATE TO BUILD UP FALSE HOPES, BEN... AND YET...
BUT, WAIT A MINUTE! THIS IS NUTTY! HOW COULD THERE BE ANY RADIO-ACTIVE HERBS CENTURIES AGO? THERE WASN'T ANY ATOMIC ENERGY IN THOSE DAYS! ANYWAY, HOW CAN WE GET BACK INTO THE PAST?? IT AIN'T EXACTLY LIKE TAKING A SUBWAY OR A BUS!!
I CAN'T ANSWER THE FIRST QUESTION, BEN... BUT I THINK I CAN ANSWER THE SECOND!
REMEMBER OUR FIRST ENCOUNTER WITH DOCTOR DOOM* MORE THAN A YEAR AGO?
AT THE CONCLUSION OF THAT ADVENTURE, DOOM'S CASTLE WAS ABANDONED BY HIM, BUT THERE IS STILL A CHANCE THAT THE MACHINE HE USED TO SEND US INTO THE PAST MAY STILL BE OPERATIONAL!
UR GALLERY OF SUPER-VILLAINS
DOCTOR DOOM
* F.F. #5 JULY...
REED, YOU OL' DICTIONARY-READIN', DOUBLE-TALKIN', RUBBER-BONED EGGHEAD! WHAT ARE WE STANDIN' AROUND JAWIN' FOR!? LET'S GO!!
BEN, YOU HOT-TEMPERED, LOUD-MOUTHED, BEETLE-BRAINED GARGOYLE... THAT'S WHAT I WAS WAITING FOR YOU TO SAY!!
4.

A SHORT TIME LATER, THE FABULOUS FOURSOME'S FAMOUS V.T.O.L. POGO PLANE* REACHES THE ALMOST INACCESSIBLE SITE OF THEIR ARCH-FOE'S NOW-DESERTED CASTLE!
THERE'S DOOM'S CASTLE NOW... STRAIGHT AHEAD!
LET'S HOPE THAT TIME MACHINE OF HIS ISN'T COMPLETELY WRECKED!
*V.T.O.L.-VERTICAL TAKE-OFF AND LANDING.
I'LL FLY OVER THE WALL AND LOWER THE DRAWBRIDGE FOR YOU THREE LANDLUBBERS!
EVERYTHING SEEMS TO BE ALMOST AS DOOM LEFT IT!
YEAH, EXCEPT THAT OL' IRON-HEAD AIN'T AROUND!
THEN, AS THE MIGHTY DRAWBRIDGE CREAKS DOWN...
HI, KIDS! IF I KNEW YOU WERE COMING, I'D HAVE BAKED A CAKE!
HEY, WE'RE IN LUCK! HERE'S THE PANEL WE STOOD ON WHEN WE TOOK OUR LITTLE TRIP! LOOKS AS GOOD AS NEW!
LUCKY FOR US THAT DOCTOR DOOM MADE ALMOST EVERYTHING FIRE-PROOF TO PROTECT HIM-SELF AGAINST YOU, JOHNNY!
THE CONTROLS WHICH HE WORKED WHILE SITTING IN HIS SPECIALLY-BUILT CHAIR ALL SEEM TO BE INTACT!
ALICIA, BABY, YOU'LL HAVE TO STAY BEHIND AND OPERATE THIS GIZMO, TO GET US THERE AND BACK! THINK YOU CAN HANDLE IT?
I'VE GOT TO, BEN! IF YOU EXPLAIN IT CAREFULLY, I'LL TRY TO DO IT BY TOUCH!
BUT, BEN... MY DARLING... IF THERE WILL BE ANY DANGER TO YOU... TO ANY OF YOU... THEN IT ISN'T WORTH IT! I COULDN'T BEAR IT IF...
FORGET IT, KID! DANGER IS OUR BUSINESS, LIKE THEY SAY IN THE MOVIES!
AND THEN, AFTER HOURS OF PRACTICE...
GOOD LUCK, YOU DEAR, WONDER-FUL FRIENDS...
REMEMBER, ALICIA... WORK THOSE BUTTONS IN EXACTLY THE PATTERN WE SHOWED YOU! IF ALL GOES WELL, WE'LL RETURN IN TWENTY-FOUR HOURS!
FAREWELL, YOU BRAVE, NOBLE, UNSELFISH ADVENTURERS! FARE-WELL, BEN... MY OWN DARLING LOVE...
5.

SECONDS LATER... OR, IS IT WEEKS... PERHAPS MONTHS, OR AGES?? THERE IS NO WAY TO KNOW WHEN THE MYSTERY OF TIME TRAVEL IS CONCERNED! BUT, SEEMINGLY WITHIN THE WINK OF AN EYE, THE COLORFUL QUARTET FIND THEMSELVES IN THE LAND OF THE ANCIENT PHAROAHS!
WE DID IT! WE'RE HERE! NOW ALL WE GOTTA DO IS FIND THAT RADIO-ACTIVE HERB AND BRING IT BACK WITH US!
I ONLY WISH IT WERE THAT EASY, BEN! I HAVE AN UNEASY FEELING ABOUT THIS CENTURY... THESE YEARS WHICH HISTORY HAS NO RECORD OF!
HOW CAN YOU BE SURE WE LANDED AT THE RIGHT TIME, REED?
BY THE CONDITION OF THE SPHINX! SEE HOW NEW IT LOOKS! IT HASN'T EVEN BEGUN TO CHIP YET!
LOOK!! ON THAT SAND DUNE AHEAD... SOME SORT OF WARRIORS!
FOR THE LUVVA MIKE! ARE THEY KIDDIN'? DO THEY THINK THEY CAN SCARE OFF THE FANTASTIC FOUR WITH A FEW OVERSIZED TOOTHPICKS?
USE YOUR HEAD, GRUESOME! THEY NEVER HEARD OF THE FF... AND THEY'RE TOSSIN' THOSE "TOOTH-PICKS" A LITTLE TOO CLOSE FOR COMFORT!
STRANGE... THEIR HELMETS DON'T SEEM TO BELONG TO THIS TIME!
THIS IS A HECKUVA TIME TO WORRY ABOUT THE CLOTHES THEY'RE WEARIN'!! WHO DO YOU THINK YOU ARE, CHRISTIAN DIOR??
STEP ASIDE, BOYS AND GIRL! LITTLE OLD TORCHY IS GONNA TAKE SOME OF THE FIGHT OUT OF THOSE GENTS!
WHEN A BUNCH OF METAL SPEARS FLY INTO A FLAMING SCREEN, THERE'S ONLY ONE THING THEY CAN DO... AND THAT'S MELT! BOY, I'LL BET I LOOK REAL IMPRESSIVE UP HERE!
FINDING THEMSELVES SPEARLESS, THE ON-RUSHING HORDE THEN TRIES A MASS ATTACK IN FORCE! BUT THEY PICK THE WRONG TARGET!
GOIN' SOMEWHERE, PLAYMATES?
6.

SUPPOSE I JUST TIE YOU UP WITH YOUR OWN ARMOR, HUH? FOR YOUR OWN PROTECTION, OF COURSE! A BUNCH OF CLUMSY GALOOTS LIKE YOU CAN HURT YOURSELVES, RUNNIN' AROUND LOOSE THAT WAY!
BEN, HURRY! HERE COME MORE OF THEM... IN CHARIOTS!
BEN'S DONE HIS SHARE, SUE! I'LL TAKE CARE OF THESE NEWCOMERS, IN MY OWN MANNER!
CAN'T GET VERY FAR WHEN SOMEONE'S HOLDING ONTO YOUR WHEELS, CAN YOU? AT LEAST YOU HAVE NICE SOFT SAND TO TUMBLE DOWN ON!
WELL! I SUPPOSE IN THESE DAYS, PEOPLE DON'T KNOW THAT IT'S IMPOLITE TO FIGHT WITH A LADY!
SO I'LL JUST STEP OUT OF THE PICTURE FOR A WHILE, UNTIL THEY GET A CHANCE TO STUDY EMILY POST!
7.

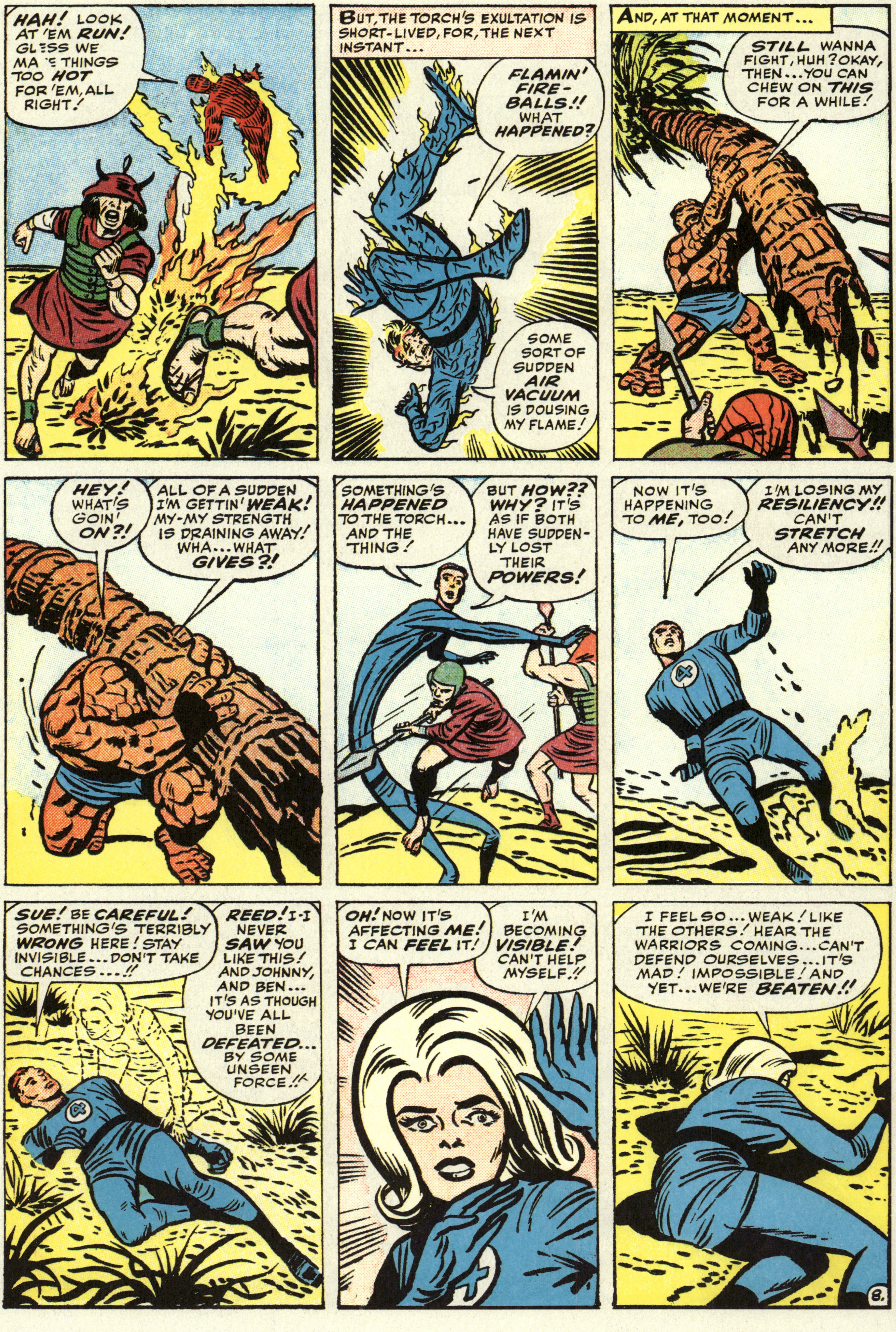

HAH! LOOK AT 'EM RUN! GLESS WE MA 'E THINGS TOO HOT FOR 'EM, ALL RIGHT!
BUT, THE TORCH'S EXULTATION IS SHORT-LIVED, FOR, THE NEXT INSTANT...
FLAMIN' FIRE-BALLS!! WHAT HAPPENED?
SOME SORT OF SUDDEN AIR VACUUM IS DOUSING MY FLAME!
AND, AT THAT MOMENT...
STILL WANNA FIGHT, HUH? OKAY, THEN... YOU CAN CHEW ON THIS FOR A WHILE!
HEY! WHAT'S GOIN' ON?!
ALL OF A SUDDEN I'M GETTIN' WEAK! MY-MY STRENGTH IS DRAINING AWAY! WHA... WHAT GIVES?!
SOMETHING'S HAPPENED TO THE TORCH... AND THE THING!
BUT HOW?? WHY? IT'S AS IF BOTH HAVE SUDDEN-LY LOST THEIR POWERS!
NOW IT'S HAPPENING TO ME, TOO!
I'M LOSING MY RESILIENCY!! CAN'T STRETCH ANY MORE!!
SUE! BE CAREFUL! SOMETHING'S TERRIBLY WRONG HERE! STAY INVISIBLE... DON'T TAKE CHANCES...!!
REED! I-I NEVER SAW YOU LIKE THIS! AND JOHNNY, AND BEN... IT'S AS THOUGH YOU'VE ALL BEEN DEFEATED... BY SOME UNSEEN FORCE!!
OH! NOW IT'S AFFECTING ME! I CAN FEEL IT!
I'M BECOMING VISIBLE! CAN'T HELP MYSELF!!
I FEEL SO... WEAK! LIKE THE OTHERS! HEAR THE WARRIORS COMING... CAN'T DEFEND OURSELVES... IT'S MAD! IMPOSSIBLE! AND YET... WE'RE BEATEN!!
8.

BUT THE FABULOUS FOURSOME HAVE STILL MORE STAGGERING SURPRISES IN STORE! FOR, WHEN THEY REGAIN CONSCIOUSNESS AGAIN, THEY FIND...
WHA... WHAT HAPPENED TO US?? WHERE ARE WE?
WE'VE BEEN BROUGHT TO A THRONE ROOM! WE'RE PRISONERS OF... THE PHAROAH!
ON YOUR FEET, CAPTIVES! YOU ARE IN THE PRESENCE OF THE AWESOME RAMA-TUT, KING OF KINGS, MASTER OF MEN, LORD OF THE SEVEN SUNS!
NOW THAT YOU KNOW WHO I AM, THERE IS NO NEED TO INTRODUCE YOURSELVES... FOR I AM QUITE FAMILIAR WITH THE FANTASTIC FOUR!
YOU KNOW US?!
AHH! I THOUGHT THAT REMARK WOULD STARTLE YOU!
REED, SOMETHING IS WRONG! HOW CAN HE KNOW ABOUT US... A THOUSAND YEARS BEFORE WE WERE BORN?
AND HE'S TALKING ENGLISH!! BEFORE THE LANGUAGE WAS EVEN INVENTED! THIS IS NUTTY!
CAN WE HAVE LANDED IN THE WRONG YEAR?? CAN THIS BE... THE FUTURE??
NO! IT IS THE PAST! THE SECRET LIES WITH RAMA-TUT HIMSELF!
YOUR MIND IS INDEED AS SHARP AS THE ANCIENT LEGENDS CLAIMED! YES, THIS IS THE PAST!
BUT I AM NOT A PART OF IT! AS YOU HAVE OBVIOUSLY GUESSED, NO ANCIENT PHAROAH FROM PRIMITIVE TIMES COULD HAVE THE POWER TO SUBDUE THE FANTASTIC FOUR!
THEN, THERE IS ONLY ONE POSSIBLE ANSWER, INCREDIBLE THOUGH IT MAY BE...
OF COURSE! THIS IS THE WEAPON WHICH SAPPED YOUR POWERS; WHICH MADE YOU MY CAPTIVES!
THIS ULTRA-DIODE RAY. INVENTED IN THE YEAR 3,000... ONE THOUSAND YEARS FURTHER IN THE FUTURE THAN YOUR OWN CENTURY!
THEN... YOU TOO ARE.. A TIME TRAVELER!!
9.

YES, I COME FROM THE YEAR 3,000.. THE GLORIOUS AGE OF ENLIGHTENMENT, THE CENTURY OF PEACE AND PROGRESS.. THE ULTIMATE IN CIVILIZATION AND CULTURE! AND I HATED IT!
"FOR I WAS THEN, AS I AM NOW, A MAN OF ACTION, AN ADVENTURER! BUT THERE WERE NO ADVENTURES IN THE YEAR 3,000...NO ENEMIES TO BATTLE, NO DRAGONS TO SLAY! ALL WAS PEACEFUL...HORRIBLY, UNBEARABLY PEACEFUL!!"
WHY WAS I BORN INTO AN AGE WHEN THE ONLY EXCITEMENT A MAN CAN FIND IS IN WATCHING 3-D STEREOVISIONS FROM A THOUSAND YEARS AGO?!!
"IT WAS WHILE WATCHING SUCH ANCIENT FILMS, PRESENTED BY OUR HISTORICAL SOCIETY, THAT I LEARNED OF THE EXISTENCE OF THE FANTASTIC FOUR! HOW I ENVIED YOUR DRAMATIC CAREERS!"
"THEN, ONE DAY, WHILE VISITING THE RUINS OF AN AMAZING ANCESTOR OF MINE, I CAME UPON WHAT WAS LEFT OF HIS GREATEST INVENTION...A TIME MACHINE!"
PART OF THE MACHINE STILL REMAINS...AND HERE ARE THE PLANS FOR ITS OPERATION!
IT WOULD BE SIMPLE FOR ME TO RECREATE IT, AND USE IT FOR MY OWN PURPOSES!
"I DEVOTED YEARS TO THE BUILDING OF THAT TIME MACHINE, FROM MY ANCESTOR'S PLANS! BUT, KNOWING THE SUPERSTITIOUS BELIEFS OF PEOPLE IN BYGONE DAYS, I SHAPED IT IN THE FORM OF A STRANGE CREATURE, IN THE FORM OF AN IDOL!"
"THEN AT LAST I WAS READY! READY TO TRAVEL TO LONG-DEAD AGES... READY TO BECOME A TIME LOOTER, WITH MY HEADQUARTERS IN ANCIENT EGYPT, WHERE, WITH MY VAST SCIENTIFIC KNOW-LEDGE, I COULD BECOME AN ABSOLUTE RULER OF MANKIND!!"
10.

"AND SO I TRAVELLED BACK INTO THE DIM PAST, BACK TO THE LAND OF ANCIENT EGYPT, IN MY MARVELOUS TIME MACHINE, WHICH WAS SHAPED LIKE AN AWESOME IDOL!"
OH, WONDER OF WONDERS! WHAT MIRACLE IS UPON US??
"BUT, DUE TO A CARELESS MISCALCULATION ON MY PART, THE MACHINE WAS DAMAGED IN LANDING, SO THAT I HAVE BEEN UNABLE TO LEAVE THIS PRIMITIVE CENTURY! ALSO, I SUFFERED A TERRIBLE INJURY AS I CRASHED!
MY EYES!! I CAN'T SEE!!
"BUT, FIRING BLINDLY AT THE DAZED NATIVES, I MADE THEM MY SLAVES! THEY OBTAINED A RARE HERB FOR ME WHICH, AFFECTED BY THE RADIATION FROM MY DAMAGED MACHINE, HAD THE POWER TO RESTORE MY EYESIGHT! I HAVE RULED HERE EVER SINCE!"
AS THE PHAROAH FROM THE FUTURE ENDS HIS STARTLING TALE, MR. FANTASTIC MAKES A SUDDEN SURPRISE MOVE...
MOST OF HIS POWER IS IN THAT AWESOME WEAPON! IF I CAN JUST SEIZE IT...!
HAH! NOT FAST ENOUGH, MY OVER-EAGER FRIEND!
NOW I'LL SHOW YOU THE UNDREAMED-OF POWER OF MY MIGHTY WEAPON!
BY BATHING YOU WITH ITS LOW-INTENSITY RAYS, IT CAN SAP YOUR WILL AND MAKE YOU MY SLAVES UNTIL I DECIDE TO REPEAT THE TREATMENT AND FREE YOU!
11

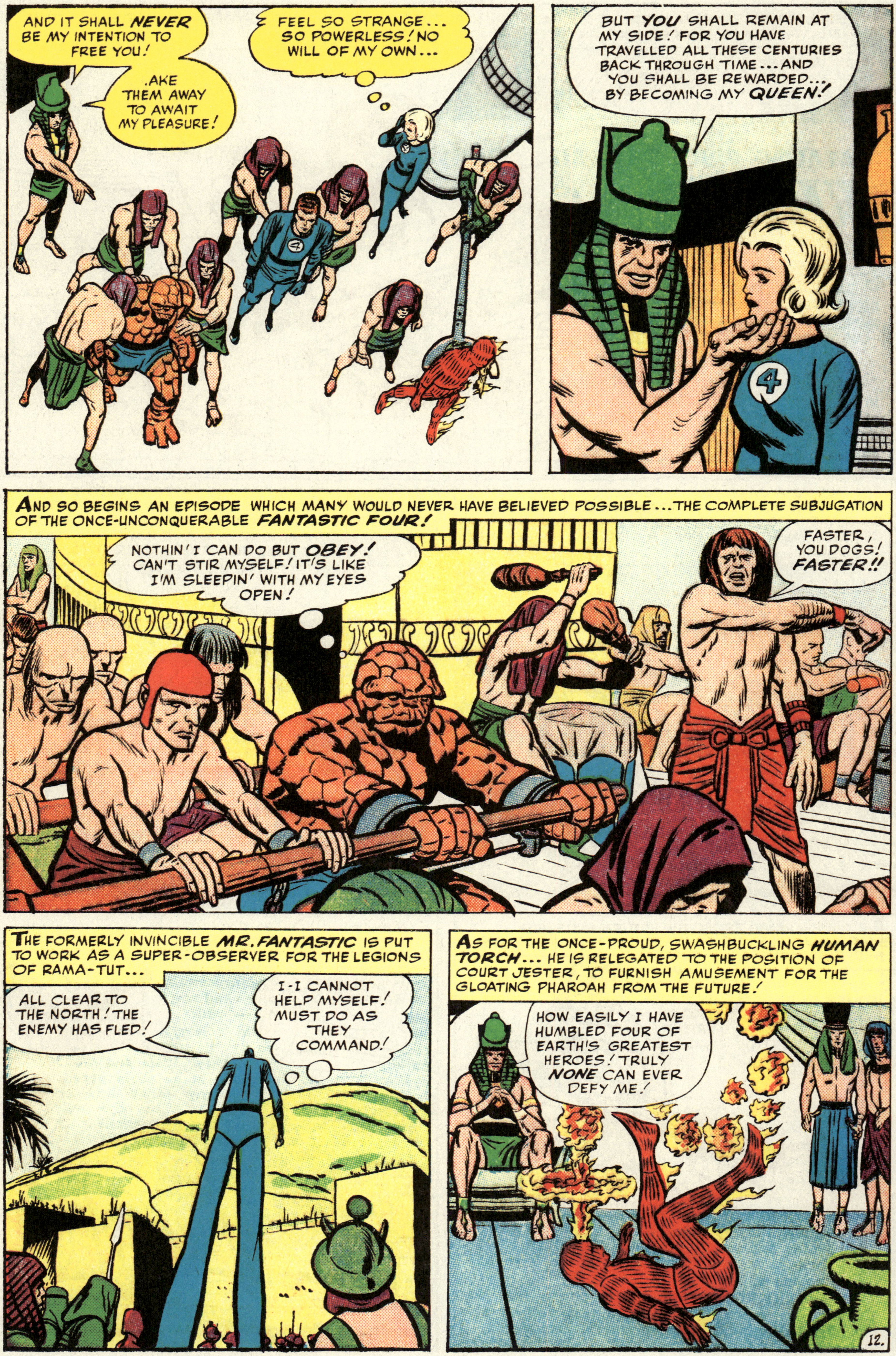
AND IT SHALL NEVER BE MY INTENTION TO FREE YOU!
.AKE THEM AWAY TO AWAIT MY PLEASURE!
FEEL SO STRANGE... SO POWERLESS! NO WILL OF MY OWN...
BUT YOU SHALL REMAIN AT MY SIDE! FOR YOU HAVE TRAVELLED ALL THESE CENTURIES BACK THROUGH TIME... AND YOU SHALL BE REWARDED... BY BECOMING MY QUEEN!
AND SO BEGINS AN EPISODE WHICH MANY WOULD NEVER HAVE BELIEVED POSSIBLE... THE COMPLETE SUBJUGATION OF THE ONCE-UNCONQUERABLE FANTASTIC FOUR!
NOTHIN' I CAN DO BUT OBEY! CAN'T STIR MYSELF! IT'S LIKE I'M SLEEPIN' WITH MY EYES OPEN!
FASTER, YOU DOGS! FASTER!!
THE FORMERLY INVINCIBLE MR. FANTASTIC IS PUT TO WORK AS A SUPER-OBSERVER FOR THE LEGIONS OF RAMA-TUT...
ALL CLEAR TO THE NORTH! THE ENEMY HAS FLED!
I-I CANNOT HELP MYSELF! MUST DO AS THEY COMMAND!
AS FOR THE ONCE-PROUD, SWASHBUCKLING HUMAN TORCH... HE IS RELEGATED TO THE POSITION OF COURT JESTER, TO FURNISH AMUSEMENT FOR THE GLOATING PHAROAH FROM THE FUTURE!
HOW EASILY I HAVE HUMBLED FOUR OF EARTH'S GREATEST HEROES! TRULY NONE CAN EVER DEFY ME!

AND, AS THE CLOCK SLOWLY DRAWS NEAR TO THE FATEFUL MOMENT WHEN THE WAITING ALICIA WILL ATTEMPT TO BRING THE FANTASTIC FOUR BACK TO THE PRESENT, SUE STORM HAS THE FINISHING TOUCHES APPLIED TO HER BRIDAL COSTUME!
THE EFFECTS OF RAMA-TUT'S RAY GUN WILL NEVER WEAR OFF!
OUR ONLY HOPE IS TO HAVE IT FIRED AT US AGAIN! BUT HOW? HOW??
EVERY FIBRE OF MY BEING WANTS TO RUN, TO FLEE, TO ESCAPE FROM THIS TERRIBLE FATE --- BUT I CANNOT! MY BODY NO LONGER OBEYS MY BRAIN'S COMMANDS!
HOW STRANGE FOR ONE ABOUT TO BECOME A QUEEN TO LOOK SO SAD!
BUT AN INSCRUTABLE FATE, WORKING IN MYSTERIOUS WAYS, CAN CHANGE THE PLANS OF ANYONE, EVEN RAMA-TUT! FOR THERE, UNDER THE HEAT OF A SUN FAR HOTTER THAN THAT OF TWENTIETH-CENTURY NEW YORK, THE BODY CHEMISTRY OF THE IMPRISONED THING UNDERGOES A SUBTLE CHANGE, UNTIL...
...AS THE RAYS GET HOTTER AND HOTTER, THE MOLECULES OF HIS BODY BEGIN TO REACT IN A STARTLING MANNER...AND ONCE MORE ONE OF THE MOST AWESOME PHYSICAL CHANGES EVER RECORDED STARTS TO TAKE PLACE...
...UNTIL, IN THE PLACE OF THE MIGHTY THING, THE NOW-NORMAL FIGURE OF BEN GRIMM APPEARS! BEN GRIMM, SLIM ENOUGH TO SLIP THROUGH THE OVERSIZED SHACKLES! BEN GRIMM, WHOSE MIND AND WILL ARE NOT AFFECTED BY THE RAY AS WAS THE THING!!
I DON'T KNOW HOW IT HAPPENED, BUT I'M BEN GRIMM AGAIN... AND I'VE GOT ONE SLIM CHANCE TO SET THE OTHERS FREE! IF ONLY I CAN REACH SHORE!
A GALLEY SLAVE HAS BROKEN FREE! SEIZE HIM!!
BUT BEN GRIMM IS ARMED WITH TWENTIETH-CENTURY MAN'S KNOWLEDGE OF JUDO AND BOXING...
I MAY NOT HAVE THE STRENGTH OF THE THING, BUT I'LL STILL GIVE YOU JOKERS A RUN FOR YOUR MONEY!
13.

FINALLY...
HE HAS LEAPED OVERBOARD! AFTER HIM!
IT IS USELESS! WE CANNOT ROW THIS CUMBERSOME VESSEL AS FAST AS HE CAN SWIM!
REACHING SHORE SAFELY, THE FRANTIC BEN GRIMM SEIZES A NEARBY CHARIOT IN ONE LAST DESPERATE EFFORT...
NOW IF I CAN JUST MAKE IT TO THE PALACE OF RAMA-TUT!
MEANWHILE, WITHIN THE PALACE GATES...
DO NOT FRET, MY LOVELY...
AT MY SIDE YOU SHALL BECOME HISTORY'S MOST ENVIED QUEEN!
THIS IS MADNESS! HERE I AM, BEING FORCED TO ENTERTAIN RAMA-TUT, WHEN I'M ACHING TO STRIKE AT HIM --- TO ATTACK HIM ... TO DESTROY HIM ... BUT I'M POWERLESS TO DO SO!
AND NOW, MY BRIDE-TO-BE, SIP YOUR NECTAR AND TOAST OUR LOVE, FOR SOON YOU SHALL BE QUEEN OF ALL THE NILE!
GUESS AGAIN, LOVER BOY!
I DID IT! NOW I'VE GOT THAT GUN OF YOURS, AND THINGS ARE GONNA START POPPIN' AROUND HERE!
ANOTHER TWENTIETH-CENTURY INTRUDER! BUT WHO? HOW? UGH!!
14

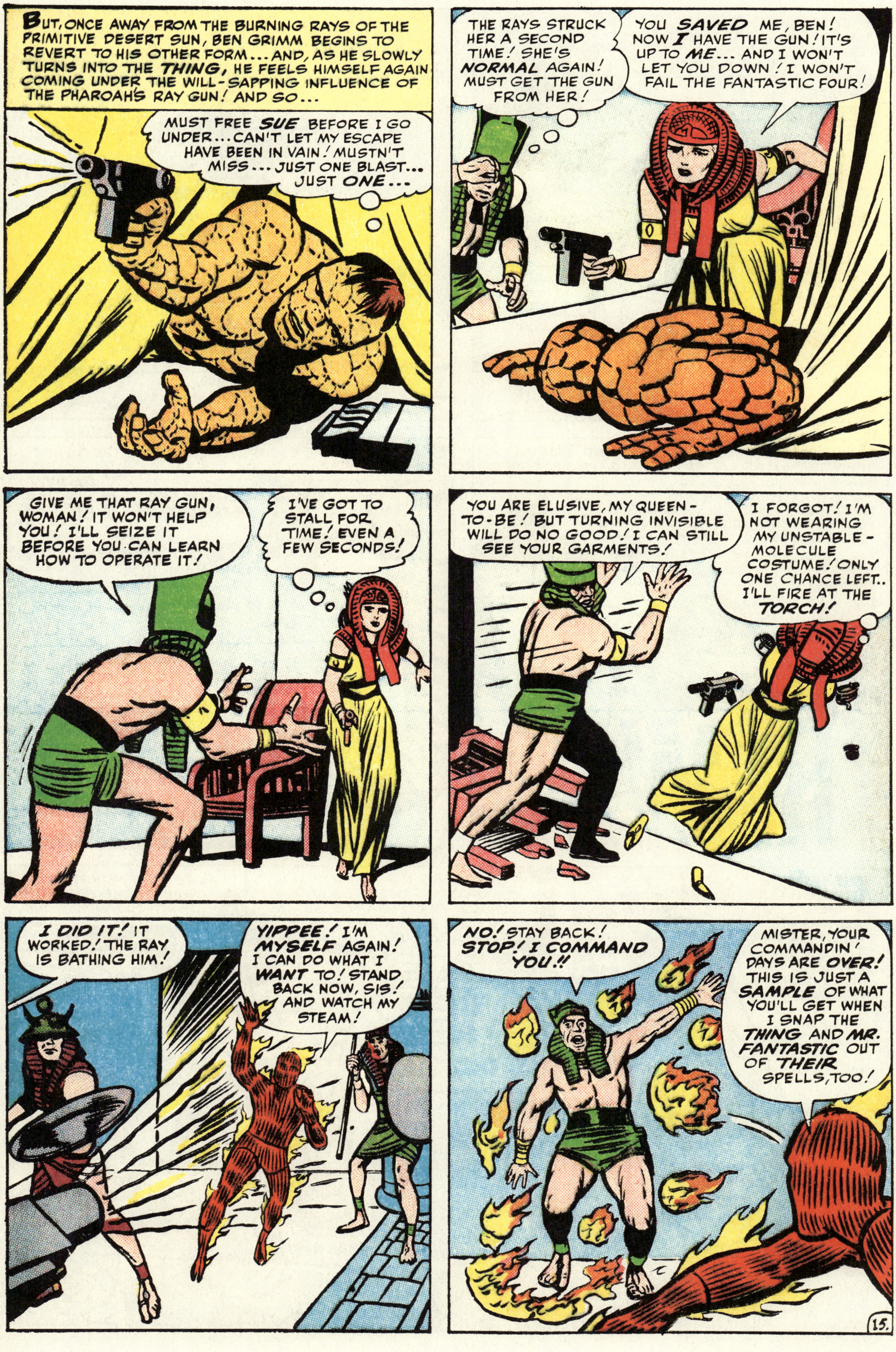

BUT, ONCE AWAY FROM THE BURNING RAYS OF THE PRIMITIVE DESERT SUN, BEN GRIMM BEGINS TO REVERT TO HIS OTHER FORM... AND, AS HE SLOWLY TURNS INTO THE THING, HE FEELS HIMSELF AGAIN COMING UNDER THE WILL-SAPPING INFLUENCE OF THE PHAROAH'S RAY GUN! AND SO...
MUST FREE SUE BEFORE I GO UNDER... CAN'T LET MY ESCAPE HAVE BEEN IN VAIN! MUSTN'T MISS... JUST ONE BLAST... JUST ONE...
THE RAYS STRUCK HER A SECOND TIME! SHE'S NORMAL AGAIN! MUST GET THE GUN FROM HER!
YOU SAVED ME, BEN! NOW I HAVE THE GUN! IT'S UP TO ME... AND I WON'T LET YOU DOWN! I WON'T FAIL THE FANTASTIC FOUR!
GIVE ME THAT RAY GUN, WOMAN! IT WON'T HELP YOU! I'LL SEIZE IT BEFORE YOU CAN LEARN HOW TO OPERATE IT!
I'VE GOT TO STALL FOR TIME! EVEN A FEW SECONDS!
YOU ARE ELUSIVE, MY QUEEN-TO-BE! BUT TURNING INVISIBLE WILL DO NO GOOD! I CAN STILL SEE YOUR GARMENTS!
I FORGOT! I'M NOT WEARING MY UNSTABLE-MOLECULE COSTUME! ONLY ONE CHANCE LEFT.. I'LL FIRE AT THE TORCH!
I DID IT! IT WORKED! THE RAY IS BATHING HIM!
YIPPEE! I'M MYSELF AGAIN! I CAN DO WHAT I WANT TO! STAND BACK NOW, SIS! AND WATCH MY STEAM!
NO! STAY BACK! STOP! I COMMAND YOU!!
MISTER, YOUR COMMANDIN' DAYS ARE OVER! THIS IS JUST A SAMPLE OF WHAT YOU'LL GET WHEN I SNAP THE THING AND MR. FANTASTIC OUT OF THEIR SPELLS, TOO!
15.

IT IS FORTUNATE THAT THE FLAMING FOOL IS TOO SOFT-HEARTED TO ATTEMPT TO SLAY ME WITH HIS FIERY POWER! HE DIDN'T SUSPECT I WAS FEELING THE WALL BEHIND ME TO TOUCH A SECRET STUD OPENING TO MY HIDDEN ESCAPE CHAMBER!
NOW, WHILE HE WASTES HIS TIME REVIVING HIS FRIENDS, I SHALL DO WHAT MUST BE DONE!
THIS PASSAGEWAY LEADS DIRECTLY TO THE CONTROL ROOM OF MY TIME MACHINE! ONCE INSIDE, I SHALL HAVE THE UPPER HAND!!
MEANWHILE, AT TORCH'S COMMAND, SUE AGAIN FIRES THE AMAZING RAY GUN, AIMING IT POINT-BLANK AT THE THING...
THAT DID IT, SIS! HE'S SNAPPING OUT OF IT AGAIN!
OHH, MY ACHIN' HEAD!
WE MUST STILL FIND REED!
BUT, BEFORE THE ESCAPEES CAN LEAVE THE PALACE, THEY SEE...
STOP THE INTRUDERS!
DEATH TO THE ENEMIES OF RAMA-TUT!
WHILE THOSE GOONS MAKE UP THEIR CORN-BALL PHRASES, THE LITTLE OL' THING WILL JUST GIVE 'EM A NICE, BIG WELCOME!
WHERE YOU RUNNIN' TO, PLAYMATES?? THERE'S LOTS MORE PARTY GAMES WE CAN PLAY IF YA HANG AROUND!
FLEE! THE MONSTROUS ONE HAS THE STRENGTH OF A THOUSAND DEMONS!
16.

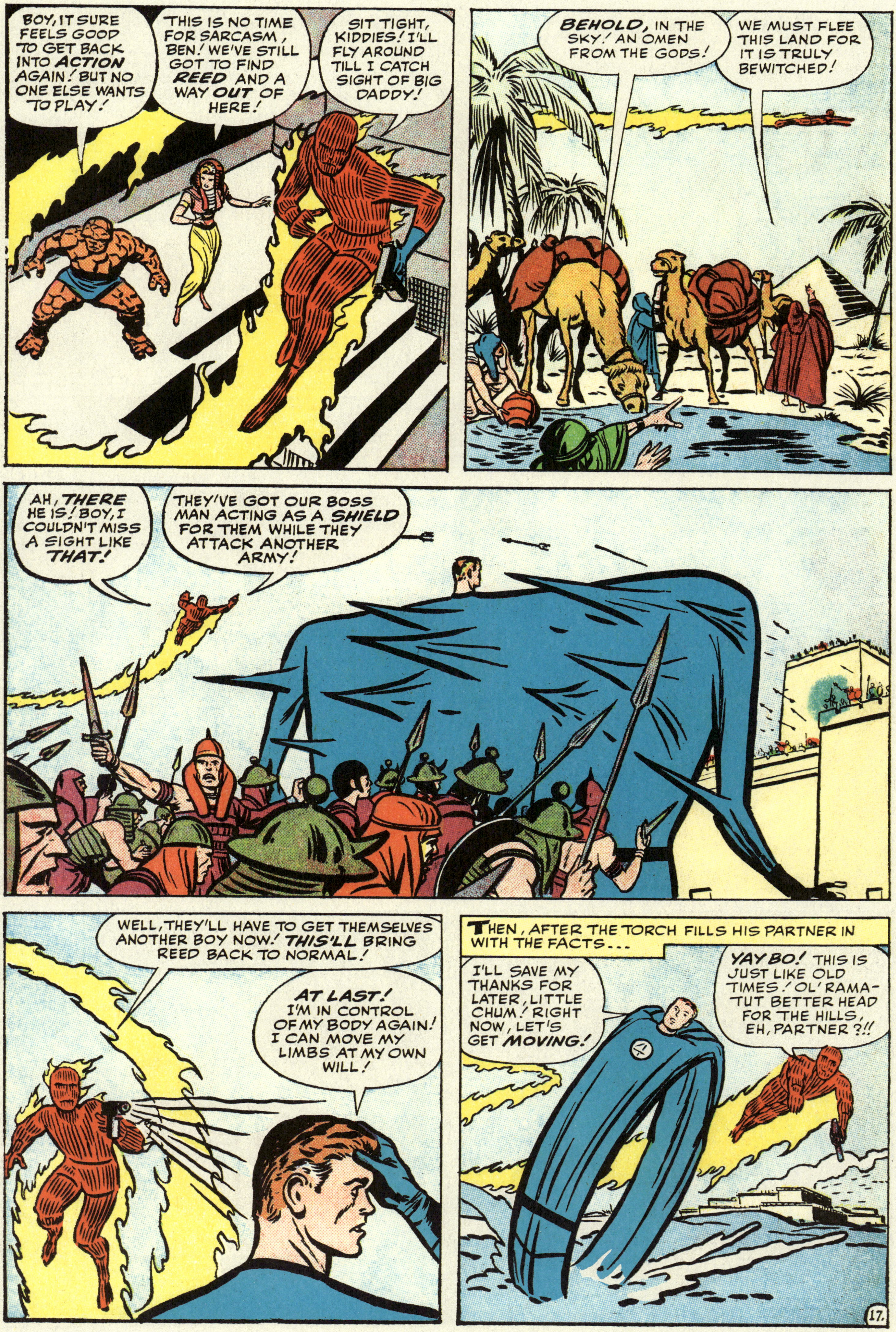

BOY, IT SURE FEELS GOOD TO GET BACK INTO ACTION AGAIN! BUT NO ONE ELSE WANTS TO PLAY!
THIS IS NO TIME FOR SARCASM, BEN! WE'VE STILL GOT TO FIND REED AND A WAY OUT OF HERE!
SIT TIGHT, KIDDIES! I'LL FLY AROUND TILL I CATCH SIGHT OF BIG DADDY!
BEHOLD, IN THE SKY! AN OMEN FROM THE GODS!
WE MUST FLEE THIS LAND FOR IT IS TRULY BEWITCHED!
AH, THERE HE IS! BOY, I COULDN'T MISS A SIGHT LIKE THAT!
THEY'VE GOT OUR BOSS MAN ACTING AS A SHIELD FOR THEM WHILE THEY ATTACK ANOTHER ARMY!
WELL, THEY'LL HAVE TO GET THEMSELVES ANOTHER BOY NOW! THIS'LL BRING REED BACK TO NORMAL!
AT LAST! I'M IN CONTROL OF MY BODY AGAIN! I CAN MOVE MY LIMBS AT MY OWN WILL!
THEN, AFTER THE TORCH FILLS HIS PARTNER IN WITH THE FACTS...
I'LL SAVE MY THANKS FOR LATER, LITTLE CHUM! RIGHT NOW, LET'S GET MOVING!
YAY BO! THIS IS JUST LIKE OLD TIMES! OL' RAMA-TUT BETTER HEAD FOR THE HILLS, EH, PARTNER?!!
17

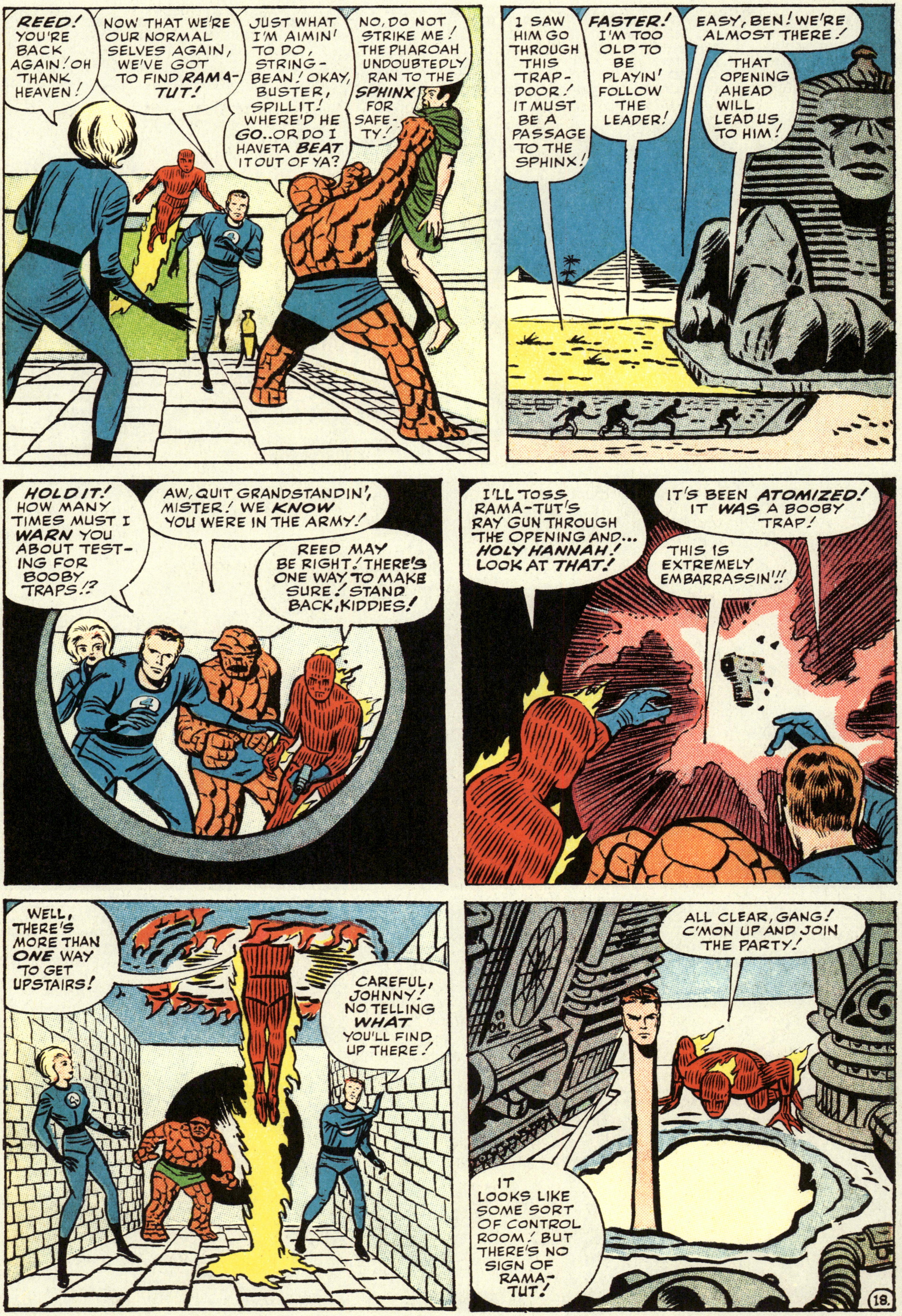
REED! YOU'RE BACK AGAIN! OH THANK HEAVEN!
NOW THAT WE'RE OUR NORMAL SELVES AGAIN, WE'VE GOT TO FIND RAMA-TUT!
JUST WHAT I'M AIMIN' TO DO, STRING-BEAN! OKAY, BUSTER, SPILL IT! WHERE'D HE GO..OR DO I HAVETA BEAT IT OUT OF YA?
NO, DO NOT STRIKE ME! THE PHAROAH UNDOUBTEDLY RAN TO THE SPHINX FOR SAFETY!
I SAW HIM GO THROUGH THIS TRAP-DOOR! IT MUST BE A PASSAGE TO THE SPHINX!
FASTER! I'M TOO OLD TO BE PLAYIN' FOLLOW THE LEADER!
EASY, BEN! WE'RE ALMOST THERE!
THAT OPENING AHEAD WILL LEAD US TO HIM!
HOLD IT! HOW MANY TIMES MUST I WARN YOU ABOUT TESTING FOR BOOBY TRAPS!?
AW, QUIT GRANDSTANDIN', MISTER! WE KNOW YOU WERE IN THE ARMY!
REED MAY BE RIGHT! THERE'S ONE WAY TO MAKE SURE! STAND BACK, KIDDIES!
I'LL TOSS RAMA-TUT'S RAY GUN THROUGH THE OPENING AND... HOLY HANNAH! LOOK AT THAT!
IT'S BEEN ATOMIZED! IT WAS A BOOBY TRAP!
THIS IS EXTREMELY EMBARRASSIN'!!
WELL, THERE'S MORE THAN ONE WAY TO GET UPSTAIRS!
CAREFUL, JOHNNY! NO TELLING WHAT YOU'LL FIND UP THERE!
ALL CLEAR, GANG! C'MON UP AND JOIN THE PARTY!
IT LOOKS LIKE SOME SORT OF CONTROL ROOM! BUT THERE'S NO SIGN OF RAMA-TUT!
18.

SAY, THERE'S SOME KIND OF SCREEN OVER THERE! IT'S STARTING TO GLOW!
CATCH ME, REED!
A PLEASURE, HONEY!
PHOOEY! I'M ALWAYS LAST IN LINE! IT'S GIVIN' ME A COMPLEX!
SUDDENLY, THE SCREEN WHICH THE TORCH HAD NOTICED, COMES TO LIFE WITH AN ENRAGED IMAGE OF RAMA-TUT!
YOU ARE MORE POWERFUL THAN I SUSPECTED! YOU CANNOT BE ALLOWED TO FRUSTRATE MY PLANS ANY LONGER! I MUST DESTROY YOU!
HAW! HOW MANY TIMES HAVE WE HEARD THAT SPEECH BEFORE?
BUT THE PHAROAH LOOKS LIKE HE AIN'T JUST WHISTLIN' DIXIE!
GET BACK! HE'S UNLEASHED A TORRENT OF WATER ON US! QUICK, JOHNNY... FLY ABOVE IT!
REED! THE ROOM WILL BE FILLED WITHIN SECONDS! HOW CAN WE ESCAPE IN TIME?
NUTS! A THING LIKE THIS CAN GIVE YA DISHPAN HANDS!
QUICK, TORCH! HURL A STREAM OF YOUR MOST INTENSE FLAME DIRECTLY AT THE OPEN WATER MAIN!
GOTCHA, REED! I'LL HAVE THE SOURCE OF THAT LITTLE BUBBLE-BATH VAPORIZED IN NO TIME!
SECONDS LATER...
YOU DID IT, JOHNNY! YOU STOPPED THE ONRUSHING WATER!
SURE! AND LOOK HOW MY LOW-INTENSITY HEAT CAN DRY OUT THE REST OF THE ROOM!
Y'KNOW SOME-THIN'? I'M BEGINNIN' TO THINK THAT NUTTY PHAROAH DOESN'T LIKE US!
THERE'S NO TELLING WHAT HE'LL TRY NEXT! WE'VE GOT TO FIND HIM, AND DEFEAT HIM SOMEHOW!
DON'T MAKE IT SOUND SO HARD, BUDDY BOY! ONE LITTLE LOVE TAP FROM YOURS TRULY WILL BE ALL IT TAKES! LET'S GO!
19.

I'LL SEARCH THE CORE OF THE SPHINX, FOLLOWING ALL THE HIDDEN CIRCUITS!
MY SYSTEM'S SHORT AND SWEET! I'LL JUST BULL MY WAY THROUGH! TRY AN' KEEP UP WITH ME, DOLL FACE!
NOW THAT MY FLAME'S HAD A FEW MINUTES TO RECHARGE ITSELF, I STILL THINK FLYIN'S THE BEST WAY!!
BUT, MINUTES LATER, DESPITE THEIR DIFFERENT ROUTES, THE FABULOUS FOURSOME ALL CONVERGE ON ONE SPOT...
WE'VE SEARCHED EVERYWHERE ELSE! RAMA-TUT MUST BE IN HERE!
YOU ARE RIGHT, RICHARDS! BUT YOU ARE TOO LATE! WITHIN SECONDS I SHALL BE GONE... TO ANOTHER DIMENSION, ANOTHER AGE, WHEREVER MY SATELLITE GLOBE TAKES ME!
QUICK, GET BACK! THIS CIRCULAR ROOM IS REALLY A MISSILE... IT'S ABOUT TO BLAST OFF!
I SHALL LEAVE MY SPHINX BEHIND, TO MYSTIFY MANKIND FOR CENTURIES TO COME! AND, WHEN I LEAVE, THE MEMORY OF MY REIGN SHALL FADE INTO OBLIVION... AS THOUGH I HAVE NEVER BEEN!
SO THAT'S WHY THERE ARE NO RECORDS OF RAMA-TUT'S STRANGE REIGN!
20.

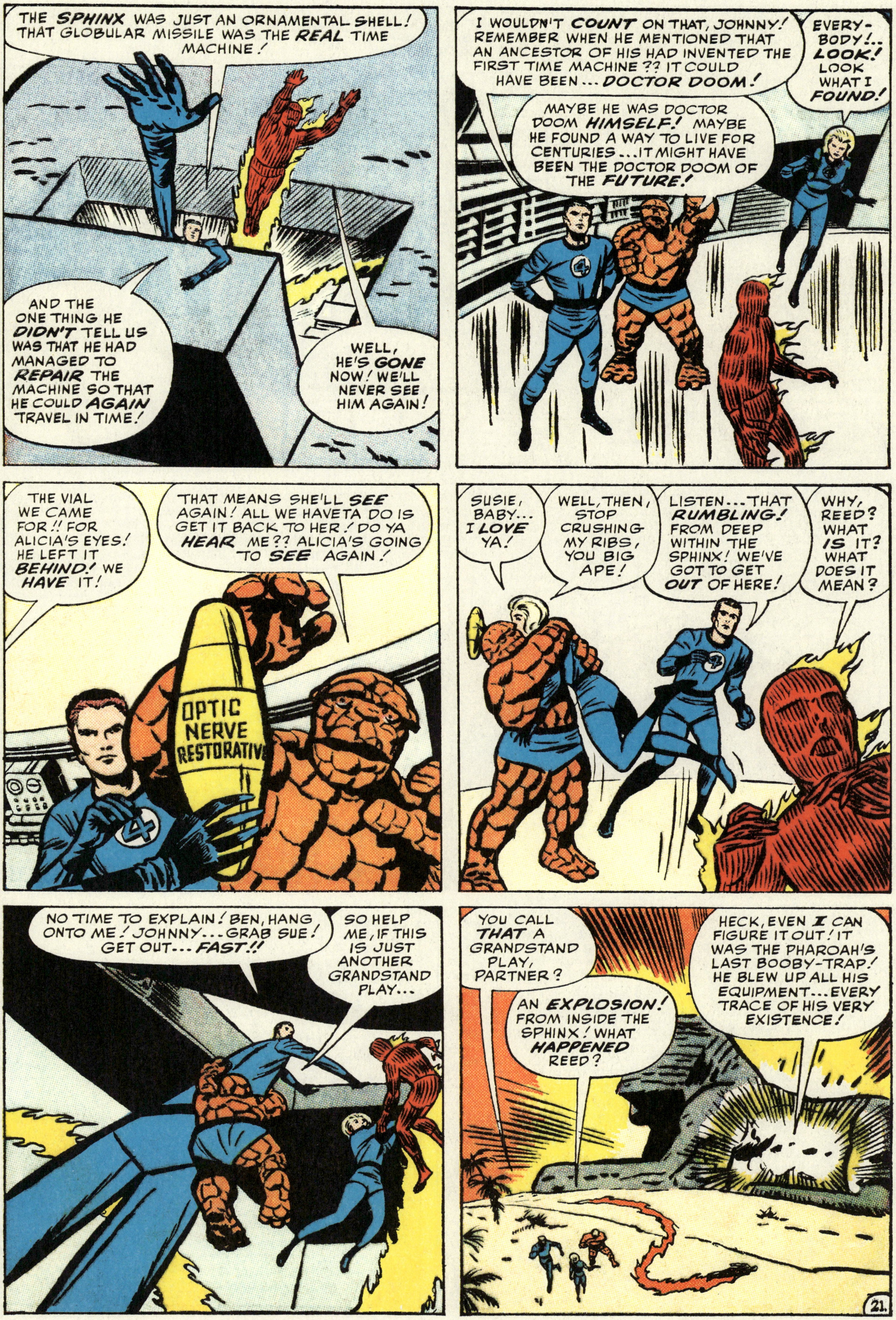
THE SPHINX WAS JUST AN ORNAMENTAL SHELL! THAT GLOBULAR MISSILE WAS THE REAL TIME MACHINE!
AND THE ONE THING HE DIDN'T TELL US WAS THAT HE HAD MANAGED TO REPAIR THE MACHINE SO THAT HE COULD AGAIN TRAVEL IN TIME!
WELL, HE'S GONE NOW! WE'LL NEVER SEE HIM AGAIN!
I WOULDN'T COUNT ON THAT, JOHNNY! REMEMBER WHEN HE MENTIONED THAT AN ANCESTOR OF HIS HAD INVENTED THE FIRST TIME MACHINE?? IT COULD HAVE BEEN... DOCTOR DOOM!
MAYBE HE WAS DOCTOR DOOM HIMSELF! MAYBE HE FOUND A WAY TO LIVE FOR CENTURIES... IT MIGHT HAVE BEEN THE DOCTOR DOOM OF THE FUTURE!
EVERYBODY!.. LOOK! LOOK WHAT I FOUND!
THE VIAL WE CAME FOR!! FOR ALICIA'S EYES! HE LEFT IT BEHIND! WE HAVE IT!
THAT MEANS SHE'LL SEE AGAIN! ALL WE HAVETA DO IS GET IT BACK TO HER! DO YA HEAR ME?? ALICIA'S GOING TO SEE AGAIN!
OPTIC NERVE RESTORATIVE
SUSIE, BABY... I LOVE YA!
WELL, THEN, STOP CRUSHING MY RIBS, YOU BIG APE!
LISTEN... THAT RUMBLING! FROM DEEP WITHIN THE SPHINX! WE'VE GOT TO GET OUT OF HERE!
WHY, REED? WHAT IS IT? WHAT DOES IT MEAN?
NO TIME TO EXPLAIN! BEN, HANG ONTO ME! JOHNNY... GRAB SUE! GET OUT... FAST!!
SO HELP ME, IF THIS IS JUST ANOTHER GRANDSTAND PLAY...
YOU CALL THAT A GRANDSTAND PLAY, PARTNER?
AN EXPLOSION! FROM INSIDE THE SPHINX! WHAT HAPPENED REED?
HECK, EVEN I CAN FIGURE IT OUT! IT WAS THE PHAROAH'S LAST BOOBY-TRAP! HE BLEW UP ALL HIS EQUIPMENT... EVERY TRACE OF HIS VERY EXISTENCE!

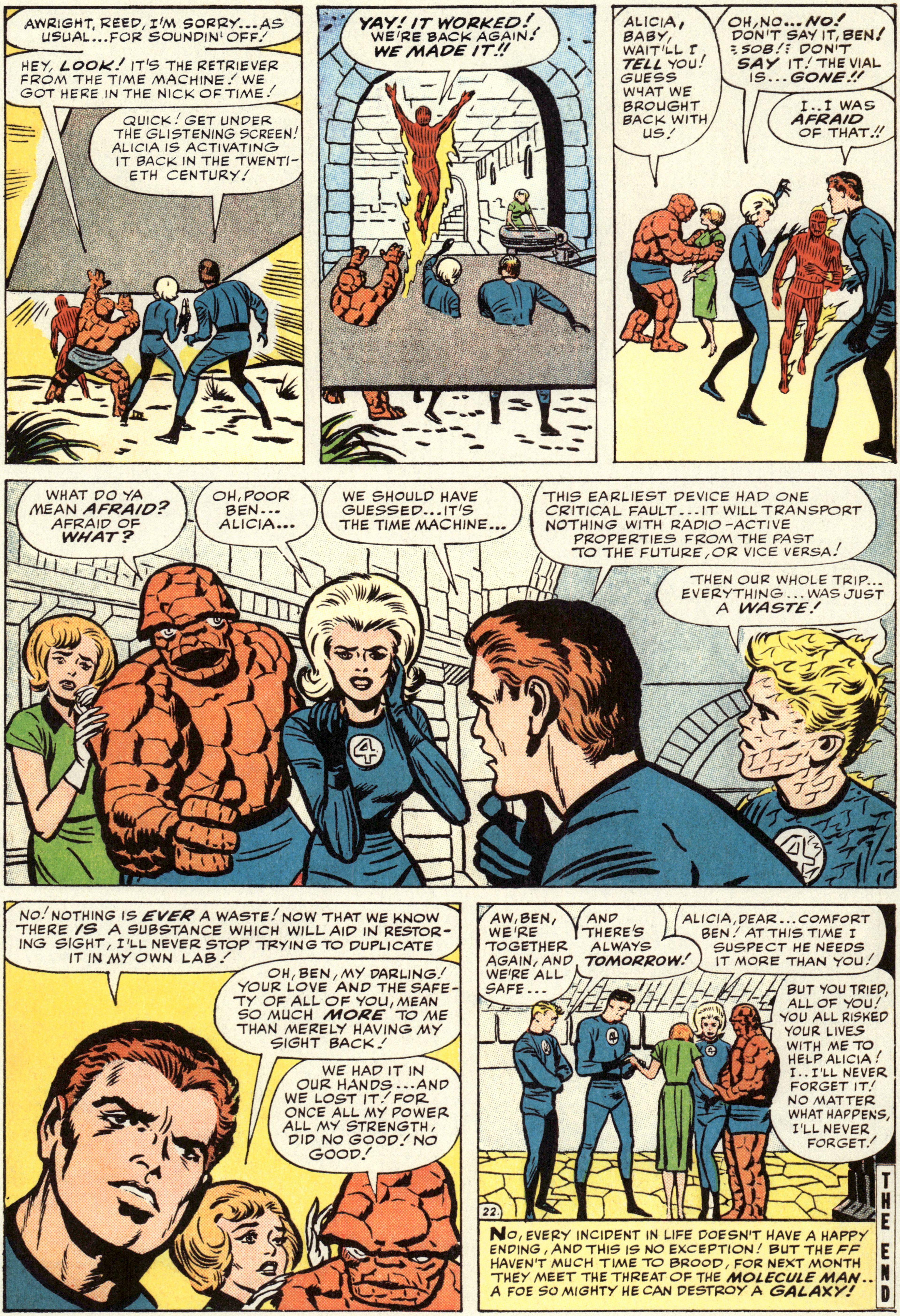

AWRIGHT, REED, I'M SORRY... AS USUAL... FOR SOUNDIN' OFF!
HEY, LOOK! IT'S THE RETRIEVER FROM THE TIME MACHINE! WE GOT HERE IN THE NICK OF TIME!
QUICK! GET UNDER THE GLISTENING SCREEN! ALICIA IS ACTIVATING IT BACK IN THE TWENTIETH CENTURY!
YAY! IT WORKED! WE'RE BACK AGAIN! WE MADE IT!!
ALICIA, BABY, WAIT'LL I TELL YOU! GUESS WHAT WE BROUGHT BACK WITH US!
OH, NO... NO! DON'T SAY IT, BEN! SOB! DON'T SAY IT! THE VIAL IS... GONE!!
I.. I WAS AFRAID OF THAT!!
WHAT DO YA MEAN AFRAID? AFRAID OF WHAT?
OH, POOR BEN... ALICIA...
WE SHOULD HAVE GUESSED... IT'S THE TIME MACHINE...
THIS EARLIEST DEVICE HAD ONE CRITICAL FAULT... IT WILL TRANSPORT NOTHING WITH RADIO-ACTIVE PROPERTIES FROM THE PAST TO THE FUTURE, OR VICE VERSA!
THEN OUR WHOLE TRIP... EVERYTHING... WAS JUST A WASTE!
NO! NOTHING IS EVER A WASTE! NOW THAT WE KNOW THERE IS A SUBSTANCE WHICH WILL AID IN RESTORING SIGHT, I'LL NEVER STOP TRYING TO DUPLICATE IT IN MY OWN LAB!
OH, BEN, MY DARLING! YOUR LOVE AND THE SAFETY OF ALL OF YOU, MEAN SO MUCH MORE TO ME THAN MERELY HAVING MY SIGHT BACK!
WE HAD IT IN OUR HANDS... AND WE LOST IT! FOR ONCE ALL MY POWER ALL MY STRENGTH, DID NO GOOD! NO GOOD!
AW, BEN, WE'RE TOGETHER AGAIN, AND WE'RE ALL SAFE...
AND THERE'S ALWAYS TOMORROW!
ALICIA, DEAR... COMFORT BEN! AT THIS TIME I SUSPECT HE NEEDS IT MORE THAN YOU!
BUT YOU TRIED, ALL OF YOU! YOU ALL RISKED YOUR LIVES WITH ME TO HELP ALICIA! I.. I'LL NEVER FORGET IT! NO MATTER WHAT HAPPENS, I'LL NEVER FORGET!
22.
THE END
NO, EVERY INCIDENT IN LIFE DOESN'T HAVE A HAPPY ENDING, AND THIS IS NO EXCEPTION! BUT THE FF HAVEN'T MUCH TIME TO BROOD, FOR NEXT MONTH THEY MEET THE THREAT OF THE MOLECULE MAN.. A FOE SO MIGHTY HE CAN DESTROY A GALAXY!

Address YOUR letters to:
LEE and KIRBY
FANTASTIC FOUR
THIRD FLOOR
655 MADISON AVE.
NEW YORK 21, N. Y.

FANTASTIC 4 FAN PAGE

Dear Stan and Jack,

I told my mother that you two read every letter you get whether it's printed or not. She said, and I quote, "I'll bet secretaries read and answer them!"

Sidney D. Evans
33 Monsignor Reynolds Way
Boston 18, Mass.

We wish we HAD "secretaries," Sid! We've got one overworked little gal who opens the letters for us, and then we read each and every one—honest!

Dear Stan and Jack,

I only have one complaint; that's about SGT. FURY AND HIS HOWLING COMMANDOS—YEECH!! What a name!!

Robert Purinton
91 Ravine Road
Medford, Mass.

No! No! No! His name is NICK—not YEECH!

Dear Stan and Jack,

Finally made up my mind to write and tell you both that it's been a pleasure to read your magazines. I remember reading SUBMARINER way back in the '40's when I was in high school. I don't read many comics, but I wouldn't miss an issue put out by MARVEL COMICS GROUP. I would love to see a lot of the "old characters" revived again. Your new character SPIDER-MAN is very interesting, to say the least, as is Dr. Strange in STRANGE TALES. Keep up the good work.

Mrs. Beryl Wright
15 Abbott St.
Worcester 2, Mass.

Thanks, Mrs. Wright. We hope you enjoy our stories as much as we enjoy our readers' letters.

Dear Stan and Jack,

Oops! You goofed again. In issue #16 on page 9 panel 7 the Thing said to Alicia "It's all right, Sue baby!" when he should have said, "It's all right, Alicia baby!" Besides that your magazine was cool as a thousand pounds of fireballs. Without the Thing the F.F. would not be half as good. So until Sue and I get married, so long!

Curtis M. Wells
913 Watt St.
Jeffersonville, Ind.

Would you believe we received HUNDREDS of letters telling us of that careless mistake? Our only alibi is—we have so many characters to keep track of, we sometimes forget our OWN names! Isn't that right, Mac? I mean JACK!

Dear Stan and Jack,

Please publish more issues like #11! The story "A Visit with the Fantastic Four" was great, and the article about the F.F.'s origin made it even better. The two-page fan mail is terrific! Please don't add any new members; it's just fine now!

Martin Jackson
4103 Westwood Drive
Anchorage, Alaska

Glad you approve, Marty—but where have you BEEN since issue #11??

Dear Stan and Jack,

I started reading your comics only a few months ago and already think they're just wonderful. But I found one mistake in your comic JOURNEY INTO MYSTERY #93. Thor's hammer's greatest power is that when he throws it, it always returns; but in this issue on page 11, you show Thor throwing his hammer away and it did not come back. Can you explain this?

John Stone
919B Suburban Pkwy.
Portsmouth, Va.

It will not return if Thor ORDERS it not to return, as he did in that instance! (It's easy to explain these things, Johnny, when we make up our own rules!)

Dear Stan and Jack,

A few months ago we were at the neighborhood newsstand looking over the different mags when suddenly I saw F.F. The artwork was so unique and the characters almost looked alive that I decided to buy it. My sister came over and said sarcastically, "Who ever heard of a stupid mag named F.F.?" She said if I wanted it I would have to buy it myself. I bought the magazine and — — it was marvelous, great and super—WOW! Later I persuaded my sister to read it by relating some of the action scenes. Well, she thinks it's the greatest mag on the newsstands. Now I don't have to buy F.F.—my sister beats me to it!

Eddie L. Malone, Jr.
P.O. Box 851
Seminole, Texas

So what'samatter? YOU can't buy one TOO??!

Dear Stan and Jack,

As a usual reader of your magnificent "Fantastic Four" I have great pleasure in telling you that all your friends in Miles enjoy such an exciting magazine. No doubt all your friends in the whole of Australia enjoy the "Fantastic Four." Keep up the good work.

Ross O'Connor
20 McNulty Street
Miles, Queensland
Australia

Ross, we're including your letter just to show off! Fans in Australia!! How ABOUT that?!!

Dear Stan and Jack,

In answer to your question of "Would you rather remain as the Thing or Ben Grimm?," I'll choose Ben Grimm. That would solve things all around, especially for me. I have a four year old daughter and every issue we go through the same old bit over the Thing.—"Mommy—what's THAT!" "That's a man, honey." "What happened to HIM?" "He was hit by these cosmic rays and . . ." "What's mic rays," "COSmic." "Osmic?" "No, COsmic." "What's osmic rays, mommy?" "That's COSmic, and I can't explain what they are." "Oh, why?"—That's just a part of our conversation, so now can you see why I want Ben back? The only way I could enjoy your wonderful mag more would be to be able to read it in peace and quiet. Oh, come on, Stan!—with your imagination you can write a good story to change the Thing back to Ben without busting up the F.F. Please???

Mrs. Jo Shelby
Box 264
Reedsburg, Wisconsin

We asked Ben for his opinion and he growled: "Hire a baby sitter!" Wotta you do with a guy like that?

CONTINUED . . .

Dear Stan and Jack,

A few days ago while checking the new comics, I saw the first issue of SGT. FURY AND HIS HOWLING COMMANDOS and passed it right by, reason being that I just don't dig war comics. But today, when I had bought most of your good comics, I took a closer look at St. Fury for a laugh. I noticed it was of the excellent MARVEL GROUP and after a quick glance at the art, I deduced that it could only be done by Jack Kirby. And since you guys haven't had a really big flop yet, I decided to find out what this one was like. When I had finished reading it, I found I was in a complete state of *shock!* This new comic had given me the greatest experience of my life! Never have I read anything as exciting! Everything about it was terrific. Even the Department on Weapons of War was surprisingly good. The entire comic was totally realistic and exciting. This is one comic that will always stay on the top of my list. Congratulations on a job well done!

Steve Griffin
1972 Morris Gate
Seaford, New York

JACK: "SGT. FURY"? Is that one of OURS?
STAN: You lunkhead, you just drew it a WEEK ago!
JACK: Gosh, who can remember that far back?!

Dear Stan and Jack,

While the F.F. is undoubtedly one of the best comic magazines on the market, it has its failings. The worst part of that is that when you do a lemon it's a doozy! I'm speaking of issues #13 and #15. Both of these were really poor, especially when contrasted to your masterpieces (like #s 4, 6, and 9). Let me take #13. In the last panel of p. 12, we are informed that in the next issue the FF will meet "one of the most powerful super-villains of all." This turns out to be "The Red Ghost." Never in my wildest flights of fancy did I dream "red" would refer to the communists!! Nor did I imagine that the tale would take place on the moon. Both of these were disappointing. Also, the cover was horrible, cluttered up with all sorts of vital announcements. (Ha!) One more thing: I've never seen a worse artist combination than Kirby and Ditko. Both are great alone, but please, let's not team them up again. Between two lemons there was a peach—#14. Though the letter pages were pretty awful, the story was great. But may I say that your courage is to be admired. You're not afraid to try new ideas, and if a new idea DOES fail, you simply change it in a later ish. You can't lose. By the way, now that the Ant-Man (formerly your worst effort) has gained the Wasp for a partner, he's great. I also think highly of the Torch and Iron Man. But, undoubtedly, aside from the FF your best hero is Thor. You broke the mold and came up with a truly unique hero. In the future I hope to see: Thor guest-star with the FF, Sub-Mariner turn hero, more F.F. adventures on earth, less of Dr. Doom. Finally, thanks again for a great magazine.

Steve Gerber
7014 Roberts Court
University City 30, Mo.

Steve would be a great letter writer if he wasn't so shy about giving opinions!

Dear Stan and Jack,

I would like to know why you don't keep back issues. You have told us you don't, but never why. I am sure it is not sheer meanness. (is it?). Is it because of the expense? I would think not, for you could charge 25¢ or more for magazines you make money on for 12¢. Well, enough guessing, just tell me, please!

Herbert L. Patterson
242 Park Ave.
Long Beach, Calif.

The answer is so simple you'd never guess . . . We haven't the ROOM to keep 'em! Any idea how much SPACE all those issues take up??

Dear Stan and Jack,

I think the most controversial dispute in your mag today is the human interest matter. Should a comic hero act like a comic hero, or should he (or she) act like a real person? The only reason that there has developed a "regulation hero" which supposedly sets the pattern is that no one has had the "guts" to try something new and perhaps a bit more practical. Thanks to the MARVEL COMICS GROUP, "You've seen one, you've seen them all" no longer applies to all comics.

Fred Romanek
4928 Enfield Ave.
Encino, California

Thanks for the philosophical approach, Freddie.

Dear Stan and Jack,

My husband and I first began reading the MARVEL mags recently. Can't decide which is our favorite—they're all excellent. But we don't see letters from any of the hundreds of Canadians who are your devoted fans. How come?

Linda and Percy Smoke
448 D'Arcy Street
Cobourg, Ontario
Canada

See? With one stroke of the pen we cement American-Canadian relations!

SPECIAL ANNOUNCEMENTS SECTION:

- **This is a big month for MARVEL! "THE AVENGERS," "X-MEN," "FANTASTIC FOUR ANNUAL," and "STRANGE TALES ANNUAL" are all on sale as you read this! We predict all four new ishes are going to be real solid HITS! So don't make liars of us, huh?**

- **Wait till you see the big change in ASTONISH #49. (On sale Aug. 1st.) ANT-MAN gains a great new power—and a new name! As for the WASP—well, see for yourself! (To celebrate the occasion, Jack Kirby himself drew this one).**

- **By the way, wanna share an "inside joke" with us? You may notice that Jack often draws crowd scenes—Well, we at MARVEL refer to the people in his crowds as "Kirby's Kast of Kharacters," and if you look closely, you'll see the same faces appearing over and over again. (Same goes for the Western covers he draws. Take a look!)**

- **Here's the result of our "Should Reed remain as leader of the FF?" poll. In favor of Reed: 6,043. Opposed to Reed: 422. 'Nuff said.**

- **Oh, we've been meaning to tell you—when writing to us, please don't say "I enjoyed the issue I just read." Please tell us the issue NUMBER so we'll know what you're referring to. Fair enough?**

- **A number of you have asked for more of DR. STRANGE, in STRANGE TALES. So, we'll have another of his off-beat tales in STRANGE TALES #114—on sale Aug. 8th. We almost hope you DON'T like him, because BOY—are those stories hard to write!!!**

- **Before we go, here's a tip for next ish—we've come up with a somewhat different super-villain for you, and for the FF! He's the MOLECULE MAN! And he's not just menacing our little ol' planet . . . oh no! He's liable to destroy the whole blamed UNIVERSE! Don't miss him!**

BOYS
12 or older
MAKE $1 to $5 WEEKLY
IN YOUR SPARE TIME
5¢ PROFIT on every GRIT you sell.
Win FREE PRIZES, Like These, Too
Sell GRIT
"America's Greatest Family Newspaper"
Enjoyed by 900,000 Families Every Week
Over 30,000 boys, 12 or older, sell GRIT every week in a few hours of their spare time — make lots of spending money — win prizes — get valuable business training.
GRIT WILL HELP YOU GET STARTED in a profitable business of your own. We will send you papers and easy-to-understand selling instructions.
You pay only for the papers you sell until you know how many to order. GRIT sells for 15c a copy. You keep 5c and send GRIT 10c for each paper you sell.
GRIT PUBLISHING CO., Williamsport, Pa.
MC 6-3
Send my first bundle of papers, selling helps and prize offers.
Name
Are You a Boy? Age Date Born Year
In Care of
Street and No. R. F. D.
Post Office State
Print Your Last Name Plainly Here
If you are a boy — 12 or older
Grab This Great Opportunity!
SEND THE COUPON NOW
in an envelope or pasted on a postcard

HYPNO-COIN
NEW - POCKET SIZE INVENTION
HELPS HYPNOTIZE IN MINUTES
IT MUST WORK FOR YOU OR MONEY BACK!
Hold the HYPNO-COIN in front of the person you want to hypnotize. Then, gently vibrate the plastic lens. This sets the hypnotic pattern into a whirling motion. A motion that is so fascinating, it captures and rivets your subject's eyes to the "Hypno-Coin". Now, proceed to give your hypnotic suggestions and commands. Get this amazing hypnotic aid complete with a FREE revealing booklet of secrets and instructions. It tells you what to say and do, how to command and re-hypnotize with the snap of a finger, how to thrill and amaze them with hypnotic stunts, feats of strength and memory, etc. Get the COIN, Booklet and large illustrated catalog for only $1.00 ppd. Sent in a plain wrapper, Money back if not delighted!
Sorry no C.O.D.s Send to:
HYPNOTIC-AIDS, A-89, 1133 Broadway, N. Y. 10, N. Y.
THRILL AND AMAZE THEM at parties and gatherings with fascinating hypnotic feats of memory, stunts, and exhibitions!
BONUS
Free!
Booklet of revealing secrets & instructions and large illustrated catalog with order!
HYPNOTIC AIDS SUPPLY CO. A-89
1133 Broadway, New York 10, N. Y.
Enclosed $1.00 Send Hypno-Coin
Name
Address
City State
only — $1.00 ppd.
MAIL TODAY

ANNUAL
72 BIG PAGES
APPROVED BY THE COMICS CODE AUTHORITY
Fantastic Four
IND.
ANNUAL
MARVEL COMICS GROUP 25¢
#1 1963
"THE UNDERSEA LEGIONS OF SUB-MARINER!"
AT LAST! SUB-MARINER FINDS HIS LONG-LOST RACE!
AND SO BEGINS THE MOST FANTASTIC BATTLE OF ALL TIME!
INSIDE THE PAGES OF THIS, THE WORLD'S GREATEST COMIC MAGAZINE!
SPIDER-MAN WAITS WITHIN THESE PAGES!!
Also: "THE ORIGIN OF THE FANTASTIC FOUR!"
THE MOST REQUESTED SAGA EVER PRINTED!
And... DON'T MISS THE AWESOME "GALLERY OF VILLAINS!"

THE FANTASTIC FOUR ANNUAL is published by CANAM PUBLISHER SALES CORP. OFFICE OF PUBLICATION: 655 MADISON AVENUE, NEW YORK, N.Y. Published annually. Copyright 1963 by Canam Publisher Sales Corp., 655 Madison Avenue, New York, N.Y. Vol. 1, No. 1, 1963 issue. Price 25¢ per copy. No similarity between any of the names, characters, persons, and/or institutions appearing in this magazine with those of any living or dead person or institution is intended, and any such similarity which may exist is purely coincidental. Printed in the U.S.A. by The Eastern Color Printing Co., Waterbury 20, Conn.

THE FABULOUS FANTASTIC FOUR PRESENT:
SUB-MARINER Versus THE HUMAN RACE!
THE LONGEST UNINTERRUPTED SUPER-EPIC OF ITS KIND EVER PUBLISHED!!
WRITTEN BY: STAN LEE
DRAWN BY: JACK KIRBY
INKING: DICK AYERS
LETTERING: ART SIMEK
X-324
1

COUNTLESS FATHOMS BENEATH THE SEA... THE MOST COLORFUL CORONATION OF ALL TIME TAKES PLACE! FOR PRINCE NAMOR, THE MIGHTY SUB-MARINER, HAS FINALLY FOUND HIS LONG-LOST UNDERSEA KINGDOM! AND HERE, AMIDST BREATHTAKING POMP AND PAGEANTRY, HE ONCE AGAIN DONS HIS ROYAL CROWN, AS HE IS ACCLAIMED NAMOR THE FIRST, PRINCE OF ATLANTIS, EMPEROR OF THE DEEP, LORD OF THE SEVEN SEAS, AND SUPREME COMMANDER OF THE UNDERSEA LEGIONS!
I VOW TO BE TRUE TO THE NAME OF NAMOR, WHICH MEANS "AVENGING SON"! I SHALL NEVER REST TILL THE INSOLENT HUMAN RACE HAS PAID FOR ITS CRIMES AGAINST OUR PEOPLE! NOW RISE, AND PLEDGE ME YOUR HEARTS, YOUR HANDS, YOUR LIVES!
ALL HAIL MIGHTY NAMOR! HAIL, PRINCE OF SUB-MARINERS! GREAT NEPTUNE HIMSELF HAS SENT THEE TO LEAD US!
2

HAIL, HAIL! ALL HOMAGE TO THE NOBLE PROTECTOR OF THE DEEP! LONG LIVE NAMOR! LONG LIVE ATLANTIS! HAIL TO THE GODS WHO HAVE RETURNED OUR MIGHTY LEADER!
WHERE YOU LEAD, WE WILL FOLLOW! WHERE YOU COMMAND, WE WILL OBEY! FOR YOU ARE TRULY NAMOR, PRINCE OF THE BLOOD, AND WE ARE YOUR SUBJECTS!
3

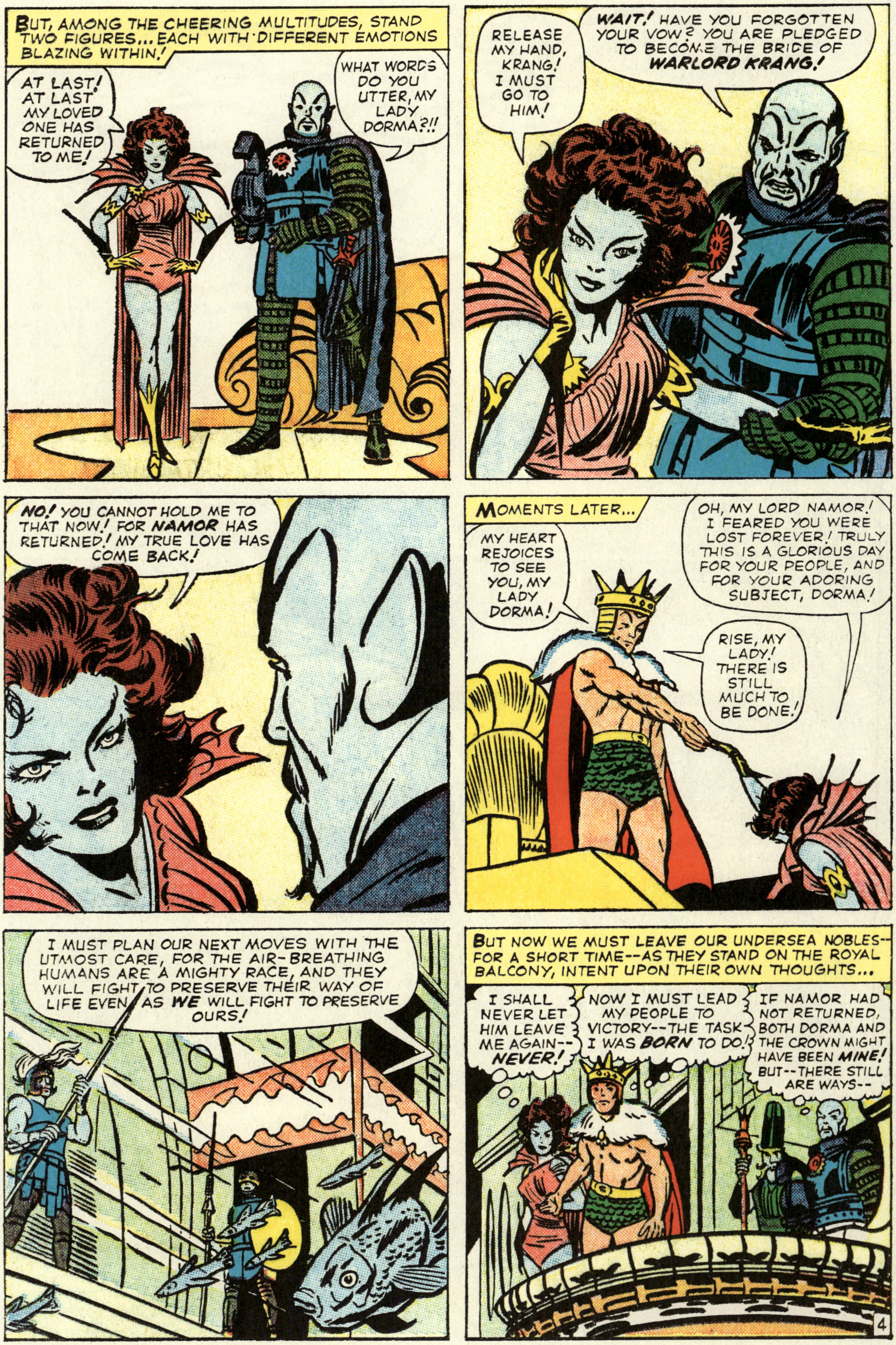
BUT, AMONG THE CHEERING MULTITUDES, STAND TWO FIGURES... EACH WITH DIFFERENT EMOTIONS BLAZING WITHIN!
AT LAST! AT LAST MY LOVED ONE HAS RETURNED TO ME!
WHAT WORDS DO YOU UTTER, MY LADY DORMA?!!
RELEASE MY HAND, KRANG! I MUST GO TO HIM!
WAIT! HAVE YOU FORGOTTEN YOUR VOW? YOU ARE PLEDGED TO BECOME THE BRIDE OF WARLORD KRANG!
NO! YOU CANNOT HOLD ME TO THAT NOW! FOR NAMOR HAS RETURNED! MY TRUE LOVE HAS COME BACK!
MOMENTS LATER...
OH, MY LORD NAMOR! I FEARED YOU WERE LOST FOREVER! TRULY THIS IS A GLORIOUS DAY FOR YOUR PEOPLE, AND FOR YOUR ADORING SUBJECT, DORMA!
MY HEART REJOICES TO SEE YOU, MY LADY DORMA!
RISE, MY LADY! THERE IS STILL MUCH TO BE DONE!
I MUST PLAN OUR NEXT MOVES WITH THE UTMOST CARE, FOR THE AIR-BREATHING HUMANS ARE A MIGHTY RACE, AND THEY WILL FIGHT TO PRESERVE THEIR WAY OF LIFE EVEN AS WE WILL FIGHT TO PRESERVE OURS!
BUT NOW WE MUST LEAVE OUR UNDERSEA NOBLES-- FOR A SHORT TIME--AS THEY STAND ON THE ROYAL BALCONY, INTENT UPON THEIR OWN THOUGHTS...
I SHALL NEVER LET HIM LEAVE ME AGAIN-- NEVER!
NOW I MUST LEAD MY PEOPLE TO VICTORY--THE TASK I WAS BORN TO DO!
IF NAMOR HAD NOT RETURNED, BOTH DORMA AND THE CROWN MIGHT HAVE BEEN MINE! BUT--THERE STILL ARE WAYS--
4

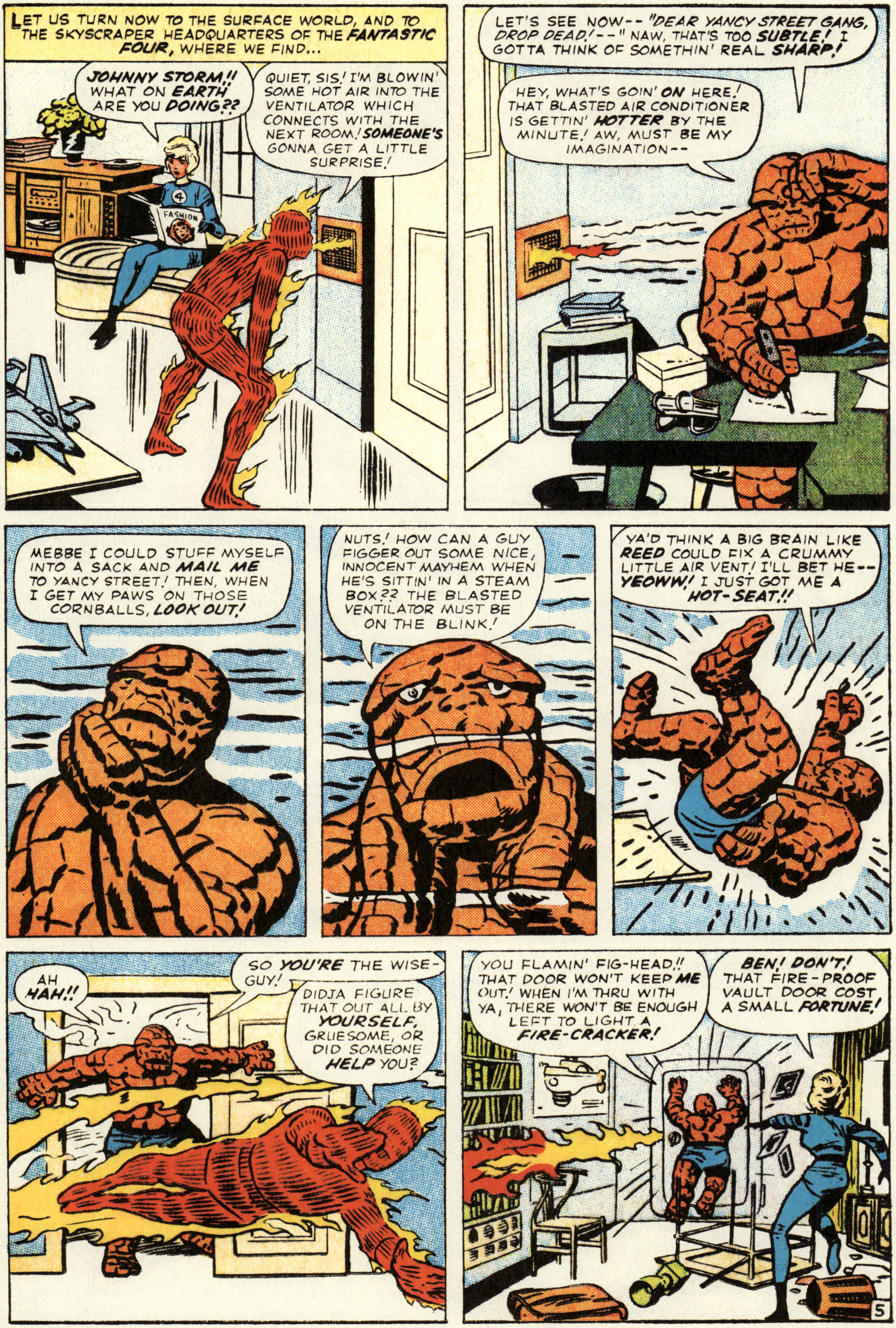
LET US TURN NOW TO THE SURFACE WORLD, AND TO THE SKYSCRAPER HEADQUARTERS OF THE FANTASTIC FOUR, WHERE WE FIND...
JOHNNY STORM!! WHAT ON EARTH ARE YOU DOING??
QUIET, SIS! I'M BLOWIN' SOME HOT AIR INTO THE VENTILATOR WHICH CONNECTS WITH THE NEXT ROOM! SOMEONE'S GONNA GET A LITTLE SURPRISE!
FASHION
LET'S SEE NOW-- "DEAR YANCY STREET GANG, DROP DEAD!--" NAW, THAT'S TOO SUBTLE! I GOTTA THINK OF SOMETHIN' REAL SHARP!
HEY, WHAT'S GOIN' ON HERE! THAT BLASTED AIR CONDITIONER IS GETTIN' HOTTER BY THE MINUTE! AW, MUST BE MY IMAGINATION--
MEBBE I COULD STUFF MYSELF INTO A SACK AND MAIL ME TO YANCY STREET! THEN, WHEN I GET MY PAWS ON THOSE CORNBALLS, LOOK OUT!
NUTS! HOW CAN A GUY FIGGER OUT SOME NICE, INNOCENT MAYHEM WHEN HE'S SITTIN' IN A STEAM BOX?? THE BLASTED VENTILATOR MUST BE ON THE BLINK!
YA'D THINK A BIG BRAIN LIKE REED COULD FIX A CRUMMY LITTLE AIR VENT! I'LL BET HE-- YEOWW! I JUST GOT ME A HOT-SEAT!!
AH HAH!!
SO YOU'RE THE WISE-GUY!
DIDJA FIGURE THAT OUT ALL BY YOURSELF, GRUESOME, OR DID SOMEONE HELP YOU?
YOU FLAMIN' FIG-HEAD!! THAT DOOR WON'T KEEP ME OUT! WHEN I'M THRU WITH YA, THERE WON'T BE ENOUGH LEFT TO LIGHT A FIRE-CRACKER!
BEN! DON'T! THAT FIRE-PROOF VAULT DOOR COST A SMALL FORTUNE!
5

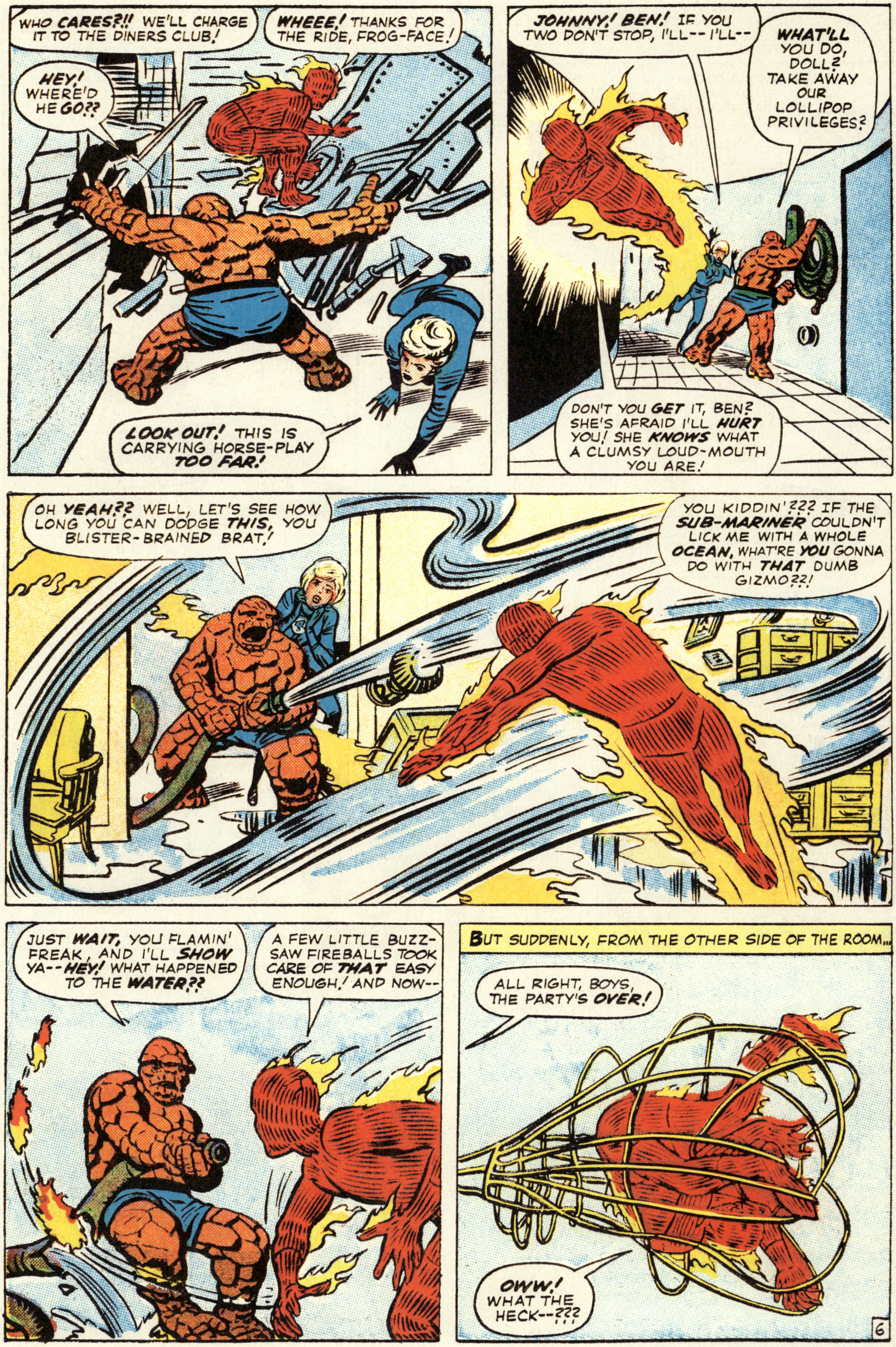
WHO CARES?!! WE'LL CHARGE IT TO THE DINERS CLUB!
WHEEE! THANKS FOR THE RIDE, FROG-FACE!
HEY! WHERE'D HE GO??
LOOK OUT! THIS IS CARRYING HORSE-PLAY TOO FAR!
JOHNNY! BEN! IF YOU TWO DON'T STOP, I'LL-- I'LL--
WHAT'LL YOU DO, DOLL? TAKE AWAY OUR LOLLIPOP PRIVILEGES?
DON'T YOU GET IT, BEN? SHE'S AFRAID I'LL HURT YOU! SHE KNOWS WHAT A CLUMSY LOUD-MOUTH YOU ARE!
OH YEAH?? WELL, LET'S SEE HOW LONG YOU CAN DODGE THIS, YOU BLISTER-BRAINED BRAT!
YOU KIDDIN'??? IF THE SUB-MARINER COULDN'T LICK ME WITH A WHOLE OCEAN, WHAT'RE YOU GONNA DO WITH THAT DUMB GIZMO??!
JUST WAIT, YOU FLAMIN' FREAK, AND I'LL SHOW YA--HEY! WHAT HAPPENED TO THE WATER??
A FEW LITTLE BUZZ-SAW FIREBALLS TOOK CARE OF THAT EASY ENOUGH! AND NOW--
BUT SUDDENLY, FROM THE OTHER SIDE OF THE ROOM...
ALL RIGHT, BOYS, THE PARTY'S OVER!
OWW! WHAT THE HECK--???
6

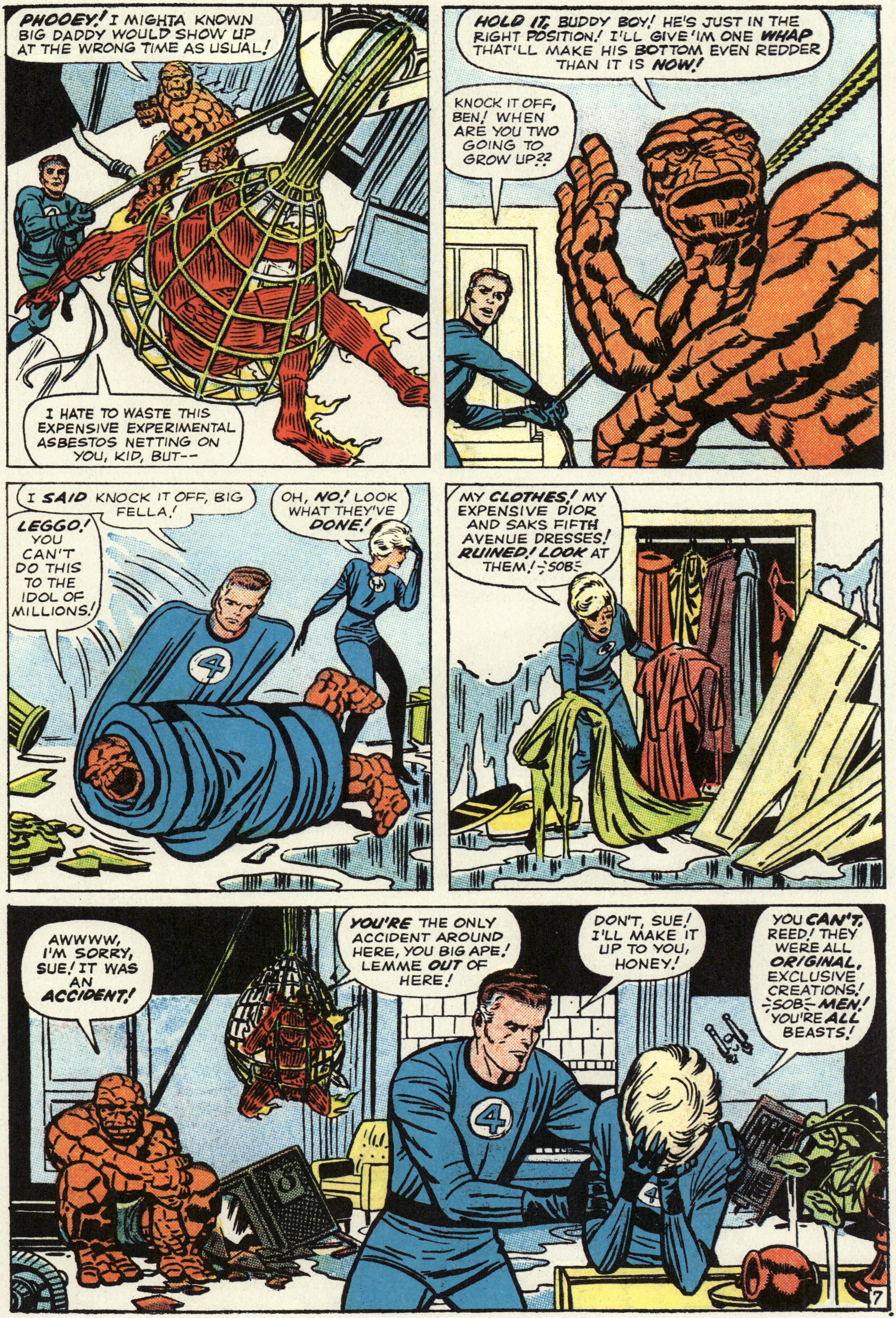
PHOOEY! I MIGHTA KNOWN BIG DADDY WOULD SHOW UP AT THE WRONG TIME AS USUAL!
I HATE TO WASTE THIS EXPENSIVE EXPERIMENTAL ASBESTOS NETTING ON YOU, KID, BUT--
HOLD IT, BUDDY BOY! HE'S JUST IN THE RIGHT POSITION! I'LL GIVE 'IM ONE WHAP THAT'LL MAKE HIS BOTTOM EVEN REDDER THAN IT IS NOW!
KNOCK IT OFF, BEN! WHEN ARE YOU TWO GOING TO GROW UP??
I SAID KNOCK IT OFF, BIG FELLA!
LEGGO! YOU CAN'T DO THIS TO THE IDOL OF MILLIONS!
OH, NO! LOOK WHAT THEY'VE DONE!
MY CLOTHES! MY EXPENSIVE DIOR AND SAKS FIFTH AVENUE DRESSES! RUINED! LOOK AT THEM! -SOB-
AWWWW, I'M SORRY, SUE! IT WAS AN ACCIDENT!
YOU'RE THE ONLY ACCIDENT AROUND HERE, YOU BIG APE! LEMME OUT OF HERE!
DON'T, SUE! I'LL MAKE IT UP TO YOU, HONEY!
YOU CAN'T, REED! THEY WERE ALL ORIGINAL, EXCLUSIVE CREATIONS! -SOB- MEN! YOU'RE ALL BEASTS!
7

FORGIVE ME, BOYS! IT--IT ISN'T LIKE ME TO GET SO EMOTIONAL!
FORGET IT, SUE! WE ALL SEEM TO BE KEYED-UP, TENSE-- I THINK WE'VE BEEN WORKING TOO HARD! WE NEED A VACATION!
HEAR THAT, TORCHY-BOY?? A VACATION!! HOW ABOUT THAT!
LOOK OUT, YOU CLUMSY LUMMOX! OWWW!
BE SERIOUS, JOHNNY! I THINK A VACATION FOR US IS A WONDERFUL IDEA!
SOME VACATION, IF THE THING COMES ALONG! BUT OKAY, I'M FOR IT!
BUT WHERE'LL WE GO? I'M NO GOL-DARNED SIGHT-SEER! I WANT A SPOT THAT SWINGS!
I THINK I HAVE THE ANSWER, KIDS!
RECENTLY ONE OF OUR NEW EXPERIMENTAL ATOMIC SUBS REPORTED THE PRESENCE OF A STRANGE SEA MONSTER IN THE MIDDLE OF THE ATLANTIC! THAT SIGHTING WAS CONFIRMED BY OTHER SUB COMMANDERS AS WELL!
"AT THE SAME TIME, A COMMERCIAL JET, ON A NEW YORK TO LONDON FLIGHT, REPORTED THE PRESENCE OF GIGANTIC, INCREDIBLE FISH COMING TO THE SURFACE IN THAT SAME AREA!"
YOU AIN'T BUYIN' THAT JAZZ, ARE YA, REED? REMEMBER, I USEDTA BE A JET-JOCKEY MYSELF, AND AFTER A LONG TOUR OF DUTY, A POLLYWOG COULD BEGIN TO LOOK LIKE A PLATTERPUSS TO THOSE GUYS!
SURE, BEN'S RIGHT--FOR ONCE! SEA MONSTERS ARE FOR COMIC BOOKS!
PERHAPS, BUT IT WILL GIVE US A CHANCE TO COMBINE BUSINESS WITH PLEASURE! FOR OUR VACATION, WE CAN TAKE A CRUISE TO THAT SAME AREA, AND SEE WHAT'S GOING ON!
8

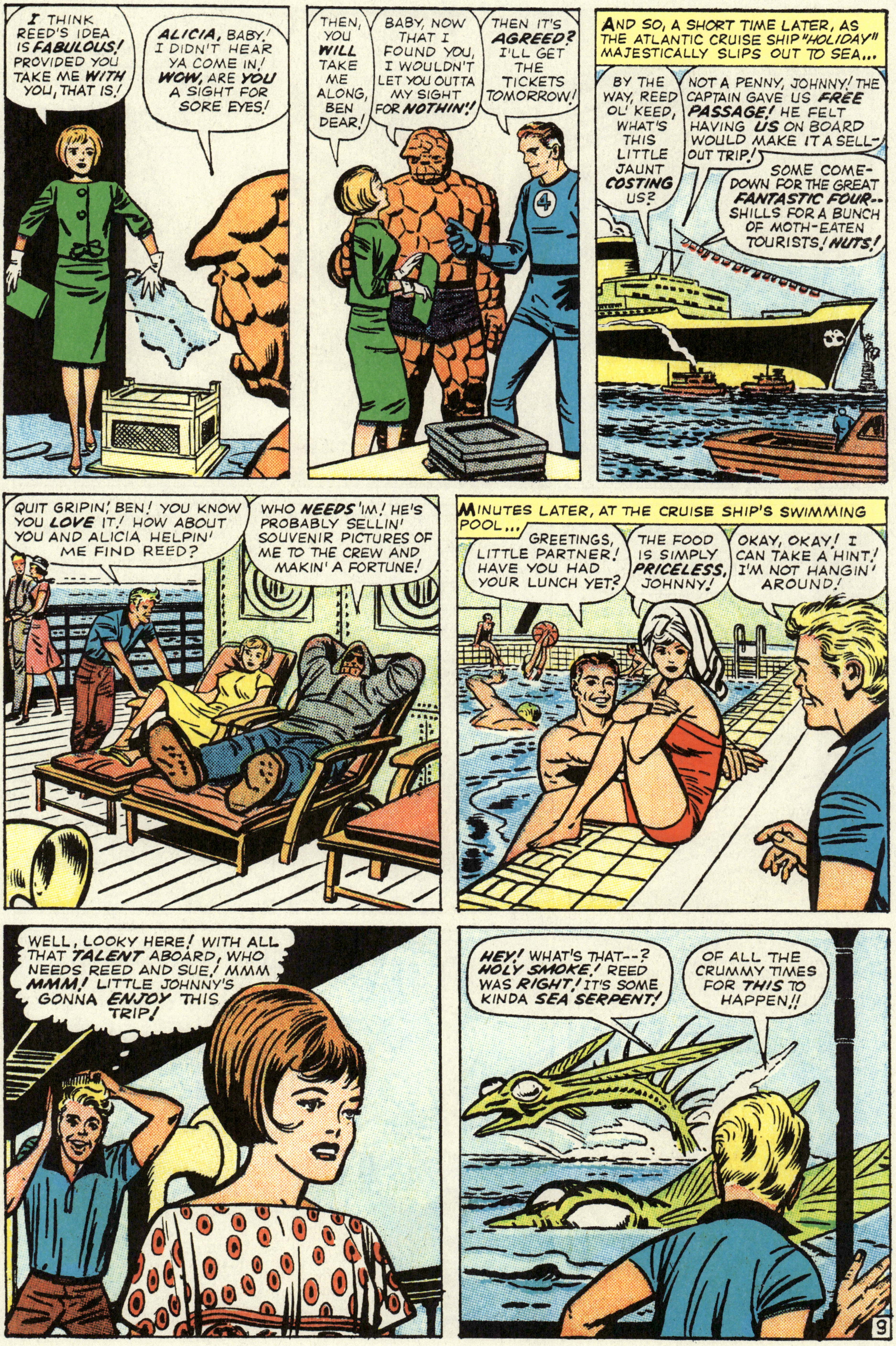
I THINK REED'S IDEA IS FABULOUS! PROVIDED YOU TAKE ME WITH YOU, THAT IS!
ALICIA, BABY! I DIDN'T HEAR YA COME IN! WOW, ARE YOU A SIGHT FOR SORE EYES!
THEN, YOU WILL TAKE ME ALONG, BEN DEAR!
BABY, NOW THAT I FOUND YOU, I WOULDN'T LET YOU OUTTA MY SIGHT FOR NOTHIN'!
THEN IT'S AGREED? I'LL GET THE TICKETS TOMORROW!
AND SO, A SHORT TIME LATER, AS THE ATLANTIC CRUISE SHIP "HOLIDAY" MAJESTICALLY SLIPS OUT TO SEA...
BY THE WAY, REED OL' KEED, WHAT'S THIS LITTLE JAUNT COSTING US?
NOT A PENNY, JOHNNY! THE CAPTAIN GAVE US FREE PASSAGE! HE FELT HAVING US ON BOARD WOULD MAKE IT A SELL-OUT TRIP!
SOME COME-DOWN FOR THE GREAT FANTASTIC FOUR-- SHILLS FOR A BUNCH OF MOTH-EATEN TOURISTS! NUTS!
QUIT GRIPIN', BEN! YOU KNOW YOU LOVE IT! HOW ABOUT YOU AND ALICIA HELPIN' ME FIND REED?
WHO NEEDS 'IM! HE'S PROBABLY SELLIN' SOUVENIR PICTURES OF ME TO THE CREW AND MAKIN' A FORTUNE!
MINUTES LATER, AT THE CRUISE SHIP'S SWIMMING POOL...
GREETINGS, LITTLE PARTNER! HAVE YOU HAD YOUR LUNCH YET?
THE FOOD IS SIMPLY PRICELESS, JOHNNY!
OKAY, OKAY! I CAN TAKE A HINT! I'M NOT HANGIN' AROUND!
WELL, LOOKY HERE! WITH ALL THAT TALENT ABOARD, WHO NEEDS REED AND SUE! MMM MMM! LITTLE JOHNNY'S GONNA ENJOY THIS TRIP!
HEY! WHAT'S THAT--? HOLY SMOKE! REED WAS RIGHT! IT'S SOME KINDA SEA SERPENT!
OF ALL THE CRUMMY TIMES FOR THIS TO HAPPEN!!
9

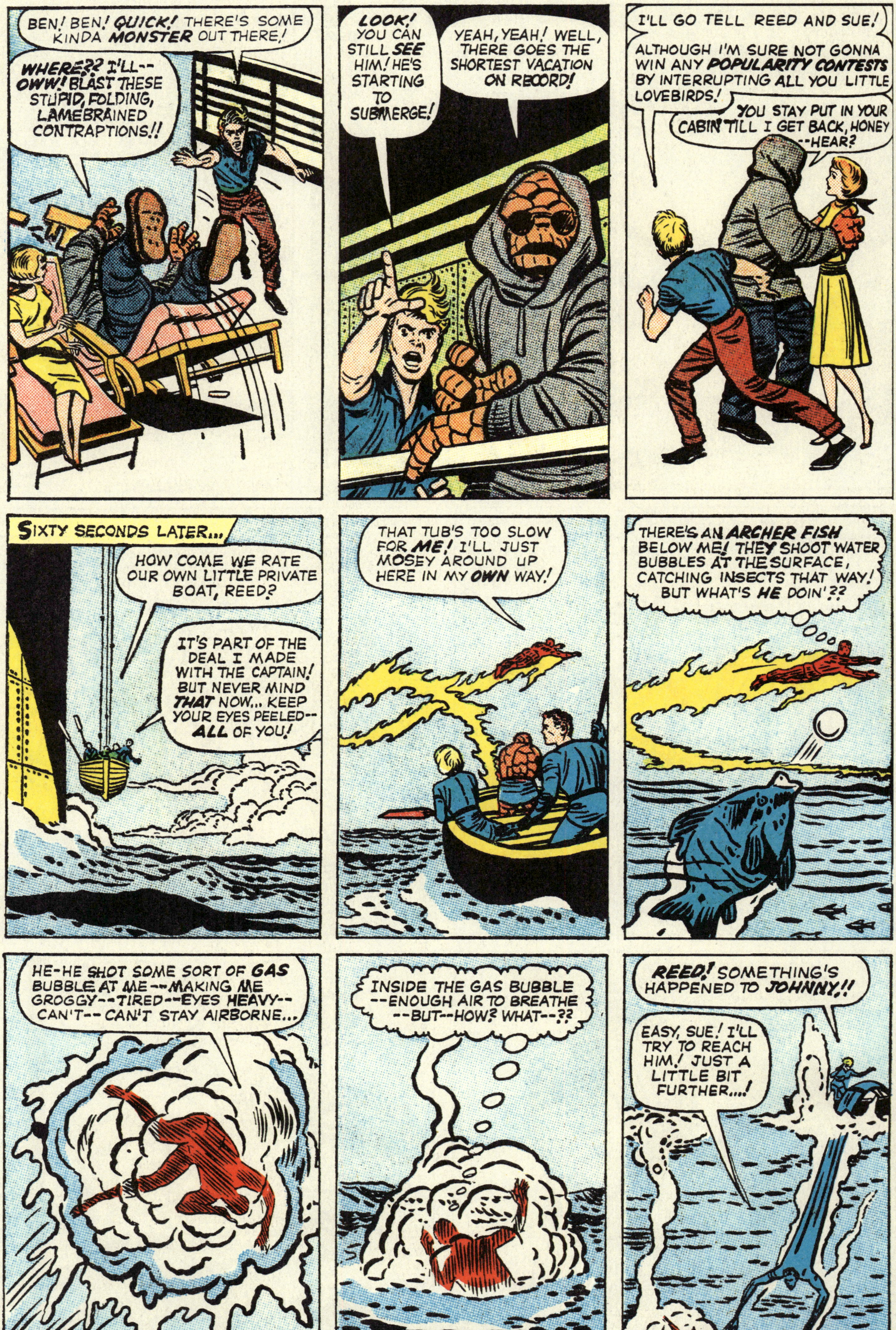

BEN! BEN! QUICK! THERE'S SOME KINDA MONSTER OUT THERE!
WHERE?? I'LL-- OWW! BLAST THESE STUPID, FOLDING, LAMEBRAINED CONTRAPTIONS!!
LOOK! YOU CAN STILL SEE HIM! HE'S STARTING TO SUBMERGE!
YEAH, YEAH! WELL, THERE GOES THE SHORTEST VACATION ON RECORD!
I'LL GO TELL REED AND SUE!
ALTHOUGH I'M SURE NOT GONNA WIN ANY POPULARITY CONTESTS BY INTERRUPTING ALL YOU LITTLE LOVEBIRDS!
YOU STAY PUT IN YOUR CABIN TILL I GET BACK, HONEY --HEAR?
SIXTY SECONDS LATER...
HOW COME WE RATE OUR OWN LITTLE PRIVATE BOAT, REED?
IT'S PART OF THE DEAL I MADE WITH THE CAPTAIN! BUT NEVER MIND THAT NOW... KEEP YOUR EYES PEELED-- ALL OF YOU!
THAT TUB'S TOO SLOW FOR ME! I'LL JUST MOSEY AROUND UP HERE IN MY OWN WAY!
THERE'S AN ARCHER FISH BELOW ME! THEY SHOOT WATER BUBBLES AT THE SURFACE, CATCHING INSECTS THAT WAY! BUT WHAT'S HE DOIN'??
HE-HE SHOT SOME SORT OF GAS BUBBLE AT ME--MAKING ME GROGGY--TIRED--EYES HEAVY-- CAN'T-- CAN'T STAY AIRBORNE...
INSIDE THE GAS BUBBLE --ENOUGH AIR TO BREATHE --BUT--HOW? WHAT--??
REED! SOMETHING'S HAPPENED TO JOHNNY!!
EASY, SUE! I'LL TRY TO REACH HIM! JUST A LITTLE BIT FURTHER....!
10

BUT, AT THAT MOMENT, THE BRILLIANT LEADER OF THE COLORFUL QUARTET IS SWEPT UP BY AN OXYGEN-FILLED, GIANT-SIZED MAGNETIC SEA SHELL!
SWOOOOSH
SOME UNDERSEA INTELLIGENCE KNOWS WE'RE HERE--AND IS ATTACKING US!!
WHILE ON THE SURFACE, A HUGE, SQUID-LIKE FISH EJECTS A LARGE MEMBRANOUS SACK WHICH COMPLETELY ENCASES THE ROWBOAT CONTAINING BEN AND SUE!
THIS OVERSIZED LAUNDRY-BAG AINT GONNA HOLD US INSIDE OF IT!
IT--IT ALL HAPPENED SO QUICKLY!
FOR THE LUVVA PETE! WE'RE BEIN' PULLED UNDER THE WATER INSIDE THIS GIZMO, BOAT AND ALL!
DON'T TRY TO TEAR IT OPEN, BEN! THERE'S AIR INSIDE IT! IF IT SHOULD RIP, WE'LL DROWN!
AND, SURROUNDED BY HIS HIGHEST-RANKING AIDES, A SILENT, REGAL FIGURE WAITS CONFIDENTLY BELOW!
YOUR MANEUVER HAS SUCCEEDED, YOUR HIGHNESS!
OF COURSE! NOW HAVE THEM PLACED INSIDE THE PLASTI-DOME COMMUNICATOR SO THAT I MAY ADDRESS THEM!
SO! WE MEET ONCE AGAIN! WELCOME, TO THE SOVEREIGN EMPIRE OF ATLANTIS!
IT'S SUB-MARINER! I HAD A FEELING YOU WERE BEHIND ALL THIS!
CONSIDER YOUR WORDS, SURFACEMEN! SPEAK WITH RESPECT WHEN ADDRESSING HIS ROYAL HIGHNESS, NAMOR THE FIRST!
YEAH? WELL, JUST WAIT! WHEN I GET THRU WITH 'IM, IT'LL BE NAMOR THE LAST!
11

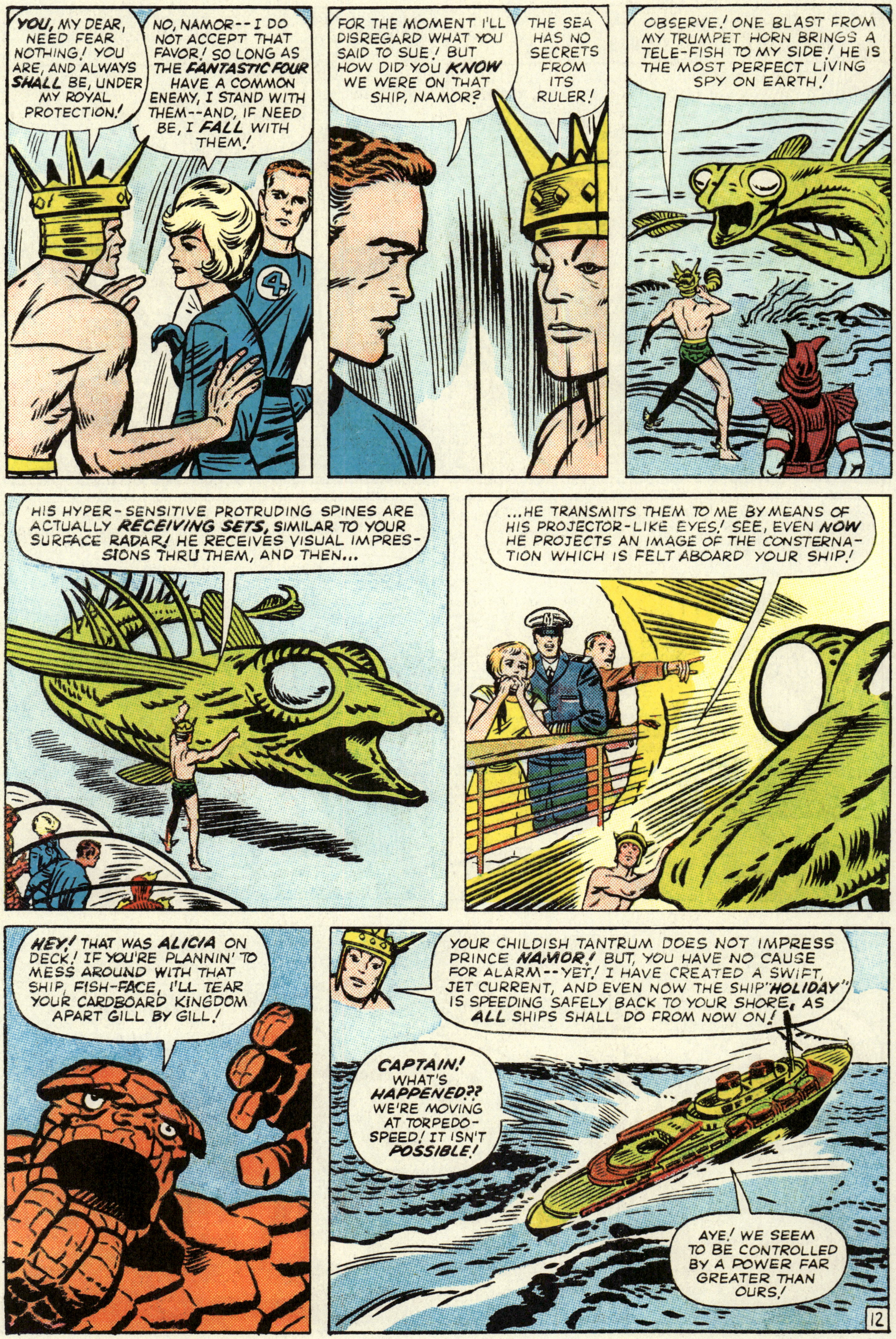
YOU, MY DEAR, NEED FEAR NOTHING! YOU ARE, AND ALWAYS SHALL BE, UNDER MY ROYAL PROTECTION!
NO, NAMOR--I DO NOT ACCEPT THAT FAVOR! SO LONG AS THE FANTASTIC FOUR HAVE A COMMON ENEMY, I STAND WITH THEM--AND, IF NEED BE, I FALL WITH THEM!
FOR THE MOMENT I'LL DISREGARD WHAT YOU SAID TO SUE! BUT HOW DID YOU KNOW WE WERE ON THAT SHIP, NAMOR?
THE SEA HAS NO SECRETS FROM ITS RULER!
OBSERVE! ONE BLAST FROM MY TRUMPET HORN BRINGS A TELE-FISH TO MY SIDE! HE IS THE MOST PERFECT LIVING SPY ON EARTH!
HIS HYPER-SENSITIVE PROTRUDING SPINES ARE ACTUALLY RECEIVING SETS, SIMILAR TO YOUR SURFACE RADAR! HE RECEIVES VISUAL IMPRESSIONS THRU THEM, AND THEN...
...HE TRANSMITS THEM TO ME BY MEANS OF HIS PROJECTOR-LIKE EYES! SEE, EVEN NOW HE PROJECTS AN IMAGE OF THE CONSTERNATION WHICH IS FELT ABOARD YOUR SHIP!
HEY! THAT WAS ALICIA ON DECK! IF YOU'RE PLANNIN' TO MESS AROUND WITH THAT SHIP, FISH-FACE, I'LL TEAR YOUR CARDBOARD KINGDOM APART GILL BY GILL!
YOUR CHILDISH TANTRUM DOES NOT IMPRESS PRINCE NAMOR! BUT, YOU HAVE NO CAUSE FOR ALARM--YET! I HAVE CREATED A SWIFT JET CURRENT, AND EVEN NOW THE SHIP "HOLIDAY" IS SPEEDING SAFELY BACK TO YOUR SHORE, AS ALL SHIPS SHALL DO FROM NOW ON!
CAPTAIN! WHAT'S HAPPENED?? WE'RE MOVING AT TORPEDO-SPEED! IT ISN'T POSSIBLE!
AYE! WE SEEM TO BE CONTROLLED BY A POWER FAR GREATER THAN OURS!

AS FOR YOU, I COMMANDED THE MONSTERS OF THE DEEP TO REVEAL THEMSELVES AT SEA, KNOWING YOU WOULD COME TO INVESTIGATE! FOR I HAVE A MESSAGE TO BE DELIVERED TO THE SURFACE WORLD-- AND I WANT YOU TO DELIVER IT! THE AIR-BREATHING HUMANS WILL BELIEVE WHAT THEY ARE TOLD BY THE FANTASTIC FOUR!
IT WOULDA BEEN CHEAPER TO SEND A TELEGRAM, YOU WATER-LOGGED HAM!
QUIET, BEN! LET HIM FINISH!
YOU MUST TELL THE UNITED NATIONS, THAT I, PRINCE NAMOR, PROCLAIM THE SEVEN SEAS AND THE SKIES ABOVE THEM AS MY IMPERIAL DOMAIN! FROM THIS DAY FORWARD, NO SURFACEMAN'S SHIP OR AIRCRAFT MAY TRESPASS ON MY KINGDOM!
NOW YOU WILL BE PLACED WITHIN A TRANSPARENT WATER-ROCKET, AND RETURNED TO AMERICA TO DELIVER MY ULTIMATUM! THE AUDIENCE IS ENDED!
NAMOR! THIS COULD MEAN WAR BETWEEN OUR TWO RACES!
YOU CAN'T REASON WITH HIM NOW, SUE! WE'LL HAVE TO BIDE OUR TIME!
I'D LIKE TO REASON WITH 'IM --WITH A BRICK!
HOLD ON TO THIS CENTER ROD, ALL OF YOU! THEY'RE FORCING TONS OF WATER PRESSURE UNDER THIS CYLINDER, TO MAKE IT RISE!
HEY! WHAT IS THIS BLAMED THINGAMAJIG??
I FEEL LIKE SOME KINDA NUT INSIDE HERE!
DON'T MOCK THEIR TECHNOLOGY, JOHNNY! IN THEIR OWN WAY, THEY SEEM TO BE AS HIGHLY ADVANCED AS WE! PERHAPS-- AND IT IS A FRIGHTENING THOUGHT-- PERHAPS EVEN MORE SO!
SEE? WHERE WE USE FLUID ROCKET PROPELLENT, THEY USE HIGHLY-CONCENTRATED WATER-PRESSURE POWER!
REED! WHAT'S HAPPENING NOW?? WE'LL DROWN!!
DON'T PANIC!! WE'LL BE ALRIGHT! THEY SIMPLY USE AN EXPANDING POD OF WATER TO ENVELOP US AND CUSHION THE SHOCK OF ORBITAL ENTRY!
YOU MEAN IT'LL SAVE US IF IT DOESN'T KILL US FIRST, HUH?
WHAT AN EGG-HEAD! REED, IF THEY EVER STRAPPED YA IN THE ELECTRIC CHAIR, YOU'D PROBABLY BE EXPLAININ' HOW THE BLAMED THING WORKS WHILE THEY PULLED THE SWITCH!
SORRY, BEN-- GUESS I DO GET LONG-WINDED AT TIMES! BUT I NEVER DREAMED NAMOR'S UNDERSEA PEOPLE WERE SO TECHNOLOGICALLY ADVANCED! THIS COULD MEAN THE GREATEST DANGER THAN THE HUMAN RACE HAS EVER FACED! IT COULD BE THE END OF HOMO SAPIENS' DOMINATION OF EARTH!
13

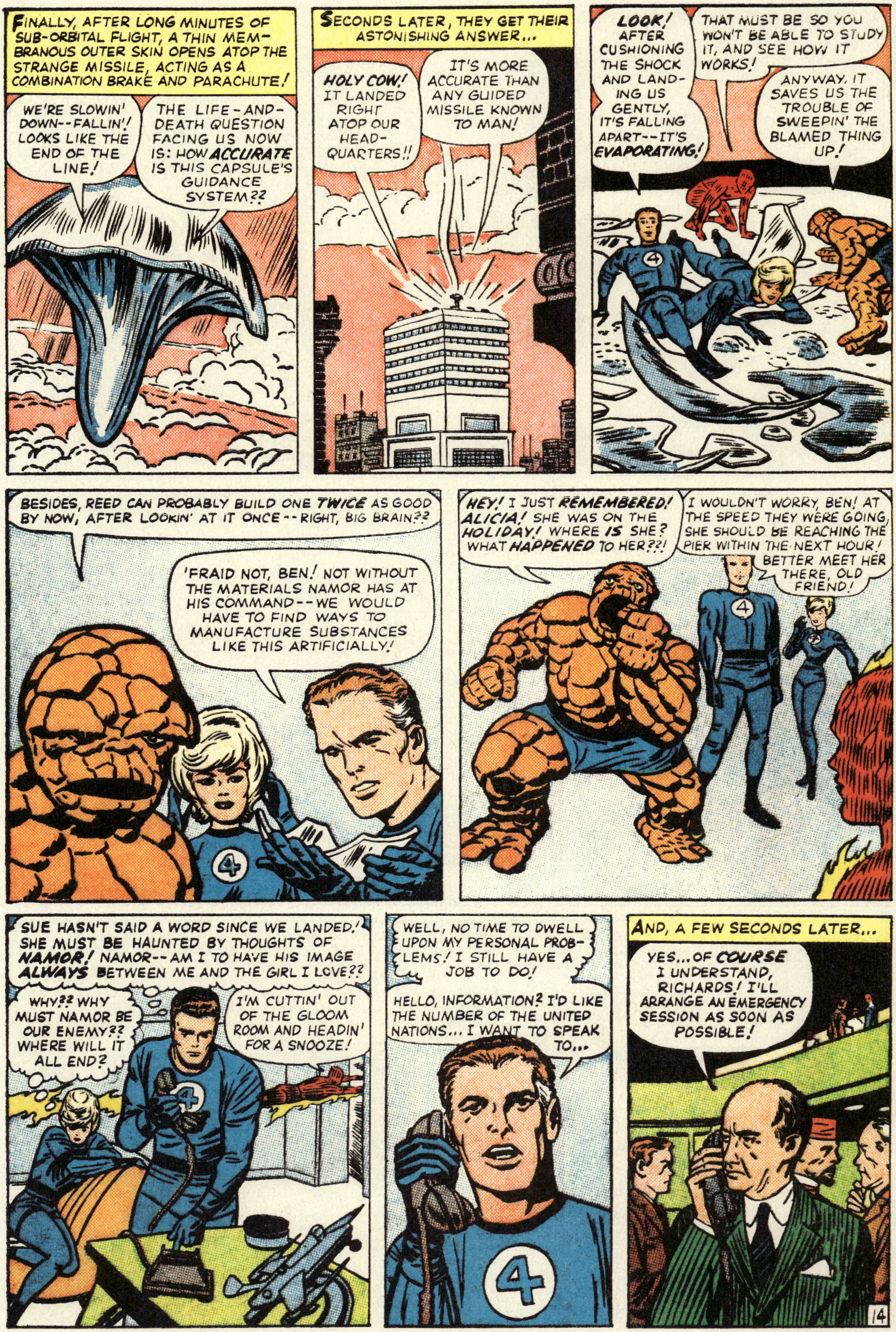
FINALLY, AFTER LONG MINUTES OF SUB-ORBITAL FLIGHT, A THIN MEMBRANOUS OUTER SKIN OPENS ATOP THE STRANGE MISSILE, ACTING AS A COMBINATION BRAKE AND PARACHUTE!
WE'RE SLOWIN' DOWN--FALLIN'! LOOKS LIKE THE END OF THE LINE!
THE LIFE-AND-DEATH QUESTION FACING US NOW IS: HOW ACCURATE IS THIS CAPSULE'S GUIDANCE SYSTEM??
SECONDS LATER, THEY GET THEIR ASTONISHING ANSWER...
HOLY COW! IT LANDED RIGHT ATOP OUR HEAD-QUARTERS!!
IT'S MORE ACCURATE THAN ANY GUIDED MISSILE KNOWN TO MAN!
LOOK! AFTER CUSHIONING THE SHOCK AND LANDING US GENTLY, IT'S FALLING APART--IT'S EVAPORATING!
THAT MUST BE SO YOU WON'T BE ABLE TO STUDY IT, AND SEE HOW IT WORKS!
ANYWAY, IT SAVES US THE TROUBLE OF SWEEPIN' THE BLAMED THING UP!
BESIDES, REED CAN PROBABLY BUILD ONE TWICE AS GOOD BY NOW, AFTER LOOKIN' AT IT ONCE--RIGHT, BIG BRAIN??
'FRAID NOT, BEN! NOT WITHOUT THE MATERIALS NAMOR HAS AT HIS COMMAND--WE WOULD HAVE TO FIND WAYS TO MANUFACTURE SUBSTANCES LIKE THIS ARTIFICIALLY!
HEY! I JUST REMEMBERED! ALICIA! SHE WAS ON THE HOLIDAY! WHERE IS SHE? WHAT HAPPENED TO HER??!
I WOULDN'T WORRY, BEN! AT THE SPEED THEY WERE GOING, SHE SHOULD BE REACHING THE PIER WITHIN THE NEXT HOUR!
BETTER MEET HER THERE, OLD FRIEND!
SUE HASN'T SAID A WORD SINCE WE LANDED! SHE MUST BE HAUNTED BY THOUGHTS OF NAMOR! NAMOR--AM I TO HAVE HIS IMAGE ALWAYS BETWEEN ME AND THE GIRL I LOVE??
WHY?? WHY MUST NAMOR BE OUR ENEMY?? WHERE WILL IT ALL END?
I'M CUTTIN' OUT OF THE GLOOM ROOM AND HEADIN' FOR A SNOOZE!
WELL, NO TIME TO DWELL UPON MY PERSONAL PROBLEMS! I STILL HAVE A JOB TO DO!
HELLO, INFORMATION? I'D LIKE THE NUMBER OF THE UNITED NATIONS... I WANT TO SPEAK TO...
AND, A FEW SECONDS LATER...
YES...OF COURSE I UNDERSTAND, RICHARDS! I'LL ARRANGE AN EMERGENCY SESSION AS SOON AS POSSIBLE!
14

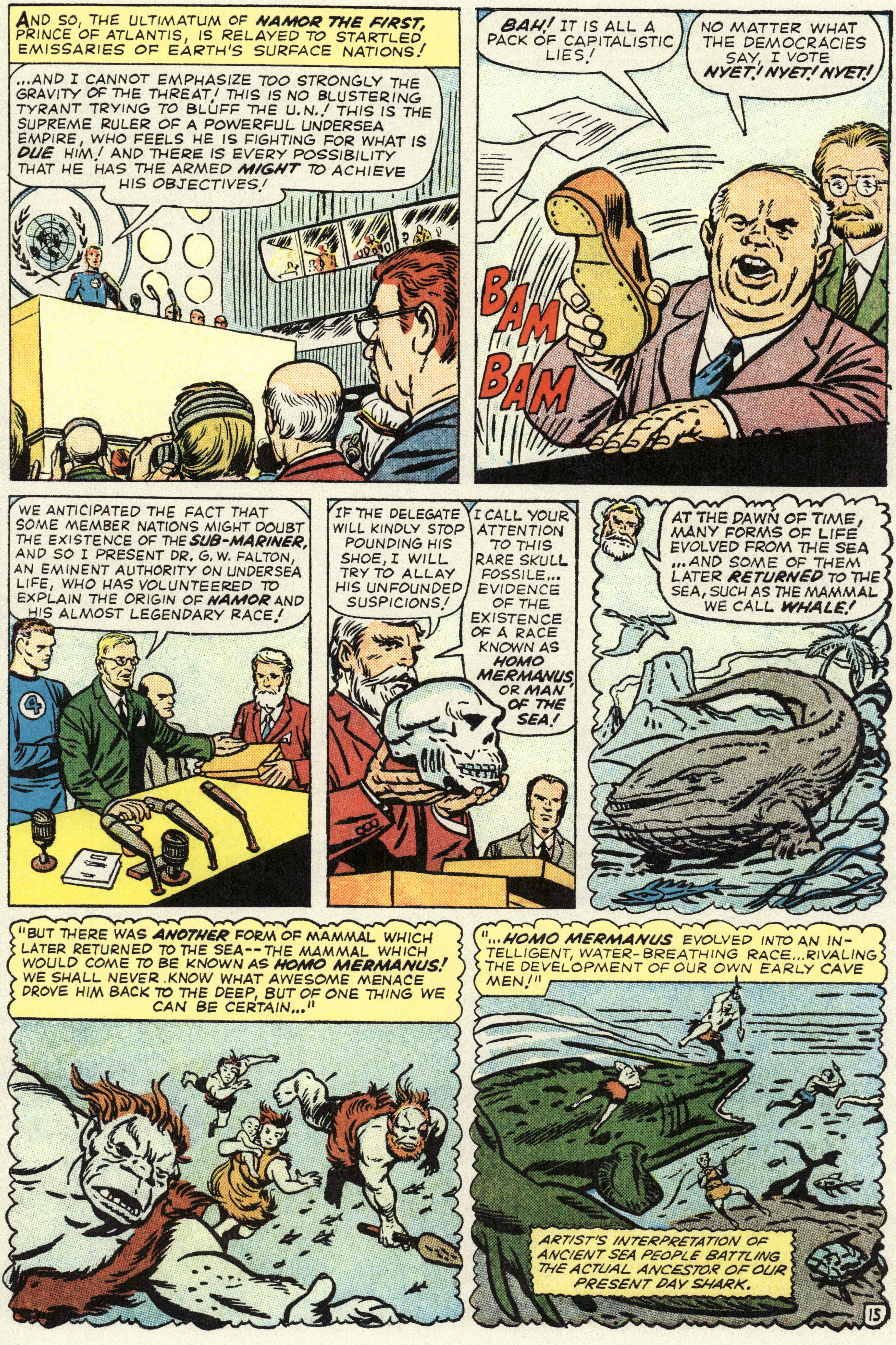
AND SO, THE ULTIMATUM OF NAMOR THE FIRST, PRINCE OF ATLANTIS, IS RELAYED TO STARTLED EMISSARIES OF EARTH'S SURFACE NATIONS!
...AND I CANNOT EMPHASIZE TOO STRONGLY THE GRAVITY OF THE THREAT! THIS IS NO BLUSTERING TYRANT TRYING TO BLUFF THE U.N.! THIS IS THE SUPREME RULER OF A POWERFUL UNDERSEA EMPIRE, WHO FEELS HE IS FIGHTING FOR WHAT IS DUE HIM! AND THERE IS EVERY POSSIBILITY THAT HE HAS THE ARMED MIGHT TO ACHIEVE HIS OBJECTIVES!
BAH! IT IS ALL A PACK OF CAPITALISTIC LIES!
NO MATTER WHAT THE DEMOCRACIES SAY, I VOTE NYET! NYET! NYET!
BAM BAM
WE ANTICIPATED THE FACT THAT SOME MEMBER NATIONS MIGHT DOUBT THE EXISTENCE OF THE SUB-MARINER, AND SO I PRESENT DR. G. W. FALTON, AN EMINENT AUTHORITY ON UNDERSEA LIFE, WHO HAS VOLUNTEERED TO EXPLAIN THE ORIGIN OF NAMOR AND HIS ALMOST LEGENDARY RACE!
IF THE DELEGATE WILL KINDLY STOP POUNDING HIS SHOE, I WILL TRY TO ALLAY HIS UNFOUNDED SUSPICIONS!
I CALL YOUR ATTENTION TO THIS RARE SKULL FOSSILE... EVIDENCE OF THE EXISTENCE OF A RACE KNOWN AS HOMO MERMANUS, OR MAN OF THE SEA!
AT THE DAWN OF TIME, MANY FORMS OF LIFE EVOLVED FROM THE SEA ...AND SOME OF THEM LATER RETURNED TO THE SEA, SUCH AS THE MAMMAL WE CALL WHALE!
"BUT THERE WAS ANOTHER FORM OF MAMMAL WHICH LATER RETURNED TO THE SEA--THE MAMMAL WHICH WOULD COME TO BE KNOWN AS HOMO MERMANUS! WE SHALL NEVER KNOW WHAT AWESOME MENACE DROVE HIM BACK TO THE DEEP, BUT OF ONE THING WE CAN BE CERTAIN..."
"...HOMO MERMANUS EVOLVED INTO AN INTELLIGENT, WATER-BREATHING RACE...RIVALING THE DEVELOPMENT OF OUR OWN EARLY CAVE MEN!"
ARTIST'S INTERPRETATION OF ANCIENT SEA PEOPLE BATTLING THE ACTUAL ANCESTOR OF OUR PRESENT DAY SHARK.
15

"CENTURIES PASSED, AND, AS THE SURFACE CAVE MEN FOUND DEEP, SHELTERED CAVES FOR THEIR MUTUAL PROTECTION, SO DID HOMO MERMANUS FIND HUGE, UNBREAKABLE SHELLS WHICH THEY CARRIED AS SHIELDS ON THEIR NOMADIC WANDERINGS... SHIELDS TO SHELTER THEM FROM THE INCONCEIVABLE DANGERS OF THE DEEP."
"AND, STILL PARALLELING THE DEVELOPMENT OF SURFACE HUMANS, THE UNDERSEA DWELLERS SOON LEARNED TO MAKE ALLIES OF CERTAIN FORMS OF MARINE LIFE, TO DOMESTICATE THEM AND TRAIN THEM, AS MAN WAS DOING ON SHORE WITH HORSES, DOGS, AND CAMELS."
"THEN, IN TIME, HOMO MERMANUS STUMBLED UPON WEAPONS OF WAR... AND THERE TOO, ALAS, THEIR HISTORY DUPLICATED OUR OWN!"
16

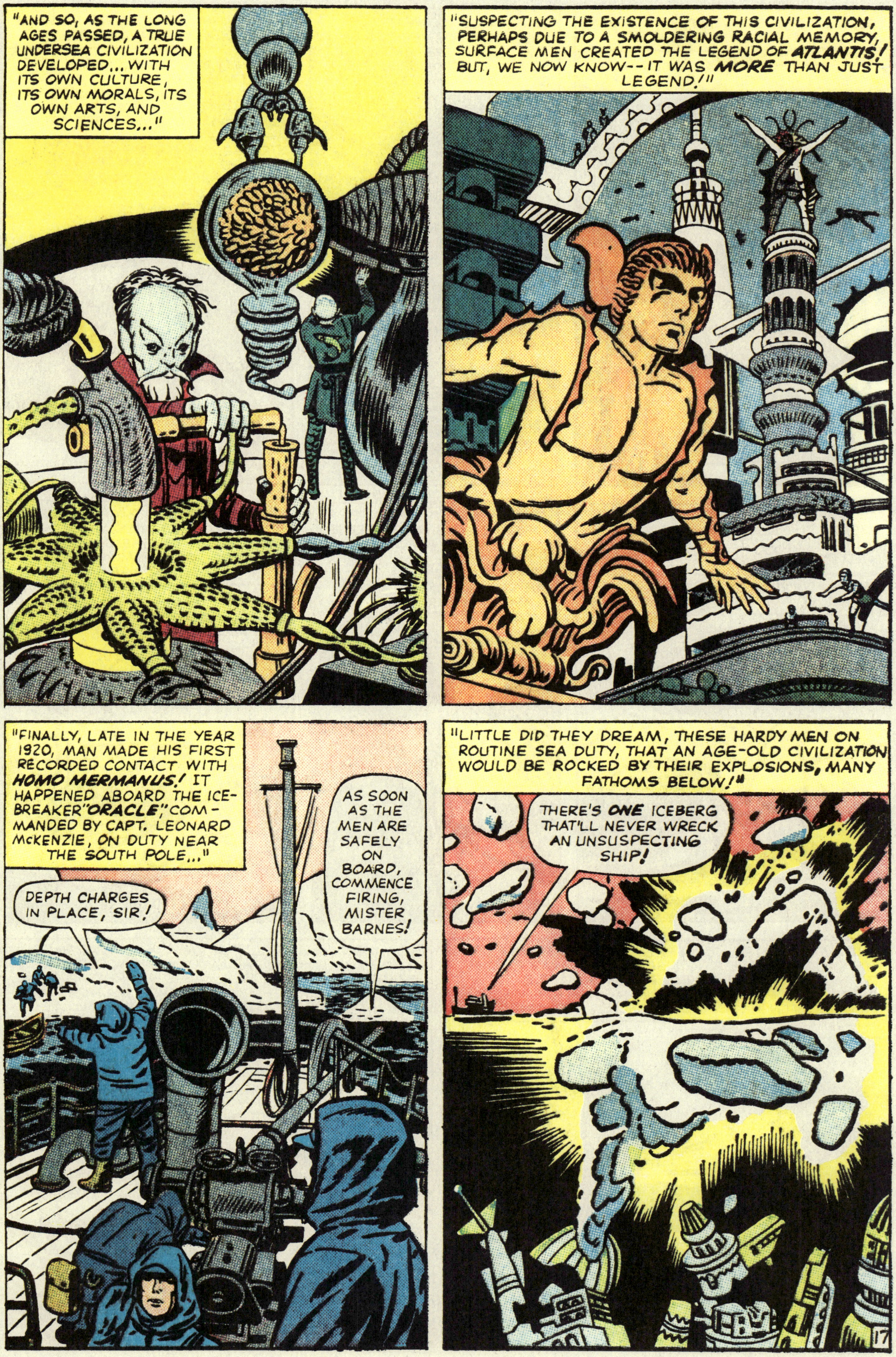
"AND SO, AS THE LONG AGES PASSED, A TRUE UNDERSEA CIVILIZATION DEVELOPED... WITH ITS OWN CULTURE, ITS OWN MORALS, ITS OWN ARTS, AND SCIENCES..."
"SUSPECTING THE EXISTENCE OF THIS CIVILIZATION, PERHAPS DUE TO A SMOLDERING RACIAL MEMORY, SURFACE MEN CREATED THE LEGEND OF ATLANTIS! BUT, WE NOW KNOW-- IT WAS MORE THAN JUST LEGEND!"
"FINALLY, LATE IN THE YEAR 1920, MAN MADE HIS FIRST RECORDED CONTACT WITH HOMO MERMANUS! IT HAPPENED ABOARD THE ICE-BREAKER "ORACLE," COMMANDED BY CAPT. LEONARD McKENZIE, ON DUTY NEAR THE SOUTH POLE..."
AS SOON AS THE MEN ARE SAFELY ON BOARD, COMMENCE FIRING, MISTER BARNES!
DEPTH CHARGES IN PLACE, SIR!
"LITTLE DID THEY DREAM, THESE HARDY MEN ON ROUTINE SEA DUTY, THAT AN AGE-OLD CIVILIZATION WOULD BE ROCKED BY THEIR EXPLOSIONS, MANY FATHOMS BELOW!"
THERE'S ONE ICEBERG THAT'LL NEVER WRECK AN UNSUSPECTING SHIP!
17

"PUZZLED BY THE SEVERITY OF THE BLAST, THE KING SENT FOR HIS DAUGHTER, PRINCESS FEN...!"
MY DEAR, I WISH YOU TO SEND A SCOUTING EXPEDITION TO INVESTIGATE THAT STRANGE EXPLOSION!
AS YOU COMMAND, MY FATHER!
THERE IS NO NEED FOR A SCOUTING PARTY! FOR SUCH A SIMPLE MISSION, I, MYSELF, SHALL MAKE THE ASCENT!
"BEING ABLE TO BREATHE OUT OF THE WATER FOR PERIODS UP TO FIVE HOURS, THE STRONG-WILLED PRINCESS SPIED THE SILENT SHIP, AND STEALTHILY CLIMBED ABOARD!"
I MUST LEARN WHAT MANNER OF CREATURES INHABIT THIS STRANGE VESSEL!
"BUT, WITHIN MINUTES, HER PRESENCE WAS DISCOVERED, AND THEN..."
IT DON'T MAKE SENSE, CAPTAIN! SHE OUGHTTA BE FROZEN SOLID IN THAT GETUP, BUT SHE AINT! AND LOOK AT THE COLOR OF HER SKIN! AND NO ONE CAN SAVVY THE LINGO SHE TALKS!
STRANGE... SHE SEEMS TO BE HAVING DIFFICULTY BREATHING! SHE KEEPS LOOKING AT THE WATER--AS THOUGH SHE WANTS TO RETURN!
"AS TIME PASSED, PRINCESS FEN CONQUERED THE HUMAN'S LANGUAGE--AND SHE CONQUERED EVEN MORE--SHE CONQUERED THE CAPTAIN'S HEART!"
SHE'S SO LOVELY... SO GENTLE... SO FRAGILE!
I SHOULD RETURN TO THE DEEP, BUT I CANNOT! I CANNOT LEAVE--HIM!
FEN, MY LOVELY STRANGER--MY MYSTERIOUS ENCHANTRESS--I MUST ASK YOU--
I KNOW YOUR QUESTION, BELOVED--AND MY HEART ANSWERS "YES"!
"AND SO, THE TWO RACES, SEPARATED FOR COUNTLESS AGES, WERE UNITED ONCE MORE--BY THE SIMPLE, UNIVERSAL CEREMONY OF--MARRIAGE!"
TILL DEATH US DO PART!
"BUT, WEEKS LATER, CONCERNED BY THE ABSENCE OF HIS DAUGHTER, THE KING DISPATCHED A WAR PARTY TO THE SURFACE! IN THE ENSUING BATTLE, CAPTAIN McKENZIE WAS SLAIN, AS THE HELPLESS PRINCESS FEN MERCIFULLY FAINTED INTO UNCONSCIOUSNESS!"
"HOWEVER, AS A RESULT OF THIS TRAGIC MARRIAGE, A SON WAS BORN TO THE GRIEVING PRINCESS! A NEW BREED OF UNDERSEA MAN--ABLE TO BREATHE BOTH AIR AND WATER! THIS WAS PRINCE NAMOR, THE SUB-MARINER, POSSIBLY THE FIRST KNOWN MUTANT OF OUR TIME! NOBLE, POWERFUL, DEDICATED... THE ONLY TRUE HUMAN AMPHIBIAN ON EARTH!"
18

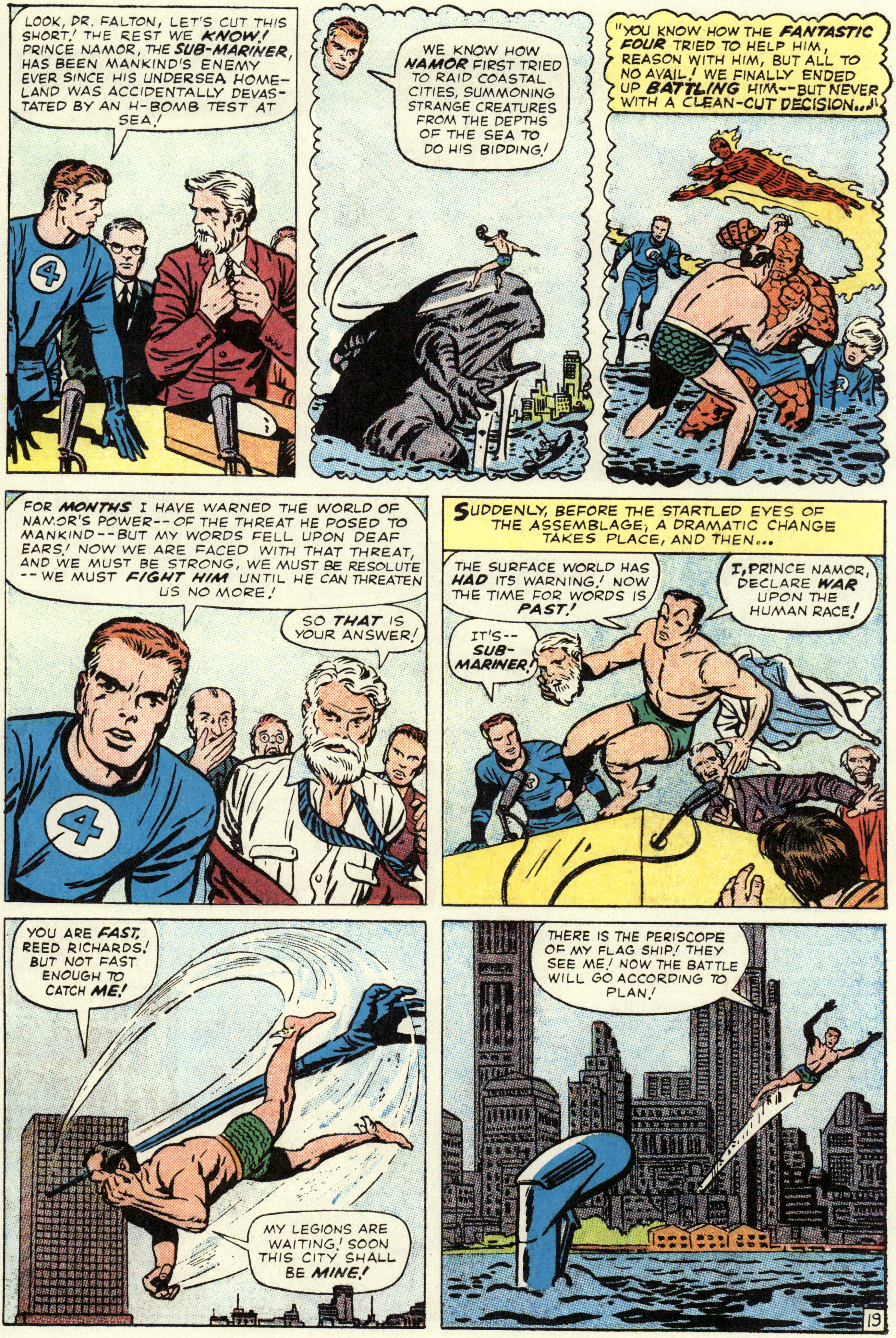
LOOK, DR. FALTON, LET'S CUT THIS SHORT! THE REST WE KNOW! PRINCE NAMOR, THE SUB-MARINER, HAS BEEN MANKIND'S ENEMY EVER SINCE HIS UNDERSEA HOME-LAND WAS ACCIDENTALLY DEVAS-TATED BY AN H-BOMB TEST AT SEA!
WE KNOW HOW NAMOR FIRST TRIED TO RAID COASTAL CITIES, SUMMONING STRANGE CREATURES FROM THE DEPTHS OF THE SEA TO DO HIS BIDDING!
"YOU KNOW HOW THE FANTASTIC FOUR TRIED TO HELP HIM, REASON WITH HIM, BUT ALL TO NO AVAIL! WE FINALLY ENDED UP BATTLING HIM--BUT NEVER WITH A CLEAN-CUT DECISION..."
FOR MONTHS I HAVE WARNED THE WORLD OF NAMOR'S POWER--OF THE THREAT HE POSED TO MANKIND--BUT MY WORDS FELL UPON DEAF EARS! NOW WE ARE FACED WITH THAT THREAT, AND WE MUST BE STRONG, WE MUST BE RESOLUTE --WE MUST FIGHT HIM UNTIL HE CAN THREATEN US NO MORE!
SO THAT IS YOUR ANSWER!
SUDDENLY, BEFORE THE STARTLED EYES OF THE ASSEMBLAGE, A DRAMATIC CHANGE TAKES PLACE, AND THEN...
THE SURFACE WORLD HAS HAD ITS WARNING! NOW THE TIME FOR WORDS IS PAST!
I, PRINCE NAMOR, DECLARE WAR UPON THE HUMAN RACE!
IT'S--SUB-MARINER!
YOU ARE FAST, REED RICHARDS! BUT NOT FAST ENOUGH TO CATCH ME!
MY LEGIONS ARE WAITING! SOON THIS CITY SHALL BE MINE!
THERE IS THE PERISCOPE OF MY FLAG SHIP! THEY SEE ME! NOW THE BATTLE WILL GO ACCORDING TO PLAN!
19

AT A SIGNAL FROM NAMOR, HIS IMPERIAL LANDING BARGES RISE TO THE SURFACE, UNLOADING THEIR DREAD CONTENTS UPON THE UNPREPARED STREETS OF THE WORLD'S GREATEST CITY!
THE ELEMENT OF SURPRISE IS WITH US! NEW YORK WILL BE OURS BEFORE THEY KNOW WHAT HAS HAPPENED!
DISPERSE!! TAKE YOUR POSITIONS!
HEY--LOOK!! WHAT GIVES?? ARE THEY FILMIN' A MOVIE, OR SOMETHING?
-GULP- THIS AINT A MOVIE, PAL! THIS IS FOR REAL!
WITHIN MINUTES, NAMOR'S SHOCK TROOPS ARE EVERYWHERE!
FIRST PHASE OF INVASION COMPLETED! NO CASUALTIES!
TAKEN COMPLETELY BY SURPRISE--HOPELESSLY OUTNUMBERED--NEW YORK'S POLICE OFFICERS FIND THEMSELVES PRISONERS OF A HOSTILE ARMY BEFORE A SHOT CAN BE FIRED!
THIS IS THE LAST OF THEM!
LOCK THEM IN THOSE CELLS!
BY EARLY AFTERNOON, THE IMPOSSIBLE IS AN ACCOMPLISHED FACT! NAMOR'S LEGIONS ARE IN COMPLETE CONTROL OF THE CAPTIVE CITY!
ROYAL
2 BIG 2
FEATURES
TODAY---

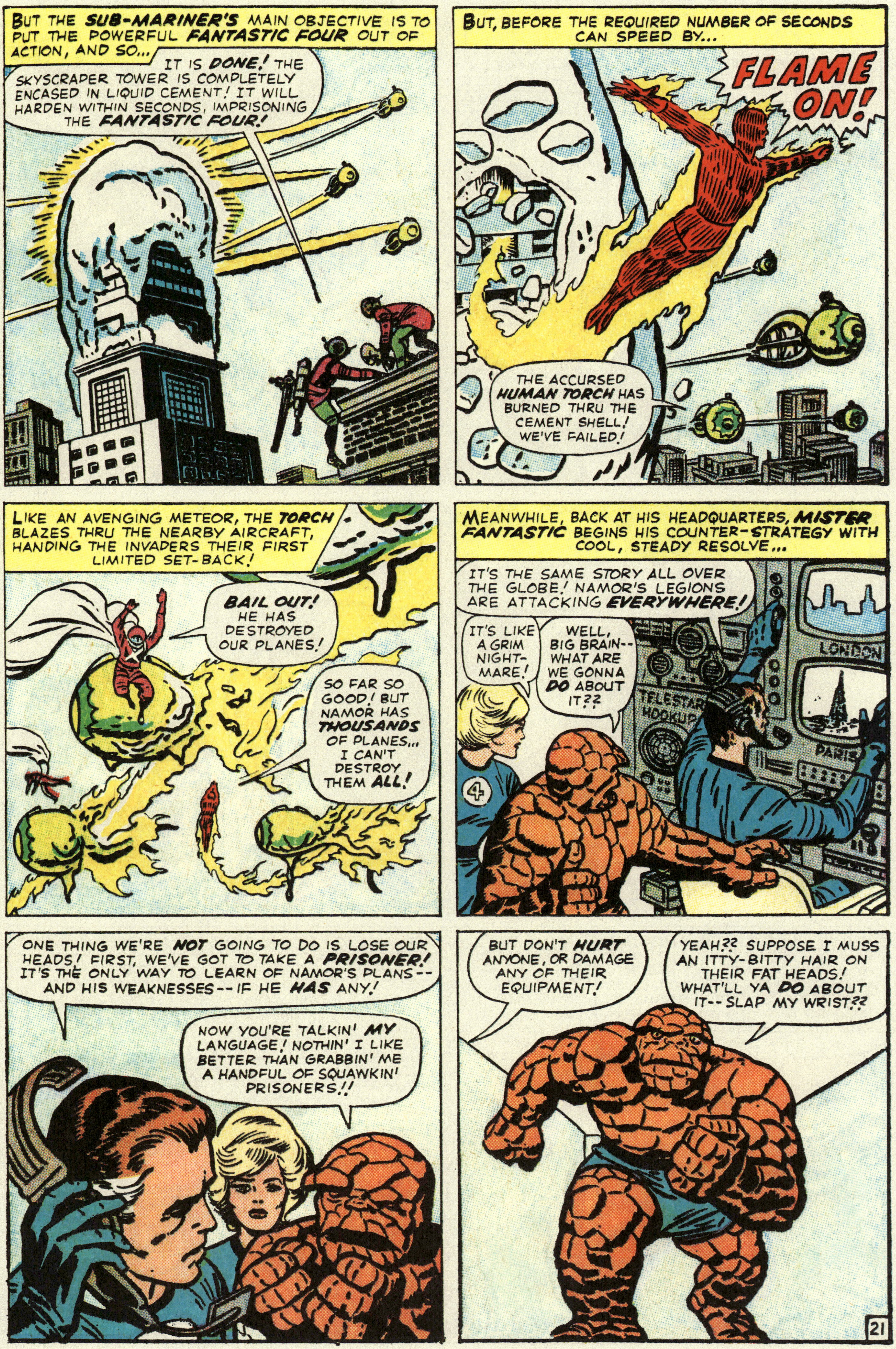

BUT THE SUB-MARINER'S MAIN OBJECTIVE IS TO PUT THE POWERFUL FANTASTIC FOUR OUT OF ACTION, AND SO...
IT IS DONE! THE SKYSCRAPER TOWER IS COMPLETELY ENCASED IN LIQUID CEMENT! IT WILL HARDEN WITHIN SECONDS, IMPRISONING THE FANTASTIC FOUR!
BUT, BEFORE THE REQUIRED NUMBER OF SECONDS CAN SPEED BY...
FLAME ON!
THE ACCURSED HUMAN TORCH HAS BURNED THRU THE CEMENT SHELL! WE'VE FAILED!
LIKE AN AVENGING METEOR, THE TORCH BLAZES THRU THE NEARBY AIRCRAFT, HANDING THE INVADERS THEIR FIRST LIMITED SET-BACK!
BAIL OUT! HE HAS DESTROYED OUR PLANES!
SO FAR SO GOOD! BUT NAMOR HAS THOUSANDS OF PLANES... I CAN'T DESTROY THEM ALL!
MEANWHILE, BACK AT HIS HEADQUARTERS, MISTER FANTASTIC BEGINS HIS COUNTER-STRATEGY WITH COOL, STEADY RESOLVE...
IT'S THE SAME STORY ALL OVER THE GLOBE! NAMOR'S LEGIONS ARE ATTACKING EVERYWHERE!
IT'S LIKE A GRIM NIGHT-MARE!
WELL, BIG BRAIN-- WHAT ARE WE GONNA DO ABOUT IT??
LONDON
TELESTAR HOOKUP
PARIS
ONE THING WE'RE NOT GOING TO DO IS LOSE OUR HEADS! FIRST, WE'VE GOT TO TAKE A PRISONER! IT'S THE ONLY WAY TO LEARN OF NAMOR'S PLANS -- AND HIS WEAKNESSES -- IF HE HAS ANY!
NOW YOU'RE TALKIN' MY LANGUAGE! NOTHIN' I LIKE BETTER THAN GRABBIN' ME A HANDFUL OF SQUAWKIN' PRISONERS!!
BUT DON'T HURT ANYONE, OR DAMAGE ANY OF THEIR EQUIPMENT!
YEAH?? SUPPOSE I MUSS AN ITTY-BITTY HAIR ON THEIR FAT HEADS! WHAT'LL YA DO ABOUT IT-- SLAP MY WRIST??
21

WELL, LOOKY HERE! DID YOU KIDDIES GET THAT LITTLE POP GUN FOR YOUR BIRTHDAY??
STAND BACK, HUMAN! NONE MAY LEAVE THIS BUILDING, BY IMPERIAL ORDER OF PRINCE NAMOR HIMSELF!
BAXTER BUILDING
MOVING WITH UNEXPECTED SPEED FOR ONE SO BULKY, THE THING JAMS HIS FIST INTO THE GUN BARREL, AND...
I HAD A HUNCH I COULD MAKE THIS PEA-SHOOTER BACKFIRE!
HEY, CURLY! YA SAID YOU WANTED A PRISONER!
HERE'S A WHOLE KABOODLE OF "VOLUNTEERS"... SO YOU CAN TAKE YOUR PICK!
I REFUSE TO DIVULGE ANYTHING EXCEPT MY NAME, RANK, AND SERIAL NUMBER!
ZAT SO?? WHAT'LL YA BET I CAN MAKE YOU CHANGE YOUR MIND??
NO NEED FOR THAT, BEN! HIS HELMET, FILLED WITH WATER, TELLS ME ALL I HAVE TO KNOW! NOW I HAVE THE ANSWER I WAS SEEKING!
4
NAMOR HIMSELF IS THE ONLY ONE WHO CAN BREATHE THE AIR AND WATER! HIS PEOPLE CANNOT LIVE IN OUR ATMOSPHERE FOR MORE THAN A SHORT TIME WITHOUT WATER! SO, ALL I NEED DO IS FIND A WAY TO EVAPORATE THE LIFE-GIVING WATER FROM THEIR HELMETS...
MEANWHILE, ON THE MALL AT CENTRAL PARK, THE VICTORIOUS PRINCE NAMOR ISSUES HIS FIRST EDICT...
EFFECTIVE IMMEDIATELY, I PROCLAIM THIS CITY UNDER MARTIAL LAW! IF ALL ORDERS ARE OBEYED, NONE WILL BE HARMED! BUT ANY DISOBEDIENCE OR DEFIANCE WILL BE MET WITH INSTANT, UNCOMPROMISING RETALIATION! SO BE IT!
I NEVER DREAMED I'D EVER BE FILMING A SCENE LIKE THIS! IN LESS THAN TWENTY-FOUR HOURS FROM THE TIME HE FIRST APPEARED, NAMOR IS TALKING TO US LIKE A CONQUEROR, TALKING TO HIS HELPLESS SUBJECTS!
WBTV
22

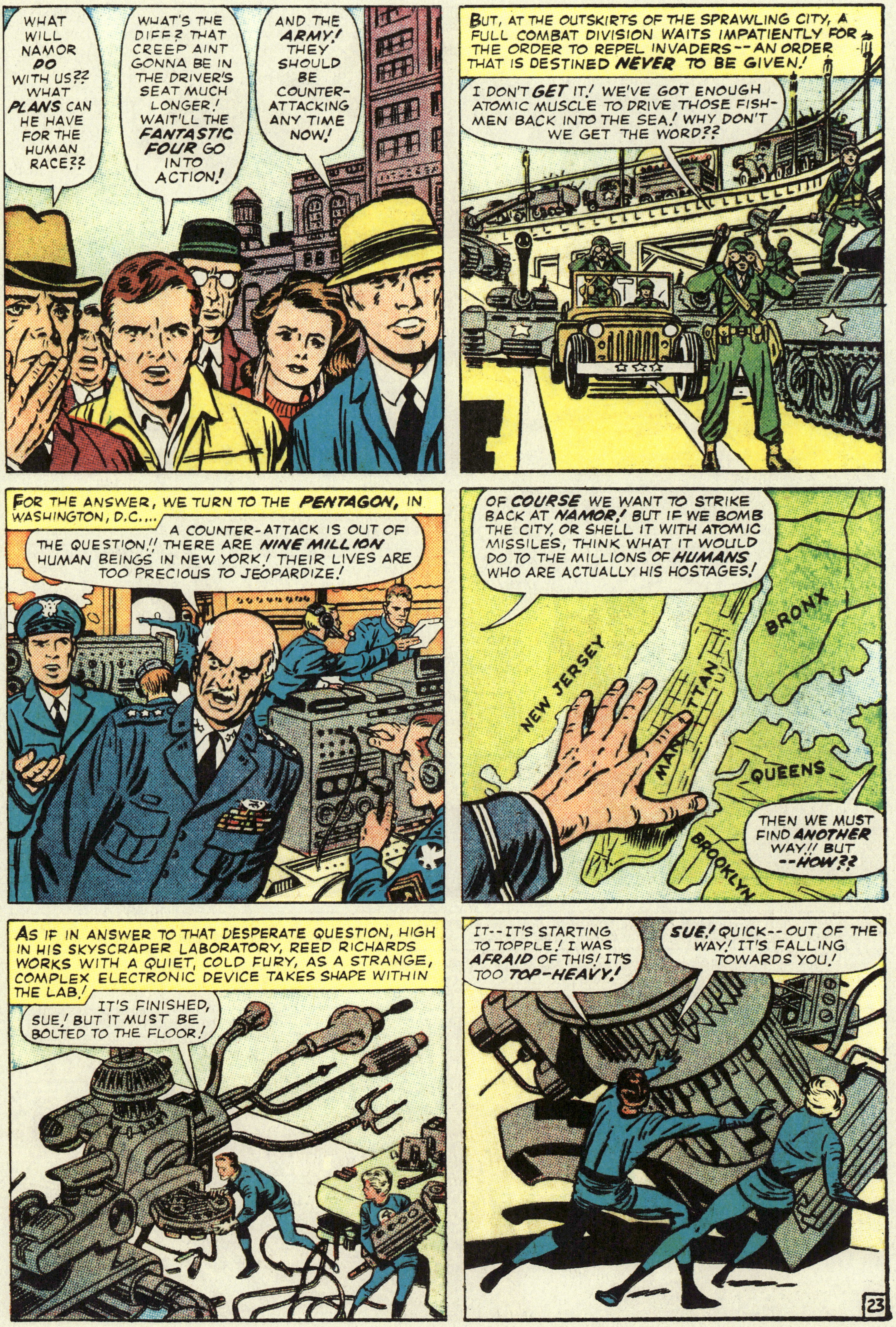

WHAT WILL NAMOR DO WITH US?? WHAT PLANS CAN HE HAVE FOR THE HUMAN RACE??
WHAT'S THE DIFF? THAT CREEP AINT GONNA BE IN THE DRIVER'S SEAT MUCH LONGER! WAIT'LL THE FANTASTIC FOUR GO INTO ACTION!
AND THE ARMY! THEY SHOULD BE COUNTER-ATTACKING ANY TIME NOW!
BUT, AT THE OUTSKIRTS OF THE SPRAWLING CITY, A FULL COMBAT DIVISION WAITS IMPATIENTLY FOR THE ORDER TO REPEL INVADERS--AN ORDER THAT IS DESTINED NEVER TO BE GIVEN!
I DON'T GET IT! WE'VE GOT ENOUGH ATOMIC MUSCLE TO DRIVE THOSE FISH-MEN BACK INTO THE SEA! WHY DON'T WE GET THE WORD??
FOR THE ANSWER, WE TURN TO THE PENTAGON, IN WASHINGTON, D.C....
A COUNTER-ATTACK IS OUT OF THE QUESTION!! THERE ARE NINE MILLION HUMAN BEINGS IN NEW YORK! THEIR LIVES ARE TOO PRECIOUS TO JEOPARDIZE!
OF COURSE WE WANT TO STRIKE BACK AT NAMOR! BUT IF WE BOMB THE CITY, OR SHELL IT WITH ATOMIC MISSILES, THINK WHAT IT WOULD DO TO THE MILLIONS OF HUMANS WHO ARE ACTUALLY HIS HOSTAGES!
BRONX
NEW JERSEY
MANHATTAN
QUEENS
BROOKLYN
THEN WE MUST FIND ANOTHER WAY!! BUT --HOW??
AS IF IN ANSWER TO THAT DESPERATE QUESTION, HIGH IN HIS SKYSCRAPER LABORATORY, REED RICHARDS WORKS WITH A QUIET, COLD FURY, AS A STRANGE, COMPLEX ELECTRONIC DEVICE TAKES SHAPE WITHIN THE LAB!
IT'S FINISHED, SUE! BUT IT MUST BE BOLTED TO THE FLOOR!
IT--IT'S STARTING TO TOPPLE! I WAS AFRAID OF THIS! IT'S TOO TOP-HEAVY!
SUE! QUICK--OUT OF THE WAY! IT'S FALLING TOWARDS YOU!
23

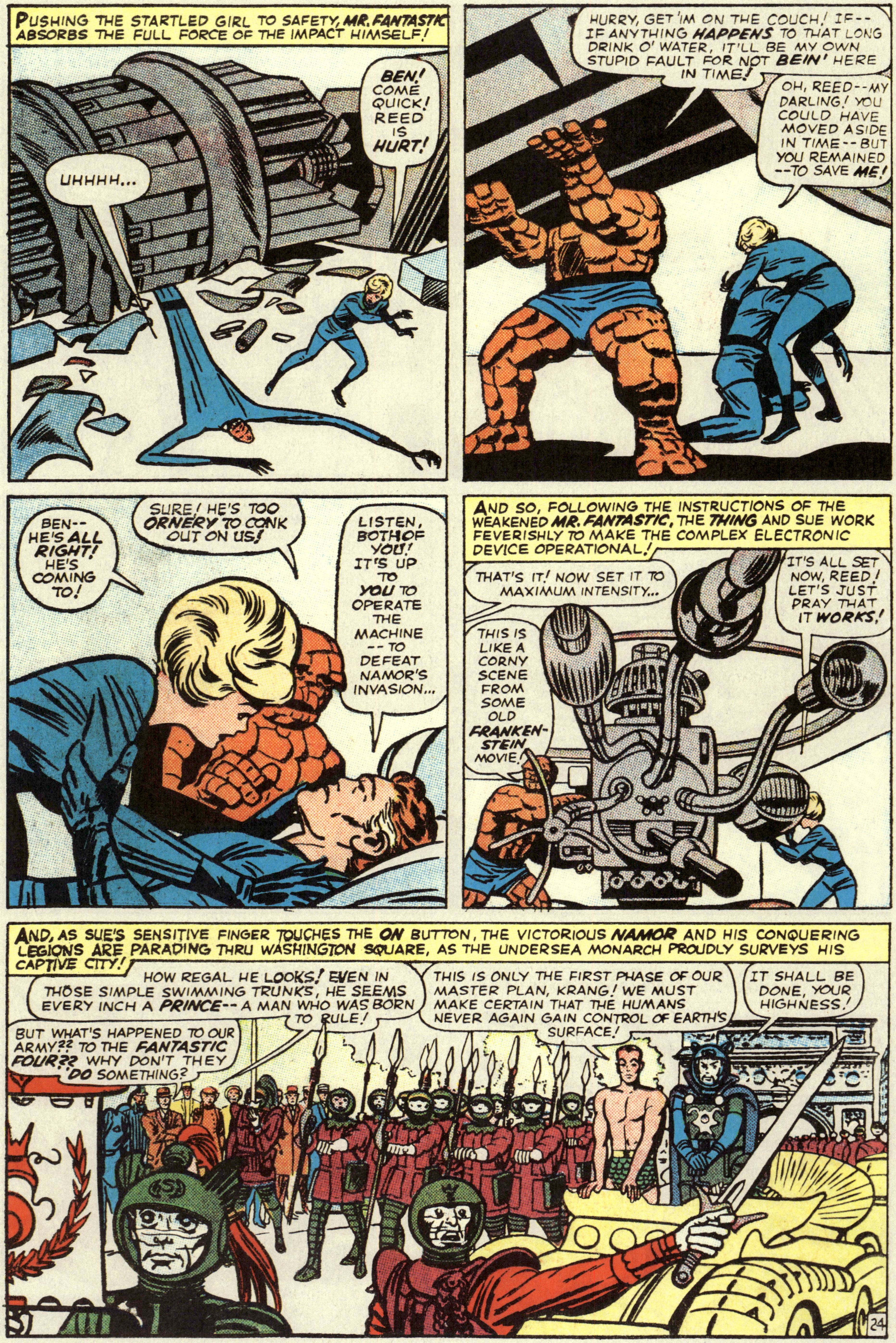
PUSHING THE STARTLED GIRL TO SAFETY, MR. FANTASTIC ABSORBS THE FULL FORCE OF THE IMPACT HIMSELF!
BEN! COME QUICK! REED IS HURT!
UHHHH...
HURRY, GET 'IM ON THE COUCH! IF-- IF ANYTHING HAPPENS TO THAT LONG DRINK O' WATER, IT'LL BE MY OWN STUPID FAULT FOR NOT BEIN' HERE IN TIME!
OH, REED--MY DARLING! YOU COULD HAVE MOVED ASIDE IN TIME--BUT YOU REMAINED --TO SAVE ME!
BEN-- HE'S ALL RIGHT! HE'S COMING TO!
SURE! HE'S TOO ORNERY TO CONK OUT ON US!
LISTEN, BOTH OF YOU! IT'S UP TO YOU TO OPERATE THE MACHINE --TO DEFEAT NAMOR'S INVASION...
AND SO, FOLLOWING THE INSTRUCTIONS OF THE WEAKENED MR. FANTASTIC, THE THING AND SUE WORK FEVERISHLY TO MAKE THE COMPLEX ELECTRONIC DEVICE OPERATIONAL!
THAT'S IT! NOW SET IT TO MAXIMUM INTENSITY...
IT'S ALL SET NOW, REED! LET'S JUST PRAY THAT IT WORKS!
THIS IS LIKE A CORNY SCENE FROM SOME OLD FRANKEN-STEIN MOVIE!
AND, AS SUE'S SENSITIVE FINGER TOUCHES THE ON BUTTON, THE VICTORIOUS NAMOR AND HIS CONQUERING LEGIONS ARE PARADING THRU WASHINGTON SQUARE, AS THE UNDERSEA MONARCH PROUDLY SURVEYS HIS CAPTIVE CITY!
HOW REGAL HE LOOKS! EVEN IN THOSE SIMPLE SWIMMING TRUNKS, HE SEEMS EVERY INCH A PRINCE--A MAN WHO WAS BORN TO RULE!
BUT WHAT'S HAPPENED TO OUR ARMY?? TO THE FANTASTIC FOUR?? WHY DON'T THEY DO SOMETHING?
THIS IS ONLY THE FIRST PHASE OF OUR MASTER PLAN, KRANG! WE MUST MAKE CERTAIN THAT THE HUMANS NEVER AGAIN GAIN CONTROL OF EARTH'S SURFACE!
IT SHALL BE DONE, YOUR HIGHNESS!
24

AT THAT VERY SECOND, A LOW, DISCORDANT HUM IS HEARD THRUOUT THE CITY, AS POWERFUL, INVISIBLE RAYS STRIKE OUT FROM THE TOWER OF THE BAXTER BUILDING, DRAINING DRY THE HELMET OF EVERY ONE OF NAMOR'S INVADING WARRIORS!
LOOK!! THE UNDERSEA SOLDIERS -- SOMETHING'S HAPPENING TO THEM!!
THAT EERIE HUM!! WHERE IS IT COMING FROM? WHAT IS IT?
MMMMMMMMMMMM
MY MEN ARE SUFFOCATING! THEIR HELMET WATER IS EVAPORATING!!
QUICK! BACK TO THE SEA! ALL OF YOU!
WITHIN MINUTES, THE ONCE-VICTORIOUS ARMY BECOMES A GASPING, WHEEZING HELPLESS HORDE!
THEY HAVE ONLY ONE OBJECTIVE --ONE GOAL-- TO REACH THE LIFE-GIVING SEA WHILE THERE STILL IS TIME!
AND SO, AS SUDDENLY AS IT HAD BEGUN, THE INCREDIBLE INVASION IS ENDED! THE CITY IS SAVED!
BUT THERE IS ONE INVADER WHO HAS NOT RETURNED TO THE SEA...
THE ACCURSED EVAPORATION RAY BLANKETED THE EARTH! MY MEN RETREATED FROM EVERY OCCUPIED CITY! ONLY MR. FANTASTIC COULD BE RESPONSIBLE!
NAMOR! I WAS EXPECTING YOU!
YOU HAVE ONLY WON THE FIRST SKIRMISH! BUT THE WAR GOES ON!
STILL IN A WEAKENED CONDITION, REED RICHARDS CANNOT MOVE FAST ENOUGH TO EVADE THE SUB-MARINER'S POWERFUL ATTACK!
I SHALL SEE TO IT THAT YOU NEVER AGAIN UPSET THE GRAND DESIGN OF MY PEOPLE!
YOU'RE A FOOL, NAMOR! YOU CAN NEVER DEFEAT THE HUMAN RACE!
25

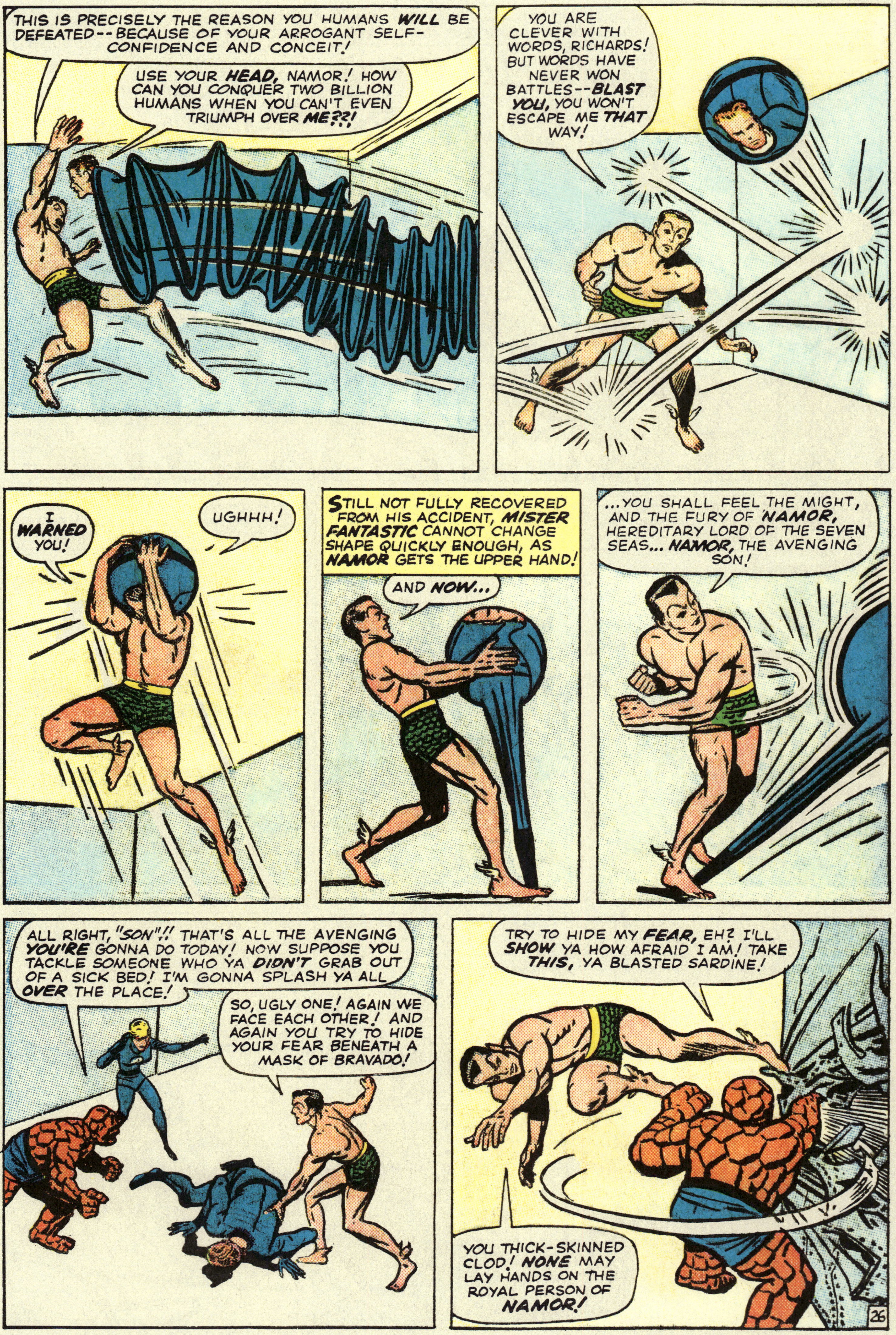
THIS IS PRECISELY THE REASON YOU HUMANS WILL BE DEFEATED--BECAUSE OF YOUR ARROGANT SELF-CONFIDENCE AND CONCEIT!
USE YOUR HEAD, NAMOR! HOW CAN YOU CONQUER TWO BILLION HUMANS WHEN YOU CAN'T EVEN TRIUMPH OVER ME??!
YOU ARE CLEVER WITH WORDS, RICHARDS! BUT WORDS HAVE NEVER WON BATTLES--BLAST YOU, YOU WON'T ESCAPE ME THAT WAY!
I WARNED YOU!
UGHHH!
STILL NOT FULLY RECOVERED FROM HIS ACCIDENT, MISTER FANTASTIC CANNOT CHANGE SHAPE QUICKLY ENOUGH, AS NAMOR GETS THE UPPER HAND!
AND NOW...
...YOU SHALL FEEL THE MIGHT, AND THE FURY OF NAMOR, HEREDITARY LORD OF THE SEVEN SEAS... NAMOR, THE AVENGING SON!
ALL RIGHT, "SON"!! THAT'S ALL THE AVENGING YOU'RE GONNA DO TODAY! NOW SUPPOSE YOU TACKLE SOMEONE WHO YA DIDN'T GRAB OUT OF A SICK BED! I'M GONNA SPLASH YA ALL OVER THE PLACE!
SO, UGLY ONE! AGAIN WE FACE EACH OTHER! AND AGAIN YOU TRY TO HIDE YOUR FEAR BENEATH A MASK OF BRAVADO!
TRY TO HIDE MY FEAR, EH? I'LL SHOW YA HOW AFRAID I AM! TAKE THIS, YA BLASTED SARDINE!
YOU THICK-SKINNED CLOD! NONE MAY LAY HANDS ON THE ROYAL PERSON OF NAMOR!
26

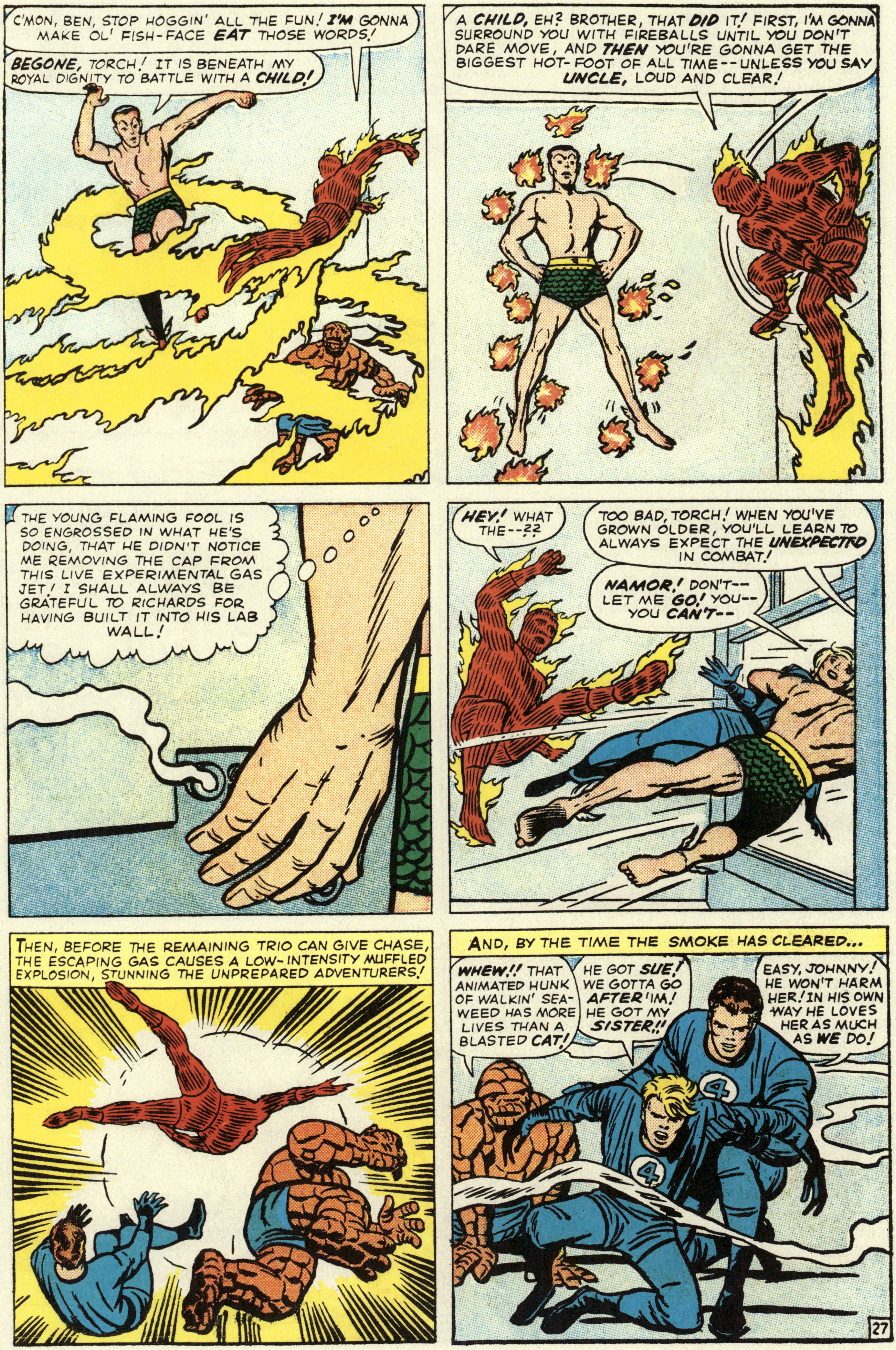
C'MON, BEN, STOP HOGGIN' ALL THE FUN! I'M GONNA MAKE OL' FISH-FACE EAT THOSE WORDS!
BEGONE, TORCH! IT IS BENEATH MY ROYAL DIGNITY TO BATTLE WITH A CHILD!
A CHILD, EH? BROTHER, THAT DID IT! FIRST, I'M GONNA SURROUND YOU WITH FIREBALLS UNTIL YOU DON'T DARE MOVE, AND THEN YOU'RE GONNA GET THE BIGGEST HOT-FOOT OF ALL TIME--UNLESS YOU SAY UNCLE, LOUD AND CLEAR!
THE YOUNG FLAMING FOOL IS SO ENGROSSED IN WHAT HE'S DOING, THAT HE DIDN'T NOTICE ME REMOVING THE CAP FROM THIS LIVE EXPERIMENTAL GAS JET! I SHALL ALWAYS BE GRATEFUL TO RICHARDS FOR HAVING BUILT IT INTO HIS LAB WALL!
HEY! WHAT THE--??
TOO BAD, TORCH! WHEN YOU'VE GROWN OLDER, YOU'LL LEARN TO ALWAYS EXPECT THE UNEXPECTED IN COMBAT!
NAMOR! DON'T-- LET ME GO! YOU-- YOU CAN'T--
THEN, BEFORE THE REMAINING TRIO CAN GIVE CHASE, THE ESCAPING GAS CAUSES A LOW-INTENSITY MUFFLED EXPLOSION, STUNNING THE UNPREPARED ADVENTURERS!
AND, BY THE TIME THE SMOKE HAS CLEARED...
WHEW!! THAT ANIMATED HUNK OF WALKIN' SEA-WEED HAS MORE LIVES THAN A BLASTED CAT!
HE GOT SUE! WE GOTTA GO AFTER 'IM! HE GOT MY SISTER!!
EASY, JOHNNY! HE WON'T HARM HER! IN HIS OWN WAY HE LOVES HER AS MUCH AS WE DO!
27

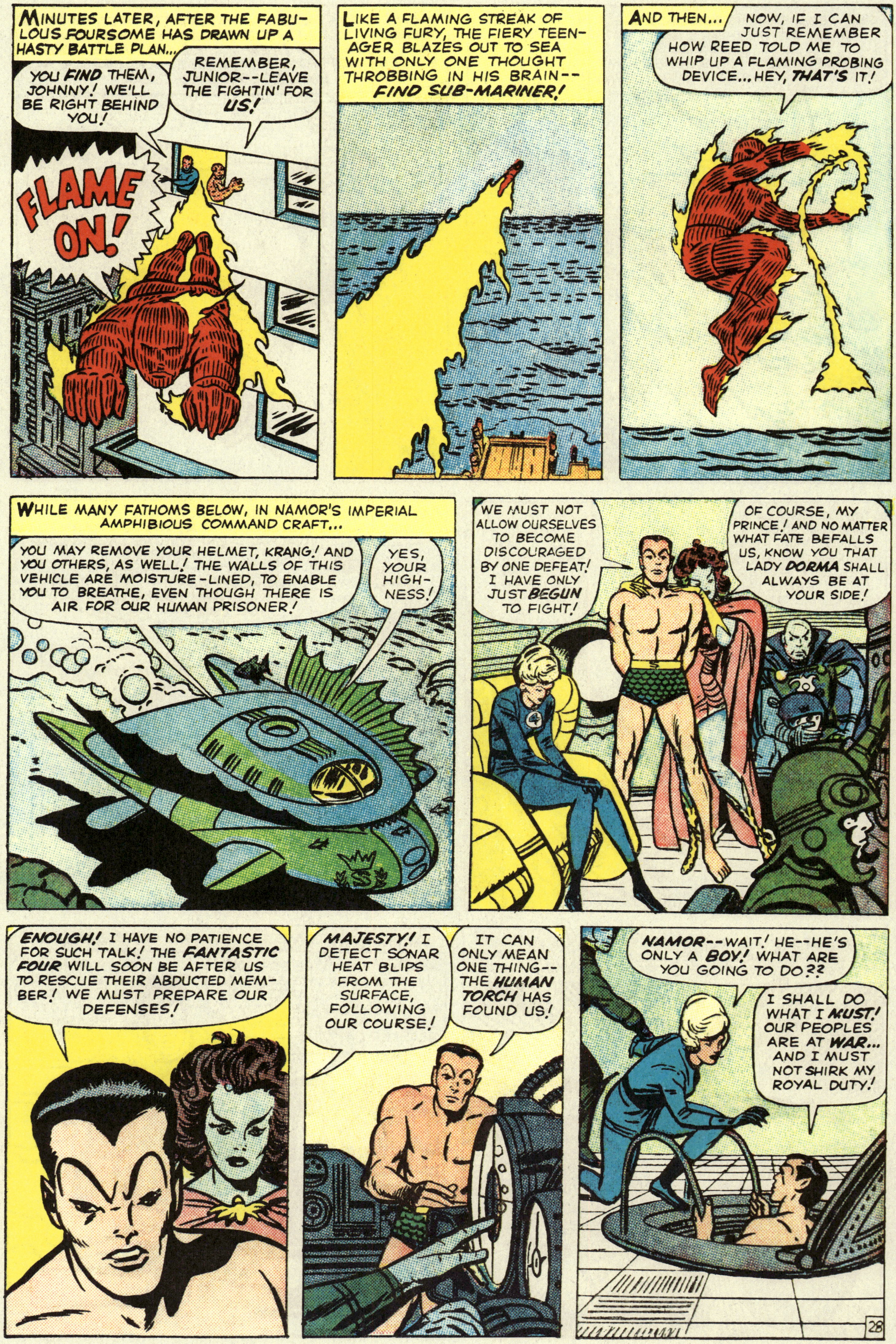
MINUTES LATER, AFTER THE FABULOUS FOURSOME HAS DRAWN UP A HASTY BATTLE PLAN...
YOU FIND THEM, JOHNNY! WE'LL BE RIGHT BEHIND YOU!
REMEMBER, JUNIOR--LEAVE THE FIGHTIN' FOR US!
FLAME ON!
LIKE A FLAMING STREAK OF LIVING FURY, THE FIERY TEEN-AGER BLAZES OUT TO SEA WITH ONLY ONE THOUGHT THROBBING IN HIS BRAIN-- FIND SUB-MARINER!
AND THEN...
NOW, IF I CAN JUST REMEMBER HOW REED TOLD ME TO WHIP UP A FLAMING PROBING DEVICE... HEY, THAT'S IT!
WHILE MANY FATHOMS BELOW, IN NAMOR'S IMPERIAL AMPHIBIOUS COMMAND CRAFT...
YOU MAY REMOVE YOUR HELMET, KRANG! AND YOU OTHERS, AS WELL! THE WALLS OF THIS VEHICLE ARE MOISTURE-LINED, TO ENABLE YOU TO BREATHE, EVEN THOUGH THERE IS AIR FOR OUR HUMAN PRISONER!
YES, YOUR HIGHNESS!
WE MUST NOT ALLOW OURSELVES TO BECOME DISCOURAGED BY ONE DEFEAT! I HAVE ONLY JUST BEGUN TO FIGHT!
OF COURSE, MY PRINCE! AND NO MATTER WHAT FATE BEFALLS US, KNOW YOU THAT LADY DORMA SHALL ALWAYS BE AT YOUR SIDE!
ENOUGH! I HAVE NO PATIENCE FOR SUCH TALK! THE FANTASTIC FOUR WILL SOON BE AFTER US TO RESCUE THEIR ABDUCTED MEMBER! WE MUST PREPARE OUR DEFENSES!
MAJESTY! I DETECT SONAR HEAT BLIPS FROM THE SURFACE, FOLLOWING OUR COURSE!
IT CAN ONLY MEAN ONE THING-- THE HUMAN TORCH HAS FOUND US!
NAMOR--WAIT! HE--HE'S ONLY A BOY! WHAT ARE YOU GOING TO DO??
I SHALL DO WHAT I MUST! OUR PEOPLES ARE AT WAR... AND I MUST NOT SHIRK MY ROYAL DUTY!
28

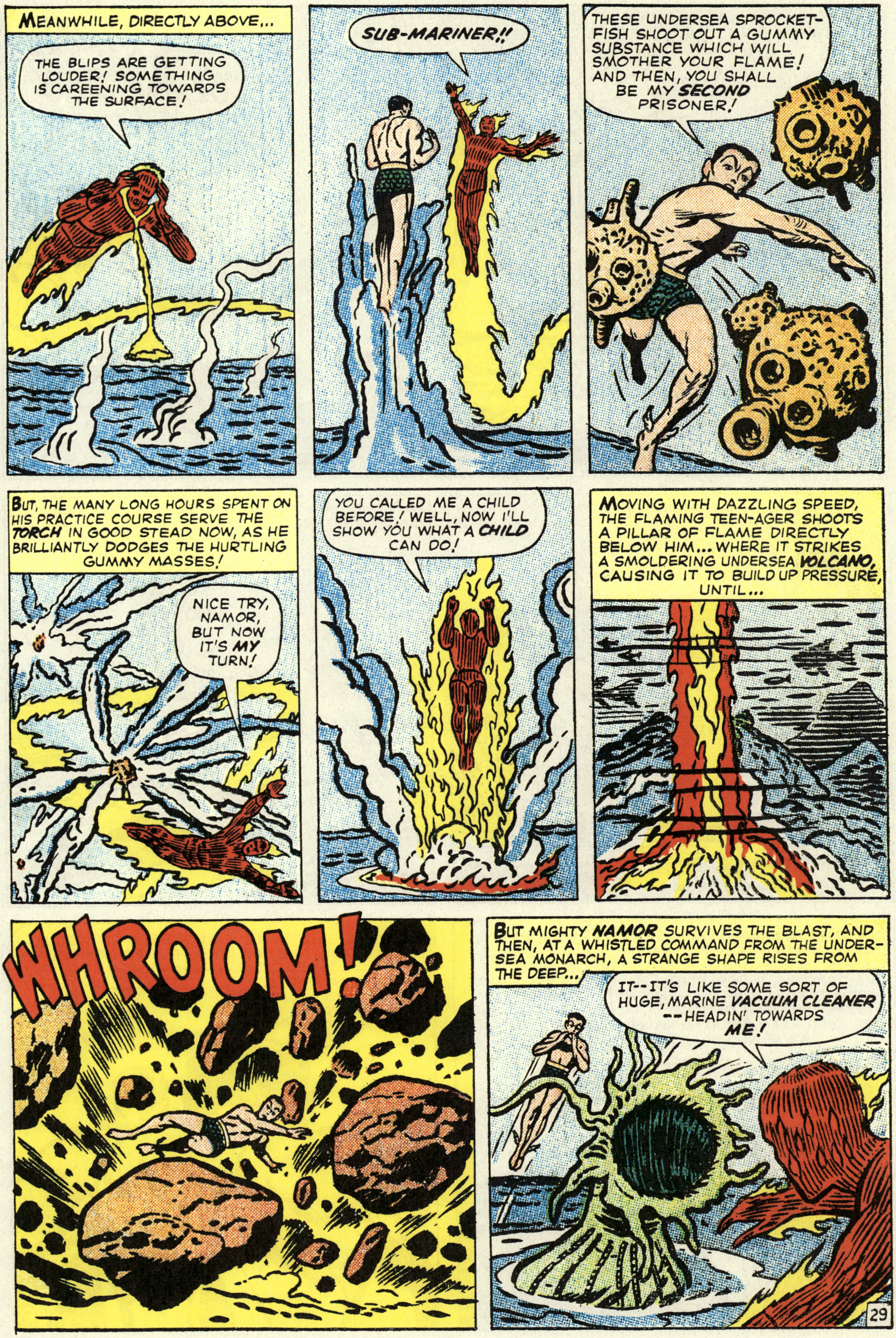
MEANWHILE, DIRECTLY ABOVE...
THE BLIPS ARE GETTING LOUDER! SOMETHING IS CAREENING TOWARDS THE SURFACE!
SUB-MARINER!!
THESE UNDERSEA SPROCKET-FISH SHOOT OUT A GUMMY SUBSTANCE WHICH WILL SMOTHER YOUR FLAME! AND THEN, YOU SHALL BE MY SECOND PRISONER!
BUT, THE MANY LONG HOURS SPENT ON HIS PRACTICE COURSE SERVE THE TORCH IN GOOD STEAD NOW, AS HE BRILLIANTLY DODGES THE HURTLING GUMMY MASSES!
NICE TRY, NAMOR, BUT NOW IT'S MY TURN!
YOU CALLED ME A CHILD BEFORE! WELL, NOW I'LL SHOW YOU WHAT A CHILD CAN DO!
MOVING WITH DAZZLING SPEED, THE FLAMING TEEN-AGER SHOOTS A PILLAR OF FLAME DIRECTLY BELOW HIM... WHERE IT STRIKES A SMOLDERING UNDERSEA VOLCANO, CAUSING IT TO BUILD UP PRESSURE, UNTIL...
WHROOM!
BUT MIGHTY NAMOR SURVIVES THE BLAST, AND THEN, AT A WHISTLED COMMAND FROM THE UNDERSEA MONARCH, A STRANGE SHAPE RISES FROM THE DEEP...
IT--IT'S LIKE SOME SORT OF HUGE, MARINE VACUUM CLEANER --HEADIN' TOWARDS ME!
29

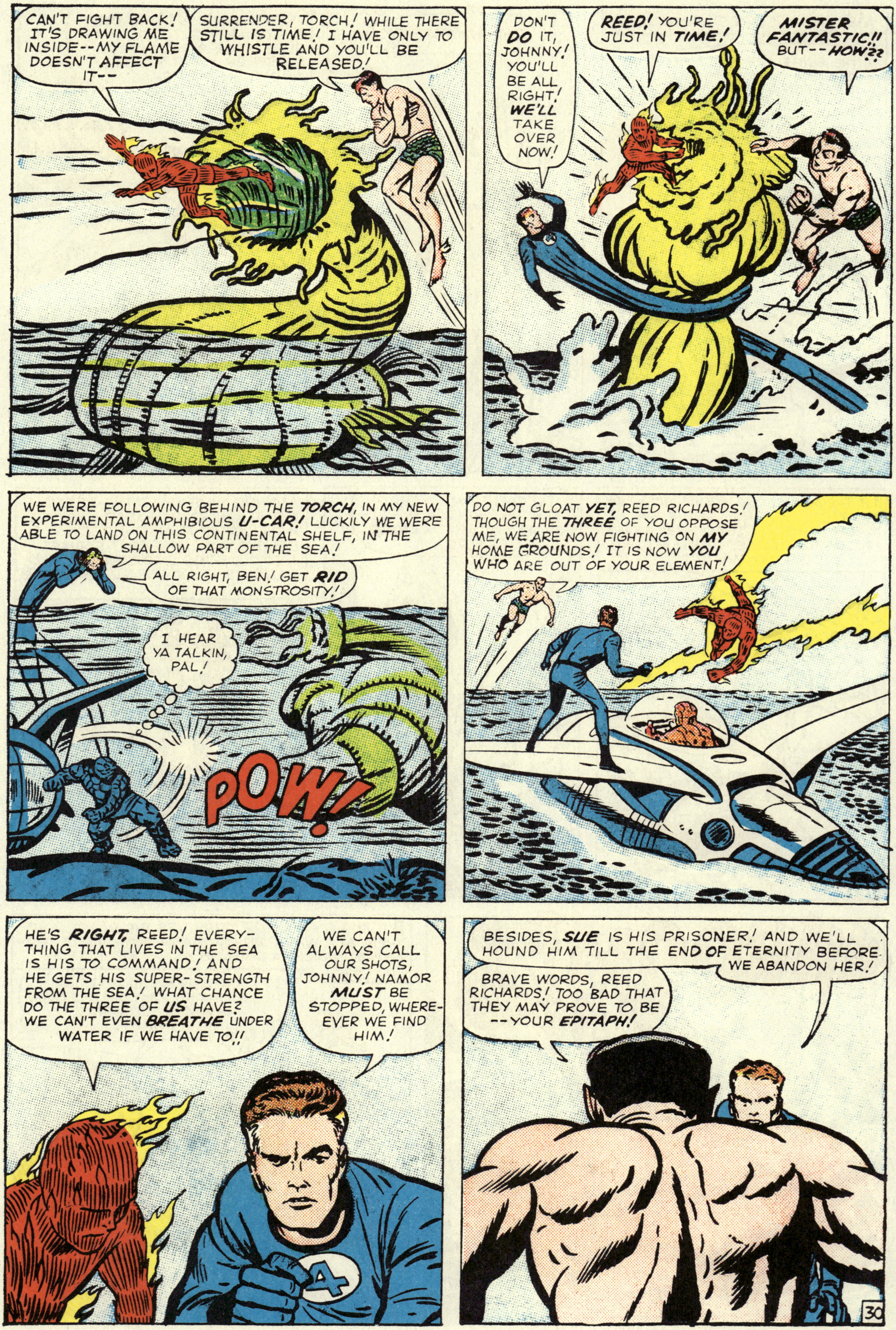
CAN'T FIGHT BACK! IT'S DRAWING ME INSIDE--MY FLAME DOESN'T AFFECT IT--
SURRENDER, TORCH! WHILE THERE STILL IS TIME! I HAVE ONLY TO WHISTLE AND YOU'LL BE RELEASED!
DON'T DO IT, JOHNNY! YOU'LL BE ALL RIGHT! WE'LL TAKE OVER NOW!
REED! YOU'RE JUST IN TIME!
MISTER FANTASTIC!! BUT--HOW??
WE WERE FOLLOWING BEHIND THE TORCH, IN MY NEW EXPERIMENTAL AMPHIBIOUS U-CAR! LUCKILY WE WERE ABLE TO LAND ON THIS CONTINENTAL SHELF, IN THE SHALLOW PART OF THE SEA!
ALL RIGHT, BEN! GET RID OF THAT MONSTROSITY!
I HEAR YA TALKIN, PAL!
POW!
DO NOT GLOAT YET, REED RICHARDS! THOUGH THE THREE OF YOU OPPOSE ME, WE ARE NOW FIGHTING ON MY HOME GROUNDS! IT IS NOW YOU WHO ARE OUT OF YOUR ELEMENT!
HE'S RIGHT, REED! EVERYTHING THAT LIVES IN THE SEA IS HIS TO COMMAND! AND HE GETS HIS SUPER-STRENGTH FROM THE SEA! WHAT CHANCE DO THE THREE OF US HAVE? WE CAN'T EVEN BREATHE UNDER WATER IF WE HAVE TO!!
WE CAN'T ALWAYS CALL OUR SHOTS, JOHNNY! NAMOR MUST BE STOPPED, WHEREEVER WE FIND HIM!
BESIDES, SUE IS HIS PRISONER! AND WE'LL HOUND HIM TILL THE END OF ETERNITY BEFORE WE ABANDON HER!
BRAVE WORDS, REED RICHARDS! TOO BAD THAT THEY MAY PROVE TO BE --YOUR EPITAPH!
30

AND THEN, AS NAMOR LANDS THE FIRST AWESOME BLOW, THE CLASH OF TITANS BEGINS!
ZOOOOM
POW!
SEIZING THE PLIABLE FORM OF REED RICHARDS, NAMOR FASHIONS A CRUDE CANDLE-SNUFFER OUT OF HIS STUNNED BODY!
COME CLOSER, TORCH --CLOSER!
JUST TRY 'N STOP ME, BIG MAN!
YOU MEAN-- LIKE THIS???
UNNGHHHH...
CAUGHT BY SURPRISE, THE TORCH'S FLAME IS SUDDENLY SNUFFED OUT-- BUT, AT THAT SPLIT-SECOND, MR. FANTASTIC REGAINS CONSCIOUSNESS, AND...
TAKE YOUR CLAMMY HANDS OFF ME, NAMOR!
REED-- GRAB ME! I'M FALLIN'!!
SNAP!
EASY, BOY! WE'LL TAKE THE PLUNGE TOGETHER --AND WE'LL BRING NAMOR WITH US!

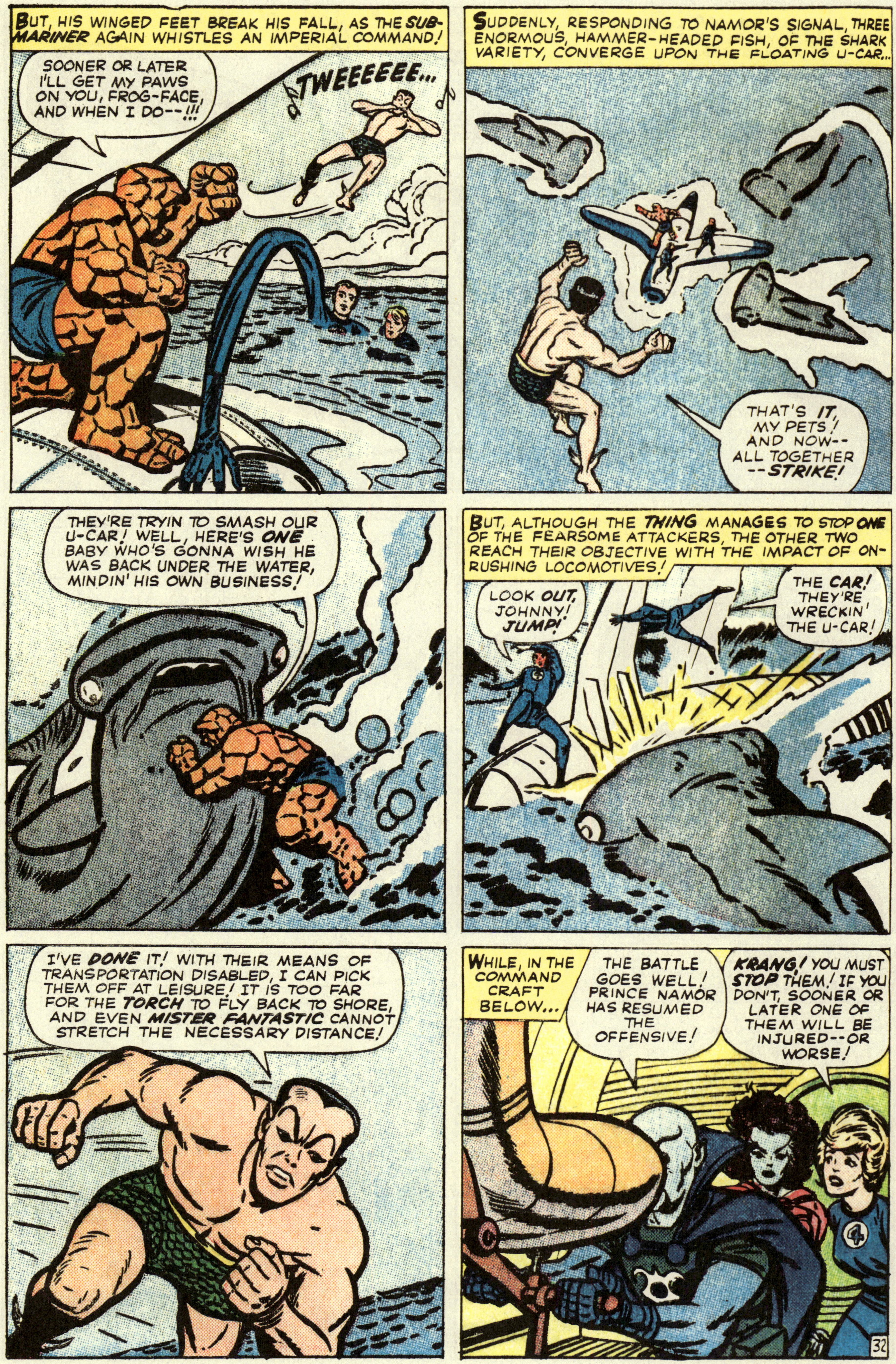
BUT, HIS WINGED FEET BREAK HIS FALL, AS THE SUB-MARINER AGAIN WHISTLES AN IMPERIAL COMMAND!
SOONER OR LATER I'LL GET MY PAWS ON YOU, FROG-FACE, AND WHEN I DO--!!!
TWEEEEEE...
SUDDENLY, RESPONDING TO NAMOR'S SIGNAL, THREE ENORMOUS, HAMMER-HEADED FISH, OF THE SHARK VARIETY, CONVERGE UPON THE FLOATING U-CAR...
THAT'S IT, MY PETS! AND NOW-- ALL TOGETHER --STRIKE!
THEY'RE TRYIN TO SMASH OUR U-CAR! WELL, HERE'S ONE BABY WHO'S GONNA WISH HE WAS BACK UNDER THE WATER, MINDIN' HIS OWN BUSINESS!
BUT, ALTHOUGH THE THING MANAGES TO STOP ONE OF THE FEARSOME ATTACKERS, THE OTHER TWO REACH THEIR OBJECTIVE WITH THE IMPACT OF ON-RUSHING LOCOMOTIVES!
LOOK OUT, JOHNNY! JUMP!
THE CAR! THEY'RE WRECKIN' THE U-CAR!
I'VE DONE IT! WITH THEIR MEANS OF TRANSPORTATION DISABLED, I CAN PICK THEM OFF AT LEISURE! IT IS TOO FAR FOR THE TORCH TO FLY BACK TO SHORE, AND EVEN MISTER FANTASTIC CANNOT STRETCH THE NECESSARY DISTANCE!
WHILE, IN THE COMMAND CRAFT BELOW...
THE BATTLE GOES WELL! PRINCE NAMOR HAS RESUMED THE OFFENSIVE!
KRANG! YOU MUST STOP THEM! IF YOU DON'T, SOONER OR LATER ONE OF THEM WILL BE INJURED--OR WORSE!
32

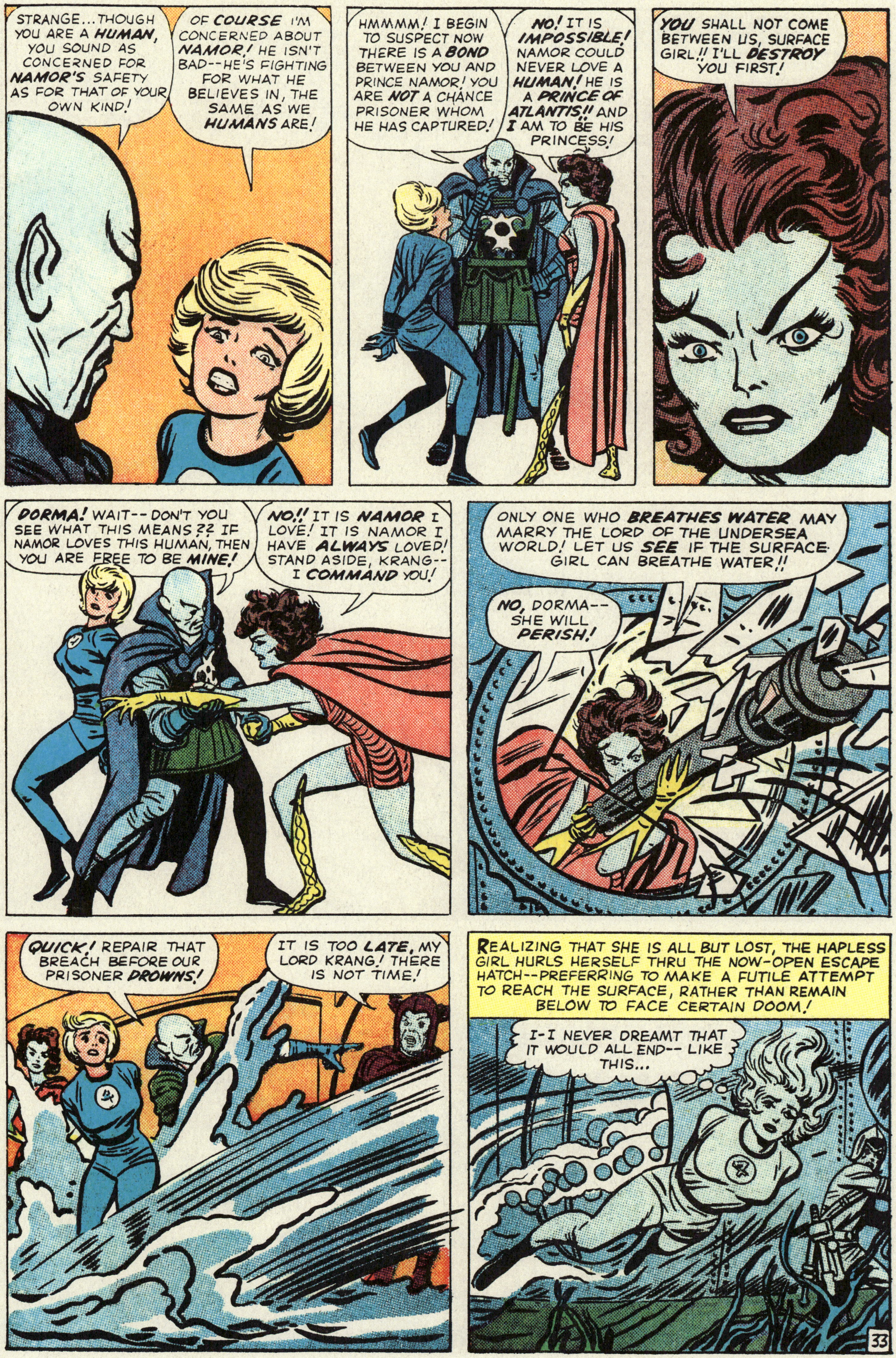
STRANGE... THOUGH YOU ARE A HUMAN, YOU SOUND AS CONCERNED FOR NAMOR'S SAFETY AS FOR THAT OF YOUR OWN KIND!
OF COURSE I'M CONCERNED ABOUT NAMOR! HE ISN'T BAD--HE'S FIGHTING FOR WHAT HE BELIEVES IN, THE SAME AS WE HUMANS ARE!
HMMMM! I BEGIN TO SUSPECT NOW THERE IS A BOND BETWEEN YOU AND PRINCE NAMOR! YOU ARE NOT A CHANCE PRISONER WHOM HE HAS CAPTURED!
NO! IT IS IMPOSSIBLE! NAMOR COULD NEVER LOVE A HUMAN! HE IS A PRINCE OF ATLANTIS!! AND I AM TO BE HIS PRINCESS!
YOU SHALL NOT COME BETWEEN US, SURFACE GIRL!! I'LL DESTROY YOU FIRST!
DORMA! WAIT-- DON'T YOU SEE WHAT THIS MEANS?? IF NAMOR LOVES THIS HUMAN, THEN YOU ARE FREE TO BE MINE!
NO!! IT IS NAMOR I LOVE! IT IS NAMOR I HAVE ALWAYS LOVED! STAND ASIDE, KRANG-- I COMMAND YOU!
ONLY ONE WHO BREATHES WATER MAY MARRY THE LORD OF THE UNDERSEA WORLD! LET US SEE IF THE SURFACE GIRL CAN BREATHE WATER!!
NO, DORMA-- SHE WILL PERISH!
QUICK! REPAIR THAT BREACH BEFORE OUR PRISONER DROWNS!
IT IS TOO LATE, MY LORD KRANG! THERE IS NOT TIME!
REALIZING THAT SHE IS ALL BUT LOST, THE HAPLESS GIRL HURLS HERSELF THRU THE NOW-OPEN ESCAPE HATCH--PREFERRING TO MAKE A FUTILE ATTEMPT TO REACH THE SURFACE, RATHER THAN REMAIN BELOW TO FACE CERTAIN DOOM!
I-I NEVER DREAMT THAT IT WOULD ALL END-- LIKE THIS...
33

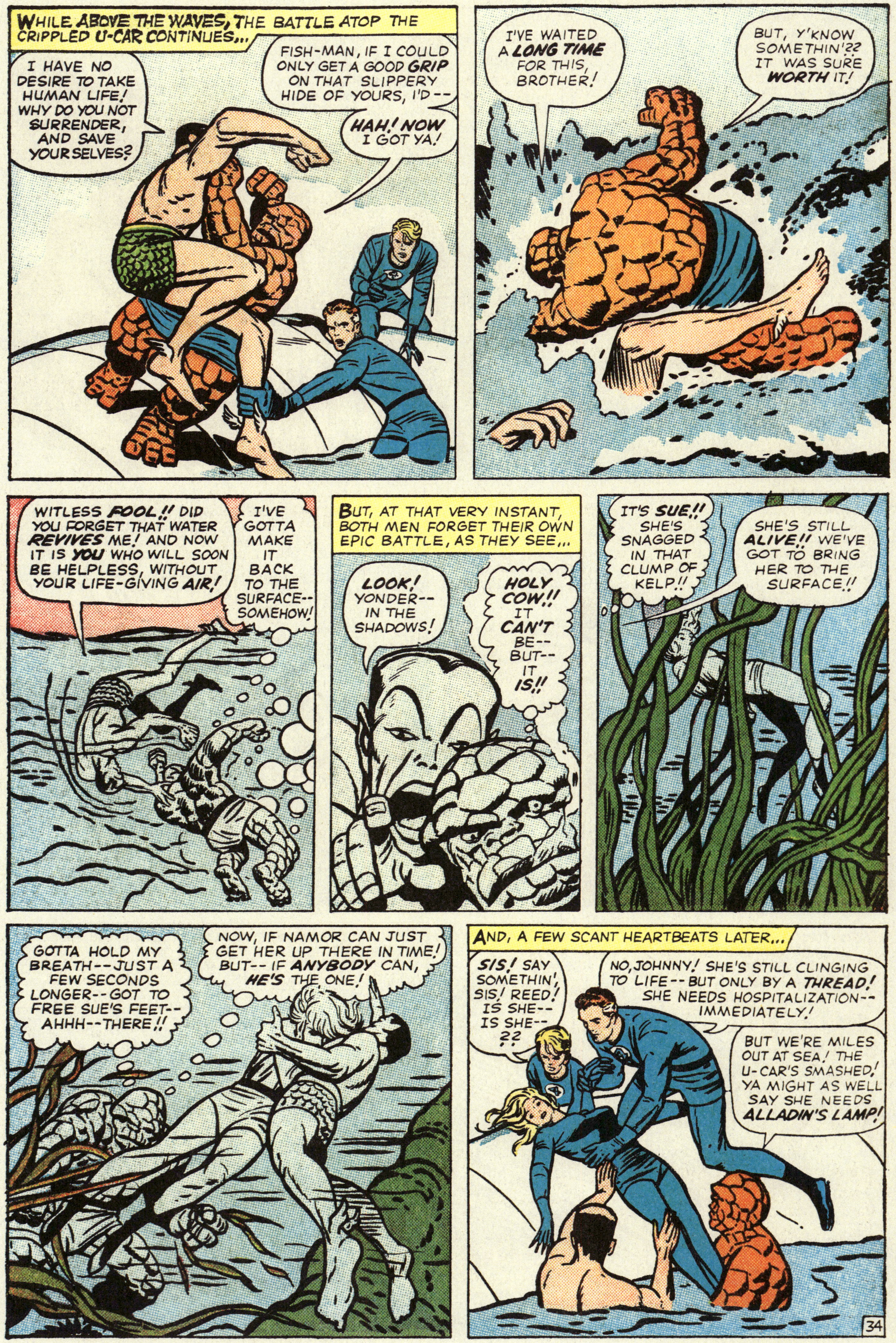
WHILE ABOVE THE WAVES, THE BATTLE ATOP THE CRIPPLED U-CAR CONTINUES,..
I HAVE NO DESIRE TO TAKE HUMAN LIFE! WHY DO YOU NOT SURRENDER, AND SAVE YOURSELVES?
FISH-MAN, IF I COULD ONLY GET A GOOD GRIP ON THAT SLIPPERY HIDE OF YOURS, I'D --
HAH! NOW I GOT YA!
I'VE WAITED A LONG TIME FOR THIS, BROTHER!
BUT, Y'KNOW SOMETHIN'?? IT WAS SURE WORTH IT!
WITLESS FOOL!! DID YOU FORGET THAT WATER REVIVES ME! AND NOW IT IS YOU WHO WILL SOON BE HELPLESS, WITHOUT YOUR LIFE-GIVING AIR!
I'VE GOTTA MAKE IT BACK TO THE SURFACE-- SOMEHOW!
BUT, AT THAT VERY INSTANT, BOTH MEN FORGET THEIR OWN EPIC BATTLE, AS THEY SEE,..
LOOK! YONDER-- IN THE SHADOWS!
HOLY COW!! IT CAN'T BE-- BUT-- IT IS!!
IT'S SUE!! SHE'S SNAGGED IN THAT CLUMP OF KELP!!
SHE'S STILL ALIVE!! WE'VE GOT TO BRING HER TO THE SURFACE!!
GOTTA HOLD MY BREATH-- JUST A FEW SECONDS LONGER-- GOT TO FREE SUE'S FEET-- AHHH-- THERE!!
NOW, IF NAMOR CAN JUST GET HER UP THERE IN TIME! BUT-- IF ANYBODY CAN, HE'S THE ONE!
AND, A FEW SCANT HEARTBEATS LATER...
SIS! SAY SOMETHIN', SIS! REED! IS SHE-- IS SHE-- ??
NO, JOHNNY! SHE'S STILL CLINGING TO LIFE -- BUT ONLY BY A THREAD! SHE NEEDS HOSPITALIZATION-- IMMEDIATELY!
BUT WE'RE MILES OUT AT SEA! THE U-CAR'S SMASHED! YA MIGHT AS WELL SAY SHE NEEDS ALLADIN'S LAMP!
34

NAMOR, IF ANYTHING HAPPENS TO SUE, THERE'LL BE NO PLACE ON LAND OR SEA WHERE YOU'LL BE SAFE FROM ME!!
QUIET! I MUST THINK!
THERE'S ONLY ONE THING THAT CAN REACH SHORE IN TIME--MY IMPERIAL COMMAND CRAFT!
REED! GRAB 'IM! HE'S TRYIN' TO ESCAPE!
NO, BEN-- NOT THIS TIME!
MOVING LIKE A MAN POSSESSED, THE MIGHTY LORD OF THE DEEP PLUNGES ONCE AGAIN INTO HIS WATERY DOMAIN...
...REACHING HIS OBJECTIVE WITHIN SECONDS!
THEY HAVE REPAIRED A BROKEN PORTHOLE! THAT MUST BE HOW SUE LEFT THE CRAFT!
STAND ASIDE--ALL OF YOU! NAMOR IS HERE!
DORMA! KRANG! QUICKLY, LEAVE THE SHIP! TAKE THE CREW WITH YOU! I WANT NO MORE WEIGHT THAN IS ABSOLUTE NECESSARY! NOW GO!
YOUR MAJESTY, EVEN A KING CANNOT SPEAK TO ME LIKE THAT! DO YOU FORGET MY OWN ROYAL LINEAGE?
BY YOUR LEAVE, MAJESTY, MAY WE HAVE SOME EXPLANATION? AS WARLORD OF ATLANTIS, I AM ENTITLED TO KNOW YOUR BATTLE PLANS!
THIS DOES NOT CONCERN BATTLE PLANS! THE SURFACE GIRL IS DYING --I MUST GET HER TO A HOSPITAL WITHIN MINUTES! NO MORE TIME FOR TALK! YOU HAVE YOUR ORDERS!
THE SURFACE GIRL!! YOU ORDER US OUT OF THE IMPERIAL CRAFT IN ORDER TO SAVE AN ENEMY!!
I KNEW IT!! YOU ARE IN LOVE HER! SHE HAS BEWITCHED YOU! BUT NOT EVEN A PRINCE OF THE BLOOD MAY BETRAY HIS PEOPLE LIKE THIS!
SILENCE, DORMA! I CLAIM IMPERIAL PRIVILEGE, AS IS MY RIGHT!
AND SO, LEAVING THE OTHERS BEHIND WITH AN AUXILIARY LIFE-CRAFT, THE LORD OF ATLANTIS TAKES SOLE COMMAND OF THE POWERFUL SHIP!
35

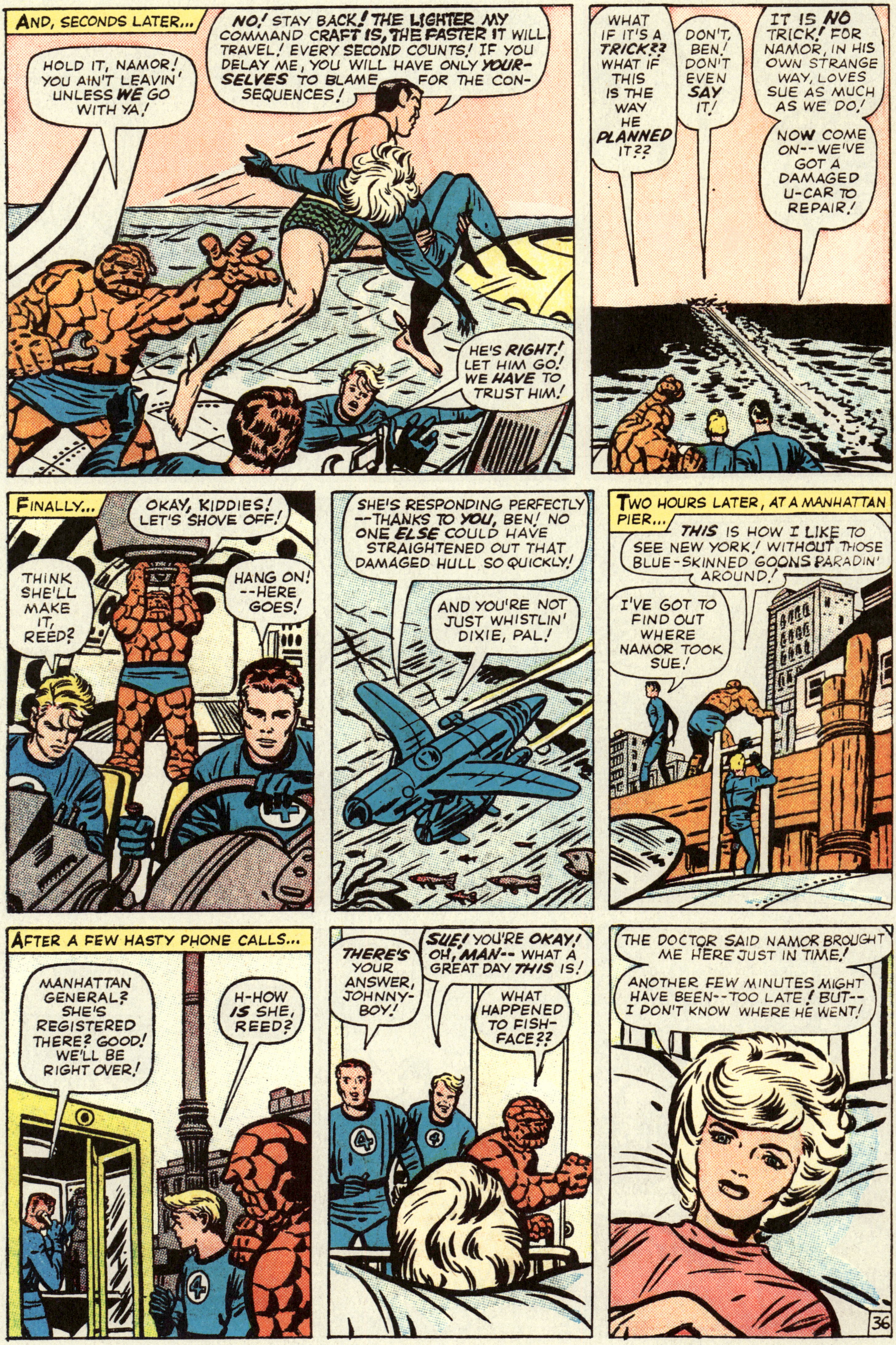

AND, SECONDS LATER...
HOLD IT, NAMOR! YOU AIN'T LEAVIN' UNLESS WE GO WITH YA!
NO! STAY BACK! THE LIGHTER MY COMMAND CRAFT IS, THE FASTER IT WILL TRAVEL! EVERY SECOND COUNTS! IF YOU DELAY ME, YOU WILL HAVE ONLY YOURSELVES TO BLAME FOR THE CONSEQUENCES!
HE'S RIGHT! LET HIM GO! WE HAVE TO TRUST HIM!
WHAT IF IT'S A TRICK?? WHAT IF THIS IS THE WAY HE PLANNED IT??
DON'T, BEN! DON'T EVEN SAY IT!
IT IS NO TRICK! FOR NAMOR, IN HIS OWN STRANGE WAY, LOVES SUE AS MUCH AS WE DO!
NOW COME ON-- WE'VE GOT A DAMAGED U-CAR TO REPAIR!
FINALLY...
OKAY, KIDDIES! LET'S SHOVE OFF!
THINK SHE'LL MAKE IT, REED?
HANG ON! --HERE GOES!
SHE'S RESPONDING PERFECTLY --THANKS TO YOU, BEN! NO ONE ELSE COULD HAVE STRAIGHTENED OUT THAT DAMAGED HULL SO QUICKLY!
AND YOU'RE NOT JUST WHISTLIN' DIXIE, PAL!
TWO HOURS LATER, AT A MANHATTAN PIER...
THIS IS HOW I LIKE TO SEE NEW YORK! WITHOUT THOSE BLUE-SKINNED GOONS PARADIN' AROUND!
I'VE GOT TO FIND OUT WHERE NAMOR TOOK SUE!
AFTER A FEW HASTY PHONE CALLS...
MANHATTAN GENERAL? SHE'S REGISTERED THERE? GOOD! WE'LL BE RIGHT OVER!
H-HOW IS SHE, REED?
THERE'S YOUR ANSWER, JOHNNY-BOY!
SUE! YOU'RE OKAY! OH, MAN-- WHAT A GREAT DAY THIS IS!
WHAT HAPPENED TO FISH-FACE??
THE DOCTOR SAID NAMOR BROUGHT ME HERE JUST IN TIME!
ANOTHER FEW MINUTES MIGHT HAVE BEEN--TOO LATE! BUT-- I DON'T KNOW WHERE HE WENT!
36

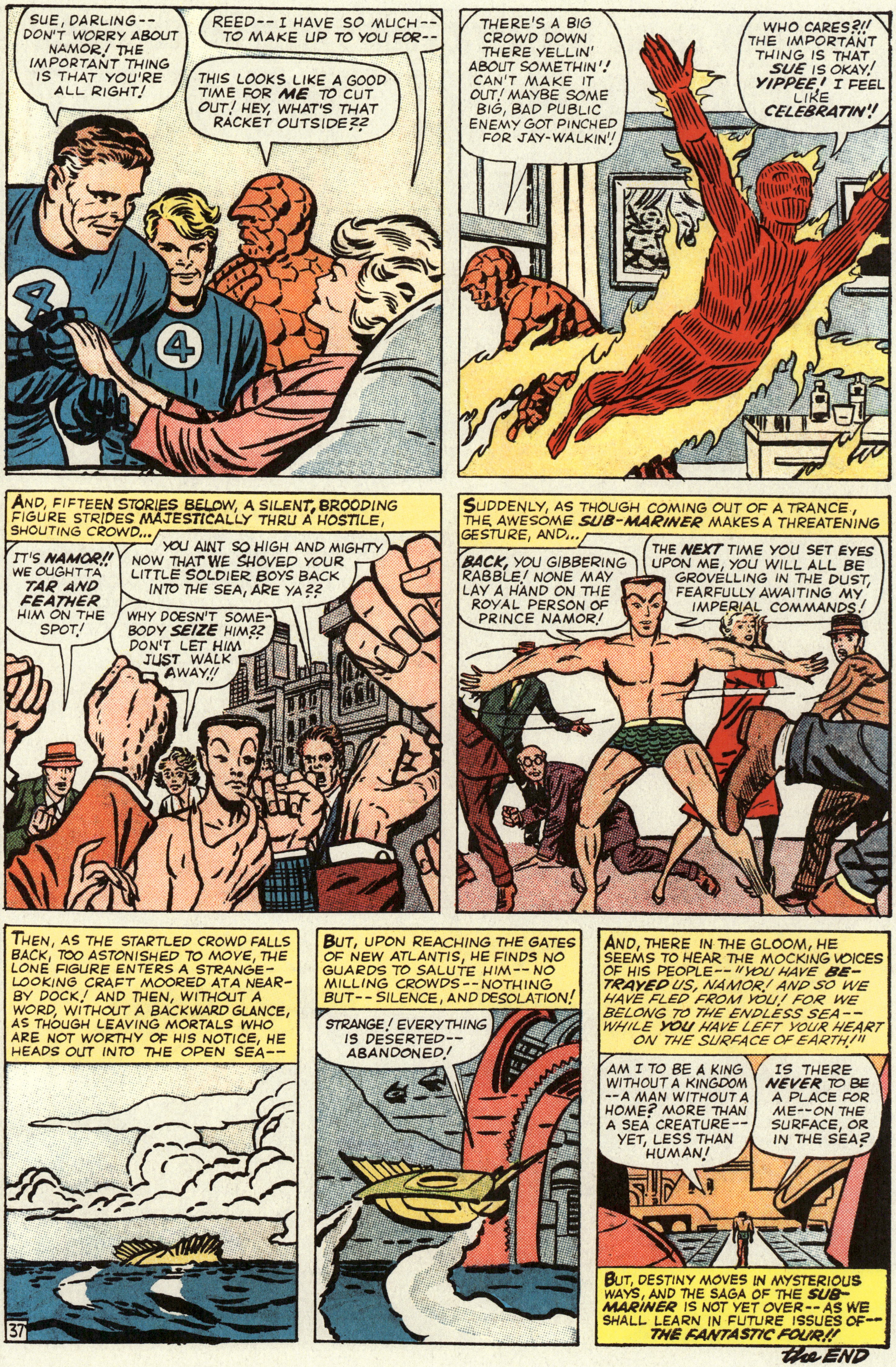
SUE, DARLING -- DON'T WORRY ABOUT NAMOR! THE IMPORTANT THING IS THAT YOU'RE ALL RIGHT!
REED -- I HAVE SO MUCH -- TO MAKE UP TO YOU FOR --
THIS LOOKS LIKE A GOOD TIME FOR ME TO CUT OUT! HEY, WHAT'S THAT RACKET OUTSIDE??
THERE'S A BIG CROWD DOWN THERE YELLIN' ABOUT SOMETHIN'! CAN'T MAKE IT OUT! MAYBE SOME BIG, BAD PUBLIC ENEMY GOT PINCHED FOR JAY-WALKIN'!
WHO CARES?!! THE IMPORTANT THING IS THAT SUE IS OKAY! YIPPEE! I FEEL LIKE CELEBRATIN'!
AND, FIFTEEN STORIES BELOW, A SILENT, BROODING FIGURE STRIDES MAJESTICALLY THRU A HOSTILE, SHOUTING CROWD...
IT'S NAMOR!! WE OUGHTTA TAR AND FEATHER HIM ON THE SPOT!
YOU AINT SO HIGH AND MIGHTY NOW THAT WE SHOVED YOUR LITTLE SOLDIER BOYS BACK INTO THE SEA, ARE YA??
WHY DOESN'T SOMEBODY SEIZE HIM?? DON'T LET HIM JUST WALK AWAY!!
SUDDENLY, AS THOUGH COMING OUT OF A TRANCE, THE AWESOME SUB-MARINER MAKES A THREATENING GESTURE, AND...
BACK, YOU GIBBERING RABBLE! NONE MAY LAY A HAND ON THE ROYAL PERSON OF PRINCE NAMOR!
THE NEXT TIME YOU SET EYES UPON ME, YOU WILL ALL BE GROVELLING IN THE DUST, FEARFULLY AWAITING MY IMPERIAL COMMANDS!
THEN, AS THE STARTLED CROWD FALLS BACK, TOO ASTONISHED TO MOVE, THE LONE FIGURE ENTERS A STRANGE-LOOKING CRAFT MOORED AT A NEARBY DOCK! AND THEN, WITHOUT A WORD, WITHOUT A BACKWARD GLANCE, AS THOUGH LEAVING MORTALS WHO ARE NOT WORTHY OF HIS NOTICE, HE HEADS OUT INTO THE OPEN SEA --
BUT, UPON REACHING THE GATES OF NEW ATLANTIS, HE FINDS NO GUARDS TO SALUTE HIM -- NO MILLING CROWDS -- NOTHING BUT -- SILENCE, AND DESOLATION!
STRANGE! EVERYTHING IS DESERTED -- ABANDONED!
AND, THERE IN THE GLOOM, HE SEEMS TO HEAR THE MOCKING VOICES OF HIS PEOPLE -- "YOU HAVE BETRAYED US, NAMOR! AND SO WE HAVE FLED FROM YOU! FOR WE BELONG TO THE ENDLESS SEA -- WHILE YOU HAVE LEFT YOUR HEART ON THE SURFACE OF EARTH!"
AM I TO BE A KING WITHOUT A KINGDOM -- A MAN WITHOUT A HOME? MORE THAN A SEA CREATURE -- YET, LESS THAN HUMAN!
IS THERE NEVER TO BE A PLACE FOR ME -- ON THE SURFACE, OR IN THE SEA?
BUT, DESTINY MOVES IN MYSTERIOUS WAYS, AND THE SAGA OF THE SUB-MARINER IS NOT YET OVER -- AS WE SHALL LEARN IN FUTURE ISSUES OF -- THE FANTASTIC FOUR!!
37
the END

A GALLERY OF THE FANTASTIC FOUR'S MOST FAMOUS FOES!
THE MOLE MAN
FROM F.F. #1 NOV.
THE MOLE MAN! NEARLY BLIND INHABITANT OF THE NETHER REGIONS OF EARTH! USING HIS STRANGE "RADAR-SENSE" INSTEAD OF EYESIGHT, AIDED BY AN AWESOME GROUP OF UNDEREARTH MONSTERS, THIS BITTER, BROODING MAN YEARS AGO LEFT EARTH'S SURFACE BECAUSE OF HIS HATRED FOR MANKIND, AND SET UP AN UNDERGROUND EMPIRE OVER WHICH HE RULED WITH TYRANNICAL POWER... UNTIL THE FANTASTIC FOUR PUT AN END TO HIS SAVAGE DREAM OF CONQUERING THE SURFACE OF EARTH!

A GALLERY OF THE FANTASTIC FOUR'S MOST FAMOUS FOES!
THE SKRULLS FROM OUTER SPACE!
FROM F.F. # 2 JAN.
THEY CALLED THEMSELVES SKRULLS! BUT, BY ANY NAME, THEY WERE A BAND OF THE MOST DANGEROUS MENACES EARTH HAD EVER FACED! ABLE TO CHANGE THEIR APPEARANCES AT WILL, THEY TOOK THE IDENTITIES OF THE FANTASTIC FOUR, AND ALMOST SUCCEEDED IN PUTTING THE BLAME FOR THEIR OWN MISDEEDS ON THE COLORFUL QUARTET! BUT THEY LEARNED, IN TIME, THAT IT TAKES MORE THAN EXPERT MIMICRY TO TURN A GROUP OF AMAZING ALIENS INTO AMERICA'S GREATEST HEROES!

A GALLERY OF THE FANTASTIC FOUR'S MOST FAMOUS FOES!
the MIRACLE MAN
FROM F.F. # 3 MAR.
HOW DO YOU FIGHT A MAN WHO CAN ACCOMPLISH MIRACLES! THAT WAS THE PROBLEM WHICH CONFRONTED THE FANTASTIC FOUR WHEN THEY FACED THE THREAT OF THE MIRACLE MAN! HE SEEMED STRONGER THAN THE THING, MORE BRILLIANT THAN MISTER FANTASTIC, MORE POWERFUL THAN THE HUMAN TORCH, AND MORE ELUSIVE THAN THE INVISIBLE GIRL! YET, OUR COLORFUL COMBO WERE TO FINALLY LEARN THAT EVEN MIRACLES ARE NOT ALWAYS WHAT THEY SEEM... NOT WHEN THEY ARE PRODUCED BY A MASTER HYPNOTIST!

A GALLERY OF THE FANTASTIC FOUR'S MOST FAMOUS FOES!
PRINCE NAMOR, THE SENSATIONAL
SUB-MARINER
FIRST APPEARED IN F.F. #4 MAY
SUB-MARINER! RULER OF THE SEAS! ROYAL PRINCE-OF-THE-BLOOD OF A MIGHTY, ALMOST LEGENDARY RACE! HIS STRENGTH IS THE STRENGTH OF MANY SURFACE-MEN, AND HIS FIGHTING HEART AND RAW COURAGE MAKE HIM AN INDOMITABLE FOE! ABLE TO BREATHE UNDER WATER, TO WITHSTAND THE CRUSHING PRESSURE OF THE OCEAN'S DEPTHS... ABLE TO FLY FOR SHORT DISTANCES AIDED BY HIS WINGED FEET... POSSESSING THE INCREDIBLE POWER OF ALL THE UNDERSEA CREATURES, PRINCE NAMOR, THE SUB-MARINER, IS THE MOST TALKED-ABOUT, MOST COLORFUL HERO-VILLAIN IN ALL OF COMICDOM TODAY!

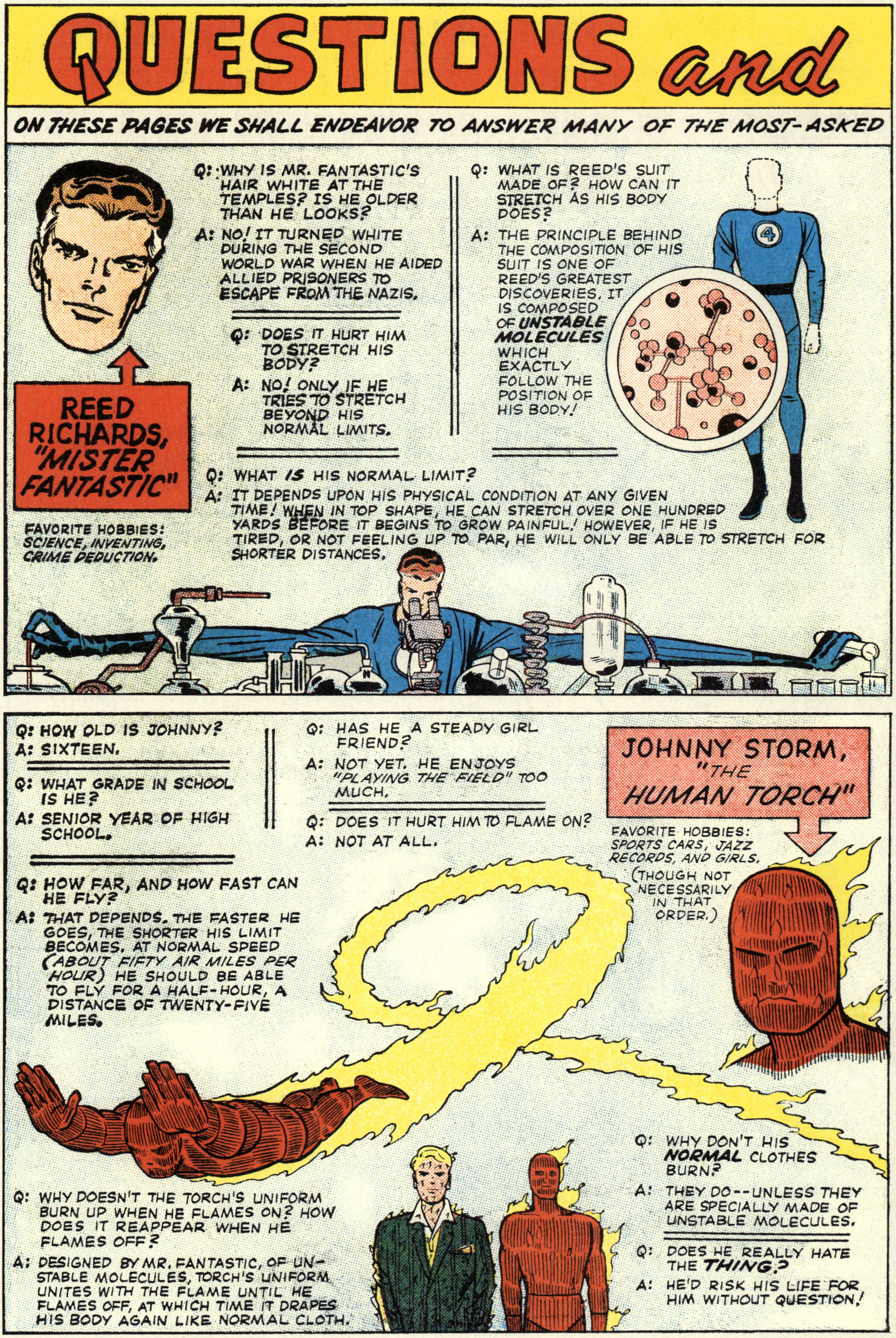

QUESTIONS and
ON THESE PAGES WE SHALL ENDEAVOR TO ANSWER MANY OF THE MOST-ASKED
REED RICHARDS, "MISTER FANTASTIC"
FAVORITE HOBBIES: SCIENCE, INVENTING, CRIME DEDUCTION.
Q: WHY IS MR. FANTASTIC'S HAIR WHITE AT THE TEMPLES? IS HE OLDER THAN HE LOOKS?
A: NO! IT TURNED WHITE DURING THE SECOND WORLD WAR WHEN HE AIDED ALLIED PRISONERS TO ESCAPE FROM THE NAZIS.
Q: DOES IT HURT HIM TO STRETCH HIS BODY?
A: NO! ONLY IF HE TRIES TO STRETCH BEYOND HIS NORMAL LIMITS.
Q: WHAT IS REED'S SUIT MADE OF? HOW CAN IT STRETCH AS HIS BODY DOES?
A: THE PRINCIPLE BEHIND THE COMPOSITION OF HIS SUIT IS ONE OF REED'S GREATEST DISCOVERIES. IT IS COMPOSED OF UNSTABLE MOLECULES WHICH EXACTLY FOLLOW THE POSITION OF HIS BODY!
Q: WHAT IS HIS NORMAL LIMIT?
A: IT DEPENDS UPON HIS PHYSICAL CONDITION AT ANY GIVEN TIME! WHEN IN TOP SHAPE, HE CAN STRETCH OVER ONE HUNDRED YARDS BEFORE IT BEGINS TO GROW PAINFUL! HOWEVER, IF HE IS TIRED, OR NOT FEELING UP TO PAR, HE WILL ONLY BE ABLE TO STRETCH FOR SHORTER DISTANCES.
Q: HOW OLD IS JOHNNY?
A: SIXTEEN.
Q: WHAT GRADE IN SCHOOL IS HE?
A: SENIOR YEAR OF HIGH SCHOOL.
Q: HAS HE A STEADY GIRL FRIEND?
A: NOT YET. HE ENJOYS "PLAYING THE FIELD" TOO MUCH.
Q: DOES IT HURT HIM TO FLAME ON?
A: NOT AT ALL.
JOHNNY STORM, "THE HUMAN TORCH"
FAVORITE HOBBIES: SPORTS CARS, JAZZ RECORDS, AND GIRLS. (THOUGH NOT NECESSARILY IN THAT ORDER.)
Q: HOW FAR, AND HOW FAST CAN HE FLY?
A: THAT DEPENDS. THE FASTER HE GOES, THE SHORTER HIS LIMIT BECOMES. AT NORMAL SPEED (ABOUT FIFTY AIR MILES PER HOUR) HE SHOULD BE ABLE TO FLY FOR A HALF-HOUR, A DISTANCE OF TWENTY-FIVE MILES.
Q: WHY DON'T HIS NORMAL CLOTHES BURN?
A: THEY DO--UNLESS THEY ARE SPECIALLY MADE OF UNSTABLE MOLECULES.
Q: WHY DOESN'T THE TORCH'S UNIFORM BURN UP WHEN HE FLAMES ON? HOW DOES IT REAPPEAR WHEN HE FLAMES OFF?
A: DESIGNED BY MR. FANTASTIC, OF UNSTABLE MOLECULES, TORCH'S UNIFORM UNITES WITH THE FLAME UNTIL HE FLAMES OFF, AT WHICH TIME IT DRAPES HIS BODY AGAIN LIKE NORMAL CLOTH.
Q: DOES HE REALLY HATE THE THING?
A: HE'D RISK HIS LIFE FOR HIM WITHOUT QUESTION!

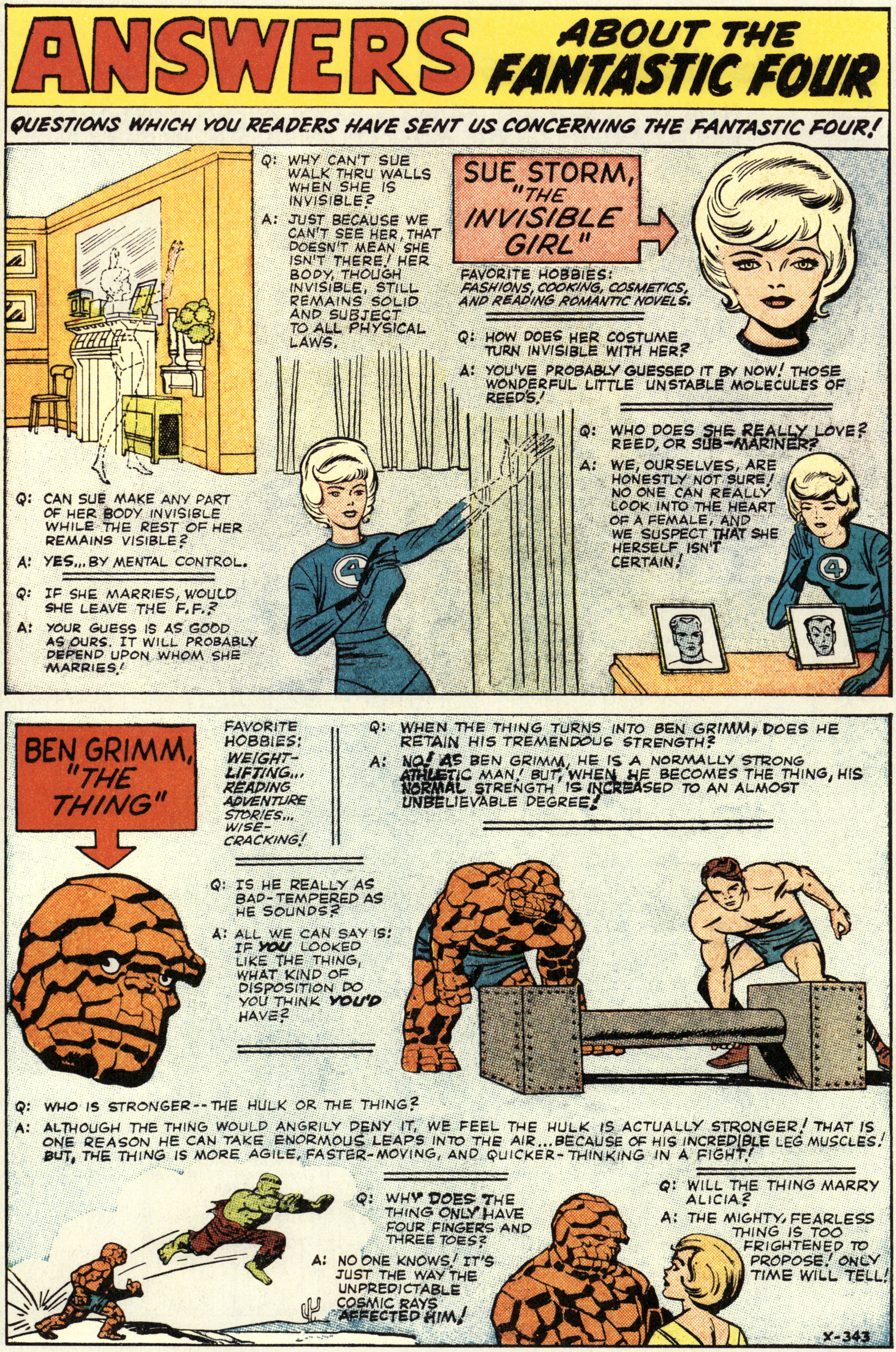
ANSWERS ABOUT THE FANTASTIC FOUR
QUESTIONS WHICH YOU READERS HAVE SENT US CONCERNING THE FANTASTIC FOUR!
Q: WHY CAN'T SUE WALK THRU WALLS WHEN SHE IS INVISIBLE?
A: JUST BECAUSE WE CAN'T SEE HER, THAT DOESN'T MEAN SHE ISN'T THERE! HER BODY, THOUGH INVISIBLE, STILL REMAINS SOLID AND SUBJECT TO ALL PHYSICAL LAWS.
SUE STORM, "THE INVISIBLE GIRL"
FAVORITE HOBBIES: FASHIONS, COOKING, COSMETICS, AND READING ROMANTIC NOVELS.
Q: HOW DOES HER COSTUME TURN INVISIBLE WITH HER?
A: YOU'VE PROBABLY GUESSED IT BY NOW! THOSE WONDERFUL LITTLE UNSTABLE MOLECULES OF REED'S!
Q: WHO DOES SHE REALLY LOVE? REED, OR SUB-MARINER?
A: WE, OURSELVES, ARE HONESTLY NOT SURE! NO ONE CAN REALLY LOOK INTO THE HEART OF A FEMALE, AND WE SUSPECT THAT SHE HERSELF ISN'T CERTAIN!
Q: CAN SUE MAKE ANY PART OF HER BODY INVISIBLE WHILE THE REST OF HER REMAINS VISIBLE?
A: YES... BY MENTAL CONTROL.
Q: IF SHE MARRIES, WOULD SHE LEAVE THE F.F.?
A: YOUR GUESS IS AS GOOD AS OURS. IT WILL PROBABLY DEPEND UPON WHOM SHE MARRIES!
BEN GRIMM, "THE THING"
FAVORITE HOBBIES: WEIGHT-LIFTING... READING ADVENTURE STORIES... WISE-CRACKING!
Q: WHEN THE THING TURNS INTO BEN GRIMM, DOES HE RETAIN HIS TREMENDOUS STRENGTH?
A: NO! AS BEN GRIMM, HE IS A NORMALLY STRONG ATHLETIC MAN! BUT, WHEN HE BECOMES THE THING, HIS NORMAL STRENGTH IS INCREASED TO AN ALMOST UNBELIEVABLE DEGREE!
Q: IS HE REALLY AS BAD-TEMPERED AS HE SOUNDS?
A: ALL WE CAN SAY IS: IF YOU LOOKED LIKE THE THING, WHAT KIND OF DISPOSITION DO YOU THINK YOU'D HAVE?
Q: WHO IS STRONGER--THE HULK OR THE THING?
A: ALTHOUGH THE THING WOULD ANGRILY DENY IT, WE FEEL THE HULK IS ACTUALLY STRONGER! THAT IS ONE REASON HE CAN TAKE ENORMOUS LEAPS INTO THE AIR... BECAUSE OF HIS INCREDIBLE LEG MUSCLES! BUT, THE THING IS MORE AGILE, FASTER-MOVING, AND QUICKER-THINKING IN A FIGHT!
Q: WHY DOES THE THING ONLY HAVE FOUR FINGERS AND THREE TOES?
A: NO ONE KNOWS! IT'S JUST THE WAY THE UNPREDICTABLE COSMIC RAYS AFFECTED HIM!
Q: WILL THE THING MARRY ALICIA?
A: THE MIGHTY, FEARLESS THING IS TOO FRIGHTENED TO PROPOSE! ONLY TIME WILL TELL!
X-343

INSIDE THE BAXTER BLDG.
NEW YORK'S MOST FAMOUS SKYSCRAPER TOWER... HEADQUARTERS OF THE MOST COLORFUL SUPER-HERO COMBO THE CIVILIZED WORLD HAS EVER KNOWN!
JUST EAST OF FIFTH AVENUE, IN MIDTOWN MANHATTAN, STANDS THE MIGHTY BAXTER BUILDING... THIRTY-FIVE STORIES HIGH!
OBSERVATORY
ANTI-VIBRATION WALL CONTAINS SPECIAL MATERIALS WHICH COMPLETELY ABSORB SHOCK OF ROCKET LAUNCHING
ROCKET SILO
FANTASTI-CAR
FANTASTI-COPTER
VEHICLE HANGARS ACCESSIBLE FROM ROOFTOP ELEVATORS AND FROM FLOORS BELOW
PHOTO ANALYSIS LAB
4
STORAGE AND SUPPLY ROOMS
PASSENGER MISSILE
LONG RANGE ICBM TYPE
POGO ORBIT PLANE
VEHICLE MAINTENANCE SHOPS
SAVE FOR FUTURE REFERENCE!
PRIVATE ELEVATOR FOR EXCLUSIVE USE BY FANTASTIC FOUR
MISSILE MONITORING ROOM
MISSILE READY ROOM ENTRANCE TO LAUNCH PAD
PROJECTION ROOM
CONFERENCE ROOM
LAUNCH PAD
GIANT MAP ROOM
ELECTRONIC LAB
BIOLOGICAL RESEARCH LAB
TECHNICAL RESEARCH LAB MACHINE SHOPS
CHEMISTRY LAB
TELESTAR-CONTINENTAL-LOCAL AND CLOSED CIRCUIT TV MONITORS
TV SENDING STUDIO
RADIO SENDING AND RECEIVING ROOM
ROCKET FIRE EXHAUST RUNS THROUGH PIPES DOWN LENGTH OF BUILDING AND DISSIPATES IN UNDER-GROUND PIPES LEADING TO RIVER
GYMNASIUM
RECREATION ROOM
RECEPTION ROOM
DINING ROOM
REED AND BEN ARE PERMANENT RESIDENTS
REED'S APARTMENT
BEN'S ROOM
TORCH AND SISTER SUE STORM COMMUTE FROM SUBURBS USE ROOMS BELOW FOR CONVENIENCE
TORCH'S ASBESTOS ROOM
SUE STORM'S ROOM

ON SALE NOW!
SURE TO BE ONE OF THE MOST TALKED-ABOUT ISSUES OF ALL!!
Here's Why...
ANNUAL
MARVEL COMICS GROUP 25¢
APPROVED BY THE COMICS CODE AUTHORITY
72 BIG PAGES
STRANGE TALES ANNUAL
IND.
#2 1963
THE AMAZING SPIDER-MAN
FACE-TO-FACE WITH...
THE HUMAN TORCH
THE LONG-AWAITED EPIC-LENGTH THRILLER IS ONLY ONE OF THE MANY WONDERFUL FEATURES WITHIN THESE UNFORGETTABLE PAGES!
THE MARVEL COMICS GROUP USHERS IN THE MARVEL AGE OF COMICS!
72 PAGES OF SUPER THRILLS!
ALL NEW: 18 PAGES of HUMAN TORCH and SPIDER-MAN!!
PLUS: TEN OF THE GREATEST FULL-LENGTH FANTASY EPICS EVER PUBLISHED!
ANOTHER WINNER FROM THE TOP-RANKING MARVEL COMICS GROUP!!

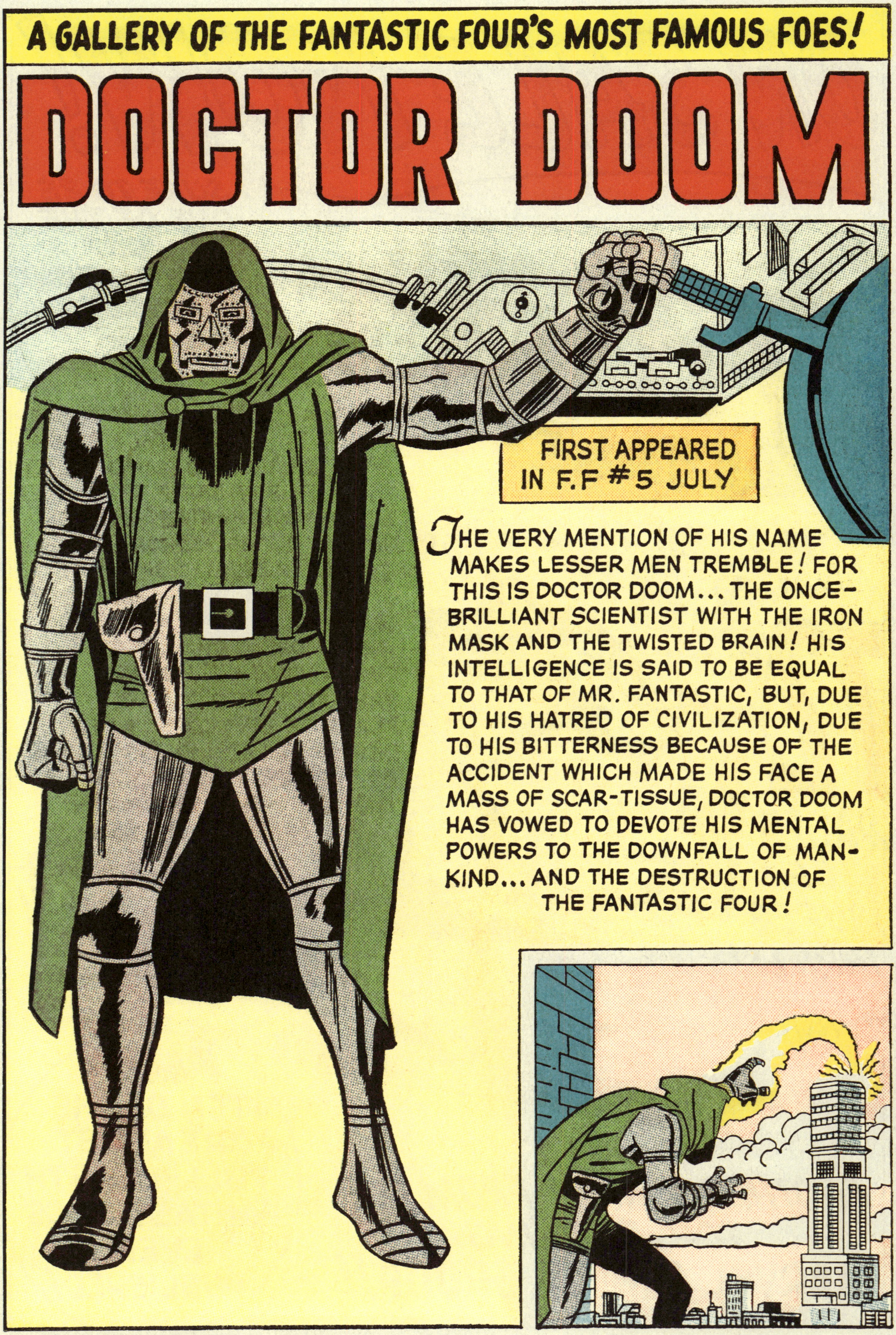
A GALLERY OF THE FANTASTIC FOUR'S MOST FAMOUS FOES!
DOCTOR DOOM
FIRST APPEARED IN F.F #5 JULY
THE VERY MENTION OF HIS NAME MAKES LESSER MEN TREMBLE! FOR THIS IS DOCTOR DOOM... THE ONCE-BRILLIANT SCIENTIST WITH THE IRON MASK AND THE TWISTED BRAIN! HIS INTELLIGENCE IS SAID TO BE EQUAL TO THAT OF MR. FANTASTIC, BUT, DUE TO HIS HATRED OF CIVILIZATION, DUE TO HIS BITTERNESS BECAUSE OF THE ACCIDENT WHICH MADE HIS FACE A MASS OF SCAR-TISSUE, DOCTOR DOOM HAS VOWED TO DEVOTE HIS MENTAL POWERS TO THE DOWNFALL OF MANKIND... AND THE DESTRUCTION OF THE FANTASTIC FOUR!

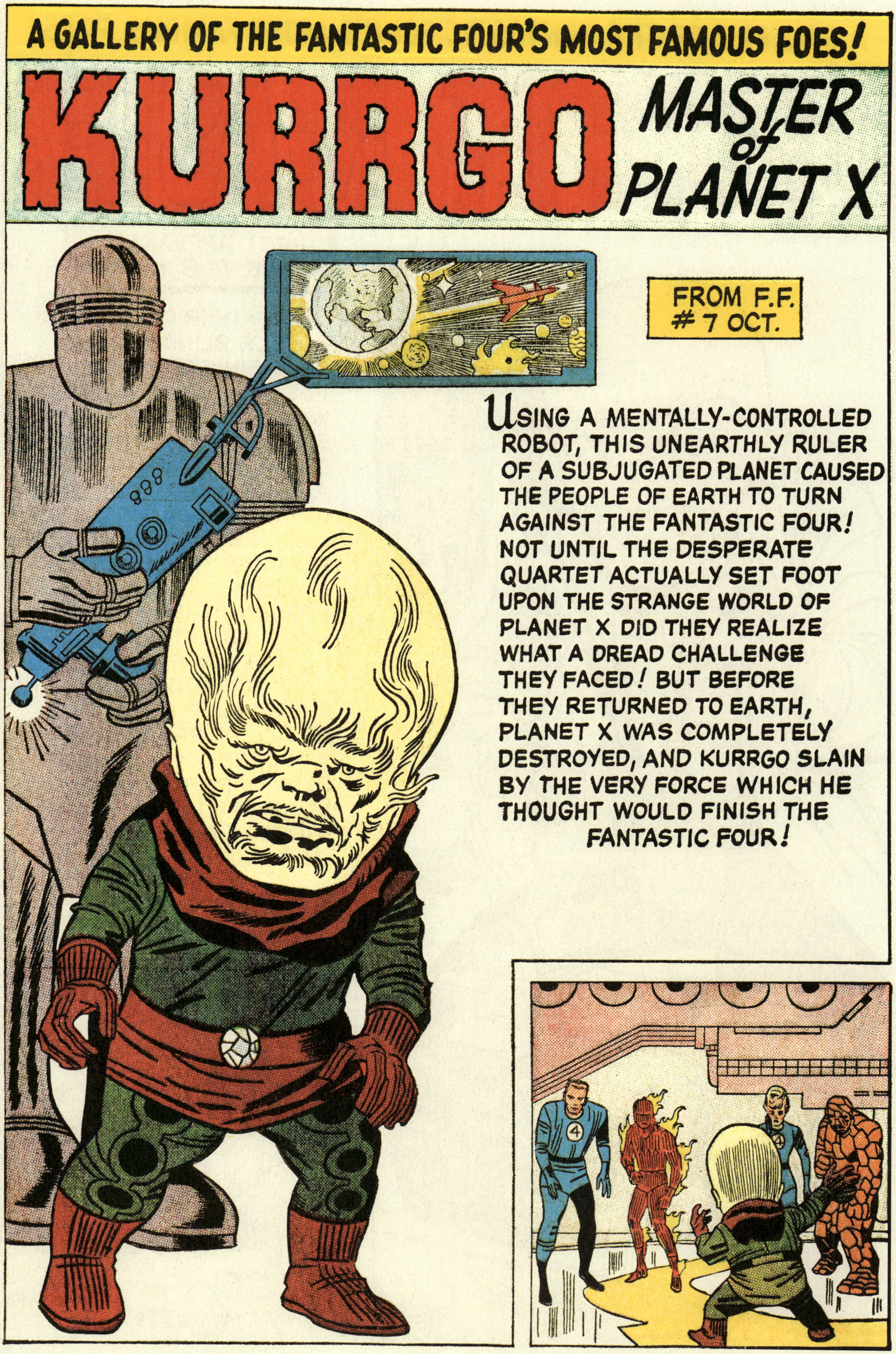
A GALLERY OF THE FANTASTIC FOUR'S MOST FAMOUS FOES!
KURRGO MASTER of PLANET X
FROM F.F. # 7 OCT.
USING A MENTALLY-CONTROLLED ROBOT, THIS UNEARTHLY RULER OF A SUBJUGATED PLANET CAUSED THE PEOPLE OF EARTH TO TURN AGAINST THE FANTASTIC FOUR! NOT UNTIL THE DESPERATE QUARTET ACTUALLY SET FOOT UPON THE STRANGE WORLD OF PLANET X DID THEY REALIZE WHAT A DREAD CHALLENGE THEY FACED! BUT BEFORE THEY RETURNED TO EARTH, PLANET X WAS COMPLETELY DESTROYED, AND KURRGO SLAIN BY THE VERY FORCE WHICH HE THOUGHT WOULD FINISH THE FANTASTIC FOUR!

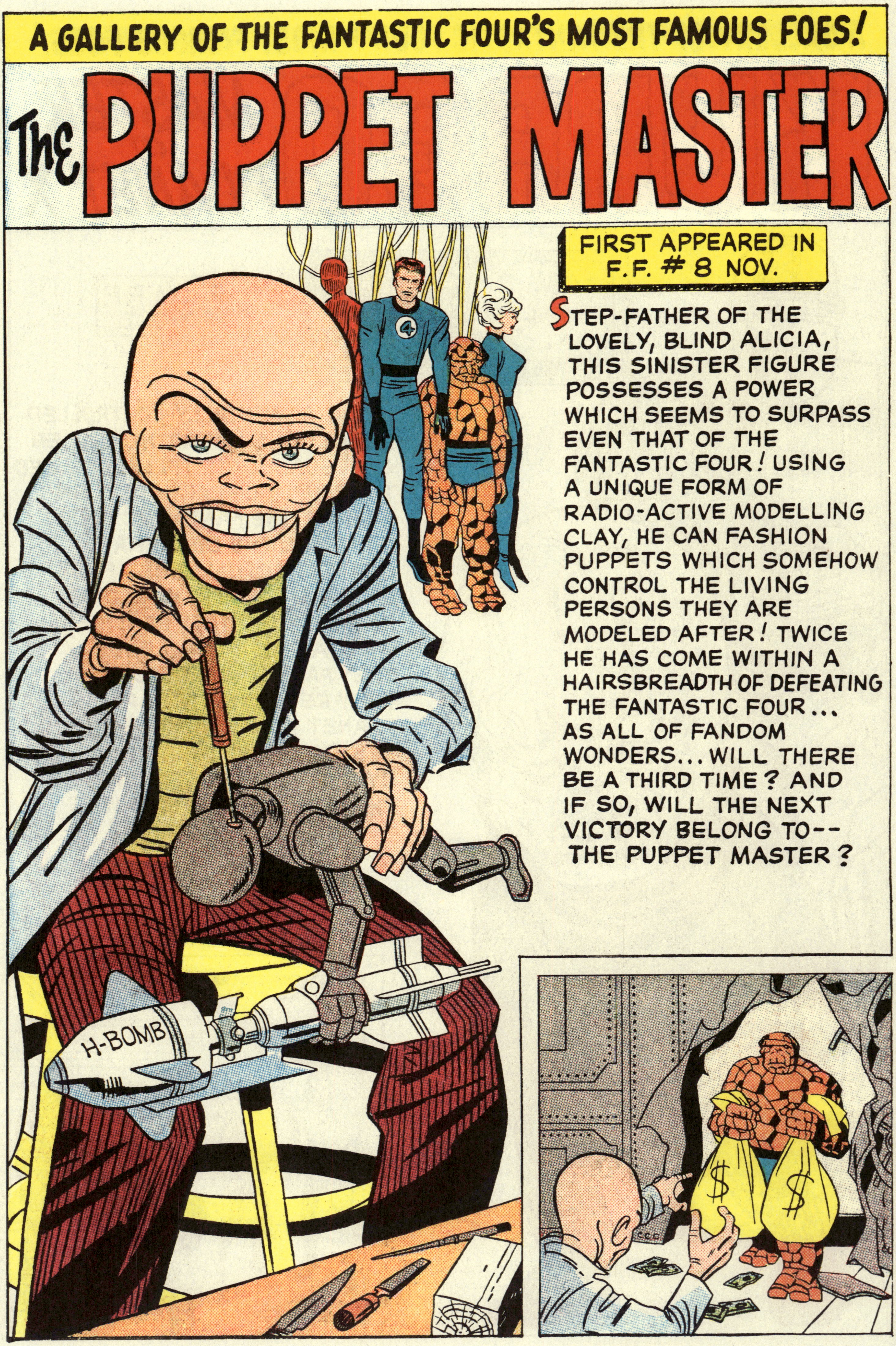
A GALLERY OF THE FANTASTIC FOUR'S MOST FAMOUS FOES!
THE PUPPET MASTER
FIRST APPEARED IN F.F. # 8 NOV.
STEP-FATHER OF THE LOVELY, BLIND ALICIA, THIS SINISTER FIGURE POSSESSES A POWER WHICH SEEMS TO SURPASS EVEN THAT OF THE FANTASTIC FOUR! USING A UNIQUE FORM OF RADIO-ACTIVE MODELLING CLAY, HE CAN FASHION PUPPETS WHICH SOMEHOW CONTROL THE LIVING PERSONS THEY ARE MODELED AFTER! TWICE HE HAS COME WITHIN A HAIRSBREADTH OF DEFEATING THE FANTASTIC FOUR... AS ALL OF FANDOM WONDERS... WILL THERE BE A THIRD TIME? AND IF SO, WILL THE NEXT VICTORY BELONG TO-- THE PUPPET MASTER?
H-BOMB
$
$

THE FABULOUS FANTASTIC FOUR MEET
SPIDER-MAN!*
I SHOULD HAVE THOUGHT OF THIS LONG AGO! I CAN PROBABLY EARN A FORTUNE BY JOINING FORCES WITH THE FANTASTIC FOUR!
THEY'LL BE REAL IMPRESSED WHEN THEY SEE HOW EASILY I CAN BREAK INTO THEIR SKYSCRAPER HEADQUARTERS!
EDITOR'S NOTE:
THIS MEMORABLE INCIDENT, ONE OF THE HIGH POINTS IN COMIC MAGAZINE HISTORY, FIRST OCCURED IN "THE AMAZING SPIDER-MAN" # 1, MARCH! IT WAS MERELY A SMALL, TWO-PAGE EPISODE WHICH BEGAN ONE OF SPIDER-MAN'S GREATEST ADVENTURES! HOWEVER, WE HAVE RECEIVED COUNTLESS REQUESTS ASKING US TO RE-DO THIS FAMOUS ENCOUNTER, BUT TO DEVOTE MORE SPACE TO IT, SHOWING IT IN ALL ITS EXCITING DETAIL! AND SO-- BECAUSE YOU REQUESTED IT...
WRITTEN BY: STAN LEE
DRAWN BY: JACK KIRBY
INKING: STEVE DITKO
LETTERING: RAY HOLLOWAY
* BY SPECIAL ARRANGEMENT WITH SPIDER-MAN MAGAZINE WHERE THIS EPISODE, BY LEE AND DITKO, FIRST APPEARED IN CONDENSED FORM!
AT THAT MOMENT, AN ALARM RINGS IN THE READY-ROOM OF THE FANTASTIC FOUR!
THE ALARM! SOMEONE IS TRYING TO SNEAK IN!
HE MUST BE SOME KINDA NUT TO THINK HE CAN TAKE US BY SURPRISE!
BRIN-NG
THERE'S HIS PICTURE ON OUR VIEWPLATE! IT'S SPIDER-MAN!
HOW OBLIGING OF THEM TO LEAVE A WINDOW OPEN FOR ME! THIS IS A BREEZE!
1

GREETINGS, GROUP! YOU SHOULDN'T MAKE IT SO EASY FOR PEOPLE TO DROP IN ON YA!
GOT NEWS FOR YOU, LOUDMOUTH: IT AINT THAT EASY!
WHA--? A PLEXI-GLASS CAGE! DROPPED FROM THE CEILING!
THIS GIZMO MAY KEEP OUT THE RIFF-RAFF, GRUESOME, BUT IT'S A JOKE TO ME!
THAT DEVICE COST US THOUSANDS! IF YOU WRECK IT...
DON'T WORRY, RUBBER-FACE! THIS SQUIRT'S GONNA BE TAUGHT SOME MANNERS RIGHT NOW!
OWW! YA BIG APE-- WHO DO YA THINK YOU'RE PUSHIN' AROUND?
DON'T FORGET YOU'RE MESSIN' WITH A GUY WHO HAS THE PROPORTIONATE STRENGTH OF A SPIDER!
NUTS! THAT'S WHAT I GET FOR PULLING MY PUNCH ON ACCOUNTA HIS SIZE!
OKAY, WISE-GUY! YOU WANNA PLAY IN THE BIG LEAGUE? I'LL GIVE YA A LITTLE SAMPLE OF WHAT TO EXPECT!
SO YOU GOT THE PROPORTIONATE STRENGTH OF A SPIDER, HUH? EVER SEE AN INSECT THAT COULD PULL A STUNT LIKE THIS??
MAYBE NOT...
BUT I'VE GOT STUNTS OF MY OWN-- LIKE STICKIN' TO THE WALL TO DODGE YOUR CLUMSY ATTEMPTS TO TRAP ME!

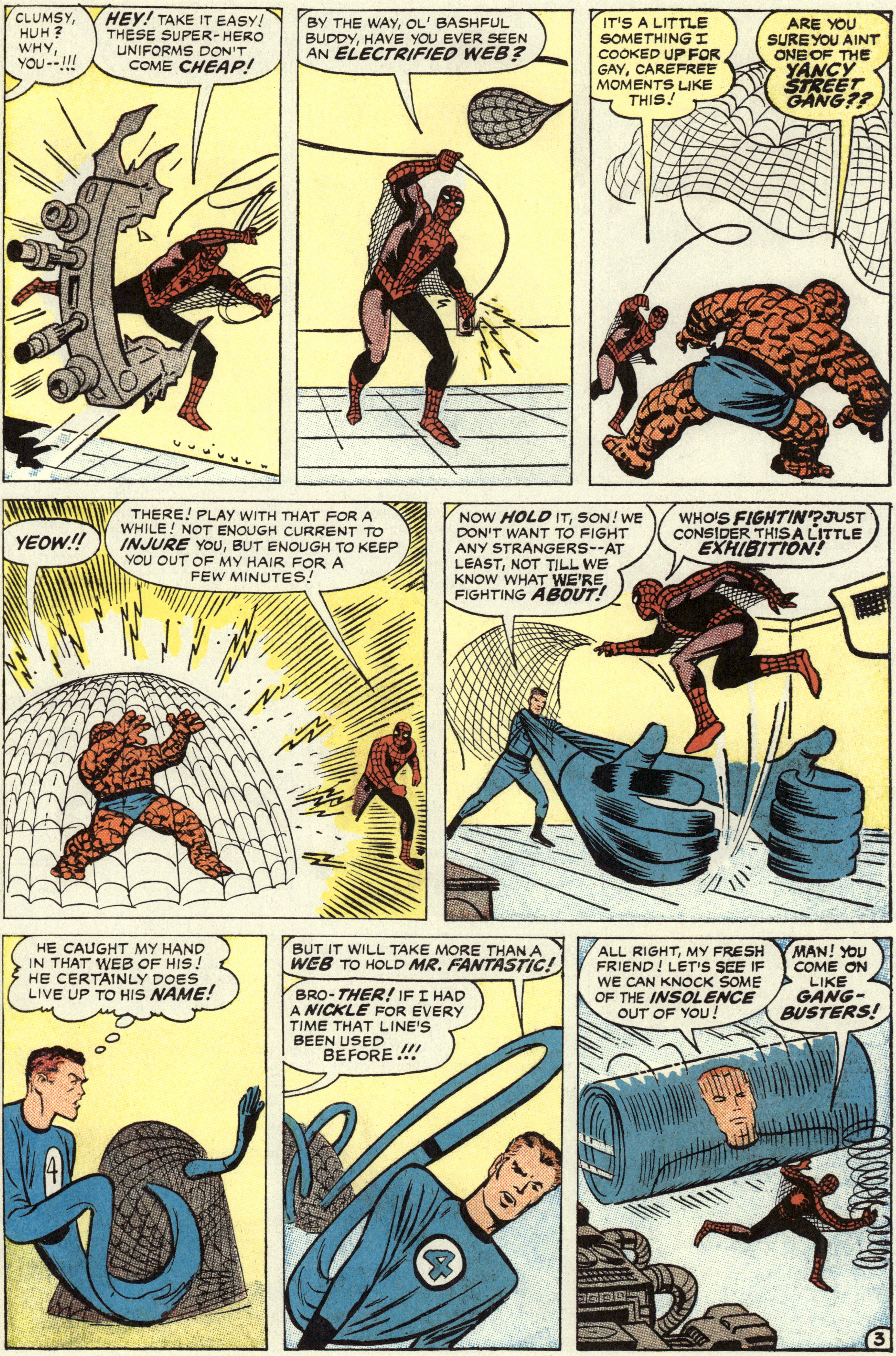
CLUMSY, HUH ? WHY, YOU--!!!
HEY! TAKE IT EASY! THESE SUPER-HERO UNIFORMS DON'T COME CHEAP!
BY THE WAY, OL' BASHFUL BUDDY, HAVE YOU EVER SEEN AN ELECTRIFIED WEB?
IT'S A LITTLE SOMETHING I COOKED UP FOR GAY, CAREFREE MOMENTS LIKE THIS!
ARE YOU SURE YOU AINT ONE OF THE YANCY STREET GANG??
YEOW!!
THERE! PLAY WITH THAT FOR A WHILE! NOT ENOUGH CURRENT TO INJURE YOU, BUT ENOUGH TO KEEP YOU OUT OF MY HAIR FOR A FEW MINUTES!
NOW HOLD IT, SON! WE DON'T WANT TO FIGHT ANY STRANGERS--AT LEAST, NOT TILL WE KNOW WHAT WE'RE FIGHTING ABOUT!
WHO'S FIGHTIN'? JUST CONSIDER THIS A LITTLE EXHIBITION!
HE CAUGHT MY HAND IN THAT WEB OF HIS! HE CERTAINLY DOES LIVE UP TO HIS NAME!
BUT IT WILL TAKE MORE THAN A WEB TO HOLD MR. FANTASTIC!
BRO-THER! IF I HAD A NICKLE FOR EVERY TIME THAT LINE'S BEEN USED BEFORE!!!
ALL RIGHT, MY FRESH FRIEND! LET'S SEE IF WE CAN KNOCK SOME OF THE INSOLENCE OUT OF YOU!
MAN! YOU COME ON LIKE GANG-BUSTERS!
3

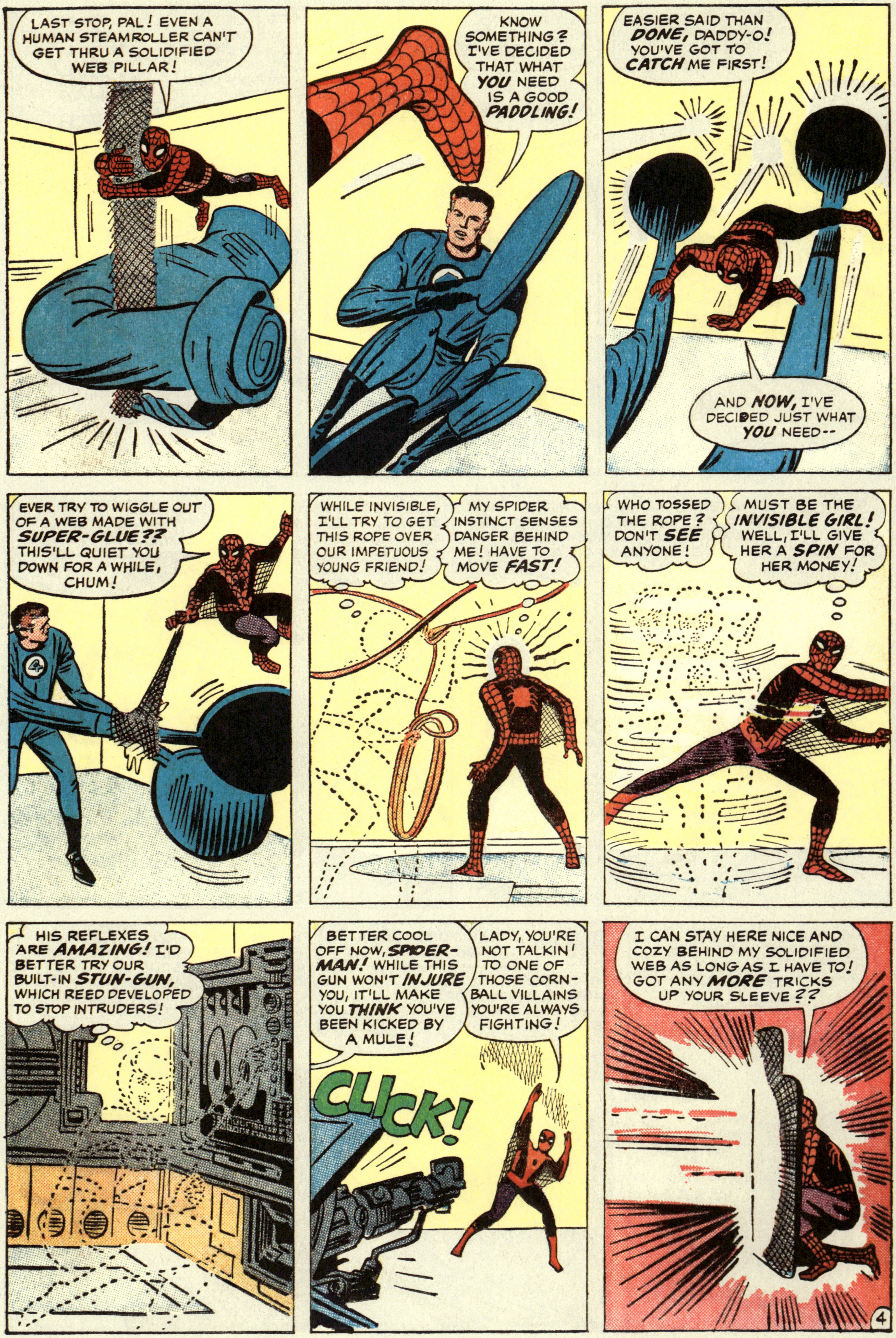

LAST STOP, PAL! EVEN A HUMAN STEAMROLLER CAN'T GET THRU A SOLIDIFIED WEB PILLAR!
KNOW SOMETHING? I'VE DECIDED THAT WHAT YOU NEED IS A GOOD PADDLING!
EASIER SAID THAN DONE, DADDY-O! YOU'VE GOT TO CATCH ME FIRST!
AND NOW, I'VE DECIDED JUST WHAT YOU NEED--
EVER TRY TO WIGGLE OUT OF A WEB MADE WITH SUPER-GLUE?? THIS'LL QUIET YOU DOWN FOR A WHILE, CHUM!
WHILE INVISIBLE, I'LL TRY TO GET THIS ROPE OVER OUR IMPETUOUS YOUNG FRIEND!
MY SPIDER INSTINCT SENSES DANGER BEHIND ME! HAVE TO MOVE FAST!
WHO TOSSED THE ROPE? DON'T SEE ANYONE!
MUST BE THE INVISIBLE GIRL! WELL, I'LL GIVE HER A SPIN FOR HER MONEY!
HIS REFLEXES ARE AMAZING! I'D BETTER TRY OUR BUILT-IN STUN-GUN, WHICH REED DEVELOPED TO STOP INTRUDERS!
BETTER COOL OFF NOW, SPIDER-MAN! WHILE THIS GUN WON'T INJURE YOU, IT'LL MAKE YOU THINK YOU'VE BEEN KICKED BY A MULE!
LADY, YOU'RE NOT TALKIN' TO ONE OF THOSE CORN-BALL VILLAINS YOU'RE ALWAYS FIGHTING!
CLICK!
I CAN STAY HERE NICE AND COZY BEHIND MY SOLIDIFIED WEB AS LONG AS I HAVE TO! GOT ANY MORE TRICKS UP YOUR SLEEVE??
4

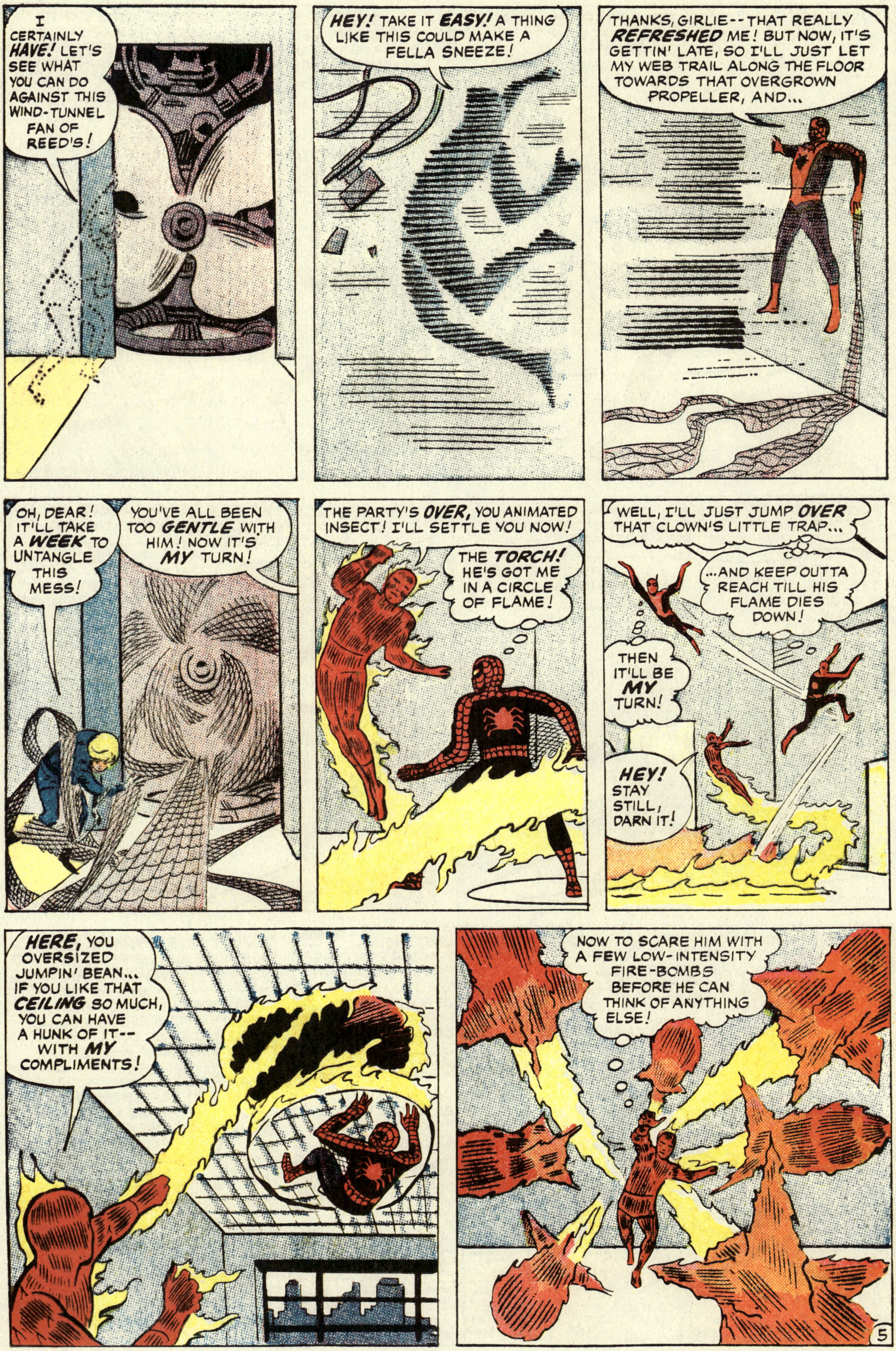
I CERTAINLY HAVE! LET'S SEE WHAT YOU CAN DO AGAINST THIS WIND-TUNNEL FAN OF REED'S!
HEY! TAKE IT EASY! A THING LIKE THIS COULD MAKE A FELLA SNEEZE!
THANKS, GIRLIE--THAT REALLY REFRESHED ME! BUT NOW, IT'S GETTIN' LATE, SO I'LL JUST LET MY WEB TRAIL ALONG THE FLOOR TOWARDS THAT OVERGROWN PROPELLER, AND...
OH, DEAR! IT'LL TAKE A WEEK TO UNTANGLE THIS MESS!
YOU'VE ALL BEEN TOO GENTLE WITH HIM! NOW IT'S MY TURN!
THE PARTY'S OVER, YOU ANIMATED INSECT! I'LL SETTLE YOU NOW!
THE TORCH! HE'S GOT ME IN A CIRCLE OF FLAME!
WELL, I'LL JUST JUMP OVER THAT CLOWN'S LITTLE TRAP...
...AND KEEP OUTTA REACH TILL HIS FLAME DIES DOWN!
THEN IT'LL BE MY TURN!
HEY! STAY STILL, DARN IT!
HERE, YOU OVERSIZED JUMPIN' BEAN... IF YOU LIKE THAT CEILING SO MUCH, YOU CAN HAVE A HUNK OF IT-- WITH MY COMPLIMENTS!
NOW TO SCARE HIM WITH A FEW LOW-INTENSITY FIRE-BOMBS BEFORE HE CAN THINK OF ANYTHING ELSE!
5

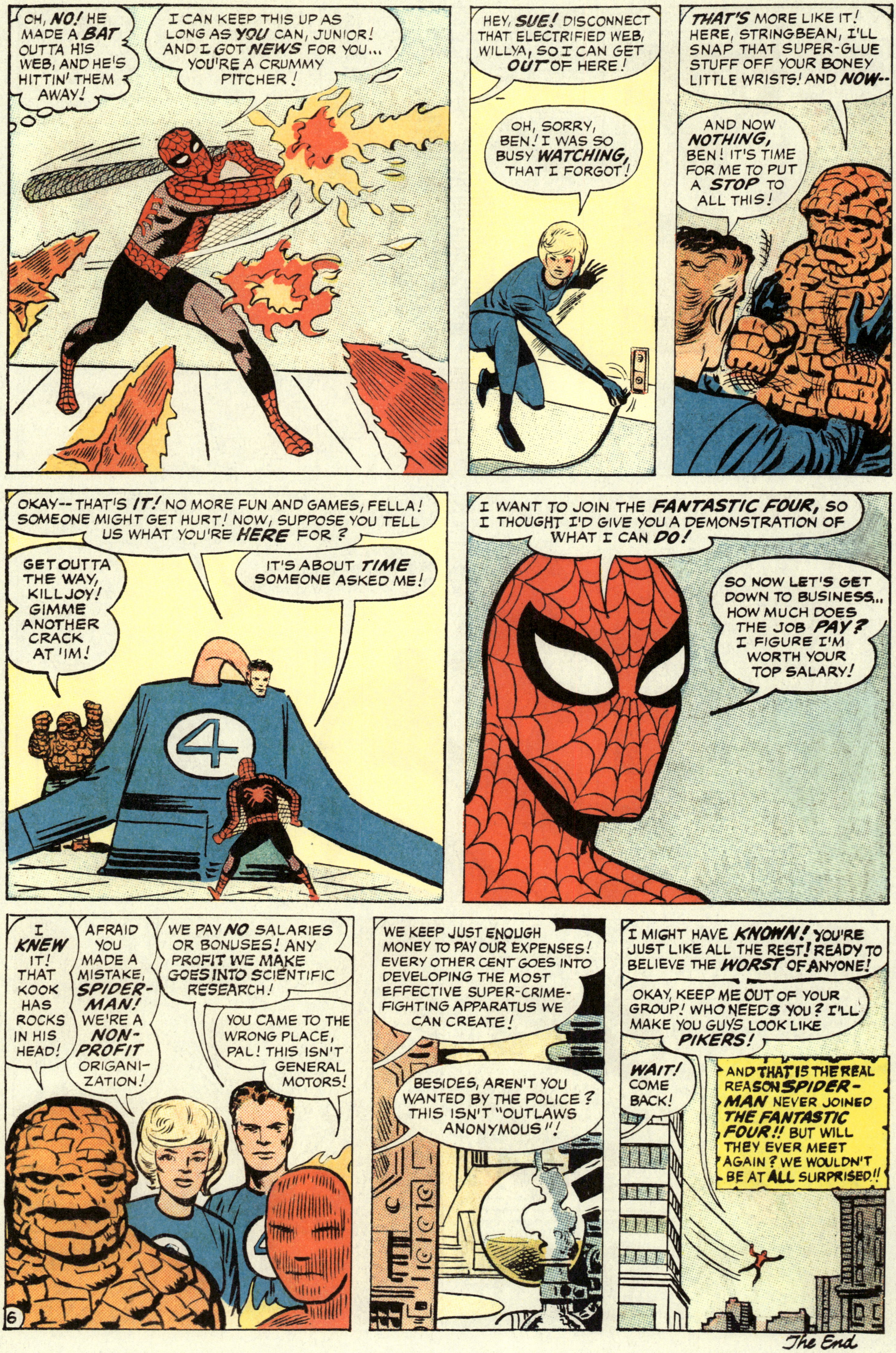

OH, NO! HE MADE A BAT OUTTA HIS WEB, AND HE'S HITTIN' THEM AWAY!
I CAN KEEP THIS UP AS LONG AS YOU CAN, JUNIOR! AND I GOT NEWS FOR YOU... YOU'RE A CRUMMY PITCHER!
HEY, SUE! DISCONNECT THAT ELECTRIFIED WEB, WILLYA, SO I CAN GET OUT OF HERE!
OH, SORRY, BEN! I WAS SO BUSY WATCHING, THAT I FORGOT!
THAT'S MORE LIKE IT! HERE, STRINGBEAN, I'LL SNAP THAT SUPER-GLUE STUFF OFF YOUR BONEY LITTLE WRISTS! AND NOW--
AND NOW NOTHING, BEN! IT'S TIME FOR ME TO PUT A STOP TO ALL THIS!
OKAY-- THAT'S IT! NO MORE FUN AND GAMES, FELLA! SOMEONE MIGHT GET HURT! NOW, SUPPOSE YOU TELL US WHAT YOU'RE HERE FOR?
GET OUTTA THE WAY, KILLJOY! GIMME ANOTHER CRACK AT 'IM!
IT'S ABOUT TIME SOMEONE ASKED ME!
I WANT TO JOIN THE FANTASTIC FOUR, SO I THOUGHT I'D GIVE YOU A DEMONSTRATION OF WHAT I CAN DO!
SO NOW LET'S GET DOWN TO BUSINESS.. HOW MUCH DOES THE JOB PAY? I FIGURE I'M WORTH YOUR TOP SALARY!
I KNEW IT! THAT KOOK HAS ROCKS IN HIS HEAD!
AFRAID YOU MADE A MISTAKE, SPIDER-MAN! WE'RE A NON-PROFIT ORIGANI-ZATION!
WE PAY NO SALARIES OR BONUSES! ANY PROFIT WE MAKE GOES INTO SCIENTIFIC RESEARCH!
YOU CAME TO THE WRONG PLACE, PAL! THIS ISN'T GENERAL MOTORS!
WE KEEP JUST ENOUGH MONEY TO PAY OUR EXPENSES! EVERY OTHER CENT GOES INTO DEVELOPING THE MOST EFFECTIVE SUPER-CRIME-FIGHTING APPARATUS WE CAN CREATE!
BESIDES, AREN'T YOU WANTED BY THE POLICE? THIS ISN'T "OUTLAWS ANONYMOUS"!
I MIGHT HAVE KNOWN! YOU'RE JUST LIKE ALL THE REST! READY TO BELIEVE THE WORST OF ANYONE!
OKAY, KEEP ME OUT OF YOUR GROUP! WHO NEEDS YOU? I'LL MAKE YOU GUYS LOOK LIKE PIKERS!
WAIT! COME BACK!
AND THAT IS THE REAL REASON SPIDER-MAN NEVER JOINED THE FANTASTIC FOUR!! BUT WILL THEY EVER MEET AGAIN? WE WOULDN'T BE AT ALL SURPRISED!!
6
The End

NOW ON SALE MONTHLY
DON'T MISS HIM!
MARVEL COMICS GROUP USHERS IN THE MARVEL AGE OF COMICS!
APPROVED BY THE COMICS CODE AUTHORITY
MARVEL
the AMAZING SPIDER-MAN
IRON MAN!
ANT-MAN!
THOR!
THE HULK!
LOOK FOR THE NEWEST WINNER FROM THE MARVEL COMICS GROUP!
ALL IN
BY THE COMICS CODE AUTHORITY
THE AVENGERS
EARTH'S MIGHTIEST SUPER-HEROES!

A GALLERY OF THE FANTASTIC FOUR'S MOST FAMOUS FOES!
The IMPOSSIBLE MAN FROM THE PLANET POPPUP
FROM F.F. #11 FEB.
THE IMPOSSIBLE MAN! THE MOST AMAZING VISITOR EARTH HAS EVER KNOWN! FROM THE PLANET POPPUP, WHERE THE EVOLUTIONARY PROCESS HAS BEEN SPEEDED UP TO SUCH A DEGREE THAT HE CAN CHANGE HIS BODY INTO ANYTHING WITH THE SPEED OF THOUGHT! A RARITY AMONG THE FANTASTIC FOUR'S FOES BECAUSE HE HASN'T A VILLAINOUS THOUGHT IN HIS HEAD! ALL HE WANTS TO DO IS HAVE FUN! BUT THE IMPOSSIBLE MAN'S IDEA OF FUN ALMOST MADE A SHAMBLES OUT OF EARTH AND FAILURES OUT OF THE FANTASTIC FOUR!

A GALLERY OF THE FANTASTIC FOUR'S MOST FAMOUS FOES!

THE INCREDIBLE HULK

FROM F.F. # 12 MAR.

POSSIBILY THE MOST POWERFUL LIVING CREATURE TO WALK THE EARTH... THIS IS THE HULK! ONLY ONE OTHER PERSON KNOWS HIS WELL-GUARDED SECRET... THE FACT THAT HE IS ACTUALLY DR. BRUCE BANNER, A SCIENTIST ALMOST AS FAMOUS AS REED RICHARDS HIMSELF! BUT, WHEN HE STEPS IN FRONT OF HIS UNIQUE GAMMA-RAY MACHINE, THE RESPECTED DR. BANNER BECOMES THE RAGING, UNCONTROLLABLE, RAMPAGING MOUNTAIN OF MUSCLE... THE INCREDIBLE HULK! FANS STILL TALK OF THE EPIC BATTLE BETWEEN THE HULK AND THE THING... AND WONDER IF THEY'LL EVER MEET AGAIN!

A GALLERY OF THE FANTASTIC FOUR'S MOST FAMOUS FOES!
THE RED GHOST AND HIS INDESCRIBABLE SUPER APES
FROM F.F. #13 APRIL
THE WARPED BRAIN OF THIS BROODING COMMUNIST SCIENTIST FIRST CONCEIVED THE IDEA OF MATCHING POWER FOR POWER WITH THE FANTASTIC FOUR BY SUBJECTING HIMSELF AND HIS TRIO OF TRAINED APES TO THE SAME COSMIC RAYS FROM WHICH THE FANTASTIC FOUR HAD DERIVED THEIR POWER! AND THEN, LOCKED IN MORTAL COMBAT, THERE WITHIN THE LOST CITY OF THE MOON, BOTH TEAMS OF SUPER-POWERFUL FOES HAD THEIR SHOWDOWN BATTLE... WITH THE FATE OF EARTH HANGING IN THE PRECARIOUS BALANCE!

A GALLERY OF THE FANTASTIC FOUR'S MOST FAMOUS FOES!

THE MAD THINKER and his AWESOME ANDROID

ANOTHER MARVEL MASTERPIECE ...
THE STRANGEST SUPER-HEROES OF ALL!
1 SEPT.
IND.
APPROVED BY THE COMICS CODE AUTHORITY
MARVEL COMICS GROUP 12¢
the X-MEN
DON'T MISS THIS FABULOUS FIRST ISSUE!
IN THE SENSATIONAL FANTASTIC FOUR STYLE!
X-MEN VERSUS MAGNETO EARTH'S MOST POWERFUL SUPER VILLAIN!!
NOW ON SALE
...IN THE FABULOUS MARVEL STYLE!

100 TOY SOLDIERS, MADE OF DURABLE PLASTIC, EACH ON ITS OWN BASE, MEASURING UP TO 4½"!

- ★ FUN TO SHOW
- ★ FUN TO TRADE
- ★ FUN TO COLLECT

PACKED in this FOOTLOCKER
TOY STORAGE BOX

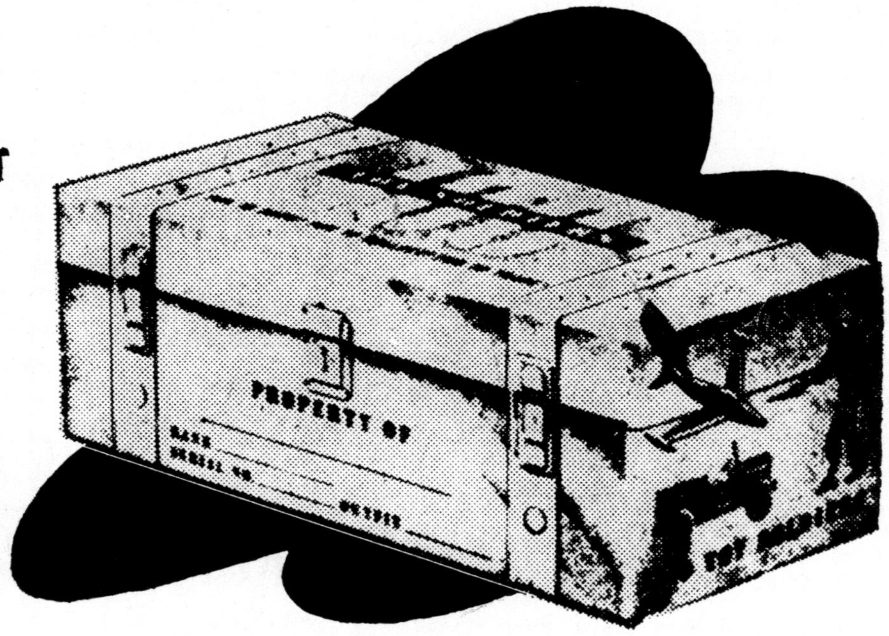

EACH FOOTLOCKER CONTAINS:

- 4 Tanks
- 4 Jeeps
- 4 Battleships
- 4 Cruisers
- 4 Sailors
- 4 Riflemen
- 8 Machinegunners
- 8 Sharpshooters
- 4 Infantrymen
- 8 Officers
- 8 Waves
- 8 Wacs
- 4 Bombers
- 4 Trucks
- 8 Jet Planes
- 8 Cannon
- 4 Bazookamen
- 4 Marksmen

100 TOY SOLDIERS, Dept. MT-1
Carle Place, Long Island, N. Y.

NO C.O.D.'s

HERE'S MY $1.25!
Rush the TOY SOLDIERS TO ME!

Name ....

Address ....

City .... **State** ....

Canada and foreign orders send $1.50 postal money order.

GIVE ME JUST ONE EVENING and I'LL TEACH YOU TO HYPNOTIZE EASILY !

Hypnotize others quickly, safely---perform any known HYPNOTIC FEAT with EASE! Amaze friends-Exert your Hypnotic Power over others - Be POPULAR and WANTED!

YES, it's true! You can hypnotize easily so QUICKLY and simply you'll be amazed! And it doesn't take special talents or long months of study. The very first day you receive this miracle GUIDE TO HYPNOTISM you'll be able to perform wonders that will astound everyone. It's that SIMPLE.... WHEN YOU KNOW HOW.

Imagine the thrill of being able to EXERT YOUR POWER OVER OTHERS. You'll be the center of attraction at parties or work. You'll be able to make others do your bidding...perform and entertain with feats that have baffled millions for years. And you'll do these wonders with EASE. For, Hypnotism is no longer a secret miracle of science but a POWER anyone can exert over another..when you know how!

25 MIRACLE LESSONS

- **HOW TO HYPNOTIZE** New Simple Technique
- **HOW TO AWAKEN SUBJECT**
- **THE POST-HYPNOTIC SUGGESTION** How to make others do your bidding after they are awakened; hypnotiz - ing by telephone.
- **HOW TO GAIN MAGNETIC NEW PERSONALITY**
- **MESMERISM** Quick technique for hypnotizing.
- **MAGNETIC HEALING** How to stop pain. Much surgery is performed by Hypnotism.
- **HOW TO HYPNOTIZE FOR MONEY**
- **CURING BAD HABITS** End sleeplessness, stop smoking, lose weight, etc.
- **POWER OF SUGGESTION**
- **HYPNOTIZE YOURSELF**
- **MAGNETIC INFLUENCE** Control others.
- **HYPNOTIZING CROWDS**
- **HOW TO ENTERTAIN**
- **MIND READING**
- **HYPNOTISM IN BUSINESS**

and much, much more is covered!

Palmer-Jones Publishers. Dept. 100
285 Market St., Newark, N. J.

SIMPLE SECRETS REVEALED AT LAST

For years the knowledge of how to produce hypnotic sleep has been so well guarded that only a few have mastered this art. But now the veil of secrecy has been lifted and the innermost SECRETS and techniques revealed for the first time. The fact is that Hypnotism is a scientific fact that anyone can learn. Once you know these secrets and methods you can bring about this strange and wonderful control that has only been used by doctors, psychiatrists and entertainers in the past. Yes, now this remarkable phenomena will be yours to use for pleasure, self-development and countless other benefits.

YOU CAN PERFORM ANY HYPNOTIC FEAT!

First, you must understand that what another person does with Hypnotism, you can also do. There isn't anything anyone has ever done with this art that you cannot do! YOU can make people cry, laugh, shout, stop smoking, recall childhood memories, act like an infant, make water taste like vinegar, get folks to sing, dance ... do a 1001 things they would never do when not UNDER YOUR POWER. And the most amazing thing of all is --- HOW EASY IT IS TO DO!

SO EASY TO MASTER!

Here at last is the most perfect, complete and easily-learned course on Hypnotism ever written. In three short, simple chapters you learn the hidden secrets of Hypnotism and how to work this scientific miracle. No long, technical, mumbo-jumbo explanations are given. The entire 25-lesson Guide to Hypnotism is written in plain, SIMPLE language that anyone can understand. After the third lesson you are able to begin performing countless techniques and powers clearly explained in the next 22 lessons. You'll learn how to cure bad habits in yourself and others, how to BUILD PERSONAL MAGNETISM, SLEEP without drugs, use Hypnotism to help STOP PAIN, stop smoking, BUILD WILL POWER, LOSE WEIGHT, IMPROVE YOUR MEMORY and so much more. And you'll learn how to MAKE MONEY with your new power by entertaining at parties, lodges, club meetings, etc. Truly, this knowledge will give you a New SURGE of CONFIDENCE and POWER unlike any you have ever known!

ACT, FEEL AND BE A NEW PERSON!

How often have you wished that you could EXERT a MAGNETIC POWER and INFLUENCE OVER OTHERS? Get people to respond to your every command, .win respect, admiration and envy from both men and women! Well, DREAM NO LONGER. It's all possible through the secret, magnetic power of Hypnotism. You'll not only be MASTER OVER OTHERS but also yourself. You can BUILD A STRONG, MAGNETIC PERSONALITY through Self-Hypnotism. You use Mesmerism to READ the MINDS of others and Plant YOUR Thoughts in their minds. You can direct yourself to ACCOMPLISH anything, as easily as you can command others. You have the power to accomplish your innermost dreams.

25 Fact-Packed LESSONS TELL ALL!

Never before has such a Complete and authentic course on Hypnotism been available at such a low price. Doctors and students have PAID hundreds of DOLLARS for personal instruction in Hypnotism, when obtainable. Knowledge such as this can be worth THOUSANDS of DOLLARS to the user over the years. Yet, due to printing economies, large press runs and also by the elimination of correspondence costs, the complete 25-Lesson Guide To HYPNOTISM is yours for only $1.98. Yes, only $1.98 for the COMPLETE COURSE bound in book form. Certainly a tiny investment for so much!

• USE FOR 30 DAYS • WITHOUT OBLIGATION!

PROVE to Yourself that YOU CAN HYPNOTIZE EASILY! Order the 25-Lesson Guide to Hypnotism today and put it to the test the very next evening. The first three chapters teach you the SECRET of Hypnotism and the 22 chapters that follow introduce you to many new WONDERS of this miraculous art. For the next 30 days as our guest, perform the WONDERS of Hypnotism among your friends, at home and at work. Then, if you don't feel it's the GREATEST VALUE you have ever received for $1.98--we don't want you to keep it. Just mail it back and the small payment you sent will be PROMPTLY refunded---no questions asked. You have nothing to lose -- amazing new POWERS TO GAIN! So order now!

CHECK HERE HYPNOTIC POWERS YOU WANT!

- [ ] INFLUENCE OTHERS
- [ ] SELF-HYPNOSIS
- [ ] CURE BAD HABITS
- [ ] LOSE WEIGHT
- [ ] STOP SMOKING
- [ ] PERFORM STUNTS, TRICKS
- [ ] DO MIND READING
- [ ] GAIN MAGNETIC PERSONALITY
- [ ] RELIEVE TENSION
- [ ] MAKE MONEY

MAIL NO-RISK FREE TRIAL COUPON!

PALMER-JONES PUBLISHERS, Dept. 100
285 Market Street, Newark, New Jersey

YES, Send me for 30-day HOME TRIAL the complete 25-Lesson GUIDE TO HYPNOTISM.

- [ ] I enclose $1.98 - payment in full - which will be refunded to me if I am not 100% delighted.

Name ____________________

Address ____________________

City ____________ Zone ___ State ________

- [ ] I agree that I will not use this power for other than proper use.

THE HISTORY

I NEVER THOUGHT IT COULD HAPPEN! RAMA-TUT'S RAY GUN HAS MADE HELPLESS SLAVES OF THE FANTASTIC FOUR!

THERE, SUSAN STORM! THERE IS WHAT HAPPENS TO THOSE WHO DEFY ME--NO MATTER WHAT POWERS THEY POSSESS!

STORYLINES & CREDITS

FANTASTIC FOUR No. 1

Cover date: November 1961
On-sale date: August 8, 1961
Cover price: 10 cents
Pages: 36

Editor: Stan Lee

Cover
Pencils: Jack Kirby
Inks: George Klein
Colors: Stan Goldberg
Letters: Art Simek (cover lettering and logo design); Sol Brodsky (logo design)

First appearance of the Fantastic Four: Mr. Fantastic / Reed Richards, Invisible Girl / Sue Storm, the Thing / Ben Grimm, and Johnny Storm / Human Torch (a reinvention of a 1939 Timely Comics character). First appearance of Mole Man.

"THE *FANTASTIC FOUR!*"
Pages: 22
Script: Stan Lee
Pencils: Jack Kirby
Inks: George Klein
Colors: Stan Goldberg
Letters: Art Simek

Dr. Reed Richards sends a flare into the sky—THE FANTASTIC FOUR—summoning the rest of his team. Sue Storm leaves a friend's house by becoming invisible and taking a cab; Ben Grimm smashes his way out of a haberdasher; Johnny Storm flies and has to fight National Guard jets that are dispatched to investigate. Flashback to their origins: Reed Richards, fiancée Sue Storm, her brother Johnny Storm, and Ben Grimm break into an aeronautical facility. In an effort to fight Communists, the four commandeer a ship that Reed has built. However, the mission is a failure, and they crash back on Earth, only to find that cosmic rays have changed them: Sue can turn invisible, Ben is a rock monster, Reed can stretch his body, and Johnny can set himself aflame and fly. They decide to use their powers for good, and name themselves Invisible Girl, the Thing, Mr. Fantastic, and the Human Torch. Back in the present, Reed shows them photos of giant holes that have opened up all over the world, and we see another one open up in Africa, swallowing an entire building. Reed pinpoints the source to a place called Monster Isle. When they arrive, they battle a three-headed monster before meeting the Mole Man. He tells them his story, and when the Thing and Invisible Girl show up, he unleashes the biggest and baddest monsters he has. The Fantastic Four fight them off, and Torch creates a rock slide to seal the entrance to Mole Man's lair.

FANTASTIC FOUR No. 2

Cover date: January 1962
On-sale date: September 28, 1961
Cover price: 10 cents
Pages: 36

Editor: Stan Lee

Cover "SKRULLS FROM OUTER SPACE!"
Pencils: Jack Kirby
Inks: George Klein
Colors: Stan Goldberg
Letters: Art Simek

First appearance of the Skrulls. Johnny's trademark phrase "Flame on!" used for the first time.

"*THE* FANTASTIC FOUR *MEET THE SKRULLS FROM OUTER SPACE!*"
Pages: 24
Script: Stan Lee
Pencils: Jack Kirby
Inks: George Klein
Colors: Stan Goldberg
Letters: John Duffy

The Thing destroys an oil rig, and then Sue Storm steals a diamond worth $10 million. The Human Torch melts a statue at its public unveiling, and Mr. Fantastic plunges the city into darkness. It's not the Fantastic Four behind these crimes, though—it's a race of alien shape-shifters known as Skrulls. The Fantastic Four are in a country cabin when they hear about the crimes, and U.S. Army soldiers show up to arrest them. The four of them go into hiding to figure out a plan to flush out the impersonators. Johnny destroys a launching platform, hoping to draw them out. The Skrulls take the bait and kidnap Johnny, who leads the rest of the FF to them, and a fight breaks out. They learn that the Skrulls have an invasion force in the atmosphere, waiting to see if the FF can be defeated first. The FF visit the mother ship and show photo evidence (panels clipped from *Strange Tales* and *Journey into Mystery*) to prove that an alien invasion would be certain doom for the Skrulls. The FF volunteer to stay behind, so the rest of the Skrull race can be safe, and are rewarded for their heroism. When they return through the atmosphere, the Thing becomes Ben Grimm again, but it's short-lived. The Fantastic Four deal with the Skrulls left on Earth by hypnotizing them to forget their previous identities; they then shape-shift to live out the rest of their days as cows.

FANTASTIC FOUR No. 3

Cover date: March 1962
On-sale date: December 12, 1961
Cover price: 12 cents
Pages: 36

Editor: Stan Lee

Cover
Pencils: Jack Kirby
Inks: Sol Brodsky
Colors: Stan Goldberg
Letters: Art Simek

First appearance of Miracle Man; cover price increases to 12 cents. The team debuts costumes and the Fantasti-car.

"*THE MENACE OF THE* MIRACLE MAN"
Pages: 23
Script: Stan Lee
Pencils: Jack Kirby
Inks: Sol Brodsky
Colors: Stan Goldberg
Letters: Art Simek

At a magic show, the Fantastic Four witness Miracle Man, who bests the Thing in a show of strength. Miracle Man decides he needs a feat to show the world his power. At home, Sue Storm shows everyone the costumes she's made for the team. On TV, they see Miracle Man bring a monster to life at a movie premiere. The police commissioner tells the FF that Miracle Man has declared war on the whole human race. The FF manages to destroy the monster, but they are quickly bested by the Miracle Man, who brags about defeating them twice. Back home, Ben and Johnny fight; Sue gets hypnotized by Miracle Man, who orders her to call the other three. When they arrive, Miracle Man is holding an oversize key that he turns into a machine gun. They pursue Miracle Man in an old car, and Mr. Fantastic stretches his body to become a wheel when a tire gets shot out. Johnny blinds Miracle Man, and then they subdue him. He brings Sue out of her trance, and Miracle Man reveals that he doesn't have powers—he's just a master of mass illusion. Johnny quits the team out of frustration, and Reed wonders what will happen if Johnny turns on them.

FANTASTIC FOUR No. 4

Cover date: May 1962
On-sale date: February 8, 1962
Cover price: 12 cents
Pages: 36

Editor: Stan Lee

Cover
"***THE COMING OF THE SUB-MARINER!***"
Pencils: Jack Kirby
Inks: Sol Brodsky
Colors: Stan Goldberg
Letters: Art Simek

Another 1939 Marvel Comics character is revived: Namor the Sub-Mariner.

"***THE COMING OF... SUB-MARINER!***"
Pages: 23
Script: Stan Lee
Pencils: Jack Kirby
Inks: Sol Brodsky
Colors: Stan Goldberg
Letters: Art Simek

Sue, Reed, and Ben separate and go out looking for Johnny; the Thing finds him working in a garage. They fight, but Johnny gets away when the Thing turns back into Ben Grimm. Johnny gets a hotel room in the Bowery with derelicts and tries to distract himself reading an old Sub-Mariner comic. There's an extremely tough, bearded guy living in the hotel; Johnny uses his flame to shave the old guy, and it turns out it's the Sub-Mariner himself, suffering from amnesia. Johnny throws the Sub-Mariner in the ocean, his memory comes back, and he remembers how the humans destroyed his home. When he returns to the surface, he vows vengeance on mankind. Johnny calls the FF, while Namor goes back in the ocean and awakens Giganto, the "largest living thing in all the world." With Giganto moving toward the city, the order is given to evacuate. Giganto begins destroying the city; the Thing finds a nuclear bomb in a military depot and straps it to his back. He plants the bomb inside Giganto and escapes just in time. Invisible Girl realizes that Namor can call more monsters from the sea with his horn, so she steals it. Namor catches her and says that he'll show mercy to the human race if she marries him. She agrees, but Johnny creates a suction vortex and sends Namor into the deepest part of the sea.

FANTASTIC FOUR No. 5

Cover date: July 1962
On-sale date: April 10, 1962
Cover price: 12 cents
Pages: 36

Editor: Stan Lee

Cover "***MEET...*** **DOCTOR DOOM!**"
Pencils: Jack Kirby
Inks: Joe Sinnott
Colors: Stan Goldberg
Letters: Art Simek

First appearance of Doctor Doom / Victor von Doom.

"**PRISONERS OF *DOCTOR DOOM!***"
Pages: 23
Script: Stan Lee
Pencils: Jack Kirby
Inks: Joe Sinnott
Colors: Stan Goldberg
Letters: Art Simek

Johnny and the Thing fight yet again when Johnny says Thing looks like the Hulk. They stop when a giant, fireproof net is draped over their building. The voice from above is that of Victor von Doom, a classmate of Reed's in college. Doom demands Sue for a hostage. He then orders the other three aboard his helicopter. At his castle, Doom tells them that he has created a time-travel device, and that he is sending them back in time to get Blackbeard's treasure for him. Doom has to stay in the present to operate the machine. Transported to the past, Reed, Johnny, and Ben disguise themselves. They're given poisoned grog and wake up in the hold of a pirate ship. They fight the pirates, who then refer to the Thing as Blackbeard. Knowing Doom would only want the treasure if it had dangerous powers, Reed divides it among the men and fills the chest with chains. Thing wants to stay behind, since in the future he's a freak, but here he's somebody. A hurricane destroys the ship, however, and Reed and Johnny find the Thing—and Blackbeard's treasure chest—washed ashore. Doom returns them to the present but is angered when he finds out they only brought back the chest (as promised) and not the treasure. Thing destroys the villain, but it's only a robot Doom. The real one is watching remotely and drains their room of oxygen, but Sue saves the day by short-circuiting the controls. Sue finds them just in time, and they break out of the castle, which is set aflame. Doom escapes.

FANTASTIC FOUR No. 6

Cover date: September 1962
On-sale date: Jun 12, 1962
Cover price: 12 cents
Pages: 36

Editor: Stan Lee

Cover "**the DIABOLICAL DUO JOIN FORCES!**"
Pencils: Jack Kirby
Inks: Dick Ayers
Colors: Stan Goldberg
Letters: Art Simek

"***CAPTIVES of the DEADLY DUO!***"
Pages: 24
Script: Stan Lee
Pencils: Jack Kirby
Inks: Dick Ayers
Colors: Stan Goldberg
Letters: Terry Szenics

Doctor Doom finds the Sub-Mariner in the ocean and proposes an alliance to defeat the Fantastic Four and all mankind. Doom gives Sub-Mariner a demonstration of his new magnetic weapon. Sub-Mariner says that he will never hurt Sue Storm, but that everyone else is fair game. In the Baxter Building, Johnny finds a photo of Sub-Mariner, so it seems that Sue reciprocates the crush. Namor shows up at the Baxter Building, and the FF all suspect a trap; they're proved right when the entire building is pulled from the ground by Doom's magnetic device. Doom, in a ship, is dragging them into space, planning to hurl the Baxter Building and the Fantastic Four into the sun. Namor, realizing he's as much a victim now as the FF, goes after Doom. Doom jumps from the ship onto a meteor, and Sub-Mariner guides the Baxter Building back to Earth and deposits it where it belongs. The FF find Doom's device in the basement, but can't remove it—Namor removes it remotely, and with Doom presumed dead, Namor puts the device in the bottom of the ocean and goes back there himself.

FANTASTIC FOUR No. 7

Cover date: October 1962
On-sale date: July 3, 1962
Cover price: 12 cents
Pages: 36

Editor: Stan Lee

Cover "THE MASTER OF *PLANET X*"
Pencils and inks: Jack Kirby
Colors: Stan Goldberg
Letters: Art Simek

First appearance of Kurrgo.

"*PRISONERS* OF KURRGO, *MASTER OF* PLANET X"
Pages: 24
Script: Stan Lee
Pencils: Jack Kirby
Inks: Dick Ayers
Colors: Stan Goldberg
Letters: Art Simek and Terry Szenics

Kurrgo, Master of Planet X, watches from across the galaxy as a ship races toward Earth to take the Fantastic Four captive. An asteroid is hurtling toward Planet X, and the only people who can stop it are the FF. The Four argue about having to go to a government dinner, while the ship from Planet X, piloted by a robot, arrives on Earth. The robot unleashes a "hostility ray" that causes people to fight and argue. The nation's lawmakers turn on the FF, declaring them menaces. The FF flee, and from their Fantasti-car, they can see the spaceship following them. At the Baxter Building, the robot approaches and shows them how society has turned against them — not just New York society, but the entire world. The robot shows them the ways society will eventually subdue the Four. They agree to go with the robot to Planet X. The Four realize they're on a doomed planet, and to save themselves they'll have to destroy the asteroid, so they hastily construct a reducing device to shrink everything and everyone on the planet by 1,000. That way everyone can fit on the only two spaceships the planet has. Just in time, the FF and the inhabitants of Planet X escape before the asteroid hits. Kurrgo, however, greedily trying to hoard the enlarging gas for himself, gets left behind on the planet.

FANTASTIC FOUR No. 8

Cover date: November 1962
On-sale date: August 9, 1962
Cover price: 12 cents
Pages: 36

Editor: Stan Lee

Cover "PRISONERS OF THE PUPPET-MASTER*!*"
Pencils: Jack Kirby
Inks: Dick Ayers
Colors: Stan Goldberg
Letters: Art Simek

First appearances of the Puppet Master and Alicia Masters.

"*PRISONERS OF THE* PUPPET MASTER*!*"
Pages: 23
Script: Stan Lee
Pencils: Jack Kirby
Inks: Dick Ayers
Colors: Stan Goldberg
Letters: Art Simek

Reed is working in his lab; Johnny and the Thing fight, then Ben quits the team. While Sue and Ben talk outside, they see a man climbing a bridge. Johnny notices the man has a glazed, trance-like look. Meanwhile, the Puppet Master has built a scale model bridge and has a toy of the man. He builds a model of the Thing out of radioactive clay, drawing him to the Puppet Master's house. Invisible Girl follows him. Puppet Master neutralizes Sue. A blind woman named Alicia Masters feels Thing's face to see what he looks like, and after disguising herself as Sue, they leave together. Puppet Master uses a doll to manipulate the prison warden. Thing and "Sue" arrive at the Baxter Building. Reed can see something is wrong with the Thing, and Thing crashes into the potion that Reed was working on — one that turns the Thing back into Ben Grimm, breaking Puppet Master's spell. They realize that "Sue" is actually the Puppet Master's daughter; Ben holds her to comfort her, but she doesn't know who he is. Quickly, he turns back into the Thing, and she's comforted as she realizes who he is. The prisoners are freed, and with her father occupied, she tries to escape. She manages to shoot off the FF signal just as the Puppet Master gains control of her again. He unleashes a monster to hold them off. They rescue her and quell the prison riot, but the Puppet Master gets away. Just as he's about to unleash one last puppet — him as king — Alicia tries to get it, but he trips over her and falls out the window to his death.

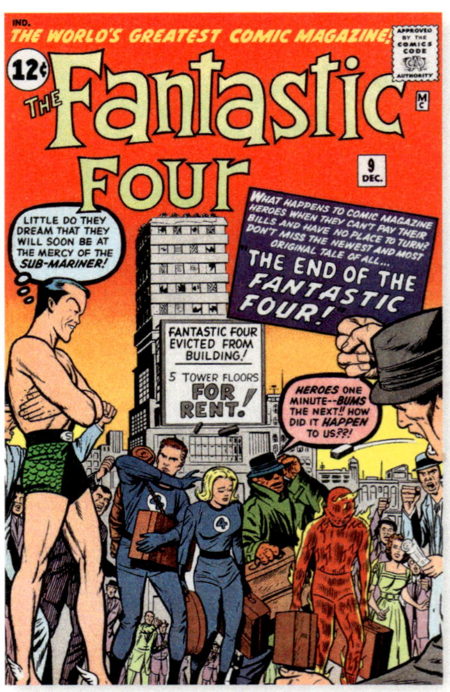

FANTASTIC FOUR No. 9

Cover date: December 1962
On-sale date: September 4, 1962
Cover price: 12 cents
Pages: 36

Editor: Stan Lee

Cover "THE END OF THE *FANTASTIC FOUR!*"
Pencils: Jack Kirby
Inks: Dick Ayers
Colors: Stan Goldberg
Letters: Art Simek

"*THE END OF THE* FANTASTIC FOUR*!*"
Pages: 23
Script: Stan Lee
Pencils: Jack Kirby
Inks: Dick Ayers
Colors: Stan Goldberg
Letters: Art Simek

Reed invests his fortune in stocks; the market crashes and leaves the Fantastic Four broke, reduced to selling their possessions to pay the bills. Namor watches a news broadcast about it. Ben tells his troubles to Alicia. Everyone tries to figure out how to make a fortune fast. They are offered a million dollars to star in a movie, but they have to hitchhike cross-country to get to Hollywood. The film's producer is... the Sub-Mariner. He's been pillaging sunken treasure and bought a movie studio. Johnny and Ben enjoy themselves. Namor takes Sue out to dinner; she asks him why he's being so generous. Namor takes Reed to an island for the first day of shooting, but it's a trap, and Namor leaves Reed behind to die at the hands of a cyclops. Namor similarly tricks Johnny, and then he decides to take on the Thing himself. The Thing turns into Ben Grimm again, and Namor knocks him out. In his office, Namor prepares to seduce Sue, but she suspects what he did, and they fight until the other three return — Ben also having become the Thing again. Sue doesn't let them pummel Namor and makes him hold up his end of the contract. The movie they make is a hit.

FANTASTIC FOUR No. 10

Cover date: January 1963
On-sale date: October 9, 1962
Cover price: 12 cents
Pages: 36

Editor: Stan Lee

Cover
"THE RETURN OF *DOCTOR DOOM!*"
Pencils: Jack Kirby
Inks: Dick Ayers
Colors: Stan Goldberg
Letters: Art Simek

Guest appearances by Stan Lee and Jack Kirby.

"*THE RETURN OF* DOCTOR DOOM!"
Pages: 23
Script: Stan Lee
Pencils: Jack Kirby
Inks: Dick Ayers
Colors: Stan Goldberg
Letters: Art Simek

The FF responds to the signal flare, but it's just Thing wanting to show them Alicia's sculptures of their villains. Sue is upset that Namor is included as a villain, and Reed is confused about Sue's feelings. In the Marvel offices, Stan Lee and Jack Kirby are trying to figure out how to continue the story when Doctor Doom walks in. He won't explain how he has returned from space, but says to get Mr. Fantastic to the Marvel offices to discuss a plot. As soon as Reed walks in, Doom gases him, and tells Lee and Kirby to send the other three members to his address. When Reed wakes up, Doom tells him he now has a working mental teleporter, which he got from a race called the Ovoids when he was lost in space. The device also allows him to switch bodies…which he promptly does—with Reed. They fight, and then the rest of the FF show up. In Doom's body, Reed's pleas go unheeded, and the FF fantasize about how they're going to put Doom away forever. Reed (Doom) suggests putting him in a special chamber that he had prepared for the FF. Back at HQ, miniaturized zoo animals run out of Reed's lab. "Reed" shows off his new reducing ray and explains that it's a way for them to maintain their powers longer, and that it might help Thing become human again. Meanwhile, Doom (Reed) breaks out of the chamber and goes to Alicia's apartment for help, but Sue is there. Alicia sees a goodness and nobility in Doom (Reed). The FF bring Doom (Reed) back to HQ and ask Reed (Doom) what to do with him. The FF trick Doom into revealing the plot, and the bodies get switched back. A fight ensues, and Doom gets hit with his reducing ray until he becomes so tiny that he disappears.

FANTASTIC FOUR No. 11

Cover date: February 1963
On-sale date: November 1, 1962
Cover price: 12 cents
Pages: 36
Editor: Stan Lee

Cover "THE IMPOSSIBLE MAN"
Pencils: Jack Kirby
Inks: Dick Ayers
Colors: Stan Goldberg
Letters: Art Simek

First appearances of Willie Lumpkin and the Impossible Man.

"A *VISIT WITH THE FANTASTIC FOUR*"
Pages: 11
Script: Stan Lee
Pencils: Jack Kirby
Inks: Dick Ayers
Colors: Stan Goldberg
Letters: Art Simek

The FF see kids playing as the Fantastic Four; when they arrive at the Baxter Building, mailman Willie "Lumpy" Lumpkin has a giant sack of fan mail for them. While reading the mail, Reed gives Thing the last attempt at a serum, and it turns him back into Ben. They answer reader questions about their past, and Reed addresses criticism that Sue doesn't contribute enough. Ben turns back into the Thing. An alarm sounds and inside a flying saucer in their hangar there's a birthday cake and party for Sue.

"THE IMPOSSIBLE MAN"
Pages: 11
Script: Stan Lee
Pencils: Jack Kirby
Inks: Dick Ayers
Colors: Stan Goldberg
Letters: Art Simek

In a "hobo jungle," the Impossible Man from the planet Poppup appears. Looking for money, the Impossible Man pops into a bank vault and helps himself. The Fantastic Four are called to a restaurant, where Impossible Man is eating a feast. He tells them where he comes from and about his ability to change into anything—a product of his swift evolutionary processes. A fight breaks out, and then the Impossible Man wreaks havoc across Manhattan until the National Guard shows up to try and help. The FF realize he's not dangerous so much as like a super powerful child. Reed decides that if everyone on Earth just ignores Impossible Man, he'll eventually get bored and go away—which is what happens, and he turns himself into a rocket and blasts off into space.

FANTASTIC FOUR No. 12

Cover date: March 1963
On-sale date: December 10, 1962
Cover price: 12 cents
Pages: 36

Editor: Stan Lee

Cover "*the FANTASTIC FOUR meet THE HULK!*"
Pencils: Jack Kirby
Inks: Dick Ayers
Colors: Stan Goldberg
Letters: Art Simek

Guest appearances by the Hulk and General Ross.

"THE INCREDIBLE HULK"
Pages: 23
Script: Stan Lee
Pencils: Jack Kirby
Inks: Dick Ayers
Colors: Stan Goldberg
Letters: Art Simek

As Thing and Alicia leave a performance by the symphony, an infantry unit surrounds the Thing and subdues him. Turns out, they mistook him—in his civilian clothes and hat—for the Hulk. General Ross shows up at FF headquarters and tells the Four that he wants them to find and destroy the Hulk. Reed, Ben, and Johnny talk about approaches to neutralizing the Hulk. Sue isn't sure how she can help, but Ross tells her "a pretty young lady can always be of help—just by keeping the men's morale up!" With General Ross, they use the revamped Fantasti-car to go to the missile site where the Hulk was last seen. They meet Bruce Banner and Rick Jones—and Bruce's assistant, Karl Kort—but the Thing gets impatient and crashes the meeting. Banner and Jones explain that something called the Wrecker has been destroying missile sites. Then, trying to return a wallet to Kort, the FF realize that he is the Wrecker, not the Hulk. The Thing tests a rocket sled, but the Wrecker sabotages it. Banner shows up and says that Kort / Wrecker abducted Rick Jones. In private, Banner turns into the Hulk. In the underground tunnels looking for Kort and Jones, the Hulk and Fantastic Four face off. During the battle, Thing finds a giant robot—the Wrecker—and realizes the Hulk is innocent. Kort is arrested, and the Hulk escapes.

FANTASTIC FOUR No. 13

Cover date: April 1963
On-sale date: January 3, 1963
Cover price: 12 cents
Pages: 36

Editor: Stan Lee

Cover "THE RED GHOST!"
Pencils: Jack Kirby
Inks: Steve Ditko
Colors: Stan Goldberg
Letters: Art Simek

First appearance of the Red Ghost / Ivan Kragoff and the Watcher.

"THE FANTASTIC FOUR *versus* THE RED *GHOST* AND HIS INDESCRIBABLE *SUPER-APES!*"
Pages: 22
Script: Stan Lee
Pencils: Jack Kirby
Inks: Steve Ditko
Colors: Stan Goldberg
Letters: Art Simek

An explosion in Reed's lab is the result of him underestimating the power of a new rocket fuel that might enable the U.S. to beat the Russians to the Moon — if the Russians don't have the technology already. In Russia, Ivan Kragoff is training apes to operate a spaceship. The FF and Kragoff — with his three apes — blast off at the same moment. While the apes are piloting the ship, Kragoff straps himself to a table to absorb cosmic rays in an attempt to become even more powerful than the FF. The Torch spies on Kragoff's ship and sees that all three apes have been given super powers by the cosmic rays. The FF reach the Moon and realize that mankind isn't the first species on the Moon. As they explore, the Thing finds the apes and Kragoff, who is now going by the name of Red Ghost and can make himself unsolid at will; they're interrupted by the Watcher. The Watcher tells them that his planet is a giant supercomputer, and that his race goes about the galaxy observing other species, and that there will be no war on the Moon — Thing and Red Ghost will have to duke it out. Inside a dead city in the Moon, Reed wants to take the noble course and work with the Red Ghost to explore the Moon as fellow members of the human race. Red Ghost refuses, and the battle begins. After fighting for a while, Red Ghost escapes and breaks into the Watcher's house, but when he is thrown out, Reed blasts him with a paralysis ray. The Watcher declares the FF victorious.

FANTASTIC FOUR No. 14

Cover date: May 1963
On-sale date: February 12, 1963
Cover price: 12 cents
Pages: 36

Editor: Stan Lee

Cover "*the* SUB-MARINER *STRIKES!*"
Pencils: Jack Kirby
Inks: Steve Ditko
Colors: Stan Goldberg
Letters: Art Simek

"THE MERCILESS PUPPET MASTER"
Pages: 22
Script: Stan Lee
Pencils: Jack Kirby
Inks: Dick Ayers
Colors: Stan Goldberg
Letters: Art Simek

The FF return from their trip to the Moon, and they are greeted as heroes. Rival fan clubs of Mr. Fantastic get into a fight, a wrestler challenges Thing, and Sue is offered a Hollywood contract. Torch creates an air funnel to pull the FF out and deposit them on the roof of their building. Reed catches Sue using a roving-eye TV, searching the ocean floor for Namor. The Puppet Master is discharged from a sanatorium and decides to use the Sub-Mariner to get even with the FF. Puppet Master forces Namor to use telepathy to contact Sue. Namor uses a hypno-fish to hypnotize Sue, encloses in her in a bubble, and takes her to the sea. Puppet Master fashions puppets of the FF. Namor appears to the FF and tells them Sue is his prisoner. Thing goes to see Alicia before leaving to face the Sub-Mariner; she convinces him to take her with them. They battle various forces in the ocean until they reach Namor, who shows them he has Sue in a glass bubble guarded by a giant octopus. Namor says he'll battle them one by one, as is the custom of his people, and so he does. While Reed is fighting Namor, Thing frees Sue. Puppet Master then tells Namor not to just defeat the FF, but to kill them. Alicia and the FF realize that Puppet Master is behind this. Namor tries to kill them, but the FF are prepared: Sue defends Namor. The octopus destroys Puppet Master's sub, freeing Namor from the mind control.

FANTASTIC FOUR No. 15

Cover date: June 1963
On-sale date: March 12, 1963
Cover price: 12 cents
Pages: 36

Editor: Stan Lee

Cover "*THE MAD THINKER AND HIS* AWESOME ANDROID!"
Pencils: Jack Kirby
Inks: Dick Ayers
Colors: Stan Goldberg
Letters: Art Simek

First appearance of the Thinker.

"*THE FANTASTIC FOUR BATTLE ...the* MAD THINKER *AND HIS* AWESOME ANDROID*!*"
Pages: 20
Script: Stan Lee
Pencils: Jack Kirby
Inks: Dick Ayers
Colors: Stan Goldberg
Letters: Art Simek

Reed sends out the flare and tells the rest of the FF that mobsters are all flocking to New York. Meanwhile, the Thinker is organizing a kingdom of crime, with him and his computers as the brain, and he's going to declare New York an independent nation, with him as the ruler. Thinker uses his brain and his computers ("calculators") to predict "everything that will happen, down to the last split-second!" Some of the gangsters question the Thinker's abilities. The Thinker has ensured that all four members of the FF received attractive job offers. When the Four immediately start squabbling, they go their separate ways — to their new jobs. After a chain of events predicted by the Thinker, he and his goons break into the FF's now-deserted head-quarters. The FF quickly get fed up with their new jobs and return home, only to find the Baxter Building turned into a giant crystal. The Thinker confronts the FF and says he is going to turn Reed's scientific research against them — and does, using Reed's inventions as weapons, before unleashing a living android the Thinker built from Reed's notes on DNA. They defeat the monster and the Thinker (with the help of Willie Lumpkin), using the one thing that the Thinker didn't prepare for: the X-factor (i.e., the unexpected).

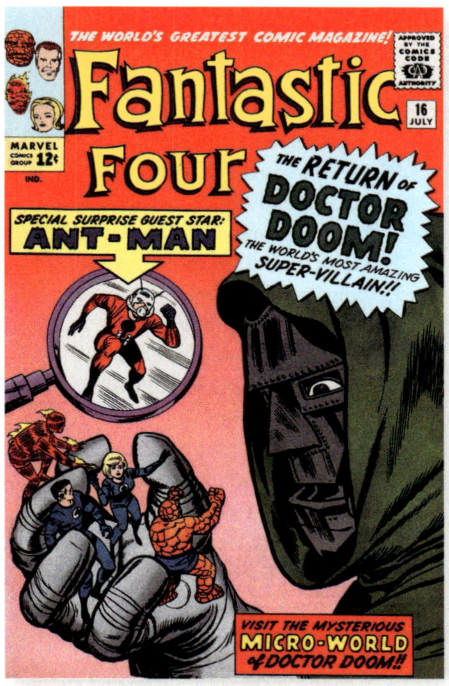

FANTASTIC FOUR No. 16

Cover date: July 1963
On-sale date: April 9, 1963
Cover price: 12 cents
Pages: 36

Editor: Stan Lee

Cover
"*THE RETURN OF* DOCTOR DOOM!"
Pencils: Jack Kirby
Inks: Dick Ayers
Colors: Stan Goldberg
Letters: Art Simek

Ant-Man guest stars.

"*THE MICRO-WORLD OF* DOCTOR DOOM!"
Pages: 22
Script: Stan Lee
Pencils: Jack Kirby
Inks: Dick Ayers
Colors: Stan Goldberg
Letters: Art Simek

Johnny foils a robbery and returns to HQ to find that Reed, Sue, and Ben have been miniaturized. They quickly return to normal size, but it turns out that in the preceding days, all four shrunk while doing normal activities. Now, a voice comes out of nowhere and threatens the FF. Reed says they should call Ant-Man to see if he can help. A network of ants gets him the message, and soon he's in the Baxter Building. He gives them special reducing and growing drops and vows to do some research in his lab. At Alicia's, Reed gives Ben his newest attempt at a cure for Ben's rocklike body, and he becomes human again (briefly). The disembodied voice of a girl warns them of Doctor Doom. Remembering that the last time they saw Doom he was shrinking, they divide Ant-Man's formula and shrink themselves. They end up in Doctor Doom's micro-world. Doom tells them of his life here, and how he took over and became its ruler. The FF strike, but Sue is captured, and Doom puts them all to sleep. When they awake, they meet the king and Princess Pearla, who had been trying to warn them about Doom, who has convinced the planet Tok to join him. Tok will use the FF as slaves. Meanwhile, Ant-Man finds the FF's place empty and follows them to the micro-world. Sue devises an escape plan: Ant-Man is captured by Doom. Sue frees him, the FF spring into action, Doom escapes, and the king agrees to let the FF use his enlarging ray so they can get back home.

FANTASTIC FOUR No. 17

Cover date: August 1963
On-sale date: May 9, 1963
Cover price: 12 cents
Pages: 36

Editor: Stan Lee

Cover "*IN THE CLUTCHES OF* DOCTOR DOOM!"
Pencils: Jack Kirby
Inks: Dick Ayers
Colors: Stan Goldberg
Letters: Art Simek

"*DEFEATED BY* DOCTOR DOOM!"
Pages: 22
Script: Stan Lee
Pencils: Jack Kirby
Inks: Dick Ayers
Colors: Stan Goldberg
Letters: Art Simek

After recapping the previous issue, Reed tests a new invention to try to find Doom. After an unsuccessful day searching, the FF ride the elevator up together, but don't notice when the janitor (Doom) puts trackers on them. They find themselves followed by floating dolls, until Reed notices trackers on their hands. They realize the janitor was Doom and that he's probably watching them. It turns out that the first part of Doom's plan was just to embarrass and confuse the FF, but the second part is to enact his vengeance and destroy them—and he'll use Alicia to do it. He kidnaps her and then threatens the U.S. with war if his demands aren't met. The President won't give in to a terrorist, so Doom begins sabotaging labs and factories ...which pleases the Russians. The government asks for the FF's help. Reed explains to the FF that the floating dolls had scanned their anatomies earlier, so Doom knows the atomic structure of the FF's bodies. Reed says that the Thing is the only one who can defeat Doom, because if he changes to Ben Grimm, his atomic structure changes, and Doom won't be able to prepare for that. He changes to Ben, penetrating Doom's defenses just before he turns back into the Thing. He lets the rest of the FF in, and they each combat Doom's traps. Doom sends them to another dimension—but it turns out he really just sent their images, as he discovers when the actual FF burst into his lab. Sue defeats Doom one on one, but he escapes. The FF rescues Alicia.

FANTASTIC FOUR No. 18

Cover date: September 1963
On-sale date: June 11, 1963
Cover price: 12 cents
Pages: 36

Editor: Stan Lee

Cover "THE ALL-POWERFUL SUPER-SKRULL!"
Pencils: Jack Kirby
Inks: Paul Reinman
Colors: Stan Goldberg
Letters: Art Simek

First appearance of the Super Skrull.

"A SKRULL WALKS AMONG US!"
Pages: 18
Script: Stan Lee
Pencils: Jack Kirby
Inks: Dick Ayers
Colors: Stan Goldberg
Letters: Art Simek

Reed and Sue test their passenger missile and head to Hawaii on a date. Meanwhile, on the Skrulls' planet, the Super Skrull is introduced to the king. He has the powers of all four members of the FF. Days later, the FF are reunited when a Skrull ship arrives in Times Square and claims the planet for the Skrull Empire. They battle the Super Skrull, who uses the FF's own powers against them, sometimes in combination (becoming invisible and shooting flame arrows, for instance). The FF has to retreat, but back in Reed's lab, Reed develops a jammer that can short-circuit the Skrull's powers—they just have to place the jammer on him. They tell the Skrull to meet them on Crater Isle, and they fly their missile to meet him there. The Skrulls turn up the Super Skrull's power to full intensity. While Reed, Johnny, and Ben engage him, Sue sneaks up and puts the jammer on him. They seal the now-powerless Super Skrull inside a cave and leave him there.

FANTASTIC FOUR No. 19

Cover date: October 1963
On-sale date: July 9, 1963
Cover price: 12 cents
Pages: 36

Editor: Stan Lee

Cover
"*AT THE MERCY OF* RAMA-TUT"
Pencils: Jack Kirby
Inks: Paul Reinman
Colors: Stan Goldberg
Letters: Art Simek

First appearance of Rama-Tut.

"PRISONERS OF THE PHAROAH!"
Pages: 22
Script: Stan Lee
Pencils: Jack Kirby
Inks: Dick Ayers
Colors: Stan Goldberg
Letters: Sam Rosen

At the Museum of Natural History, Reed finds a hieroglyph indicating that during a short period in Egyptian history, there was a radioactive potion that could cure blindness. He calls the Thing and Alicia to headquarters to tell them about it. They return to Doom's abandoned castle and find that his time-travel device is still there and working. It means Alicia will have to stay behind to operate it, and she transports the FF to the time period in ancient Egypt where Reed thinks the cure can be found. The FF are immediately attacked by warriors who seem to be from the wrong time period. As the battle progresses, the FF slowly begin losing their powers and becoming weak. They are taken to the chambers of Rama-Tut, who is revealed to be a time traveler from the year 3000. He was bored of peace, and, looking for action, found the remains of and restored a time machine, and prepared to become a time looter. When he landed in Egypt, he was blinded, but still managed to enslave the natives, and found a cure for his sight. The four are subjugated by Rama-Tat's ray gun and forced to work for and entertain. Under the sun's heat, the Thing changes back to Ben Grimm, slips his shackles and escapes. Ben frees Sue just as he's turning back into the Thing; Sue frees the Torch. Mr. Fantastic is being used as a human shield from attackers, but the Torch frees him. Reunited in the core of the Sphinx, they avoid booby traps while they look for Rama-Tut, who blasts off in a missile. Rama-Tut blows up his lab, and the FF return to the present, but the vial of optic restorative doesn't transport with them.

FANTASTIC FOUR ANNUAL No. 1

Cover date: 1963
On-sale date: July 2, 1963
Cover price: 25 cents
Pages: 76

Editor: Stan Lee

Cover "THE UNDERSEA LEGIONS OF *SUB-MARINER!*"
Pencils: Jack Kirby
Inks: Dick Ayers
Colors: Stan Goldberg
Letters: Art Simek

"*SUB-MARINER Versus* THE HUMAN RACE!"
Pages: 37
Script: Stan Lee
Pencils: Jack Kirby
Inks: Dick Ayers
Colors: Stan Goldberg
Letters: Art Simek

Namor is crowned "prince of Atlantis, emperor of the deep, lord of the seven seas, and supreme commander of the undersea legions." Lady Dorma breaks up with Warlord Krang, as her true love Namor has returned. Meanwhile, Johnny and the Thing get in a fight that makes a mess of the FF's headquarters. Sue gets very upset, calling all men "beasts." Reed decides they all need a vacation and uses sightings of sea monsters as an excuse to take a cruise and relax and investigate. Alicia joins them, and Johnny immediately spots a sea serpent. The FF brought a special boat and lower themselves into the sea to investigate, but they're rounded up individually and taken to Namor. He orders them to inform the U.N. that he proclaims the seven seas and the skies above them as his domain, which means no ships or aircraft are allowed there from now on. They're returned to America, but Alicia is left behind on the cruise ship. Namor's message is relayed to the U.N. An oceanographer relays the origins of Namor and Atlantis to them. The expert, however, is just Namor in disguise, and he signals his ships to surface and for the forces of Atlantis to take over New York City. Reed realizes Namor is the only one who can breathe air. As the army tries to figure out what to do to stop the Atlanteans, Reed devises a new invention, but he gets hurt and it's up to Sue and the Thing to put it into operation. A hum is heard across the city, which dissolves the water in the Atlanteans' helmets, forcing them to jump into the sea. Namor fights Mr. Fantastic, the Thing, and the Torch, but escapes to Atlantis with Sue. Then it's Thing, Mr. Fantastic, and the Torch for round two. Sue escapes Namor's ship, and Namor helps her to the surface, but she needs a hospital. Namor saves her, the rest of the FF make it to the hospital, and Namor finds himself without a kingdom.

"A GALLERY OF THE FANTASTIC FOUR'S MOST FAMOUS FOES!"
Pages: 4
Script: Stan Lee
Pencils: Jack Kirby
Inks: Sol Brodsky
Colors: Stan Goldberg
Letters: Ray Holloway

"QUESTIONS *and* ANSWERS *ABOUT THE FANTASTIC FOUR*"
Pages: 2
Script: Stan Lee
Pencils: Jack Kirby
Inks: Sol Brodsky
Colors: Stan Goldberg
Letters: Art Simek

"*INSIDE THE BAXTER BLDG.*"
Pages: 1
Script: Stan Lee
Pencils: Jack Kirby
Inks: Sol Brodsky
Colors: Stan Goldberg
Letters: Art Simek

"A GALLERY OF THE FANTASTIC FOUR'S MOST FAMOUS FOES!"
Pages: 3
Script: Stan Lee
Pencils: Jack Kirby
Inks: attributed to Sol Brodsky and Jack Kirby
Colors: Stan Goldberg
Letters: Ray Holloway

"THE FABULOUS FANTASTIC FOUR MEET SPIDER-MAN!"
Pages: 6
Script: Stan Lee
Pencils: Jack Kirby
Inks: Steve Ditko
Colors: Stan Goldberg
Letters: Ray Holloway

The FF / Spider-Man fight sequence from *Amazing Spider-Man* No. 1 is recounted.

"A GALLERY OF THE FANTASTIC FOUR'S MOST FAMOUS FOES!"
Pages: 4
Script: Stan Lee
Pencils: Jack Kirby
Inks: Sol Brodsky (Impossible Man); Dick Ayers (Mad Thinker); attributed to Jack Kirby and Sol Brodsky
Colors: Stan Goldberg
Letters: Ray Holloway and Art Simek

(*Opposite*) Quickly a fan-favorite, the Fantastic Four would earn their own dedicated fanzine/newsletter by 1963.

"TORCH"
It's Fantastic
(THE FANTASTIC FOUR NEWSLETTER)
SUB-MARINER
DOC DOOM
the "THING"
"MR FANTASTIC"
"INVISIBLE GIRL"
Cover design and illustration by
Fred Romanek

AT LAST! SUB-MARINER FINDS HIS LONG-LOST RACE!
AND SO BEGINS THE MOST FANTASTIC BATTLE OF ALL TIME!
INSIDE THE PAGES OF THIS, THE WORLD'S GREATEST COMIC MAGAZINE!

BIOGRAPHIES

A highlight of **DICK AYERS**'s early years was his cocreation of spooky, masked Western hero Ghost Rider for Magazine Enterprises. His Atlas debut was in pre-Code horror, and he was attached to many successful Westerns, drawing *Wyatt Earp*, *Two-Gun Kid*, and *Rawhide Kid*, and, later, during the Marvel Age of Comics, a new version of Ghost Rider. His inking on Jack Kirby's pencils defined the look of the early Marvel Age. Ayers inked a wide variety of titles, including *Captain America*, *Avengers*, *X-Men*, and *Fantastic Four*. During the '60s and early '70s, he specialized in Marvel war and Western comics, such as *Sgt. Fury*, *Gunhawks*, *Captain Savage*, and *Combat Kelly*. And in the late '70s, Ayers moved to DC Comics, where he did notable work on *Jonah Hex*. He was inducted into the Eisner Awards Hall of Fame in 2007 and passed away in May 2014.

SOL BRODSKY was Stan Lee's right-hand man during the rise of the Marvel Age of Comics, and, according to his boss, he could "do everything," including inking *Fantastic Four* No. 3–4. Brodsky was just a teenager when he started his career as a penciler and inker for Marvel in 1942, but he began in earnest after World War II, working on teen titles. By the Atlas period he worked on war and spy comics, as well as being a prime post-Code cover artist. At the "Atlas implosion of 1957," Brodsky left Marvel to start *Cracked Magazine* and helped other artists find work at Charlton Comics. By 1964, Martin Goodman's company rehired him to be Lee's production manager. Over the next 20 years, he would become a vice president in the company, overseeing Marvel UK and other special projects. Brodsky passed away in 1984 at the age of 61.

Born Max Finkelstein, **CARL BURGOS** will always be remembered as the creator of the Human Torch. Through 1942, he told dozens of Torch stories, and created the Thunderer in *Daring Mystery Comics*. He was drafted during World War II, and upon his return he joined the Timely Comics staff. Burgos would later help revive the Torch during the Atlas Era, as well as doing the odd genre story. He was a major post-Code cover artist, becoming the unofficial cover editor of the company in the '50s. During the Marvel Age, he penciled three issues of *Tales to Astonish* featuring Giant-Man, and drew a story starring Johnny Storm, the new Human Torch, in *Strange Tales* No. 123. Burgos died in 1984.

STEVE DITKO's individualistic style, imaginative designs, and consummate storytelling are legendary. Learning the ropes under instructor Jerry Robinson at the Cartoonists and Illustrators School, Ditko entered the field in 1953, drawing science fiction and horror tales for outfits such as Prize Publications and Charlton. In 1956, he found work at Atlas, soon collaborating with Stan Lee on a series of offbeat fantasy stories. Along with Jack Kirby, Ditko was instrumental in launching the Marvel Age, cocreating Spider-Man and Dr. Strange with Lee. After leaving Marvel in 1966, Ditko's accomplishments included creating or cocreating Hawk and Dove, Creeper, and Shade, the Changing Man for DC, and the Question at Charlton, and illustrating lush black-and-white stories for Warren Publishing's horror line. On his own, Ditko explored his philosophical beliefs with creations such as Mr. A, the Mocker, and Static. Avoiding the spotlight, his reluctance to exploit his creations or interact in public earned him the label "the J. D. Salinger of comics." Ditko instead chose to concentrate on writing essays and drawing self-published comics. His status in the history of comics as a unique thought-provoking innovator is assured. He died in 2018.

One of the pioneers of comics' Golden Age, **BILL EVERETT** created Namor, the Sub-Mariner, a character whose brash passions emulated the writer/artist's fascination with the sea. Alongside Carl Burgos's Human Torch, the Sub-Mariner's anarchic, violent debut in the first issue of *Marvel Comics* helped set the pace for the rise of Timely and the super hero genre. Everett would draw Namor in four different eras: his Golden Age origins, a mid-'50s Atlas revival, various issues of *Tales to Astonish*, and a beautiful nine-issue run before his death in 1973. His other feature credits include brilliant and gruesome pre-Code horror in the 1950s, Atlas's *Marvel Boy* and *Venus*, and the first issue of *Daredevil*.

STAN GOLDBERG was an indispensable part of Timely/Atlas from the waning days of the '40s through the Silver Age. Initially a staff colorist in 1949, Goldberg began penciling women's humor titles like *Kathy*, *Patsy Walker*, *Chili*, and *Millie the Model* in Dan DeCarlo's house style. Goldberg was one of Stan Lee's few staffers as the Marvel Age of Comics ramped up, and he designed color schemes for *Spider-Man*, *Fantastic Four*, *Hulk*, and others. In the early '70s, he joined DeCarlo at Archie Comics, drawing the kids of Riverdale until 2010. He died in 2014 at age 82.

The son of Lithuanian immigrants and an itinerant during his Depression-era youth, **MARTIN GOODMAN** could never have known he would become an integral figure in the evolution of a new art form. From his humble start working under publishing pioneer Louis Silberkleit at various companies, Goodman showed business acumen. In the late '30s, the "comic book" gave him another publishing outlet, and he amped up the super hero trend with anthologies stuffed with a parade of new four-color characters. He hired his wife's cousin, Stan Lee, to first manage Timely, then Atlas, and later Marvel as his flagship comic book outlets, while also maintaining a line of men's, film, sports, and other general interest magazines. Goodman passed away in 1992.

DON HECK may lack the boisterous acclaim imparted to some of his Atlas contemporaries, but his work is an indelible part of that era's legacy. His dramatic covers for Comic Media's '50s-era horror titles drew the attention of Stan Lee, who hired him to work for Atlas in 1955, where Heck tackled all genres, his romance art garnering the most enthusiastic reviews. During the Marvel Age, Don drew the first Iron Man story (Jack Kirby drew the cover), creating the look of Tony Stark and his supporting cast. Heck drew early Ant-Man and Giant-Man, and a long run on *The Avengers* during their "Kooky Quartet" era. Heck also worked on such Gold Key Comics titles as *Voyage to the Bottom of the Sea* and *The Man from U.N.C.L.E.* From the '70s to the early '90s, he drew *Batgirl*, *Justice League of America*, *Wonder Woman*, and *Flash*. He passed away from lung cancer in 1995.

Born Jacob Kurtzberg in 1917 in New York's Lower East Side, **JACK KIRBY** would become one of comics' most legendary creators through an utterly distinctive style combining bombastic layouts, dynamic figurework, and untrammeled imagination. An early collaboration with Joe Simon produced Captain America for Timely. At National, the duo delivered the Newsboy Legion, Boy Commandos, Sandman, and Manhunter. After serving in World War II, Kirby and partner Joe Simon established the romance genre with *Young Romance*. In 1958, he began drawing war stories, Westerns, and an overwhelming array of monsters for Atlas titles. Kirby drew the first "Marvel Age" comic, *Fantastic Four* No. 1, joining writer Stan Lee on that title for a 10-year run for the ages. In that time, he also cocreated Avengers, X-Men, Incredible Hulk, Ant-Man, Sgt. Fury and His Howling Commandos, S.H.I.E.L.D., and Thor, leaving his unmistakable stamp on the characters. At DC, he invented the New Gods mythos, and a mid-'70s return to Marvel produced *Eternals*, *Machine Man*, *2001: A Space Odyssey*, and new takes on cocreations Captain America and the Black Panther. Kirby collaborated with Stan Lee for a final time on the Silver Surfer graphic novel. During the late '70s, he ventured into television animation, producing storyboards for *Fantastic Four* and *Thundarr the Barbarian*. In the 1980s, he created his last new characters, including Captain Victory and Silver Star. The King — as he had been called for decades—passed away in 1994.

GEORGE KLEIN penciled and inked almost exclusively for Timely/Atlas from 1941 to the late '50s, leaving Marvel for DC right at the start of the Silver Age. One key credit that is long unacknowledged was his (probable) inking of Jack Kirby on *Fantastic Four* No. 1–2. Klein returned to Marvel in 1968, where Kirby, Gene Colan, and John Buscema oversaw his exceptional inking. He passed away in 1969.

In the seven decades since reporting to work at Timely as an editorial assistant, **STAN LEE** became the most recognized figure in comics. Born Stanley Martin Lieber in 1922 to Romanian immigrants in New York City, Lee went from writing text pieces to full-length stories, to becoming head writer, editor, and art director while managing the company for cousin-in-law Martin Goodman. During the Atlas Era of the '50s, he oversaw the company's lines of genre material — including war, crime, romance, humor, and funny animal — and in 1961 launched the Marvel Age. With a small stable of handpicked artists at his side, Lee cocreated and wrote super hero comics starring the Fantastic Four, Spider-Man, the X-Men, the Avengers, Doctor Strange, Daredevil, Ant-Man, Giant-Man, and the Hulk, building a shared universe where they could flourish in the imaginations of young readers. The worldwide fan community he built through his comics — at conventions, on the college circuit, and in the media — has remained fiercely loyal through the years. Lee was still active in the industry with various comics and media projects, and movie cameos, until his death in 2018.

Ukrainian immigrant **JACOB "JACK" S. LIEBOWITZ** became pulp printer Harry Donenfeld's accountant in 1929, then his business manager and partner in acquiring National Allied Publications from its financially strapped owner, Malcolm Wheeler-Nicholson, in 1937. The foresighted Liebowitz spearheaded the acquisition of Superman and, with Donenfeld, became the first comics publisher to aggressively license and promote its properties, putting Superman on radio in 1940, making him a star of cartoons in 1941 and movie serials in 1948, and putting him on television in 1953. Liebowitz changed the company's name to National Comics, then National Periodical Publications before taking the company public in 1961. In 1967, he engineered the sale of NPP to Kinney National Services (later Time Warner).

PAUL REINMAN broke into comics in 1940, drawing Green Lantern in *All-American Comics*, and Whizzer, Falcon, and Patriot for Timely. An Atlas stalwart, he produced excellent artwork on numerous horror and war stories and was one of the small cadre of artists retained by Stan Lee after the 1957 implosion, becoming an early inker on Jack Kirby's *X-Men* and *Hulk*. Reinman had a brief stint at Archie Comics, drawing their super hero line in the early 1960s, and returned to Marvel in the late 1960s as an inker, penciler, and an uncredited colorist throughout the 1970s. Some of his last work was assisting John Romita Sr. on *Amazing Spider-Man*.

ART SIMEK spent almost three decades lettering comics and designing logos at Marvel. From the waning days of the Atlas Era through the Bronze Age, he formed a one-two punch with Sam Rose, filling word balloons in virtually every title Marvel published.

JOE SIMON was Timely's first staff editor. While sharing a studio with Jack Kirby, artist Simon cocreated Captain America in 1940, a stirring

symbol of American idealism and pride during the war-torn decade that followed. His partnership with Kirby also produced such noted characters as the Sandman, the Boy Commandos, and the Newsboy Legion for DC, and the horror comic *Black Magic* for Prize Publications. In the '50s, Simon and Kirby started Mainline Publications. Their Fighting American was a sometimes tongue-in-cheek homage to Captain America, who had been recently revived by Atlas. In 1990, Simon provided a compelling account of his contributions to modern comic book history with *The Comic Book Makers*, an autobiography written with his son, Jim. He passed away in 2011 at age 98.

Called "the best inker in the business" and "one of the nicest guys in comics," **JOE SINNOTT** was, along with Stan Lee and Jack Kirby, one of the trinity of virtuosos that lifted *Fantastic Four* into the firmament of comics history. He started his career working across the many genres of the Atlas Era, often doing double-duty on pencils and inks. One of Sinnott's favorite assignments was drawing the biographical stories for *Treasure Chest*, comics that were distributed throughout the Catholic school system in the 1950s and '60s. By the Marvel Age, Sinnott was almost exclusively dedicated to inking duties, eventually providing finishes to nearly every title in the Silver Age Marvel canon. His first job on *Fantastic Four* was on issue No. 5, inking Jack Kirby's first pencils of Doctor Doom. He wouldn't return to Marvel's flagship title until *Fantastic Four* No. 44, but when he did, he was there to stay. He inked just about every issue of *Fantastic Four* until John Byrne took over the book with No. 232.

(*Above*) In another example of Lee and Kirby having fun with the fans, this panel from *Fantastic Four* No. 10 show the collaborators toiling away in their Madison Avenue offices on the next issue, hoping to come up with a villain as memorable as Doctor Doom.

(*Page 700*) These sketches, found on the back of a page of original artwork from issue No. 3, show Stan Lee exploring what would become the Fantastic Four's emblem. Perhaps scribbled during a brainstorming session with Marvel's production manager, Sol Brodsky, Stan first deconstructs Kirby's proposed monogram 'FF' (visible in the unpublished panels on page 649) before settling on the minimal '4' that evokes the team's Space Age '60s origins.

THE COMICS The majority of the comics included in this volume were photographed from the collection of Shelton Drum. A comic collector since childhood, Drum began aggressively hunting out his favorite issues during the mid-1960s, after noticing that *Amazing Spider-Man* No. 1 was selling for the then-unbelievable price of 10 dollars. He also began purchasing three of every Marvel comic being published, using the extras to trade for gaps in his collection. In 1980 Shelton opened the Heroes Aren't Hard to Find store in Charlotte, North Carolina. That store and its satellite locations grew to become one of the largest and most well-known comics retailers in the country. In 1982 he launched Heroes Convention, and it quickly established itself as a "must" on the summer convention schedule, drawing fans, exhibitors, and creators from every region of the country.

THE CGC Most of the comic books photographed for this volume were evaluated and graded by the Certified Guaranty Company LLC. When it was founded in 2000, CGC revolutionized the comic book marketplace by providing clear, objective, and impartial assessments of authenticity and grade. Each comic was encased in a CGC state-of-the-art holder, which combines superior optics and advanced archival materials to provide the best in display and preservation. A tamper-evident seal and numerous security features provide an even higher level of confidence. Today CGC is the world's largest and most trusted third-party grading service for comics, trading cards, magazines, concert posters, and related collectibles.

THE REPRODUCTIONS Rather than recolor the original production artwork (as has been done in previous decades' reprints of classic comics), TASCHEN has attempted to create an ideal representation of these books as they were produced at the time of publication. Beginning with high grade, top-quality comics sourced with the assistance of the CGC, we made super-high resolution photographs of each page as printed more than half a century ago, then used modern retouching techniques to correct problems with the era's inexpensive, imperfect printing. This included improved and balanced ink densities and color matching, proper registration of the four-color printing and correction of thick/thin lines resulting from the flexible plates "smudging." The end result is a finished product—as if hot off of a world-class printing press, produced without economic or time-pressure constraints—that we are confident readers, fans, artists, and collectors alike will love.

THE ACKNOWLEDGMENTS At Marvel, thanks are due to Joe Hochstein, Sven Larsen, Brian Overton, Rickey Purdin, Jeremy West, and Jeff Youngquist. At the CGC, thanks to Mike Browne, Brittany McManus, Matt Nelson, and Harshen Patel. Thanks are also due to Josh Baker, Bob Bretall, Aaron Caplan, Nick Caputo, Dan Carr, Gill Champion and POW!, Andrew Lewis, John Morrow, John Nee, Barry Pearl, Cory Sedlmeier, Karla Southern, Tellshiar, Roy Thomas, Michael Vassallo, Nina Wiener, Scott Bryan Wilson, and Sarah Southard.

Foreword Mike Massimino
"The World's Greatest Comic Magazine" Mark Waid

Additional images courtesy of: Gold, Glen: 25; Imaged by Heritage Auctions, ha.com: 27, 30, 33, 37; TAM Collection: 23 (top right); Tellshiar: 36, 695; Vassallo, Michael: 17 (left).

Endnotes

1. Gerard Jones, ***Men of Tomorrow: Geeks, Gangsters, and the Birth of the Comic Book*** (New York: Basic Books, 2004).
2. Jon B. Cooke, ed., "Stan the Man and Roy the Boy: A Conversation Between Stan Lee and Roy Thomas" ***Comic Book Artist*** No. 2 (Raleigh: TwoMorrows Publishing, 1998).
3. Jordan Raphael and Tom Spurgeon, ***Stan Lee and The Rise and Fall of the American Comic Book*** (Chicago: Chicago Review Press, 2003): 72.
4. Mark Evanier, ***Kirby: King of Comics*** (New York: Abrams ComicArts, 2008): 88.
5. Leonard Pitts, Jr., ***Stan Lee: Conversations*** (Jackson: University Press of Mississippi, 2007): 87.
6. Stan Lee, ***Excelsior!: The Amazing Life of Stan Lee*** (New York: Fireside, 2002): 112.
7. Lee, ***Excelsior!: The Amazing Life of Stan Lee***: 113.
8. John Morrow, ***Kirby & Lee, Stuf' Said*** (Raleigh: TwoMorrows Publishing, 2018): 19.
9. Morrow, ***Kirby & Lee, Stuf' Said***: 23.
10. Tom Brevoort, "Lee & Kirby: Fantastic Four # 1, Part Two" (February 2019), https://tombrevoort.com/2019/02/02/lee-kirby-fantastic-four-1-part-two/.
11. Roy Thomas, ***The Comicollector*** No. 1 (September 1961).
12. Pitts, Jr., ***Stan Lee: Conversations***: 181.

Editor: Steve Korté, New York
Captions: Jermaine McLaughlin, New York
Photography: Daniel Gray, Charlotte

EACH AND EVERY TASCHEN BOOK PLANTS A SEED!
TASCHEN is a carbon neutral publisher. Each year, we offset our annual carbon emissions with carbon credits at the Instituto Terra, a reforestation program in Minas Gerais, Brazil, founded by Lélia and Sebastião Salgado. To find out more about this ecological partnership, please check: taschen.com/zerocarbon
INSPIRATION: UNLIMITED. CARBON FOOTPRINT: ZERO.

To stay informed about TASCHEN and our upcoming titles, please subscribe to our free magazine at www.taschen.com/magazine, follow us on Instagram and Facebook, or e-mail your questions to contact@taschen.com.

TASCHEN GmbH
Hohenzollernring 53, D-50672 Köln
taschen.com

Printed in Italy
ISBN 978-3-8365-8231-5
ISBN Famous First Edition 978-3-8365-9425-7
ISBN Collector's Edition 978-3-8365-9219-2

YOU DON'T HAVE TO MAKE A SPEECH, BIG SHOT! WE UNDER-STAND! WE'VE GOTTA **USE** THAT POWER TO HELP MANKIND, RIGHT?
RIGHT, BEN, RIGHT!

I'M CALLING MYSELF THE HUMAN TORCH-- AND I'M WITH YOU ALL THE WAY!
SAME GOES FOR ME... THE INVISIBLE GIRL!
THERE'S ONLY ONE STILL MISSING... BEN!!